ANNUAL REVIEW OF MICROBIOLOGY

ANNUAL REVIEW OF MICROBIOLOGY

MORTIMER P. STARR, *Editor*
University of California, Davis

JOHN L. INGRAHAM, *Associate Editor*
University of California, Davis

ALBERT BALOWS, *Associate Editor*
Center for Disease Control, Atlanta

VOLUME 34

1980

ANNUAL REVIEWS INC. 4139 EL CAMINO WAY PALO ALTO, CALIFORNIA 94306

ANNUAL REVIEWS INC.
Palo Alto, California, USA

REPRINTS The conspicuous number aligned in the margin with the title of each article in this volume is a key for use in ordering reprints. Available reprints are priced at the uniform rate of $1.00 each postpaid. The minimum acceptable reprint order is 5 reprints and/or $5.00 prepaid. A quantity discount is available.

International Standard Serial Number: 0066-4227
International Standard Book Number: 0-8243-1134-5
Library of Congress Catalog Card Number: 49-432

PRINTED AND BOUND IN THE UNITED STATES OF AMERICA

Annual Review of Microbiology
Volume 34, 1980

CONTENTS

THE JOURNEY, NOT THE ARRIVAL, MATTERS, *Roger Y. Stanier* 1

VIRUS-LIKE PARTICLES OF YEAST, *Jeremy A. Bruenn* 49

FLAGELLAR STRUCTURE AND FUNCTION IN EUBACTERIA, *R. N. Doetsch and R. D. Sjoblad* 69

RECENT TAXONOMIC DEVELOPMENTS AND CHANGES IN MEDICAL MYCOLOGY, *Michael R. McGinnis* 109

MODIFIED BASES IN BACTERIOPHAGE DNAS, *R. A. J. Warren* 137

NATURAL β-LACTAM ANTIBIOTICS, *Hatsuo Aoki and Masakuni Okuhara* 159

OXYGEN AND HYDROGEN IN BIOLOGICAL NITROGEN FIXATION, *Robert L. Robson and John R. Postgate* 183

NITROGEN METABOLITE REGULATION OF ANTIBIOTIC BIOSYNTHESIS, *Yair Aharonowitz* 209

MUTAGENICITY AND CARCINOGENICITY OF MYCOTOXINS: DNA BINDING AS A POSSIBLE MODE OF ACTION, *Avishay-Abraham Stark* 235

ORE LEACHING BY BACTERIA, *D. G. Lundgren and M. Silver* 263

CHLAMYDIAE, *Julius Schachter and Harlan D. Caldwell* 285

THE IMMUNOLOGICAL ACTIVITIES OF BACTERIAL PEPTIDOGLYCANS, *D. E. S. Stewart-Tull* 311

DISEASES OF HUMANS (OTHER THAN CHOLERA) CAUSED BY VIBRIOS, *Paul A. Blake, Robert E. Weaver, and Dannie G. Hollis* 341

PROTEINS OF THE OUTER MEMBRANE OF GRAM-NEGATIVE BACTERIA, *M. J. Osborn and H. C. P. Wu* 369

CHEMICAL AND FUEL PRODUCTION BY ANAEROBIC BACTERIA, *J. G. Zeikus* 423

PLASMID-MEDIATED FACTORS ASSOCIATED WITH VIRULENCE OF BACTERIA TO ANIMALS, *Lynn P. Elwell and Patricia L. Shipley* 465

Some Aspects of Structure and Function in N_2-Fixing Cyanobacteria, *W. D. P. Stewart* 497

Antibiotics From *Micromonospora*, *Gerald H. Wagman and Marvin J. Weinstein* 537

Natural Populations of the Genus *Staphylococcus*, *Wesley E. Kloos* 559

Chemically Defined Antiviral Vaccines, *Ruth Arnon* 593

Defective Interfering Influenza Viruses, *Debi P. Nayak* 619

Genetics of *Erwinia* Species, *Arun K. Chatterjee and Mortimer P. Starr* 645

The Genus *Spiroplasma*, *Robert F. Whitcomb* 677

Indexes

Author Index 711

Subject Index 744

Cumulative Index of Contributing Authors, Volumes 30–34 757

Cumulative Index of Chapter Titles, Volumes 30–34 759

OTHER REVIEWS OF MICROBIOLOGICAL INTEREST

From the *Annual Review of Biochemistry,* Volume 49 (1980):

Crawford, I. P., Stauffer, G. V. *Regulation of Tryptophan Biosynthesis*

Weinberg, R. A. *Integrated Genomes of Animal Viruses*

Petes, T. D. *Molecular Genetics of Yeast*

From the *Annual Review of Genetics,* Volume 14 (1980):

Egel, R., Kohli, J., Thuriaux, P., Wolf, K. *Genetics of the Fission Yeast Schizosaccharomyces pombe*

Gorovsky, M. A. *Genome Organization and Reorganization in Tetrahymena*

McCarty, M. *Reminiscences of the Early Days of Transformation*

Mount, D. W. *The Genetics of Protein Degradation in Bacteria*

Willetts, N., Skurray, R. *The Conjugation System of F-Like Plasmids*

From the *Annual Review of Medicine,* Volume 31 (1980):

Meyer, R. D., Finegold, S. M. *Legionnaires' Disease*

Smith, J. W., Wolfe, M. S. *Giardiasis*

From the *Annual Review of Pharmacology and Toxicology,* Volume 20 (1980):

Smith, R. A., Sidwell, R. W., Robins, R. K. *Antiviral Mechanisms of Action*

From the *Annual Review of Phytopathology,* Volume 18 (1980):

Pérombelon, M. C. M., Kelman, A. *Ecology of the Soft Rot Erwinias*

Yoder, O. C. *Toxins in Pathogenesis*

Drew, M. C., Lynch, J. M. *Soil Anaerobiosis, Microorganisms, and Root Function*

Roger Stanier

Ann. Rev. Microbiol. 1980. 34:1–48

THE JOURNEY, NOT THE ARRIVAL, MATTERS

❖1768

Roger Y. Stanier

Institut Pasteur, 28 rue du Dr Roux, 75724 Paris Cedex 15, France

---

CONTENTS

Canadian Childhood: 1916–1936 1
Marking Time: 1936–1939 6
The Hopkins Marine Station, Pacific Grove: 1939–1942 8
Return to Canada: 1942–1945 10
Second European Interlude: 1945–1946 10
Transition: Indiana University 11
Berkeley: 1947–1971 12
Genesis of The Microbial World, 1952 13
Abuse of Power: The Naval Biological Laboratory 14
Biochemistry Without Tears: Sequential/Simultaneous Induction 19
Biochemistry With Tears: Mandelate Pathway 23
Experiments With Purple Nonsulfur Bacteria 23
The genesis of the "chromatophore" concept 23
Regulation of pigment synthesis 27
A General Role for Carotenoid Pigments 29
Experiments with the blue-green mutant 29
Diphenylamine as a specific inhibitor of carotenogenesis by Rhodospirillum rubrum 30
The role of carotenoid pigments in conferring photoprotection on chemoheterotrophs (including man) 32
The Role of Organic Substrates in Photoheterotrophy 33
The Mechanism of Streptomycin Action 34
Cellular Differentiation in the Caulobacters 35
Taxonomic Excursions: The Aerobic Pseudomonads 37
Departure From Berkeley, 1971 40
Towards a General Definition of Procaryotes: What to do About the Cyanobacteria? 40
Envoi 45

Canadian Childhood: 1916–1936

I was born in Victoria, British Columbia, then a small Canadian provincial capital, halfway through the first cataclysmic War of the 20th century. Survivors used to refer to it, with unconscious irony, as the "Great" War.

0066-4227/80/1001-0001$01.00

As one who grew up during the '20s and '30s on the isolated Canadian periphery, largely protected from the Great Depression, I experienced a faint afterglow of Victorian optimism. I believed that science and culture would go hand in hand to the common enrichment of civilization. The passage of events during this dark and terrible century has long since shattered this illusion.

I recall Victoria as being sharply stratified fifty years ago. There was a minority of British gentry—primarily a first-generation influx, attracted by the mild and beautiful surroundings—with its own peculiar *esprit de classe.* The gentry coexisted alongside of a large majority of native Canadians, democratic and egalitarian. Both my parents belonged to the gentry. My father had emigrated in 1888, at the age of 17. Blessed with a numerous Victorian family, my grandfather sold his farms in Shropshire during the agricultural depression of the '80s, and (somewhat imprudently) sent his oldest son to Canada in order to find out whether prairie wheat-growing would provide the answer to his financial embarrassments. The response being favorable, he emigrated with his family to Moosomin (Saskatchewan). It was an interesting experiment in natural selection. Needless to say, the Victorian gentry went to the wall, faced with pioneering conditions and the cruel Saskatchewan winter. Profoundly discouraged, my grandfather stuck it out for two or three years and re-emigrated to Britain, accompanied by his second wife and young children. The family of the first wife, now adults, were left to fend for themselves. The girls opted for marriage with the few neighboring gentry who had successfully survived (any other marital fate would have been unthinkable). The boys had varied careers: an unsuccessful prospector, an employee of an insurance company, and a doctor. My father was the doctor. He hadn't even completed his secondary education and had a hard struggle. Aided in part by a generous brother-in-law, he completed medicine at the University of Toronto in 1901. Much later (1912) he spent a year at the Mayo Clinic and specialized in the new science of radiology. In fact, he opened the first private practice of diagnostic radiology in western Canada in 1913, 18 years after Röntgen's discovery.

My mother emigrated in 1912. She was in her early 30s. My grandmother, long widowed, had two girls, of whom the older (my aunt) had married a Montana rancher, himself of British origin. He had "weak lungs," and the doctors counselled a dry and elevated climate. An excellent counsel: he lived to 97. After some years of childlessness, my aunt announced her pregnancy. My grandmother then took decisive steps. Having stored all her household effects, she set out for British Columbia, accompanied by the younger daughter, who later became my mother. Trained as a teacher with excellent references, my mother had no difficulty in finding a good job, at the Misses Gordon's private school in Vancouver.

My mother's education had been excellent: a private school (Cheltenham), followed by three years at Cambridge where she studied English literature. However, she didn't qualify for a degree. In 1900, Oxford and Cambridge withheld the honor from women. Trinity College (Dublin) was quick to profit from such remarkable sexual discrimination. They announced to all female Oxbridge graduates that an MA degree was theirs for the asking (accompanied, needless to say, by a hefty registration fee). Bizarrely, my mother was thus an MA from Trinity College, even though she had graduated with a BA from Cambridge.

I've often speculated about my grandmother's motives for this extraordinary migration to Canada. Life on a Montana ranch was both primitive and isolated in those days. Still, nothing prevented my aunt from completing her pregnancy and giving birth to her child in a nearby Montana town with good medical facilities. I suspect that there was one unspoken but overriding sentiment: my grandmother's deeply held British patriotism. Despite his impeccable origins in the Manx squirearchy, my uncle Heywood Daly had taken wholeheartedly to a Montana rancher's life, with all that implies concerning social outlook (i.e. extreme conservatism and rugged independence). Indeed, he eventually became almost indistinguishable from the native product. My grandmother was thoroughly displeased by this disaffection from the standards expected of the British gentry. It perhaps entered her mind that by conducting the delivery north of the border she would determine that the newborn at least was Canadian (then a second-rate synonym for British) and not American. So it was. My cousin John (born 1912) was actually British-educated, having been shipped "home" at the tender age of 14 to enter a grim public school, Sedbergh on the Yorkshire moors, where he passed four sad and lonely years, handed round during vacations to our British relatives. John proved to be an extraordinary character for whom I had great respect and affection. Returning to British Columbia, he became a good commercial fisherman and worked both effectively and unceasingly for the welfare of the fishing community and for a variety of educational and social causes (the social causes, mainly left of center). He detested the United States for its wealth and power, which he judged were put to bad uses.

My parents were married in 1915. The marriage proved a disaster from the outset. I was considerably scarred by the overt parental conflicts. When my sister was born in 1919, I developed convincing symptoms of subacute bacterial endocarditis, then invariably fatal. All the clinicians in Victoria were brought to my bedside and mournfully concurred in the prognosis. Of course, reliable diagnostic procedures—blood cultures and electrocardiograms—were still in the future. I was quite unnecessarily immobilized from the age of 3 until I was 4½ and then slowly began to "recover."

In 1921 my father resigned his radiological practice and retired to his country house by the sea, some 30 miles north of Victoria. He was only 50, and the motives for retirement were probably mixed: concern for my health, then deemed precarious; a fear (well-founded) of radiological hazards; and lastly, a suspicion that he was about to be recruited, as by far the best qualified, for resident radiologist at a Victoria hospital. My father was a typical private enterprise physician. To work for a mere salary, subject to the rules of the hospital administrator and accountable for regular hours, was profoundly distasteful.

The enforced propinquity of my parents didn't lead to harmony: quarrels (of some violence) were almost daily occurrences. Always prone to believe that he was an authority on general conduct (we jokingly called his epistles "Lord Chesterfield's letters"), my father grew increasingly authoritarian with his family, thus inducing in me a deep sense of inadequacy, reinforced by my miserable school years. Indeed, it was relieved only at the age of 23, when Kees van Niel restored by his affection and confidence the belief that I might really amount to something. It is certainly not the least part of the debt that I owe to this beloved friend and teacher.

There remained the question of my education. The local elementary day school was ruled out: only a private boarding school could qualify. Hence I was shipped at the age of 7 to St. Christopher's School in Victoria, where I spent 2 years. In 1925 I was introduced at the age of 9 to Shawnigan Lake School where I spent five long and hellish years. This resident penal colony, then presided over by C. W. Lonsdale, combined in one unpalatable mixture poor food, virtually unheated classrooms and dormitories, Anglican principles, and hard labor (the elaborate garden was entirely constructed by work teams of helpless boys), together of course with a rigorous classical education and ferocious discipline, corporal punishment being the rule.

Most of the teachers were genuine British imports. They retained titles earned through the "Great" War (e.g. "Captain" Ellison, "Captain" Levien). A curious custom, attributable to the social snobbery of those years. In the 1914–1918 war, an "officer" was ipso facto a "gentleman"; other ranks were not.

Underfed, chronically cold, poor at games and intermittently beaten, I implored my parents to cut this particular educational experience short; it fell on deaf ears. I owe my liberation to an accident. In 1930 my father arrived by chance to find me in the infirmary with an undiagnosed case of pneumonia. A glance at the telltale temperature chart and a summary auscultation revealed the diagnosis. Furious, he wrapped me in a blanket and carried me away. I was never to return.

Complicated by pleurisy, the convalescence was slow in pre-penicillin days, and I spent the best part of three months in bed. Fortunately, at least one parent was convinced that Shawnigan Lake School might be hazardous to my health.

In 1930, the tenants who had rented our house in Victoria gave up the lease. This enabled my mother, who had two children of school age to educate, to economize by placing us in day schools, and to make ends meet by taking in boarders. My father preferred to remain in the country, a quasi separation which, I suspect, was a great relief to them both. Thus my final year prior to matriculation was spent (at last!) at a public day school, the Oak Bay High School, a happy experience after the barbarism of Shawnigan.

I fear that I have painted too bleak a portrait of my father. Although my parents were comparatively poor and although I was educated in the depths of the Great Depression, they never stinted on my education, even when I hesitated and marked time for several years. For this, I'm profoundly grateful.

Curiously, the five years at Shawnigan Lake sensitized me in another direction. In 1936 I became immediately aware of the evils of National Socialism, which mirrored at the level of a whole nation some of the salient aspects of my school years: the loss of freedom, the sadism, the brutality.

I graduated from high school in 1931 at the age of 15. Thereafter, I enrolled in Victoria College, the local junior college, for three years, vainly trying to catch up with my precocity. The college was small—some 200–300 students—and housed in temporary quarters. The locale was a stone "castle" in deplorable Victorian taste, late residence for local magnates, the Dunsmuirs. No money had been wasted to convert it to educational purposes. As I recall, larger classes were attended in the ballroom, decorated in white and gold woodwork, with an elaborate parquet floor.

I shall always be deeply grateful for the education that Victoria College then afforded, thanks to a handful of devoted and first-rate teachers. Jeannette Cann and Ruth Humphrey taught me all the English that I know. Mme Sanderson-Mongin, witty and vivacious, struggled Canute-like with the terrible accents of Victorians. Walter Gage [then a very young man, subsequently President of the University of British Columbia (U.B.C.)] proved a masterly exponent of elementary mathematics. Only physics and chemistry were poorly taught. Forewarned, I avoided them.

Jeff Cunningham, housed in a temporary wooden annex, was responsible for my gradually awakening interest in biology. A classical zoologist, he drove us to observe, dissect and depict with rigor and precision. Viewed in retrospect, the training was somewhat limited and old-fashioned, but he taught us to work with enthusiasm and passion.

Meanwhile, my parents hovered anxiously over my future career. However, a being so drained of self-confidence scarcely merited the hovering. Of one thing I was convinced: a medical career (which my father clearly favored) was closed to me. The reason was simple if ignoble: I couldn't stand the sight of blood.

Unwarily, I confessed that literature and history were my preferred subjects, only to be greeted by hoots of derision (how would the boy make his living?). I therefore invented a more devious plan. At U.B.C. where I transferred during my junior and senior years, I would major in bacteriology. This had two advantages: it fitted in with my biological interests and it was a para-medical discipline, apt to meet favor in my father's eyes. And that, dear reader, constitutes the narrow path of how I became a microbiologist.

When I reached U.B.C. at Vancouver in 1934, only 1500 students were enrolled. I put myself down for the honors program in bacteriology. This gave me a first taste of research (an undergraduate thesis on marine agar-digesting bacteria), but necessarily narrowed my training. Unfortunately, the chemistry courses that I did take were atrociously taught and old-fashioned. My mounting enthusiasm about the research project delayed graduation until late July 1936. I received first class honors, a modest encouragement.

Marking Time: 1936–1939

My father had invested in a small insurance policy for me, which matured when I was 18. In 1936, I decided to visit Europe and repair my chemistry deficiency at the University of Munich. Needless to say, I had an extremely vague notion of the phenomenon of National Socialism. It didn't take me many months to decide that this once great university had been destroyed. Political direction was in the hands of Nazi bullies; professors (those that had survived the Jewish purge) were cowed and deferential; sinister rumors circulated about Dachau, an early prototype of concentration camps; most disturbing of all, the pace of Nazi rearmament was feverish. I decided that it was useless to continue. This left me several months of freedom, from which I profited by travelling widely in Britain, France, Italy and Czechoslovakia, convinced that if and when I returned, Europe would be in ruins.

In reality, the outbreak of war was only two or three years away. This is a war that Britain nearly lost and that effectively abolished her claim to the status of a Great Power. My British relatives—a fair sample of the British nation—refused to look reality in the face and displayed a truly incredible complacency, faced with the coming storm. Cassandra-like I made myself highly unpopular (I was an intolerable young adult: conceited and cocksure, a consequence of my basic insecurity) by predicting almost to the year the outbreak of a potentially disastrous war if nothing were done to confront National Socialism. In retrospect, it was almost too late. Subsequent historical assessment has pointed to the Nazi reoccupation of the Rhineland (1936) as the watershed, when a joint declaration of war by the allied Franco-British-Czech forces could have led to the occupation of Germany without risk and succeeded in toppling National Socialism. I am a great believer in precedents. The terrible evils for which National Socialism was the model in the 1930s and '40s have gone reverberating down into the later 20th century, and somehow palliated (if that be the correct word) the shock of subsequent monstrosities.

It is no merit that on a few months acquaintance with Nazism, a young and very inexperienced Canadian made so accurate a prognosis of the fate of Europe. This has taught me a useful lesson on the short-sightedness of politicians, whether they be of right, left or center, and specifically bearing on US policy (because I lived in that country nearly 30 years). I select, more or less at random, particular instances: the Loyalty Oath, which almost wrecked the University of California and produced deep, long-lasting and bitter cleavages during the ominous heyday of McCarthyism; the brutal, sanctimonious and ultimately disastrous policy pursued during the late '60s in south Vietnam and Cambodia by Nixon and Kissinger; the ostrich-like energy policy in the '70s.

In 1937 I decided that Europe was doomed. The only reasonable chance of pursuing graduate study was in the U.S. I chose the University of California, Berkeley (UCB) largely for the irrelevant reason that I had close friends there, Mike and Ruth Lerner. As I look back on it, I was exceptionally lucky. The waiver of the nonresident tuition fee (later a major roadblock to all foreign nationals) was then in the hands of C. B. Lipman, at that time Dean of Graduate Studies. A personal interview of five minutes with Dean Lipman was granted, and I was exempted. Other fees were nominal.

I enrolled in the bacteriology department, then a poor choice. The principal researches conducted, under the auspices of A. P. Krueger, were on preDelbrückian phage growth, which didn't interest me. The younger sister campus, University of California, Los Angeles (UCLA), enquired at Berkeley for a teaching assistant, and I was selected for the term 1938–1939. It was my first paid job. However, something of much greater importance lay in store. A graduate student (I can't recall who) casually told me of a remarkable summer course in microbiology, conducted by C. B. van Niel at the Hopkins Marine Station of Stanford University. The time fitted, and by sheer chance, I enrolled. There were only five students in the class, and Mike Doudoroff served as teaching assistant. I recall that he dashed in and out of the classroom in buccaneer style, a black eyepatch well fitting his Armenian features. He was then engaged in the isolation of "dim" mutants of luminous bacteria and couldn't spare the time to get dark-adapted.

After two years of marking time, my fate was decided in a few days. It took less than a week to conclude that van Niel was the ideal master and teacher; general microbiology was to be my domain. Perhaps I may quote from van Niel (117) concerning his famous "program" of research (largely fulfilled, by the way):

> Soon after my arrival, Dr. Walter K. Fisher enquired about the research program that I intended to develop. I explained that my interests covered a broad spectrum, comprising the morphology, taxonomy, ecology, physiology and biochemistry of the bacteria, fungi, algae and protozoa. And because the fundamental problems pertained to freshwater and soil organisms, as much as to marine forms, it seemed to me unwise to restrict my attention to the latter, whose only distinguishing feature was their occurrence in salt water (a misjudgement, by the way, although it would take the work of R. A. MacLeod (60) to reveal it). The response was gratifying simple and direct: "You go right ahead, doctor". On this basis, I have conducted my "program" at the Hopkins Marine Station.

There was only one snag about my plans: that teaching assistantship at UCLA. I discussed the problem with van Niel, who offered as consolation that a master's thesis (an extension of my undergraduate thesis) wouldn't come amiss. After several days happily spent in the van Niel home, I departed with reluctance to Los Angeles.

In fact, the year spent at UCLA was far from wasted. I discovered a rich and varied source of marine agar-decomposing bacteria in the daily seawater count plates routinely prepared by my friend Syd Rittenberg, then an assistant of Claude Zobell at the Scripps Institution of La Jolla. The base (peptone) was nutritionally complex, hence to a degree nonselective. I succeeded in isolating two agar-decomposing *Cytophaga* strains, both nutritionally unspecialized and with complex growth factor requirements. The "classical" cellulose-decomposing cytophagas, largely studied by Winogradsky (122), were presumed to be strictly restricted to one substrate (cellulose). They proved to be very difficult to purify, and considerable uncertainties with regard to their taxonomic affinities persisted. On the other hand, the nutritionally unspecialized marine cytophagas were easy to purify since they grew well on a clear agar medium, and this led to the unambiguous demonstration of the method of locomotion: gliding movement. With the rashness of youth, I unhesitatingly assigned them to the only major group unicellular nonphototrophic gliders then known: the myxobacteria (84).

The Hopkins Marine Station, Pacific Grove: 1939–1942

I returned to the Marine Station with an extraordinary sense of freedom in the summer of 1939. In the summer course of 1938, van Niel had displayed all the as yet unfathomed riches of general microbiology; now, given enough insight and imagination, it was up to us to profit by them. I'd already jotted down some interesting problems in my notebook and was eager to come to grips with them.

Parenthetically, I've at no time run dry on ideas. In retrospect, I skated somewhat lightly and superficially over what later proved to be major problems of molecular biology [e.g. the characterization with Schachman & Pardee of what would be subsequently called 70S ribosomes (76) and the mechanism of streptomycin dependence (83)]. But that's the inevitable penalty paid by foxes, who like to skim the cream off a diversity of promising subjects, and not be hedgehogs, who labor patiently over one big topic through decades.

In view of my weakness (this is not a gross exaggeration) in the physical sciences, I lazily chose the first part of van Niel's celebrated "program": the morphology and taxonomy of microorganisms. That was one of the great incidental benefits of thesis work at the Marine Station. Since van Niel saw the problems of general microbiology *sensu lato,* one had the sense of a virtually unlimited choice and an interested and sympathetic interlocutor. I chose the "classical" cellulose-decomposing cytophagas. A new key to the purification of the group had recently been discovered by H. L. Jensen (42). This combined a very finely divided cellulose preparation and poured plates of dilute (0.8%) agar. The rationale was simple: the cytophagas, being gliders, can migrate readily through weak agar gels. This is the only way to gain access to the insoluble nutrient (cellulose), since there is no diffusible enzyme and cellulose can be attacked only by cell-to-substrate contact.

Using this technique, I purified several strains. To my surprise, cellulose was not the sole substrate as had heretofore been claimed (88). Filter-sterilized sugars (notably glucose and cellobiose) would support growth. Even 40 years later, I must admit that I'm still uncertain of the interpretation, as well as of the curious predilection of the cytophagas for direct cell-to-nutrient contact. In view of the permease hypothesis (then a decade away), conceivably the wild types of the cytophagas possess only a single permease (i.e. a cellulose permease), and are thus truly obligate cellulose decomposers. Additional permeases for glucose and cellobiose may be acquired by mutation and selection. Some indications of this emerged much later (May Kihara Ornston, unpublished experiments).

The three years spent at Pacific Grove were among the happiest and most productive of my life. I completed my taxonomic survey of the agar-decomposing bacteria (85); I characterized the nutritional requirements of the cellulolytic chytrid, *Rhizophlyctis rosea,* which had emerged in enrichment cultures and which I was the first to purify (86); I identified *Streptomyces coelicolor* as an agar-decomposer and traced its structural variations by using this property as a marker (87).

Of one paper I'm somewhat less than proud: "The main outlines of bacterial classification" (109). All the more so, as with much special pleading, I persuaded van Niel to append his name to it. He never as a matter of principle co-authored articles of which he hadn't shared directly in research—a good lesson for all of us. I suppose he construed it as a purely theoretical paper, in which he was morally justified to share. It should be construed as the last gasp (at least in bacteriology) of speculative, "phylogenetic" system-building before molecular biology took over and brought some solid facts to the assessment of evolutionary relationships.

Return to Canada: 1942–1945

In 1942, I was appointed Junior Research Bacteriologist at the National Research Council of Canada. My job was to explore the production of 2,3-butanediol (a precursor of synthetic rubber) by fermentation. Since Canada had a vast wheat surplus, it appeared reasonable to use the starch-fermenting *Bacillus polymyxa,* which could grow (albeit with relatively low butanediol yields) on unhydrolyzed wheat mashes (1, 56).

Jackson W. Foster, whom I'd known as a postdoctoral fellow at the Marine Station, had entered Merck & Co., Inc., and was responsible for extending an invitation to me, early in 1944, to join a Canadian subsidiary, Merck & Co., Ltd (Montreal). The technology of penicillin production—including that key device, the submerged fermentation process—was then being developed, and Merck had a critical role. The acetone-butanol fermentation, which was conducted in 10,000 gallon tanks and had hitherto been assumed to maintain sterility satisfactorily, had major flaws in it, as evidenced by the frequency of phage infections. One could not guarantee sterility by this means; and absolute sterility was a sine qua non of the penicillin process. A good deal of reflection was therefore expended (mainly by Merck) on the principles of fermenter design. Accordingly, when I was invited to establish the penicillin industry in Canada, the know-how (absolutely typical) had been developed south of the border. Although my title was director of penicillin production, I had little to do with the processes of extraction and assay. My principal job was to grow the inoculum and take the all-important precautions that guaranteed sterility in the fermenters. Accordingly, it is a testimony to a technologically superior process that during the 18 months of my tenure, the bulk of penicillin produced in Canada had the Merck label.

Second European Interlude: 1945–1946

I had yearned for a return to peace and to my microbiological activities. After all, when one considers the tortuous pathway that I'd followed, some 4 years of active research at the age of nearly 30 wasn't much to show.

Awarded a Guggenheim fellowship, I set off in relief late in 1945 for Great Britain, to the laboratory of Marjorie Stephenson and the biochemistry department of Cambridge.

Marjorie Stephenson and Ernest Gale, her second in command, were well-trained biochemists. By then, it was too late to remedy what should have been a solid foundation in biochemistry, constructed on a solid foundation in chemistry. There remained an admission of defeat: enrollment in the undergraduate course of biochemistry. My ignorance of biochemistry was profound (largely because I'd profited from the enormous freedom of choice at the Marine Station and didn't acquire the basic knowledge). This soon made itself felt.

I owe one long friendship to my stay of six months at Cambridge: E. G. Pringsheim, the pioneer of algal pure cultures. Professor at the German University of Prague, he escaped 10 days before the Nazi occupation, bringing his collection with him, and took up exile with F. E. Fritsch, the distinguished algologist who then occupied a chair at the University of London. When the bombing of London started in earnest, Pringsheim was evacuated to Cambridge where he occupied one large room in the Botany School, his only technician being his wife, Olga. I reveal no secrets by stating that Cambridge has a certain reputation for stand-offishness. To be landed with an elderly and distinguished Jewish refugee who had no earlier connection with the University was a bit much to stomach. At all events, Pringsheim was totally isolated and very unhappy. He welcomed me with open arms and taught me much about algology in general and algal cultures in particular.

Looking a long way forward, I dedicated our monograph on pure cultures of unicellular cyanobacteria (1971) to Pringsheim's memory, about 6 months after his death at 88.

For the second half of the Guggenheim in 1946, I began to look for a site where one could do the style of microbiology to which I had become accustomed. I chose the Rothamsted Experimental Station in Harpenden (Herts), where H. G. Thornton headed the microbiology department. There I worked in peace, and reasonably effectively. The result was the isolation and characterization of *Cytophaga johnsonae,* a chitinolytic (though nutritionally unspecialized) nonfruiting myxobacterium (90).

Transition: Indiana University

I'd already agreed to an offer from the University of California, where I was destined to pass more than 20 years (1947–1971) of highly productive work. Nevertheless, out of prudence, I had accepted a prior offer from the University of Indiana. This was necessarily transient (1946–1947). It was marked by a deep inner personal crisis; in fact, I was so profoundly disturbed and shaken that work was impossible. Hence I prefer to pass over this unhappy, unproductive year in silence.

Berkeley: 1947–1971

Until the advent of Mike Doudoroff (appointed shortly before World War II), the bacteriology department at UCB had a staff with predominantly medical interests engaged in either medical or paramedical research. Mike was responsible for introducing a vannielian flavor to the introductory courses, skillfully adapting the experimental work of van Niel's course to much larger classes. It was at his urging, I suspect, that an invitation was extended to me in 1946 to strengthen the nonmedical aspects of the departmental program. I accepted with alacrity. The prospect of Mike as a colleague was very pleasing. Moreover, I'd been yearning for a return to the blessed Californian climate for almost five years. We were subsequently joined (1949–1961) by Ed Adelberg. Ed had had no previous courses in microbiology. However, we overlooked that, in view of his knowledge of biochemical genetics. He accepted the challenge and developed into an excellent teacher, both at the elementary and advanced levels.

Two extremely valuable additions to our research team should now be mentioned: Norberto Palleroni (Argentinian) and Germaine Cohen-Bazire (French). Both spent long periods (14 and 16 years, respectively) in our department, supported by extramural research funds. Accordingly, the professorial triumvirate (Adelberg-Doudoroff-Stanier) was backed up, with extraordinary effectiveness, by a nonteaching research staff (Palleroni and Cohen-Bazire).

When I look back at the period of 1949–1961, it is with a considerable sense of nostalgia. Ed, Mike and I formed an ideal working team, particularly after we moved to the fifth floor of the Life Sciences Building in 1950–1951. It should be recalled that the span of two decades—roughly, 1947–1967—represented the Golden Age of American extramural research grants. Our principal sources were the American Cancer Society, the National Science Foundation, the Office of Naval Research and the National Institutes of Health. Without exception, these agencies interpreted their funding mission in a remarkably broad-minded way. Here I'd like to pay tribute to the intelligent and self-effacing officials (Bill Consolazio, above all) who made our paths easy.

All three of us agreed on a policy of pooled research grants (no doubt illegal in these stricter days). A predoctoral or postdoctoral visitor would be "adopted" by anyone who happened to be in funds, and the problem of punctilious book-balancing was not enforced. Moreover, there gradually grew up between us an affection and esteem that proved absolutely vital for intellectual communication. We insisted, when the fifth floor was renovated, on a room in which we held a coffee-and-doughnuts hour and where we discussed with absolute freedom and at length our own and others' results.

As far as I'm aware, the policy of extramural fund-pooling was unique among the inhabitants of the enormous Life Sciences Building. It continued between Mike and me until my departure for France in 1971. At last report (1978) the old coffee room has been demolished, in favor of more "useful" space.

It was Mike who finally encouraged me to dip my toes in the cold waters of biochemistry. An excellent carbohydrate chemist, he freely conceded the terrible quality of his biochemical training and confessed that he emerged from it thinking that glycogen was a lipid!

Of course, an element of chance favored this close collaboration. One was propinquity: we were neatly packed into the northwest corner of the fifth floor. But a considerable spirit of generosity[1] and a respect for the rights of others were essential ingredients as well. Furthermore, there were marked complementarities. Ed revealed magnificent administrative talents, which led him to the vice-chairmanship (and subsequently to the chairmanship) of the department. Mike and I had none. Ed planned in full detail the internal architecture of our installation on the fifth floor.

When Ed received the offer of the chairmanship of microbiology at Yale in 1961, Mike and I knew instinctively that a wonderful decade was about to end. At all events, things were never quite the same again. For a variety of reasons, we failed to establish the intellectual rapport with his successors that was shared with Ed.

Genesis of The Microbial World, 1952

Ed, Mike, and I used to grouse intermittently about the very inferior quality of elementary bacteriology textbooks. Only one was intellectually respectable: A. T. Henrici's *The Biology of Bacteria.* This was much out of date, until Erling Ordal volunteered, as an act of piety to his revered late Professor, to prepare a second edition. Poor Erling! The sacrifice was great, since he had a terror of writing. There had been some discussion with W. H. Freeman about writing a book ourselves that would place general microbiology in the context of biology. Molecular biology was about to make its appearance. We were acutely aware of the low level set by any "standard" elementary bacteriology text, compared to any good text of general biology;

[1]Here a recollection intrudes. When Mike was elected to membership in the National Academy of Sciences for his great biochemical achievements (the mode of action of sucrose phosphorylase; the Entner-Doudoroff pathway), he confessed to me in the privacy of his office that the pleasure was somehow spoilt for him, because I couldn't be elected too (this was statutory: Canadian residents in the US were ineligible for regular membership in the NAS). Needless to say, I was deeply touched. At last report (1979), I've been elected a Foreign Associate.

however, the discussion was tentative, and didn't proceed to the signing of a contract. Ed Adelberg was in fact the midwife of this enterprise. One of the Prentice-Hall scouts dropped in and (as I suspect that they all do with their "contacts") asked if anyone were prepared to write a microbiology text. Ed remarked that Mike and I were the obvious candidates and arranged a meeting. We stated that we'd already been thinking of writing a book for W. H. Freeman and Company but let him tell us of the advantages of changing publishers. He persuaded us of the immense marketing and advertising power that Prentice-Hall represented; and we lightheartedly signed, all three, on the dotted line.

Abuse of Power: The Naval Biological Laboratory

In the 1920s and '30s, Berkeley was the first site of big-time experimental physics, presided over by the extremely ambitious E. O. Lawrence. Out of the cyclotron, which represented a quantitative change, it was natural that there developed the giant Manhattan Project, first directed by J. Robert Oppenheimer, one of the physics professors at UCB. By chance, Berkeley thus became the administrative center of atomic weaponry. In the immediate postwar years (with the accompanying hysteria of McCarthyism) I don't think it was recognized how seriously the university deviated from the traditional area of free thought and free inquiry. After all, the drama unfolded offstage, as it were. Financing of Livermore and Los Alamos was governmental, and rigid security measures were an obvious necessity. The university was reduced to the status neatly characterized by one observer of "a benevolent absentee landlord".

My experience with an analogous small-scale enterprise, the Naval Biological Laboratory (NBL), is worth recounting. The brainchild of Professor A. P. Krueger (who held a naval reserve commission), the NBL was discreetly camouflaged, but was in reality an agency of bacteriological warfare until 1969. When I arrived in 1947, the NBL was established on the fifth floor of the Life Sciences Building. Mike and I (soon to be joined by Ed Adelberg) shared crowded quarters on the third floor. Our protests about the nonacademic fifth floor occupants were greeted with soothing noises by Professor Krueger. The NBL would shortly move to more commodious quarters at the Oakland Naval Supply Center, leaving a very rich harvest of scientific equipment. Neither promise was fulfilled. The NBL continued to occupy fifth floor quarters until 1950–1951; and these were stripped to the bare walls before evacuation.

Moreover, I gradually became aware that loyalty to the goals of the NBL, rather than to those of the Department of Bacteriology in Berkeley, ran very deep. I've never accepted the principle of bacteriological warfare, a dirty business (albeit enormously less effective in destroying lives and sowing lethal mutations than nuclear warfare). Hence, I readily signed an unofficial manifesto organized by Martin Pollock, condemning bacteriological warfare. The specific occasion, as I recall, was the annual meeting of the Society for General Microbiology; I'd been invited to London to participate in the symposium. To be honest, I had no illusions that signing a manifesto would have the slightest effect, but preferred to make a public stand. This received a minimal amount of newspaper coverage. But on my return to Berkeley, a furious colleague attacked me on the curious grounds of "disloyalty", and strongly hinted that if I deemed bacteriological warfare hazardous for our health, I should move north of the US-Canadian border.

A critical faculty meeting occurred in 1957. The post of Director of the NBL was vacant, and Professor S. S. Elberg, who was then both chairman of the department and Acting Director of the NBL (a most improper conjunction, when I think about it), was charged with recruitment. He had unearthed a seemingly promising candidate, whom I shall call X. However, X demurred and proposed that the Directorship be sweetened with a full Professorship in the department. After discusssion, Professor Elberg thought that he had obtained prior approval for this from Clark Kerr, then Berkeley's Chancellor. His preparations thus completed, the faculty was summoned. Needless to say, neither Mike nor I had been apprised of what lay ahead. Though full professors, we were after all adjudged to be "disloyal".[2]

The meeting was decidedly stormy. Professor Elberg insisted that we vote on the qualities of the candidate for the professorial half of his appointment. To tell the truth, both Mike and I had a low opinion of the talents of X, but were reluctant to sprinkle gasoline on the flames and insisted on a prior vote over the principle of the dual appointment. The upshot was a long letter to Clark Kerr. I think it's important as a policy statement, and for that reason I've left it largely intact:

March 1, 1957
Chancellor Clark Kerr
3335 Dwinelle Hall
Berkeley Campus

Dear Chancellor Kerr:

The purpose of this memorandum is to acquaint you with our views concerning the establishment of a titular professorship in our department for the Director of the Naval

[2]This "disloyalty" with respect to Mike should be revealed. One night Mike loudly made a series of provocative remarks at the Alameda Naval Air Officers' Club, whither Krueger had invited us. The site was ill-chosen. Some overzealous officer(s) reported him to the FBI, and the inevitable hearing followed. As a result, Mike was permanently disqualified (though an American citizen) from all panels dealing with extramural funding by the US government. My "disloyalty", of course, was the *lèse majesté* of the signature publicly condemning bacteriological warfare.

Biological Laboratory. In our opinion, such an appointment raises very important problems of academic policy. We are asking our chairman, who does not agree with our views to forward this memorandum to you, with his own comments.

At a recent staff meeting, Professor Elberg informed us of the negotiations concerning the directorship of the N.B.L. which he had undertaken in his capacity as its acting director. He stated that the post could not be adequately filled until, on your initiative, it was made more attractive by the addition of a titular full professorship in the Department of Bacteriology; further, that a candidate suitable to the needs of the post had now been found and nominated. Professor Elberg therefore wished, in his capacity as departmental chairman, to inform us that the nomination had been made, and to explain to us what he considered to be the qualifications of the candidate for the professorial half of his prospective dual appointment. Since this was the first occasion on which either the position or the candidate had been discussed in a staff meeting of our department, we took the view, to which we still adhere, that we had no desire to consider the professional qualifications of the candidate until we had been given an opportunity to consider the question of policy. Professor Elberg initially took the view that the policy decision had been made administratively, and could therefore not be profitably discussed by us. There was, nonetheless, a discussion of policy, which was sufficient to reveal serious differences of opinion among the members of our department.

As you know, the N.B.L. is not administratively a part of the Department of Bacteriology of the College of Letters and Science, and the selection of a new director for this organization is therefore a matter neither of departmental nor of college concern. On the other hand, the addition of a new full professor to our department is a matter of direct and vital interest to both department and college. It is in this academic context that we wish to discuss the principles involved in the proposed dual position.

A full professorship on the Berkeley campus is rightly regarded as one of the highest positions which the academic world has to offer, and is not therefore something to be lightly given. We feel most strongly that the linking of a full professorship to the directorship of the N.B.L., an organization which has no formal connections with the academic life of the campus, is a flagrant misuse of this academic title. To put the matter bluntly, the full professorship is here being used as a recruiting device to facilitate the filling of a rather unattractive post, which also happens to be under the control of the university administration.

The appointment has a most important bearing on the development of our department. In the long run, the primary factor which determines the eminence of a department in Berkeley is the judgement exercised by its members in nominating additions to their numbers. The faculty review committee can eliminate the manifestly unfit, but has no power to initiate first-rate appointments. In our department, we are agreed that proposals for regular new appointments should reflect the collective judgement of the existing faculty. However, the present proposed appointment by its very nature does not and cannot reflect such a collective departmental judgement. The real job to be filled is the directorship of N.B.L., and factors wholly irrelevant to the professorship—security clearance, acceptability to the Office of Naval Research, ability to work harmoniously with Navy personnel—are of paramount importance in governing the choice of a candidate. If the post automatically carries professorial rank, the members of the department are placed in an impossible position. Either they have to accept as a colleague (of the highest academic rank), a man in whose selection they have not played the slightest role; or they have to oppose the professorial appointment, and thereby influence the selection of a director for the N.B.L., which is none of their business. Once appointed, the new director of the N.B.L and professor of bacteriology is free to participate in all departmental decisions. A voting member will have been added to our department who is not of our choice, who is not directly and closely concerned with our academic affairs, and who is not even necessarily a scientist of the caliber that we would have sought if we had exercised our collective judgement. This can greatly influence the future evolution of a small department such as ours.

Furthermore, the appointment establishes a precedent which, if acted on, could further directly modify the composition of our department in future years. Positions at the N.B.L. do not carry job security, and this obviously makes the recruitment and retention of a first-rate scientific staff well-nigh impossible. In the case of the director, the proposed professorial appointment removes this insecurity from one position of the N.B.L. If the new director is anxious, as he should be, to build his staff on a higher scientific level and a more permanent basis, he will be foolish if he does not press for an extension of the precedent already created in his own case. If he alleges that X can be attracted to N.B.L. only if a titular associate professorship is also granted, on what logical grounds can a refusal be based? In this fashion, the composition of our faculty could be very easily changed most drastically by the addition of titular (but voting) faculty members having the most tenuous associations with the Berkeley campus.

Lastly, we should like to examine the probable contributions of the new titular professor to campus life. The directorship of the N.B.L. is a full-time job; there is no doubt of that. If the director is himself an active scientist he will certainly wish to maintain his own research program, an activity that could be reasonably expected to occupy any part of his time not devoted to administrative work. It therefore seems most probable that the director of the N.B.L., working at some distance from the campus, will be able to come to the campus only at rare intervals. At the very maximum, he might undertake one seminar. We do not think that the department stands to gain much scholastically from this almost empty, absentee professorship. Nor is its holder likely to contribute to the welfare of the university community through committee work, since his remoteness from the campus will preclude his obtaining the familiarity with academic and campus problems that is so essential to effective committee work, and that is gained only by participation in the day-to-day life of the campus. Thus we conclude that neither their campus nor the department would derive benefits from the proposed appointment at all commensurate with the academic privilege conferred and with the academic dangers implicit in such an appointment.

We regret that we are forced to raise this issue so late in the day, and would certainly have written to you earlier had we been fully cognizant of the situation that was developing. Irrespective of the scientific qualifications of the man now proposed as the director of the N.B.L., we are convinced that the policy of a dual appointment is academically most undesirable. Since it will clearly affect the future of our department, and eventually perhaps of other departments on the campus, we should like to urge that the faculty be given an opportunity to offer its opinion on the policy before any appointment is specifically considered.

Yours sincerely,

Michael Doudoroff
Professor of Bacteriology

R. Y. Stanier
Professor of Bacteriology

Fortunately, Clark Kerr retreated on his decision, using the time-worn (and time-wasting) device of the ad hoc committee. The committee reasonably recommended a separation between the directorship of the NBL and the full professorship. X, the much-touted candidate, decided to accept the directorship after all.

The sequel is instructive. X, faced with an administrative structure of considerable complexity and of even greater red tape, proved a disastrous administrator. He was unprotected by tenure and was therefore dismissed after only one year.

One additional facet of the NBL story was publicly revealed 25 years later (*San Francisco Chronicle:* 23.12.1976). In 1950–1951, the Army was responsible for an extensive series of air-borne microbial dispersals over major American cities. The marker was then presumed to be nonpathogenic (*Serratia marcescens*). Later experiments have revealed that this particular species does have pathogenic potential, notably in patients with a very low level of natural resistance. Within a week of the air-borne dispersal, a mini-epidemic of *Serratia marcescens* infections (including one death) broke out at the old Stanford Hospital. So exceptional were *Serratia* infections at the time, that a team of medical investigators published an article about it in a journal of international standing, the *Annals of Internal Medicine* (119). What was the response of the staff of NBL, who well knew of the air dispersal experiment? To alert responsible public health officials and epidemiologists? Not at all. This was a secret of state, undisclosed until 1976.

In order not to be accused of bias, I enclose an editorial opinion (*San Francisco Chronicle:* 24.12.1976).

THE ARMY'S SECRET

MORE THAN 25 years ago the Army secretly conducted germ warfare tests at various locations throughout the country, including San Francisco. It released quantities of bacteria into the air around this city to test the dispersal of airborne microbes.

Shortly after the tests, doctors at the old Stanford Hospital here reported an epidemic of bacterial infections. One patient, Edward Nevin, patriarch of a widely known San Francisco family, died of such an infection.

A causal relation between the Army testing and Mr. Nevin's death cannot be made, since the medical records have long been destroyed, but the Nevin family is understandably upset, and willing to draw the inference that had there not been the testing, the death would not have occurred.

ONE FAMILY MEMBER, Edward Nevin III, said, "the Department of the Army completely disregarded the dignity of the individual. There is absolutely no justification in our society to act in reckless disregard of the very people it is supposed to protect".

There is a tendency to agree with the family's views, but that must be tempered by the knowledge that it is impossible at this late date to establish to a certainty that the death of Edward Nevin Sr. and the tests were directly related.

But there is no need for temperance in pointing out the Army's arrogance in conducting the tests without first notifying any non-military health officials, epidemiologists or bacteriologists that it was planning to put microbes into the air.

And the arrogance continues to this day, with an Army spokesman maintaining that the results of the tests made a quarter century ago are still classified. We can rightly wonder what else the Army has done—or may still be doing—to an unwitting civilian populace.

Biochemistry Without Tears: Sequential/Simultaneous Induction

Many aerobic bacteria and fungi can use aromatic compounds as sole sources of carbon and energy, a nutritional character that reflects the operation of specialized metabolic pathways through which these substrates are converted to aliphatic intermediary metabolites. One of the major microbial pathways for the utilization of aromatic compounds is the β-ketoadipate pathway. It provides a mechanism for the utilization of many different primary substrates (e.g. tryptophan, mandelate, vanillate, quinate, benzoate, phenanthrene, naphthalene, anthracene) and has a very wide taxonomic distribution, both among bacteria and fungi.

Thirty years ago, our ignorance of the major pathways leading to the dissimilation of aromatic substrates was profound: the metabolism of mandelate, benzoate, p-OH-benzoate, and phenol were blank points on the map. In 1947 I decided—somewhat rashly, in view of my biochemical ignorance—to tackle this problem. I should recall that techniques for the preparation of active, cell-free extracts were likewise lacking. All that biochemists could do was to isolate and characterize possible intermediates that accumulated in liquid media, supplemented with an aromatic compound. W. Charles Evans had detected two promising diphenolic substances, using cultures of "Vibrio 01"[3], later identified as *Acinetobacter calcoaceticus* by Baumann (4): catechol (accumulated from benzoate) and photocatechuate (accumulated from p-OH benzoate) (22).

Kilby (53) isolated and characterized β-ketoadipate, a six-carbon β-ketoacid that accumulated in phenol-grown cultures of "*Vibrio* 01". This proved to be a key discovery. It eventually gave its name to one of the major dissimilatory pathways leading from aromatic compounds.

At least, I'd learnt the use of warburg vessels. I soon noticed a striking effect on the kinetics of O_2 consumption by resting cells of fluorescent pseudomonads in the presence of aromatic substrates. Grown on any nonaromatic substrate, O_2 uptake by resting cells got off to a sluggish start, its rate increasing progressively with time.

Grown on any aromatic substrate, resting cells oxidized it immediately at a rapid and constant rate. I soon began to experiment systematically with

[3]"Simultaneous adaptation" was rebaptized a few years later (16) as "sequential induction". This term is not really appropriate, since analysis of patterns of induction has revealed that there is a high degree of simultaneity about it. As an example, only two inducers in the *Acinetobacter* β-ketoadipate pathway trigger the synthesis of no less than 6 enzymes.

fluorescent pseudomonads, grown on ("adapted" to) a variety of aromatic substrates, and observed a significant pattern. Mandelate-grown cells, for example, were "adapted" not only to mandelate, but to a whole chain of potential metabolic intermediates; benzoyl formate, benzaldehyde, and benzoate. Benzoate-grown cells, on the other hand, were not: they were "unadapted" to the components of the mandelate pathway. It was obvious that this would be of potential value in clarifying the specific metabolic pathways. I therefore announced the principle of "simultaneous adaptation" (89).[3] With hindsight, I was remarkably lucky in the choice of organisms and the choice of substrates.

First, fluorescent pseudomonads readily synthesize a whole battery of enzymes in resting cell suspensions (try that with *E. coli* and see how far you get!). Second, at least with aromatic substrates, there were no problems of permeability (permeability problems began to rear their ugly heads when the pathway led through the muconic acids and the lactones). Third, the β-ketoadipate pathway is long and complex; it is likewise entirely inducible, down to the point of metabolic convergence with the Krebs cycle. Last, I was fortunate in the specificity of induction, generally very high. The specific patterns of induction enabled me easily to discriminate between benzoate- and *p*-0H-benzoate-grown cultures and thus to determine that the β-ketoadipate pathway consists of two parallel, convergent branches. Dried preparations of benzoate- and *p*-OH benzoate-grown cells, although inactive on their respective substrates, oxidized the two diphenolic compounds catechol and protocatechuate stoichiometrically to β-ketoadipate (80, 107). There was an absolute dependence on the patterns of prior growth: thus, benzoate-grown dried cells oxidized exclusively catechol, and *p*-OH-benzoate-grown dried cells oxidized exclusively protocatechuate.

It is no accident that Suda, Hayaishi & Oda (112) grasped the same principle (which they termed "successive adaptation") in the course of study of the complex inductive dissimilatory pathway leading from L-tryptophan, some two years later. Strictly on the principle of successive adaptation, the following pathway was postulated:

L-tryptophan → L-kynurenine → anthranilate → catechol → ?

I first encountered Osamu Hayaishi in the fall of 1949 when he drew to our attention the valuable paper by Suda, Hayaishi & Oda. At that time, he was on the way to the University of Wisconsin, on a Rockefeller Fellowship, to work with D. E. Green.

In the meantime, Martha Tsuchida and I had been tackling independently the problem of the dissimilatory metabolism of tryptophan (108). We proposed an alternate pathway likewise based on the principle of simultaneous adaptation:

$$\begin{array}{l} \text{D-tryptophan} \rightarrow \text{D-kynurenine} \searrow \\ \qquad\qquad\qquad\qquad\qquad\qquad\qquad \text{kynurenate} \\ \text{L-tryptophan} \rightarrow \text{L-kynurenine} \nearrow \end{array}$$

We got no further for lack of appropriate intermediates. It was evident that the two pathways diverged; this was perhaps not surprising, since one was mediated by a fluorescent pseudomonad and the other by a nonpigmented "*Pseudomonas* sp." (identified 15 years later as *P. acidovorans*).

In short, I had a tryptophan problem ready made for Osamu. I arranged with the Rockefeller authorities to bring him for four months to Berkeley. I've never worked so hard before or after. We managed to publish five papers dealing with tryptophan metabolism! (100–104).

It had already become evident that active, cell-free preparations were imperative. We tried a variety of methods: acetone drying, vacuum drying over P_2O_5, autolysis of heavy cell suspensions. Fortunately, grinding with powdered alumina proved both simple and effective. It remained so until more expensive gadgets (the Raytheon sonic oscillator and the French pressure cell) replaced it.

Osamu had already described a catechol-oxidizing enzyme, "pyrocatechase" (35). After partial purification, pyrocatechase was found to catalyze oxidation of catechol with an uptake of 2 atoms of oxygen and with formation of an acid that appeared to be identical with *cis, cis*-muconate. A crude, cell-free catechol-oxidizing system of very similar properties, which likewise oxidized catechol with an uptake of 2 atoms of oxygen and produced β-ketoadipate in stoichiometric amounts, had already been prepared. I could see that Osamu was somewhat uneasy about the identification of β-ketoadipate. To me, the explanation seemed simple:

1. catechol + O_2 $\xrightarrow{(\textit{pyrocatechase})}$ muconate
2. muconate + H_2O $\xrightarrow{(\textit{unknown enzymes})}$ β-ketoadipate.

Late in our work, I was greatly surprised to discover that Osamu had conserved about 5 mg of muconate, the postulated intermediate. Since we were working with active, crude extracts that readily oxidized catechol to β-ketoadipate, I proposed popping the entire 5 mg of muconate in a cell-free extract to see whether it would really be converted to the β-ketoacid. Osamu rather weakly assented. Horrors! It didn't work! I should have recognized the elements of a culture conflict. Osamu should have replied,

"No! Not on your life!" He actually replied with a "Yes", meaning "No". For some days, there was a noticeable coolness about the laboratory as Osamu mourned his lost muconate. Fortunately, the explanation was soon forthcoming. At that time, the stereochemistry of the 3 muconates was unclear. Elvidge et al (21) discovered the third geometrical isomer of muconic acid, which had the *cis, trans* configuration. It was further shown that the all-*cis* isomer is unstable in aqueous solution and readily isomerizable to the stable *cis-trans* form. Thus, it is probable that most of the data reported for *cis, cis*-muconate were really obtained on the *cis-trans* isomer. Finally, Evans & Smith (23) examined the enzymic behavior of the 3 muconic acids: the biological specificity was high; only the *cis, cis* isomer was an intermediate in the enzymatic dissimilation of catechol to β-ketoadipate.

The conclusion was now clear: Hayaishi & Hashimoto had indeed purified the catechol-oxidizing enzyme to the step where only muconate was detectable as a product; but the *cis, cis*-muconate originally produced underwent isomerization during the course of isolation to the *cis-trans* isomer, biologically inactive.

Meanwhile, I'd characterized (in collaboration with D. L. MacDonald) β-carboxymuconate (59), a highly unstable homologue of *cis, cis*-muconate that occurs in the protocatechuate branch of the pathway.

Katagiri & Hayaishi (48) made a major contribution to the β-ketoadipate pathway: characterization of the terminal steps, likewise inducible with aromatic substrates. Activation with CoA led to β-ketoadipyl-CoA. A subsequent thiolytic cleavage produced the net reaction:

$$\beta\text{-ketoadipate} + \underset{\longrightarrow}{\text{CoASH}} \text{ succinate} + \text{acetyl-CoA.}$$

Six carbon atoms, directly derived from the aromatic nucleus, were thus made available for oxidation via the Krebs cycle.

The full biochemical details (see Figure 1) of the catechol and protocatechuate branches of the pathway were not elucidated for some 10 years. They entailed some very difficult chemistry in which hitherto unknown and chemically unstable lactones were implicated. On both the chemical and enzymological levels, these reactions owed much to my former student, L. N. Ornston (63–65), particularly with respect to the protocatechuate branch. Nick purified, isolated, and characterized the component enzymes. Furthermore, he devised highly sensitive and specific assay methods, applicable to crude cell-free extracts, that permitted assay of each component enzyme. This established the β-ketoadipate pathway as an object of choice for comparative regulatory studies (105). Analyses of this aspect were largely conducted in our laboratory at Berkeley, by José Cánovas (9, 10), Mark Wheelis (7), Michael Kemp (50), and Ben Johnson (46, 47). One interesting and significant fact emerged. Throughout the procaryotes, the β-ketoadipate pathway was metabolically identical. The patterns of regulation (nature of the inducer-substrates; specific enzymes subject to their control) were also identical, provided that two closely related organisms (e.g. *Pseudomonas aeruginosa* and *P. putida*) were compared. However, they differed in many respects when one transcended generic boundaries (e.g. *Pseudomonas, Acinetobacter, Alcaligenes*). We concluded that specific patterns of regulation that govern a common pathway appeared to represent a generic property, not a specific one (8).

Biochemistry With Tears: Mandelate Pathway

In our experiments with dried cells, we'd observed a significant oxygen uptake at the expense of racemic (DL-) mandelic acid. This corresponded to one mole per mole of mandelate furnished, theoretically sufficient to oxidize the racemate completely to benzoic acid.

Awarded a Guggenheim Fellowship for 1951–1952, I decided to visit the laboratory of I. C. Gunsalus at the University of Illinois. I'd known Gunny early in my scientific career and counted on his patience and understanding to take a long-deferred cold plunge into biochemistry. The experience lasted a total of six months. We discovered the fractionation of the mandelate complex into soluble and particulate components (33). The washed particle fraction converted L(+) mandelate to benzoyl formate, with an oxygen uptake of 1 atom/mole (99). All four remaining enzymes, namely mandelate racemase (which converted both isomers into a racemic mixture), benzoylformate carboxylase, and two benzaldehyde dehydrogenases—one linked to NAD, the other to NADP—were soluble (34). We'd detected no less than five distinct, inducible enzymes. Subsequent experiments on induction by George Hegeman, one of my students (36–38), pointed very strongly to the entire mandelate pathway enzymes as being coordinately induced. All five enzymes were induced by atrolactate, a nonmetabolizable substrate analog (34).

Experiments With Purple Nonsulfur Bacteria

THE GENESIS OF THE "CHROMATOPHORE" CONCEPT In 1950, Howard Schachman invited Arthur Pardee and myself (68, 76) to collaborate on ultracentrifugal analyses of enzymatically active, cell-free bacterial preparations. We were quite frankly on a fishing expedition: if the ultracentrifuge of Howard Schachman revealed the expected continuum of macromolecules, we could abandon it, at little or no cost in time and effort.

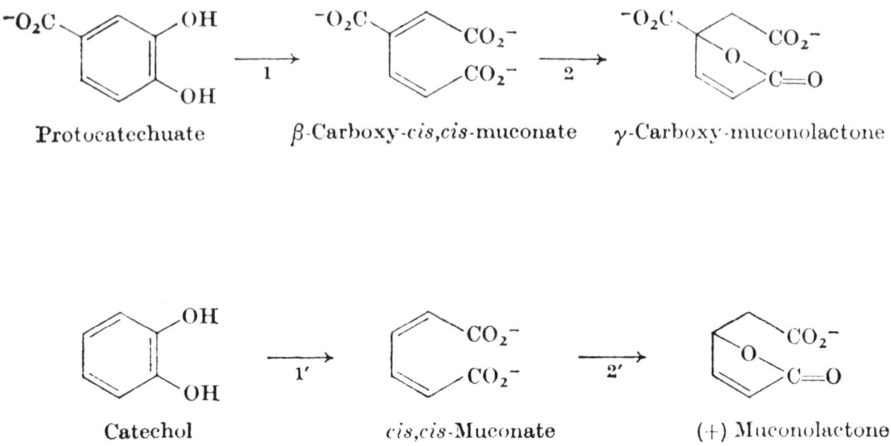

To our stupefaction, the ultracentrifuge displayed marked discontinuities, and discontinuities with very similar sedimentation patterns in all the bacteria examined. One major component was purified, and identified by Arthur Pardee as a ribonucleoprotein. It was subsequently characterized as a 45S subunit of the 70S ribosome.

A further surprise awaited us. An extract of *Rhodospirillum rubrum,* grown anaerobically in the light and therefore richly endowed with photopigments, showed a particulate structure of very great size (~ 190S) (68). It should be recalled that various lines of evidence (25, 26, 49, 58) had converged: the photopigments of the purple and green bacteria were presumed to be soluble chromoproteins. Nobody had proposed their particulate nature. Coupled with its very striking monodispersity, this led us into a major error of interpretation: the notion of a system of particles both physically isolated and internally localized, like beans in a bag—in a word, the "chromatophore" concept. We'd even computed the number of chromatophores per cell: approximately 5000. In summary, we'd grossly underestimated the comminutive effects of harsh methods of extraction (e.g. alumina grinding, sonication) on the integrity of membrane structure. I have to confess that even when Tuttle & Gest (115) demonstrated that the preparation of a lysate by a gentler, enzymatic procedure (lysozyme and polymyxin treatment) liberated very few chromatophores and thus pointed clearly to the photosynthetic membrane system as a topologically complex continuum, we didn't really believe them. Only when ultrastructural studies with partly depigmented cells (exposed to high light intensities) had revealed the peripheral nature and physical continuity of the so-called "chromatophores" (12) were we convinced.

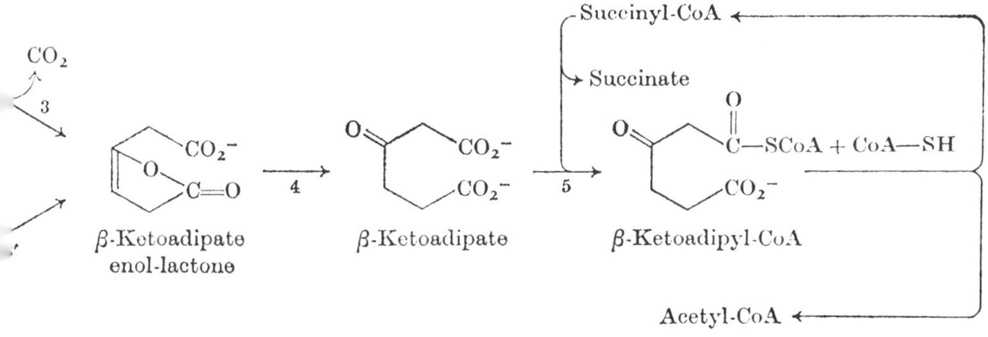

Figure 1 The parallel, convergent step-reactions of the β-ketoadipate pathway in bacteria.

There was an additional reason for our stubborn scepticism. For the first time, Frenkel (27) observed a variety of photophosphorylations, both cyclic and noncyclic, with chromatophore preparations from *R. rubrum.* This confirmed our belief that, in view of this striking photosynthetic function, the chromatophores were not simply artifacts of cell breakage.

Another aspect of the problem confronted us: the "disappearance" of chromatophores in aerobically grown depigmented cells. *R. rubrum* is a facultative photoheterotroph; cultivating it aerobically in the dark (under conditions of chemotrophy) resulted in a progressive bleaching of bacteriochlorophyll and carotenoids, to the stage where the cells appear almost totally depigmented. This is readily reversible phenotypically: placed under anaerobic conditions in the light, the totality of the cells regain pigmentation. Ultracentrifugation of cell-free extracts prepared from such depigmented cells revealed no trace of the distinctive sedimentation boundary (~190S) characteristic of photosynthetically grown cells.

At the time, the conditions responsible for such environmentally induced changes in the pigment system of purple bacteria were virtually unexplored. Van Niel (116) summed up the few facts in his comprehensive monograph on the nonsulfur purple bacteria:

> The environmental conditions may considerably influence the composition of the pigment system of purple bacteria. The most striking effects are no doubt exerted by light and oxygen. As a rule pure cultures grown aerobically in the dark produce only little pigment. The more restricted the oxygen supply in such cases, the more pronounced also is the pigmentation. The most abundant pigmentation occurs, however, in illuminated cultures, where it seems little, if at all, influenced by oxygen. In view of the fact that oxygen does not participate in the metabolism of suspensions of non-sulfur purple bacteria in the light, the relative independence of pigment production from oxygen

tension is not surprising, though admittedly conclusions drawn from experiments with non-growing bacteria need not hold true for cultures in which multiplication takes place. What has been here remarked concerning the effects of environmental conditions on pigment formation is based entirely on visual observations. No careful quantitative studies have yet been made on the pigments of the Athiorhodaceae.

In 1951–1952, I spent the end of a sabbatical year with Jacques Monod. Monod's policy was to place his promising postdoctorals in a good American laboratory. Perhaps rightly, he mistrusted the constricting effects of a purely French education. One promising postdoctoral, Germaine Cohen-Bazire was ready for expatriation. By chance, an advertisement for a Merck Fellowship (tenable in the United States) turned up in my mail. Since I knew of the situation, I passed this to Germaine, warning her that the prospects were somewhat uncertain since only one Merck fellowship was proposed for the whole of Europe. Jacques soon heard of it. He summoned me to his office, and posed the crucial question: "Are you willing to accept Germaine in your laboratory?" I was taken aback by such frankness and managed to stammer, "Yes." As it turned out, she failed to gain the Merck fellowship. The lucky contestant was Milton Salton, who also elected to work in Berkeley with me. I was thus placed in an embarrassing position, in view of the leading question of Jacques. I began to cast about for a suitable project for 1953–1954, this time financed by extramural grant funds. It should be tailor-made for Germaine, who had studied in depth the kinetics of β-galactosidase synthesis. Accordingly, it was natural, in view of my preoccupations, that I selected the regulation of pigment synthesis in nonsulfur purple bacteria. I therefore became responsible for Germaine. The extramural grant was for one year. As fate would have it, she remained a member of our research team for a full 16 years (1955–1971).

The so-called nepotism rule grossly discriminated against faculty wives with high professional qualifications. It was "Kinder, Kirche, Küche" for them; they were relegated to the kitchen, to become unpaid domestic help. Upon our marriage in 1956, the nepotism rule loomed large. Fortunately, Germaine escaped this fate. Not that the nepotism rule was relaxed; quite the contrary. Mike agreed to help us, for he detected a loophole. By volunteering to co-sponsor and co-sign Germaine's extramural research proposals, he would count me out (as an official husband, anyway). Incidentally, it says much for the spirit of confidence and generosity that reigned in the department. This "gray" arrangement persisted until 1971 when Germaine and I left Berkeley permanently, to join the Institut Pasteur. It served two most successful purposes: first, it produced a lot of good science; and second, it preserved Germaine's self-repect.

Thus, the first quantitative study on the kinetics of pigment synthesis by the nonsulfur purple bacteria was launched. The team consisted of Germaine and myself, later joined by Bill Sistrom who had just finished his thesis. The experimental material was chosen (*Rhodospirillum rubrum* and *Rhodopseudomonas sphaeroides*). They were both reasonably rapid growers and good aerobes. Some way along in our studies, we were fortunate in selecting a spontaneous mutant, the so-called green mutant of *R. sphaeroides.* It had late blocks in carotenoid synthesis and synthesized two compounds of identical absorption spectra: neurosporene and hydroxyneurosporene. Quantitative pigment extraction and measurement was at the same time both rapid and precise: methanolic extraction, followed by measurements at two wavelengths (775 nm for bacteriochlorophyll; 468 nm for the two neurosporenes). The turbidity at 680 nm (the minimum in the light-absorbing pigments) was selected as a criterion of growth.

REGULATION OF PIGMENT SYNTHESIS The photosynthetic pigment system of nonsulfur purple bacteria consists of bacteriochlorophyll and one or more carotenoid pigments. Our initial observation (14) was that although bacteriochlorophyll and carotenoids differed greatly in chemical structure (and hence, presumably, in biosynthetic origin), their synthesis appeared to be grossly coupled by any environmental factors that we cared to impose on the cell. One could say that bacteriochlorophyll synthesis was finely tuned, and carotenoid synthesis was coarsely tuned. As an illustration, imposition of aerobic conditions, irrespective of whether one at the same time imposed light or darkness, permanently and totally arrested bacteriochlorophyll synthesis, whereas it reduced by 80–90% carotenoid synthesis. Here, I shall be primarily concerned with the remarkable phenomenon of fine tuning of the regulation of bacteriochlorophyll synthesis, as indeed have been most subsequent workers.

The response of a cell suspension growing anaerobically in the light under steady-state conditions to an abrupt increase of light intensity was striking. This had no effect on the growth rate, provided that the cell suspension was exposed to a saturating light intensity. However, bacteriochlorophyll synthesis was totally arrested, without the accumulation of any obvious intermediates (e.g. porphyrins, Mg porphyrins) in the growth medium. The response of a cell suspension growing under steady-state conditions to an abrupt decrease of light intensity was equally striking. A decrease of light intensity resulted in a very marked increase in the differential rate of bacteriochlorophyll synthesis. As a result, the bacteriochlorophyll content of the cells rose to that characteristic of the lower light intensity: in effect, to each particular light intensity under anaerobic conditions there corresponded a specific, differential rate of bacteriochlorophyll synthesis.

Even in the presence of light, the introduction of air completely arrested bacteriochlorophyll synthesis. This was maintained as long as aerobic conditions persisted. Consequently, when a culture that was growing exponentially under anaerobic conditions in the light was exposed to air, a regular dilution of bacteriochlorophyll occurred. After four or five generations, the cells were photosynthetically incompetent, even if they had been illuminated continuously. When so-called "bleached" cells were exposed once more to anaerobiosis and light, they went into a profound lag (lasting often 24 hr or more). The duration of the lag was governed primarily by the degree to which the pigment system had been attenuated during the preceding period of aerobic growth. However, when cells were exposed in the dark to low oxygen tension, pigment synthesis resumed and fully photosynthetically competent cells were obtained (13).

Other environmental factors were explored: the chemical nature of the organic substrate, the concentration of bicarbonate, and the temperature. All had their specific effects on the differential rates of bacteriochlorophyll synthesis.

In brief, these quantitative observations established that purple bacteria have a very finely tuned system for the regulation of bacteriochlorophyll synthesis that responds with remarkable precision and sensitivity to any perturbation of the environment.

What was the nature of this regulation? On the purely physiological level, the answer was easy: "The effects of light on the differential rate of chlorophyll and carotenoid synthesis can be completely and simply explained (sic!) by the assumption that the regulatory factor is the level of oxidation of some component of the (electron) carrier system. When the carrier is highly reduced, pigment synthesis proceeds at a high differential rate; when the carrier is oxidized, pigment synthesis diminishes, eventually becoming zero at some critical level of oxidation of the carrier" (96).

This was written 23 years ago, accompanied by a simple diagram to explain the situation. To be frank, we were completely unaware of the extraordinary complexities of the pathway of pyrrole synthesis in *R. sphaeroides.* June Lascelles in a recent review (55) estimated that the three biosynthetic products were bacteriochlorophyll, hemes, and corrinoids (respectively, Mg, Fe, and Co branches) at approximate concentrations of 25, 0.3, and 0.07 nm/mg dry weight. None of these three pathways—enzymatically highly complex—has been mapped in detail. Lascelles (55) concluded her introduction with a characteristically wry confession of defeat. "Having made apologies, the reviewer will now attempt to fit together the few facts, hoping that the empty acres will encourage further experimenters."

A General Role for Carotenoid Pigments

EXPERIMENTS WITH THE BLUE-GREEN MUTANT (31, 79) *Rhodopseudomonas sphaeroides* appeared to be a promising candidate for obtaining pigment mutants, to judge from the spontaneous appearance of the green mutant. Accordingly, I proposed to Dr. Mary Griffiths, who had recently joined the laboratory as postdoctoral research associate, the project of isolating UV-induced pigment mutants. She succeeded beyond my expectations in isolating 50 independent mutants, largely blocked in the pathway of carotenoid synthesis (32). Our attention soon focused on the so-called blue-green phenotype, devoid of colored carotenoids, but accumulating a colorless C_{40} precursor, phytoene. Grown anaerobically in the light, the growth of the blue-green mutant was low: about half that of the wild type. We attributed this to the somewhat lower specific bacteriochlorophyll content (about 70–80% of the wild type), coupled with the accumulation of a complex mixture of water-soluble bacteriochlorophyll precursors (most of which we failed to identify). Thanks to its low photosynthetic growth rate, we were plagued by numerous reversions until, after about a year, we succeeded in isolating a relatively stable clone. Aerobically in the dark, the growth rate of the mutant was identical to that of the wild type.

To our complete surprise, however, exposure of photosynthetically grown cells of the blue-green mutant to light and air revealed a much more severe physiological derangement. Photosynthetically grown cells were rapidly killed, and bacteriochlorophyll was destroyed.

We soon determined that the death of the blue-green mutant and the destruction of its bacteriochlorophyll required the *simultaneous* presence of both light and air. If shielded from light at the same time that it was exposed to air, it behaved exactly as did the wild type. Moreover, a simple experiment with infrared filters pointed very strongly to bacteriochlorophyll as the photosensitizer (79). Bacteriochlorophyll has a clearcut infrared peak in vivo between 800 and 900 nm; it is completely separated from all other components of the pigment system. The experiment was simple, and decisive: during the initial period of anaerobic growth, the light intensities were progressively adjusted until the two cultures—one placed behind the infrared filter, the other exposed to white light—were growing photosynthetically at identical rates. Air was then introduced. Over at least 3 hr, kinetics of bacteriochlorophyll destruction were identical, and the arrest of growth (an index of photokilling) was total.

DIPHENYLAMINE AS A SPECIFIC INHIBITOR OF CAROTENOGENESIS BY RHODOSPIRILLUM RUBRUM Our studies with the blue-green mutant of *Rhodopseudomonas sphaeroides* suggested that the carotenoid pigments characteristically associated with the photosynthetic apparatus performed an essential physiological function; protection of the cell from the deleterious effects of bacteriochlorophyll-catalyzed photooxidations.[4]

A much more powerful argument could, however, be adduced. A specific depletion by diphenylamine of carotenoid pigments accompanied by a massive accumulation of weakly colored or colorless precursors (notably phytoene) could be produced without a change of genotype in the purple bacterium, *R. rubrum.* Under these conditions, cells of *R. rubrum* become almost devoid of colored carotenoids but retain a normal bacteriochlorophyll content. Exposed to light and air, such cells display the characteristic symptoms of photosensitivity (death and bacteriochlorophyll destruction). However, in *R. rubrum,* carotenoid depletion through the effect of diphenylamine is readily reversible. If carotenoid-depleted cells are suspended in buffer in the light without diphenylamine, a rapid synthesis of colored carotenoids begins immediately, at the expense of most of the accumulated, endogenous colorless precursors. The restoration of colored carotenoids is accompanied by a rapid diminution of the induced photosensitivity (15).

Neither Germaine nor I were carotenoidologists. We enlisted Tom Nakayama as our expert, and he confirmed the accumulation in massive amounts of phytoene, phytofluene, ζ-carotene, and neurosporene in *R. rubrum* prior to the removal of diphenylamine.

It was then we recognized that we had on our hands a key problem with respect to carotenoid biosynthesis. These were precisely the postulated precursors—highly saturated carotenoid hydrocarbons—proposed by the Porter-Lincoln sequence. I should recall that the pathway of carotenoid biosynthesis was subject to considerable controversy at that time. This was in no small measure due to a poor choice of biological material: the tomato plant. The leaves were green, reflecting a normal pathway of carotenogenesis; only the ripe fruits changed in color in the mutants, no doubt as a response to secondary branchpoints in the pathway of carotenogenesis. These changes were, without question, attributable to "mutations". I queried Gordon Mackinney—one of the doubters of the Porter-Lincoln se-

[4]The coupled photooxidative damage and lethality exemplified by the blue-green mutant of *R. sphaeroides* is a special case. In phytoene-containing phototrophic eucaryotes, the photooxidative damage is not necessarily lethal, being confined to the chloroplast. As a secondary consequence, this leads to albinism and not to photokilling (i.e. the so-called *ghost* mutation in tomato plants).

quence, though he had no very satisfactory hypothesis to replace it—concerning the properties of the recently discovered *ghost* in gene in tomatoes, which led to phytoene accumulation in the leaves: "Gordon, just what sort of a plant does the *ghost* gene produce?" "Funny that you should ask that, Roger. I should characterize it as a sort of witches'-broom." Then I understood. The *ghost* gene mutant plant was actually grafted on normal plants: the plant was phenotypically an albino, since chlorophyll was destroyed by photooxidation. The *ghost* gene was the *sole* mutation that reflected a lesion introduced in the primary pathway of carotenoid biosynthesis!

Through the diphenylamine experiments in *R. rubrum,* we were certain that we had a lovely system for the study of the chemistry of carotenoid biosynthesis. When we discussed our observations with Kees van Niel, he came up with the ideal solution: Synnøve Liaaen-Jensen, an expert carotenoid chemist. Recently married, young, and charming, she had been awarded a Styri fellowship and didn't know what to do with it. Her original intention had been to work with L. Zechmeister; Zeichmeister was retiring, and she'd been advised in turn to work with Kees van Niel. We explained our observations to Synnøve. She had only six months of her fellowship to share with us. She undertook the careful qualitative and quantitative analyses of the very complex interconversions of the carotenoid pigments in *R. rubrum* (44). Sometimes there were no less than 15 intermediates and final products! We had, however, one ace in the hole: after the removal of diphenylamine, the net synthesis of total carotenoids in buffered suspensions was negligible. Thus, we had simply to add up the total carotenoid balance—accumulations as well as disappearances—to arrive at a sound bookkeeping. The answer was unambiguous: the much-questioned Porter-Lincoln sequence really existed. Curiously, only phytoene (the major colorless carotenoid hydrocarbon that was accumulated in the diphenylamine grown cells of *R. rubrum*) was metabolically inert. The following scheme concorded excellently with our results:

phytofluene → zeta-carotene → neurosporene →
lycopene → P481 (a hitherto unidentified carotenoid hydrocarbon)
(introduction of O-CH_3 groups) → spirilloxanthin.

The real bottleneck was in equipment: we had a manually operated Beckman DU. Only during the last days of her stay was Synnøve able to run a few spectra on a homemade, recording DU, generously put at our disposal by Joe Nielands. The data, quantitative and qualitative, represent a triumph for the manual operation of a DU and the patient skill of Synnøve (45).

Synnøve was one of our greatest success stories—if that term isn't too presumptuous. She rapidly and successfully completed her doctoral dissertation (43) on the theme originally chosen at Berkeley, characterizing in detail the numerous metabolic intermediates that were left indeterminate after her all too brief stay in Berkeley. Indeed, she was the first woman in Norway to receive the honor of a doctorate in organic chemistry. She acceded to the Chair of Organic Chemistry at the University of Trondheim, which she today occupies with high distinction.

THE ROLE OF CAROTENOID PIGMENTS IN CONFERRING PHOTOPROTECTION ON CHEMOHETEROTROPHS (INCLUDING MAN) Carotenoid pigments have an exceptionally wide natural distribution. Their function in conferring photoprotection on all phototrophic organisms was sufficiently explained by our preceding experiments. We began to wonder about the role of carotenoid pigments in chemoheterotrophs. True, the potential candidates as photosensitive pigments (e.g. porphyrins) were present at far lower concentrations than in phototrophs. Accordingly, we proposed to Riyo Kunisawa a comparative study on a typical chemoheterotroph, *Corynebacterium poinsettiae.* This test organism was selected because its carotenoid pigment composition was well characterized (54). Riyo first isolated a colorless (phytoene-containing) mutant, which was duly exposed to light and air in comparative experiments. At first, there was no selective killing of the colorless mutant. We thought the experiment had failed, until we took into account the rather low concentrations of potential photosensitizers. We then repeated the experiment, this time in the presence of an artificial photosensitizer, toluidine blue, and with all appropriate controls. The results were decisive: the colorless mutant duly died, whereas the pigmented one survived.

A parallel experiment was conducted by Mickey Mathews and Bill Sistrom (61): a comparison of the yellow wild type of *Sarcina lutea* and a colorless, phytoene-accumulating mutant. This time, a far higher light intensity was employed (direct sunlight), and it was unnecessary to add an artificial photosensitizer. The mutant was killed, whereas the pigmented wild type survived.

Mickey Mathews-Roth had medical training. During her postdoctoral stay with us, she discussed the possibility of carotenotherapy in human patients suffering from light-sensitive metabolic diseases.

A series of experiments followed on the oral administration of carotenoid pigments in experimental animals, subject to induced photosensitization. The marked protection that ensued encouraged her to launch carotenotherapy in humans subject to erythropoietic protoporphyria (62). Such patients, treated with large quantities of β-carotene, administered orally, acquired an increased tolerance to sunlight. Thanks to the initiative of Mickey Mathews-Roth, I may claim a modest footnote in medical history for the symptomatic alleviation of some porphyriacs by carotenotherapy.

The Role of Organic Substrates in Photoheterotrophy

In 1957–1959, I was awarded a research professorship by the Miller Institute. Two whole years to devote to research, without teaching, committee work, or other distractions! Faced with so much freedom, at first I panicked. The intellectual paralysis lasted a long, painful year. I was saved from disaster by Germaine, who made an astute observation. Examining microscopically two parallel cultures of *R. sphaeroides,* both grown anaerobically in the light on acetate and on malate, she noted a remarkable difference.

The acetate-grown cells were stuffed with refractile granules, whereas the malate-grown cells were completely clear. She identified the inclusion bodies in acetate-grown cells as poly-β-hydroxybutyrate. Although later recognized to be very widely distributed as a procaryotic primary reserve material (24, 121), it has been almost completely neglected, save by a particular school of French microbiologists led by Lemoigne at the Pasteur Institute (57). That is why Germaine had no trouble in identifying it.[5]

Germaine had unlocked the key—long rusty—to the role of primary reserve materials in assimilatory processes in general, including their role in anoxygenic photosynthesis. As if to add to the confusion, there were not one but two products of primary assimilation in purple bacteria, neither of which had been chemically identified before. They were on slightly different oxidation levels: poly-β-hydroxybutyrate, more reduced and a derivative of the fatty acid pathway; and a carbohydrate, more oxidized, and designated conventionally "(CH_2O)". The specific patterns of primary assimilation were in turn strongly influenced by the chemical nature of the substrate, as Germaine had observed.

The carbohydrate reserve material, "(CH_2O)", was presumably a polysaccharide. It was soon identified as glycogen (98).

I'd like to go back some fifteen years when I was a graduate student at Pacific Grove (1939–1942). These were precisely the years where the fa-

[5]Its neglect can be partly attributed to very peculiar solubility properties. Poly-β-hydroxybutyrate represents a class of cell constituents that is particularly elusive by the standard procedures for cell fractionation. Applied to cells that contained the polymer, these procedures resulted in its seeming inclusion in the protein fraction. Only a total nitrogen determination (which was not habitual) would have revealed it as a major, nonnitrogenous component. An illustration suffices. In detailed studies on oxidative assimilation (which included tracer methods) by *Pseudomonas saccharophila,* Wiame & Doudoroff (120) completely failed to identify this major assimilatory product. Once it had been chemically identified, Doudoroff & Stanier (20) had no difficulty in determining that in *P. saccharophila* some 60–90% of the assimilated carbon was accumulated in the cell as poly-β-hydroxybutyrate.

mous so-called "unified theory" of photosynthesis was developed by Kees van Niel. Moreover, I'd assisted at the very polite, unwritten controversy between Gaffron and van Niel (indeed, almost unspoken, because Hans Gaffron had surrendered his position prematurely in 1935).[6] Meditating the new data, which had replaced the vague designation "more cell material" with precise chemical formulae, it flashed through my mind one day, during the coffee hour, that maybe Kees van Niel had been wrong and Hans Gaffron had been right about the paths of photoassimilation in nonsulfur purple bacteria. So certain was I, that I wrote a few idealized equations on the blackboard. Now all that remained was to do the tracer experiments, which were essentially confirmatory (98).

After the lapse of almost 45 years, it is difficult to determine what the Gaffron-van Niel controversy was really about. I think it was the relative importance attributable to CO_2 fixation: although a dark process, it was deemed essential for all modes of photosynthesis, oxygenic and anoxygenic. Gaffron, on the other hand, espoused a direct photoassimilation of organic substrates, a notion that became fashionable only when the motive force (photophosphorylation) was revealed.

Gaffron had discovered a highly significant reaction: the photometabolism of acetate, accompanied by a net H_2 uptake:

$$2n \text{ acetate} + n\ H_2 \xrightarrow{\text{light}} (C_4H_6O_2)_n + 2n\ H_2O.$$

As presented by Gaffron, the acetate-H_2 reaction suggests a role for the organic substrate quite different from that postulated by van Niel: a *photoreductive assimilation of acetate,* completely divorced from CO_2 fixation. Looking at the matter with hindsight, Gaffron failed to establish his postulated role for organic substrates, simply because he failed to determine the chemical role played by $(C_4H_6O_2)_n$. Had he been familiar with the papers of Lemoigne's group, the affair would have been easy. Indeed, the tracer techniques that we used would have been essentially confirmatory.

The Mechanism of Streptomycin Action

I had one chronic complaint about the Berkeley graduate students: a singular lack of initiative in proposing thesis topics. Paradoxically, when a graduate student did display his initiative in this respect, I was lukewarm. The proposer was C. R. Spotts, and the proposal had to do with the mode of action of streptomycin. I remarked to Charles Spotts that many highly

[6]Gaffron (28) has published his reminiscences of this period, which are both historically and psychologically fascinating.

competent scientists were hard after this particular grail, and that it was probably a hopeless proposition. Nevertheless, Spotts persisted. I retreated a bit, and struck a bargain: if he didn't come up with some interesting and original results within six months, I'd reserve the right to change the theme of the thesis to one of my choice.

In *Escherichia coli* there were three known alternate responses to streptomycin: sensitivity, resistance (sometimes termed "indifference"), and dependence. Furthermore, analysis had shown these to be multiple alleles of a single genetic locus. We chose dependence as by far the most interesting case: an antibiotic, magically transformed into a growth factor.

We therefore decided to characterize the withdrawal symptoms provoked by depletion of streptomycin in streptomycin dependent mutants—in accordance with Lwoff's classic studies on growth factors.

Charles was a hard worker and before the six months had elapsed, he began to produce some very interesting results. The only embarrassing thing was their diversity. I used to tremble when yet another nugget of miscellaneous information was laid on my desk. In short, I hadn't the faintest clue of an explanatory hypothesis.

In due course, Charles was awarded his doctorate—still, I blush to recall, without an explanatory hypothesis. All that his thesis contained was a long series of meticulously executed experiments on the epiphenomena associated with streptomycin deprivation.

At that time (1960–1961) I had a sabbatical leave due, which I intended to spend in Paris. Charles had a postdoctoral fellowship, which he planned to spend with Georges Cohen in the Laboratoire d'Enzymologie at Gif. The road from Paris to Gif is only an hour's drive, and I fully intended to wrest an explanatory hypothesis out of Charles Spotts and his thesis work. I still remember that we sat in the library during a long day, reviewing piece by piece the data. All of sudden, it clicked (83). The only coherent working hypothesis—albeit complex, and constructed largely on indirect evidence—was that a protein in the 70s ribosome had been genetically modified, becoming dysfunctional when streptomycin was absent in the dependent mutant.

Cellular Differentiation in the Caulobacters

The genus *Caulobacter* was created in 1935 by Henrici & Johnson (39) to accommodate a distinctive, but previously unrecognized, group of unicellular, stalked bacteria. Although Henrici & Johnson did not cultivate *Caulobacter,* one representative of the group had been isolated in 1905, and three additional strains were later obtained in pure culture. The isolation of these bacteria was in principle simple. All were strict aerobes and chemoheterotrophs, that grew on a dilute peptone-YE medium. In 1960 I suggested the

Caulobacter group to Jeanne Stove (later Poindexter) as a doctoral thesis problem. I was encouraged by Dr. Barbara Bachmann, at that time Teaching Associate in our department. She had herself been interested in caulobacters but had lacked the time to pursue their study. She generously provided the six pure cultures that she had obtained, and guided the research in the early stages.

From water samples and other sources, we enlarged the collection to some 50 strains. This was a great relief; I always felt more comfortable with large strain collections, since this enabled the investigators to pick the ideal experimental material. We selected CB2 and CB15, two strains of *Caulobacter crescentus,* which could grow reasonably rapidly in a strictly defined medium. Most of the caulobacter strains we had isolated were slow-growing, multiple auxotrophs. Strains CB2 and CB15 have been the favorite objects for numerous researches ever since.

Two different kinds of cells occur in any *Caulobacter* culture, in roughly equal proportions: stalked cells and swarmers. The swarmer bears a single polar flagellum and is microscopically indistinguishable from a small, straight, or curved, Gram-negative bacterium—a *Vibrio* or *Pseudomonas*—except for the presence of a secreted substance, occasionally observable at the base of the flagellum. This so-called "holdfast" confers on the cell nonspecific adhesion to a wide variety of solid objects.

The second type of cell (stalked cells) bears a stalk at one pole in place of a flagellum and is therefore by definition immotile. The stalk is much thinner than the body of the cell and can be barely resolved by light microscopy. Consequently, the detailed interpretation of its structure and its relation to the cell became possible only as a result of electron microscopy. The stalk is not a secreted structure, but a tubular outgrowth of the cell itself. The only secreted element is the holdfast, which occupies the distal end of the stalk. Division of a stalked cell gives rise to two unlike sister cells: a basal stalked cell and an apical swarmer. Previous accounts implied that the transition of a swarmer to a stalked cell was a consequence of its attachment. According to this interpretation, the swarmer→ stalked cell transition was a facultative event in the life cycle, essentially conditioned by environmental factors. We found that this was incorrect: stalk formation was an obligatory stage in the morphogenesis of each swarmer, whether attached or not. This crucial observation was made with ridiculous ease. The dimorphic cells in a *Caulobacter* culture could be physically separated from another by centrifugation. Swarmers formed a firm, well-packed pellet in a centrifugal field; stalked cells formed a looser, supernatant layer, apparently because the semi-rigid stalks impeded close packing. It was rather simple to synchronize *Caulobacter* cells at relatively high densities by repeated centrifugations in the cold (111). In a liquid culture subsequently inoculated with a population that consisted largely of swarmers, nearly all the members of the population developed stalks before there was any increase in viable count.

We also followed the evolution of cell populations in microcultures. When a stalked cell divided, giving rise to two dimorphic sister cells, division of the stalked cell invariably preceded that of the swarmer. However, once the swarmer had formed a stalk, division times were comparable with those of the original stalked sibling. The division time of a swarmer (110–120' under our conditions of growth) represented the time required (20–25') for the conversion of swarmer to stalk cell, added to the time of division of the stalk cell (90–95').

Despite the 50-odd strains assembled by Jeanne Poindexter, the classification of *Caulobacter* was remarkably complex. I was reluctant to approve the monograph for publication and recommended that she pursue an additional postdoctoral year, taken with Kees van Niel, where she completed and rounded out this work. Jeanne's monograph, published in 1964 (71), is now the standard reference on the *Caulobacter* group and is still a mine of information.

Another graduate student, Jean Schmidt, pursued studies primarily on the characterization of caulobacter phages. All told, she isolated 23 phages, falling into 7 highly diverse groups, with respect to host ranges, serological properties, and RNA or DNA content. The caulobacters emerged as a completely isolated group, with respect to host-phage interactions (77).

John Gerhart had made an interesting observation: stalk elongation was dependent on phosphate starvation. Whereas the stalk length in cultures with unlimited phosphate was typically 2–3 μm (approximately the length of the cell), the stalk lengthened to 18–20 μm in cultures with no added phosphate. One ecological mystery was solved: the extraordinary stalk length of enrichment cultures of caulobacters, dependent on a very feeble nutrient enrichment (0.01% peptone) of tapwater. This proved to be an effect of phosphate limitation. Jean Schmidt turned these observations to good account by her elegant radioautographic studies. She showed that synthesis of all components of the stalk (i.e. cell wall, cell membrane, and membranous inclusions) take place de novo in a sharply localized region, at or very close to the junction of the stalk with the cell (78).

Taxonomic Excursions: The Aerobic Pseudomonads

Over the course of years, we had accumulated a large and diverse collection of aerobic pseudomonads, mostly listed under the uniformative rubric:

Pseudomonas sp. Some strains synthesized the characteristic yellow-green fluorescent water-soluble pigment: these were classified as "*P. fluorescens*". Since the taxonomy of the aerobic pseudomonads had remained more or less static for at least a decade, I decided to become a taxonomist myself. This is one of the very few decisions on which I didn't consult Mike Doudoroff beforehand. Mike was initially sceptical and at first held back. However, the growing fascination of *Pseudomonas* taxonomy soon engulfed him. Only Norberto Palleroni, a taxonomist himself, was enthusiastic. This encouraged me to proceed with what would eventually prove a very long and laborious enterprise.

The essential problem with *Pseudomonas* taxonomy was simple: the diagnostic tests then in current use did not yield a sufficiently broad picture of phenotypic traits to permit a satisfactory definition of species. In reality, only one species, *P. aeruginosa,* was sufficiently well characterized (moreover, on very slender phenotypic grounds) to be recognizable.

The array of diagnostic tests largely originated from those described for coliform bacteria, a fact that explains the heavy dependence on acid production in carbohydrate broth cultures incubated under semianaerobic conditions. Hugh & Leifson (41a) had already observed that standard methods for detecting acid production in carbohydrate media were unreliable for aerobic pseudomonads, and they had modified this procedure by the simple device of greatly diminishing the peptone concentration of culture media. Many of the aerobic pseudomonads are powerful ammonifiers, so that cultures with the standard peptone concentration may become alkaline, even though the carbohydrate is extensively decomposed. However, a much more general criticism of this heavy dependence on carbohydrate utilization could be made. The aerobic pseudomonads are nutritionally versatile organisms. A good taxonomic methodology was likely to be one which probes deeply their most striking and ecologically significant group character (not shared to any appreciable degree by the coliform bacteria)—the ability to use a wide variety of organic compounds as sole carbon and energy sources for aerobic growth. The foundations of this approach were laid half a century ago by den Dooren de Jong (19) in a study of many strains, both fluorescent and nonfluorescent.

Accordingly, the methodology (essentially borrowed from den Dooren de Jong) imposed itself. Every strain was tested for its ability to use as sole source of carbon and energy 146 different organic compounds. To reduce the sheer manual labor involved, the tests were conducted by replica plating.

A few other, carefully selected tests of physiological or biochemical nature were included: denitrification, accumulation of poly-β-hydroxybutyrate, temperature relations, nitrogen sources and specific growth factor requirements,[7] cytochrome difference spectra, chemolithotrophic growth at the expense of H_2,[8] arginine metabolism (particularly tests for arginine dihydrolase), ring fission mechanisms, and mean DNA base composition (our friend Manley Mandel took care of this systematically for all our strains).

The collection of aerobic pseudomonads that we had isolated by enrichment (some 50 strains all told) soon proved much too limited for so ambitious a taxonomic enterprise. Consequently, we launched an emergency call for additional strains; the original monograph contained detailed published descriptions of about 270 cultures (106). By gradual accretion,[9] the collection was enlarged and eventually amounted to about 1000 cultures.

Out of this vast accumulation of data, we saw with delight the true taxonomic structure of the aerobic pseudomonads emerging (2, 72, 95, 106). Twenty-nine species all told, where hundreds of nomenspecies had previously obscured the view. Indeed, results were so clear-cut that we didn't need to resort to numerical taxonomy. I quote my succinct summary: "The resultant data have revealed many hitherto unrecognized characters of taxonomic significance. As a consequence, it has become possible to recognize among biotypes examined a limited number of species which can be clearly distinguished from one another by multiple, unrelated phenotypic traits".

One major technique that we hadn't mastered was the relatively new one of DNA/DNA reassociation in vitro. Consequently, Norberto familiarized himself with it in the laboratory of Brian MacCarthy at the University of Washington (66). The first results were encouraging. Those clusters that we had grouped together intuitively on phenotypic grounds (e.g. the fluorescent pseudomonads) shared common DNA/DNA reassociations and thus became grouped together on genetic grounds. However, many of the genetic relations proved too remote to pick up by the technique of DNA/DNA reassociation in vitro. Here, Norberto and Riyo Kunisawa collaborated[10]

[7]These were rare among aerobic pseudomonads. One specific case emerged: a methionine requirement was universal in *P. maltophilia*.

[8]None of the numerous strains of aerobic pseudomonads chosen at random displayed the character of chemolithotrophic growth with H_2. This led Mike to propose an interesting thesis on the so-called "Hydrogen bacteria", which he suggested to Diana Halaus. She used the same taxonomic techniques as in our work on the aerobic pseudomonads. These bacteria proved to be a distinctive and highly heterogeneous subgroup variously classified in the genera *Pseudomonas, Alcaligenes,* and *Paracoccus* (17). This entailed the abandonment of the physiological genus *Hydrogenomonas* (18), of which (perhaps fortunately) no type species had been conserved.

[9]Also included were Paul Baumann's collections of the *Moraxella* (3) and *Acinetobacter* (4) groups, which he studied by methods essentially analogous to ours.

[10]After my departure from Berkeley.

on a systematic study of rRNA/DNA reassociations (67) susceptible to detect much more remote genetic homologies. The aerobic pseudomonads are represented by no less than 5 rRNA/DNA homology groups, most of them sufficiently unrelated so that DNA/DNA reassociations are no longer adequate to reveal genetic homologies. This is, I like to think, the culmination of our most ambitious and rewarding taxonomic enterprise.

Departure From Berkeley, 1971

In 1971 after many hesitations, I decided to leave Berkeley for the Institut Pasteur in Paris. My motives were evenly balanced: political and academic. Already in 1964, Berkeley had been at the boiling point with the Free Speech Movement (a foretaste of May 1968). There followed a more or less continuous succession of minor academic disturbances, extending over four to five years, some interspersed with random violence and destruction. I mourned over the burnt-out Wheeler Auditorium with its elaborate and irreplaceable coffered ceiling. More ominously, there loomed the figure of Ronald Reagan, who threatened (having rapidly ousted the President, Clark Kerr) to tighten the screws on the University. In short, I was thoroughly disenchanted with academic life. My disenchantment with political life was no less. It can be summarized by a *New Yorker* cartoon, just prior to the election of Richard Nixon. An individual walks along, and in his thought pattern is inscribed: *President* Nixon, *President* Nixon, *President* Nixon . . ., as if to savor all the incredulity of this contingency.

Elie Wollman, at the International Congress in Mexico City, invited me to the Pasteur Institute. The new building in Molecular Biology was under construction, and Georges Cohen and I were invited to fill the space, formerly occupied by Jacques Monod and François Jacob in the old building. It was a very tempting offer. Both Germaine and I had retained our original French and Canadian citizenships, so there were no ties of allegiance to be dissolved. Moreover, the choice of a research institute, rather than a university, found considerable favor in my eyes. I posed two conditions: first, that I should confine my research activities to the cyanobacteria; and second, that I should invite Rosmarie Rippka to accompany us. Trained as a technician in Germany, she had been for some years working with our group, and had demonstrated her remarkable flair for research.

Towards a General Definition of Procaryotes: What to do About the Cyanobacteria?

One of the intellectual scandals of general microbiology was an absence of a clear definition of the bacteria. Here was a group of remarkable diversity, mimicking in development the fungi (i.e. actinomycetes), the cellular slime molds (i. e. the myxobacteria), the fission yeasts (any large, chemoheterotrophic unicellular bacterium, dividing by binary fission). The functional diversity of the bacteria was shown most strikingly by a simple enumeration of their metabolic properties: photosynthetic or nonphotosynthetic; motile by any of three different mechanisms, or permanently immotile; multiplying by transverse fission, by budding, or by the formation of conidia or gonidia. I was deeply puzzled about this. Any good general microbiologist would assign a typical *Streptomyces* without hesitation to the "bacteria". In a very early paper, published with Kees van Niel, I came to grips with this major question, albeit with seemingly inconclusive results (109). It has remained for me a nagging question, and I have returned to it repeatedly (91–94, 110) over the years.

Even at that time (1941) it seemed probable that the so-called "blue-green algae", which performed typical oxygenic photosynthesis, should be included in the assemblage of bacteria.

What to call this great bacterial assemblage, which was essentially a kingdom? I hesitated, and fixed on Haeckel's term the Monera, for want of something better. André Lwoff drew my attention to Chatton's taxonomic dichotomy, printed in a rare publication (11): "procaryotes" for bacteria and blue-green algae; "eucaryotes" for all the rest of cellular organisms whether plants, animals, or protists. I adopted these terms with enthusiasm; indeed, this has now become a part of standard terminology.

Secondly, how to define the procaryotes? This was not easy. In 1941 it seemed to me that the discriminatory properties were all negative: absence of true nuclei (the essence of the procaryotic definition); absence of sexual reproduction; absence of plastids.

I was tempted to add a fourth discriminatory character: absence of vacuoles. However, Kees dissuaded me, warning that Petter had observed structures called "gas vacuoles" in *Halobacterium* (70).

Joshua Lederberg shot down in flames my second discriminatory character, by showing sexual recombination in *E. coli.* It proved to be a "sexual reproduction" of a most remarkable type, not elucidated for some 15 years.

Parenthetically, most terms used in both eucaryotic and procaryotic contexts are deeply ambiguous, since they apply to nonhomologous elements: (gas) *vacuole, nucleus, sexual reproduction* and *flagellum* are all typical examples.

The advent of a novel technique, electron microscopy, associated with the development of satisfactory fixation procedures and techniques of thin sectioning, shed a flood of new light on the structure and function of cells, both eucaryotic and procaryotic. A distinctive attribute of the eucaryotic cell was the abundance of specialized, internal unit membrane systems: Endoplasmic reticulum, Golgi apparatus, vacuoles, nucleus, lysosomes, mitochondria, and (in phototrophic eucaryotes) the chloroplasts were all surrounded and enclosed by unit membranes. These enabled eucaryotes to develop specific functions such as phagocytosis and pinocytosis, the secretion of a variety of materials via the Golgi system, intracellular digestion, the ability to maintain cellular endosymbionts, and a marked mobility of cytoplasm, manifested (in wall-less cells) by directed streaming and ameboid movement (94).

The panoply of functional attributes characteristic of the procaryotic cell were both limited and by no means universally distributed. Among them were the "gas vacuoles", to which van Niel had objected in 1941. Nothing could reveal more strikingly the deeply ambiguous application of a single term, *vacuole,* in a procaryotic and a eucaryotic context. As electron microscopy showed, the so-called "gas vacuoles" were composed of minute gas cylinders with conical ends (gas vesicles). The gas vacuole was a compound organelle, a unit of flotation in some planktonic, aquatic procaryotes. The isolation and purification of gas vesicles showed that they consisted of pure protein(s), as contrasted with the eucaryotic vacuole, the boundaries of which are a complex lipoprotein matrix (i.e. a typical unit membrane).

After some controversy, the distinctive functional attribute of nitrogen fixation was generally recognized to be a procaryotic character. Nitrogen fixation has an unexpectedly wide distribution: the *nif* genes are encoded by a majority of cyanobacteria, both heterocystous and nonheterocystous, by purple bacteria, and by a wide diversity of chemoheterotrophs. A third additional procaryotic character (though far from universal) should be recognized: synthesis of the reserve material, poly-β-hydroxybutyrate.

These data are summarized in Table 1, in which I have included the cyanobacteria. As an inspection of the table makes clear, the cyanobacteria conform overwhelmingly to the definition of procaryotes on the basis of a large number of multiple discriminatory characters, the most significant being positive: possession of 70S ribosomes as the agents of protein synthesis and of a cell wall composed of the distinctive heteropolymer, peptidoglycan. These two characters go far to explain the nature of selective toxicity of many antibiotics, so important in chemotherapy.

Cyanobacteria display an identical antibiotic sensitivity spectrum. Experience has shown that antibiotic treatments with the aim of reducing potential bacterial contaminants are virtually useless.

The cyanobacteria perform oxygenic photosynthesis, indistinguishable in machinery and reaction mechanisms from typical "plant" photosynthesis. One-hundred and fifty years ago, they were left without much question to the botanists, apart from some shrewd and isolated pioneers, such as F.

Table 1 Some genetic and cytoplasmic differences among eucaryotes, procaryotes, and cyanobacteria

	Eucaryotes	Procaryotes	Cyanobacteria
Genetic differences			
Nucleoplasm, membrane-bounded	+	–	–
Presence of nucleolus	+	–	–
Mitosis	+	–	–
DNA localized in mitochondria (and chloroplasts, in the case of phototrophs)	+	–	–
Mechanism of genetic recombination:			
Gametic fusion	+	–	–
Formation of partial diploids by unidirectional transfer of DNA	–	+	?
Cytoplasmic differences			
Endoplasmic reticulum	+	–	–
Golgi apparatus	+	–	–
Lysosomes	+	–	–
Mitochondria	+	–	–
Chloroplasts	v[a]	–	–
Ribosomes:			
Cytoplasmic	80S	70S	70S
Organellar[b]	70S	–	–
Wall containing peptidoglycans[c]	–	+	+

[a]Confined to phototrophic eucaryotes.
[b]Confined to chloroplasts and mitochondria.
[c]Exception: the *Mollicutes*.

Cohn and E. G. Pringsheim who were familar alike with the bacteria and the cyanobacteria and who continued to emphasize their affinities with the bacteria.

This was only natural, in view of the classical definition of the term algae as encompassing all oxygenic phototrophs of simple general structure. The definition of algae had become dependent on a purely physiological property: the performance of oxygenic photosynthesis. The botanists had resolutely ignored the ever-mounting evidence that cyanobacteria were procaryotes and had to be treated as such. Here was a truly major procaryotic photosynthetic line, of very wide dispersal and diversity, virtually unexplored microbiologically. This became evident to me about 1963.

As a result, cyanobacteriology (if I may coin the term) had been gently static for 100 years. In fact cyanobacterial research was basically concerned with two elements, both descriptive: ecology (for the cyanobacteria had been revealed as major components in several ecosystems) and taxonomy.

Neither ecological nor taxonomic research with cyanobacteria could be resolved in a decisive fashion.

A familiar botanical complaint was that it was "very difficult" (if not impossible) to axenize cyanobacteria. Indeed, nobody questioned the difficulties. Their unusually low growth rates, coupled with their obligate photoautotrophy and the frequently copious slime formation, complicated the task. But in any group composed predominantly of obligate photo- or chemoautotrophs, the complaint had a familiar ring. Time, patience and, above all, microbiological skill had a part to play. I judged that to axenize the cyanobacteria was a prime consideration: only the provision of numerous pure cultures could launch cyanobacteriology in a progressive course. At this juncture, I was fortunate in encountering Mary Mennes Allen. Trained at Wisconsin, she'd acquired a deep curiosity about blue-greens. She was initially enrolled as a graduate student in the Botany Department at Berkeley. Alas! no faculty member was willing to share her enthusiasms. She came to see me in some distress. At that time, I was Chairman of the Group in Microbiology, and I accepted her for graduate work, but with two provisos. First, she would work with nothing but blue-greens; and second, she would do all she could to obtain pure cultures. Mary Allen responded with enthusiasm. She succeeded in axenizing over 20 strains. Indeed, her pure cultures constituted the start of our collection. She launched us on a series of investigations that lasted almost 20 years. In restrospect, I can heartily recommend the leisurely exploration of a hitherto neglected branch of procaryotes. It was delightful. Almost any question one might ask, whether major or minor, could be answered by: "I don't know".

There still remain many unanswered questions about the cyanobacteria. Nonetheless, I'd like to list some of the insights gained during the last 15 years from the work of our laboratory (97).

1. An explanation (at least partial) of the frequently encountered cyanobacterial character of obligate autotrophy: (*a*) absence of specific permeases directed against the limited list of sugars that support cyanobacterial growth; (*b*) absence of α-ketoglutarate dehydrogenase that makes the tricarboxylic acid cycle inoperative[11] (82). The sole means of oxidizing sugars to completion is through the oxidative pentose phosphate cycle and consequently via the two key enzymes, glucose-6-phosphate dehydrogenase and 6-phosphogluconate dehydrogenase, both of which are strictly NADP-linked. The cyanobacteria possess a distinctive attribute: oxygen-linked respiration passes through NADPH, not through NADH (69).

The absence of a specific glucose permease was first deduced on the basis of indirect evidence (69). It has now been confirmed by a detailed study (5).

[11]Shared by some obligate chemolithotrophs and methylotrophs (81).

2. Comparative chemical studies on the fatty acid composition of cyanobacteria, both filamentous and unicellular strains (51, 52).

3. Chemical studies on the phycobiliproteins (29, 30). These were started with the help and collaboration of a skilled protein chemist, Alex Glazer, during a highly profitable sabbatical visit to Berkeley during our last year at the University.

4. Analyses of the chemical composition and ultrastructure of cyanobacterial phycobilisomes (6, 114).

5. The discovery and characterization of a unique unicellular cyanobacterium, lacking thylacoids (75).

6. The occurrence and distribution of chromatic adaptation among cyanobacteria (113).

7. The study of an entire order, the Pleurocapsales (118), on the basis of pure cultures and their patterns of growth and development.

8. Revelation of a widespread distribution of the genes encoding for nitrogen fixation in nonheterocystous cyanobacteria (74). This was accomplished by a special technique of induction that ensured strict anaerobiosis.

9. Our taxonomic conclusions have been epitomized by a recent publication in the Journal of General Microbiology, running to almost 100 pages. This comprises the strain histories, properties, and generic assignments of 176 pure cultures (73) together with genome sizes and mean DNA base compositions on the same collection (40, 41).

Envoi

A quotation—from memory—out of the capacious store of aphorisms of André Lwoff:

"Au fond, la recherche scientifique, c'est une activité ludique."

The historical factors that converged to define science for me as *une activité ludique* during the last four decades (ca 1940–1980) are not, alas, likely to be repeated. The attentive reader will note that the dates of my activity coincide, more or less precisely, with the second great revolution in the history of biology: that of molecular biology.

My own *activité ludique* wasn't in this heroic domain, perhaps as a result of a certain inherent laziness, both physical and intellectual. However, I should like to emphasize that there really were microbiological treasures, simply waiting to be picked up. Let me recapitulate: the regulation of pigment synthesis by nonsulfur purple bacteria; the role of carotenoid pigments as agents of photoprotection; the life cycle of *Caulobacter;* the path of carbon in photoheterotrophy; the definition of bacteria as procaryotes; the cyanobacteria, like a sleeping beauty, just emerging from a profound coma of 150 years. All this was virgin territory. Lately, it's become somewhat trampled and overcrowded.

I should also add that two of these decades (ca 1947–1968) coincided with a time when extramural funds were at their peak.

Lastly, I'm profoundly grateful to all those—graduate students, postdoctoral fellows, and research associates—who contrived to make my path an easy one. My special thanks go to Miss Annick Sciot who patiently typed from manuscript many versions of this account.

I've had a very good journey. It's the arrival that counts now.

Literature Cited

1. Adams, G. A., Stanier, R. Y. 1945. *Can. J. Res.* 23:1–9
2. Ballard, R. W., Palleroni, N. J., Doudoroff, M., Stanier, R. Y., Mandel, M. 1970. *J. Gen. Microbiol.* 60:199–214
3. Baumann, P., Doudoroff, M., Stanier, R. Y. 1968. *J. Bacteriol.* 95:58–73
4. Baumann, P., Doudoroff, M., Stanier, R. Y. 1968. *J. Bacteriol.* 95:1520–41
5. Beauclerk, A. A. D., Smith, A. J. 1978. *Eur. J. Biochem.* 82:187–97
6. Bryant, D. A., Guglielmi, G., Tandeau de Marsac, N., Castets, A. M., Cohen-Bazire, G. 1979. *Arch. Microbiol.* 123:113–27
7. Cánovas, J. L., Johnson, B. F., Wheelis, M. L. 1968. *Eur. J. Biochem.* 3:305–11
8. Cánovas, J. L., Ornston, L. N., Stanier, R. Y. 1967. *Science* 156:1695–99
9. Cánovas, J. L., Stanier, R. Y. 1967. *Eur. J. Biochem.* 1:289–300
10. Cánovas, J. L., Wheelis, M., Stanier, R. Y. 1968. *Eur. J. Biochem.* 3:293–304
11. Chatton, E. 1937. *Titres et Travaux Scientifiques (1906–1937), Sète, 1937,* ed. E. Sottano
12. Cohen-Bazire, G., Kunisawa, R. 1960. *Proc. Natl. Acad. Sci. USA* 46:1543–53
13. Cohen-Bazire, G., Kunisawa, R. 1963. *J. Cell Biol.* 16:401–19
14. Cohen-Bazire, G., Sistrom, W. R., Stanier, R. Y. 1957. *J. Cell. Comp. Physiol.* 49:25–68
15. Cohen-Bazire, G., Stanier, R. Y. 1958. *Nature* 181:250–54
16. Cohn, M., Monod, J., Pollock, M. R., Spiegelman, S., Stanier, R. Y. 1953. *Nature* 174:513–16
17. Davis, D. H., Doudoroff, M., Stanier, R. Y., Mandel, M. 1969. *Int. J. Syst. Bacteriol.* 19:375–90
18. Davis, D. H., Stanier, R. Y., Doudoroff, M., Mandel, M. 1970. *Arch. Mikrobiol.* 70:1–13
19. den Dooren de Jong, L. E. 1926. *PhD thesis. Rotterdam: Nijgh & van Ditmar*
20. Doudoroff, M., Stanier, R. Y. 1959. *Nature* 183:1440–42
21. Elvidge, J. A., Linstead, R. P., Sims, P., Orkin, B. A. J. 1950. *Chem. Soc. Rev.* p. 2235–41
22. Evans, W. C. 1947. *Biochem. J.* 41:373–82
23. Evans, W. C., Smith, B. S. W. 1951. *Biochem. J.* 49 (Proc. Biochem. Soc., X–XI)
24. Forsyth, W. G. C., Hayward, A. C., Roberts, J. R. 1958. *Nature* 182:800
25. French, C. S. 1940. *J. Gen. Physiol.* 23:409–81
26. French, C. S. 1940. *J. Gen. Physiol.* 23:483–94
27. Frenkel, A. W. 1954. *J. Am. Chem. Soc.* 76:5568
28. Gaffron, H. 1963. In *Bacterial Photosynthesis,* ed. H. Gest, A. San Pietro, L. P. Vernon. Ohio: Antioch Press Yellow Springs. 523 pp.
29. Glazer, A. N., Cohen-Bazire, G. 1971. *Proc. Natl. Acad. Sci. USA* 68:1398–1401
30. Glazer, A. N., Cohen-Bazire, G., Stanier, R. Y. 1971. *Arch. Mikrobiol.* 80:1–18
31. Griffiths, M., Sistrom, W. R., Cohen-Bazire, G., Stanier, R. Y. 1955. *Nature.* 176:1211–15
32. Griffiths, M., Stanier, R. Y. 1956. *J. Gen. Microbiol.* 14:698–715
33. Gunsalus, I. C., Gunsalus, C. F., Stanier, R. Y. 1953. *J. Bacteriol.* 66:538–42
34. Gunsalus, C. F., Stanier, R. Y., Gunsalus, I. C. 1953. *J. Bacteriol.* 66:548–53
35. Hayaishi, O., Hashimoto, K. 1950. *Med. J. Osaka Univ.* 2:33–36
36. Hegeman, G. D. 1966. *J. Bacteriol.* 91:1140–54
37. Hegeman, G. D. 1966. *J. Bacteriol.* 91:1155–60
38. Hegeman, G. D. 1966. *J. Bacteriol.* 91:1161–67
39. Henrici, A. T., Johnson, D. E. 1935. *J. Bacteriol.* 30:61–93
40. Herdman, M., Janvier, M., Rippka, R., Stanier, R. Y. 1979. *J. Gen. Microbiol.* 111:73–88

41. Herdman, M., Janvier, M., Waterbury, J. B., Rippka, R., Stanier, R. Y., Mandel, M. 1979. *J. Gen. Microbiol.* 111:63–71
41a. Hugh, R., Leifson, E. 1953. *J. Bacteriol.* 66:24–26
42. Jensen, H. L. 1940. *Proc. Linn. Soc. NSW* 65:543–56
43. Jensen, S. L. 1962. *The constitution of some bacterial carotenoids and their bearing on biosynthetic problems.* Kgl Nor. Vidensk. Selsk. Skr., N° 8, Trondheim
44. Jensen, S. L., Cohen-Bazire, G., Nakayama, T. O. M., Stanier, R. Y. 1958. *Biochim. Biophys. Acta* 29:477–98
45. Jensen, S. L., Cohen-Bazire, G., Stanier, R. Y. 1962. *Nature* 192: 1168–72
46. Johnson, B. F., Stanier, R. Y. 1971. *J. Bacteriol.* 107:476
47. Johnson, B. F., Stanier, R. Y. 1971. *J. Bacteriol.* 107:468–75
48. Katagiri, M., Hayaishi, O. 1957. *J. Biol. Chem.* 226:439–48
49. Katz, E., Wassink, E. C. 1939. *Enzymologia* 7:97–112
50. Kemp, M. B., Hegeman, G. D. 1968. *J. Bacteriol.* 96:1488–99
51. Kenyon, C. N., Rippka, R., Stanier, R. Y. 1972. *Arch. Mikrobiol.* 83:216–36
52. Kenyon, C. N., Stanier, R. Y. 1970. *Nature* 227:1164–66
53. Kilby, B. A. 1948. *Biochem. J.* 43:5
54. Kunisawa, R., Stanier, R. Y. 1958. *Arch. Mikrobiol.* 31:146–56
55. Lascelles, J. 1978. In *The Photosynthetic Bacteria,* eds. R. K. Clayton, W. R. Sistrom. New York: Plenum. 946 pp.
56. Ledingham, G. A., Adams, G. A., Stanier, R. Y. 1945. *Can. J. Res.* 23:48–71
57. Lemoigne, M. 1927. *Ann. Inst. Pasteur Paris* 41:148–65
58. Lubimenko, V. 1921. *C. R. Acad. Sci.* 173:365–67
59. MacDonald, D. L., Stanier, R. Y., Ingraham, J. L. 1954. *J. Biol. Chem.* 210:809–20
60. MacLeod, R. A. 1965. *Bacteriol. Rev.* 29:9–23
61. Mathews, M. M., Sistrom, W. R. 1959. *Nature* 184:1892–94
62. Mathews-Roth, M. M., Pathak, M. A., Fitzpatrick, T. B., Harber, L. C., Kass, E. H. 1970. *N. Engl. J. Med.* 282:1231–34
63. Ornston, L. N. 1966. *J. Biol. Chem.* 241:3787–94
64. Ornston, L. N. 1966. *J. Biol. Chem.* 241:3795–99
65. Ornston, L. N. 1966. *J. Biol. Chem.* 241:3800–10
66. Palleroni, N. J., Ballard, R. W., Ralston, E., Doudoroff, M. 1972. *J. Bacteriol.* 110:1–11
67. Palleroni, N. J., Kunisawa, R., Contopoulou, R., Doudoroff, M. 1973. *Int. J. Syst. Bacteriol.* 23:333–39
68. Pardee, A. B., Schachman, H. K., Stanier, R. Y. 1952. *Nature* 169:282–84
69. Pelroy, R. A., Rippka, R., Stanier, R. Y. 1972. *Arch. Mikrobiol.* 87:303–22
70. Petter, H. F. M. 1931. *Proc. Natl. Acad. Sci. Amsterdam.* 34:1417–23
71. Poindexter, J. S. 1964. *Bacteriol. Rev.* 28:231–95
72. Redfearn, M. S., Palleroni, N. J., Stanier, R. Y. 1964. *J. Gen. Microbiol.* 43:293–313
73. Rippka, R., Deruelles, J., Waterbury, J. B., Herdman, M., Stanier, R. Y. 1979. *J. Gen. Microbiol.* 111:1–61
74. Rippka, R., Waterbury, J. B. 1977. *FEMS Microbiol. Lett.* 2:83–86
75. Rippka, R., Waterbury, J. B., Cohen-Bazire, G. 1974. *Arch. Microbiol.* 100:419–36
76. Schachman, H. K., Pardee, A. B., Stanier, R. Y. 1952. *Arch Biochem. Biophys.* 38:245–60
77. Schmidt, J. M., Stanier, R. Y. 1965. *J. Gen. Microbiol.* 39:95–107
78. Schmidt, J. M., Stanier, R. Y. 1966. *J. Cell Biol.* 28:423–36
79. Sistrom, W. R., Griffiths, M., Stanier, R. Y. 1956. *J. Cell. Comp. Physiol.* 48:473–516
80. Sleeper, B. P., Tsuchida, M., Stanier, R. Y. 1950. *J. Bacteriol.* 59:129–33
81. Smith, A. J., Hoare, D. 1977. *Bacteriol. Rev.* 41:419–48
82. Smith, A. J., London, J., Stanier, R. Y. 1967. *J. Bacteriol.* 94:972–83
83. Spotts, C. R., Stanier, R. Y. 1961. *Nature* 192:633–37
84. Stanier, R. Y. 1940. *J. Bacteriol.* 40:619–35
85. Stanier, R. Y. 1941. *J. Bacteriol.* 42:527–59
86. Stanier, R. Y. 1942. *J. Bacteriol.* 43:499–520
87. Stanier, R. Y. 1942. *J. Bacteriol.* 44:555–70
88. Stanier, R. Y. 1942. *Bacteriol. Rev.* 6:143–96
89. Stanier, R. Y. 1947. *J. Bacteriol.* 54:339–48
90. Stanier, R. Y. 1947. *J. Bacteriol.* 53:297–315
91. Stanier, R. Y. 1954. In *Cellular Metabolism and Infections,* ed. E. Racker, pp. 3–24. New York: Academic

92. Stanier, R. Y. 1961. *Ann. Inst. Pasteur Paris* 101:297–312
93. Stanier, R. Y. 1964. In *The Bacteria,* ed. I. C. Gunsalus, R. Y. Stanier, pp. 445–64. New York: Academic
94. Stanier, R. Y. 1970. *Symp. Soc. Gen. Microbiol.* 20:1–38
95. Stanier, R. Y. 1976. *Bull. Inst. Pasteur Paris* 74:255–70
96. Stanier, R. Y., Cohen-Bazire, G. 1957. *Symp. Soc. Gen. Microbiol.* 7:56–89
97. Stanier, R. Y., Cohen-Bazire, G. 1977. *Ann. Rev. Microbiol.* 31:225–74
98. Stanier, R. Y., Doudoroff, M., Kunisawa, R., Contopoulou, R. 1959. *Proc. Natl. Acad. Sci. USA* 43:1246–60
99. Stanier, R. Y., Gunsalus, I. C., Gunsalus, C. F. 1953. *J. Bacteriol.* 66:543–47
100. Stanier, R. Y., Hayaishi, O. 1951. *Science* 114:326–30
101. Stanier, R. Y., Hayaishi, O. 1951. *J. Bacteriol.* 62:367–75
102. Stanier, R. Y., Hayaishi, O. 1951. *J. Bacteriol.* 62:691–709
103. Stanier, R. Y., Hayaishi, O. 1952. *J. Biol. Chem.* 195:735–40
104. Stanier, R. Y., Hayaishi, O., Tsuchida, M. 1951. *J. Bacteriol.* 62:355–66
105. Stanier, R. Y., Ornston, L. N. 1973. *Adv. Microb. Physiol.* 9:89–152
106. Stanier, R. Y., Palleroni, N. J., Doudoroff, M. 1964. *J. Gen. Microbiol.* 43:159–271
107. Stanier, R. Y., Sleeper, B. P., Tsuchida, M., MacDonald, D. L. 1950. *J. Bacteriol.* 59:137–51
108. Stanier, R. Y., Tsuchida, M. 1949. *J. Bacteriol.* 58:45–60
109. Stanier, R. Y., van Niel, C. B. 1941. *J. Bacteriol.* 42:437–66
110. Stanier, R. Y., van Niel, C. B. 1962. *Arch. Mikrobiol.* 42:17–35
111. Stove, J. L., Stanier, R. Y. 1962. *Nature* 196:1189–92
112. Suda, M., Hayaishi, O., Oda, Y. 1950. *Med. J. Osaka Univ.* 2:21-31
113. Tandeau de Marsac, N. 1977. *J. Bacteriol.* 130:82–91
114. Tandeau de Marsac, N., Cohen-Bazire, G. 1977. *Proc. Natl. Acad. Sci. USA* 74:1635–39
115. Tuttle, A. L., Gest, H. 1959. *Proc. Natl. Acad. Sci. USA* 45:1261–69
116. van Niel, C. B. 1944. *Bacteriol. Rev.* 8:1–118
117. van Niel, C. B. 1967. *Ann. Rev. Microbiol.* 21:1–30
118. Waterbury, J. B., Stanier, R. Y. 1977. *Bacteriol. Rev.* 42:2–44
119. Wheat, R. P., Zuckerman, A., Rantz, L. A. 1952. *Ann. Intern. Med.* 90:79–86
120. Wiame, J. M., Doudoroff, M. 1951. *J. Bacteriol.* 62:187–93
121. Williamson, D. H., Wilkinson, J. F. 1958. *J. Gen. Microbiol.* 19:198–209
122. Winogradsky, S. 1929. *Ann. Inst. Pasteur Paris* 43:549–633

Ann. Rev. Microbiol. 1980. 34:49–68

VIRUS-LIKE PARTICLES OF YEAST

❖1769

Jeremy A. Bruenn

Division of Cell and Molecular Biology, State University of New York at Buffalo, Buffalo, New York 14260

CONTENTS

INTRODUCTION ... 49
The Killer Character ... 50
The killing reaction ... 51
Other killer systems ... 51
ScV as a model system ... 52
PHYSICAL PROPERTIES OF ScV PARTICLES ... 52
CAPSID POLYPEPTIDES ... 55
ScV RNAs ... 56
Structure ... 56
Sizes of L and M ... 57
Defective Interfering ScV dsRNAs ... 59
TRANSLATION PRODUCTS OF ScV RNAs ... 61
ScV RNA POLYMERASE ... 62
NUCLEAR GENES ... 64
ScV "Provirus" ... 65
SUMMARY ... 66

INTRODUCTION

There are now numerous examples of virus-like particles (VLPs) in fungi. These VLPs are known to contain double-stranded RNAs (dsRNAs), a limited number of capsid polypeptides, and a capsid-associated RNA polymerase activity. They are generally transmitted solely by mating (or hyphal fusion); no extracellular particles are present. Fungal VLPs have been reservedly dignified with the title "virus," specifically mycovirus (75), although they lack the criterion of infectivity normally associated with the term virus (63). Yeast VLPs are better characterized than any other fungal

0066-4227/80/1001-0049$01.00

virus particles: in fact, only in this case has a VLP dsRNA been shown directly to code for a VLP polypeptide (44). Consequently, the nomenclature followed for the fungal "viruses" is followed in this review: yeast VLPs are designated ScV, for *Saccharomyces cerevisiae* virus.

The Killer Character

The discovery of ScV began in a rather roundabout way by the discovery of the "killer" phenomenon in *S. cerevisiae.* Bevan and collaborators discovered that certain strains of yeast inhibited the growth of other strains in medium of pH somewhat lower than that normally used for yeast (8, 65). Wild-type killer strains are immune to the effects of the diffusable toxin that they produce (8, 65). Killer yeasts occur in genera other than *Saccharomyces* as well (26, 72).

Strains of *S. cerevisiae* generally fall into three categories with respect to their killer phenotype: wild-type killers, sensitives, and neutrals (9, 83). Killer strains (K^+R^+) both produce toxin and are immune to its effects. Sensitives (K^-R^-) do not produce toxin and are sensitive to its effects. Neutrals (K^-R^+) do not produce toxin but are resistant to its effects. These traits are inherited cytoplasmically: that is, a diploid formed by mating a haploid K^-R^- with a haploid K^+R^+ results in a K^+R^+ diploid that upon subsequent meiosis produces only K^+R^+ haploid segregants. The killer character can also be cured by treatments known not to cause nuclear mutations, such as simple heat treatment (97) or low concentrations of cycloheximide (31), but not by treatments known to affect mitochondrial DNA inheritance, such as ethidium bromide (31). Inheritance of the killer character, except in special circumstances (102), is independent of that of mitochondria (3) and does not influence the inheritance of mitochondrial genes (110). The genetic entity conferring the killer character is now known to be a dsRNA.

Berry & Bevan (7) first described a double-stranded RNA in yeast, later known as P1 or L, that was first (incorrectly) associated with the killer character by Vodkin & Fink (90). Bevan and collaborators demonstrated the association of killer with a second dsRNA (P2 or M) that was present only in association with L (10, 66). A third type of dsRNA (S) is present in suppressive sensitive strains: that is, K^-R^- strains which when mated to K^+R^+ strains give almost entirely K^-R^- segregants (84, 88, 91). All of these dsRNAs are now known to be separately encapsidated in virus-like particles (ScV) with the same major capsid protein (18, 37, 39, 40, 49; K. A. Bostian, J. A. Sturgeon, and D. J. Tipper, personal communication). L is about 4.5 kbp and M about 1.8 kbp (see ScV RNAs). L encodes the major capsid protein and M the toxin polypeptide (12, 44). The observed killer phenotypes (inherited cytoplasmically), their designated genotypes, and their molecular nature are enumerated in Table 1. Note that in each case, L is present if M or S is present.

The term "killer factor" is synonymous with the killer toxin produced by strains harboring the "killer character." The "killer character" is a functional M dsRNA, or viral particles containing M: ScV-M, as they will be designated in this review.

THE KILLING REACTION Killing was first shown to be mediated by a diffusable product of killer cells (8) that contained a protein moiety (22, 105). Toxin bound to cell membranes is responsible for killing (24), apparently by causing an irreversible change in the plasma membrane that results in the loss of intracellular ions and ATP (23–25, 81). The toxin is a single polypeptide of 11,000 to 12,000 daltons (determined by SDS-polyacrylamide gel electrophoresis) or of 109 amino acid residues (determined by amino acid composition), stable only in the pH range 4.2–4.6 and lacking carbohydrate (71). The toxin polypeptide is encoded by M (12). The existence of this toxin is primarily responsible for the ease with which both nuclear and cytoplasmic mutations affecting the maintenance and expression of ScV-M have been isolated, and thus for the genetic dissection of the virus and the nuclear genes involved in its replication, transcription, and translation.

OTHER KILLER SYSTEMS A somewhat less well-characterized and more complex killer system exists in the smut fungus *Ustilago maydis.* Here, wild-type killer strains have VLPs of several types, containing dsRNAs varying from about 90 bp to about 4.2 kbp (30, 54, 57, 108). Killer, neutral, sensitive, and suppressive-sensitive strains exist (55, 56, 59). The toxin is a polypeptide (36, 53) of 9–11,000 daltons (57) that appears to be encoded by

Table 1 Killer cytoplasmic genotypes

Phenotype	Genotypic designation	Molecular nature	Original description
K^+R^+ (wild-type killer)	KIL-k	Wild-type M	8, 65
K^-R^- (sensitive)	KIL-o	No M	8, 9, 65, 83
K^-R^+ (neutral)	KIL-n	Point mutation or small deletion of M	9, 83
K^-R^- suppressive sensitive	KIL-s	Large deletion of M (S)	84
K^+R^- suicide	KIL-s, k	S and M both present	91
K^-R^- diploid dependent	KIL-d	Unknown	98
K^-R^- *ski* dependent	KIL-sd	Unknown	87b

a dsRNA of about 1 kbp (57). Capsid protein(s) and possibly replicase protein(s) appear to be encoded by a dsRNA of about 4.2 kbp (56). Clearly the *Ustilago maydis* killer system is remarkably similar to ScV, even to the sizes of the toxin polypeptide and the sizes of the two dsRNAs encoding the toxin and the capsid polypeptides.

SCV AS A MODEL SYSTEM The ScV complex is useful as a model system in several respects. For instance, ScV-L is the simplest known dsRNA virus: there are no other cases of a singly segmented dsRNA virus sufficient unto itself for replication, although there are examples of multiply segmented genomes of lower net complexity. The genetic dissection of ScV-M and the nuclear genes affecting its expression and maintenance is a unique opportunity to understand the relationship between a virus and its host cell. The fungal viruses in general, and ScV in particular, offer an unexampled opportunity to explore the nature of persistent infections in organisms in which persistent infection is the rule rather than the exception. Finally, ScV exhibits the generation of defective interfering (DI) particles whose genomic structure is accessible to sequence determination. Since DI particles seem to play an important role in viral pathogenesis (45, 46), the study of DI particles in ScV may shed light on viral infections of higher organisms, including those of man.

PHYSICAL PROPERTIES OF ScV PARTICLES

The discovery of dsRNAs in yeast naturally prompted the search for virus-like particles (VLPs) in the expectation that these dsRNAs were the genome of a fungal virus similar to those already demonstrated in many fungal genera. Berry & Bevan (7) were unable to detect VLPs in thin sections of yeast or in the supernatant of cells disrupted by freeze pressing. The first report of L-containing VLPs (ScV-L) was by Buck et al (18); it was followed by the report of Herring & Bevan (39), which also reported the existence of VLPs containing M (ScV-M), separable by sucrose density gradient centrifugation from ScV-L. The known physical properties of yeast VLPs are summarized in Table. 2. ScV-L, the best characterized of the particles, has a $s_{20,w}$ of about 160, a density in CsCl of 1.41, and a A_{260}/A_{280} ratio of about 1.5. Electron microscopy of ScV-L by a number of investigators (2, 18, 39, 44) has demonstrated particles roughly 40 nm across, some of which have a crudely hexagonal outline (Figure 1) [e.g. see (94)]. Such an outline would be consistent with an icosohedral particle.

If we make certain assumptions, we can calculate the probable total molecular weight of ScV-L and predict the physical properties of ScV-M that have not been extensively documented. We assume that ScV-L and

Table 2 Physical properties of ScV particles

ScV	$s_{20,w}$	Density CsCl (g/cc)	Size (nm)	A_{260}/A_{280}	Ref.
ScV-L	160	—	33–35	1.4	18
ScV-L	150	—	39	—	39
ScV-L	—	—	35[a]	—	94
ScV-L	162	1.40	40	1.6	2
ScV-L	160	1.42	—	—	70
ScV-L	—	—	40	—	44
ScV-L	—	1.40–1.42	35–41	1.5–1.6	49, 73
ScV-empty	102	1.29	—	0.95	2
ScV-empty	101	—	—	0.75	18
ScV-empty	110	1.32	—	—	70
ScV-M	—	1.36–1.38	—	1.2	49, 73
ScV-M	—	—	39	—	39
ScV-S	—	1.36–1.38	—	1.3	49, 73

[a] From the calibrated photograph in Figure 6, rather than from the text, which assigns a value of about 50 nm (94).

ScV-M have the same major capside polypeptide, ScV-P1, which constitutes 98% or more of the particle protein (see discussion of VLP polypeptides) and only one molecule of either S or M per particle. We further assume that the density of L or M in CsCl is 1.9 g/cc (82). If

n = number of monomers of ScV-P1 in ScV-L or ScV-M
M_M = molecular weight of M = 1.2×10^6 g/m (see VLP RNAs)
M_L = molecular weight of L = 3.1×10^6 g/m (see VLP RNAs)
S_v = CsCl density of VLP
S_n = CsCl density of RNA = 1.9 g/cc
S_p = CsCl density of VLP protein (empty capsid) = 1.31
M_{P1} = molecular weight of ScV-P1 = 88,000 g/m (see capsid polypeptides),

then the weight fraction of RNA in ScV-L is (64)

$$F_L = \frac{S_n}{S_v} \frac{S_v - S_p}{S_n - S_p} = 0.228$$

and the number of ScV-P1 polypeptides in ScV-L is

$$n_L = \frac{\frac{M_L}{F_L} - M_L}{M_{P1}}, \text{ or } \quad n_L = 119.$$

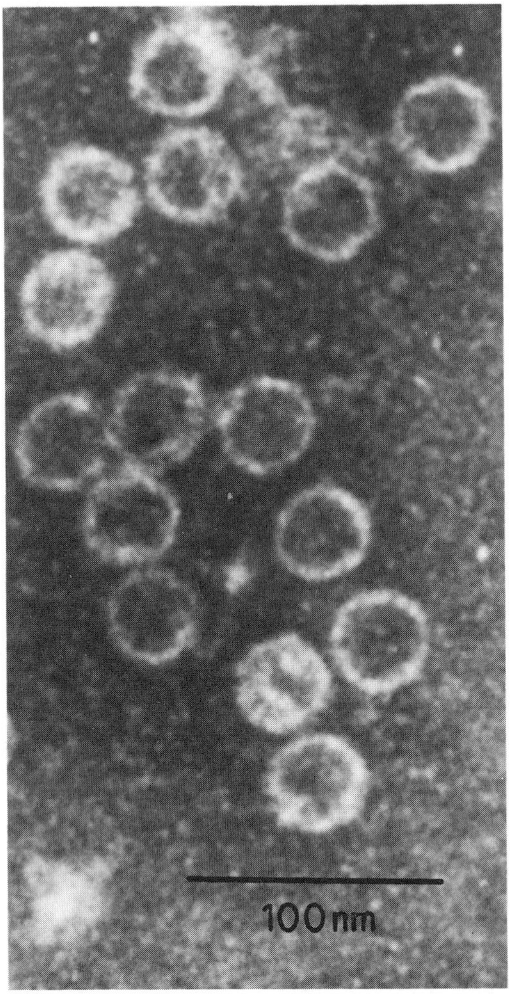

Figure 1 ScV-L particles isolated by CsCl density gradient centrifugation (D. F. Pietras and J. A. Bruenn, unpublished observations).

The estimated number of ScV-P1 polypeptides in ScV-L is thus about 120 per particle. If we assume that ScV-M is composed of the same number of ScV-P1 polypeptides (see capsid polypeptides), we can calculate the expected density of ScV-M, which turns out to be 1.35–1.36. Values of 1.36–1.38 for ScV-M (49, 73) are in agreement with this theoretical value. Particle sizes calculated in this way are 13.6×10^6 daltons for ScV-L and 11.7×10^6 daltons for ScV-M, which would make them barely separable by sucrose gradient centrifugation, as observed (39). ScV-L would be 22.8%

RNA and ScV-M 10.3% RNA. VLPs containing the smaller S, or suppresive dsRNAs present in some strains (see VLP RNAs section) have CsCl densities similar to those of ScV-M (49, 73). The number of estimated molecules of ScV-P1 in the ScV particle is consistent with the assumption that it is a simple icosohedron composed of 60 structural units, each made of 2 molecules of ScV-P1. This type of structure has been proposed for a *Penicillium stoloniferum* virus (19).

Clearly, ScV is similar to the component viruses of other fungi, which, typically, are dsRNA viruses of $s_{20,w}$ of 140–170, CsCl densities of 1.3 to 1.45, sizes of 30–40 nm, molecular weights in the range of 13 X 10^6, dsRNA components of 0.06 X 10^6 to 3 X 10^6 daltons separately encapsidated, and RNA contents of 10–15% (see 60, 61, 75, 107).

If we assume, as is probably the case (70), that both L and M are always encapsidated, then we can calculate the minimum number of ScV particles per cell. As a fraction of total yeast RNA, L and M constitute 1–5 X 10^{-3} of RNA in most strains (12, 44, 91, 101). One strain has about 10 times as much dsRNA (3 X 10^{-2}) (70). If we assume, as did Wickner (99), 50 μg/10^8 cells total RNA (11), we arrive at 100 to 3000 molecules of dsRNA per cell, of which some 90% are L (91, 101). This puts a lower limit on the number of ScV particles per cell. In at least one strain of yeast, there may be as many as 30,000 ScV particles per cell, as judged by electron microscopy of thin sections (94). This last study also clearly locates the ScV particles in the cytoplasm, outside cytoplasmic organelles.

The ScV particles have been shown to be immunologically unrelated to viruses from *Penicillium stoloniferum, Aspergillus foetidus,* and *Aspergillus niger* (18).

CAPSID POLYPEPTIDES

There appears to be only one major capsid polypeptide in ScV particles (40, 44, 70). Oliver et al (70) found that the major capsid polypeptide (about 90% of the total protein) migrated somewhat slower than bovin serum albumin (67,000 mol wt) on SDS-polyacrylamide gels and estimated its molecular weight at 75,000. There were no polypeptide markers of molecular weights greater than that of bovine serum albumin on their SDS-polyacrylamide gel, and there were only three markers *in toto,* so this estimate can not be considered entirely reliable. Oliver et al (70) also found two minor capsid polypeptides of estimated molecular weights 53,000 and 37,000. None of these polypeptides was glycosylated.

Hopper et al (44) found only one major capsid polypeptide in ScV-L particles: a polypeptide which migrated slightly faster than phosphorylase

A (92,000) on 7.5 or 10% SDS-polyacrylamide gels. They have assigned a molecular weight of 88,000 to this protein, designated ScV-P1. The amino acid composition of this polypeptide has been determined. Hopper et al (44) and Bostian et al (12) have found only this polypeptide in ScV-L; although there are always minor components present in the ScV-L fractions of sucrose gradients, these vary from preparation to preparation. The size of ScV-P1 has been confirmed in two other laboratories (G. R. Fink, personal communication; J. Bruenn, unpublished). Current estimates are that ScV-P1 constitutes at least 98% of the protein in ScV-L (K. A. Bostian, personal communication).

ScV-P1 is also the major capsid polypeptide in ScV-M particles; SDS-polyacrylamide gel electrophoresis of ScV-M and ScV-L proteins or ScV-L protein alone reveals only ScV-P1 (40). Sucrose gradient separation of ScV-L and ScV-M, SDS-polyacrylamide gel electrophoresis of ScV-M polypeptides, and tryptic peptide analysis of the resulting major band confirms that the major polypeptide in ScV-M is also ScV-P1 (K. A. Bostian, J. A. Sturgeon, and D. J. Tipper, personal communication). ScV-M and ScV-L also have immunological cross-reactivity (37). There may, nevertheless, be differences between ScV-M and ScV-L capsid polypeptides, because the particles have not been sufficiently purified to detect minor components. There is reason to suspect such differences from what is already known of the replication of L and M (see section on nuclear genes), so resolution of this question is desirable.

Penicillium chrysogenum virus (PcV) also has one sizable major capsid polypeptide (125,000 mol wt) (109), although the other fungal viruses so far characterized have a more complex capsid structure (see 75). All the physical properties of PcV are very similar to those of ScV: PcV has dsRNAs of about 2×10^6 mol wt (17, 68, 106), a sedimentation coefficient of 150S, a density in CsCl of 1.35 g/cc (13), and a size of about 35–40 nm (13).

ScV RNAs

Structure

Like the fungal viruses, yeast VLPs contain double-stranded RNAs. That they are completely double-stranded has been established by resistance to pancreatic RNase at high salt concentrations (7, 10, 90), pink staining with toluidine blue (7), the sharpness of the melting profile of L ($T_m = 99.3$°C in $1 \times$ SSC buffer) (10), induction of interferon in mouse cells (7, 10), cellulose chromatography (10, 32, 90), denaturing gel electrophoresis (10, 16, 33, 43), 5' end analysis (15), electron microscopy (16, 33, 43, 86), RNAse III sensitivity (90, 91) and base composition (16). There might be small single-stranded regions at the 3' or 5' ends, but the extensive single-stranded regions suggested originally by Vodkin et al (91) are clearly ruled out by this accumulation of data.

Recent determinations of the base compositions of some ScV dsRNAs are consistent with complete double-strandedness (16). T_1 fingerprint analysis (16) and pancreatic RNAse fingerprint analysis (Bruenn, unpublished) have also demonstrated the absence of any poly (A) tract longer than 10 nucleotides in any of these RNAs. Shalitin & Fischer (77) have reported the specific binding of 50% of L and M to poly (U) Sepharose in the presence of 0.5% sarkosyl. This result would be consistent with short stretches of Poly (A) (less than 30 nucleotides in length) accessible to the poly (U) (77).

Electron microscopy under partially denaturing conditions demonstrates an A-U rich sequence of about 0.2 kbp in length located approximately in the center of M (33). T_1 fingerprint analysis fails to demonstrate any sequence homology between L and M (16), although their ultimate 5' terminal nucleotides are identical and they have some 3' end homology (see below).

The 5' ends of both L and M are pppGp (15), in contrast to the blocked 5' ends characteristic of reovirus (28, 67), ssRNA plant virus RNA (111), higher eucaryotic mRNAs (1), or yeast mRNA (85). No 5' ends have been determined for any of the fungal virus dsRNAs, although Szekely & Loviny (87) have shown that some of these dsRNAs are not susceptible to 5' end labelling with polynucleotide kinase. The 3' ends of L, M, and five S dsRNAs have been sequenced (16a). The 3' ends of each dsRNA are heterogeneous and consist of two different groups of sequences, each group being a family of related sequences. M and S dsRNAs have the same two families of 3' termini; L has a different set of 3' termini, one of which has partial homology to one 3' terminus of M.

Sizes of L and M

Size estimates of the ScV dsRNAs have been made by native gel electrophoresis in agarose or polyacrylamide (2, 10, 16, 91, 101), by denaturing gel electrophoresis in the methyl-mercury agarose system of Bailey & Davidson (6; 16, 33, 43) or in formamide-polyacrylamide (10), by sucrose gradient centrifugation (10), by band spreading in equilibrium cesium sulfate gradient centrifugation (43), by electron microscopy (16, 33, 43, 86) and by 5' end determination (16) (Table 3). Each of these methods has disadvantages that lead to some uncertainty in the sizes of L and M.

Size determination by native gel electrophoresis in the presence of marker dsRNAs can only be as accurate as the knowledge of the sizes of the marker dsRNAs. Of those dsRNAs used for sizing of L and M (*Aspergillus foetidus* virus dsRNAs, bacteriophage ϕ6 dsRNAs, *Penicillium chrysogenum* virus dsRNAs, and reovirus dsRNAs), only the reovirus dsRNAs have been sized by a physical method independent of comparison to other RNAs (78). For

Table 3 Sizes of ScV RNAs[a]

Native gel electro-phoresis	Denaturing gel electro-phoresis	Sucrose gradient centrifugation	Equilibrium density gradient centrifugation	Electron microscopy	5′ end deter-mination	Ref.
Size estimates of L (kbp)						
3.6	4.4–5.2	3.8–4.5	—	—	—	10[b]
4.8	—	—	—	—	—	41[b]
4.4	—	—	—	—	—	100[c]
3.6	—	—	—	—	—	91[d]
3.7	—	—	—	—	—	2[e]
—	—	—	—	4.3	—	86[f]
—	4.5–5.2	—	4.9–5.2	4.4	—	43[g]
4.1	4.3	—	—	4.3	4.5–4.8	16[h]
Size estimates of M (kbp)						
2.0	—	1.5–2.0	—	—	—	10[b]
2.5	—	—	—	—	—	100[c]
2.0	—	—	—	—	—	91[d]
1.9	—	—	—	—	—	2[e]
—	—	—	—	1.8	—	86[f]
—	1.7	—	—	1.9	—	33[i]
1.9	1.8	—	—	1.8	1.7	16[h]

[a] Sizes in base pairs are calculated from gel electrophoresis and centrifugation molecular weights (given in the references) using the base compositions of L and M (16); for the sodium salts of L and M, values given are 687.0 g/mol/bp and 687.6 g/mol/bp respectively. Sizes from electron microscope measurements are all normalized from the given (or calculated) values in microns to base pairs, using a value of 3.0×10^{-10} m/bp (58).

[b] dsRNA markers were from *Aspergillus foetidus* virus; ssRNA marker was yeast rRNA.

[c] dsRNA markers from bacteriophage $\phi 6$.

[d] dsRNA markers from reovirus.

[e] dsRNA markers from *Penicillium chrysogenum* virus.

[f] Calibration against a grating replica (no internal standards).

[g] ssRNA markers for gel electrophoresis were HeLa cell rRNAs. Internal standard for electron microscopy was G4 RF DNA.

[h] dsRNA markers were from reovirus; ssRNA markers were yeast rRNAs. Internal standard for electron microscopy was SV40-relaxed circular DNA.

[i] Internal standard for electron microscopy was PSC101 DNA. ssRNA markers for gel electrophoresis were yeast rRNAs.

example, bacteriophage $\phi 6$ dsRNAs have been sized by denaturing gel electrophoresis with bromegrass mosaic virus RNAs and by electron microscopy (see below) (76). *Aspergillus foetidus* virus (AfV) dsRNAs have been sized by comparison with reovirus dsRNAs (21), and the sizes of AfV dsRNAs have recently been revised upward by 33% (41). Accurate size determination can only be based on comparison to standards with very accurately known sizes, preferably to RNAs of known sequence. This is practical if comparison is made to single-stranded RNAs of known length, e.g. the yeast rRNAs. Such a comparison has been made for L and M by denaturing gel electrophoresis (10, 16, 33). These results give consistently higher values for the size of L and consistently lower values for the size of M than comparison of the native dsRNAs to reovirus RNAs, for example (16, 91). Sucrose gradient centrifugation is intrinsically less accurate than gel electrophoresis and suffers the same deficiency in its dependence on marker RNAs. Electron microscopy by a number of investigators has given very consistent results (16, 33, 43, 86), with generally accepted values of 1.31 μm for the length of L and 0.55 μm for the length of M. Unfortunately, conversion to base pairs requires knowledge of the unit spacing of the RNA double-helix, which has been variously estimated from 2.73 Å/bp (5) to 3.17 Å/bp (34). These uncertainties translate to uncertainties of at least 15% in the number of base pairs in L and M. One group has attempted to eliminate this uncertainty by calibrating the electron microscopy with the size of M determined by denaturing gel electrophoresis (33), which only makes the result of the electron microscopy dependent on the accuracy of the gel electrophoresis. Another group has attempted to calibrate the electron microscopy of L by sizing of L with equilibrium density gradient centrifugation (43). This last method is one of the two physical methods entirely independent of comparison with other ds-or ssRNAs that have been applied to sizing of the yeast VLP dsRNAs. The size of L determined by this method is considerably higher than that determined by denaturing gel electrophoresis against markers of known length (16) or by electron microscopy, using the most popular value for the RNA double helix nucleotide spacing [3 Å (58)]. It would be instructive to see the equilibrium sedimentation method applied to size determination of a double-stranded RNA whose size has been determined by some independent physical means (e.g. a reovirus RNA). Finally, the sizes of L and M have been determined from 5' end analysis, a method which measures the amount of radioactivity in the 5' ends (pppGp) as a proportion of the total radioactivity in a given sample of RNA and divides the result into the number (8) of phosphates in ends per molecule (16). This procedure suffers from inaccuracies on the high side due to poor recovery of 5' ends and on the low side due to poor scintillation counting efficiencies of the larger spots on the electrophoregram containing most of the radioactivity (the end products of complete hydrolysis—Ap, Gp, Cp, and Up). The 5' end determinations have given results on the high end of the spectrum of values for L and on the low end of the spectrum of values for M. In the absence of actual sequence determination or electron microscopy of other double-stranded RNAs of known sequence, the sizes of L and M can only be estimated. The present data, placing more weight on the methyl-mercury agarose gel sizing, the electron microscopy, and the 5' end determinations, indicate about 4.3–4.8 kbp for L and 1.7–1.9 kbp for M.

Defective Interfering ScV dsRNAs

Suppressive sensitive strains of yeast were originally isolated by Somers (84). These strains are similar to simple sensitive strains in that killer functions have been lost: that is, they possess neither killer toxin nor resistance to killer toxin. These changes are not in the nuclear genome, but in the cytoplasmic killer determinant (84). However, in contrast to strains lacking killer functions (KIL-o), suppressive strains behave like suppressive cytoplasmic petites in crosses: suppressive x wild-type killer gives primarily sensitive segregants, as well as toxin-sensitive diploids (84). In current terminology suppressive strains are (KIL-s) (104).

Vodkin et al (91) and Tzen et al (88) demonstrated the presence of new dsRNAs (S) in suppressive strains. Smaller than M, these dsRNAs apparently replaced M, since the suppressive strains uniformly lacked M. All suppressive strains continued to have L. The original parent strain of all the suppressive strains used by Vodkin and collaborators was T132B, a strain with L, M, and an S dsRNA of 0.25×10^6 daltons (91). This strain appeared to both produce toxin and to be susceptible to it. Since T132B frequently segregated (KIL-s) cells and rarely segregated (KIL-k) cells, it was probably the existence of the former that gave T132B its "suicide" phenotype. Suppressive dsRNAs are also encapsidated in ScV particles (37, 49) which are designated ScV-S (see section on physical properties of VLPs).

Since ScV-S appears to replace ScV-M whenever the two are present in the same cytoplasm, ScV-S particles appear to be analogous to the defective interfering (DI) particles of animal viruses (45, 46). This hypothesis presumes that S and M are replicated by the same proteins and that they are therefore under the same genetic control and possess similar replicase recognition sites. There is now considerable structural evidence and some genetic evidence in favor of this hypothesis.

Several S dsRNAs have been extensively analyzed by two groups. All appear to be entirely double stranded by the criteria of electron microscopy, methyl-mercury agarose denaturing gel electrophoresis, and base composition (16, 33, 86). They consist of two size classes: S3, S14, and S733 of 0.7–0.8 kbp (16, 33, 49, 86) and S1, S4, S2, and S17 of 1.3–1.5 kbp (16, 16a, 33, 49, 86).

All of these S dsRNAs are derived from M, as demonstrated by T_1 fingerprint analysis for S1, S3, S14, and S733 (16, 49), by electron microscope heteroduplex analysis for S1, S3, and S4 (33), and by 3' end sequence analysis for S1, S2, S14, S17, and S733 (16a). S1 is a tandem duplication of S3 (16,33) and S4 may be derived from S1 by a small internal deletion (about 50 bp). Fried & Fink estimated that 0.50 kbp of S3 are derived from one end of M and 0.22 kbp from the other (33). The process which results in the duplication of S3 occurs constantly in strains which contain ScV-S3, since such strains always have S1 (16). The 3' termini of S1, S3, S733, S14, and M are identical for at least the first 23 nucleotides at one end (16, 16a) and at least the first 34 nucleotides at the other (16a, 49); therefore the sequence homology at the ends detected by heteroduplex mapping extends to the ultimate 3' nucleosides. S1, S3, and S733, numerous generations after the original isolation of the suppressive parents, have diverged somewhat from their original sequences, since they possess new T_1 oligonucleotides not present in M (16, 49). This generation of new sequence variants after prolonged replication is similar to the evolution of sequence variants in vesicular stomatitis virus persistent infections (42).

The structure of S dsRNAs—that is, their derivation from the ends of their parental dsRNA by internal deletion—is similar to the evolution of some animal virus DI viral RNAs. These are due to internal deletions of the parental RNA (35, 52, 69), deletions of the 3' end of the parental RNA (47, 62), or deletions of the 5' end of the parental RNA (50, 51).

Several collections of suppressive mutants have been made, and in each case, the suppressive sensitive strains have at least one S dsRNA (as judged by gel electrophoresis) smaller than M (88, 93; Wickner, personal communication). Vodkin, for instance, characterized some 14 suppressive strains and found S dsRNAs ranging from about 540 bp to 1.46 kbp (93). Three of these, S2, S14, and S17, are among those characterized in detail (see above).

There are numerous nuclear mutations that affect the replication of M but have no effect on the replication of L (104) (see section on nuclear genes). The effect of only one of these on the replication of S dsRNAs has been determined (84). The recessive allele of this nuclear gene (m) when present in haploid cells prevents the replication of either M or S, but is harmless toward L. The similar genetic control of M and S is as expected if the explanation of the suppressive phenotype is the competition of ScV-S and ScV-M for cellular replication factors (16, 49).

TRANSLATION PRODUCTS OF ScV RNAs

Although yeast strains having neither ScV-L nor ScV-M and strains having only ScV-L exist, there are no strains with ScV-M or ScV-S that simultaneously lack ScV-L. This conspicuous association of ScV-M and ScV-S particles with ScV-L particles and the presence of the same major capsid protein in ScV-M and ScV-L naturally generated the supposition that L encoded the major capsid protein of ScV. Hopper et al (44) have directly demonstrated the verity of this proposition by in vitro translation of denatured L dsRNA. A product is made in the wheat-germ translation system that precipitates with anti ScV γ-globulin, coelectrophoreses with authentic ScV-P1 in SDS-polyacrylamide gels, and has tryptic peptides labelled with ^{35}S-methionine of the same chromatographic characteristics as those of ScV-P1. Some larger polypeptides precipitated with anti-ScV γ-globulin are also made. These may be read-through polypeptides or pre-processing intermediates. Some smaller polypeptides precipitating with anti-ScV may be premature termination fragments of ScV-P1 (44). No in vitro translation product of L is currently a likely candidate for a capsid-associated replicase or transcriptase activity (44), although such might be expected (see section on nuclear genes and ScV RNA polymerase).

Since the presence of M is a necessary (though not sufficient) condition for the expression of the killer phenotype (10, 66, 88, 91), M might be expected to code for the killer toxin and for proteins involved in toxin immunity. The purification of the killer toxin (ScV-P4) (71) has made possible a direct test of this hypothesis. Bostian et al have made anti-ScV-P4 serum for the immunoprecipitation of in vitro polypeptides made in response to added denatured M (12). Denatured M efficiently directs the synthesis of a polypeptide of 32,000 daltons which is precipitated by anti-ScV-P4 γ-globulin and contains all but one of the seven tryptic peptides of ScV-P4 (12,000 mol wt). The in vitro product also contains four tryptic peptides not found in ScV-P4. None of the M in vitro translation products are immunoprecipitated with anti-ScV γ-globulin. A minor M in vitro product of 30,000 daltons is not immunoprecipitated with anti-ScV-P4 γ-globulin. M from (KIL-n) strains also directs the synthesis of a 32,000 dalton protein cross-reacting with ScV-P4. Consequently, neutral strains probably have point mutations (or small deletions) of M. Denatured S dsRNAs (S1, S3, and S4: see ScV RNAs section) program the synthesis of an 8,000 dalton protein without apparent immunological cross-reactivity to ScV-P4. In sum, M encodes the toxin polypeptide, which is probably the result of posttranslational processing of a 32,000 dalton precursor. This processing may be similar to that of mammalian secretory protein precursors (79) or to that of viral precursor polypeptides subsequently cleaved to a number of viral polypeptides, each with a distinct role in infection (89). According to either model, the M toxin prepolypeptide might include an immunity protein, a replicase, or a transcriptase, in addition to the toxin polypeptide.

ScV RNA POLYMERASE

SCV-L and ScV-M particles possess a single-stranded RNA polymerase activity (41, 95). This activity is insensitive to DNase, α-amanitin, and actinomycin D, but sensitive to ethidium bromide and pyrophosphate (95). It requires all four ribonucleoside triphosphates and magnesium ion (95). The major product of the reaction in ScV-L particles is a single-stranded RNA of approximately the molecular weight of a denatured strand of L (41, 95), which appears to be entirely complementary to only one of the two strands of L (14, 38, 41). Some 4% of the incorporated radioactivity produced by ScV-L particles appeared to be double-stranded L, by criteria of cellulose chromatography and native gel electrophoresis (41). This RNA might consist of short nascent strands of ssRNA still held to the template dsRNA by the polymerase complex, despite phenol extraction. If so, methyl-mercury denaturing gels of the complex would result in small radioactive ssRNAs, rather than the full-sized transcripts expected of a true dsRNA in vitro product. No such experiment has yet been published.

The ScV RNA polymerase activity is not dependent on S-adenosyl methionine (SAM), nor is it stimulated by SAM (M. J. Leibowitz, personal communication; V. Brennan, L. Bobek, and J. Bruenn, unpublished). The product of the in vitro reaction is uncapped (Bobek and Brennan, unpublished). *Penicillium stoloniferum* virus S RNA polymerase is also SAM independent (20).

Particle-associated RNA polymerases have now been described for a number of fungal viruses (4, 27, 68, 74). Buck (20) has proposed a model for the replication of fungal virus dsRNAs. The viral polymerase would initiate synthesis at either 3' end, synthesizing a ssRNA that would remain in the particle. The polymerase would then switch template strands and synthesize the complementary ssRNA, creating a viral particle with two complete dsRNAs. Cellular proteases would release the dsRNAs with polymerase attached; the polymerase would then transcribe the message strand for translation and the free double-stranded RNAs would finally be encapsidated. Present experimental evidence is consistent with this hypothesis, but not conclusive. One critical element of the hypothesis is that single-stranded products of transcription remain encapsidated in the particles, as has been observed for *Penicillium stolinoferum* virus (27) and for *Aspergillus foetidus* virus (74). The in vitro ssRNA synthesized by ScV, however, appears to be extruded from the particles (95).

Presently, the preferred model for replication of ScV particles is that established for reovirus. The reovirus transcriptase activity is activated by a partial uncoating of virus particles in lysozomes; the transcriptase synthesizes ssRNAs in a conservative mode that act as mRNAs for the synthesis of viral proteins; these same ssRNAs serve as templates for the synthesis of complementary strands within nascent virions; these partially completed virions now continue the cycle of ssRNA synthesis; finally, virions cease ssRNA synthesis upon completion of their outer capsids (48, 80).

In ScV replication, as in the replication of the fungal viruses, there must be some means by which the number of virus particles per cell is limited sufficiently that cellular death does not ensue, possibly by synchronization of virus replication and cell division. Evidence of host control of ScV replication is that replication of ScV dsRNAs is confined to the G1 phase of the cell cycle (V. A. Zakian and W. Fangman, personal communication).

NUCLEAR GENES

The presence of ScV-M wild-type particles confers on their host cells an easily recognizable phenotype: the ability to secrete killer toxin and to resist its effects. ScV-L particles confer no such recognizable phenotype. Consequently, the search for chromosomal mutations affecting yeast virus-like particles has been confined to those that affect inheritance or expression of M. None of the mutations presently characterized has any noticeable effect on L.

There are three general classes of nuclear mutations affecting the killer character: mutations that eliminate both the ability to kill and the resistance to toxin (*mak*) (31, 83, 96, 101, 104); mutations that eliminate the ability to kill but have no effect on resistance to toxin (*kex*) (56, 96, 100); and mutations eliminating resistance to toxin but not the capacity for killing (*rex*) (96). Note that K^+R^- strains grow normally above pH 4.6.

The *mak* mutants owe their phenotype to the loss of M in *mak* haploids or in *mak/mak* diploids (99). Since M codes for the killer toxin and probably for a protein necessary for toxin resistance (see section on translation products of ScV RNAs), the immediate cause of the K^-R^- phenotype of *mak* mutants is evident. Mutants of the *mak* type were first isolated by Somers & Bevan (83) and were designated *m;* these are now known to be mutations in the same gene designated *mak* 10 by Wickner (104). There are now some 26 *mak* genes established by complementation and mapping (99, 104), only one of which (*pets*) affects the maintenance of the mitochondrial genome as well as that of ScV-M (31). Some *mak* mutations appear to be highly pleiotropic: for instance, *spe2* mutants, which lack the ability to synthesize polyamines and are thus defective in meiosis, are also unable to maintain M (29). Some of these mutations must affect gene products utilized jointly (or sequentially) in some cellular processes necessary for maintenance of M: for instance, there are dominant suppressors of *mak*7 (known as KRB-1 mutations) that also suppress *pets* (103) and *ski* mutations that suppress many *mak* mutations (87a, 87b, 87c). It seems likely that additional types of *mak* mutants will be found.

The rather spectacular multiplicity of nuclear genes affecting the maintenance of M remains to be explained. None of the *mak* mutations affects the maintenance of L (66, 99), but at least one affects the maintenance of S (84). The selective effect on M could be explained as a ScV dosage effect: if the *mak* mutations resulted in limiting concentrations of proteins necessary for replication of both types of ScV, but ScV-L competed more efficiently for the limiting proteins, then the observed selective loss of M (or of S dsRNAs with similar replication recognition sequences) might be observed. A more tenable explanation would be that M and S require for their replication or encapsidation a number of cellular proteins not required by L. This hypothesis would seem to require different 3' and 5' end sequences (replication and packaging recognition sequences) in L versus M and S, as has been observed (16a).

The number of *kex* loci seems much more finite. In fact, Wickner and collaborators (100) have isolated some 30 or more independent mutants of this class and all had alterations of one of two genes (*kex*1 and *kex*2). The *kex*2 mutations have rather drastic pleiotropic effects, preventing sporulation in homozygous diploids and secretion of α-factor pheromone or response to a-factor II pheromone by α-*kex*2 haploids (59). The *kex* mutants do not lose either L or M (100) and are probably altered in processing of toxin precursor polypeptides or in secretion of toxin (12). The phenotype of the *kex*2 mutants is certainly consistent with a membrane defect.

The *rex* mutants have not been thoroughly characterized, but these might also be membrane mutants in which a site for the immunity protein was lacking, but the corresponding membrane site for toxin protein remained.

ScV "Provirus"

There have been two reports of nuclear DNA copies of the ScV RNAs in wild-type killer strains (77, 92). Both are probably apocryphal. Shalitin & Fischer used as a hybridization probe for DNA sequences homologous to L and M a crude "poly (A)" fraction from a poly (U) Sepharose column (77). Even if this contained some 50% dsRNA (as claimed) their hybridization results are easily explained as hybridization of the contaminating RNAs. Vodkin used as a hybridization probe a "dsRNA" fraction isolated on CF11 cellulose columns containing L dsRNA (92). His preparations were probably contaminated with fragments of ribosomal RNA, which are known to be present in CF11 "dsRNA" fractions isolated from RNase-treated whole-cell RNA (M. Vodkin, personal communication). Shalitin & Fischer reported some 35 nuclear genes hybridizable to their probe: Vodkin's data indicated approximately 10 nuclear genes hybridizable to his probe (38). Both results are consistent with rRNA contamination of the RNA probes. Wickner & Leibowitz (103), using dsRNA purified by CF11 chromatography and acrylamide gel electrophoresis and labelled in vitro with [^{125}I], have been unable to find any yeast DNA sequences homologous to L or to M. Hastie et al (38), using either [^{32}P] in vivo labelled L purified by Cf11 chromatography and agarose gel electrophoresis or the α-[^{32}P]-ATP in vitro labelled product of the ScV-L RNA polymerase reaction, have shown that there are fewer than 0.075 copies of L per yeast nuclear genome and possibly fewer than 0.025 copies of L per nuclear genome.

SUMMARY

ScV is a simple dsRNA virus with two, separately encapsidated dsRNAs. Like fungal virus particles, ScV particles are communicated from cell to cell only by mating. The larger viral dsRNA (L) encodes the major capsid protein. The smaller (M) encodes a toxin lethal to strains without ScV-M particles. L and M have little sequence homology, and ScV-M particles are dependent on ScV-L particles for the synthesis of their capsid polypeptide and possibly for the synthesis of replicase and transcriptase polypeptides. Internal deletions of M result in defective-interfering particles containing fragments of M (ScV-S particles). ScV-M and ScV-S particles are dependent for their replication on products of the nuclear genome that are not necessary for replication of ScV-L particles. ScV-L and ScV-M particles are known to possess an RNA polymerase activity, the primary product of which is complementary to one of the strands of the template dsRNA. ScV-S dsRNAs diverge in sequence from their parental RNAs as do the RNAs of animal viruses replicated in persistent infections. In sum, ScV possesses all the attributes (except infectivity) of a genuine segmented dsRNA virus and exhibits, in a simple model system, phenomena of defective interfering particles, persistent infection, helper viruses, and complex (and analyzable) genetic interaction between host cell and virus.

Literature Cited

1. Adams, J. M., Cory, S. 1975. *Nature New Biol.* 255:28–40
2. Adler, J., Wood, H. A., Bozarth, R. F. 1976. *J. Virol.* 17:472–76
3. Al-Aidroos, K., Somers, J. M., Bussey, H. 1973. *Mol. Gen. Genet.* 122:323–30
4. Alaoui, R., Jacquemin, J. M., Boccardo, G. 1974. *Acta Virol.* 18:193–202
5. Arnott, S., Fuller, W., Hodgson, A., Prutton, I. 1968. *Nature* 220:561–64
6. Bailey, J. M., Davidson, N. 1976. *Anal. Biochem.* 70:75–85
7. Berry, E. A., Bevan, E. A. 1972. *Nature New Biol.* 239:279–80
8. Bevan, E. A., Makower, M. 1963. In *Genetics Today,* ed. S. J. Geerts, 1:202–3. New York: Macmillan
9. Bevan, E. A., Somers, J. M. 1969. *Genet. Res.* 14:71–77
10. Bevan, E. A., Herring, A. J., Mitchell, D. J. 1973. *Nature* 245:81–86
11. Bohlke, K. W., Friesen, J. D. 1975. *J. Bacteriol.* 121:429–33
12. Bostian, K. A., Hopper, J. E., Rogers, D. T., Tipper, D. J. 1979. *Cell.* In press
13. Bozarth, R. F., Wood, H. A. 1971. *Phytopathology* 61:886
14. Brennan, V., Hastie, N., Bruenn, J. 1978. *9th Int. Conf. Yeast Gen. Mol. Biol., Rochester, NY, Abstr. 321*
15. Bruenn, J., Keitz, B. 1976. *Nucleic Acids Res.* 3:2427–36
16. Bruenn, J., Kane, W. 1978. *J. Virol.* 26:762–72

16a. Bruenn, J., Brennan, V. 1980. *Cell.* In press

17. Buck, K. W., Chain, E. B., Himmelweit, F. 1971. *J. Gen. Virol.* 12:131–39
18. Buck, K. W., Lhoas, P., Street, B. K. 1973. *Biochem. Soc. Trans.* 1:1141–42
19. Buck, K. W., Kempson-Jones, G. F. 1974. *J. Gen. Virol.* 22:441–45
20. Buck, K. W. 1975. *Nucleic Acids Res.* 2:1889–1902
21. Buck, K. W., Ratti, G. 1975. *J. Gen. Virol.* 27:211–24
22. Bussey, H. 1972. *Nature New Biol.* 235:73–75
23. Bussey, H., Sherman, D. 1973. *Biochim. Biophys. Acta* 298:868–75
24. Bussey, H., Sherman, D., Somers, J. M. 1973. *J. Bacteriol.* 113:1193–97
25. Bussey, H. 1974. *J. Gen. Microbiol.* 82:171–79

26. Bussey, H., Skipper, N. 1975. *J. Bacteriol.* 124:476–83
27. Chater, K. F., Morgan, D. H. 1974. *J. Gen. Virol.* 23:307–17
28. Chow, N. L., Shatkin, A. J. 1975. *J. Virol.* 15:1057–64
29. Cohn, M. S., Tabor, C. W., Tabor, H., Wickner, R. B. 1978. *J. Biol. Chem.* 253:5225–27
30. Day, P. R., Anagnostakis, S. L. 1973. *Phytopathology* 63:1017–18
31. Fink, G. R., Styles, C. A. 1972. *Proc. Natl. Acad. Sci. USA* 69:2846–49
32. Franklin, R. M. 1966. *Proc. Natl. Acad. Sci. USA* 55:1504–11
33. Fried, H. M., Fink, G. R. 1978. *Proc. Natl. Acad. Sci. USA* 75:4224–28
34. Granboulan, N., Franklin, R. M. 1966. *J. Mol. Biol.* 22:173–77
35. Guild, G. M., Stollar, V. 1977. *Virology* 77:175–88
36. Hankin, L., Puhalla, J. E. 1971. *Phytopathology* 61:50–53
37. Harris, M. S. 1978. *Microbios* 21:161–76
38. Hastie, N. D., Brennan, V., Bruenn, J. A. 1978. *J. Virol.* 28:1002–5
39. Herring, A. J., Bevan, E. A. 1974. *J. Gen. Virol.* 22:387–94
40. Herring, A. J., Bevan, E. A. 1975. In *Molecular Biology of Nucleocytoplasmic Relationships,* Chap. 3.6, pp. 149–54
41. Herring, A. J., Bevan, E. A. 1977. *Nature* 268:464–66
42. Holland, J. J., Grabau, E. A., Jones, C. L., Semler, B. L. 1979. *Cell* 16:495–504
43. Holm, C. A., Oliver, S. G., Newman, A. M., Holland, L. E., McLaughlin, C. S., Wagner, E. K., Warner, R. C. 1978. *J. Biol. Chem.* 253:8332–36
44. Hopper, J. E., Bostian, K. A., Rowe, L. B., Tipper, D. J. 1977. *J. Biol. Chem.* 252:9010–17
45. Huang, A. S., Baltimore, D. 1970. *Nature* 266:325–27
46. Huang, A. S. 1977. *Bacteriol. Rev.* 41:811–21
47. Johnson, L. D., Lazzarini, R. A. 1977. *Virology* 77:863–66
48. Joklik, W. K. 1974. In *Comprehensive Virology* 2:231–34. New York: Plenum
49. Kane, W., Pietras, D., Bruenn, J. A. 1979. *J. Virol.* 32:692–96
50. Keene, J. D., Rosenberg, M., Lazzarini, R. A. 1977. *Proc. Natl. Acad. Sci. USA* 74:1353–57
51. Keene, J. D., Schubert, M., Lazzarini, R. A., Rosenberg, M. 1978. *Proc. Natl. Acad. Sci. USA* 75:3225–29
52. Kennedy, S. I. T. 1976. *J. Mol. Biol.* 108:491–511
53. Koltin, Y., Day, P. R. 1975. *Appl. Microbiol.* 30:694–96
54. Koltin, Y., Day, P. R. 1976. *Proc. Natl. Acad. Sci. USA* 73:594–98
55. Koltin, Y., Day, P. R. 1976. *Genetics* 82:629–37
56. Koltin, Y. 1977. *Genetics* 86:527–34
57. Koltin, Y., Kandel, J. S. 1978. *Genetics* 88:267–76
58. Langridge, R., Gomatos, P. J. 1963. *Science* 141:694–98
59. Leibowitz, M. J., Wickner, R. B. 1976. *Proc. Natl. Acad. Sci. USA* 73:2061–65
60. Lemke, P. A., Nash, C. H. 1964. *Bacteriol. Rev.* 38:29–56
61. Lemke, P. A. 1976. *Ann. Rev. Microbiol.* 30:105–45
62. Leppert, M., Kort, L., Kolakofsky, D. 1977. *Cell* 12:539–52
63. Luria, S. E., Darnell, J. E. 1967. *General Virology.* New York: Wiley. 512 pp. 2nd ed.
64. Luria, S. E., Darnell, J. E., Baltimore, D., Campbell, A. 1978. *General Virology.* New York: Wiley. 578 pp. 3rd ed.
65. Makower, M., Bevan, E. A. 1963. In *Genetics Today,* ed. S. J. Geerts, 1:202. New York: Macmillan
66. Mitchell, D. J., Herring, A. J., Bevan, E. A. 1976. *Heredity* 37:129–34
67. Miura, K. I., Watanabe, K., Sugiura, M. 1974. *J. Mol. Biol.* 86:31–48
68. Nash, C. H., Douthart, R. J., Ellis, L. F., Van Franke, R. M., Burnett, J. P., Lemke, P. A. 1973. *Can. J. Microbiol.* 19:97–103
69. Nomoto, A., Jacobson, A., Lee, Y. F., Dunn, J., Wimmer, E. 1979. *J. Mol. Biol.* 128:179–96
70. Oliver, S. G., McCready, S. J., Holm, C., Sutherland, P. A., McLaughlin, C. S., Cox, B. S. 1977. *J. Bacteriol.* 130:1303–9
71. Palfree, G. E., Bussey, H. 1979. *Eur. J. Biochem.* 93:487–93
72. Philliskirk, G., Young, T. W. 1975. *Antonie van Leeuwenhoek* 34:1–18
73. Pietras, D. F., Bruenn, J. A. 1976. *Int. J. Biochem.* 7:173–79
74. Ratti, G., Buck, K. W. 1975. *Biochem. Biophys. Res. Commun.* 66:706–11
75. Saksena, K. N., Lemke, P. A. 1978. In *Comprehensive Virology* 12:103–43. New York: Plenum
76. Semancik, J. S., Vidaver, A. K., Van Etten, J. L. 1973. *J. Mol. Biol.* 78:617–25
77. Shalitin, C., Fischer, I. 1975. *Biochim. Biophys. Acta* 414:263–72
78. Shatkin, A. J., Sipe, J. D., Loh, P. 1968. *J. Virol.* 2:986–91

79. Shields, D., Blobel, G. 1978. *J. Biol. Chem.* 253:3753–56
80. Silverstein, S. C., Christman, J. K., Acs, G. 1976. *Ann. Rev. Biochem.* 45:375–408
81. Skipper, N., Bussey, H. 1977. *J. Bacteriol.* 129:668–77
82. Sober, H. A., ed. 1970. *Handbook of Biochemistry with Selected Data for Molecular Biology.* Cleveland: Chem. Rubber. 1622 pp. 2nd ed.
83. Somers, J. M., Bevan, E. A. 1968. *Genet. Res.* 13:71–83
84. Somers, J. M. 1973. *Genetics* 74:571–79
85. Sripati, C. E., Groner, Y., Warner, J. R. 1976. *J. Biol. Chem.* 251:2898–2904
86. Sweeney, T. K., Tate, A., Fink, G. R. 1976. *Genetics* 84:27–42
87. Szekely, M., Loviny, T. 1975. *J. Mol. Biol.* 93:79–87
87a. Toh-E, A., Guerry, P., Wickner, R. B. 1978. *J. Bacteriol.* 136:1002–7
87b. Toh-E, A., Wickner, R. B. 1979. *Genetics.* 91:673–82
87c. Toh-E, A., Wickner, R. B. 1980. *Proc. Natl. Acad. Sci. USA.* In press
88. Tzen, J. C., Somers, J. M., Mitchell, D. J. 1974. *Heredity* 33:132
89. Villa-Komaroff, L., Guttman, N., Baltimore, D., Lodish, H. F. 1975. *Proc. Natl. Acad. Sci. USA* 72:4157–61
90. Vodkin, M. H., Fink, G. R. 1973. *Proc. Natl. Acad. Sci. USA.* 70:1069–72
91. Vodkin, M., Katterman, F., Fink, G. R. 1974. *J. Bacteriol.* 117:681–86
92. Vodkin, M. 1977. *J. Virol.* 21:516–21
93. Vodkin, M. 1977. *J. Bacteriol.* 132: 346–48
94. Weber, H., Lindner, R. 1975. *Z. Allg. Mikrobiol.* 15:631–38
95. Welsh, J. D., Leibowitz, M. J. 1978. *9th Int. Conf. Yeast Genet. Mol. Biol., Rochester,* Abstr. 320
96. Wickner, R. B. 1974. *Genetics* 76: 423–32
97. Wickner, R. B. 1974. *J. Bacteriol.* 117: 1356–57
98. Wickner, R. B. 1976. *Genetics* 82:273–85
99. Wickner, R. B. 1976. *Bacteriol. Rev.* 40:757–73
100. Wickner, R. B., Leibowitz, M. J. 1976. *Genetics* 82:429–442
101. Wickner, R. B., Leibowitz, M. J. 1976. *J. Mol. Biol.* 105:427–43
102. Wickner, R. B. 1977. *Genetics* 87: 441–52
103. Wickner, R. B., Leibowitz, M. J. 1977. *Genetics* 87:453–69
104. Wickner, R. B. 1978. *Genetics* 88: 419–25
105. Wood, D. R., Bevan, E. A. 1968. *J. Gen. Microbiol.* 51:115–26
106. Wood, H. A., Bozarth, R. F. 1972. *Virology* 47:604–9
107. Wood, H. A. 1973. *J. Gen. Virol.* 20:61–85
108. Wood, H. A., Bozarth, R. F. 1973. *Phytopathology* 63:1019–21
109. Yamashita, S., Doi, Y., Yora, K. 1975. *Proc. 1st Intersectional Congr. Int. Assoc. Microbiol. Soc.* 3:340–50
110. Young, R. A., Perlman, P. S. 1975. *J. Bacteriol.* 124:290–95
111. Zimmern, D. 1975. *Nucleic Acids Res.* 2:1189–1201

Ann. Rev. Microbiol. 1980. 34:69–108

FLAGELLAR STRUCTURE AND FUNCTION IN EUBACTERIA

◆1770

R. N. Doetsch and R. D. Sjoblad

Department of Microbiology, University of Maryland, College Park, Maryland 20742

CONTENTS

INTRODUCTION 69
NEW METHODS FOR OBSERVING FLAGELLA AND MOTILITY 70
The Flagellar Organelle 70
Motile Individual Organisms and Populations 73
FLAGELLAR STRUCTURE 77
The Filament 77
The Hook 84
The Basal Structure 85
FLAGELLAR BIOMECHANICS 88
BIOLOGICAL ASPECTS OF MOTILITY 93
Environmental Influences on Motile Populations 93
Flagellar Diversity 101
CONCLUDING REMARKS 103

INTRODUCTION

Important functions served by translational movement in eubacteria include aiding in attachment to surfaces, conferring an essential character to forms having cyclic developmental phases, escaping from predators or unfavorable environments, entering into symbiotic relationships, and maintenance in physiologically optimal environments. Motility is not essential to survival, however, and many well-known bacteria are nonmotile, yet maintain themselves without apparent disadvantage.

The ideal arena for investigating eubacterial motility functions would be the natural environment; however, techniques for performing in situ studies are poorly developed. Therefore, attempts have been made to extrapolate conclusions from artificial laboratory experiments to natural conditions.

0066-4227/80/1001-0069$01.00

Certain aspects of eubacterial motility have been studied at suborganismal levels. Included here are the origin and insertion of flagella, flagellar fine structure, and macromolecular assembly. In order to avoid possible erroneous generalizations concerning motile functions, the widest range of specimens must be examined. In contrast to relatively crude methods applied to organismal studies of eubacterial movement, sophisticated instrumentation has been employed for studies on molecular aspects of the flagellar organelle.

This review considers publications concerning eubacterial movement from 1972 to the present. The literature appearing in this brief time is awesome in bulk, and apparently every facet of the field has been probed. Recent excellent reviews make it unnecessary to consider certain areas. These include spirochaetal movement (33), mechanisms of chemotactic phenomena (2, 17, 21, 107, 135), and the genetics of flagellar formation (75, 167). Besides swimming, certain bacteria exhibit gliding and twitching movements, and Henrichsen's essay (67) is still useful.

Bacterial flagella and movements mediated by them have been used as models for studying protein synthesis, morphogenesis, and organelle development, and molecular aspects of sensory reception and information processing. These are outside the scope of this review, which focuses mainly on biological aspects of eubacterial flagella and movement.

We consider work done on flagella and on motility characteristics of individual organisms and populations. Current ideas concerning flagellar fine structure of a variety of eubacteria are summarized, including hook, filament, sheath, and basal apparatus. Biomechanical aspects of the eubacterial flagellum are appraised, and this is followed by an account of current work dealing with biological aspects of eubacterial motility in relation to environmental influences on motile populations.

NEW METHODS FOR OBSERVING FLAGELLA AND MOTILITY

The Flagellar Organelle

Determination of flagellar distribution and morphology using light microscopy is a useful and necessary operation in identifying, for example, certain Gram-negative nonfermentative bacteria. Flagella staining is reputed to be an art rather than a scientific procedure since it is erratic and often exasperating. Consequently, modifications of original methods, some of which trace their ancestry to Robert Koch, are continuously reported in the hope that they will obviate the difficulties encountered.

Two hazards are the apparent extreme fragility of flagellar attachment to the organism and the fact that flagellar cross sections (12–20 nm) lie below the limits of ordinary light microscope resolution (~ 200nm). Walc-Pokrzywnicki (190) puts great emphasis on scrupulous cleaning of microscope slides using soap and water, dichromate-sulfuric acid solutions, and the like. Curiously, no one, it appears, has investigated systematically the use of optical foams or detergents for this task. This author (190) maintains that formalin-fixed bacteria (absolute alcohol, 9 parts; 40% (vol/vol) formaldehyde, 1 part) are required for best results. The tannic acid mordant is unstable and its use leads to erratic results if not carefully prepared and applied. Use of ammoniacal silver nitrate has been revived (142, 190), modified by employing a sodium thiosulfate wash (190). The width of stained flagella depends on the action of ferric tannate mordant, and not the strength of the silver solution.

West et al (192) also modified Rhodes' technique (142) by eliminating "... precleaning of slides, the dilution step of the organism into distilled water, and the use of a saturated aqueous solution of aniline as a portion of the mordant." The flagella of 42 of 43 cultures of Gram-negative nonfermentative organisms are readily stained using the procedures recommended.

Leifson's old method (101) continually attracts variations. Clark (39) claims his modifications are used "... as easily as the Gram stain method." This is accomplished by making subtle quantitative changes in the staining reagent and mordant formulations. He reports that flagella of bacteria taken directly from 24 and 48 h blood agar plates are easily and reliably stained. Success has been reported (40) following substitution of 6% (wt/vol) tannic acid for 3% (wt/vol).

Modifications of Gray's method (61) have been made by Mayfield & Inniss (117). In addition to altering reagent concentrations, they advise use of a syringe fitted with a 0.22 μm (pore diameter) cellulose membrane filter, thus allowing for filtration of combined mordant-staining reagent prior to direct application on a slide. A small amount (one loopful) of culture suspended in distilled water is covered with a cover slip, and the filtered stain applied to its edge. The slide is examined using phase-contrast or bright-field optics, and the simultaneously mordanted and stained flagella are "... easily visible after one minute." We found this technique useful in observing flagella of bacteria suspended in liquid marine media or in artificial seawater.

Another modification (62) of Gray's method extends the staining time to 15 to 20 min and successfully reveals the flagella of phytopathogenic bacteria (*Erwinia* and *Pseudomonas*).

There has been a marked improvement of techniques employed for visualizing flagellar bundles (fascicles) of living bacteria using light microscopy. Macnab & Koshland (110) claim that it is possible to observe *individual* flagella of living bacteria using a high intensity arc lamp (75 W high-pressure xenon) and efficient dark-field optics. However, they note, "... individual flagella could sometimes be seen fleetingly. . . ." It is more likely that flagellar fascicles rather than individual flagella are visualized clearly, especially since the overall magnification of the optical systems ranges from 250 to 625X. The flagellum (17–19 nm in cross section) of *Pseudomonas stutzeri* is observed "without difficulty." Macnab (105) claims it is erroneous to assume that because bacterial flagella have a cross section of ~ 15 nm, they cannot be seen. The limit, he argues, is one of resolution, and not detection. He recommends a short-arc xenon, mercury, or xenon-mercury lamps of 75 W-arc or higher. He uses a Hanovia 500 W xenon arc lamp (959-C 98) in a light housing (Oriel 6140) with an adjustable collimating lens system (48 mm + 1.0), a tempered-glass heat filter (Optical Industries 03 FHA 02) and a yellow filter (Optical Industries GG495), together with a dark-field condenser (Zeiss Ultracondenser NA 1.2 to 1.4), a medium-power (40X) Zeiss dry fluorite objective (NA 0.75), and a Zeiss wide angle Kpl eyepiece (10 or 16X). Because of the low light scattering power of flagella, great care is required in adjusting all elements of the system. Macnab points out that "... no photographic film can match the capabilities of the human eye in terms of sensitivity, dynamic range, and perception of the form of a moving object." Indeed, his photographs reveal flagellar bundles and not individual flagella.

Helical transformations of flagellar bundles have been studied (87) using a Nikon SKR microscope, dark-field microscopy (Olympus DC condenser, NA 1.2 to 1.33) and a Ushio 100 W mercury lamp. Photographs of images obtained with a 40X Olympus oil immersion apochromatic objective (NA 1.0) and a Nikon 10X eyepiece were taken with a Nikon EMF camera. Hotani (71) uses a 500 W Ushio mercury arc lamp equipped with a collimator (Ushio UI501C) and a yellow filter. He states that it is possible to observe single flagellar filaments of *Salmonella* when examined with a 40X Olympus apochromatic objective, a 15X Olympus eyepiece, and an Olympus DC paraboloid dark-field condenser (NA 1.20 to 1.33). In order to photograph a *single* flagellum, an exposure time of 1 sec or longer is required, and since Brownian motion prevents obtaining clear pictures of free-floating elements, it is necessary to focus on those which form weak attractive associations with the glass surface of the microscope slide.

Hotani (72) has made a frame analysis of cinematographs (16mm) of video-tape pictures obtained by reconstituting moving images of single flagellar filaments from motile *Salmonella* (strains SJ 25 and SJ 814) as viewed with dark-field microscopy. He reports that flagellar filaments attach to a glass surface only at one end (the H-end). When helical filaments are subjected to viscous flow of a methyl cellulose solution, they rotate as a result of the generated hydrodynamic torque. The average torque for rotating filaments on glass in viscous fluids at a flow rate of 15 μm sec^{-1} is calculated as between 5×10^{-12} and 1×10^{-13} dyn cm.

A great number of publications on electron microscopic studies of bacterial flagella have appeared since 1972, and these will be considered in the section on flagellar structure.

Motile Individual Organisms and Populations

A tracking microscope that automatically remains focused on an individual swimming bacterium was described as early as 1971 (15). The observation chamber can be displaced in the *x, y,* and *z* coordinates in such a way that the position of the organism appears fixed in the microscope field. Coordinate shifts, in the presence of gradients of attractant or repellent chemicals, are recorded. Using this technique (20) for observing chemotactic responses of *Escherichia coli,* it was discovered that when proceeding up-gradient of an attractant the organisms' motions are characterized by "runs," or periods of smooth translational movement, whereas down-gradient movements exhibit abrupt translational and directional changes termed "tumbles" or "twiddles." Observations of this kind and others (22) have led to a marked increase of interest in the possibility of using bacterial sensory phenomena as models for cellular behavioral studies.

Lovely et al (103) also have developed a tracking microscope. They use a large sample cuvette (10 X 10 X 46 mm) which permits tracking in stable, defined gradients of chemotactic stimulants. The instrument is servo-controlled by a human operator and utilizes motors. The bacteria, contained in a 1 cm path spectrometer cuvette attached to an *x-y-z* micromanipulator, are monitored for directional changes by micrometer screws driven by stepping motors. Tracking an individual bacterium involves exact opposition of its velocities, so that it appears stationary. The operator controls three potentiometers, two by means of a "joystick," and the third by a foot pedal. Voltage from a potentiometer controls speed and direction of the corresponding stepping motors. The position of each potentiometer thus determines the velocity of the sample cuvette along the corresponding coordinate axis. Continuous monitoring by the observer retains the image of the individual bacterium on the eyepiece cross hairs of the horizontally mounted microscope. Three sets of up/down counters digitally follow the position of the motors. A fourth set, driven by a crystal oscillator, provides a time base. Whenever a record of time and position coordinates is desired, the contents of the counters are transferred to latch circuits and then to paper tape for subsequent computer analysis. Bacteria are visualized in dark-field using 16X eyepieces and a special 32X objective (UM K50) which has an unusually large free working distance (7 mm) to allow observation throughout the cuvette depth.

Cinematography is useful for obtaining permanent dynamic records of bacterial motion. Time-lapse "tracks" of individual motile bacteria developed on film were made a decade ago by Vaituzis & Doetsch (186). Since that time a number of other tracking techniques have been developed.

Tracking techniques (186) have been used (53) to study swarming phenomena in *Proteus.* Two kinds of tracks are found. Some appear relatively thick, bright, and corkscrew-like, and others are thin and faint. It is concluded that the former are produced by the rotation of *Proteus* long-forms about their longitudinal axes, thereby describing a relatively wide arc due to the curvature of these organisms. Short, nonswarming organisms are rods and so rotate more closely around their axes, thereby producing a thinner track.

The hydrodynamics and energetics of helical swimming in *Spirillum* have been analyzed with medium-speed cinematography (194). The spirilla are placed within a petroleum-ringed slide preparation and photographed with a Milliken DBM-55 cine camera at speeds of 100 to 300 frames sec $^{-1}$. Dark-field conditions are obtained by means of a camera-pulsed xenon-arc lamp in conjunction with a Zeiss WL microscope equipped with a dark-field apochromatic 40X objective. The film, depicting the motion of flagellar fascicles, is analyzed from tracings made on a parallax-corrected triad film reader.

Such analyses reveal that the aft end of spirilla shows a flagellar bundle that roughly describes a helix (see also 78). This observed geometry is consistent with the expected curvature for a real attached fiber that is bent backward under uniform stress. In order to produce a forward motion the body and/or bundle must propagate a traveling wave that can push the fluid continuously, thereby generating a viscous fluid reaction in the direction of the rotation axis.

Cinematographic analysis of *Salmonella* and *Pseudomonas* movements were made by Asakura and associates (159, 161, 198). These workers employ Pathe M or Bolex RX cameras, 250 or 500 W mercury-arc lamps as illumination sources, and a variety of optical systems to investigate the ratio of propulsive velocity to the frequency of bodily rotation, and also the frequency of wave propagation along flagellar filaments. For the former, a dark-ground condenser (NA 1.2 to 1.4), a Nikon achromat objective (100X), a Nikon HK 5X eyepiece, and a Nikon EFM 16-C beam splitter are used. A film speed of 32 frames sec^{-1} and an exposure time of 1/72 sec are used. In a few instances two cine cameras are connected to a Nikon triocular microscope, and the movement of the bacteria is recorded simultaneously with the two cameras at film speeds of 48 and 80 frames sec^{-1}, respectively. Exposure times are 1/120 and 1/180 sec. In both studies the frames of a cinematograph are successively projected on a screen and the position and shape of the bacterial body are traced. In 12 successive cinematographic frames it is seen that helical waves of flagella propagate distally. The propulsive velocity is calculated from the tracings. For the second problem, an Olympus beam-splitter receives the image from an Olympus HFT microscope equipped with a dark-field condenser DC-W (NA 1.2 to 1.4), an apochromat objective H1 40X (NA 1.0), and a photographic eyepiece FK (6.7X). The magnification at the film is 214X. A framing speed of 12 sec^{-1} and an exposure of 1/33 sec is adopted. In both studies 20% Mohr's salts, or glass filters are used to absorb heat. In some experiments with *Salmonella,* medium viscosity is increased with methylcellulose to obtain improved pictures of flagellar bundles.

Stroboscopic techniques have proven useful in the hands of Koshland and associates (171, 181). A quantitative method was developed for measuring the tumble frequency of individual bacteria during chemotactic responses. The microscope, attached to a camera, is focused on the slide surface and 0.8 sec exposure photographs are taken at various time intervals with dark-field illumination and a high pressure xenon-arc lamp with a 5 Hz flashing rate. An orange long-pass band filter (Corning 3-69) excludes blue light, which causes spurious photoresponses at high intensities. Kodak 2475 high contrast film is developed and projected onto white paper. Tracks of "runs" and "tumbles" of individual bacteria are clearly depicted.

Salmonella typhimurium was observed in dark-field and photographed (0.8 sec exposures at 6.0 sec intervals, one flash per two sec) with a stroboscopic high-pressure xenon-arc lamp (181). Smoothly swimming bacteria are depicted by tracks that appear as dotted lines, whereas tumbling bacteria appear as splotches of light. These markers are used to evaluate chemotactic responses and gradient sensing.

Schneider & Doetsch (152) utilize a television tape recorder (Panasonic NV-504) to store the microscope image scanned by a television camera coupled to a monitor (Electrohome EMV-23AG). Thus, either "live" or recorded images of individual motile bacteria can be studied. The television camera (Concord MTC-21) is joined to a Zeiss II photomicroscope supplied with a 60 W illumination source. A "phase 2" system is used with a Zeiss Neofluar objective lens (40X) to furnish an image of a dark organism against a light background. The television tape is played back to measure velocities, and the paths of individual bacteria are traced with a marking pencil on a grid of heavy transparent plastic sheet.

An apparatus for determining the rate and direction of "tethered" *E. coli* has been developed (92). The images from dark-field microscopy (Nikon Model L with 20X objective, 15X eyepiece and ¼X lens) are coupled to a television camera (National WV-200), monitor (Ikegami PM-97T), and tape recorder (Ikegami TVR-321J) in the manner described above (152). The playback image is passed through an image-splitter plus two graded filters and transformed into two electrically sinusoidal signals having a 90° phase difference. Rotation rate is determined from the frequency of the signal, and the direction of rotation is detected from the phase shift between two signals. The apparatus has a range of rotation detection rates from 1.3 to 17 rps in the steady state. Change of direction of rotation has to be less than 15 rps to be detected.

Movements of motile populations have been investigated by studying the time dependence of the fluctuating intensity of scattered light from systems in which the number of organisms varies with time (146). Nossal & Chen (128) use laser light intensity correlation spectroscopy to study oxygen taxis of *E. coli* K12. If a chemotactic source is located in the plane defined by the incident laser beam and the detected scattered beam, with Θ the scattering angle and α the angle between the source and incident beam, then the photocount in a short time interval is proportional to the intensity of the scattered light at that time. Thus, if the photomultiplier is passed through a real-time autocorrelator, information is obtained in the form of a time correlation function. In this way, swimming velocities for populations of responding and nonresponding bacteria are distinguished.

Intensity fluctuation spectroscopy (IFS) is sensitive primarily to the rotational component of bacterial movement (147). It is argued that although IFS is not directly sensitive to translational speed of motile organisms, it is still useful because it facilitates study of rotational movement in work on flagellar action and chemotaxis. The coherent light from a Spectra-Physics 125 He Ne laser (6,328 Å) has been used to illuminate a heavy suspension (absorbance $\sim$ 0.5) of swimming bacteria, and a detector (Saicor 43A correlator) measures the dynamics of fluctuation of scattered light (147). The far-field intensity as a function of time is related to the number of scatterers occupying the scattering volume at any time and to the position of the fluctuating diffraction pattern generated (13). Since bacterial dimensions are of the same order as the wavelengths of incident light, the average dynamic properties of a large population of particles or bacteria, due, for example, to twisting and wobbling and translation velocities, are detected. Temperature dependence of *E. coli* motility rates also have been studied using IFS (13).

Theoretical aspects of IFS have been considered (29, 147, 173) but, practically, this technique will probably not become common in the near future.

FLAGELLAR STRUCTURE

Over the past decade, enormous advances have been made in uncovering the structural features of this organelle. Techniques of modern biochemical and biophysical research have been brought to bear on the investigation of flagella, and it is perhaps a truism to state that presently we know much more about the physical and chemical characteristics of this organelle than we do about how it functions. Obviously, analytical techniques are easier to use on isolated and purified flagella than on those attached to a normal living organism.

Wide use of electron microscopy has led to the convention of subdividing the bacterial flagellum into three morphologically and chemically distinct parts designated as filament, hook, and basal structure. We consider here advances made recently in our knowledge of each of these.

The Filament

The section of the flagellum between hook and distal end is known as the filament. Unsheathed filaments average around 20 nm in diameter and 10 to 20 μm in length. With the exception of "straight," and "curly" or "coiled" mutants, most flagella appear to possess a waveform of constant amplitude when viewed as flattened two-dimensional projections, but the form in living organisms is that of a semirigid helix. Some exceptions have been observed. The flagellar fascicle form of *Thiospirillum jenense,* for instance, has a scythe-like configuration whose individual elements lack waveform. Also, the flagellar fascicle of *Aquaspirillum fasciculus* has the ability to "coil up like springs," and exhibits helical wave propagation (175).

On the other hand, studies of reconstituted *Salmonella* flagellar filaments, using quasi-elastic scattering of laser light (59), have led to the conclusion that the bacterial flagellum is "very stiff." The flexural rigidity for straight-type flagella is calculated to be of the order of 10^{-15} dyn/cm^2. F-actin has a value of 1.5×10^{-17} dyn/cm^2, i.e. 100-fold less than the rigidity of *Salmonella* flagella. The strength of secondary bonds between flagellins in a flagellum and between G-actins in F-actin would be of the same order of magnitude if one takes into account the differences in number of strands and in geometrical shapes, that is, a cylinder versus a twisted filament.

The principal, and perhaps only, biochemical species comprising the filament is a protein called flagellin. There appears to be considerable variation in the molecular weights of flagellins of various eubacteria, and representative values range from 33 $\times$ 10^3 for *Bacillus subtilis,* to 51 to 57 $\times$ 10^3 for *Salmonella* spp., and 60 $\times$ 10^3 for *E. coli* (93). It is characteristic of flagellins that cysteine and tryptophan are absent, and that ϵ-*N*-methyl lysine occurs only in *Salmonella* flagella (81).

In an investigation of *Proteus* flagella (28) it is concluded that the flagellin protomers are wedge shaped and lined up at regular intervals of 52 Å in roughly axially parallel strands. Eight of these strands are combined to form a hollow cylinder. The flagellin subunits are tilted at a 30° angle to the filament axis, and the hollow central core is approximately 3 nm in diameter. It is suggested (30, 31) that flagellin molecules from different strains of *Salmonella* all have nearly the same shape. Small configurational changes are believed to account for various observed differences in curvature and twist of the filament. These polymorphic transitions can be induced by changes in pH, by variations in a few residues in the polypeptide chain, or by external viscous forces.

Scanning electron microscopy (SEM) reveals typical helical shapes of *S. typhimurium* and *Pseudomonas aeruginosa* flagella only in specimens fixed with glutaraldehyde, but not in those fixed in osmium tetroxide (4). *S. typhimurium* flagella are successfully preserved for SEM using a thin agar layer method, which avoids unnecessary pipetting and centrifuging. The organisms are fixed best in 1% (wt/vol) glutaraldehyde in 0.15 M cacodylate buffer (pH 7.2). Dehydration with ethanol, rather than acetone, induces morphological alterations in the filament so that the typical helical form is absent (116).

Vandermolen & Williams (188), using SEM techniques similar to the Japanese workers (116), report that some *Proteus mirabilis* organisms in the swarming stage are equipped with more than 1,000 flagella, although at this point individual cell lengths range from 50 to 100 μm. It is difficult to imagine how such a proliferation of flagella would be useful. Armitage & Smith (10), observing flagellar proliferation during swarmer differentiation in *P. mirabilis,* report that the flagella increased from 3 to 150 per unit cell volume, which represents an increase in the cell surface area occupied by flagella from 0.02 to 1.0%. This may require a reorganization of the proteins and lipopolysaccharides of the outer membranes to accommodate and stabilize the filaments. This possibility is indicated by the increase in swarmer cell permeability (9).

Filament fine structure studies continue to reveal interesting information. Although flagella substructure is revealed in most studies, Czajkowski et al (43) report its absence in attached flagella of *P. mirabilis* and *B. subtilis.* They use either potassium phosphotungstate or uranyl acetate in their negative stains, but close-to-focus high resolution electron micrographs reveal no regular structures. It is suggested that "... the granular patterns observed by using out-of-focus pictures of the flagella represent optical artifacts." It is not denied that X-ray diffraction or ultracentrifugal and other analytical techniques show bacterial flagella to consist of subunits; however, the results suggest that conventional high resolution electron microscopy of flagellar filaments does not always reveal subunits in flagella, particularly when great care is used in handling them and when beam damage is avoided—precautions earlier studies may not have included.

Detailed filament substructure studies on *Pseudomonas rhodos* 9-6 reveal that this bacterium produces two kinds of filaments (150, 151). "Plain" flagella, 13 nm in diameter, are composed of "globular subunits like normal bacteria." These consist of 9 large-scale helical rows of subunits intersecting 4 small scale helices of pitch angle 25°. In addition, there are "complex" flagella, which have a conspicuous helical sheath 18 nm in diameter consisting of three close-fitting helical bands, each about 4.7 nm wide. The bands are separated by axial intervals 4.7 nm wide at an angle of 27°. The interval core substructure is similar but not identical to that of the plain filaments. Both kinds of filaments are observed on single organisms. Plain flagella have a 37×10^3 dalton subunit, separable into two isoproteins, and the complex flagella has only a 55×10^3 dalton protein.

The filament structure of *Rhizobium lupini* H13-3 is 16 nm in diameter and consists of a cylindrical core (11 nm diameter), surrounded by three close-fitting bands of helical "sheath" (149). These bands are 4.9 nm wide and separated by axial intervals, also 4.9 nm, at an angle of 31°. This filament has a 43×10^3 dalton protein representing both core and helical sheath, and thus differs from the complex filaments of *P. rhodos.*

Sheathed filaments have been described for bacteria of the genera *Bdellovibrio, Vibrio, Pseudomonas, Proteus,* and *R. lupini* H13-3. Sheath material varies in size and degree of structural organization, and the relation between sheath and motility is unknown. Yang et al (197) purified the "core" of the sheathed filament of *Vibrio cholerae* Inaba V86, and report that it is composed of a single protein subunit of molecular weight 45×10^3 g/mol and that it has a density of 1.3 g/cm^3. Ferritin-labeled antibody prepared against purified core reacts with the intact filament, and not with the cell surface, suggesting that the sheath in this instance is not an extension of the outer wall. Interestingly, flagellar core antibody also immobilizes viable cholera organisms. On the other hand, Mulholland et al (126) report that *V. cholerae* Inaba CA 401 has a filament sheath that is antigenically different from its core protein. There is some confusion regarding the word "core," since Sleytr & Glauert (169) see "empty" cores in filaments of freeze-etched preparations of *Clostridium thermohydrosulfuricum.* They use the word to describe the hollow appearance of the half-cylinders observed in the filaments. Schmitt et al (151) state that the complex flagellar filament of *P. rhodos* 9–6 is "sheathed" by a super-folded triple helix fixed onto the core structure. This helical band differs from other reported sheaths which generally appear to be closely applied outer cell wall extensions, easily separated from the underlying filament. Perhaps some other term ought be applied to the *P. rhodos* complex filaments, as they are clearly structurally different.

Lawn et al (100) using standard electron microscopy techniques have examined the flagellar filaments of 50 *E. coli* strains and distinguish six principal morphotypes (A to F). Type A filaments are thin and have a featureless surface; their most prominent character is a series of helical, almost longitudinal grooves. Type B filaments have a prominent surface pattern of diagonal striations suggesting subunits arranged helically. Type C also has diagonal striations, but these are not as prominent as in Type B. Type D filaments show a serrated profile with the points all inclined towards one pole of the filament. Types E and F have gaps, which could be filled with uranyl acetate, between the surface and central core. The surface layer at the edge appears as loops that occasionally seem to connect with diagonal striations across the filament surface, suggesting the presence of sheath-like helical strands wound around it. Type E differs from Type F in the space between successive loops at one edge ($\sim$ 20 nm). A few *E. coli* strains have filaments not resembling any of the above morphotypes. Lawn (99) reports that the observed differences in diameter and surface structure are accompanied by considerable variations in flagellin molecular weights, ranging from 37 to 69 $\times 10^3$. Lawn et al (100) claim that regularity of structure and its reproducibility in different isolates of the same H serotype demonstrates the usefulness of their technique; but they warn that because filaments are susceptible to acid dissociation, the use of aldehyde fixation and uranyl acetate may reflect a surface structure altered by the acid pH or by reaction with a charged heavy metal-containing ion.

Flagellar filaments of Gram-negative, aerobic, hydrogen bacteria, including *Alcaligenes eutrophus, A. paradoxus, A. ruhlandii, Pseudomonas flava, P. pseudoflava, P. facilis, Aquaspirillum autotrophicum, Paracoccus denitrificans,* and *"Corynebacterium" autotrophicum,* have been investigated by Aragno et al (7). They distinguish three types of filament fine structure based on the angle (α), the subunits made with the axis (A), and the axes tangential to the left (L) and right (D) oblique rows of subunits. Type I is interpreted as a hexagonal arrangement of roughly iso-diametrical subunits. Type II is also considered to represent a hexagonal arrangement of subunits, but these are elongated in the direction of A. Type III filaments have a periodically undulating sheath. No helical sheath structure could be detected in the hydrogen bacteria studied.

Straight filament mutants from *Salmonella typhimurium* SJ814 have been studied by O'Brien & Bennett (130) using electron microscopy and optical diffraction techniques. Underfocused pictures of uranyl acetate stained filaments reveal that they possess globular subunits 5 nm in diameter, close packed in a hexagonal or near-hexagonal lattice. If the external filament diameter is taken as 20 nm, then the number of longitudinal rows of subunits would be in the range of 8 to 12. The structure of normal, wavy filaments of *S. typhimurium* SJ814 is similar to that of the mutant straight form, but it has long-pitch helical rows running nearly parallel to its filament length. In any case, the number of longitudinal or near-longitudinal subunit rows is the same (~ 11). The selection rule, $L = 15\,\text{n} + 82\,m$, where L is the layer-line number, n, the order of the Bessel function, and m is zero or any integer, positive or negative, yields n $= 11$ when $L = 1$, and n $=$ 5 when $L = 7$. These parameters define a helix of 82 subunits in 15 turns, or just under 11 subunits in two turns. O'Brien & Bennett (130) conclude that "... the most obvious difference in substructure between normal and straight flagella is the inclination of the long-pitch helical rows to the length of the flagellum, that is, the degree of 'twist' of the rows. In normal flagella these rows run at least 2° to the length of the flagellum and their helical pitch is about 2.5 nm. In straight flagella the corresponding parameters are about 7° and 0.4 nm." Exposure of normal flagellated *P. aeruginosa* PJ106 to *p*-fluorophenylalanine results in the production of straight filaments (176), but no fine structure investigation has been done on these. Helical flagella from *Salmonella* and *Escherichia* become straight in the presence of 0.5 M citric acid at below pH 4.0 (89). Contrarily, straight filaments from *Salmonella* SJ814 become helical shaped under the same conditions. It has been determined that the basic (1-start) helix in straight filaments is right-handed. However, optical diffraction and X-ray diffraction studies reveal that the near-longitudinal rows of subunits in citric acid-induced straight flagella tilt at a 2 to 3° angle with respect to the flagellar axis. This inclination appears to be left-handed. It is concluded that there must be two types of straight flagella.

Iino et al (77) report that *S. typhimurium* SJ4020 appears to have five filament forms in phase 2 (one of two antigenic types of flagella in enteric bacteria), depending upon the method of specimen preparation. Without formalin fixation the "N" form (L $= 1.01$ μm, $\lambda = 0.92$ μm, h $= 0.16$ μm) is predominant. When a suspension in deionized water is negatively stained with uranyl acetate or phosphotungstate, more than 90% of the filaments observed are "N," and the remainder are "C" (L $= 1.38$ μm, $\lambda = 1.10$ μm, h $= 0.36$ μm) or "S" (L $= 0.76$ μm, $\lambda = 0.72$ μm, h $= 0.10$ μm) forms. Only rarely does an "O" (straight) form appear. The waveforms appearing as minor fractions increase with the time that the suspensions are maintained in water. Furthermore, uranyl acetate enhances the increase of "C" forms, whereas phosphotungstate does not. The "M" form (L = 0.52 μm, λ = 0.50 μm, h = 0.04 μm) is seen when the specimen is held for 3 h in deionized water at 23°C and negatively stained with phosphotungstate. The investigators conclude that each waveform represents a stable structure to which a polymorphous filament can convert. Asakura (11) postulates that the percentage difference in length of the outermost and innermost lines (α) seen in electron micrographs of negatively stained filaments represents the difference between the outermost and innermost strands, and α is proportional to the curvature of the filament helix. The average of the angles of the outermost and innermost lines to the axis of the helix ($\Delta\Theta$) represents the degree of twist of the longitudinal strands. When Iino et al (77) compare α and $\Delta\Theta$ values for polymorphous mutant filaments simple geometrical relationships are obtained, except with the "O" form. There is a relative constancy of α, and the increase of $\Delta\Theta$ relates to the decrease of L in the range of 2 to 7° as follows: "M" ($\alpha = 5.53\%$, $\Delta\Theta = 6.76°$), "S" ($\alpha = 5.05\%$, $\Delta\Theta = 4.48°$), "N" ($\alpha = 4.77\%$, $\Delta\Theta = 3.30°$), and "C" ($\alpha = 5.52\%$, $\Delta\Theta = 2.09°$). Hence, these authors propose that the relationships are indications that the four waveforms result from changes in the amount of twisting of the longitudinal strands around the axis of the filament, without significant changes in the relative lengths of the outermost and innermost strands. As the longitudinal strands become more twisted, L, λ, and h become smaller. Asakura & Iino (12) suggest that homogeneous polymers of a single kind of flagellin are themselves polymorphic in nature, alternating between several discrete stable forms. Under certain environmental conditions the stability of each form is determined by the nature of the flagellin. The polymorphism of filaments experimentally observed by Iino et al (77) seems to verify this hypothesis.

Kondoh & Yanagida (94) find that the helical arrangement of subunits in straight flagellar filaments of *E. coli* K 12, strains W3623 and N17–7, is different in some details from those of *Salmonella* mutants reported by Asakura & Iino (12) and O'Brien & Bennett (130). Using optical diffraction and filtering methods for analyzing electron micrographs of negatively stained filaments, Kondoh & Yanagida (94) state that these consist of a 1-start basic helix with 11 subunits in two turns with a pitch of 2.6 nm. One class of rows of subunits runs closely parallel to the filament axis. The angle of the near-axial rows to the filament axis is 0° for *E. coli* straight filaments, but 7° for *Salmonella.* In addition, the axial repeat is 5.2 nm for the former, but 39.2 nm for the latter.

A series of investigations on the flagellin of *Bacillus subtilis* (37, 48, 156) has been undertaken in which the entire amino acid sequence eventually was established. The primary structure shows no obvious regularities or major repetitions of homologous sequences, and hydrophobic residues are distributed randomly in the sequence. The NH_2-terminal region (residues 1 to 101) possesses a net charge of +6, the middle region (residues 102 to 203) a net charge of –9, and the COOH-terminal region (residues 204 to 304) a net charge of –4; hence, the charge distribution is asymmetric.

Flagellin has been used as a model self-assembly system. High and low pH, urea, guanidine, and detergents are among the agents that dissociate filaments into their constituent protomers, the flagellins. These molecules may be reassociated to form filaments practically indistinguishable from the original, and hence this process is of value in determining factors of filament assembly. Kagawa (82) finds the flagellin of *Salmonella* strain SJ25 can be polymerized (by sodium deoxycholate at 60°C) into long filaments which differ from normal in that they have no large-scale periodicity and are quite stable to high temperatures, acid and alkali. This new structure, named "P" by Hotani et al (73), was first observed after polymerization of flagellin with a soluble membrane fraction derived from deflagellated *Salmonella* SJ25. "P" filaments can be reversibly converted to ordinary flagella, and thus they also must consist of flagellin molecules having an intact primary structure (70). "P" filaments are straight, are not of uniform thickness (less than normal filaments), and appear to have a rough surface. They are similar in appearance to pili and hence they are designated as "P" filaments (73). Further work by Kagawa (82) suggests, however, that they differ from pili in their secondary structures. Wakabayashi et al (189) have studied "P" filaments by X-ray diffraction and find no regular layer-line reflection, suggesting that practically no order exists in the arrangement of flagellin molecules comprising them. The cross-β structure is predominant in the "P" filament, but normal flagella filaments have practically none. Bacterial pili have an ordered structure with respect to subunit arrangement, and, therefore, "P" filaments are not similar to pili at the molecular level.

Salmonella flagella filaments have been frequently used in reconstitution and reaggregation studies as indicated above. Monomeric flagellin solutions, produced by exposing sheared and purified flagella filaments to disaggregating agents, can be induced to regenerate the original filament by seeding with small fragments of the filament, produced by ultrasonic disintegration. This work (71, 87) adds considerably to knowledge concerning the nature of the combining site and intermolecular forces involved in protomer-protomer interaction (148).

In vitro polymerization experiments using *Salmonella* flagellin reveal that the monomer binds to the distal end of the filament and, in turn, serves as part of the nucleus for polymerization of the next monomer. Incorporation of the monomer is accompanied by its configurational change. Iino (75) points out that a conformational change of flagellin molecules upon their assembly confers structural polarity to the filament and confines the assembly to the distal end. It is assumed that the growth of filaments in vivo is reflected by in vitro observations. Temperature, pH, ionic strength, flagellin concentration, and the nature of the flagellar filaments control the process. Kamiya & Asakura (87) find that reconstituted filaments of *Salmonella* SJ670 are left-handed helices with a pitch of 2.3 μm at pH 7.0, but when the pH is 4.7 they are transformed into close coils with a pitch of 0.5 μm. Further lowering of the pH converts these coiled filaments into curly, right-handed helices with a pitch of 1.1 μm. These transformations are rapid and reversible. Helical transformations may occur in the filaments of living bacteria, and it has been proposed that the "tumbling" movements of swimming organisms may be caused by a transient conversion of normal to curly filaments accompanied by a rotation change (107). Further work by Kamiya & Asakura (88) reveals that similar helical transformations occur at alkaline pH values.

The physicochemical characteristics of different flagellins have been described, including that of *Caulobacter crescentus* (95, 96), *E. coli* (99, 118), *Bacillus subtilis* (118, 168), and *Salmonella* (93).

The Hook

The section of flagellum between filament and basal structure is known as the hook. It is short, slightly curved, and has a diameter somewhat greater than the filament. The word "hook" seems inappropriate for describing this structure since it appears to be a bent or slightly curved segment, but the term is sanctioned by use. The hook appears to be less variable in length than the filament and ranges from 70 to 90 nm. It consists principally of a single polypeptide subunit. In *E. coli* (85, 165) the hook protein has a molecular weight around 42×10^3, but that of *Bacillus subtilis* hooks is reported as 33×10^3 (51). The major hook protein has been assigned no formal name, but it obviously differs from flagellin. Low pH, urea, and other flagellin solvents have little effect on the hook, and it is antigenically distinct from flagellin. *Hag* mutants of *E. coli* are incapable of synthesizing filaments but do make hook and basal structures (51).

Polyhook mutants of *E. coli* (165) and *S. typhimurium* (136) have been described. *C. crescentus* (ATCC 19089) polyhook protein has a molecular weight of 72×10^3 (158). These structures, designated as "superhooks," are homologous with normal hooks but much longer (5). The mutants lack ability to terminate the hook structure assembly and synthesize flagellin very slowly. Few polyhooks bear filaments, but "tethered" nonfilament polyhook mutants display cell rotation. The genetics and chemistry of hooks have been thoroughly reviewed (68, 167).

Raska et al (141) state that "plain" flagellar hooks of *Pseudomonas rhodos* 9–6 are cone-shaped, 70 nm long and 13 to 21.5 nm wide, and consist of helically wound subunits. The hooks of "complex" flagella are curved cylindrical structures 180 to 190 nm long, 15 to 16 nm wide, and consist of globulin subunits. Such hooks consist of a tubular sheath of helically arranged monomers of 43×10^3 daltons, and an inner core 5 nm wide.

Kagawa et al (83) report that polyhooks which are derived from nonmotile mutants of *Salmonella* and *Escherichia* and are helix-shaped under physiological conditions (pH 7.0) can be transformed to straight filaments when the pH is decreased to 3.2 or lower. This helical to straight transformation is reversible. They also find that a "doughnut" shaped polyhook can be produced by heating at 75°C at pH 8.2 in the absence of salts. The authors speculate that at 75°C polyhooks form close coils, and when shortened to the length of about one turn (~ 0.3 μm) an intrafilamentous head-to-tail association occurs, thereby forming doughnut-shaped entities.

Kagawa et al (84) find that *Salmonella* serotypes possess hooks which share common antigenicity. This raises the interesting question as to why flagellar filaments appear antigenically diverse, whereas hooks appear homogenous. *Salmonella* hook antisera will not immobilize a given serotype, but filament antisera will, and it is suggested that bacteria possessing new mutant H-antigens can "escape" the immunological defense of the host better than those carrying preexisting H-antigen. Therefore filament mutations are selectively advantageous, whereas hook antigen mutations are selectively neutral.

The precise function of the hook is unknown. It has been suggested that it may act as a "universal joint" at the base of the filament, thus allowing efficient transmission of rotational motion to the rest of the structure (167). Macnab (107) speculates that the marked curvature of the hook might serve in orienting the filament by flexibly coupling it to the cell body so that a lateral filament could operate in a bundle on the long axis of the cell. Nothing has been reported on the structural rigidity of the hook. If it is rigid, it would define the cone of revolution described by a rotating filament, but no hookless mutant has been isolated to test the requirement of the hook for translational motion. The hook may serve as the initiation point for polymerization of flagellin into the filament structure (141, 196), but this has not been demonstrated.

The Basal Structure

The proximal eubacterial terminal structure is the most complex part of flagella. On the basis of detailed electron microscope work on isolated and intact flagella of several different bacteria, a model basal structure has been developed. In Gram-negative organisms, such as *E. coli,* four discs or rings are bound to the terminal part of the flagellum ("rod") below the hook. These rings have been named (49, 50) and they are located as follows: the "L" ring, associated with the lipopolysaccharide outer wall; the "P" ring, associated with the peptidoglycan layer; the "S" ring, lying between the cytoplasmic membrane and the peptidoglycan layer; and the "M" ring, attached to the cytoplasmic membrane. The rings appear paired, and the "L" and "P" rings are separated (in *E. coli*) by a 9 nm gap; at a distance of 12 nm are situated the paired "S" and "M" rings, separated by only 3 nm. The "rod" on which these four rings are associated is about one-half the diameter of the filament. Basal structures of *Bacillus subtilis* flagella are similar to those of *E. coli,* except that they have only one pair of rings, analogous to the "S" and "M" rings. The suggested functions of these structures are considered in the section on biomechanics, and in these terms the "M" ring is a rotor, the "S" ring, a stator, and "P" and "L" are bushings.

Coulton & Murray (41, 42) have made an extensive study of the cell envelope regions associated with the basal structure of *Aquaspirillum serpens.* They find a series of up to seven concentric rings and an inner collar that forms a plate 90 nm in diameter located on the inner leaflet of the outer cell envelope. The "L" ring also is inserted into this envelope. The "P" ring is positioned exterior to the peptidoglycan layer and possibly indented or modified by it. Most interesting is the observation that the "M" ring has regular splayed fibrils emanating from it. Coulton & Murray (41, 42) suggest that these may be membrane-associated and serve as anchorage structures. The "M" ring is believed to be situated below the cytoplasmic membrane, but the "S" ring lies within it. These observations reinforce the need for study of a variety of bacteria to expand our understanding of flagellar basal structure and function. It is important to remember that one or more strategic components of the basal structure might not survive the rigors of specimen preparation, and the work of Coulton & Murray (41, 42) confirms the possible hazards of generalizations based on the examination of only a few specimens.

Hoeniger et al (69) have described a "polar organelle" of *Sphaerotilus natans.* The subpolar flagellar tuft (10 to 30 filaments) is inserted into this structure, which consists of an inner layer joined by spokes to the cytoplasmic membrane. The latter is unusually dense where it contacts the polar organelle. Chalcroft et al (36) report that the flagellar tuft of *Selenomonas ruminantium* originates from a specialized organelle derived from the cytoplasm and cytoplasmic membrane. This structure appears as a flattened sac in the middle of the concave side of the organism, and it is bounded by a unit membrane. The organelle occupies about one-third the length of the concave side and is always associated with the "bullet-shaped" flagellar bases. A polar organelle was first described by Murray & Birch-Anderson (127) for *A. serpens.*

Flagellar basal membranes never have been observed in dividing selenomonads and are seen only in those not dividing (91). It is assumed that the "polar organelle" or "flagellar basal membranes" are functionally equivalent in the various organisms showing them. The structure might function in the synthesis of flagella precursors, might aggregate such precursors (flagellin?) into morphologically distinct organelles, or perhaps might supply energy to the flagella.

The relationships believed to exist between flagellar basal structures and cell wall elements may have to be modified for organisms other than eubacteria. Recently, for example, Black et al (26) have described flagellar motility in *Thermoplasma acidophilum.* Demonstration of functioning flagella in a wall-less prokaryote suggests that current notions of flagellar operation need to be reexamined.

In the natural transformation of *C. crescentus* from a motile swarmer to a stalked organism, the intact flagellum is released into the environment (157). Filament, hook, and rod are easily observed, but curiously, the latter completely lacks the usual ring structures. It is possible that these remain with the organism after development of the stalk or that they are released undetected into the medium. The filament of *C. crescentus* also is of interest in that, unlike most eubacteria, it consists of two different flagellin subunits (25 and 27 $\times$ 10^3 daltons) which are immunologically cross-reactive (95, 96).

Laboratory preparations of intact *C. crescentus* flagella obtained from lysed organisms have been found by Johnson et al (79) to possess a basal structure somewhat different from that observed in other Gram-negative bacteria. It consists of five rings mounted on a rod. Two of the rings (rings I and II) are in the hook-proximal upper set, and three rings (two narrow, one wide) are in the lower set. The diameters of the upper rings are 32 and 21 nm. The three lower rings (III, IV and V) are all 21 nm in diameter, although ring V (proximal) is thicker than rings III and IV. Since *C. crescentus* periodically sheds its flagellum, ring V might be involved in the release mechanism, but this does not rule out the possibility that it could function as a rotation mechanism.

Fein (55) proposes that in flagellar morphogenesis a certain degree of localized peptidoglycan hydrolysis is required for assembly and insertion of rings in bacteria such as *Bacillus subtilis* 168 and *B. licheniformis* 6346. Poorly lytic mutants show impaired motility as well as defective flagellar morphogenesis. The basal structure is believed to be involved in the assembly and function of the organelle. The regulation of surface structure formation is a complex process and, as noted by Marino et al (114) for *C. crescentus,* involves "... controlling (A) the time of synthesis of the precursor subunits, (B) the assembly of the defined structure, (C) the location of structure information which may reflect both the synthesis and assembly processes, and (D) coordination with the cell division cycle."

FLAGELLAR BIOMECHANICS

Studies with *E. coli* tethered to microscope slides or to each other via specific flagellar component antibodies provide evidence that these bacteria swim by rotation of their helical flagella (166). Tethered polyhook mutants and tethered mutants with straight flagella are observed to rotate 360° around an axis through one end of the bacterial body. The direction of body rotation is normally counterclockwise (CCW); however, the bacteria occasionally reverse direction for several turns. The rotation of the flagellar filament at the point of insertion into the bacterial body is inferred from the observations on the spinning of the soma.

The change in the direction of body rotation from the normal CCW bias to a clockwise (CW) bias is induced by addition of chemical repellents. CCW rotation is induced by the addition of chemical attractants (97). It is concluded that the chemotactic responses in *E. coli* are effected by a change in the direction of flagellar rotation and that tumbles are caused by CW rotation and smooth swimming by CCW rotation of left-handed (LH) helical filaments. Observations of the movement of the peritrichously flagellated bacterium, *Salmonella typhimurium,* are also consistent with the possession of LH helical filaments rotating in CCW direction (110). The normal flagella of living *Bacillus* are also LH helical filaments (191).

A monoflagellated bacterium, *Pseudomonas citronellolis,* does not tumble, but rather changes direction by "backing up" after a period of straight swimming. The bodies of tethered *P. citronellolis* also rotate in a biased CCW direction, and addition of repellents increases the frequency of oscillation between CCW and CW rotation (180). Macnab (107) has outlined the evidence that wave propagation by helical flagella is caused by rotation of the filaments at the base and not by cyclic conformational changes of individual filaments. Yet, he notes that "... a direct demonstration of flagellar rotation is still lacking and would be reassuring to have."

The normal LH flagella of *Salmonella* have a wavelength of 2.3 μm but "curly" configurations with a wavelength of 1.1 μm also are encountered (138). Normal isolated flagella can be converted to curly flagella (e.g. by varying pH) and this represents a transition from a LH to a RH (right-handed) helical configuration (160). The transition also has been observed with motile *Salmonella* under dark-field light microscopy. Recent evidence shows that filament conversion from a LH to a RH mode is part of the tumbling responses (104, 111).

The rotary mechanism implies the presence of a "motor" at the flagellar base, which intermittently reverses from CCW to CW rotation. Normally, the motor is assumed to run in a CCW mode, resulting in CCW rotation of LH helical filaments. During tumbling the motor reverses to a CW rotation, imparting enough torsion to convert the filaments to the RH helical form. "The chaotic motion of the cell body, in reaction to a number of flagella which are rotating and in transition (from LH to RH configuration) constitutes the tumble." (110).

The propelling unit in peritrichously flagellated bacteria during smooth swimming is a flagellar bundle, as observed with dark-field microscopy (137). The bundle is aligned with the long axes of the organisms and with the direction of travel. The formation of the flagellar fascicle is theoretically feasible on the basis of viscous flow and the elastic properties of the filaments (6). During runs, individual flagella pump fluid away from the organism, creating a viscous flow which drags the filaments into a single bundle. It is proposed that tumbling may be generated by "running the flagella in reverse." The feasibility that a fascicle of semirigid LH helical filaments rotating in a CCW direction will not entangle as long as wave propagation is away from the points of attachment has been explored theoretically and demonstrated by a working model (106). The fascicle, representing a compact in-phase agglomeration of individual rotating flagella, can operate indefinitely in this mode or until a right-handed torque is applied at the point of flagella attachment. Change of rotation from LH to RH should cause the bundle to jam, yet this is not observed (i.e. in "tumbling"). Instead the bundle disperses as the individual filaments fly apart (110). Apparently, the flagellar bundle becomes destabilized (unwinds) as the polymorphic transition occurs; however, the mechanics of the process of flying apart of the flagellar bundle can only be guessed at in the absence of high speed, high resolution, cinematographic studies of the phenomenon (32).

Videotapes of tethered flagella undergoing polymorphic transitions have been made by Macnab (107). He noted that the transition at any instant is "... confined to a quite local region and propagates positively, i.e. away from the point of attachment." Thus, a filament in transition possesses a proximal RH segment that becomes longer and a LH distal segment that becomes shorter as the localized transition region propagates away from the point of tethering. Calladine has reassessed some details of his model flagellum (30, 31) and believes that a version in which the bistable feature is at a "corner" of the subunit is consistent with the geometry of normal and curly filaments. Distortion of the packing of interconnected subunits is consistent with the geometry at a change in waveform junction in a single filament containing two distinct waveforms (e.g. as in the transition from a LH to RH helix) (32). Subunit packing mechanics also can explain the discontinuous changes of sign in curvature and other features observed when individual flagella are flattened in electron microscopy preparations. Further, the mechanical behavior of subunit assembly makes possible an explanation for the formation of straight polymer from normal *Salmonella* flagellin at high concentrations of NaCl as observed by Kamiya & Asakura (86).

As mentioned above, RH helical filaments rotating CW would not jam (105) and, further, if the conversion is complete in all the flagella, the bacteria should swim smoothly. Recently, mutants of *S. typhimurium* LT2 (*che U* mutants) have been isolated that swim smoothly by CW rotation of RH flagellar fascicles (90). The *che U* mutants show inverted chemotactic behavior, as they are attracted by repellents and are repelled by attractants for the wild-type strain. A theoretical explanation for the molecular aspects of the inverted behavioral responses has been forwarded (90, 143).

Hypotheses on the operation of the flagellar motor center on the functional aspects of the observed structures comprising the basal body (see section on flagellar structure). Most attention has been focused on how the innermost ring, the M ring, might function with the S ring in generating torque. Berg (16, 18) and Läuger (98) assume that the S ring is attached to the peptidoglycan layer of the cell wall and that torque is generated between the S and M rings. The M ring, mounted in the rod, is assumed to rotate in the cytoplasmic membrane. However, the S ring of *E. coli* may be located in the periplasmic space (50). The possibility that torque may be generated at the contact area between the outer cylindrical surface of the axial rod and the inner cylindrical surface of the M ring has recently been suggested (108).

Since functioning flagella have been demonstrated in a wall-less microorganism, *T. acidophilum,* (26), possession of a cell wall is not essential for motility in all flagellated bacteria. The coordination, uncoordination, and recoordination of the flagellar fascicles located at opposite poles of certain *Spirillum* spp. pose some puzzling questions in the search for a unified theory on the mechanism of prokaryotic propulsion by flagella (34). In normal motility both fascicles of *Spirillum volutans* rotate in the same direction, causing the spiral body to rotate in the opposite direction (122); when the fascicles reorient from a "head-tail" to "tail-head" configuration (presumably caused by a reversal of the flagellar "motors"), *S. volutans* swims in the opposite direction. Certain chemicals can render *S. volutans* immobile by causing each of the fascicles to rotate in opposite directions. Two major types of uncoordination have been observed, with both fascicles either in the head orientation ("dual-head") or both in the tail orientation ("dual-tail") (122). A further type of uncoordination has been described ("dual-straight-tail") in which both polar bundles project outward in a plane longitudinal to the helical soma. This type of coordination apparently involves "unusually narrow cones of revolution" (34).

In most cases, removal of the uncoordinating chemical agent results in flagellar fascicle recoordination. Although it has not yet been possible to determine the direction of rotation of flagellar fascicles in the uncoordinated state, it has been observed that the bundle is rotating at a lower speed than in the coordinated state (34). Doetsch (52) has proposed that the various types of flagella bundle alignments may be explained by the production of an electrically asymmetric cell (dipole state) as a stimulus causes local membrane depolarization at one pole of the spirillum. Theories concerning the mechanism of flagellar rotation have to account for the situation where two motors on the same organism rotate simultaneously in opposite directions.

An inhibitor which specifically inactivates CW rotation of tethered *S. typhimurium* is formed in autoclaved nutrient broth, in citrate-containing media, or in citrate autoclaved at neutral pH (172). Continuous washing of tethered bacteria with solutions containing the inactivator results in a gradual and irreversible inhibition of CW rotation. Thus, the phenomenon is unlike the transient suppression caused by chemical attractants. The precise nature of inhibitory action is unknown. Spudich & Koshland (172) state, inhibitors could "... provide a useful probe into the molecular mechanism of bacterial chemotaxis." Similar inactivators, if they could be found, might also be useful in studying the uncoordination and recoordination of fascicles of bipolarly flagellated bacteria such as *S. volutans*.

The energy source for flagellar rotation is derived not from adenosine triphosphate (ATP) hydrolysis but rather from the electrochemical potential of protons across the membrane (i.e. proton-motive force, PMF). The evidence for this conclusion recently has been summarized by Macnab (107), and thus our discussion is not intended to be comprehensive. PMF can be defined as the amount of work done by a single proton as it moves across a membrane. Both the transmembrane potential ($\Delta\psi$) and the transmembrane pH (ΔpH) contribute to the total PMF. Disturbance of both, with ionophores or uncouplers, abolishes motility in an actively metabolizing peritrichously flagellated strain of *Streptococcus* (113). The *Streptococcus* strain becomes immotile when starved for glucose; however, motility (tumbling) is restored when it is exposed either to an artificial $\Delta\psi$ or an artificial ΔpH. "Runs" occur if an attractant is added upon establishing the PMF. A significant level of ATP synthesis ($>$750 pmol/mg dry weight) is not required for motility resumption, since starved streptococci preincubated with arsenate or *N,N'*-dicyclohexyl-carbodiimide also resume motility upon PMF imposition. Similar results have been obtained with *Bacillus subtilis* (47), *Escherichia coli* (131), and *Rhodospirillum rubrum* (14). It is possible that an efflux of internal hydroxyl ions constitutes the PMF, but this phenomenon cannot be distinguished from the influx of protons (65).

Hypotheses have been forwarded to explain how PMF drives the flagellar motor. It has been suggested that torque is generated as protons are channeled through the contact surface between the S and M rings (98). Alternatively, protons may be translocated through the area where the outer cylindrical surface of the axial filament comes in contact with the inner cylindrical surface of the S ring (108). Macnab (108) has critically reviewed the existing theoretical explanations on the coupling of PMF to motor rotation. It remains to be determined if protons are used directly by the motor and also how the electrical and chemical potential of protons (or possibly other ionic species) is coupled to mechanical rotation. Further, the ability of the motor to change rotational direction has to be accounted for when considering the mechanism of the chemomechanical transduction process.

It is clear that transient alterations in bacterial membrane potential cause changes in swimming behavior of bacteria. However, the relationship between membrane potential alteration and chemotaxis is not so clear. While chemical attractants and repellents induce a transient hyperpolarized membrane state in *E. coli* (178), a strong attractant (L-alanine) for *Bacillus subtilis* shows no effect on the membrane potential (124). It is difficult to believe that these observations can be explained by fundamental differences between the chemotaxis mechanisms of Gram-negative and Gram-positive bacteria. It appears that the observed differences may reside in the relatively slow, indirect methods that are assumed to measure membrane potential, or perhaps may result from experimental artifacts.

A more rapid, direct approach has been used by Armitage & Evans (8) to measure membrane potential in *Rhodospeudomonas sphaeroides.* Membrane-associated carotenoids of this photosynthetic bacterium undergo an electrochromic absorption shift that is linearly related to a change in membrane potential. The authors assume that the absorption spectrum is "... caused by the pumping of protons across the membrane." Both chemical attractants and repellents cause an increase in the membrane potential of *Rhodospeudomonas sphaeroides* as shown by the absorption shift in the carotenoid pigments. An inital rapid rise in membrane potential ($t_{1/2} \sim$ 75–100 msec) is induced by the chemicals. A fast decay phase ($t_{1/2} \sim 300$ msec) is followed by a slower decay phase (1.5–2.0 min) as the potential returns to a steady level. Inability to find a change in membrane potential with *Bacillus subtilis* may have been due to methodological limitations.

This part of the chemotactic signal may have occurred " . . . as a very fast transient, outside the range of their slow measuring system" (8).

BIOLOGICAL ASPECTS OF MOTILITY

Environmental Influences on Motile Populations

Bacteria in natural ecosystems are constantly subjected to fluctuations in chemical and physical environmental parameters. In situ effects of these factors on motility of naturally occurring prokaryote populations are difficult to measure and, thus, current knowledge is derived largely from controlled laboratory studies.

A variety of prokaryotic flagellates are found in soil and aquatic environments and also in association with higher organisms in these ecosystems. Motile bacteria are readily isolated from such diverse habitats as deep ocean trenches, rumen contents, and periodontal areas. It is not obvious that possession of motor organelles provides a competitive advantage for prokaryotes, since nonmotile bacteria survive quite well in various environments. Yet, active motility may allow an organism to take advantage of nutrients present in wider areas of its milieu.

The argument that survival advantages are conferred upon flagellated bacteria is strengthened by the absolute dependence of tactic responses on the possession of motility. Taxes may result in the accumulation of motile bacteria in physiologically favorable environments or may prevent accumulation in unfavorable environments. Tactic responses in bacteria have received much attention and, thus, our discussion will consider only some of the possible ecological consequences of these behavioral phenomena.

The fundamental question concerning bacterial chemotaxis relates to the correlation of laboratory-based behavior with bacterial responses in natural habitats. Laboratory assays typically compare the number of organisms entering a microcapillary containing a test chemical to the number entering a capillary without the chemical. Responses of high population densities ($\sim 10^8$ organisms/ml) of a pure culture suspended in a defined chemotaxis medium do not reflect the complex chemical, physical, and biological interactions that certainly exist in natural habitats.

Yet, some possible generalizations can be made with the data available from laboratory studies. For example, a general correlation has been noted between negative chemotaxis and avoidance of toxic chemicals (170, 182). There also is evidence that positive chemotaxis is generally related to the accumulation of bacteria in favorable (e.g. nutrient-containing) environments. Since most heterotrophic bacteria are attracted to a wide variety of chemicals, including many carbohydrates and amino acids, it is difficult to postulate that a specific chemical would function as an ecological determinant for this behavioral response. Thus, positive chemotaxis would probably function in aiding these bacteria to find, or remain in, areas containing any of a variety of nutrients.

Not all nutrients are attractants, and uptake and metabolism of a chemical are not essential for attraction (1). In general, however, *E. coli* is attracted to amino acids it can oxidize (121). Further studies with other bacteria are needed to confirm that chemical attractants generally serve as nutrients. Perhaps investigations with chemoautotrophic bacteria would help establish this relationship. We have evaluated positive chemotaxis in the sulfur-oxidizing chemoautotroph, *Thiobacillus thioparus.* Ammonium, nitrate, and thiosulfate ions, which can serve as nitrogen and sulfur sources, are the only attractants recognized by this organism; carbohydrates and amino acids fail to elicit any response. It is suggested that motile prokaryotes exhibiting only limited chemotactic responses may be useful model organisms in studying the survival value of positive chemotaxis.

Only one study has attempted to appraise this (139). When a motile chemotactic strain of *Proteus mirabilis* and a nonchemotactic motile mutant are inoculated in a semisolid, amino acid medium, the chemotactic strain reaches a significantly higher population density after 14 h. Both organisms grow at the same initial rate in the semisolid medium, and both strains attain the same final population density when mixed in broth culture where, presumably, no gradients exist. However, since the mutant strain displays "more frequent tumbling" than the chemotactic wild type, these results may only reflect the competitive advantage that the "normal" swimmer has in exploiting the amino acid nutrients in a semisolid medium.

Positive chemotaxis may limit the dispersal of flagellated *Actinoplanes brasiliensis* spores (132). The spores are attracted to chloride, bromide, and seawater but do not respond to other ions nor to a variety of organic compounds that support growth. The motile phase of *A. brasiliensis* is transient and attraction to seawater may limit the dispersal of spores away from sandy soils near seashores.

Experiments failed to show that the predatory bacterium, *Bdellovibrio bacteriovorus,* is attracted to components in exudates of host Gram-negative bacteria, indicating that chemotaxis is not directly involved (174). *Bdellovibrio bacteriovorus* is attracted to a number of amino acids and positive chemotaxis may act indirectly by "... enabling bdellovibrios to locate environments containing nutrients that would relieve their starvation as well as attract and support the growth of potential prey cells."

Motile, iron-containing bacteria are found in diverse aquatic environments. A recent, exciting discovery reveals that these bacteria can orient and swim along geomagnetic lines of force (27). Motility is required for magnetotaxis, and accumulations of "magnetococci" occur at the south magnetic focus of a magnet and not at the north magnetic pole (125). The biological role or roles of magnetotaxis are unclear. While most magnetotactic bacteria have been observed in aquatic sediments, Moench & Konetzka (125) found high concentrations of a magnetococcus in the water column of a sewage oxidation pond. A magnetotactic spirillum isolated from a freshwater swamp has been mass cultured in its magnetic as well as in its nonmagnetic state (56).

Very little is known about the existence of chemical sex attractants in bacteria. Under defined experimental conditions, motile Hfr *Salmonella typhimurium* are attracted by F organisms (24). The F bacteria may produce a sex attractant specific for the Hfr mating type. Recipient organisms of the nonmotile bacterium *Streptococcus faecalis* produce a heat-stable protein that causes mating aggregates to form when donor and recipient are mixed (54). It appears premature to label this factor as analogous to a "sex pheromone," as suggested by Saunders (144), especially since no active movement of the bacterium would be involved. However, the results should stimulate the search for chemical signals in other motile mating pair bacterial systems.

Other responses that influence the behavior of motile prokaryotes include taxes to air (aerotaxis) and to light (phototaxis). Positive aerotaxis is usually considered to result from the movement of an organism up a gradient of O_2, but may also result from movement down a gradient of CO_2 (66). The latter possibility apparently has not been considered in most studies of aerotaxis in bacteria. *Spirillum volutans* in capillary tubes with an oxidizable substrate forms bands in response to self-created oxygen gradients (35). The rate of band migration is directly related to the rate of respiration. Oxygen uptake and oxidative phosphorylation are required for band formation, and intracellular ATP levels may regulate the aerotactic response, possibly by influencing flagellar activity.

Finger-like zoogloea consisting of bacteria embedded in a viscous, gelatinous matrix are common in organic rich polluted environments. The predominant bacteria in zoogloeae are polarly flagellated (184). A study on the formation of wastewater zoogloeae (185) indicates that the finger-like projections elongate in water toward an air : water interface.

Comprehensive consideration of phototaxis in photosynthetic prokaryotes is beyond the scope of this review; however, the effect of light on nonphotosynthetic bacteria will be discussed. Phototaxis in *S. volutans* was observed as early as 1920 (122). Recently, it has been shown that aerobically grown *R. rubrum*, containing no detectable bacteriochlorophyll, move toward a strong light stimulus (64). Interference due to thermotaxis has to be considered in such studies; however, phototaxis of *R. rubrum* is observed even after the light is passed through a heat-absorbing filter.

Exposure of *S. typhimurium* (110), *Pseudomonas citronellolis* (179), or *E. coli* (180) to intense light results in an increase in the tumbling frequency of these bacteria. Short pulses of light (390–530 nm) initiate continuous tumbling, whereas longer exposures induce smooth swimming and eventually paralysis. The minium intensity of white light that causes 80% or more of *S. typhimurium* to constantly tumble is 0.9 $J/cm^2/sec$ (180). After approximately 5 sec exposure the organisms exhibit a smooth swimming phase and they become paralyzed at about 30 sec exposure. An intensity of 0.09 $J/cm^2/sec$ is sufficient to cause constant tumbling of *S. typhimurium* when the bacteria are incubated with 2.5×10^{-6} M proflavin, a photoreducible dye. This light intensity (equivalent to 77.4 $cal/cm^2/h$) is well within the range that may reach and penetrate surface waters of natural ecosystems. A value of 100 $cal/cm^2/h$ has been given as an approximation of the radiation from the sun and sky with the sun at zenith (177). Thus, the light-induced responses may under certain conditions (e.g. in coastal surface waters containing high humic acid levels) be of ecological importance by affecting the swimming behavior of motile bacteria.

Motile behavior of bacteria also may be affected by temperature. When placed in a linear temperature gradient of 17–39°C, *E. coli* forms a dense band at approximately 30°C, suggesting a thermotactic response (112). When incubated at constant temperatures, maximum tumbling frequency occurs at 34°C and very little tumbling is observed at 20 or 39°C. Motility tracks become more curved at the higher temperatures. The average swimming speed of *E. coli* generally increases as temperature is increased, but a slight decrease in speed is noted at 34°C, where tumbling occurs more frequently. A sudden temperature drop from 30 to 20°C induces a temporary increase (30 sec) in the tumbling frequency, whereas a quick rise in temperature (from 27 to 34°C) results in a rapid, transient decrease in tumbling frequency. Smooth swimming mutants show no change in motile behavior as temperature is increased or decreased. The formation of an oxygen gradient and the accompanying bacterial chemotaxis to oxygen complicate conclusions that can be made on thermotaxis in *E. coli.* However, it is clear that tumbling frequency of this bacterium can be modulated by temperature.

The effect of temperature on a wide variety of variously flagellated bacteria has been studied with a precision temperature-controlled chamber (154). All species observed moved five to seven times as fast at 50°C than at 10°C, and the marked increase in translational velocity occurred regardless of the original incubation temperature. Temperature jumps over a range of ± 30°C could be achieved in less than 1 sec with the apparatus. Temperature drops induced periods of transient tumbling (2 to 10 sec) in the peritrichously flagellated organisms studied and more frequent reversal of direction in the polarly flagellated species. Upward temperature jumps induced transient periods of accelerated velocities. A partial capacity for temperature adaptation was noted since, "... the greatest average translational velocity at any given observation temperature occurred when the organisms were grown at temperatures less than the optimum." It is theorized that temperature drops may result in membrane depolarization.

Many classical descriptive studies have referred to the attachment of prokaryotes to surfaces at solid-liquid interfaces. Recent application of SEM has confirmed that a variety of microorganisms may attach to inert surfaces in aquatic and terrestrial systems, as well as to surfaces of other microorganisms, plants and animals. Remarkably little is known about the initial mechanisms of prokaryote adherence, including the possible involvement of flagella as attachment devices. Certain Gram-negative bacteria have been tethered to glass slides via specific flagellar antibodies (166). However, the adhesion also may occur naturally (119) or with selected bacterial flagellar mutants (74).

Adhesion of bacteria to intestinal surfaces may be initiated by chemotactic responses. A pepsin digest of rabbit intestinal mucosa inhibits the association of *Salmonella enteritidis* and cholera vibrios with rabbit intestine (57). A subsequent report shows that the intestine extract also neutralizes a positive chemotactic response of *Vibrio cholerae, E. coli,* and *S. typhimurium* to the villous surface of pieces of mouse or rabbit intestine (3). Nonchemotactic motile mutants of the three bacterial species do not accumulate at the intestinal surfaces.

Recent evidence indicates that the gradient which attracts *V. cholerae* to the mucosal surface of rabbit or germ-free mouse intestinal slices originates in the area at the base of the villi (58). A chemotactic parent strain accumulates in the mucus gel at the basal area between villi, whereas a nonchemotactic mutant derived from the parent strain does not. The parent strain also is attracted by twenty amino acids. Yet, it is too early to conclude that these compounds are responsible for causing *V. cholerae* to associate rapidly with intestinal mucus gels. An in vivo evaluation of the virulence of the nonchemotactic mutants versus wild-type bacteria may help to confirm a relationship between chemotaxis and disease. Recently, a chemotactic strain of *V. cholerae* has been shown to associate strongly with the mucosa of rabbit ileal loops (58). A nonchemotactic mutant associates with the mucosa to a significantly lower degree in these in vivo studies.

Motile forms of plant pathogenic bacteria may more readily reach favorable sites for infection. The role of bacterial motility in plant invasiveness has been studied with *Pseudomonas phaseolicola,* the agent of halo blight disease in the common bean (134). Folar bacterial pathogens, such as *P. phaseolicola,* usually invade through natural plant openings (stomata, hydathodes, or nectaries) when these areas are moist or under high humidity. Motile strains of *P. phaseolicola* applied externally to plant leaves cause up to twelve times as many lesions as do mutants with paralyzed flagella (134).

Certain bacteriophages adsorb to motile bacteria by first attaching to host flagella. Phage χ of enteric bacteria (123), phage PBS-1 of *Bacillus subtilis* (140), phage 7–7–1 of *Rhizobium lupini* (102), phage ϕ6 of swarmer cells of *Caulobacter vibriodes* (80), and ϕ Cp 34 of *C. vibriodes* and *Caulobacter crescentus* swarmers (60) have been identified as flagellotropic phages.

Electron microscopic observations show that these DNA-containing bacteriophages possess a short fiber or fibers at the free end of their tail which initially attaches to the filament of the host flagellum. Although difficult to demonstrate experimentally, the phage particles apparently move to the base of the flagellum where they inject their DNA into the host (145). In all cases nonflagellated host strains or mutants are resistant to infection by flagellotropic phages. Attachment of phages to host flagella is not necessarily specific since PBS-1 of *Bacillus subtilis* also attaches to flagella of resistant *Bacillus* species (193).

The *E. coli:* phage χ system has received the most attention. Infection of the host soon results in its immobilization. The phage cannot infect paralyzed mutants whose flagella do not rotate (123), but they do adsorb to, and infect, bacterial mutants that possess rotating straight or curly flagella (76, 123).

Suspending *Caulobacter* in 10% (wt/vol) polyethylene glycol blocks motility but has no effect on growth (60). Phage ϕ Cp 34 does not attach to host flagella in this viscous medium, which may suggest that flagellar motion is needed for phage adsorption. Alternatively, the polyethylene glycol may directly interfere with the interaction of the phage with host flagella. No data were presented showing the effects of lesser concentrations of the viscous agent on *Caulobacter* infection by phage ϕ Cp 34.

Recently, 23 motile *E. coli* mutants have been isolated that are resistant to phage χ (74). Four of these mutants were studied further and found to have altered flagellin. Two of the mutants move normally, one tumbles at high frequency, and the other exhibits a high degree of natural tethering (presumably by the flagella) to surfaces of glass slides. Host range mutants of phage χ which attach to flagella of the above host mutants have been isolated, indicating that a defined configuration of χ tail fiber recognizes a specific area of flagellar filament. It has been proposed that phage χ moves along the filament like a "nut on a bolt"; the threads are the grooves between the helical rows of flagellin molecules (19). If flagellotropic phages move along rotating host filaments to the hook region, the initial attachment must be reversible.

It is not clear at what point motility of host bacteria ceases. However, a high multiplicity of infection "may lead to an immediate cessation of flagellar rotation owing to a sudden increase of the torque applied, thus preventing phages from reaching their final receptor at the flagellar base" (102).

The host range of phage 7–7–1 is limited to *R. lupini* H 13–3, a strain with 5 to 10 complex peritrichous flagella per bacterium (149). Phage 7–7–1 does not attach to nonmotile mutants with polyhooks (102).

Chemicals can affect the swimming velocity of motile bacteria. Serine and galactose increase the mean velocity of *E. coli* and *S. typhimurium* (109, 129). The increase is probably not mediated by chemoreceptors, since a galactose taxis mutant is similarly stimulated. The velocity of *B. subtilis* 60015 is increased from an average of 11.5 $\mu m/sec^{-1}$ to as much as 24.0 $\mu m/sec^{-1}$ upon the addition, at 10 mM, of a variety of amino acids (46). Some of the best motility stimulants (i.e. L-glutamic acid and L-lysine) are not attractants for *B. subtilis* 60015 (187). D-Amino acids, also not attractants (187), are nearly as effective as L-isomers in increasing bacterial velocity (46). The amino acid stimulants also greatly lengthen the time span over which *B. subtilis* remains motile. L-Glutamine, a motility stimulant, increases the percentage of motile bacteria in a population from an initial 85 to 94%; however, it is believed that this velocity enhancement is not due to an increase in the number of motile organisms. Further, the action of the amino acids probably is not due to a general effect on bacterial metabolism, since no relationship between increased velocity and change in intracellular ATP levels or oxygen consumption is observed.

Exogenously supplied cyclic adenosine 3',5'-monophosphate (cyclic AMP) stimulates flagella synthesis of certain bacteria (195). Migration of *Escherichia coli* S-26 in glass tubes containing a semisolid medium is enhanced by addition of 1–3 mM cyclic AMP (115). 8-Hydroxycyclic AMP also stimulates population migration, although to a lesser extent. Cyclic GMP (cyclic guanosine 3',5'-monophosphate) at 1–3 mM inhibits the motility of *E. coli* S-26, and it also competitively inhibits the stimulant effect of cyclic AMP.

Neurotransmitters, which have been implicated in cyclic AMP increase in mammalian sympathetic nerve systems, also stimulate *E. coli* population migration. The biogenic amines, dopamine and histamine, at concentrations as low as 1 μM, are among the most potent stimulants. The higher concentration (1–3 mM) of exogenously supplied cyclic AMP needed to elicit a detectable response is probably due to the low permeability of this chemical. Acetylcholine, which can increase cyclic GMP levels in mammalian cells, inhibits migration at a concentration of 1 mM. Adrenergic blocking agents, antihistamines, and neuroleptics inhibit *E. coli* migration when added at concentrations greater than 40 μM. The drugs do not inhibit bacterial growth at those concentrations.

This evidence indicates that levels of intracellular cyclic AMP and cyclic GMP can regulate bacterial motility. It will be of interest to evaluate whether the relatively high levels of amino acids (10 mM) that increase the mean velocity of bacteria (46) affect intracellular levels of cyclic AMP or cyclic GMP. Possibly, the above observations also will have to be included in the present models that attempt to define the molecular biology of motility and chemotaxis in bacteria.

Aliphatic alcohols, at concentrations as high as 10^{-2} M, induce continuous states of uncoordinated translational movement in *Pseudomonas fluorescens, Rhodospirillum rubrum,* and *Alcaligenes faecalis* (25). Normal motility patterns are resumed upon removal of the alcohols. The frequency of reversals in *P. fluorescens* generally increased with an increase in the length of the alkyl moiety of the alcohols.

The effect of pressure on bacterial motility has been studied with pure cultures of *E. coli, Serratia marinorubra, Proteus mirabilis, Salmonella typhosa,* and *Bacillus licheniformis* (120). Movement of these bacteria is progressively inhibited as pressure is increased. None of the bacteria are motile at 306 atm or greater, even though they multiply at these pressures. Further experiments with *E. coli* show that flagellar synthesis is inhibited at high pressures.

Motility of flagellated bacteria is influenced by the viscosity of the suspending medium. Shoesmith (164) observed an initial velocity increase with a slight increase in viscosity. Translational movement reaches a maximum value and then decreases as the viscosity is further increased. Studies by Schneider & Doetsch (153), with variously flagellated bacteria, confirm and extend the above observations and show that the response is a general behavioral phenomenon among motile bacteria. Polarly flagellated bacteria show maximum velocities at lower viscosities than peritrichously flagellated bacteria. Viscosities beyond 2 to 5 centipoise (cp) are sufficient to cause a decrease in bacterial velocity (153). Greenberg & Canale-Parola (63) have determined that bacterial species (including *Pseudomonas aeruginosa, A. serpens,* and *E. coli*) are immobilized at 60 cp, "a relatively low viscosity."

Two bacteria have been isolated from nature which are able to migrate through agar gels (63). One of these organisms, identified as *Spirillum gracile,* reaches a maximum velocity, in polyvinylpyrrolidone, at 2 cp and becomes immobilized at 1000 cp. The other bacterium, a flexible, Gram-negative, aerobic, rod-shaped bacterium (0.4 by 8 to 12 μm), has a maximum velocity at 6.5 cp and the minimum immobilizing viscosity is greater than 1000 cp. The data with the latter show that a bacterium need not be helical in order to move through viscous solutions.

Eubacteria grown in viscous media do not appear to change their flagellar arrangements (153). Nevertheless, certain modifications of the flagellar cone of revolution are observed. Greenberg & Canale-Parola (63) suggest that certain flagellated bacteria possess the ability to swim through environments of relatively high viscosity because they possess a specialized type of motility apparatus suited to the conditions of their habitats.

The gel-like structure of solutions containing viscous agents with long, unbranched chains (e.g. methylcellulose or polyvinylpyrrolidone) may explain the observed increase in velocity at low viscosities of 1–8 cp (23). Perhaps the efficiency of flagellar propulsion is "enhanced by the gel-like structure of these solutions." Helical, flagellated bacteria (e.g. *Spirillum*) may swim more rapidly in dilute viscous media (153) because the gel-like structure of these solutions reduces the "circumferential slip" of the helix that is observed when the bacteria are propelled through nonviscous solutions (23).

Bacterial velocity is not increased in solutions (circa 2 cp) containing dextran as a viscous agent (164). It is suggested (23) that viscous solutions containing highly branched polymers do not change the solution hydrodynamics as do unbranched polymers.

Flagellar Diversity

The arrangement of flagella on a given organism is constant; indeed, this characteristic is used for taxonomic purposes. There are, however, some cases where variation of flagella distribution and wavelength occurs. *Pseudomonas mendocina* and *Pseudomonas stutzeri,* as young cultures on solid complex media, form lateral flagella of shorter wavelength than the polar flagella normally produced (133). Seelinger & Welshimer (155) state that *Listeria* is peritrichous at 20 to 25°C, but at 37°C forms only polar flagella. Variation in flagellar arrangement and/or wavelength on a given organism is found among certain *Aeromonas, Photobacterium,* and *Vibrio* species (45). These authors defined "variable flagellation" as follows: "... when both polar and lateral flagella, morphologically distinct, are present in the same organism although not necessarily on the same cell." In contrast, "mixed flagellation" would be used in cases where polar and lateral flagella occur on the same individual.

Vibrio alginolyticus (45) has a single, sheathed, polar flagellum with a wavelength of $\sim$ 1.5 μm and a thickness of 25 nm when grown in liquid medium, whereas on solid medium lateral flagella ($\lambda = 0.9$ μm, thickness = 15 nm) are predominant. If the incubation temperature of agar cultures is 40°C or above, lateral flagella are markedly reduced in number, but polar flagella are less affected by higher temperatures. On semisolid media (<0.5% agar), lateral flagella are rarely seen. These investigators suggest that lateral flagella are important aids in holding organisms to a solid surface, whereas when living free, the production of lateral flagella would be wasteful since locomotion could be adequately accomplished with a single polar flagellum. Furthermore, it is believed that *V. alginolyticus* achieves a "polymeric bridging" by the production of lateral flagella, enabling it to adhere to surfaces. This reasoning would apply to the majority of marine bacteria reported to have variable flagellation. On the other hand, Meadows (119) reports similar behavior patterns in the ability of bacteria to attach to glass surfaces, regardless of whether they are polarly flagellated (*Aeromonas liquefaciens* NCIB 9233, *P. fluorescens* NCIB 9046) or peritrichously flagellated (*E. coli* NCTC 8196, *Flavobacterium* sp. NCMB 292).

Additional chemical factors affecting flagellation of *V. alginolyticus* have been reported (44). On agar media with more than 4% NaCl, the number of lateral flagella decreases with increasing salt concentration, and in liquid media with 6.0 to 9.0% NaCl, organisms with polar tufts of 2 to 4 sheathed or unsheathed flagella are seen. In liquid media with 0.1 to 0.3% boric acid, or 0.05 to 0.1% $Al(OH)_3$, organisms tend to produce lateral flagella in addition to the normally formed polar flagella. The lateral and polar flagella of *Vibrio parahaemolyticus* are found to be antigenically distinct (162). Palleroni et al (133) theorize that two sets of genetic determinants might govern, respectively, the production of polar and lateral flagella. The "signal" to which bacteria respond in this manner is unknown but certainly constitutes a fascinating area for investigation.

Ulitizur (183) has found that the development of lateral flagella in *V. alginolyticus* NCMB 1803 depends on a complex relationship between temperature, salt concentration, and pH. He reports that the organisms grew well over a temperature range of 20 to 44°C, but no lateral flagella developed above 20°C at NaCl concentations above 0.7%. At 30 to 46°C, increasing amounts of NaCl are required for formation of lateral flagella. At pH 6.0, *V. alginolyticus* forms lateral flagella at 37°C in 1% NaCl, but at least 3% NaCl is required at pH 9.0. The sheathed polar flagellum is produced at all temperatures (20 to 46°C) and salinities (0.5 to 5.0%). It is possible that the sheath may serve to protect and conserve the flagellum.

Chatterjee (38) observes that lateral flagella of *V. parahaemolyticus* appear more susceptible to mechanical agitation than the polar. It is further noted that 37°C cultures show monotrichous polar flagella, but 22°C cultures consist mainly of laterally flagellated organisms. Shinoda & Okamoto (163) designate the flagella of *V. parahaemolyticus* as "M" (polar, monotrichous) and "L" (lateral). The latter develop at both 25 and 37°C on solid medium, but not in liquid or semisolid media. "L" flagella formation is depressed by lowering pH and by transferral from solid to liquid media. Although *V. parahaemolyticus* possesses "L" flagella at 37°C after 3 h, overnight cultures do not, and the authors believe that "L" flagella spontaneously detach and decompose at high temperatures.

From the results of deBoer et al (44, 45), Ulitizur (183), and Shinoda & Okamoto (163), "L" flagella appear directly related to swarming and attachment on solid media and also to swimming in liquid media, if not attached. Contrarily, the "M" flagellum is a locomotory organelle only in liquid media.

CONCLUDING REMARKS

Knowledge regarding eubacterial flagella has expanded more in the past nine years than in the previous seventy. New structural details have been described and recent evidence shows the mechanics of bacterial flagellar operation differs from that of other protist locomotory organelles. One cannot fail to be impressed with the vast and expensive armamentarium of laboratory apparatus that has been brought to bear on all aspects of flagella and motion problems. Yet, limitations and hidden assumptions attendant upon such complicated machinery may not always be realized, and theories built on sophisticated approaches ought be susceptible to treatment with "Occam's razor."

In spite of all the technological advances, the "experimentum crucis" with regard to rotational movement of flagella remains to be done, and the available optical evidence may be tinged with a faint suspicion of "trompe l'oeil." The operation of sheathed flagella of Gram-negative bacteria also may present problems for the rotary theory of flagellar motion, since the sheath appears to be an extension of the outer cell wall. Accordingly, either the flagella must rotate within the sheath or the sheath must rotate. Neither of these possibilities appears attractive. A universal function applied to the basal structures, thus far described for a limited number of bacteria, will have to await further testing with a wider range of more diverse organisms.

Behavioral studies in bacteria have provoked similar studies in other organisms such as algae, fungi, and protozoa. It is more likely that the eukaryotes, rather than the bacteria, would serve as useful models for sensory responses of more complex animals, including man. A possible exception is that of magnetic sensing in bacteria, which may have a counterpart in bees and migratory birds.

The ecological roles of bacterial taxes can only be inferred from data of laboratory studies, which typically measure responses of single species to a particular physical or chemical stimulus. Hopefully, results from in vitro studies with an ever increasing diversity of bacteria will provide a valuable conceptual base for future in situ or in vivo ecological studies, as well as for more complex laboratory assays. Unfortunately, microbial ecologists have been relatively slow in exploring the possibility that tactic responses may act as significant, or perhaps even major, ecological determinants for naturally occurring microbial populations.

The discovery that amino acid sequences in flagellin confer different charge polarities to regions of the filament may have implications for the study of flagella as organelles of attachment to surfaces. Further, such observations make it conceivable that certain bacteria might aggregate by means of flagella-flagella contact, and in our laboratory evidence has been obtained with a marine pseudomonad that supports this contention.

Further work needs to be done to confirm the modus operandi of flagellotropic bacteriophages. It is difficult to believe that phages can attach to flagella rotating at ~ 3000 rpm. Perhaps the attachment stage occurs when the flagella reverse direction. Further, the possibility that pili have a role in the flagellotropic phage phenomenon should be investigated.

The mighty mass of published materials relating to flagella, motility and associated elements causes one to pause in awe at the accomplishments of this decade. We can only hope that the quantity will shortly make clear problems and phenomena that still appear opaque. Perhaps it is a question of being too close to the forest to see the trees, but in any event, let us hope that we will find "nature as she is and not as we imagine her to be."

ACKNOWLEDGMENTS

The authors wish to thank T. M. Cook and R. M. Cole for reading and criticizing the entire manuscript. We are also grateful to E. Taylor and D. Stewart for providing useful references.

Literature Cited

1. Adler, J. 1969. *Science* 166:1588–97
2. Adler, J. 1975. *Ann. Rev. Biochem.* 44:341–56
3. Allweiss, B., Carey, K. E., Dostal, J., Edwards, T. F., Freter, R. 1977. *Nature* 266:448–50
4. Amako, K., Umeda, A. 1977. *J. Gen. Microbiol.* 98:297–99
5. Ames, G. F., Spudich, E. N., Nikaido, H. 1974. *J. Bacteriol.* 117:406–16
6. Anderson, R. A. 1975. In *Swimming and Flying in Nature,* ed. T. Y. Wu, C. J. Brokaw, C. J. Brennan, 1:45–56. New York: Plenum. 422 pp.
7. Aragno, M., Walther-Maurschat, A., Mayer, F., Schlegel, H. G. 1977. *Arch. Mikrobiol.* 114:93–100
8. Armitage, J. P., Evans, M. C. W. 1979. *FEBS Lett.* 102:143–46
9. Armitage, J. P., Rowbury, R. J., Smith, D. G. 1975. *J. Gen. Microbiol.* 89:199–202
10. Armitage, J. P., Smith, D. G. 1978. *FEMS Microbiol. Lett.* 4:163–65
11. Asakura, S. 1970. *Adv. Biophys.* 1:99–155
12. Asakura, S., Iino, T. 1972. *J. Mol. Biol.* 64:251–68
13. Banks, G., Schaefer, D. W., Alpert, S. S. 1975. *Biophys. J.* 15:253–61
14. Belyakova, T. N., Galgolev, A. N., Skulachev, V. P. 1976. *Biokhimiya* 41:1478–83

15. Berg, H. C. 1971 *Rev. Sci. Instrum.* 42:868–71
16. Berg, H. C. 1974. *Nature* 249:77–79
17. Berg, H. C. 1975. *Ann. Rev. Biophys. Bioeng.* 4:119–36
18. Berg, H. C. 1975. *Nature* 254:389–92
19. Berg, H. C., Anderson, R. A. 1973. *Nature* 245:380–82
20. Berg, H. C., Brown, D. A. 1972. *Nature* 239:500–4
21. Berg, H. C., Purcell, E. M. 1977. *Biophys. J.* 20:193–219
22. Berg, H. C., Tedesco, P. M. 1975. *Proc. Natl. Acad. Sci. USA* 72:3235–39
23. Berg, H. C., Turner, L. 1979. *Nature* 278:349–51
24. Bezdek, M., Soska, J. 1972. *Folia Microbiol. Prague* 17:366–69
25. Biddle, C., Doetsch, R. N. 1974. *Can. J. Microbiol.* 20:1063–65
26. Black, F. T., Freundt, E. A., Vinther, O., Christiansen, C. 1979. *J. Bacteriol.* 137:456–60
27. Blakemore, R. 1975. *Science* 190: 377–79
28. Bode, W., Engel, J., Winklmair, D. 1972. *Eur. J. Biochem.* 26:313–27
29. Boon, J. P., Nossal, R., Chen, S. H. 1974. *Biophys. J.* 14:847–64
30. Calladine, C. R. 1975. *Nature* 255: 121–24
31. Calladine, C. R. 1976. *J. Theor. Biol.* 57:469–89
32. Calladine, C. R. 1978. *J. Mol. Biol.* 118:457–80
33. Canale-Parola, E. 1978. *Ann. Rev. Microbiol.* 32:69–99
34. Caraway, B. H., Krieg, N. R. 1972. *Can. J. Microbiol.* 18:1749–59
35. Caraway, B. H., Krieg, N. R. 1974. *Can. J. Microbiol.* 20:1367–78
36. Chalcroft, J. P., Bullivant, S., Howard, B. H. 1973. *J. Gen. Microbiol.* 79: 135–46
37. Chang, J. Y., Delange, R. J., Shaper, J. H., Glazer, A. N. 1976. *J. Biol. Chem.* 251:695–700
38. Chatterjee, B. D. 1974. *Indian J. Med. Res.* 62:1455–58
39. Clark, W. A. 1976. *J. Clin. Microbiol.* 3:632–34
40. Cook, J. H., Southern, P. M. 1975. *IRCS Med. Sci.* 3:238–39
41. Coulton, J. W., Murray, R. G. E. 1977. *Biochim. Biophys. Acta* 465:290–310
42. Coulton, J. W., Murray, R. G. E. 1978. *J. Bacteriol.* 136:1037–49
43. Czajkowski, J., Soltesz, V., Weibull, C. 1974. *J. Ultrastruct. Res.* 46:79–86
44. De Boer, W. E., Golten, C., Scheffers, W. A. 1975. *Antonie van Leeuwenhoek J. Microbiol. Serol.* 41:385–403
45. De Boer, W. E., Golten, C., Scheffers, W. A. 1975. *Neth. J. Sea Res.* 9:197–213
46. De Jong, M. H., van der Drift, C., Stumm, C., Arends, J. J. A. 1977. *Arch. Mikrobiol.* 13:153–58
47. De Jong, M. H., van der Drift, C., Vogels, G. D. 1976. *Arch. Mikrobiol.* 111:7–11
48. Delange, R. J., Chang, J. Y., Shaper, J. H., Glazer, A. N. 1976. *J. Biol. Chem.* 251:705–11
49. DePamphilis, M. L., Adler, J. 1971. *J. Bacteriol.* 105:384–95
50. DePamphilis, M. L., Adler, J. 1971. *J. Bacteriol.* 105:396–407
51. Dimmitt, K., Simon, M. I. 1971. *J. Bacteriol.* 108:282–86
52. Doetsch, R. N. 1972. *J. Theor. Biol.* 35:55–66
53. Douglas, C. W. I. 1979. *J. Med. Microbiol.* 12:195–99
54. Dunny, G. M., Brown, B. L., Clewell, D. B. 1978. *Proc. Natl. Acad. Sci. USA* 75:3479–83
55. Fein, J. E. 1979. *J. Bacteriol.* 137:933–46
56. Frankel, R. B., Blakemore, R. P., Wolfe, R. S. 1979. *Science* 203:1355–56
57. Freter, R., Jones, G. W. 1976. *Infect. Immun.* 14:246–56
58. Freter, R., O'Brien, P. C. M., Macsai, S. 1979. *Am. J. Clin. Nutr.* 32:128–32
59. Fujime, S., Maruyama, M., Asakura, S. 1972. *J. Mol. Biol.* 68:347–59
60. Fukuda, A., Miyakawa, K., Iba, H., Okada, Y. 1976. *Virology* 71:583–92
61. Gray, P. H. H. 1926. *J. Bacteriol.* 12:273–74
62. Grebenyuk, M. V., Gvozdyak, R. I. 1972. *Mikrobiol. Zh. Kiev* 34:655–56
63. Greenberg, E. P., Canale-Parola, E. 1977. *J. Bacteriol.* 132:356–58
64. Harayama, S., Iino, T. 1976. *J. Gen. Microbiol.* 94:173–79
65. Harold, F. M. 1977. *Ann. Rev. Microbiol.* 31:181–203
66. Hauser, D. C. R., Petrylak, D., Singer, G., Levandowsky, M. 1978. *Nature* 273:230–31
67. Henrichsen, J. 1972. *Bacteriol. Rev.* 36:478–503
68. Hilmen, M., Simon, M. 1976. In *Cell Motility,* ed. R. Goldman, T. Pollard, J. Rosenbaum, *Cold Spring Harbor Conf.* 3A:35–45
69. Hoeniger, J. F. M., Tauschel, H. D., Stokes, J. L. 1973. *Can. J. Microbiol.* 19:309–13
70. Hotani, H. 1971. *J. Mol. Biol.* 57: 575–81

71. Hotani, H. 1976. *J. Mol. Biol.* 106: 151–66
72. Hotani, H. 1979. *J. Mol. Biol.* 129: 305–18
73. Hotani, H., Asakura, S., Iino, T. 1969. *Biochim. Biophys. Acta* 194:572–83
74. Icho, T., Iino, T. 1978. *J. Bacteriol.* 134:854–60
75. Iino, T. 1977. *Ann. Rev. Genet.* 11: 161–82
76. Iino, T., Mitani, M. 1967. *J. Gen. Microbiol.* 49:81–88
77. Iino, T., Oguchi, T., Kuroiwa, T. 1974. *J. Gen. Microbiol.* 81:37–45
78. Jarosch, R. 1972. *Protoplasma* 75: 465–69
79. Johnson, R. C., Walsh, M. P., Ely, B., Shapiro, L. 1979. *J. Bacteriol.* 138: 984–89
80. Jollick, J. D., Wright, B. L. 1974. *J. Gen. Virol.* 22:197–205
81. Joys, T. M., Kim, H. 1978. *Microbios Lett.* 7:65–68
82. Kagawa, H. 1973. *Biochim. Biophys. Acta* 317:114–22
83. Kagawa, H., Aizawa, S. I., Awakura, S. 1979. *J. Mol. Biol.* 129:333–36
84. Kagawa, H., Asakura, S., Iino, T. 1973. *J. Bacteriol.* 113:1474–81
85. Kagawa, H., Owaribe, K., Asakura, S., Takahashi, N. 1976. *J. Bacteriol.* 125: 68–73
86. Kamiya, R., Asakura, S. 1974. *J. Mol. Biol.* 87:55–62
87. Kamiya, R., Asakura, S. 1976. *J. Mol. Biol.* 106:167–86
88. Kamiya, R., Asakura, S. 1977. *J. Mol. Biol.* 108:513–18
89. Kamiya, R., Asakura, S., Wakabayashi, K., Namba, K. 1979. *J. Mol. Biol.* 131:725–42
90. Khan, S., Macnab, R. M., Defranco, A. L., Koshland, D. E. Jr. 1978. *Proc. Natl. Acad. Sci. USA* 75:4150–54
91. Kingsley, V. V., Hoeniger, J. F. M. 1973. *Bacteriol. Rev.* 37:479–521
92. Kobayasi, S., Maeda, K., Imae, Y. 1977. *Rev. Sci. Instrum.* 48:407–10
93. Kondoh, H., Hotani, H. 1974. *Biochim. Biophys. Acta* 336:117–39
94. Kondoh, H., Yanagida, M. 1975. *J. Mol. Biol.* 96:641–52
95. Lagenaur, C., Agabian, N. 1976. *J. Bacteriol.* 128:435–44
96. Lagenaur, C., Agabian, N. 1977. *J. Bacteriol.* 132:731–33
97. Larsen, S. H., Reader, R. W., Kort, E. N., Tso, W-W., Adler, J. 1974. *Nature* 249:74–77
98. Läuger, P. 1977. *Nature* 268:360–62
99. Lawn, A. M. 1977. *J. Gen. Microbiol.* 101:121–30
100. Lawn, A. M., Ørskov, I., Ørskov, F. 1977. *J. Gen. Microbiol.* 101:111–19
101. Leifson, E. 1951. *J. Bacteriol.* 62:377–89
102. Lotz, W., Acker, G., Schmitt, R. 1977. *J. Gen. Virol.* 34:9–17
103. Lovely, P. S., Dahlquist, F. W., Macnab, R. M., Koshland, D. E. Jr. 1974. *Rev. Sci. Instrum.* 45:683–86
104. Macnab, R. M. 1975. *Proc. 1st Int. Congr. Int. Assoc. Microbiol. Soc.* 1:674–83
105. Macnab, R. M. 1976. *J. Clin. Microbiol.* 4:258–65
106. Macnab, R. M. 1977. *Proc. Natl. Acad. Sci. USA* 74:221–25
107. Macnab, R. M. 1978. *CRC Crit. Rev. Biochem.* 5:291–343
108. Macnab, R. M. 1979. *Trends Biochem. Sci.* 4:N10–13
109. Macnab, R. M., Koshland, D. E. Jr. 1972. *Proc. Natl. Acad. Sci. USA* 69:2509–12
110. Macnab, R. M. Koshland, D. E. Jr. 1974. *J. Mol. Biol.* 84:399–406
111. Macnab, R. M., Ornston, M. K. 1977. *J. Mol. Biol.* 112:1–30
112. Maeda, K., Imae, Y., Shioi, J-I., Oosawa, F. 1976. *J. Bacteriol.* 127: 1039–46
113. Manson, M. D., Tedesco, P., Berg, H. C., Harold, F. M., van der Drift, C. 1977. *Proc. Natl. Acad. Sci. USA* 74:3060–64
114. Marino, W., Ammer, S., Shapiro, L. 1976. *J. Mol. Biol.* 107:115–30
115. Maruyama, H. B., Azuma, H. 1976. *J. Cyclic Nucleotide Res.* 2:129–38
116. Matsuguchi, M., Takeya, K., Umeda, A., Amako, K., Watabe, T., Aita, S. 1977. *J. Electron Microsc.* 26:343–44
117. Mayfield, C. I., Inniss, W. E. 1977. *Can. J. Microbiol.* 23:1311–13
118. McDonough, M. W., Smith, S. E. 1976. *Microbios.* 16:49–54
119. Meadows, P. S. 1971. *Arch. Microbiol.* 75:374–81
120. Meganathan, R., Marquis, R. E. 1973. *Nature* 246:525–27
121. Mesibov, R., Adler, J. 1972. *J. Bacteriol.* 112:315–26
122. Metzner, P. 1920. *Jahrb. Wiss. Bot.* 59:325–412
123. Meynell, E. W. 1967. *J. Gen. Microbiol.* 25:253–90
124. Miller, J. B., Koshland, D. E. Jr. 1977. *Proc. Natl. Acad. Sci. USA* 74:4752–56
125. Moench, T. T., Konetzka, W. A. 1978. *Arch. Mikrobiol.* 119:203–12
126. Mulholland, A., Larson, A. D., Hart, L. T., Eubanks, E. R. 1978. *Abstr. Annu. Meet. Am. Soc. Microbiol.* 78:40

127. Murray, R. G. E., Birch-Anderson, A. 1963. *Can. J. Microbiol.* 9:393–401
128. Nossal, R., Chen, S. H. 1972. *Opt. Commun.* 5:117–22
129. Nossal, R., Chen, S. H. 1973. *Nature* 244:253–54
130. O'Brien, E. J., Bennett, P. M. 1972. *J. Mol. Biol.* 70:133–52
131. Padan, E., Zilberstein, D., Rottenberg, H. 1976. *Eur. J. Biochem.* 63:533–41
132. Palleroni, N. J. 1976. *Arch Mikrobiol.* 110:13–18
133. Palleroni, N. J., Doudoroff, M., Stanier, R. Y., Solanes, R. E., Mandel, M. 1970. *J. Gen. Microbiol.* 60:215–31
134. Panopoulos, N. J., Schroth, M. N. 1974. *Phytopathology* 64:1389–97
135. Parkinson, J. S. 1977. *Ann. Rev. Genet.* 11:397–414
136. Patterson-Delafield, J., Martinez, R. J. 1973. *Arch. Mikrobiol.* 90:107–20
137. Pijper, A. 1962. *J. R. Microsc. Soc.* 81:61–66
138. Pijper, A., Neser, M. L., Abraham, G. 1956. *J. Gen. Microbiol.* 14:371–80
139. Pilgram, W. K., Williams, F. D. 1976. *Can. J. Microbiol.* 22:1771–73
140. Raimondo, L. H., Lundh, N. P., Martinez, R. J. 1968. *J. Virol.* 2:256–64
141. Raska, I., Mayer, F., Edelbluth, C., Schmitt, R. 1976. *J. Bacteriol.* 125:679–88
142. Rhodes, M. E. 1958. *J. Gen. Microbiol.* 18:639–48
143. Rubik, B. A., Koshland, D. E. Jr. 1978. *Proc. Natl. Acad. Sci. USA* 75:2820–24
144. Saunders, J. R. 1978. *Nature* 275: 692–94
145. Schade, S. A., Adler, J., Ris, H. 1967. *J. Virol.* 1:597–609
146. Schaefer, D. W. 1973. *Science* 180:1293–95
147. Schaefer, D. W., Banks, G., Alpert, S. S. 1974. *Nature* 248:162–63
148. Schalch, W., Bode, W. 1975. *Biochim. Biophys. Acta* 405:292–305
149. Schmitt, R., Bamberger, I., Acker, G., Mayer, F. 1974. *Arch. Mikrobiol.* 100:145–62
150. Schmitt, R., Raska, I., Mayer, F. 1972. *Zentralbl. Bakteriol. Parasitenkd. Infectionskr.* 220:347–50
151. Schmitt, R., Raska, I., Mayer, F. 1974. *J. Bacteriol.* 117:844–57
152. Schneider, W. R., Doetsch, R. N. 1974. *Appl. Microbiol.* 27:283–84
153. Schneider, W. R., Doetsch, R. N. 1974. *J. Bacteriol.* 117:696–701
154. Schneider, W. R., Doetsch, R. N. 1977. *Appl. Environ. Microbiol.* 34:695–700
155. Seeliger, H. P. R., Welshimer, H. J. 1974. In *Bergey's Manual of Determinative Bacteriology,* ed. R. E. Buchanan, N. E. Gibbons, pp. 593–96. Baltimore: Williams & Wilkins. 1246 pp.
156. Shaper, J. H., Delange, R. J., Martinez, R. J., Glazer, A. N. 1976. *J. Biol. Chem.* 251:701–4
157. Shapiro, L., Maizel, J. V. 1973. *J. Bacteriol.* 113:478–85
158. Sheffery, M., Newton, A. 1979. *J. Bacteriol.* 138:575–83
159. Shimada, K., Ikkai, T., Yoshida, T., Asakura, S. 1976. *J. Mechanochem. Cell Motil.* 3:185–94
160. Shimada, K., Kamiya, R., Asakura, S. 1974. *Nature* 254:332–34
161. Shimada, K., Yoshida, T., Asakura, S. 1975. In *Swimming and Flying in Nature,* ed. T. Y. Wu, C. J. Brokaw, C. J. Brennan, 1:31–43. New York: Plenum. 422 pp.
162. Shinoda, S., Honda, T., Takeda, Y., Miwatani, T. 1974. *J. Bacteriol.* 120:923–28
163. Shinoda, S., Okamoto, K. 1977. *J. Bacteriol.* 129:1266–71
164. Shoesmith, J. G. 1960. *J. Gen. Microbiol.* 22:528–35
165. Silverman, M., Simon, M. 1972. *J. Bacteriol.* 112:986–93
166. Silverman, M., Simon, M. 1974. *Nature* 249:73–74
167. Silverman, M., Simon, M. I. 1977. *Ann. Rev. Microbiol.* 31:397–419
168. Simon, M. I., Emerson, S. U., Shaper, J. H., Bernard, P. D., Glazer, A. N. 1977. *J. Bacteriol.* 130:200–4
169. Sleytr, U. B., Glauert, A. M. 1973. *Nature* 241:542–43
170. Smith, J. L., Doetsch, R. N. 1969. *J. Gen. Microbiol.* 55:379–91
171. Spudich, J. L., Koshland, D. E. Jr. 1975. *Proc. Natl. Acad. Sci. USA* 72:710–13
172. Spudich, J. L., Koshland, D. E. Jr. 1979. *J. Bacteriol.* 139:442–47
173. Stock, G. B., Carlson, F. D. 1975. See Ref. 161, pp. 57–68
174. Straley, S. C., Conti, S. F. 1977. *J. Bacteriol.* 132:628–40
175. Strength, W. J., Isani, B., Linn, D. M., Williams, F. D., Vandermolen, G. E., Laughon, B. E., Krieg, N. R. 1976. *Int. J. Syst. Bacteriol.* 26:253–68
176. Suzuki, T., Iino, T. 1977. *J. Bacteriol.* 129:527–29
177. Sverdrup, H. U., Johnson, M. W., Fleming, R. H., eds. 1942. *The Oceans. Their Physics, Chemistry and General Biology.* New Jersey: Prentice Hall. 1087 pp.
178. Szmelcman, S., Adler, J. 1976. *Proc. Natl. Acad. Sci. USA* 73:4387–91

179. Taylor, B. L., Koshland, D. E. Jr. 1974. *J. Bacteriol.* 119:640–42
180. Taylor, B. L., Koshland, D. E. Jr. 1975. *J. Bacteriol.* 123:557–69
181. Taylor, B. L., Koshland, D. E. Jr. 1976. *J. Supramol. Struct.* 4:343–53
182. Tso, W-W., Adler, J. 1974. *J. Bacteriol.* 118:560–76
183. Ulitzur, S. 1975. *Arch. Mikrobiol.* 104:285–88
184. Unz, R. F., Dondero, N. C. 1967. *Can. J. Microbiol.* 13:1671–82
185. Unz, R. F., Farrah, S. R. 1976. *Water Res.* 10:665–72
186. Vaituzis, Z., Doetsch, R. N. 1969. *Appl. Microbiol.* 17:584–88
187. Van der Drift, C., De Jong, M. H. 1974. *Arch. Mikrobiol.* 96:83–92
188. Vandermolen, G. E., Williams, F. D. 1977. *Can. J. Microbiol.* 23:107–12
189. Wakabayashi, K., Yamaguchi, T., Kagawa, H. 1974. *J. Mol. Biol.* 83:545–49
190. Walc-Pokrzywnicki, Z. 1973. *Zentralbl. Bakteriol. Parasitenkd. Infectionskr.* 223:240–43
191. Weibull, C. 1949. *Ark. Kemi* 1:573–75
192. West, M., Burdash, N. M., Freimuth, F. 1977. *J. Clin. Microbiol.* 6:414–19
193. Wilson, J. J., Takahashi, I. 1978. *Can. J. Microbiol.* 24:1–8
194. Winet, H., Keller, S. R. 1976. *J. Exp. Biol.* 65:577–602
195. Yakuta, T., Gots, J. S. 1976. *J. Bacteriol.* 103:513–16
196. Yamaguchi, S., Iino, T., Kuroiwa, T. 1972. *J. Gen. Micriobiol.* 70:299–303
197. Yang, G. C. H., Schrank, G. D., Freeman, B. A. 1977. *J. Bacteriol.* 129: 1121–28
198. Yoshida, T., Shimada, K., Asakura, S. 1975. *J. Mechanochem. Cell Motil.* 2:87–98

Ann. Rev. Microbiol. 1980. 34:109–35

RECENT TAXONOMIC DEVELOPMENTS AND CHANGES IN MEDICAL MYCOLOGY

◆1771

Michael R. McGinnis

Clinical Microbiology Laboratories, North Carolina Memorial Hospital; Department of Bacteriology and Immunology, University of North Carolina, Chapel Hill, North Carolina 27514

CONTENTS

INTRODUCTION 109
DIVISION ASCOMYCOTA 112
DIVISION BASIDIOMYCOTA 114
DIVISION FUNGI IMPERFECTI 115
Class Blastomycetes 116
Class Hyphomycetes 118
DIVISION ZYGOMYCOTA 128
CONCLUSION 131

INTRODUCTION

During the past several years, many new and exciting developments in the taxonomy of the medically important fungi have occurred. A number of the major genera and species have been reevaluated, some redefined, and others named as new taxa. Many of these changes are a result of a more clear understanding of conidiogenesis and morphogenesis, a better appreciation of metabolic pathways and nucleic-acid-base composition, and newer methods for quantitative and qualitative analysis of the various cellular components of the fungi.

Many biologists believe that at least five kingdoms (196, 197) are necessary for the classification of all types of living things. In the classification of the Kingdom Fungi adopted here, the kingdom contains five divisions:

0066-4227/80/1001-0109$01.00

Chytridiomycota, Zygomycota, Ascomycota, Basidiomycota, and Fungi Imperfecti (Deuteromycota). Organisms previously classified as fungi—that is, labyrinthulids, mycetozoans, oomycetes, plasmodiophoromycetes, and thraustochytrids—are placed in the Kingdom Protista, if this classification of the Kingdom Fungi is followed. Fungi are eukaryotic organisms characterized by absorptive nutrition, usually zygotic meiosis, by cell walls that are typically chitinous, unicellular or filamentous elements, and by synthesis of lysine by the L-α-adipic acid biosynthetic pathway (122).

Taxonomy is a dynamic science that is concerned with the synthesis of data obtained from biochemistry, cytology, genetics, morphology, and physiology into a useful and practical classification system. Owing to its dynamic nature, taxonomy can never be stable because as new data become available, they must be integrated into our classification systems. The value of these data and their impact upon classification depends upon the judgement, experience, and expertise of each taxonomist. Every mycologist is entitled to his or her own opinions and approaches to the identification of fungi, the relative importance of characters, the classification system adopted, and the interpretation of the International Code of Botanical Nomenclature (ICBN) (165). The acceptance or rejection of terminology and characteristics used in mycology "... is arrived at by consensus, which seems little influenced by reasoned arguments or pronouncements by individuals or committees." (109). Such individual freedoms are limited in Bacteriology, where the Subcommittees on Taxonomy recommend to the Judicial Commission (101) nomenclatural changes and interpretations of the International Code of Nomenclature of Bacteria, changes in names, conservation of names, rejection of names, and the minimal standards for the description of new taxa, which include the characters to be used and the methods for their assessment.

The relative value of the different characters used in mycology varies from one group of fungi to another. For example, the echinulate nature of the macroconidia of *Microsporum* is an important generic characteristic, whereas in the genus *Cladosporium,* the various species may form conidia that are either echinulate or smooth. Linnaeus (104) summarized this basic concept by stating: "Characters that in one genus are strong enough to establish a genus, in another are not in the least necessary. The character does not establish the genus, but the genus the character. The character flows from the genus, not the genus from the character. The character does not exist so that the genus may be made, but so that the genus may be recognized."

In contrast to taxonomy, nomenclature is concerned with insuring that all fungi are named in a uniform and consistent manner. The rules governing nomenclature are clearly stated in the ICBN. These permit only a minimum of personal judgement. Even though all of the rules may not be acceptable to everyone, they must be adhered to. Unfortunately, this basic concept is occasionally forgotten.

Many mycologists do not agree with Article 9.5 (ICBN) which states that type specimens of names of taxa cannot be living cultures. The majority of taxonomic studies utilize living cultures; thus they should be accepted as types. It has been recently proposed (180) that Article 9.5 should be changed so that living cultures can be designated as types. These would have to be lyophilized and deposited in a major culture collection, and isotypes would have to be sent to at least one additional culture collection.

Article 13 (ICBN) establishes 1 January 1821 as the starting date for the FUNGI CAETERI, 1 May 1753 for lichens, and 31 December 1801 for rusts, smuts, and the Gasteromycetes. The starting date of 1 January 1821 for the FUNGI CAETERI needs to be revised (71, 91) because it causes a great deal of confusion with older names. Unfortunately, any starting date will cause some confusion. Several proposals for emending Article 13 have been recently made in *Taxon* (180). Until this Article is changed, 1 January 1821 must be used.

Of special interest to medical mycologists is Article 59 (ICBN) which governs the names of fungi with polymorphic (pleomorphic) life cycles. According to a proposed revision of Article 59 made at the Second International Mycological Congress, when an anamorphic phase is named, it will have to be typified by a single anamorph (180). This single anamorph should be the most stable, unique, and distinctive form. The term anamorph is defined as an organ of asexual or somatic reproduction, either specialized or generalized, but neither morphologically nor karyologically sexual. A teleomorph is a reproductive organ that is specialized morphologically or karyologically for generating meiospores or their homologues, whether by normally sexual or parthenogenetic means. The holomorph is the whole fungus and includes all of its anamorphs, or all of its anamorph(s) and teleomorph, or its teleomorph (195). The teleomorphic name becomes the name for the whole fungus.

Yeast workers tend to approach taxonomy in a slightly different manner than most other mycologists. Type cultures have always been maintained by zymologists in place of type specimens or descriptions. When a type culture is lost, a neotype culture is designated as its replacement. After an anamorph is connected to a teleomorph, the former is typically discarded and the entire yeast is then referred to by its teleomorphic name. This is often applied inconsistently. For example, the commonly encountered yeast *Candida pseudotropicalis* (anamorph) is called *C. pseudotropicalis* rather than *Kluyveromyces marxianus* (teleomorph).

DIVISION ASCOMYCOTA

The Ascomycetes are characterized by the formation of asci and ascospores. Those fungi that have characteristics in common with the Ascomycetes, but do not form asci and ascospores as far as we know, are classified in the Division Fungi Imperfecti. For convenience, the Ascomycetes can be divided into two basic groups, yeasts and filamentous Ascomycetes.

Ascomycetous yeasts are a heterogeneous group of fungi, even though they superficially appear to be homogeneous. During their life cycle, they contain a unicellular form. The various yeasts are distinguished from each other on the basis of cell division and conidiogenesis (28, 185), ascus formation, ascospore morphology, mating studies, physiological data (6, 105), lipid composition (140), carbohydrate composition (192), enzyme profiles (99), electrophoretic patterns (51), DNA base compositions (mol% G+C) (52, 168), DNA-DNA hybridizations, cell-wall composition (8, 55), temperature limits (181), and other kinds of data. Owing to the fact that the majority of ascomycetous yeasts are not important as etiologic agents of disease, they will not be considered in this review.

A number of filamentous Ascomycetes and their anamorphs are extremely important pathogens of man and animals. There is a trend towards relying more heavily upon anamorphs as a character to distinguish the various ascomycetous genera (84, 113, 185). For example, the ascomycete *Ceratocystis* produces a *Sporothrix* asexual form. Von Arx (185) restricts the genus *Ceratocystis* to those species with *Chalara* anamorphs. For those species that form a *Sporothrix, Graphium,* or similar form, von Arx adopts the genus *Ophiostoma* instead of *Ceratocystis.* The perithecia of the genera *Ceratocystis* and *Ophiostoma* are so morphologically alike, *Ophiostoma* is generally considered by most mycologists to be a synonym of *Ceratocystis.* Such an approach results in anatomical and biological species concepts being used interchangeably. This raises the question of how much significance should be placed upon the use of anamorphs in characterizing ascomycete genera.

Much of the traditional classification of the Ascomycetes is based upon the development of their ascocarps and centrum (central portion of the ascocarp) (50, 108, 187). Other types of data—such as ascus development, ascospore morphology, mating studies (133), cell-wall composition (8, 191), carotenoid pigments (177), and mol% G+C content (168)—have been used to circumscribe taxa. These types of data have been applied in numerical taxonomic systems (33, 40) for comparing and contrasting many genera and species.

The genus *Ajellomyces* was proposed by McDonough & Lewis in 1968 for the sexual form of *Blastomyces dermatitidis* (115). These authors placed the genus *Ajellomyces* in the Gymnoascaceae, and characterized the teleomorph as having thick-walled, spiraling hyphae that radiated from a common center in the gymnothecium (a loosely organized ascocarp with random asci). From the spirals, a secondary network of swollen, thin-walled hyphae developed. The small asci, which were described by McDonough & Lewis as being globose to subglobose, contained eight, globose, hyaline ascospores. While working with *Histoplasma capsulatum,* Kwon-Chung (92, 93) discovered its teleomorph and established the new ascomycetous genus *Emmonsiella.* Later, she concluded that *H. capsulatum* var. *capsulatum* and *H. capsulatum* var. *duboisii* formed a single teleomorph, *E. capsulata* (96). The genus *Emmonsiella* was distinguished by her from *Ajellomyces* by having pyriform to clavate asci and a network of thin-walled, non-swollen secondary peridial hyphae. The ascocarp initials were also considered to be distinctive (94). McGinnis & Katz (123) studied the type specimens and living cultures of *A. dermatitidis* and *E. capsulata.* These authors reported that the asci of *A. dermatitidis* were actually clavate to pyriform and that the initiation of the gymnothecium in both genera is basically the same. The principal difference between these two genera involved swollen versus non-swollen secondary peridial hyphae. As a result of their study, McGinnis & Katz considered *Emmonsiella* to be a synonym of *Ajellomyces* and transferred *E. capsulata* to the genus *Ajellomyces* as *A. capsulatus* (as *"capsulata"*).

Dermatophytes that form gymnothecia are classified in either the genus *Nannizzia* or *Arthroderma.* These genera are distinguished from each other on the basis of their peridial hyphae. *Arthroderma* forms peridial hyphae that consist of pronounced dumbbell-shaped cells, whereas *Nannizzia* forms cells at the periphery of the gymnothecia that are only slightly constricted. In practice, the genera are distinguished from each other mainly by their anamorphs; *Nannizzia* by *Microsporum* and *Arthroderma* by either *Trichophyton* or *Chrysosporium.* The identification of the various species in the genera *Nannizzia* and *Arthroderma* relies so heavily upon the particular *Microsporum* or *Trichophyton* anamorph, that if the anamorph was absent, the teleomorph could not be identified to species in many instances. The separation of the genera *Nannizzia* and *Arthroderma* is somewhat analogous to the situation that occurred with *Ajellomyces* and *Emmonsiella.* The genera *Nannizzia* and *Arthroderma* could be considered congeneric. If necessary, *Nannizzia* could be maintained as a subgenus of *Arthroderma.* Additional support of this possible disposition is furnished by the fact that the ontogeny of the holothallic conidia of *Microsporum* and *Trichophyton* (28) is essentially identical. Only their outer cell-wall thickness and the presence or absence of echinulations distinguishes them. Traditionally, *Nannizzia* and *Arthroderma* are maintained as separate genera.

The taxonomy surrounding the genus *Neotestudina* is somewhat confused. The genus was established by Segretain & Destombes for *N. rosatii,* an etiologic agent of mycetoma (159). Von Arx (183) studied *N. rosatii* and presented a detailed summary of its ascostromata, bitunicate asci, and ascospore morphology. In their study of *Zopfia,* Hawksworth & Booth (67) considered *Neotestudina* to be a synonym of *Zopfia* and proposed the new combination *Z. rosatii.* Using scanning electron microscopy, Hawksworth (66) has reevaluated the generic concepts in the Testudinaceae. Based upon ascospore morphology, he concluded that *Neotestudina* was the proper genus for *N. rosatii,* not *Zopfia.* The ascospores of *N. rosatii* were characterized by Hawksworth as being two-celled, variable in shape, less than 50 μm in length, without furrows, smooth, and with a germ pore at each end. Thus, the proper name for this etiologic agent of mycetoma is *N. rosatii.*

In 1899, Saccardo & Sydow (153) established the genus *Allescheria* for a fungus previously known as *Eurotiopsis gayoni.* Twenty-three years later, Shear (160) described the species *A. boydii,* which he proposed for an etiologic agent of a mycetoma (16). Shear also described *Scedosporium* (as *Cephalosporium boydii*) and *Graphium* (as *Dendrostilbella boydii*) conidial states. In 1970, Malloch (112) concluded that *E. gayoni,* which was the type species for the genera *Eurotiopsis* and *Allescheria,* was a synonym of *Monascus.* This conclusion was based upon the facts that the ascocarps of *E. gayoni* were small, the cultures were red, the ascospores and conidia were described as being hyaline or pinkish, the fungus was isolated from flour, and that in 1903, it was demonstrated that *Monascus* had more than one eight-spored ascus in each ascocarp. The fungus Shear described as *A. boydii* was clearly different from *E. gayoni* because it produced large ascocarps, pale brown colonies, orange- to copper-colored ascospores, dematiaceous conidia, and occasionally synnemata. Since *A. boydii* was distinctive and could not be accommodated in any known genus, Malloch proposed for *A. boydii,* the new genus *Petriellidium,* which now contains seven species.

DIVISION BASIDIOMYCOTA

During the past several years, basidiomycetous teleomorphs for some yeasts belonging to the genera *Candida, Cryptococcus, Rhodotorula,* and *Torulopsis* have been found. These include such basidiomycetous genera as *Filobasidium, Filobasidiella, Leucosporidium,* and *Rhodosporidium.*

The genus *Filobasidiella,* which was established for *F. neoformans,* is the teleomorph of *Cryptococcus neoformans* (95). Kwon-Chung has reported that the chains of basidiospores arise from the basidium in a basipetal manner. Four nuclei apparently remain inside the basidium (97) during basidiospore production. Maintaining *Filobasidiella* separate from *Filobasidium* can be questioned. Not all mycologists would agree that single versus chains of basidiospores is a substantial generic characteristic. It is important to note that most *Cryptococcus* anamorphs associated with Basidiomycetes are formed by *Filobasidium.* The situation involving *Filobasidiella* and *Filobasidium* is somewhat similar to *Exoascus* and *Taphrina. Taphrina* once included those species having many-spored asci, whereas *Exoascus* included species having eight-spored asci. *Exoascus* is now considered to be a synonym of *Taphrina.*

DIVISION FUNGI IMPERFECTI

The Division Fungi Imperfecti is a heterogeneous assemblage of phylogenetically diverse fungi that are classified together for convenience. Since sexual reproductive structures are unknown, these fungi are classified primarily upon morphological grounds and differences in their modes of conidiogenesis. This approach has been derived from the work of Saccardo (148, 149), Hughes (70), Tubaki (174, 175), Subramanian (170), Barron (7), and others. Following the First International Workshop-Conference on the Classification of Fungi Imperfecti held at Kananaskis, Canada (83), it was hoped that the recommended terminology for describing conidium development and conidiogenesis, as well as the tentative ontogenetically based classification system, would resolve many of the taxonomic problems encountered when purely morphological characteristics are used for the classification of the Fungi Imperfecti. The work of Cole & Samson (28), Madelin (111), and others in the area of conidiogenesis clearly shows that conidiogenesis is extremely variable and cannot be used as the sole basis for classification, as originally hoped. Recently, there has been a renewed interest in classifying these fungi on the basis of either actual or hypothesized ascomycetous or basidiomycetous affinities (113, 185).

Many techniques are being applied to the taxonomy of the Fungi Imperfecti. Scanning and transmission electron microscopy have shown relationships between structures and their ontogeny that were previously unrealized (28). Biochemical methods such as chromatography, electrophoresis, spectrophotometry, nuclear magnetic resonance spectroscopy, X-ray diffraction, mass spectrometry, pyrolysis, and enzymatic analysis are contributing valuable taxonomic data (39). Percent G+C content (37, 64, 168), DNA-DNA reassociation (168), and physiological data have become increasingly important taxonomic criteria, especially in the yeasts. Numerical taxonomy (33, 41), cell-wall composition (8, 191), and carbohydrate composition (189, 192) are interesting approaches.

Class Blastomycetes

Berlese (12) established the genus *Torulopsis* in 1894 for *T. rosea.* He characterized it as follows: "Active cells had an ellipsoidal form; they were indistinguishable from the common *Saccharomyces ellipsoideus:* however, when placed on a plaster cone, in a few days, it becomes perfectly spherical, and its cytoplasm, at first homogenous, become condensed in a large central globule that was highly refringent and oily in appearance, while the residual protoplasm became pink." The genus *Torulopsis* was later defined by Saccardo (150) as "Cellulae ellipsoideae vel globosae, continuae, non apiculatae nec catenulatae hyalinae v. laete coloratae. Mycelium nullum. Endosporae nullae. Fermentationem alcoholicam excitat." Since neither a type culture nor specimen were apparently saved, the description of *Torulopsis* is the type (Article 9.3, ICBN). Owing to the absence of a type culture, Lodder & Kreger-van Rij (106) designated *T. colliculosa* to be the type species for *Torulopsis.* Thus, *Torulopsis* Lodder & Kreger-van Rij, which is based upon the species *T. colliculosa,* is a later homonym (Article 48.1, ICBN) and must therefore be rejected (Article 64.1, ICBN) unless it is conserved (Article 48.2, ICBN). This is an excellent example of the confusion that can result when the ICBN is disregarded. If a living culture is necessary, then a neotype should be designated for *T. rosea* rather than a new genus.

The genus *Candida* was originally described by Berkhout (11) in 1923: "Diagnosis: few hyphae, prostrate, breaking up into shorter or longer pieces. Conidia, arising by budding from the hyphae or on top of each other; are small and hyaline." The genus was conserved (145) in order to resolve the confusion surrounding it and the genus *Monilia.* It is noteworthy that *Candida* was specifically conserved against *Syringospora* Quinq., 1868. The reintroduction of *Syringospora* by van der Walt (178, 179) as a basidiomycetous genus and the use of *Syringospora* as an ascomycetous genus by von Arx et al (188) are misapplications of the name *Syringospora.* Article 59 (ICBN) states that a genus based upon an asexual form (anamorph) cannot be used as the name for a sexual form (teleomorph). The original description and illustrations of *Syringospora* and *Oidium albicans* clearly show that *Syringospora* was based upon an asexual form. The type of *Syringospora* is *O. albicans* Robin since *S. robinii* was explicitly a renaming of *O. albicans.* Thus, the name *Syringospora* refers only to the asexual state represented by its type. Article 59 also states that Ascomycetes and Basidiomycetes must be characterized by the presence of asci or basidia, respectively. This Article neither implies nor states that nuclear behavior is acceptable for determining ascomycetous or basidiomycetous affinities. Van der Walt's interpretation that *S. albicans* is a basidiomycete, based upon nuclear studies, and his conclusion that the large cells of *S. albicans* are basidia are obviously in error. If van der Walt and von Arx et al believe that sexual spores are produced by van der Walt's neotype isolate of *S. albicans,* then a new genus should have been established rather than emending *Syringospora,* a *nomen rejiciendum.*

Yarrow & Meyer (198) have recently proposed that *Candida* be emended to include species without pseudohyphae. They considered *Torulopsis* to be a synonym of *Candida.* If the proposal of Yarrow & Meyer is accepted on taxonomic grounds, then *Torulopsis* is the correct generic name, not *Candida.* Since *Candida* was not specifically conserved against *Torulopsis,* and these two genera are based upon different types, the rule of priority must be applied. *Torulopsis* was validly and effectively described several years prior to *Candida.* Owing to the wide acceptance of both genera, a proposal to conserve *Candida* against *Torulopsis* would serve no useful purpose. It is this author's feeling that the two genera are not congeneric and that they can be differentiated primarily by the presence or absence of pseudohyphae as defined by Lodder (105).

Kwon-Chung and Bennett (98) have recently proposed that *Cryptococcus neoformans* should be divided into two species, *C. neoformans* and *C. bacillisporus. Cryptococcus bacillisporus* was established for isolates of *C. neoformans* that were of the B and C serotypes, formed a *Filobasidiella bacillispora* teleomorph, and had differences in their creatinine metabolism and ammonia formation. It appears best to consider *C. neoformans* and *C. bacillisporus* conspecific. The differences presented by Kwon-Chung et al are not sufficient to justify two separate species.

The taxonomy of *Sarcinosporon inkin* (78, 89) and *Fissuricella filamenta* (139) is in a state of flux. The genus *Sarcinosporon* was established for *Sarcinomyces inkin* Oho by King & Jong in 1975, who also considered *Prototheca filamenta* to be a synonym of *Sarcinosporon inkin* (89). In 1977, Pore et al (139) described the new genus *Fissuricella* for *P. filamenta* because they felt their isolates were significantly different from the concept King & Jong proposed for *Sarcinosporon.* Pore et al considered *Sarcinomyces inkin* Oho, the type species for the genus *Sarcinosporon,* to be a synonym of their fungus *F. filamenta.* If Pore et al believed that *Sarcinomyces inkin* Oho is a synonym of *F. filamenta,* then their genus must be treated as a synonym of *Sarcinosporon* since both genera would be based upon the same species. Judging from their paper, Pore et al apparently meant to say *Sarcinomyces inkin* Oho *sensu* King et Jong, *non Sarcinomyces inkin* Oho, is a synonym of *F. filamenta.* Additional study will be necessary before this problem is resolved.

Some medical mycologists incorrectly designate *Malassezia* as a synonym of *Pityrosporum* (105). There is little doubt that *Malassezia* and

Pityrosporum are congeneric. Since *Malassezia* was validly and effectively published several years prior to *Pityrosporum, Pityrosporum* is a synonym of *Malassezia. Pityrosporum orbiculare* and *P. ovale* are synonyms of *M. furfur,* whereas *P. pachydermatis* is a synonym of *M. pachydermatis* (60).

Class Hyphomycetes

While studying *Cephalosporium* and some similar genera, Gams (53) concluded that the generic name *Cephalosporium* is a *nomen dubium* and should be replaced by the older name *Acremonium.* He expanded the concept of *Acremonium* to include species that produced conidia in either balls, chains, or both, from cylindrical phialides. As defined by Gams, *Acremonium* has become a heterogeneous genus consisting of slow to medium growing fungi that produce one-celled (rarely two-celled) phialoconidia in balls or chains from thin-walled phialides. This extremely broad concept has not been accepted by all mycologists. For example, *Gliomastix* is not usually accepted as a synonym of *Acremonium* as proposed by Gams. Using acid-phenol electrophoretic data for a number of isolates of *Acremonium,* Chesson et al (24) concluded that their data do not support the sections proposed by Gams.

Several species of medical interest previously classified in *Cephalosporium* are now considered to be species of *Acremonium.* The principal ones include *A. falciforme (C. falciforme), A. Kiliense (C. acremonium* in part, *C. infestans, C. kiliense, C. madurae), A. potronii (C. potronii), A. recifei (C. recifei),* and *A. roseo-griseum (C. roseo-griseum). Cephalosporium acremonium,* which is often cited in the medical mycological literature, has been used to encompass any isolate with elliptical conidia measuring 1–1.5 $\times$ 4 μm that formed white colonies, which became rose-colored with age. Gams treated this fungus in part as a synonym of six species of *Acremonium* and one species of *Verticillium* (53).

In 1972, Subramanian (171) established the new genus *Sagrahamala,* which was based upon *Torula luzulae.* Subramanian believed the genus was necessary for some species that Gams (53) included in his section *Gliomastix* of the genus *Acremonium* and the monophialidic species of *Paecilomyces.* The genus *Sagrahamala* was characterized by producing true chains of persistent, basipetal, one-celled, dry, seceding conidia. Gams (54) has recently rejected Subramanian's genus and his basic concept that conidia may be either in true or false chains. Instead, Gams believes that the correct concept is based on whether the chains of conidia produced by these fungi have connectives between conidia.

Gams agrees with Subramanian that the monophialidic species of *Paecilomyces* are distinct from the genus *Acremonium* (54, 172). Owing to the fact that Gams considers *Sagrahamala* to be a synonym of *Acremonium,* he established the new genus *Sagenomella* for those members of *Acremonium* that produce connected conidial chains, sympodially proliferating phialides, and phialides that often have a centrally swollen portion. Gams included the monophialidic species of *Paecilomyces* in his genus *Sagenomella.* Until the concepts of true versus false chains (171) and connected versus disconnected chains (54) are reevaluated, there will continue to be disagreement concerning the best disposition of the monophialidic species of *Paecilomyces.*

Aureobasidium pullulans has often been used as a collecting point for black yeasts in general. This identification is often incorrect because many of the black yeasts seen in medical mycology laboratories are actually species of *Phaeococcus.* De Hoog (41) established the genus *Phaeococcus* in 1977 to accommodate non-filamentous black yeasts that produce restricted, glistening, black colonies composed of thick-walled, dark olivaceous brown, globose to ellipsoidal budding cells which may occur in chains. The genus *Phaeococcus* is often an anamorph associated with genera such as *Exophiala* and *Wangiella.*

The taxonomy surrounding the genus *Aureobasidium* and its synonym *Pullularia* is complex (29, 30, 41). Utilizing scanning electron microscopy, Pechak & Crang (136) have reported that the conidia produced along the hyphae by *A. pullulans* are blastic and that they are released by a double septum mechanism. Many isolates of *Aureobasidium* produce a *Scytalidium* anamorph consisting of dematiaceous arthroconidia. The genus *Aureobasidium* is recognized by the presence of hyaline, one-celled conidia that are produced laterally along the hyphae, whether a *Scytalidium* anamorph is present or not. In her monograph of *Aureobasidium,* Hermanides-Nijhof (41) defined *Aureobasidium* in part as producing numerous one-celled conidia in a synchronized manner. Those species previously included in *Aureobasidium* that produced conidia in a basipetal manner she assigned to the genus *Hormonema.* The distinction between *Aureobasidium* and *Hormonema* is not always evident by direct microscopic observation. Until additional data are available, it appears best to maintain *Hormonema* as a synonym of *Aureobasidium.*

In 1888, Costantin & Rolland (31) proposed the genus *Blastomyces* for a white mold they isolated from bear dung. Their fungus, *B. luteus,* is identical to *Chrysosporium merdarium* (19). Gilchrist & Stokes in 1896 (57) isolated a white mold from a patient with blastomycosis that they tentatively considered to be a species of *Oidium.* In 1898, they proposed the new genus and species *Blastomyces dermatitidis* for their fungus (58). After studying their paper, it is evident that Gilchrist & Stokes were unaware that the genus *Blastomyces* had been previously proposed for a different mold. The generic name *Blastomyces* Gilchrist et Stokes, 1898 is a homonym and must be rejected (Article 64, ICBN). The generic name *Blastomyces* can be used only if it is conserved (Article 14, ICBN).

The genus *Chrysosporium* can be defined (162) as forming " . . . aleurioconidia terminally, at the ends of short or long lateral branches, or directly on the sides of the hyphae. Intercalary aleurioconidia occur in some species, and these integrade with alternate arthroconidia." While studying the genus *Chrysosporium* and similar hyphomycetes, Carmichael (19) transferred *B. dermatitidis* to *Chrysosporium*. He proposed the new combination *C. dermatitidis* because he felt that the conidia produced by *B. dermatitidis* were typical of those produced by other members of the genus *Chrysosporium*. Carmichael also suggested that the generic name *Zymonema* is available for *B. dermatitidis* if mycologists find *Chrysosporium* taxonomically unacceptable. Neither of these proposals have been accepted by most medical mycologists. Utilizing exoantigens, Kaufman & Standard (82) have concluded that *B. dermatitidis* is different from the species of *Chrysosporium* they studied.

Carmichael (19), Padhye & Carmichael (134), and McGinnis (122) consider the genus *Emmonsia* to be a synonym of *Chrysosporium*. The genus *Emmonsia* was established by Ciferri & Montemartini (26) for a hyphomycete originally isolated from the lungs of wild rodents and described as *Haplosporangium parva*. This was necessary because the genus *Haplosporangium* was originally established for a zygomycete. *Emmonsia brasiliensis* and *E. ciferrina* are best considered synonyms of *C. pruinosum*, and *E. parva* and *E. crescens* as synonyms of *C. parvum*. These species differ from other species of *Chrysosporium* in part by producing extremely large cells (adiospores) in lung tissue or at elevated temperatures on laboratory media. It could be argued that *Emmonsia* should be maintained as a distinct genus, as are the genera *Blastomyces, Coccidioides,* and *Histoplasma*. The conidial anamorph of these latter genera could be assigned to the genera *Chrysosporium, Malbranchea,* and *Sepedonium* or *Chrysosporium,* respectively. If the genera *Blastomyces, Coccidioides, Histoplasma,* and *Paracoccidioides* are to be maintained, they will have to be defined upon their tissue form, not their conidial anamorph in culture at 25°C.

The genus *Cladosporium* contains two major pathogens, *C. bantianum* and *C. carrionii*. There is considerable disagreement among medical mycologists regarding the relationship between the species *C. bantianum* and *C. trichoides*. *Cladosporium bantianum* was originally described as *Torula bantiana* by Saccardo in 1912 (152). The fungus Saccardo studied was isolated from a patient who had cerebral phaeohyphomycosis. In 1952, Emmons (13) described the new species, *C. trichoides,* for a fungus isolated from a patient who also had cerebral phaeohyphomycosis. Emmons was unaware that Saccardo had previously described a similar fungus as a species of *Torula.* Borelli (14) studied Saccardo's type specimens and in 1960 transferred *T. bantiana* to the genus *Cladosporium* as *C. bantianum.* He also considered *C. trichoides* to be a synonym of *C. bantianum.* Emmons et al (47) disagree with Borelli because they feel that the infection, colony color, conidial chain length, and size range for the conidia were significantly different in the two species. I have had the opportunity to study Saccardo's original materials, the type culture of *C. trichoides,* and several other isolates identified as either *C. trichoides* or *C. bantianum.* It is my belief that Borelli is correct and *C. trichoides* is a synonym of *C. bantianum.* The lesions and histopathology of Banti's original case (5, 167) are compatible with the one Binford et al (13) reported. Since temperature, light, and medium composition have a profound effect upon colony color, length of conidial chains, and size of conidia, the differences reported between these two species are within the limits of acceptible variation for a single species. The original photomicrographs taken by Saccardo show conidial chains longer than those reported in the original description. Emmons et al (47) also noted that the conidia tended to be larger in some isolates upon primary recovery, becoming smaller under cultivation. Thus, *C. bantianum* is the most appropriate name for this fungus. Borelli & Marcano (15) have recently established the new species *C. castellanii* as another etiologic agent of tinea nigra. McGinnis & Padhye (125) studied *C. castellanii* and concluded that it was a synonym of *Stenella araguata,* a phytopathogen found in Venezuela.

In their study of the genus *Malbranchea,* Sigler & Carmichael (162) referred to the mycelial form of *Coccidioides immitis* as the *Malbranchea* state of *C. immitis.* This is a logical way of referring to the conidial anamorph, since *C. immitis* was originally described solely on the basis of spherules containing endospores in tissue (144). The generic name *Coccidioides* was suggested by Stiles (144), but formally proposed by Rixford & Gilchrist (144), who believed that their organism was a protozoan. Over the years, the concept of *C. immitis* has been broadened to include both the tissue (spherules) and conidial (alternating arthroconidia) forms. In essence, *Coccidioides,* as well as *Blastomyces, Histoplasma* and *Paracoccidioides,* are not individual genera defined by a single morphological form, but are genera defined by a combination of different anamorphs. The mold form of *Coccidioides* can be distinguished from other species of *Malbranchea* by the development of spherules and by specific exoantigens (73).

While studying erythrasma, Lang in 1879 (100) introduced the genus *Epidermidophyton* for the organism he saw in human skin. It is difficult to determine from his original description what he saw, but it may have been an artifact. The name *Epidermidophyton* is of no value, but it stands as an earlier homonym (Article 65, ICBN) because the name was once treated as a fungus. In 1881, Mégnin (127) established the genus *Epidermophyton* for *E. gallinae,* which is now considered to be *Microsporum gallinae.* Thus, *Epidermophyton* Mégnin is a synonym of *Microsporum.* Sabouraud (146) defined the genus *Epidermophyton* in 1907 to include isolates that formed thick-walled, robust, hyaline, terminal, several-celled conidia that often occurred in clusters. His concept of *Epidermophyton* was based upon *E. inguinale,* which is now accepted as a synonym of *E. floccosum.* There is no doubt that *E. floccosum* and *M. gallinae* are entirely different fungi that belong in separate genera. *Epidermophyton* Mégnin, 1881 and *Epidermophyton* Sabouraud, 1907 are illegitimate and must be rejected because they are homonyms (Article 64.1, ICBN) of Lang's genus. Loeffler (107) proposed that *Epidermophyton* Sabouraud, 1907 (147) should be conserved against *Epidermophyton* Mégnin, 1881 and *Epidermidophyton* Lang, 1879. His proposal for conservation was rejected by the Special Committee for Fungi and Lichens of the International Botanical Congress. Steps are being taken to have the genus *Epidermophyton* Sabouraud reconsidered for conservation. In anticipation that *Epidermophyton* Sabouraud, 1907 will be conserved, it can be used for the species *E. floccosum* and *E. stockdaleae.*

Until recently, the genus *Exophiala* was essentially unknown to most medical mycologists. The genus is characterized by the development of cylindrical to lageniform, pale brown annellides that produce one- to several-celled, hyaline to brown annelloconidia in a ball. In 1977, McGinnis and Padhye (121, 124) studied *Phialophora jeanselmei* and *P. gougerotii;* they proposed that *P. jeanselmei* should be transferred to *Exophiala* as *E. jeanselmei,* that *P. gougerotii* in the sense of Borelli and other contemporary mycologists represents misidentified isolates of *E. jeanselmei,* and that *P. gougerotii* in the original sense of Matruchot is a synonym of *Sporothrix schenckii.* In addition, McGinnis (117) considers the fungus described as *P. spinifera* to be *E. spinifera.* Since *E. spinifera* produces distinctive annellides, it seems inappropriate to consider it a species of *Rhinocladiella* as proposed by de Hoog (41). *Rhinocladiella* is characterized by sympodial conidiophores. Recently, McGinnis (120) has disagreed with Hermanides-Nijhof's treatment of the fungus commonly known as *Cladosporium werneckii.* Owing to its annellides which may be either integrated within the hyphae or as yeast cells or both, this fungus should be referred to as *E. werneckii* as originally proposed by von Arx (182). McGinnis also pointed out that *Microsporum mansonii* is a synonym of *Malassezia furfur* since its original description was based upon a fungus seen in lesions of pityriasis versicolor, not tinea nigra. The type culture of *Microsporum mansonii* studied by de Hoog (41) and others is an isolate that was incorrectly considered by Castellani (120) to be the same organism he saw in skin lesions. This culture apparently originated several years after the name *M. mansonii* was proposed by Castellani. The living culture of this fungus appears to represent an undescribed species of *Wangiella.*

Owing to its polymorphic nature, the taxonomy of the genus *Fonsecaea* is extremely complex and confusing. Negroni proposed the genus *Fonsecaea* in 1936 for the etiologic agent of a case of chromoblastomycosis. He (129, 130) designated *Hormodendrum pedrosoi* Brumpt, 1922 as the type species for his new genus. Negroni's Figures 2 and 3 (129) clearly show sympodial conidiophores giving rise to one-celled primary conidia, primary conidia giving rise to secondary conidia in a sympodial arrangement, and some development that is compatible with the genus *Cladosporium.* The apices of many of the conidiophores illustrated are swollen with distinct denticles. This is not compatible with the genus *Rhinocladiella* as Nannfeldt (128) described it [Figure 43 in (128)]. I have had the opportunity to see the type material for *Rhinocladiella* and the neotype culture of *F. pedrosoi. Rhinocladiella* tends to produce its conidia along much of the conidiophore, and secondary conidia are absent. Thus, *Fonsecaea* and *Rhinocladiella* are not congeneric as proposed by de Hoog (41) and Schol-Schwarz (157).

Carrión & Emmons (22, 48) reported the presence of phialides in *F. compacta* and *F. pedrosoi.* The phialides were described as being typical of those formed by *Phialophora verrucosa.* Owing to this observation, Redaelli & Ciferri in 1942 (142) transferred *F. compacta* and *F. pedrosoi* to the genus *Phialophora.* Since the sympodial conidiogenous cells are so distinctive, they should be used to characterize *Fonsecaea* rather than the rare phialides occasionally produced by some isolates. The *Rhinocladiella*-like form often associated with *Fonsecaea* is usually referred to as *Acrotheca*-like. This is an error since *Acrotheca* is a synonym of *Ramularia,* an entirely different hyphomycete.

Fonsecaea compacta was first proposed by Carrión in 1935 (20). This proposal was invalid because a Latin diagnosis was not provided. The name *F. compacta* was validated in 1940 when Carrión provided the required Latin diagnosis (21). De Hoog (41) suggested that its morphology is similar to *Xylohypha.* I have studied *X. curta* and *F. compacta* and found that these two fungi are quite different. *Fonsecaea compacta* is similar to *Cladosporium chlorocephalum* (114). There is no doubt that *F. compacta* does belong in the genus *Fonsecaea.* The compact conidial heads consisting of subglobose to ovoid, catenulate conidia with blunt bases are quite different from *F. pedrosoi.*

Members of the genus *Geotrichum* typically form moist, yeast-like, flat, white colonies. Sigler & Carmichael (162) prefer to restrict the moist colonial morphology and the formation of chains of hyaline, slimy arthroconidia by segmentation of undifferentiated hyphae to *Geotrichum*. Similar isolates producing dry colonies with large amounts of aerial hyphae would be excluded from *Geotrichum*. Von Arx et al (188) expanded the concept of *Geotrichum* to include isolates that may form blastoconidia, and made the new combinations *G. capitatum, G. fermentans,* and *G. penicillatum* for *Trichosporon capitatum, T. fermentans,* and *T. penicillatum,* respectively. Weijman (192) studied the carbohydrate composition of *Geotrichum, Trichosporon,* and several other genera and concluded that "... *Geotrichum* has to be restricted to fungi with ascomycetous affinities and *Dipodascus* perfect states, whereas *Trichosporon* is suitable for the accommodation of basidiomycetous fungi related to *Filobasidium* and *Filobasidiella.*" Among the species accepted in *Geotrichum,* Weijman omitted *G. candidum,* the type species for the genus *Geotrichum.* Von Arx (186) believes that the genus *Trichosporon* must be restricted to species with dolipore septa, some of which have proven to be anamorphs of *Hyphopichia.* Von Arx (184) has transferred *Endomyces geotrichum,* the sexual form of *G. candidum,* as well as similar teleomorphs to the genus *Dipodascus.* If we accept the approach of von Arx, von Arx et al, and Weijman, the identification of *Geotrichum* and *Trichosporon* on morphological grounds—that is, the presence or absence of blastoconidia—will not be attainable in many instances. From a practical point of view, this author prefers to accept the approach of Sigler & Carmichael (162) and King & Jong (90) and restrict the genus *Geotrichum* to those isolates that produce hyphae and arthroconidia, and the genus *Trichosporon* to those isolates producing hyaline hyphae, blastoconidia, and arthroconidia.

While working in the Panama canal zone, Darling (34) designated the etiologic agent of a new infection (attributed to a protozoan) as *Histoplasma capsulatum* without culturing it. The fungal nature of *H. capsulatum* was finally proven in 1934 by de Monbreun (43), even though it was suggested by da Rocha-Lima twelve years earlier (35). The genus *Histoplasma* is primarily defined by the presence of small intracellular yeasts in tissue; it contains two species, *H. capsulatum* var. *capsulatum, H. capsulatum* var. *duboisii,* and *H. farciminosum.* When the genus *Histoplasma* is characterized on the basis of a yeast form, either in tissue or at 37°C in the laboratory, *H. farciminosum* can be accommodated very nicely in the genus. If the genus is defined by the distinctive conidia, then *H. farciminosum* does not belong in *Histoplasma* (3). Serological studies (166) have shown that all of these species have antigens in common.

Sigler et al (163) recently described *Renispora flavissima* as a new member of the Gymnoascaceae. This fungus produces a conidial form that is morphologically indistinguishable from *H. capsulatum.* It differs from *H. capsulatum* by forming yellow colonies that neither produce microconidia nor convert to a yeast form at 37°C. The conidia are 6–11 μm and are either spiny, coarsely tuberculate, or occasionally smooth-walled. These authors designated the anamorph as the *Chrysosporium* state of *R. flavissima.* They also consider the mold form of *H. capsulatum* to be the *Chrysosporium* state of *Ajellomyces capsulatus. Sepedonium* is differentiated by these authors from *Chrysosporium* by having larger, usually 15–25 μm, golden-yellow conidia, an accessory phialoconidial anamorph, and a teleomorph (when present) in the Hypocreaceae instead of the Gymnoascaceae. *Renispora* differs from *Ajellomyces* by lacking coiled appendages and having ascospores with a different shape. The placement of the conidial forms of *Blastomyces dermatitidis, H. capsulatum,* the anamorph of *R. flavissima,* and those species previously assigned to *Emmonsia* in the genus *Chrysosporium* (19, 163) has merit. Some earlier serological studies (81, 103) have reported that some of these fungi have antigens in common.

Among the Mycelia Sterilia, the genera *Madurella* and *Paracoccidioides* must be considered. Like so many of the older genera of medically important fungi, *Madurella* and *Paracoccidioides* were based upon the type of mycoses that they caused and their morphology in tissue. In 1905, while studying material from a mycetoma, Brumpt (18) established the genus *Madurella* for the fungus he saw producing black granules in tissue. It was not until 1912 (17) that *M. mycetomatis* was first isolated. Since mycetoma is a Greek word, its genitive in Latin is *mycetomatis,* not *mycetomi.* Some isolates identified on clinical and mycological grounds in culture that superficially resemble *M. mycetomatis* may produce phialides like those seen in the genus *Phialophora.* It should be obvious that these isolates cannot be included in the genus *Madurella* because it is illogical to classify an isolate that is producing conidia in the order Mycelia Sterilia.

With reference to *Paracoccidioides,* Splendore in 1912 (164) proposed the name *Zymonema brasiliense* for a fungus that produced a yeast form characterized by multiple budding in tissue. The fungus was first isolated by Lutz (110) four years earlier even though it was not named. It was placed in its current genus by de Almeida (36) in 1930. Some isolates of *P. brasiliensis* are occasionally found that produce conidia compatible with those seen in the genus *Chrysosporium* (122).

Dermatophytes in the genera *Microsporum* and *Trichophyton* have been classified on the basis of biochemical data (161), serology (138), nutritional requirements (56, 137), colony morphology, microscopic morphology, and the type of clinical disease produced (141). Since these genera are characterized in part by large, multicelled conidia, it seems illogical to include species such as *T. soudanense* and *T. yaoundei* in the genus *Trichophyton,* as they do not form macroconidia. Historically, they are classified in the genus *Trichophyton* simply because they cause ringworm. If their one-celled conidia were used for classification purposes, they could be accommodated in *Chrysosporium* under Carmichael's concept of that genus (19). Cole & Samson (28) have characterized the development of both the macro- and microconidia, produced by some of the members of *Microsporum* and *Trichophyton,* as holothallic in origin. This is in contrast to some isolates of the Gymnoascaceae referred to as *Chrysosporium* spp. which Cole & Samson reported are blastic in origin. For fungi such as *T. soudanense* and *T. yaoundei,* it would be helpful to know whether their conidia are blastic or thallic. Such species might be best placed in the genus *Chrysosporium.* The genera *Microsporum* and *Trichophyton* are distinguished from each other on the basis of their macroconidia with thick outer cell walls having echinulations, and thin outer cell walls without echinulations, respectively.

The genus *Mycocentrospora* should be mentioned because of its close resemblance to *Cercospora.* While studying a case of phaeohyphomycosis in Asia, Emmons et al (49) identified the etiologic agent as *C. apii.* Chupp (25) questioned whether their fungus was actually a *Cerospora.* His feelings were that it was not a member of the genus *Cercospora.* Deighton & Mulder (42) studied Emmons's fungus and concluded that it was a misidentified isolate of *M. acerina.* These authors have resolved the confusion surrounding *M. acerina* and the misidentified isolate known as *C. apii.*

The genus *Phialophora* was established for *P. verrucosa* by Medlar (126). Medlar characterized the genus by having dematiaceous phialides with distinct collarettes that produced balls of one-celled conidia. Some mycologists have incorrectly attributed the genus to Thaxter (126). There is no doubt that Thaxter did the taxonomy, but the generic name *Phialophora* was formally proposed by Medlar. In 1970, Schol-Schwarz (158) revised the genus *Phialophora* and included a number of species in *Phialophora* that could be accommodated nicely elsewhere. Cole & Kendrick in 1973 (27) re-studied *Phialophora* and defined it more closely to the original concept of Medlar. They considered phialides with a distinct constriction at the base of the collarette to be characteristic of *Phialophora,* and they maintained the genus *Margarinomyces* for isolates that formed phialides which merged into collarettes without a constriction. They also concluded that chlamydospores are not produced by *Phialophora* as suggested by Schol-Schwarz.

Zweibel & Wang (199) have recently addressed the question whether *P. americana* should be maintained as a synonym of *P. verrucosa.* Based upon morphological observations, electrophoretic and pathogenicity data, these authors concluded that Hughes's (71) treatment of *P. americana* and *P. verrucosa* as separate species is correct. Isolates having shallow collarettes would be included in *P. verrucosa,* whereas isolates with a high frequency of deep collarettes would be placed in *P. americana.* Zweibel & Wang also demonstrated that both species have pathogenic abilities. Additional study will be necessary before this question can be resolved.

The *P. hoffmannii* complex (119) represents one problem group that has not been adequately treated. The colonies are often ochraceous, amber, to pale grey in color. The phialides with non-flared collarettes and colonies that may not be dematiaceous suggest that this complex might be better classified elsewhere, such as in *Acremonium* or a similar genus. De Hoog (41) considered *P. heteromorpha* to be a variety of *Exophiala jeanselmei.* McGinnis (121) and Wang (190) have studied the type material of *P. hetermorpha* and believe it should be maintained as a species of *Phialophora.*

One fungus that has caused considerable taxonomic confusion is the anamorph of *Petriellidium boydii,* which is often referred to as *Monosporium apiospermum* for lack of a better name. In 1911, Saccardo (151) described the etiologic agent isolated from a case of mycetoma as *M. apiospermum.* In his discussion, Saccardo suggested that this species should have its own genus, for which the generic name *Scedosporium* was mentioned. The discussion of *Scedosporium* was clearly a diagnosis. The genus *Scedosporium* was effectively but invalidly published because Saccardo, having suggested the new genus, retained the species in *Monosporium.* A generic name is invalid if the author who proposes it does not accept and use it in his original publication (Article 34.1, ICBN). In 1919, Castellani & Chalmers (23) prepared what must be considered a minimum diagnosis for the genus *Scedosporium* and attributed the generic name to Saccardo. As a result, they validated the genus *Scedosporium* and proposed the new combination *S. apiospermum.* Thus, the correct citations are *Scedosporium* Saccardo ex Castellani et Chalmers, 1919 and *S. apiospermum* (Saccardo) Castellani et Chalmers, 1919. The generic name *Monosporium* is unacceptable for *S. apiospermum* because it is illegitimate; its type was included in three earlier genera (71). I have had the opportunity to study the type material of *S. apiospermum.* It is essentially the same as the type material Shear (160) preserved in 1922 for *Cephalosporium boydii* and *Dendrostilbella boydii,* the anamorphs he described for *Petriellidium boydii* (as *Allescheria boydii*). The type material of *C. boydii* shows single conidia and balls of conidia at the apices of cylindrical conidiogenous cells. Care must be exercised in identifying isolates as *P. boydii* solely upon the *Scedosporium* anamorph. *Scedosporium* is associated with several genera and species other than *P. boydii.*

The genus *Sporothrix* was proposed in 1900 by Hektoen & Perkins (68) for a fungus isolated from a case of sporotrichosis. In 1906, de Beurmann and Gougerot (38) transferred *S. schenckii* to the genus *Sporotrichum.* For some unexplainable reason, the genus *Sporothrix* was ignored from that time on. In 1958, Hughes (71) designated *Sporotrichum aureum* to be the lectotype for the genus *Sporotrichum.* Shortly afterward, Carmichael (19) pointed out that *Sporothrix* forms sympodial conidiophores with hyaline conidia, whereas *Sporotrichum* forms large, golden-brown conidia. In addition, *Sporotrichum* produces broad hyphae with clamp connections. Thus, *Sporothrix* is distinctively different from members of the genus *Sporotrichum.* Care must be exercised in using dimorphism as the sole means of distinguishing *Sporothrix schenckii* from other species of *Sporothrix.* Taylor (173) found several *Sporothrix* anamorphs of *Ceratocystis* species that could produce a yeast form like *S. schenckii.* The yeast forms were morphologically similar to *S. schenckii,* as well as being pathogenic for mice.

Among the dematiaceous fungi of medical interest, the polymorphic black yeasts are probably the most difficult to define. One of these fungi is the pathogen Kano described as *Hormiscium dermatitidis* in 1934 and again in 1937 (79, 80). This fungus was usually referred to as a species of either *Fonsecaea, Phialophora,* or *Rhinocladiella* until McGinnis (116, 118) proposed the new genus *Wangiella* for it. The genus *Wangiella* was based primarily upon phialides without collarettes (by light microscopy). During his study of the genus *Exophiala,* de Hoog (41) transferred *W. dermatitidis* to *Exophiala.* This was done because de Hoog observed both annellides and phialides in *W. dermatitidis.* If one considers the annellides to be more typical and distinctive rather than the phialides, then de Hoog's treatment of this fungus is best. Owing to the facts that the phialides are more stable, unique, and distinctive, that the yeast form does not produce the muzzle cells that occur in some species of *Exophiala,* that the colonies are distinctively wet, black, yeast-like, and sticky to the touch, and that the fungus can grow at 40°C, *Wangiella* is the most logical genus for this fungus. Preliminary work with exoantigens are also showing differences between *W. dermatitidis* and some members of *Exophiala* (P. G. Standard, unpublished data).

DIVISION ZYGOMYCOTA

The class Phycomycetes was established a number of years ago to accommodate most of the lower fungi. As our knowledge of these organisms expanded, the class Phycomycetes rapidly became obsolete and was replaced by a number of new classes (1). The majority of these organisms are now classified in the Kingdom Protista by many mycologists (132). Since the class Phycomycetes is so vague, the archaic term phycomycosis has no value. Mycoses caused by Zygomycetes are usually referred to as either zygomycosis, mucormycosis, or entomophthoromycosis (4). Zygomycosis is the preferred term since it can encompass the latter two terms.

The Zygomycetes are distinguished from each other on the basis of sexual and asexual forms. There are no formal Fungi Imperfecti among the Zygomycetes because the anamorphs formed by these fungi are so distinctive, that is, the sporangia, sporangiola, spores, and conidia. Zygospores have a restricted taxonomic value; they are primarily valuable at the family and ordinal levels (10). Since the bulk of the isolates are apparently heterothallic, zygospores are not commonly seen. Within the various genera, there are some species that are not known to produce zygospores. As more sexual states are found, especially in the Mucorales, they may become important in realizing phylogenetic relationships at the family and generic levels.

In order to appreciate the taxonomy of the Zygomycetes, it is important to have a firm grasp of several terms that are used to characterize their teleomorphs and anamorphs. Spores are propagules that arise by either meiosis or mitosis. Meiosis precedes the formation of ascospores and basidiospores, but occurs normally in zygospores, presumably, some time after their maturity. In the case of asexual reproduction, they are formed within a merosporangium, sporangium, or sporangiolum following a cleavage process. In contrast, conidia are asexual propagules that are usually deciduous, and they are not formed within merosporangia, sporangia, or sporangiola. Some mycologists incorrectly refer to sporangiola as conidia when they contain a single sporangiospore. These structures are reduced sporangia (10, 28) and not conidia in the strict sense. Arthroconidia (69, 72) and yeast-like cells producing blastoconidia (102) are occasionally produced by some Zygomycetes, especially members of the genus *Mucor.* Since these kinds of conidia are relatively rare, they have little taxonomic value. Griffiths (63) has proposed that the term chlamydospore be restricted to thick-walled propagules (intercalary in origin) and that it should not include azygospores. In the Zygomycetes, as well as in the other major groups of fungi, the term chlamydospore has often been applied to many different structures (83). There is a trend for other types of data to be incorporated into our classification system for these fungi. These data include cell-wall composition (8, 193), antigenic relationships (62, 77), mol% G+C content (168), enzymatic profiles (59, 65, 135, 169), ultrastructure (28), mating studies (65, 154, 156, 194), physiological data (75), and temperature requirements (155).

The genus *Absidia* contains a single human pathogen, *A. corymbifera. Absidia corymbifera* and *A. ramosa* were considered by many to represent two distinct species distinguished from each other on the basis of subspherical versus elongate sporangiospores, respectively. Nottebrock et al (131) reviewed the controversial taxonomy surrounding these two species and concluded that they are conspecific. This conclusion has been widely accepted. While conducting mating studies and temperature investigations in the genus *Cunninghamella,* Weitzman & Crist (194) discovered that the human pathogenic isolates previously identified as *C. elegans* were misidentified. They concluded that these isolates were actually *C. bertholletiae.* Their observations agree with the conclusion of Reinhardt et al (143) that *C. elegans* is not pathogenic for man.

There is some confusion surrounding *Rhizopus stolonifer.* Based upon priority, *R. nigricans* is a synonym of *R. stolonifer.* Ajello (4) and Reinhardt et al (143) have clearly pointed out that *R. stolonifer* is not a pathogen of man. A number of the isolates recovered from opportunistic infections that were identified as this species have been reidentified as *R. arrhizus* and *R. oryzae.* Jones & Kaufman (77) and the British Society for Mycopathology (2) have suggested that these two latter species may be conspecific. Zycha et al (200), Inui et al (75), and Dabinett & Wellman (32) have maintained them as separate species. Additional study is needed before this problem can be resolved.

Recently, Schipper (155) transferred *Mucor pusillus* to the genus *Rhizomucor* as *R. pusillus.* This decision was based partly upon the ability of *R. pusillus* to grow at 55°C and to produce stolons and rhizoids. Unlike *Rhizopus* species, the sporangiophores repeatedly branch in *Rhizomucor pusillus.* In contrast to species of *Absidia, R. pusillus* has globose sporangia without apophyses. Schipper et al observed that the ornamentation of the zygospores of *R. pusillus* is distinctive (156).

The genus *Basidiobolus* was established by Eidam in 1886 (46) to accommodate *B. ranarum* and *B. lacertae.* The first documented human infection caused by *Basidiobolus* was reported by Joe et al (76) in 1956 from Indonesia. Based upon the present of zygospores with undulating outer cell walls, Emmons (76) identified the etiologic agent as *B. ranarum.* Judging from Figures 10–12 in (76), it is difficult to determine the surface topography of all the zygospores they illustrated. Zygospores with both smooth and undulating walls appear to be present. Drechsler (45) obtained a subculture of the Indonesian isolate from Emmons and concluded that it was either an undescribed species or a variant of *B. meristosporus.* This conclusion was based in part upon Drechsler's observation that the zygospores had smooth outer walls. It should be noted that the fungus received by Drechsler from Emmons (A1238) bears a different accession number than the one (NIH 2505) given to the American Type culture Collection (ATCC 14052). According to Dr. Kwon-Chung at NIH, NIH 2505 was deposited after A1238. Both of these isolates are reported to be from the original Indonesian case (76). Emmons et al (47) now consider this fungus to be *B. haptosporus.*

The principal characteristics that have been used to distinguish the various species of *Basidiobolus* include the presence or absence of a *Streptomyces*-like odor, growth at different temperatures, and the surface topography of the zygospore outer wall. Traditionally, isolates having a *Streptomyces*-like odor and zygospores with an undulating cell wall were identified as *B. ranarum. Basidiobolus haptosporus* and *B. meristosporus* have been distinguished from *B. ranarum* by having zygospores with smooth walls and an absence of a *Streptomyces*-like odor, the former two being distinguished from each other by temperature studies (61). Hutchison et al (74) and King (88) have shown that temperature requirements, zygospore wall topography, and the presence or absence of a *Streptomyces*-like odor are extremely variable characteristics and are not useful in distinguishing taxa. King also noted that a human isolate produced a *Streptomyces*-like odor and smooth-walled zygospores (ATCC 14052), while a second human isolate (ATCC 16109) formed zygospores that had both smooth and undulating walls. In the original description of *B. ranarum,* Eidam (46) clearly illustrated both smooth- and undulating-walled zygospores [compare Figures 7–9, 12 and 6, 13 and 14, Plate 12 in (46)]. In fact, Drechsler (44) has illustrated smooth- and undulating-walled zygospores in *B. ranarum* [compare Figures 3 G, H and 3 E, F in (44)]. Drechsler also illustrated zygospores of *B. haptosporus* [Figure 4 I, K in (44)] that are nearly identical to the one Eidam illustrated of *B. lacertae* [Figure 23, Plate 12 in (46)].

A taxonomic revision of the genus *Basidiobolus* is needed. Based upon morphology, it appears best to consider *B. haptosporus, B. heterosporus, B. lacertae, B. magnus, B. meristosporus, B. myxophilus,* and *B. philippinensis* as synonyms of *B. ranarum.* The percent of total fatty acid content in *B. haptosporus, B. heterosporus,* and *B. ranarum* is essentially the same (176), which adds additional support to the above conclusion. *Basidiobolus microsporus,* which was described by Benjamin in 1962 (9), is readily distinguished from *B. ranarum* by the production of exogenous microspores.

There is no debate regarding the current classification of *Conidiobolus coronatus* and *C. incongruus.* At one time, *C. coronatus* was considered to be a member of the genus *Entomophthora* (as *E. coronata*). The papers by King (85–88) should be consulted for additional information.

CONCLUSION

Many taxonomic problems have been resolved during the past several years owing to a better appreciation and understanding of conidiogenesis, morphogenesis, metabolic pathways, and the cellular components of the fungi. Several problem areas still exist, which require additional data before they can be adequately resolved. A better appreciation of anamorph-teleomorph connections will aid mycologists in understanding the whole fungus. As new antifungal agents become available for the treatment of the mycoses, it will become more important in the future that medically important fungi be clearly and concisely defined. Recent advances in fungal taxonomy will undoubtedly aid medical mycologists in achieving this important goal.

ACKNOWLEDGMENTS

I would like to thank Mrs. Lynne Sigler and Drs. Libero Ajello, Jerry Benny, J. W. Carmichael, Barry Katz, Michael Rinaldi, and Donald P. Rogers for their many helpful comments and suggestions.

Literature Cited

1. Ainsworth, G. C. 1973. In *The Fungi An Advanced Treatise,* ed. G. C. Ainsworth, F. K. Sparrow, A. S. Sussman, 4A:1–7. New York/London: Academic. 621 pp.
2. Ainsworth, G. C., Austwick, P. K. C., Barlow, A. J. E., Cruickshank, C. N. D., Gentles, J. C., Mackenzie, D. W. R., Stockdale, P. M. 1977. *Nomenclature of fungi pathogenic to man and animals. Memorandum No. 23,* pp. 1–26. London: Her Majesty's Stationary Office. 4th ed.
3. Ajello, L. 1968. *Mykosen* 11:507–14
4. Ajello, L., Dean, D. F., Irwin, R. S. 1976. *Mycologia* 68:52–62
5. Banti, G. 1911. *Atti Accad. Med. Fis. Fiorentina,* p. 49
6. Barnett, J. A., Pankhurst, R. J. 1974. *A New Key to the Yeasts.* Amsterdam/London: North-Holland. 273 pp.
7. Barron, G. L. 1968. *The Genera of Hyphomycetes from Soil.* Baltimore: Williams & Wilkins. 364 pp.
8. Bartnicki-Garcia, S. 1968. *Ann. Rev. Microbiol.* 22:87–108
9. Benjamin, R. K. 1962. *Aliso* 5:223–33
10. Benjamin, R. K. 1979. In *The Whole Fungus,* ed. B. Kendrick, 2:573–621. Ottawa: Natl. Mus. Can. 793 pp.
11. Berkhout, M. 1923. De schimmelgeslachten *Monilia, Oidium, Oospora* and *Torula.* PhD thesis. Univ. Utrecht. 71 pp.
12. Berlese, A. N. 1894. *G. Vitic. Enol.* 3:52–55
13. Binford, C. H., Thompson, R. K., Gorham, M. E., Emmons, C. W. 1952. *Am. J. Clin. Pathol.* 22:535–42
14. Borelli, D. 1960. *Riv. Anat. Patol. Oncol.* 17:615–22
15. Borelli, D., Marcano, C. 1973. *Castellania* 1:151–54
16. Boyd, M. F., Cutchfield, E. D. 1921. *Am. J. Trop. Med.* 1:215–89
17. Brault, J. 1912. *Ann. Dermatol. Syphiligr. Ser. 5* 3:333–43
18. Brumpt, E. 1905. *C. R. Seances Soc. Biol. Paris* 58:997–99
19. Carmichael, J. W. 1962. *Can. J. Bot.* 40:1137–73
20. Carrión, A. L. 1935. *P. R. J. Public Health Trop. Med.* 10:543–45
21. Carrión, A. L. 1940. *P. R. J. Public Health Trop. Med.* 15:340–61
22. Carrión, A. L., Emmons, C. W. 1935. *P. R. J. Public Health Trop. Med.* 11:114–15
23. Castellani, A., Chalmers, A. J. 1919. *Manual of Tropical Medicine.* New York: William Wood. 2436 pp. 3rd ed.
24. Chesson, A., Morgan, J. J., Codner, R. C. 1978. *Trans. Br. Mycol. Soc.* 70:345–61
25. Chupp, C. 1957. *Mycologia* 49:773–74
26. Ciferri, R., Montemartini, A. 1959. *Mycopathol. Mycol. Appl.* 10:303–16
27. Cole, G. T., Kendrick, B. 1973. *Mycologia* 65:661–88
28. Cole, G. T., Samson, R. A. 1979. *Patterns of Development in Conidial Fungi.* London: Pitman. 190 pp.
29. Cooke, W. B. 1959. *Mycopathol. Mycol. Appl.* 12:1–45
30. Cooke, W. B. 1962. *Mycopathol. Mycol. Appl.* 17:1–43
31. Constantin, M., Rolland. 1888. *Bull. Soc. Mycol. Fr.* 4:153–57
32. Dabinett, P. E., Wellman, A. M. 1973. *Can. J. Bot.* 51:2053–64
33. Dabinett, P. E., Wellman, A. M. 1978. *Can. J. Bot.* 56:2031–49
34. Darling, S. T. 1906. *J. Am. Med. Assoc.* 46:1283–85
35. da Rocha-Lima, H. 1912. *Zentralbl. Bakteriol. Parasitenkd. Infektionskr.* 67:233–49

36. de Almeida, F. 1930. *An. Fac. Med. Univ. São Paulo* 5:125–39
37. de Bertoldi, M. 1976. *Can. J. Bot.* 54:2755–68
38. de Beurmann, L., Gougerot, H. 1906. *Ann. Dermatol. Syphiligr.* 7:837–64, 914–22, 993–1006
39. de Hoog, G. S., ed. 1979. *Centraalbureau voor Schimmelcultures, 75 Years Culture Collection.* Baarn: Centraalbur. Schimmelcult. 61 pp.
40. de Hoog, G. S. 1979. See Ref. 10, pp. 215–39
41. de Hoog, G. S., Hermanides-Nijhof, E. J. 1977. *Stud. Mycol.* 15:1–222
42. Deighton, F. C., Mulder, J. L. 1977. *Trans. Br. Mycol. Soc.* 69:326–27
43. de Monbreun, W. A. 1934. *Am. J. Trop. Med.* 14:93–124
44. Drechsler, C. 1956. *Mycologia* 48: 655–76
45. Drechsler, C. 1958. *Am. J. Bot.* 45: 632–38
46. Eidam, E. 1886. *Beitr. Biol. Pflanz.* 4:181–251
47. Emmons, C. W., Binford, C. H., Utz, J. P., Kwon-Chung, K. J. 1977. *Medical Mycology.* Philadelphia: Lea & Febiger. 592 pp. 3rd ed.
48. Emmons, C. W., Carrión, A. L. 1936. *P. R. J. Public Health Trop. Med.* 11:703–10
49. Emmons, C. W., Joe, L. K., Eng, N. T., Pohan, A., Kertopati, S., van der Meulen, A. 1957. *Mycologia* 49:1–10
50. Fennell, D. I. 1973. See Ref. 1, pp. 45–68
51. Franke, R. G. 1973. *Bull. Torrey Bot. Club* 100:287–96
52. Fuson, G. B., Price, C. W., Phaff, H. J. 1979. *Int. J. Syst. Bacteriol.* 29:64–69
53. Gams, W. 1971. *Cephalosporium-artige Schimmelpilze (Hyphomycetes).* Stuttgart: Fischer. 262 pp.
54. Gams, W. 1978. *Persoonia* 10:97–112
55. Gander, J. E. 1974. *Ann. Rev. Microbiol.* 28:103–19
56. Georg, L. K., Camp, L. B. 1957. *J. Bacteriol.* 74:113–21
57. Gilchrist, T. C., Stokes, W. R. 1896. *Bull. Johns Hopkins Hosp.* 7:129–33
58. Gilchrist, T. C., Stokes, W. R. 1898. *J. Exp. Med.* 3:53–78
59. Gleason, F. H. 1971. *Mycologia* 63: 906–10
60. Gordon, M. A. 1979. *Sabouraudia* 17:305–9
61. Greer, D. L., Friedman, L. 1966. *Sabouraudia* 4:231–41
62. Greer, D. L., Friedman, L. 1966. *Sabouraudia* 5:7–13
63. Griffiths, D. A. 1974. *Nova Hedwigia Z. Kryptogamenkde.* 25:503–47
64. Guého, E. 1979. *Antonie van Leeuwenhoek J. Microbiol. Serol.* 45:199–210
65. Havens, P. L. 1976. *Mycotaxon* 4: 218–32
66. Hawksworth, D. L. 1979. *Can. J. Bot.* 57:91–99
67. Hawksworth, D. L., Booth, C. 1974. *Mycol. Pap.* 135:1–38
68. Hektoen, L., Perkins, C. F. 1900. *J. Exp. Med.* 5:77–89
69. Hesseltine, C. W., Ellis, J. J. 1973. See Ref. 1, 4B:187–217
70. Hughes, S. J. 1953. *Can. J. Bot.* 31:577–659
71. Hughes, S. J. 1958. *Can. J. Bot.* 36:727–836
72. Hughes, S. J. 1971. In *Taxonomy of Fungi Imperfecti,* ed. B. Kendrick, pp. 7–36. Toronto/Buffalo: Univ. Toronto. 309 pp.
73. Huppert, M., Sun, S. H., Rice, E. H. 1978. *J. Clin. Microbiol.* 8:346–48
74. Hutchison, J. A., King, D. S., Nickerson, M. A. 1972. *Mycologia* 64:467–74
75. Inui, T., Takeda, Y., Iizuka, H. 1965. *J. Gen. Appl. Microbiol.* 11:1–121 (Suppl.)
76. Joe, L. K., Eng, N. T., Pohan, A., van der Meulen, H., Emmons, C. W. 1956. *Arch. Dermatol.* 74:378–83
77. Jones, K. W., Kaufman, L. 1978. *J. Clin. Microbiol.* 7:97–103
78. Jong, S. C., King, D. S. 1976. *Mycotaxon* 3:397–400
79. Kano, K. 1934. *Aichi Igakkai Zasshi* 41:1657–73
80. Kano, K. 1937. *Arch. Dermatol. Syphilol.* 176:282–94
81. Kaufman, L., Blumer, S. 1966. *J. Bacteriol.* 91:1434–39
82. Kaufman, L., Standard, P. 1978. *Curr. Microbiol.* 1:135–40
83. Kendrick, B. 1971. See Ref. 72, pp. 1–309
84. Kendrick, B., DiCosmo, F. 1979. See Ref. 10, pp. 283–410
85. King, D. S. 1976. *Can. J. Bot.* 54:45–65
86. King, D. S. 1976. *Can. J. Bot.* 54:1285–96
87. King, D. S. 1977. *Can. J. Bot.* 55: 718–29
88. King, D. S. 1979. *Mycologia* 71:731–45
89. King, D. S., Jong, S. C. 1975. *Mycotaxon* 3:89–94
90. King, D. S., Jong, S. C. 1977. *Mycotaxon* 6:391–417
91. Korf, R. P., Kohn, L. M. 1979. *Mycotaxon* 9:521–22
92. Kwon-Chung, K. J. 1972. *Science* 175:326

93. Kwon-Chung, K. J. 1972. *Science* 177:368–69
94. Kwon-Chung, K. J. 1973. *Mycologia* 65:109–21
95. Kwon-Chung, K. J. 1975. *Mycologia* 67:1197–1200
96. Kwon-Chung, K. J. 1975. *Mycologia* 67:980–90
97. Kwon-Chung, K. J. 1976. *Mycologia* 68:821–33
98. Kwon-Chung, K. J., Bennett, J. E., Theodore, T. S. 1978. *Int. J. Syst. Bacteriol.* 28:616–20
99. Lachance, M., Phaff, H. J. 1979. *Int. J. Syst. Bacteriol.* 29:70–78
100. Lang, E. 1879. *Vjschr. Dermatol. Syphiligr.* 11:257–63
101. Lapage, S. P., Sneath, P. H. A., Lessel, E. F., Skerman, V. B. D., Seeliger, H. P. R., Clark, W. A., eds. 1976. *International Code of Nomenclature of Bacteria and Statutes of the International Association of Microbiological Societies.* Washington: Am. Soc. Microbiol. 180 pp.
102. Lara, S. L., Bartnicki-Garcia, S. 1974. *Arch. Microbiol.* 97:1–16
103. Li, M., Garrison, R. G., Dodd, H. 1967. *Mycopathol. Mycol. Appl.* 33:353–63
104. Linnaeus, C. 1751. *Philosophia Botanica.* Stockholm: Godofr. Kiesewetter, 362 pp. 1st ed.
105. Lodder, J., ed. 1970. *The Yeasts, a Taxonomic Study.* Amsterdam: North-Holland. 1385 pp. 2nd ed.
106. Lodder, J., Kreger-van Rij, N. J. W. 1952. *The Yeasts, a Taxonomic Study.* Amsterdam: North-Holland. 713 pp.
107. Loeffler, W. 1976. *Taxon* 25:208–10
108. Luttrell, E. S. 1973. See Ref. 1, pp. 135–219
109. Luttrell, E. S. 1979. See Ref. 10, pp. 241–64
110. Lutz, A. 1908. *Bras. Med.* 22:121–24, 141–44
111. Madelin, M. F. 1979. See Ref. 10, pp. 63–80
112. Malloch, D. 1970. *Mycologia* 62: 727–40
113. Malloch, D. 1979. See Ref. 10, pp. 153–65
114. Mason, E. W., Ellis, M. B. 1953. *Mycol. Pap.* 56:1–127
115. McDonough, E. S., Lewis, A. L. 1968. *Mycologia* 60:76–83
116. McGinnis, M. R. 1977. *Mycotaxon* 5:353–63
117. McGinnis, M. R. 1977. *Mycotaxon* 5:337–40
118. McGinnis, M. R. 1977. *Mycotaxon* 6:367–69
119. McGinnis, M. R. 1978. *Pan Am. Health Org. Sci. Publ. No. 356,* pp. 37–59
120. McGinnis, M. R. 1979. *Sabouraudia* 17:145–54
121. McGinnis, M. R. 1979. *Mycopathologia* 65:79–87
122. McGinnis, M. R. 1980. *Laboratory Handbook of Medical Mycology.* New York: Academic. In press
123. McGinnis, M. R., Katz, B. 1979. *Mycotaxon* 8:157–64
124. McGinnis, M. R., Padhye, A. A. 1977. *Mycotaxon* 5:341–52
125. McGinnis, M. R., Padhye, A. A. 1978. *Mycotaxon* 7:415–18
126. Medlar, E. M. 1915. *J. Med. Res.* 32:507–21
127. Mégnin, M. 1881. *C. R. Seances Soc. Biol. Paris* 33:404–5
128. Melin, E., Nannfeldt, J. A. 1934. *Sven. Skogsvårdsfören. Tidskr.* 32:397–585
129. Negroni, P. 1936. *Rev. Inst. Bacteriol. Buenos Aires* 7:419–26
130. Negroni, P. 1936. *Rev. Soc. Argent. Biol.* 12:180–84
131. Nottebrock, H., Scholer, H. J., Wall, M. 1974. *Sabouraudia* 12:64–74
132. Olive, L. 1975. *The Mycetozoans.* New York/London: Academic. 293 pp.
133. Padhye, A. A. 1975. *Pan. Am. Health Org. Sci. Publ. No. 304,* pp. 111–17
134. Padhye, A. A., Carmichael, J. W. 1968. *Mycologia* 60:445–47
135. Peberdy, J. F., Turner, M. 1968. *J. Gen. Microbiol.* 51:303–12
136. Pechak, D. G., Crang, R. E. 1977. *Mycologia* 69:783–92
137. Philpot, C. M. 1977. *Sabouraudia* 15: 141–50
138. Philpot, C. M. 1978. *Sabouraudia* 16: 247–56
139. Pore, R. S., D'Amato, R. F., Ajello, L. 1977. *Sabouraudia* 15:69–78
140. Rattray, J. B. M., Schibeci, A., Kidby, D. K. 1975. *Bacteriol. Rev.* 39:197–231
141. Rebell, G., Taplin, D. 1970. *Dermatophytes. Their Recognition and Identification.* Coral Gables: Univ. Miami Press. 124 pp. 2nd ed.
142. Redaelli, P., Ciferri, R. 1942. *Tratt. Micopatol. Umana* 5:584–612
143. Reinhardt, D. J., Kaplan, W., Ajello, L. 1970. *Infect. Immun.* 2:404–13
144. Rixford, E., Gilchrist, T. C. 1896. *Johns Hopkins Hosp. Rep.* 1:209–68
145. Rogers, D. P. 1953. *Mycologia* 45: 312–22
146. Sabouraud, R. 1907. *Arch. Méd. Exp. Anat. Pathol.* 19:565–86, 737–66
147. Sabouraud, R. 1910. *Les Teignes.* Paris: Masson & Cie. 855 pp.

148. Saccardo, P. A. 1886. *Sylloge Fungorum.* 4:1–807
149. Saccardo, P. A. 1906. *Sylloge Fungorum* 18:1–838
150. Saccardo, P. A. 1906. *Sylloge Fungorum* 18:495
151. Saccardo, P. A. 1911. *Ann. Mycol.* 9:249–57
152. Saccardo, P. A. 1912. *Ann. Mycol.* 10:310–22
153. Saccardo, P. A., Sydow, P. 1899. *Sylloge Fungorum* 14:464
154. Schipper, M. A. A. 1978. *Stud. Mycol.* 17:1–52
155. Schipper, M. A. A. 1978. *Stud. Mycol.* 17:53–71
156. Schipper, M. A. A., Samson, R. A., Staplers, J. A. 1975. *Persoonia* 8:321–28
157. Schol-Schwarz, M. B. 1968. *Antonie van Leeuwenhoek J. Microbiol. Serol.* 34: 119–52
158. Schol-Schwarz, M. B. 1970. *Persoonia* 6:59–94
159. Segretain, G., Destombes, P. 1961. *C. R. Acad. Sci.* 253:2577–79
160. Shear, C. L. 1922. *Mycologia* 14:239–43
161. Schechter, Y., Landau, J. W., Dabrowa, N., Newcomer, V. D. 1968. *J. Invest. Dermatol.* 51:165–76
162. Sigler, L., Carmichael, J. W. 1976. *Mycotaxon* 4:349–488
163. Sigler, L., Gaur, P. K., Lichtwardt, R. W., Carmichael, J. W. 1979. *Mycotaxon* 10:133–41
164. Splendore, A. 1912. *Bull. Soc. Pathol. Exot.* 5:313–19
165. Stafleu, F. A., Demoulin, V., Greuter, W., Hiepko, P., Linczevski, I. A., McVaugh, R., Meikle, R. D., Rollins, R. C., Ross, R., Schopf, J. M., Voss, E. G. 1978. *International Code of Botanical Nomenclature Adopted by the Twelfth International Botanical Congress, Leningrad, July 1975.* Utrecht: Bohn, Scheltema & Holkema. 457 pp.
166. Standard, P. G., Kaufman, L. 1976. *J. Clin. Microbiol.* 3:191–99
167. Stigliani, R. 1961. *Arch. Vecc. Firenze* 36:329–43
168. Storck, R., Alexopoulos, C. J. 1970. *Bacteriol. Rev.* 34:126–54
169. Stout, D. L., Shaw, C. R. 1973. *Mycologia* 65:803–8
170. Subramanian, C. V. 1962. *Bull. Bot. Surv. India* 4:249–59
171. Subramanian, C. V. 1972. *Curr. Sci.* 41:43–49
172. Subramanian, C. V., Pushkaran, M. 1975. *Kavaka* 3:77–99
173. Taylor, J. J. 1970. *Mycopathol. Mycol. Appl.* 42:233–40
174. Tubaki, K. 1958. *J. Hattori Bot. Lab.* 20:142–244
175. Tubaki, K. 1963. *Ann. Rep. Inst. Ferment. Osaka* 1:25–54
176. Tyrrell, D. 1967. *Can. J. Microbiol.* 13:755–60
177. Valadon, L. R. G. 1976. *Trans. Br. Mycol. Soc.* 67:1–15
178. van der Walt, J. P. 1969. *Antonie van Leeuwenhoek J. Microbiol. Serol.* Suppl. 35:A1–2
179. van der Walt, J. P. 1970. *Mycopathol. Mycol. Appl.* 40:231–43
180. van Warmelo, K. T. 1979. *Taxon* 28: 424–31
181. Vidal-Leiria, M., Buckley, H., van Uden, N. 1979. *Mycologia* 71:493–501
182. von Arx, J. A. 1970. *The Genera of Fungi Sporulating in Pure Culture.* Lehre: Cramer. 288 pp.
183. von Arx, J. A. 1971. *Persoonia* 6: 365–69
184. von Arx, J. A. 1977. *Antonie van Leeuwenhoek J. Microbiol. Serol.* 43:333–40
185. von Arx, J. A. 1979. See Ref. 10, pp. 201–13
186. von Arx, J. A. 1979. See Ref. 10, pp. 555–71
187. von Arx, J. A., Müller, E. 1975. *Stud. Mycol.* 9:1–159
188. von Arx, J. A., Rodrigues de Miranda, L., Smith, M. T., Yarrow, D. 1977. *Stud. Mycol.* 14:1–42
189. von Arx, J. A., Weijman, A. C. M. 1979. *Antonie van Leeuwenhoek J. Microbiol. Serol.* 45:547–55
190. Wang, C. J. K. 1979. See Ref. 10, pp. 81–91
191. Weijman, A. C. M. 1976. *Antonie van Leeuwenhoek J. Microbiol. Serol.* 42: 315–24
192. Weijman, A. C. M. 1979. *Antonie van Leeuwenhoek J. Microbiol. Serol.* 45: 119–27
193. Weijman, A. C. M., Meuzelaar, H. L. C. 1979. *Can. J. Bot.* 57:284–91
194. Weitzman, I., Crist, M. Y. 1979. *Mycologia* 71:1024–33
195. Weresub, L. K., Hennebert, G. L. 1979. *Mycotaxon* 8:181–86
196. Whittaker, R. H. 1969. *Science* 163:150–60
197. Whittaker, R. H., Margulis, L. 1978. *BioSystems* 10:3–18
198. Yarrow, D., Meyer, S. A. 1978. *Int. J. Syst. Bacteriol.* 28:611–15
199. Zweibel, S. M., Wang, C. J. K. 1978. *PAHO Sci. Publ. No. 356,* pp. 91–100
200. Zycha, H., Siepmann, R., Linnemann, G. 1969. *Mucorales eine Beschreibung Aller Gattungen und Arten Dieser Pilzgruppe.* Lehre: Cramer. 355 pp.

Ann. Rev. Microbiol. 1980. 34:137–58

MODIFIED BASES IN BACTERIOPHAGE DNAs

❖1772

R. A. J. Warren

Department of Microbiology, University of British Columbia, Vancouver, British Columbia, Canada, V6T 1W5

CONTENTS

INTRODUCTION 137
MODIFIED BASES IDENTIFIED IN BACTERIOPHAGE DNAs 138
DETECTION AND IDENTIFICATION OF MODIFIED BASES IN DNA 139
EFFECTS OF MODIFIED BASES ON THE PHYSICAL-CHEMICAL PROPERTIES OF DNA 140
BIOSYNTHESIS OF DNAs CONTAINING MODIFIED BASES 142
Phages in Which a Base is Replaced Completely With a Modified Base 143
Bacteriophage T4 143
Bacteriophage φe 144
Bacteriophage PBS2 145
Bacteriophage XP12 146
Phages in Which a Base is Partially Replaced With a Modified Base 146
Bacteriophage SP15 146
Bacteriophage SP10 147
Bacteriophage φW14 147
BIOLOGICAL CONSEQUENCES OF BASE MODIFICATION 148
Nuclease Susceptibility 148
Transcription 149
Replication 150
DNA Conformation and Recognition 151
DNA Packaging 152
Other Consequences 152
MODIFIED BASES MAY NOT BE ESSENTIAL FOR BIOLOGICAL ACTIVITY 153
MODIFIED BASES IN OTHER ORGANISMS 154
CONCLUDING REMARKS 154

INTRODUCTION

This review considers bacteriophage DNAs in which all or a major proportion of one of the four bases found commonly in DNA is replaced by a modified base. It does not consider the methylated bases that are found in

0066-4227/80/1001-0137$01.00

small amounts in DNA and that function usually to protect DNA against specific restriction endonucleases.

The first modified base in a bacteriophage DNA, 5-hydroxymethylcytosine (hmCyt), was discovered 27 years ago (154). It played a crucial role in the development of the biochemistry of T-even phage-infected *Escherichia coli* (20, 125). Since then, modified bases have been found in a variety of other bacteriophages. They are of interest from the point of view of their biochemistry and, more recently, their effects on DNA conformation and function. The biosynthesis of some of these bases has been reviewed extensively (20, 47, 88, 91). This review emphasizes the more recent developments in modified base biochemistry and considers also some of their effects on DNA structure and function.

MODIFIED BASES IDENTIFIED IN BACTERIOPHAGE DNAs

The structures of the modified bases that have been identified in phage DNAs are given in Figure 1. Doubtless, others will be identified as more phage DNAs are examined. The presence of a modified base usually alters the physical properties of a DNA (see the next section), and the properties of some phage DNAs suggest the presence of as yet unidentified modified bases (3, 150).

The phages discussed in this review are listed in Table 1. T4 is taken as representative of the three T-even phages, ϕe as representative of a group of identical phages which includes SP8, ϕe, SP01, and SP82G (138).

In some phages, the modified base may carry further substituents. In T4 DNA, glucose molecules are attached to the hmCyt residues, 70% of them by α-glycosidic bonds, 30% of them by β-glycosidic bonds (75). In SP15 DNA, the 4-hydroxyls in the dihydroxypentyl sidechains carry three glucose molecules, as maltose and glucose-1-phosphate (11, 142). In SP10 DNA, the γ-carboxyls of the glutamyl sidechains carry an as yet unidentified hydrophilic substituent containing a primary amine (M. Mandel, personal communication). However, the hydroxymethyl groups in ϕe (2), the uracils in PBS2 (2, 140), and the putrescinyl groups in ϕW14 (R. A. J. Warren, unpublished observations) are not further substituted.

The possibility that a modified base in DNA can carry a substituent such as glucose or an amine complicates the assignment of a structure to the base. The bases are released from DNA by acid hydrolysis under conditions that will allow hydrolysis of glycosidic bonds. Thus, the modified base obtained from T4 DNA is hmCyt, not the glucosylated derivates. However, if the substituent is attached to the modified base by an acid-stable bond, the so-called hypermodified (44) base is released by acid hydrolysis. The struc-

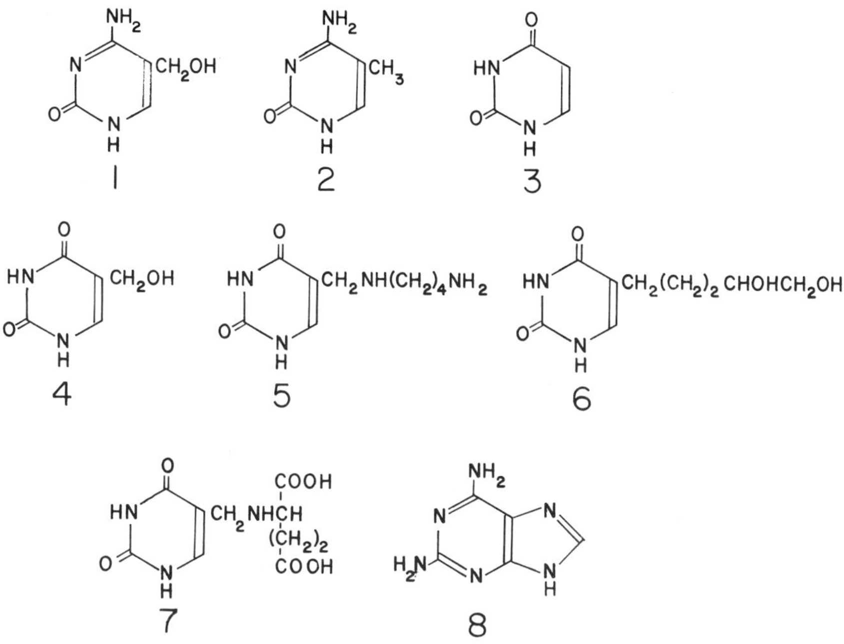

Figure 1 Structures of modified bases in phage DNAs: 1. 5-hydroxymethylcytosine (hmCyt); 2. 5-methylcytosine (mCyt); 3. uracil (Ura); 4. 5-hydroxymethyluracil (hmUra); 5. α-putrescinylthymine (putThy); 6. 5-dihydroxypentyluracil (dhpUra); 7. α-glutamylthymine (gluThy); 8. 2-aminoadenine (nAde).

tures shown in Figure 1 are the bases released from DNA by acid hydrolysis. It should be borne in mind that the properties of the DNA in question are determined by the structure of the modified base as it is found in the DNA. This structure can be determined by enzymatic hydrolysis of the DNA to nucleotides or nucleosides and characterization of any unusual product.

DETECTION AND IDENTIFICATION OF MODIFIED BASES IN DNA

The base composition of DNA is designated usually as the mol% G+C. This can be determined by measuring the thermal transition temperature of the DNA (87), the buoyant density of the DNA (122), or by hydrolysis of the DNA and quantification of the bases.

The presence of a modified base is often indicated or suggested by a discrepancy in the mol% G+C for a DNA as determined by the first two of these methods (see Table 1 and the references given therein). Subsequent chemical and/or enzymatic hydrolysis usually releases an unusual base or nucleotide. Some modified bases appear to be unstable during hydrolysis in perchloric acid, e.g. hmCyt (154), hmUra (54), dhpUra (86), and putThy (67). However, the two former bases may simply be discarded as perchlorate esters during removal of the excess perchloric acid from the hydrolysates (M. Mandel, personal communication).

If one of the normal bases is reduced in or missing from a DNA, it is very likely that the unknown base is a derivative of the missing base and will base pair in the same way (see Table 1). This obviously defines the types of structure to be expected and greatly simplifies the interpretation of the NMR spectra of the more complex bases (10, 67). The simpler structures can usually be identified by chromatography, ultraviolet spectrophotometry, and mass spectometry.

EFFECTS OF MODIFIED BASES ON THE PHYSICAL-CHEMICAL PROPERTIES OF DNA

The presence of a modified base can alter the properties of a DNA. In some cases these changes can be related directly to the structures of the modified bases; in other cases, only indirectly. Studies with synthetic polynucleotides show quite clearly that methylation of a base serves to lower the buoyant density and to increase the thermal transition temperature of a given double-helical polymer (41, 59, 126, 156); the magnitude of the observed effect depends on base sequence (41, 126). The properties of PBS2 DNA, in which Ura replaces Thy, and of XP12 DNA, in which mCyt replaces Cyt, agree with these observations (Table 1). However, for alkyl substituents other than methyl, the correlation does not hold: the thermal transition temperature for T3 DNA in which most of the thymine is replaced with 5-ethyluracil is lower than that for normal T3 DNA (103). Furthermore, modification of the apolar character of a pyrimidine 5-methyl substituent will alter its influence on helix stability (126) and buoyant density. The thermal transition temperature of ϕe DNA, in which hmUra replaces Thy, is lower, whereas the buoyant density is higher than expected (Table 1). Therefore, alkyl groups larger than methyl, and polar substituents seem to destabilize the double helix. However, although the buoyant density of glucosylated T4 DNA is slightly higher than expected, its thermal transition temperature is that expected for a DNA of 34 mol% G+C (Table 1). The presence of a charged group on a modified base will further complicate its effects on DNA, as for example, in ϕW14 and SP15 DNAs (Table 1). The thermal transition temperature of ϕW14 DNA is higher than expected because the amino groups on the putrescinyl sidechains can neutralize some

Table 1 Properties of phage DNAs containing modified bases

Phage	Host	DNA molecular weight ($\times 10^{-6}$)	Mol % G+C		Base change	Extent of change[a] (%)	T_m^b		Buoyant density[c]		References
			Phage	Host			Ob-served	Ex-pected[d]	Ob-served	Ex-pected[d]	
T4	*Escherichia coli*	110	34	50	5-hmCyt for Cyt	100	84	84	1.700	1.694	61, 87, 122, 154
ϕe	*Bacillus subtilis*	100	39	43	5-hmUra for Thy	100	77.5	85.3	1.742	1.703	54, 119, 138
PBS2	*B. subtilis*	150	28	43	Ura for Thy	100	76.5	81.5	1.722	1.690	51, 74, 128, 129
χP12	*Xanthomonas oryzae*	30	67	64	5-mCyt for Cyt	100	101.5	95.4	1.710	1.726	29, 68
S2L	*Synechococcus elongatus*	28	69	70	2-nAde for Ade	100	101.9	98.3	1.731	1.728	60
SP15	*B. subtilis*	250	42	43	5-dhpUra for Thy	41	61.7	86.2	1.761	1.702	10, 86, 139
SP10	*B. subtilis*	59[e]	43	43	α-gluThy for Thy	15–20	81.5	86.9	1.723	1.703	66, 77
ϕW14	*Pseudomonas acidovorans*	92	51[f]	67	α-putThy for Thy	50	99.3	90.3	1.666	1.716	9, 102

[a] The extent to which the modified base replaces the normal base.
[b] Thermal transition temperatures are extrapolated to the value in 0.15 M NaCl.
[c] Buoyant densities in neutral CsCl, assuming a value of 1,710 g ml^{-1} for *E. coli* DNA.
[d] These are the values expected for a DNA of the same mol % G+C and of normal composition.
[e] Not reported, but may be the value given [K. Bott, personal communication in (6)].
[f] M. Mandel, personal communication.

of the phosphate negative charges, thereby reducing negative charge repulsion. The buoyant density of this DNA is very low, probably because the methylene groups in the sidechains, like the methyl group in Thy, have a direct effect on density and the amino groups exclude cesium ions in a CsCl gradient. On the other hand, the thermal transition temperature of SP15 DNA is very low because the extra phosphates on the dihydroxypentyl sidechains increase negative charge repulsion; the buoyant density of this DNA is very high, probably because of the phosphate and glucose molecules attached to the dihydroxypentyl sidechains.

The properties of ϕW14 and S2L DNAs suggest that ionic bonds, such as those between the putrescinyl amines and phosphates, are more effective than extra hydrogen bonds in stabilizing the double helix. The thermal transition temperature for ϕW14 DNA is 9.0°, that for S2L only 3.6° higher than expected (Table 1).

The presence of a modified base can affect the chemical stability of a DNA. ϕW14 and SP15 DNAs are alkali-labile: ϕW14 DNA fragments (77); SP15 DNA loses glucose-1-phosphate, fragments, and decreases in buoyant density (86, 99). The chemical basis of such lability has not been elucidated. The buoyant density of SP10 DNA decreases during storage at physiological pH (9).

BIOSYNTHESIS OF DNAs CONTAINING MODIFIED BASES

The pattern of DNA synthesis in a phage-infected cell relative to the uninfected cell will reflect the characteristics of the phage in question. The amount of DNA synthesized during the latent period will depend on the size of the viral genome and the burst size. If infection leads to a significant increase in the rate of DNA synthesis, then the rate of synthesis of DNA precursors may increase, too. If the relative amounts of the deoxynucleoside triphosphates in the intracellular pool reflect the base composition of the DNA, these amounts may change if the base composition of the phage is very much different from that of the host. If the phage DNA contains a modified base that is not found in the uninfected cell and that is synthesized at the mononucleotide level, the phage genome must encode the enzymes necessary for the formation of the deoxynucleoside triphosphate of the base, and the enzymes and/or other proteins necessary for the exclusion of the normal base from the phage DNA. If the modified base does not replace a normal base completely, it can be synthesized at the mononucleotide level or at the polynucleotide level by modification of the normal base.

Phages in Which a Base is Replaced Completely With a Modified Base

BACTERIOPHAGE T4 The biochemistry of hmCyt synthesis is understood in considerable detail. It has been reviewed extensively (20, 88, 91); these reviews should be consulted for details and for references other than those cited in this section. The route of biosnythesis ensures exclusion of Cyt from T4 DNA (Figure 2). Most of the dCMP required as the substrate for the dCMP hydroxymethylase is derived from dCDP and dCTP by the action of the phage-coded dCTPase-dUTPase. This removes dCTP which would otherwise serve as a substrate for DNA polymerization. The dCMP formed is converted partly to hmdCMP by the hydroxymethylase and partly to dUMP by the phage-coded dCMP deaminase. Some dCMP arises from the mononucleotides released by total degradation of host DNA following infection; about 35% of these mononucleotides are incorporated into phage DNA. Although the rate of DNA synthesis increases about 10-fold following infection, there is little if any increase in the size of the deoxyribonucleotide pools (89). This means that there must be an increased rate of flow of DNA precursors through the pools. Host DNA contains 50, T4 DNA 34 mol% G+C. The dCMP deaminase helps to bring about a shift in the ratio of Thy to Cyt deoxyribonucleotides in the pools following infection: Thy and hmCyt deoxyribonucleotides are found in infected cells in the precise ratio (2:1) at which they occur in T4 DNA (34). Infection with amber mutants defective in dCMP deaminase gives a ratio of 0.5 (16).

There is some regulation of pyrimidine deoxyribonucleotide biosynthesis in T4-infected cells (5, 37, 90, 93) which appears to involve a multienzyme complex (93). Evidence for such a complex has accumulated during the last few years (15, 17, 21, 33, 34, 43, 93, 101, 111, 112, 124, 132, 133, 152, 153). Much of this work was reviewed recently (93). The composition of the complex is still unclear: it may contain the T4-specified enzymes dCMP hydroxymethylase, thymidylate synthase, dCTPase/dUTPase, ribonucleoside diphosphate reductase, deoxynucleoside monophosphate kinase, and dCMP deaminase, together with the host enzyme, nucleoside diphosphate

Figure 2 Reactions involved in the incorporation of hmCyt into, and the exclusion of Cyt from, T4 DNA. Phage-specified enzymes⟶; host-specified enzyme -→. Enzymes: 1 dCTPase; 2 dCMP hydroxymethlase; 3 deoxynucleoside monophosphate kinase; 4 nucleoside diphosphate kinase; 5 DNA polymerase.

kinase (93); or it may contain the first four enzymes given above, together with the T4-specified enzymes, DNA polymerase and β-glucosyl transferase, and the products of the T4 genes 32 or 44, and 45 (43). The complex serves to channel the pyrimidine deoxynucleotide precursors to the replication forks of growing T4 DNA (43, 93, 111). It helps to explain the paradox of an increase in the rate of DNA synthesis without an increase in the sizes of the precursor pools: the local concentrations of intermediates in such a complex can be significantly higher than their concentrations in the pools (93). Although much of the evidence supporting the existence of this enzyme complex has been obtained in vitro, using plasmolyzed cells and carefully fractionated cell-free extracts, there is in vivo evidence for its existence (15, 17, 34, 132, 133). Much of this depends on an ingenious assay for pyrimidine deoxyribonucleotide formation in infected cells: in a thymine-requiring host, the only enzymes catalyzing the release of tritium from [5-^{3}H]uracil are the T4-specified dCMP hydroxymethylase and thymidylate synthase (132).

It should be pointed out that several of the T4 early enzymes involved in pyrimidine deoxynucleotide biosynthesis are not part of the complex described above (93). Although dihydrofolate reductase is not found in the complex, it is found as an integral part of the T4 baseplate (64, 92, 98), probably complexed with the T4 thymidylate synthase (65), which is also a baseplate component (12, 63, 65). It is intriguing that the T4 thymidylate synthase is a component of two apparently distinct multiprotein complexes —one enzymatically active, the other seeming to fulfill a primarily structural role.

All of the hydroxymethyl groups in T4 DNA are substituted—70% of them with α-glucosidic, 30% of them with β-glucosidic groups (75). The glucose molecules are attached after DNA polymerization (31), but it is probable that glucosylation is coupled fairly tightly to replication (95). The α-glucosyl groups are not distributed randomly along the DNA sequence: neighboring purine nucleotides appear to hinder glucosylation, especially when linked to the 3' position of the hmCyt residue (81). T4 encodes an α- and a β-glucosyl transferase, and these enzymes show some sequence specificity (22).

BACTERIOPHAGE ϕe The biochemistry of hmUra biosynthesis in ϕe-infected *Bacillus subtilis* is fairly well understood and has been reviewed recently (47, 88, 91). As with hmCyt/Cyt in T4 DNA, the route of biosynthesis ensures the exclusion of Thy from ϕe DNA (Figure 3). In this case, however, most of the dUMP required as the immediate precursor of hmdUMP arises de novo. Thy nucleotides cannot be converted to hmUra nucleotides, and the phage encodes a protein inhibitor of the host thymidy-

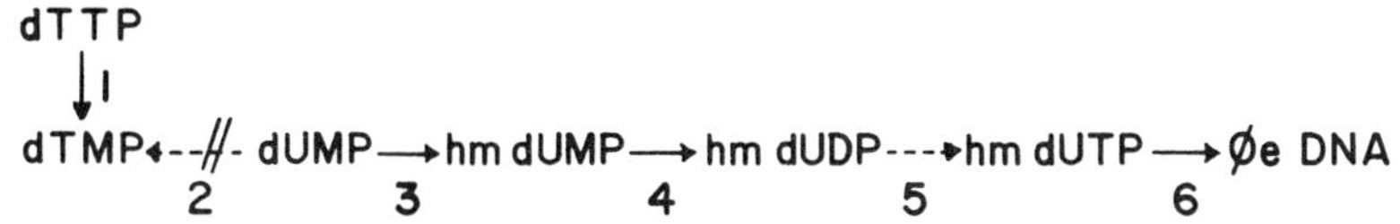

Figure 3 Reactions involved in the incorporation of hmUra into, and the exclusion of Thy from, ϕe DNA. Phage-specified enzymes ⟶; - - → host-specified enzymes. Enzymes: 1 dTTPase; 2 thymidylate synthase; 3 dUMP hydroxymethylase; 4 deoxynucleoside monophosphate kinase; 5 nucleoside diphosphate kinase; 6 DNA polymerase.

late synthase (45, 118), presumably to channel dUMP toward the hydroxymethylase. The phage also encodes a dTTPase/dUTPase which converts dTTP to dTMP (28, 116). ϕe infection leads to a cessation of host DNA synthesis (83, 117) but the host DNA is not degraded to acid-soluble fragments (117). This means that the deoxyribonucleotides in ϕe DNA are synthesized entirely de novo.

ϕe DNA has a slightly lower G+C content than the host DNA (Table 1). Phage infection induces the synthesis of a dCMP deaminase (118). This enzyme could serve to adjust slightly the relative levels of the pyrimidine nucleotides in the DNA precursor pools.

Unlike the glucosylated hydroxymethyl groups of T4 DNA, the hydroxymethyl groups in ϕe are not substituted (2).

BACTERIOPHAGE PBS2 The biosynthesis of a DNA containing Ura instead of Thy (Figure 4) poses an additional problem: besides the exclusion of Thy and the incorporation of Ura, the phage must ensure also that the Ura-containing DNA is not degraded. The deamination of Cyt in DNA produces Ura, and cells have evolved a mechanism to reduce the frequency of such transition mutations. The enzyme uracil-DNA glycosylase eliminates Ura residues from DNA by cleaving the appropriate glycosidic bonds (78, 80), and *B. subtilis* contains this enzyme (26, 135, 136). When PBS2 infects *B. subtilis,* Ura is not released from the phage DNA unless phage-specific protein synthesis is inhibited (25). Under normal conditions, infection leads to inhibition of the uracil-DNA glycosylase activity (38, 135, 136). The inhibitor is a small, heat-stable protein (57). The incorporation of Ura into cellular DNA is also reduced by the presence of dUTPases. *B. subtilis* contains a dUTPase that is specific for dUTP (28, 137), and PBS2 induces a protein inhibitor of this enzyme (49, 106a, 137).

Thy is excluded from PBS2 by the action of several enzymes. A phage-specified dTMPase removes dTMP. A phage-specified dUMP kinase appears to serve a dual purpose, since the phosphorylation of dUMP will remove the substrate of the host thymidylate synthase (137). Although the activity of dTTPase increases following infection, it is not clear if this is phage-specified. The level of dTTP declines to less than 10% of the preinfection level within 5 min of infection (49).

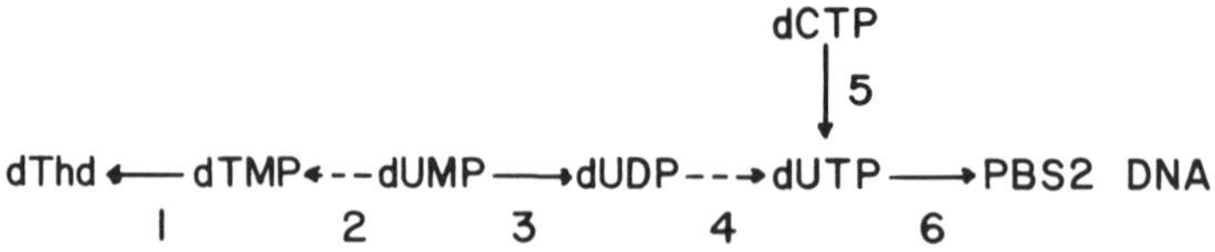

Figure 4 Reactions involved in the incorporation of Ura into, and the exclusion of Thy from, PBS2 DNA. Phage-specified enzymes ⟶; host-specified enzymes - - →. Enzymes: 1 dTMPase; 2 thymidylate synthase; 3 deoxynucleoside monophosphate kinase; 4 nucleoside diphosphate kinase; 5 dCTP deaminase; 6 DNA polymerase.

A phage-specified dCTP deaminase, which is inhibited by dTTP (134), provides 30–50% of the Ura in PBS2 DNA (49, 115); the remainder arises by reduction of uridine nucleotides (49) by host enzymes. Up to 20% of the Ura may be provided by the host dCMP deaminase (115). dUTP appears 10 min after infection and the level increases until the onset of phage DNA synthesis 10 min later (49). Host DNA synthesis is inhibited (114) but the DNA is not degraded extensively (49), so the nucleotides in PBS2 DNA are synthesized entirely de novo. The G+C content (28 mol%) of PBS2 DNA is significantly less than that of the host DNA (43 mol%), and the combined activities of the host dCMP deaminase and the phage-specified dCTP deaminase could serve to adjust the levels of the pyrimidine deoxynucleotides accordingly.

BACTERIOPHAGE XP12 Relatively little is known about the biosynthesis of mCyt in XP12 DNA. dCMP methyltransferase activity is detectable in extracts of infected but not of uninfected cells (69). The purified enzyme (32) uses formaldehyde and dCMP or CMP (but not dUMP) in a reaction that oxidizes the required tetrahydrofolate to dihydrofolate (32, 69). Since XP12 appears also to encode a thymidylate synthase (30), the need for dihydrofolate reductase activity will be increased considerably following infection. Host DNA synthesis is inhibited, but the DNA is not degraded extensively (30).

Phages in Which a Base is Partially Replaced With a Modified Base

So far, all the phages falling into this category have a partial replacement of Thy. (Table 1). Since the methyl group of Thy is unreactive, is Thy or some other Ura derivative the precursor of the modified base? Does the modification occur at the precursor or polynucleotide level? Furthermore, it is important to know if the modification is random or sequence-specific.

BACTERIOPHAGE SP15 The dhpUra in SP15 DNA is made at the precursor level: infected cells contain the deoxynucleoside triphosphate of this base (143). At least part of the dihydroxypentyl sidechain comes from ribose (144). The synthesis of SP15 DNA is inhibited by flurodeoxyuridine (fldUrd) and the inhibition is overcome by dThd (14, 143). This suggests that the Thy in SP15 DNA is formed at the precursor level by a thymidylate synthase. The glucose molecules found on mature SP15 DNA are attached to the dihydroxypentyl sidechains at the polynucleotide level (143). Host DNA is not degraded extensively, so the precursors are synthesized de novo.

SP15 DNA is very unusual in that its synthesis involves five, not four, deoxynucleoside triphosphate precursors. Does the DNA polymerase involved recognize sequence and incorporate Thy and dhpUra at defined loci or is the incorporation random? If it is random, why would the observed ratio of the two bases in the DNA have persisted? This ratio is not fixed because it is changed when the DNA is synthesized in the presence of certain inhibitors (see later).

BACTERIOPHAGE SP10 The work on the biosynthesis of SP10 DNA has been done with SP10c, a clear-plaque derivative. The biosynthesis of SP10c DNA is not inhibited by fldUrd (84); dThd incorporation stops permanently after infection of a thy$^-$ host strain (84); dTTPase activity appears after infection (84) and dTTP falls eventually to $<5\%$ of the pre-infection levels (85); thymidylate synthase activity decreases 70% after infection (151). This means that the Thy in SP10c DNA is made at the polynucleotide level by a novel, phage-specific mechanism. dUMP hydroxymethylase activity appears after infection (151). Although hmdUMP is converted to hmdUTP by extracts of uninfected cells, hmdUMP is not converted to hmdUDP. However, extracts of infected cells catalyze the latter reaction (151). Infected cells contain hmdUTP, and it is proposed that hmdUTP and not dTTP is a substrate for SP10c DNA replication (24). dUTP is absent before and after infection (85). It is possible that hmUra in the DNA is also a precursor of gluThy, since extracts of infected cells do not phosphorylate gludTMP (151). Although 85–90% of the host DNA is degraded to acid-soluble fragments before lysis of the infected cell, only 2% of the Ade and 0.25% of the Thy in host DNA is nuclease-resistant (i.e. encapsulated) by lysis (84). This means that there is little, if any, incorporation into SP10c DNA of nucleotides from the host DNA (84).

BACTERIOPHAGE ϕW14 The thymine in ϕW14 DNA also is synthesized at the polynucleotide level: the incorporation of dThd stops permanently after the infection of a thy$^-$ host, dTTPase activity appears, there is no dTTP in the cells when phage DNA synthesis reaches its maximal rate, and phage DNA synthesis is not inhibited by fldUrd (K. L. Maltman et al, accepted for publication).

Like gluThy in SP10c, putThy appears also to be synthesized at the polynucleotide level because putThy mononucleotides are not detectable in infected cells (K. L. Maltman et al, accepted for publication). Thy is not a precursor of putThy because both bases are labelled equally by [2,3-^{3}H]serine (58). Infected-cell extracts have dUMP hydroxymethylase activity (58; J. Neuhard et al, accepted for publication), hmdUTP is present in infected cells, and pulse-labelled replicating phage DNA contains low but detectable levels of hmUra after acid hydrolysis (J. Neuhard et al, accepted for publication). This suggests that hmUra is the precursor of Thy and putThy at the polynucleotide level. *Pseudomonas acidovorans* is impermeable to putrescine, but ornithine penetrates the cells and is converted to putrescine (56). Ornithine labels specifically the putThy residues in ϕW14 DNA (108). Host DNA synthesis stops after infection, but the DNA is not degraded to acid-soluble fragments.

It is interesting that SP10, with a Gram-positive host, and ϕW14, with a Gram-negative host, should both have Thy partially replaced with a hypermodified base with a secondary amine at C-5 of the pyrimidine ring, and that in both phages, Thy and the hypermodified base appear to be formed from hmUra at the polynucleotide level.

BIOLOGICAL CONSEQUENCES OF BASE MODIFICATION

The modified bases in phage DNAs could have a variety of functions, such as protecting the DNAs from host and phage nucleases, serving as signals for transcription and replication of the DNAs, and facilitating the packaging and/or injection of the DNAs.

Nuclease Susceptibility

The DNA of T4 faces a variety of nucleases inside the infected cell, including both host enzymes whose function is to inactivate foreign DNA and T4 enzymes whose function is to degrade host DNA. Glucosylation protects the viral DNA from the action of one or more host nucleases in vivo (39, 46, 113); hmCyt by itself is insufficient to protect newly synthesized hmCyt-containing *E. coli* DNA made in toluenized cells (36), or phage fd DNA made in vitro with hmCyt instead of Cyt in one strand (35). Glucosylation of the hmCyt-containing fd DNA affords protection (35). Glucosylated T4 DNA is resistant also to cleavage by many sequence-specific restriction endonucleases from other procaryotes (7, 13, 55).

Since T4 has evolved a mechanism for degradation of host DNA, it must avoid self-destruction by distinguishing its own genetic material from that of the host (62). Hydroxymethylation of the Cyt residues protects T4 DNA from degradation by T4-coded nucleases specific for Cyt-containing DNA (120, 121). Such a protective mechanism is not obligatory for a phage that degrades the host DNA, however. Many phages that do not have modified bases in their DNAs degrade host DNA extensively. Little is known regarding the protective effect of other modified bases against host nucleases. Mutants of ϕe in which up to 20% of the hmUra is replaced with Thy are viable (see later), suggesting that the function of hmUra may not be protection against nucleases. In those DNAs with only a partial replacement of thymine, there must be either inactivation of host nucleases following infection, or protection of specific sequences recognized by host nucleases, or a lack of restriction by the host for other reasons. Phage ϕ29 DNA does not contain modified bases, but it is resistant to a variety of sequence-specific endonucleases, apparently because the DNA lacks the sequences recognized by these enzymes (52). On the other hand, PBS2 and ϕe DNAs are cleaved by *Eco* R1 (6) and several other sequence-specific endonucleases (7), but the rate of cleavage by enzymes recognizing A-T-containing sequences is reduced by the presence of the modified bases (7).

Transcription

The entire transcription program of T4 DNA is carried out by the host RNA polymerase (RNAP) [see (109) for a review]. The immediate early genes are transcribed by the unmodified enzyme. Since all the hmCyt residues in T4 DNA are glucosylated, the glucosyl groups do not interfere with the recognition of promoter regions by the *Escherichia coli* RNAP. The transcription of all other T4 genes is mediated by phage-modified forms of the host RNAP (109). Substitution of Cyt for hmCyt in T4 DNA blocks true late gene expression, primarily at the level of transcription but also at the level of translation; early gene expression is unaffected (109). However, the hmCyt requirement is not absolute (see later). The β-glucosyl groups may play a special transcriptional role throughout infection. Wild-type T4 grows poorly on a rifampicin-resistant mutant of *E. coli,* giving indistinct plaques; "distinct plaque" mutants carry mutations in the β-glucosyl transferase gene (96). However, this dependence is not absolute because T4 can produce progeny in nonglucosylating hosts such as *Shigella* and certain *E. coli* mutants (113).

The transcription of ϕe also is carried out by the host RNAP, again using phage-modified forms of the enzyme (which show template preferences for homologous hmUra-containing DNA) for the production of certain transcripts (47, 109). The hmUra residues appear not to be essential for transcription because ϕe mutants that contain up to 20% of the hmUra replaced with Thy (27, 83, 117) are viable. Presumably, this substitution is random.

Transcription in PBS2-infected cells is complex. The phage DNA has little or no template activity with the host RNAP (82). Rifampicin and streptolydigin do not inhibit the PBS2 infective cycle, even if added before infection; actinomycin D, however, is inhibitory (106, 114). PBS2-infected cells contain a new phage-specified rifampicin-resistant, actinomycin D-sensitive RNAP which is active with PBS2 DNA and poly (dA-dT) as templates, but which is relatively inactive with other templates (19, 107). The enzyme is 10 times more active with PBS2 DNA as a template than with ϕe DNA, but the activity with poly (dA-dT) shows that the activity is not limited to Ura-containing DNA (19). The enzyme is unusual among phage-specified RNAPs in having five subunits, all of which are phage-specified and none of which appear before the middle of the lytic cycle (18). It preferentially and asymetrically transcribes PBS2 late genes (18). PBS2 early transcription does not require phage-specific protein synthesis, even though it is rifampicin resistant (18). RNAP activity has not been detected in PBS2 particles (107) and the nature of the early transcription events remains unclear.

SP15 and SP10 transcription is sensitive to rifampicin and streptolydigin throughout the infective cycles (23, 84). In each case there are two waves of phage-specific RNA synthesis during the infective cycle. Either the host RNAP, or modified forms of it, can transcribe DNAs containing hypermodified pyrimidines, or these phages encode drug-sensitive RNAPs. In DNAs such as those of SP15, SP10, and ϕW14 in which Thy is only partially replaced, it is essential to know the distribution of the hypermodified bases within the DNAs. If the distribution is not random, the modified bases could affect the specificity of transcription.

Replication

Both the T4 and the *E. coli* DNA polymerases (DNAPs) can use dCTP or hmdCTP as a substrate under the appropriate conditions in vitro. The host enzyme may discriminate in vivo, but the phage enzyme can produce Cyt-containing (97) and even Ura-containing progeny (145). Thus, the phage-specified DNAP does not require hmCyt as a substrate or in the template. The incorporation of hmCyt instead of Cyt in T4-infected cells depends on the elimination of dCTP and the use of an enzyme complex to channel the pyrimidine deoxynucleotide precursors to the DNA replication complex. The ϕe DNA replication enzymes do not distinguish between Thy and hmUra in vivo because Thy can replace some of the Ura in ϕe DNA (27, 83, 117), but hmUra is not incorporated into the DNA of a thy$^-$ host (100). The purified SP01 (similar to ϕe) DNAP incorporates dTTP, dUTP, and hmdUTP with equal efficiency (155). The *Bacillus subtilis* replication enzymes use dTTP preferentially to dUTP, but the PBS2-specified enzyme is equally active with either substrate (105). The purified *B. subtilis* DNAP III uses dUTP as a substrate and Ura-containing DNA as a template (48). Overall, it seems that the modified bases are not significant factors in DNA replication.

DNA Conformation and Recognition

The C-5 of the pyrimidine ring lies to one side of the major groove when DNA is in the double-helical B form. Quite bulky groups can be attached to this position without distorting the structure of a space-filling model of B form DNA, e.g. glucosylated hydroxymethyl groups in T4, dihydroxypentyl groups carrying sugar phosphates in SP15. Substitution at C-5 can influence certain DNA-protein interactions: e.g. uracil-DNA glycosylases recognize uracil but not thymine residues in DNA. If methyl groups are considered to be signals, then PBS2 has no signals, XP12 DNA has a signal on every pyrimidine, and the other DNAs under discussion have a variety of modified signals. It is probable that the protein-DNA contacts occur predominantly in the major groove of the DNA in the *E. coli* RNAP-*lac* promotor complex (53) and in the *lac* repressor-*lac* operator complex (40).

Telestability (the stabilization or destabilization of one region of a DNA double helix by an adjacent region) may be important in DNA-protein interactions (147). Sequence isomeric DNAs are defined as DNAs with the same nucleotide composition but different sequences. Studies with high molecular weight DNA polymers of defined repeating nucleotide sequences show sequence isomeric DNAs to have different and characteristic properties. This means that measurements made with natural DNAs are, in effect, composite measurements on various types of sequences (147). The extent to which one DNA region can influence the thermostability of adjacent regions will depend on the range and magnitude of their cooperative interactions, and work with synthetic polymers shows such interactions can extend over a distance of 35 base pairs (147).

Modified bases can alter drastically the behavior of sequence isomeric DNAs (147), and the increased thermostability caused by the binding of certain drugs is extended to the nonbinding regions of synthetic polymers (147). Such observations are immediately relevant to the DNAs of phages like SP15, SP10, and ϕW14. In ϕW14 DNA, for example, even though putThy represents only 12% of the bases, the effect of the amine-phosphate interactions could be enhanced by telestabilization, and the thermal transition temperature is unusually high (Table 1). Conversely, the increased negative charge repulsion in SP15 DNA could be enhanced, and in this case the thermal transition temperature is unusually low (Table 1).

Modified bases could alter the extent of hydration of DNA, since an AT base pair can bind one or two more water molecules than a GC base pair (42). For AT base pairs, the greatest atom exposure is exhibited by the thymine methyl groups, but only when the DNA is in the B form (1). Methyl groups are hydrophobic, and their exposure in the major groove would tend to encourage water-water aggregation and thus exert pressure on the major groove to remain wide (1). This means that AT rich DNAs will tend to adopt the B form, and that hydrophilic substituents at the C-5 of pyrimidines could alter the DNA conformation.

DNAs with modified base are potentially powerful tools for studying telestability, DNA conformation, and various aspects of protein-DNA interaction. However, relatively little has been done in this regard. SP8 DNA (related to ϕe) is in the B form in fibers at 75% relative humidity [R. Langridge, quoted in (54)]. PBS2 DNA gives normal B form diffraction patterns (73), even though Ura may not base-stack like Thy (104). T4 DNA appears to prefer the B form in fibers (8), but steric hindrance may be a factor here because the major groove is deeper and narrower in the A than it is in the B form. ϕW14 DNA, on the other hand, appears to be stabilized in the A form in fibers because this allows the formation of ionic bonds between putrescinyl amines and phosphates (D. G. Goodwin, et al, submitted for publication).

DNA Packaging

Modified bases in various phage DNAs are not essential for packaging of the DNAs into phage heads. PBS2 (127), SP15 (130), and SP10 (131) are generalized transducing phages. This means that there is no discrimination during packaging against host DNA which lacks the appropriate modified base. ϕe DNA containing up to 20% of the hmUra replaced with Thy is packaged normally (83); T4 DNA lacking glucose (113), or containing Cyt instead of hmCyt (97) or containing Thy, Ura, Cyt, and hmCyt (145), is packaged normally.

Other Consequences

Thymine-dimers are formed during UV irradiation of DNA. The modified Thys in phage DNAs may also photodimerize. putThy dimerizes with itself, with Thy, and with Ura when irradiated in frozen aqueous solution. It also undergoes internal cyclization followed by breakdown to uracil (E. Kulikowska and D. Shugar, personal communication) in a reaction analogous to that undergone by 5-ethyluracil (66). Furthermore, irradiation of ϕW14 DNA results in the elimination of some of the putrescinyl groups (J. Botelho, unpublished observation). The photochemistry of bases like dhpUra, gluThy and putThy is potentially of great interest.

The deamination of Cyt to Ura causes transition mutations, but the frequency of such mutations is reduced by the combined action of uracil-DNA glycosylase and repair enzymes. In the case of T4, deamination of hmCyt will produce hmUra, which is not a substrate for uracil-DNA glycosylase (79, 80), and T4 shows a higher than expected rate of mutation following heat-induced deamination of Cyt (4). In PBS2, although Cyt may be deaminated to Ura, infection leads to an inhibition of the host uracil-

DNA glycosylase activity (38, 135, 136). PBS2 DNA has an exceptionally low G+C content (28 mol%), and it has been pointed out that all permissible G·C → A·U transitions may have occurred already in this phage during evolution, so that a strong selective pressure would be exerted against further genetic drift of this kind (79). The rate of Cyt deamination-induced mutation has not been measured in PBS2. In phage XP12, the deamination of mCyt will give Thy, which, of course, is not a substrate for uracil-DNA glycosylase.

MODIFIED BASES MAY NOT BE ESSENTIAL FOR BIOLOGICAL ACTIVITY

Cyt is excluded from T4 DNA by the phage-specified dCTPase which converts dCTP, the precursor of Cyt in DNA, to dCMP. The phage-specified dCMP hydroxymethylase removes the dCMP by converting it to hmdCMP. The dCTPase is an essential gene product. When *E. coli* is infected under nonpermissive conditions with a T4 mutant defective in dCTPase, Cyt is incorporated into T4 DNA but viable progeny are not produced because this DNA is fragmented by the T4-specified nucleases that hydrolyze Cyt-containing DNA (71). A triple mutant of T4, defective in dCTPase and two of the T4 endonucleases, directs the synthesis of intact T4 DNA containing Cyt and hmCyt, but progeny are not produced because there is little, if any, synthesis of late proteins (70). The presence of Cyt in T4 DNA impairs the synthesis of late proteins (50, 72, 76).

However, mutation in a fourth gene in this type of mutant, the *alc* gene, allows the production of T4 DNA containing only Cyt (123). In a pentuple mutant of T4 which lacks dCMP hydroxymethylase, dCTPase, endonuclease II, and endonuclease IV and which is also alc^{-}, a small burst of progeny is produced whose DNA contains only Cyt (97), even though late transcription is still somewhat impaired. It seems, then, that there is not an absolute requirement for hmCyt in T4 gene expression, but that it is required for optimal expression. The availability of Cyt-containing T4 DNA has allowed the cloning of fragments of the T4 genome (94, 141, 148). Furthermore, the replication of such T4 multiple mutants in strains of *E. coli* defective in dUTPase and uracil-DNA glycosylase yields viable progeny in which the DNA contains Cyt, hmCyt, Thy, and Ura (145). A T4 multiple mutant that allows the incorporation of Cyt into T4 DNA and that does not disrupt the host nucleoid appears unable to discriminate between host and phage DNA during packaging because it transduces host genes with a fairly high frequency (149).

Mutants of ϕe lacking the phage-specified dTTPase produce normal bursts of viable progeny in which up to 20% of the hmUra is replaced with Thy (27, 83, 117), showing that a full complement of hmUra is not essential for the replication, transcription, and packaging of ϕe DNA. The PBS2-specified inhibitor of the host dUTPase is poorly active in vitro at pH 9.7. If the pH of the medium for PBS2 infection is increased from 7.0 to 8.85, there is a marked decrease in the synthesis of phage DNA, and few progeny phage are produced. The DNA made at pH 8.85 contains roughly equal amounts of Thy and Ura but it is not clear if this is packaged efficiently into particles (106a).

The synthesis of SP15 DNA is inhibited by fldUrd; the inhibition is overcome by exogenous dThd. As the concentration of dThd added to the inhibited culture is increased, the amount of dThd in the DNA increases, that of hpUra decreases, and the buoyant density of the DNA is lower than usual (14). Although the DNA yield can be as high as 70% of normal, the yield of phage is about 30% because of a reduced burst size. Since particles containing the Thy-enriched DNA are infective, it seems that the normal DNA is packaged preferentially. However, Thy-enriched DNA is also packaged and is expressed efficiently in subsequent infections (14). Thy and dhpUra are formed at the precursor level in SP15-infected cells (143) and then are incorporated into DNA in a fixed ratio (86). Since this ratio can be changed by the addition of fldUrd and dThd, how is it kept constant in uninhibited cultures?

MODIFIED BASES IN OTHER ORGANISMS

The presence of a modified base is not restricted to bacteriophage DNAs. In the dinoflagellate *Gyrodinium cohnii,* 38% of the Thy is replaced with hmUra; as might be expected, this lowers the expected thermal transition temperature and increases the buoyant density of the DNA. The hmUra is not dispersed uniformly in the DNA (110). The route of hmUra biosynthesis in *G. cohnii* is of great interest because HmdUrd is strongly cytostatic for a variety of mammalian cell lines, and it is lethal for mice in vivo (146).

CONCLUDING REMARKS

In some bacteriophage DNAs, one of the four bases found commonly in DNA is replaced with a modified base. In most cases, the H-bonding properties of the modified base are the same as those of the base it replaces. The replacement can be complete or partial.

Recent investigations of the routes of biosynthesis of modified bases have revealed a variety of interesting biochemical phenomena. In T4, several phage-specified enzymes have multiple roles as catalytic agents and as components of multienzyme complexes and/or particle structural components. SP15 DNA is synthesized from five rather than four nucleotide precursors. The Thy in SP10 and ϕW14 DNAs is synthesized at the polynucleotide level.

The modified bases may not be essential to phages T4, ϕe, and SP15, but their presence appears to be required for maximal gene expression or for maximal DNA packaging. Nonetheless, DNAs containing modified bases could be used to advantage in studying various aspects of DNA conformation, function, and photochemistry.

ACKNOWLEDGMENTS

Dr. John L. Ingraham suggested that I write this review. I thank him for his inspiration and encouragement. I thank Drs. Manley Mandel, Jan Neuhard, David Shugar, and Harry Witmer for communicating results prior to publication, and Kirk Maltman and Dr. Bob Miller for moral support. Research from my laboratory is supported by the National Scientific and Engineering Research Council of Canada (Operating Grant A3686).

Literature Cited

1. Alden, C. J., Kim, S.-H. 1979. *J. Mol. Biol.* 132:411–34
2. Alegria, A. H., Kahan, F. M. 1968. *Biochemistry* 7:1132–40
3. Alexandrushkina, N. I., Kirnos, M. D., Magradze, N. M., Zamchuk, L. A., Goldfarb, D. M., Vanyushin, B. F. 1978. *Bioorg. Chem.* 4:1191–96 (In Russian)
4. Baltz, R. H., Bingham, P. M., Drake, J. W. 1976. *Proc. Natl. Acad. Sci. USA* 73:1269–73
5. Berglund, O. 1972. *J. Biol. Chem.* 247:7276–81
6. Berkner, K. L., Folk, W. R. 1977. *J. Biol. Chem.* 252:3185–93
7. Berkner, K. L., Folk, W. R. 1979. *J. Biol. Chem.* 254:2551–60
8. Bloomfield, V., Crothers, D. M., Tinoco, I. Jr. 1974. *Physical Chemistry of Nucleic Acids.* New York: Harper & Row. 517 pp.
9. Bott, K., Strauss, B. 1965. *Virology* 25:212–25
10. Brandon, C., Gallop, P. M., Marmur, J., Hayashi, H., Nakanishi, K. 1972. *Nature* 239:71–72
11. Brandon, C. R. 1974. *Structure of the unusual pyrimidine nucleotide in Bacillus subtilis SP-15 DNA.* PhD thesis. Yeshiva Univ., New York. 229 pp.
12. Capco, G. R., Mathews, C. K. 1973. *Arch. Biochem. Biophys.* 158:736–43
13. Carlson, K., Nicolaisen, B. 1979. *J. Virol.* 31:112–23
14. Casella, E., Markewych, O., Dosmar, M., Witmer, H. 1978. *J. Virol.* 28: 753–66
15. Chao, J., Leach, M., Karam, J. 1977. *J. Virol.* 24:557–63
16. Chiu, C.-S., Ruettinger, T., Flanegan, J. B., Greenberg, G. R. 1977. *J. Biol. Chem.* 252:8603–8
17. Chiu, C.-S., Tomich, P. K., Greenberg, G. R. 1976. *Proc. Natl. Acad. Sci. USA* 73:757–61
18. Clark, S. 1978. *J. Virol.* 25:224–37
19. Clark, S., Losick, R., Pero, J. 1974. *Nature* 252:21–24
20. Cohen, S. S. 1968. *Virus-Induced Enzymes.* New York: Columbia Univ. Press. 315 pp.
21. Collinsworth, W. L., Mathews, C. K. 1974. *J. Virol.* 13:908–15
22. de Waard, A., Ubbink, T. E. C. M., Beukman, W. 1967. *Eur. J. Biochem.* 2:303–8
23. Dosmar, M., Markewych, O., Witmer, H. 1977. *J. Virol.* 21:924–31
24. Dosmar, M., Witmer, H. 1979. *Curr. Microbiol.* 2:361–64
25. Duncan, B. K., Warner, H. R. 1977. *J. Virol.* 22:835–38
26. Duncan, J., Hamilton, L., Friedberg, E. 1976. *J. Virol.* 19:338–45
27. Dunham, L. F., Price, A. R. 1974. *J. Virol.* 14:709–12
28. Dunham, L. F., Price, A. R. 1974. *Biochemistry* 13:2667–72
29. Ehrlich, M., Ehrlich, K., Mayo, J. A.

1975. *Biochim. Biophys. Acta* 395: 109–19
30. Ehrlich, M., Lin, F.-S., Ehrlich, K., Brown, S. L., Mayo, J. A. 1977. *J. Virol.* 23:517–23
31. Erikson, R. L., Szybalski, W. 1964. *Virology* 22:111–24
32. Feng, T. Y., Tu, J., Kuo, T. T. 1978. *Eur. J. Biochem.* 87:29–36
33. Flanegan, J. B., Chiu, C.-S., Greenberg, G. R. 1977. *J. Biol. Chem.* 252:6031–37
34. Flanegan, J. B., Greenberg, G. R. 1977. *J. Biol. Chem.* 252:3019–27
35. Fleischman, R. A., Campbell, J. L., Richardson, C. C. 1975. *Fed. Proc.* 34:554
36. Fleischman, R. A., Richardson, C. C. 1971. *Proc. Natl. Acad. Sci. USA* 68:2527–31
37. Fleming, W. H., Bessman, M. J. 1967. *J. Biol. Chem.* 242:363–71
38. Friedberg, E. C., Ganesan, A. K., Minton, K. 1975. *J. Virol.* 16:315–21
39. Fukasawa, T. 1964. *J. Mol. Biol.* 9: 525–36
40. Gilbert, W., Mazam, A., Mirzabekov, A. 1976. In *Control of Ribosome Synthesis,* ed. N. Kjeldgaard, O. Maaloe, pp. 139–48. New York: Academic
41. Gill, J. E., Mazrimas, J. A., Bishop, C. C. Jr. 1974. *Biochim. Biophys. Acta* 335:330–48
42. Goldblum, A., Perahia, D., Pullman, A. 1978. *FEBS Lett.* 91:213–15
43. Greenberg, G. R., Chiu, C.-S. 1978. *Fed. Proc.* 37:1409
44. Hall, R. H. 1971. *The Modified Nucleosides in Nucleic Acids.* New York: Columbia Univ. Press. 451 pp.
45. Haslam, E. A., Roscoe, D. H., Tucker, R. G. 1967. *Biochim. Biophys. Acta* 134:312–26
46. Hattman, S. 1964. *Virology* 24:333–48
47. Hemphill, H. E., Whiteley, H. R. 1975. *Bacteriol. Rev.* 39:257–315
48. Hitzeman, R. A., Price, A. R. 1978. *J. Virol.* 28:697–709
49. Hitzeman, R. A., Price, A. R., Neuhard, J., Møllgaard, H. 1978. In *DNA Synthesis: Present and Future,* ed. I. Molineux, M. Kohiyama. New York: Plenum. 1161 pp.
50. Hosoda, J., Levinthal, C. 1968. *Virology* 34:709–27
51. Hunter, B. I., Yamagishi, H., Takahashi, I. 1967. *J. Virol.* 1:841–42
52. Ito, J., Roberts, R. J. 1979. *Gene* 5:1–7
53. Johnsrud, L. 1978. *Proc. Natl. Acad. Sci. USA* 75:5314–18
54. Kallen, R. G., Simon, M., Marmur, J. 1962. *J. Mol. Biol.* 5:248–50
55. Kaplan, D. A., Nierlich, D. P. 1975. *J. Biol. Chem.* 250:2395–97
56. Karrer, E., Warren, R. A. J. 1974. *Can. J. Microbiol.* 20:469–71
57. Katz, G. E., Price, A. R., Pomerantz, M. J. 1976. *J. Virol.* 20:535–38
58. Kelln, R. A., Warren, R. A. J. 1973. *J. Virol.* 12:1427–33
59. Kirk, J. T. O. 1967. *J. Mol. Biol.* 28:171–72
60. Kirnos, M. D., Khudyakov, I. Y., Alexandruschinka, N. I., Vanyushin, B. F. 1977. *Nature* 270:369–70
61. Klotz, L. C., Zimm, B. H. 1972. *J. Mol. Biol.* 72:779–800
62. Koerner, J. F., Snustad, D. P. 1979. *Microbiol. Rev.* 43:199–223
63. Kozloff, L. M., Crosby, L. K., Lute, M. 1975. *J. Virol.* 16:1409–19
64. Kozloff, L. M., Crosby, L. K., Lute, M., Hall, D. H. 1975. *J. Virol.* 16:1401–8
65. Kozloff, L. M., Lute, M., Crosby, L. K. 1977. *J. Virol.* 23:637–44
66. Krajewska, E., Shugar, D. 1971. *Science* 173:435–37
67. Kropinski, A. M. B., Bose, R. J., Warren, R. A. J. 1973. *Biochemistry* 12: 151–57
68. Kuo, T.-T., Huang, T.-C., Teng, M.-H. 1968. *J. Mol. Biol.* 34:373–75
69. Kuo, T.-T., Tu, J. 1976. *Nature* 263:615
70. Kutter, E., Beug, A., Sluss, R., Jensen, L., Bradley, D. 1975. *J. Mol. Biol.* 99: 591–607
71. Kutter, E. M., Wiberg, J. S. 1968. *J. Mol. Biol.* 38:395–411
72. Kutter, E. M., Wiberg, J. S. 1969. *J. Virol.* 4:439–53
73. Langridge, R. J., Marmur, J. 1964. *Science* 143:1450–51
74. Lauer, G. D., Klotz, L. C. 1976. *J. Virol.* 18:1163–64
75. Lehman, I. R., Pratt, E. A. 1960. *J. Biol. Chem.* 235:3254–59
76. Levinthal, C., Hosada, J., Shub, D. 1967. *The Molecular Biology of Viruses,* ed. J. S. Colter, W. Paranchych. New York: Academic. 730 pp.
77. Lewis, H. A., Miller, R. C. Jr., Stone, J. C., Warren, R. A. J. 1975. *J. Virol.* 16:1375–79
78. Lindahl, T. 1974. *Proc. Natl. Acad. Sci. USA* 71:3649–53
79. Lindahl, T. 1979. *Prog. Nucleic Acid Res. Mol. Biol.* 22:135–92
80. Lindahl, T., Ljungquist, S., Siegert, W., Nyberg, B., Sperens, B. 1977. *J. Biol. Chem.* 252:3286–94
81. Lunt, M. R., Siebke, J.-C., Burton, K. 1964. *Biochem. J.* 92:27–36
82. Maia, J. C. C., Kerjan, P., Szulmajster, F. 1971. *FEBS Lett.* 13:269–74

83. Marcus, M., Newlon, M. C. 1971. *Virology* 44:83–93
84. Markewych, O., Boghosian, A., Dosmar, M., Ende, D., Witmer, H. 1977. *J. Virol.* 21:84–95
85. Markewych, O., Casella, E., Dosmar, M., Witmer, H. 1979. *J. Virol.* 29:61–68
86. Marmur, J., Brandon, C., Neubort, S., Ehrlich, M., Mandel, M., Konvicka, J. 1972. *Nature* 239:68–70
87. Marmur, J., Doty, P. 1962. *J. Mol. Biol.* 5:109–18
88. Mathews, C. K. 1971. *Bacteriophage Biochemistry.* New York: Van Nostrand Reinhold. 373 pp.
89. Mathews, C. K. 1972. *J. Biol. Chem.* 247:7430–38
90. Mathews, C. K. 1976. *Arch. Biochem. Biophys.* 172:178–87
91. Mathews, C. K. 1977. In *Comprehensive Virology,* ed. H. Fraenkel-Conrat, R. R. Wagner, 7:179–294. New York: Plenum
92. Mathews, C. K., Crosby, L. K., Kozloff, L. M. 1973. *J. Virol.* 12:75–78
93. Mathews, C. K., North, T. W., Reddy, G. V. P. 1979. *Adv. Enzyme Regul.* 17:133–56
94. Mattson, T., van Houwe, G., Bolle, A., Selzer, G., Epstein, R. H. 1977. *Mol. Gen. Genet.* 154:319–26
95. McNicol, L. A., Goldberg, E. B. 1973. *J. Mol. Biol.* 76:285–301
96. Montgomery, D. L., Snyder, L. R. 1973. *Virology* 53:349–58
97. Morton, D., Kutter, E. M., Guttman, B. S. 1978. *J. Virol.* 28:262–69
98. Mosher, R. A., DiRenzo, A. B., Mathews, C. K. 1977. *J. Virol.* 23:645–58
99. Neubort, S., Marmur, J. 1973. *J. Virol.* 12:1078–84
100. Nishihara, M., Friedman, M., Aposhian, H. V. 1969. *J. Virol.* 3:164–70
101. North, T. W., Stafford, M. E., Mathews, C. K. 1976. *J. Virol.* 17:973–82
102. Okubo, S., Stodolsky, M., Bott, K., Strauss, B. 1963. *Proc. Natl. Acad. Sci. USA* 50:679–86
103. Pietrzykowska, I., Shugar, D. 1967. *Acta Biochim. Pol.* 14:169–81
104. Plesiewicz, E., Stepien, E., Bolewska, K., Wierzchowski, K. L. 1976. *Nucleic Acids Res.* 3:1295–1306
105. Price, A. R., Cook, S. J. 1972. *J. Virol.* 9:602–10
106. Price, A. R., Frabotta, M. 1972. *Biochem. Biophys. Res. Commun.* 48:1578–85
106a. Price, A. R., Frato, J. 1975. *J. Biol. Chem.* 250:8804–11
107. Price, A. R., Hitzeman, R., Frato, J., Lombardi, K. 1974. *Nucleic Acids Res.* 1:1497–1502
108. Quail, A., Karrer, E., Warren, R. A. J. 1976. *J. Gen. Virol.* 33:135–38
109. Rabussay, D., Geiduschek, E. P. 1977. See Ref. 91, 8:1–196
110. Rae, P. M. M. 1973. *Proc. Natl. Acad. Sci. USA* 70:1141–45
111. Reddy, G. V. P., Mathews, C. K. 1979. *J. Biol. Chem.* 253:3461–67
112. Reddy, G. V. P., Singh, A., Stafford, M. E., Mathews, C. K. 1977. *Proc. Natl. Acad. Sci. USA* 74:3152–56
113. Revel, H. R., Luria, S. E. 1970. *Ann. Rev. Genet.* 4:177–92
114. Rima, B. K., Takahashi, I. 1973. *Can. J. Biochem.* 51:1219–24
115. Rima, B. K., Takahashi, I. 1979. *J. Gen. Microbiol.* 112:127–33
116. Roscoe, D. H. 1969. *Virology* 38:520–26
117. Roscoe, D. H. 1969. *Virology* 38:527–37
118. Roscoe, D. H., Tucker, R. G. 1966. *Virology* 29:157–66
119. Rosenberg, E. 1965. *Proc. Natl. Acad. Sci. USA* 53:836–41
120. Sadowski, P. D., Hurwitz, J. 1969. *J. Biol. Chem.* 244:6182–91
121. Sadowski, P. D., Hurwitz, J. 1969. *J. Biol. Chem.* 244:6192–98
122. Schildkraut, C. L., Marmur, J., Doty, P. 1962. *J. Mol. Biol.* 4:430–43
123. Snyder, L., Gold, L., Kutter, E. 1976. *Proc. Natl. Acad. Sci. USA* 73:3098–3102
124. Stafford, M. E., Reddy, G. V. P., Mathews, C. K. 1977. *J. Virol.* 23:53–60
125. Stent, G. S. 1963. *Molecular Biology of Bacterial Viruses.* San Francisco: Freeman. 474 pp.
126. Szer, W., Shugar, D. 1966. *J. Mol. Biol.* 17:174–87
127. Takahashi, I. 1963. *J. Gen. Microbiol.* 31:211–17
128. Takahashi, I., Marmur, J. 1963. *Nature* 197:794–95
129. Takahashi, I., Marmur, J. 1963. *Biochem. Biophys. Res. Commun.* 10:289–92
130. Taylor, M. J., Thorne, C. B. 1963. *J. Bacteriol.* 86:452–61
131. Thorne, C. B. 1962. *J. Bacteriol.* 83:106–11
132. Tomich, P. K., Chiu, C.-S., Wovcha, M. G., Greenberg, G. R. 1974. *J. Biol. Chem.* 249:7613–22
133. Tomich, P. K., Greenberg, G. R. 1973. *Biochem. Biophys. Res. Commun.* 50:1032–38
134. Tomita, F., Takahashi, I. 1969. *Biochim. Biophys. Acta* 179:18–27

135. Tomita, F., Takahashi, I. 1975. *J. Virol.* 15:1073–80
136. Tomita, F., Takahashi, I. 1975. *J. Virol.* 15:1081–87
137. Tomita, F., Takahashi, I. 1976. In *Microbiology 1976,* ed. D. Schlessinger, pp. 315–18. Washington, DC: Am. Soc. Microbiol.
138. Truffaut, N., Revet, B., Soulic, M.-O. 1970. *Eur. J. Biochem.* 15:391–400
139. Tyreyar, F. J., Taylor, H. J., Lawton, W. D., Goldberg, I. D. 1969. *J. Bacteriol.* 100:1027–36
140. Ulbricht, T. L. V., Rogers, G. T., Takahashi, I. 1966. *Biochem. Biophys. Res. Commun.* 22:141–43
141. Velten, J., Fukada, K., Abelson, J. 1976. *Gene* 1:93–106
142. Walker, M. S. 1977. *Studies of the biosynthesis of the hypermodified base in bacteriophage SP15 deoxyribonucleic acid.* PhD thesis. Univ. Texas, Houston. 134 pp.
143. Walker, M. S., Mandel, M. 1978. *J. Virol.* 25:500–9
144. Walker, M. S., Mandel, M. 1978. *J. Virol.* 25:695–97
145. Warner, H. R., Duncan, B. K. 1978. *Nature* 272:32–34
146. Waschke, S., Reefschläger, J., Bärwolff, D., Langen, P. 1975. *Nature* 255: 629–30
147. Wells, R. D., Blakesly, R. W., Burd, J. F., Chan, H. W., Dodgson, J. B., Hardies, S. C., Horn, G. T., Jensen, K. F., Larson, J. E., Nes, I. F., Selsing, E., Wartell, R. M. 1977. *CRC Crit. Rev. Biochem.* 4:305–40
148. Wilson, G. G., Tanyashin, V. I., Murray, N. E. 1977. *Mol. Gen. Genet.* 156:203–14
149. Wilson, G. G., Young, K. K. Y., Edlin, G. J., Konigsberg, W. 1979. *Nature* 280:80–82
150. Winston, V., Thompson, T. L. 1976. *Bacteriol. Proc.* p. 234
151. Witmer, H., Dosmar, M. 1978. *Curr. Microbiol.* 1:289–92
152. Wovcha, M. G., Chiu, C.-S., Tomich, P. K., Greenberg, G. R. 1976. *J. Virol.* 20:142–56
153. Wovcha, M. G., Tomich, P. K., Chiu, C.-S., Greenberg, G. R. 1973. *Proc. Natl. Acad. Sci. USA* 70:2196–2200
154. Wyatt, G. R., Cohen, S. S. 1953. *Biochem. J.* 55:774–82
155. Yehle, C. O., Ganesan, A. T. 1973. *J. Biol. Chem.* 248:7456–63
156. Zmudzka, B., Bollum, F. J., Shugar, D. 1969. *Biochemistry* 8:3049–59

Ann. Rev. Microbiol. 1980. 34:159–81

NATURAL β-LACTAM ANTIBIOTICS

❖1773

Hatsuo Aoki and Masakuni Okuhara

Research Laboratories, Fujisawa Pharmaceutical Co., Ltd., Osaka, Japan

CONTENTS

INTRODUCTION 160
Occurrence of β-Lactam Antibiotics in Nature 160
Classification of β-Lactam Antibiotics 161
PENICILLINS AND CEPHALOSPORINS 161
Occurrence of Penicillins and Cephalosporins 161
History of Development 162
Fermentation and Isolation 163
Biosynthesis 165
Biological Activities 166
CEPHAMYCINS (7-METHOXYCEPHALOSPORINS) 168
Discovery and Isolation of β-Lactam Antibiotics from Streptomyces 168
Fermentation and Biosynthesis 168
Biological Activities 170
NOCARDICINS 170
Screening Procedure and Occurrence 170
Fermentation and Isolation 171
Physical and Chemical Properties 172
Biosynthetic Studies 172
Biological Activities 172
THIENAMYCINS AND OLIVANIC ACIDS 173
Occurrence of Thienamycins and Related Substances 173
Fermentation and Isolation 174
Physical and Chemical Properties 174
Biological Activities 175
CLAVULANIC ACID 176
Screening Procedure for β-Lactamase Inhibitors and Discovery of Clavulanic Acid 176
Fermentation and Isolation 176
Chemical Characteristics 177
Biological Activities 177
CONCLUDING REMARKS 177

0066-4227/80/1001-0159$01.00

INTRODUCTION

Occurrence of β-Lactam Antibiotics in Nature

The β-Lactam structure is not frequently encountered in nature; only a limited number of compounds of this group have been reported: pachystermines from a higher plant, *Pachysandra terminalis* (70); wild-fire toxin from a bacterium, *Pseudomonas tabaci* (117); two antimetabolites from a *Streptomyces* species (113); anticancer antibiotics, phleomycins and bleomycins from *Streptomyces verticillus* (118); and so-called β-lactam antibiotics.

β-Lactam antibiotics are characterized chemically by the presence of a β-lactam ring in their structures and biologically by their inhibitory effect on the biosynthesis of essential structural components of bacterial cell wall (120). These structural components are absent in mammalian cells, so that their selective inhibition has no effect on metabolism of animals cells.

In 1929, Fleming (40) noticed antibacterial activity of a fungal metabolite and reported some characteristics of the active principle, which he named penicillin after the producing strain, *Penicillium notatum.* Elucidation of the structure of penicillin by Abraham et al (4) showed this antibiotic has a β-lactam ring in its molecule. Low toxicity and excellent antibacterial activity of penicillin attracted the attention of numerous researchers and clinicians. Cephalosporin C, the second member of the β-lactam antibiotics, was found in 1953 (96). The availability of the nuclei of penicillin and cephalosporin, 6-aminopenicillanic acid (6-APA) and 7-aminocephalsoporanic acid (7-ACA), has led to the production of many thousands of semisynthetic penicillins and cephalosporins (50, 105, 106, 112, 126), some of which are among the most important chemotherapeutic agents now used to treat bacterial infections.

For a long time in the history of β-lactam antibiotics, only penicillins and cephalosporins had been known to be produced in fermentation broths of microorganisms. Penicillins were found to be produced by several species of fungi and one strain of *Streptomyces.* Only a limited number of strains had been known to produce cephalosporin C. The importance of β-lactam antibiotics has spurred researchers, especially in pharmaceutical companies, to undertake screening programs directed toward the discovery of this group of antibiotics. A number of new screening procedures have been devised and reported (11). A screening method using β-lactam antibiotic–super-susceptible mutants of bacteria resulted in the discovery of several novel types of β-lactams, such as nocardicins and Ps-5. This method also played a role in detecting a wide variety of eukaryotic molds and prokaryotic actinomycetes which produce cephalosporin ring (cephem) and penicillin ring (penam) compounds. Test of β-lactamase inhibitory activity led to the discovery of clavulanic acid and olivanic acids.

Classification of β-Lactam Antibiotics

β-Lactam antibiotics can be classified into six groups according to their structural characteristics. All β-lactam antibiotics, except nocardicins, are derivatives of bicyclic ring systems. The penicillin ring system (penam) contains a four-membered β-lactam ring fused with a five-membered thiazolidine ring. The cephalosporin ring system (cephem) consists of a four-membered β-lactam ring fused with an unsaturated six-membered dihydrothiazine ring. Cephamycins have a methoxy group at the 7 position of the cephem ring. Clavulanic acid differs from penicillin in so far as the β-lactam ring is fused with a five-membered oxazolidine ring instead of a thiazolidine ring. It has no acyl amide side chain at the 6 position of the nucleus, but has a hydroxyethylidene substituent at the 2 position. Nocardicins are monocyclic β-lactams that have a unique acyl group attached to the amino function of the nucleus. In thienamycins and olivanic acids, the β-lactam ring is fused with a five-membered pyrroline ring (desthia-carbapenem). A structural feature that is common to all of these natural β-lactam antibiotics is the carboxy group on the carbon adjacent to the β-lactam nitrogen (Figure 1).

PENICILLINS AND CEPHALOSPORINS

Occurrence of Penicillins and Cephalosporins

Penicillins and cephalosporins are extensively reviewed (8, 41, 94, 127) because of their clinical utility and their biologically and chemically interesting properties.

From the early stage of research, two penicillins, penicillin G and penicillin F, were known to be produced in the fermentation broth of *Penicillium*. Penicillin G and F proved to be benzylpenicillin and pentenylpenicillin, respectively. Subsequent research showed that the quantity and quality of the penicillins synthesized by *Penicillium chrysogenum* depend on the ingredients of the fermentation medium. Addition of a variety of side-chain precursors to the fermentation medium resulted in the production of corresponding penicillins (16, 18). Natural penicillins (Table 1) are produced by either true fungi (eukaryote) (67, 76) or *Streptomyces* (prokaryote) (67). For a long time only a few strains of molds had been known to produce cephalosporin C. Recent studies using β-lactam–super-susceptible mutants of bacteria (72, 74, 77) have demonstrated, however, that a considerable number of genera of eukaryotic fungi other than *Cephalosporium* or *Emericellopsis* produce cephalosporin C and related compounds. Reports are accumulating on the fermentation production of cephem compounds by wild isolates and also by mutant organisms derived from cephalosporin C–producing strains (42, 52, 66, 68, 73, 107, 121) (Table 2). Production of cephalosporins from *n*-paraffin was also reported (75).

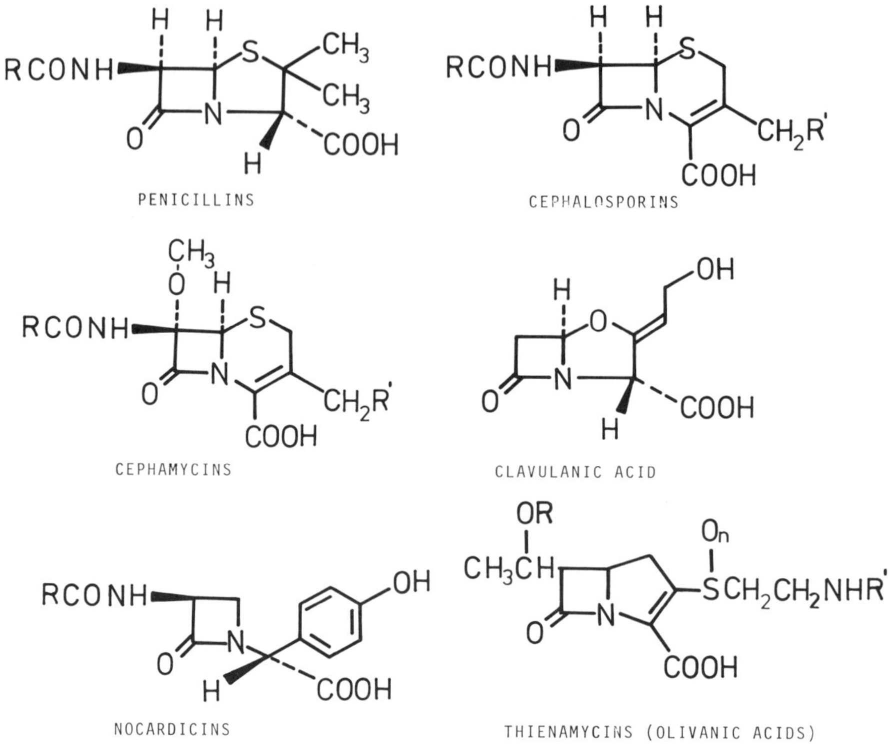

Figure 1 Natural β-lactam antibiotics.

History of Development

In 1929, Fleming noticed anti-*Staphylococcus* sp. activity of a metabolite of *Penicillium notatum* contaminating an agar plate and examined the properties of the active principle (40). It was, however, in 1940 that the chemotherapeutic efficacy of penicillin was demonstrated in mice and then in man by Abraham et al (3). The β-lactam structure of the antibiotic was first reported by Abraham et al in 1943 (4). Production of the nucleus of the penicillin molecule, 6-APA, was achieved by fermentation with no side-chain precursor added (14), by hydrolysis of benzylpenicillin by bacterial amidases (69, 110) and by chemical synthesis. The discovery of 6-APA marked the dawn of a new era of semisynthetic β-lactam antibiotics; various compounds with excellent chemotherapeutic activity appeared, starting with the 6-APA. In 1953, Newton & Abraham (96) discovered cephalosporin C among the metabolic products of a strain, *Cephalosporium acremonium,* which had been isolated in 1945 by Brotzu from a sewage outfall at Cagliari (20). In 1959, the structure of cephalosporin C was

Table 1 Natural penicillins

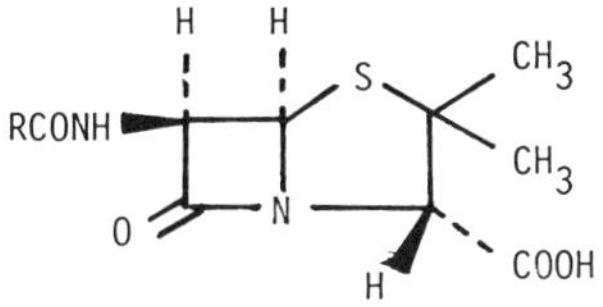

Generic Name	R (N-Acyl side chain)
Penicillin G	$C_6H_5CH_2$-
Penicillin F	$CH_3CH_2CH{=}CHCH_2$-
Dihydropenicillin F	$CH_3(CH_2)_4$-
Penicillin K	$CH_3(CH_2)_6$-
Penicillin X	p-OH-C_6H_4-CH_2-
Penicillin V	$C_6H_5OCH_2$-
Penicillin N	HO_2C-CH(NH_2)(CH_2)$_3$- (D)
Isopenicillin N	HO_2C-CH(NH_2)(CH_2)$_3$- (L)
KPN	HO-(CH_2)$_3$-

proposed by Abraham & Newton (5) and confirmed by X-ray crystalographic analysis (53). Production of the cephalosporin nucleus, 7-ACA, has also led to the semisynthesis of many thousands of cephalosporin antibiotics.

Fermentation and Isolation

The most important fungus for commercial production of penicillins is *Penicillium chrysogenum;* remarkable improvements in productivity have been achieved over the last thirty years by selecting high yield mutants (31, 35) and by improving medium compositions and fermentation conditions. Penicillins with relatively nonpolar side chains are obtained from fermentation with *Penicillium chrysogenum* in the presence of appropriate precursors (16, 18). These penicillins are readily extracted with organic solvents.

Table 2 Natural cephem compounds

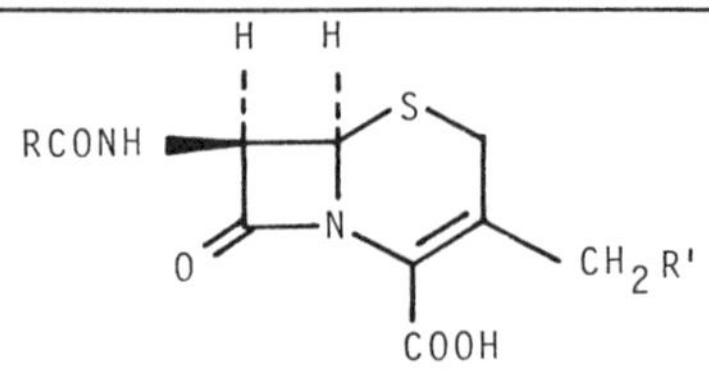

Generic Name	R	R'	References
Cephalosporin C	$HO_2C\text{-}CH(NH_2)(CH_2)_3\text{-}$	$\text{-}OCOCH_3$	5
Deacetyl-cephalosporin C	$HO_2C\text{-}CH(NH_2)(CH_2)_3\text{-}$	-OH	42
Deacetoxy-cephalosporin C	$HO_2C\text{-}CH(NH_2)(CH_2)_3\text{-}$	-H	52
A 16886 A	$HO_2C\text{-}CH(NH_2)(CH_2)_3\text{-}$	$\text{-}OCONH_2$	93
C 43219	$HO_2C\text{-}CH(NH_2)(CH_2)_3\text{-}$	$\text{-}SC(CH_3)_2CH(NH_2)CO_2H$	68
F-1	$HO_2C\text{-}CH(NH_2)(CH_2)_3\text{-}$	$\text{-}SCH_3$	66
N-Acetyl-deacetoxy-cephalosporin C	$HO_2C\text{-}CH(NH\text{-}COCH_3)\text{-}(CH_2)_3\text{-}$	-H	121
Compound a	$HO_2C\text{-}(CH_2)_3\text{-}$	-H	75
b		-OH	
c		$\text{-}OCOCH_3$	

Penicillin N is produced by strains of *Cephalosporium* and *Streptomyces.* Penicillin N–producing microorganisms have not yet been found to produce any other penicillin and do not respond to addition of side-chain precursors into the medium. This penicillin is hydrophilic and can not be extracted with organic solvents.

As cephalosporin C–producing microorganisms had been substantially limited until recently, the descendants of Brotzu's strain have been employed in almost all works of commercial fermentations. Although the main product is cephalosporin C, in fermentation with improved mutants smaller quantities of penicillin N, deacetylcephalosporin C, and sometimes deacetoxycephalosporin C are also produced. Cephalosporin C is a hydrophilic compound which can be extracted by the use of ion exchange resins and nonionic macroporous adsorption resins.

Biosynthesis

Extensive reviews exist on the biosynthesis of penicillins and cephalosporins (2, 7, 13, 29, 67, 85, 124). The molecular units that comprise penicillins and cephalosporins were known to be L-cysteine, L-valine, and an appropriate side-chain precursor. Penam and cephem antibiotics can be classified into two groups with regard to their biosynthetic patterns, which are designated as *Penicillium* type and *Cephalosporium* type (85). The *Penicillium* type leads to the production of penicillins with nonpolar acyl side chains derived from mono-substituted acetic acids. The penicillin nucleus, 6-APA, and isopenicillin N with a δ-(L-α-aminoadipyl) side chain accumulate in the fermentation broth in the absence of side-chain precursor. All organisms of this type are eukaryotic molds. In contrast, in the *Cephalosporium* type of fermentation, only one type of penicillin with δ-(D-α-aminoadipyl) side chain is produced independently or along with cephalosporin C. Trace amounts of 6-APA are sometimes detectable in the fermentations broth of *Emericellopsis* and *Cephalosporium.* Most strains of *Streptomyces* which produce cephem compounds belong to this type. 7-Aminocephalosporanic acid has not yet been detected in the fermentation, nor is any other cephalosporin with different acyl side chain produced by addition of side-chain precursor to the fermentation medium.

Since the discovery of a tripeptide, δ-(α-aminoadipyl) cysteinylvaline, in small amounts in the mycelium of *Penicillium chrysogenum* (12) and *Cephalosporium acremonium* (87), this tripeptide has been considered to be the key intermediate of biosynthetic pathway of β-lactam antibiotics. The tripeptide was shown to be of LLD-configuration (9, 26, 39, 87). In the cell-free system of *Cephalosporium acremonium* (87), a small amount of radioactivity from [^{14}C]valine was found to be incorporated in Penicillin N (17, 37). Incorporation was also observed when LLD-tripeptide, labeled in either the methyl groups or the α-position of its valine moiety, was used as a precursor (39). No incorporation was detected from either LLL or DLD tripeptides. Penicillin N-negative mutants were isolated by Shirafuji et al (114) from *Cephalosporium acremonium*; some of them accumulated a disulfide dimer of LLD-tripeptide in the fermentation broth. Bauer (15) reported the biosynthesis of the tripeptide by cell-free extract of *Penicillium chrysogenum.* These results indicate the LLD-tripeptide may be a precursor of penicillin N and/or cephalosporin C in *Cephalosporium* type of fermentation. It has also been suggested that penicillin N is a precursor of the common penicillins produced by *Penicillium* type. Later investigation showed that isopenicillin N is the hypothetical precursor of choice. Labels from isopenicillin N and phenylacetyl coenzyme A were found to be incorporated into benzylpenicillin in the extract of *Penicillium chrysogenum* (38).

The mechanisms concerning ring formation in the biosynthesis of the β-lactam antibiotics have not yet been elucidated. But some information was obtained as to the stereochemistry of the cyclization in the biosynthesis of benzylpenicillin by *Penicillium chrysogenum* (1, 78, 79, 131) and of cephalosporin C by *Cephalosporium acremonium* (58, 95).

Kohsaka & Demain (80) recently demonstrated that penicillin N stimulated the formation of cephalosprorin-like compound in the cell-free lysate of protoplasts of *Cephalosporium acremonium* under the condition of high aeration. Yoshida et al (130) have ascertained this conversion by the use of *Cephalosporium* mutants blocked in the synthesis of the β-lactam antibiotics. Using thin-layer chromatography and paper electrophoresis, they also identified the product of the cell-free reaction as deacetoxycephalosporin C. The precise mechanism of conversion of penam ring into cephem is, however, still unknown.

The terminal steps in cephalosporin biosynthesis have been elucidated by the use of blocked mutants (108). Mutants blocked in the final steps in cephalosporin biosynthesis were isolated. Some of them accumulated deacetylcephalosporin C (42, 45), and others were found to accumulate deacetoxycephalosporin C (44, 107) in the fermentation broths. Cell-free extract of the parent strain converted deacetoxycephalosporin C into cephalosporin C, but extracts of the blocked mutants were incapable of this conversion (41, 43). Cephalosporin C–negative mutants were analyzed for the accumulation of penicillin N, deacetoxycephalosporin C, deacetylcephalosporin C, and cephalosporin C (107). Patterns of accumulation were consistent with a biosynthetic pathway involving sequential conversion of penicillin N to cephalosporin C through deacetoxycephalosporin C and deactylcephalosporin C (Figure 2). A hydroxylase that converts deacetoxycephalosporin C to deacetylcephalosporin C (46, 86, 122) and an acetyl transferase that transfers acetyl function from acetyl Co A to deacetylcephalosporin C (43) have been reported.

Biological Activities

The natural penicillins vary considerably in their intrinsic antibacterial activity (91). Benzylpenicillin was most widely used for therapy of Gram-positive bacterial infections because of its high activity against pyogenic cocci. As benzylpenicillin is unstable in acidic solution and destroyed by gastric acid, it is used only through parenteral routes. Phenoxymethylpenicillin is more resistant to gastric acid and can be administered through oral routes. The usefulness of natural penicillins had decreased because of

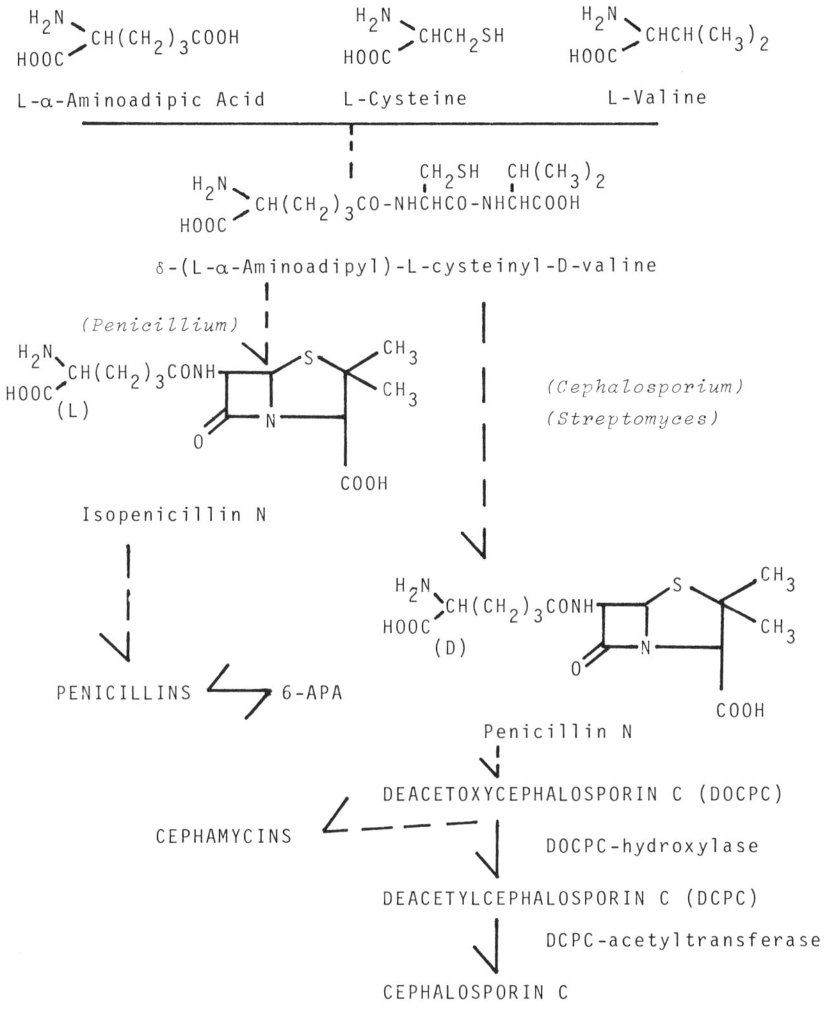

Figure 2 Biosynthetic pathway of penicillins and cephalosporins.

the emergence of penicillin-resistant staphylococci which produce β-lactamase, the enzyme that destroys these antibiotics. Cephalosporin C shows a wide range of activity and is effective against many penicillin-resistant strains of *Staphylococcus aureus* (6). Intrinsic antibacterial activity is, however, not satisfactory; it is about equivalent to benzylpenicillin against Gram-negative bacilli, but considerably less active against Gram-positive bacteria. The importance of penicillin and cephalosporin is not in their intrinsic activity but in their usefulness as starting material for semisynthetic antibiotics. Synthetic chemical research programs based on modification of the acyl side chain have yielded a large number of new penicillins and cephalosporins, some of which are exceedingly superior to the parent compounds and are among the most important chemotherapeutic agents currently in clinical use.

CEPHAMYCINS (7-METHOXYCEPHALOSPORINS)

Discovery and Isolation of β-Lactam Antibiotics from Streptomyces

In the early stages of β-lactam research, only one strain of *Streptomyces* had been reported to produce penicillin N. No cephalosporin C had been found to be produced by any prokaryote. The possibility that penicillin N may be associated with biosynthesis of cephalosporin compounds prompted searches for new penicillin N–producing organisms of Actinomycetales. In 1971, the screening program at Lilly Research Laboratories (93) resulted in the discovery of three new cephem antibiotics in fermentation broths of *Streptomyces. Streptomyces lipmanni* produced a cephem antibiotics with a methoxy group at C-7 position. A novel species, *Streptomyces clavuligerus* (51), yielded two new antibiotics, cephalosporin (A-16886-A) and 7-methoxycephalosporin (A-16886-B), with carbamoyloxymethyl function at C-3 position. Both of the strains also produced penicillin N. Simultaneously, researchers at Merck Sharp & Dohme Company found that several species of *Streptomyces* produce 7-methoxycephalosporins (115). They named this group of antibiotics cephamycin A, B, and C. Cephamycin C was found to be identical with A-16886-B. More recently, C-2801-X was isolated (47, 48) from a fermentation broth of new species of Streptomyces, *Streptomyces heteromorphus* and *Streptomyces panayensis,* which also contained cephamycin A and B. The structure of 2801 X is identical to that of cephamycin B except for an additional hydroxy group on the phenyl moiety. Several related antibiotic substances have also been reported (60, 61) (Table 3).

Fermentation and Biosynthesis

The stimulatory effect of methionine on production of cephalosporins and penicillin N by *Cephalosporium* has been well documented (30, 103). Radioactivity was incorporated into cephalosporin C from ^{35}S-labeled methionine without dilution. In the case of *Streptomyces,* however, the enhancing effect of methionine on cephamycin production has not been reported. Label from [^{14}C]methionine is reported to be incorporated into 7-methoxy function of the cephamycin molecule. Whitney et al (128) reported that

Table 3 Natural 7-Methoxycephem compounds

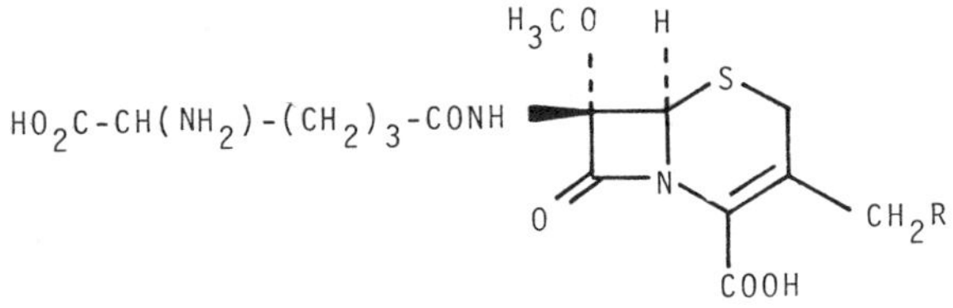

Generic Name	R	Reference
Cephamycin C (A-16886 B)	$-OCONH_2$	115
A-16884 A	$-OCOCH_3$	93
Cephamycin A	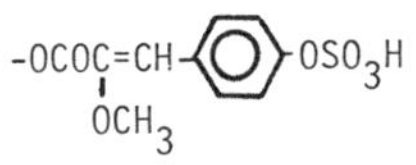	115
Cephamycin B	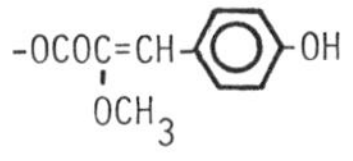	115
C-2081 X	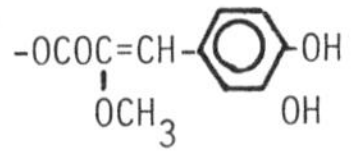	48
SF-1623	$-S-SO_3H$	61
WS-3442 D	-H	60

label from α-aminoadipic acid, valine, and cysteine is incorporated into 7-methoxycephalosporin by *Streptomyces clavuligerus* to a significant degree. The tripeptide, δ-(α-aminoadipyl) cysteinylvaline has also been found in the mycelium of *Streptomyces clavuligerus* and *Streptomyces lipmanii* (8). Thus, cephamycins seem to be synthesized principally in the same way as cephalosporin C and penicillin N.

There are two distinct pathways for microbial synthesis of the amino acid, lysine (71). In higher fungi, lysine is synthesized through the homocitrate pathway in which α-aminoadipic acid is an intermediate. α-Aminoadipic acid is provided in this way in cephalosporin and penicillin fermentation with eukaryotic molds. In prokaryotes, on the other hand, lysine biosynthesis proceeds through diaminopimelic acid, and α-aminoadipic acid is derived from lysine. The incorporation of radioactivity was reported from D,L-[1-^{14}C]lysine into A-16886-B by *Streptomyces clavuligerus* (128). This clearly indicates the origin of α-aminoadipic acid in *Streptomyces* is different from that in eukaryotes and related to bacterial pathway. Brewer et al demonstrated that in *Streptomyces clavuligerus,* O-carbamyltransferase converts 3-hydroxymethylcephalosporins into carbamoylcephalosporins. This enzyme requires carbamoyl phosphate as a substrate (19). O'Sullivan et al reported that the oxygen atoms of the methoxy group, as well as exocyclic methylene group at C-3 position, are derived from molecular oxygen (102).

Biological Activities

Cephamycin A, B (28, 88), and C-2801 X are fairly active in vitro against Gram-positive and certain Gram-negative bacteria. Cephamycin C has weaker activity against Gram-positive bacteria, but against Gram-negative bacilli it is more active than cephamycin A and B and is essentially as active as cephalosporin C or semisynthetic antibiotics such as cephaloridine or cephalothin. Cephamycins are quite resistant to hydrolysis by cephalosporinases produced by bacteria resistant to cephalosporins. Cephamycin C is active in vitro against clinically isolated strains such as *Proteus sp., Providencia sp.,* and *Escherichia coli.* Though the intrinsic activity of cephamycin C is not sufficient as a clinical agent when compared with excellent activity of some semisynthetic cephalosporins and penicillins, it is useful as a starting material for production of semisynthetic 7-methoxycephalosporin antibiotics (101).

NOCARDICINS

Screening Procedure and Occurrence

A screening program for β-lactam antibiotics by Fujisawa Pharmaceutical Co. led to the discovery of monocyclic β-lactam antibiotic, nocardicin (10). Mutant strains of *Escherichi coli* and *Pseudomonsa aeruginosa* which are specifically supersensitive to penicillin and cephalosporin as test organisms were used (11). The antibiotic is produced by a strain of *Nocardia,* which has been designated *Nocardia uniformis* subsp. *tsuyamanensis.* Several related compounds have been detected in the nocardicin culture by the use of a nocardicin C (hydrogenated nocardicin A)–super-susceptible mutant of *Pseudomonas aeruginosa.* They are isolated and characterized (55, 83); their structures (49) are shown in Table 4.

Table 4 Nocardicins

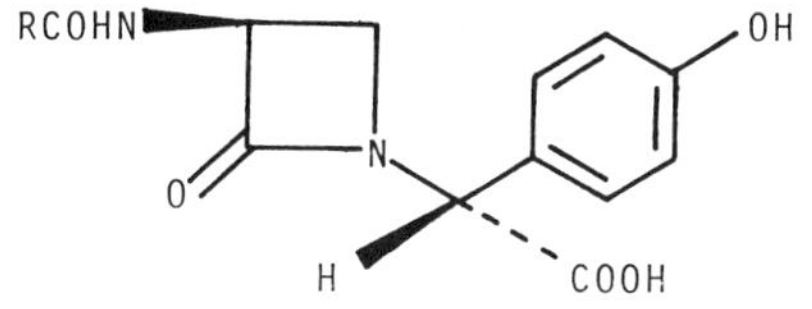

Name	R
Nocardicin A	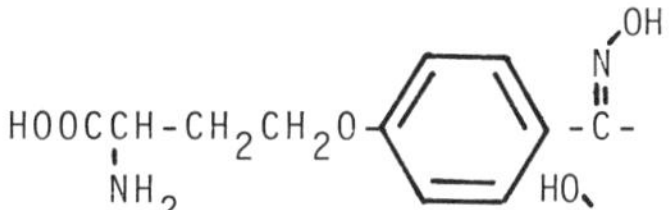
Nocardicin B	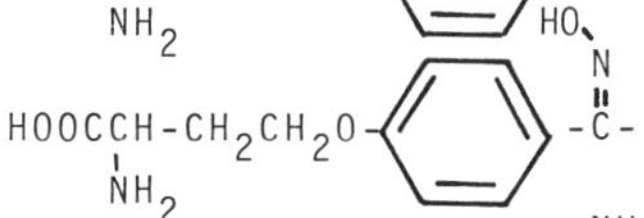
Nocardicin C	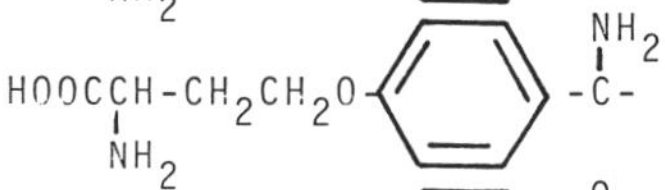
Nocardicin D	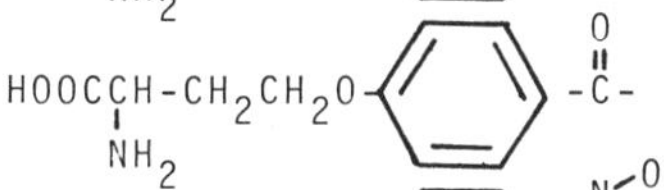
Nocardicin E	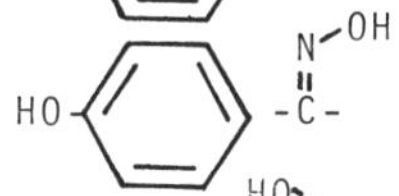
Nocardicin F	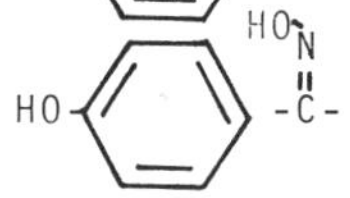
Nocardicin G	

Fermentation and Isolation

Nocardicins are produced under aerobic submerged conditions with *Nocardia uniformis* subsp. *tsuyamanensis* or *Streptomyces alcalophilus* sp. nov. (E. Iguchi et al, unpublished data). Addition of an amino acid, tyrosine, in the production medium showed a marked stimulatory effect on nocardicin production (56, 92). Nocardicins are isolated and purified by nonionic macroporous adsorption resins. Separation of nocardicin components is achieved by the use of column chromatography with adsorption resin, silicic acid, and cellulose powder.

Physical and Chemical Properties

Nocardicin A is an acidic substance, soluble in alkaline solutions. The antibiotic is extremely stable in acidic or alkaline solutions. Nocardicin shows lower β-lactam absorption band in the infrared (IR) when compared with other natural β-lactam antibiotics. The carbonyl band in the infrared is considered a predictor of the strain on the β-lactam ring (32), so the lower IR frequency of nocardicin suggests the low reactivity of the β-lactam ring of the antibiotic; this may explain its moderate antibacterial activity, resistance to hydrolysis by β-lactamases, lack of immunogenicity and cross-reactivity with penicillin and cephalosporin, and weak binding of ^{14}C-labeled nocardicin A to penicillin-binding proteins of *Escherichi coli* (K. Kunugita et al, unpublished data).

Biosynthetic Studies

Addition of D- or L-tyrosine in the medium showed a marked stimulatory effect on nocardicin production. Hosoda et al (56) reported that the radioactivity was efficiently incorporated into nocardicin molecule from L-[U–^{14}C] tyrosine, L-[U-^{14}C] serine, [U-^{14}C] glycine, L-[U-^{14}C] alanine, and [U-^{14}C] homoserine, but the label was not incorporated from L-[1–^{14}C] tyrosine. After degradation of labeled nocardicin A and examination of degradative products, they have clearly demonstrated that radioactivity from serine, alanine, and glycine is incorporated into β-lactam ring, tyrosine into aromatic moieties, and homoserine into the 3-amino-3-carboxypropoxy moiety of the antibiotic. A biosynthetic pathway of nocardicin, which is quite different from that of penicillins and cephalosporins, was proposed as illustrated in Figure 3. The nocardicin nucleus, 3-aminonocardicinic acid, has not been found in the fermentation broth, but this compound can be prepared from nocardicin C by bacterial amidases (82).

Biological Activities

Nocardicin A exerts a modest antibacterial activity (97) against Gram-negative bacteria including *Pseudomonas aeruginosa, Serratia marcescens,* and indole-positive and -negative *Proteus* spp. The antibiotic has no significant in vitro activity against *Staphylococcus aureus* or *Escherichia coli.* No cross-resistance was seen between nocardicin A and other β-lactam antibiotics examined. The in vitro activity of nocardicin A against *Pseudomonas aeruginosa* and *Proteus* spp. was greatly influenced by the assay medium used (81). Sodium chloride was found to be the most potent antagonist of its activity. Some amino acids, sugars, and divalent cations also antagonize nocardicin activity. This antibiotic has stronger in vivo activity than can be expected from its demonstrated in vitro effect. This can be explained by the

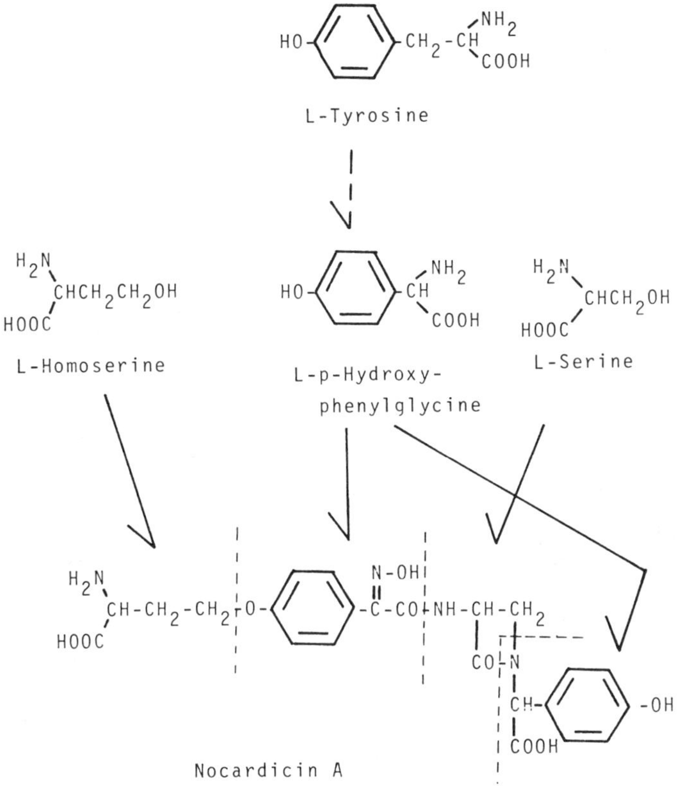

Figure 3 Biosynthetic pathway of nocardicin.

synergy of its antibacterial activity and the body defense mechanisms of experimental animals (90).

THIENAMYCINS AND OLIVANIC ACIDS

Occurrence of Thienamycins and Related Substances

In 1976 thienamycin, the first member of a related series of desthia-carbapenem antibiotics, was reported (63, 65). This antibiotic was found in the culture broth of a new species, *Streptomyces cattleya*. *N*-Acetylthienamycin has also been reported (64) to be produced in the same fermentation broth. Four additional isomeric *N*-acetylthienamycins were reported to be produced by *Streptomyces flavogriseus* and *Streptomyces olivaceus* (23, 25, 116). They have been identified as *N*-acetyl-6-epithienamycin (epithienamycin A), *N*-acetyl-8-epithienamycin (epithienamycin C), and the dehydro analogues which are unsaturated in the *N*-acetylcysteamine side chain (epithienamycin B and D) (Table 5.) At Beecham Research Laboratories, researchers engaged in screening for naturally occurring inhibitors of β-lactamase discovered that various strains of *Streptomyces* produce a family of β-lactamase inhibitors that have been referred to as olivanic acid complex (24). The chemical structure of the compounds of this family, MM 4550, MM 13902, and MM 17880 was reported in 1977 (22, 24, 27, 54). They proved to belong to the desthia-carbapenem antibiotics. One of the β-lactamase inhibitors produced by *Streptomyces flavoviridis*, MC-696-SY-2, (123) has been reported to have a structure closely related to that of MM 4550 (59). Most recently, an antibiotic, Ps-5, was reported (98, 99) from *Streptomyces cremeus* subsp. *auratilis.*

Fermentation and Isolation

Thienamycin is produced in the culture filtrate of *Streptomyces cattleya* as a component of a complex of β-lactam antibiotics including penicillin N, cephamycin A, and *N*-acetyl derivative of thienamycin (65). Extraction and purification of this extremely unstable antibiotic were achieved by the use of ion exchange resins, such as Dowex 50, Dowex 1, and macroporous adsorption resins such as Amberlite XAD-2. Olivanic acids, MM 4550, MM 13920, and MM 17880 are coproduced by several strains of *Streptomyces olivaceus* and closely related species (24). This group of antibiotics is detected by the use of a β-lactamase inhibition test. Fermentation production of this antibiotic complex requires a relatively low nitrogen content and a high C/N ratio and is stimulated by the addition of a trace amount of cobalt ion in the production medium. Isolation of these antibiotics from culture filtrate and separation of each antibiotic component were achieved by column chromatography on QAE Sephadex (54). Ps-5 is produced by *Streptomyces cremeus* subsp. *auratilis* and detected by the use of *Comamonas terrigena* B-996, a cephalothin–super-susceptible mutant of *Comamonas terrigena* IFO 12865 (99). Extraction and purification were carried out by the use of several ion exchange and nonionic macroporous adsorption resins.

Physical and Chemical Properties

Thienamycin is a very unstable substance (65). Optimum stability is between pH 6 and 7, declining with unusual rapidity outside of this range. Inactivation accelerates as concentration of the antibiotic is increased above approximately 10 mg/ml. It is susceptible to inactivation by dilute solution of hydroxylamine or cysteine. Stereochemical characteristic of thienamycin (Table 5) is that the substituent about the azetidinone ring has the *trans*-configuration, as opposed to the *cis*-configuration observed among the

Table 5 Thienamycins and related compounds

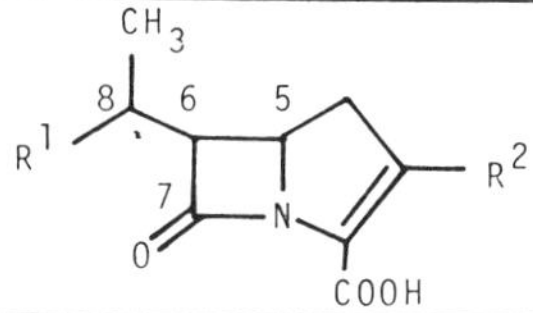

Generic Name	R^1	R^2	C5,C6,C8 Configuration	β-Lactam Configuration	References
Thienamycin	-OH	$-SCH_2CH_2NH_2$	R,S,R	trans	65
N-Acetylthienamycin	-OH	$-SCH_2CH_2NHCOCH_3$	R,S,R	trans	64
Epithienamycin A (MM 22380)	-OH	$-SCH_2CH_2NHCOCH_3$	R,R,S	cis	23
Epithienamycin B (MM 22382)	-OH	$-SCH{=}CHNHCOCH_3$	R,R,S	cis	23
Epithienamycin C	-OH	$-SCH_2CH_2NHCOCH_3$	R,S,S	trans	25
Epithienamycin D (MM 22383)	-OH	$-SCH{=}CHNHCOCH_3$	R,S,S	trans	23
Epithienamycin E (MM 13902)	$-OSO_3H$	$-SCH{=}CHNHCOCH_3$	R,R,S	cis	23
Epithienamycin F (MM 17780)	$-OSO_3H$	$-SCH_2CH_2NHCOCH_3$	R,R,S	cis	23
MM 4550 (MC696 SY2 A)	$-OSO_3H$	$-S-CH{=}CHNHCOCH_3$	R,R,S	cis	23
Ps-5	-H	$-SCH_2CH_2NHCOCH_3$	not reported	not reported	98

natural β-lactam antibiotics, such as penicillin, cephalosporin, and nocardicin. The *trans*-configuration is also observed with *N*-acetylthienamycin and epithienamycin C and D. Olivanic acids are also unstable in aqueous solution outside of a narrow pH range and rapidly inactivated by addition of hydroxylamine or cysteine. Olivanic acids have *cis*-configuration at C6-C5 position (23).

Biological Activities

Thienamycin exhibits a potent and broad spectrum activity against Gram-negative bacilli and Gram-positive cocci, including many isolates which are resistant to currently available β-lactam antibiotics (119, 125). It also shows excellent activity against certain anaerobic bacteria. Epithienamycin A and

B have biological activity comparable to *N*-acetylthienamycin, whereas C and D possess relatively low antibacterial activity but better stability to β-lactamases. Neither stereochemistry (*cis* or *trans* at C6-C5) nor double bond in the *N*-acetylcysteamine moiety seems to have significant effect on biological activity. Though only limited data are available, C8-stereochemistry seems to affect the biological activity. Olivanic acids (54) inhibit a number of different types of β-lactamases of various bacterial origins in a progressive manner and show synergy with β-lactam antibiotics that are sensitive to β-lactamases. MM 13902 and MM 17880 have good antibacterial activity on Gram-positive and -negative bacteria, whereas MM 4550 is less active as an antibiotic. Ps-5 (111) has potent antibacterial activity against a wide spectrum of Gram-positive and -negative bacteria and also shows an inhibitory effect on β-lactamases produced by various bacteria (100). Its antibacterial activity is reported to be unaffected by inoculum size in in vitro assay, which is not the case in thienamycin.

CLAVULANIC ACID

Screening Procedure for β-Lactamase Inhibitors and Discovery of Clavulanic Acid

The majority of pathogenic bacteria that are resistant to penicillins and cephalosporins owe their resistance to the production of a β-lactamase that inactivates the antibiotics. Inhibitors of this β-lactamase would exhibit synergy with β-lactam antibiotics that are susceptible to the enzyme. This is the principle of the method employed for discovery of β-lactamase-inhibitors in Beecham Laboratories (21). One such inhibitor, called clavulanic acid, has been found to be produced by *Streptomyces clavuligerus,* an actinomycete producing cephamycins (21, 109). The compound was isolated and shown to be a novel fused β-lactam, different from any of the natural β-lactam antibiotics so far reported.

Fermentation and Isolation

Clavulanic acid (109) is produced by *Streptomyces clavuligerus* together with cephamycin C, deacetoxycephalosporin C, and penicillin N in submerged culture using a complex nutrient medium. It is extracted with an organic solvent such as *n*-butanol at an acidic pH and reextracted from the organic solvent into water at neutral or alkaline pH. Purification of the antibiotic is achieved by the use of chromatography on permutit FFIP resin, Bio-Rad Bio-Gel P2, and Whatman CC 31 cellulose columns and is obtained as sodium salt. The biosynthesis of clavulanic acid was investigated (36) and it was shown that the carbon skelton of [1, 3-^{13}C] glycerol is incorporated intact into the β-lactam carbons and that the remaining five carbons are derived from α-ketoglutarate.

Chemical Characteristics

Clavulanic acid has a bicyclic ring system as found in penicillins and cephalosporins; however, it has no amino acyl side chain, it has oxygen instead of sulfur, and it contains a hydroxyethylidene substituent in the oxazolidine ring (57).

Biological Activities

Clavulanic acid is effective against a wide spectrum of Gram-positive and -negative bacteria but the level of activity is relatively low (109). It is, however, a potent inhibitor of various β-lactamases including those found in *Escherichia coli* (plasmid-mediated), *Klebsiella pneumoniae, Proteus mirabilis,* and *Staphylococcus aureus;* but cephalosporinase type of β-lactamases from *Pseudomonas aeruginosa, Enterobacter cloaccae,* and chromosomally determined *E. coli* lactamases are less well inhibited. The progressive and irreversible character of β-lactamase inhibition by clavulanic acid is reported (34, 84). In the presence of low concentration of clavulanic acid, many strains of *Staphylococcus aureus, Klebsiella,* and *Escherichia coli* are rendered susceptible to penicillins and cephalosporins but some bacteria do not respond well to clavulanic acid plus penicillins or cephalosporins (33, 62, 89, 104). The combined effect of clavulanic acid and cephalosporins is also shown on certain anaerobic bacteria resistant to β-lactam antibiotics (129).

CONCLUDING REMARKS

The extensive studies of β-lactam antibiotics has been stimulated by the clinical importance of a large number of semisynthetic agents derived from penicillin and cephalosporin. For a long time, however, only two types of β-lactam antibiotics (penam and cephem compounds) had been known to be produced by relatively limited number of microorganisms. Recent development of screening procedures by use of novel techniques has resulted in the discovery of various new types of β-lactam antibiotics. Isolation and use of β-lactam–super-susceptible mutants of bacteria contributed to the discovery of β-lactam antibiotics that might have otherwise eluded detection, such as nocardicins, and new cephem and penam compounds from a wide variety of fungi. A procedure for detecting β-lactamase inhibitors also played a role in the discovery of clavulanic acid and olivanic acids.

The additional role of novel microbial cultures appears particularly pertinent in the discovery of thienamycin, which is produced by the hitherto undescribed species of *Streptomyces.*

New β-lactam antibiotics will contribute to the advancement of our knowledge about the biosynthesis and biological activity of this interesting group of compounds. Also, some of them will prove to be important starting material for semisynthetic chemotherapeutic agents of clinical utility. The advances in β-lactam antibiotic research seem to justify our faith in the versatility of microorganisms in elaborating novel types of compounds that have not been known to man.

Literature Cited

1. Aberhart, D. J., Lin, L. J., Chu, J. Y. R. 1975. *J. Chem. Soc. Perkin Trans.* 1:2517–23
2. Aberhart, D. J. 1977. *Tetrahedron* 33:1545–59
3. Abraham, E. P., Chain, E., Fletcher, C. M., Gardner, A. D., Heatley, N. G., Jennings, M. A., Florey, H. W. 1941. *Lancet* 2:177–88
4. Abraham, E. P., Chain, E., Baker, W., Robinson, R. 1943. *PEN Report No. 103,* 22nd October 1943
5. Abraham, E. P., Newton, G. G. F. 1961. *Biochem. J.* 79:377–93
6. Abraham, E. P. 1962. *Pharmacol. Rev.* 14:473–500
7. Abraham, E. P. 1977. In *Recent Advances in the Chemistry of β-Lactam Antibiotics,* ed. J. Elks, pp. 1–11. London: Burlington House
8. Abraham, E. P. 1977. *Jap. J. Antibiot.* 30: S1–26 (Suppl.)
9. Adriaens, P., Meesschaert, B., Wuyts, W., Vanderhaeghe, H., Eyssen, H. 1975. *Antimicrob. Agents Chemother.* 8:638–42
10. Aoki, H., Sakai, H., Kohsaka, M., Konomi, T., Hosoda, J., Kubochi, Y., Iguchi, E., Imanaka, H. 1976. *J. Antibiot.* 29:492–500
11. Aoki, H., Kunugita, K., Hosoda, J., Imanaka, H. 1977. *Jpn. J. Antibiot.* 30: S207–17 (Suppl.)
12. Arnstein, H. R. V., Artman, M., Morris, D., Toms, E. J. 1960. *Biochem. J.* 76:353–57
13. Arnstein, H. R. V., Grant, P. T. 1960. *Bacteriol. Rev.* 20:133–47
14. Batchelor, F. R., Doyle, F. P., Naylor, J. H. C., Rolinson, G. N. 1959. *Nature* 183:257–58
15. Bauer, K. 1970. *Z. Naturforsch.* 25:1125–29
16. Behrens, O. K., Corse, J., Edwards, J. P., Garrison, L., Jones, R. G., Soper, Q. F., Van Abeele, F. R., Whitehead, C. W. 1948. *J. Biol. Chem.* 175:793–809
17. Bost, P. E., Demain, A. L. 1977. *Biochem. J.* 162:681–87
18. Brandl, E., Margreiter, H. 1954. *Österr. Chem. Ztg.* 55:11–21
19. Brewer, S. J., Boyle, T. T., Turner, M. K. 1977. *Biochem. Soc. Trans.* 5: 1026–29
20. Brotzu, G. 1948. *Lav. Ist. Ig. Cagliari,* pp. 1–11
21. Brown, A. G., Butterworth, D., Cole, M., Hanscomb, G., Hood, J. D., Reading, C., Rolinson, G. N. 1976. *J. Antibiot.* 29:668–69
22. Brown, A. G., Corbett, D. F., Eglington, A. J., Howarth, T. T. 1977. *J. Chem. Soc. Chem. Commun.* 1977: 523–25
23. Brown, A. G., Corbett, D. F., Eglington, A. J., Howarth, T. T. 1979. *J. Antibiot.* 32:961–63
24. Butterworth, D., Cole, M., Hanscomb, G., Rolinson, G. N. 1979. *J. Antibiot.* 32:287–94
25. Cassidy, P. J., Stapley, E. O., Goegelman, R., Miller, T. W., Arison, B. H., Albers-Schönberg, G., Zimmerman, S. B., Birnbaum, J. 1977. *Proc. Intersci. Conf. Antimicrob. Agents Chemother. 17th, No. 81* (Abstr.)
26. Chan, J. A., Huang, F-C., Sih, C. J. 1976. *Biochemistry* 15:177–80
27. Corbett, D. F., Eglington, A. J., Howarth, T. T. 1977. *J. Chem. Soc. Chem. Commun.* 1977:953–54
28. Daoust, D. R., Onishi, H. R., Wallick, H., Hendlin, D., Stapley, E. O. 1973. *Antimicrob. Agents Chemother.* 3: 254–61
29. Demain, A. L. 1959. *Adv. Appl. Microbiol.* 1:23–47
30. Demain, A. L., Newkirk, J. F. 1962. *Appl. Microbiol.* 10:321–25
31. Demain, A. L. 1973. *Adv. Appl. Microbiol.* 16:177–202
32. Demarco, P. V., Nagarajan, R. 1972. See Ref. 41, pp. 311–69
33. Dumon, L., Adriaens, P., Anne, J., Eyssen, H. 1979. *Antimicrob. Agents Chemother.* 15:315–17
34. Durkin, J. P., Viswanatha, T. 1978. *J. Antibiot.* 31:1162–69

35. Elander, R. P. 1976. *Microbiology-1976,* ed. D. Schlessinger, pp. 517–21. Washington: Am. Soc. Microbiol.
36. Elson, S. W., Oliver, R. S. 1978. *J. Antibiot.* 31:586–592
37. Fawcett, P. A. 1975. *PhD thesis.* Oxford Univ.
38. Fawcett, P. A., Usher, J. J., Abraham, E. P. 1975. *Biochem. J.* 151:741–46
39. Fawcett, P. A., Usher, J. J., Huddleston, J. A., Bleaney, R. C., Nisbet, J. J., Abraham, E. P. 1976. *Biochem. J.* 157:651–60
40. Fleming, A. 1929. *Br. J. Exp. Pathol.* 10:226–36
41. Flynn, E. H., ed. 1972. *Cephalosporins and Penicillins.* New York/London: Academic
42. Fujisawa, Y., Shirafuji, H., Kida, M., Nara, K., Yoneda, M., Kanzaki, T. 1973. *Nature New Biol.* 246:154–55
43. Fujisawa, Y., Kanzaki, T. 1975. *Agric. Biol. Chem.* 39:2043–48
44. Fujisawa, Y., Kitano, K., Kanzaki, T. 1975. *Agric. Biol. Chem.* 39:2049–55
45. Fujisawa, Y., Shirafuji, H., Kida, M., Nara, K., Yoneda, M., Kanzaki, T. 1975. *Agric. Biol. Chem.* 39:1295–1301
46. Fujisawa, Y., Kikuchi, M., Kanzaki, T. 1977. *J. Antibiot.* 30:775–77
47. Fukase, H., Hasegawa, T., Hatano, K., Iwasaki, H., Yoneda, M. 1976. *J. Antibiot.* 29:113–20
48. Hasegawa, T., Hatano, K., Fukase, H., Iwasaki, H. 1975. *Jpn. Patent No. 50–53594* (Published, unexamined)
49. Hashimoto, M., Komori, T., Kamiya, T. 1976. *J. Antibiot.* 29:890–901
50. Hashimoto, M., Kamiya, T. 1977. *Jpn. J. Antibiot.* 30: S218–29 (Suppl.)
51. Higgens, C. E., Kastner, R. E. 1971. *Int. J. Syst. Bacteriol.* 21:326–31
52. Higgens, C. E., Hamill, R. L., Sands, T. H., Hoehn, M. M., Davis, N. E., Nagarajan, R., Boeck, L. D. 1974. *J. Antibiot.* 27:298–300
53. Hodgkin, D. C., Maslen, E. N. 1961. *Biochem. J.* 79:393–402
54. Hood, J. D., Box, S. J., Verall, M. S. 1979. *J. Antibiot.* 32:295–304
55. Hosoda, J., Konomi, T., Tani, N., Aoki, H., Imanaka, H. 1977. *Agric. Biol. Chem.* 41:2013–20
56. Hosoda, J., Tani, N., Konomi, T., Ohsawa, S., Aoki, H., Imanaka, H. 1977. *Agric. Biol. Chem.* 41:2007–12
57. Howarth, T. T., Brown, A. G., King, T. J. 1976. *J. Chem. Soc. Chem. Commun.* 1976:266–67
58. Huddleston, J. A., Abraham, E. P., Young, D. W., Morecombe, D. J., Sen, P. K. 1978. *Biochem. J.* 168:705–7
59. Iinuma, K., Naganawa, H., Kondo, S., Ohno, M., Umezawa, H. 1977. *J. Antibiot.* 30:770–72
60. Imanaka, H., Hosoda, J., Jomon, K., Ueda, I., Morino, D., Sakai, H. 1974. *Jpn. Patent No. 49–26488* (Published, unexamined)
61. Inoue, S., Shomura, T., Kojima, M., Ogawa, Y., Watanabe, H., Kondo, Y., Saito, K., Yamada, Y., Niida, T. 1975. *Jpn. Pat. No. 50–82291* (Published, unexamined)
62. Jackson, R. T., Harris, L. F., Alford, R. H. 1978. *Antimicrob. Agents Chemother.* 14:118–25
63. Kahan, J. S., Kahan, F. M., Goegelman, R., Currie, S. A., Jackson, M., Stapley, E. O., Miller, T. W., Miller, A. K., Hendlin, D., Mochales, S., Hernandez, S., Woodruff, H. B. 1976. *Proc. Intersci. Conf. Antimicrob. Agents Chemother. 16th, No. 227* (Abstr.)
64. Kahan, J. S., Kahan, F. M., Goegelman, R., Stapley, E. O., Hernandez, S. 1977. *Ger. Offen. 2, 652, 681*
65. Kahan, J. S., Kahan, F. M., Goegelman, R., Currie, S. A., Jackson, M., Stapley, E. O., Miller, T. W., Miller, A. K., Hendlin, D., Mochales, S., Hernandez, S., Woodruff, H. B., Birnbaum, J. 1979. *J. Antibiot.* 32:1–12
66. Kanzaki, T., Fukita, T., Shirafuji, H., Fujisawa, Y., Kitano, K. 1974. *J. Antibiot.* 27:361–62
67. Kanzaki, T., Fujisawa, Y. 1976. *Adv. Appl. Microbiol.* 20:159–201
68. Kanzaki, T., Fukita, T., Kitano, K., Katamoto, K., Nara, K., Nakao, Y. 1976. *J. Ferment. Technol.* 54:720–25
69. Kaufmann, W., Bauer, K. 1960. *Naturwissenschaften* 47:474–75
70. Kikuchi, T., Uyeo, S. 1967. *Chem. Pharm. Bull.* 15:549–70
71. Kirkpatrick, J. R., Doolin, L. E., Godfrey, O. W. 1973. *Antimicrob. Agents Chemother.* 4:542–50
72. Kitano, K., Kintaka, K., Suzuki, S., Katamoto, K., Nara, K., Nakao, Y. 1975. *J. Ferment. Technol.* 53:327–38
73. Kitano, K., Fujisawa, Y., Katamoto, K., Nara, K., Nakao, Y. 1976. *J. Ferment. Technol.* 54:712–19
74. Kitano, K., Kintaka, K., Nakao, Y. 1976. *J. Ferment. Technol.* 54:696–704
75. Kitano, K., Kintaka, K., Suzuki, S., Katamoto, K., Nara, K., Nakao, Y. 1976. *J. Ferment. Technol.* 54:683–95
76. Kitano, K., Kintaka, K., Suzuki, S., Katamoto, K., Nara, K., Nakao, Y. 1976. *J. Ferment. Technol.* 54:705–11
77. Kitano, K. 1977. *J. Takeda Res. Lab.* 36:(1/2)105–92

78. Kluender, H., Bradley, C. H., Sih, C. J., Fawcett, P. A., Abraham, E. P. 1973. *J. Am. Chem. Soc.* 95:6149–50
79. Kluender, H., Huang, F-C., Fritzberg, A., Schnoes, H., Sih, C. J., Fawcett, P., Abraham, E. P. 1974. *J. Am. Chem. Soc.* 96:4054–55
80. Kohsaka, M., Demain, A. L. 1976. *Biochem. Biophys. Res. Commun.* 70: 465–73
81. Kojo, H., Mine, Y., Nishida, M., Yokota, T. 1977. *J. Antibiot.* 30:926–31
82. Komori, T., Kunugita, K., Nakahara, K., Aoki, H., Imanaka, H. 1978. *Agric. Biol. Chem.* 42:1439–40
83. Kurita, M., Jomon, K., Komori, T., Miyairi, N., Aoki, H., Kuge, S., Kamiya, T., Imanaka, H. 1976. *J. Antibiot.* 29:1243–45
84. Labia, R., Peduzzi, J. 1978. *Biochim. Biophys. Acta* 526:572–79
85. Lemke, P. A., Brannon, D. R. 1972. See Ref. 41, pp. 370–437
86. Liersch, M., Nüesch, J., Treichler, H. J. 1976. In *Proc. 2nd Int. Symp. Genet. Ind. Microorg.*, ed. K. D. MacDonald, pp. 179–95. London: Academic
87. Loder, P. B., Abraham, E. P. 1971. *Biochem. J.* 123:471–76
88. Miller, A. K., Celozzi, E., Pelak, B. A., Stapley, E. O., Hendlin, D. 1972. *Antimicrob. Agents Chemother.* 2:281–86
89. Miller, J. M., Baker, C. N., Thornsberry, C. 1978. *Antimicrob. Agents Chemother.* 14:749–96
90. Mine, Y., Nonoyama, S., Kojo, H., Fukada, S., Nishida, M., Goto, S., Kuwahara, S. 1977. *J. Antibiot.* 30: 932–37
91. Molitor, H., Graessle, O. E. 1950. *Pharmacol. Rev.* 2:1–60
92. Mori, S., Ohsawa, S., Aoki, H., Imanaka, H. 1977. *Jpn. Pat. No. 52-64494* (Published, unexamined)
93. Nagarajan, R., Boeck, L. D., Gorman, M., Hamill, R. L., Higgens, C. E., Hoehn, M. M., Stark, W. M., Whitney, J. G. 1971. *J. Am. Chem. Soc.* 93:2308–10
94. Naylor, J. H. C. 1973. In *Advances in Drug Research,* ed. N. J. Harper, A. B. Simmonds, pp. 1–105. London/New York: Academic
95. Neuss, N., Nash, C. H., Baldwin, J. E., Lemke, P. A., Grutzner, J. B. 1973. *J. Am. Chem. Soc.* 95:3797–98
96. Newton, G. G. F., Abraham, E. P. 1956. *Biochem. J.* 62:651–58
97. Nishida, M., Mine, Y., Nonoyama, S., Kojo, H., Goto, S., Kuwahara, S. 1977. *J. Antibiot.* 30:917–25
98. Okamura, K., Hirata, S., Okumura, Y., Fukagawa, Y., Shimauchi, Y., Kouno, K., Ishikura, T., Lein, J. 1978. *J. Antibiot.* 31:480–82
99. Okamura, K., Hirata, S., Koki, A., Hori, K., Shibamoto, N., Okumura, Y., Okabe, M., Okamoto, R., Kouno, K., Fukagawa, Y., Shimauchi, Y., Ishikura, T., Lein, J. 1979. *J. Antibiot.* 32:262–71
100. Okamura, K., Sakamoto, M., Fukagawa, Y., Ishikura, T., Lein, J. 1979. *J. Antibiot.* 32:280–86
101. Onishi, H. R., Daoust, D. R., Zimmerman, S. B., Hendlin, D., Stapley, E. O. 1974. *Antimicrob. Agents Chemother.* 5:38–48
102. O'Sullivan, J., Aplin, R. T., Stevens, D. M., Abraham, E. P. 1979. *Biochem. J.* 179:47–52
103. Ott, J. L., Godzeski, C. W., Pavey, D., Farran, J. D., Horton, D. R. 1962. *Appl. Microbiol.* 10:515–23
104. Paisley, J. W., Washington, J. A. II. 1978. *Antimicrob. Agents Chemother.* 14:224–27
105. Price, K. E. 1977. In *Structure Activity Relationships Among the Semisynthetic Antibiotics,* ed. D. Perlman, pp. 1–59. New York/San Francisco/London: Academic
106. Price, K. E. 1977. See Ref. 105, pp. 61–86
107. Queener, S. W., Capone, J. J., Raude, A. B., Nagarajan, R. 1974. *Antimicrob. Agents Chemother.* 6:334–37
108. Queener, S. W., Sebek, O. K., Vézina, C. 1978. *Ann. Rev. Microbiol.* 32:593–636
109. Reading, C., Cole, M. 1977. *Antimicrob. Agents Chemother.* 11:852–57
110. Rolinson, G. N., Batchelor, F. R., Butterworth, D., Cameronwood, J., Cole, M., Eustace, G. C., Hart, M. V., Richards, M., Chain, E. B. 1960. *Nature* 187:236–37
111. Sakamoto, M., Iguchi, H., Okamura, K., Hori, S., Fukagawa, Y., Ishikura, T., Lein, J. 1979. *J. Antibiot.* 32:272–79
112. Sassiver, M. L., Lewis, A. 1977. See Ref. 105, pp. 87–160
113. Scannell, J. P., Pruess, D. L., Blount, J. F., Ax, H. A., Kellett, M., Weiss, F., Demny, T. C., Williams, T. H., Stempel, A. 1975. *J. Antibiot.* 28:1–6
114. Shirafuji, H., Fujisawa, Y., Kida, M., Kanzaki, T., Yoneda, M. 1979. *Agric. Biol. Chem.* 43:155–60
115. Stapley, E. O., Jackson, M., Hernandez, S., Zimmerman, S. B., Currie, S. A., Mochales, S., Mata, J. M., Woodruff, H. B., Hendlin, D. 1972. *Antimicrob. Agents Chemother.* 2:122–31
116. Stapley, E. O., Cassidy, P., Currie, S. A., Daoust, D., Goegelman, R., Her-

nandez, S., Jackson, M., Mata, J. M., Miller, A. K., Monaghan, R. L., Tunac, J. B., Zimmerman, S. B., Hendlin, D. 1977. *Proc. Intersci. Conf. Antimicrob. Agents Chemother. 17th, No. 80* (Abstr.)
117. Stewart, W. W. 1971. *Nature:* 229: 174–78
118. Takita, T., Muraoka, Y., Yoshioka, T., Fujii, A., Maeda, K., Umezawa, H. 1972. *J. Antibiot.* 25:755–58
119. Tally, F. P., Jacobus, N. V., Gorbach, S. L. 1978. *Antimicrob. Agents Chemother.* 14:436–38
120. Tomasz, A. 1979. *Ann. Rev. Microbiol.* 33:113–37
121. Traxler, P., Treichler, H. J., Nüesch, J. 1975. *J. Antibiot.* 28:605–6
122. Turner, M. K., Farthing, J. E., Brewer, S. J. 1978. *Biochem. J.* 173:839–50
123. Umezawa, H., Mitsuhashi, S., Hamada, M., Iyobe, S., Takahashi, S., Utahara, R., Osato, Y., Yamazaki, S., Ogawara, H., Maeda, K. 1973. *J. Antibiot.* 26: 51–54
124. Vandamme, E. J. 1977. *Adv. Appl. Microbiol.* 21:89–123
125. Weaver, S. S., Bodey, G. P., LeBlanc, B. M. 1979. *Antimicrob. Agents Chemother.* 15:518–21
126. Webber, J. A., Ott, J. L. 1977. See Ref. 105, pp. 167–337
127. Wheeler, W. J. 1977. *Lloydia* 40: 519–42
128. Whitney, D. J., Brannon, D. R., Mabe, J. A., Wicker, K. J. 1972. *Antimicrob. Agents Chemother.* 1:247–51
129. Wüst, J., Wilkins, T. D. 1978. *Antimicrob. Agents Chemother.* 13:130–33
130. Yoshida, M., Konomi, T., Kohsaka, M., Baldwin, J. E., Herchen, S., Singh, P., Hunt, N. A., Demain, A. L. 1978. *Proc. Natl. Acad. Sci. USA* 75:6253–6257
131. Young, D. W., Morecombe, D. J., Sen, P. K. 1977. *Eur. J. Biochem.* 75:133–47

Ann. Rev. Microbiol. 1980. 34:183–207

OXYGEN AND HYDROGEN IN BIOLOGICAL NITROGEN FIXATION

❖1774

Robert L. Robson and John R. Postgate

Unit of Nitrogen Fixation, University of Sussex, Brighton, BN1 9RQ, United Kingdom

---

CONTENTS

INTRODUCTION 184
INVOLVEMENT OF OXYGEN 184
Effects of Oxygen on Nitrogen-Fixing Systems 184
Protection of the Nitrogen-Fixing System From Oxygen in Vivo 186
Mechanisms of Protection From Oxygen in Azotobacter 186
Respiratory protection 186
Conformational protection 188
Oxygen Regulation of Nitrogenase Synthesis 190
Microaerobic Nitrogen Fixation 191
Xanthobacter (Corynebacterium) autotrophicus and X. (Mycobacterium) flavus 191
Azospirillaceae 191
Rhizobiaceae 192
Methanotrophs 192
Phototrophs 192
Other bacteria 192
Relative oxygen tolerance 192
Conformational Protection in Microaerophilic Diazotrophs 193
Role of Gum 193
The Nodule as an Oxygen-Restricting Compartment 193
Heterocysts as Oxygen-Restricting Compartments 194
Other Protective Strategies 194
INVOLVEMENT OF HYDROGEN 194
Hydrogen as a Substrate for Nitrogen Fixation 195
Hydrogen as an Inhibitor of Nitrogenase 195
The Hydrogen-Deuterium "Exchange" Reaction 195
Hydrogen Evolution by Purified Nitrogenase 197
Hydrogenase in Nitrogen-Fixing Bacteria 199
Hydrogenase and the Recycling of "Waste" Hydrogen 201
Removal of inhibitory hydrogen 201
Enhancement of respiratory protection 201
Provision of ATP and/or reducing power 202
CONCLUSIONS 202

0066-4227/80/1001-0183$01.00

INTRODUCTION

Understanding of biological nitrogen fixation, an exclusively microbiological process, has developed almost explosively in the last two decades. The appearance of numerous books, reviews, and published symposia (e.g. 124, 131–133, 176, 202) testify to the rapid and sometimes spectacular advances that have occurred in the chemistry, enzymology, physiology, microbiology, ecology, and genetics of the process. It is no longer possible to review even these subdivisions adequately in the space available, so we have chosen to concentrate on two aspects of the physiology of nitrogen fixation where important developments have occurred in the last few years.

As background to our review we remind readers of certain features of nitrogen fixation which we shall take for granted since documentation is available in any advanced text on the subject. The enzyme consists of two metalloproteins, both of which are essential for activity. The larger, the MoFe protein, binds the reducible substrate and might be termed the "true" nitrogenase (68) and the smaller, the Fe protein, interacts with ATP and Mg^{2+} in a hydrolytic reaction. Both proteins are irreversibly destroyed by oxygen, the Fe protein most rapidly in vitro, and protection of these proteins from damage by oxygen is one of the overriding principles of the physiology of nitrogen fixation (e.g. 150). Nitrogenase can release H_2 from H_2O and this reaction accompanies reduction of N_2 but not necessarily reduction of N_2 analogues such as C_2H_2. H_2 also inhibits nitrogenase function in vivo with most systems studied so far, though the inhibition is rarely total. O_2 inhibits nitrogenase synthesis in many organisms such as *Klebsiella pneumoniae* or *Bacillus polymyxa,* which then behave like anaerobes or, at best, microaerophiles, if obliged to fix N_2. NH_3, the product of N_2 fixation, represses nitrogenase synthesis at the level of transcription of the *nif* gene cluster. Finally, all free-living nitrogen-fixing bacteria and many symbiotic nitrogen-fixing systems contain the enzyme hydrogenase. In *Desulfovibrio, Clostridium pasteurianum,* and *K. pneumoniae,* normal reversible hydrogenases are present, but in *Azotobacter* and those rhizobia which possess hydrogenase, the dominant enzyme is of the irreversible, uptake class (62).

The literature survey for this review closed in October 1979.

INVOLVEMENT OF OXYGEN

Effects of Oxygen on Nitrogen-Fixing Systems

Both the MoFe and Fe proteins of nitrogenase are irreversibly damaged by O_2, and special anoxic handling techniques are required for their purification and study (70). Fe proteins are the more sensitive: those from *Klebsiella pneumoniae* and *Azotobacter chroococcum* have half lives in air of ca 45 s, that of *A. vinelandii* loses 57% of activity in 2 min; *C. pasteurianum* Fe protein is inactivated by air in 5 min with the concomitant oxidation of two sulfhydryl groups and one S^{2-} group (see 50). ATP augments the O_2 sensitivities of Fe proteins from *K. pneumoniae* and *A. chroococcum* (52, 206). O_2-inactivated proteins have no electron paramagnetic resonance (EPR) spectrum and the Mössbauer spectrum of O_2-inactivated *K. pneumoniae* protein resembles that of reduced ferredoxin. Several distinct phases may be associated with O_2 inactivation; the initial stages result not in destruction of the FeS center but in subtle change that renders the protein incapable of accepting electrons (171). The α-helical content of both *K. pneumoniae* and *C. pasteurianum* Fe proteins decreased when O_2-damaged as shown by circular dichroism (CD) spectroscopy (29, 51); oxidation by air increased 420-nm absorption of Fe proteins from *C. pasteurianum, A. vinelandii, A. Chroococcum,* and *K. pneumoniae* (see 50).

MoFe proteins are less sensitive to O_2. Controlled oxidation by O_2 while retaining activity is possible, although prolonged exposure causes irreversible inactivation. MoFe proteins from *C. pasteurianum* were still 30% active after 1 h exposure to air while those of *A. vinelandii* and *A. chroococcum* have half lives of 10 min, *K. pneumoniae* 8 min, and *Rhizobium japonicum* 4.5 min (see 50). EPR spectroscopy indicates that exposure to O_2 results in a sequence of changes probably associated with various oxidation states of the Fe atoms (34, 57, 73, 143, 172); these findings are further amplified by the effects of O_2 on its Mössbauer spectrum (97, 171). O_2 increases the 460 nm absorption (51, 194, 211); small oxidative changes in the α-helical content of *C. pasteurianum* MoFe proteins occur (29) and prolonged exposure to air caused loss of S^{2-}, Mo, and Fe (83). X-ray absorption edge fine structure spectroscopy (EXAFS) indicates that Mo-O bonding is found only after O_2 inactivation (30–32). The FeMo cofactor, which can be extracted from MoFe protein, reactivates nitrogenase activity in various mutants and is more O_2 labile than the Fe protein (166).

All the data recently reviewed (50) are consistent with the view that O_2 lability of these proteins involves metal-S centers in each protein which participate in either substrate binding or electron transfer. Oxygen reduction probably proceeds by a univalent pathway in which O_2^-, H_2O_2 followed by OH^- and possibly singlet oxygen are generated; some of these species are more reactive than O_2 and may contribute greatly to oxidative damage. While the Fe protein from *C. pasteurianum* could be 50% oxidized (as judged by increase in 440 nm absorbance) before inactivation occurred, in the presence of superoxide dismutase and catalase, 97% oxidation resulted in loss of only 19% activity indicating that superoxide or peroxide were responsible in part for inactivation (125).

The nitrogenase proteins are not the only components of the nitrogen-fixing systems which are O_2 sensitive. Electron carriers to nitrogenase are usually either ferredoxins or flavodoxins (207). Both can show autoxidation and sometimes irreversible oxidative damage. Flavodoxin hydroquinone, believed to be the primary electron donor to *Azotobacter* nitrogenase, is rapidly autoxidized (208) and may, like other flavin hydroquinones, generate O_2^- on autoxidation. In living aerobic cells, the natural oxygen lability of the nitrogen-fixing systems might be augmented by the generation of O_2^- in response to extreme oxygenation.

Protection of the Nitrogen-Fixing System From Oxygen in Vivo

Despite the O_2 lability of nitrogenase proteins in vitro, the capacity to fix N_2 is found in obligate aerobes and oxygenic photosynthetic prokaryotes as well as in obligate and facultative anaerobes. For all N_2-fixing organisms O_2 is potentially inhibitory to growth and such protective mechanisms as exist are only conditionally effective. Among aerobic N_2-fixing organisms we distinguish between those capable of initiating growth on N_2 in an environment initially equilibrated with air (aerobic N_2 fixation) and those which only initiate growth at subatmospheric O_2 concentrations (microaerobic N_2 fixation). Much of our understanding of mechanisms for protection of nitrogenase from O_2 derives from studies with *Azotobacter* and with those cyanobacteria that overcome the special problem arising from their simultaneous photosynthetic O_2-evolution.

Mechanisms of Protection From Oxygen in Azotobacter

RESPIRATORY PROTECTION It has long been known that O_2 inhibits growth of *Azotobacter* species when fixing N_2 (19, 121, 160, 189) and that N_2 fixation is more efficient at low O_2 tensions (98, 144). The finding that *A. vinelandii,* given excess O_2, consumed more carbon source than required to satisfy its energy requirement for growth led Phillips & Johnson (147) to propose that respiration functioned as an "O_2-wasting" system.

More detailed studies with *A. chroococcum* (35, 36), often employing chemostat cultures, confirmed the O_2 sensitivity of N_2-fixing populations and also the decrease in nitrogen-fixing efficiency with increasing aeration. Increased aeration elicited an increase in respiration and a decrease in the Y_C substrate and Y_{O_2} while maintaining a low dissolved O_2 tension, indicating that the respiratory system adapted to limit the diffusion of O_2 into the organism. This mechanism was termed respiratory protection. Consistent with this view, both C-limited and P-limited N_2-fixing populations were hypersensitive to O_2. P-limited cultures showed an apparent loss of viability during O_2 stress when tested on N-free media but not on a medium containing NH_4^+ (108), indicating that nitrogenase was irreversibly damaged when respiration failed to keep pace with increased oxygenation.

Respiratory protection entails adaptation of the respiratory system in response to increased oxygenation. Respiratory rates in azotobacters may attain very high values (199) and as a consequence, energy conservation efficiency is lowered, which has been expressed variously as a decrease in Y_C, Y_{O_2}, or efficiency of nitrogen fixation vis a vis carbon substrate, or as an increase in the maintenance energy requirement (35, 36, 45, 126–128).

Numerous studies show that the protective response partly depends on subtle adjustments in the composition and functioning of the respiratory chain, which is itself complex. It has been studied most fully in *A. vinelandii* and has been reviewed elsewhere (66, 86). Aspects apparently important to respiratory protection are the following.

1. Terminal "branching" occurs after cytochrome *b,* providing two alternative major routes of electrons to O_2. Only one (cytochromes *b* through c_4, c_5 to a_1o) and not the other (cytochromes *b* to *d*) is associated with an energy conservation site (site III).
2. There is an obligatory central segment (ubiquinone to cytochrome *b*) which provides energy conservation site II.
3. Only one of the associated dehydrogenases, NADH oxidase, is associated with an energy conservation site (site I), whereas NADPH and malate oxidases are not.

No new components are induced by growth on N_2 in either *A. vinelandii* or *A. chroococcum* (35, 36, 47, 102), although changes in absolute and relative amounts of cytochromes are observed. Generally, increased aeration decreases the overall concentration of cytochromes except cytochrome *d* (1, 47, 64, 112, 135, 182) and simultaneously elevates the activities of one or more of the respiratory chain dehydrogenases (1).

Therefore, unless growth is limited by O_2, the dominant terminal branch, that from cytochromes *b* to *d,* bypasses energy conservation site III. Studies with membrane vesicles (1, 88) or with whole organisms (44, 87) show a loss in energy conservation site I in highly aerated populations. The mechanism is not clear, but the degree of uncoupling at site I is determined by the degree of reduction of ubiquinone (105). Also, a fourth energy conservation site may be associated with the uptake hydrogenase in *Azotobacter* (105, 210) and its efficiency of energy coupling is lowered by excess O_2, possibly as a result of inhibition of hydrogenase (105). Specific "energy-slip" reactions may contribute to decreases in efficiency of energy conservation because discrepancies exist between the degrees of uncoupling provided by loss of sites I and III and the observed decreases in Y_C substrate values (66, 74).

The factors which control the respiratory rate are probably several and may depend upon cultural conditions. Control may be exerted at the level of the respiratory chain. The O_2 tension in the culture may influence respiration rate: the values of K_m for the O_2 of the terminal oxidases [(18 μM for cytochrome *d,* 3 μM for cytochrome *o* (82)] lie in the range (15 to 30 μM) found in steady-state N_2-fixing cultures (35, 36). The respiratory chain is probably subject to respiratory control in *Azotobacter,* as even exogenous ATP influences the respiratory rate of *A. chroococcum* (204); the failure of respiration to adapt following O_2 stress in P-limited chemostat populations of *A. chroococcum* (108) supports this view. In isolated membranes from *A. vinelandii,* respiratory control at the obligatory energy conservation site II is influenced by the "electron-pressure" across the transport chain. Increases in the ratio of activities of terminal oxidases with respect to dehydrogenases reduces respiratory control at this site (89). Therefore, increased aeration may weaken respiratory control. Evidence obtained using isolated membranes (1, 105) indicates that the activities of the associated dehydrogenases limit the flow of electrons along the respiratory chain, a conclusion also supported by the reduction in content of some cytochromes observed upon increased oxygenation. Therefore, the increases in specific activities of these dehydrogenases with increased aeration may have a significant influence on the respiratory rate in vivo (1, 64).

Obviously, other factors may also limit or control the metabolic flux. Poor carbon substrates may lower the potential respiration rate; glycollate, which only supports growth in *A. chroococcum* if NH_4^+ is present (103), is probably an extreme example of this kind. Sucrose-grown batch cultures of *A. vinelandii* respire more rapidly with pyruvate than with sucrose, implying that sucrose transport or early steps in its metabolism limit the respiration rate with this substrate (64).

A number of studies indicate that oxygen metabolism is closely integrated with general cell metabolism (64, 103, 179). Detailed examination of the catabolism of *Azotobacter beijerinckii* (25, 85, 165, 175, 195) indicates that increased oxygenation increases the specific activities of key catabolic enzymes of the Entner & Doudoroff pathway and tricarboxylic acid (TCA) cycle, as well as decreasing the specific activities of enzymes involved in poly-β-hydroxybutyrate (PHB) synthesis.

In conclusion, respiratory protection in *Azotobacter* results not from some simple mechanism but rather from an orchestrated series of changes which have both kinetic and genetic bases.

CONFORMATIONAL PROTECTION Studies on the influence of O_2 on N_2 fixation in chemostat cultures of *A. chroococcum* led to the proposal (35) that, in addition to active protection by respiration, O_2 stress could cause nitrogenase in vivo to assume a conformation in which it was protected from O_2, though unable to reduce N_2. N_2 fixation could be totally inhibited by excess oxygenation (switch-off), and activity returned rapidly when aeration was lowered (switch-on) without nitrogenase synthesis de novo (46, 47, 204). The switched-off condition was taken to be an expression of the conformationally protected state. Excessive O_2 stress inactivated nitrogenase by specific damage to the Fe protein (47).

The O_2 stability of *Azotobacter* nitrogenase in crude extracts (17, 95, 96) was also considered to be a manifestation of the conformationally protected state (47). Initially there was no evidence whether conformational protection resulted from some specific relative orientation of the two nitrogenase proteins themselves or from association of both with one or more stabilizing factors. The possibility of involvement of membranes was considered (139, 152) but later questioned (79, 145). Some stabilization was obtained by addition of various crude extract fractions (95, 205) or divalent cations (206).

Studies of partially purified O_2-stable preparations from *Azotobacter* have shown that conformational protection results from association with a third protein. In *A. vinelandii,* stability resulted from an association between the nitrogenase proteins and another FeS protein (63, 65, 158). The protein (*A. vinelandii* FeSII) had been purified and characterized much earlier (40, 90, 141, 167). It has a reported molecular weight of 24,000, possibly contains more than one polypeptide chain (191), contains an Fe_2S_2 center, is aerotolerant and has optical, EPR, and CD spectra similar to those of spinach ferredoxin. On reduction, it accepts a single electron per pair of Fe atoms; its E'_0 of -225 mV is considerably less negative than that of spinach ferredoxin but is similarly pH independent. A more highly purified but still O_2-stable form of nitrogenase from *A. chroococcum* also contains a protective FeS protein in an equimolar stoichiometric complex with the nitrogenase proteins. Its molecular weight is 14,000 but in many details resembles the FeS protein II from *A. vinelandii.* It was protective in reconstitution experiments (154).

Neither protective protein is considered to participate in electron transfer to nitrogenase, nor do they markedly stabilize the separate nitrogenase components; although electron transfer occurs from the reduced Fe protein of nitrogenase to these proteins there is no evidence for a tight complex between them (191; R. N. F. Thorneley and R. L. Robson, unpublished). Protection also depends on the presence of Mg^{2+}, which may also induce considerable aggregation of nitrogenase, giving rise to the so-called particulate form of the enzyme observed in crude extracts (17, 95). Whether aggregation provides additional protection is not known. Though O_2-induced "switch-off" of activity was earlier thought to be an expression of conformational protection, this is not necessarily true. Flavodoxin is the putative electron donor to nitrogenase in *Azotobacter,* and deflection of electrons from nitrogenase by rapid autoxidation of flavodoxin hydroquinone may explain the switch-off phenomenon (158, 208). If so, the inclusion of an extremely O_2-sensitive but O_2-stable electron carrier in the electron transfer steps to nitrogenase may be an important element in the mechanism of conformational protection, since it may act as an O_2 sensor. The sequence of events leading to the conformationally protected nitrogenase in vivo will probably be resolved when a full understanding has been gained of the interactions in vitro between flavodoxin, nitrogenase components, and protective proteins, with particular reference to the redox states of the various proteins at various stages of oxidation. The protective protein may also regulate nitrogenase activity in *Azotobacter vinelandii* (158), as was suggested by the early physiological experiments, but its presence is not obligatory for nitrogenase activity.

Oxygen Regulation of Nitrogenase Synthesis

Repression of nitrogenase synthesis by O_2 has been observed in *Klebsiella pneumoniae, Rhizobium* 32H1, and *Azotobacter chroococcum*—organisms representing the spectrum of oxygen tolerance. It may be a general phenomenon, ensuring that wasteful synthesis of nitrogenase is avoided.

As O_2 stress causes loss of nitrogenase activity in vivo, evidence for O_2 repression must depend on determinations of the rate of synthesis of the enzyme; pulse-labelling techniques are probably the most reliable.

O_2 repression was first observed in *K. pneumoniae* and was suggested by observations that aerobic N_2 fixation did not occur (146). These observations were considerably strengthened by the finding that O_2 exposure of organisms resulted in the loss of immunologically detectable nitrogenase (180) and were confirmed by pulse-labelling studies (48) in which the half life for decay of synthesis of nitrogenase polypeptides in air was approximately 11 min, similar to that for NH_4^+ repression.

In *A. chroococcum,* pulse-labelling studies revealed that, when respiratory protection was overburdened by excess O_2, synthesis of nitrogenase was repressed. O_2 repression was more rapid than was observed for *K. pneumoniae* and was considerably faster than NH_4^+ repression. O_2 probably also repressed synthesis of the putative electron donor flavodoxin but did not appear to affect the concentration of the protective protein (155).

In *Rhizobium* strain 32H1, using antiserum prepared against *R. japonicum* MoFe protein, MoFe protein cross-reacting material could not be detected in highly aerobic chemostat cultures (6), although some cross-reacting material was observed in aerobic batch culures of *R. japonicum* (10). Recently pulse-labelling studies confirm O_2 repression of nitrogenase in *R. japonicum* (H. Hennecke, personal communication).

The mechanism of O_2 repression in *K. pneumoniae* will probably be resolved in the near future, largely as a result of the rapid progress in our understanding of the genetics of nitrogen fixation in this organism. Questions pertinent to O_2 regulation are as follows. Is it mediated by the same mechanism as NH_4^+ repression or is the mechanism related to the more general genetic regulation by O_2 of respiratory enzymes, etc? What is the O_2 sensing mechanism and are all the *nif* gene products repressed by O_2?

Developments in our understanding of genetic regulation of the *nif* cluster have been reviewed recently (119) and include the use of *lac*Z fusions within *nif* genes as a means of studying their expression. This clearly is a significant advance for the study of O_2 regulation, as constitutive mutants may be studied without the interference normally associated with inactivation of nitrogenase by O_2. In the *nif* cluster, in which a minimum of 15 genes have been identified, one or possibly two genes, designated as *nif* A/L, are involved in regulation. The product of *nif*A is required for *nif* expression, whereas a revertant of a mutation in *nif*L is not subject to O_2 repression to the same extent as the parent strain (C. K. Kennedy and S. Hill, unpublished data). This suggests that the product of *nif*L is involved in O_2 regulation in this organism.

Microaerobic Nitrogen Fixation

Though respiratory protection has been most studied in *Azotobacter*, respiration per se can obviously be protective in any organism capable of aerobic metabolism. Most genera of aerobic diazotrophs are more sensitive to O_2 than azotobacters and appear to lack the highly developed and rapid response to O_2 stress shown by *Azotobacter* (108). Failure to recognize the prevalence of such O_2 sensitivity has sometimes led to confusion regarding their physiology or failure to detect fixation at all. Examples of aerobic diazotrophs which are microaerophilic when fixing N_2 include the following.

XANTHOBACTER (CORYNEBACTERIUM) AUTOTROPHICUS AND X. (MYCOBACTERIUM) FLAVUS The hydrogen-oxidizing nitrogen-fixing bacteria have been grouped in a new genus *Xanthobacter* (117a, 197), and all show only microaerobic fixation: optimal growth at 0.05 atm O_2 (61) and inhibition by 0.13 atm O_2 (38) have been quoted. *X. flavus* (as *M. flavum* 301) was thought to require other organisms (58) or organic N (114) to fix N_2 but since axenic cultures grew well without fixed N in continuous culture it is likely that these apparent prerequisites were simply expressions of microaerophily (9).

AZOSPIRILLACEAE These grow well in air with NH_4^+ but diazotrophy is microaerobic and the organisms, in semisolid media, form a pellicle below the meniscus. No adaptive response to O_2 stress comparable to respiratory protection was observed in *A. brasilense* (129, 137).

RHIZOBIACEAE That the "slow-growing" rhizobia (*R. japonicum,* cowpea species) can grow diazotrophically *ex planta* on solid (104, 118, 142) or liquid (6, 91, 187) media is well established. The organisms are exceptionally O_2 sensitive and the apparent requirement for two substrates (104, 118, 142) is simply a reflection of the need for a rapidly respirable substrate (6). No adaptive response to O_2 stress was detected (6); the need for fixed N in diazotrophic culture has not been eliminated (60) and may not be entirely explicable in terms of O_2 sensitivity.

METHANOTROPHS These show only microaerobic diazotrophy (37, 39). The initial enzyme of methane oxidation, methane monooxygenase (75, 106) consumes O_2; in *Methylospira capsulatus* its activity is augmented in response to increased O_2, and the organisms show hypersensitivity to O_2 if methane is replaced by methanol as growth substrate. Therefore the enzyme probably contributes significantly to the protection of nitrogenase (33).

PHOTOTROPHS The filamentous cyanobacterium *Plectonema boryanum* was the first to be recognized (177) of a substantial group of nonheterocystous cyanobacteria which show only microaerobic diazotrophy (see review by W. D. P. Stewart in this volume). Nitrogen fixation by the photosynthetic anaerobe *Rhodopseudomonas capsulata* shows some degree of oxygen tolerance, attributed to H_2-based respiratory protection (see below).

OTHER BACTERIA *Thiobacillus ferrooxidans* shows only microaerobic diazotrophy (115); the spasmodic nature of reports of diazotrophic arthrobacters may have a similar cause since *Arthrobacter fluorescens* is very O_2 sensitive (23). *Derxia gummosa,* though a member of the Azotobacteriaceae, shows greater O_2 sensitivity than azotobacters (76); *Klebsiella pneumoniae,* though normally regarded as an obligatory anaerobic diazotroph, can be grown with air if its respiration scavenges dissolved O_2 effectively (77, 78, 100).

RELATIVE OXYGEN TOLERANCE The dissolved O_2 tension (dO_2) in a culture of a diazotroph is the resultant of the respiration rate and oxygen solution rate. It is influenced by many factors including the geometry of the culture vessel, the substrate being utilized, the population density, and the temperature. Values of dO_2 are of little value for a precise comparison of oxygen tolerance between species but we record some published data for steady state dO_2 since they illustrate the ranges customarily encountered:

cowpea rhizobium strain 32H1, ~ 1 μM (6); *X. autotrophicus* 9229, 4.4 μM (7); *A. brasilense,* ~ 8 μM (129); *A. lipoferum,* ~ 7 μM (138); *Methylosporus capsulatus* Bath, 9.8 μM (33); *A. chroococcum* (N_2 limited) 20 μM (36), P limited 10 μM (36, 108); *A. chroococcum* (probably O_2 limited despite exceptional oxygenation) < 3 μM (80). Values of over 60 μM (188) or 100 μM (23) are difficult to credit.

Conformational Protection in Microaerophilic Diazotrophs

The concept of conformational protection in *Azotobacter* arose from four main observations: regulation of nitrogenase according to the time of exposure to O_2 in chemostats; decreased activity at higher O_2 concentration in the "bell-shaped curve" relating activity to pO_2; existence of oxygen tolerance in crude nitrogenase preparations; reversible inactivation of nitrogenase by O_2 stress (switch on-off) (150). The process has not been widely sought in other organisms. Switch on-off need not imply conformational protection (see above) but oxygen tolerant subcellular particles with nitrogenase activity imply conformational protection (e.g. 9), provided that residual intact cells are excluded. Postgate (151) recorded that the diazotrophic anaerobes *Clostridium pasteurianum* and *K. pneumoniae* could be harvested in air without damage to their nitrogenase, whereas *Desulfovibrio desulfuricans* could not; this fact implies passive protection of nitrogenase in vivo in the first two but not in the latter organism.

Role of Gum

Most diazotrophs cultivated in air form abundant extracellular polysaccharides (gum) which may help to generate a locally microaerobic environment. This topic has not been studied systematically in aerobic or microaerophilic diazotrophs, though non-gummy mutants exist of *A. vinelandii, A. chroococcum,* and *Derxia gummosa* which seem to have no special O_2 sensitivity (22, 211; F. O. Pedrosa, J. Döbereiner and M. G. Yates, submitted for publication). In conditions in which *K. pneumoniae* would grow diazotrophically in air, Wilcockson (198) could find no correlation between gumminess and O_2 tolerance.

The Nodule as an Oxygen-Restricting Compartment

Leghemoglobin is essential for effective nitrogen-fixing legume symbioses and without it fixation is slow or absent. Work by the Canberra group, in particular, has rationalized the role of leghemoglobin as an oxygen transport protein which delivers O_2 for aerobic diazotrophy by the bacteroids yet which, because of its high affinity for O_2, prevents the local dO_2 from reaching concentrations damaging to nitrogenase. Physiological experiments with bacteroids as well as kinetic data for O_2 uptake by leghemoglobin and the bacteroid respiratory oxidase are consistent with this view, as is the marked oxygen sensitivity of rhizobial fixation *ex planta*; details will not be given here as a comprehensive review has been published recently (41). The legume nodule thus emerges as a physiological compartment for protecting nitrogenase from oxygen as well as for supplying bacteroids with photosynthate. Leghemoglobin is a sophistication rather than essential, because *Parasponia* (*Trema*) forms functional nodules without leghemoglobin and its physiological equivalents have not (yet) been described in *Frankia* or cyanobacterial associations. Diffusion barriers partially contribute to oxygen restriction in nodules, and respiratory protection involving hydrogenase probably occurs within the bacteroids (below).

Heterocysts as Oxygen-Restricting Compartments

Oxygenic photosynthetic bacteria (Cyanobacteria) have a special problem in protecting nitrogenase because photoevolution of O_2 augments any normal environmental O_2 stress. Stewart (see review in this volume) has reviewed evidence that the heterocysts of certain filamentous cyanobacteria are compartments in which access of O_2 to nitrogenase is restricted in various ways. With the exception of *Gloeocapsa,* nonheterocystous cyanobacteria are microaerophilic and photosensitive in diazotrophic culture. We refer readers to Dr. Stewart's chapter for more details.

Other Protective Strategies

Clustering of the marine cyanobacteria *Trichodesmium* has been held to protect those inside the cluster for oxygen and thus facilitate nitrogen fixation within the cluster (24). Temporal separation of nitrogen fixation from photosynthesis is one of the proposals (59) to account for the oxygen tolerance of the coccoid cyanobacterium, *Gloeocapsa.*

Casual associations with aerobic heterotrophs must surely protect the nitrogenase of diazotrophs in many natural environments of high C/N ratio.

INVOLVEMENT OF HYDROGEN

Hydrogen is directly involved in nitrogenase action in four ways. It can be an oxidizable substrate for nitrogen fixation; it inhibits nitrogen fixation; nitrogenase can catalyze the formation of HD from deuterium; nitrogenase can evolve H_2 from water. In addition, the enzyme hydrogenase is usually present alongside nitrogenase and is now known to augment the efficiency of nitrogen fixation. The involvement of H_2 is thus complex and multiple; the topic features in recent symposia on both nitrogen fixation (132, 133) and hydrogen metabolism (159) and has been the subject of a symposium in its own right (192).

Hydrogen as a Substrate for Nitrogen Fixation

Mortenson (122) showed that the hydrogenase of *Clostridium pasteurianum* donated electrons to clostridial nitrogenase in vitro. Hydrogen and hydrogenase preparations, with a viologen dye substituting for a ferredoxin or flavodoxin, are sometimes useful alternatives to sodium dithionite, deazaflavin, or chloroplast preparations for laboratory studies on nitrogenase (e.g. 196). Whether hydrogen contributes to nitrogen fixation in living clostridia is not clear, but it probably does so in the cyanobacteria (see 11). In *Klebsiella pneumoniae,* Hill (78) found no contribution by exogenous H_2, but Yates & Walker (212) have evidence that H_2 augments acetylene reduction by intact *Azotobacter chroococcum.* The discovery of nitrogen fixation among certain of the hydrogen bacteria, the group now designated *Xanthobacter* (*Corynebacterium*) *autotrophicus* (197), now provides unequivocal evidence for hydrogen-supported nitrogen fixation in vivo: such facultative autotrophs are capable of exploiting H_2/O_2 reactions for both CO_2 and N_2 fixation.

Hydrogen as an Inhibitor of Nitrogenase

Hydrogen has been known since the mid-1930s to inhibit nitrogen fixation, as Wilson (201) amusingly described. Hydrogenase was once thought to be directly involved but the effect could be demonstrated in nodules lacking hydrogenase activity. More recent biochemical studies have shown that H_2 inhibition of nitrogenase can take place in vitro and that it is specific to N_2 reduction: H_2 does not inhibit acetylene reduction or hydrogen evolution, for example (see 21, 72, 84), nor does ATP hydrolysis cease (67). Most authorities agree that H_2 inhibition is competitive (see 21) which, according to conventional enzymological dogma, would imply reversible competitive binding of H_2 to the N_2-fixing site. H_2 will displace bound N_2 from certain Mo dinitrogen complexes (3). However reversible competitive binding may be too simplistic an interpretation, because H_2 inhibition and the H/D reaction, both N_2-specific, have mechanistic features in common. This point is amplified in the next section.

The Hydrogen-Deuterium "Exchange" Reaction

H/D "exchange" by soybean nodules is greater under N_2 than under He (5, 81). This finding implied that nitrogenase catalyzed H/D "exchange," an unexpected reaction since N_2 reduction itself is irreversible and no $^{15}N_2/^{14}N_2$ exchange occurs (see 72). Burris (21) described earlier studies;

despite doubts (94), the consensus is that, both in nodules and *Azotobacter,* the reaction is only significant when N_2 is being reduced, not when acetylene, other N_2 analogues, or H^+ are the reducible substrates. The reaction occurs with nitrogenase preparations freed of contaminating hydrogenase; it requires ATP and is inhibited by CO. Levels of N_2 well below the apparent K_m for NH_4 formation induce maximum HD formation (15); even N_2 contaminating Ar or He can induce the reaction. Hardy & Burns (71) suggested that N_2 specificity implied formation of an intermediate dinitrogen hydride capable of H/D exchange and favored a species at the diimide level of oxidation, a view shared by Schrauzer (161) on the basis of H/D formation during reductive decomposition of a molybdenum thiol complex. Bulen (15) concluded that HD was the product of "a D_2-induced decomposition of a labile intermediate in N_2 reduction" because electrons were apparently consumed in HD formation. For example, the following futile cycle would yield HD and regenerate N_2 from a bound diimide intermediate while consuming two electrons, one per HD produced:

$$E + N_2 \rightarrow E{:}N_2 \xrightarrow[\substack{2e \\ 2H^+}]{+\,ATP} E{:}N_2H_2 \xrightarrow{+\,D_2} \begin{matrix} E{:}N_2 \\ +\,2HD \end{matrix} \rightarrow E + N_2$$

Whatever the mechanism, the "exchange" reaction is not an exchange at all, but an inhibitory side reaction induced by exogenous D_2. Obviously H_2 would mimic D_2, so a reaction scheme of this kind accounts for both HD "exchange" and H_2 inhibition. Further work by the Kettering Group (18, 130, 178) has supported this mechanism: the reaction is shown by highly purified *Azotobacter vinelandii* nitrogenase; it consumes one electron/HD; its extent is influenced by component ratio and ATP supply; hydrazine, a poor but real substrate for nitrogenase, does not augment HD formation. The reaction was not entirely N_2 dependent: in the putative absence of N_2, HD formation to about 6% of the maximum was reported. In the mechanism above, D_2 or H_2 reacts directly with the intermediate dinitrogen hydride without interaction with the solvent. Consistent with this view, Burgess et al (18) found little T_2O when the atmosphere was labelled with T_2: 98% of HD arose without solvent interaction. A conceivable intermediate is that demonstrated by Thorneley, Eady & Lowe (185) but it is probably not diimide (183). The idea that an intermediate in N_2 reduction is involved arises from the N_2 specificity of HD formation. Interpretation in terms of reductive formation of enzyme hydrides can be put forward, in which the bound protons are leaving groups for N_2 binding but can also interact with D_2 or H_2. A hypothesis along these lines, which encompasses N_2 specificity, has been proposed by Chatt (27).

Hydrogen Evolution by Purified Nitrogenase

Nitrogenase, in the absence of a substrate such as nitrogen, discharges the hydrogen ion to form gaseous hydrogen, an irreversible reaction which consumes ATP. First observed with crude nitrogenase preparations (16), it is shown by the purest nitrogenase preparations obtained so far; the nitrogenase of *Rhodospirillum rubrum* requires activation for this as for other functions (see 136).

That H_2 evolution has mechanistic differences from N_2 reduction has been likely since the early discovery (14, 20) that the H_2-evolving function of nitrogenase is insensitive to CO, though the reduction of N_2, C_2H_2, and other nitrogen analogues is inhibited by this gas. CO insensitivity also tends to exclude any close mechanistic relationship to the H_2 inhibition and HD formation reactions just discussed. Differential inhibition of acetylene reduction over H_2 evolution was observed by Eady et al (49) when structural analogues of ATP were introduced into functioning enzyme preparations. ATP interacts with the Fe protein of nitrogenase, so these observations imply a second role for ATP, interacting with the MoFe protein probably at the $N_2(C_2H_2)$-binding site. They might also imply that the geometry or location of the H^+-binding site is different. On the other hand, ATP analogues may have nonspecific actions on electron distribution between H^+ and other substrates simply by lowering the effective ATP concentration at the functioning enzyme; but other data (186) support an involvement of ATP with the MoFe protein.

Smith et al (173) studied hybrid nitrogenase composed of Fe protein from *C. pasteurianum* + MoFe protein from *K. pneumoniae* and showed that, though linear H_2 evolution took place immediately after the reaction was initiated, acetylene reduction showed a lag of some minutes. N_2 reduction showed a longer lag (170). Thorneley & Eady (184) found a similar lag in C_2H_2 or N_2 reduction, during which a concomitant burst of H_2 evolution took place, using homologous *K. pneumoniae* nitrogenase at low temperatures (10°C) or with a marked imbalance of Fe to MoFe protein. These findings suggest that an activation state of nitrogenase is necessary for C_2H_2 or N_2 reduction, which is not needed for H_2 evolution. H_2-evolving nitrogenase shows a small but distinctive EPR signal which is bleached by C_2H_2 but enhanced by N_2 (113, 209); in mechanistic schemes for interpreting the EPR signals observable in functioning nitrogenase (113), a different species is regarded as reacting with H^+ from that which reacts with C_2H_2 or N_2. The various EPR signals may represent different activation states of the enzyme or different allosteric forms, or both: all are assignable to Fe atoms in the MoFe protein.

H_2 evolution persists in the presence of alternative substrates such as cyanide or isocyanide according to early experiments (93), but acetylene suppresses H_2 evolution almost completely (e.g. 73). Rivera-Ortez & Burris (153) studied the effects of N_2, CN^- and C_2H_2 on H_2 evolution in detail and concluded that N_2, unlike CN^- or C_2H_2, "could not compete completely with H^+ for electrons." H_2 evolution accompanies nitrogen reduction by even the purest nitrogenase preparations, even under 6 atm of N_2 (67). It represents a wastage of biological energy as ATP; the question arises whether it is an intrinsic property of the enzyme system. Low levels of ATP supply augmented H_2 evolution over nitrogen reduction with crude *A. vinelandii* nitrogenase (67), and many workers have observed that the proportion of H_2 evolved by purified nitrogenase under nitrogen is influenced by the ratio of the Fe protein to the MoFe protein, since deficiency of Fe protein tends to increase H_2 evolution (e.g. 184). Thorneley & Eady (184) observed a greater proportion of H_2 evolution at 10 than at 30°C with purified *K. pneumoniae* nitrogenase. Yates & Walker (212) reported that a combination of low ATP and high relative MoFe protein greatly increased the ratio of H_2 evolved to N_2 reduced by purified *A. chroococcum* nitrogenase. In no experiment was less than 1 mol H_2 formed/mol N_2 reduced by the cell free enzyme; low levels of H_2 evolved by intact cells could be accounted for as hydrogen recycled by hydrogenase. That hydrogen evolution seems never to be less than 1 mol/mol N_2 reduced in vitro suggests that this is a stoichiometric minimum: that nitrogen reduction, unlike acetylene reduction, necessarily involves a hydrogen evolution step. The question was posed by Orme-Johnson (140) and discussed by Schrauzer (162), Nikonova & Shilov (134), Yates & Walker (212), and Chatt (27); chemical interpretations of H_2 evolution under N_2 have been proposed along two lines. Chatt (27) considered preliminary reduction of protons to hydrides, two of which groups (as H_2) are displaced when N_2 binds; others favor disproportionation of a dinitrogen hydride intermediate at the diimide level of oxidation; the discussion resembles that concerned with HD formation and H_2 inhibition. Spontaneous disproportionation of an intermediate would, however, require a ratio of H_2-evolved to N_2-reduced of less than 1. H_2 evolution under N_2 appears to be mechanistically different from the CO-insensitive H_2 evolution that occurs in the absence of N_2; it is not simply a matter of competition with H^+ for electrons but is an intrinsic part of the N_2 reduction process. It follows that the simple 6 electron stoichiometry for nitrogen fixation ($N_2 + 6H^+$ 6e $2NH_3$) is incorrect; whether Schrauzer's (162) formulation ($N_2 + 8H^+$ 8e $2NH_3 + H_2$) is a correct representation of the enzymic stoichiometry remains to be established.

Hydrogenase in Nitrogen-Fixing Bacteria

The hydrogenase-nitrogenase correlation (200, 201) can be paraphrased in this form: all nitrogen-fixing bacteria possess hydrogenase but not all organisms which have hydrogenase fix nitrogen. The correlation was always imperfect because hydrogenase was rarely demonstrable in legume nodules. Since nitrogenase is now known to evolve H_2 and to catalyze HD formation, thus simulating two of the properties of a reversible hydrogenase, some earlier evidence for the presence of hydrogenase might seem suspect but, after tests with dyestuffs, the correlation has held up in all instances for which it has been claimed.

Hydrogenase is present in anaerobic nitrogen-fixing bacteria such as *Clostridium pasteurianum, Klebsiella pneumoniae,* or *Desulfovibrio desulfuricans,* whether fixing nitrogen or not. In these organisms a conventional reversible hydrogenase is present, though recently unidirectional hydrogenase has also been reported in *C. pasteurianum* (28). Bothe et al (11) reviewed its distribution in cyanobacteria, where photoevolution of H_2 complicates the picture, but this reaction seems to be assignable to nitrogenase. Cyanobacterial hydrogenase seems to be unidirectional and constitutive, inhibited by CO and C_2H_2. Its synthesis is apparently augmented by H_2, but since O_2 influences hydrogenase contents in many organisms (101), the evidence that H_2 "induction" is not a result of depletion of photoproduced O_2 by H_2 is not always convincing. Light-dependent and light-independent H_2/O_2 reactions exist, and low levels of reverse hydrogenase activity have been detected in *Anabena.* Hydrogen metabolism in cyanobacteria is discussed more extensively by Stewart (see review in this volume).

Hydrogenase is constitutive in photosynthetic anaerobes such as *Rhodospirillum rubrum* and *Rhodopseudomonas capsulata,* though growth conditions influence its activity (see 120); however, a connection between expression of hydrogenase and nitrogen fixation genes may exist in *Rhodopseudomonas acidophila* (168). Hydrogenase is present in aerobic heterotrophs and Wilson's group presented evidence that hydrogenase of *Azotobacter* was partly regulated in parallel with nitrogenase: that N_2-fixing populations had higher hydrogenase activities than NH_4- or NO_3-grown populations (107). These experiments were made with batch cultures and activity was much influenced by phase of growth. A reexamination in our laboratories with chemostat cultures in which ancillary parameters such as growth rate, pH, and population density can be made more strictly comparable, indicated that hydrogenase and nitrogenase activities were regulated simultaneously by ammonia in carbon-limited *Azotobacter chroococcum* (210) but that ancillary parameters had considerable effects: N_2- or O_2 -limited chemostat cultures had relatively low activities and evolved H_2 (193, 212); sulfate-limited cultures had similar low hydrogenase activities with either N_2 or NH_4^+ as N sources, suggesting that carbon-source (catabolite) repression of hydrogenase synthesis overrides ammonia regulation in all but C-limited populations. The hydrogenase of *A. chroococcum* is located in vesicles (105) but has been solubilized and partly purified (190). Lespinat, Gerster & Berlier (109) used D_2 as a tracer to indicate augmentation of hydrogenase activity in *A chroococcum* by oxygen; Berndt & Wölfle (8) showed that a low pO_2 favored hydrogenase formation by *X. autotrophicus;* growth phase influences hydrogenase formation in this organism, but differently from *A. vinelandii* (148).

Hydrogenase is probably present in nonleguminous nodules. Rhizobia seemed to be the one exception to Wilson's hydrogenase-nitrogenase correlation because hydrogenase was rarely demonstrable in legume nodules. Dixon (43) reviewed the situation: when present, the enzyme is unidirectional and relatively insoluble; it links to O_2, redox dyes, or ferricyanide. Only certain strains of rhizobia have the genetic information (now called *hup* genes) for uptake hydrogenase synthesis; the bacterial genotype determines the presence of hydrogenase, though the plant host and growth conditions influence *hup* expression in nodules. Loss of hydrogen via nitrogenase consumes ATP and is an energy drain, so possession of hydrogenase might be expected to augment nodule efficiency. This subject has been extensively studied by H. J. Evans and his colleagues (e.g. 26, 56, 157, 163, 164). *R. japonicum* includes natural hydrogenase-positive (Hup^+) and hydrogenase-negative (Hup^-) strains that can be distinguished by a simple tetrazolium test (116); the former perform best in greenhouse and growth chamber tests (2). *Rhizobium leguminosarum* includes types with insufficient hydrogenase to recycle the gas completely; slow-growing rhizobia and nonleguminous symbioses tend not to evolve H_2 at all.

Progress has been summarized by Evans et al (54–56), including extraction of particulate hydrogenase from *R. japonicum* bacteroids and study of its properties (156). Two extractable hydrogenases, one stimulated by ATP, have been reported in soybean and lupin bacteroids (181). Hydrogenase is formed by free-living rhizobia (110, 116). H_2 in the atmosphere sometimes augments hydrogenase formation, and oxygen or carbon sources tend to diminish hydrogenase formation (169). Carbon source repression is antagonized by cyclic AMP (111). Ribulose biphosphate carboxylase is derepressed, along with the uptake hydrogenase of Hup^+ *R. japonicum* (169); this combination renders the organism capable of microaerobic chemoautotrophic growth under H_2 (69). Hup^- mutants of Hup^+ *R. japonicum* have been prepared (117) and should facilitate quantitation of the role of hydrogenase, as well as allowing genetic manipulation of *hup* genes. Hup^- mutants did not grow chemoautotrophically (69). Other naturally Hup^+

bacteria might also be able to grow chemoautotrophically; F. O. Pedrosa, J. Dobereiner and M. G. Yates (Submitted for publication) have shown that *Derxia* species can do this but not *A. chroococcum* or *Beijerinckia indica.*

Hydrogenase and the Recycling of "Waste" Hydrogen

Though nitrogenase evolves H_2 in vitro, even when N_2 is being fixed, growing batch cultures of *Azotobacter* do not, though chemostat cultures may do so (193). Hardy & Burns (71) and Bulen (see 149) suggested that the uptake hydrogenase of *Azotobacter* "scavenged" H_2 formed by nitrogenase; Dixon (42) suggested a scavenging function for hydrogenase in nodules and proposed reasons which will be discussed later. Evidence that hydrogenase does scavenge the H_2 formed by nitrogenase is now overwhelming. In *Azotobacter* it is based on selective inhibition of hydrogenase in vivo by acetylene and/or CO (174), a procedure which works with cyanobacteria (13) but not *Rhizobium japonicum* (156) nor *Xanthobacter autotrophicus* (8). In *R. japonicum* the evidence depends on comparison of natural or mutant Hup^- strains with Hup^+ strains (see 54–56). With photosynthetic anaerobes, sequential H_2 evolution and H_2 uptake has been demonstrated (92; see also 120). The fact that hydrogenase scavenges H_2 in vivo may thus be taken for granted and the important question becomes why? Dixon (42, 43) suggested that hydrogenase in legume nodules, when present, might have any or all of three functions: protection against H_2 inhibition, enhancement of respiratory protection, supplementary energy generation for nitrogen fixation. None of these functions excludes any of the others; energy generation could be oblique, by recovering ATP through the H_2/O_2 reaction, and/or direct, with H_2 acting as electron donor for nitrogen fixation. These functions will be discussed separately.

REMOVAL OF INHIBITORY HYDROGEN Dixon (42, 43) was inclined to dismiss this function in rhizobia because of the fugacity of the H_2 molecule, but Mortenson (123) regarded it as "a major purpose of hydrogenase." Walker & Yates (193) found that H_2 evolution by *A. chroococcum* did not accelerate in air after the hydrogenase was irreversibly inhibited by a pulse of C_2H_2 and concluded that H_2 would not accumulate sufficiently to inhibit N_2 reduction.

ENHANCEMENT OF RESPIRATORY PROTECTION Any substrate that enhances the respiration rate may augment respiratory protection. A definitive test for enhancement is a shift of the graph of nitrogenase activity plotted against dissolved oxygen tension to higher pO_2 values. Ruiz-Argueso, Emerich & Evans (156) presented evidence that hydrogen, through hydrogenase, augmented respiratory protection in *R. japonicum* bacteroids; Walker & Yates (193, 212) showed that exogenous H_2 decreased the oxygen sensitivity of *A. chroococcum* nitrogenase, but only when the carbon source (mannitol) was in short supply; Bothe, Tennigkeit & Eisbrenner (12) showed that exogenous H_2 decreased O_2 sensitivity of nitrogenase in *Anabena variabilis;* it is reasonable to suppose that hydrogenase and hydrogen augment respiratory protection in other organisms, including *Rhodopseudomonas capsulata* (see 120).

PROVISION OF ATP AND/OR REDUCING POWER Dixon (42) reported H_2-dependent ATP generation by *R. leguminosarum* bacteroids. Ruiz-Argueso, Emerich & Evans (156) considered that hydrogen and hydrogenase provided both reducing power and energy (ATP) in *R. japonicum* bacteroids; the subsequent demonstration that Hup^+ *R. japonicum* strains grow autotrophically by the H_2/O_2 reaction (69) entirely vindicated their conclusions. Walker & Yates (193) reported that acetylene at concentrations too low to inhibit hydrogenase was reduced by *A. chroococcum* using H_2 as hydrogen donor (provided O_2 was present) but did not establish H_2-supported ATP generation. H_2 augments acetylene reduction in *Anabena* species (4, 203) in the presence of air; H_2 can couple to nitrogenase anaerobically in *A. variabilis* and *A. cylindrica* (12, 53). The fact that *Rhodopseudomonas capsulata* grows autotrophically with H_2, CO_2, and N_2 (99) removes any doubt that H_2 and hydrogenase couple to nitrogenase but Meyer, Kelley & Vignais (120) regarded energy and reductant generation as a minor function of recycled hydrogen compared with respiratory protection of nitrogenase.

CONCLUSIONS

The overriding importance of oxygen exclusion for the process of biological nitrogen fixation began to make sense in the late 1960s, and abundant evidence has accumulated since then to confirm this prerequisite. The possession of hydrogenase now makes sense as well; though it is physiologically less essential, it not only conserves energy for the microbe but augments the effectiveness of its oxygen exclusion processes.

ACKNOWLEDGMENTS

We thank Dr. M. G. Yates for checking the manuscript and acknowledge permission to quote unpublished material from Dr. Susan Hill, Dr. Christina Kennedy, Dr. H. Hennecke and Dr. M. G. Yates.

Literature Cited

1. Ackrell, B. A. C., Jones, C. W. 1971. *Eur. J. Biochem.* 20:29–35
2. Albrecht, S. L., Maier, R. J., Hanus, F. J., Russell, S. A., Emerich, D. W., Evans, H. J. 1979. *Science* 203:1255–57
3. Archer, L. J., George, T. A. 1973. *J. Organomet. Chem.* 54:C25
4. Benemann, J. R., Weare, N. M. 1974. *Science* 101:401–8
5. Bergersen, F. J. 1963. *Aust. J. Biol. Sci.* 16:669–80
6. Bergersen, F. J., Turner, G. L., Gibson, A. H., Dudman, W. F. 1976. *Biochim. Biophys. Acta* 444:164–74
7. Berndt, H., Ostwal, K. P., Lalucat, J., Schumann, C., Meyer, F., Schlegel, H. G. 1976. *Arch. Microbiol.* 108:17–26
8. Berndt, H., Wölfle, D. 1978. See Ref. 159, pp. 327–52
9. Biggins, D. R., Postgate, J. R. 1969. *J. Gen. Microbiol.* 56:181–93
10. Bishop, P. E., Evans, H. J., Daniel, R. M., Hampton, R. O. 1975. *Biochim. Biophys. Acta* 381:248–56
11. Bothe, H., Distler, E., Eisbrenner, G. 1978. *Biochimie* 60:277–89
12. Bothe, H., Tennigkeit, J., Eisbrenner, G. 1977. *Arch. Microbiol.* 114:43–49
13. Bothe, H., Tennigkeit, J., Eisbrenner, G., Yates, M. G. 1977. *Planta* 133: 237–42
14. Bulen, W. A. 1965. In *Non-Heme Iron Proteins; Role in Energy Conversion,* ed. A. San-Pietro, pp. 261–88. Yellow Springs: Antioch. 473 pp.
15. Bulen, W. A. 1976. See Ref. 131, 1:177–86
16. Bulen, W. A., Burns, R. C., LeComte, J. R. 1965. *Proc. Natl. Acad. Sci. USA* 53:532–39
17. Bulen, W. A., LeComte, J. R. 1966. *Proc. Natl. Acad. Sci. USA* 56:979–86
18. Burgess, B. K., Wherland, S., Stiefel, E. I., Newton, W. E. 1980. In *Molybdenum Chemistry of Biological Significance,* ed. W. E. Newton, S. Otsuka. New York: Plenum. In press
19. Burk, D. 1930. *J. Phys. Chem.* 34:1195–1209
20. Burns, R. C. 1965. See Ref. 14, pp. 289–97

20a. Burns, R. C., Hardy, R. W. F. 1975. *Nitrogen Fixation in Bacteria and Higher Plants.* New York: Springer. 189 pp.

21. Burris, R. H. 1971. See Ref. 149, pp. 105–60
22. Bush, J. A., Wilson, P. W. 1959. *Nature* 184:381
23. Cacciari, I., Lippi, D., Bordeleau, L. M. 1979. *Can. J. Microbiol.* 25:746–51
24. Carpenter, E. J., Price, C. C. 1976. *Science* 191:1278–80
25. Carter, I. S., Dawes, E. A. 1979. *J. Gen. Microbiol.* 110:393–400
26. Carter, K. R., Kennings, N. T., Hanus, J., Evans, H. J. 1978. *Can. J. Microbiol.* 24:307–11
27. Chatt, J. 1980. See Ref. 176. In press
28. Chen, J. S. 1978. See Ref. 159, pp. 57–82
29. Chen, J. S., Multani, J. S., Mortenson, L. E. 1973. *Biochim. Biophys. Acta* 310:51–59
30. Cramer, S. P., Gillum, W. O., Hodgson, K. O., Mortenson, L. E., Stiefel, E. I., Chisnel, J. R., Brill, W. J., Shah, V. K. 1978. *J. Am. Chem. Soc.* 100:3814–19
31. Cramer, S. P., Hodgson, K. O., Gillum, W. O., Mortenson, L. E. 1978. *J. Am. Chem. Soc.* 100:3398–3407
32. Cramer, S. P., Hodgson, K. O., Stiefel, E. I., Newton, W. 1978. *J. Am. Chem. Soc.* 100:2748–61
33. Dalton, H. 1980. See Ref. 176. In press
34. Dalton, H., Morris, J. A., Wood, M. A., Mortenson, L. E. 1971. *Biochemistry* 10:2066–72
35. Dalton, H., Postgate, J. R. 1969. *J. Gen. Microbiol.* 54:463–73
36. Dalton, H., Postgate, J. R. 1969. *J. Gen. Microbiol.* 56:307–19
37. Dalton, H., Whittenbury, R. 1976. *Arch. Microbiol.* 109:147–51
38. De Bont, J. A. M., Leitjen, M. W. N. 1976. *Arch. Microbiol.* 107:235–40
39. De Bont, J. A. M., Mulder, E. G. 1974. *J. Gen. Microbiol.* 83:113–21
40. Dervartanian, D. V., Shethna, Y. I., Beinert, H. 1969. *Biochim. Biophys. Acta* 194:548–63
41. Dilworth, M. J., Appleby, C. A. 1979. See Ref. 70, pp. 691–764
42. Dixon, R. O. D. 1972. *Arch. Microbiol.* 85:193–201
43. Dixon, R. O. D. 1978. *Biochimie* 60: 233–36
44. Downs, A. J., Jones, C. W. 1975. *FEBS Lett.* 60:42–46
45. Drozd, J. W. 1978. *FEMS Microbiol. Lett.* 3:47–49
46. Drozd, J. W., Postgate, J. R. 1970. *J. Gen. Microbiol.* 60:427–29
47. Drozd, J., Postgate, J. R. 1970. *J. Gen. Microbiol.* 63:63–73
48. Eady, R. R., Issack, R., Kennedy, C., Postgate, J. R., Ratcliffe, H. D. 1978. *J. Gen. Microbiol.* 104:277–85
49. Eady, R. R., Kennedy, C., Smith, B. E., Thorneley, R. N. F., Yates, G., Postgate, J. R. 1975. *Biochem. Soc. Trans.* 3:488–92

50. Eady, R. R., Smith, B. E. 1979. See Ref. 70, pp. 399–490
51. Eady, R. R., Smith, B. E., Cook, K. A., Postgate, J. R. 1972. *Biochem. J.* 128: 655–75
52. Eady, R. R., Smith, B. E., Thorneley, R. N. F., Yates, M. G., Postgate, J. R. 1975. In *Nitrogen Fixation by Free-living Micro-organisms,* ed. W. D. P. Stewart, *International Biological Programme* 6:377–88. London: Cambridge Univ. Press
53. Eisbrenner, G., Bothe, H. 1979. *Arch. Microbiol.* 123:37–45
54. Evans, H. J., Emerich, D. W., Ruiz-Argueso, T., Albrecht, S. L., Maier, R. J., Simpson, F., Russell, S. A. 1978. See Ref. 159, pp. 287–306
55. Evans, H. J., Emerich, D. W., Ruiz-Argueso, T., Maier, R. J., Albrecht, S. L. 1980. See Ref. 132a. In press
56. Evans, H. J., Ruiz-Argueso, T., Jennings, N. T., Hanus, J. 1977. In *Genetic Engineering for Nitrogen Fixation,* ed. A. Hollaender, pp. 33–55. New York: Plenum. 538 pp.
57. Evans, M. C. W., Telfer, A., Smith, R. V. 1973. *Biochim. Biophys. Acta* 310: 344–52
58. Fedorov, M. W., Kalininskaya, T. A. 1961. *Mikrobiologiya* 30:9–14
59. Gallon, J. R., LaRue, T. A., Kurz, W. G. W. 1975. *Can. J. Microbiol.* 19: 321–23
60. Gibson, A. H., Scowcroft, W. R., Child, J. J., Pagan, J. D. 1976. *Arch. Microbiol.* 108:45–54
61. Gogotov, J. N., Schlegel, H. G. 1974. *Arch. Microbiol.* 97:359–62
62. Gray, C. T., Gest, H. 1965. *Science* 148:186–92
63. Haaker, H., Scherings, G., Veeger, C. 1977. See Ref. 133, pp. 271–85
64. Haaker, H., Veeger, C. 1976. *Eur. J. Biochem.* 63:499–507
65. Haaker, H., Veeger, C. 1977. *Eur. J. Biochem.* 77:1–10
66. Haddock, B. A., Jones, C. W. 1977. *Bacteriol. Rev.* 41:47–99
67. Hadfield, K. L., Bulen, W. A. 1969. *Biochemistry* 8:5103–8
68. Hagerman, R. V., Burris, R. H. 1978. *Proc. Natl. Acad. Sci. USA* 75:2699–2702
69. Hanus, F. J., Maier, R. J., Evans, H. J. 1979. *Proc. Natl. Acad. Sci. USA.* 76:1788–92
70. Hardy, R. W. F., Bottomly, F., Burns, R. C., eds. 1979. *A Treatise on Dinitrogen Fixation, Sect. I, II.* New York: Wiley. 812 pp.
71. Hardy, R. W. F., Burns, R. C. 1968. *Ann. Rev. Biochem.* 37:331–58
72. Deleted in proof
73. Hardy, R. W. F., Burns, R. C., Parshall, G. W. 1971. *Adv. Chem. Ser.* 100: 219–47
74. Harrison, D. E. F. 1976. *Adv. Microb. Physiol.* 14:247–313
75. Higgins, I. J., Quayle, J. R. 1970. *Biochem. J.* 118:201–8
76. Hill, S. 1971. *J. Gen. Microbiol.* 67: 77–85
77. Hill, S. 1976. *J. Gen. Microbiol.* 93: 333–45
78. Hill, S. 1976. *J. Gen. Microbiol.* 95:297–312
79. Hill, S., Drozd, J. W., Postgate, J. R. 1972. *J. Appl. Chem. Biotechnol.* 22: 541–58
80. Hine, P. W., Lees, H. 1976. *Can. J. Microbiol.* 22:611–18
81. Hoch, G. E., Schneider, K. C., Burris, R. H. 1960. *Biochim. Biophys. Acta* 37:273–79
82. Hoffman, P. S., Morgan, T. V., Dervartanian, D. V. 1979. *Eur. J. Biochem.* 100:19–27
83. Huang, T. C., Zumft, W. G., Mortenson, L. E. 1973. *J. Bacteriol.* 113: 884–90
84. Hwang, J. C., Chen, C. H., Burris, R. H. 1973. *Biochim. Biophys. Acta* 292:256–70
85. Jackson, F. A., Dawes, E. A. 1976. *J. Gen. Microbiol.* 97:303–12
86. Jones, C. W. 1977. *Symp. Soc. Gen. Microbiol.* 27:23–59
87. Jones, C. W., Brice, J. M., Downs, A. J., Drozd, J. W. 1975. *Eur. J. Biochem.* 52:265–71
88. Jones, C. W., Brice, J. M., Wright, V., Ackrell, B. A. C. 1973. *FEBS Lett.* 29:77–81
89. Jones, C. W., Erickson, S. K., Ackrell, B. A. C. 1971. *FEBS Lett.* 13:33–35
90. Ke, B., Bulen, W. A., Shaw, E. R., Breeze, R. H. 1974. *Arch. Biochem. Biophys.* 162:301–9
91. Keister, D. L. 1975. *J. Bacteriol.* 123:1265–68
92. Kelley, B. C., Meyer, C., Gandy, C., Vignais, P. 1977. *FEBS Lett.* 81:281–85
93. Kelly, M. 1968. *Biochem. J.* 107:1–6
94. Kelly, M. 1968. *Biochem. J.* 109: 322–24
95. Kelly, M. 1969. *Biochim. Biophys. Acta* 171:9–22
96. Kelly, M. 1969. *Biochim. Biophys. Acta* 191:527–40
97. Kelly, M., Lang, G. 1970. *Biochim. Biophys. Acta* 223:86–104

98. Khmel, I. A., Gabinskaya, K. N., Jerusalimsky, N. D. 1965. *Mikrobiologiya* 34:689–94
99. Klemme, J. H. 1968. *Arch. Mikrobiol.* 64:29–42
100. Klucas, R. 1972. *Can. J. Microbiol.* 18:1845–50
101. Kluyver, A. J., Manten, A. 1942. *Antonie van Leeuwenhoek* 8:71–85
102. Knowles, C. J., Redfearn, E. R. 1968. *Biochim. Biophys. Acta* 162:348–55
103. Kurz, W. G. W., LaRue, T. A. 1973. *Can. J. Microbiol.* 19:321–24
104. Kurz, W. G. W., LaRue, T. A. 1975. *Nature* 256:407–9
105. Laane, C., Haaker, H., Veeger, C. 1979. *Eur. J. Biochem.* 97:369–77
106. Leadbetter, E. R., Foster, J. W. 1959. *Nature* 184:1428–29
107. Lee, S. B., Wilson, P. W. 1943. *J. Biol. Chem.* 151:377–85
108. Lees, H., Postgate, J. R. 1973. *J. Gen. Microbiol.* 75:161–66
109. Lespinat, P. A., Gerster, R., Berlier, Y. 1978. *Biochimie* 60:339–41
110. Lim, S. T. 1978. *Plant Physiol.* 62: 609–11
111. Lim, S. T., Shanmugam, K. T. 1979. *Biochim. Biophys. Acta* 584:479–92
112. Lisenkova, L. L., Khmel, I. A. 1967. *Mikrobiologiya* 36:905–11
113. Lowe, D. J., Eady, R. R., Thorneley, R. N. F. 1978. *Biochem. J.* 173:277–90
114. Lvov, N. P. 1963. *Izv. Akad. Nauk Arm. SSSR Biol. Nauki* 2:270–82
115. Mackintosh, M. E. 1978. *J. Gen. Microbiol.* 105:215–18
116. Maier, R. J., Campbell, N. E. R., Hanus, J., Simpson, F. B., Russell, S. A., Evans, H. J. 1978. *Proc. Natl. Acad. Sci. USA* 75:3258–62
117. Maier, R. J., Postgate, J. R., Evans, H. J. 1978. *Nature* 276:494–95
117a. Malik, K. A., Klaus, D. 1979. *Int. J. Syst. Bacteriol.* 29:283–87
118. McComb, J. A., Elliott, J., Dilworth, M. J. 1975. *Nature* 256:409–10
119. Merrick, M., Dixon, R., Eady, R., Hill, S., Kennedy, C., Iaccarino, M. 1980. See Ref. 176. In press
120. Meyer, J., Kelley, B. C., Vignais, P. M. 1978. *Biochimie* 60:245–60
121. Meyerhof, O., Burk, D. 1928. *Z. Phys. Chem. Abt. A* 139:117–42
122. Mortenson, L. E. 1964. *Proc. Natl. Acad. Sci. USA* 52:272–79
123. Mortenson, L. E. 1978. *Biochimie* 60: 219–24
124. Mortenson, L. E., Thorneley, R. N. F. 1979. *Ann. Rev. Biochem.* 48:387–418
125. Mortenson, L. E., Walker, M. N., Walker, G. A. 1976. See Ref. 131, 1:117–49
126. Nagai, S., Aiba, S. 1972. *J. Gen. Microbiol.* 73:531–38
127. Nagai, S., Nishizawa, Y., Aiba, S. 1969. *J. Gen. Microbiol.* 59:163–69
128. Nagai, S., Nishizawa, Y., Onodera, M., Aiba, S. 1971. *J. Gen. Microbiol.* 66:197–203
129. Nelson, L. M., Knowles, R. 1978. *Can. J. Microbiol.* 24:1395–1403
130. Newton, W. E., Bulen, W. A., Hadfield, K. L., Stiefel, E. I., Watt, G. D. 1977. See Ref. 133, pp. 119–30
131. Newton, W. E., Nyman, C. J. 1976. *Proc. 1st Int. Symp. Nitrogen Fixation.* Vols. 1, 2. Pullman, Wash: Washington State Univ. Press. 311 pp.
132. Newton, W. E., Orme-Johnson, W. H. 1980. *Nitrogen Fixation,* Vol. 1: *Free-living Systems and Chemical Models.* Baltimore: Univ. Park press. 416 pp.
132a. Newton, W. E., Orme-Johnson, W. H. 1980. *Nitrogen Fixation.* Vol. 2: *Symbiotic Associations and Blue-Green Algae.* Baltimore: Univ. Park Press. 352 pp.
133. Newton, W., Postgate, J. R., Rodriguez-Barrueco, C. 1977. *Recent Developments in Nitrogen Fixation.* London: Academic. 622 pp.
134. Nikonova, L. A., Shilov, A. E. 1977. See Ref. 133, pp. 41–52
135. Nishizawa, Y., Nagai, S., Aiba, S. 1971. *J. Gen. Appl. Microbiol.* 17:131–40
136. Nordlund, S. , Eriksson, U. 1979. *Biochim. Biophys. Acta* 547:429–37
137. Okon, Y., Albrecht, S. L., Burris, R. H. 1976. *J. Bacteriol.* 127:1248–54
138. Okon, Y., Houchins, J. P., Albrecht, S. L., Burris, R. H. 1977. *J. Gen. Microbiol.* 98:87–93
139. Oppenheim, J., Fisher, R. J., Marcus, L., Wilson, P. W. 1970. *J. Bacteriol.* 101:292–96
140. Orme-Johnson, W. H. 1977. See Ref. 56, pp. 317–32
141. Orme-Johnson, W. H., Beinert, H. 1969. *J. Biol. Chem.* 244:6143–48
142. Pagan, J. D., Child, J. J., Scowcroft, W. R., Gibson, A. H. 1975. *Nature* 256:406–7
143. Palmer, G., Multani, J. S., Zumft, W. G., Mortenson, L. E. 1972. *Arch. Biochem. Biophys.* 153:325–32
144. Parker, C. A. 1954. *Nature* 173:780–81
145. Pate, J. L., Shah, V. K., Brill, W. J. 1973. *J. Bacteriol.* 114:1346–50
146. Pengra, R. M., Wilson, P. W. 1958. *J. Bacteriol.* 75:21–25
147. Phillips, D. H., Johnson, M. J. 1961. *J.*

Biochem. Microbiol. Technol. Eng. 3:277–309
148. Pinkwart, M., Bahl, H., Reimer, M., Wölfle, D., Berndt, H. 1979. *FEMS Microbiol. Lett.* 6:177–81
149. Postgate, J. R. 1971. In *The Chemistry and Biochemistry of Nitrogen Fixation,* ed. J. R. Postgate, pp. 185–86. London: Plenum. 326 pp.
150. Postgate, J. R. 1974. In *The Biology of Nitrogen Fixation,* ed. A. Quispel, pp. 663–86. Amsterdam: North Holland. 769 pp.
151. Postgate, J. R. 1974. In *Evolution in the Microbial World,* ed. M. J. Carlile, J. J. Skehel, *Symp. Soc. Gen. Microbiol.* 24:263–92
152. Reed, D. W., Toia, R. E., Raveed, D. 1974. *Biochem. Biophys. Res. Commun.* 58:20–26
153. Rivera-Ortez, J. M., Burris, R. H. 1975. *J. Bacteriol.* 123:537–45
154. Robson, R. L. 1979. *Biochem. J.* 181:569–75
155. Robson, R. L. 1979. *FEMS Microbiol. Lett.* 5:259–62
156. Ruiz-Argueso, T., Emerich, D. W., Evans, H. J. 1979. *Arch. Microbiol.* 121:199–206
157. Ruiz-Argueso, T., Hanus, J., Evans, H. J. 1978. *Arch. Microbiol.* 116:113–18
158. Scherings, G., Haaker, H., Veeger, C. 1977. *Eur. J. Biochem.* 77:621–30
159. Schlegel, H. G., Schneider, K. 1978. *Hydrogenase: Their Catalytic Activity, Structure and Function,* Göttingen: Goltze KG. 453 pp.
160. Schmidt-Lorenz, W., Rippel-Baldes, A. 1957. *Arch. Mikrobiol.* 28:45–68
161. Schrauzer, G. N. 1974. *J. Less-Common Met.* 36:275–86
162. Schrauzer, G. N. 1977. See Ref. 133, pp. 109–18
163. Schubert, K. R., Engelke, J. A., Russell, S. A., Evans, H. J. 1978. *Plant Physiol.* 60:651–54
164. Schubert, K. R., Jennings, N. T., Evans, H. J. 1978. *Plant Physiol.* 61:398–401
165. Senior, P. J., Dawes, E. A. 1971. *Biochem. J.* 125:55–66
166. Shah, V. K., Brill, W. J. 1973. *Biochim. Biophys. Acta* 305:445–54
167. Shethna, Y. I., Dervartanian, D. V., Beinert, H. 1968. *Biochem. Biophys. Res. Commun.* 31:862–68
168. Siefert, E., Pfennig, N. 1978. *Biochimie* 60:261–65
169. Simpson, F. B., Maier, R. J., Evans, H. J. 1979. *Arch. Microbiol.* 123:1–8
170. Smith, B. E., Eady, R. R., Thorneley, R. N. F., Yates, M. G., Postgate, J. R. 1977. See Ref. 133, pp. 191–204
171. Smith, B. E., Lang, G. 1974. *Biochem. J.* 137:169–80
172. Smith, B. E., Lowe, D. J., Bray, R. C. 1972. *Biochem. J.* 130:641–43
173. Smith, B. E., Thorneley, R. N. F., Eady, R. R., Mortenson, L. E. 1976. *Biochem. J.* 157:439–47
174. Smith, L. A., Hill, S., Yates, M. G. 1976. *Nature* 262:209–10
175. Stephenson, M. P., Jackson, F. A., Dawes, E. A. 1978. *J. Gen. Microbiol.* 109:89–96
176. Stewart, W. D. P., Gallon, J. R., eds. 1980. *Nitrogen Fixation. Ann. Proc. Phytochem. Soc. Eur., 18th.* London: Academic. In press
177. Stewart, W. D. P., Lex, M. 1970. *Arch. Mikrobiol.* 73:250–60
178. Stiefel, E. I., Burgess, B. K., Wherland, S., Newton, W. E., Corbin, J. L., Watt, G. D. 1980. See Ref. 132, pp. 211–22
179. Still, G. G., Wang, C. H. 1964. *Arch. Biochem. Biophys.* 105:126–32
180. St. John, R. T., Shah, V. K., Brill, W. J. 1974. *J. Bacteriol.* 119:266–69
181. Suzuki, T., Maruyama, Y. 1979. *Agric. Biol. Chem.* 43:1833–39
182. Swank, R. T., Burris, R. H. 1969. *Biochim. Biophys. Acta* 180:473–89
183. Thorneley, R. N. F., Chatt, J., Eady, R. R., Lowe, D. J., O'Donnell, M. J., Postgate, J. R., Richards, R. L., Smith, B. E. 1980. See Ref. 132, pp. 171–94
184. Thorneley, R. N. F., Eady, R. R. 1977. *Biochem. J.* 167:457–61
185. Thorneley, R. N. F., Eady, R. R., Lowe, D. J. 1978. *Nature* 272:557–58
186. Thorneley, R. N. F., Lowe, D. J., Eady, R. R., Miller, R. W. 1979. *Biochem. Soc. Trans.* 7:633–36
187. Tjepkema, J., Evans, H. J. 1975. *Biochem. Biophys. Res. Commun.* 65: 625–28
188. Tsai, J. C., Aladegbami, S. L., Vela, G. R. 1979. *J. Bacteriol.* 139:639–45
189. Tschapek, M., Giambiagi, N. 1955. *Arch. Mikrobiol.* 21:376–90
190. Van der Werf, A., Yates, M. G. 1978. See Ref. 159, pp. 307–26
191. Veeger, D., Laane, C., Scherings, G., Matz, L., Haaker, H., Van Zeeland-Wolbers, L. 1980. See Ref. 132, pp. 11–38.
192. Vignais, P. M. 1978. *Biochimie 60:* Pt. 3, pp. 217–341
193. Walker, C. C., Yates, M. G. 1978. *Biochimie* 60:225–31
194. Walker, M., Mortenson, L. E. 1973. *Biochem. Biophys. Res. Commun.* 54: 669–76
195. Ward, A. C., Rowley, B. I., Dawes, E. A. 1971. *J. Gen. Microbiol.* 102:61–68

196. Ware, D. A. 1972. *Biochem. J.* 130:301–2
197. Wiegel, J., Wilke, D., Baumgarten, J., Opitz, R., Schlegel, H. G. 1978. *Int. J. Syst. Bacteriol.* 28:573–81
198. Wilcockson, J. 1977. *J. Gen. Microbiol.* 101:311–17
199. Williams, A. M., Wilson, P. W. 1954. *J. Bacteriol.* 67:353–60
200. Wilson, P. W. 1958. In *Encyclopedia of Plant Physiology,* ed. W. Rutland, 8:9–47. Berlin:Springer. 1310 pp.
201. Wilson, P. W. 1969. *Proc. R. Soc. London Ser. B* 172:319–25
202. Winter, H. C., Burris, R. H. 1976. *Ann. Rev. Biochem.* 45:409–26
203. Wolk, C. P., Wojciuch, E. 1971. *Planta* 97:126–34
204. Yates, M. G. 1970. *J. Gen. Microbiol.* 60:393–40
205. Yates, M. G. 1970. *FEBS Lett.* 8:281–85
206. Yates, M. G. 1972. *Eur. J. Biochem.* 29:386–92
207. Yates, M. G. 1977. See Ref. 133, pp. 219–70
208. Yates, M. G., Jones, C. W. 1974. *Adv. Microb. Physiol.* 11:97–135
209. Yates, M. G., Lowe, D. J. 1976. *FEBS Lett.* 72:121–26
210. Yates, M. G., Partridge, C. D. P., Walker, C. C., Van der Werf, A., Campbell, F. C., Postgate, J. R. 1980. See Ref. 176. In press
211. Yates, M. G., Planque, K. 1975. *Eur. J. Biochem.* 60:467–76
212. Yates, M. G., Walker, C. 1980. See Ref. 132, pp. 95–110

Ann. Rev. Microbiol. 1980. 34:209–33

NITROGEN METABOLITE REGULATION OF ANTIBIOTIC BIOSYNTHESIS

❖1775

Yair Aharonowitz

Department of Microbiology, The George S. Wise Faculty of Life Sciences, Tel Aviv University, Tel Aviv, Israel

CONTENTS

INTRODUCTION 210
RELATIONSHIP BETWEEN GROWTH AND ANTIBIOTIC PRODUCTION 211
NITROGEN METABOLISM AND ANTIBIOTIC BIOSYNTHESIS 212
Nitrogen Nutrition and Antibiotic Production 212
The Origin of the Nitrogen Atom in the Antibiotic Molecule 213
Direct precursors 213
Nitrogen transfer reactions 214
Regulatory Functions Exerted by Primary Nitrogen Metabolites 216
GENERAL NITROGEN METABOLITE REGULATION 217
Microbial Nitrogen Assimilatory Mechanisms 217
The Involvement of Glutamine Synthetase in Regulation of Degradative Pathways 218
Metabolic Regulation of Catabolic Reactions by Ammonia in Fungi 219
NITROGEN METABOLITE REGULATION IN ANTIBIOTIC PRODUCTION 220
Antibiotic Biosynthesis in Streptomycetes 220
β-Lactam antibiotics 220
Nourseothricin 221
Erythromycin 222
β-Lactam Antibiotic Biosynthesis in Fungi 222
Cephalosporin C 222
Penicillin 223
TRANSPORT CAPACITY AND AMINO ACID POOL COMPOSITION 224
Ammonium Transport 224
Ammonium Effect on Amino Acid Transport in Fungi 225
Control of Amino Acid Transport in Bacteria 225
Intracellular Concentrations of Free Amino Acids During the Growth Cycle 226

0066-4227/80/1001-0209$01.00

ANTIBIOTIC PRODUCTION, PROTEOLYSIS, AND SPORULATION 227
CONCLUDING REMARKS 229

INTRODUCTION

Microorganisms are able to synthesize a great variety of metabolites that are required for growth, development, and survival. To gain selective advantages, highly developed mechanisms for the regulation of metabolic processes have evolved that enable organisms to respond to and to utilize as efficiently as possible the nutrients that are normally available in the environment. Thus, the presence of a required metabolite, in excess, generally results in the repression and/or inhibition of enzymes leading to its own synthesis, with the concomitant decrease in the concentration of intermediates that are part of its biosynthetic pathway. Changes in enzyme profiles, biosynthetic intermediates, and end products may in turn lead to alterations in growth rate or biomass. In microorganisms that undergo differentiation these changes may give rise to new forms and molecular organization.

Among the great variety of metabolites produced by microorganisms, the antibiotics have attracted the special interest of scientists for many years. Their diversity and complexity, their presence in detectable amounts in a number of different species, and the fact that as yet no specific biological function can be attributed to many of them, have made antibiotics the subject of very intense research efforts.

From the standpoint of commercial production of antibiotics, an organism with the least stringent regulatory restrictions is the organism of choice. Such an organism will "waste" a great deal of the available nutritional resources in order to overproduce and excrete a particular product that can subsequently be recovered (26). Production is increased through a combination of strain improvement and adjustment of physiological and growth conditions. Although some attempts have been made to study genetic and metabolic regulatory mechanisms operating in the biosynthesis of antibiotics, industrial development relies primarily on an empirical approach.

This review focuses on those regulatory mechanisms that control the assimilatory and catabolic processes that may result in increased availability of precursors for antibiotic synthesis. In this regard, the evidence for nitrogen involvement in the regulation of antibiotic biosynthesis is emphasized. In addition, the notion that the level of nitrogen-containing catabolites may act as a determining factor in the initiation and rate of antibiotic biosynthesis is discussed in the light of recent findings concerning the general control mechanism operating in catabolite repression and induction. The reader is referred to a series of reviews dealing with the genetics of antibiotic biosynthesis (55, 89), the regulation of biosynthesis (27, 33, 75), and the relationship between growth and production (114).

RELATIONSHIP BETWEEN GROWTH AND ANTIBIOTIC PRODUCTION

In order to gain some insight into the control of antibiotic synthesis, several basic questions have to be answered. (*a*) When are the specific "antibiotic synthetases" formed, and how is their formation controlled? (*b*) What are the primary metabolic activities required to supply precursors for the antibiotic molecule? (*c*) How do these two systems operate in a coordinated fashion enabling antibiotic synthesis to proceed efficiently?

It has been very difficult to answer these questions, primarily because most of the specific antibiotic synthetases have yet to be described. Furthermore, the systems are complicated by the diversity in metabolic origin and chemical structure of antibiotics.

Some of the earliest observations relating to antibiotic production came from studies of fermentation kinetics in batch culture. The growth curve could be divided into the growth phase (trophophase) and the production phase (idiophase) (19). In certain cases, enzymes of antibiotic biosynthesis are repressed during the trophophase and derepressed during the transition to idiophase. Repression in trophophase was observed for enzymes involved in biosynthesis of streptidine (116), tylosin (78), actinomycin (47), and gramicidin S (109). In the case of actinomycin the repression has been attributed to carbon catabolite repression (47). In most cases, however, the basis for lack of biosynthetic activity is not known. Possibly, antibiotic synthetases are present but inactive during trophophase. This was found to be the case in growing cells that produce patulin (20). In addition, resting cells prepared from a growing culture of *Streptomyces griseus* synthesized candicidin in the presence of chloramphenicol, though none was produced by growing cells of the same age (70). Similarly, the specific ability of resting cells of *Cephalosporium acremonium* to produce penicillin N reached a peak during rapid growth on a variety of sugars, even though only little antibiotic was found in the fermentation broth at that time (27).

Aharonowitz & Demain (4, 5) studied the effect of carbon and nitrogen sources on growth and β-lactam antibiotic production in the actinomycete *Streptomyces clavuligerus.* It was shown that a change in the carbon source, from an amino acid or organic acid to glycerol, shifted antibiotic production from a growth-associated mode to production during idiophase (4). Similar shifts were brought about by the addition of increasing concentrations of ammonium ions to a culture in which an amino acid was the major nitrogen source (5). It was suggested that conditions favoring catabolism of certain nutrient molecules influence biosynthesis of antibiotics by enhancing catabolic processes that increase the level of antibiotic precursors. These favorable conditions would be created, for example, by limiting concentrations of ammonium, carbon, sulfur, or a required amino acid; this could trigger the catabolism of protein molecules by proteases and thus provide free amino acid precursors to the metabolic pool (75).

If antibiotic synthetases are present during growth and if the precursors of the antibiotic are primary metabolites, a posttranscriptional control system for secondary metabolism may determine the activity of the antibiotic synthetases. Such a control system might affect rate of antibiotic production, specific production per unit of biomass, excretion of product, and timing of antibiotic biosynthesis. Under such conditions, the levels of available precursors may be the major factor in connecting primary to secondary metabolism. The concentration of precursors in the intracellular pool should determine the rate of secondary metabolite biosynthesis when such concentrations are in the range of the K_m values of the antibiotic synthetases.

NITROGEN METABOLISM AND ANTIBIOTIC BIOSYNTHESIS

Nitrogen atoms are present in many antibiotic molecules and as such are usually derived from nitrogen-containing primary metabolites (12). In the subsequent section some of the possible interrelationships between primary nitrogen metabolism and the biosynthesis of antibiotics, as derived from nutritional studies, are considered.

Nitrogen Nutrition and Antibiotic Production

Many findings show that antibiotic production is influenced by the state of nitrogen in the culture medium. In the production of streptomycin by *Streptomyces griseus,* soybean meal was found to be a very effective source of nitrogen (36). This is a cheap and commercially available source and has the advantage of a slow breakdown during the fermentation process. Proline was found to be one of the best nitrogen sources in streptomycin production (127) and was used in combination with ammonium salts. When *Streptomyces niveus* was grown on chemically defined medium that contained proline in addition to ammonium sulfate as sources of nitrogen, the ammonium ions were utilized prior to proline; novobiocin production occurred only after the consumption of the ammonium ions (63). Increasing the concentration of ammonium sulfate resulted in an inhibition of novobiocin production by 90%. Substitution of ammonium sulfate in the medium by high concentration of proline resulted in much higher yields of novobiocin (63). In the production of gramicidin S by *Bacillus brevis,* a combination of five amino acids was required for good growth, yet the further addition of phenylalanine was required for high gramicidin S production (113).

Williams & Katz (126) described a chemically defined medium for production of actinomycin D by *Streptomyces parvulus.* They found that although a number of L-amino acids were favorable sources of nitrogen for actinomycin D synthesis when used singly, the combination of L-histidine and L-glutamic acid yielded the highest titer. Inorganic nitrogen sources such as nitrates, nitrite, and several ammonium salts resulted in much less antibiotic production. Several types of nitrogen compounds were tested as sole nitrogen sources for cephalosporin production by *Streptomyces clavuligerus* in a defined minimal medium (5). It was found that supplementation with certain amino acids or urea was best for antibiotic production. Asparagine and glutamine gave rise to the highest levels of cephalosporin while arginine was almost as effective. Although ammonium ions supported only a somewhat lower growth rate than asparagine, antibiotic production was very poor with the inorganic nitrogen source. It appears that some kind of "ammonium repression" of antibiotic production occurs in many fermentations when ammonium is supplied in excess.

The Origin of the Nitrogen Atom in the Antibiotic Molecule

In considering the flow of nitrogen along the various pathways of antibiotic biosynthesis, we must distinguish between those reactions in which a nitrogen-containing precursor such as an amino acid is incorporated intact into the antibiotic molecule and those in which only the nitrogen atom of the primary metabolite is transferred by an antibiotic-specific reaction to a specific intermediate.

DIRECT PRECURSORS The metabolism of amino acids, purines, and pyrimidines provides the nitrogenous precursors for antibiotic biosynthesis. Specific amino acids have been shown to be direct precursors for many peptide antibiotics found in the fermentation broth of various *Bacillus* (59) and *Pseudomonas* (69) species. One representative example is the biosynthesis of the cyclic decapeptide gramicidin S by *Bacillus brevis.* This antibiotic can be produced by a cell-free extract containing the five specific amino acids present in the antibiotic; the amino acids are activated and incorporated into the final antibiotic molecule (109). A protoplast system derived from *B. licheniformis* produces the peptide antibiotic bacitracin when the six constitutive amino acids are present (102). L-valine is a precursor of the D-valine moiety of the actinomycin molecule in *Streptomyces antibioticus* (58). It is now evident that cysteine is incorporated intact into the penicillin molecule by *Penicillium chrysogenum* (8), while valine provides the nitrogen atom for the thiazolidine ring (104). Similar results were found for cephalosporin C produced by *Cephalosporium acremonium* (1). The antifungal antibiotic pyrolnitrin, produced by various species of *Pseudomonas,* serves as an example of incorporation of an intact amino acid to form a nonpeptide antibiotic. Addition of tryptophan to the culture medium increases pyrolnitrin production; by using ^{15}N-tryptophan in which the various nitrogen atoms were labeled specifically, both indole nitrogen and the amino nitrogen of tryptophan were shown to be incorporated into the antibiotic molecule (41). Puromycin is a purine glycoside antibiotic containing dimethyl adenine and ribosamine linked to *o*-methyltyrosine (130). Such a molecule serves as an example for the involvement of nitrogen-containing intermediates originating from both nucleotides and amino acids.

In the fermentation broth of different *Bacillus* species, multiple forms of an antibiotic are generally produced simultaneously (59). Thus, supplementation with one of the amino acids can direct the biosynthetic process in such a way that the antibiotic formed preferentially will be the one rich in the exogenously added amino acid (59). An example is the biosynthesis of the antibiotic actinomycin by species of *Streptomyces:* different actinomycins are synthesized when the organisms are grown in the presence of one or another of the four isomers of isoleucine (128).

Conditional mutants have been obtained (25) which produce antibiotics only in the presence of a specific intermediate or its analogs. Such mutants are termed "idiotrophs" (81). Thus Nagaoka & Demain (81) obtained an idiotroph of the streptomycin-producing *S. griseus,* which could produce streptomycin only in the presence of streptidine. Feeding 2-deoxystreptidine resulted in production of a new antibiotic called streptomutin. In such a way, new antibiotics can be found in which the nitrogen atoms in a new antibiotic are located in different positions. The uptake of such precursors by the cell can be a target for regulation of antibiotic synthesis by nitrogen.

NITROGEN TRANSFER REACTIONS One of the examples of the involvement of nitrogen transfer reactions in antibiotic biosynthesis is the biosynthesis of the moieties of the aminocyclitol antibiotics. The compounds in this group include the aminated inositol derivatives streptamine, actinamine, 2-deoxystreptamine, bluensidine, and streptidine (94). The best studied biosynthetic path to an aminocyclitol is that of streptidine of the antibiotic streptomycin. The introduction of nitrogen atoms into streptomycin intermediates pertains mainly in the steps between *myo*-inositol and streptidine.

In the conversion of 2-keto-*myo*-inositol to the intermediate bluensamine, L-glutamine was found to be the best amino donor for the transamination reaction (120). The aminotransferase catalyzing this reaction could have evolved either from a catabolic or an anabolic aminotransferase acting on aminosugars that have configurations similar to aminocyclitols. In fact, the aminating enzyme, L-glutamine: keto-*scyllo*-inositol aminotransferase is relatively nonspecific (117). Other amino donors include *scyllo*-inosamine, *myo*-inosamine, streptamine, and 2-deoxystreptamine. At higher concentrations, both L-alanine and L-glutamate can serve as weak amino donors. After bluensamine is activated by phosphorylation with ATP, an amidino group of arginine is transferred to *o*-phosphorylinosamine. The enzyme L-arginine: inosaminephosphate amidinotransferase uses mainly arginine and canavanine as amidino donors (118). The second guanidino group of streptidine is synthesized by an analogous set of reactions. The *N*-amidino-3-keto-*scyllo*-inosamine is transaminated to *N*-amindinostreptamine. This reaction has been shown to occur in extracts of *Streptomyces bikiniensis* (119) and is most active with alanine as amino donor. Once again, the formation of streptidine-6-phosphate is brought about by an amidinotransferase enzyme using arginine as amidino donor (123). Walker & Walker (121) have found that cell-free extracts from strains producing streptomycin, gentamicin, and neomycin (21) all catalyze transaminations with the 1-amino group of 2-deoxystreptamine and streptamine, as well as with aminodeoxy-*scyllo*-inositol, indicating that the 3-amino moiety of 2-deoxystreptamine is added first and that a single aminotransferase is responsible for both transaminations.

Amino- and amidinotransferases have been shown to catalyze reactions leading to the biosynthesis of indolmycin by *Streptomyces griseus* (41), with the two nitrogen atoms of the aminooxazolinone system originating from the amidino group of arginine. The latter is transferred as an intact unit, i.e. without separating the two nitrogen atoms (131). The biosynthetic pathway also involves transamination of tryptophan to indolepyruvate, followed by methylation of the latter to give 3-methylindolepyruvic acid.

The involvement of carbamylation in antibiotic biosynthesis is indicated by studies on novobiocin production. The nitrogen of the carbamyl group attached to the noviose ring arises from metabolic nitrogen, presumably from glutamine, which in bacteria and fungi serves as the amino source for carbamyl phosphate (62).

When the activities in antibiotic biosynthesis discussed above are considered as targets for nitrogen regulation, it becomes obvious that the presence of adequate concentrations of the amino and amidino donors, such as glutamine, alanine, glutamate, and arginine respectively, is crucial for these enzymes to operate. The amino- and amidinotransferases might be induced or derepressed by specific substrates or structural analogs. Or, if the enzymes have already been synthesized, an increased concentration of the substrates might enable them to operate at their maximal rate. In this regard, the exogenous addition of arginine to intact mycelia of *Streptomyces griseus* and *S. bikiniensis* results in the accumulation of *o*-phosphorylstreptidine (119), a streptomycin-specific intermediate. Similar effects were observed when glutamine and asparagine were used (124).

Regulatory Functions Exerted by Primary Nitrogen Metabolites

In addition to their direct involvement in primary metabolite interconversions leading to antibiotic production, certain amino acids have been shown to function in the regulation of secondary metabolite synthesis (33). For example, addition of tryptophan to *Claviceps* producing ergot alkaloids results in elevated levels of the first enzyme of the ergot alkaloid biosynthetic pathway, dimethylallyltryptophan (DMAT) synthetase (64). It was suggested that the induction effect mediated by tryptophan, or a derivative thereof, involves de novo synthesis of the enzyme. In a different set of experiments, it was observed that cephalosporin C biosynthesis in *Cephalosporium acremonium* is enhanced by the addition of methionine (32). By using methionine analogs and mutants blocked in reactions between cysteine and methionine, methionine's effect on antibiotic production was shown to be due to a regulatory effect, rather than to its role as a sulfur donor (31, 34).

A high penicillin-producing strain of *Penicillium chrysogenum* has been found to produce elevated levels of acetohydroxyacid synthetase, the first enzyme in the valine biosynthetic pathway (49). One of the sites for inhibition by valine, originally present in the enzyme of the parent strain, has been lost by mutation; the allosteric site, for which valine is a strictly noncompetitive inhibitor, remains. Thus, the overproduction of penicillin in this strain may be attributed to these changes which might ensure the supply of valine required for elevated penicillin synthesis (49). In fungi, one of the intermediates of lysine biosynthesis, α-aminoadipic acid (AAA), is also involved in penicillin biosynthesis. Feedback inhibition by lysine of the first enzyme of lysine biosynthesis (homocitrate synthetase) limits production of AAA, thus indirectly inhibiting penicillin production (28, 72, 76, 77). In *Streptomyces,* AAA is a catabolic product of lysine (60). It was found that addition of lysine to a culture of *S. clavuligerus* stimulates antibiotic production. Furthermore, a large number of *S. clavuligerus* mutants resistant to concerted feedback inhibition of aspartokinase by lysine and threonine produce elevated levels of β-lactam antibiotics (S. Mendelovitz and Y. Aharonowitz, in preparation).

GENERAL NITROGEN METABOLITE REGULATION

The preceding section deals primarily with specific regulatory effects of nitrogen-containing metabolites on antibiotic production. Nevertheless, the main metabolic function of these metabolites will by necessity be subject to more general or pleotropic modes of regulation which are common to many procaryotic and eucaryotic cells.

One feature of such regulation is that a single factor can activate the transcription of many different operons having the same physiological function (73). It may be argued that such mechanisms, by their regulation of the synthesis of certain proteins, control cellular functions that are not essential to the organism under all growth conditions. If such functions are involved directly or indirectly in antibiotic biosynthesis, the mechanism controlling them becomes highly relevant. A common function for such operons may be the supply of carbon and energy or nitrogen. For example, cAMP and the cAMP receptor protein (CRP) have been shown to activate the promoters of a wide variety of genes concerned with transport and utilization of energy and carbon source (83, 93). In addition, other proteins involved in a variety of cell functions have been shown to be under the same control (83). In the following paragraphs, those general modes of regulation operating in bacterial and fungal systems that control nitrogen metabolism will be briefly surveyed.

Microbial Nitrogen Assimilatory Mechanisms

In many species of microorganisms ammonia is assimilated by either one of two metabolic pathways. When high concentrations of ammonia are available, the enzyme glutamate dehydrogenase (GDH) catalyzes the reductive amination of 2-ketoglutarate to give L-glutamate. This enzyme possesses a low affinity for ammonia and operates primarily when high concentrations of ammonia are available in the medium. However, when the ammonia supply is restricted, the enzyme glutamine synthetase (GS) catalyzes the ATP-dependent production of glutamine from ammonia and glutamate. In addition to the GDH reaction, glutamate can be formed by several alternative routes. The enzyme glutamate synthase (GOGAT) (108) can catalyze the reaction of glutamine with 2-ketoglutarate to form two molecules of glutamate. Thus, the combined reaction of GS and GOGAT results in the net assimilation of ammonia to form one molecule of glutamate at the expense of one molecule of ATP (108). In addition, glutamate can be formed by catabolic degradation of other amino acids and by transamination reactions catalyzing the transfer of amino groups from these amino acids to 2-oxoglutarate (110).

The Involvement of Glutamine Synthetase in Regulation of Degradative Pathways

Tyler (110) has recently summarized the present state of knowledge concerning regulation of nitrogen assimilation in enteric bacteria. As a result of an extensive biochemical and genetic study, it has been postulated that a general control element mediates the formation of a wide array of enzymes involved in the assimilation of nitrogen into glutamate and glutamine. The molecule glutamine synthetase itself has been implicated as one such control element on the basis of the following experimental observations. (*a*) When nitrogen becomes growth-limiting, the synthesis of glutamine synthetase is elevated (11, 15, 16, 86). (*b*) When histidine is added as a sole source of nitrogen in the presence of an alternative carbon source, catabolic degradation of the amino acid occurs. This degradation was inhibited by high ammonia (87). In contrast, high ammonia does not interfere with amino acid degradation when the latter is required as a sole source of carbon and energy. Results using a variety of mutants of *Klebsiella aerogenes* suggested that the control element monitoring the state of nitrogen in the growth medium is the GS itself. (*c*) Finally, Tyler et al (111) tested the transcription of the *hut* (histidine utilization) specific message in vitro and found that the addition of cAMP and CRP together causes an eightfold increase in transcription of *hut* specific message. Nonadenylylated GS (the form present in nitrogen-limited cells) could replace cAMP and CRP in the assay. Adenylylated GS (the form present in cells grown with excess nitrogen) does not cause a significant stimulation of transcription (111). These results, taken together, provide strong evidence for the role of GS in the regulation of nitrogen catabolic pathways.

The enzymes involved in the utilization of arginine are controlled by GS (43). Thus, synthesis of the catabolic N^2-acetylornithine 5-aminotransferase (ACOAT) of *K. aerogenes* was found to be subject to catabolic repression exerted by glucose when ammonia was present in excess (43). However, when these cells were deprived of nitrogen, the biosynthesis of this enzyme escaped catabolic repression. The activation observed was mediated by GS as shown by the fact that mutants affected in the regulation or synthesis of GS were also affected in the control of ACOAT formation. It is worth noting that cells capable of degrading arginine were also able to produce ornithine from arginine (45). Friedrich & Magasanik (46) studied agmatine degradation in *K. aerogenes* and showed that the synthesis of agmatinase and of 4-aminobutyrate aminotransferase was activated by GS. A similar amidinotransferase has been described in streptomycin producers of *Streptomyces* species (122), although the possible correlation between this enzyme and GS levels in Streptomycetes has not been investigated.

As described above, similar aminotransferases and amidinotransferases are involved in the biosynthesis of certain antibiotics such as aminocyclytols (94). In addition, the peptide antibiotic bacitracin, which is produced by *Bacillus* species, contains ornithine as a constituent. In this organism, ornithine is an intermediate in both anabolic and catabolic routes of arginine metabolism. The two enzymes metabolizing ornithine in both these pathways, ornithine carbamoyltransferase (the enzyme involved in biosynthesis of arginine) and ornithine δ-aminotransferase (involved in arginine degradation) were studied, along with arginase. Induction of both anabolic and catabolic routes of arginine metabolism was observed when the cells stopped growing and started to produce the antibiotic (90). Of interest was the finding that the highest yield of bacitracin was obtained from a mutant with a genetic block in ornithine 5-aminotransferase. The mutation increases the availability of ornithine for the antibiotic synthesis since it cuts off the degradation of ornithine to glutamate and proline (90). It would be of interest to approach the study of antibiotic synthesis in this system, in which antibiotic synthesis is shown to be dependent on transfer of nitrogen atoms from the arginine molecule, in the light of the result with *Klebsiella aerogenes* (43, 45, 46).

Studies on the correlation between levels of GS and degradative enzymes have led to the conclusion that syntheses asparginase (91) and urease (44), enzymes catalyzing utilization of proline (87) in *Klebsiella aerogenes* or γ-aminobutyric acid in *E. coli* (129) as well as nitrogen-fixation in a variety of organisms (54, 105, 125), are activated by GS. For several other nitrogen-fixing bacterial groups, only circumstantial evidence for GS involvement in induction of nitrogenase was reported (57, 61, 71, 112).

Metabolic Regulation of Catabolic Reactions by Ammonia in Fungi

Ammonia or certain of its metabolic products have been shown to repress the synthesis of some enzymes of nitrogen catabolic pathways in *Aspergillus nidulans, Neurospora crassa,* and certain yeasts (84). This effect of ammonium has been termed "ammonium repression" (9) and was shown to control a number of systems, such as the catabolism of purines (100), arginine (10, 35), and histidine (56), transport of urea (37), and synthesis of extracellular proteases (23), and nitrogen reductase (84).

The specific control elements in this general mode of nitrogen catabolite repression are not yet well characterized. However, some key observations point to several possibilities. Dubois et al (35) proposed that in *Saccharomyces cerevisiae* the NADP-dependent glutamate dehydrogenase (GDH) complexed with ammonia and 2-ketoglutarate plays a direct role in nitrogen metabolite repression. This suggests a role for NADP-GDH similar to that proposed by Magasanik (73) for glutamine synthetase. Arst & Cove (9) have concluded from their observations in *Aspergillus nidulans* that a product of a gene, *areA,* is required for the synthesis of nitrogen-catabolic enzymes and that ammonium repression involves an interference with the action of this positive regulatory factor. In recent reports on nitrogen repression in *Neurospora crassa,* Dantzig et al (23a) observed that nitrogen metabolites (other than ammonium) appear to be responsible for the mediation of "ammonium repression." This was supported by the observation that in *N. crassa,* the *am* mutant, which lacks NADP-GDH activity, was derepressed for synthesis of nitrate reductase, even in the presence of ammonium. However, certain amino acids, including arginine, asparagine, and glutamate, could still repress nitrate reductase in this *am* mutant. The involvement of glutamine in nitrogen metabolite repression was further studied in glutamine-requiring auxotrophs of *N. crassa* (85). It was shown that in such *gln-a* mutants, neither glutamate nor glutamate plus ammonium were as effective in repressing nitrate reductase as glutamine. In a similar mutant of *N. crassa* which possesses a much reduced GS, nitrate reductase was freed from ammonium repression (38). These observations strongly suggest that the effect of ammonium on nitrate reductase induction is probably the result of its conversion to glutamine.

NITROGEN METABOLITE REGULATION IN ANTIBIOTIC PRODUCTION

Antibiotic Biosynthesis in Streptomycetes

β-LACTAM ANTIBIOTICS The effect of nitrogen metabolism on the production of cephalosporins by *Streptomyces clavuligerus* has recently been reported (5). Antibiotic production in this strain had previously been shown to be affected by the phosphate (3) and carbon (2) state of the medium. When the effect of various organic and inorganic nitrogen-containing compounds on antibiotic production was studied, a negative effect of excess ammonium was observed. The addition of ammonium to cultures grown on asparagine, glutamine, and other amino acids as nitrogen source resulted in suppression of antibiotic production (5). The ammonium effect can be explained either by the inhibition of the "antibiotic synthetases" or, alternatively, by an effect at some other step(s) that is required for synthesis of antibiotics. In order to distinguish between these alternatives, excess amounts of ammonium were added at different times during the growth period and antibiotic production was monitored (5). The ammonium effect expressed itself early in the growth phase. Furthermore, no inhibition was found at any time when ammonium was added after the onset of antibiotic production. It appears from this observation that inhibition of antibiotic synthesis by ammonium is not due to inhibition of the antibiotic synthetase activity. Rather, an earlier process is affected, which might involve either the biosynthesis of the antibiotic synthetases or other metabolic steps required to enhance production.

The various ammonium-assimilatory reactions of *S. clavuligerus* were investigated during the growth and productive phase (2). Both GS and GOGAT, as well as reductive amination of α-keto acids, were studied. As described above for other microbial systems, GS in *S. clavuligerus* was repressed when ammonium was in excess. Although GDH was not detected, alanine dehydrogenase (ADH) levels were enhanced under conditions of excess ammonium. An alternative assimilatory function for ADH was also suggested (6), based on the observation that high levels of ADH were found only when cells were grown in the presence of ammonia. When different amino acids were used in place of ammonia, only alanine elicited an increase in ADH. In this case, a catabolic function for ADH was suggested (6). Of interest were the findings that GS activity reached a peak during late stages of growth when ammonia was depleted from the medium; no adenylylated form of the enzyme could be detected under any of the conditions investigated (N. Shuster and Y. Aharonowitz, unpublished).

The relationship between GS activity, cephalosporin titers, and specific cephalosporin production in *S. clavuligerus* showed that the highest specific production was obtained under those growth conditions that led to high GS activity. When cells were grown on media containing ammonium in excess, both GS activity and specific production decreased (2). In contrast, growing the cells in nitrogen-limiting concentrations of ammonium resulted in a lower biomass with increased specific production.

NOURSEOTHRICIN In view of the interrelationship observed between nitrogen metabolism and antibiotic synthesis, the results obtained by Gräfe et al (50–52) are of interest. It was found that *o*-aminobenzoic acid (OABA) stimulated the production of the antibiotic nourseothricin by *Streptomyces noursei* (13). The addition of OABA caused a switch from one metabolic state, in which catabolism of amino acids is preferred, towards another state in which enhanced amino acid biosynthesis using ammonium was observed (52). The GS activity in *S. noursei* (51) is repressed by excess ammonium and derepressed when the ammonium disappears from the medium. Alanine addition markedly increased the ADH activity, and if ammonium and alanine were added simultaneously, GS was elevated. These observations have led to further investigations of the conditions and mechanisms that cause the switch in metabolism. The working hypothesis is that limitation of amino acid uptake, together with oxidative deamination, can remove nitrogencatabolites that might repress antibiotic synthesis. It was suggested that OABA inhibited amino acid catabolism, thereby enhancing antibiotic production (50). The experimental evidence appears to support this hypothesis; the transition from the state of low ADH, low GS, and high levels of GDH to a state in which ADH and GS activities are high was effected by increasing the concentration of the nitrogen source in the medium. In contrast, a decrease in ammonium was shown to induce the transition in the opposite direction. The same could also be achieved by the addition of different aminobenzoic acids known to stimulate production. Furthermore, a similar effect was brought about by agents known to affect the Redox potential of the cell (52).

ERYTHROMYCIN A more specific role for ADH in antibiotic production was reported in the biosynthesis of erythromycin by *Streptomyces erythreus* (99). A selective utilization of alanine for growth and antibiotic production was associated with high NAD-ADH activity. The enzyme is substrate-inducible, but the induction is not specific; glutamate serves equally well as an inducer. ADH activity was shown to be repressed by glucose or propanol, but 48 h after propanol addition a "derepression" occurred. In a noninduced culture, ADH activity decreased and a constant concentration of alanine in the mycelium was observed when cells were in the stationary phase. This suggested either the participation of an additional enzymatic system in the regulation of alanine metabolism or a shift in the anabolic-catabolic equilibrium of the cell (99). Unfortunately, the behavior of other enzymes involved in nitrogen metabolism was not reported.

It would be of interest to see how those physiological conditions leading to a simultaneous decrease in cephalosporin production and ADH in *S. clavuligerus* (6) affect erythromycin biosynthesis in *S. erythreus.* Furthermore, the observations made with *S. clavuligerus* grown on alanine and high concentration of ammonium as the nitrogen source showed decreased GS activity, increased catabolic ADH activity, and decreased cephalosporin production (2, 6), whereas in *S. noursei* alanine and excess ammonium caused an increase of both enzyme activities. Such discrepancies complicate our ability to interpret the observations and establish a general scheme. The use of different organisms, products, and different growth conditions is probably the reason for these contradictory results.

β-Lactam Antibiotic Biosynthesis in Fungi

CEPHALOSPORIN C For all three amino acids [α-aminoadipic acid (AAA), cysteine, and valine] which make up the cephalosporin C molecule produced by *Cephalosporium acremonium* (1), glutamate is expected to supply the α-amino nitrogen. Thus, the correlation between the specific activity of GDH and cephalosporin C biosynthesis was investigated in producing mutants of *C. acremonium* (88). In one line of mutants NADP-GDH was derepressed (or induced) during the stationary growth phase. This line of mutants stems from a high producing parent mutant. It was suggested that increased synthesis of GDH during the stationary phase may remove a nitrogen limitation on cephalosporin C synthesis by ensuring an adequate supply of L-glutamate for the transamination of α-ketoadipic acid, 3-phosphopyruvic acid, and α-ketoisovalerate to produce AAA, serine (for cysteine synthesis), and valine (88). It would be of interest to test this hypothesis by investigating a mutant isolated directly from the wild type (impaired in glutamate biosynthesis) for improved cephalosporin production. *Saccharomyces cerevisiae* (96) and *Neurospora crassa* (103) have been shown to possess two enzymes: a NAD-GDH with a catabolic role and NADP-GDH which is implicated in glutamate biosynthesis. High levels of NADP-GDH were shown to be invariably associated with low levels of the NAD-specific GDH and vice versa. It would be of interest to follow these two activities under different growth conditions in relation to antibiotic production.

PENICILLIN Penicillin production by *Penicillium chrysogenum* has very recently been shown to be under nitrogen control (S. Sanchez, personal communication). Maximal penicillin production was found only when low ammonium concentrations were added. Under these conditions GS activity and the glutamine concentration in the pool were high. When ammonium concentration was increased, the opposite results were observed. Glutamine was found to stimulate penicillin production when added to resting cells previously grown in low ammonium. In addition, when the glutamine analog, methionine sulfoximine, was added, it supported growth and antibiotic production, even though GS activity was inhibited. A role for glutamine as an amino donor for the synthesis of at least one of the amino acids connected with the penicillin structure has been proposed (S. Sanchez, personal communication). However, a different role for glutamine can be suggested, based on the role of glutamine as an element involved in nitrogen metabolite repression (discussed above) (73, 110). Thus, when cells are in a resting state, catabolic enzyme activities can be derepressed or induced and subsequently repressed by addition of glutamine. A biosynthetic role for glutamine in penicillin biosynthesis is further supported by the recent observations made with nitrogen-starved conidia of *Neurospora crassa* (40). An induction of GS synthesis was found in conidia that were nutritionally deprived. The addition of ammonia or glutamine resulted in the accumulation of glutamate and arginine. Evidence indicating degradation of glutamine with subsequent formation of glutamate and glutamine (resynthesis), as a necessary step for the synthesis and accumulation of arginine from exogenous glutamine, was presented. A model was proposed suggesting that in non-growing conidia of *N. crassa* a cycle occurs in which glutamine is degraded and resynthesized. The advantage of such a cycle would be the utilization of carbon and nitrogen for the synthesis of amino acids in general and for the synthesis and accumulation of arginine and/or glutamine in particular (40). If such a cycle occurs in the penicillin-producing fungi, it would support a role for glutamine in penicillin synthesis suggested above. Further studies on the structure and function of eucaryotic GS have recently been published (24).

TRANSPORT CAPACITY AND AMINO ACID POOL COMPOSITION

One interesting feature of the uptake of nutrients from the environment is its control by intracellular metabolites which act as regulatory effectors (84). Any change in the balance of transport control mechanisms (due to changes in the physiological growth conditions or genetic modifications) will result in changes in transport kinetics and will affect the accumulation or release of metabolites that function in primary as well as secondary metabolism.

It is outside the scope of this article to discuss the studies of nitrogen uptake in depth. A few general regulatory processes that might be relevant for the study of antibiotic biosynthesis will be discussed.

Ammonium Transport

Since ammonium has been implicated as a participant in nitrogen metabolite repression and regulation of antibiotic production, it is relevant to mention some of the factors that influence its uptake. In *Penicillium chrysogenum* (53), the rate of ammonium uptake increased dramatically when cells were starved for nitrogen. Both glutamine and asparagine were shown to inhibit its uptake. Similar results were observed in *Saccharomyces cerevisiae* (97), although there was no significant derepression of this transport system during nitrogen starvation. The isolation and characterization of low transport mutants in *Aspergillus nidulans* (84) gave rise to the suggestion that the intracellular concentration of ammonia regulates transport both by inhibition and by repression of the synthesis of some protein components of the uptake system. The regulation of ammonium transport by asparagine and glutamine is further supported by a study of ammonia and L-amide content of the intracellular pool in the filamentous fungus *Stemphylum botrysum* (17), which shows that L-amides, rather than ammonia, regulate the transport system for ammonium.

Ammonium Effect on Amino Acid Transport in Fungi

The effect of ammonium on amino acid uptake was studied in several systems. In *Saccharomyces cerevisiae* (98) ammonium could prevent the increase in rate of amino acid uptake initially brought about by nitrogen starvation. Comparison of a mutant that lacks the anabolic NADP-GDH and another mutant that lacks NADP-GDH and possesses derepressed levels of the catabolic NAD-GDH led to the suggestion that the inhibition of amino acid transport by ammonium ions results from the uptake of the latter into the cell. The subsequent incorporation of ammonium ions into the α-amino groups of glutamate and other amino acids indicates that anabolic NADP-GDH inhibits amino acid transport by virtue of its enzymatic activity rather than its function as a regulatory element. These observations contrast with those suggesting a direct role of NADP-GDH in nitrogen metabolite repression (35). The involvement of the regulatory gene *areA* (9) in ammonium repression was discussed above.

Control of Amino Acid Transport in Bacteria

Kustu et al (65) have recently presented evidence for general nitrogen control over amino acid transport. They found that the synthesis of both GS and transport proteins in *Salmonella typhimurium* is elevated either when nitrogen is limited in the growth medium or as a result of the introduction into the strain of nitrogen-regulating mutations. The mutations map quite close to the structural gene for GS, and it was suggested that they were located in a regulatory gene *glnR* (65).

Amino acid transport is not exclusively controlled by the availability of nitrogen in the growth medium. Alper & Ames (7) reported that the availability of carbon and energy also affects the transport of amino acids in a general way. They showed that *Salmonella typhimurium* mutants lacking either adenyl cyclase or CRP were partially resistant to a variety of antibiotics and inhibitory analogs of normal bacterial energy and carbon sources. It was suggested that these transport systems are all under positive control by cAMP and that cAMP acts as a signal molecule for energy and carbon deprivation. Furthermore, the permeases for aromatic amino acids are also under cAMP control (7). According to these authors, as the cells increase the cAMP concentration in response to carbon and energy starvation, the concentration of the cAMP-CRP complex rises and new operons can be activated according to a special hierarchy that exists in the affinities of different promoters to the cAMP-CRP complex.

Of special interest is the effect of cAMP on amino acid transport in streptomycetes. Ring et al (95) have shown that in resting cells of *Streptomyces hydrogenans,* exogenous cAMP and dibutyryl-cAMP stimulate the active uptake of 2-aminobutyric acid and a variety of amino acids. Further studies (66) provided evidence that cells grown under various conditions exhibited different transport capacities for several amino acids. These differences were observed regardless of the presence or absence of amino acids in the growth media.

Intracellular Concentrations of Free Amino Acids During the Growth Cycle

Modulation of cell structure and function in response to environmental variations reflect changes in genetic expression which are mediated by the interaction of intracellular substances acting through control systems (107). Therefore, the relationship between environmental conditions, growth cycle, and the intracellular concentrations of free amino acids in the cellular pool is an interesting subject for further studies.

It was shown by Tempest & Meers (107) that all free amino acid pools of various bacteria and certain yeasts were similar in that they contain only a limited range of detectable amino acids; in general, those pools in Gram-positive bacteria and yeasts have 5 to 20 times higher the concentrations than the pools in Gram-negative bacteria. Glutamate invariably predominated and generally accounted for over 50% of the total amino acid content of the pool. Brown & Stanley (18) presented evidence to show that the size and composition of such pools are environmentally controlled and may be considered essential for cell function under the imposed culture conditions. The concentration of NaC1 has the most marked effect on pool composition. In microorganisms such as streptomycetes, which undergo differentiation, the concentrations of all extractable amino acids are altered during the growth of the culture (66). It was shown that the individual alterations were neither strictly synchronized nor did they occur to the same extent for each amino acid. Appreciable concentrations of free amino acids were found only in stationary or slowly growing cells, whereas during the rapid growth phase the level was quite low. The uptake capacity was lowest when the pool size was at its maximum, and increased when the pool size was lowered. It was therefore suggested that in rapidly growing cells, the transport capacities and biosynthetic systems are growth-rate limiting. Thus, the supply of amino acids may be rate limiting for protein synthesis (66). These observations may explain some of the reasons for the trophophase-idiophase kinetics that characterized many of the fermentations conducted in batch culture (19). Furthermore, the increased transport capacity accompanying the increase in growth rate found in streptomycetes grown in continuous cultures raises the possibility that amino acid uptake is tightly coupled to macromolecular biosynthesis (66). This may explain the inability, in some instances, to detect appreciable amounts of secondary metabolites in continuously growing cultures.

ANTIBIOTIC PRODUCTION, PROTEOLYSIS, AND SPORULATION

A temporal relationship between peptide antibiotic production, appearance of intracellular serine proteases, and sporulation has been observed in certain *Bacillus* species (58, 105, 115). This observation led to the isolation of mutants simultaneously impaired in sporulation, antibiotic synthesis, and proteolytic activity. Furthermore, it was found that certain *B. cereus* mutants blocked in both sporogenesis and antibiotic production were protease negative (108), while sporulation and protease negative mutants were also blocked in antibiotic production (68). A mutant from *B. cereus* was isolated and found to possess altered intracellular protease, lower turnover rate, and an inability to process properly the precursors for spore coat synthesis (22). Quite recently, *B. brevis* mutants were described which have lost the ability to produce linear gramicidin; these mutants produced defective spores. Of interest was the finding that the defect could be overcome by the addition of linear gramicidin during the early stages of sporulation (80). Nevertheless, other mutants have been characterized in which gramicidin S synthesis is defective, yet sporulation is normal (29).

In a study of the synthesis of the polypeptide antibiotic mycobacillin by *B. subtilis* (14), it was found that mutant strains blocked in mycobacillin production produced less exoproteases regardless of their ability to sporulate. However, those mutants blocked in sporulation which produced effective proteases were not always mycobacillin producers. The need for a minimal level of exoprotease formation for elaboration of mycobacillin was suggested. A coordinate relationship was found between sporulation, serine protease production, and the antibiotic cephamycin C synthesis in *Streptomyces lactamdurans* (48). It was found that antibiotic production and serine protease formation were coordinately regulated. The relationship was quantitative; mutants that failed to produce serine protease also failed to produce cephamycin C. Moreover, mutants that produced abnormally high levels of the antibiotic produced equally elevated levels of serine protease. Of interest was the observation that mutants which failed to produce aerial mycelium also failed to synthesize the antibiotic and serine protease.

In a similar study, the effect of ammonium was investigated (2). It was found that in the β-lactam antibiotic producer *Streptomyces clavuligerus*, grown on a chemically defined medium, antibiotic production followed an increase in the total extracellular proteolytic activity when asparagine was the sole nitrogen source. However, substituting asparagine by ammonium drastically repressed both antibiotic and extracellular protease formation. In the latter case, although the growth rate was lower, the culture ultimately reached the same final cell mass (2) (Y. Aharonowitz and J. Piret, unpublished observations). Of interest was the similarity between the kinetics of appearance of GS (discussed above), extracellular proteases, and cephalosporin production, even with respect to the ammonium repression.

Freese et al (42) have recently reported that partial purine deprivation can cause sporulation of *Bacillus subtilis* in the presence of excess ammonium, glucose, and phosphate. Purine deprivation could be achieved either by using leaky purine mutations or by growing non-leaky purine auxotrophs supplemented with small amounts of required precursor. These results suggest the possibility of using similar mutations in order to avoid the ammonium effect in antibiotic production. Vitkovic & Sadoff (115) provided evidence that the antibiotic bacitracin may be a catabolic product of a preexisting, more complex molecule. These authors described a sporulation-specific seryl protease from *Bacillus licheniformis.* The action of this protease on antibiotic-free extracts of *B. licheniformis* cells yielded a peptide that was identified as bacitracin by its biological activity, spectral properties, and co-chromatography with purified bacitracin.

What might be the role of proteolytic enzymes in the process of antibiotic production? Szulmajster (106) suggested that two main functions may be currently attributed to the intracellular proteases in spore development. One concerns the extensive turnover of proteins occurring during sporulation, and the other, posttranscriptional modifications of preexisting vegetative proteins. Based on the observations discussed above, it is tempting to suggest that the same two functions may contribute to the initiation of antibiotic-specific gene expression with the concomitant increase of required antibiotic precursors. Thus if starvation for carbon, nitrogen, a required amino acid, or sulfur stimulates proteolysis (79), the regulation of such a system might be an interesting target for study of nitrogen regulation of antibiotic production.

In regard to the relationship between GS and sporulation, mutants isolated from *Bacillus subtilis* and *B. megaterium* displayed both GS and asporogenous phenotypes. Revertants either to prototrophy or to the ability to sporulate were studied, and a relationship between GS and sporulation was indicated. This relationship could not be entirely attributed to the catalytic properties of GS (92). In a different study (82) undertaken to investigate GS and GOGAT activities during growth and sporulation of *B. subtilis,* it was reported that GS activity was unaltered during the onset of sporulation. Using a different experimental approach (30), it was shown that the levels of GS, GDH, and arginase during growth and sporulation of *B. licheniformis* on various nitrogen sources did not change in such a way as to suggest a special function for any of these enzymes in the regulation of sporulation. Thus, even though GS plays a central role in nitrogen metabolism and regulation of gene expression in the enterics, no conclusive evidence for the direct involvement of GS in regulation of antibiotic production and differentiation in spore-forming organisms has yet been forthcoming.

There could be several reasons for a close connection between sporulation, antibiotic production, and proteases. One is that many of the mutants discussed above may be pleotropic mutants derived by mutation in a gene responsible for a common regulatory function (25, 101). The other possibility is that spore formation is the product of a linear sequence of events which includes antibiotic production and proteolysis in its earliest stages (74). A genetic alteration in one of these early steps should thus prevent the expression of subsequent functions in the pathway.

CONCLUDING REMARKS

This review summarizes results that suggest a correlation between the capacity of a given organism to synthesize an antibiotic molecule and the physiological state of the culture with respect to nitrogen metabolism. Controls operating at the level of primary nitrogen metabolism may also determine the efficiency of the antibiotic biosynthetic machinery. In this regard, the controls involving the glutamine synthetase molecule and other regulatory gene products operating in procaryotes (110), the mechanism termed "nitrogen metabolite repression" in fungi (9), and the special role suggested for glutamine in fungal systems (23a, 40) are particularly noteworthy. Several approaches to the study of nitrogen metabolite control in antibiotic production have been described in this review:

1. Nitrogen control at the catabolic level
2. Regulation at the biosynthetic level; glutamate, glutamine, antibiotic-specific precursors, and regulatory effectors.
3. Transport of nitrogen metabolites
4. Modulation of intracellular concentration of free metabolites
5. Protein turnover and degradation
6. Regulation of antibiotic "synthetase" formation.

Control of antibiotic biosynthesis probably occurs at the level of transcription, translation, and posttranslation. In fact, regulatory signals from nitrogen metabolism elicit effects at each level, although the nature of these signals remains to be determined. Nevertheless, it should be stressed that the expression of specific genes involved in antibiotic biosynthesis is most likely controlled by a host of different signals in which nitrogen metabolite control is just one candidate.

The integration of several lines of research into an overall picture of the regulation of antibiotic production would appear to be a difficult (if not impossible) task. Only fragmentary evidence is available on specific enzymes. In addition, most of the producing microorganisms can not yet be manipulated genetically. This is complicated by the fact that in many instances the same or structurally similar antibiotic is produced by different genera (67), whereas in most cases the producing strain excretes an array of related antibiotics (12). Nevertheless, since most of these secondary metabolites originate from primary metabolites common to most living cells, a more fruitful comparison of results should become possible by (*a*) using standardized growth conditions, (*b*) choosing defined media, and (*c*) studying different genera that produce similar antibiotics (i.e. β-lactam production by fungi and actinomycetes).

It is clear that the elucidation of regulatory mechanisms controlling antibiotic production will provide basic elements currently missing in industrial development of antibiotics: (*a*) a more logical basis for determining optimal physiological and growth conditions leading to maximum antibiotic production, and (*b*) an additional intellectual framework on which to base genetic modifications leading to strain improvement.

Acknowledgments

I wish to express my appreciation to Dr. David Gutnick for his critical reading and excellent editorial assistance in preparing this review, to Arnold L. Demain and Eugene Rosenberg for their critical reading, and to T. Gutnick for typing. My thanks also to Dr. S. Sanchez, who made his results available to me prior to publication.

The research in my laboratory was supported by a grant from the United States-Israel Binational Science Foundation (BSF).

Literature Cited

1. Abraham, E. P., Newton, G. G. F. 1967. In *Antibiotics II, Biosynthesis,* ed. D. Gottlieb, P. D. Shaw, pp. 1–16. Berlin: Springer. 466 pp.
2. Aharonowitz, Y. 1978. In *Genetics of Industrial Microorganisms,* ed. O. K. Sebek, A. I. Laskin, pp. 210–17. Washington DC: Am. Soc. Microbiol. 283 pp.
3. Aharonowitz, Y., Demain, A. L. 1977. *Arch. Microbiol.* 115:169–173
4. Aharonowitz, Y., Demain, A. L. 1978. *Antimicrob. Agents Chemother.* 14: 159–64
5. Aharonowitz, Y., Demain, A. L. 1979. *Can. J. Microbiol.* 25:61–67
6. Aharonowitz, Y., Friedrich, C. G. 1980. *Arch. Microbiol.* 125:137–42
7. Alper, M. D., Ames, B. N. 1978. *J. Bacteriol.* 133:149–57
8. Arnstein, H. R. V., Grant, P. T. 1954. *Biochem. J.* 57:360
9. Arst, H. N., Cove, D. J. 1973. *Mol. Gen. Genet.* 126:111–41
10. Bartnik, E., Guzewska, J., Weglenski, P. 1973. *Mol. Gen. Genet.* 126:85–92
11. Bender, R. A., Magasanik, B. 1977. *J. Bacteriol.* 132:100–5
12. Berdy, J. 1974. *Adv. Appl. Microbiol.* 18:309–406

13. Bocker, H., Thrum, H. 1966. In *Antibiotics—Advances in Research, Production and Clinical Use,* ed. M. Herold, Z. Gabriel, pp. 584–87. London: Butterworths; Prague: UCS Medical Press
14. Bose, R., Ray, B., Bose, S. K. 1979. *Folia Microbiol. Prague* 24:373–75
15. Brenchley, J. E., Baker, C. E., Patil, L. G. 1975. *J. Bacteriol.* 124:182–89
16. Brenchley, J. E., Prival, M. J., Magasanik, B. 1973. *J. Biol. Chem.* 248:6122–28
17. Briman, A., Barash, I. 1980. *J. Gen. Microbiol.* 116:201–6
18. Brown, C. M., Stanley, S. O. 1972. *J. Appl. Chem. Biotechnol.* 22:363–89
19. Bu'Lock, J. D., Powell, A. J. 1965. *Experientia* 21:55–56
20. Bu'Lock, J. D.,Shepherd, D., Winstanley, D. J. 1969. *Can. J. Microbiol.* 15:279–85
21. Chen, Y., Walker, J. B. 1977. *Biochem. Biophys. Res. Commun.* 77:688–92
22. Cheng, Y. E., Aronson, A. T. 1977. *Proc. Natl. Acad. Sci. USA* 74:1254–58
23. Cohen, B. L. 1972. *J. Gen. Microbiol.* 71:293–99
23a. Dantzig, A. H., Zurowski, W. K., Ball, T. S., Nason, A. 1978. *J. Bacteriol.* 133:671–79
24. Darila, G., Sanchez, F., Palacios, R., Mora, J. 1978. *J. Bacteriol.* 134:693–98
25. Daum, S. J., Lemke, J. R. 1979. *Ann. Rev. Microbiol.* 33:241–65
26. Demain, A. L. 1972. *J. Appl. Chem. Biotechnol.* 22:345–62
27. Demain, A. L., Kennel, Y. M., Aharonowitz, Y. 1979. In *Microbial Technology: Current State, Future Prospects,* ed. A. T. Bull, D. C. Ellwood, C. Ratledge, 29:163–85. London: Soc. Gen. Microbiol., Cambridge Univ. Press. 422 pp.
28. Demain, A. L., Masurekar, P. S. 1974. *J. Gen. Microbiol.* 82:143–51
29. Demain, A. L., Piret, J. M. 1978. In *Spores VII,* ed. G. Chambliss, J. C. Vary, p. 17. Washington DC: *Am. Soc. Microbiol.*
30. Donohue, T. J., Bernlohr, R. W. 1978. See Ref. 29, pp. 293–98
31. Drew, S. W., Demain, A. L. 1973. *Biotech. Bioeng.* 15:743–54
32. Drew, S. W., Demain, A. L. 1975. *Antimicrob. Agents Chemother.* 8:5–10
33. Drew, S. W., Demain, A. L. 1977. *Ann. Rev. Microbiol.* 31:343–56
34. Drew, S. W., Winstanley, D. J., Demain, A. L. 1976. *Appl. Environ. Microbiol.* 31:143–45
35. Dubois, E., Grenson, M., Wiame, J. M. 1974. *Eur. J. Biochem.* 48:60.–16
36. Dulaney, E. L. 1948. *J. Bacteriol.* 56:305–13
37. Dunn, E., Pateman, J. A. 1972. *Heredity* 29:129
38. Dunn-Coleman, N. S., Tomsett, A. B., Gratt, R. H. 1979. *J. Bacteriol.* 139:697–700
39. Deleted in proof
40. Espin, G., Palacios, R., Mora, J. 1979. *J. Gen. Microbiol.* 115:59–68
41. Floss, H. G., Chang, C. J., Mascaretti, O.,Shimada, K. 1978. *Planta Med.* 34: 345–80
42. Freese, E., Heinze, J. E., Galliers, E. M. 1979. *J. Gen. Microbiol.* 115:193–205
43. Friedrich, B., Friedrich, C. G., Magasanik, B. 1978. *J. Bacteriol.* 133:686–91
44. Friedrich, B., Magasanik, B. 1977. *J. Bacteriol.* 131:446–52
45. Friedrich, B., Magasanik, B. 1978. *J. Bacteriol.* 133:680–85
46. Friedrich, B., Magasanik, B. 1979. *J. Bacteriol.* 137:1127–33
47. Gallo, M., Katz, E. 1972. *J. Bacteriol.* 109:659–67
48. Ginther, C. L. 1979. *Antimicrob. Agents Chemother.* 15:522–26
49. Goulden, S. A., Chattaway, W. F. 1969. *J. Gen. Microbiol.* 59:111–18
50. Gräfe, U., Bocker, H., Reinhardt, G., Thrum, H. 1978. *Z. Allg. Mikrobiol.* 18:479–86
51. Gräfe, U., Bocker, H., Thrum, H. 1977. *Z. Allg. Mikrobiol.* 17:201–9
52. Gräfe, U., Bocker, H., Thrum, H. 1979. *Z. Allg. Mikrobiol.* 19:235–46
53. Hackette, S. L., Skye, G. E., Burton, C. E., Segel, H. 1970. *J. Biol. Chem.* 245:4241–50
54. Hillmer, P., Fahlbusch, K. 1979. *Arch. Microbiol.* 122:213–18
55. Hopwood, D. A., Merrick, M. J. 1977. *Bacteriol. Rev.* 41:595–635
56. Hynes, M. J. 1974. *J. Bacteriol.* 120: 116–23
57. Jones, B. L., Monty, K. J. 1979. *J. Bacteriol.* 139:1007–13
58. Katz, E. 1967. See Ref. 1, pp. 276–341
59. Katz, E., Demain, A. L. 1977. *Bacteriol. Rev.* 41:449–74
60. Kirkpatrick, J. R., Doolin, L. E., Godfrey, O. W. 1973. *Antimicrob. Agents Chemother.* 4:542–50
61. Kleinschmidt, J. A., Kleiner, D. 1978. *Eur. J. Biochem.* 89:51–60
62. Kominek, L. A. 1967. See Ref. 1, pp. 231–39
63. Kominek, L. A. 1972. *Antimicrob. Agents Chemother.* 1:123–34
64. Krupinski, V. M., Robbers, J. E., Floss, H. G. 1976. *J. Bacteriol.* 125:158–65

65. Kustu, S. G., McFarland, N. C., Hui, S. P., Esmon, B., Ames, G. F.-L. 1979. *J. Bacteriol.* 138:218–34
66. Langheinrich, W., Ring, K. 1976. *Arch. Microbiol.* 109:227–35
67. Lechevalier, H. A. 1975. *Adv. Appl. Microbiol.* 19:25–45
68. Leighton, T. G., Doi, R. H., Warren, A. J., Kelln, R. A. 1973. *J. Mol. Biol.* 76:103–22
69. Leisinger, T., Margraff, R. 1979. *Microbiol.Rev.* 43:422–42
70. Liras, P., Villaneuva, J. R., Martin, J. F. 1977. *J. Gen. Microbiol.* 102:269–77
71. Ludwig, R. A. 1978. *J. Bacteriol.* 135:114–23
72. Lugano, J. M., Revilla, G., Villaneuva, J. R., Martin, J. F. 1979. *J. Gen. Microbiol.* 115:207–11
73. Magasanik, B. 1976. *Prog. Nucleic Acid Res. Mol. Biol.* 17:99–115
74. Mandelstam, J. 1969. *Symp. Soc. Gen. Microbiol.* 19:377–402
75. Martin, J. F. 1977. *Adv. Biochem. Eng.* 6:105–27
76. Masurekar, P. S., Demain, A. L. 1972. *Can. J. Microbiol.* 18:1045–48
77. Masurekar, P. S., Demain, A. L. 1974. *Antimicrob. Agents Chemother.* 6: 366–68
78. Matern, H., Brillinger, G. V., Pape, H. 1973. *Arch. Mikrobiol.* 88:37–48
79. Miller, C. G. 1975. *Ann. Rev. Microbiol.* 29:485–504
80. Mukherjee, P. K., Paulus, H. 1977. *Proc. Natl. Acad. Sci. USA* 74:780–84
81. Nagaoka, K., Demain, A. L. 1975. *J. Antibiot.* 28:627–35
82. Pan, F. L., Coot, J. G. 1979. *J. Gen. Microbiol.* 112:373–77
83. Pastan, I., Adhya, S. 1976. *Bacteriol Rev.* 40:527–51
84. Pateman, J. A., Kinghorn, J. R. 1976. In *The Filamentous Fungi, Biosynthesis and Metabolism,* ed. J. C. Smith, D. R. Berry, 2:159–237. London: Arnold. 520 pp.
85. Premakumar, R., Sorger, G. J., Gooden, D. 1979. *J. Bacteriol.* 137: 1119–26
86. Prival, M. J., Brenchley, J. E., Magasanik, B. 1973. *J. Biol. Chem.* 248: 4334–44
87. Prival, M. J., Magasanik, B. 1971. *J. Biol. Chem.* 246:6288–96
88. Queener, S. W., McDermott, J., Radue, A. B. 1975. *Antimicrob. Agents Chemother.* 7:646–51
89. Queener, S. W., Sebek, O. K., Vézina, C. 1978. *Ann. Rev. Microbiol.* 32:593–636
90. Raczynska-Bojanowska, K. 1974. *Postepy Hig. Med. Dosw.* 28:499–514
91. Resnick, A. D., Magasanik, B. 1976. *J. Biol. Chem.* 251:2722–28
92. Reysset, G., Bott, K. F., Aubert, J.-P. 1978. See Ref. 30, pp. 271–76
93. Rickenberg, H. V. 1974. *Ann. Rev. Microbiol.* 28:353–69
94. Rinehart, K. L., Stroshane, R. M. 1976. *J. Antibiot.* 29:319–53
95. Ring, K., Langheinrich, W., Ehle, H., Foit, B. 1977. *Arch. Microbiol.* 115: 199–205
96. Roon, R. J., Even, H. L. 1973. *J. Bacteriol.* 116:367–73
97. Roon, R. J., Even, H. L., Dunlop, P., Larimore, F. L. 1975. *J. Bacteriol.* 122:502–9
98. Roon, R. J., Larimore, F., Levy, J. S. 1975. *J. Bacteriol.* 124:325–31
99. Roszkowski, J., Rafalski, A., Raczynska-Bojanowska, K. 1969. *Acta Microbiol. Pol. Ser. B* 1(18):59–68
100. Scazzocchio, O., Darlington, A. J. 1968. *Biochim. Biophys. Acta* 166: 557–68
101. Schaffer, P. 1969. *Bacteriol. Rev.* 33: 48–71
102. Snoke, J. E. 1960. *J. Bacteriol.* 81: 986–89
103. Stachow, C. S., Sanwal, B. D. 1967. *Biochim. Biophys. Acta* 139:294–307
104. Stevens, C. M., De Long, C. W. 1958. *J. Biol. Chem.* 230:991
105. Streicher, S. L., Shanmugam, K. T., Ausubel, F., Morandi, C., Goldberg, R. B. 1974. *J. Bacteriol.* 120:815–21
106. Szulmajster, J. 1979. *Trends Biochem. Sci.* 4:18–22
107. Tempest, D. W., Meers, J. L. 1970. *J. Gen. Microbiol.* 64:171–85
108. Tempest, D. W., Meers, J. L., Brown, C. M. 1970. *Biochem. J.* 117:405–7
109. Tomino, S., Yamada, M., Itoh, H., Kurahashi, K. 1967. *Biochemistry* 6: 2552–60
110. Tyler, B. 1978. *Ann. Rev. Biochem.* 47:1127–62
111. Tyler, B., DeLeo, A. B., Magasanik, B. 1974. *Proc. Natl. Acad. Sci. USA* 71: 225–29
112. Upchurch, R. G., Elkan, G. H. 1978. *J. Gen. Microbiol.* 104:219–25
113. Vandamme, E. J., Demain, A. L. 1976. *Antimicrob. Agents Chemother.* 10: 265–73
114. Vanek, Z., Mikulik, K. 1978. *Folia Microbiol. Prague* 23:309–28
115. Vitkovic, L., Sadoff, H. L. 1977. *J. Bacteriol.* 131:897–905
116. Walker, J. B. 1978. In *Cyclitols and Phosphoinositides,* ed. W. Wells, F. Ei-

senberg Jr., pp. 423–38. New York: Academic
117. Walker, J. B. 1979. *Folia Microbiol. Prague* 24:286–91
118. Walker, J. B., Hnilica, V. S. 1964. *Biochim. Biophys. Acta* 89:473–82
119. Walker, J. B., Walker, M. S. 1967. *Biochemistry* 6:3821–29
120. Walker, J. B., Walker, M. S. 1968. *Biochim. Biophys. Acta* 170:219–20
121. Walker, J. B., Walker, M. S. 1969. *Biochemistry* 8:763–70
122. Walker, J. B., Walker, M. S. 1970. *Methods Enzymol.* 17A:1012–15
123. Walker, M. S., Walker, J. B. 1965. *Biochim. Biophys. Acta* 97:397–98
124. Walker, M. S., Walker, J. B. 1967. *Biochim. Biophys. Acta* 136:272–78
125. Wall, J. D., Gest, H. 1979. *J. Bacteriol.* 137:1459–63
126. Williams, W. K., Katz, E. 1977. *Antimicrob. Agents Chemother.* 11:281–90
127. Woodruff, H. B., Ruger, M. 1948. *J. Bacteriol.* 56:315–21
128. Yajima, T., Mason, K. T., Katz, E. 1975. *Antimicrob. Agents Chemother.* 7:773–80
129. Zaboura, M., Halpern, Y. S. 1978. *J. Bacteriol.* 133:447–51
130. Zähner, H., Maas, W. K. 1972. In *Biology of Antibiotics.* New York: Springer. 125 pp.
131. Zee, L., Hornemann, U., Floss, H. G. 1975. *Biochem. Physiol. Pflanz.* 168: 19–25

Ann. Rev. Microbiol. 1980. 34:235–62

MUTAGENICITY AND CARCINOGENICITY OF MYCOTOXINS: DNA Binding as a Possible Mode of Action

❖1776

Avishay-Abraham Stark

Department of Biochemistry, Tel Aviv University, Tel Aviv, Israel

CONTENTS

INTRODUCTION 235
RELATIONSHIP BETWEEN GENETIC ACTIVITY AND CARCINOGENICITY OF MYCOTOXINS OTHER THAN AFLATOXINS 237
GENETIC ACTIVITY OF MYCOTOXINS FOR WHICH CARCINOGENICITY HAS NOT YET BEEN REPORTED 244
AFLATOXINS AND RELATED COMPOUNDS 248
Introduction 248
Structure-Activity Relationship in Aflatoxins and Related Compounds 248
Mutagenicity of Aflatoxins and Related Compounds 250
Nature of the Mutations Induced by Aflatoxins 251
Cellular Functions Affecting Mutagenesis by Aflatoxins 251
RELATIONSHIP BETWEEN NUCLEIC ACID BINDING, CARCINOGENICITY, AND GENETIC ACTIVITY OF MYCOTOXINS 252
Mycotoxins Other Than Aflatoxins 252
Aflatoxins and Sterigmatocystin 253
Organotropism and Species Specificity of Carcinogenicity of AFB_1 As Related to Nucleic Acid Binding 254
Nature of AFB_1- and Sterigmatocystin-DNA Adducts 255
CONCLUDING REMARKS 257

INTRODUCTION

Environmental carcinogenesis today is a matter of great concern and a field of extensive research, mainly due to the realization that the etiologies of

0066-4227/80/1001-0235$01.00

most human cancers reside in environmental factors (93) and that certain chemicals can induce cancer. It is easy to envision exposure to carcinogenic chemicals through diet, occupation, or habits; the likelihood of being afflicted with cancer thus becomes a function of one's life style.

Due to historical reasons, all early and most current research concerning carcinogenic chemicals focused on the properties of synthetic compounds. A substantial amount of evidence, accumulated during the past two decades, points to the importance of *naturally occurring* carcinogens (95, 102, 127, 187, 189) as health hazards. Most of these carcinogens are secondary metabolites of microorganisms and plants. Most relevant to man are those compounds occurring in plants which are used as foods, medicines, and beverages.

Of special interest are the *mycotoxins,* a versatile family of secondary fungal metabolites eliciting toxicity (mycotoxicoses) in man and animals. Mycotoxins are intimately associated with almost every food or feed and can be produced by contaminating fungi at every stage of harvesting, production, and storage of food. It is now well established that, among other ill-effects, several mycotoxins induce cancer in experimental animals; one mycotoxin has been implicated as carcinogenic for humans. Carcinogenicity of mycotoxins has been reviewed (36, 37, 95, 102, 127, 187, 189).

The extensive work of Ames and his colleagues (1–3, 89–92) and of many other groups which established a strong correlation between the carcinogenic and mutagenic properties of chemicals has had an enormous impact in the field of chemical and environmental carcinogenesis. It has lent strong support for the hypothesis that somatic mutations play an important role in the formation of tumors (13, 68) and has permitted rapid and inexpensive means for screening of chemicals with potential carcinogenicity. Today, there is an abundance of short-term tests for potential carcinogenicity. Among those that have been used to detect activity of mycotoxins are the Rec effect (differential toxicity to wild-type and rec$^-$ strains of *Bacillus subtilis*), mutation induction in yeast, induction of chromosomal aberration and DNA breaks in mammalian cells in tissue culture, dominant-lethal effects and teratogenicity in animals, and binding of mycotoxins to nucleic acids.

It is suggested here that the term *genetic activity,* (15) rather than mutagenicity, be used for the description of compounds affecting the genetic material, not necessarily by induction of proper mutations. The reader is referred to the series, *Chemical Mutagens, Principles and Methods for Their Detection,* Vols. 1–5, ed. A. Hollander Plenum Press, New York, and reference (90) for a detailed description and analysis of genetic activity tests.

Many mycotoxins have been assayed in the above-mentioned systems and a considerable number of them proved to be genetically active (55, 102, 162). It should be noted, though, that carcinogenic mycotoxins, especially those belonging to the aflatoxin series, are capable of interaction with cellular macromolecules other than nucleic acids (4, 17, 51, 52, 86, 199). This suggests that processes leading to tumor formation may not depend solely on the genetic activity of such mycotoxins. It is difficult to imagine, however, how the persistent loss or change of response to growth control functions (genetically transmitted through many generations) would not involve the genetic material, at least in the initiation of the process. This review is thus focused on the relationship between genetic and carcinogenic activities of mycotoxins and on some molecular aspects of their interactions with the genetic material. Further studies will hopefully enable us to evaluate the relevance of RNA and/or protein-carcinogen interactions to the initiation or propagation of the formation of tumors.

RELATIONSHIP BETWEEN GENETIC ACTIVITY AND CARCINOGENICITY OF MYCOTOXINS OTHER THAN AFLATOXINS

Fourteen mycotoxins are recognized as carcinogens. Tables 1 and 2 summarize information concerning the carcinogenicity and genetic activities of the various mycotoxins and clearly show that, with the exception of the oligopeptide cyclochlorotin, each carcinogenic mycotoxin is genetically active. The inclusion of embryotoxicity, teratogenicity, and mutagenicity in evaluation of the carcinogenic potential of mycotoxins has been already emphasized by Hayes (55). Table 1 also includes tests for induction of macrolesions, e.g. chromosomal aberrations, chromosome breaks, effects on the mitotic apparatus, and microlesions, such as binding to nucleic acids and induction of single- or double-strand breaks in DNA as indicators for genetic activity of mycotoxins. The high correlation between genetic and carcinogenic activity (93%) is obtained only when all aspects of genetic activity are considered. The limitation of individual assay systems in detecting genetic activity is obvious. Although the Ames test reveals mutagenicity of some 71% of carcinogenic mycotoxins, it is 100% effective only in the unique aflatoxin groups and much less effective (43%) in other carcinogenic mycotoxins (Tables 1, 2). The yeast system revealed mutagenicity in four out of eight tested carcinogenic mycotoxins and was not superior to the Ames test except in the case of patulin. It is important to develop further the yeast test because it is one of the simplest eukaryotic microorganisms

Table 1 Carcinogenicity and genetic activity of mycotoxins other than aflatoxins

			Mutagenicity in microorganisms *S. typhimurium* TA strains					
Mycotoxin	Carcinogenicity	Teratogenicity	1935	1537	1538	98	100	TM677[a]
Citrinin	+ In nephritic rats; induced with dichlorophenylsuccinimide; synergist in forming renal tumors in rats induced with DMN. (134)	? Mice (58a)	–	–	–	–	–	NT
Cyclochlorotin	+ Rat, mouse (38, 138, 153, 170, 171)	NT	NT	NT	NT	–	–	–
Ergot alkaloids	NT	NT	NT	NT	NT	NT	NT	NT
Fusarenon-X	NT	NT	NT	NT	NT	–	+[b]	NT
Griseofulvin	+ Mouse (25, 39, 61); synergist with 3-MCA (7)	+ Rat (67, 129)	–	–	–	–	–	NT
Kojic acid	NT	Chick embryo (66)	–	–	–	+	–	NT
Luteoskyrin	+ Mouse (69, 99, 171)	NT	NT	+[c]	NT	–	–	–
Mycophenolic acid	NT	NT	–	–	–	–	–	NT
Nivalenol	NT	NT	NT	NT	NT	NT	NT	NT
Ochratoxin A	+ Rat liver when fed with sterculic acid (33); negative, rat (113)	+ Rat, mouse (56, 97, 104), hamster (60), chick embryo (48); negative, chick (96, 197)	–	–	+[d]	–	–	NT
Patulin	+ Mouse, by injection (26); negative by feeding (37, 109)	+ Chick (20); negative, mouse (114)	–	–	–	–	–	NT

Reference	Yeast (ref.)	Rec effect *B. subtilis* (ref.)	Mutagenicity in higher organisms	Interaction with nucleic acids: Binding	Interaction with nucleic acids: DNA breaks	Other genetic effects
71, 179, 194	– (71)	+ (62, 158)	NT	NT	NT	NT
141	NT	– (158)	NT	NT	NT	NT
	NT	NT	Dominant lethal effect, mouse (118)	NT	NT	+ Chromosomal aberrations, mouse, human (116, 117); negative in hamster (87) or human lymphocytes, administered in vivo in human volunteers (152)
100, 154, 155, 159	+ (156)	– (158)	Negative 8AG^{r}[a], mouse (166, 168)	NT	±HeLa (169)	NT
71, 75[g], 179, 194	– (71)	– (158)	Negative, micronucleus test (75)	NT	NT	+ Interference with microtubule formation (176)
179	NT	NT	NT	NT	+ (66)	Chromosomal breaks, rat liver cells in tissue culture (66)
141, 165	+ (160)	+ (62, 158)	Negative 8AG^{r}, mouse (166, 168)	DNA (120, 161, 163, 164)	±HeLa (169)	+ Chromosomal aberrations, Ehrlich ascites tumor cells (124)
179	NT	NT	+ 8AG^{r}, mouse (166, 168)	NT	+ mouse, (84, 166. 168)	Anti-tumor agent (18, 183, 184), DNA synthesis inhibition (84)
	+ (156)	– (158)	+ radiomimetic damage (147, 157)	NT	NT	NT
71, 179, 194	– (71)	– (158)	Negative, 8 AG^{r} mouse (168)	NT	NT	+ Abnormal mitosis in monkey kidney epithelial cells (142)
71, 179, 194	+ (88)	+ (62, 158) + (80)[e]	+ 8AG^{r}, mouse (114); negative mouse (166) and negative dominant lethal effect, mouse (114)	NT	+HeLa (169) mouse (166, 168)	Chromosomal aberrations or breaks in salamander, avian (132), human (185), plant (115)

Table 1 *(Continued)*

Mycotoxin	Carcinogenicity	Teratogenicity	Mutagenicity in microorganisms *S. typhimurium* TA strains 1935	1537	1538	98	100	TM677[a]
Patulin-cystein adduct	NT	+ Mouse (20)	NT	NT	NT	–	–	NT
Penicillic acid	+ Local (SC) mouse, rat (27–29); negative by feeding (37)	Negative, mouse (55)	NT	–	–	–	–	NT
Rubratoxin-B	Negative, rat (190)	+ Mouse (59, 70)	–	–	–	–	–	NT
Rugulosin	+ Mouse, rat (37)	NT	–	+[c]	NT	–	–	+[b]
T -2 Toxin	+ Rat (128)	+ Mouse (138)	–	–	–	–	NT	NT
Zeralenone	Possible etiology (promotion ?) of tumors in lab animals (feed contaminant ?) (126)	Negative, rat, mouse, swine (55)	–	–	–	–	–	NT

Mutagenic activity in *S. typhimurium* was in the presence of mammalian metabolizing systems.
NT = Not tested.
[a] 8-Azaguanine resistance marker.
[b] Without metabolic activation.
[c] D. F. Liberman, personal communication.
[d] Mixture of Ochratoxin A + B.
[e] Weak positive effect in *E. coli* pol A vs. pol A+.
[f] Zearalenol-B is positive in Rec effect test, *B. subtilis*.
[g] Negative also in TA1530, 1539.

that can be readily cultivated and screened for mutations. Perhaps the use of UV-sensitive strains might improve the sensitivity of this system.

The Rec effect in *B. subtilis* has proved useful in assaying mycotoxins. A correlation of 67% was found between carcinogenicity and the positive Rec effect. However, results were often reported semiquantitatively and obtained in the absence of metabolizing systems. Quantitative Rec assay made in suspension and the inclusion of microsomal fractions should improve this assay.

Taken together, all three microbial assays reveal an 85% level of correlation between carcinogenicity and genetic activity among the carcinogenic

Reference	Yeast (ref.)	Rec effect *B. subtilis* (ref.)	Mutagenicity in higher organisms	Interaction with nucleic acids: Binding	Interaction with nucleic acids: DNA breaks	Other genetic effects
173	NT	NT	NT	NT	NT	NT
71, 179, 194	– (71)	+ (62, 158)	+ 8AG^r mouse (166, 168)	NT	+HeLa (169) mouse (166, 168)	NT
71, 194	– (71)	– (158)	+ Dose response dominant lethal effect, mouse (42)	DNA, RNA (57, 103)	+HeLa (169)	+ Chromosomal aberrations, *Allium cepa* (115)
141, 165	+ (160)	+ (62, 158)	NT	DNA (120, 161, 163–164)	NT	NT
71, 154, 177	– (71)	– (158)	Negative in Drosophila, sex-linked lethal test (136a)	NT	(–) *Allium* (81) (–) HeLa (169)	c-Mitotic agent in *Allium cepa* (81)
10, 71	– (71)	+ (10,[f] 62, 158)	NT	NT	NT	Regulates sexual production of peritrichia (193a, 193b)

mycotoxins, the exceptions being griseofulvin, T-2 toxin, and cyclochlorotin. The addition of mutagenicity assays in mammalian cells and tests for other types of genetic activity as described in Table 1 make cyclochlorotin the only carcinogenic mycotoxin undetectable in short-term tests. Whichever screening regime is chosen, it should mainly, though not only, rely on a proper mutation-induction test; it should not rely on assays based on differential toxicity to pol$^-$ or rec$^-$ strains or on other tests that involve the assay of biological phenomena related to the particular cell population being challenged, rather than to the genetic descendents of this population, e.g. the induction of lysogenic phage [inductest (102)]. The Rec effect may serve as a useful second choice test. Inductest employment in mycotoxin screening has been infrequent, its dependence on mammalian metabolism is, at best, equivocal even for a potent carcinogen mutagen such as AFB_1 (see below), and it cannot, therefore, be properly evaluated until further tested.

It seems, therefore, that a combination of the Ames, yeast, and Rec assays, in screening mycotoxins, should be effective in unmasking potential

Table 2 Carcinogenicity, genetic activity and DNA binding properties of aflatoxins and related compounds

Compound	Carcinogenicity Animal: organ [dose] (reference)	Mutagenicity (% of activity of AFB_1)				in vitro DNA binding (% of AFB_1 activity)	Existence of 2–3 double bond
		S. typhimurium					
		TA98	TA100	*N. Crassa*	Rec effect *B. subtilis*		
AFB_1	Rat: liver, kidney, colon. Trout, guppy, duck, ferret, mouse. Monkey: liver. Sheep: nose [0.5–1.5 ppm, oral] (14, 191). Man (?): liver (172, 188)	100 (194)	100 (53) 5 (179)[a]	100 (108)	+ (62, 158)	100 (53)	+
AFL	Trout: liver, 1/2 tumor activity of AFB_1 (125)	23 (194)	NT	NT	NT	NT	+
AFG_1	Rat: liver, kidney. Duck: liver [1–3 ppm, oral] (14, 191)	3.3 (194)	8.3 (53)	12 (108)	+ (62, 158)	18.3 (53)	+
AFM_1	Rat, trout: liver, 1/3 tumor activity of AFB_1 in trout. Less tumorigenic than AFB_1 in rat (136, 193)	3.2 (194)	2.3 (53)	NT	– (62, 158)	2.6 (53)	+
$AFLH_1$	NT	2.0 (194)	NT	NT	NT	NT	+
AFQ_1	Non-tumorigenic in trout (191)	1.2 (194)	1.7 (53)	NT	NT	1.6 (53)	+
AFB_2	Weakly active, rat liver [at 150 × AFB_1 dose] (191)	0.2 (194)	0.5 (53)	NT	– (62, 158)	1.0 (53)	–
AFP_1	NT	0.1 (194)	1.8 (53)	NT	NT	0 (53)	+
AFG_2	Inactive in trout (6)	0.1 (194)	1.0 (53)	NT	– (62, 158)	0 (53)	–
AFB_{2a}	NT	0.0 (194)	NT	NT	NT	NT	–
Sterigmatocystin	Rat: liver [10–100 ppm, oral] (106, 112, 113), 1/100 to 1/10 tumorigenicity of AFB_1 (29, 113)	10.7 (196) 12.9 (159)	10[b]	NT	+ (62, 158)	20–30[c] (40)	+

0-Acetylsterigmatocystin	Rat: liver [10 ppm, oral]	8.7 (159)	NT	NT	+ (62, 158)	NT	+
0-Acetyldihydrosterigmato-cystin	NT	NT	NT	NT	– (62, 158)	NT	–
Versicolorin A	NT	5.8 (196) 0.3 (179)[e]	0.1 (179)[d]	NT	NT	NT	+
Versiconal acetate	NT	0.21 (196)	NT	NT	NT	NT	–
Averufin	NT	0.19 (196)	NT	NT	NT	NT	–
Norsolorinic acid	NT	0.18 (196)	NT	NT	NT	NT	–
5-Methylsterigmatocystin	NT	+ [f, h]	NT	NT	NT	NT	+
Demethylsterigmatocystin	NT	+ [f, g, h,]	NT	NT	NT	NT	+
Sterigmatin	NT	+ [f, h]	NT	NT	NT	NT	+
6,8-Dimethylversicolorin	NT	+ [f, h]	NT	NT	NT	NT	+
Austocystin A	NT	84 (179)	19 (179)	NT	NT	NT	+
Austocystin D	NT	0 (179)	0.7 (179)	NT	NT	NT	+
Austdiol	NT	0 (179) 0.17 (179)[e]	0.01 (179)	NT	NT	NT	–
AFB_1-N^7GUA adduct	NT	±[i]		NT	NT	NT	–

A part of the table was adapted from (194, 196). Some relative activity values were calculated from (159, 179).
NT = Not tested.

[a] Nonactivated AFB_1 was mutagenic to TA100, 5% of activated AFB_1 activity.

[b] A. A. Stark, unpublished.

[c] Determined by quantitation of nonradioactive N^7-GUA-ST adduct as major product (40).

[d] Versicolorin A also mutagenic (without metabolic activation) to TA100, 1.7% of nonactivated AFB_1 (179).

[e] Without metabolic activation, % of nonactivated AFB_1.

[f] Not quantitated against AFB_1. Defined as strong or fairly strong mutagens.

[g] Without metabolic activation.

[h] M. Nagao, T. Hamasaki, M. Yamasaki, I. Hatsuda, T. Sugimura, unpublished data.

[i] N^7-guanine adduct of AFB_1 was very slightly mutagenic to strains TA100 and TM677 at 500–1000 × AFB_1 doses (A. A. Stark, unpublished data).

carcinogens. A laboratory dealing with biological effects of mycotoxins could easily and inexpensively devise a setup including five *Salmonella* tester strains, two yeast, and two *B. subtilis* strains needed for this purpose.

GENETIC ACTIVITY OF MYCOTOXINS FOR WHICH CARCINOGENICITY HAS NOT YET BEEN REPORTED

Genetic activity has been observed in numerous mycotoxins. It would not be surprising to find among them several carcinogens, since many of them are structurally similar to other carcinogenic and genetically active mycotoxins. Thirteen bisfuran-containing compounds related to aflatoxins (Table 2) are mutagenic; mutagenic anthraquinones emodin, skyrin, lumiluteoskyrin, and rubroskyrin are closely related to the carcinogens rugulosin and luteoskyrin. An interesting feature among some of the anthraquinone mycotoxins is their genetic activity in the absence of mammalian metabolism. This property may be attributed to their capacity of binding to nucleic acids in the absence of metabolizing systems (see below). However, some of them do require metabolic activation: skyrin and emodin in *Salmonella* strain TA1537 (178; D. F. Liberman, personal communication). Emodin 1, (8)-monoglucoside required, in addition to mammalian microsomes, the presence of an extract of rat-cecal bacteria in order to mutagenize the same strain (12). Another point of interest is the similarity of the anthraquinone moieties in the mutagens emodin, skyrin, versicolorin A, and many other members of the aflatoxin series. Kojic acid and mycophenolic acid are genetically active in a number of systems and so are the epoxy-trichothecenes fusarenon-X and nivalenol. Other epoxy-trichothecenes such as satratoxin-H (81, 136a) and diacetoxyprenol are genetically active. They are structurally related to the carcinogenic trichothecene T-2 toxin. All these mycotoxins are, therefore, of interest and should be tested in proper assay systems for carcinogenicity. The same applies for austdiol, austocystin, other members of the aflatoxin series, viridicatumtoxin (179), the mutagen streptonigrin (74), and the teratogens alternariol, cytochalasin B, and cytochalasin D (8, 133).

Two mollicellins, depsidone mycotoxins from *Chaetomium mollicellum,* are mutagenic to *Salmonella.* There is no structural resemblance between these and other genetically active mycotoxins. It was suggested that their mutagenic activity resides in an 0-methyl group in the position *ortho* to a 3-methylbutenoic moiety (140). They have not been tested in other short-term tests.

It is difficult to make a decision concerning zearalenone at this stage: it is positive (as zearalenol-b) in the Rec assay, non-teratogenic to rat, mouse, or swine, and non-mutagenic in bacterial systems. However, it was considered as a possible cause of tumors in laboratory animals, probably through feed contamination. Thorough tests for carcinogenicity should be conducted with this compound, since analogous substances are used as animal-feed additives. The hormone-like activity of zearalenol indicates that it might be active as a tumor promoter.

In addition to genetically active mycotoxins, some fifty fungal metabolites possessing *antitumor* activities are known. This list includes trichothecenes, anthraquinones, peptides, diketopiperazines, macrolides, and lactones (44). Most of them were shown to interfere mainly with DNA and RNA metabolism. Considering the fact that most antitumor agents are carcinogenic themselves, one might expect to find carcinogenicity and genetic activities among these as well.

There are suggestions that compounds isolated from fungal species used in the food industry may possess genetic activity, e.g. *Penicillium roqueforti* (62–64, 130, 131, 158), *P. camemberti* (47), *Agaricus bisporus* (151), or *Gyromytra esculenta* (150, 174). The available information is not sufficient for the evaluation of the risk involved in ingestion of foods containing these fungi, especially in view of reports of failure to isolate toxins from, or elicit toxicity with, strains actually used for food production (72, 143).

Finally, listed below are mycotoxins which have been found to be non-mutagenic in *Salmonella* or the Rec assays and which have not been reported as possessing any other genetic activity. Iridoskyrin, islandicin, xanthocillin-X-dimethylether, chrysophanol, pibasterol (141) tryptoquivaline, tryptoquivalone, cyclopiazonic acid, secalonic acids D and F (179; A. A. Stark, unpublished data), mollicellins A, B, D, F, G, and H (140), AFB_{2a} (194), fumitremogen B, 0-methylsterigmatocystin, TR_2toxin (179) oosporein, verruculogen, viriditoxin (71), moniliformin, monoacetoxy- and triacetoxyprenol, deoxynivalenol, 3-acetyl-deoxynivalenol (177) were not mutagenic to *Salmonella.* Citeroviridin, erythroskyrin, fusaric acid, butenolide, and oosponol were negative in the Rec assay (62, 158).

Effects of mycotoxins on DNA, RNA, and protein synthesis have been extensively studied and are often referred to as possible explanations for their carcinogenicity or genetic activity. With this in mind we shall explore the binding of mycotoxins to nucleic acids as a possible mode of action for mycotoxins in causing mutations and, probably, cancer. The reader should turn to other reviews (19, 186) for information concerning the various biochemical responses to mycotoxins.

The structures of most mycotoxins described in this review are shown in Figure 1. The reader should refer to the figure whenever necessary.

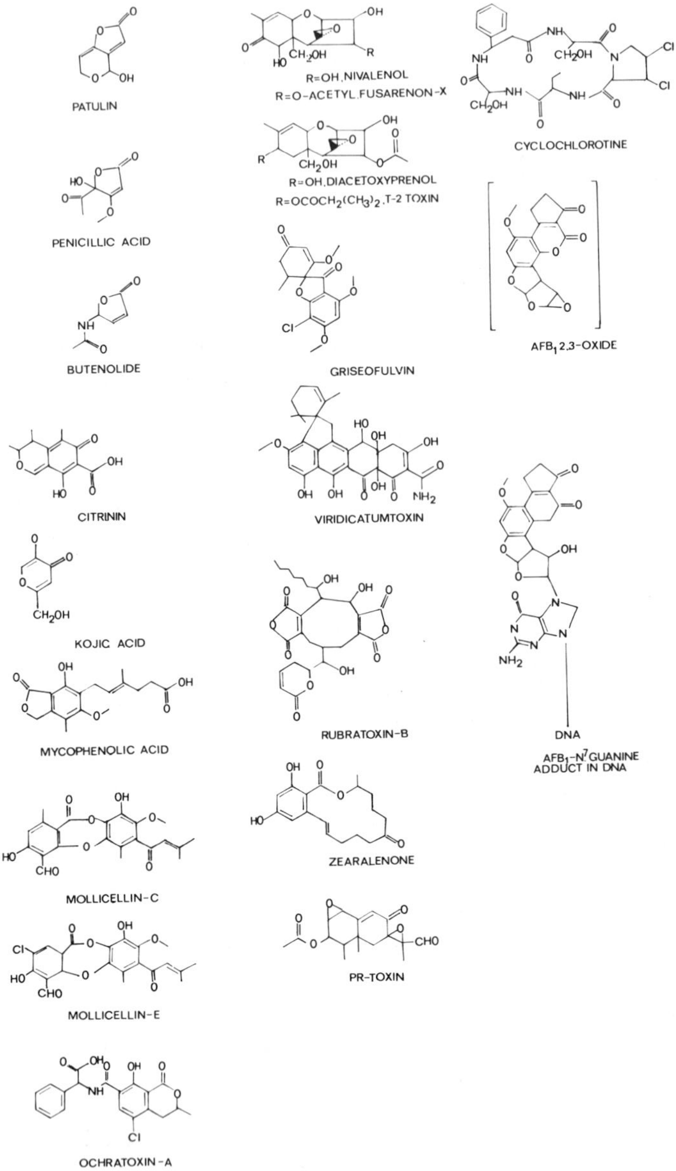

Figure 1 Structures of genetically active and carcinogenic mycotoxins.

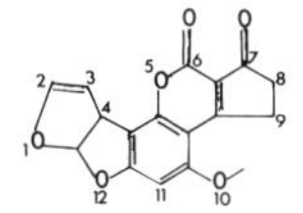

AFB_1

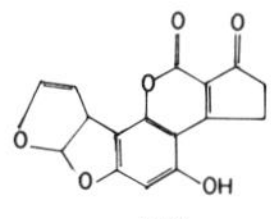

AFP_1

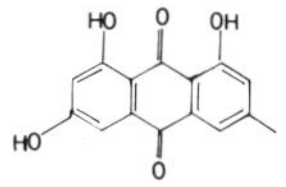

EMODIN

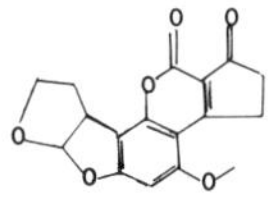

AFB_2

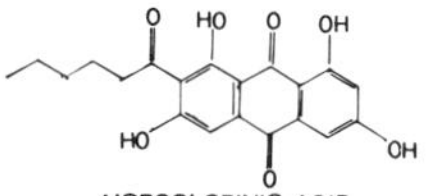

NORSOLORINIC ACID

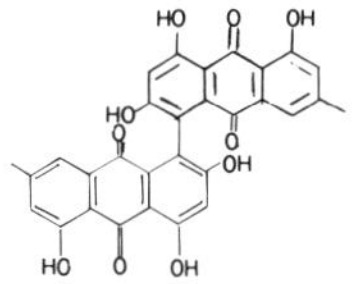

SKYRIN

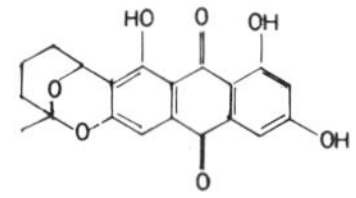

AVERUFIN

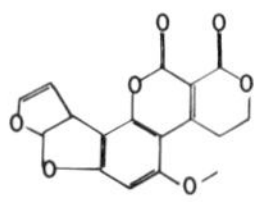

AFG_1

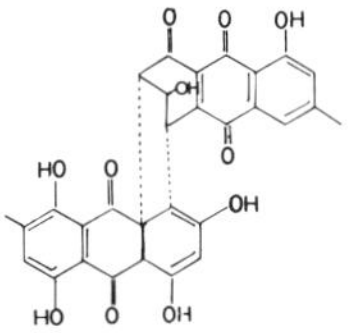

RUBROSKYRIN

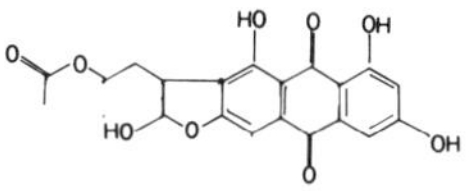

VERSICONAL-ACETATE

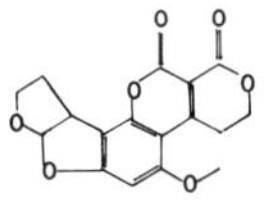

AFG_2

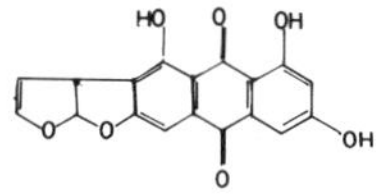

VERSICOLORIN-A

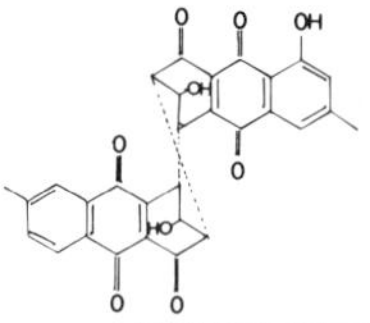

LUMILUTEOSKYRIN

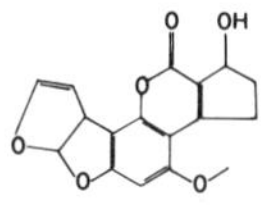

AFL

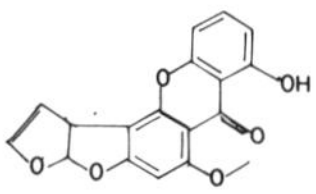

STERIGMATOCYSTIN

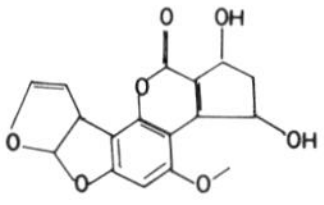

$AFLH_1$

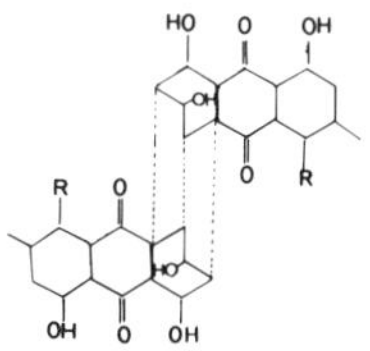

R=OH, LUTEOSKYRIN
R=H, RUGULOSIN

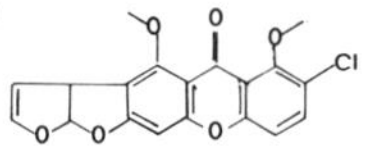

AUSTOCYSTIN-A

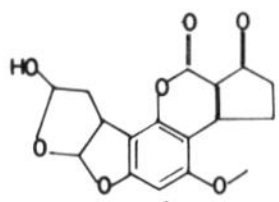

AFB_{2a}

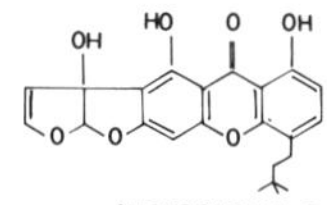

AUSTOCYSTIN-D

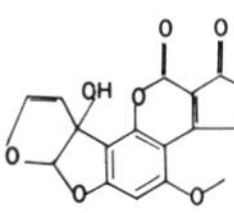

AFM_1

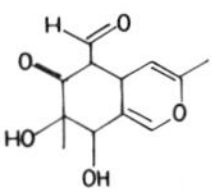

AUSTDIOL

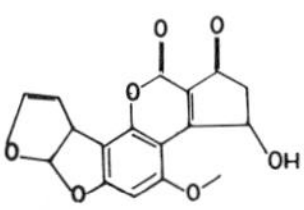

AFQ_1

AFLATOXINS AND RELATED COMPOUNDS

Introduction

The most thoroughly studied group of mycotoxins, in so far as carcinogenicity is concerned, is that of aflatoxins and their related compounds. Several carcinogens and potent mutagens belong to this group, of which Aflatoxin B_1 (AFB_1) is the most potent. The carcinogenicity of AFB_1, demonstrated shortly after its discovery, prompted research into almost every aspect of its biosynthesis, production, chemistry, metabolism, biological activities, epidemiology, and molecular biology. AFB_1 has thus become the "*E. Coli* of mycotoxins." A detailed review of the vast literature concerning carcinogenicity of aflatoxins and their related metabolites is beyond the scope of this paper and the reader is advised to refer to other well-documented sources (186, 188, 189). Hence, carcinogenicity and genetic activity of aflatoxins will be discussed here mainly in terms of aflatoxin binding to DNA.

A substantial amount of evidence for the existence of a cause-effect relationship between the incidence of liver cancer in humans and the ingestion of aflatoxin has led to the conclusion that aflatoxin is carcinogenic for humans. The widespread presence of aflatoxin creates serious environmental and economic problems. AFB_1 dissemination in human food has been associated epidemiologically with geographical areas having a high incidence of primary liver cancer (172, 188). Primary liver cancer in Kenya, Swaziland, Mozambique, and Thailand (0.7 to 25.4 cases/10^5/year) could be correlated with daily AFB_1 intake (3.5 to 222.4 ng/kg body weight/day) to give a crude dose-response pattern (172, 189). As shown in Table 2, other aflatoxin biogenetic precursors and metabolites are also carcinogenic. The principal target organ is the liver, but other organs are also susceptible.

Structure-Activity Relationship in Aflatoxins and Related Compounds

Metabolism of aflatoxins is considered a prerequisite for carcinogenicity and for most of the diverse biological activities of aflatoxins. It is now well-established that the chemical site implicated as responsible for the biological activities of aflatoxins and related compounds is the C_2-C_3 double bond in the dihydrofurofuran moiety of these molecules (Figure 1). Reduction of this bond, yielding 2,3-dihydro AFB_1 (AFB_2) results in a 200–500-fold decrease in mutagenicity and some 150-fold decrease in carcinogenicity. The same is true for AFG_1 and its 2,3-dihydro form, AFG_2 (Table 2). Weak carcinogenicity of AFB_2 may, however, be explained by the capacity of certain (duck) liver microsomes (but not mouse, rat, or human microsomes) to oxidize AFB_2, in vitro, to AFB_1 in appreciable amounts (170). Indeed, the lethal potency of AFB_2 in duck (one quarter that of AFB_1) is higher than in other animals. The hypothesis that AFB_2 activation occurs through oxidation to AFB_1 is further supported by the evidence that AFB_2 forms nucleic acid adducts that are chromatographically indistinguishable from AFB_1 adducts (144).

The existence of the double bond in the furan moiety is sufficient to elicit mutagenicity: 2-(*N*-ethylcarbamyolhydroxymethyl) furan, consisting of a simple substituted furan ring, was shown to be mutagenic to *Salmonella typhimurium* TA100 after activation with postmitochondrial supernatant and to be capable of in vitro covalent binding to DNA (50; A. A. Stark, unpublished data).

Structure differences in the moieties attached to the bisfuran (e.g. coumarin in AFB_1, xanthone in sterigmatocystin, anthraquinone in versicolorin A) markedly affect biological activity of the molecules (Table 2, Figure 1). Carcinogenicity, mutagenicity, and DNA binding capacity of AFB_1 far surpass that of other metabolites containing a C_2-C_3 unsaturated bond. The exceptional affinity of AFB_1 to DNA is discussed below.

The intermediate compound (ultimate carcinogen/mutagen) in the metabolic activation of aflatoxin has been postulated to be the 2,3-oxide derivative (Figure 1). This notion draws support from the following lines of evidence. AFB_1-2,3-dihydrodiol was isolated from acid hydrolysate of DNA- or rRNA-AFB_1 adducts formed in vivo or in vitro (45, 144, 145). Dihydrodiol is the expected product of the hydrolysis of AFB_1-2,3-oxide. Second, AFB_1-2,3-dichloride, a compound similar in its reactivity to the putative 2,3-oxide form, displayed reactivity and mutagenicity typical for the metabolite formed by liver microsomes (146). Third, structural analysis of the AFB_1-DNA and sterigmatocystin-DNA adducts revealed that the N^7 atom of guanine in DNA and C_2 atom of AFB_1 or sterigmatocystin were responsible for the principal adducts formed in vivo or in vitro (40, 41). Oxidation at the C_2-C_3 site renders the C_2 atom of AFB_1 or sterigmatocystin electron deficient, thus enabling an effective electrophilic attack at the proper, sterically available N^7 atom of guanine (23, 40, 41, 79, 119).

In addition, indirect biochemical evidence for the involvement of an epoxide moiety in the biologically active form of aflatoxins is shown by the fact that the addition of the epoxide-hydrase inhibitor 1,1,1,trichloropropane-2,3-oxide (TCPO) to microsomal preparations markedly increased the mutagenicity of AFB_1 (108). Epoxide hydrase catalyzes the hydrolysis of epoxides to form the respective diols. TCPO also inhibits the formation of

AFB_1-dihydrodiol (19). It should be noted that AFB_1-2,3-oxide has not been isolated, most probably due to the extremely short half-life of this highly reactive molecule.

Mutagenicity of Aflatoxins and Related Compounds

AFB_1 is one of the most potent naturally occurring mutagens. It can induce mutations in bacterial, algal, fungal, and insect species (35, 107) and in mammalian (31, 34, 73, 107) and human cells in tissue culture (32, 111). The reader is referred to reviews concerning the genetic aspects of aflatoxin mutagenesis for further details (107, 108).

Mutagenicity of aflatoxins and related compounds is almost invariably obtained in the presence, but not in the absence, of mammalian metabolizing systems. The principal role of epoxidation at the C_2-C_3 portion as a prerequisite for activity is discussed above. However, mutagenic and genetic activity of aflatoxin in the absence of mammalian metabolism in various systems not known to possess analogous enzymatic activities have been reported: AFB_1 and AFG_1 mutagenized vegetatively growing cultures, but not resting conidia of *Neurospora crassa* (108). [Metabolically activated AFB_1 did mutagenize the resting conidia (108)]. Weak mutagenicity of nonactivated AFB_1 and versicolorin A have also been reported (159, 179). Nonactivated AFB_1, AFG_1, and sterigmatocystin were positive in the *B. subtilis* Rec assay (158). Other examples are the in vitro induction of mutations in transforming DNA of *Bacillus subtilis* by crystaline AFB_1 or AFG_1 (85) and the induction of prophage in lysogenic *Bacillus magaterium* (78, 180), *Escherichia coli* (107), and *Staphylococcus aureus* (77). However, others specify the need of metabolic activation for phage induction by AFB_1, AFG_1, and sterigmatocystin in *E. coli* (98). The latter work showed also that induction by AFB_1 was tenfold more effective than by AFG_1 and was generally increased in an excision repair-deficient strain of *E. coli*. The effectiveness of the interaction of nonactivated aflatoxins with nucleoproteins such as histones was found to be similar or even greater than with DNA (8, 137). It is thus possible that prophage induction could occur either through binding of aflatoxin to the phage repressor (a protein with high affinity to DNA), thereby decreasing its affinity and, resulting in facile dissociation of the repressor-DNA complex, or via binding to DNA, rendering the binding site inaccessible to interaction with the phage repressor protein. It should be noted that genetic effects with nonactivated aflatoxins were obtained at concentrations exceeding by far those required for the induction of cancer or mutations in the presence of metabolizing systems. It is impossible to decide, in the absence of additional data, whether (*a*) nonmodified aflatoxins are indeed weak mutagenic agents, (*b*) various microorganisms do possess some limited capacity of aflatoxin metabolism or (*c*) Rec effect and phage induction are aflatoxin-dependent but involve different molecular mechanisms.

Nature of the Mutations Induced by Aflatoxins

Point mutations are the predominant type of genetic lesions caused by aflatoxins: 94 and 92% of mutations in *N. crassa* induced by AFB_1 and AFG_1, respectively, are point mutations (16, 107, 108). *S. typhimurium* TA100 is three- to fortyfold more susceptible to mutagenesis by AFB_1, sterigmatocystin versicolorin A, and autocystin D than strain TA98 (179; A. A. Stark, unpublished).

However, AFB_1 was shown to induce frameshift mutations in *Salmonella* (46, 91) and deletions and intragenic alterations in *N. crassa* (16, 108). Of all the mycotoxins belonging to the aflatoxin group (Table 2), austocystin A showed the highest potency as a frameshift mutagen (179).

Cellular Functions Affecting Mutagenesis by Aflatoxins

As will be shown later, mutations arise as a consequence of interactions between aflatoxins and DNA. However, cellular functions play a crucial role in determining whether a premutational lesion caused by aflatoxins would lead to mutational events or not. Involvement of various DNA repair processes appears to be the principal factor in the determination of the fate of these premutational lesions. In general, the presence of error-free excision repair systems decreases AFB_1 mutagenicity regardless of the nature of the mutation induced, suggesting that the UV correndonuclease responsible for the initial incisions at sites of bulky lesions is able to efficiently recognize and excise AFB_1-containing lesions. A functional Rec A gene product protects the cells from the toxic effects of AFB_1; Rec A^- strains of *B. subtilis* and *E. coli* (46, 158) are more sensitive to killing by AFB_1 than their corresponding parent strains.

Aflatoxin-mediated mutagenesis is enhanced by the presence of plasmid pKM101. This plasmid somehow amplifies the activity of inducible error-prone repair system(s) (175). However, there is evidence substantiating the capacity of metabolically activated AFB_1 or the DNA lesions caused by activated AFB_1 to act as inducer(s) of error-prone repair via an SOS mechanism in bacterial cells and an SOS-like state in mammalian cells. AFB_1 induces prophage in lysogens of *E. coli* (98), causes Weigle-like reactivation of UV-irradiated λ phage in *E. coli* (49) and of UV-irradiated SV40 in monkey kidney cells (121); it induces DNA repair in diploid human fibroblasts and in SV40-transformed human fibroblasts, but not in the repair deficient mutants of *Xeroderma pigmentosum* cells (122). Nonactivated AFB_1, AFG_1, AFB_2, and AFG_2 do not induce DNA repair in permeabilized *E. coli* cells (149).

RELATIONSHIP BETWEEN NUCLEIC ACID BINDING, CARCINOGENICITY, AND GENETIC ACTIVITY OF MYCOTOXINS

Mycotoxins Other Than Aflatoxins

It is well established that chemical carcinogens form DNA, RNA, and protein adducts both in vivo and in vitro, and in many cases the level of macromolecular binding is correlated with the likelihood of tumor formation (58, 93, 94). Carcinogenic mycotoxins are no exception to this. Several carcinogenic and genetically active mycotoxins were shown to react either covalently or non-covalently with nucleic acids.

Spectral shifts in the UV were observed following in vitro interaction of nonactivated rubratoxin B with RNA and DNA and indicated binding of this mycotoxin to nucleic acids (57). Disaggregation of polysomes was also observed with rubratoxin B, possibly due to its interaction with RNA (103). The ability of this mycotoxin to interact with nucleic acids correlates well with its pronounced genetic activity expressed as teratogenicity and induction of dominant-lethal mutations and DNA breaks in mammalian systems. No carcinogenicity or mutagenicity in microbial systems were, however, reported for rubratoxin B (Table 1).

The anthraquinone-dimer carcinogens luteoskyrin and rugulosin were also found to bind in vitro to DNA in the absence of metabolizing systems. The binding required Mg^{2+} or Mn^{2+} ions, occurred with single- or double-stranded DNA, and caused shifts in the spectra of the mycotoxins (9, 105, 120, 161, 163, 164). Here again, DNA binding properties correlated well with genetic activities (Table 1). The mutagen skyrin binds to viral RNA and to DNA without metabolic activation in the presence of Mg^{2+}. Skyrin-DNA-Mg^{2+} complexes differ from those of luteoskyrin and rugulosin in that they dissociate upon gel filtration (198). The number of covalent bonds connecting the anthraquinone moities in these mycotoxins appears to determine their ability to form polychelates with divalent cations and to strongly bind to nucleic acids (Figure 1): skyrin, containing one bond, reacts weakly and does not form polychelates, whereas luteoskyrin and rugulosin, containing three bonds, form polychelates and stable complexes with nucleic acids.

In view of the reaction types described above, luteoskyrin and rugulosin might elicit genetic effects through non-covalent, intercalative interactions with DNA. The fact that both mutagenize *S. typhimurium* TA1537, a strain revertible by frameshift mutagens, supports this suggestion. It is not known, however, whether the observed in vitro phenomena are the only, or even the major, reaction types leading to genetic activity or carcinogenicity in vivo.

Indications for interactions of other genetically active mycotoxins can be found in the ability of patulin, penicillic acid, and fusarenon-X to cause DNA breaks (Table 1). Additional information concerning these is not available. Mycophenolic acid also causes DNA breaks; but since it depletes cells of almost all of their GTP (84), breaks might reflect perturbation of DNA synthesis.

Aflatoxins and Sterigmatocystin

Two types of interactions were found to occur between aflatoxins and nucleic acids: non-covalent, weak and reversible binding (137) requiring the mere presence of mycotoxin and nucleic acid, and irreversible covalent binding requiring mammalian metabolizing systems.

Non-covalent binding of AFB_1 to DNA was demonstrated in numerous cases. The reaction rate is inversely proportional to ionic strength: affinity of AFB_1 to DNA decreased with an increase in potassium phosphate concentration from 10 to 600 mM or in NaCl from 15 to 150 mM (65, 137). It was suggested that such non-covalent binding involves intercalation and hydrogen bonding with guanine residues. Double-stranded DNA binds AFB_1 more effectively than single-stranded DNA or RNA (43, 137). AFG_1 and AFG_2 similarly bind to DNA, albeit to a degree lesser than that of AFB_1, as judged by spectral shifts (21, 22).

Although no specific secondary structural changes occur in nonmetabolized AFB_1 complexes with DNA, analysis of melting profiles indicate an increase in interaction between DNA strands mediated by AFB_1 (8, 21, 22). In parallel with the above reactions, genetic activity of aflatoxins in the absence of mammalian metabolism has been observed in a number of cases (see above). In agreement with the intercalation hypothesis is the finding that as much as 35% of the mutations produced in vitro by nonactivated AFB_1, or AFG_1 in transforming DNA of *B. subtilis* reverted at frequencies less than 10^{-8} and were considered as deletions (85). However, nonactivated AFB_1 and versicolorin A mutagenized *Salmonella* strains TA100 rather than TA98 (179).

Most of the carcinogenic and genetic activities of aflatoxins and related compounds have been observed with metabolically activated mycotoxins;

they correlate well with their covalent binding to macromolecules with specific preference to DNA. The presence of the C_2-C_3 unsaturated bond is crucial; reduction at this position results invariably in marked decrease of DNA binding capacity of AFB_1 and AFG_1 (Table 2). A remarkable correlation exists therefore between carcinogenicity, mutagenicity, and the extent of covalent binding among the various aflatoxins, their metabolites, and biogenetic precursors (Table 2). Another case in point is the quantitative relationship between the extent of AFB_1 covalently bound to DNA and the induction of mutations to 8-azaguanine resistance ($8AG^r$) in *S. typhimurium* strain TM677 (139). DNA purified from mutagenized cells containing 15 and 22 AFB_1 residues per genome was associated with induced $8AG^r$ mutant frequencies of 4.9 and 9.6×10^{-4}, respectively. Assuming that the target size for 8AG resistance consists of about 5300 base pairs, it was estimated that a given AFB_1 residue has a probability of 3 to 4% of inducing a mutational event (139). It was also found that covalent binding of AFB_1 to transforming DNA and subsequent transformation of *Streptococcus pneumoniae* produced various antibiotic-resistance mutations in the recipient cells and that the degree of mutagenesis was proportional to the degree of AFB_1 covalent binding to the transforming DNA (A. A. Stark and C. N. Giroux, unpublished). Mutations occurred at or near AFB_1 binding sites: cells transformed with streptomycin-resistant, AFB_1-modified DNA were subsequently grown in the presence of streptomycin. An increase in mutation frequency was observed for fusidic acid resistance (a marker closely linked to streptomycin resistance) but not in rifampin resistance (an unlinked marker). Increase in mutant frequency was observed in both loci in the absence of streptomycin selection (Stark and Giroux, unpublished).

Organotropism and Species Specificity of Carcinogenicity by AFB_1 As Related to Nucleic Acid Binding

Similar to AFB_1-mediated mutagenesis, organotropism and species specificity of AFB_1-mediated carcinogenesis is reflected by the extent of differential covalent binding of AFB_1 metabolites to DNA observed in the appropriate organ or species (192). In Fischer rats, which are highly susceptible to AFB_1 carcinogenesis, the levels of the principal AFB_1-DNA adducts (see below) in the primary target organ (liver) were tenfold higher than those found in DNA of the kidney, an organ not susceptible to AFB_1 carcinogenesis in this strain (23, 192) (Table 3). When mice, a species resistant to AFB_1 carcinogenesis, were challenged with equitoxic doses of AFB_1, liver DNA contained sixfold more AFB_1-DNA adducts than kidney DNA; however

Table 3 Organotropism and species specificity of AFB_1: Comparison of in vivo binding levels of AFB_1 in liver and kidney DNA from the rat and the mouse

	Liver		Kidney	
	Rat	Mouse	Rat	Mouse
DNA binding extent[a, b]				
AFB_1 residues/10^6 nucleotides	114	1.9	12.6	7.8
Relative binding[c]	60	1.0	6.6	4.1

[a] Adapted from Wogan et al (1979) (Reference 192). Numbers presented are combined binding values of the various adducts appearing as distinct peaks in high pressure liquid chromatography HPLC of acid hydrolysis products of DNA modified by AFB_1 in vivo.

[b] The major adduct in all cases was 2.3-dihydro-2-(N^7-guanyl)-3-hydroxy AFB_1.

[c] Binding extent of AFB_1 metabolites to mouse liver DNA in vivo was arbitrarily designated as unity.

the extent of binding was 86-fold lower than that found in rat liver. The main reason for such organ and species specificity seems to reside in differential oxidative metabolism in the various animals. For example, aflatoxicol (AFL) is a stable AFB_1 metabolite which can be readily reduced back to AFB_1, thus serving as a reservoir of AFB_1. Those species, such as the rat and the trout (83), in which AFL happens to be the major AFB_1-metabolite are also more susceptible to AFB_1 carcinogenesis (195). Conversion of AFL to AFB_1 may also explain the high potency of AFL as a mugaten for *Salmonella* in a system using rat liver microsomes for metabolic activation.

Nature of AFB_1- and Sterigmatocystin-DNA Adducts

Except for a limited number of AFB_1 and sterigmatocystin adducts, the structures of mycotoxin adducts with DNA have not yet been elucidated. Chromatography of acid hydrolysis products of AFB_1 or sterigmatocystin-modified DNA yielded 10 to 14 distinct peaks, indicating a multiplicity of reactions of these mycotoxins with various DNA nucleotides (40, 41, 192). The preference of guanine as a principal target for AFB_1 attack was evidenced by the high reactivity towards G-C rich regions in DNA (54); moreover, each purine residue can serve as a target for covalent AFB_1 binding, guanine being a better target than adenine (24).

Invariably, the major AFB_1-DNA adduct found in each and every in vivo or in vitro system is 2,3-dihydro-2-(N^7-guanyl)-3 hydroxy AFB_1 (Figure 1). It was found in the DNA of rat liver and kidney, mouse liver and kidney (23, 192), *S. typhimurium* (139), human bronchus and colon (5), and calf thymus (41). Analogously, the major sterigmatocystin-DNA adduct proved to be 2,3-dihydro-2-(N^7-guanyl)-3 hydroxy ST (40). These adducts consist of 60–90% of the covalently bound mycotoxin to DNA. The structure of the major adducts point out again that the C_2-C_3 unsaturated bond is the reactive moiety of aflatoxins and strongly supports the notion that the exo-2,3 oxide is the reactive (ultimate) metabolite. AFB_2-DNA adducts are identical to those of AFB_1, possibly due to the oxidation of AFB_2 to AFB_1 (119, 144).

N^7 of guanine is a prime target for many other mutagens and carcinogens due to its steric availability. Substitution at this site introduces a positive charge in the imidazole ring where the adduct is bound to DNA and renders the glycosidic bond labile to acid hydrolysis (135), leading to facile depurination at this site. Alkylation at N^7 with small groups (methyl, ethyl) and subsequent depurination are not considered to be mutagenic (135). However, it is not known whether substitutions with a bulky residue, such as AFB_1 or sterigmatocystin, would be mutagenic.

Mild alkaline hydrolysis results in imidazole-ring opening (41, 79). The structure of the open-ring adduct has not been established rigorously; however, this adduct may have important implications in mutagenesis, since the glycosidic bond is stable, thus increasing the probability that such lesions lead to mutations.

It is not to be implied here that the major AFB_1-DNA adduct need constitute the major type of premutational lesion. Since the efficiency of AFB_1 mutagenesis is 3-4% (see above), it is possible that some other, minor adduct(s), as yet structurally unidentified, form the principal premutational lesion.

In addition to sites susceptible to facile depurination, modifications of adenines and guanines in DNA by AFB_1 create alkali-labile lesions at the site of the modified bases (24): a ^{32}P-end-labeled, 168 base-pair DNA restriction fragment from the *lac* promoter-operator region, with known base sequence, was reacted in vitro with metabolically activated AFB_1, followed by alkali or piperidine treatment and gel electrophoresis. The lengths of the cleavage products were the same as those produced by alkali-induced breakage of the same sequences of DNA which had been modified with dimethyl sulfate. The identity of the reactions of dimethyl sulfate and AFB_1 with DNA suggests that the site of adenine modification occurred at N^3 (24). The authors suggested that breakage of the phosphodiester bond at the site of modification by AFB_1 might lead to the elimination of the modified purine, thus causing deletion. Supporting this hypothesis is the ability of AFB_1 to revert *S. typhimurium* strains TA1537 and TA1538, which probably revert by deletion of a G-C pair or two bases, G and C. However, the missense-containing strain TA100 is just as effectively reverted by AFB_1.

Although all purines were accessible to attack by AFB_1, modification rates of individual purines varied. This indicates that the interaction of AFB_1 with DNA probably involves nucleotides closely situated to the purine being attacked, i.e. AFB_1 may manifest a certain degree of sequence specificity. Preliminary evidence supports this suggestion. After formation of a covalent bond between C-2 of AFB_1 and N^7 of guanine, AFB_1 may be situated in the major groove of DNA in a conformation that enables the C-6 and C-7 carbonyl oxygens to form hydrogen bonds with amino hydrogens located on the second succeeding base from the modified one (J. M. Essigmann and G. Büchi, personal communication, from model building studies of an AFB_1-DNA). This hypothesis predicts that elimination of one carbonyl oxygen would reduce binding efficiency. Indeed, deoxo AFB_1, lacking the C-7 carbonyl oxygen, was about twofold less mutagenic to *S. typhimurium* TA100 and TM677 (A. Stark, unpublished). Similar DNA-carcinogen models were constructed in order to formulate a feasible mechanism for the interaction of mutagenic fluorene derivatives with DNA; these models show the requirement of a covalent bond at C-8 of guanine and hydrogen bonding at C-4 amino group of an adjacent cytosine residue (76).

Other circumstantial evidence emerges from the study of the differential distribution of $8AG^r$ mutants arising from transport deficiency (*gxu* locus) and purine biosynthesis deregulation (purine over production) among spontaneous and AFB_1-induced $8AG^r$ mutant populations of *S. typhimurium* (A. A. Stark and D. F. Liberman, unpublished).

CONCLUDING REMARKS

An alarming number of mycotoxins possess carcinogenic, mutagenic, and other activities affecting, in one way or another, the genetic apparatus. The reason for this phenomenon is obscure; nevertheless, the fact that most of them are naturally occurring environmental pollutants intimately associated with human food and animal feed should be of great concern and prompt further intensive research in this field. A combination of short-term genetic activity tests was shown to be useful in detecting potential carcinogenic properties of mycotoxins. Data summarized here are compatible with the notion that interaction of mycotoxins with nucleic acids may be a possible explanation for their genetic and carcinogenic activities. Aflatoxins and related metabolites were shown to constitute a useful model for the study of the relationship between the structure, metabolism, and biological activities of chemical carcinogens. The study of the structural nature of other mycotoxins-DNA adducts and their relationship to mutagenicity/-carcinogenicity is urgently needed, especially in those cases where metabolic activation seems not to be required. In addition, molecular biology studies of the genetic effects of carcinogenic mycotoxins should concentrate on systems involving mammalian, (preferably human) cells in tissue culture.

Finally, immediate steps should be taken in order to eliminate hazardous compounds such as griseofulvin from pharmacists' drug lists or physicians' list of prescription antibiotics.

NOTE ADDED IN PROOF The ability of AFB_1 to mutagenize transforming DNA of *B. subtilis* in the absence of microsomal activating systems (85) is explained by the fact that under the reaction conditions employed [high concentrations of AFB_1, incubation at elevated temperatures (up to 53° C) for long periods of time (220 min) in the presence of light], AFB_1 did bind covalently to DNA (V. M. Maher, personal communication). Photoactivation and subsequent binding of AFB_1 to DNA has been recently established (Shieh, J-C., Song, P-S. 1980. *Cancer Res.* 40:689–95).

Literature Cited

1. Ames, B. N. 1979. *Science* 204:587–93
2. Ames, B. N., Durston, W. E., Yamasaki, E., Lee, F. D. 1973. *Proc. Natl. Acad. Sci. USA* 70:2281-85
3. Ames, B. N., McCann, J., Yamasaki, E. 1975. *Mutat. Res.* 31:347–63
4. Ashoor, S. A., Chu, F. S. 1975. *Biochem. Pharmacol.* 24:1799–1805
5. Autrup, H., Essigmann, J. M., Croy, R. G., Trump, B. F., Wogan, G. N., Curtis, C. 1979. *Cancer Res.* 39:694–98
6. Ayers, J. L., Lee, D. J., Wales, J. H., Sinnhuber, R. O. 1971. *J. Natl. Cancer Inst.* 46:561–64
7. Barich, L. L., Schwarz, J., Barich, D. 1962. *Cancer Res.* 22:53–62
8. Black, H. S., Jirgensons, B. 1967. *Plant Physiol.* 42:731–35
9. Bouhet, J. C., Chuong, P. P. V. 1976. *3rd IUPAC Symp. Mycotoxins Foodstuffs* (Abstr. 70)
10. Boutibonnes, P., Loquet, C. 1979. *IRCS Med. Sci.* 7:204
11. Brown, M. H., Szczech, G. M., Purmalis, B. P. 1976. *Toxicol. Appl. Pharmacol.* 37:331–38
12. Brown, J. P., Dietrich, P. S. 1979. *Mutat. Res.* 66:9–24
13. Burdette, W. J. 1955. *Cancer Res.* 15:201–26
14. Butler, W. H., Greenblatt, M., Lijinsky, W. 1969. *Cancer Res.* 29:2206–11
15. Callen, D. F., Mohn, G. R., Ong, T-M. 1977. *Mutat. Res.* 45:7–11
16. Callen, D. F., Ong, T-M. 1978. *Mutat. Res.* 49:371–76
17. Campbell, C. T., Hayes, J. R., Newberne, P. M. 1978. *Cancer Res.* 38:4569–73
18. Carter, S. B., Franklin, T. J., Jones, D. F., Leonard, B. J., Mills, S. D., Turner, R. W., Turner, W. B. 1969. *Nature* 223:848
19. Chu, F. S. 1977. *Adv. Appl. Microbiol.* 22:83–143
20. Ciegler, A., Beckwith, A. C., Jackson, L. K. 1976. *Appl. Environ. Microbiol.* 31:664–67
21. Clifford, J. I., Rees, K. R. 1966. *Nature* 209:312–13
22. Clifford, J. I., Rees, K. R. 1967. *Biochem. J.* 102:65–75
23. Croy, R. G., Essigmann, J. M., Reinhold, V. N., Wogan, G. N. 1978. *Proc. Natl. Acad. Sci. USA* 75:1745–49
24. D'Andrea, A. D., Haseltine, W. A. 1978. *Proc. Natl. Acad. Sci. USA* 75:4120–24
25. De Matteis, F., Donnelly, A. J., Runge, W. J. 1966. *Cancer Res.* 26:721–26
26. Dickens, F., Jones, H. E. H. 1961. *Br. J. Cancer* 15:85–100
27. Dickens, F., Jones, H. E. H. 1963. *Br. J. Cancer* 17:100–8
28. Dickens, F., Jones, H. E. H. 1965. *Br. J. Cancer* 19:392–403
29. Dickens, F., Jones, H. E. H., Waynforth, H. B. 1966. *Br. J. Cancer* 20:134–44
30. Deleted in proof
31. Dolimpio, D. A., Green, S., Legator, M., Jacobson, C. B. 1966. *3rd Int. Congr. Hum. Genet.* 26: (Abstr.)

32. Dolimpio, D. A., Jacobson, C., Legator, M. 1968. *Proc. Soc. Exp. Biol. Med.* 127:559–62
33. Doster, R. C., Sinnhuber, R. O., Wales, J. H., Lee, D. J. 1971. *Fed. Proc.* 30:578
34. Elis, J., DiPaolo, J. A. 1967. *Arch. Pathol.* 83:53–57
35. El-Zawahri, M., Moubasher, A., Morad, M., El-Kady, I. 1977. *Ann. Nutr. Aliment.* 31:854–66
36. Enomoto, M. 1978. In *Toxicology, Biochemistry and Pathology of Mycotoxins,* ed. K. Uraguchi, M. Yamazaki, pp. 239–62. New York: Wiley
37. Enomoto, M., Saito, N. 1972. *Ann. Rev. Microbiol.* 26:279–312
38. Enomoto, M., Ueno, I. 1974. In *Mycotoxin,* ed. I. F. H. Purchase, p. 303. Amsterdam: Elsevier
39. Epstein, S. S., Andrea, J., Joshi, S., Mantel, N. 1967. *Cancer Res.* 27:1900–6
40. Essigmann, J. M., Barker, L. J., Fowler, K. W., Francisco, M. A., Reinhold, V. N., Wogan, G. N. 1979. *Proc. Natl. Acad. Sci. USA* 76:179–83
41. Essigmann, J. M., Croy, R. G., Nadzan, A. M., Busby, W. F. Jr., Reinhold, V. N., Büchi, G., Wogan, G. N. 1977. *Proc. Natl. Acad. Sci. USA* 74:1870–74
42. Evans, M. A., Wilson, B. J., Harbison, R. D. 1975. *Pharmacology* 17:248
43. Fujimoto, S., Ohba, Y. 1975. *J. Biochem.* 77:187–95
44. Fuska, J., Proska, B. 1976. *Adv. Appl. Microbiol.* 20:259–370
45. Garner, R. C. 1973. *Fed. Eur. Biochem. Soc. Lett.* 36:261–64
46. Garner, R. C., Wright, L. M. 1973. *Br. J. Cancer* 28:544–51
47. Gibel, W., Wegner, K., Wildner, G. P. 1971. *Arch. Geschwulstforsch.* 38:1–6
48. Gilani, S. H., Bancroft, J., Reily, M. 1978. *Toxicol. Appl. Pharmacol.* 46:543–46
49. Goze, A., Sarasin, A., Moulé, Y., Devoret, R. 1975. *Mutat. Res.* 28:1–7
50. Guengerich, F. P. 1977. *Biochem. Pharmacol.* 26:1909–15
51. Gurtoo, H. L., Bejba, N. 1974. *Biochem. Biophys. Res. Commun.* 61:735–42
52. Gurtoo, H. L., Campbell, T. C. 1974. *Mol. Pharmacol.* 10:776–89
53. Gurtoo, H. L., Dahms, R. P., Paigen, B. 1978. *Biochem. Biophys. Res. Commun.* 81:965–72
54. Gurtoo, H. L., Dave, C. V. 1975. *Cancer Res.* 35:382–89
55. Hayes, A. W. 1979. *Mycopathologia* 65:29–41
56. Hayes, A. W., Hood, R. D., Lee, H. C. 1974. *Teratology* 9:93–98
57. Hayes, A. W., Watson, S. A. 1977. *J. Toxicol. Environ. Health* 2:639–50
58. Heidelberger, C. 1975. *Ann. Rev. Biochem.* 44:79–121
58a. Hood, R. D., Hayes, A. W., Scammell, J. G. 1976. *Food Cosmet. Toxicol.* 14:175–78
59. Hood, R. D., Innes, J. E., Hayes, A. W. 1973. *Bull. Environ. Contam. Toxicol.* 10:200–7
60. Hood, R. D., Naughton, M. J., Hayes, A. W. 1976. *Teratology* 13:11–14
61. Hurst, W. E., Paget, G. E. 1963. *Br. J. Dermatol.* 75:105–12
62. Kada, T., Tutikawa, K., Sadaie, Y. 1972. *Mutat. Res.* 16:165–74
63. Kader, M. M. A., Zaki, A. H., El-Kirdassi, Z. H. M., El-Kammah, B., Bosselia, A. A. 1969. *J. Egypt. Med. Assoc.* 52:764–74
64. Kader, M. M. A., Zaki, A. H., El-Kirdassi, Z. H. M., Shoeb, Z. E., Eissa, M. H. 1970. *Grasas Aceites Seville* 21:197–201
65. King, A. M. Q., Nicholson, B. H. 1967. *Biochem. J.* 104:69P
66. Kinosita, R., Ishiko, T., Sugiyama, S., Seto, T., Igarasi, S., Goetz, I. E. 1968. *Cancer Res.* 28:2296–2311
67. Klin, M. F., Beall, J. R. 1972. *Science* 175:1483–84
68. Knudson, A. G. 1977. *Cancer* 39:1882–86
69. Kobayashi, Y. Uraguchi, K., Sakai, F., Tatsuno, T., Tsukioka, M., Noguchi, Y., Tsunoda, H., Miyake, M., Saito, M., Enomoto, M., Shikata, T., Ishiko, T. 1959. *Proc. Jpn. Acad.* 35:501–6
70. Koshakji, R. P., Wilson, B. J., Harbison, R. D. 1973. *Res. Commun. Chem. Pathol. Pharmacol.* 5:584–91
71. Kuczuk, M., Benson, P. M., Heath, H. E., Hayes, A. W. 1978. *Mutat. Res.* 53:11–20
72. Lafont, P., Lafont, J., Payen, J., Chany, E., Bertin, G., Frayssinet, C. 1976. *Food Cosmet. Toxicol.* 14:137–39
73. Langenbach, R., Freed, H. J., Huberman, E. 1978. *Proc. Natl. Acad. Sci. USA* 75:2864–67
74. Lapshinskaya, O. A. 1970. *Antibiotiki Moscow* 15:494
75. Léonard, A., Poncelet, F., Grutman, G., Carbonelle, E., Fabry, L. 1979. *Mutat. Res.* 68:225–34
76. Levin, D. E., Barnes, W. S., Klekowski, E. 1979. *Chem. Biol. Interact.* 63:1–10
77. Levine, A., Moreau, P. L., Sedgwick, S. G., Devoret, R., Adhya, S., Gottesman, M., Das, A. 1978. *Mutat. Res.* 50:29–35

78. Lillehoj, E. B., Ciegler, A. 1970. *Appl. Microbiol.* 20:782–85
79. Lin, J. K., Miller, J. A., Miller, E. C. 1977. *Cancer Res.* 37:4430–38
80. Lindroth, S., von Wright, A. 1978. *Appl. Environ. Microbiol.* 35:1003–7
81. Linnainmaa, K., Sorsa, M., Ilus, T. 1979. *Hereditas* 90:151–56
82. Linville, G. P., Shepard, T. H. 1972. *Nature New Biol.* 236:246
83. Loveland, L. M., Nixon, J. E., Pawlowski, N. E., Eisele, T. A., Libby, L. M., Sinnhuber, R. O. 1979. *J. Environ. Pathol. Toxicol.* 2:707–18
84. Lowe, J. K., Brox, L., Henderson, J. F. 1977. *Cancer Res.* 37:736–43
85. Maher, V. M., Summers, W. C. 1968. *Nature* 225:68–70
86. Mainigi, K. D., Soroff, S. 1977. *Cancer Res.* 37:4304–12
87. Matter, B. E. 1976. *J. Int. Med. Res.* 4:382–92
88. Mayer, W. M., Legator, M. S. 1969. *J. Agric. Food Chem.* 17:454–56
89. McCann, J., Ames, B. N. 1976. *Proc. Natl. Acad. Sci. USA* 73:950–54
90. McCann, J., Ames, B. N. 1978. In *Mutagenesis,* ed. W. G. Flamm, M. A. Mehlman, pp.87–180. New York: Halstead
91. McCann, J., Choi, E., Yamasaki, E., Ames, B. N. 1975. *Proc. Natl. Acad. Sci. USA* 72:5135–39
92. McCann, J., Spingarn, N. E., Kobori, J., Ames, B. N. 1975. *Proc. Natl. Acad. Sci. USA* 72:979–83
93. Miller, E. C. 1978. *Cancer Res.* 38:1479–96
94. Miller, E. C., Miller, J. A. 1966. *Pharmacol. Rev.* 18:805–38
95. Miller, J. A. 1973. In *Toxicants Occurring Naturally in Foods,* pp. 508–49. Washington: Natl. Acad. Sci.
96. Mintzlaff, H. J., Christ, W. 1972. *Fleischwirtschaft* 52:1174
97. Moré, J., Galtier, P. 1974. *Ann. Rech. Vet.* 5:167–78
98. Moreau, P., Bailone, A., Devoret, R. 1976. *Proc. Natl. Acad. Sci. USA* 73:3700–4
99. Morooka, N., Nakano, N., Uchida, N. 1966. *Jpn. J. Med. Sci. Biol.* 19:293–303
100. Nagao, M., et al 1976. *Proc. 4th Meet. Jpn. Assoc. Mycotoxicol.* 9:41–43
101. Deleted in proof
102. Nagao, M., Sugimura, T., Matsushima, T. 1978. *Ann. Rev. Genet.* 12:117–59
103. Neely, W. C., Siraj, M. Y., Smith, L. B., Hayes, A. W. 1977. *J. Assoc. Off. Anal. Chem.*
104. Nesheim, S. 1976. *Adv. Chem. Ser.* 149:276–95
105. Ohba, Y., Fromageot, P. 1967. *Eur. J. Biochem.* 1:147–51
106. Ohtsubo, K., Saito, M., Kimura, H., Tsuruta, O. 1978. *Food Cosmet. Toxicol.* 16:143–51
107. Ong, T-M. 1975. *Mutat. Res.* 32:35–53
108. Ong, T-M. 1978. In *Toxins, Animal, Plant and Microbiol,* ed. P. Rosenberg, pp. 791–99. New York: Pergamon
109. Osswald, H., Frank, H. K., Komitowaski, D., Winter, H. 1978. *Food Cosmet. Toxicol.* 16:243–47
110. Deleted in proof
111. Promchainant, C., Baimai, V., Nondasuta, A. 1972. *Mutat. Res.* 16:373–80
112. Purchase, I. F. H., Van der Watt, J. J. 1968. *Food Cosmet. Toxicol.* 6:555–56
113. Purchase, I. F. H., Van der Watt, J. J. 1970. *Food Cosmet. Toxicol.* 8:289–95
114. Reddy, C. S., Chan, P. K., Hayes, A. W. 1978. *Toxicology* 11:219–23
115. Reiss, J. 1975. *Cytologia* 40:703–8
116. Roberts, G. T., Rand, M. J. 1977. *Mutat. Res.* 56:59–68
117. Roberts, G. T., Rand, M. J. 1977. *Mutat. Res.* 48:205–14
118. Roberts, G. T., Rand, M. J. 1978. *Mutat. Res.* 50:317–25
119. Roebuck, B. D., Siegel, W. G., Wogan, G. N. 1978. *Cancer Res.* 38:999–1002
120. Ruet, A., Sentenac, A., Simon, E. J., Bouhet, J. C., Fromageot, P. 1973. *Biochemistry* 12:2318
121. Sarasin, A. R., Hanawalt, P. C. 1978. *Proc. Natl. Acad. Sci. USA* 75:346–50
122. Sarasin, A. R., Smith, C. A., Hanawalt, P. C. 1977. *Cancer Res.* 37:1786–93
123. Deleted in proof
124. Schachtschabel, D. O., Zilliken, F., Saito, M., Foley, G. E. 1969. *Exp. Cell Res.* 57:19-28
125. Schoenhard, G. L. 1974. PhD thesis. Oregon State Univ.
126. Schoental, R. 1974. *Cancer Res.* 34:2419–20
127. Schoental, R. 1976. In *Chemical Carcinogens,* ed. C. E. Searle, pp.626–89. Washington DC: Ann. Chem. Soc.
128. Schoental, R., Joffe, A. Z., Yagen, B. 1979. *Cancer Res.* 39:2179–89
129. Scott, F. W., de La Hunt, A., Schutz, R. D., Bistner, S. I., Riis, R. C. 1975. *Teratology* 11:79–86
130. Scott, P. M., Kennedy, B. P. C. 1976. *J. Agric. Food Chem.* 24:865–68
131. Scott, P. M., Menien, M. A., Polonsky, J. 1976. 1976. *Experientia* 32:140–42
132. Sentein, R. 1955. *C. R. Soc. Biol.* 149:1621–22
133. Shepard, T. H., Greenway, J. C. 1977. *Teratology* 16:131–36

134. Shinohara, Y., Arai, M., Hirao, K., Sugihara, S., Nakanishi, K. 1976. *Gann* 67:147–55
135. Singer, B. 1975. *Prog. Nucleic Acid Res. Mol. Biol.* 15:219–84
136. Sinnhuber, R. O., Lee, D. J., Wales, J. H., Landers, M. K., Keyl, A. C. 1970. *Fed. Proc.* 29:568
136a. Sorsa, M., Linnainmaa, K., Ilus, T. 1978. *Mutat. Res.* 53:267
137. Sporn, M. B., Dingman, C. W., Phelps, H. L., Wogan, G. N. 1966. *Science* 151:1539–41
138. Stanford, G. K., Hood, R. D., Hayes, A. W. 1976. *Res. Commun. Chem. Pathol. Pharmacol.* 10:743–46
139. Stark, A. A., Essigmann, J. M., Demain, A. L., Skopek, T. R., Wogan, G. N. 1979. *Proc. Natl. Acad. Sci. USA* 76:1343–47
140. Stark, A. A., Kobbe, B., Matsuo, K., Büchi, G., Wogan, G. N., Demain, A. L. 1978. *Appl. Environ. Microbiol.* 36:412–20
141. Stark, A. A., Townsend, J. M., Wogan, G. N., Demain, A. L., Manmade, A., Ghosh, A. C. 1978. *J. Environ. Pathol. Toxicol.* 2:313–24
142. Steyn, P. S., Vleggaar, R., DuPreez, N. P., Blyth, A. A., Seegers, J. C. 1975. *Toxicol. Appl. Pharmacol.* 32:198–203
143. Still, P. E., Wein, R. D., Smalley, E. B., Strong, F. M. 1972. *Fed. Proc.* 31:733 (Abstr. 2910)
144. Swenson, D. H., Lin, J. K., Miller, E. C., Miller, J. A. 1977. *Cancer Res.* 37:172–81
145. Swenson, D. H., Miller, J. A., Miller, E. C. 1973. *Biochem. Biophys. Res. Commun.* 53:1260–67
146. Swenson, D. H., Miller, J. A., Miller, E. C. 1975. *Cancer Res.* 35:3811–23
147. Tatsuno, T. 1968. *Cancer Res.* 28:2393–96
148. Deleted in proof
149. Thielmann, H. W., Gersbach, H. 1978. *Z. Krebsforsch.* 92:177–214
150. Toth, B. 1975. *Cancer Res.* 35:3693–97
151. Toth, B., Nagel, D., Patil, K., Erickson, J., Antonson, K. 1978. *Cancer Res.* 38:177–80
152. Tsuchimoto, I., Stadler, G. R. 1976. *Arzneim. Forsch.* 26:2101–3
153. Ueno, I., Saito, M., Enomoto, M., Uraguchi, K. 1973. *Proc. Jpn. Cancer Assoc. 32nd Ann. Meet. Osaka,* p. 187
154. Ueno, Y. 1976. *IUPAC Mycotoxin Symp., Paris, Ann. Nutr. Aliment.*
155. Ueno, Y. 1977. *Pure Appl. Chem.* 49:1737–45
156. Ueno, Y., Ueno, I., Iitor, Y., Tsunoda, H., Enomoto, M., Ohtsubo, K. 1971. *Jpn. J. Exp. Med.* 41:521–39
157. Ueno, Y., Fukushima, K. 1968. *Experientia* 24:1032–33
158. Ueno, Y., Kubota, K. 1976. *Cancer Res.* 36:445–51
159. Ueno, Y., Kubota, K., Ito, T., Nakamura, Y. 1978. *Cancer Res.* 38:536–42
160. Ueno, Y., Nakajima, M. 1974. *Chem. Pharm. Bull.* 22:2258–62
161. Ueno, Y., Platel, A., Fromageot, P. 1967. *Biochim. Biophys. Acta* 134:27–36
162. Ueno, Y., Ueno, I. 1978. See Ref. 36, pp. 172–88
163. Ueno, Y., Ueno, I., Mizumoto, K., Tatsuno, T. 1968. *J. Biochem.* 63:395–97
164. Ueno, Y., Ueno, I., Tatsuno, T. 1966. *Seikagaku* 38:687
165. Ueno, Y., Yanai, M. 1978. In *Toxicology and Biochemistry of Mycotoxins,* ed. K. Uraguchi, M. Yamazaki, p. 177. New York: Halstead
166. Umeda, M. 1977. In *Mycotoxin in Human and Animal Health,* ed. J. V. Rodricks, C. W. Hesseltime, M. A. Mehlman, pp. 713–29. Park Forest South, Ill: Pathotox
167. Deleted in proof
168. Umeda, M., Tsutsui, T., Saito, M. 1977. *Gann* 68:619–25
169. Umeda, M., Yamamoto, J., Saito, M. 1972. *Jpn. J. Exp. Med.* 42:527–35
170. Uraguchi, K., Sakai, F., Tsukioka, M., Noguchi, Y., Tatsuno, M. 1961. *Jpn. J. Exp. Med.* 31:435–61
171. Uraguchi, K., Saito, M., Noguchi, Y., Takahashi, K., Enomoto, M., Tatsuno, T. 1972. *Food Cosmet. Toxicol.* 10:193–207
172. Van Rensburg, S. J., Van der Watt, J. J., Purchase, I. F. H., Pereira-Continho, L., Markham, R. 1974. *S. Afr. Med. J.* 48:2508a–d
173. Von Wright, A., Lindroth, S. 1978. *Mutat. Res.* 58:211–15
174. Von Wright, A., Niskanen, A., Pyysalo, H. 1977. *Mutat. Res.* 56:105–10
175. Walker, G. C. 1978. *J. Bacteriol.* 133:1203–11
176. Weber, K., Wehland, J., Herzog, W. 1976. *J. Mol. Biol.* 102:817–29
177. Wehner, F. C., Marasas, W. F. O., Thiel, P. G. 1978. *Appl. Environ. Microbiol.* 35:659–62
178. Wehner, F. C., Thiel, P. G., du Rand, M. 1979. *Appl. Environ. Microbiol.* 37:658–60
179. Wehner, F. C., Thiel, P. G., Van Rensburg, S. J., Demasius, I. P. C. 1978. *Mutat. Res.* 58:193–203

180. Whittaker, B. L., Chipley, J. R. 1979. *Appl. Environ. Microbiol.* 37:554–58
181. Deleted in proof
182. Deleted in proof
183. Williams, R. H., Lively, D. H., DeLong, D. C., Cline, J. C., Sweeney, M. J., Poore, G. A., Larsen, S. H. 1968. *J. Antibiot.* 21:463–64
184. Wilson, B. J. 1971. In *Microbial Toxins,* ed. A. Ciegler, S. Kadis, S. J. Ajl, 6:459–521. New York: Academic
185. Withers, R. E. G. 1965. In *Proc. Symp. Mutat Process,* ed. Z. Landa, pp. 359–64. Czech. Acad. Sci.
186. Wogan, G. N. 1973. *Methods Cancer Res.* 7:309–44
187. Wogan, G. N. 1974. In *The Physiopathology of Cancer,* ed. F. Homburger, pp. 64–109. Basel: Karger
188. Wogan, G. N. 1976. In *Hepatocellular Carcinoma,* ed. K. Okuda, R. L. Peters, pp. 25–41. New York: Wiley
189. Wogan, G. N. 1977. In *Environmental Cancer, Adv. Mod. Toxicol.,* ed. H. F. Kraybill, M. A. Mehlman, 3:263–90. New York: Wiley
190. Wogan, G. N., Edwards, G. S., Newberne, P. M. 1971. *Toxicol. Appl. Pharmacol.* 19:712–20
191. Wogan, G. N., Edwards, G. S., Newberne, P. M. 1971. *Cancer Res.* 31:1936–42
192. Wogan, G. N., Essigmann, J. M., Croy, R. G., Busby, W. F. Jr., Groopman, J. D., Stark, A. A. 1979. In *Int. Symp. Princess Takamatsu Cancer Res. Fund, 9th, Tokyo.* In press
193. Wogan, G. N., Paglialunga, S. 1974. *Food Cosmet. Toxicol.* 12:681–85
193a. Wolf, J. C., Mirocha, C. J. 1973. *Can. J. Microbiol.* 19:725–34
193b. Wolf, J. C., Mirocha, C. J. 1977. *Appl. Environ. Microbiol.* 33:546–60
194. Wong, J. J., Hsieh, D. P. H. 1978. *Proc. Natl. Acad. Sci. USA* 73:2241-44
195. Wong, J. J., Hsieh, D. P. H. 1978. *Science* 200:325–27
196. Wong, J. J., Singh, R., Hsieh, D. P. H. 1977. *Mutation Res.* 44:447–50
197. Yamazaki, M., Suzuki, S., Sakakibara, Y., Miyaki, K. 1971. *Jpn. J. Med. Sci. Biol.* 24:245
198. Yoshikazu, Y., Nakata, M., Suzuki, N. 1976. *J. Pestic. Sci.* 1:107–14
199. Yu, F-L. 1977. *J. Biol. Chem.* 252:3245–51

Ann. Rev. Microbiol. 1980. 34:263–83

ORE LEACHING BY BACTERIA ♦1777

D. G. Lundgren

Biology Department, Syracuse University, Syracuse, New York 13210

M. Silver

Center for Mineral and Energy Technology, Ottawa, Ontario, Canada K1A-G1

CONTENTS

INTRODUCTION 263
THEORY AND APPLICATION OF BACTERIAL LEACHING 264
Direct Mechanism 265
Indirect Mechanism 266
MICROBIAL INVOLVEMENT 267
Overview 267
Iron-Oxidizing Thiobacilli 267
LEACHING METHODS 271
Research Applications 271
Commercial Applications 271
Parameters Affecting Bacterial Leaching 272
Temperature 272
pH 273
Oxidation-reduction potential 273
Composition of the leaching medium 273
Particle size and substrate concentration 275
MICROBIAL METAL EXTRACTIONS 275
Copper 275
Uranium 277
Other Metals 278
CONCLUDING REMARKS 280

INTRODUCTION

The elements iron and sulfur circulate in the biosphere through specific paths from environment to organisms and back to the environment. Certain paths only involve microorganisms and it is here that biological reactions of relevance in leaching of metals from mineral ores occur (28). Of major importance are bacterial oxidations of iron, elemental sulfur, and mineral

0066-4227/80/1001-0263$01.00

sulfides; these organisms have evolved an unusual mode of existence and it is known that their oxidative reactions have assisted man from times of the early Phoenicians and Romans. Natural metal leaching has been practiced in Spain, Peru, Canada, France, the United States, and other countries, without knowing the contributions of microorganisms in the processes (13, 130). Only during the last three decades have we begun to understand microbial metal dissolution phenomena.

The writers of this review were encouraged by the expanding interest in both basic and applied aspects of bacterial leaching. During the last four years, three international conferences, held on different continents, have focused on various facets of microbial ore extractions (101, 106, 115). There have also been recent reviews of the subject area which emphasize the potential future revolutionary changes bacteria could have on the mining of metallic minerals (13, 92, 107, 130, 142, 143, 145).

THEORY AND APPLICATION OF BACTERIAL LEACHING

Metals can be dissolved from insoluble minerals directly by the metabolism of microorganisms or indirectly by the products of their metabolism. The biological reactions involved in extractive metallurgy are primarily oxidations of sulfur or mineral sulfides. Many metals may be leached from the corresponding sulfides and it is this process that has been utilized in the commercial leaching operations using microorganisms. Uranium ores do not exist as sulfides; they usually occur as insoluble oxides; whether or not they are directly attacked by bacteria is still unproven. Uranium is, however, closely associated with pyrite (FeS_2) and is affected through indirect action by bacteria forming ferric sulfate:

$$UO_2 + Fe_2(SO_4)_3 \rightarrow UO_2SO_4 + 2FeSO_4. \qquad 1.$$

The uranyl sulfate can be recovered from solution by ion exchange or solvent extraction (54).

A generalized reaction is often used to express the biological oxidation of a mineral sulfide involved in leaching (130).

$$MS + 2O_2 \xrightarrow{\text{microorganism}} MSO_4 \qquad 2.$$

where M is a bivalent metal.

The leaching process is the end result of the bacteria acting upon the mineral sulfide, which serves as an energy source in the presence of other nutrients.

Direct Mechanism

Some microorganisms are capable of direct oxidative attack on mineral sulfides. Scanning electron micrographs have revealed that numerous bacteria attach themselves to the surface of sulfide minerals in solutions supplemented with nutrients (10, 11, 141). Results indicate that bacteria dissolve a sulfide surface of the crystal by means of cell contact. Lundgren & Tano (83) have discussed the nature of the cell surface of a mineral sulfide-oxidizing bacterium and have presented a model to explain iron and sulfide oxidation. Microbial cells have also been shown to attach to metal hydroxides (75).

Silverman (120) concluded that at least two roles were performed by bacteria in the solubilization of minerals. One role involved the ferric-ferrous cycle (indirect mechanism), whereas the other involved physical contact of the organism with the insoluble sulfide crystals and was independent of the ferric-ferrous cycle. Insoluble sulfide minerals can be degraded by microorganisms in the absence of ferric iron under conditions that preclude any likely involvement of a ferrous-ferric cycle (98). Present evidence from research using soluble sources of sulfide and reduced iron substrates supports the idea that iron and sulfide can be simultaneously oxidized by bacteria (8, 38, 77, 78) and that both oxidative processes contribute to metal leaching.

Although many aspects of the direct attack by bacteria on mineral sulfides remain unknown, it is apparent that specific iron and sulfide oxidizers must play an important role. Microbial involvement is influenced by the chemical nature of both the aqueous and solid crystal phases (11). Bacteria appear to attach specifically to the sulfide moiety of mineral rock surfaces, which are the regions that contain the energy supply for the bacteria. Attachment and sulfide oxidation result in pitting of the mineral surface. The extent of surface corrosion varies from crystal to crystal and is related to the orientation of the mineral (10, 11, 141). A metabolite that aids the dissolution of the mineral sulfide may also be produced (10). This substance was postulated to act either by: (*a*) oxidation of Fe^{2+}, (*b*) solubilization of molecular sulfur on the surface of crystals, or (*c*) direct attack on crystallized mineral sulfide surfaces.

Attachment of bacteria to surfaces of pyrite (FeS_2) and chalcopyrite ($CuFeS_2$) is followed by biological reactions. For pyrite, the following reactions are believed to take place:

$$FeS_2 + 3\tfrac{1}{2}O_2 + H_2O \rightarrow FeSO_4 + H_2SO_4, \quad 3.$$

$$2FeSO_4 + \tfrac{1}{2}O_2 + H_2SO_4 \xrightarrow{\text{bacteria}} Fe_2(SO_4)_3 + H_2O, \quad 4.$$

$$FeS_2 + Fe_2(SO_4)_3 \rightarrow 3FeSO_4 + 2S, \quad 5.$$
$$2S + 3O_2 + 2H_2O \xrightarrow{\text{bacteria}} 2H_2SO_4. \quad 6.$$

The reactions with chalcopyrite are:

$$2CuFeS_2 + 8\tfrac{1}{2}O_2 + H_2SO_4 \xrightarrow{\text{bacteria}} 2CuSO_4 + Fe_2(SO_4)_3 + H_2O, \quad 7.$$
$$CuFeS_2 + 2Fe_2(SO_4)_3 \rightarrow CuSO_4 + 5FeSO_4 + 2S. \quad 8.$$

The sulfur formed in Reaction 8 can be oxidized by Reaction 6.

Although the catalytic role of bacteria in these reactions is generally accepted, surface attachment is not obligatory for leaching of pyrite or chalcopyrite. The presence of sufficient numbers of bacteria in the solutions in juxtaposition to the reacting surface is adequate to indirectly support the leaching process.

Indirect Mechanism

Silverman & Ehrlich (121) have discussed the role of ferric sulfate solutions and oxygen in the oxidation of mineral sulfides. Minerals such as galena (PbS), chalcopyrite ($CuFeS_2$), bornite (Cu_5FeS_4), and sphalerite (ZnS) are oxidized more rapidly than pyrite and marcasite (FeS_2), whereas covellite (CuS), chalcocite (Cu_2S) and molybdenite (MoS_2) are oxidized more slowly (121, 137, 138). Ferric ion, either alone or in combination, is the most important chemical species involved in the indirect attacks on sulfide minerals (44). Reactions to explain the involvement of ferric iron are:

$$\text{(aerobic) } MeS + 2Fe^{3+} + H_2 + 2O_2 \rightarrow Me^{2+} + 2Fe^{2+} + SO_4^{=} + 2H^+, \quad 9.$$
$$\text{(anaerobic) } Fe_2(SO_4)_3 + FeS_2 \rightarrow 3FeSO_4 + 2S. \quad 10.$$

In the presence of iron-oxidizing bacteria, the ferrous iron produced by these reactions can be oxidized to ferric ion, thereby establishing a cyclic process. Thus the oxidative attack involves two steps: (*a*) the chemical interaction of ferric iron with the sulfide material (123) and (*b*) the regeneration of ferric iron by the bacteria.

There is a very slow rate of abiotic ferrous iron oxidation at low pH values, but the oxidation is greatly accelerated in the presence of iron-oxidizing bacteria; a factor of 10^5 to 10^6 times has been estimated (146). There is little doubt that under some conditions ferric iron plays a positive role in indirect mechanisms of oxidative attack on sulfide metals, and the possibility exists that, with copper-containing minerals, complex cuprous ions may play a similar role (107). Duncan & Walden (41) have shown that the addition of ferrous sulfate has no effect upon the release of copper from chalcopyrite.

MICROBIAL INVOLVEMENT

Overview

The contribution of microbiological activity to the degradation of sulfide minerals has been unequivocally demonstrated (27). The dominant organisms are those possessing the ability to oxidize iron and reduced sulfur compounds and to tolerate high metal iron concentrations and low acidity (6, 7, 37, 145, 148). To a lesser extent, the involvement of a number of heterotrophic bacteria, fungi, yeasts, algae, and protozoa are found (21, 36, 46, 89). Ralph (107) has presented a reasonable explanation of the varied microbial population associated with sulfide oxidations and has proposed a likely microbial succession in sulfide environments which is influenced by physical and chemical characteristics of the mineral components. Attention has been given to the importance of the pH of the environment; below pH 4.5, organisms that can derive energy from the oxidation of ferrous iron predominate. At pH values around 4.5, a filamentous iron-oxidizing bacterium, *Metallogenium,* can grow (153, 154). The organism's role in leaching reactions is unknown, but it may function as an important pH-succession organism in the environment. Above pH 5, where the chemical oxidation of ferrous iron is rapid and where the effectiveness of the coupling of energy for the ferrous-ferric reaction is diminished, organisms such as *Gallionella* may be extremely important (62, 63). Details of the specific actions of these heterotrophic or mixotrophic microorganisms is sparse, and a full understanding of the organisms' role in sulfide oxidation must await results of further laboratory studies utilizing novel culture procedures (107).

The principal acid-generating microorganism affiliated with mineral leaching is *Thiobacillus ferrooxidans,* which oxidizes both reduced sulfur and iron compounds in acid conditions. Spherical lobate thermophilic chemolithotrophs (7, 14, 15, 73) associated with sulfide minerals can also oxidize both reduced iron and sulfur compounds. The taxonomy of these is not yet clear. Thermophilic, iron-oxidizing thiobacillus-like bacteria have also been isolated (16, 17, 18). Norris & Kelly (104) have discussed the role of different thiobacilli in pyrite oxidation when cultured alone and in mixed culture.

Iron-Oxidizing Thiobacilli

More is known about the general physiology and metabolism of iron-oxidizing thiobacilli than any other organisms associated with metal extraction. Studies have been motivated by applied interest in commercial leaching and in the chemolithotrophic character of these bacteria. Recent reviews of the biochemistry and physiology of *T. ferrooxidans* have focused on the organism's role in hydrometallurgical processes (13, 107, 128, 130) and its involvement in the biogeochemical processes of iron cycling (82).

The influence of microorganisms on metal leaching is physiological (e.g. as catalysts) and is a consequence of the organism's mode of metabolism. This metabolism involves the oxidation of a suitable substrate and is carried out at the expense of certain nutrients taken into the bacteria in support of growth. The energy source for *T. ferrooxidans* is reduced iron, which is stable in acid solutions. Physiologically, the following events occur: ferrous iron is oxidized with the release of electrons (20, 26, 77)

$$2Fe^{2+} \rightarrow 2Fe^{3+} + 2e^{-}, \qquad 11.$$

the reducing potential of which is then available for the reduction of molecular oxygen

$$\tfrac{1}{2}O_2 + 2e^{-} + 2H^{+} \rightarrow H_2O. \qquad 12.$$

The pair of electrons transferred yields enough energy to insure the formation of ATP when coupled to oxidative phosphorylation:

$$ADP + P_i \rightarrow ATP. \qquad 13.$$

In the process of electron transfer there are a number of Fe^{2+}-dependent cytochrome reductions. Although *T. ferrooxidans* grows optimally at pH 2, its internal pH approaches neutrality and maintains a transmembrane pH gradient of 4.5 (30–32). Ingledew and associates (67, 68) have calculated the membrane potential to be –10 mV and the electrochemical proton activity difference to be 256 mV; this value is adequate to support the formation of ATP. Energy conservation has been shown in *T. ferrooxidans* to result from the classical chemiosmotic ATPase reaction which couples the entry of protons down the transmembrane pH gradient to the synthesis of ATP (67, 68). The following overall reactions involving iron are expressions of the cell's metabolism:

$$4FeSO_4 + 2H_2SO_4 + O_2 \rightarrow 2Fe_2(SO_4)_3 + 2H_2O, \qquad 14.$$
$$2Fe_2(SO_4)_3 + 12H_2O \rightarrow 4Fe(OH)_3 + 6H_2SO_4. \qquad 15.$$

Ferric sulfate, the product of the oxidation, reacts with water to form ferric hydroxide and sulfuric acid. Reaction 15 is spontaneous and leads to a net increase in acid in the environment. Furthermore, the reaction is important in maintaining an electron-proton balance during the oxidation of iron. Various ferric hydroxide complexes result, as reactions occur between ferric hydroxide and sulfates. These reactions lead to the formation of jarosite, which appears as yellowish and brownish red precipitates following the oxidation of iron and is commonly referred to as "yellow-boy." The hydroxide-sulfate complexes have a buffering capacity that controls the pH of the environment, thereby affecting the reactions of iron. Some energy substrates of *T. ferrooxidans* are insoluble even at low pH values, and this makes their biochemical oxidation difficult. In these environments, the direct association of the organism with the substrate is important. Further, the localization of the appropriate oxidases in the cytoplasmic membrane provides the proper topology to allow electron transfer to occur at the cell's periphery. A rationale for the oxidation of insoluble substrates by procaryotic organisms has been offered (48).

Two other important reactions for autotrophic growth, the formation of reducing power and the fixation of CO_2, are dependent upon the energy-generating processes of metabolism. The reduction of pyridine nucleotides (NADH, NADPH) provides the organism with reducing power and is generated from the oxidation of ferrous iron. Energy is also required to move the electrons against a redox potential gradient of +.38V (cytochrome *c*) to −.34V for the NAD/NADH couple (pH 2.9).

$$NAD^+ + 2e^- + 2H^+ + 2ATP \rightarrow NADH + H^+ + 2ADP + 2Pi, \quad 16.$$
$$NADH + H^+ + NADP^+ \rightarrow NAD^+ + NADPH + H^+. \quad 17.$$

This aspect of the metabolism of *T. ferrooxidans* has received very little study.

The CO_2 fixation reactions in *T. ferrooxidans* are coupled to the production of energy from Fe^{2+} oxidation. The two major reactions are controlled physiologically, and all of the organism's need for carbon can be supplied through CO_2 fixation (52, 88). The pathway for CO_2 assimilation is a reductive pentose phosphate cycle that includes two characteristic enzymatic reactions: (*a*) phosphorylation of ribulose 5-phosphate, catalyzed by phosphoribulose kinase, to yield ribulose 1,5-diphosphate, and; (*b*) ribulose-1,5 bisphosphate carboxylase, which catalyzes a reaction between one molecule of CO_2 and one molecule of ribulose 1,5-diphosphate with a concomitant dismutation to yield two molecules of 3-phosphoglyceric acid (35, 88).

Under certain growth situations, the carbon needs of the organism can be met by compounds other than CO_2. Although a number of laboratory studies have shown the adaptability of iron-grown cultures to the use of organic substrates for energy and carbon, little is known about the organism's capacity for heterotrophy and/or mixotrophy in nature. It is assumed that prior to growth on organic substrates, synthesis of new enzymes is necessary. Enzyme synthesis would depend upon substrate concentration, pH, temperature, and other environmental parameters (147). It has been shown that a number of enzyme systems in iron-grown cells are repressed or induced, depending upon growth conditions (125, 147). When *T. ferrooxidans* is adapted to heterotrophy, the organism can permanently lose its ability to oxidize iron, which is unusual among microbial adaptation mechanisms. The possibility exists that such bacterial physiological variations are really due to mixtures of closely associated organisms possessing these diverse characteristics that predominate when the organisms are grown under different environmental conditions. One of these was isolated, characterized, and named *Thiobacillus acidophilus* (57, 105). Different strains of *T. ferrooxidans* vary in their ability to oxidize metal sulfides (119). These variations are reflected in differences in the base ratios of the DNA of populations grown on different substrates (117).

Like the biochemistry of iron oxidation, the biochemistry and physiology of inorganic sulfur oxidation by thiobacilli is well characterized. Silver (117) and Ralph (107) have summarized the relevance of sulfur oxidations to metal leaching. The various reduced sulfur compounds studied include soluble compounds such as S^{2-}, H_2S, $S_2O_3^{2-}$, SO_3^{2-}, $S_4O_6^{2-}$, $n(S\text{-}S)^{2-}$. Insoluble sulfur compounds include elemental sulfur and many sulfide minerals (113).

A general scheme relating most of the known oxidative reactions of sulfur compounds by thiobacilli is:

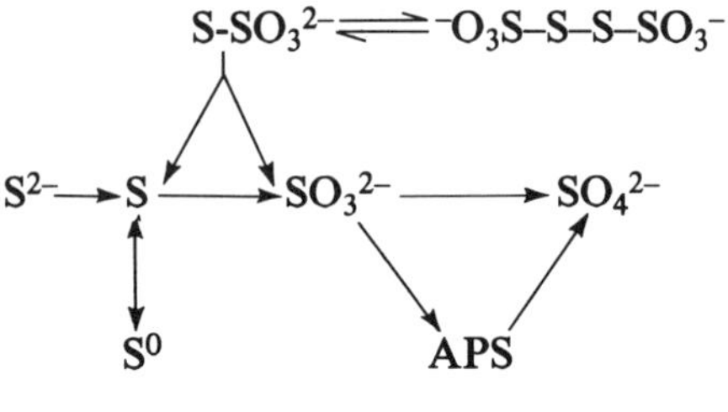

When sulfide or sulfur, common substrates in sulfide mineral leachings, is the substrate for oxidation, it enters the central pathway. Sulfide oxidation proceeds in two stages; in the first stage, sulfide loses two electrons mediated by a sulfide oxidase, and polymerization of the resulting sulfur atoms occurs. The oxidation of the short-chain polysulfide to polymeric sulfur compounds then follows (99). The polysulfides are thought to be membrane associated. Membrane fractions prepared from acidophilic sulfur-grown *T. ferrooxidans* oxidize soluble sulfide (126). Sulfur is oxidized to sulfite, which in turn can be oxidized by one of two pathways.

Although most of the attention of microbial leaching has centered upon the oxidation of iron and sulfur, it is important to remember that successful leaching depends as well upon other aspects of growth of the appropriate organisms. Besides an energy source and carbon (CO_2), *T. ferrooxidans* requires nitrogen, phosphate, sulfate, and trace metals; the general nutrition has been reviewed (13, 47, 130, 149).

LEACHING METHODS

Research Applications

The object of small-scale laboratory investigations is to determine the extent and rate of the alteration of the minerals in these ores. To this end, the laboratory investigations should be geared initially towards the optimum leaching conditions and subsequently towards simulating methods for proposed commercial implementation. Early laboratory studies used stationary vessels of crushed ore and liquid media containing bacteria (109), or ore-filled columns with or without solution percolation (24, 51, 90); neither method provided sufficient oxygen transfer. Respirometer vessels were also used which, although providing sufficient aeration, were limited by the extremely small sample volume (5). Vessels agitated either by stirring (40) or by shaking (43) provided superior aeration. Larger scale experiments could also be conducted in tanks and fermentors (29, 95) in which the leaching parameters could be controlled (59).

Extraction in columns, either with or without circulation of the leaching medium, simulates heap and dump leaching. Although percolation results in better transfer of the dissolved nutrients to the bacteria and facilitates the removal of solubilized products and toxic waste materials, percolation still might not fulfill the high oxygen requirements of the bacteria. Dual stage column percolation experiments have been performed in which the column effluents were treated to remove metabolic products and to regenerate a suitable leaching solution, as well as the bacteria suspended therein (34, 91), thereby giving better yields.

Commercial Applications

The predominant commercial methods used in bacterial extraction of ores are dump and heap leaching (56, 116). In dump leaching, very large quantities of low-grade, run-of-the-mine ores or waste rock are deposited on impermeable ground, usually in valleys. Leach solutions are introduced either naturally or more often by spraying, flooding, or injecting through vertical pipes. The fluid percolates to the bottom where the pregnant solution is collected for concentration of the metal values. Heap leaching is similar but smaller in scale, using finer and more concentrated ore deposited in mounds on prepared drainage pads. Heap leaching is also used for the extraction of metal values from the swell of underground mines. Metal values are also extracted from the stopes of underground mines.

Leaching solutions are brought in contact with the broken ore by percolation (54), alternate flooding and dewatering (152), spraying and hosing (86, 87, 116), or by the injection of leach solutions (152). The pregnant liquors are then recovered either from the sumps or at recovery wells. This method is applicable not only in new mines but also in abandoned operations in which up to 30% of the metal values may remain underground in the walls and pillars.

Tank and vat leaching can be done on ores of sufficiently high grade and values to justify the higher capital costs incurred in this procedure. Although currently not practiced in the extraction of metals, procedures have been proposed (59, 64, 95, 96, 132).

Parameters Affecting Bacterial Leaching

Like all other life processes, the leaching of ores by microbes is influenced by environmental factors. These will be dealt with individually.

TEMPERATURE All processes based on the transformation of minerals by microorganisms are confined to a limited range of temperatures, despite the fact that growth of various bacteria has been observed between –18 and 105°C (151). Increasing temperature results not only in the usual augmentation in the chemical reaction rate but also, within limits, in faster microbial metabolism. Although the lower temperature limits of the metabolic activity of the iron-oxidizing bacteria have not as yet been established, active bacterial iron oxidation in soils and in mines has been noted at about 10°C, and the lower limit of this activity is generally accepted to be the freezing point of water. Optimal leaching of metal sulfide ores and oxidation of ferrous iron by these bacteria has been determined to occur between 25 and 45°C (29, 93); 55°C is the limit of biological oxidation, and only chemical oxidation occurs above this temperature. The temperature coefficients (Q_{10}) and the energies of activation (E_a) have been determined, between 23 and 32°C, to be around 2 and to be between 11.7 and 16.3 kcal/mol respectively for ZnS (140), $FeSO_4$ (60, 81), Cu_2S, and CuS (112); the energies of inactivation (E_i) for these substrates, between 40 and 45°C, are between 53.3 and 61.5 kcal/mol respectively (60, 112, 140). Thermophilic iron-oxidizing bacteria have also been isolated from sulfide mineral-bearing environments that might represent a natural succession to *T. ferrooxidans*, as localized temperatures increase because of the exothermic oxidation of pyrite (6). Both rod-shaped and lobate spherical iron and sulfur-oxidizing bacteria have been isolated from these and other sources that possess temperature minima of 30 to 55°C and maxima of 50°C to more than 90°C (17).

pH *T. ferrooxidans* is active in the pH range of 1.5–5 (120) with a maximum of about 6 (90) and a minimum of about 1 without adaptation of the culture (145). Optimum pH is between 1.0 and 2.5 for the oxidation of ferrous iron (60, 85), zinc sulfide (140), cobalt sulfide (129), chalcopyrite (90, 110, 111), chalcocite (112), covellite (66, 112), galena (76, 127), and pyrite (2). *T. ferrooxidans* has been adapted to grow at lower pH values (71, 146) at which the formation of basic ferric sulfate jarosite is decreased.

Spherical thermophilic bacteria of the *Sulfolobus* type have been shown to be active between pH values of 1 and 6 (19) with pH optima between 2 and 3 (20, 33) when they use elemental and reduced sulfur and iron compounds as substrates. A number of thermophilic thiobacilli have also been isolated with various pH optima between 2 and 9 (80) when the substrates are ferrous iron, sulfide minerals, elemental sulfur, and reduced sulfur compounds.

OXIDATION-REDUCTION POTENTIAL The oxidation-reduction potential (*Eh*), is a measure of the tendency of a substance to accept or donate electrons and is used to measure the oxidizing ability of a given environment. The indirect oxidation that results in solubilization of minerals by ferric iron is highly dependent upon this factor (44). During the oxidation of ferrous iron by *T. ferrooxidans,* the oxidation-reduction potential might be expected to increase toward that of the ferric-ferrous system, which is +747 mV at 25°C. In reality, this value is rarely approached, except at very low iron concentrations or at high acidity, because oxidized iron is precipitated from the medium as jarosite. *Eh* values between +190 and +550 mV have been measured during this oxidation (58). Similarly, the *Eh* has been observed between +220 and +515 mV (102, 111, 112) and between +340 and +540 mV (25, 54, 55, 95) during the oxidation of metal sulfides and the extraction of uranium, respectively, by the iron-oxidizing thiobacilli.

COMPOSITION OF THE LEACHING MEDIUM Growth media for the iron-oxidizing thiobacilli have been described (13, 23, 79, 122, 130, 149); these media contain excess concentrations of all the required nutritional salts, including ammonia, sulfate, potassium, phosphate, magnesium, and calcium. Other trace element requirements are usually fulfilled by impurities in the constituents of the media. The energy source, ferrous sulfate, may be replaced by minerals containing iron or sulfur, and the carbon source is supplied in the air as carbon dioxide. Although ferric iron has been suggested to serve as an oxidant (21), oxygen is generally regarded as the only agent to fulfill this role. These growth media have been widely used in laboratory studies, but they are obviously too expensive for use in large scale mining operations. From an economic standpoint, it is desirable to identify those nutrients needed to be added to the leaching solution to form a practical leaching medium. The organism's requirement for sulfur and acidic environment is fulfilled by sulfate, a product or byproduct of the oxidation of sulfide minerals and ferrous iron respectively. Potassium, calcium, and magnesium are also present in operational leaching media in excess of the minimal requirements needed for growth. Phosphate and ammonia are the only medium constituents not ubiquitous to the leaching solutions. However, phosphate is supplied whenever the mineral apatite is present in the ores, and ammonia may be residual from blasting or milling operations. Nutritional studies have shown that the concentrations of these latter two components affect the rate and yield of zinc extractions (140, 148).

The iron-oxidizing thiobacilli are strictly aerobic, and limitations in oxygen availability affect the rates of ferrous iron oxidation (60) and metal extraction (59). Optimization of aeration has been accomplished by increasing the mass transfer of oxygen (59, 60). The volumetric oxygen transfer coefficient (K_{1a}) decreases from 200 h^{-1} in sterile conditions to 46 h^{-1} during the growth of *T. ferrooxidans* at the expense of ferrous iron as substrate (59, 127).

The concentration of carbon dioxide affects leaching; when the levels were increased, ferrous iron oxidation (9, 100, 114) and metal extraction from sulfide minerals (22, 140) were stimulated. Conversely, when carbon dioxide was removed, the rate of pyrite oxidation decreased (24).

Ferric iron is not only the product of the oxidation of ferrous iron and iron-containing sulfide minerals, but it is also a very effective oxidant of both sulfide and oxide minerals (44). Extraction of copper from covellite and chalcocite is stimulated by concentrations of 10^{-4} to 10^{-2}M iron (66, 112). Thus, both the direct and indirect mechanisms can occur simultaneously. Excess ferric sulfate precipitates cover the ore surfaces, thus impeding bacterial and chemical oxidation (60, 69, 93, 116). Regrinding of the leach residue allows the resumption of leaching on the freshly exposed surfaces (96, 111, 129).

Ferrous iron and metal sulfide oxidations by iron-oxidizing thiobacilli are remarkably insensitive to metal ion concentrations. These bacteria can tolerate aluminum (0.37M), zinc (0.15M), cobalt (0.17M), manganese (0.18M), copper (0.16M), chromium (0.1M), and uranium (0.01M) (13, 145, unpublished results). Tolerances are lower to silver (10^{-9}M to 10^{-5}M), mercury (0.05M), and molybdenum (0.03M), and the oxides of selenium, tellurium, and arsenic are inhibitory (13). High concentrations of both ferrous and ferric ions cause a kinetically complex inhibition of ferrous iron oxidation (72).

Although low concentrations of surfactants accelerate the oxidation of copper sulfide minerals (22, 39), higher concentrations are inhibitory (49, 134, 150) because they reduce surface tension (134) and decrease the mass transfer of oxygen (1). Flotation and solvent extraction reagents are also inhibitory (136, 144), as are various sugars (118) and keto acids (12).

PARTICLE SIZE AND SUBSTRATE CONCENTRATION Greater yields and extraction rates of metals from ores occur when the specific surface area of the ore is increased by reducing particle size (130). Size reduction increases the availability of substrate, and in practice, the degree of lixiviation is directly proportional to the surface area of the particles. Decreasing particle size of low grade ores below a critical dimension can, however, increase the surface area of the gangue relative to the substrate and is thus equivalent to the dilution of the substrate (49). The concentration of solid substrate is expressed as the pulp density or as the solid : liquid ratio. Increasing the mass results in more available substrate and thus tends to increase the absolute quantity of metal values solubilized. Extraction rates may decrease, however, when the solid : liquid ratio is high because of the interference of the solids with the mass transfer of nutrients, especially oxygen and carbon dioxide, to the organisms (130).

MICROBIAL METAL EXTRACTIONS

As stated previously, a number of minerals may be oxidized directly by bacteria or indirectly by ferric ions. Both mechanisms usually operate simultaneously in nature and in commercial metal extractions.

Copper

The most commonly investigated minerals of copper are chalcopyrite ($CuFeS_2$), chalcocite (Cu_2S), and covellite (CuS). All can be leached by both direct bacterial attack and/or by ferric iron as the oxidant. For the iron-containing mineral chalcopyrite, both mechanisms occur simultaneously and are difficult to separate. The following sequence of reactions describes chalcopyrite oxidation in the presence of bacteria.

$$48\ CuFeS_2 + 204\ O_2 + 24\ H_2SO_4 \rightarrow 48\ CuSO_4 + 24\ Fe_2(SO_4)_3 + 24\ H_2O, \quad 18.$$

$$12\ CuFeS_2 + 24\ Fe_2(SO_4)_3 \rightarrow 12\ CuSO_4 + 60\ FeSO_4 + 24\ S^0, \quad 19.$$

$$60\ FeSO_4 + 30\ H_2SO_4 + 15\ O_2 \rightarrow 30\ Fe_2(SO_4)_3 + 30\ H_2O, \quad 20.$$
$$24\ S^0 + 24\ H_2O + 36\ O_2 \rightarrow 24\ H_2SO_4, \quad 21.$$
$$30\ Fe_2(SO_4)_3 + 120\ H_2O \rightarrow 20\{H[Fe(SO_4)_2 \cdot 2\ Fe(OH)_3]\} + 50\ H_2SO_4, \quad 22.$$

$$60\ CuFeS_2 + 255\ O_2 + 90\ H_2O \rightarrow 60\ CuSO_4 + 20\{H[Fe(SO_4)_2 \cdot 2\ Fe(OH)_3]\} + 20\ H_2SO_4. \quad 23.$$

It is doubtful that the initial attack on this mineral is through dissolution, owing to its very low solubility (61). *T. ferrooxidans* has been reported to oxidized monovalent copper, as well as iron and sulfur (53, 103). Iron and copper exist in chalcopyrite in both oxidized and reduced valencies (155); these and the sulfide moiety are readily oxidized either by bacteria directly (Reaction 18), by ferric iron initially present (Reaction 19), or by ferric sulfate formed by bacterial oxidation (Reaction 20). The resulting ferrous iron and elemental sulfur can subsequently be oxidized by bacteria (77, 78) as shown in Reactions 20 and 21. During the initial phase of oxidation (Reactions 18–20), sulfate is consumed and the pH tends to rise, causing the precipitation of ferric sulfate and basic sulfate salts of copper such as antlerite (119). Ferric sulfate is hydrolyzed in a slow reaction (69) to secondary iron minerals, such as jarosite, with the regeneration of sulfate (Reaction 15).

In early studies of chalcopyrite leaching in single-stage laboratory columns (24), the yield of solubilized copper was generally disappointing. Typical recoveries from this process were 25% in 60 days (108), 40% in 70 days, and 60% in 470 days (90). Razzell & Trussell (109, 110) recovered 45% of the copper from chalcopyrite using a stationary culture test. These yields were improved using agitation in reaction tanks; recoveries from different experiments ranged from 35% in 33 days (40), 72% in 12 days and 100% in 26 days (39), 59% in 5 days (42), 60% in 4 days and 79% in 6 days (137) and 55% in 12 days (111). Bruynesteyn and coworkers (22) recovered 50–60% of the copper from chalcopyrite in 4–6 days using an aerated tank. Yields could be improved to 80–96% by regrinding and leaching the residues (22, 111).

Other copper sulfide minerals can be leached by *T. ferrooxidans*. Chalcocite is oxidized to copper sulfate with digenite (Cu_9S_5) and covellite (CuS) as intermediates:

$$10\ Cu_2S + 2\ H_2SO_4 + O_2 \rightarrow 2\ Cu_9S_5 + 2\ CuSO_4 + 2\ H_2O, \quad 24.$$
$$2\ Cu_9S_5 + 8\ H_2SO_4 + 4\ O_2 \rightarrow 10\ CuS + 8\ CuSO_4 + 8\ H_2O, \quad 25.$$
$$10\ CuS + 20\ O_2 \rightarrow 10\ CuSO_4, \quad 26.$$

$$10\ Cu_2S + 10\ H_2SO_4 + 25\ O_2 \rightarrow 20\ CuSO_4 + 10\ H_2O. \quad 27.$$

Both digenite and covellite are oxidized by *T. ferrooxidans* to $CuSO_4$ (103, 112). As sulfate is consumed, the pH tends to rise with the precipitation of antlerite and, if not adjusted, will reach values detrimental to bacterial oxidation (119).

Bacterial oxidation on these minerals was first investigated by Bryner and coworkers (24) and later by others (66, 103). They found that copper was solubilized from chalcocite and covellite, both in the absence and presence of iron; the optimum concentration of iron was 4–20 mM (66, 112). Ferric iron can oxidize these minerals to $CuSO_4$ according to the following reactions:

$$Cu_2S + 2\ Fe_2(SO_4)_3 \rightarrow 2\ CuSO_4 + 4\ FeSO_4 + S^0, \qquad 28.$$

$$CuS + Fe_2(SO_4)_3 \rightarrow CuSO_4 + 2\ FeSO_4 + S^0, \qquad 29.$$

$$Cu_9S_5 + 9\ Fe_2(SO_4)_3 \rightarrow 9\ CuSO_4 + 18\ FeSO_4 + 5\ S^0. \qquad 30.$$

Generally, less than complete solubilization of the copper from these minerals occurs, which is due to the precipitation of secondary minerals, principally jarosite; the latter deposits on the surface of the mineral particles, blocking the oxidative action of both the bacteria and ferric iron.

Copper sulfides occur naturally, almost always in the presence of iron sulfide minerals, such as pyrite and pyrrhotite, which can also be oxidized by *T. ferrooxidans* and ferric iron (see Reactions 3, 4, 5). Thus, the leaching of sulfide minerals that do not contain iron can be affected either negatively or positively by iron.

Copper selenide (CuSe) is oxidized by *T. ferrooxidans* (135); copper sulfate and elemental selenium are formed according to the reaction

$$2\ CuSe + 2\ H_2SO_4 + O_2 \rightarrow 2\ CuSO_4 + 2\ Se^0 + 2\ H_2O. \qquad 31.$$

Uranium

The standard free energy change (20.6 kcal/mol) and the oxidation-reduction potential for the tetravalent-hexavalent uranium system (446 mV) are similar to those of the ferrous-ferric system (17.8 kcal/mol and 747 mV respectively). Uranium oxidation proceeds more rapidly in the presence of iron-oxidizing thiobacilli than in the presence of ferric iron alone (59, 65), suggesting that a supplementary oxidation of uranium occurs which is catalyzed by bacteria. Recent calorimetric (124) and respirometric (70) investigations support the thesis that tretravalent uranium is oxidized by *T. ferrooxidans* according to the reaction:

$$2\ UO_2 + O_2 + 2\ H_2SO_4 \rightarrow 2\ UO_2SO_4 + 2\ H_2O. \qquad 32.$$

Insoluble tetravalent uranium is also oxidized to the soluble hexavalent state by ferric sulfate, as stated for Reaction 1.

During the 1960s, uranium extraction mediated by the iron-oxidizing thiobacilli had been investigated in mining operations in Canada (50, 86, 87) and the United States (53) and in laboratory experiments (3, 4, 54, 64, 65, 94, 95, 97). The ferric iron required for the oxidation of the tetravalent uranium is supplied through the biological oxidation of either soluble ferrous iron or iron-containing sulfide minerals present in the uranium ore (4, 58, 64). The applicability of leaching uranium using iron-oxidizing bacteria and the influence of various parameters have been investigated. Using percolation columns, recoveries of uranium up to 90% were achieved from finely ground low-grade ores, i.e. 85% of the uranium was recovered from an ore with particle size of 6.3 mm in 20 weeks (3, 4), 80–90% from an ore with a particle size of 4 mm in 20 weeks (65). Fisher (50) obtained uranium extraction yields of 35–55% and 49–79% in 30 and 60 days, respectively, on ores with particle sizes of 0.8–12.7 mm. Using a two-stage system in which ore crushed to less than 3 mm was leached by percolation at 50°C and the iron reoxidized by *T. ferrooxidans* in a separate reaction vessel at 30°C, Manchee (91) recovered over 90% of the available uranium. The retention time of the replaceable ore-filled columns was 10 days. Derry and colleagues (34) have discussed a similar in-plant process. A six-stage semi-continuous counter-current decantation system was successful in recovering over 90% of the uranium with a retention time of 31 h (95). Uranium solubilization of 67% was achieved in a stirred aerated fermentor in 9 days; recoveries were increased to 87% upon regrinding the residue and releaching it for another 9 days (59). Uranium extraction in shake flasks was also effective; the leaching process was completed in 5–10 days (58, 127).

Microorganisms other than *T. ferrooxidans* such as the iron-oxidizing sulfolobus-like thermophiles (13), the thermophilic thiobacilli (80), and other thiobacilli (74) have been proposed to be suitable for uranium extraction.

Other Metals

T. ferrooxidans is able to oxidize stibnite (Sb_2S_3) (119, 133, 135); *Stibiobacter senarmontii* was isolated and shown to use as energy sources stibnite and senarmontite (Sb_4O_6) (81). Stibnite is oxidized directly to antimony (III) sulfate by *T. ferrooxidans* (135); the antimony (III) sulfate is then partially hydrolyzed to insoluble antimony (III) oxide sulfate or oxidized to antimony (V) sulfate, which is subsequently hydrolyzed to insoluble antimony (V) dioxide sulfate.

$$Sb_2S_3 + 6\ O_2 \rightarrow Sb_2(SO_4)_3, \tag{33.}$$
$$Sb_2(SO_4)_3 + 2\ H_2O \rightarrow (SbO)_2SO_4 + 2\ H_2SO_4, \tag{34.}$$
$$Sb_2(SO_4)_3 + O_2 + 2\ H_2SO_4 \rightarrow Sb_2(SO_4)_5 + 2\ H_2O, \tag{35.}$$
$$Sb_2(SO_4)_5 + 4\ H_2O \rightarrow (SbO_2)_2SO_4 + 4\ H_2SO_4. \tag{36.}$$

S. senarmontii uses the oxidation of trivalent antimony to the pentavalent form for energy generation (84). Although *T. ferrooxidans* assimilates carbon dioxide in the presence of stibnite (119), it has not been proven whether it is the oxidation of the antimony or the sulfide moiety or both which this bacterium uses as an energy source.

Gallium sulfide (Ga_2S_3) is oxidized to gallium sulfate ($Ga_2(SO_4)_3$) in a reaction analogous to that of stibnite (131). In addition, the sulfides of gallium (131) and bismuth (Bi_2S_3) (130) are oxidized by ferric iron according to the reaction:

$$M_2S_3 + 3\ Fe_2(SO_4)_3 \rightarrow M_2(SO_4)_3 + 6\ FeSO_4 + 3\ S^0. \tag{37.}$$

Both simple and complex sulfides of arsenic are reported to be used as substrates by *T. ferrooxidans.* These include orpiment (As_2S_3) (45), enargite [$Cu_3(As, Sb)S_4$] (47), and arsenopyrite (FeAsS) (47). Arsenopyrite is directly oxidized by bacteria:

$$2\ FeAsS + 7\ O_2 + 2\ H_2O \rightarrow 2\ FeAsO_4 + 2\ H_2SO_4 \tag{38.}$$

and by ferric sulfate

$$2FeAsS + Fe_2(SO_4)_3 + 4\ H_2O + 6\ O_2 \rightarrow 2\ H_3AsO_4 + 4\ FeSO_4 + 3\ H_2SO_4. \tag{39.}$$

The arsenate reacts with the ferric sulfate

$$2\ H_3AsO_4 + Fe_2(SO_4)_3 \rightarrow 2\ FeAsO_4 + 3\ H_2SO_4 \tag{40.}$$

to form the insoluble ferric arsenate.

Among other insoluble metal sulfides oxidized by *T. ferrooxidans* are those of cadmium, mineralogically known as greenockite (137), cobalt (sycoporite) (128, 129, 137), lead (galena) (76, 119, 127, 139), nickel (millerite) (42, 43, 107, 127, 128), and zinc (sphalerite) (42, 90, 21, 128, 130, 137). The rates of bacterial oxidation of some of these and of the copper sulfides covellite and chalcocite are dependent upon their solubility constants (138).

A more complex sulfide mineral of nickel, pentlandite, is oxidized directly by *T. ferrooxidans* (130) according to the reaction:

$$8(Ni,Co,Fe)_9S_8 + 141\ O_2 + 26\ H_2SO_4 \rightarrow 36(Ni,Co)SO_4 + 18\ Fe_2(SO_4)_3 + 26\ H_2O. \quad 41.$$

The sulfates of cadmium, cobalt, nickel, and zinc are soluble, whereas that of lead, mineralogically known as anglesite, is insoluble and precipitates (76).

Although molybdenum is generally toxic to *T. ferrooxidans,* this bacterium does oxidize molybdenite (23) by the reaction

$$2\ MoS_2 + 9\ O_2 + 6\ H_2O \rightarrow 2\ H_2MoO_4 + 4\ H_2SO_4. \quad 42.$$

Ehrlich has recently reviewed a number of inorganic oxidations catalyzed by bacteria (48).

CONCLUDING REMARKS

From the literature it is apparent that much has been learned about microbial leaching and the potential of the organisms for leaching. Regardless of the present limited applications of microbes for leaching, the future appears promising. We can look forward to new modifications of the leaching process including: (*a*) redesigning of heap dumps to include finger dumps to exercise natural aeration and artificial aeration with compressed air; (*b*) genetic manipulation of chemolithotrophic bacteria to fit the optimum conditions needed for successful leaching or the application of naturally selected higher-yielding organisms: (*c*) vat leaching to allow more controls for optimizing leaching and improving pollution control and (*d*) the use of ore concentrates for leaching.

Literature Cited

1. Aiba, S., Humphrey, A. E., Millis, N. F. 1965. *Biochemical Engineering,* pp. 92–127. New York: Academic. 1st ed.
2. Atkins, A. S. 1978. See Ref. 101, pp. 403–26
3. Audsley, A., Daborne, G. R. 1963. *Trans. Inst. Min. Metall.* 72:235–46
4. Audsley, A., Daborne, G. R. 1963. *Trans. Inst. Min. Metall.* 72:247–54
5. Beck, J. V. 1960. *J. Bacteriol.* 79:502–9
6. Beck, J. V. 1967. *Biotechnol. Bioeng.* 9:487–97
7. Beck, J. V. 1969. In *Fermentation Advances,* ed. D. Perlman, pp. 747–71. New York/London: Academic
8. Beck, J. V., Brown, D. G. 1968. *J. Bacteriol.* 96:1433–34
9. Beck, J. V., Shafia, F. M. 1964. *J. Bacteriol.* 88:850–57
10. Bennett, J. C., Tributsch, H. 1978. *J. Bacteriol.* 134:310–17
11. Berry, V. K., Murr, L. E. 1978. See Ref. 101, pp. 103–36
12. Borichewski, R. M. 1967. *J. Bacteriol.* 93:597–99
13. Brierley, C. L. 1978. *Crit. Rev. Microbiol.* 6:207–62
14. Brierley, C. L., Brierley, J. A. 1973. *Can. J. Microbiol.* 19:183–88
15. Brierley, C. L., Murr, L. E. 1973. *Science* 179:488–90

16. Brierley, J. A. 1978. *Appl. Environ. Microbiol.* 36:523–25
17. Brierley, J. A., Lockwood, S. J. 1977. *FEMS Microbiol. Lett.* 2:163–65
18. Brierley, J. A., Norris, P. R., Kelly, D. P., LeRoux, N. W. 1978. *Eur. J. Appl. Microbiol. Biotechnol.* 5:291–99
19. Brock, T. D., Brock, K. M., Belly, R. T., Weiss, R. L. 1972. *Arch. Mikrobiol.* 84:54–68
20. Brock, T. D., Darland, G. K. 1970. *Science* 169:1316–18
21. Brock, T. D., Gustafson, J. 1976. *Appl. Environ. Microbiol.* 32:567–71
22. Bruynesteyn, A., Duncan, D. W., Walden, C. C. 1971. *Can. Metall.* 10:57–63
23. Bryner, L. C., Anderson, R. 1957. *Ind. Chem. Eng.* 49:1721–24
24. Bryner, L. C., Beck, J. F., Davis, D. B., Wilson, D. G. 1954. *Ind. Eng. Chem.* 46:2578–92
25. Celada, J., Lara-Gomez, J. 1965. *J. Inorg. Nucl. Chem.* 27:2561–62
26. Cobley, J. G., Haddock, B. A. 1975. *FEBS Lett.* 60:29–33
27. Colmer, A. R., Hinkle, M. F. 1947. *Science* 106:252–56
28. Corrans, I. J., Harris, B., Ralph, B. J. 1972. *J. S. Afr. Inst. Min. Metall.* 72:221–30
29. Corrick, J. D., Sutton, J. A. 1965. *US Dep. Inter. Bur. Mines Rep. No. 6714.* 22 pp.
30. Cox, J. C., Boxer, D. H. 1978. *Biochem. J.* 174:497–502
31. Cox, J. C., Nicholls, D. G., Ingledew, W. 1979. *Biochem. J.* 178:195–200
32. Cox, J. C., Aasa, R., Malmstrom, B. G. 1978. *FEBS Lett.* 93:157–60
33. DeRosa, M., Gambocorta, A., Bu'lock, J. D. 1975. *J. Gen. Microbiol.* 86:156–64
34. Derry, R., Garrett, K. H., LeRoux, N. W., Smith, S. E. 1976. In *Geology, Mining and Extractive Processing of Uranium,* ed. M. L. Jones, pp. 56–62. London: Inst. Min. Metall.
35. Din, G. A., Suzuki, I., Lees, H. 1967. *Can. J. Microbiol.* 13:1413–20
36. Dugan, P. R. 1975. *Ohio J. Sci.* 75:266–79
37. Duncan, D. W., Bruynesteyn, A. 1971. *Can. Min. Metall. Bull.* 64:32–36
38. Duncan, D. W., Landesman, J., Walden, C. C. 1967. *Can. J. Microbiol.* 13:397–403
39. Duncan, D. W., Trussell, P. C. 1964. *Can. Metall. Q.* 3:43–55
40. Duncan, D. W., Trussell, P. C., Walden, C. C. 1964. *Appl. Microbiol.* 12:122–26
41. Duncan, D. W., Walden, C. C. 1972. In *Developments in Industrial Microbiology,* ed. E. D. Murray, 13:66–75. Washington DC: Am. Inst. Biol. Sci.
42. Duncan, D. W., Walden, C. C., Trussell, P. C. 1966. *Can. Min. Metall. Bull.* 59:1075–79
43. Duncan, D. W., Walden, C. C., Trussell, P. C., Lowe, E. A. 1967. *Trans Soc. Min. Eng. AIME* 238:1–7
44. Dutrizac, J. E., MacDonald, R. J. C. 1974. *Miner. Sci. Eng.* 6:59–100
45. Ehrlich, H. L. 1963. *Econ. Geol.* 58:991–94
46. Ehrlich, H. L. 1963. *J. Bacteriol.* 86:350–52
47. Ehrlich, H. L. 1964. *Econ. Geol.* 59:1306–11
48. Ehrlich, H. L. 1978. *Geomicrobiology* 1:65–83
49. Ehrlich, H. L., Fox, S. I. 1967. *Biotechnol. Bioeng.* 9:471–85
50. Fisher, J. R. 1966. *Trans. Can. Inst. Min. Metall.* 69:167–71
51. Fletcher, A. W. 1970. *Trans. Inst. Min. Metall.* 79:247–52
52. Gale, N. L., Beck, J. V. 1967. *J. Bacteriol.* 94:1052–60
53. Gardner, J., Ritchie, M. I. 1967. *Eng. Min. J.* 168:106–7
54. Gow, W. A., McCreedy, H. H., Ritcey, G. M., McNamara, V. M., Harrison, V. F., Lucas, B. H. 1971. In *Recovery of Uranium, pp. 195–211. Vienna: Int. At. Energy Agency*
55. Gromova, L. A., Pereverzew, N. A., Karavaiko, G. I. 1978. *Mikrobiologiya* 47:239–41
56. Groudev, S. N., Genchev, F. N., Gaidarjiev, S. S. 1978. See Ref. 101, pp. 253–74
57. Guay, R., Silver, M. 1975. *Can. J. Microbiol.* 21:281–88
58. Guay, R., Silver, M., Torma, A. E. 1976. *Eur. J. Appl. Microbiol.* 3:157–67
59. Guay, R., Silver, M., Torma, A. E. 1977. *Biotechnol. Bioeng.* 19:727–40
60. Guay, R., Torma, A. E., Silver, M. 1975. *Ann. Microbiol.* 126B:209–19
61. Habashi, F. 1978. *Chalcopyrite—Its Chemistry and Metallurgy,* p. 63. New York: McGraw Hill Int. 165 pp.
62. Hanert, H. 1973. *Arch. Microbiol.* 88:225–43
63. Hanert, H. 1974. *Arch. Microbiol.* 96:59–74
64. Harrison, V. F., Gow, W. A., Hughson, M. R. 1966. *J. Met.* 18:1189–94
65. Harrison, V. F., Gow, W. A., Ivarson, K. C. 1966. *Can. Min. J.* 87: 64–67
66. Imai, K., Sakaguchi, H., Sugio, T.,

Tano, T. 1973. *J. Ferment. Technol.* 51:865–70
67. Ingledew, W. J., Cox, J. C., Halling, P. J. 1977. *FEMS Microbiol. Lett.* 2: 193–97
68. Ingledew, W. J., Cox, J. C., Jones, R. W., Garland, P. B. 1978. In *Frontiers of Biological Energetics, Electrons to Tissues,* ed. P. L. Dutton, J. S. Leigh, A. Scarpa, 1:334–41. New York: Academic
69. Ivarson, K. C. 1973. *Can. J. Soil. Sci.* 53:315–23
70. Ivarson, K. C. 1980. *Curr. Microbiol.* In press
71. Kelly, D. P., Eccleston, M., Jones, C. A. 1977. See Ref. 115, pp. 126–32
72. Kelly, D. P., Jones, C. A. 1978. See Ref. 101, pp. 19–44
73. Kelly, D. P., Norris, P. R., Brierley, C. L. 1979. *Soc. Gen. Microbiol. Q.* 6:510
74. Kelly, D. P., Tuovinen, O. H. 1975. *Plant Soil* 43:77–93
75. Kennedy, J. F., Barker, S. A., Humphreys, J. D. 1976. *Nature* 261:242–44
76. Kingma, J., Silver, M. 1980. *Appl. Environ. Microbiol.* 39:635–41
77. Landesman, J., Duncan, D. W., Walden, C. C. 1966. *Can. J. Microbiol.* 12:25–33
78. Landesman, J., Duncan, D. W., Walden, C. C. 1966. *Can. J. Microbiol.* 12:957–64
79. Leathen, W. W., Braley, S. A., McIntyre, L. D. 1953. *Appl. Microbiol.* 1:61–64
80. LeRoux, N. W., Wakerley, D. S., Hunt, S. D. 1977. *J. Gen. Microbiol.* 100:197–201
81. Lundgren, D. G. 1975. *Ohio J. Sci.* 75:280–87
82. Lundgren, D. G., Dean, W. 1979. In *Biogeochemical Cycling of Mineral-Forming Elements,* ed. P. A. Trudinger, P. J. Swain, pp. 211–51. Amsterdam New York: Elsevier
83. Lundgren, D. G., Tano, T., 1978. See Ref. 101, pp. 151–66
84. Lyalikova, N. N. 1974. *Mikrobiologiya* 43:941–43
85. MacDonald, D. G., Clark, R. H. 1970. *Can. J. Chem. Eng.* 48:669–76
86. MacGregor, R. A. 1966. *Can. Inst. Min. Metall. Bull.* 59:583–87
87. MacGregor, R. A. 1969. *Min. Eng.* 51:54–55
88. Maciag, W. J., Lundgren, D. G. 1964. *Biochem. Biophys. Res. Commun.* 17:603–7
89. Madgwick, J. C., Ralph, B. J. 1977. See Ref. 115, pp. 85–91. Weinheim, Germany: Verlag Chemie
90. Malouf, E. E., Prater, J. D. 1961. *J. Met.* 14:353–56
91. Manchee, R. J. 1977. *Trans. Inst. Min. Metall.* 86:126–33
92. Manchee, R. J. 1979. *Trends Biol. Sci.* 4:77–80
93. Marchlenwitz, B., Schwartz, W. 1961. *Z. Allg. Mikrobiol.* 1:100–14
94. Matic, M., Mrost, M. 1964. *S. Afr. Ind. Chem.* 18:127–33
95. McCreedy, H. H., Harrison, V. F., Gow, W. A. 1969. *Can. Inst. Min. Metall. Bull.* 62:135–40
96. McElroy, R. O., Bruynesteyn, A. 1978. See Ref. 101, pp. 375–87
97. Miller, R. P., Napier, E., Wells, R. A. 1963. *Trans. Inst. Min. Metall.* 72: 217–34
98. Mizoguchi, T., Sato, T., Okabe, T. 1976. *J. Ferment. Technol.* 54:181–91
99. Moriarty, D. J. W., Nicholas, D. J. D. 1969. *Biochim. Biophys. Acta* 184: 114–23
100. Moss, J. F., Andersen, J. E. 1968. *Aust. Inst. Min. Metall. Proc.* 225:15–25
101. Murr, L. E., Torma, A. E., Brierley, J. A., eds. 1978. *Metallurgical Applications of Bacterial Leaching and Related Microbiological Phenomena.* New York: Academic. 526 pp.
102. Napier, E., Wood, R. G., Chambers, L. A. 1968. In *Symposium On Advances In Extractive Metallurgy,* pp. 942–57. London: Inst. Min. Metall.
103. Nielsen, A. M., Beck, J. V. 1972. *Science* 175:1124–26
104. Norris, P. R., Kelly, D. P. 1978. *FEMS Microbiol. Lett.* 4:143–46
105. Proteau, G., Silver, M. 1978. *Can. J. Microbiol.* 24:1158–63
106. Ralph, B. J. 1980. In *Conf. Biogeochem. Min. Ind. Environ. Pollut. Leaching Conf., Aust. Acad. Sci. Canberra, Australia.* In press
107. Ralph, B. J. 1979. In *Biogeochemical Cycling of Mineral-Forming Elements,* ed. P. A. Trudinger, P. J. Swain, pp. 369–96. Amsterdam/New York: Elsevier
108. Razzell, W. E. 1962. *Can. Min. Metall. Bull.* 55:190–91
109. Razzell, W. E., Trussell, P. C. 1963. *Appl. Microbiol.* 11:105–10
110. Razzell, W. E., Trussell, P. C. 1963. *J. Bacteriol.* 85:595–603
111. Sakaguchi, H., Silver, M., Torma, A. E. 1976. *Biotechnol. Bioeng.* 18:1091–1101
112. Sakaguchi, H., Torma, A. E., Silver, M. 1976. *Appl. Environ. Microbiol.* 31:7–10
113. Sato, M. 1960. *Econ. Geol.* 55:1202–31
114. Schnaitman, C. A., Lundgren, D. G. 1965. *Can. J. Microbiol.* 11:23–27

115. Schwartz, W., ed. 1977. *Conference Bacterial Leaching, GBF Monogr. No. 4.* Weinheim, Germany: Verlag Chemie. 270 pp.
116. Sheffer, H. W., Evans, L. G. 1968. *Copper Leaching Practices in the Western United States, US Bur. Mines Rep. No. 8341.* 57 pp.
117. Silver, M. 1978. See Ref. 101, pp. 3–17
118. Silver, M., Margalith, P., Lundgren, D. G. 1967. *J. Bacteriol.* 93:1765–69
119. Silver, M., Torma, A. E. 1974. *Can. J. Microbiol.* 20:141–47
120. Silverman, M. P. 1967. *J. Bacteriol.* 94:1046–51
121. Silverman, M. P., Ehrlich, H. K. 1964. *Adv. Appl. Microbiol.*, 6:153–206. New York: Academic
122. Silverman, M. P., Lundgren, D. G. 1959. *J. Bacteriol.* 77:642–47
123. Singer, P. C., Stumm, W. 1970. *Science* 167:1121–23
124. Soljanto, P., Tuovinen, O. H. 1980. See Ref. 106. In press
125. Tabita, R., Lundgren, D. G. 1971. *J. Bacteriol.* 108:328–37
126. Tano, T., Lundgren, D. G. 1978. *Appl. Environ. Microbiol.* 36:1198–1205
127. Tomizuka, N., Yagisawa, M. 1978. See Ref. 101, pp. 321–44
128. Torma, A. E. 1971. *Rev. Can. Biol.* 30:209–16
129. Torma, A. E. 1975. *Canada Patent No. 960,463*
130. Torma, A. E. 1977. *Adv. Biochem. Eng.*, ed. T. K. Ghose, A. Frechter, N. Blackebrough, 6:1–37. New York: Springer
131. Torma, A. E. 1978. *Can. J. Microbiol.* 24:888–91
132. Torma, A. E. 1978. See Ref. 101, pp. 375–87
133. Torma, A. E., Gabra, G. G. 1977. *Antonie van Leeuwenhoek J. Microbiol. Serol.* 43:1–6
134. Torma, A. E., Gabra, G. G., Guay, R., Silver, M. 1976. *Hydrometallurgy* 1: 301–9
135. Torma, A. E., Habashi, F. 1972. *Can. J. Microbiol.* 18:1780–81
136. Torma, A. E., Itzkovitch, I. J. 1976. *Appl. Environ. Microbiol.* 32:102–7
137. Torma, A. E., Legault, G. 1973. *Ann. Microbiol.* 124A:111–21
138. Torma, A. E., Sakaguchi, H. 1978. *J. Ferment. Technol.* 56:173–78
139. Torma, A. E., Subramanian, K. N. 1974. *Int. J. Miner. Process.* 1:125–34
140. Torma, A. E., Walden, C. C., Branion, R. M. R. 1970. *Biotechnol. Bioeng.* 12:501–17
141. Tributsch, H. 1976. *Naturwissenschaften* 63:88
142. Trudinger, P. A. 1971. *Miner. Sci. Eng.* 3:13–25
143. Tuovinen, O. H. 1972. *At. Energy Rev.* 10:251–58
144. Tuovinen, O. H. 1978. *Eur. J. Appl. Microbiol. Biotechnol.* 5:301–4
145. Tuovinen, O. H., Kelly, D. P. 1972. *Z. Allg. Mikrobiol.* 12:311–46
146. Tuovinen, O. H., Kelly, D. P. 1973. *Arch. Mikrobiol.* 88:285–98
147. Tuovinen, O. H., Kelly, D. P., Dow, C. S., Eccleston, M. 1978. See Ref. 101, pp. 61–81
148. Tuovinen, O. H., Niemela, S. I., Gyllenberg, H. G. 1971. *Antonie van Leeuwenhoek J. Microbiol. Serol.* 37:489–96
149. Tuovinen, O. H., Panda, F. A., Tsuchiya, H. M. 1979. *Appl. Environ. Microbiol.* 37:954–58
150. Tuttle, J. H., Dugan, P. R. 1976. *Can. J. Microbiol.* 22:719–24
151. Valentyne, J. R. 1967. *Ann. NY Acad. Sci.* 108:342–53
152. Wadsworth, M. E. 1975. In *Symposium of Inplace Leaching and Solution Mining,* ed. Y. S. Kim. Reno:Sch. Mines
153. Walsh, F., Mitchell, R. 1972. *J. Gen. Microbiol.* 72:369–76
154. Walsh, F., Mitchell, R. 1972. *Environ. Sci. Technol.* 6:809–12
155. Wycoff, R. W. G. 1970. *Bull. Soc. Fr. Mineral. Cristallogr.* 93:120–22

Ann. Rev. Microbiol. 1980. 34:285–309

CHLAMYDIAE

❖1778

Julius Schachter[1]

G. W. Hooper Foundation, University of California, San Francisco, California 94143

Harlan D. Caldwell

F. I. Proctor Foundation, University of California, San Francisco, California 94143

CONTENTS

INTRODUCTION 286
TAXONOMY 287
MICROBIOLOGY 289
Initiation of Infection 289
Growth Cycle 291
Morphologic aspects 291
Metabolic aspects 292
Action of antimicrobial agents 293
Chlamydial Antigens 294
Genus-specific antigens 294
Species-specific antigens 295
Serotype-specific antigens 296
Virulence Factors Related to Antigenic Structure 297
CLINICAL SPECTRUM OF HUMAN CHLAMYDIAL INFECTIONS 297
Chlamydia psittaci 297
Chlamydia trachomatis 298
Ocular 298
Male genital tract 298
Female genital tract 299
Concomitant infections with the Gonococcus 300
Neonatal 301
EPIDEMIOLOGY 302
Chlamydia psittaci 302
Avian infections 302
Mammalian infections 303

[1]Requests for reprints should be addressed to Dr. Schachter

0066-4227/80/1001-0285$01.00

Human infections 303
Chlamydia trachomatis 304
LABORATORY DIAGNOSIS 305
CONCLUDING REMARKS 306

INTRODUCTION

In the early 1970s, interest in chlamydiae increased considerably as their role in genital tract disease became clearer (37, 81, 84). It is ironic that *Chlamydia trachomatis* should achieve its greatest measure of recognition as a cause of nongonococcal urethritis. As we enter the 1980s, it appears that this disease will ultimately be recognized as the least important of human infections with *C. trachomatis.* Throughout this century there have been flurries of interest in the chlamydiae as certain etiologic associations were made (84). In the past they were considered to be large viruses that caused relatively uncommon diseases such as psittacosis and lymphogranuloma venereum (LGV) or endemic diseases in exotic areas (e.g. trachoma in North Africa). Increased awareness of the clinical significance of human chlamydial infections in all parts of the world, including industrialized nations, has been paralleled by interesting basic observations on the biology of these unique organisms (10, 68).

It is likely that the chlamydiae are among the most ubiquitous parasites within the animal kingdom. Virtually all avian species, most domestic mammals, and many feral mammals have been shown to be natural hosts for *C. psittaci* infections (62). It is likely that the chlamydiae infecting the lower mammals are of poor infectivity for humans. Enormous quantities of agent are shed in the feces or discharges from infected sheep, cattle, and cats and contaminate the human environment, but only rare case reports have suggested that humans become infected with these particular chlamydiae. Avian chlamydiae, on the other hand, are infectious to man. They cause the human disease psittacosis, which is still a significant occupational hazard to workers in the poultry industry (28).

Just as *C. psittaci* strains seem to be well adapted to birds and lower mammals, *C. trachomatis* seems to be specifically adapted to humans. Several hundred million people have trachoma, which is a chronic keratoconjunctivitis. The disease is holoendemic in many developing countries where virtually all infants and young children acquire the infection. In industrialized countries certain *C. trachomatis* serotypes are now recognized to be among the most common sexually transmitted pathogens. While most of the sexually transmitted diseases caused by *C. trachomatis* are relatively mild and involve mucous membranes (cervicitis, urethritis, and occasionally conjunctivitis), systemic complications are recognized. The awareness of newly recognized diseases has reached the level where the claim has been made, with justification, that the clinical spectrum of sexually transmitted chlamydial infections approaches that of gonococcal infections (14). Some of the systemic diseases associated with sexually transmitted chlamydiae are epididymitis, Bartholinitis, acute salpingitis, and probably perihepatitis. In addition to horizontal transmission by sexual means, vertical transmission also occurs. Exposed neonates contract chlamydial infections when passing through the infected cervix and may develop conjunctivitis and/or pneumonia. This review emphasizes information that has accrued in the past decade on this interesting group of organisms.

TAXONOMY

Chlamydiae were called large viruses when they were first seen in association with the psittacosis outbreak of 1929. Earlier, the agents had been thought to be protozoans when the typical intracytoplasmic inclusions were seen in the conjunctival scrapings. Because these agents are obligatory intracellular parasites and are relatively small (the elementary body is approximately 300–350 nm in diameter and close to the limits of resolution of the light microscope), they had been thought to be viruses. Bedson and Meyer, two pioneer students of the organism, both felt uncomfortable with this designation and discussed the bacterial nature of the psittacosis agent. It remained, however, for the work of Stanier and Lwoff in differentiating between viruses and bacteria for the definition of chlamydiae as bacteria to be made (based in large part on the studies of Moulder and his colleagues) (65, 66). Basic characteristics of these microorganisms are summarized in Table 1.

Over the years the chlamydiae have been known by a variety of names (reviewed by Page) (74). The currently accepted taxonomic classification of the chlamydiae is far from ideal. However, it does provide for useful differentiation of these agents based on laboratory tests that can be performed relatively easily. Because of their unique growth cycle, the chlamydiae have been placed in their own order, Chlamydiales (75). There is one family, Chlamydiaceae, and one genus, *Chlamydia,* with two species, *C. psittaci* and *C. trachomatis.* The two species are differentiated on the basis of sulfonamide susceptibility and glycogen accumulation (or iodine staining) within the inclusion. *C. psittaci* strains are sulfa resistant and iodine-stain negative, whereas *C. trachomatis* strains are susceptible to sulfonamides and their inclusions stain with iodine. Relative sulfonamide resistance is known to occur in LGV (*C. trachomatis*) strains and, conversely, susceptibility has been observed in *C. psittaci* strains.

Table 1 Properties of chlamydiae, viruses, and bacteria[a]

	Chlamydiae	Viruses	Bacteria
Size (nm)	Ca 350	15–350	300–3,000
Shape	Coccoid	Symmetrical	Varied
Obligatory intracellular parasites	+	+	–
Nucleic acids	2	1	2
Complex cell wall	+	–	+
Muramic acid	–	–	+
Reproductive mode	Complicated cycle and fission	Eclipse-synthesis-assembly	Fission
Sensitivity to sulfonamides or antibiotics	+	–	+
Ribosomes	+	–	+
Metabolic enzymes	+	–	+
Energy production	–	–	+

[a]Reproduced with permission of PSG Publishing Co., Inc., from Schachter, J. and Dawson, C. R. (1978) *Human Chlamydial Infections.*

Each species includes a wide variety of microorganisms with different biological and serologic properties. For example, *C. trachomatis* strains include the mouse pneumonitis strain and 15 serotypes of human origin (37). Four of these serotypes have been regularly associated with hyperendemic, potentially blinding trachoma (A, Ba, B, and C) whereas types D through K have usually been associated with sexually transmitted infections and sporadic cases of conjunctivitis. The lymphogranuloma venereum strains, serotypes L-1, L-2, and L-3 of *C. trachomatis,* are more invasive in the human host and may be differentiated in tissue culture systems on the basis of regular cell-to-cell transmission or serial infection without mechanical assistance. Thus the LGV strains produce plaques in susceptible (such as L-929 cells) cell culture monolayers (7). They also appear to have different receptor sites than the other *C. trachomatis* strains (53). Preliminary studies indicate that there are some differences in the plasmid DNA of LGV and other *C. trachomatis* strains (55).

Thus, it seems likely that there are at least three separate species included within the current designated species of *C. trachomatis.* The trachoma-inclusion conjunctivitis strains (serotypes A through K) comprise one species, the lymphogranuloma strains (serotypes L-1, L-2, and L-3) comprise the second species, and the apparently unrelated mouse pneumonitis strain represent the third species. Creation of new species on such grounds would remedy the awkward situation where the researcher must continually stipulate which *C. trachomatis* isolates are being examined or discussed.

C. psittaci strains also include a large number of serotypes (6) and possess different biological properties including, most practically, the ability to produce diseases in humans and in hosts of economic importance. However, there are no simple and systematic means of differentiating these strains within the laboratory.

Validity of the separation of the two species is supported by the difference in the G+C DNA ratios of *C. trachomatis* (45%) and *C. psittaci* (41%) (51). There appears to be relatively little (< 11%) DNA homology between the two species (102). The chlamydiae have a very small genome compared to most bacterial species. At 6–8.5 $\times 10^5$ base pairs, the genome is approximately half the size of *Neisseria* or rickettsial DNA and one quarter the size of *Escherichia coli* DNA (50). These observations are based on studies performed with relatively few strains of chlamydiae; several workers have suggested that some of the results of G+C ratio of the two species represent a spectrum of values that overlaps (35). The failure to demonstrate DNA homology between the two species is surprising. On inductive grounds it is hard to avoid the conclusion that *C. trachomatis* and *C. psittaci* must be descended from a common ancestor. Clearly, there are differences in specific antigen structure, folic acid metabolism, and glycogen accumulation. However, the similarities are far more striking: a genus-specific antigen, a common (and unique) growth cycle, the size and shape of particles, the properties relevant to virulence and host-cell interaction, metabolism, etc. It is tempting to postulate that from a common origin some diversity developed during long adaptation to specific hosts (*C. trachomatis* to humans, *C. psittaci* to mammals and birds). Thus, one would expect some genetic relatedness between these two species.

MICROBIOLOGY

Initiation of Infection

In naturally occurring chlamydial infections, there appear to be some differences in the ability of chlamydial strains to infect different cell types. *C. trachomatis* strains (other than LGV) appear to infect columnar epithelial cells, and most diseases they cause reflect transmission along the mucous membrane surfaces containing these susceptible cells. *C. psittaci* strains, on the other hand, appear to have a broader host cell spectrum and are often found in macrophages.

The initial contact between the infecting agent and the host cell involves heat-sensitive sites on the chlamydiae and, at least as far as *C. psittaci* is concerned, trypsin-sensitive sites on the host cell (17). Recent results suggest that *N*-acetylglucosamine is involved in the attachment because wheat germ agglutinin, a lectin having this specificity, inhibits and competes with the attachment process for *C. psittaci* (6BC strain) and an LGV strain of *C. trachomatis* (54). For other *C. trachomatis* strains, there appear to be relatively specific receptor sites that can be removed by treatment with neuraminidase (53). Attachment may also be enhanced by changing surface charge; for example, pretreatment of cultures with DEAE dextran enhances attachment and the organism can be eluted by heparin treatment (11, 41). Once attached, the agent enters the cell by a phagocytic process (32). Because chlamydiae are obligatory intracellular parasites, it is highly advantageous for them to induce phagocytosis by host cells. This phagocytosis is preferential because chlamydiae are ingested more quickly than other bacteria or inert particles (18). This efficient ingestion by a nonprofessionally phagocytic host cell is induced by the chlamydiae. The chlamydiae share with many obligatory intracellular parasites the ability to inhibit the normal host cells' defense mechanisms. Although they enter the cell through a phagocytic process and are present within a phagosome throughout their developmental cycle, the phagosome does not fuse with lysosomes until very late in the cycle (32, 48). The prevention of lysosomal fusion is directed by chlamydial surface antigens and is apparently dependent upon live replicating chlamydiae. Heat-killed or antibody-treated chlamydiae are also phagocytized, but phagolysosomal fusion occurs. It is not yet clear whether the antibody treatment used to identify chlamydial activities is restricted to those apparently specific effects or if the results simply reflect exposure of the cell to a dead organism (e.g. antibody-treated chlamydiae could be killed by a complement-dependent mechanism). The chlamydia-infected cell appears healthy until relatively late in the developmental cycle. Then some phagolysosomal fusion may occur at the end stage when newly developed infectious particles are released from the infected cell.

For a number of years there appeared to be conflicting data in the literature concerning the effects of chlamydial infection on host cell replication. Some reports discuss replication of the infected host cells, whereas others indicate that chlamydial infection prevents multiplication of the host cell and completely diverts its synthetic capabilities to the metabolic requirements of the chlamydiae (15, 44, 67, 71). It is now recognized that the differences in these two sets of results reflect differences in multiplicity of infection (MOI). Where chlamydiae are used to infect cells at very high MOI ($>$ 100), toxic results are obtained and the host cells die in the absence of chlamydial replication. When lower, but still relatively high MOI (10–50) is used to infect the cells, the toxic effect is not observed and the chlamydiae are capable of multiplying within the host cell; however, the host cell is damaged to the stage where its replication is impaired (48). At low MOI ($<$ 1 infectious unit per cell), inclusions develop within the cells; however, they can still divide, and daughter cells may or may not be infected. Thus, one cell may divide and one daughter will be free of infection while the other can be killed by the infectious process. In some instances, both daughter cells can be infected.

Growth Cycle

MORPHOLOGIC ASPECTS The chlamydial particle remains intact within the phagosome. The elementary body (diameter ca 350 nm) undergoes some sort of reorganization so that within 6–8 hr it has changed to what is called the reticulate particle or initial body. These larger (800–1,000 nm) particles are metabolically active, synthesize macromolecular material, and multiply by binary fission until approximately 18 hr postinfection. At this stage of replication, initial bodies may continue multiplying by fission, but some undergo another reorganization, by which they become elementary bodies on a 1:1 ratio. These elementary bodies are then released from the inclusion and from the host cell to infect other cells. Electron microscopy has shown that both particle types have two distinct trilaminar cell membranes (Figure 1) (4, 60, 61).

The chemical composition of the cell wall of the elementary body is quite similar to that of Gram-negative bacteria. The cell wall of the reticulate particle contains less phospholipid and lacks cysteine and methionine (58, 61). The initial bodies are highly labile and do not survive outside the host

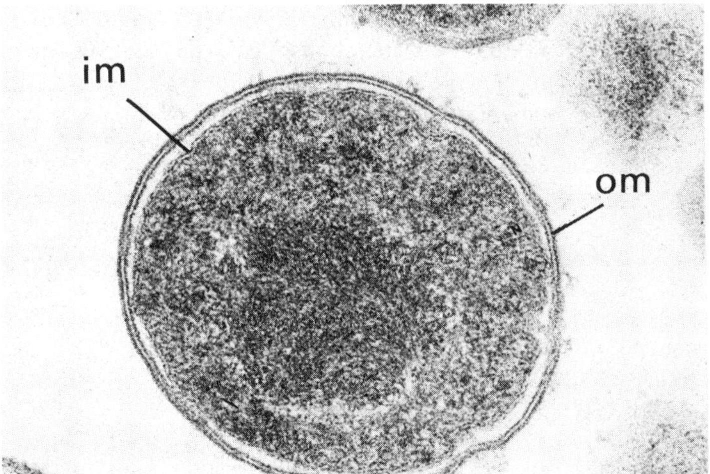

Figure 1 Electron photomicrograph of a thin section of a *C. trachomatis* elementary body (strain L2/434). The trilaminar outer membrane (OM) and inner cytoplasmic membrane (IM) of the elementary body are illustrated (X 118,000).

cell. The elementary bodies are relatively stable in extracellular environments. It is likely that these two forms of chlamydiae represent evolutionary adaptation to the intracellular or extracellular environment (Table 2).

The theory that *C. psittaci* and *C. trachomatis* descended from a common ancestor would predict that initial bodies will be virtually identical throughout the genus. The elementary bodies, being extracellular, would be exposed to selective pressures such as antibody and host cell membrane structure. The evolution to more efficient parasitism would result in antigenic heterogeneity, specific receptor sites, etc. The initial bodies being sheltered from these pressures would probably be found to possess genus-specific antigens and the same basic membrane structures that facilitate transport of nutrients. To date, there are no findings that are inconsistent with this description, but sufficient data have not yet been obtained to validate the hypothesis.

METABOLIC ASPECTS The major studies of nutritional requirements of chlamydiae were conducted by Morgan and associates (64). They found that *C. psittaci* (6BC strain) did not need any components that were not required for the growth of the host cell. Chlamydiae are sensitive to inhibitors of protein synthesis early in the developmental cycle. Although it is hard to study chlamydial metabolism against the larger background of host cell metabolism, it has been shown that protein synthesis peaks approximately 10–15 hr after infection when multiplication of chlamydial particles occurs. By selective inhibition of metabolism of either the parasite or host cell (cycloheximide inhibits the synthetic capabilities of the mammalian cell lines and chloramphenicol inhibits protein synthesis of chlamydiae), it was

Table 2 Properties of chlamydial particles

Property	Elementary body	Reticulate particle
Size	200–400 nm	600–1,000 nm
Rigid cell wall	+	–
Extracellular stability	+	–
Serotype-specific antigens	+	–
Species-specific antigens exposed	–	+
DNA	nucleoid	dispersed
RNA/DNA ratio	<1	3–4
Infective	+[a]	–
Induce phagocytosis	+[a]	–
Inhibit phagosome fusion	+[a]	–
Toxicity	+[a]	–
Metabolic activity	–	+
Replication	–	+

[a] Properties apparently blocked by specific antibody.

possible to separate the net production of proteins or nucleic acids of chlamydiae from the cell background at different times (2, 3). As expected, RNA and DNA synthesis peak at the 15–25 hr period when agent multiplication is highest (91). The log phase lasts approximately 10 hr. The availability of some metabolites, such as isoleucine, may be growth limiting (42). Host protein synthesis is not inhibited by chlamydial infection. The use of cycloheximide or emetine clearly shows that host protein synthesis is not required for the development of chlamydiae (2, 11). However, since chlamydiae are recovered at higher titers from selectively inhibited cells, there may be some competition for nutrients between the protein-synthesizing systems of the organism and those of the host cell. RNA synthesis is required earlier in the developmental cycle than DNA synthesis. RNA would be involved in metabolic processes; new RNA is not required when the second reorganization (from reticulate form to elementary body) takes place relatively late in the growth cycle (94).

Chlamydiae contain fatty acids different from those found in some host cells. For example, phosphatidylglycerol is a major component of the 6BC strain and is not found in some mammalian cells (MK2) that support its growth (56). Glycogen is accumulated in the inclusions of *C. trachomatis* strains, peaking approximately 48–60 hr after infection. *C. psittaci* strains synthesize glycogen, but levels are much lower than with *C. trachomatis* strains (31). The significance of this glycogen that accumulates in the inclusions, but is not necessarily part of the chlamydial particle, is not known.

Chlamydial metabolism has been reviewed in depth elsewhere (10, 65, 66). The most significant observation has been the failure to detect any chlamydial metabolic pathway that results in generation of energy, although chlamydiae have considerable biosynthetic capability. Thus, Moulder has called them "energy parasites" that use the host cell's ATP for their own metabolism.

ACTION OF ANTIMICROBIAL AGENTS Chlamydiae are susceptible to a wide variety of antimicrobial agents (84). They are susceptible to most of the broad spectrum antibiotics. Tetracyclines are highly active against the chlamydiae. Erythromycin also is effective in eradicating chlamydial infections. Penicillins are highly active in vitro but are not clinically useful. They inhibit cell wall synthesis of most bacteria and similarly interfere with the replication of chlamydial reticulate particles, resulting in large bizarre forms and preventing ultimate development of elementary bodies (52). Penicillins act on *Chlamydia,* even though muramic acid appears to be absent in chlamydial particles (or, if present, is there in trace amounts that could not have structural significance) (34). Thus, the chlamydial peptidoglycan differs in composition from peptidoglycans of other bacteria. As expected, inhibitors of cell wall synthesis affect division of reticulate forms and are inactive late in the growth cycle. By definition, *C. trachomatis* strains are susceptible to sulfonamides, whereas most *C. psittaci* strains are resistant. Rifampicin, powerful inhibitor of nucleic acid synthesis, is highly active against chlamydiae, although resistance to rifampicin can be developed quite easily by chlamydiae in the laboratory (12, 49).

Chlamydial Antigens

Knowledge of the architecture and chemistry of chlamydial antigens is rather rudimentary, mainly because it is difficult to obtain adequate quantities of organisms required for the conventional physicochemical fractionation procedures routinely employed for antigenic analysis. Consequently, the limited information currently available on the chemical nature and molecular location of chlamydial antigens has largely been obtained indirectly from serologic studies. It is becoming increasingly evident, however, that the *Chlamydia* are antigenically complex organisms, possessing antigens of genus, species, and subspecies (serotype) specificity (Table 3).

GENUS-SPECIFIC ANTIGENS All members of the genus share a heat-stabile (100° C for 30 min), common antigen, referred to as the "chlamydial group antigen." The group antigen is readily extracted with ethyl ether, sodium lauryl sulfate, or sodium deoxycholate. Early investigations suggested a lipocarbohydrate nature for the antigen because its ability to fix complement was lost after removal of lipid or by periodate oxidation. Only recently, however, has the group antigen been characterized. Dhir et al isolated a large water-soluble polysaccharide ($0.2–2.0 \times 10^6$ mol wt) after alkaline hydrolysis of partially purified ethyl ether–extracted antigen (25).

Table 3 Properties of chlamydial antigens

Antigenic specificity	Chemical characterization of purified antigen	Comments
Genus (group) specific	Acidic polysaccharide $\approx 10^6$ mol wt	1. Heat stable CF antigen; 2. at least 3 antigens by immunodiffusion
Species-specific	Protein—1.5×10^5 mol wt	Heat labile, minimum of 18 *C. trachomatis* antigens found by two dimensional immunoelectrophoresis; 15 for *C. psittaci*
Type-specific	Protein—$2.7–3.2 \times 10^4$ mol wt	Microimmunofluorescence, neutralization of toxicity and infectivity; *C. trachomatis* has 15 serotypes; many for *C. psittaci*

The isolated polysaccharide failed to fix complement but was capable of inhibiting complement fixation by crude antigen. The antigen was precipitable by immunodiffusion analysis and reacted as a single antigen when tested against *C. psittaci* or *C. trachomatis* hyperimmune antiserum. The immunodominant determinant of the isolated component was identified as an acidic polysaccharide glycosidically bound to serologically inactive neutral carbohydrates. The immunodominant antigen was similar but not identical to 2-keto-3-deoxyoctanoic acid of *Salmonella* lipopolysaccharide.

Other, as yet uncharacterized, genus-specific antigens have been detected. A single cross-reacting group antigen was shared between the *C. psittaci* (Cal-10) and *C. trachomatis* (LGV-434) strains (21). This antigen is not the acidic polysaccharide group antigen described previously, since its antigenicity is destroyed by heating at 100° C for 30 min.

SPECIES-SPECIFIC ANTIGENS Species-specific antigens are shared by all members of a chlamydial species. Evidence for such antigens has been demonstrated by direct fluorescent antibody staining, indirect hemagglutination with extracts of extensively sonicated organisms, and immunodiffusion analysis of sonicated extracts of organisms pretreated with deoxycholate (23, 26, 97). Crossed immunoelectrophoresis of extracts of *C. psittaci* strain Cal-10 and *C. trachomatis* strain LGV-434 organisms solubilized with Triton X-100 has resolved as many as 18 species-specific antigenic components, 15 of which were heat labile and protease susceptible (21). The apparent protein nature and the dependence on nonionic detergent for maintaining solubility suggests that chlamydial species-specific antigens are predominantly membrane-associated antigens. The interspecies antigenic heterogeneity observed by crossed immunoelectrophoresis correlates well with the DNA homology studies that showed less than 11% interspecies homology, whereas homology was as great as 95% between DNA of strains within the same species. Crossed immunoelectrophoresis of Triton X-100–solubilized LGV-434 antigens identified an immunodominant antigen that was consistently precipitated by sera of patients with proven *C. trachomatis* infections (20). Monospecific rabbit antiserum against this antigen was used for indirect fluorescent antibody staining of chlamydial infected cells. The antigen was shown to be common to all 15 *C. trachomatis* serotypes but was not shared by the mouse pneumonitis strain or *C. psittaci* strains. This *C. trachomatis* species-specific antigen was purified to homogeneity by immunoadsorbtion using monospecific antibody (19). The antigen was shown to be a protein with a subunit molecular weight of 1.55×10^5, whose antigenicity was destroyed by heating at 56° C for 30 min or by treatment with pronase. This antigen appears to be highly immunogenic and is common to all *C. trachomatis* strains, making it an attractive candidate for a serologic test antigen. Similarly, purified reticulate bodies appear to be species specific by immunofluorescence and may be useful in serology (105).

SEROTYPE-SPECIFIC ANTIGENS Subspecies antigens are determinants common only to certain chlamydial isolates within a species and have been referred to as serotype-specific antigens. Considerable interest has been paid to this group of antigens because of their important biological characteristics. Subspecies antigens have been detected in a variety of in vivo and in vitro serological tests that have been used to serologically classify chlamydial isolates. The observation of Rake and Jones that large intravenous inoculations of viable *Chlamydia* could cause a "toxic" death in mice (mortality not accounted for by replication of the organism) led to a serological method for the differentiation of chlamydiae according to type-specific antigens. Manire & Meyer observed that pretreatment of *C. psittaci* with hyperimmune antisera was capable of neutralizing toxicity and that this neutralization was strain specific and could be used to differentiate between isolates of *C. psittaci* organisms (57). A mouse toxicity prevention test (MTPT) was utilized to serologically classify ocular trachoma strains of *C. trachomatis* by Bell et al (13). Wang, Grayston & Alexander extended these observations and found that the MTPT could be used to serologically classify a number of *C. trachomatis* isolates into distinct serotypes (1, 98).

Type-specific antigens have also been demonstrated by immunofluorescence. Nichols & McComb, using cross-adsorption of hyperimmune antisera, demonstrated three distinct immunological groups of *C. trachomatis* isolates (70). Wang & Grayston developed an indirect microimmunofluorescence (micro-IF) test for the simultaneous comparison of *C. trachomatis* strains using terminal dilutions of antisera (99). This test gave serological groupings identical to those that had been previously described using the MTPT; to date, 15 distinct antigenic serotypes of *C. trachomatis* have been identified (37).

In addition to their importance as serotyping antigens, subspecies antigens appear to play a major role in the development of protective immunity to *C. trachomatis* infections (46, 100). The fact that these antigens are detected by micro-IF and can be neutralized by antiserum must reflect their surface location on the infective elementary body (45). The chemical nature of subspecies-specific antigens is poorly understood, and conflicting evidence concerning the nature of these antigens has been reported. Protective antigens that function in the MTPT were found to be labile to trypsin treatment, to be heat stable, and to have no essential lipid components (101). However, Dhir et al found that antigens reactive with early type-specific rabbit serum were present in the lipid fraction from chloroform methanol water partitioning (26). In their studies, antigenicity was not destroyed by trypsin, pronase, or periodate treatment; this would suggest that the antigen detected by immunofluorescence may be lipoid hapten that is strongly bound to protein. On the other hand, Sacks & MacDonald isolated a type-specific antigen from *C. trachomatis* serotype A and characterized the antigen as a heat-labile, pronase-sensitive surface protein antigen with an apparent subunit molecular weight of 27,000 (78). The type specificity of the antigen was demonstrated by its ability to bind only homologous antibody obtained from either hyperimmune rabbit antisera or serum from trachoma-infected owl monkeys. The discrepancies concerning the chemical nature of *C. trachomatis* type-specific antigens most likely reflect the varying test systems in which the physicochemical characteristics of these antigens have been analyzed.

Virulence Factors Related to Antigenic Structure

In addition to their important immunological characteristics, recent evidence suggests that surface antigens are also important biologically; they operate as chlamydial virulence factors that are functional in the early events of the infectious process. Many features of the *Chlamydia*-host cell interaction, discussed in the section on the growth cycle, must reflect surface antigen structure.

Limited studies indicate that homologous or homotypic antibody can block or neutralize chlamydial attachment, induced phagocytosis, inhibition of phagolysosomal fusion, toxicity, and infectivity. It seems unlikely that a single serotype-specific determinant would control all these biologic properties that are common to the genus. Perhaps the serotype-specific antigens are terminal determinants of a common complex macromolecule. This would explain why only monotypic antisera are able to neutralize or block all these chlamydial functions. The actual relationship of subspecies-specific antigens and chlamydial virulence factors, if it exists, awaits further studies on the biochemical and immunological characterization of the chlamydial outer membrane.

CLINICAL SPECTRUM OF HUMAN CHLAMYDIAL INFECTIONS

Chlamydia psittaci

Human psittacosis occurs in two forms: a severe pneumonia or a systemic, toxic form of infection without respiratory tract involvement (84). Fever, muscle aches and pains, chills, and severe headache are characteristic of both forms. Clinically inapparent infections are known to occur and have been demonstrated serologically.

Chlamydia trachomatis

OCULAR Trachoma is a chronic conjunctivitis with a marked follicular reaction and papillary hypertrophy of the conjunctiva (84). Corneal involvement is characteristic and pannus (neovascularization) at the superior limbus is regularly found. Follicles may develop at the corneal periphery and result in the development of Herbert's pits. As a result of necrosis of the follicles, the conjunctiva may develop scars. Over years these scars contract and turn in the upper eyelid, resulting in abrasion of the cornea by eyelashes. These lesions, called trichiasis and entropion, are the blinding lesions of trachoma. The cornea is damaged, both mechanically and by secondary infection, resulting in blindness. The pathogenesis of blinding trachoma is dependent upon the interaction or the combined effects of *C. trachomatis* infection and secondary bacterial pathogens (*Haemophilus* spp. and *Moraxella* spp.); with persistent or multiple reinfection it is possible that hypersensitivity also plays a role in this disease.

Inclusion conjunctivitis in the adult is an acute follicular conjunctivitis, whereas in the infant it is more commonly a mucopurulent conjunctivitis. In either instance, it tends to be self-limiting, although persistent ocular infections with chlamydiae have been recognized (47, 63). Visual loss as a result of this infection has rarely been reported. Micropannus and sheet scarring of the conjunctiva may be found in infants who have been treated inappropriately or whose treatment has been delayed. The spectrum of disease in infants ranges from very mild mucopurulent conjunctivitis to severe, frankly purulent conjunctivitis that is clinically indistinguishable from gonococcal ophthalmia neonatorum. The incubation period for most ocular *C. trachomatis* infections is approximately 1–2 weeks.

MALE GENITAL TRACT *C. trachomatis* infection in men is the most common identified cause of nongonococcal urethritis (NGU) (43, 81). Although the urethritis usually results in a scant mucoid discharge, the disease cannot be clearly distinguished from gonococcal urethritis on clinical grounds; a spectrum from absence of discharge to frankly purulent discharge is recognized. Chlamydiae can be recovered from approximately 35–50% of men with NGU. Lacking the facilities to demonstrate chlamydial infection (this usually requires a tissue culture laboratory, because isolation of the agent is the only efficient means of diagnosing this infection), the clinician most often establishes a diagnosis of NGU by excluding gonorrhea. The patient is then treated with the tetracycline (1 g/day for 14 days or 2 g/day for 7 days), which is active against both chlamydiae and *Ureaplasma urealyticum;* the latter is the best candidate for the etiology of nonchlamydial NGU. Long-lasting tetracyclines such as minocycline or doxycycline are also effective; erythromycin and sulfonamides are effective against chlamydial urethritis but are not recommended for treatment of NGU except where tetracyclines cannot be used. Just as gonorrhea is a sexually transmitted infection and calls for epidemiologic treatment of contacts, chlamydial infections call for a similar approach. Approximately one third of female partners of men with NGU have chlamydial infection of the cervix and two thirds or more of women whose male partners have chlamydial urethritis will have chlamydial infection of the cervix. Clinically inapparent infections occur and, as is characteristic with sexually transmitted diseases, if one studies disease in women, one often identifies inapparent infections in their male contacts (and vice versa). *C. trachomatis* is recognized as a major cause of what has been called idiopathic epididymitis (14). The agents have been recovered from epididymal aspirates at higher rates than *Neisseria gonorrhoeae*. Chlamydial proctitis is recognized and *C. trachomatis* has been recovered from the pharynx of homosexual men (36) (although the clinical significance of the observation is not clear).

FEMALE GENITAL TRACT Most chlamydial infections of the female genital tract involve the cervix. The infection may be clinically inapparent or may result in a severe cervicitis. Chlamydiae do not cause vaginitis, as they do not appear to parasitize any cells in the vaginal wall. Chlamydiae are recognized causes of urethritis and proctitis in women (27, 63). The prevalence of chlamydial infection of the female urethra is greater than has been previously recognized (73). These infections, associated with dysuria, may not involve the cervix. Thus it is important to sample the urethra, as well as the cervix, for isolation attempts.

C. trachomatis has been recovered from the pharynx of women but the clinical significance of this observation is not clear (82). *C. trachomatis* appears to be a significant cause of nongonococcal acute salpingitis (59). In Sweden chlamydiae have been recovered from fallopian tube specimens collected by laparoscopy of women with acute salpingitis. It does not appear that *Chlamydia* make the same contribution to salpingitis in the United States where gonococcal salpingitis still appears to predominate.

The discrepancy between results obtained in Sweden and those obtained in the United States may be more apparent than real. In Sweden the specimens were collected by biopsy of the fallopian tubes and this procedure has not yet been applied in the United States. However, in Seattle, 20% of women with acute salpingitis were shown to seroconvert with chlamydial antigens (30). Unpublished studies in San Francisco (R. Sweet and J. Schachter) are in agreement: 8 (22%) of 36 women with acute salpingitis not only seroconverted, showing fourfold or greater rises to chlamydial antigens, but also had the very high antibody titers often associated with systemic chlamydial infection. Similar results have been obtained in England (96).

Chlamydiae have also been recovered from inflamed Bartholin glands (24). Serologic evidence has been obtained indicating that chlamydiae may be involved in the etiology of perihepatitis (69) (Fitz-Hugh-Curtis syndrome), but isolation data are still needed.

The role of chlamydiae in infertility (caused by epididymitis in men and salpingitis in women) requires evaluation. In addition, systemic complications of chlamydial infection of the cervix in pregnant women may be important. Postpartum salpingitis has been associated with chlamydial infection of the cervix and with inclusion conjunctivitis in the newborn. The role of *C. trachomatis* in endometritis is not clear but deserves elucidation. In mammals, *C. psittaci* may infect cells lining the uterus and may interfere with implantation, thereby affecting fertility by another means (16). It is not known whether *C. trachomatis* has this ability. In addition, the possibility that chlamydiae may infect trophoblasts and thus be involved in fetal wastage also deserves investigation.

CONCOMITANT INFECTIONS WITH THE *GONOCOCCUS* It has been found that chlamydial infection occurs in 20–30% of all women attending VD clinics. The highest rates (up to 60%) are found in women with gonorrhea. This dual infection also occurs commonly in men. In England, about one third of men with gonococcal infection also have chlamydial infection, whereas in the United States about 20% of men with gonorrhea have dual infection (43, 72, 76). The significance of this observation lies in the fact that these men tend to develop postgonococcal urethritis (PGU). *C. trachomatis* is clearly the major cause of PGU and 60–100% of men with double infection will develop PGU if they receive penicillin treatment for their gonorrhea (43, 72, 76). It is largely in recognition of the significance of these dual infections (since these men come back for treatment or have been considered treatment failures) that the recent Center for Disease Control (CDC) recommendations for treatment of gonorrhea have included tetracycline (5 day X 2g/day) as a first-choice treatment for gonorrhea. Although this regimen has not been validated as efficacious in treating chlamydial infection, it is likely to show significant results in reducing cases of PGU. The 5-day course may be ineffective in treating some chlamydial infections (although this has not yet been studied) in and of itself, but it may still be effective in preventing PGU since it is likely that many of these men have acquired both infections at the same exposure and that a shorter course of therapy might abort a developing chlamydial infection.

NEONATAL The infant passing through the infected birth canal may acquire a chlamydial infection that manifests itself as conjunctivitis (81, 84). This disease was recognized in the early 1900s; systemic complications, such as pneumonia, were first reported in 1975 (88).

Chlamydial pneumonia of infants is a disease that has been characterized by the elegant studies of Beem and his colleagues at the University of Chicago (8, 9, 95). It is typically found in infants between 1 and 3 months of age (the age range is 2 weeks to 4 months, with most cases occurring in the second month of life) and follows a chronic afebrile course. The syndrome is quite characteristic. The infants have tachypnea (occasionally apnea) and a staccato cough without the inspiratory whoop of pertussis. Many of the infants (approximately 50%) will have a history of conjunctivitis or will have conjunctivitis upon examination. Serous otitis media is recognized as a complication and chlamydiae have been recovered, as the sole pathogen, from the nasopharynx, throat, and lung biopsies of infants with this pneumonia (5, 8). In addition, they may be recovered from feces or from rectal swabs, although no enteric disease has been observed (86). *C. trachomatis* can be readily cultured from nasopharyngeal aspirates of infants with pneumonia, although some workers have had less success in using swabs (41). There have been a number of cases where chlamydiae were recovered from lung biopsies and where specimens obtained from the upper respiratory tract were negative (5). Prospective studies have confirmed the observation that very high levels of IgM antibodies to *C. trachomatis* accompany pneumonia but not inclusion conjunctivitis or inapparent infections (8, 87). Given vagaries of tissue sampling, it seems likely that serologic methods may be the means of choice in diagnosing this pneumonia.

Prevalence studies indicate that 30–50% of pneumonias in the first 6 months of life are caused by chlamydial infections (41, 81). Approximately 25% of these infants also have viral infections, but the clinical course of the disease does not seem to be significantly modified by the presence of the viruses and seems to be due to *Chlamydia* (95). Upper respiratory tract infection commonly accompanies conjunctivitis in infants and does not invariably result in pneumonia. Prospective studies have shown that inapparent respiratory tract infection may occur in the absence of conjunctivitis. The number of prospective studies performed on neonatal chlamydial infections have yielded remarkably concordant results (22, 33, 39, 81, 87). Approximately 60–70% of all newborn infants exposed to *Chlamydia* during passage through the birth canal will acquire chlamydial infection as determined by serologic testing (Table 4). Twenty-five to fifty percent of the infants at risk will develop inclusion conjunctivitis of the newborn and 10–20% of the infants will develop pneumonia. The greatest difference among the prospective studies has been the prevalence of chlamydial infection in the cervices of women attending the different clinics. The chlamydial infection rates have ranged from 2 to 13%. This wide range probably reflects the socioeconomic status of the clientele of these clinics, as chlamydial infection is much higher in clinics serving unwed mothers from lower socioeconomic backgrounds. However, it is clear that chlamydial infections are among the most common perinatally acquired infections and that they are an order of magnitude higher than herpes simplex virus, group B streptococcus, toxoplasmosis, etc. Systemic chlamydial infections occur both in infants with conjunctivitis and in infants without antecedent eye infection (87). Thus, the likelihood of preventing chlamydial pneumonia by use of antichlamydial ocular prophylaxis is slim. Silver nitrate drops are ineffective in preventing chlamydial infection. It has been postulated that changing from standard Credé prophylaxis to either tetracycline or erythromycin ointment might prevent chlamydial infection (80, 81). Preliminary results indicate that erythromycin ointment does prevent chlamydial conjunctivitis, which is far more common than gonococcal ophthalmia neonatorum (40). It is unlikely that it will prevent pneumonias (as had been previously speculated) because it is clear that the chlamydiae may be introduced through sites other than the eye.

EPIDEMIOLOGY

Chlamydia psittaci

AVIAN INFECTIONS Most avian infections are transmitted among the natural hosts by a combination of horizontal and vertical means (84). In birds the infections are largely of the gastrointestinal tract and the agent is shed in feces, although infectious respiratory tract discharges also occur. Thus, nestlings may be infected by their parents and then may carry the agent for many years. Inapparent, latent infections may be activated by

Table 4 Prospective studies on chlamydial infection in infants

		Exposed infants develop		
Ref	Maternal infection rate	Inclusion conjunctivitis	Pneumonia	Any infection
(22)	18/124 (12.7%)	9/18 (50%)	NS[a]	12/18 (67%)
(33)	30/340 (8.8%)	8/18 (44%)	2/18 (11%)	11/18 (61%)
(81)	25/500 (5%)	10/25 (40%)	NS[a]	NS[a]
(87)	36/900 (4%)	7/20 (35%)	4/20 (20%)	14/20 (70%)
(39)	6/322 (2%)	2/6 (33%)	1/6 (17%)	4/6 (67%)

[a] NS = not studied.

stress; healthy shedders may infect avian contacts. Clinically inapparent infections are common (latency is a characteristic of many chlamydial infections). While it is relatively easy to understand or postulate transmission chains in birds under natural conditions, it has been difficult to understand the epidemiology of *C. psittaci* infections in poultry. These birds are not raised in the nest but are raised under highly artificial, carefully timed sequences where entire harvests are made of flocks cycled through an area where only birds of that cohort are to be found. It has been postulated that environmental contamination may result in spread of chlamydiae or that ectoparasites may be involved in transmitting chlamydiae. *C. psittaci* are quite hardy and may persist in dried litter for many months. Despite recovery of chlamydiae from naturally and artificially infected ectoparasites, these insects have yet to be shown to have a role in transmission (29). Intriguing are the observations of Grimes who has shown that grackles, inapparently infected with chlamydiae, shed large quantities of agent in their feces (38). It is tempting to postulate that these and possibly other avian species may act as feral amplifying hosts, introducing chlamydia into turkey ranches, etc, where morbidity may be economically disastrous (as well as presenting a significant public health hazard).

C. psittaci isolated from avian species comprise many serotypes and also may be differentiated by experimental host range and pathogenicity patterns.

MAMMALIAN INFECTIONS At some time in the natural infective process in most domestic mammals, chlamydial strains can be recovered from the intestines (93). These strains are often shed in feces, occasionally at very high titer. It is likely that many chlamydial infections of mammals are transmitted by this route. Since chlamydiae cause a large variety of diseases in mammals, including conjunctivitis and pneumonitis, other modes of spread must also occur. Chlamydiae have been recovered from semen samples, and sexual transmission is obviously a potential mode.

Human infections are rarely epidemiologically associated with *C. psittaci* infections in mammals. Some cases of human infection with the agent of feline pneumonitis or bovine chlamydiae have been reported (84, 89).

C. psittaci recovered from domestic mammals seem to comprise two major serotypes that may be associated with disease-producing potential and biological properties of the agent (83, 92).

HUMAN INFECTIONS Human psittacosis occurs in two epidemiologic settings. The disease is an occupational hazard within the poultry industry and individuals working in poultry processing plants are at particular risk (28, 84). The other human infections result from exposure to pet birds or occasionally to feral birds. These cases tend to be sporadic (although point source outbreaks have been noted), whereas the outbreaks in the poultry industry tend to be larger point source outbreaks (but, conversely, sporadic cases are recognized). The birds implicated in infecting humans may be clinically ill, may have lesions apparent only at autopsy, or may have no signs of infection.

Prevention of human cases associated with pet birds is largely dependent on prevention of avian infection by chemoprophylaxis. Imported exotic avian species are supposed to be treated at licensed quarantine stations before the birds are introduced into commerce. Although effective means of treating these birds with feed containing tetracycline exist, it has been shown that inadequately treated birds are often released from quarantine stations and have been implicated as sources of human infection (90).

Chlamydia trachomatis

There are two major epidemiologic patterns of *C. trachomatis* infections (84). Although the pattern of transmission in industrialized countries may differ from that observed in developing nations, the distinctions between the two are not absolute. Both infectious chains may occur in either type of society.

In developing nations, trachoma, the world's leading cause of preventable blindness, affects hundreds of millions of people and has caused blindness in millions. Active infection occurs mainly in children and the disease follows familial patterns. Trachoma is particularly difficult to deal with from a public health viewpoint because the blinding complications of the disease take years to develop and blindness often occurs 25 or more years after the active disease. Topical ocular chemotherapy with tetracycline ointment is effective in minimizing the severity of trachoma and therefore in reducing its blinding complications. The finding that topical treatment is often temporarily effective but that most of the treated children are rapidly reinfected, together with the observations concerning chlamydial pneumonia in the United States, has led to the hypothesis that *C. trachomatis* infections in young children in hyperendemic trachoma areas may be systemic (85). Although the disease association with systemic infection is not yet clear, we and our colleagues have recovered *C. trachomatis* from conjunctiva, nasopharynx, oropharynx, and rectal specimens from infants with trachoma in Egypt (Schachter et al, unpublished findings). This provides a rationale for the treatment failures with topical antibiotics, for we do not have to hypothesize exogenous reinfection from missed (untreated) cases within the community. It is apparent that the children can reinfect themselves, since topical treatment cannot be expected to eradicate infection at the other sites.

In industrialized countries, most transmission of chlamydial infection is sexual. Chlamydiae are found in the genital tracts of many patients attending venereal disease clinics. They are not part of the normal flora of the male or female genital tract, although approximately 1–2% of sexually active men and 5% of sexually active women may harbor these agents. If infective genital tract discharges reach the conjunctiva, inclusion conjunctivitis, an acute follicular conjunctivitis may develop. The infected cervix is a site for transmission of chlamydial infection to newborn infants. Prospective studies have indicated that approximately 70% of infants passing through an infected cervix acquire the chlamydial infection and 35–50% of the exposed infants will develop conjunctivitis. Studies from Denmark have suggested that some of the infants with conjunctivitis have persistent infections and may be a focus for person-to-person transmission to other children (63). Systemic infections have been observed in as high as 20% of exposed infants, with pneumonia being the most serious recognized consequence.

LABORATORY DIAGNOSIS

The increased awareness of the clinical significance of human infections with *Chlamydia trachomatis* has emphasized the need for efficient methods of diagnosing these infections. Unfortunately, simple and inexpensive diagnostic procedures are not available. The cytologic techniques used for demonstrating inclusions may play a useful role in the diagnosis of trachoma or other ocular infections but are of limited use in diagnosing genital tract infections. Serologic tests are not particularly useful in diagnosis unless patients are selected on the basis of first disease episode. In high risk populations, such as patients attending venereal disease clinics, the background or prevalence rate of seroreactors is so high ($> 60\%$) as to make serodiagnosis extremely difficult (79). The chronic nature of many chlamydial infections makes it very difficult to demonstrate rising antibody titers when testing paired (acute and convalescent) serum specimens. The exception to this is in diagnosing chlamydial pneumonia in infants; high IgM antibodies are virtually always found in patients with this disease (8, 87). In all other instances, the method of choice for diagnosing the chlamydial infection is direct isolation of the agent in tissue culture systems. The systems of choice appear to be iododeoxyuridine- or cycloheximide-treated McCoy cells (77, 103). Clinical specimens must be centrifuged into the cells, which are then incubated for 48–72 hr and examined microscopically for the presence of inclusions after the monolayers have been stained by iodine, Giemsa, or immunofluorescent procedures. Unfortunately, this procedure requires a tissue culture laboratory and is not routinely available.

The tissue culture isolation procedure is simple enough to be introduced into bacteriology laboratories if the appropriate cells grown on coverslips can be supplied commercially. The procedure requires only inoculation of the collected specimen into the cells by centrifugation and replacement of the media with cycloheximide-containing medium; the cells can then be examined microscopically by iodine or Giemsa stains after 48–72 hr incubation. Although commercial availability of materials would be a significant step forward, it would not be the quantum leap that is required for easier diagnosis of chlamydial infection; this would require an innovative breakthrough in the existing technology.

In addition, there are a number of problems associated with the technique which requires rigorous standardization. Some types of swabs have been found to be toxic to *Chlamydia* and there is great need for an improved transport media. Also, some fetal calf sera used in the tissue culture media may be toxic, may reverse the cycloheximide effect, or may have antichlamydial activity. Although the *Chlamydia* isolation procedures in tissue culture present a great improvement over the yolk sac isolation procedures that were available in the past, it is clear that a major improvement in technology is required. Since chlamydiae appear to be genetically unrelated to other microorganisms and to possess unique antigens, it is possible that diagnostic procedures based on detection of chlamydial nucleic acids or antigens in clinical specimens may be developed; such procedures would allow diagnoses to be established more easily.

CONCLUDING REMARKS

We should not be complacent about our current knowledge of *C. trachomatis* infections. Given the revelations of the past decade, it is predictable that further expansion of the clinical spectrum will take place in the next ten years. The role of chlamydiae in the following conditions must be defined: respiratory disease and pneumonia in children and adults; maternal complications of pregnancy; nongonococcal proctitis in homosexual and heterosexual populations; and enteric disease associated with chlamydial infection of the gut. Each of these clinical conditions represents a disease complex where chlamydial etiology could logically be expected.

The simplest way to picture the pathogenesis of chlamydial infections is to consider them as parasites of columnar epithelial cells. In anatomic sites, where they reach these cells either by autogenous spread or by person-to-person transmission, they are likely to cause disease. These conditions are usually local, but systemic spread may occur. A fertile area for research may be disease in immunosuppressed individuals; animal experiments have shown that local chlamydial infections may become more invasive if the immune response is suppressed (104).

It will be interesting to see if research efforts expand the clinical spectrum of chlamydial infections. In any case, it is hoped that further research will provide simplification of laboratory techniques to allow routine diagnosis of these infections. Studies on chlamydial structures and their functions should provide further insight into the *Chlamydia*-host cell interaction and may provide clues on methods to prevent infection.

ACKNOWLEDGMENTS

The cooperation of Mary L. Chiappino and Dr. Barbara A. Nichols (F. I. Proctor Foundation, University of California) in providing the authors with the electron photomicrograph is gratefully acknowledged.

This work was supported by Public Health Service grants EY-03046, EY-01205, EY-02216 from the National Eye Institute, AI-14540 from the National Institute of Allergy and Infectious Diseases, and HD-12271 from the National Institute of Child Health and Human Development.

Literature Cited

1. Alexander, E. R., Wang, S-P., Grayston, J. T. 1967. *Am. J. Ophthalmol.* 63:1469–78
2. Alexander, J. J. 1968. *J. Bacteriol.* 95:327–32
3. Alexander, J. J. 1969. *J. Bacteriol.* 97:653–57
4. Anderson, D. R., Hopps, H. E., Barile, M. F., Bernheim, B. C. 1965. *J. Bacteriol.* 90:1387–1404
5. Arth, C., Von Schmidt, B., Grossman, M., Schachter, J. 1978. *J. Pediatr.* 93:447–49
6. Banks, J., Eddie, B., Sung, M., Sugg, N., Schachter, J., Meyer, K. F. 1970. *Infect. Immun.* 2:443–47
7. Banks, J., Schachter, J. 1978. *Infect. Immun.* 20(3):864–66
8. Beem, M. O., Saxon, E. M. 1977. *N. Engl. J. Med.* 296:306–10
9. Beem, M. O., Saxon, E. M., Tipple, M. 1979. *Pediatrics* 63(2):198
10. Becker, Y. 1978. *Microbiol. Rev.* 42(2): 274–306
11. Becker, Y., Asher, Y. 1972. *J. Bacteriol.* 109:966–70
12. Becker, Y., Asher, Y., Himmel, N., Zakay-Rones, Z. 1969. *Nature* 224: 33–34
13. Bell, S. D., Snyder, J. C., Murray, E. S. 1959. *Science* 130:626–27
14. Berger, R. E., Alexander, E. R., Monda, G. D., Ansel, J., McCormack, G., Holmes, K. K. 1978. *N. Engl. J. Med.* 298:301–4
15. Bose, S. K., Liebhaber, H. 1979. *Infect. Immun.* 24(3):953–57
16. Bowen, R. A., Spears, P., Storz, J., Seidel, G. E. 1978. *J. Infect. Dis.* 138:95–98
17. Byrne, G. I. 1976. *Infect. Immun.* 14:645–51
18. Byrne, G. I., Moulder, J. W. 1978. *Infect. Immun.* 19(2):598–606
19. Caldwell, H. D., Kuo, C. C. 1977. *J. Immunol.* 118:437–41
20. Caldwell, H. D., Kuo, C. C., Kenny, G. E. 1975. *J. Immunol.* 115:969–75
21. Caldwell, H. D., Kuo, C. C., Kenny, G. E. 1975. *J. Immunol.* 115:963–68
22. Chandler, J. W., Alexander, E. R., Pheiffer, T. A., Wang, S-P., Holmes, K. K., English, M. 1977. *Acad. Ophthalmol. Otolaryngol.* 83:302–8
23. Collins, A. R., Barron, A. L. 1970. *J. Infect. Dis.* 121:1–8
24. Davies, J. A., Rees, E., Hobson, D., Karayiannis, P. 1978. *Br. J. Vener. Dis.* 54(6):409–13
25. Dhir, S. P., Hakomori, S., Kenny, G. E., Grayston, J. T. 1972. *J. Immunol.* 109:116–22
26. Dhir, S. P., Wang, S-P., Grayston, J. T. 1971. *Trachoma and Related Disorders,* pp. 133–41. The Netherlands: Excerpta Medica. 587 pp.
27. Dunlop, E. M. C., Vaughn-Jackson, J. D., Darougar, S., Jones, B. R. 1972. *Br. J. Vener. Dis.* 48:425–28
28. Durfee, P. T., Pullen, M. M., Currier, R. W., Parker, R. L. 1975. *J. Am. Vet. Med. Assoc.* 167:804–8

29. Eddie, B., Meyer, K. F., Lambrecht, F. L., Furman, D. P. 1962. *J. Infect. Dis.* 110:231–37
30. Eschenbach, D. A., Buchanan, T. M., Pollock, H. M., Forsyth, P. S., Alexander, E. R., Lin, J. S., Wang, S-P., Wentworth, B. B., McCormack, W. M., Holmes, K. K. 1975. *N. Engl. J. Med.* 293:166–71
31. Fan, V. S. C., Jenkin, H. M. 1970. *J. Bacteriol.* 104:608–9
32. Friis, R. R. 1972. *J. Bacteriol.* 110:706–21
33. Frommell, G. T., Rothenberg, R., Wang, S-P., McIntosh, K., Wintersgill, C., Allaman, J., Orr, I. 1979. *J. Pediatr.* 95(1):28
34. Garrett, A. J., Harrison, M. J., Manire, G. P. 1974. *J. Gen. Microbiol.* 80:315–18
35. Gerloff, R. K., Ritter, D. B., Watson, R. O. 1966. *J. Infect. Dis.* 116:197–202
36. Goldmeier, D., Darougar, S. 1977. *Br. J. Vener. Dis.* 53:184–85
37. Grayston, J. T., Wang, S-P. 1975. *J. Infect. Dis.* 132:87–105
38. Grimes, J. E. 1978. *Avian Dis.* 22(2): 308–12
39. Hammerschlag, M. R., Anderka, M., Semine, D. Z., McComb, D., McCormack, W. M. 1979. *Pediatrics* 64(2):142
40. Hammerschlag, M. R., Chiang, W. T., Chandler, J. W., English, M., Alexander, E. R. 1979. In *19th Intersci. Conf. Antimicrob. Agents Chemother. Meet. No. 524* (Abstr.)
41. Harrison, H. R., English, M. G., Lee, C. K., Alexander, E. R. 1978. *N. Engl. J. Med.* 298(13):702–8
42. Hatch, T. P. 1975. *Infect. Immun.* 12:211–20
43. Holmes, K. K., Handsfield, H. H., Wang, S-P., Wentworth, B. B., Turck, M., Anderson, J. B., Alexander, E. R. 1975. *N. Engl. J. Med.* 292:1199–206
44. Horoschak, K. D., Moulder, J. W. 1978. *Infect. Immun.* 19(1):281–86
45. Howard, L. V. 1975. *Infect. Immun.* 11(4):698–703
46. Jawetz, E., Rose, L., Hanna, L., Thygeson, P. 1965. *J. Am. Med. Assoc.* 194:620–32
47. Jones, B. R. 1964. *Br. J. Vener. Dis.* 40:3–18
48. Kellogg, K. R., Horoschak, K. D., Moulder, J. W. 1977. *Infect. Immun.* 18(2):531
49. Keshishyan, H. L., Hanna, L., Jawetz, E. 1973. *Nature* 244:173–74
50. Kingsbury, D. T. 1969. *J. Bacteriol.* 98:1400–1
51. Kingsbury, D. T., Weiss, E. 1968. *J. Bacteriol.* 96:1421–23
52. Kramer, M. J., Gordon, F. B. 1971. *Infect. Immun.* 3:333–41
53. Kuo, C. C., Wang, S-P., Grayston, J. T. 1973. *Infect. Immun.* 8:74–79
54. Levy, N. J. 1979. *Infect. Immun.* 25(3): 946
55. Lovett, M.A., Kuo, C. C., Holmes, K. K., Falkow, S. 1979. *19th Intersci. Conf. Antimicrob. Agents Chemother. Meet. No. 6* (Abstr.)
56. Makino, S., Jenkin, H. M., Yu, H. M., Townsend, D. 1970. *J. Bacteriol.* 103:62–70
57. Manire, G. P., Meyer, K. F. 1950. *J. Infect. Dis.* 86:241–50
58. Manire, G. P., Tamura, A. 1967. *J. Bacteriol.* 94:1178–83
59. Mardh, P-A., Ripa, T., Svensson, L., Westrom, L. 1977. *N. Engl. J. Med.* 296:1377–79
60. Matsumoto, A., Manire, G. P. 1970. *J. Bacteriol.* 104:1332–37
61. Matsumoto, A., Manire, G. P. 1970. *J. Bacteriol.* 101:278–85
62. Meyer, K. F. 1967. *Am. J. Ophthalmol.* 63:1225–46
63. Mordhorst, C. H., Wang, S-P., Grayston, J. T. 1978. *J. Am. Med. Assoc.* 239(17):1765–71
64. Morgan, H. R., Bader, J. P. 1954. *J. Exp. Med.* 99:451–60
65. Moulder, J. W. 1964. *The Psittacosis Group as Bacteria.* New York: Wiley. 95 pp.
66. Moulder, J. W. 1966. *Ann. Rev. Microbiol.* 20:107–30
67. Moulder, J. W. 1969. *Bioscience* 19:875–82
68. Moulder, J. W. 1974. *J. Infect. Dis.* 130:300–6
69. Muller-Schoop, J., Wang, S-P., Schlapfer, H. U., Lammli, J., Knoblauch, M., Ammann, R. 1978. *Schweiz. Med. Wochenschr.* 108:1067
70. Nichols, R. L., McComb, D. E. 1964. *J. Exp. Med.* 120(4):639–54
71. Officer, J. E., Brown, A. 1960. *J. Infect. Dis.* 107:283–99
72. Oriel, J. D., Reeve, P., Thomas, B. J., Nicol, C. S. 1975. *J. Infect. Dis.* 131:376–82
73. Paavonen, J. 1979. *Sex. Trans. Dis.* 6(2):69–71
74. Page, L. A. 1966. *Int. J. Syst. Bacteriol.* 16:223–52
75. Page, L. A. 1974. *Bergey's Manual of Determinative Bacteriology,* pp. 914–28. Baltimore: Williams & Wilkins. 8th ed.
76. Richmond, S. J., Hilton, A. L., Clarke,

S. K. R. 1972. *Br. J. Vener. Dis.* 48:437–44
77. Ripa, K. T., Mardh, P-A. 1977. *Nongonococcal Urethritis and Related Infections,* pp. 323–27. Washington D.C: Am. Soc. Microbiol.
78. Sacks, D. L., MacDonald, A. B. 1979. *J. Immunol.* 122(1):136–39
79. Schachter, J. 1976. *Manual of Clinical Immunology.* pp. 494–99. Washington D.C: Am. Soc. Microbiol.
80. Schachter, J. 1977. *Sex. Transm. Dis.* 4:116–18
81. Schachter, J. 1978. *N. Engl. J. Med.* 298:428–35, 490–95, 540–49
82. Schachter, J., Atwood, G. 1975. *J. Am. Vener. Dis. Assoc.* 2:12
83. Schachter, J., Banks, J., Sugg, N., Sung, M., Storz, J., Meyer, K. F. 1975. *Infect. Immun.* 11:904–7
84. Schachter, J., Dawson, C. R. 1978. *Human Chlamydial Infections.* Littleton, Mass: Publ. Sci. Group. 273 pp.
85. Schachter, J., Dawson, C. R. 1979. *Lancet* 1:702–3
86. Schachter, J., Grossman, M., Holt, J., Sweet, R., Spector, S. 1979. *J. Infect. Dis.* 139(2):232–34
87. Schachter, J., Holt, J., Goodner, E., Grossman, M., Sweet, R., Mills, J. 1979. *Lancet* 2:377–80
88. Schachter, J., Lum, L., Gooding, C. A., Ostler, B. 1975. *J. Pediatr.* 87:779–80
89. Schachter, J., Ostler, H. B., Meyer, K. F. 1969. *Lancet* 1:1063–65
90. Schachter, J., Sugg, N., Sung, M. 1978. *J. Infect. Dis.* 137(1):44–49
91. Schechter, E. M. 1966. *J. Bacteriol.* 91:2069–80
92. Spears, P., Storz, J. 1979. *Infect. Immun.* 24(1):244
93. Storz, J. 1971. *Chlamydia and Chlamydia-Induced Diseases.* Springfield, Ill: Thomas. 358 pp.
94. Tamura, A., Iwanaga, M. 1965. *J. Mol. Biol.* 11:97–108
95. Tipple, M. A., Beem, M., Saxon, E. 1979. *Pediatrics* 63(2):192
96. Treharne, J. D., Ripa, K. T., Mardh, P. A., Svensson, L., Westrom, L., Darougar, S. 1979. *Br. J. Vener. Dis.* 55(1):26
97. Vedros, N. A. 1967. *J. Immunol.* 99:1183
98. Wang, S-P., Grayston, J. T. 1963. *J. Immunol.* 90:849–56
99. Wang, S-P., Grayston, J. T. 1970. *Am. J. Ophthalmol.* 70:367–74
100. Wang, S-P., Grayston, J. T., Alexander, E. R. 1967. *Am. J. Ophthalmol.* 63:1615–30
101. Wang, S-P., Kenny, G. E., Grayston, J. T. 1967. *Am. J. Ophthalmol.* 63:1443
102. Weiss, E., Schramek, S., Wilson, N. N., Newman, L. W. 1970. *Infect. Immun.* 2:24–28
103. Wentworth, B. B., Alexander, E. R. 1974. *Appl. Microbiol.* 27:912–16
104. White, H. J., Rank, R. G., Soloff, B. L., Barron, A. L. 1979. *Infect. Immun.* 26(2):728–35
105. Yong, E. C., Chinn, J. S., Caldwell, H. D., Kuo, C-C. 1979. *J. Clin. Microbiol.* 10(3):351–56

Ann. Rev. Microbiol. 1980. 34:311–40

THE IMMUNOLOGICAL ACTIVITIES OF BACTERIAL PEPTIDOGLYCANS

❖1779

D. E. S. Stewart-Tull

Department of Microbiology, University of Glasgow,
Glasgow G61 1QH, Scotland

CONTENTS

INTRODUCTION 311
Relationship between Bacteria and Mammals 311
Structure of Peptidoglycan 312
Immune Response or Tolerance? 313
IMMUNOPOTENTIATING EFFECTS OF PEPTIDOGLYCAN 314
Freund Adjuvant 314
Peptidoglycan Adjuvants 316
Naturally occurring substances 316
The minimal chemical structure of peptidoglycan adjuvant 321
ANTIGENICITY OF PEPTIDOGLYCAN 326
ADVERSE BIOLOGICAL ACTIVITIES 327
Polyarthritis in Rats 327
Induction of Autoimmune Diseases 328
Pyrogenicity 329
IMMUNOTHERAPY OF CANCER 330
ACTIVATION OF CELLS BY PEPTIDOGLYCAN COMPLEXES 332
SUMMARY 335

INTRODUCTION

Relationship between Bacteria and Mammals

In the uterus, with the exception of diseases caused by transplacental transmission, a fetus grows in a relatively sterile environment. During parturition the neonate is exposed to bacteria while passing through the cervical canal and vagina, and within a few days it begins to acquire a characteristic bacterial flora. "Man becomes the habitat of a very rich microbial flora. The skin, the mucous membranes, the intestines and the genital organs offer a

0066-4227/80/1001-0311$01.00

feeding ground for bacteria of all kinds" (106). The bacteria may be commensal or symbiotic, e.g. lactobacilli, which produce the acidic environment of the vagina and prevent colonization by many pyogenic species, and coliforms, which produce vitamins or micronutrients in the gut. Nevertheless, the mammalian host possesses a variety of nonimmunological, first-line defense mechanisms, such as lysozyme in tears, oily skin secretions, mucus in the respiratory, intestinal, and genitourinary tracts, and acidity in the stomach—all of which enable it to control these vast hordes of bacteria present on the surfaces of the body. This complex equilibrium between host and bacteria is destroyed when pathogenic species overcome the first line of defense, invade the tissues, and cause an inflammatory reaction. The bacteria are engulfed by the polymorphonuclear leukocytes, killed, and partially digested within the phagolysosome. The complete process whereby this occurs is unknown; however, it has been established that lysozyme acts on the peptidoglycan of the cell wall and that the hydrogen peroxide-dependent myeloperoxidase, in the presence of chloride ions, removes peptides from the cell wall. The mycobacterial cell wall will be protected from enzymic attack in the phagolysosome by the associated lipid components of the outer surface layers. It is likely that this is why *Mycobacterium tuberculosis* survives and multiples in polymorphonuclear leukocytes.

However, the D-amino acids present the macrophages with a catabolic problem. Oxidative deamination by a D-amino acid oxidase occurs in the liver and kidneys. Whether α,ϵ-diaminopimelic acid (DAP) is catabolized is doubtful because this amino acid can be isolated from lymph nodes. The DAP was detected by the author in hilar and mediastinal lymph nodes obtained *post mortem* from a healthy human being. Recent evidence (128) showed that when ^{14}C-labelled synthetic *N*-acetylmuramyl-L-alanyl-D-isoglutamine (Ac Mur-L-Ala-D-$GluNH_2$) was injected in saline into mice, it was rapidly excreted in the urine. After 2 hr some 75–95% of the labelled muramyldipeptide was recovered in an unaltered state. However, appreciable amounts were retained in the liver where it was degraded into predominantly *N*-acetylmuramic acid. The elimination of the synthetic muramyldipeptide was retarded when it was incorporated into a water-in-mineral-oil emulsion; 45% remained in the injected paw after 24 hr. There is no evidence to show whether *N*-acetylmuramic acid is stored in tissues during life as has been found with DAP.

Structure of Peptidoglycan

The cell walls of bacteria are formed from a number of polymeric components, each of which possesses immunological properties, e.g. teichoic acids and lipopolysaccharides. In Gram-positive organisms peptidoglycan (murein, mucopeptide, glycopeptide) is the major component of the cell wall.

It consists of a glycan backbone with alternating β1-4-linked residues of *N*-acetyl-D-glucosamine and muramic acid. The latter is usually *N*-acetylated (129), but in mycobacterial and some nocardial species the *N*-acetyl group is oxidized to give the *N*-glycolated form (4, 19). Muramic acid acts as the linking substance between peptides and sugars through an amide bond at the carboxyl group of the D-lactic acid ether at C-3 (137). Some of the muramic acid in the mycobacterial cell wall was present as muramic acid-6-phosphate (75, 98). This unique residue is able to link both peptides and lipopolysaccharide (arabinogalactan-mycolic acid) to the glycan. The peptide is composed of alternating L-and-D-amino acids. Glutamic acid and alanine, invariably present as the second and fourth amino acids in the stem tetrapeptide, are in the D-configuration (69, 138), which is not normally found in nature. The first amino acid is always L-alanine; a variety of amino acids, including DL 2,6-diaminopimelic acid, occupy the third position (66, 67, 179).

In the Gram-negative cell wall the peptidoglycan covalently linked to lipoprotein molecules forms a unimolecular rigid layer between the outer membrane and the cytoplasmic membrane of the cell envelope (55). The *N*-acetylmuramic acid residues are linked to stem tetrapeptides composed of L-alanyl-D-isoglutamyl-(L)*meso*diaminopimelyl (L)-D-alanine. Approximately two thirds of these stem peptides are cross-linked through D-alanyl-(D)*meso*diaminopimelate linkages.

In addition to the glycan-stem peptide structure, different types of cross-linkage occur in which the amino acceptor is either the ω-amino group of a dibasic amino acid in position three (Type A) or the amino group of a C-terminal dibasic amino acid linked to the α-carboxyl group of D-glutamate in position two (Type B). So far, four type A and two type B structures have been found (54, 140).

A detailed discussion of peptidoglycan structure is not possible in this short review and the reader is referred to two comprehensive articles by Tipper & Wright (159) and Wright & Tipper (180).

Immune Response or Tolerance?

In the vertebrate, after exposure to a foreign substance, a humoral immune response may occur in which there is differentiation of T and B effector cells leading to antibody synthesis. Apart from the T *helper* cells (T_H) that interact with B cells in the production of antibodies, evidence is accumulating that T *suppressor* cells (T_S) are important in specifically inhibiting antibody formation. A general role for the T_S cells in the regulation of immune responses and tolerance has been postulated. Tolerance is induced when exposure to a specific antigen does not lead to antibody synthesis but instead leads to suppression or inactivation of lymphocytes. Low zone tolerance is induced by the effect of small quantities of antigen on the T-cell population, and high zone tolerance by a massive dose of antigen (112). T_S cells are formed in response to antigens with repeating antigenic determinants. The continuous exposure of individuals, from birth, to peptidoglycans (with repeating disaccharide units) from indigenous bacteria resident in the respiratory and gastrointestinal tracts could explain tolerance in adult life by a T_S cell mechanism. Tolerance can also be induced by high doses of polysaccharides or polypeptides with D isomers of amino acids that saturate the receptors on the surface of B cells. The binding may be reversible if a glycoside residue is involved, but, as noted above, mammals do not possess proteases that attack polypeptides of D-amino acids. Therefore, if peptidoglycan binds to the cell surface through the stem peptide, it could lead to irreversible B-cell inactivation and tolerance. The binding of mycobacterial peptidoglycolipids and glycopeptides (both containing peptidoglycan) to mammalian cell membranes was examined by Stewart-Tull et al (148). The affinity for membranes was reversible, but some glycopeptide remained attached to the cell membrane. As will be shown later, these peptidoglycolipids and glycopeptides cause immunosuppression or immunopotentiation, depending on the dose and timing of the injection in relation to a separate protein antigenic stimulus. In addition, Stewart-Tull and McInroy (unpublished observation) were unable to detect antibodies against the mycobacterial adjuvant component in any guinea pig sera by precipitation or complement fixation tests. The question arises as to how the immunogenic peptidoglycan-containing substances stimulate the immune responses to other protein antigens but not to themselves. Further investigations are required before definite conclusions can be reached; however, it seems probable, since the basic peptidoglycan structures are so similar, that the host will show some tolerance to a wide variety of bacteria. Immune responses do occur in human beings; for example, secretory IgA agglutinins to a wide range of commensal bacteria have been demonstrated (6, 104) and peptidoglycan antibodies are present in preimmune sera (63, 139).

IMMUNOPOTENTIATING EFFECTS OF PEPTIDOGLYCAN

Freund Adjuvant

The original observations of Freund and his colleagues revealed that the presence of tubercle bacilli in the mineral oil component of a water-in-oil emulsion containing protein antigen stimulated increased precipitin titers to the protein antigen. Guinea pigs also showed a delayed hypersensitivity reaction to the protein antigen (50, 52). Since this time, Freund complete adjuvant (FCA) has been used in innumerable studies, reviewed by Stewart-Tull (147). It was obvious that attention would be directed towards the active component of the mycobacterial cells responsible for adjuvant activity (immunopotentiation). A chloroform-soluble wax produced an effect similar to that obtained with whole organisms, and increased antiovalbumin antibody titers were produced (131, 173). This adjuvant-active wax material was chemically analyzed and consisted of mycolic acid esters bound to a polysaccharide (arabinose, galactose, and mannose residues) and a heptapeptide (2 α,ϵ-diaminopimelic acid, 2 D-glutamic, 1 D-alanine and 2 L-alanine) linked to hexosamines (7, 8), i.e. the wax was a peptidoglycolipid. Earlier studies (71, 72) indicated that the peptide moiety was linked to the glycolipid through galactosamine. However, the similarity between components of the peptidoglycolipid and the mycobacterial cell wall (39) was obvious and it was found that muramic acid was present and functioned in the same manner in the peptidoglycolipid (151). Numerous studies revealed that the structure of the peptidoglycolipid (Figure 1), was based on a repeating peptidoglycan monomer linked to a glycolipid (20, 21, 76, 98, 100, 108, 151). After thirty years the relation between adjuvant activity and the cell wall was established (83, 151). The biological events that occurred after the injection of peptidoglycolipid and a protein antigen in a water-in-mineral oil emulsion into guinea pigs were summarized by White (170, 171). The formation of an epithelioid-macrophage granuloma at the site of injection, a cell-mediated immune response to the protein antigen, an increase in the levels of circulating antibody with an associated increase of IgG_1 and IgG_2 immunoglobulin, and the ability to stimulate an experimental autoimmune disease were recognized criteria of an adjuvant response (83, 85, 89, 149, 152, 171, 173, 174). Adjuvant-active mycobacterial fractions caused proliferation of macrophages, with epithelioid cell morphology, in a local granuloma (169) that was formed through an immunological stimulus (172). A delayed hypersensitivity reaction to the protein antigen, usually ovalbumin, was measured in the corneal response. Guinea pigs that were sensitized by the injection of 200 μg peptidoglycolipid from *Mycobacterium tuberculosis* $H_{37}R_v$ and 2.0 mg ovalbumin in a water-in-oil emulsion and that were subsequently challenged with ovalbumin showed a thickened opaque, greyish-white cornea (173, 174). Peptidoglycolipid (400 μg) released from *M. bovis* BCG (bacillus Calmette-Guérin) cell walls also stimulated a delayed corneal response to lysozyme and ovalbumin (83). In such animals the antiovalbumin levels could be as high as 2–5 mg of antibody protein per milliliter of serum.

A scheme of testing mycobacterial peptidoglycolipid adjuvants was used by Koga et al (80) in the mouse. The adjuvant preparations were injected intraperitoneally and the number of plaque-forming cells in the spleen was

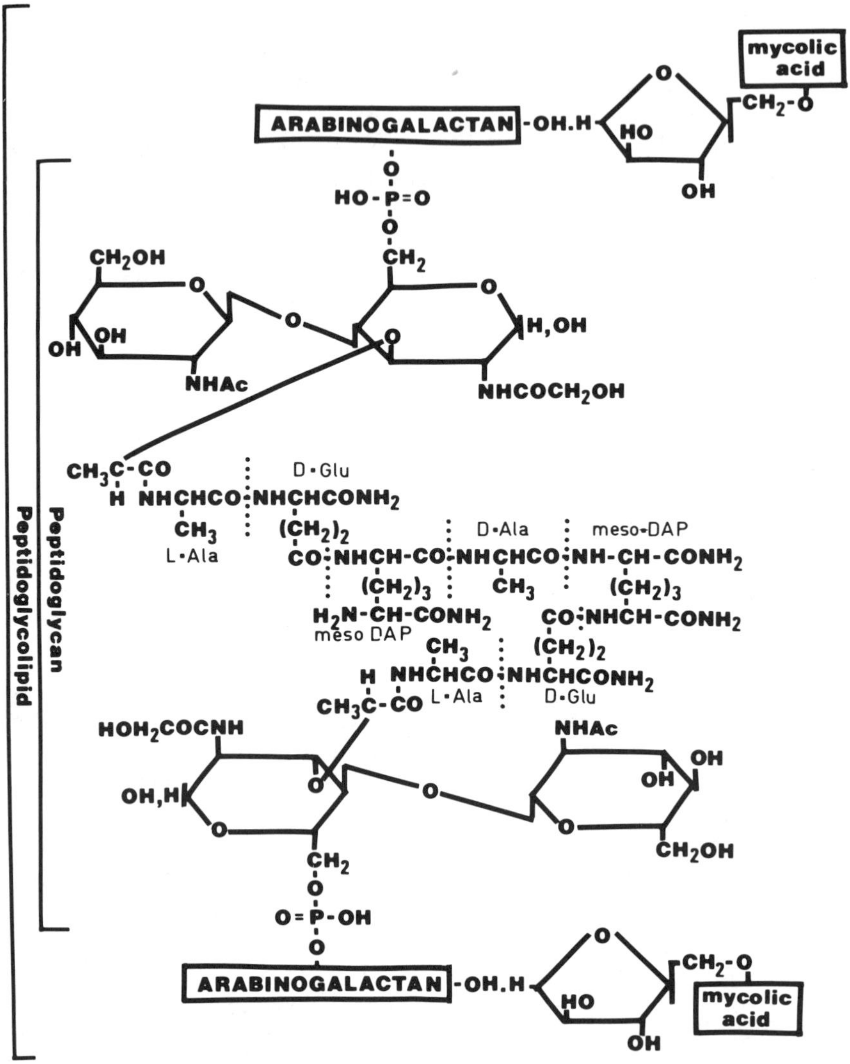

Figure 1 The structure of mycobacterial peptidoglycan and peptidoglycolipid.

determined at various time intervals. This procedure has been used recently to test some of the water-soluble adjuvants of peptidoglycan origin.

Peptidoglycan Adjuvants

NATURALLY OCCURRING SUBSTANCES As an extension of the peptidoglycolipid studies, Holton & Schwab (68) demonstrated for the first time that peptidoglycan, isolated from the cell walls of β-hemolytic streptococci, stimulated increased levels of antibovine serum albumin (BSA) in rabbits. The whole cell walls were less active and no conclusive evidence was obtained to indicate the induction of a delayed hypersensitivity reaction. This study showed that the lipid component of the mycobacterial peptidoglycolipid was not an important constituent of the adjuvant. Although partially delipidated *Mycobacterium tuberculosis, M. bovis, M. smegmatis,* and *M. phlei* organisms stimulated an adjuvant response, totally delipidated cells and cell wall glycopeptide were inactive (173). However, the cell walls of *M. bovis* BCG, high molecular weight cell wall fractions of *M. smegmatis* (85, 89) and *M. tuberculosis* $H_{37}R_v$ (5), and the cell wall glycopeptide, probably a peptidoglycan monomer (149), produced an adjuvant response to ovalbumin.

A number of water-soluble preparations were isolated from whole cells or cell walls of mycobacteria (2, 65, 91, 110, 149). Water-soluble adjuvant (WSA), an arabinogalactan linked to peptidoglycan with a molecular weight of 20,000, was isolated from *M. smegmatis* (2) or *Nocardia opaca* (3) cell walls by lysozyme digestion and gel filtration. This material induced delayed-type hypersensitivity against ovalbumin in guinea pigs sensitized with 1.0 μg of WSA and 2.5 mg of ovalbumin in a water-in-oil emulsion.

Rabbits injected with the synthetic polypeptide poly(Tyr,Glu)-poly(DL-Ala)poly(Lys) in aqueous solution containing 500 μg of WSA did not produce increased levels of antibody. However, when injected with Freund incomplete adjuvant an increased response was found after 31 days, which was equivalent to the response found with Freund complete adjuvant. An almost twofold increase in antibody was obtained when the WSA was added to FCA plus antigen (101). The additive effect of mycobacterial organisms and WSA may be explained by the dose of adjuvant in FCA; if the dose was below the optimum level, the WSA would be expected to increase the adjuvant response.

In saline the WSA showed low levels of adjuvant activity (10, 11). When mice were injected subcutaneously with 50 μg of BSA, together with 100 or 300 μg of WSA in saline, and thirty days later were given a booster injection of 100 μg of BSA, the humoral antibody response was greatly depressed (30). After acylation of WSA with phthalic or succinic anhydride, the products sodium phthalyl-WSA and succinylated-WSA were highly active and stimulated the humoral antibody response against both BSA and influenza vaccine when administered in saline (10). It was concluded that the conformation of the native WSA prevented the expression of the adjuvant activity in saline. This conformation of the molecule could be altered by phthalylation or succinylation in such a manner as to expose the active portion of the molecule (10). It is difficult to make direct comparisons between this series of experiments and those of White and his colleagues (170, 171, 173, 174) because, as originally defined, it was the effect of an adjuvant substance on the primary antibody response that was monitored.

An equivalent weight of 75 μg of cell walls was required to produce a similar result (2). A polysaccharide-peptidoglycan (POLY-PA) fraction obtained from *M. tuberculosis* by autolysis produced a similar effect against ovalbumin (110, 165, 166). Although 200–500 μg of native POLY-PA were used, only 20 μg of acetylated PA were required to produce an adjuvant response. The reverse was found with acetylated peptidoglycolipid; the adjuvant activity was reduced and the dosage had to be increased to at least 1.0 mg in the sensitizing injection mixture (136, 157). Subsequently, the POLY-PA was conjugated to either lauric or palmitic acid (109). Palmitic acid-POLY-PA from *M. tuberculosis* Test increased the delayed type hypersensitivity to azobenzenearsonate-acetyl-L-tyrosine when injected in a water-in-oil emulsion. The effect of the palmitic acid conjugation was more significant when guinea pigs were injected with ovalbumin in saline. Previously it was believed that mycobacterial adjuvants were active only in the presence of mineral oil. However, these results complement the findings of Coon & Hunter (37) who showed increased immunogenicity of BSA conjugated to lauric acid.

As mentioned above, one should not confuse the adjuvant effect on the primary antibody response with the effect on the secondary response. This is demonstrated by the effect of POLY-PA and its derivatives on the production of antiinfluenza antibodies in rabbits. The animals were injected intramuscularly with 2.0 ml of saline containing 128 hemagglutinating units of influenza vaccine and 1.0 mg of the mycobacterial preparation in saline. The human influenza antigen (strain B/Massachusetts/3/66) consisted of β-propiolactone-inactivated virions purified by zonal centrifugation which were obtained from the Institut Mérieux, France. After 21 days the maximum titer of antiinfluenza antibodies in the primary response was 1/80 in an animal given POLY-PA laurate; the majority were insignificant (<1/10). When the rabbits were given a booster injection of the same mixtures and the antibody titers measured 7 days later, it was noted that POLY-PA laurate-stimulated animals showed titers of 1/160–1/2560 (109). The majority of titers were low (1/40–1/160) in animals receiving native POLY-PA from *M. tuberculosis* $H_{37}R_a$ or Test or POLY-PA-palmitate. It may be of significance in this respect that in my own laboratory the repetitive injection of the adjuvant substance always reduces the titer of antibody. During routine antibody production the booster injection in rabbits is always given without adjuvant.

A mycobacterial adjuvant and antitumor factor (MAAF) was prepared from *M. bovis* BCG by hydrogenolysis products (65), but it was surprising that this fraction did not contain muramic acid. Subsequently, an adjuvant-active fraction (MAF3) was isolated from hydrogenolysis products of *M. tuberculosis* Aoyama B, which was a heteropolymer of the cell wall with a molecular weight of 16,000 (91). Although this material stimulated increased levels of IgG_2 antibody and induced a delayed response to ovalbumin in guinea pigs, it was conceded that it was not a pure cell wall fraction.

A glycopeptide was isolated from the culture fluid of *M. tuberculosis* (149) by the fractionation method of Seibert et al (143). This glycopeptide was a monomeric polymer of peptidoglycan, had a molecular weight of 35,000, and was water-soluble. Elevated primary immune responses were found with serum antibody N levels (591–857) comparable to those stimulated by the cell walls of *M. bovis* BCG (484–1156) and in excess of those stimulated by peptidoglycolipid from *M. tuberculosis* (199–707) (149).

With this background, numerous groups began to investigate the adjuvant properties of peptidoglycan. Peptidoglycan was isolated from *Moraxella glucidolytica, Neisseria perflava, Escherichia coli* RE600, and *Proteus vulgaris* (119–121) and was tested for an adjuvant effect against azobenzenearsonate-*N*-acetyl-L-tyrosine. Although the peptidoglycans were similar in structure, equivalent biological effects were found with 200 μg of *Proteus vulgaris,* 50 μg of *Moraxella glucidolytica,* 10 μg of *Neisseria perflava,* and 100 μg of *E. coli.* The cell walls of *Corynebacterium parvum* and *Bacillus megaterium* were found to increase the number of plaque-forming cells in the spleen after injection of antigen one day later (122).

Kotani and his colleagues (85, 89) investigated the immunological adjuvant activity of cell walls from 21 species of Gram-positive bacteria (Table 1). Since the mycobacterial adjuvants possessed peptidoglycan, it was reasonable to propose that bacterial cell walls would generally show activity in the stimulation of elevated antibody levels and induction of delayed hypersensitivity. Some of the antiovalbumin levels were much higher than I had found with mycobacterial adjuvants, e.g. enzyme digests of *Staphylococcus aureus,* 1103 μg; *Streptococcus pyogenes,* 1092 μg; *Streptococcus mutans,* 912 μg. These digests produced strongly positive corneal delayed-type hypersensitivity reactions. This may be explained in part by the fact that the animals were exsanguinated 7–10 days after corneal and skin testing for delayed-type hypersensitivity and the 100–200 μg of ovalbumin used in these tests would trigger a secondary response. In addition, it was somewhat surprising that, weight for weight, the responses seemed to be variable (116–1243—antibody N). The cell walls of lysozyme-susceptible *Micrococcus luteus* NCTC 2665 and lysozyme-resistant *Staphylococcus epidermidis* ATCC155 were inactive. With the synthetic antigen azobenzenearsonate-*N*-acetyl-L-tyrosine, the peptidoglycan and the *N*-acetylmuramyltetrapeptide from *S. epidermidis* (45) were found to be adjuvant active (48). An endopeptidase digest of *S. epidermidis, M. luteus,* and *Corynebacterium poinsettiae* cell walls released components able to stimulate the immune response against ovalbumin (86). Why is it that one cell wall is more active than another? As pointed out previously, the conformation of the adjuvant molecule may be an important factor in the expression of adjuvant activity. Kotani and his colleagues (86) helped to explain the lack of adjuvant activity in the cell walls of some species. The cell walls of *Microbacterium lacticum* (peptidoglycan type-B1α), *Eubacterium limosum* (B2α), *Corynebacterium poinsettiae* (B2β), *C. betae* (B2β), and *C. insidiosum* (B2γ) were inactive as adjuvants, and *Arthrobacter atrocyaneus* (A3 α) was only weakly active. The first amino acid residue linked to muramic acid was glycine or L-serine and not L-alanine. The cross linkages were through the α-carboxyl group of the D-glutamic acid or threo-3-hydroxyglutamic acid, in the second position of one peptide, with the carboxyl group of the C-terminal D-alanine in the fourth position of another peptide. In group A peptidoglycans the α-carboxyl group of the D-glutamic acid is amidated (140, 159), but in the peptidoglycan of *Arthrobacter atrocyaneus* it is substituted by glycine amide. It does seem that the α-carboxyl group of the D-glutamic acid is important in the determination of adjuvant activity.

Azobenzenearsonate-*N*-acetyl-L-tyrosine is naturally more immunogenic than ovalbumin, which would indicate that the test antigen may influence the ability of an adjuvant-active substance to affect the immune response (Table 1).

Attempts to solubilize the immunologically active component of the cell walls were done with the peptidoglycan-degrading enzymes L-11 (77), L-3 (116), mutanolysin (186), and Chalaropsis B (58). The enzymatic cell wall digests of *Staphylococcus aureus, Streptococcus pyogenes* Gr. A, *Streptococcus salivarius, Streptococcus mutans, Streptococcus faecalis, Lactobacillus plantarum,* and *Bacillus megaterium* stimulated increased levels of antibodies and induced delayed-type hypersensitivity to ovalbumin. It was interesting that both the *N*-acetylglucosaminylribitol teichoic acid-glycan-

Table 1 Delayed hypersensitivity reactions to ovalbumin and azobenzenearsonate-*N*-acetyl-L-tyrosine (111)

	Delayed skin reactions to:	
	Ovalbumin mm^2 (skin reaction ratio of test/control after 48 hr)	Azobenzenearsonate-*N*-acetyl-L-tyrosine mm^2 (no reaction in control animals after 24 hr)
Crude WSA from *C. parvum* + Freund incomplete adjuvant	25.6	89.0
Freund complete adjubant containing *M. tuberculosis* $H_{37}R_a$	38.5	91.0

oligopeptide of *S. aureus* and the glucosylribitol teichoic acid-oligosaccharide-peptide of *L. plantarum,* high molecular weight polymeric structures, were highly active. However, it was unfortunate that these preparations were pyrogenic in rabbits.

THE MINIMAL CHEMICAL STRUCTURE OF PEPTIDOGLYCAN ADJUVANT In 1971 Edgar Lederer (97) pointed out that "the task of the chemist will be to degrade mycobacterial cell walls by gentle, mostly enzymatic methods, to try to isolate the simplest type of molecule having still one or another of the 'desirable activities'; this work must of course be pursued in close contact with competent biologists. At the same time syn-

Table 2 Immunopotentiating activities associated with bacterial cell walls

Cell walls containing peptidoglycan from:	Stimulation of immunoglobulin production	Induction of cell-mediated immunity
Staphylococcus aureus	+++	+++
S. epidermidis	+	–
Streptococcus mutans	+++	+++
S. faecalis	+++	++
S. faecium	+++	+++
S. lactis	+++	+++
S. bovis	+++	+++
S. pyogenes	++	+++
S. thermophilus	+++	+++
Mycobacterium bovis BCG	+++	+++
M. smegmatis	+++	+++
Lactobacillus plantarum	+++	+++
Nocardia asteroides	++	+++
Bacillus megaterium	+++	++
Clostridium botulinum	++	++
Streptomyces fradiae	++	++
S. lavendurae	++	++
Micrococcus luteus (lysodeikticus)	–	–
Corynebacterium parvum	+++	++
C. poinsettiae	–	–
C. betae	–	–
C. insidiosum	–	–
C. granulosum	+++	–
Proteus vulgaris	+++	+++
Neisseria perflava	+++	+++
Microbacterium lacticum	–	–
Eubacterium limosum	–	–
Arthrobacter atrocyaneus	–	–

thetic model compounds will have to be prepared so as to be able to obtain, finally, active compounds by total synthesis."

The main emphasis in research was thus directed towards the smallest constituent of the peptidoglycan that would stimulate an adjuvant response. *N*-acetylglucosamine-*N*-glycolylmuramic acid-L-Ala-D-Glu-meso-DAP-D-Ala was isolated from *Mycobacterium smegmatis* (1) and from *M. tuberculosis* strain Peurois (70) and these were shown to possess an adjuvant effect. Since other peptidoglycans were adjuvant active, it was apparent that the activity of the mycobacterial adjuvant was not dependent on *N*-acetylglucosamine, the *N*-glycolyl group of the muramic acid, the amidation of free carboxyl groups of D-glutamic acid, or the presence of *meso*-DAP, which could be replaced by L-lysine.

The C-terminal D-Ala of the peptide was removed and the *N*-acetylglucosamine cleaved from the glycan of *E. coli* by Ellouz et al (45). The resultant disaccharide-tripeptide was adjuvant active at a dose level of 25 μg with ovalbumin as adjuvant. After amidase action the disaccharide and tetrapeptide were released and these were inactive. A synthetic tetrapeptide was also inactive (45, 89). When azobenzene arsonate-*N*-acetyl-L-tyrosine was used as antigen, the tetrapeptide was reported to have activity (48; Figure 2). This interpretation may be explained by the immunogenicity of the synthetic antigen (Table 1).

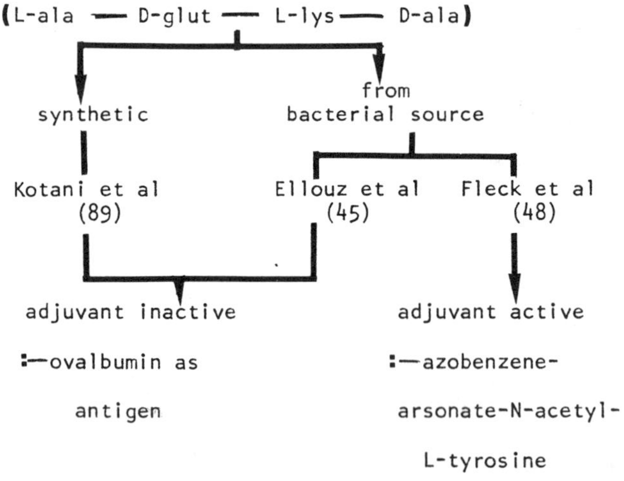

Figure 2 Adjuvant activity of tetrapeptide monomer; this was inactive when ovalbumin was the antigen and active when azobenzenearsonate-*N*-acetyl-L-tyrosine was the antigen.

The importance of the peptide moiety was shown by (123) the immunopotentiating effect of the tetra- and tripeptides of *B. megaterium* cell walls conjugated to Sepharose 4B with cyanogen bromide. The complete cell walls of *B. megaterium* or *Corynebacterium parvum* (1.0 mg) produced significant results (1% level) when injected intraperitoneally into mice one day after the antigen. On the other hand, conjugated peptide-Sepharose 4B was effective when administered four days prior to the injection of antigen.

N-acetylmuramyltripeptides were obtained from nucleotide precursors of cell wall synthesis, with cycloserine as inhibitor of synthesis. Both the DAP-containing (*Bacillus cereus*) and lysine-containing (*S. epidermidis*) preparations were strongly adjuvant active (25 μg dose).

The scene was set for the final attack by chemists on the minimal structure, and *N*-acetylmuramyl-L-alanyl-D-isoglutamine was synthesized (92, 105; Figure 3). The muramyldipeptide (MDP) stimulated increased levels of antibody and induced delayed-type hypersensitivity to ovalbumin at much lower doses than the whole bacilli used in Freund's complete adjuvant (45, 89). The inclusion of MDP in a water-in-oil emulsion containing ovalbumin stimulated the production of the IgG_2 class of immunoglobulins (95) previously shown by White et al (174) to be a feature of the mycobacterial adjuvant.

The passive hemagglutination titers increased in the secondary response after injection of MDP and BSA in saline. In addition, Kotani et al concluded (87) that the lack of adjuvant activity in group B peptidoglycans could not be explained by the replacement of L-alanine (first amino acid) with L-serine or glycine in MDP since this caused an increase and decrease respectively in the adjuvant activity of the substituted muramyldipeptide. Muramyldipeptides (MurNAc-L-ala-IsoGlu and MurNAc-L-ala-D-glu) in-

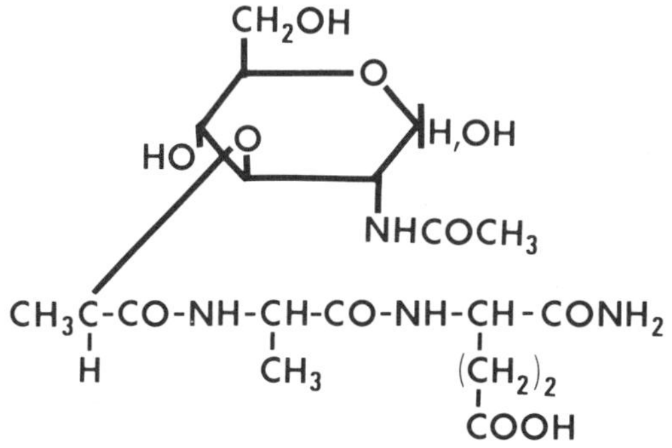

Figure 3 The structure of *N*-acetylmuramyl-L-alanyl-D-isoglutamine.

duced a strong delayed-type response in rats after injection of 0.1 mg of ovalbumin and 0.1 mg of MDP in Freund incomplete adjuvant (156).

The problem of making comparisons between studies measuring the primary and secondary immune responses was reinforced by the results of stimulating anti-BSA antibodies in mice. The MDP was introduced in aqueous solution by various routes with the primary subcutaneous injection of 0.5 mg of BSA. A booster injection of 0.1 mg of BSA was given on day 30 to stimulate the secondary response; anti-BSA antibodies were measured by passive hemagglutination. As shown in Figure 4 there was a significant increase in the titers of antibody after the booster injection (31). This also confirmed the ability of MDP to act as an adjuvant in mice in an aqueous medium (11). *N*-acetylmuramyldipeptide or 6-O-stearoyl-*N*-acetymuramyldipeptide (100 μg) injected into guinea pigs in Freund incomplete adjuvant containing 50 μg azobenzenearsonate-*N*-acetyl-L-tyrosine stimulated a delayed hypersensitivity response to the antigen after 14 days. Skin tests were done using 100 μg of azobenzenearsonate-α-amylase. These two substances also increased the production of antibodies against bacterial α-amylase (16, 181). The synthetic 6-O-mycoloyl-*N*-acetylmuramyldipeptide (50 μg) (92) and 6-O-mycoloyl-*N*-acetylmuramyl-L-seryl-D-isoglutamine (162) were also adjuvant active, but 6-O-mycoloyl-*N*-acetylmuramic acid was inactive (182).

6-O-lauroyl, 6-O-stearoyl or 6-O-docosanoyl-*N*-acetyl-L-alanyl-D-isoglutamine were adjuvant active in guinea pigs when administered in liposomes composed of lecithin and cholesterol (10:10 μmoles) (84).

An effect of MDP which could be exploited was the stimulation of resistance to virulent *Klebsiella pneumoniae* infection in mice (33). The mice were injected with 1×10^4 *K. pneumoniae* i.m. one day after the injection of either 100 μg of MDP i.v. or 2.0 mg of MDP per os; 72 and 67% respectively of infected mice survived. Subsequently seventeen analogues of part of the peptidoglycan were found to be ineffective in increasing this resistance to *K. pneumoniae* infection (34). The importance of the L-Ala-D-Glu in the synthetic glycopeptide was recognized because they were essential to produce the anti-*Klebsiella* activity. Adjuvant activity was removed by altering the structure of the D-glutamyl residue (12, 127).

After glycosidation with *p*-aminophenol (PAP), the PAP-MDP formed lost the ability to protect mice against *K. pneumoniae* infections; however, cross-linking of PAP-MDP with glutaraldehyde produced a polymeric form Pol (PAP-MDP) that was more active than MDP (126). These findings suggest that some additional structural features, besides L-Ala-D-Glu, are important for the stimulation of resistance to *K. pneumoniae* in mice.

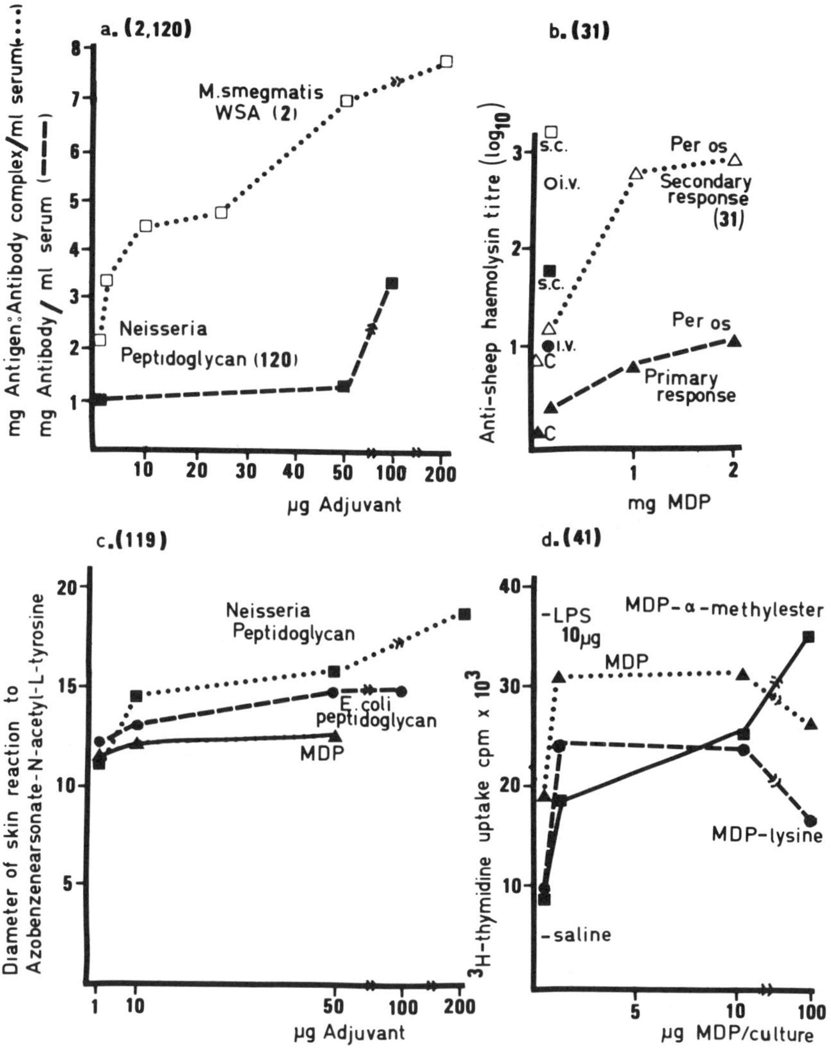

Figure 4 The effect of adjuvant dosage on (*a*) and (*b*) the stimulation of increased antibody levels, (*c*) induction of cell-mediated immunity, and (*d*) spleen cell mitogenicity. Note the difference between the primary and secondary immune responses in the presence of MDP. In (*b*) C., i.v., and s.c. are control, intravenous and subcutaneous; closed and open symbols represent the primary and secondary responses respectively.

ANTIGENICITY OF PEPTIDOGLYCAN

Purified peptidoglycan of Gram-negative bacteria was poorly immunogenic for rabbits and it was necessary to use SDS-treated cell walls to prepare antipeptidoglycan sera (124). The peptidoglycans of *Proteus vulgaris, Escherichia coli, Moraxella glucidolytica,* and *Neisseria perflava* which were adjuvant-active (119–121) gave reactions of identity. Inhibition studies with synthetic peptides revealed that the specificity of the antibody was directed against the tetrapeptide; the C-terminal portion *meso*DAP-D-ala was immunodominant. Weak cross-reactions were found among peptidoglycans of *Streptococcus faecium, Micrococcus luteus,* and *Corynebacterium poinsettiae* that possessed peptides with the C-terminal portions L-lys-D-ala or L-homoserine-D-ala.

With the Gram-positive cell walls of Group A variant streptococci, the antibody recognized the immunodominant D-ala-D-ala of the non-cross-linked pentapeptide (141). The D-ala-D-ala did not cause inhibition with the antiserum against Gram-negative cell walls (124).

Antisera were prepared in rabbits against pepsin-treated streptococci or human serum albuminpentapeptide. In addition a specific antimuramic acid immunoglobulin was isolated from an anti-*M. luteus* serum. The binding of [^{14}C]*N*-acetylmuramyl-L-alanyl-D-isoglutamine ([^{14}C]MDP) and *N*-acetylmuramyl-L-alanyl-D-isoglutaminyl-L lysyl [^{125}I]D-alanine (MDP-L-lys [^{125}I]D-ala) to these immunoglobulins was examined. Whereas the labelled MDP-L-lys-D-ala bound to antistreptococcal sera (35–40% precipitated) and to anti-HSA-pentapeptide (68% precipitated), less than 1% of [^{14}C] MDP was bound to these sera (9, 13). This study confirmed the immunogenicity of the C-terminal dipeptide.

It is interesting that the *N*-terminal portion of these peptides L-ala-D-glu was not the immunodominant portion of the peptidoglycan but was found to be essential in the minimal adjuvant structure. In view of our previous studies which did not reveal antibodies against peptidoglycan in guinea pigs injected with peptidoglycolipid in water-in-oil emulsions, it would seem that in the native mycobacterial cell wall the immunogenic *meso*-DAP-D-ala was present as a cryptic epitope.

Only 7% of MDP-L-lys [^{125}I]D-Ala and 0.23% of [^{14}C] MDP were precipitated by anti-*N*-acetylmuramic acid serum which confirmed that in the glycan *N*-acetylglucosamine was more immunogenic than *N*-acetylmuramic acid (132). Sera against *M. luteus* do contain antibodies with a high specificity for *N*-acetylmuramic acid, probably due to the fact that 50% of the muramic acid residues in *M. luteus* are unsubstituted and have a free carboxyl group. *N*-acetylmuramic acid ethylamide failed to inhibit, whereas *N*-acetylmuramic acid inhibited the agglutination of *M. luteus* peptidoglycan by anti-*M. luteus* serum (142).

Antibodies to peptidoglycan were demonstrated in the sera of patients infected with Group A variant streptococci as well as in normal human serum (64). However, five sera from patients with streptococcal disease and eighty normal sera failed to precipitate either MDP or MDP-L-lys-D-ala (13). The initial reaction was due to a different specificity—possibly the C-terminal dipeptide or the interpeptide-bridging peptides (di- or tri L-alanine in the group A streptococcus).

It should be remembered that the peptidoglycan is not equivalent to the whole cell wall and a mosaic of antigens will be presented to the host, e.g. staphylococcal protein A (144), teichoic acids (29, 79). Consequently, an immunological response to a particular cell wall will depend upon the stereochemical arrangement of the antigenic components.

It is surprising that so few specific antigens of the cell walls have been examined (38), but with synthesized specific antigens it would be possible to produce antisera specific for particular organisms.

ADVERSE BIOLOGICAL ACTIVITIES

For thirty years during the search for the minimal structural component required to stimulate the immune response, investigators were also attempting to remove a variety of harmful biological effects that would preclude the use of a bacterial preparation in a vaccine.

Polyarthritis in Rats

After the injection of water-in-oil emulsions containing mycobacterial organisms (130, 164) or peptidoglycolipid (177), Lewis rats were found to develop a severe polyarthritis. Cell walls from *Mycobacterium bovis* BCG (15) or *M. smegmatis* (14) produced a similar effect. Both the cell walls and the high-molecular weight peptidoglycan derivatives prepared by enzymic degradation were strongly arthritogenic. Cell walls from *M. bovis* BCG, *Corynebacterium diphtheriae, Streptomyces lavendulae, Streptomyces fradiae,* and *Lactobacillus plantarum* were active, whereas the cell walls of *Bacillus megaterium, Streptococcus pyogenes,* and *Micrococcus luteus* were inactive. In particular, the adjuvant-active enzyme digests of *Staphylococcus aureus* produced an intense polyarthritis in rats (81).

The water-soluble WSA and Neo-WSA obtained from cell walls by lysozyme treatment (3, 10, 14, 158, 160), the POLY-PA (110), and the glycopeptide (149) did not produce a polyarthritis in rats. It was significant that the synthetic muramyldipeptide and the numerous analogues were also devoid of arthitogenic activity.

It has been suggested that the length of the glycan chain is the important factor in the induction of polyarthritis in Lewis rats. A high molecular weight fraction prepared with the L-11 enzyme and *Streptomyces globisporus* enzyme (a mixture of endo-*N*, O-diacetylmuramidase and endo-*N*-acetylmuramidase) with a short glycan chain did not cause polyarthritis (149). This supports the concept of activity related to glycan length.

Induction of Autoimmune Diseases

A demyelinating encephalomyelitis in monkeys was induced after the injection of homologous brain tissue in a Freund complete adjuvant emulsion (73, 74, 114, 115, 176). The animals developed neurologic symptoms of blindness, ataxia, nystagmus, and paralysis of the limbs. Thrombosis, perivascular cuffing, and demyelination were found in the brain and spinal cord. Similar results were found in guinea pigs, but the symptoms were less severe with mycobacterial organisms (53, 82) and peptidoglycolipid (163, 175). It was concluded that the active mycobacterial factor was a cell wall component (36). The active encephalitogenic factor of brain tissue seems to be a hepta- or nonapeptide (93, 117, 118). Antibodies against this factor were detected in the sera of either patients with multiple sclerosis or individuals immunized with BCG (47).

Recent reports will have caused frustration to research workers who have attempted for so many years to produce a safe adjuvant substance. Experimental allergic encephalomyelitis was induced in guinea pigs with an encephalitogenic heptapeptide or myelin basic protein injected with 100 μg or 12.5 μg, respectively, of the water-soluble peptidoglycan complex (tetrasaccharide-heptapeptide) from *Mycobacterium tuberculosis* $H_{37}R_a$ (167, 168) or with WSA (94). A more significant report indicated that 100 μg of *M. tuberculosis* organisms or as little as 1.0 μg of muramyldipeptide stimulated allergic encephalomyelitis in guinea pigs (117, 118). T-lymphocytes were required as effector cells in the encephalitogenic lesions induced by MDP. It is extremely unfortunate that it has not been possible to separate the adjuvant-active component of peptidoglycan from the encephalomyelitis-inducing component. The α and γ carboxyl groups of the D-isoglutaminyl residue seem to be critical for biological activity once again, because, as found with the adjuvant response, there was no stimulation of encephalomyelitis with muramyl-L-alanine. From an optimistic viewpoint it is worth noting that allergic encephalomyelitis is only induced in the presence of Freund incomplete adjuvant. It would be essential to establish that the lack of encephalomyelitis-inducing activity of MDP in aqueous solution is associated with an increase in the adjuvant response.

An orchiepididymitis was also induced in guinea pigs after injection of sperm extract or a sperm autoantigen in a water-in-oil emulsion containing the synthetic watersoluble MDP. Specific antibodies and delayed hypersensitivity reactions were produced against the sperm antigens, but these were not obtained in the absence of the emulsion (161). The lesions were similar to those obtained with Freund complete adjuvant (51). Fifty micrograms of WSA and 50 μg of retinal protein in a water-in-oil emulsion induced a uveoretinitis in guinea pigs, but MDP was not very effective (90). The MDP (100 μg) plus 50 μg of retinal protein in aqueous solution, when injected two and a half months before the complete adjuvant-containing retinal antigen, reduced the incidence of uveoretinitis. The induction of tolerance by MDP to protein antigens is worthy of more attention.

Pyrogenicity

A 10 ml volume of pyrogen-free physiological saline containing a peptidoglycan or cell wall sample is injected intravenously into rabbits; if the rectal temperature rises by more than 0.6°C the specimen is pyrogenic. Earlier studies showed that staphylococcal and streptococcal peptidoglycans were pyrogenic (61, 62, 135).

The peptidoglycans of *Staphylococcus aureus, S. epidermidis, Streptococcus pneumoniae,* groups A, B, and L streptococci, *Spirillum serpens,* and *Escherichia coli* were pyrogenic (134). It was found that repeated injections of peptidoglycan resulted in the induction of tolerance to the fever effect, but the intravenous injections caused degenerative changes in the heart.

However, Heymer & Rietschel (62) pointed out that such cardiac lesions are due to the activity of poorly degradable cell walls rather than peptidoglycan. The highly adjuvant-active high molecular weight preparations from cell walls caused significant fever reactions in rabbits. For example, 250 μg of *Lactobacillus plantarum* fraction IA caused an increase of between 1.1 and 2.2°C; the IE fraction was less pyrogenic with a temperature increase of 1.0°C at the same dose. The *Streptococcus mutans* BHTR-6 fraction caused a temperature increase of 1.0–1.5°C over the dose range 100–500 μg per rabbit. The mycobacterial glycopeptide increased the rabbit's temperature by 0.5°C, even at the 500-μg dose, and was designated as a nonpyrogen. Having shown that the high molecular peptidoglycan preparations were pyrogenic, Kotani et al (88) examined synthetic *N*-acetylmuramyl peptides. Both MDP and *N*-acetylmuramyl-L-alanyl-D-isoglutamine were not pyrogenic, even at a dose level of 875 μg per rabbit (17, 162). The 6-O-mycoloyl derivative seemed to possess a greater activity for the induction of cell-mediated immunity than for the stimulation of circulating antibodies. Similar findings were reported with analogues of MDP (44) and with NAcMur-L-Ala-D-glu(NH_2)OMc and NAcMur-*N*-methyl-L-ala-D-glu-

NH_2 (125). It does not seem that pyrogenicity has as yet been definitely implicated as part of the mechanism of the adjuvant response.

IMMUNOTHERAPY OF CANCER

One reason for the expansion of the whole field of adjuvant research stems from the original work of Halpern et al (57) and Biozzi et al (27) which showed that BCG could cause suppression or regression of tumor growth. Rats were injected with 130 μg of dry BCG and were challenged 8 days later with either 1.75×10^7 T-8 tumor cells i.v. or 50 mg of tumor tissue implanted subcutaneously. When compared to control animals, a twofold decrease in tumor size in BCG-inoculated animals was recorded. Mice injected with BCG survived for longer periods than uninoculated control animals after challenge with 5×10^6 i.v. or 1×10^7 i.p. Ehrlich's ascites tumor cells. BCG-inoculated HA/1 CR Swiss female mice after challenge with Ehrlich's ascites tumor cells survived for 13 days after the death of control mice. On the other hand, when the solid sarcoma-180 tumor was used the BCG inoculated animals were completely protected at the same stage. But if C57 hybrid female mice were used, the protective effect of BCG was not observed.

Injection of tumor cells and BCG together induced a specific cell-mediated response in guinea pigs (187). An effective tumor vaccine for guinea pigs contained a mixture of 6×10^6 living BCG organisms and 1.5×10^6 Line 10 hepatoma ascites cells (23).

A specific tumor immunity was induced in guinea pigs when BCG was replaced with cell walls of *M. bovis* BCG in a water-in-oil emulsion containing hepatoma cells (188). Purified cell walls of *Mycobacterium kansasii* in physiological saline also protected mice against Ehrlich's ascites and lymphoid leukaemia; the effect was greater than that found with *M. bovis* BCG-killed cells (32). Thirty micrograms of cell walls of *M. bovis* BCG, *M. tuberculosis* $H_{37}R_v$, or *M. kansasii* were sufficient to cause regression of established tumors (189).

The cell walls of *M. smegmatis, Nocardia asteroides,* and *Corynebacterium parvum* did not possess tumor-suppressive properties. In addition, treatment of BCG cell walls with proteolytic enzymes, organic solvents, acid or alkali reduces anti-tumor activity (107, 189). The efficacy of *M. tuberculosis* $H_{37}R_a$-delipidated cell walls (150 μg in a water-in-oil emulsion) in reducing the size of established tumors increased from 33 to 83% of cases when 150 μg of mycobacterial cord factor (trehalose-6,6-dimycolate) was included in the injection mixture. Non-peptidoglycan substances do possess anti-tumor activity so the regression of tumors in 83% of animals may be due to a synergistic effect between two active anti-tumor substances.

Bekierkunst et al (26) reported suppression of urethan-induced lung adenomas and growth of Ehrlich's ascites cells after i.v. injection of cord factor (184). It should be noted that in saline suspension *M. bovis* BCG cell walls with or without cord factor induced a low degree of anti-tumor activity against L1210 murine leukaemia (96).

The cell walls of *Nocardia rubra* were highly effective in suppressing the growth of fibrosarcoma cells in BALB/c mice (18, 162).

Hiu (65) observed that 90% of F_1 hybrid mice (DBA/2 X C57B1/6) injected with 1 X 10^7 leukemic L1210 cells survived when 250 μg of mycobacterial adjuvant and anti-tumor factor (MAAF) were injected one hour later. Subsequently this injection was repeated on four occasions at three day intervals. Various water-soluble natural and synthetic peptidoglycan preparations were tested.

If 250–500 μg of POLY-PA from *M. tuberculosis* strain Test or an acetylated-PA from *M. tuberculosis* $H_{37}R_a$ were injected into rabbits 24 hr prior to the injection of Shope fibroma virus, the size of the local tumors was reduced (166). The water-soluble glycopeptide (149) was examined for its ability to suppress growth of Ehrlich's ascites tumors in ddY mice; 200-μg repetitive injections at three-day intervals protected 50% of the mice. The water-soluble peptidoglycan derivatives were less effective than *M. bovis* BCG cell walls in preventing the growth of a solid tumor implant, melanoma B_{16} (147).

N-acetylmuramyl-L-alanyl-D-isoglutamine or *N*-acetylmuramyl-L-alanyl-D-glutamic acid at the 200-μg dose level did not protect mice against L1210 murine leukemia if they were injected in saline (96). Either 100 μg of MDP or 6-O-stearoyl-*N*-acetylmuramyldipeptide were mixed with melanoma B_{16} tumor cells in an oil-in-water emulsion and injected into C57BL/6J mice; however, there was no suppression of the tumor growth (16, 181, 183).

Because of the immunotherapeutic effects of *M. bovis* BCG in producing regression of certain tumors, the significance of a synergic effect between mycolic acids and the adjuvant-active peptidoglycan was examined by introducing hydrophobic groups into the hydrophilic MDP (92). Synthetic 6-O-mycoloyl-MDP preparations (100 μg) either in phosphate-buffered saline or attached to oil droplets were mixed with 1 X 10^6 fibrosarcoma tumor cells and transplanted intradermally into SWM/MS mice. Twenty-three days after inoculation 6-O-mycoloyl-MDP, 6-O-nocardomycoloyl-MDP, and 6-O-corynomycoloyl-MDP caused suppression of tumor growth in 77, 62, and 37% of the mice respectively. These synthetic 6-O-mycoloyl-MDP preparations did not possess anti-tumor activity in phosphate-buffered saline (17, 162). The importance of other polymeric cell wall components is indicated again, and one wonders whether the chemists will turn their attention to an increasing number of chemical substitutions of muramyldipeptide.

From the various animal studies it is apparent that variable responses occur from one animal species to another and from one genetical strain to another. Both sex and age of the animals have been shown to cause variability in the ability of BCG to affect the growth of the tumor or tumor cells. Similarly, the type of experimental tumor chosen for the challenge influences the apparent protective ability of the bacterial cancer immunotherapeutic preparation.

Most adjuvant substances suppress the immune response when administered in very high doses or in repetitive injections with lower doses. Therefore, great caution must be exercised so that immunosuppression is not inadvertently stimulated in cancer patients due to the overzealous administration of a microbial or synthetic anti-tumor substance. Indeed, in a pilot study done ten years ago in Glasgow it was found that many elderly cancer patients were unable to produce a cell-mediated immune response to DNCB even before immunotherapy (H. Singh, personal communication). But, as Woodruff (178) indicated, it would be premature to abandon an immunotherapeutic approach to cancer treatment and it remains for research groups to painstakingly explore the beneficial effects of the anti-tumor substances.

For further information on cancer immunotherapy there are several detailed reviews (24, 25, 28, 49, 56, 59, 102, 103, 146).

ACTIVATION OF CELLS BY PEPTIDOGLYCAN COMPLEXES

It is obvious that the area of biological activity of peptidoglycan and peptidoglycan complexes at the cellular level is confused by the many controversial reports that have appeared in the past five years. For virtually every report of a positive action against macrophages and B and T lymphocytes, it is possible to find an antagonistic report. Heymer (60) stated, "this is not surprising, especially because of the complex structure of peptidoglycan molecules, the different methods of preparing peptidoglycan and the different animal or cell species that have been used in the various assay systems."

As mentioned throughout this paper, there are a variety of factors which will influence the outcome of biological action. The purity, size, chemical composition, and amphipathic nature of the individual peptidoglycan preparations must be known before one assay can be compared with another. It is important to know whether a particular species of test animal has been exposed previously to the peptidoglycan and whether there are specific differences in the reactions between one animal species and another. Stewart-Tull (147) stressed the need for defining biological systems in a particular animal species and asked the questions: "Is the reaction which occurs in a guinea-pig necessarily the same as that found in man or a mouse?" and "Is a mouse reaction indicative of a similar reaction in man?"

Apart from the occurrence of gross cellular interactions, it was apparent that membrane interactions with the peptidoglycan complexes would be important. The mycobacterial water-soluble glycopeptide showed an affinity for the cell membranes of peritoneal macrophages and lymphocytes, and a direct correlation between adjuvanticity and affinity for membranes was established (42, 43). An affinity of the same glycopeptide for IgG_2 guinea pig immunoglobulin was found (153), and later the dual interaction with cell membrane and IgG_2 was used as the basis for a mechanism of cell cooperation in the adjuvant response (148).

Peritoneal macrophage cells from guinea pigs, injected with oil droplet vaccines containing 1.5 mg of *Mycobacterium bovis* BCG-cell walls, killed 95% of *Listeria monocytogenes* in vitro. Cell free supernates from the preparation of activated macrophages also killed 73% of *Listeria monocytogenes.* Lymphocytes from animals injected with cell wall, when added to normal macrophages in vitro, activated the macrophages and caused 74% killing of the test organisms. It was concluded that the lymphocytes were stimulated by the BCG cell walls to produce lymphokines which induced macrophage activation (78). Intraperitoneal injection of BCG stimulated an increased activity of acid phosphatase and increased phagocytosis of *L. monocytogenes,* but no effect was found if the BCG were injected intravenously (185). The variety of peptidoglycan preparations that are known to act as mitogens is large and includes *Bacillus megaterium, E. coli* (40), *L. monocytogenes* (35), *Nocardia rubra, Mycobacterium* spp. (133), *Nocardia* spp., *Corynebacterium* spp. (16), *Staphylococcus aureus, Staphylococcus epidermidis, Streptococcus sanguis, Streptococcus salivarius, Streptococcus mutans,* and *Lactobacillus plantarum* (154).

Modollel et al (113) showed that the peptidoglycan substance WSA increased the number of antibody-forming cells against the thymus-independent DNP-dextran. In addition, WSA was active in the absence of T-lymphocytes; lymphoid cells were treated with antiserum or were obtained from nu/nu mice that lack a thymus, so it appeared that WSA did not act primarily on T cells. Their experiments also failed to demonstrate stimulation of mouse spleenic lymphocytes by 1–50 μg/ml of WSA.

Macrophages or lymphocytes were pre-incubated with WSA for 24 hr without antigen; subsequently, these cell suspensions were washed and the opposite type of untreated cells and sheep erythrocytes were added to each. In the test with WSA-treated macrophages, 1350 antibody-forming cells/10^6 cells were counted; with WSA-treated lymphocytes, only 500 antibody-forming cells were counted. The strains of mice used in this study were NMR1/Han, C3H, and C3H/nunu. This piece of work indicated the importance of the macrophage, and the suggestion was made that WSA induced macrophages to produce a lymphocyte-activating factor. Further evidence for the activation of macrophages came from the comparison of *N*-acetylmuramyl-L-Ala-D-isoglu with *N*-acetylmuramyl-L-Ala-L-isoglu in a carbon clearance test in C3H, CF1, and C57BL mice. The former adjuvant-active preparation caused a significant increase in the phagocytic activity of macrophages, whereas its diastereomer did not (155). In studies with MDP, Fevrier et al (46) showed that although T helper cells were necessary for the stimulation of B cells, the immediate target cell was the macrophage. These experiments were done in DBA/2 and C57BL/6 mice.

Other studies (16, 40, 145) showed that high molecular weight, water-soluble peptidoglycans were B-cell mitogens in Balb/c mice, but the low molecular weight peptidoglycan or MDP were nonmitogenic. Similar results were obtained by Rook & Stewart-Tull (133); the adjuvant-active *M. tuberculosis* glycopeptide, monomeric or dimeric peptidoglycan, was nonmitogenic for Balb/c inbred mice spleen cells, whereas the long-chain polymer peptidoglycolipid was mitogenic. This indicated that mitogenicity was not a necessary prerequisite for an adjuvant response. Subsequently, Damais, Parant & Chedid (41) cultured spleen cells of DBA/2 and Balb/c mice in a serum-free medium supplemented with 2-mercaptoethanol and found increased blast cell formation and uptake of [^{3}H]thymidine with peptidoglycan from *B. megaterium,* and Neo-WSA from *M. smegmatis;* however, WSA and MDP were still inactive. But if the MDP was incubated with cells for five days, [^{3}H]thymidine uptake was significantly increased. The effect was most marked with DBA/2, Balb/c, or Balb/c nu/nu mice and less obvious with C6AK hybrids. With ICR mice spleen cells (154) in a medium containing 10% fetal bovine serum, the MDP was mitogenic; it was suggested that these mice were high responders to the mitogenic effect of monomeric peptidoglycan unit. The result with nu/nu mice indicates the B cell is the target cell for MDP activity; however, Löwy, Bona & Chedid (99) found that MDP increased the efficiency of sheep erythrocyte-educated T cells in CBA mice. Cooperation between T and B lymphocytes was required for the adjuvant response stimulated by MDP. These workers concluded that T-derived lymphocytes, and not macrophages, were responsible for the adjuvant effect of MDP.

These various in vitro studies have gone full circle and evidence has accumulated which implicates macrophages and B and T cells as the target cells in the mammalian response to peptidoglycan derivatives. We know that such derivatives are immunoregulatory, both potentiating or suppressing the immune response, but we must wait for the in vivo mechanisms of action to be clearly elucidated.

SUMMARY

It is clear that the determinant of the peptidoglycan required for potentiation of the immune response is specific for a particular peptidoglycan or group of peptidoglycans. In view of the wide range of different adjuvant substances, it was not expected that one simple structure common to all bacterial peptidoglycans would be found. There is still a need to explain the lack of activity associated with some peptidoglycans. In addition, it will be important to investigate the reason why one peptidoglycan will produce a biological effect at a much lower dose level than another peptidoglycan, even though they are structurally very similar. The purity of each preparation is of paramount importance in this respect because, as we have seen, the addition of a hydrophobic mycoloyl moiety onto the synthetic MDP drastically alters its biological activity. Consequently, it must be shown that peptidoglycans are free from additional cell wall polymers, e.g. arabinogalactans and mycolic acid in mycobacterial preparations.

How is it that, weight-for-weight, one does not witness an increase in biological activity with purification of the active component? It would be expected that in the classical Freund adjuvant the activity of the mycobacterial component would be whole organisms $<$ peptidoglycolipid $<$ peptidoglycan (WSA) $<$ muramyldipeptide, but this has not been shown conclusively (Figure 4).

Nevertheless, the search for modified synthetic peptidoglycan adjuvants could provide the means to manufacture useful vaccines since it is known that an immune response can be stimulated by smaller quantities of antigen in the presence of adjuvant. The aqueous medium versus water-in-oil emulsion conflict remains to be investigated further and there is a need for the development of suitable oils to replace the crude mixtures of mineral oils currently available (150).

A serious impediment to any rapid advances in the use of peptidoglycan adjuvants was the association of autoimmune phenomena and toxicity with the muramyldipeptide. These studies must be repeated to confirm the reports of adverse reactions because it is doubtful that any pharmaceutical company would risk using a peptidoglycan adjuvant if the toxicity remained. However, with the potential development of these substances as cancer immunotherapeutic agents, it will be a worthwhile challenge.

Further exploration of the immunodepressive effect caused by repeated administration of peptidoglycan adjuvant mixtures should be done because herein may lie the explanation for the paucity of good bacterial vaccines. Repeated injections of whole cell vaccines containing peptidoglycan and/or lipopolysaccharide, both adjuvants, would progressively decrease the levels of immunity.

Literature Cited

1. Adam, A., Ciorbaru, R., Ellouz, F., Petit, J-F., Lederer, E. 1974. *Biochem. Biophys. Res. Commun.* 56:561–67
2. Adam, A., Ciorbaru, R., Petit, J-F., Lederer, E. 1972. *Proc. Natl. Acad. Sci. USA* 69:851–54
3. Adam, A., Ciorbaru, R., Petit, J-F., Lederer, E., Chedid, L., Lamensans, A., Parant, F., Parant, M., Rosselet, J. P., Berger, F. M. 1973. *Infect. Immun.* 7:855–61
4. Adam, A., Petit, J-F., Wietzerbin-Falszpan, J., Sinay, P., Thomas, D. W., Lederer, E. 1969. *FEBS Lett.* 4:87–92
5. Amar, C., Vilkas, E. 1974. *Proc. Symp. Immunostimul. Bact. Inst. Pasteur, Paris*
6. Asquith, P., ed. 1979. *Immunology of the Gastrointestinal Tract.* Churchill Livingstone: Edinburgh. 348 pp.
7. Asselineau, J. 1949. *C. R. Acad. Sci.* 229:791–94
8. Asselineau, J., Buc, H., Jollès, P., Lederer, E. 1958. *Bull. Soc. Chim. Biol.* 40:1953–64
9. Audibert, F., Carelli, C., Jolivet, M., Reichert, C., Chedid, L. 1978. *Rencontre Biologique,* pp. 35–42. Paris: Varia.
10. Audibert, F., Chedid, L. 1976. *Infect. Immun.* 14:1263–68
11. Audibert, F., Chedid, L., Lefrancier, P., Choay, J. 1976. *Cell. Immunol.* 21: 243–49
12. Audibert, F., Chedid, L., Lefrancier, P., Choay, J., Lederer, E. 1977. *Ann. Immunol. Paris* 128:653–61
13. Audibert, F., Heymer, B., Gros, C., Schleifer, K. H., Seidl, P. H., Chedid, L. 1978. *J. Immunol.* 121:1219–22
14. Audibert, F., Parant, M., Petit, J-F., Adam, A. 1973. *C. R. Acad. Sci.* 277:2097–2100
15. Azuma, I., Kanetsuna, F., Kada, Y., Takashima, T., Yamamura, Y. 1972. *Jpn. J. Microbiol.* 16:333–36
16. Azuma, I., Sugimura, K., Taniyama, T., Yamawaki, M., Yamamura, Y., Kusumoto, S., Okada, S., Shiba, T. 1976. *Infect. Immun.* 14:18–27
17. Azuma, I., Sugimura, K., Yamawaki, M., Uemiya, M., Kusumoto, S., Okada, S., Shiba, T., Yamamura, Y. 1978. *Infect. Immun.* 20:600–7
18. Azuma, I., Taniyama, T., Yamawaki, M., Sugimura, K., Yamamura, Y. 1976. *Gann* 57:733–36
19. Azuma, I., Thomas, D. W., Adam, A., Ghuysen, J. M., Bonaly, R., Petit, J-F., Lederer, E. 1970. *Biochim. Biophys. Acta* 208:444–51
20. Azuma, I., Yamamura, Y., Misaki, A. 1969. *J. Bacteriol.* 98:331–33
21. Azuma, I., Yamamura, Y., Misaki, A. 1970. *5th Jt. Meet. Tuber. Panel Jpn. US Tokyo Proc.,* p. 15
22. Azuma, I., Yamawaki, M., Ogura, T., Yoshimoto, T., Tokuzen, R., Hirao, F., Yamamura, Y. 1978. *Gann* 21:73–86
23. Bartlett, G. L., Zbar, B. 1972. *J. Natl. Cancer Inst.* 48:1709–26
24. Bast, R. C., Zbar, B., Borsos, T., Rapp, H. J. 1974. *N. Engl. J. Med.* 290: 1413–20
25. Bast, R. C., Zbar, B., Borsos, T., Rapp, H. J. 1974. *N. Engl. J. Med.* 290: 1458–69
26. Bekierkunst, A., Levij, I. S., Yarkoni, E., Vilkas, E., Lederer, E. 1971. *Infect. Immun.* 4:245–55
27. Biozzi, G., Stiffel, C., Halpern, B. N., Mouton, D. 1959. *C. R. Soc. Biol.* 153:987–89
28. Borsos, T., Rapp, H. J., eds. 1973. *Natl. Cancer Inst. Monogr. 39.* Washington DC: Natl. Inst. Health. 276 pp.
29. Burger, M. M. 1966. *Proc. Natl. Acad. Sci. USA* 56:910–17
30. Chedid, L., Audibert, F., Lefrancier, P., Choay, J., Lederer, E. 1976. *Proc. Natl. Acad. Sci. USA* 73:2472–75
31. Chedid, L., Audibert, F., Parant, M. 1976. *Rencontre Biologique,* pp. 67–72. Paris: Expansion Sci.
32. Chedid, L., Lamensans, A., Parant, F., Parant, M., Adam, A., Petit, J-F., Lederer, E. 1973. *Cancer Res.* 33:2187–95
33. Chedid, L., Parant, M., Parant, F. 1977. *C. R. Acad. Sci.* 284:405–8
34. Chedid, L., Parant, M., Parant, F., Lefrancier, P., Choay, J., Lederer, E. 1977. *Proc. Natl. Acad. Sci. USA* 74:2089–93
35. Cohen, J. J., Rodriguez, G. E., Kind, D. P., Campbell, P. A. 1975. *J. Immunol.* 114:1132–34
36. Colover, J., Consden, R. 1956. *Nature* 177:749–50
37. Coon, J., Hunter, R. 1973. *J. Immunol.* 110:183–90
38. Cummins, C. S. 1962. *J. Gen. Microbiol.* 28:35–50
39. Cummins, C. S., Harris, H. 1958. *J. Gen. Microbiol.* 18:173
40. Damais, C., Bona, C., Chedid, L., Fleck, J., Nauciel, C., Martin, J. P. 1975. *J. Immunol.* 115:268–71
41. Damais, C., Parant, M., Chedid, L. 1978. *Cell. Immunol.* 34:49–56
42. Davies, M., Stewart-Tull, D. E. S. 1973. *Immunology* 25:1–9
43. Davies, M., Stewart-Tull, D. E. S. 1980. *Immunology.* Submitted

44. Dinarello, C. A., Elin, R. J., Chedid, L., Wolff, S. M. 1978. *J. Infect. Dis.* 138:760–67
45. Ellouz, F., Adam, A., Ciorbaru, R., Lederer, E. 1974. *Biochem. Biophys. Res. Commun.* 59:1317–25
46. Fevrier, M., Birrien, J. L., Leclerc, C., Chedid, L., Liacopoulos, P. 1978. *Eur. J. Immunol.* 8:558–62
47. Field, E. J., Caspary, E. A., Ball, E. J. 1963. *Lancet* 2:11–13
48. Fleck, J., Mock, M., Tytgat, F., Nauciel, C., Minck, R. 1974. *Nature* 250:517–18
49. Frappier, A. 1972. *Bull. Acad. Natl. Med. Paris* 156:36–43
50. Freund, J., Bonanto, M. V. 1946. *J. Immunol.* 52:231–34
51. Freund, J., Lipton, M. M., Thompson, G. E. 1953. *J. Exp. Med.* 97:711–26
52. Freund, J., McDermott, K. 1942. *Proc. Soc. Exp. Biol. Med.* 49:548–53
53. Freund, J., Stern, E. R., Pisani, T. M. 1947. *J. Immunol.* 57:179–94
54. Ghuysen, J-M. 1968. *Bacteriol. Rev.* 33:425–64
55. Ghuysen, J-M. 1977. In *Membrane Assembly and Turnover,* ed. G. Poste, pp. 463–596. Amsterdam: Elsevier
56. Griffith, A. H., Regamey, R. H., eds. 1978. *Int. Symp. Biol. Prep. Treat. Cancer, Devel. Biol. Stand. 38.* Basel: Karger
57. Halpern, B. N., Biozzi, G., Stiffel, C., Mouton, D. 1959. *C. R. Soc. Biol.* 153:919–23
58. Hash, J. 1963. *Arch. Biochem. Biophys.* 102:379–88
59. Hersh, E. M., Gutterman, J. U., Marligit, G. 1973. *Immunotherapy of cancer in man. Scientific basis and current status.* Springfield, Ill: Thomas
60. Heymer, B. 1975. *Z. Immunitaetsforsch. Exp. Klin. Immunol.* 149:245–57
61. Heymer, B., Bültmann, B., Haferkamp, O. 1971. *J. Immunol.* 106:858–61
62. Heymer, B., Rietschel, E. T. 1977. In *Microbiology,* ed. D. Schlessinger, pp. 344–49. Washington, DC: Am. Soc. Microbiol.
63. Heymer, B., Schachenmayr, W., Bültmann, B., Spanel, R., Haferkamp, O., Schmidt, W. C. 1973. *J. Immunol.* 111:478–84
64. Heymer, B., Schleifer, K. H., Read, S., Zabriskie, J. B., Krause, R. M. 1976. *J. Immunol.* 117:23–26
65. Hiu, I. J. 1972. *Nature* 238:241–42
66. Hoare, D. S., Work, E. 1955. *Biochem. J.* 61:562–68
67. Hoare, D. S., Work, E. 1957. *Biochem. J.* 65:441–47
68. Holton, J. B., Schwab, J. H. 1966. *J. Immunol.* 96:134–38
69. Ikawa, M., Snell, E. E. 1956. *Biochim. Biophys. Acta* 19:576–78
70. Jollès, P., Migliore-Samour, D., Maral, R., Floc'h, F., Werner, G. H. 1975. *Z. Immunitaetsforsch. Exp. Klin. Immunol.* 149:331–40
71. Jollès, P., Nguyen-Trung-Luong-Cros, H., Lederer, E. 1960. *Biochim. Biophys. Acta* 43:559–61
72. Jollès, P., Samour, D., Lederer, E. 1962. *Arch. Biochem. Biophys. Suppl.* 1: 283–89
73. Kabat, E. A., Wolf, A., Bezer, A. E. 1946. *Science* 104:362–63
74. Kabat, E. A., Wolf, A., Bezer, A. E. 1947. *J. Exp. Med.* 85:117–30
75. Kanetsuna, F. 1968. *Biochim. Biophys. Acta* 158:130–43
76. Kanetsuna, F., San Blas, G. 1970. *Biochim. Biophys. Acta* 208:434–43
77. Kato, K., Kotani, S., Matsubara, T., Kogami, J., Hashimoto, S., Chimori, M., Kazekawa, I. 1962. *Biken J.* 5:127–31
78. Kelly, M. T. 1976. *Cell. Immunol.* 26:254–63
79. Knox, K. W., Wicken, A. J. 1973. *Bacteriol. Rev.* 37:215–57
80. Koga, T., Ishibashi, T., Sugiyama, K., Tanaka, A. 1969. *Int. Arch. Allergy. Appl. Immunol.* 36:233–44
81. Koga, T., Kotani, S., Narita, T., Pearson, C. M. 1976. *Int. Arch. Allergy Appl. Immunol.* 51:206–13
82. Kopeloff, L. M., Kopeloff, N. 1947. *J. Immunol.* 57:229–37
83. Kotani, S., Hashimoto, S., Matsubara, T., Kato, K., Harada, K., Kojami, J., Kitaura, T., Tanaka, A. 1963. *Biken J.* 6:181–96
84. Kotani, S., Kinoshita, F., Morisaki, I., Shimono, T., Okunaga, T., Takada, H., Tsujimoto, M., Watanabe, Y., Kato, K., Shiba, T., Kusumoto, S., Okada, S. 1977. *Biken J.* 20:95–103
85. Kotani, S., Narita, T., Stewart-Tull, D. E. S., Shimono, T., Watanabe, Y., Kato, K., Iwata, S. 1975. *Biken J.* 18:77–92
86. Kotani, S., Watanabe, Y., Kinoshita, F., Kato, K., Perkins, H. R. 1977. *Biken J.* 20:87–90
87. Kotani, S., Watanabe, Y., Kinoshita, F., Morisaki, I., Kato, K., Shiba, T., Kusumoto, S., Tarumi, Y., Ikenaka, K. 1977. *Biken J.* 20:39–45
88. Kotani, S., Watanabe, Y., Shimono, T., Harada, K., Shiba, T., Kusumoto, S.,

Yokogawa, K., Taniguchi, M. 1976. *Biken J.* 19:9–13
89. Kotani, S., Watanabe, Y., Shimono, T., Narita, T., Kato, K., Stewart-Tull, D. E. S., Kinoshita, F., Yokogawa, K., Kawata, S., Shiba, T., Kusumoto, S., Tarumi, Y. 1975 *Z. Immunitaetsforsch. Exp. Klin. Immunol.* 149:302–19
90. Kozak, Y. de, Audibert, F., Thillaye, B., Chedid, L., Faure, J. P. 1979. *Ann. Immunol. Paris* 130:29–32
91. Kumazawa, Y., Shibusawa, A., Suzuki, T., Mizunoe, K. 1976. *Jpn. J. Microbiol.* 20:183–90
92. Kusumoto, S., Okada, S., Shiba, T., Azuma, I., Yamamura, Y. 1976. *Tetrahedron Lett.* 47:4287–90
93. Lamoureux, G., Thibeault, G., Richer G., Bernard, C. 1972. *Union Med. Can.* 101:674–80
94. Lebar, R., Voisin, G. A. 1974. *Ann. Immunol. Paris* 125:911–16
95. Leclerc, C., Audibert, F., Chedid, L. 1978. *Immunology* 35:963–70
96. Leclerc, C., Lamensans, A., Chedid, L., Drapier, J-C., Petit, J-F., Wietzerbin, J., Lederer, E. 1976. *Cancer Immunol. Immunother.* 1:227–32
97. Lederer, E. 1971. *Pure Appl. Chem.* 25:135–65
98. Liu, T. Y., Gotschlich, E. C. 1967. *J. Biol. Chem.* 242:471–76
99. Löwy, I., Bona, C., Chedid, L. 1977. *Cell. Immunol.* 29:195–99
100. Markovits, J., Vilkas, E., Lederer, E. 1971. *Eur. J. Biochem.* 18:287–91
101. Maron, R., Mozes, E., Fuchs, S., Sela, M., Chedid, L. 1978. *Ann. Immunol. Paris* 129:489–97
102. Mathé, G. 1971. *Adv. Cancer Res.* 14:1–36
103. Mathé, G., Thompson, R. B. 1973. *Dis. Colon Rectum* 16:341–57
104. McClelland, D. B. L., Samson, R. R., Parkin, D. M., Shearman, D. J. C. 1972. *Gut* 13:450–58
105. Merser, C., Sinay, P., Adam, A. 1975. *Biochem. Biophys. Res. Commun.* 66:1316–22
106. Metchnikoff, E. 1905. *Immunity in Infective Disease.* Transl. F. G. Binnie, London: Cambridge Univ. Press (From Russian)
107. Meyer, T. J., Ribi, E. E., Azuma, I., Zbar, B. 1974. *J. Natl. Cancer Inst.* 52:103–11
108. Migliore, D., Jollès, P. 1968. *FEBS Lett.* 2:7–9
109. Migliore-Samour, D., Floc'h, F., Maral, R., Werner, G. H., Jollès, P. 1977. *Immunology* 33:477–84
110. Migliore-Samour, D., Jollès, P. 1972. *FEBS Lett.* 25:301–4
111. Migliore-Samour, D., Koronzis, M., Jollès, P., Maral, R., Floc'h, F., Werner, G. H. 1974. *Immunol. Commun.* 3:593–603
112. Mitchison, N. A. 1964. *Proc. R. Soc. London Ser. B* 161:275–92
113. Modolell, M., Luckenbach, G. A., Parant, M., Munder, P. G. 1974. *J. Immunol.* 113:395–403
114. Morgan, I. M. 1946. *J. Bacteriol.* 51:614
115. Morgan, I. M. 1947. *J. Exp. Med.* 85:131–40
116. Mori, Y., Kato, K., Matsubara, T., Kotani, S. 1960. *Biken J.* 3:139–49
117. Nagai, Y., Akiyama, K., Kotani, S., Watanabe, Y., Shimono, T., Shiba, T., Kusumoto, S. 1978. *Cell. Immunol.* 35:168–72
118. Nagai, Y., Akiyama, K., Suzuki, K., Kotani, S., Watanabe, Y., Shimono, T., Shiba, T., Kusumoto, S., Ikuta, F., Takeda, S. 1978. *Cell. Immunol.* 35:158–67
119. Nauciel, C., Fleck, J., Martin, J-P., Mock, M. 1973. *C. R. Acad. Sci. Ser. D* 276:3499–3500
120. Nauciel, C., Fleck, J., Martin, J-P., Mock, M., Nguyen-Huy, H. 1974. *Eur. J. Immunol.* 4:352–56
121. Nauciel, C., Fleck, J., Mock, M., Martin, J-P. 1973. *C. R. Acad. Sci. Ser. D* 277:2841–44
122. Nguyen-Dang, T., Hayat, M., Chenu, E., Janot, M-M. 1973. *C. R. Acad. Sci. Ser. D* 277:1717–20
123. Nguyen-Dang, T., Janot, M-M. 1975. *C. R. Acad. Sci.* 281:1777–79
124. Nguyen-Huy, H., Nauciel, C., Wermuth, C-G. 1976. *Eur. J. Biochem.* 66:79–84
125. Parant, M. 1979. *Springer Semin. Immunopathol.* 2:101–18
126. Parant, M., Damais, C., Audibert, F., Parant, F., Chedid, L., Sache, E., Lefrancier, P., Choay, J., Lederer, E. 1978. *J. Infect. Dis.* 138:378–86
127. Parant, M., Parant, F., Chedid, L. 1978. *Proc. Natl. Acad. Sci. USA* 75:3395–99
128. Parant, M., Parant, F., Chedid, L., Yapo, A., Petit, J-F., Lederer, E. 1979. *Int. J. Immunopharmocol.* 1:35–41
129. Park, J. T. 1952. *J. Biol. Chem.* 194:897–904
130. Pearson, C. M., Wood, F. D. 1959. *Arthritis Rheum.* 2:440–59
131. Raffel, S., Arnaud, L. E., Dukes, D., Huang, J. S. 1949. *J. Exp. Med.* 90:53–71

132. Rolicka, M., Park, J. T. 1969. *J. Immunol.* 103:196–203
133. Rook, G. A. W., Stewart-Tull, D. E. S. 1976. *Immunology* 31:389–96
134. Rotta, J. 1975. *Z. Immunitaetsforsch. Exp. Klin. Immunol.* 149:230–44
135. Rotta, J., Bednář, B. 1969. *J. Exp. Med.* 130:31–45
136. Saito, R., Tanaka, A., Sugiyama, K., Azuma, I., Yamamura, Y., Kato, M., Goren, M. B. 1976. *Infect. Immun.* 13:776–81
137. Salton, M. R. J. 1960. In *The Bacteria* 1:97. New York: Academic
138. Salton, M. R. J. 1964. *The Bacterial Cell Wall.* London: Elsevier. 293 pp.
139. Schachenmayr, W., Heymer, B., Haferkamp, O. 1975. *Z. Immunitaetsforsch. Exp. Klin. Immunol.* 149:179–86
140. Schleifer, K. H., Kandler, O. 1972. *Bacteriol. Rev.* 36:407–77
141. Schleifer, K. H., Krause, R. M. 1971. *J. Biol. Chem.* 246:986–93
142. Schleifer, K. H., Seidl, H. P. 1977. See Ref. 62, pp. 339–43
143. Seibert, F. B., Soto-Figueroa, E., Du Four, E. H. 1955. *Am. Rev. Tuberc.* 71:704–21
144. Sjöquist, J., Movitz, J., Johansson, I-B., Hjelm, H. 1972. *Eur. J. Biochem.* 30:190–94
145. Specter, S., Friedman, H., Chedid, L. 1977. *Proc. Soc. Exp. Biol. Med.* 155:349–52
146. Stanton, M. F., ed. 1972. *Natl. Cancer Inst. Monogr. 35, Conf. Immunol. Carcinog.* Washington, DC: Natl. Inst. Health. 477 pp.
147. Stewart-Tull, D. E. S. 1981. In *The Biology of Mycobacteria,* ed. C. Ratledge, J. L. Stanford. London: Academic
148. Stewart-Tull, D. E. S., Davies, M., Jackson, D. M. 1977. *Immunology* 34:57–67
149. Stewart-Tull, D. E. S., Shimono, T., Kotani, S., Kato, M., Ogawa, Y., Yamamura, Y., Koga, T., Pearson, C. M. 1975. *Immunology* 29:1–15
150. Stewart-Tull, D. E. S., Shimono, T., Kotani, S., Knights, B. A. 1976. *Int. Arch. Allergy Appl. Immunol.* 52:118–28
151. Stewart-Tull, D. E. S., White, R. G. 1964. *J. Gen. Microbiol.* 34:43–49
152. Stewart-Tull, D. E. S., White, R. G. 1967. *Immunology* 12:349–59
153. Stewart-Tull, D. E. S., Wilkinson, P. C., White, R. G. 1965. *Immunology* 9:151–60
154. Takada, H., Kotani, S., Kusumoto, S., Tarumi, Y., Ikewaka, K., Shiba, T. 1977. *Biken J.* 20:81–85
155. Tanaka, A., Nagao, S., Saito, R., Kotani, S., Kusumoto, S., Shiba, T. 1977. *Biochem. Biophys. Res. Commun.* 77:621–27
156. Tanaka, A., Saito, R., Sugiyama, K., Morisaki, I., Kotani, S., Kusumoto, S., Shiba, T. 1977. *Infect Immun.* 15:332–34
157. Tanaka, A., Tanaka, K., Hagimoto, D., Sugiyama, K. 1967. *Int. Arch. Allergy Appl. Immunol.* 32:224–35
158. Timsit, J., Giroud, J-P., Chedid, L., Audibert, F., Parant, M. 1976. *J. Pharmacol.* 7:577–84
159. Tipper, D. J., Wright, A. 1979. In *The Bacteria,* ed. I. C. Gunsalus, N. L. Ornston, J. R. Sokatch, 7:291–426. New York: Academic
160. Toullet, F., Audibert, F., Chedid, L., Voisin, G. A. 1974. *Ann. Immunol. Paris* 125:901–10
161. Toullet, F., Audibert, F., Voisin, G. A., Chedid, L. 1977. *Ann. Immunol. Paris* 128:267–69
162. Uemiya, M., Sugimura, K., Kusama, T., Saiki, I., Yamawaki, M., Azuma, I., Yamamura, Y. 1979. *Infect Immun.* 24:83–89
163. Waksman, B. H., Adams, R. D. 1953. *J. Infect. Dis.* 93:21–27
164. Waksman, B. H., Pearson, C. M., Sharp, J. T. 1960. *J. Immunol.* 85:403–17
165. Werner, G. H., Maral, R., Floc'h, F., Migliore-Samour, D., Jollès, P. 1975. *Biomedicine* 22:440–52
166. Werner, G. H., Maral, R., Floc'h, F., Migliore-Samour, D., Jollès, P. 1974. *C. R. Acad. Sci.* 278:789–92
167. Westall, F. C., Thompson, M., Migliore-Samour, D., Jollès, P. 1975. *Eur. J. Immunol.* 5:504–5
168. Westall, F. C., Thompson, M., Migliore-Samour, D., Jollès, P. 1975. *Immunol. Commun.* 4:353–59
169. White, R. G. 1959. In *Mechanisms of hypersensitivity,* ed. J. H. Shaffer, G. A. LoGrippo, M. W. Chase. Churchill: London
170. White, R. G. 1965. In *Wound Healing,* ed. C. Illingworth, pp. 27–41. Churchill: London
171. White, R. G. 1965. In *Molecular and Cellular Basis of Antibody Formation,* ed. J. Sterzl, p. 71. Prague: Czech. Acad. Sci.
172. White, R. G. 1971. *Scott. Med. J.* 16:280–89
173. White, R. G., Bernstock, L., Johns, R.

G. S., Lederer, E. 1958. *Immunology* 1:54–66
174. White, R. G., Jollès, P., Samour, D., Lederer, E. 1964. *Immunology* 7: 158–71
175. White, R. G., Marshall, A. H. E. 1958. *Immunology* 1:111–22
176. Wolf, A., Kabat, E. A., Bezer, A. E. 1947. *J. Neuropathol. Exp. Neurol.* 6:333–57
177. Wood, F. D., Pearson, C. M., Tanaka, A. 1969. *Int. Arch. Allergy Appl. Immunol.* 35:456–67
178. Woodruff, M. F. A. 1978. See Ref. 56, pp. 573–80
179. Work, E. 1957. *Nature* 179:841–47
180. Wright, A., Tipper, D. J. 1979. See Ref. 159, pp. 427–85
181. Yamamura, Y., Azuma, I., Sugimura, K., Kusumoto, S., Shiba, T. 1976. *Proc. Jpn. Acad.* 52:58–62
182. Yamaura, Y., Azuma, I., Sugimura, K., Yamawaki, M., Uemiya, M., Kusumoto, S., Okada, S., Shiba, T. 1976. *Gann* 67:867–77
183. Yamamura, Y., Azuma, I., Sugimura, K., Yamawaki, M., Uemiya, M., Kusumoto, S., Okada, S., Shiba, T. 1977. *Proc. Jpn. Acad.* 53:63–66
184. Yarkoni, E., Wang, L., Bekierkunst, A. 1974. *Infect Immun.* 9:977–84
185. Yarkoni, E., Wang, L., Bekierkunst, A. 1977. *Infect Immun.* 16:1–8
186. Yokogawa, K., Kawata, S., Yoshimura, Y. 1972. *Agric. Biol. Chem.* 36:2055–65
187. Zbar, B., Bernstein, I. D., Rapp, H. J. 1971. *J. Natl. Cancer Inst.* 46:831–39
188. Zbar, B., Rapp, H. J., Ribi, E. E. 1972. *J. Natl. Cancer Inst.* 48:831–35
189. Zbar, B., Ribi, E., Meyer, T., Azuma, I., Rapp, H. J. 1974. *J. Natl. Cancer Inst.* 52:1571–77

Ann. Rev. Microbiol. 1980. 34:341–67

DISEASES OF HUMANS (OTHER THAN CHOLERA) CAUSED BY VIBRIOS[1]

❖1780

Paul A. Blake

Enteric Diseases Branch, Bacterial Diseases Division, Bureau of Epidemiology, Center for Disease Control, Atlanta, Georgia 30333

Robert E. Weaver and Dannie G. Hollis

Special Bacteriology Section, Clinical Bacteriology Branch, Bacteriology Division, Bureau of Laboratories, Center for Disease Control, Atlanta, Georgia 30333

CONTENTS

INTRODUCTION 342
ISOLATION AND IDENTIFICATION 342
Isolation 342
Identification 343
NON-O GROUP 1 *VIBRIO CHOLERAE* 346
Introduction 346
Clinical Features 346
Ecology 347
Pathogenicity 348
Epidemiology 350
VIBRIO PARAHAEMOLYTICUS 352
Introduction 352
Clinical Features 352
Ecology 353
Pathogenicity 353
Epidemiology 355
VIBRIO VULNIFICUS 357
Introduction 357
Clinical Features 358
Ecology 359
Pathogenicity 359
Epidemiology 359

VIBRIO ALGINOLYTICUS 360
Introduction 360
Clinical Features 360
Ecology 362
Pathogenicity 362
Epidemiology 362
OTHER VIBRIOS POSSIBLY PATHOGENIC FOR MAN 362
Group F (EF6) Vibrios 362
Vibrio metschnikovii (Enteric Group 16) 363
CONCLUSION 363

INTRODUCTION

Vibrio cholerae O-group 1, the organism that causes cholera, has historically been the vibrio of greatest interest to clinicians, microbiologists, public health officials, and epidemiologists. Other vibrios were simply dismissed as "non-agglutinable vibrios" (NAGs) (they did not agglutinate in *V. cholerae* O-group 1 antiserum) or as "non-cholera vibrios" (NCVs). Sometimes these terms were used to indicate all vibrios other than the epidemic strains that cause cholera; in other cases they were used to describe only those vibrios that were biochemically similar to the epidemic strains. Early attempts to create order in the chaotic world of the vibrios included the efforts of Heiberg (34) in 1936 to classify them into six groups by their fermentation of several sugars. However, not until microbiologists began to sort out separate species from the "wastebasket" NCV/NAG terminology did it become apparent that these vibrios included several species that are often pathogenic for humans and that have distinct clinical features, ecologic niches, pathogenic mechanisms, and epidemiologic characteristics. These species now include *V. parahaemolyticus, V. vulnificus, V. alginolyticus,* the non-O group 1 portion of the *V. cholerae* species, and two *Vibrio* species of uncertain pathogenicity for humans—group F (EF6) vibrios and *V. metschnikovii* (enteric group 16) (Table 1). The field is evolving rapidly, and there are still many basic questions to be answered. This review summarizes the current status of knowledge about disease associated with vibrios other than O-group 1 *V. cholerae.*

ISOLATION AND IDENTIFICATION

Isolation

Many cases of gastroenteritis caused by *Vibrio* species are probably missed by bacteriology laboratories that use only routine enteric media for primary isolation of agents of gastroenteritis. Both *Vibrio* species (*V. cholerae* and *V. parahaemolyticus*) that definitely cause gastroenteritis, as well as the other vibrios listed in Table 1, can be isolated from stool specimens by direct inoculation of thiosulfate citrate bile salts sucrose (TCBS) agar. Isolation

Table 1 Summary of features of diseases (other than cholera) caused by vibrios

Organism	Principal reservoirs	Disease	Principal vehicles of transmission	Host risk factors
V. cholerae (non-01)	Unknown ? coastal sea-water; ? fresh water; ? man, animals	Gastroenteritis	Food, water	None well-established
		Soft-tissue infections	? water	Wounds
		Septicemia	? seafoods	Cirrhosis and other underlying disease
V. parahaemolyticus	Coastal seawater, seafoods	Gastroenteritis	Seafoods	None well-established
		Soft-tissue infections	Seawater	Wounds
V. vulnificus	Probably coastal seawater and seafoods	Soft-tissue infections	Seawater	Wounds
		Septicemia	Seafoods	Cirrhosis and other underlying disease
V. alginolyticus	Seawater	Soft-tissue infections	Seawater	Wounds
		Ear infections	Seawater	Perforated tympanic membrane, earlier ear infections
Group F (EF6) *Vibrio*	Unknown	Gastroenteritis (?)	Unknown	Unknown
V. metschnikovii (enteric group (16)	Unknown	Gastroenteritis (?)	Unknown	Unknown

of the various *Vibrio* species from extraintestinal sites does not require use of selective media. Most of the media used to culture blood and wounds contain at least 0.5% NaCl, which supports growth of the halophilic organisms. Detailed descriptions of methods for isolating vibrios have been published (29, 31).

Identification

Vibrios are facultative anaerobes that are usually oxidase positive and that ferment glucose without forming gas (95). With the exception of *V. metschnikovii* (56), *Vibrio* species can be differentiated from Enterobacteriaceae by the oxidase reaction. However, the oxidase reaction should be tested on growth from nonselective media because false-negative reactions have been obtained in tests of growth of *V. cholerae* (68) and *Aeromonas hydrophila* (74) from selective media.

V. cholerae can be differentiated from the other species of *Vibrio* and from group F by its lack of a requirement for more than trace amounts of NaCl in growth media. If an organism must have NaCl, it will not grow in a medium such as methyl red–Voges-Proskauer (MR-VP) broth that does not contain NaCl, but it will grow well on most of the commonly used media such as Trypticase soy agar or heart infusion agar. The requirement for NaCl can be confirmed by obtaining growth on NaCl-deficient media to which NaCl has been added in a final concentration of 0.5 to 1%.

Other oxidase-positive organisms found in clinical specimens, which, like *V. cholerae*, ferment glucose and do not require added NaCl in growth media, include *Aeromonas hydrophila, Plesiomonas shigelloides,* and *Chromobacterium violaceum;* all will grow on MacConkey agar. *V. cholerae* can be differentiated from these species by the arginine dihydrolase reaction (Table 2). Additional characteristics of *V. cholerae* are listed in Table 3.

The NaCl-requiring *Vibrio* species can be divided into two groups by the arginine dihydrolase and ornithine decarboxylase reactions. *V. parahaemolyticus, V. alginolyticus,* and *V. vulnificus* are arginine negative and ornithine positive or variable. *V. anguillarum* (a species common in seawater but not known to be pathogenic for humans), *V. metschnikovii,* and group F are arginine positive or variable and ornithine negative (Table 3). To obtain proper dihydrolase and decarboxylase reactions in the Moeller medium, NaCl must be added to a final concentration of at least 0.5 to 1% (35, 86).

The most useful characteristics for differentiating *V. parahaemolyticus, V. alginolyticus,* and *V. vulnificus* are growth in 10% NaCl; production of acid from lactose, sucrose, and arabinose; and results of O-nitrophenyl-β-D-galactopyranoside (ONPG) and Voges-Proskauer tests (Table 3). The Voges-Proskauer medium must be supplemented with NaCl to a final concentration of 3%.

The most useful reactions for differentiating *V. anguillarum* and group F are acid from arabinose and gas from glucose. *V. anguillarum* is negative in both reactions. Group F strains produce acid from arabinose and vary in production of gas from glucose.

Table 2 Differentiation of *Vibrio cholerae* from three other oxidase-positive, glucose-fermenting, nonhalophilic organisms[a]

Organisms	Reactions: L-lysine decarboxylase	L-arginine dihydrolase	L-ornithine decarboxylase
Vibrio cholerae	+[b]	–	+
Aeromonas hydrophila	–[c]	+	–
Plesiomonas shigelloides	+	+	+
Chromobacterium violaceum	–	+	–

[a] Based on data from Special Bacteriology Section, Center for Disease Control, and Hugh & Sakazaki (41).
[b] + = 90% or more positive at 48 hr.
[c] – = 0–9% positive at 48 hr.

Table 3 Characteristics of vibrio species and group F[a]

Test	*Vibrio cholerae*	*Vibrio parahaemolyticus*	*Vibrio alginolyticus*	*Vibrio vulnificus*	*Vibrio anguillarum*[b]	Group F	*Vibrio metschnikovii*[b]
Growth in 0% NaCl	+[c]	–[d]	–	–	–	–	–
Lysine decarboxylase	+	+	+	+	v[e]	–	v
Arginine dihydrolase	–	–	–	–	v	+	+
Ornithine decarboxylase	+	+	v	+	–	–	–
Growth in 10% NaCl	–	–	+	–	–	–	–
Lactose, acid	v	–	–	+ or (+)[f]	–	–	v
ONPG	+[b]	–	–	+	v	+	v
Sucrose, acid	+	–	+	–	+	+	+
Voges-Proskauer	v	–	+	–	v	v	+
Arabinose, acid	–	+	–	–	–	+[b]	–
Gas from glucose	–	–	–	–	–	v	–
Oxidase	+	+	+	+	+	+	–
Nitrate reduction	+	+	+	+	+	+	–
Glucose, acid	+	+	+	+	+	+	+
Maltose, acid	+	+	+	+	v	+	+
Mannitol, acid	+	+	+	v	+	+	+
Xylose, acid	–	–	–	–	–	–	–
Catalase	+	+	+	+	+	v	+
Indole	+	+	+	+	v	v	v
Urease	–	–	–	–	–	–	–
Sensitivity to 0/129[g]							
10 μg	+	–	–	+	+	–	+
150 μg	+	+	+	+	+	+	+

[a]Data, except where noted, from the Special Bacteriology Section, CDC: *V. cholerae,* 82 strains; *V. parahaemolyticus,* 160 strains; *V. alginolyticus,* 58 strains; *V. vulnificus,* 47 strains; group F, 25 strains.

[b]Data from Lee et al (56).

[c]+ = 90% or more positive at 48 hr.

[d]– = less than 10% positive at 48 hr.

[e]v = 10–89% positive at 48 hr.

[f]+ or (+) = 90% or more positive or delayed positive, 3–7 days.

[g]2,4-diamino-6,7-diisopropyl pteridine phosphate; data from J. V. Lee, personal communication, March 7, 1980.

Reactions within heavily lined boxes are considered the most important differential characteristics as indicated in the text.

V. metschnikovii is differentiated from *V. anguillarum* and group F by the fact that it is oxidase negative and does not reduce nitrate.

NON-O GROUP 1 *VIBRIO CHOLERAE*

Introduction

Vibrios that are biochemically similar to the epidemic strains of *V. cholerae* but do not agglutinate in *V. cholerae* O-group 1 antiserum have been referred to in the past as non-agglutinable vibrios (NAGs) or as non-cholera vibrios (NCVs). They are now included in the species *V. cholerae* (40), and in this review they will be referred to as non-O group 1 *V. cholerae* or non-O1 *V. cholerae.* These organisms have caused outbreaks and sporadic cases of gastrointestinal illness and in a few instances have been isolated from persons with extraintestinal disease.

Clinical Features

The characteristic features of gastrointestinal illness caused by non-O1 *V. cholerae* cannot be described with any confidence; two or more syndromes may be associated with these organisms. There have been only two reported outbreaks in which the clinical features were described. In an outbreak in Czechoslovakia in 1965 (1), 100% of the patients had diarrhea, 25% had vomiting, 11% had low-grade fever, and none had blood or mucus in their stools. The illness lasted 1–2 days. In an outbreak among airplane passengers arriving in Australia in 1973, most had diarrhea, vomiting, and severe abdominal cramps, and a few had low-grade fever (22). The illness usually lasted 18–24 hr.

In the reported descriptions of sporadic cases, one cannot be certain that the organism isolated caused the illness. In 1965 McIntyre et al (59) reported on 19 persons with sporadic cases of diarrheal illness in Bangladesh; stool cultures of these patients yielded a heavy growth of non-O1 *V. cholerae.* Some of the patients had severe dehydrating diarrhea, and 50% required intravenous fluid therapy. In 1979 Spira et al in Bangladesh (102) published a detailed description of 14 cases of diarrheal illness in adults from whom non-O1 *V. cholerae* were the only potential pathogens isolated. In addition to diarrhea, the patients had vomiting (100%), abdominal pain (71%), temperatures higher than 100°F (43%), and muscle cramps (21%). The mean duration of diarrhea was 42.1 hr, the mean stool volume was 60 cc/kg, and quantitative cultures of the patients' stools found a mean of 3–4 $\times 10^8$ vibrios/ml. None of the stools studied from the 14 had more than 5 fecal leukocytes/hpf, and only 1 had more than 5 fecal red blood cells/hpf.

In reports from the United States, however, blood and mucus were often found in stools. Hughes et al (43) reported on 13 persons with sporadic cases of diarrhea in the United States from whom non-O1 *V. cholerae* were isolated; associated symptoms included abdominal cramps (92%), nausea (77%), vomiting (69%), chills (64%), fever (58%), mucus in stools (30%), and bloody stools (8%). The illness lasted an average of 7 days. Since these cases were reported to the Center for Disease Control (CDC), they probably represented the most severe end of a spectrum of disease. Two of three persons subsequently reported on from Florida (18) had bloody stools. Thus, while some persons with non-O1 *V. cholerae* gastroenteritis have a severe dehydrating cholera-like illness, many have fever and some have bloody diarrhea, both of which are unusual for adults with cholera.

Treatment of severe dehydrating non-O1 *V. cholerae* gastroenteritis should focus on oral and/or intravenous rehydration. Antibiotics (particularly tetracycline) have been shown to decrease the severity and duration of cholera, but the value of antibiotic therapy of non-O1 *V. cholerae* gastroenteritis has not been determined.

In contrast to toxigenic *V. cholerae* O1 strains that do not cause extraintestinal disease, at least 18 instances of isolating non-O1 *V. cholerae* from human sources other than feces have been reported (2, 28, 33, 43, 79, 84). The sources have included bile or gallbladder (two), blood (five, including a patient with isolates from blood, a wound, and cerebrospinal fluid), infected wounds (four), ears (four), sputum (two), an appendix (one), peritoneal fluid (one), and cerebrospinal fluid (one). Although the pathogenic significance of the organisms is uncertain in some of these cases, they appear to have had a pathogenic role in at least seven cases—the five persons with septicemias (43, 79, 84) and two with wound infections (43). Those with septicemias had preexisting underlying disease [cirrhosis (two), kwashiorkor, leukemia, and severe peripheral vascular disease]. The ear infections included three cases of otitis media and one of otitis externa.

Ecology

Non-O1 *V. cholerae* strains are widely distributed in the environment in Europe, Asia, and the United States. They have been found in sewage, sewage-contaminated surface water, estuarine waters (both sewage-contaminated and apparently free from fecal contamination), seafoods, and animals (9, 88, 94).

Studies of the ecology of non-O1 *V. cholerae* in Germany, the United States, and England have generally demonstrated that the organisms are found in brackish surface waters, are more numerous during the warmer months, and are not necessarily associated with sewage contamination. They appear to be autochthonous estuarine bacterial species. In German rivers, there were more non-O1 *V. cholerae* in the summer, and the organisms were associated with water that had a pH greater than 7.5 and a salinity of 0.01% (100 mg NaCl/liter) or greater (70). In another German study, the organisms were detected in 22% of 100-ml samples of seawater collected from the Baltic Sea over a 3-year period and were present even when the coliform count was very low (69). The incidence was lowest during the first two quarters of the year (15%) and highest during the third quarter (36%). In the United States, Kaper et al detected non-O1 *V. cholerae* organisms of many serotypes throughout much of Chesapeake Bay (51). Most came from water with a salinity of 0.4–1.7%; they were not apparently correlated with the presence of fecal coliforms and were found throughout the year in low numbers, generally 1–10 cells per liter. In England, Bashford et al (6) found large numbers of non-O1 *V. cholerae* in surface waters in Kent, including a drainage ditch where the possibility of sewage contamination was considered to be negligible. As in Germany, more of the organisms were apparently present in the summer. Thus, at least some non-O1 *V. cholerae* appear to be free-living in the environment, but the pathogenicity of such free-living strains for humans is unknown.

Pathogenicity

The most comprehensive study of the pathogenic mechanisms of non-O1 *V. cholerae* was performed by Spira et al (102). They used a battery of assays to characterize the biologic activity of 110 isolates from patients with diarrheal illness, persons with non-diarrheal illness, and the environment. These assays were (*a*) production of diarrhea and death in the infant rabbit by whole culture, (*b*) ability to cause fluid accumulation in the rabbit ileal loop using 1. whole culture and 2. culture filtrates, (*c*) rabbit skin permeability activity, (*d*) induction of morphologic changes in Chinese hamster ovary (CHO) and adrenal cells, and (*e*) induction of fluid accumulation in the suckling mouse assay by culture filtrates. Four patterns of biologic activity were observed:

1. Production of a cholera toxin (CT)-like toxin [positive infant rabbit, ileal loop (both whole culture and filtrate), rabbit skin, and CHO/adrenal cell assays].
2. Production of a heat-stable toxin [positive ileal loop (both whole culture and filtrate) and infant mouse assays].
3. "Enteritis" (positive infant rabbit and/or ileal loop with whole culture assays) without production of either toxin.
4. No activity in any of these assays.

Spira & Daniel (101) subsequently compared the patterns of biologic activity of 18 strains from feces of persons with diarrheal illness in Bangladesh and 18 presumably free-living strains from relatively unpolluted portions of the aquatic environment in Bangladesh. All of the fecal isolates had some activity in these assays (33% produced CT-like toxin and 67% were in the "enteritis" group), and 67% of the environmental isolates had no activity (33% were in the "enteritis" group, and none produced CT-like toxin) ($p < .0001$, Chi-square test). Thus, there were considerable differences between human and environmental strains, but there was also some overlap in the "enteritis" group. None of these 36 strains had heat-stable toxin-like activity, but 2 strains from Chesapeake Bay discussed in Spira et al's earlier report (102) had such activity.

The CT-like toxin produced by some strains of non-O1 *V. cholerae* is very similar but not identical to CT (101, 114, 115). Some strains appear to produce more than one toxin (115).

The ability of non-O1 *V. cholerae* to produce CT-like toxin appears to be clinically relevant. Spira & Daniel found that 6 patients with toxigenic isolates had more severe illness than 12 with nontoxigenic isolates: the weight loss of members of the former group was greater (mean 5.6 vs 1.7%), their admission serum specific gravity was higher, their diarrhea lasted longer (mean 50 vs 35 hr), and their stool volume was greater (mean 103 vs 41 cc/kg) (101). Significant antitoxin titer rises were found in two of three patients with toxigenic isolates, but none were found in the eight patients with nontoxigenic isolates ($p = 0.055$) (Fisher's 2-tailed exact test).

Using the rabbit brush border assay, Spira et al (102) found that, in the 18 strains from persons with diarrhea in Bangladesh, the mean number of vibrios adhering per brush border was roughly but significantly related to the stool volume of the patient from whom the strain was isolated. Toxigenic isolates demonstrated relatively high brush border adherence.

A number of investigators have described a hemorrhagic effect of filtrates from some non-O1 *V. cholerae* in the skin of guinea pigs and rabbits (72). This hemorrhagic factor can usually be diluted sufficiently to permit detection of the vascular permeability factor (PF) in rabbit skin tests. Its significance for human disease is unknown.

Robins-Browne et al have described a non-O1 *V. cholerae* isolate from the blood of a child in South Africa with fever but no gastroenteritis (84). This organism was positive in the CHO cell assay and positive in the rabbit skin test. Although the organism was not invasive in the Sereny test, it invaded the rabbit ileal mucosa when the ligated rabbit ileal loop test was performed. Furthermore, it was cultured from the blood, liver, and spleen of two rabbits enterally infected with the organism. We do not know what proportion of non-O1 *V. cholerae* strains have this invasive property or its significance for human disease.

The studies by Spira and others demonstrate that non-O1 *V. cholerae* can produce diarrhea not only by producing toxin similar to that produced by *V. cholerae* O1 but also by other as yet ill-defined mechanisms. Currently, there is no assay (other than human feeding experiments) or group of assays with which to determine confidently the potential of a given strain to be an enteric pathogen for humans.

Epidemiology

Non-O1 *V. cholerae* have been isolated from the stools of persons with diarrheal illnesses who were infected in Asia, Africa, Europe, North America, and South America. The proportion of diarrheal illness associated with these organisms in these areas is unknown. No non-O1 *V. cholerae* were isolated from 385 persons with diarrhea in Mexico City in 1966–1967 (106), although they have been isolated from travelers returning from Mexico. In Bangladesh, non-O1 *V. cholerae* were isolated on direct plating from 3% (34/1120) of persons hospitalized at the Cholera Research Laboratory because of diarrheal illness during the early 1960s and from only .01% (1/6951) of well persons (59). Gastrointestinal disease caused by non-O1 *V. cholerae* probably occurs in many countries where it has not been reported. Outbreaks and sporadic cases have occurred, but large epidemics and pandemics like those caused by *V. cholerae* O1 have not been reported.

The non-fecal isolates from humans have been reported from the United States, Europe, and Africa (2, 28, 33, 43, 79, 84).

Little is known about the seasonality of non-O1 *V. cholerae* disease. In the United States, most domestically acquired cases occur during the warmer months.

Studies of sporadic cases of diarrheal illness associated with isolation of non-O1 *V. cholerae* from stools in the United States (1972–1979) have found that the patients frequently have a history of consumption of mollusks, especially raw oysters; the incubation period is usually less than 48 hr. Oysters were shown epidemiologically to be the vehicle of transmission on the only occasion when a case-control study was done (18); in that instance, at least some of the oysters came from beds with elevated fecal coliform counts. Mollusks are theoretically a good vehicle of transmission because they are filter-feeding organisms and can concentrate bacteria.

Studies of three outbreaks [Czechoslovakia (1), the Sudan (110), and Australia (22)] showed that the vehicle of transmission was food in two instances (potatoes and an egg and asparagus salad) and water (polluted well water) in one. The incubation periods in the three outbreaks were 20–30 hr, less than four days, and 5–38 (mean of 11.5) hr.

Most likely, transmission is almost exclusively by contaminated food or water. In the outbreak in the Sudan in 1968 (110), despite poor sanitary conditions and large numbers of infected persons, no further cases occurred four days after the well suspected of causing the epidemic was closed. No secondary cases were observed and no person-to-person transmission was evident. Non-O1 *V. cholerae* organisms multiply readily in a variety of foods and thus can reach the presumably high numbers needed to cause infection (83).

The source of infection is unknown for most cases of extraintestinal disease. Some persons have a history of recent exposure to seawater.

The reservoir of non-O1 *V. cholerae* strains that cause human disease is unknown. The organisms appear to survive and multiply in the environment, but whether or not such free-living strains are pathogenic for man is unknown. Humans may be the principal reservoir, and the organisms in food and water that cause disease may have come from an infected human. A human chronic carrier state for non-O1 *V. cholerae* may occur; in the United States the organism has been isolated from bile (43), raising the possibility of chronic biliary tract infections, and a study of sailors arriving in the Soviet Union showed that the carrier state could last 60 or more days (116).

A question of considerable epidemiologic significance is whether "transformation" of somatic antigen can occur in the natural environment, i.e. can non-O1 *V. cholerae* become *V. cholerae* O1? This was claimed in a preliminary report (8), but no other investigators have been able to reproduce such changes (32), and no such changes have been known to occur in nature.

Two serotyping systems for non-O1 *V. cholerae* based on the O antigen are widely used. In both systems, the epidemic strain of *V. cholerae* is designated O-group 1. The system developed by Sakazaki et al included 60 serotypes by 1976 (96). The system developed by Smith & Goodner at the Vibrio Research Laboratory (VRL) recognized 72 serotypes by 1979 (98). Studies at CDC showed that each system included some serotypes not included in the other, and many serotypes in each system appeared to correspond to serotypes in the other (23). Neither system has thus far determined any marked differences in the serotypes of isolates from human and non-human sources (89, 98). However, comprehensive systematic studies on this subject have not yet been published.

In 1936, Heiberg (34) classified vibrios into six groups by their fermentation of sucrose, mannose, and arabinose; two more groups were added by Smith & Goodner in 1965 (99). Non-O1 *V. cholerae* meeting the minimal criteria for vibrios fall into at least four of the eight groups (98). There is no apparent correlation between serotypes of the non-O1 *V. cholerae* and their Heiberg groups (98). Since the serotyping systems were developed,

Heiberg grouping has been of little practical value in studying non-O1 *V. cholerae.*

VIBRIO PARAHAEMOLYTICUS

Introduction

V. parahaemolyticus was first recognized as a cause of food poisoning in Japan in the early 1950s. In the past decade it has been found to be an important cause of diarrheal illness in many parts of the world, and it has occasionally been associated with extraintestinal disease.

Clinical Features

Two clinical syndromes have been described for patients with *V. parahaemolyticus*-associated gastroenteritis. The cardinal manifestation of the most commonly described syndrome is watery diarrhea. In eight *V. parahaemolyticus* outbreaks in the United States (3), the clinical manifestations included diarrhea (98%), abdominal cramps (82%), nausea (71%), vomiting (52%), headache (42%), fever (27%), and chills (24%). Temperature rarely exceeded 38.9°C. The illness was usually self-limited, with a median duration of three days. In severe cases, dehydration, hypotension, and acidosis may occur (58). A dysenteric syndrome with mucoid or sanguinous stools has been described in several countries. In Calcutta, India, one study showed that one quarter of 60 hospitalized patients with *V. parahaemolyticus*-associated gastroenteritis had blood and mucus in their stools (97). All eight persons involved in an outbreak in Bangladesh (42) had liquid stools, severe abdominal cramps, nausea, and vomiting. The six most severely ill persons had gross blood in their stools; on microscopic exam, these stools contained numerous red blood cells and polymorphonuclear leukocytes. The median duration of illness was 2.5 days.

Although severe cases of *V. parahaemolyticus*-associated gastroenteritis requiring hospitalization do occur, the illness is usually mild or moderate. Deaths have not been reported in the United States; however, in Japan, of 81,534 cases reported between 1965 and 1974, 31 (0.04%) deaths were recorded (62). Most patients do not require antimicrobial therapy, but those with severe or protracted cases may benefit from treatment with tetracycline (4).

The first published indication that *V. parahaemolyticus* might cause extraintestinal infections appeared in 1969, when Twedt et al reported that 14 strains of halophilic vibrios isolated from extraintestinal sites of patients in the United States and submitted to CDC were *V. parahaemolyticus* or closely related organisms (105). Zen-Yoji et al subsequently found that 6 of the 14 organisms were indeed *V. parahaemolyticus* (111). By 1976 CDC had received 18 *V. parahaemolyticus* isolates from extraintestinal sites (35). Between 1970 and mid-1979, at least nine case reports of extraintestinal infections associated with isolation of *V. parahaemolyticus* were published (14, 60, 73, 78, 85, 103, 108, 113). However, two of these (85, 113) were subsequently reported to be caused by *V. vulnificus* (lactose-fermenting *Vibrio*) (35, 109).

In the seven reported instances in which *V. parahaemolyticus* was isolated from extraintestinal sites, five isolates were from wounds of the feet or legs, one was from an ear, and one was from blood. The patient with septicemia had preexisting underlying disease (cirrhosis); he had diarrhea followed by chills and fever, and three blood cultures all yielded *V. parahaemolyticus* (103). The pathogenic significance of the organism in some of the other cases is uncertain, but it probably caused some of the illnesses. It was isolated from pus from an infected foot laceration in pure culture (60) and from synovial fluid from a patient with synovitis of the knee who had suffered a puncture wound near the patella (78). All of the patients recovered except for the one with septicemia; he died of hepatic failure, which probably was not directly related to his infection.

Ecology

V. parahaemolyticus is part of the normal flora of estuarine and other coastal waters throughout most of the world. It has been isolated from seawater, sea mud, or seafoods in Asia, North America, Australia, New Zealand, Africa, Hawaii, and Europe. It has also been isolated from fresh water and freshwater fish in India (24).

V. parahaemolyticus absorbs onto chitin and onto copepods (minute crustacean animals) (49); most of the organisms in water are associated with zooplankton. In three temperate regions—Japan (64), Korea (19), and the United States (48)—large numbers of *V. parahaemolyticus* organisms can be isolated from seawater in summer but not in winter. However, the organism can be isolated from sediment even in winter (48). *V. parahaemolyticus* apparently passes the winter in sediment, is released from the bottom in the spring and becomes attached to zooplankton, and then proliferates as the water temperature rises (50).

Pathogenicity

In 1968, Sakazaki et al (90) reported that the ability of *V. parahaemolyticus* to cause hemolysis on Wagatsuma agar (the Kanagawa phenomenon) was associated with gastrointestinal illness. They found that 96.5% of isolates from patients with diarrhea were hemolytic (Kanagawa-positive), compared to only 1% of isolates from seafoods and seawater. Subsequent experience has confirmed this very close association between Kanagawa positivity and gastrointestinal illness. However, isolates from extraintestinal infections tested at CDC have been found to be Kanagawa-negative. To our knowledge, the only reported extraintestinal isolate that proved to be Kanagawa-positive was from a patient with septicemia whose illness began with diarrhea (103).

The Kanagawa reaction is caused by a heat-stable direct hemolysin with a molecular weight of approximately 42,000 (38). The heat-stable hemolysin is cytotoxic to human FL cells in cell culture (92), cardiotoxic in vivo for mice (36), and cardiotoxic in vitro for mouse heart cells (36). Although changes have been described in the electrocardiograms of acutely ill patients (39), the clinical importance of the heat-stable hemolysin is unknown. Live *V. parahaemolyticus* does not induce intestinal fluid accumulation in infant rabbits (15). Sakazaki et al (91) found that 14 (88%) of 16 living cultures of Kanagawa-positive strains produced dilation and inflammation in the ligated rabbit ileal loop test, whereas only seven (22%) of 32 Kanagawa-negative strains were positive in the test. Sections of the gut loop of a positive test revealed mucosal disarray with necrosis, ulceration, and hemorrhage. Although they and others found that cell-free filtrates from both Kanagawa-positive and Kanagawa-negative strains concentrated by lyophilization produced positive rabbit ileal loops, this response has been attributed to the high (>20%) concentrations of NaCl produced by the concentration method (45). Culture filtrates and whole-cell lysates did not produce positive adult rabbit ileal loop responses when tested by Johnson & Calia (45).

Donta & Smith (25) found that filtrates from cultures of *V. parahaemolyticus* strains from patients with gastroenteritis did not effect either morphologic changes or steroidogenesis in Y-1 adrenal cells. However, Honda et al detected a heat-labile factor in culture filtrates of Kanagawa-positive *V. parahaemolyticus* organisms that produces a reaction in CHO cells similar to that produced by cholera toxin (37). The reason for the disparate findings is unclear.

There is some evidence that *V. parahaemolyticus* invades the intestinal tissue of humans; ulceration of the rectosigmoid was observed in one US patient (13), and leukocytes and blood have been observed in the stools of patients in Bangladesh (42). Kanagawa-positive, but not Kanagawa-negative, organisms can penetrate the intestinal epithelium of infant rabbits (15). All are Sereny test negative (15). Carruthers observed that while both Kanagawa-positive and Kanagawa-negative *V. parahaemolyticus* can cause cytotoxic effects on HeLa cell cultures, Kanagawa-positive organisms act more rapidly (16). Nonviable preparations have no effect on HeLa cells.

Ohashi et al (71) developed a reversed passive hemagglutination test which they found to be a more sensitive method than Wagatsuma agar to detect the heat-stable hemolysin responsible for the Kanagawa reaction. They found that all Kanagawa-positive isolates from humans with diarrheal disease, 32 (51%) of 63 Kanagawa-negative isolates from feces of humans with diarrhea, and none of 96 Kanagawa-negative isolates from seafoods and kitchen swabs produced the hemolysin.

Carruthers found that Kanagawa-positive *V. parahaemolyticus* adheres rapidly to HeLa cells and to human fetal intestinal (HFI) cells, whereas Kanagawa-negative *V. parahaemolyticus* does not adhere to HeLa cells and adheres to HFI cells at a much slower rate (17).

Although it is possible to detect antihemolysin antibodies (antibodies against the thermostable direct hemolysin produced by Kanagawa-positive strains of *V. parahaemolyticus*) in specimens from many patients 5–10 days after admission, many patients with typical cases have no increase in titer, and this test is not currently used for diagnosing illness (67).

Despite extensive study of the pathogenic mechanisms of *V. parahaemolyticus,* we do not yet understand how it causes gastrointestinal disease in humans.

Epidemiology

During the last decade, *V. parahaemolyticus*-associated gastroenteritis has been reported in North America, Central America, Africa, Europe, and Asia. Extraintestinal infections have been reported in North America, Europe, Asia, and Australia. In only a few countries have surveys given any indication of the importance of the organism as a cause of gastrointestinal illness (63). In Calcutta, India, in a one-year study of 3,433 diarrheal stools, *V. parahaemolyticus* was isolated from 378 (11%). In two studies in Indonesia, the organism was isolated from 2.6 and 3.7% of patients with gastroenteritis. In Thailand, 10.7% (850/7930) of stools from patients with diarrhea at an infectious disease hospital yielded the organism. In Vietnam, *V. parahaemolyticus* was isolated from 8.5–15% of patients with diarrheal illnesses. In Korea, 3 (1.5%) of 199 persons with enteric infections had the organism isolated from their stools. In Japan (1965–1974), 24% (81, 534/345,738) of reported cases of food poisoning were attributed to *V. parahaemolyticus.* The organism was isolated from only 0.3% of 2,000 healthy Japanese (112). In the United States, except in occasional large outbreaks (3, 55), *V. parahaemolyticus* is rarely isolated from patients with gastroenteritis; however, the incidence of the disease is unknown because most laboratories do not use culture media appropriate for isolating vibrios from stools.

Marked seasonality of the disease has been noted in the United States (3), Thailand (63), and Japan (63). In the United States and Japan, outbreaks of the disease occur almost exclusively during the warm summer and early fall months; in Bangkok, Thailand, the proportion of persons with diarrheal illness from whom *V. parahaemolyticus* is isolated varies from 3.9% in the relatively cool month of January to 22.6% in the warm month of September. This seasonal variation may reflect both enhanced opportunity for *V. parahaemolyticus* to multiply in unrefrigerated foods during the summer months and the increased prevalence of *V. parahaemolyticus* in the environment during warm weather. Extraintestinal isolations also appear to occur during the warm months: the four cases with known dates occurred in June–October.

V. parahaemolyticus—associated gastroenteritis appears to be transmitted exclusively by food, usually raw or cooked seafood, although sometimes other foods presumably cross-contaminated by raw seafood have been thought to transmit the infection. In India, a study showed that one third of 60 patients with *V. parahaemolyticus*-associated gastroenteritis denied having eaten fish or shellfish during the previous seven days (97).

Several mechanisms have contributed to *V. parahaemolyticus*-associated food poisoning (3). In outbreaks involving raw seafoods, food naturally contaminated with small numbers of vibrios was held unrefrigerated long enough to allow organisms to proliferate to very large numbers. Outbreaks involving boiled shrimp have been attributed to failure to cook the shrimp at temperatures high enough to kill vibrios. Other outbreaks have been attributed to contamination of cooked seafood by raw seafood, followed by inadequate refrigeration.

The generation time of *V. parahaemolyticus* has been reported to be as short as nine minutes under ideal conditions (52), enabling the organism to multiply very rapidly in mishandled foods and quickly reach the rather large infecting dose; the ID_{50} has been determined in volunteer studies to be about 10^5–10^7 organisms for persons given antacids (93). The optimum temperature for growth is 37°C, although it will grow well at 25–44°C.

Five of the six persons with wound and ear infections had a history of recent exposure to seawater, and the sixth person was in an airplane crash near a seacoast. No history of exposure was given for the person with diarrhea and septicemia (103), who was presumably infected by the oral route.

The principal reservoir for *V. parahaemolyticus* is seafoods and seawater, usually in coastal areas. However, in Calcutta, India, *V. parahaemolyticus* has been isolated from river water, pond water, and freshwater fish (24).

Although persons with asymptomatic infections have been found, there are no reports of long-term carriage of the organism, and there is no evidence that infected foodhandlers have been a source of the organism in disease outbreaks.

In most common-source outbreaks of *V. parahaemolyticus*-associated gastrointestinal disease in Asia and the United States in which patients did not have bloody stools, the incubation period has ranged from 4 to 96 hr, with a mode of 15 hr (3, 66). However, the incubation period may be shorter for the dysenteric illness caused by *V. parahaemolyticus;* in a small outbreak in Bangladesh, incubation periods ranged from 20 min to 9 hr, with a median of 2.5 hr (42). The reason for the apparently shorter incubation period for dysenteric illness has not been explained. For extraintestinal infections, the incubation period is usually one to two days (12).

By 1976, 12 O-antigens (heat-stable somatic antigens) and 59 K-antigens (capsular or envelope antigens) had been identified (65). Many different serotypes have been found throughout the world, and the most common serotypes vary from place to place. No particular serotypes have been strongly associated with the Kanagawa phenomenon or with human illness. Thus, for practical purposes, determining *V. parahaemolyticus* serotypes is useful chiefly in epidemiologic studies of outbreaks.

VIBRIO VULNIFICUS

Introduction

Beginning in 1964, the Special Bacteriology Section of CDC occasionally received isolates from extraintestinal sites that were at first thought to be variants of *V. parahaemolyticus* but were later differentiated from *V. parahaemolyticus* by several biochemical reactions, including fermentation of lactose, and were referred to as the lactose-fermenting (L+) *Vibrio* (35, 109). This *Vibrio* has been shown by deoxyribonucleic acid reassociation experiments to be a separate species (20). Baumann et al studied 14 L+ *Vibrio* strains from CDC, assigned them to a group they designated C-2 (7), and then named them *Beneckea vulnifica* (82). This name has not been widely used, and Farmer (27) has proposed that the species be called *Vibrio vulnificus,* the name that we will use here. By mid-1979, reports of 41 cases of *V. vulnificus*-associated infection had been published (11, 30, 57, 61, 85, 104, 113), including two cases that were initially identified as *V. parahaemolyticus*-associated infections (85, 113) and four that were identified only as halophilic vibrios (cases 1 and 2 of Reference 104; cases 2 and 3 of Reference 30).

Clinical Features

Data for 39 of the cases mentioned above were included in our description of the clinical characteristics and epidemiology of *V. vulnificus* isolates submitted to CDC between 1964 and 1977 (11). The cases had two distinctly different clinical presentations. Fifteen illnesses began with signs of infection in a preexisting wound or ulcer (the "wound-infection" group). Twenty-four illnesses initially had no apparent primary focus of infection and began with systemic symptoms suggestive of septicemia—the abrupt onset of chills, fever, and/or prostration (the "primary-septicemia" group).

The patients with wound infections rapidly developed swelling and erythema around a recent wound or, in one case, a chronic stasis ulcer. The lesions often extended to involve adjacent areas, vesicles or bullae appeared (33%), and necrosis (27%) sometimes ensued. *V. vulnificus* was isolated from all cultured wounds. Some patients had fever (80%) and chills (46%) after signs of a wound infection appeared, and three had positive blood cultures. One third of the patients with wound infections had underlying disease—diabetes (two), alcoholism (one), chronic congestive heart failure and stasis ulcers (one), and leukemia and diabetes (one). All were treated with antibiotics to which *V. vulnificus* is susceptible (35), and many had their lesions debrided or incised and drained. Most were recovering within several days, and only one death occurred; the patient with leukemia developed lymphangitis, bacteremia, high fever, and shock, and died 36 hr after onset.

The patients with "primary septicemia" usually first noticed malaise followed by chills (82%), fever (92%), and prostration. Shortly after the onset of chills and fever, some had vomiting (21%) and diarrhea (17%). One third had hypotension (systolic blood pressure $\leq$ 80 mm Hg) at some point in the first 12 hr after admission. Metastatic cutaneous lesions appeared in 75%, usually within 36 hr after the onset of illness. Most commonly, erythematous or ecchymotic areas appeared on one or more extremities (usually the lower), bullae or vesicles formed, and necrotic ulcers later formed. A few patients had generalized papular or maculopapular eruptions. *V. vulnificus* was isolated from the blood of most (83%) of the patients with the primary septicemia syndrome; it was also isolated from the lesions of many (56%) of those with secondary cutaneous lesions, suggesting that the lesions were probably caused by hematogenous seeding of vibrios to the affected areas. Preexisting hepatic disease (including four cases of hemochromatosis) was noted for 75% of these patients, and five of the other six had known underlying disease: alcohol abuse or alcoholism (three), thalassemia major (one), and diabetes (one). Forty-six percent died, including all six patients with hypotension on admission and all four with hemochromatosis.

Thirty-eight percent of the patients with primary septicemia underwent surgical procedures—debridement (four), incision and drainage (one), fasciotomy (one), and leg amputation (three)—and all were treated with antibiotics to which *V. vulnificus* is susceptible. Most of those who survived became afebrile within several days. Most of the deaths were of persons who were already desperately ill when antibiotic therapy was begun; the median interval from onset of therapy to death was one day. The deaths appeared to be caused by intractable shock secondary to Gram-negative sepsis.

Ecology

Little is known of the geographic distribution and ecology of this organism. CDC has received isolates from water from a bay in Guam and from an oyster thought to have been harvested from the Gulf of Mexico. The reservoir of the organism in nature is apparently seawater, where it is probably part of the normal marine flora like the closely related *V. parahaemolyticus* (48).

Pathogenicity

The pathologic findings associated with wound infections caused by *V. vulnificus* have not been well described. However, a detailed description of the autopsy findings for a person with an apparent case of primary septicemia in Japan has been published (57). Microscopic examination of bullous skin lesions showed acute necrosis in the upper dermis without inflammatory cellular response, acute inflammation and necrosis of the fibroadipose tissue in the lower dermis and around the vessels, and transmural acute necrotizing vasculitis in subcutaneous tissue without thrombosis. The patient also had acute necrotizing epididymitis and orchitis, and acute splenitis with Gram-negative bacterial invasion. Necrotizing vasculitis was also noted in a leg amputated from one of the patients in the United States (30).

V. vulnificus has been studied in animal models by Poole & Oliver (77). They found that subcutaneous injections of the organisms into mice caused severe local infections with gross edema followed by tissue necrosis and death. The edema appeared to be caused by massive vascular leakage of plasma proteins, and death apparently was caused by generalized loss of intravascular fluid with hemoconcentration and hypotension. Although force-feeding *V. vulnificus* to mice caused no disease, injection into ligated rabbit and rat ileal loops caused bacteremia and death.

Epidemiology

V. vulnificus infections have been reported from Japan (57), Belgium (61), and 16 states in the United States (11). All but three of the US cases occurred in the period May to October, the warmer half of the year. Most of the patients were males over 40 years of age.

The US wound infections appeared to have been caused by contamination by seawater (12 patients) or saltwater crabs (two patients); only one of the patients had no known history of such contacts. Significantly more patients with wound infections than patients with septicemic onset had been in recent contact with seawater ($p<0.001$). Many patients with septicemic onset appeared to have been infected by eating raw oysters; significantly more patients with primary septicemia than patients with wound infections were known to have eaten raw oysters within one week of onset of illness ($p<0.001$), and all 19 patients who had septicemic onset and known oyster-eating habits often ate raw oysters (11). The median incubation periods were 12 hr for wound infections and 16 hr for primary septicemias.

VIBRIO ALGINOLYTICUS

Introduction

V. alginolyticus was not thought to be pathogenic for humans until 1973, when six isolates from tissue infections that had been reported by Twedt et al (105) in 1969 to be *V. parahaemolyticus* were found by Zen-Yoji et al (111) to be *V. alginolyticus.* In the same year, Von Graevenitz & Carrington (108) published the first case report, that of an ear infection apparently caused by *V. alginolyticus.* By mid-1979, at least 20 case reports of infections associated with *V. alginolyticus* isolates had been published (26, 33, 60, 73, 75, 76, 86, 87, 100, 108). In addition, in 1978 Prociv reported isolating *V. alginolyticus* from 20 wound infections in Western Australia (80). Hollis et al at CDC reported in 1976 that they had received 42 strains of *V. alginolyticus* from human extraintestinal sources for identification (35), but some of these strains came from patients whose case reports had already been published.

In some of the reported incidents, as when *V. alginolyticus* was isolated in pure culture from blood or wounds, the organism probably caused disease. However, when chronic ulcers and external otitis were present and when multiple potential pathogens were isolated, it is not clear whether *V. alginolyticus* caused the disease.

Clinical Features

Little detail about clinical features is given in most of the 20 case reports. The isolates came from wounds (nine), cutaneous ulcers (two), a burn, and ear drainage (eight); the patient with isolates from burns also had an isolate from blood.

The wounds were of the legs and feet (six), fingers (two), and scalp (one). Seven of the injuries occurred while swimming or at the seashore. The lesions, when described, were generally swollen and erythematous. Prociv wrote that most of 20 wound infections in Australia were "associated with a varying degree of cellulitis and a seropurulent exudate" (80). Five of the nine case reports of wound infections stated that *V. alginolyticus* was isolated from the wound in pure culture. None of the patients were reported to have chronic underlying disease, and none were seriously ill. Most of the patients were treated with a systemic antibiotic, usually one to which the organism was resistant, and with debridement or incision and drainage of the wound; all recovered. Of Prociv's 20 patients with wound infections, none were treated with antibiotics and most infections had cleared within one or two days after becoming apparent. Thus, it is not possible to determine from the published reports the effect of treatment with antibiotics to which the organism is susceptible.

One of the isolates from cutaneous ulcers came from a man with sickle cell anemia and chronic leg ulcers (86). When examined, he had serosanguinous fluid draining from bilateral malleolus ulcers and fever (temperature of 37.8°C); a culture of one of the ulcers yielded *V. alginolyticus* and *Staphylococcus aureus.* The other isolate from a cutaneous ulcer came from a man with chronic venous insufficiency of the right leg (75). When examined, he had a tender, erythematous 1.5-cm leg ulcer of four weeks' duration but he had no history of trauma to the area. *V. alginolyticus, Staphylococcus aureus,* and *Klebsiella pneumoniae* were isolated in culture. The effect of antibiotic therapy on these two patients was unclear.

The isolate from blood came from a woman who sustained severe burns in a boat explosion and was subsequently immersed in seawater (26). Despite intensive care, she died five days later. On the third day after the accident, some of her burns became macerated and she developed "clinical symptoms indicating a septic condition" (26). Although cultures of the surface of the burns yielded multiple organisms, *V. alginolyticus* was isolated in pure culture from biopsy specimens of burns and from blood.

Three of the isolates from ears came from patients with acute otitis media (60, 73, 108). All three patients had perforated tympanic membranes and developed purulent discharges. *V. alginolyticus* was isolated in pure culture from two patients (60, 73), and a few colonies of anaerobic diphtheroids and *Staphylococcus epidermidis* were also isolated from the third. They were treated with erythromycin (108) or tetracycline (60, 73), antibiotics to which these organisms were susceptible in vitro, and recovered uneventfully. Two isolates came from patients with external otitis (33, 87). One patient had had previous acute attacks; at the time of the reported acute attack, culture of a swab of the ear yielded a profuse pure growth of *V. alginolyticus* (87). The other patient had a draining chronic external otitis; an atypical *V. alginolyticus* was only one of several species isolated (33). No clinical details are given for three patients from whom isolates were obtained from ears (76); *V. alginolyticus* was the only organism isolated from two of these persons.

Ecology

Seawater is the normal habitat for *V. alginolyticus,* and it has been isolated from seawater and seafood in many parts of the world (5, 47, 54, 81, 107). Studies by Baross & Liston of oysters in Washington State showed that *V. alginolyticus* was rarely found in winter, but the counts rose rapidly with increasing water temperature, and the organism was abundant in summer (5). The minimum growth temperature for *V. alginolyticus* is 8°C (5).

Pathogenicity

The pathogenic mechanisms of *V. alginolyticus* have received little attention. To our knowledge, no studies have been done to determine if isolates from human infections can be differentiated from environmental isolates.

Epidemiology

V. alginolyticus is reported to have been isolated from extraintestinal sites from persons exposed in Australia (60, 80), Europe (33, 73, 87), Mexico (100), Hawaii (76), and all three coasts of the United States (26, 75, 86, 108). The infections with reported dates occurred in months when seawater is relatively warm. Seventeen (85%) of the 20 patients were male. The 18 patients whose ages were known ranged in age from 8 to 44, with a median age of 22.

All 11 persons with cutaneous infections and known exposures had been exposed to seawater shortly before the onset of clinical signs of infection; the incubation period is stated for only one patient, for whom it was 24 hr (86). The incubation period in Prociv's series of 20 *V. alginolyticus* wound infections in Australia was also 24 hr (80). Of the seven patients with ear infections and known exposures, six had been swimming in the sea shortly before onset, and one denied any recent exposure to seawater (108). The incubation period (5 days) was reported for one patient (60).

OTHER VIBRIOS POSSIBLY PATHOGENIC FOR MAN

Group F (EF6) Vibrios

Lee et al have described a group of *Vibrio*-like organisms that probably constitute a new species, and they have designated it group F (56). They report that these organisms are widely distributed in the marine and estuarine environment around Britain, and they have received similar strains from patients with diarrhea who were infected in Bangladesh, Bahrain, and Jordan. These organisms appear to be similar or identical to organisms designated group EF6 at CDC.

The clinical features and epidemiology of disease associated with isolation of this group of organisms have not yet been well defined, but some information is available from the International Center for Diarrhoeal Disease Research in Bangladesh (ICDDR,B) (formerly the Cholera Research Laboratory). In 1976–1977, hundreds of cases of diarrheal illness associated with isolation of group F vibrios occurred in Dacca and in the area around Matlab in rural Bangladesh. The organism was rarely isolated before and has rarely been isolated since this period. Approximately half the patients were children less than 5 years of age (46). Studies of family members of infected persons showed that group F vibrios were present in the stools of less than 1%. The clinical symptoms were similar to those of cholera, except that some patients had blood and mucus in their stools and some had abdominal pain and fever (46).

Nine strains from ICDDR,B tested at CDC were negative in the adrenal cell, infant mouse, and Sereny tests. Other investigators have reported that the organism kills mice when injected intraperitonially and produces a heat-labile toxin that causes fluid accumulation in ligated rabbit ileal loops (44). Currently, it is not certain that the organism is a pathogen.

Vibrio metschnikovii (Enteric Group 16)

Lee et al (56) state that the organism called *Vibrio metschnikovii* by Lee, and Enteric Group 16 by CDC, is widely distributed in rivers, estuaries, and sewage and that it has been isolated from the intestines of humans and other animals. However, there is currently no published evidence that the organism causes disease in humans or other animals. CDC has received Enteric Group 16 organisms for identification that were isolated from shrimp and and from the blood of an elderly woman with gallbladder disease.

CONCLUSION

Vibrio infections cannot be prevented unless we know how they are transmitted. Although gaps in our knowledge about the transmission of these infections remain, seafoods eaten cooked or raw and/or seawater are clearly important vehicles of transmission for non-O1 *V. cholerae, V. parahaemolyticus, V. vulnificus,* and *V. alginolyticus.*

When seafoods are eaten cooked, preventing infection is simple; regardless of *Vibrio* content, such foods will be safe if they are cooked at high enough temperatures to sterilize them and if they are protected from cross-contamination after cooking and then held until eaten at temperatures too cold ($\leq$4°C) or too hot ($\geq$60°C) to permit multiplication of vibrios. A common problem is that seafoods that are considered cooked by traditional criteria are not sterile (10, 53).

When seafoods are eaten raw, prevention of *Vibrio* infections is difficult, and it may be impossible to guarantee that any raw seafood is totally safe. Current programs to minimize the risk from eating raw shellfish, particularly oysters, attempt to prevent consumption of shellfish that have been subjected to fecal contamination. When successful, such programs should prevent hepatitis A, typhoid fever, viral gastroenteritis, and other diseases caused by contamination by human feces. However, this approach is probably ineffective against organisms that are pathogenic for man and that are probably part of normal estuarine flora: *V. vulnificus, V. parahaemolyticus,* and possibly non-O1 *V. cholerae.* It may be prudent for persons with underlying disease such as cirrhosis or leukemia to avoid raw seafood altogether, since these persons seem to be far more likely than others to have septicemia after eating raw seafood. The clustering of *V. vulnificus* and non-O1 *V. cholerae* disease during warm weather suggests that the risk is greatest in those months, whether because of greater numbers of vibrios in warm seawater or multiplication of vibrios in mishandled seafoods after harvesting. Perhaps even healthy persons anxious to minimize the risks of foodborne *Vibrio* infections should not eat raw seafoods during the warm summer and fall months. Direct measurement of the numbers and types of vibrios in shellfish and shellfish waters as suggested by Colwell & Kaper (21) may eventually be a useful adjunct to fecal coliform counts in determining when raw shellfish from a growing area present relatively little hazard to consumers. However, much more work on the ecology, epidemiology, and pathogenicity of *Vibrio* species must be done before such *Vibrio* counts can be considered for incorporation into shellfish regulations.

Prevention of *Vibrio* wound infections may be impossible, since injuries frequently occur during recreational and occupational exposures to seawater, and most seawater contact occurs when the water is warm. Thorough cleansing of wounds after exposure to seawater or raw seafoods might prevent disease, but the effectiveness of this measure has not been evaluated. Swimmers with preexisting ear disease could probably prevent otitis by keeping seawater out of their ears.

The importance of *Vibrio* infections as a cause of morbidity and mortality in the United States, and thus the importance of taking preventive measures, is still unknown. Certainly the small numbers of vibrios isolated from persons with infections and submitted to CDC for identification represent only a small fraction of the number of infections that occur. The numbers of strains of non-O1 *V. cholerae, V. vulnificus, V. alginolyticus,* and *V.*

parahaemolyticus submitted to CDC each year have increased dramatically in the past decade, a pattern which must represent primarily increased ascertainment rather than increased incidence of disease. Heightened awareness of clinicians, microbiologists, and epidemiologists about the existence of these pathogens and the settings in which they should be suspected, and collaboration between these professions, can lead to better understanding and control of *Vibrio* infections in the coming decade.

Literature Cited

1. Aldova, E., Laznickova, K., Stepankova, E., Lietava, J. 1968. *J. Infect. Dis.* 118:25–31
2. Back, E., Ljunggren, A., Smith, H. Jr. 1974. *Lancet* 1:723–24
3. Barker, W. H. Jr. 1974. *Lancet* 1:551–54
4. Barker, W. H. Jr., Gangarosa, E. J. 1974. *Ann. Rev. Med.* 25:75–81
5. Baross, J., Liston, J. 1970. *Appl. Microbiol.* 20:179–86
6. Bashford, D. J., Donovan, T. J., Furniss, A. L., Lee, J. V. 1979. *Lancet* 1:436–37
7. Baumann, P., Baumann, L., Reichelt, J. L. 1973. *J. Bacteriol.* 113:1144–55
8. Bhattacharji, L. M., Bose, B. 1964. *Indian J. Med. Res.* 52:777–86
9. Bisgaard, M., Sakazaki, R., Shimada, T. 1978. *Acta Pathol. Microbiol. Scand. Sect. B* 86:261–66
10. Blake, P. A., Allegra, D. T., Snyder, J. D., Barrett, T. J., McFarland, L., Caraway, C. T., Feeley, J. C., Craig, J. P., Lee, J. V., Puhr, N. D., Feldman, R. A. 1980. *N. Engl. J. Med.* 302:305–9
11. Blake, P. A., Merson, M. H., Weaver, R. E., Hollis, D. G., Heublein, P. C. 1979. *N. Engl. J. Med.* 300:1–5
12. Blake, P., Weaver, R., Hollis, D. 1977. *Program Abstr. 17th Intersci. Conf. Antimicrob. Agents Chemother., New York, 1977* (Abstr. No. 377)
13. Bolen, J. L., Zamiska, S. A., Greenough, W. B. III. 1974. *Am. J. Med.* 57:638–41
14. Bowmer, E. J., Woollacott, P. J. V., Greenwood, R. C. 1977. *Can. Dis. Wkly. Rep.* 3:97–98
15. Calia, F. M., Johnson, D. E. 1975. *Infect. Immun.* 11:1222–25
16. Carruthers, M. M. 1975. *J. Infect. Dis.* 132:555–60
17. Carruthers, M. M. 1977. *J. Infect. Dis.* 136:588–92
18. Center for Disease Control. 1979. *Morb. Mortal. Wkly. Rep.* 28:571–77
19. Chun, D., Chung, J. K., Seol, S. Y., Tak, R. 1974. *Am. J. Trop. Med. Hyg.* 23:1125–30
20. Clark, W. A., Steigerwalt, A. G. 1977. *Int. J. Syst. Bacteriol.* 27:194–99
21. Colwell, R. R., Kaper, J. 1977. In *Bacterial Indicators/Health Hazards Associated with Water,* ed. A. W. Hoadley, B. J. Dutka, pp. 115–25. Spec. Tech. Publ. 635. Am. Soc. Test. Mater., Philadelphia. 356 pp.
22. Dakin, W. P. H., Howell, D. J., Sutton, R. G. A., O'Keefe, M. F., Thomas, P. 1974. *Med. J. Aust.* 2:487–90
23. Davis, B. R., Brenner, D. J., Balows, A. 1977. *Abstr. 13th Jt. Conf. Cholera US-Jpn. Coop. Med. Sci. Prog.,* p. 66 (Abstr.)
24. De, S. P., Banerjee, M., Deb, B. C., Sengupta, P. G., Sil, J., Sirkar, B. K., Sen, D., Ghosh, A., Pal, S. C. 1977. *Indian J. Med. Res.* 65:21–28
25. Donta, S. T., Smith, D. M. 1974. *Infect. Immun.* 9:500–5
26. English, V. L., Lindberg, R. B. 1977. *Am. J. Med. Technol.* 43:989–93
27. Farmer, J. J. III. 1979. *Lancet* 2:903
28. Fearrington, E. L., Rand, C. H. Jr., Mewborn, A., Wilkerson, J. 1974. *Ann. Intern. Med.* 81:401
29. Feeley, J. C., Balows, A. 1974. *Manual of Clinical Microbiology,* ed. E. H. Lennette, E. H. Spaulding, J. P. Truant, pp. 238–45. Washington DC: Am. Soc. Microbiol. 970 pp. 2nd ed.
30. Fernandez, C. R., Pankey, G. A. 1975. *J. Am. Med. Assoc.* 233:1173–76
31. Furniss, A. L., Lee, J. V., Donovan, T. J. 1978. *The Vibrios.* Public Health Lab. Serv. Monogr. Ser. No. 11. London: Her Majesty's Stationery Office. 58 pp.
32. Gangarosa, E. J., Mosley, W. H. 1974. In *Cholera,* ed. D. Barua, W. Burrows, p. 392. Philadelphia: Saunders
33. Hansen, W., Crokaert, F., Yourassowsky, E. 1979. *J. Clin. Microbiol.* 9:152–53
34. Heiberg, B. 1936. *J. Hyg.* 36:114–17

35. Hollis, D. G., Weaver, R. E., Baker, C. N., Thornsberry, C. 1976. *J. Clin. Microbiol.* 3:425–31
36. Honda, T., Goshima, K., Takeda, Y., Sugino, Y., Miwatani, T. 1976. *Infect. Immun.* 13:163–71
37. Honda, T., Shimizu, M., Takeda, Y., Miwatani, T. 1976. *Infect. Immun.* 14:1028–33
38. Honda, T., Taga, S., Takeda, T., Hasibuan, M. A., Takeda, Y., Miwatani, T. 1976. *Infect. Immun.* 13:133–39
39. Honda, T., Takeda, Y., Miwatani, T. 1977. *Jpn. J. Med. Sci. Biol.* 30:84–86
40. Hugh, R., Feeley, J. C. 1972. *Int. J. Syst. Bacteriol.* 22:123
41. Hugh, R., Sakazaki, R. 1972. *J. Conf. Public Health Lab. Dir.* 30:133–37
42. Hughes, J. M., Boyce, J. M., Aleem, A. R. M. A., Wells, J. G., Rahman, A. S. M. M., Curlin, G. T. 1978. *Am. J. Trop. Med. Hyg.* 27:106–12
43. Hughes, J. M., Hollis, D. G., Gangarosa, E. J., Weaver, R. E. 1978. *Ann. Intern. Med.* 88:602–6
44. Huq, M. I., Khan, M. U., Aziz, K. M. S., Brenner, D. J. 1979. *Abstr. 15th Jt. Conf. Cholera US-Jpn. Coop. Med. Sci. Prog., Bethesda, 1979,* p. 68 (Abstr.)
45. Johnson, D. E., Calia, F. M. 1976. *J. Infect. Dis.* 133:436–40
46. Kahn, M. 1979. *See Ref. 44, p. 70 (Abstr.)*
47. Kampelmacher, E. H., Van Noorle Jansen, L. M., Mossel, D. A. A., Groen, F. J. 1972. *J. Appl. Bacteriol.* 35:431–38
48. Kaneko, T., Colwell, R. R. 1973. *J. Bacteriol.* 113:24–32
49. Kaneko, T., Colwell, R. R. 1975. *Appl. Microbiol.* 29:269–74
50. Kaneko, T., Colwell, R. R. 1975. *Appl. Microbiol.* 30:251–57
51. Kaper, J., Lockman, H., Colwell, R. R., Joseph, S. W. 1979. *Appl. Environ. Microbiol.* 37:91–103
52. Katoh, H. 1965. *Jpn. J. Bacteriol.* 20:94–99
53. Koff, R. S., Sear, H. S. 1967. *N. Engl. J. Med.* 276:737–39
54. Kristensen, K. K. 1974. *Nord. Veterinaermed.* 26:188–96
55. Lawrence, D. N., Blake, P. A., Yashuk, J. C., Wells, J. G., Creech, W. B., Hughes, J. H. 1979. *Am. J. Epidemiol.* 109:71–80
56. Lee, J. V., Donovan, T. J., Furniss, A. L. 1978. *Int. J. Syst. Bacteriol.* 28: 99–111
57. Matsuo, T., Kohno, S., Ikeda, T., Saruwatari, K., Ninomiya, H. 1978. *Acta Pathol. Jpn.* 28:937–48
58. Mazumder, D. N. G., Ghosh, A. K., De, S. P., Sirkar, B. K. 1977. *Indian J. Med. Res.* 66:180–88
59. McIntyre, O. R., Feeley, J. C., Greenough, W. B. III, Benenson, A. S., Hassan, S. I., Saad, A. 1965. *Am. J. Trop. Med. Hyg.* 14:412–18
60. McSweeney, R. J., Forgan-Smith, W. R. 1977. *Med. J. Aust.* 1:896–97
61. Mertens, A., Nagler, J., Hansen, W., Gepts-Friedenreich, E. 1979. *J. Clin. Microbiol.* 9:233–35
62. Miwatani, T., Takeda, Y. 1976. *Vibrio parahaemolyticus: A Causative Bacterium of Food Poisoning,* p. 23. Tokyo: Saikon. 149 pp.
63. Miwatani, T., Takeda, Y. 1976. See Ref. 62, pp. 23–28
64. Miwatani, T., Takeda, Y. 1976. See Ref. 62, pp. 36–37
65. Miwatani, T., Takeda, Y. 1976. See Ref. 62, pp. 46–49
66. Miwatani, T., Takeda, Y. 1976. See Ref. 62, pp. 104–9
67. Miwatani, T., Takeda, Y. 1976. See Ref. 62, pp. 108–9
68. Morris, G. K., Merson, M. H., Huq, I., Kibrya, A. K. M. G., Black, R. 1979. *J. Clin. Microbiol.* 9:79–83
69. Muller, G. 1977. *Zentralbl. Bakteriol. Parasitenkd. Infektionskr. Hyg. Abt. I. Orig. Reihe B* 165:487–97
70. Muller, H. E. 1978. *Zentrabl Bakteriol. Parasitenkd. Infektionskr. Hyg. Abt. I Orig. Reihe B* 167:272–84
71. Ohashi, M., Ohta, K., Tsuno, M., Zen-Yoji, H. 1978. *Proc. 13th Jt. Conf. Cholera US-Jpn. Coop. Med. Sci. Prog., Atlanta, 1977,* pp. 403–13
72. Ohashi, M., Shimada, T., Fukumi, H. 1972. *Jpn. J. Med. Sci. Biol.* 25:179–94
73. Olsen, H. 1978. *Acta Pathol. Microbiol. Scand. Sect. B* 86:247–48
74. Overman, T. L., D'Amato, R. F., Tomfohrde, K. M. 1979. *J. Clin. Microbiol.* 9:244–47
75. Pezzlo, M., Valter, P. J., Burns, M. J. 1979. *Am. J. Clin. Pathol.* 71:476–78
76. Pien, F., Lee, K., Higa, H. 1977. *J. Clin. Microbiol.* 5:670–72
77. Poole, M. D., Oliver, J. D. 1978. *Infect. Immun.* 20:126–29
78. Porres, J. M., Fuchs, L. A. 1975. *Clin. Orthop. Relat. Res.* 106:245–47
79. Prats, G., Mirelis, B., Pericas, R., Verger, G. 1975. *Ann. Intern. Med.* 82:848–49
80. Prociv, P. 1978. *Med. J. Aust.* 2:296
81. Reali, D., Caroli, G., Filippi, S., Simonetti, S. 1977. *Ann. Sclavo* 19:455–63
82. Reichelt, J. L., Baumann, P., Baumann, L. 1976. *Arch. Microbiol.* 110:101–20

83. Roberts, D., Gilbert, R. J. 1979. *J. Hyg.* 82:123–31
84. Robins-Browne, R. M., Still, C. S., Isaacson, M., Koornhof, H. J., Appelbaum, P. C., Scragg, J. N. 1977. *Infect. Immun.* 18:542–45
85. Roland, F. P. 1970. *N. Engl. J. Med.* 278:1306
86. Rubin, S. J., Tilton, R. C. 1975. *J. Clin. Microbiol.* 2:556–58
87. Ryan, W. J. 1976. *J. Clin. Pathol.* 29:1014–15
88. Sack, R. B. 1973. *J. Infect. Dis.* 127:709–12
89. Sakazaki, R., Shimada, T. 1977. *Jpn. J. Med. Sci. Biol.* 30:279–82
90. Sakazaki, R., Tamura, K., Kato, T., Obara, Y., Yamai, S., Hobo, K. 1968. *Jpn. J. Med. Sci. Biol.* 21:325–31
91. Sakazaki, R., Tamura, K., Hakamura, A., Kurata, T., Gohda, A., Kazuno, Y. 1974. *Jpn. J. Med. Sci. Biol.* 27: 35–43
92. Sakurai, J., Honda, T., Jinguji, Y., Arita, M., Miwatani, T. 1976. *Infect. Immun.* 13:876–83
93. Sanyal, S. C., Sen, P. C. 1974. *Proc. Int. Symp. Vibrio parahaemolyticus, Tokyo, 1973,* pp. 227–30
94. Sanyal, S. C., Singh, S. J., Tiwari, I. C., Sen, P. C., Marwah, S. M., Hazarika, U. R., Singh, H., Shimada, T., Sakazaki, R. 1974. *J. Infect. Dis.* 130:575–79
95. Shewan, J. M., Vernon, M. 1974. *Bergey's Manual of Determinative Bacteriology,* ed. R. E. Buchanan, N. E. Gibbons, pp. 340–55. Baltimore: Williams & Wilkins. 1246 pp. 8th ed.
96. Shimada, T., Sakazaki, R. 1977. *Jpn. J. Med. Sci. Biol.* 30:275–77
97. Sirkar, B. K., Deb, B. C., De, S. P., Ghosh, A., Pal, S. C. 1976. *Indian J. Med Res.* 64:1576–80
98. Smith, H. L. Jr. 1979. *J. Clin. Microbiol.* 10:85–90
99. Smith, H. L. Jr., Goodner, K. 1965. *Proc. Cholera Res. Symp., Honolulu, 1965, Public Health Serv. Publ. No. 1328,* pp. 4–8. Washington DC: US Gov. Print. Off.
100. Spark, R. P., Fried, M. L., Perry, C., Watkins, C. 1979. *Ann. Clin. Lab. Sci.* 9:133–38
101. Spira, W. M., Daniel, R. R. 1980. *Proc. 15th Jt. Conf. Cholera US-Jpn. Coop. Med. Sci. Prog., Bethesda, 1979,* pp. 440–58
102. Spira, W. M., Daniel, R. R., Ahmed, Q. S., Huq, A., Yusuf, A., Sack, D. A. 1979. *Proc. 14th Jt. Conf. US-Jpn. Coop. Med. Sci. Prog., Karatsu, 1978,* pp. 137–53
103. Tay, L., Yu, M. 1978. *Singapore Med. J.* 19:89–92
104. Thorsteinsson, S. B., Minuth, J. N., Musher, D. N. 1974. *Lancet* 2:1283–84
105. Twedt, R. M., Spaulding, P. L., Hall, H. E. 1969. *J. Bacteriol.* 98:511–18
106. Varela, G., Olarte, J., Perez-Miravete, A., Filloy, L. 1971. *Am. J. Trop. Med. Hyg.* 20:925–26
107. Vasconcelos, G. J., Stang, W. J., Laidlaw, R. H. 1975. *Appl. Microbiol.* 29:557–59
108. Von Graevenitz, A., Carrington, G. O. 1973. *Infection* 1:54–58
109. Weaver, R. E., Ehrenkranz, N. J. 1975. *Arch. Intern. Med.* 135:197
110. World Health Organization. 1969. *WHO Wkly. Epidemiol. Rec.* 44:10
111. Zen-Yoji, H., LeClair, R. A., Ohta, K., Montague, T. S. 1973. *J. Infect. Dis.* 127:237–41
112. Zen-Yoji, H., Sakai, S., Terayama, T., Kudo, Y., Ito, T., Benoki, M., Nagasaki, M. 1965. *J. Infect. Dis.* 115:436–44
113. Zide, N., Davis, J., Ehrenkranz, N. J. 1974. *Arch. Intern. Med.* 133:479–81
114. Zinnaka, Y., Fukuyoshi, S. 1974. *Proc. 9th Jt. Cholera Res. Conf. US-Jpn. Coop. Med. Sci. Prog. Grand Canyon, 1973,* pp. 61–81
115. Zinnaka, Y., Fukuyoshi, S., Okamura, Y. 1973. *Proc. 8th Jt. Conf. US-Jpn. Coop. Med. Sci. Prog. Tokyo, 1972,* pp. 116–23
116. Zubko, V. I., Zheleznyak, L. D. 1973. *Zh. Mikrobiol. Epidemiol. Immunobiol.* 50:72–74

Ann. Rev. Microbiol. 1980. 34:369–422

PROTEINS OF THE OUTER MEMBRANE OF GRAM-NEGATIVE BACTERIA

❖1781

M. J. Osborn and H. C. P. Wu

University of Connecticut Health Center, Farmington, Connecticut 06032

INTRODUCTION 370
NOMENCLATURE OF MAJOR PROTEINS 370
PORIN PROTEINS 371
Genetics and Regulation of Porin Proteins 371
E. coli matrix proteins 371
"New membrane proteins" of E. coli 375
Porins of Salmonella typhimurium 376
Structure and Function of Porin Proteins 376
Pore-forming proteins 377
Functional properties of porin proteins 379
Structure-function relationships 381
MAJOR NON-PORIN PROTEINS 384
The OmpA Protein 384
Protein a (3b) 386
Murein Lipoprotein 387
MOLECULAR ORGANIZATION OF MAJOR PROTEINS IN THE OUTER MEMBRANE 388
Topology of Major Proteins 389
Protein-Protein Interactions 390
Protein-Lipopolysaccharide Interactions 391
Protein-Peptidoglycan Interactions 391
Interaction with Periplasmic Proteins: LamB-MalE Proteins 393
BIOSYNTHESIS AND ASSEMBLY INTO THE OUTER MEMBRANE 393
Biosynthesis of Outer Membrane Proteins 393
Precursor forms of outer membrane proteins 393
Site of synthesis of outer membrane and periplasmic proteins 394
Kinetics of assembly of outer membrane proteins 396
Genetic Determinants of the Localization of Proteins in the Outer Membrane 397
Mechanism of Protein Export in Escherichia coli 398
The role of signal sequence in protein export 398
Signal peptidase 405
Other components of the export machinery 406
Energetics of protein export 407
Common vs unique pathways for the assembly of proteins destined for the cytoplasmic membrane, outer membrane, and periplasmic space 408

0066-4227/80/1001-0369$01.00

Regulation of the Synthesis and Assembly of Outer Membrane Proteins 410
INDEPENDENT ASSEMBLY OF OUTER MEMBRANE COMPONENTS 412
A MODEL FOR THE ASSEMBLY OF OUTER MEMBRANE PROTEINS 414

INTRODUCTION

The outer membrane of Gram-negative bacteria is a highly specialized structure that lies outside the cytoplasmic membrane and peptidoglycan layer and forms the interface between the cell and its external environment. Thus, the outer membrane constitutes a physical and functional barrier between the cell body and its surroundings which effectively controls access of solutes and external agents to the cytoplasmic membrane. The major function of the membrane as a barrier to antibiotics, detergents, and other toxic chemicals is necessarily accompanied by permeability properties that allow entry of nutrient solutes from the medium. In addition, the function of outer membrane components as receptors for bacteriophages and bacteriocins implies a role in uptake of macromolecules; a possible analogous function may be inferred in cell-cell interactions during F-mediated conjugation. The specialized functions of the membrane are reflected in its composition, which includes the cellular lipopolysaccharide and a limited number of highly characteristic and unusual major proteins. The physical location of the outer membrane poses unique problems in biogenesis, arising from the necessity to assemble an ordered and asymmetric membrane structure external to the cell proper and segregated from cellular biosynthetic machineries. Thus, proteins and lipids synthesized in, or in association with, the cytoplasmic membrane must be specifically targeted, translocated, and integrated into the outer membrane in such a way as to achieve not only the correct composition but also the proper orientation and intermolecular interactions.

This review focuses on the major proteins of the outer membrane of *Escherichia coli* and *Salmonella typhimurium* and emphasizes recent advances in this rapidly growing area related to function and biogenesis of the outer membrane. More detailed discussions of many of these topics, as well as aspects of outer membrane structure and function not considered here, will be found in the volume on outer membrane edited by Inouye (99) and other recent reviews (21, 51, 110, 264).

NOMENCLATURE OF MAJOR PROTEINS

Identification and genetic analysis of major outer membrane proteins of *E. coli* has been carried out simultaneously by many laboratories, using different strains, a variety of SDS-polyacrylamide gel electrophoresis systems for separation of polypeptides, and a large number of different phages, colicins, and toxic agents for selection of mutants. The resulting multiplicity of nomenclatures was probably unavoidable, particularly in view of the formidable technical difficulties in purification of these rather intractable proteins, establishment of their homogeneity, and crossmatching of their identities between laboratories. However, structural and genetic characterization of most of the major proteins has now advanced to the point where a uniform and rational nomenclature is possible as well as desirable. We strongly support the proposal of Reeves (192) and Lee et al (122) that the proteins be named in accordance with the standard nomenclature established for their structural genes in current linkage maps (3,203), and we employ this terminology here. Thus the OmpA protein is the product of the omp*A* gene and so on. Known genetic loci for major proteins of *E. coli* and *S. typhimurium* and the corresponding nomenclatures are collated in Table 1; the reader is referred to the recent reviews of Reeves (192) for a more detailed discussion of the system. Evidence for the indicated gene functions is summarized in the following section. It should be noted that it is not yet clear whether the known *nmp* loci which are involved in expression of the so-called new membrane proteins of *E. coli* are structural or regulatory in nature; therefore the names suggested by Lee et al (122), NmpA-B and NmpC, are tentative. In addition, the name *murein lipoprotein* or *lipoprotein,* for the product of the *lpp* gene is unambiguous and well established, and there would seem to be no advantage to changing this usage. The term *matrix protein* was originally applied to the OmpF protein of *E. coli* B (197) and has more recently been expanded into *matrix porins* to refer to the several constitutively expressed pore-forming proteins of *E. coli* and *S. typhimurium,* OmpC, D, and F. *Matrix porins* would indeed appear to be convenient as a descriptive trivial name for the family of abundant pore-forming proteins that have allied physical and functional properties. By these criteria, the family of matrix porins would logically include the *new membrane proteins* recently defined in *E. coli* and perhaps the LamB protein as well. However, the more specialized primary function of the latter in permeation of maltose oligosaccharides distinguishes it from other known major porins, and the term *matrix porin* might better be restricted to those proteins that normally function as general pores in permeation of hydrophilic solutes across the outer membrane.

PORIN PROTEINS

Genetics and Regulation of Porin Proteins

E. COLI MATRIX PROTEINS Mutants lacking one or both of the classical matrix porins of *E. coli* K12, proteins Ia(1a,b,0–9) and Ib (1b,c,0–8), can be readily selected by resistance to specific phages or tolerance to bacterio-

Table 1 Recommended genetic nomenclature for major outer membrane proteins of *E. coli* and *S. typhimurium* (122, 192)

	Map position (units)			Protein nomenclature								
				Previous designations *E. coli*[a]								Recommended uniform
Gene	*E. coli*	*S. typhimurium*	Gene function	B	F	H	I	L	M	S	*S. typhimurium*	nomenclature
ompA (*tolG, con, tut*)[b]	21	21	S[c]	B	TolG	II*	7	D	0–11	3a	33K	OmpA
ompB (*cry*)	74	74	R									
ompC (*par, meoA*)	47	46	S	A_2		Ib	4	c	0–8	1b	36K	OmpC
ompD	—[d]	28	S(?)								34K	OmpD
ompF (*tolF, colB, coa, cry*)	21	21	S	A_1	TolF	Ia	4	b	0–9	1a	35K	OmpF
nmpA	82.2	—[d]	?		E	Ic		e		NmpA		NmpA–B[e]
nmpB	8.6	—[d]	?							NmpB		
nmpC	12	—[d]	?							NmpC		NmpC[e]
lamB	90		S								44K	LamB
lpp (*mlpA, lpm, lpo*)	36.5		S	F		IV	11		0–18			Murein lipoprotein

[a] B = Bragg (19), F = Foulds (61), H = Henning (86), I = Inouye (51), L = Lugtenberg (135), M = Mizushima (272), S = Schnaitman (210).
[b] Previous gene designations are parenthesized.
[c] S = structural, R = regulatory, ? = not known.
[d] No gene product corresponding to locus has been identified.
[e] Tentative name, pending identification of structural gene locus.

cins (reviewed in 192). Genetic analyses of such mutants have defined three loci (Table 1), now designated *ompB, ompC, and ompF* (3). Mutations at *ompF* [21 min, previously *tolF* (61), *tut* (85), or *cry* (11, 258)] result in a Ia^-Ib^+ phenotype, characterized by tolerance to bacteriocin JF246 (61) and resistance to phages TuIa (89) and T2 (81). Conversely, mutants at *ompC* [47 min, previously *par* (5) or *meoA* (251)] are Ia^+Ib^- and are resistant to phages PA-2 and the related hybrid hy-2 (5) and Mel (251). In addition, a third class of mutants, multiply colicin tolerant (204) and resistant to OmpF- and/or OmpC-specific phages (28, 89, 252), map at a separate locus at 74 min, designated *ompB* (204). Such mutants may lack either or both of the OmpC and OmpF proteins. Since mutants in outer membrane proteins most frequently lack the affected polypeptide altogether, unequivocal identification of structural genes has been difficult and the functions of *ompB, C,* and *F* in expression of the proteins have only recently been clarified.

The variability of phenotype in *ompB* mutants and the close structural and functional relationship between the OmpC and OmpF proteins initially led to the hypothesis that both polypeptides were derived from a common structural gene, *ompB,* the product of which was subject to posttranslational modification by the products of *ompF* and *ompC* to yield the corresponding proteins (5). However, it is now clear that proteins Ia and Ib differ at multiple internal positions in amino acid sequence (95) and therefore necessarily represent separate gene products. Recent genetic evidence strongly supports identification of *ompF* and *ompC* as the structural genes and *ompB* as a regulatory locus controlling the level of expression of the two structural gene products. Merodiploids of *S. typhimurium* carrying an *E. coli* F'$ompF^+$ have been shown to express the *E. coli* OmpF protein in addition to the 34K, 35K, and 36K polypeptides normally present (205). Replacement of the *ompF* region of *E. coli* K12 with the corresponding segment of the *S. typhimurium* chromosome resulted in replacement of the *E. coli* protein with a doublet pair of polypeptides related to the *Salmonella* 35K protein (205). It is not understood why expression of the presumptive *Salmonella* OmpF protein in *E. coli* K12 should result in production of two apparently abnormal or altered polypeptide products. The structural role of *ompC* has been established both by identification of *ompC* mutants producing altered OmpC protein (246) and by construction of *ompC-lac* operon fusions (77).

Information on regulation of *ompC* and considerable clarification of the function of *ompB* has recently come from the elegant studies of Hall & Silhavy (77) on *ompB*::Mu*c*ts insertions and *ompC-lac* fusions. Expression of β-galactosidase in *ompC-lac*$^+$ operon fusion strains reflected the known regulatory properties of the OmpC protein. Enzyme activity was modulated by growth medium in a manner similar to OmpC (5, 136) and was reduced by introduction of an *ompB* allele. Interestingly, transfer of *ompB* (and *ompB*::Mucts) alleles of the OmpC(p-)OmpF(p-) type into fusion strains resulted in maximal reduction (14- to 31-fold) of β-galactosidase and abolition of the response to growth medium, while those alleles that expressed OmpF protein had a quantitatively lesser effect (5- to 17-fold) on β-galactosidase activity, and modulation by growth medium was retained. Expression of β-galactosidase was reduced in trans in merodiploids of the type *ompB*::Mucts *ompC*$^+$*lacZ*/F'*ompC-lac*$^+$ but was normal in the corresponding *ompB*$^+$ diploids, suggesting that the *ompC* gene product is not involved in transcriptional autoregulation. The results strongly suggest that *ompB*$^+$ specifies a diffusible positive regulatory element acting at the transcriptional level. To account for the differing phenotypes of *ompB* mutants, Hall & Silhavy have further suggested that *ompB* may code for two functions: one required simply to turn on the structural gene, the second modulating its quantitative level of expression in response to environmental factors. Similar analyses of the role of *ompB* in regulation of *ompF* are still lacking; existing data establish that expression of the OmpF protein also requires *ompB* function (28, 89, 204, 252), but findings in several laboratories suggest that it may be unwise to assume a unitary mode of action for the *ompB* locus.

Recent evidence suggests that the *ompB* region is extremely complex. Wanner et al (262) have reported isolation of a pleiotropic mutant, called *perA,* that produces severely reduced amounts of alkaline phosphatase, at least six other periplasmic proteins, and three major outer membrane proteins, including the OmpF protein. The OmpC protein is markedly overproduced. *PerA* proved to be 97–98% linked to *ompB* by P1 transduction. However, *ompB* mutations do not, in general, affect synthesis of alkaline phosphatase, and the genetic evidence led to the conclusion that *perA* is a separate gene. Studies on *phoA-lac* operon fusions indicated that the *perA* mutation affects production of alkaline phosphatase at a posttranscriptional level, and it was concluded that the mutation may block some step in the secretory process. Another group of mutants in the *ompB* region with unusual regulatory properties has been isolated (C. Wandersman, F. Moreno, and M. Schwartz, personal communication) by selection for resistance to phage TP1. This phage can use both LamB (λ-receptor) and OmpF proteins as receptor (260). The mutation maps very close to *ompB*, results in loss of the OmpF protein but not OmpC, and markedly reduces the expression of *lamB* in uninduced, but not in induced, cells. Wandersman et al suggest that these TP1 resistant mutants may be analogous to *perA;* however, protein and operon fusions indicate that these mutations affect transcription of *lamB* (and other genes of the maltose operons). The genetic and functional relationship of the TP1-resistant and PerA phenotypes to each other and to the "classical" OmpB phenotypes is a question of obvious current interest and importance. The evidence now available has at least begun to define the genetic and functional complexity of the region and to suggest the potential scope of its effects on expression of envelope proteins.

"NEW MEMBRANE PROTEINS" OF E. COLI Mutants that are deficient in both the OmpC and OmpF proteins are now known to exhibit pleiotropic deficiencies in nutrient transport (8, 138). The transport-defective phenotype is readily suppressed by extragenic mutations that result in expression of an electrophoretically distinct new outer membrane protein with porin function (62, 89, 187, 249). Three such suppressor loci have been identified: *nmpA* (62, 187), *nmpB* (187), and *nmpC* (187) (Table 1). The protein first described by Henning et al (67, 89) in *ompB* mutants as Ic and protein e of van Alphen et al (137, 245, 249) appear to be identical to the NmpA protein of Pugsley & Schnaitman (187) and protein E of Foulds & Chai (28, 62, 63). A close structural relationship between the NmpA and OmpF proteins was initially suggested by sequence identity of the N-terminal octapeptides (89). However, Lee et al (122) have recently shown that the two proteins differ in isoelectric point, apparent molecular weight, peptide profiles, and phage inactivation patterns. Assessments of immunological cross-reactivity have yielded discrepant results (29, 187). Most interestingly, the new protein produced by *nmpB* mutants was identical to that of *nmpA* strains by all criteria employed (187). At present there is no information as to which (if either) of the two loci represents the structural gene or as to the function of the second, nonstructural locus. Further, the NmpC protein, although quite different from the OmpC, OmpF, and NmpA-B proteins by the above criteria, was closely related structurally and immunologically to protein 2 of Schnaitman (48, 210) which appears as a product of lysogenic conversion by phage PA-2 (5).

The genes that determine expression of the *nmpA-B* product and the NmpC protein appear to be silent in wild-type K12 strains [though similar proteins may be expressed in clinical isolates (122)], and the nature of the mutations that result in expression of the new membrane proteins is not yet known. Their expression appears to be independent of the functional state of *ompB, ompC,* and *ompF* (63, 122, 135, 187). In addition, expression of the new membrane proteins is not modulated by medium osmolarity (122), a function associated with *ompB* (136). The NmpC protein is, however, subject to catabolite repression, as is its phage-directed counterpart, protein 2 (122, 186). Expression of genes determining new membrane proteins may be under negative control by more or less conventional regulatory elements independent of the *ompB* system; however, it is possible that more interesting mechanisms of chromosomal switching, such as inversion or insertion excision, may be involved in activation of *nmp* genes. Porin-deficient mutants are at a severe growth disadvantage, particularly at low nutrient concentrations such as might be found in nature, and the potential advantage of reduplication of porin genes has been pointed out by several authors (63, 122, 245). It is not entirely clear what advantage might be conferred by expressing such multiple genes alternatively rather than simultaneously; given that the total amount of these very abundant proteins which can be successfully incorporated into the membrane is limited, it may be more feasible for the cell to control the total rate of porin synthesis by maximal transcription of one gene set, rather than by down-regulated transcription of all.

PORINS OF SALMONELLA TYPHIMURIUM *S. typhimurium* LT-2 contains four major outer membrane proteins in the 33K–36K mol wt region of SDS gels, of which three, at 34K, 35K and 36K, have been identified as porins (239, 240). Expression of these is regulated by an *ompB* locus homologous to that of *E. coli* (183). The 33K protein is homologous to the OmpA protein of *E. coli* (231). Nurminen et al (169) have isolated mutants lacking the 34K and/or 36K proteins by phage resistance; resistance to phage PH51 (108, 217) yielded mutants lacking the 34K protein, while PH105 (108, 217) and P221 selected for the 36K-negative phenotype. Mutants specifically lacking the 35K protein have not yet been reported. Mapping data (Table 1) indicate that the 35K protein is genetically homologous to the OmpF protein of *E. coli* (205) and the 36K species to the OmpC protein [P. H. Mäkelä, cited in (231)]. In addition to mutations at *ompC* (47 units, near *malA*), 36K-negative isolates were also obtained which mapped at the position of *ompB* (79 units, near *malD*) as well as at a third unidentified locus. Mutants in the 34K protein mapped at a new locus, *ompD* (34 units, near *trp*), which has as yet no counterpart in *E. coli* [P. H. Mäkelä, cited in (231)].

Structure and Function of Porin Proteins

The concept is now well established that the permeability properties of the outer membrane control access of solutes to the periplasm and inner membrane and that transit of hydrophilic solutes across the outer membrane is accomplished by a battery of proteins which form transmembrane channels of varying degrees of specificity. These proteins appear to fall into three general functional categories. The first consists of a family of major outer membrane proteins, the so-called porins (158), which form general hydrophilic pores, i.e. fixed aqueous channels that allow passive nonspecific diffusion of solutes across the membrane. These pore proteins do not appear to interact directly with permeable solutes with any measurable affinity, and selectivity is primarily determined by the hydrated radius of the solute relative to that of the pore. A second class of pore-forming proteins, of which the LamB and Tsx proteins (λ-receptor and T6 receptor) are known examples, have rather more specific function. These two proteins are responsible for specific permeation of oligosaccharides of the maltose series (235) and nucleosides (80), respectively, but they appear to act as pores rather than carrier proteins in the classic sense. The pore-forming proteins are to be distinguished from outer membrane transport proteins of the third class, which are called into play for uptake of certain solutes that are relatively large in size and likely to be present in the medium at low concentrations. In these cases, exemplified in *E. coli* by outer membrane receptors for vitamin B_{12} and iron siderophores, the protein is a required component of a unique and highly specific transport system; it interacts with the transported substrate directly with high affinity and may itself take part in catalysis of substrate translocation. The function of these specific outer membrane transport proteins is complex and is still incompletely understood. These fascinating systems are the subject of excellent recent reviews by Braun (21), Kadner & Bassford (110), and Konisky (117) and are not further discussed here.

PORE-FORMING PROTEINS The pioneering studies of Nikaido and Nakae and their co-workers demonstrated the existence of hydrophilic pores across the outer membrane (43, 163, 166) and established the function of the OmpC and F proteins in pore formation in vivo (8, 166) and in reconstituted membrane systems in vitro (158, 159). This elegant work constituted a major advance in understanding the structure and function of the outer membrane; new information on the function of outer membrane porins continues to accumulate at a rapid pace. The role of OmpC, D, and F proteins in permeation in vivo has been established in several laboratories. Thus, mutants of *Salmonella typhimurium* lacking both the OmpC and D proteins showed a 7- to 20-fold reduction in the role of permeation of cephaloridine into the periplasm (166); mutants of *E. coli* B and K12 resistant to copper proved to be deficient in the OmpF, and OmpC and F, proteins respectively (138); and a group of mutants of *Escherichia coli* B/r isolated by von Meyenberg in 1971 (256) as pleiotropically transport defective (*kmt* mutants) were identified as *ompB* mutants deficient in the *ompF* product (8). In contrast to *E. coli* B, which normally expresses *ompF* as the only major porin, the full-blown pleiotropic transport-defective phenotype is observed in K12 strains only when both OmpC and OmpF proteins are eliminated, i.e. in *ompCompF* double mutants and in some *ompB* mutants (62, 138, 187).

In addition to the OmpC, D, and F proteins that are expressed constitutively, a number of conditionally expressed proteins have been shown to act as porins, including the "new membrane proteins," NmpA-B and C (29, 187, 249), and protein 2 (186). The LamB protein (λ-receptor), although genetically and physiologically a component of the specific maltose transport system, also has some functional properties of a general pore. Lambda-resistant mutants lacking the LamB protein are characterized by reduced rates of uptake of maltose and maltotriose and by loss of the ability to utilize higher maltodextrins as carbon source (24, 235, 236, 261). However, the protein shows no detectable affinity for its transport substrates either in the intact membrane or in purified form (235), and the evidence indicates that it is capable of functioning as a more general pore in vivo (257) and in vitro (17, 160). The properties described for the LamB pore are similar, but not identical, to those of the OmpF porin of *E. coli* B (see below). The homolog of the LamB protein in *S. typhimurium* has recently been identified (177, 179) as a 44K outer membrane protein induced by maltose. The protein is immunologically related to the λ-receptor (though incapable of inactivating the phage), but its porin activity has not yet been described. A more specific pore function in permeation of nucleosides has been ascribed to the Tsx protein (T6 receptor) of *E. coli* (80, 120). T6-resistant mutants lacking the protein show impaired transport of nucleosides even though *omp* genes are expressed (80, 120, 156), and the amount of Tsx protein is co-regulated with nucleoside uptake systems (120). That the protein functions as a pore rather than as a carrier was inferred from observations that nucleoside substrates do not compete with each other for uptake nor inhibit adsorption of T6 (80, 120). However, reconstitution of pore function with purified protein in vitro has not yet been described.

The phenotype of porin-deficient mutants strongly suggests that pore formation is a specific function of these proteins and not a nonspecific attribute of outer membrane proteins in general. This suggestion is confirmed by the findings that neither murein lipoprotein nor the OmpA protein confers porin activity in vesicle systems (159) and that outer membrane permeability is unaffected in a mutant totally lacking lipoprotein (165). Reduced transport of some amino acids has been observed under certain conditions in *ompA* mutants of *E. coli* (142), but it seems more likely that the defect arises as a secondary consequence of effects of the *ompA* mutation on the molecular organization of the outer membrane (see below).

It would be predicted that porin proteins must occur as major components in the outer membrane of all Gram-negative bacteria, and some information on porins of non-enteric organisms has begun to emerge. Two major outer membrane proteins of *Proteus mirabilis* with apparent molecular weights of 39K and 36K have been shown to have porin activity in synthetic bilayer vesicles (167), although the specificity of the reconstituted pores was not examined in detail. The porin(s) of *Pseudomonas aeruginosa* are of particular interest in light of the early observations of Decad & Nikaido (43) that the outer membrane of plasmolyzed cells was permeable to saccharides of at least 4000 daltons. More recent studies of Hancock & Nikaido (79) have confirmed this high permeability limit in reconstituted systems. It was postulated that these larger pores may be advantageous to an organism that is both lipolytic and proteolytic, in permitting uptake of micellar lipids or large peptides into the periplasmic space for subsequent degradation.

FUNCTIONAL PROPERTIES OF PORIN PROTEINS Both the permeability properties of porin-deficient mutants and the characteristics of pores reconstituted from individual purified proteins indicate that the OmpC, D, and F porins all act as general hydrophilic pores, allowing transmembrane diffusion of a wide spectrum of solutes of molecular weights below about 600 (8, 138, 158–162, 239, 240). It should be emphasized, however, that permeability measurements in reconstituted phospholipid vesicle systems have generally been restricted to equilibrium values of the transmembrane distribution of the solute, and not to rates of permeation. For this reason, pore properties in vitro cannot necessarily be equated to function in vivo. For example, pores reconstituted in vitro from OmpC, D, or F proteins are fully permeable to maltose (340 daltons) (161, 162, 239, 240), and omp^+ *lamB* mutants are indeed able to utilize maltose at high concentrations; however, such mutants are clearly defective in maltose uptake when the concentration of the saccharide is reduced to micromolar levels (24, 235, 236, 261). Presumably, the size of these pores is sufficiently small to reduce significantly the effective rate constant for maltose diffusion relative to that of the LamB pore.

With the above caveat in mind, the evidence currently available supports the conclusion that Omp C, D, and F porins are effective in conferring permeability to sugars and disaccharides (158, 159, 161, 162, 239, 240), amino acids (161, 162, 239, 240) [and presumably di- and tripeptides (184)], inorganic ions (14, 15, 138, 198, 207), and β-lactams (166). Although the functional properties of the OmpC and OmpF pores are broadly overlapping, they are not identical. Uptake of nucleotides at low concentrations is specifically mediated by the OmpF protein (11, 249, 267); this protein also appears to play the major role in *tsx*-independent nucleoside permeation (249, 267) and in uptake of chloramphenicol (61) and tetracycline (35). The new membrane proteins, NmpA-B and NmpC, appear to have functional properties similar to their *omp* counterparts. The NmpA-B protein, is similar to OmpF in restoration of nucleotide uptake (187, 249) but does not enhance adenosine uptake in *tsx* mutants (245). The phage-directed protein 2 is also effective in restoring amino acid and sugar uptake in porin-deficient *ompB* mutants (186).

Studies on the functional characteristics of the LamB pore have given some paradoxical results which suggest that factors other than simple Stokes radius may significantly influence solute permeation. In vivo results clearly establish that the LamB protein mediates uptake of maltodextrins as large as maltoheptaose (261) and can successfully act as a nonspecific pore for glucose and lactose (257). However, LamB was ineffective in restoring permeability of *omp* mutants to histidine and 6-aminopenicillanic acid (257). Some discrimination with respect to amino acids and nucleosides also appeared to operate in vitro, and it is curious that the cut-off size for saccharides in vesicles containing LamB was 550–650 daltons (160), even though the pore must accommodate maltodextrins of 1150 daltons (maltoheptaose) in vivo. The possibility that the periplasmic MalE protein may act cooperatively with LamB in permeation of maltodextrins (261) is discussed below. Additional evidence that the reconstituted LamB channel can discriminate even among saccharides of similar size has recently been presented by Luckey & Nikaido (134b), who employed a new kinetic assay of permeation based on liposome swelling. The relative rates of permeation of various disaccharides were found to differ by as much as 40-fold, and it was postulated that weak interaction of solutes with configuration-specific site(s) in the channel may effect the observed selectivity. Estimates of the effective diameter of the channel from measurements of ion conductivity by pore proteins incorporated into planar lipid membranes have indicated that the channel formed by LamB protein is somewhat larger than that of OmpF (17).

Detailed understanding of the functional specificities of the various porins with respect to solute structure will require methods for kinetic analysis of permeation. Rates of nutrient assimilation in vivo are generally not limited by outer membrane permeability because of the vast excess of porin proteins present in the membrane of wild-type cells (8, 166). Hydrolysis of permeant substrates by periplasmic enzymes can be employed to give rates of permeation in vivo, provided that the periplasmic hydrolase is present in sufficient excess. This technique was employed by Payne & Gilvarg (184) over ten years ago in analyses of the envelope barrier to diffusion of oligopeptides; more recently, it has been developed by Nikaido and co-workers (166) for analysis of the function of major porins in permeation of β-lactam antibiotics. However, the approach is restricted to substrates of periplasmic enzymes, and more general techniques applicable to systems reconstituted from individual purified proteins in vitro are necessary. Incorporation of porins into planar lipid bilayers (207) and the liposome swelling technique (134b) represent important developments in this direction.

STRUCTURE-FUNCTION RELATIONSHIPS As a class, the major porins (OmpC, D, and F proteins, Nmp proteins, LamB, Protein 2) share a number of unusual physical properties that are relevant to their structural and functional organization in the membrane. These include resistance to denaturation by SDS at temperatures below 85–100°C, resistance to proteolysis, a strikingly high content of β-structure in the native state, extremely strong self-association, and the characteristic association with peptidoglycan following extraction of cell envelope with SDS at nondenaturing temperatures (5, 48, 63, 66, 137, 162, 187, 197, 239, 240, 271, 272). Ultrastructural analysis of the peptidoglycan-associated matrix protein of *E. coli* B (OmpF) and reconstitution of such complexes with purified *E. coli* OmpC and F proteins have given considerable insight into the nature of the self-association characteristic of these proteins. Steven et al (229) employed electron microcopy and image processing of negatively stained specimens to determine the architecture of the complex isolated from *E. coli* by extraction of bacteria with 2% SDS at 70°C. The protein covers the surface of the peptidoglycan in a periodic monolayer arranged according to 3-fold symmetry on a hexagonal lattice with a 7.7 nm repeat. Yamada & Mizushima (268, 269) were able to reconstitute a similar hexagonal lattice structure by deposition of purified OmpC or OmpF protein on isolated peptidoglycan sacculi in the presence of lipopolysaccharide and Mg^{2+}. Although no ordered structure was formed by reconstitution on peptidoglycan lacking bound lipoprotein (268) and although the OmpF and OmpC proteins are more easily released from lipoprotein-free peptidoglycan by salt extraction (46), the presence of bound (or free) lipoprotein, or even peptidoglycan itself, is not required either for formation or maintenance of the hexagonal lattice structure. Vesicles formed from lipopolysaccharide, OmpF protein, and Mg^{2+} in the complete absence of peptidoglycan showed an ordered lattice structure very similar to that of the peptidoglycan complex (268). In addition, the lattice structure is retained, and indeed its long range order increased, after digestion of the isolated peptidoglycan complex with lysozyme (198) or isolation of the protein from spheroplasts (198). Thus, the ordered hexagonal lattice is based on strong protein-protein interactions intrinsic to the porin structure. The role of lipopolysaccharide is not yet understood, but functional interaction of OmpC and OmpF proteins with lipopolysaccharide is well established (see below).

Results obtained by a variety of techniques support the conclusion that the native porin proteins have a trimer subunit structure and that this is the miminal functional pore-forming unit. Analyses by sedimentation equilibrium in SDS of proteins purified under conditions minimizing aggregation have yielded trimer molecular weights for the OmpF protein from *E. coli* B (162, 198), the OmpC and F proteins of K12 (272), the OmpC, D, and F species of *S. typhimurium* (240), and the LamB protein (183). This is consistent with ultrastructural analyses of the peptidoglycan-associated form of OmpF, which indicated that the unit cell of the hexagonal lattice structure is most probably composed of three polypeptide chains (229). The native, soluble trimer species were fully active in reconstitution of pore function in vesicles (162, 239) and planar lipid membranes (198). The trimers could be dissociated to monomers by heating in SDS or by extremes of pH, but these were irreversibly inactivated with respect to reconstitution of porin activity or trimer structure (162, 239). Dissociation was accompanied by a large increase in SDS binding, loss of β-structure, and increase in frictional coefficient, all indicative of unfolding and denaturation (162, 198, 240). It is worth noting that because the trimer molecules are fairly globular and bind considerably less SDS than normal (162, 198, 272), their migration in SDS gel electrophoresis under nondenaturing conditions is anomalous. For example, the OmpF trimer of *E. coli* B (109,000 daltons) migrated at an apparent molecular weight of 80K in the SDS-polyacrylamide gel system of Nakae (162), and the K12 OmpC trimer actually moved faster than the heat-denatured monomers in SDS-urea gels (272).

Cross-linking studies confirm the trimer structure of soluble OmpC (181, 272) and OmpF proteins (181) and have also provided evidence that the OmpC, OmpF, and LamB proteins exist as trimers in the outer membrane (96, 181, 182, 194). In the intact membrane, however, considerable amounts of higher oligomers were also detected, with presumptive hexamers and nonamers predominating over intermediate species (182). This evidence suggests that the self-association into ordered arrays which is characteristic of these proteins in vitro may also be a major determinant of their molecular organization in the membrane in vivo. Two laboratories have approached, with conflicting results, the interesting question of whether the closely related porins OmpC and OmpF form only homotrimers when both are simultaneously expressed in the cell or whether they are capable of interacting to form heterotrimer pore structures. Palva & Randall (182) cross-linked intact cells with a cleavable cross-linking reagent under conditions in which only dimers were produced, and they concluded on the basis of two-dimensional SDS gel electrophoresis before and after cleavage that only homodimers were present. Ichihara & Mizushima (96) employed a one-dimensional SDS-urea gel system which clearly resolved cross-linked dimers and trimers of OmpC from those of OmpF to show that the products of cross-linking by dimethylsuberimidate included substantial amounts of hybrid dimers and trimers. However, in these experiments cross-linking was carried out after solubilization of the porin proteins in order to obviate inter-trimer reactions; no hybrid formation was observed when extracts, each containing only one of the two proteins, were mixed before cross-linking.

Incorporation of porin proteins into planar lipid bilayer membranes provides an additional and very interesting technique that permits sensitive measurements of membrane conductance dependent on the ion-permeable protein pore. Benz et al have described reconstitution of ion channels into planar films of oxidized cholesterol by simple addition of detergent solutions of the OmpF protein of *E. coli* B (14, 15) or LamB (17) to the bathing medium. From measurements of single-channel conductance and permeability to large organic ions, minimum channel diameters of 0.8 nm and 1.3 nm were estimated for the OmpF and LamB pores, respectively. A more sophisticated and elegant method for forming planar membranes in the absence of detergents and solvents and with well-controlled protein content has been developed by Schindler & Rosenbusch (207) for analysis of structural and functional properties of the OmpF channel. Phospholipid vesicles containing known amounts of protein are spread at an air-water interface, and the resulting monolayer is then apposed to a second monolayer of pure phospholipid over a circular aperture to form a planar bilayer membrane of well-defined composition. In spite of the differences between the two techniques, the estimated channel diameters were similar. It is of interest that functional membranes could be formed in the absence of added or protein-associated lipopolysaccharide. From detailed analyses of conductance as a function of protein content and applied voltage, Schindler & Rosenbusch (207) have further concluded that the OmpF channels exist in two states, open and closed, which are in equilibrium, that channel opening is voltage induced and voltage controlled, and that the pores exhibit a high degree of cooperativity among themselves. The latter presumably implies that intermolecular interactions within a self-associated array of trimers play a significant role in function. The minimal inducible unit at low protein concentrations corresponded to three unit channels, which, however, relaxed in three separate steps. This finding, together with observations (198) that at extremely low protein concentration (20 trimers per membrane) the maximum conductance corresponded to approximately three unit channels per trimer incorporated, led to the hypothesis that the trimer protein molecule contains three functional channels, i.e. one per monomer. Previous ultrastructural analyses of the peptidoglycan-associated form of the protein were consistent with this interpretation (229). The evidence that the channels can be closed and opened in response to applied voltage is particularly provocative in light of known requirements for an energized inner membrane in other outer membrane functions [*tonB*-dependent specific permeation systems, reviewed in (21, 110, 117)] and the finding that a Donnan potential exists across the outer membrane (230).

Ultimately, the unique physical and functional properties of porin proteins must be referred back to the primary sequence of the polypeptides; the recent completion by Henning and co-workers (34) of the primary structure of the OmpF protein of *E. coli* B/r is an important advance. In spite of the extreme hydrophobicity of the native protein, the sequence is marked by an absence of long contiguous stretches of hydrophobic residues; the longest nonpolar sequence uninterrupted by charged residues is an 11-residue segment in the middle of the chain (residues 184–194). That the polypeptide lacks a linear hydrophobic sequence long enough to span the membrane (20 residues) is perhaps not surprising, given the trimeric nature of functional unit and the additional strong protein-protein interactions among trimers. The chain does appear to consist of three regions of differing polarity: a hydrophilic region from residue 1 to 82 (51.2% polarity), a relatively nonpolar central segment from residue 83 to 194 (33.9% polarity), and a second more hydrophilic region (48% polarity) extending to the C-terminus at residue 340. Calculations of β-sheet content predicted that much of the β-structure lies in the C-terminal half of the polypeptide, but the calculated values underestimated the actual amount of β-sheet as determined by circular dichroism and infrared spectroscopy (197). In addition, calculation predicted 20% α-helix, which is far higher than the amount observed in the native protein (197). In general, the sequence presents no very obvious clues to the topology of the protein. However, this sequence contrasts strikingly with those of some classic intrinsic membrane proteins, such as glycophorin, the M13 coat protein, and the LacY protein (M protein) (25a), which are marked by an extended hydrophobic "membrane segment" capable of spanning the lipid bilayer, and it serves to reemphasize that there is no single paradigm for the structural organization of transmembrane proteins.

MAJOR NON-PORIN PROTEINS

The OmpA Protein

The OmpA protein was initially characterized in *Escherichia coli* as a major outer membrane polypeptide that exhibited anomalous heat modifiable migration in SDS polyacrylamide gels (19, 210) and as the only major polypeptide that was sensitive to protease cleavage in isolated cell envelope fractions (86, 90, 193, 213). The possibility that the OmpA protein might be heterogeneous or exist in multiple forms was suggested by the finding that two-dimensional isoelectric focusing–SDS gel electrophoresis of cell envelopes showed as many as 12 spots identifiable as the OmpA protein (90, 206). Some of these multiple species may result from the posttranslational oxidation of lysyl residues in vivo (47, 149). However, most of the apparent heterogeneity can be explained by partial renaturation and aggregation of the polypeptide during the isoelectric focusing step (90).

Recent evidence has convincingly established that the OmpA protein of *E. coli* is a transmembrane protein, and this presumably will also be true in *Salmonella typhimurium.* The *E. coli* protein acts as receptor for phages TuII*(84, 85) and K3 (143, 244) and is therefore exposed at the external face of the membrane. Exposure at the periplasmic face was initially deduced from observations that cleavage of the protein by trypsin or pronase occurs only when the inner surface of the membrane is made accessible to the protease (i.e. in isolated membrane or membrane-peptidoglycan fractions) (90, 193, 213). Definitive evidence has now come from cross-linking experiments (57, 58, 178) that showed direct cross-linking of the OmpA protein to peptidoglycan in whole cells as well as in envelope fractions. Until recently, it appeared that the OmpA protein of *S. typhimurium* might not be exposed at the external surface of the membrane. Kamio & Nikaido (111) used CNBr-activated dextran as a non-permanent probe for proteins exposed at the outer surface; they found that many of the major and minor polypeptides, including the OmpC, D, and F proteins, reacted readily but that OmpA did not. In addition, no phages have yet been found that use the OmpA protein of *S. typhimurium* as receptor. However, Stocker et al (231) have recently shown that the protein acts as receptor for bacteriocin 4–59 (78).

The physiological functions of the OmpA protein are still not completely understood. *OmpA* mutants are deficient in F-pilus mediated conjugation (221), and observations that isolated OmpA protein inhibits conjugation (212, 244) suggest that the protein functions directly in promoting formation or maintenance of mating pairs and not via some indirect effect on the molecular organization of the outer membrane. However, the precise role of the protein remains to be established. Recent studies on mutants multiply deficient in outer membrane proteins (228) strongly suggest that the OmpA protein plays a significant role in maintenance of cell morphology and outer membrane integrity, possibly through interactions with peptidoglycan (see below). This may account for the reported pleiotropic effects of *ompA* mutations on outer membrane transport functions, including reduced rates of ferrichrome-mediated iron transport (39) and amino acid uptake (142).

It is well established that the *ompA* gene is the structural gene for the protein (3, 192), and there is as yet no evidence for a separate regulatory locus analogous to *ompB.* All known mutations that result in loss of the protein in *E. coli,* including amber mutations (90), map at the *ompA* locus, as do mutants that produce an identifiably altered OmpA protein (90, 144). The gene has also been identified and mapped to the same chromosomal position in *S. typhimurium* (231). In addition, transfer of episomes carrying the *E. coli ompA* gene into *S. typhimurium* and *Proteus mirabilis* resulted in hybrids that contained the *E. coli* protein in the outer membrane and were sensitive to phage TuII* (41). Finally, Henning et al (88) have recently succeeded in cloning the gene from *E. coli* K12 on a 7.5 megadalton *Eco*RI fragment using phage λ as vector. The gene was expressed during the lytic cycle of the recombinant phage, and $ompA^+$ plaques could be identified by a rapid and sensitive replica printing technique employing radioiodinated anti-OmpA antibody. The $ompA^+$ *Eco*RI fragment was transferred from the λ-vector into the plasmid pSC101, and the recombinant plasmid was used to demonstrate synthesis of OmpA protein in minicells. Expression of pSC101-$ompA^+$ in minicells of an *ompA* strain resulted in synthesis of large amounts of envelope-bound OmpA protein and a second immunologically related polypeptide of slightly higher apparent molecular weight (~ 35,000) which is probably the biosynthetic precursor of OmpA.

There is no evidence that expression of the *ompA* gene is regulated at the transcriptional level, but some limit appears to exist on the total amount of OmpA and other major proteins that can be incorporated into the outer membrane; overproduction of OmpA protein may exert some type of post-transcriptional feedback on production of these proteins (41, 88). Datta et al (41) found that although *ompA*/F'-$ompA^+$ heterogenotes expressed both the mutationally altered and wild-type proteins, wild-type diploid homogenotes ($ompA^+$/F'-$ompA^+$) showed no gene dosage effect; the amounts of OmpA protein recovered from the membrane were identical in haploid and diploid. In contrast, diploidy for lipoprotein resulted in the expected increase in expression (152). Amplification of $ompA^+$ in *ompA* strains carrying the pSC101-$ompA^+$ plasmid had a somewhat different but related effect (88). In these strains, OmpA protein was increased about twofold, but the membrane contained considerably reduced amounts of OmpC, OmpF, and LamB proteins as well as lipoprotein. The relationship of this phenomenon to possible mechanisms of biosynthesis and assembly of outer membrane proteins is considered below.

Protein a (3b)

This 40K polypeptide, designated "protein *a*" by Lugtenberg et al (135) and 3b by Schnaitman (210), is expressed at fairly high levels by *E. coli* K12 but has remained something of a mystery, genetically and functionally. The protein has now been mapped to 12.5 min (53a), and intriguing clues to its function have recently emerged from two laboratories. Fiss et al (59a) have identified as protein *a* an outer membrane protein that catalyzes in vitro conversion of the outer membrane receptor for ferric enterobactin from an apparent molecular weight of 81K to 74K. The nature of the modification is not yet known, but the evidence suggests that protein *a* is most probably a protease. A second, and apparently independent, role for protein *a* in regulation of capsular polysaccharide biosynthesis has come from work of Gayda & Markovitz (71). These workers have cloned a 2 megadalton *Eco*RI fragment in plasmid pSC101 that specifies protein *a* and inhibits capsular polysaccharide synthesis in *capR*(*lon*) mutants. Plasmid mutants no longer repressing capsule synthesis were deficient in synthesis either of protein *a* or of two lower molecular weight polypeptides (25K and 14.5K) also specified by the 2 megadalton DNA fragment (69). The results indicated that protein *a* is one of several proteins involved in the complex regulation of capsular polysaccharide production. Synthesis of protein *a* is known to be temperature dependent (136, 145, 210), and it is possible that the mucoid phenotype of wild-type K12 strains at low temperature is in part related to the decreased synthesis of protein *a* under these conditions. Gayda et al (70) have also presented evidence from inhibitor studies for a biosynthetic precursor of protein *a,* and additional studies on hybrid plasmids expressing the gene in *capR* minicells have suggested that the *capR*$^+$ product is necessary for conversion of the precursor to the mature form of protein *a* (69). The specific function of protein *a* in regulation of capsular polysaccharide formation and the relationship of this to the findings of Fiss et al (59a) are not yet clear.

Murein Lipoprotein

Murein lipoprotein is an unusual polypeptide that bears lipid substituents at the N-terminus and is in part covalently bound at the C-terminus to peptidoglycan. The lipoprotein appears to be highly conserved among *Enterobacteriaceae* (164); the sequence of the polypeptide from *Serratia marcescens* differs from that of *E. coli* only in the C-terminal heptapeptide (98a). Bound and free forms of lipoprotein are also present in *Proteus mirabilis,* although compositional (114) and immunological (164) analyses indicate a greater divergence of sequence. Occurrence of murein lipoprotein is not limited to the enteric family; both free and bound forms of the protein have recently been identified in *Pseudomonas aeruginosa* (150).

Genetic evidence strongly supports the hypothesis that murein lipoprotein plays a primarily structural role in stabilization of the cell envelope. However, the protein is not essential. A lipoprotein deletion mutant (*lpo*) of *E. coli* K12 isolated by Hirota et al (93) showed increased blebbing of outer membrane, alterations in barrier function, increased sensitivity to EDTA, and evagination of outer membrane at division septa (64, 234), but no gross defects in cell growth or morphology. The phenotype appears to arise largely from loss of the peptidoglycan-bound form of the protein, and a missense mutant that contains greatly reduced amounts of bound lipoprotein (127, 266) has similar properties (270). The *lpo* mutation has no obvious effect on functional assembly of porin protein (57, 165), and the role of lipoprotein in vivo in the organization of these proteins in the membrane remains open.

The biosynthesis and functional significance of the lipid substituents at the N-terminal cysteine of lipoprotein remain problems of considerable interest. Recent studies have established that the glycerol moiety of the thioether-linked diglyceride residue is derived from the nonacylated glycerol of phosphatidylglycerol (32, 33). The mechanisms of N- and O-acylation of the glycerylcysteine residue are not yet known. Interestingly, mutational replacement of the C-subterminal arginine 57 by cysteine [*lpp*-1 (101)] prevents O-acylation at the N-terminus, resulting in a lipoprotein that contains only the amide-linked fatty acid (199). The finding is consistent with the hypothesis (100) that the two ends of the molecule may be in proximity during synthesis and maturation of the protein in the cytoplasmic membrane. It is assumed that the three fatty acyl chains at the N-terminus are integrated into the hydrocarbon region of the outer membrane and interact with hydrocarbon chains of the bilayer (20, 51), but their importance for the functional organization of the polypeptide in the membrane is not entirely clear. Covalent attachment of lipoprotein to peptidoglycan appears to be normal in the *lpp*-1 mutant in spite of the acyl deficiency and the alteration in charge of the C-terminus (101), suggesting that the mutant protein is correctly integrated and oriented in the membrane. On the other hand, a mutation within the signal sequence of prolipoprotein that prevents processing and maturation of the precursor (127, 266) results in a severe reduction in the bound form of the protein, although the mutant prolipoprotein is successfully incorporated into the outer membrane. Whether the defect in cross-linking to peptidoglycan should be attributed to an abnormal conformation or orientation arising from the absence of the lipid substituents or to the continued presence of the signal peptide is not known. The biogenesis and structural organization of lipoprotein in the outer membrane are discussed in later sections of this review.

MOLECULAR ORGANIZATION OF MAJOR PROTEINS IN THE OUTER MEMBRANE

Figure 1 presents a schematic cross-section of the outer membrane based on nearest neighbor analyses and studies on functional interactions. It is assumed that the lipid constituents are arranged in an asymmetric bilayer structure with lipopolysaccharide distributed exclusively in the external leaflet (154) and phospholipid predominantly if not entirely in the inner leaflet (222).

Topology of Major Proteins

That the major porin proteins must span the membrane was initially inferred from their function as phage receptors (40, 89, 251) plus their characteristic association with peptidoglycan in SDS-extracted envelopes (197) and is now obvious from their function as transmembrane pores. The evidence that OmpA protein is transmembranous is also convincing. Exposure at the external surface is apparent from its activity as receptor for phages TuII* (84, 85) and K3 (143, 221) in *E. coli* and bacteriocin 4-59 in *S. typhimurium* (231); however, it is curious that the *Salmonella* OmpA protein was not reactive with the impermeant probe, CNBr-dextran (111). Proteolytic cleavage of OmpA dependent on accessibility of the periplasmic aspect of the membrane to proteases (90, 193, 213) indicated that the protein must also be exposed at the inner face of the membrane, and this is confirmed by evidence of direct interaction with peptidoglycan in vivo (57, 58, 194) (see below). Identity of the N-terminal hexapeptide sequences of the intact protein and its large membrane-bound cleavage product led to the conclusion that the protease-sensitive region is C-terminal (90, 213). The orientation of the OmpC, D, and F proteins in the membrane has not yet been established, but the observed accessibility of a LamB-β-galactosidase hybrid protein to fluorescent anti-β-galactosidase in intact cells indicates that the C-terminus of the hybrid protein is external (220).

In freeze-fracture electron microscopy, the outer fracture face of outer membrane is characteristically studded with a dense array of intramembra-

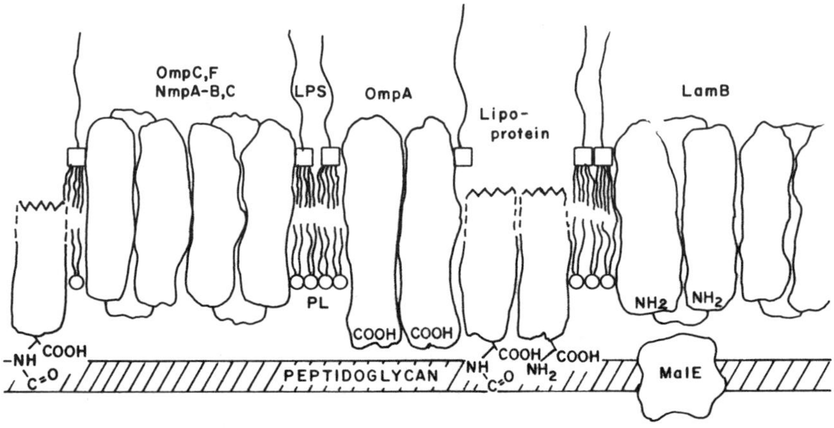

Figure 1 Schematic representation of the molecular organization of major proteins in the outer membrane of Gram-negative bacteria.

nous particles 4 to 10 nm in diameter (9a, 120a, 168, 169, 214, 222, 247, 253, 263). The particle density is closely correlated with the amounts of the transmembrane proteins, OmpA, C, D, and F (120a, 169, 214, 247, 248, 253), and the evidence strongly suggests that the particles represent individual lipopolysaccharide-protein complexes. X-ray diffraction studies (82, 243) are also consistent with the presence of protein assemblies of 10 nm diameter.

The extent to which murein lipoprotein penetrates the membrane remains uncertain. Conformational studies on isolated lipoprotein indicate an extremely high content of α-helix (80–88%) (25, 123), and it is assumed that a similar conformation exists in the outer membrane. Braun (20, 25) has postulated that the protein is anchored to the inner leaflet of the membrane by its N-terminal acyl chains, with the bulk of the polypeptide extending in two α-helices from the membrane to the underlying peptidoglycan. However, it is now apparent that mutant lipoproteins which lack some or all of the N-terminal lipid substituents are firmly integrated into the membrane (101, 127, 129, 130), and the polypeptide must therefore penetrate at least the inner leaflet of the bilayer. DiRienzo et al (51) have discussed a modification of the original model of Inouye (98) in which three lipoprotein chains form a transmembrane superhelix associated with each porin monomer. Direct evidence for the model is still lacking. Lipoprotein is reactive with antibody in deep-rough mutants (23), but the antibodies are directed against the periplasmically oriented C-terminal region of the protein. Techniques for differential incorporation of nuclear magnetic resonance (NMR) (124a) and electron paramagnetic resonance (EPR) (125) probes into the C-terminal region of lipoprotein in the intact membrane have been developed, but probes for regions of the molecule in possible association with the hydrophobic interior of the membrane are not yet available.

Protein-Protein Interactions

Nearest neighbor analyses using cross-linking techniques support the conclusion that self-association of porin trimers into ordered aggregates occurs in vivo as well as in vitro (178, 180–182, 194); they have further revealed nearest neighbor association of OmpA protein and lipoprotein with themselves and each other (194). Surprisingly, evidence for direct interaction of lipoprotein with porin in vivo is meager. Direct cross-linking of OmpC or OmpF proteins to lipoprotein has not been reported in intact cells or envelope fractions (180–182, 194). Some differences have been observed in EPR spectra of lipoprotein spin-labeled at the C-subterminal position in intact cells of OmpC-, OmpF-deficient mutants as compared to wild type (125); but whether these reflect direct porin-lipoprotein interaction or indirect effects on the environment of the C-terminal region of lipoprotein is not yet certain. Although the presence of bound lipoprotein clearly influences the association and reassociation of porins with peptidoglycan in SDS-extracted sacculi (198, 268, 271), lipoprotein is not required for formation or maintenance of porin supramolecular structure and function (158–163, 198). The available evidence in no way excludes the possibility of direct association of lipoprotein with porin polypeptides within the hydrophobic interior of the bilayer, but the question of the nature and role of the postulated interaction in vivo remains an open and important one.

Protein-Lipopolysaccharide Interactions

Interaction of matrix porins and the OmpA protein with lipopolysaccharide appears to be important both in biological function and in assembly of these proteins into the outer membrane, but the function of lipopolysaccharide in these processes is still poorly understood. Possible roles in assembly of the membrane are considered below. Dependence on lipopolysaccharide has been demonstrated for in vitro inhibition of conjugation by the OmpA protein (212, 244) and for reconstitution of phage receptor activities of OmpA (40, 244), OmpC (40), and OmpF (40, 81) proteins. In addition, in vitro inactivation of T4, whose receptor specificity is conferred by lipopolysaccharide, also requires OmpC protein (65, 87, 157). Direct protein-lipopolysaccharide interactions have been shown by protection of isolated OmpA protein from denaturation and nonspecific proteolytic degradation by lipopolysaccharide (213) and by binding studies with OmpA (208) and OmpC and F proteins (208, 271). Indeed, binding of lipopolysaccharide to OmpC and F porins is sufficiently tenacious to withstand previously established purification procedures, and the isolated proteins contain 3 mol lipopolysaccharide per mole polypeptide unless the purification is carried out at high ionic strength (198, 272). In most cases, lipid A substitutes effectively for intact lipopolysaccharide in reconstitution of biological function (40, 213, 269), suggesting that the relevant interactions are largely hydrophobic. However, interactions of both lipid and polysaccharide regions with the OmpC protein are indicated by recent studies of Yamada & Mizushima (269) on effects of lipopolysaccharide on the hexagonal lattice structure of the protein. Although lattice formation was supported by lipid A or fatty acids, the lattice constant was significantly reduced when heptoseless lipopolysaccharide or these lipids were substituted for the normal K12 lipopolysaccharide.

Protein-Peptidoglycan Interactions

Anchorage of the outer membrane to the underlying peptidoglycan is crucial for maintenance of the structural and functional integrity of the outer membrane. Although the bound form of lipoprotein undoubtedly plays a major role in this attachment, noncovalent interaction of the OmpA protein with peptidoglycan also appears to be important. In lipoprotein mutants of *E. coli* the weakened association of membrane with peptidoglycan results in exaggerated blebbing of outer membrane vesicles from the surface, especially in low Mg^{2+} media (64, 234, 270). However, cell shape is maintained, and the physical association of peptidoglycan with outer membrane is not grossly disrupted. The phenotype resembles that of *lkyD* mutants of *S. typhimurium,* in which formation of large outer membrane blebs over nascent septa is correlated with a decrease in the bound form of lipoprotein (64). In both *lpp* and *lkyD* mutants, the defect in structural integrity is accompanied by alterations in the barrier function of the membrane, including leakage of periplasmic proteins and moderately increased sensitivity to antibiotics and detergents (64, 93, 270).

The somewhat unexpected importance of the OmpA protein in outer membrane peptidoglycan associations is dramatically demonstrated in *ompAlpp*(*lpo*) double mutants of *E. coli* K12 (228, 270). Recovery of *ompA* mutants in strains containing the *lpp* mutation or deletion was possible only in media containing high Mg^{2+} concentrations (5–10 mM), and 30 mM Mg^{2+} or Ca^{2+} was required for optimal growth. Even under these conditions, the mutants exhibited complete detachment of the outer membrane from peptidoglycan, blebbing of vesicles from the outer membrane, and major aberrations in barrier function and cell morphology. Cross-linking studies confirm that the function of OmpA protein is mediated at least in part by direct interactions with peptidoglycan (57, 58). Cross-linking of OmpA protein to peptidoglycan has been observed both in wild-type (57, 58) *E. coli* and in *lpp* deletion mutants (57). It is important that in the latter strains, OmpA was the only protein to be cross-linked to peptidoglycan and that 30 to 100% of the OmpA protein (depending on the strain) was recovered in the cross-linked peptidoglycan fraction.

Although the association of matrix porins with peptidoglycan in SDS-extracted sacculi led to the assumption that these proteins must be major participants in outer membrane–peptidoglycan interactions, recent evidence suggests that direct association with peptidoglycan in vivo may be rather limited. The extent of cross-linking of OmpC and F proteins to peptidoglycan observed in wild-type cells was much lower than that of OmpA (10% vs 30–100%), and no cross-linking of the porin proteins to peptidoglycan was found in *lpp* deletion mutants (58). The results suggest that either bound-form lipoprotein is necessary for interaction of OmpC and F with peptidoglycan or that the cross-linking occurs indirectly through lipoprotein. The influence of matrix porins on the structural integrity of the membrane also seems to be limited. In contrast to the major morphological abnormalities of *ompAlpp* mutants, mutants of *E. coli* lacking OmpC and F proteins in addition to lipoprotein appeared to show no greater structural defect than their lipoprotein-negative parent (228). However an increased extent of outer membrane blebbing has been observed in *ompCompDlpp*$^+$ mutants of *S. typhimurium* (134a).

Interaction with Periplasmic Proteins: LamB-MalE Proteins

The hypothesis that direct interaction of periplasmic binding proteins with outer membrane porins may be important in at least some transport functions is suggested by recent studies of Wandersman et al (261) on mutants with impaired transport of maltodextrins (Dex$^-$). Selection for a Mal$^+$Dex$^-$ phenotype yielded, in addition to the expected class of *lamB* mutants, a class of mutants mapping in *malE,* the structural gene for the periplasmic binding protein. The defect in maltodextrin transport in these *malE* mutants could not be accounted for by loss of substrate binding activity by the periplasmic protein, and the results strongly suggested that transport of maltodextrins across the outer membrane was the step impaired. It was postulated that permeation of dextrins through the outer membrane involves cooperation of the periplasmic MalE protein with the outer membrane porin. Whether this cooperative function is mediated by direct association of the two proteins is not yet known.

BIOSYNTHESIS AND ASSEMBLY INTO THE OUTER MEMBRANE

Biosynthesis of Outer Membrane Proteins

PRECURSOR FORMS OF OUTER MEMBRANE PROTEINS It is now well established that many, but not all, outer membrane and periplasmic proteins are synthesized in molecular forms larger than the mature proteins. Four approaches have led to identification of these precursor molecules:

1. In vitro translation products of mRNA for an inner membrane protein (M13 coat protein) (116), outer membrane proteins (lipoprotein, λ-receptor) (102, 189), and periplasmic proteins (alkaline phosphatase, maltose-binding protein, arabinose-binding protein) (97, 189, 211) are larger in size than the corresponding in vivo mature proteins.
2. Precursor proteins can be synthesized and accumulated in vivo through the uncoupling of synthesis and processing. This has been achieved by the use of a specific inhibitor (94, 103), nonspecific membrane perturbants (50, 70, 76, 121, 215), and by the overproduction of precursor protein due to gene amplification (88).
3. Sequencing of structural genes for inner membrane, outer membrane, and periplasmic proteins has revealed the presence of DNA sequence

encoding the peptide extension at the NH_2-terminus of the exported protein (37, 83, 232, 233).

4. A mutant outer membrane protein has been isolated as the uncleaved precursor protein (127, 129).

That these proteins, which are a few thousand daltons larger than the corresponding mature proteins in vivo, represent true biosynthetic precursors for outer membrane and periplasmic proteins is supported by the following evidence. Pulse-chase data have revealed that the precursor for arabinose-binding protein can be chased into the mature form. Removal of phenethyl alcohol or globomycin is followed by the conversion of the precursor of OmpF and OmpC proteins or prolipoprotein into the mature species (75, 94, 103). The precursor of OmpA protein is accumulated by cells containing a non-fluid membrane; upon restoration of normal lipid fluidity, the precursor of OmpA protein is processed (50). A mutant prolipoprotein has been characterized which contains an NH_2-terminal sequence identical to that of the in vitro wild-type translation product except for a single amino acid (127, 129). These observations plus the fact that the NH_2-terminal extensions are initiated as methionine while the mature proteins begin with a variety of amino acids not preceded by methionine (Table 2) provide strong evidence that the precursor proteins are the primary translation products in vivo for outer membrane and periplasmic proteins.

Table 2 shows amino acid sequences of the peptide extensions in precursors of outer membrane and periplasmic proteins as deduced by protein or DNA sequencing. The general features of these sequences conform rather well with the known sequences at the NH_2-termini of secretory proteins in eucaryotic cells (74). A stretch of hydrophilic amino acids at the NH_2-terminus is followed by a hydrophobic segment of 10–12 amino acids. The transient nature, the hydrophobicity, and the amino-terminal location of this peptide segment constitute the common features of the so-called leader sequence or signal sequence in secretory proteins. In a later section we shall critically examine the evidence which supports the notion that these sequences are recognized in *E. coli* cells as signals for export.

SITE OF SYNTHESIS OF OUTER MEMBRANE AND PERIPLASMIC PROTEINS A number of features distinguishes the synthesis of outer membrane and periplasmic proteins from that of cytoplasmic proteins. Differential sensitivities towards inhibitors of protein synthesis provided the first clue that the synthesis of outer membrane and periplasmic proteins may utilize different biosynthetic machineries from those for cytoplasmic proteins (92, 185, 258). Recent evidence also indicates that outer membrane

Table 2 Amino terminal sequences of membrane and periplasmic proteins

Precursor of	Localization	Amino Acid Sequence	References
Lipoprotein	OM	MET LYS ALA THR LYS LEU VAL LEU GLY ALA VAL ILE LEU GLY SER THR LEU LEU ALA GLY ▼ CYS	102
λ-receptor	OM	(MET) MET ILE THR LEU ARG LYS LEU PRO LEU ALA VAL ALA VAL ALA ALA GLY VAL MET SER ALA GLN ALA MET ALA ▼ VAL	37,83
Maltose Binding Protein	P	MET LYS ILE LYS THR GLY ALA ARG ILE LEU ALA LEU SER ALA LEU THR THR MET MET PHE SER ALA SER ALA LEU ALA ▼ LYS	12
β-lactamase	P	MET SER ILE GLN HIS PHE ARG VAL ALA LEU ILE PRO PHE PHE ALA ALA PHE CYS LEU PRO VAL PHE ALA ▼ HIS	233
Arabinose Binding Protein	P	MET LYS ___ THR LYS LEU VAL LEU GLY ALA VAL ILE LEU THR ALA GLY LEU SER ___ GLY ALA ___ ALA ▼ GLU	265
fd Phage Major Coat Protein	CM	MET LYS LYS SER LEU VAL LEU LYS ALA SER VAL ALA VAL ALA THR LEU VAL PRO MET LEU SER PHE ALA ▼ ALA	232
fd Phage Minor Coat Protein	CM	MET LYS LYS LEU LEU PHE ALA ILE PRO LEU VAL VAL PRO PHE TYR SER HIS SER ▼ ALA	cited in 100
M Protein (lacY protein)	CM	MET TYR TYR LEU LYS ASN THR ASN PHE TRP MET PHE GLY LEU PHE PHE PHE PHE TYR PHE PHE ILE MET GLY ALA	25A

▼ denotes the site of proteolytic cleavage during the conversion of precursor protein to its mature form.

and periplasmic proteins are preferentially synthesized on membrane-bound polysomes (26, 188). This observation would be consistent with a co-translational mode of assembly of outer membrane and periplasmic proteins, as envisioned in the signal hypothesis (16). It has been reported that M13 phage coat protein and lipoprotein are synthesized on free polysomes (116). However these two proteins are exceptionally small in size and it is conceivable that polysomes synthesizing these proteins are more readily released from the membrane during in vitro fractionation.

KINETICS OF ASSEMBLY OF OUTER MEMBRANE PROTEINS Inasmuch as ribosomes have not been seen in the periplasmic space, it is reasonable to assume that polysomes actively engaged in the synthesis of outer membrane proteins are bound to the inner cytoplasmic membrane. It might then be expected that completed outer membrane polypeptides would reside transiently in the cytoplasmic membrane prior to translocation to the outer membrane. However, earlier attempts to detect completed outer membrane proteins in the cytoplasmic membrane fraction by pulse labeling were unsuccessful (22, 124).

Ito et al (107) first reported a difference in the rate of appearance of pulse-labeled polypeptides in the cytoplasmic membrane, outer membrane, and periplasmic space. At 30°C, the assembly of cytoplasmic membrane proteins was completed within 30 sec after labeling. The assembly of outer membrane and periplasmic proteins required 1–2 min and 5 min respectively. At 20°C, the times required for the assembly of inner membrane, outer membrane and periplasmic proteins were 1.5–2 min, 3–4 min, and more than 10 min respectively. The assembly of outer membrane and periplasmic proteins is more affected by reduced membrane fluidity than that of inner membrane proteins (107). At 30°C, assembly of outer membrane proteins in elaidate-grown cells of an unsaturated fatty acid auxotroph takes much more than 10 min, as compared to 3 min for oleate-grown cells. This difference in the rate of assembly of proteins destined for three different locations may reflect a difference in their biosynthetic machineries or assembly pathways.

Lin & Wu have confirmed and extended the work of Ito et al on the kinetics of assembly of cytoplasmic and outer membrane proteins in *E. coli* (132). At 25°C, the assembly of bulk cytoplasmic membrane proteins was completed within 30 sec, whereas the assembly of bulk outer membrane proteins required approximately 3 min to be completed. There was an inverse relationship between the rate of assembly and the apparent molecular weight of individual membrane proteins. The rate of assembly of cytoplasmic membrane proteins is two to three times faster than that of outer membrane proteins of similar molecular weight. Among the major outer membrane proteins, the assembly of OmpF and OmpC proteins into the outer membrane was unusually slow. Attempts to detect pools of outer membrane proteins in the soluble fraction or cytoplasmic membrane fraction of the pulse-labeled sample were unsuccessful. The assembly of pulse-labeled OmpF and OmpC proteins into the outer membrane was inhibited by the addition of chloramphenicol during the chase. These results strongly suggest that the rate-limiting step in the assembly of outer membrane proteins lies in the elongation of nascent chains. Given this conclusion, the slower rate of assembly of nascent proteins into the outer membrane implies that the rate of synthesis of outer membrane protein is slower than that of soluble and cytoplasmic membrane proteins. This possibility is supported by studies on the assembly of lipoprotein into the outer membrane (128). The rate of synthesis of lipoprotein was estimated to be about 14 sec per molecule at 25° C, which is significantly slower than that expected for soluble proteins [20 amino acids per sec at 37° C (59, 60)].

Pulse-chase experiments have further revealed that a small but significant amount of newly synthesized lipoprotein, immunoprecipitable with antisera against purified lipoprotein, can be found in the cytoplasmic membrane fraction (128). The nascent lipoprotein detected in the cytoplasmic membrane in a 10 sec pulse was already processed and could be chased into the outer membrane. The mature lipoprotein contains one tyrosine at the 56th residue and one isoleucine at the 7th residue (20). A pulse-labeling experiment using [^{3}H]tyrosine and [^{14}C]isoleucine was carried out by Lin et al (128) to follow the relative age of lipoprotein molecules in the inner and outer membrane fractions during the pulse. The [^{3}H]tyrosine/[^{14}C]isoleucine ratio of lipoprotein in the outer membrane was much higher than that in the cytoplasmic membrane. This difference in the [^{3}H]tyrosine/[^{14}C] isoleucine ratio of lipoprotein between the inner and outer membranes indicates that the lipoprotein molecules in the cytoplasmic membrane are younger in age than those in the outer membrane; furthermore, the transfer of completed lipoprotein molecules from the site of synthesis to the outer membrane is extremely rapid, sequential, and irreversible.

Genetic Determinants of the Localization of Proteins in the Outer Membrane

It is assumed that information necessary and sufficient for determining subcellular localization of a given protein resides both in the amino acid sequence of the primary translation product and in other components with which the particular protein will interact on its way to final destination. To define the domain of the polypeptide structures important for the targeting process, Beckwith, Silhavy and co-workers have exploited the elegant technique of gene fusion to produce hybrid proteins (6, 7, 218–220). Using three proteins of the maltose and maltodextrins transport system which have three distinct noncytoplasmic localizations, Beckwith et al have succeeded in fusing a soluble marker enzyme, β-galactosidase, with varying lengths of the NH_2-terminal segment of the proteins encoded by the *malE, malF,* and *lamB* genes. The *malE* gene encodes a periplasmic maltose-binding protein (115), the *lamB* gene codes for an outer membrane protein that functions as porin for the transport of maltose and maltodextrins (236) and as receptor for bacteriophage λ (191), and the *malF* gene product is localized in the cytoplasmic membrane (218). The results of this important series of papers can be summarized as follows (218):

1. Gene fusions between *lacZ* and *malE, malF* or *lamB* containing only small portions (10%) of *malE, malF,* or *lamB* genes produce hybrid proteins that remain localized in the cytoplasm (Table 3). For β-galactosidase to be partially located in a noncytoplasmic compartment, the fusion product must contain a significant segment (20% or more) of the NH_2-terminal portion of the *malE, malF,* or *lamB* gene product.
2. Gene fusions between *malF* and *lacZ* containing large portions of *malF* produce hybrid proteins, the major fraction of which are located in the cytoplasmic membrane.
3. *LamB-lacZ* fusions containing large portions of the *lamB* gene produce hybrid proteins, 80% of which are localized in the outer membrane—the subcellular location of the *lamB* gene product.
4. *MalE-lacZ* fusions containing major portions of the *malE* gene produce hybrid proteins associated with cytoplasmic membrane, but not in the periplasm where the *malE* gene product belongs.

These results indicate that information which directs a protein to a noncytoplasmic location is contained within the NH_2-terminal end of that protein. The presence of this information is capable of bringing a very large cytoplasmic protein, β-galactosidase, to a noncytoplasmic location. One of the most important questions to be answered is the minimal amount of information necessary and sufficient for correct targeting. The obvious candidate is the so-called signal sequence known to be present in many exported proteins, including outer membrane and periplasmic proteins.

Mechanism of Protein Export in Escherichia coli

THE ROLE OF SIGNAL SEQUENCE IN PROTEIN EXPORT Recent genetic and biochemical studies on protein export in *E. coli* have led to the following conclusions regarding the role of signal sequence in protein export.

Table 3 Amino terminal sequence of hybrid proteins encoded by *lamB-lacZ* or *malE-lacZ* fused genes

Sequence	Localization	References
1 2 3 4 5 6 7 8 9 10 11 12 13 14 15 16 17 18 19 MET ILE GLU ALA ALA HIS GLU LYS ARG GLU SER LEU ALA ALA HIS PRO PRO PHE ALA 27 28 29 30 31 32 33 34 (residues 12–19) lamB signal sequence (1–2) / μ sequence (3–11) / lacZ sequence (12–19)	Cytoplasm	6
1 2 3 4 5 6 7 8 9 10 11 12 13 14 15 16 17 18 19 20 21 22 23 24 25 26 27 28 MET ILE THR LEU ARG LYS LEU PRO LEU ALA VAL ALA VAL ALA ALA GLY VAL MET SER ALA GLN ALA MET ALA VAL ASP PHE HIS lamB signal sequence (1–25) / lamB sequence (26–40) 29 30 31 32 33 34 35 36 37 38 39 40 41 42 43 44 45 46 47 48 49 50 GLY TYR ALA ARG SER GLY ILE GLY TRP THR GLY ARG GLY VAL THR GLN LEU ASN ARG LEU ALA ALA 20 21 22 23 24 25 26 27 28 29 (residues 41–50) lacZ sequence (41–50)	Cytoplasm	6,151
1 2 3 4 5 6 7 8 9 10 11 12 13 14 15 16 17 18 19 20 MET LYS ILE LYS THR GLY ALA ARG ILE LEU ALA LEU SER ALA SER PRO GLY VAL THR GLN 19 20 21 22 23 (residues 16–20) malE signal sequence (1–14) / lacZ sequence (16–20)	Cytoplasm	6,12
1 2 3 4 5 6 7 8 9 10 11 12 13 14 15 16 17 18 19 20 21 22 23 24 25 26 27 28 29 MET LYS ILE LYS THR GLY ALA ARG ILE LEU ALA LEU SER ALA LEU THR THR MET MET PHE SER ALA <u>ASP</u> ALA LEU ALA LYS ILE (GLU) malE signal sequence (1–26) / malE sequence (27–47) 30 31 32 33 34 35 36 37 38 39 40 41 42 43 44 45 46 47 48 49 50 51 52 53 54 55 56 57 58 59 GLU GLY LYS LEU VAL ILE TRP ILE ASN GLY ASP LYS GLY TYR ASN GLY (ILE) ALA (GLU) (VAL) LEU ALA ALA HIS PRO PRO PHE ALA SER TRP 25 26 27 28 29 30 31 32 33 34 35 36 (residues 48–59) lacZ sequence (48–59)	Cytoplasmic Membrane	6,12

1. *An intact signal sequence is necessary but not sufficient for protein export.* Table 3 summarizes the amino-terminal sequence of *lamB-lacZ* and *malE-lacZ* hybrid proteins and their subcellular localization. Hybrid proteins having a partial signal sequence of λ-receptor or maltose-binding protein are not exported (6, 12). This observation, plus the fact that mutants altered in the signal sequence of *lamB* and *malE* are defective in protein export (see below), strongly suggests that an intact signal sequence is necessary for the initiation of export. However, a signal sequence alone is not sufficient for the completion of this vectorial transport process (151). The size and/or the primary structure of the remaining portion of the protein molecule may also dictate the overall efficacy of this process. This is evidenced by the failure of *E. coli* cells to export a *lamB-lacZ* hybrid protein that contains the complete signal sequence (24 amino acids) plus the first 15 residues of the LamB protein. This hybrid protein is entirely cytoplasmic in location and its signal sequence is intact. It is possible that export of this hybrid protein is initiated but aborted due to additional structural requirements of the protein-export machinery. On the other hand, a *malE-lacZ* hybrid protein containing the complete signal sequence plus the first 21–23 residues of the maltose-binding protein is bound to the cytoplasmic membrane. The difference in the efficiency of export of these two hybrid proteins is intriguing and may reflect a difference in the export machineries for the λ-receptor and the maltose-binding protein. The notion that the signal sequence is not solely responsible for the targeting of proteins to different subcellular compartments is also suggested by the fact that the signal sequence of prolipoprotein is strikingly homologous to that of arabinose-binding protein (Table 2). Unique features in the structures of mature proteins must be responsible for the localization of lipoprotein in the outer membrane and arabinose-binding protein in the periplasm.

2. *Mutants altered in the signal sequence of outer membrane or periplasmic proteins are defective in protein export.* The first mutant of an exported protein with an altered signal sequence to be identified contains a point mutation resulting in the replacement of glycine with aspartic acid at the 14th residue of prolipoprotein (127, 129). As a result of this single amino acid substitution, all of the posttranslational modifications of prolipoprotein are aborted. This mutant prolipoprotein is not processed, nor modified by the addition of glyceryl and acyl moieties and is not attached to the murein sacculus (266). It is, nevertheless, assembled into the outer membrane, albeit with a decreased rate and efficiency (130). That the defect in posttranslational modifications of the mutant prolipoprotein and its anomalous subcellular localization results from this single mutation is evidenced by the normal structure and distribution of lipoprotein in spontaneous revertants (127, 129).

A general procedure for selecting mutants altered in the signal sequence of an exported protein has been one of the major outgrowths of the gene fusion approach pioneered by Beckwith and his co-workers. Many of the gene fusions between *lacZ* and *lamB* or between *lacZ* and *malE* show a very characteristic phenotype, i.e. inducer (maltose)-sensitive growth. Among the maltose-resistant mutants of the various Mal^s *malE-lacZ* or Mal^s *lamB-lacZ* fusions were found those that confer maltose resistance (Mal^r) and simultaneously prevent noncytoplasmic localization of the hybrid protein. Furthermore, after these mutations were recombined into an otherwise wild-type *malE* or *lamB* gene, they prevented the correct localization of the wild-type gene product. Such mutations mapped extremely early in their respective genes and resulted in the accumulation of the precursor form in vivo, with a molecular weight corresponding to the precursor synthesized in vitro (4, 55, 56).

The DNA sequence of 15 such mutations which are in the portion of the *lamB* gene encoding the λ-receptor signal sequence has been determined (54). The results of the sequencing are shown in Table 4. The eight point mutations represent single base changes in four distinct base pairs of the DNA. Three of the deletions are internal to the DNA sequence encoding the signal sequence and the remaining four deletions cover this region of the DNA but are not confined to it. Similar mutations have been isolated and characterized for the maltose-binding protein (12) (Table 4). A closer examination of the amino acid alterations in the signal sequence of λ-receptor and maltose-binding protein reveals a striking common feature. The four different single amino acid substitutions in the λ-receptor signal sequence and four of the five amino acid changes in the maltose-binding protein signal sequence are all changes from hydrophobic or weakly hydrophilic amino acids to charged residues (arg, lys, asp, glu). All of these changes occur in the hydrophobic segment of the signal sequence. In both systems, multiple instances of the same mutational events are isolated. These results strongly support an essential role of the hydrophobic segment in the export process. It is also possible that only changes in a defined subset of the signal sequence amino acids will drastically affect export. Some of these mutations may prevent export by changing the secondary structure of the signal sequence. This may be particularly true for the small deletion mutation in the λ-receptor signal sequence or in the replacement of leu by pro at position 10 of the maltose-binding protein signal sequence. The deletion and point mutations clearly demonstrate that the NH_2-terminal basic hydrophilic segment at the beginning of the signal sequence is not sufficient for protein export; no export-defective mutations have been found in this segment of the signal sequence in either λ-receptor or maltose-binding protein. The fact that all of the export-defective mutations so far examined lead to alterations in the signal sequence but not elsewhere in the proteins suggests that the signal sequence is the major, if not the only, determinant required to initiate the process of protein export. More extensive analysis of mutants altered in the signal sequence and their revertants will provide further insights into the mechanism of protein localization.

It should be noted that the mutation in the signal sequence of the prolipoprotein mentioned above also affects the hydrophobic segment, changing glycine at the 14th position to a negatively charged amino acid, aspartic acid. While this alteration does prevent proteolytic processing of prolipoprotein and affects the subcellular distribution of the mutant prolipoprotein, it does not drastically affect the translocation of uncleaved prolipoprotein into the outer membrane (130). This discrepancy may be attributed to the small size of prolipoprotein compared with that of λ-receptor and maltose-binding protein precursors. It is conceivable that the interaction of the mutated signal sequence with the cytoplasmic membrane may be stable enough to allow the export of a small protein such as lipoprotein, whereas a larger precursor protein may have a greater probability of dissociating from the export machinery before the completion of its synthesis. Alternatively, it has been suggested that the apparent extreme stability of the lipoprotein mRNA may permit more rounds of mRNA translation which would compensate for the weakened interaction between the mutated signal sequence and the cytoplasmic membrane (254).

3. *Cleavage of the signal sequence is not required for transport of protein through the cytoplasmic membrane.* It has been suggested that proteolytic processing of the precursors is essential for the translocation of outer membrane proteins through the cytoplasmic membrane (51). This appears unlikely in view of the recent studies on the assembly of outer membrane proteins. In addition to the uncleaved mutant prolipoprotein that is translocated to the outer membrane at only a slightly reduced rate (130), the Tra proteins encoded by F-sex factor do not seem to undergo proteolytic processing upon export to the outer membrane (1). Further, under conditions in which the processing of precursors for OmpF, OmpC, and OmpA proteins is prevented by treatment with phenethyl alcohol or by reducing the membrane fluidity, the unprocessed precursor forms of these major outer membrane proteins appear to have passed through the cytoplasmic membrane (50, 75). Translocation of proteins across the microsomal membrane without a concomitant cleavage of the signal sequence has been demonstrated for viral glycoprotein (18) and ovalbumin (134, 176).

4. *Assembly of outer membrane and periplasmic proteins is co-translational.* Two features of the signal sequence suggest that it plays an essential role in the initiation of the formation of membrane-bound polysomes: the hydrophobicity of the sequence which allows a stable association with the

Table 4 Mutations in the signal sequence of outer membrane and periplasmic proteins

Protein	Alterations in Amino Acid Sequence	References
Lipoprotein	MET LYS ALA THR LYS LEU VAL LEU GLY ALA VAL ILE LEU GLY SER THR LEU LEU ALA GLY CYS ▼ SER SER	127,129
	↓ ASP (at GLY, position 14)	
λ-Receptor	(MET) MET ILE THR LEU ARG LYS LEU PRO LEU ALA VAL ALA VAL ALA ALA GLY VAL MET SER ALA GLN ALA MET ALA ▼ VAL ASP PHE	54,56
	↓ ASP (at VAL), ↓ GLU (at ALA), ↓ GLU (at ALA), ↓ ARG (at MET)	
	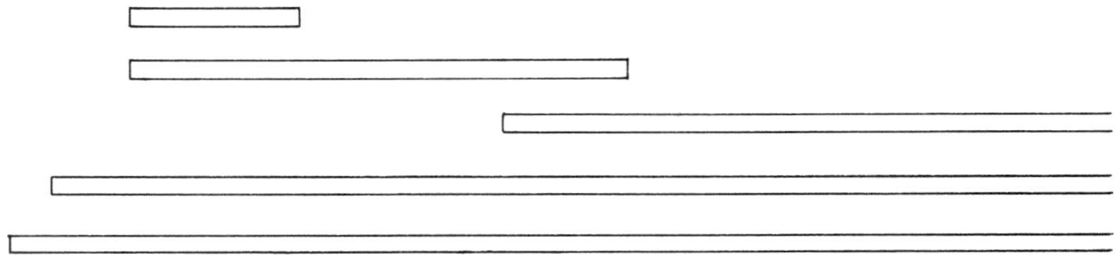	
Maltose Binding Protein	MET LYS ILE LYS THR GLY ALA ARG ILE LEU ALA LEU SER ALA LEU THR THR MET MET PHE SER ALA SER ALA LEU ALA ▼ LYS ILE GLU	6,12
	↓ PRO (at LEU), ↓ GLU (at ALA), ↓ LYS (at THR), ↓ ARG (at MET), ↓ ARG (at PHE)	

▼ denotes the site of proteolytic cleavage during the conversion of precursor protein to its mature form. ↓ denotes the amino acid alteration in signal sequence mutants.

cytoplasmic membrane (255), and its strategic location at the NH_2-terminus of a nascent chain. These two features provide the basis of postulating a co-translational mode of assembly of membrane or secretory proteins. Post-translational assembly of proteins containing transient leader sequence has been reported in both procaryotic and eucaryotic cells (27, 36, 38, 52, 73, 91, 106, 139, 196), and the two mechanisms need not be mutually exclusive. Nevertheless, the following observations tend to favor the possibility that the signal sequence in precursor proteins is involved in co-translational assembly of outer membrane and periplasmic proteins. It is possible that the mechanism of assembly of proteins into the cytoplasmic membrane may be distinct from those for extracellular proteins.

(*a*) Outer membrane and periplasmic proteins have been shown to be synthesized on membrane-bound polysomes (26, 188).

(*b*) Extracellular labeling of nascent alkaline phosphatase traversing the cytoplasmic membrane provided direct evidence that exported proteins may traverse the cytoplasmic membranes as growing chains (227).

(*c*) Mutants selected for defective export contain point or deletion mutations clustered within or extended into the signal sequence of λ-receptor or maltose-binding protein (12, 54). If the signal sequence is involved posttranslationally to alter the folding of a secretory protein (264), one might expect to find export-defective mutants with altered sequences within the mature protein and an intact signal sequence. This has not yet been found. This negative result suggests that structural alterations outside the signal sequence do not often affect the initiation of the export process.

(*d*) Kinetic evidence indicates that the processing of the precursor is extremely rapid. The export of outer membrane protein following its synthesis is so rapid that the distinction between co- and posttranslational assembly becomes kinetically moot. In the case of lipoprotein, it has been shown that the order of transfer of lipoprotein from the site of synthesis to the outer membrane is the same as that of chain completion of nascent molecules (128).

(*e*) The length and the general features of the signal sequences in the precursor forms of inner membrane, outer membrane, and periplasmic proteins are very similar to those found in secretory proteins that are translocated across the microsomal membrane co-translationally (74, 100). On the other hand, the transient signal sequences in proteins which are targeted for other organelles and assembled posttranslationally appear larger in size and may be quite different in primary and secondary structures (27, 36, 38, 52, 91, 139, 209, 259). This difference in the structures of the leader sequences might be expected teleologically so that the nascent chains of the latter class of proteins would not be attached to the microsomal membrane via the amino-terminal segment during their synthesis. Whether such divergence in the structures of leader sequences exists in inner membrane, outer membrane, and periplasmic proteins of *E. coli* remains to be seen.

(*f*) The suppression of export deficiency due to alterations in the signal sequence of LamB or maltose-binding protein by a second-site mutation mapped in a region of *E. coli* genome coding for ribosomal proteins (218) is consistent with a direct ribosome-membrane interaction during co-translational assembly of outer membrane and periplasmic proteins.

During phage M13 infection, the coat proteins are inserted asymmetrically into the cytoplasmic membrane of the infected cells. Later in the infectious process, newly synthesized procoat protein is assembled into the same membrane and the signal sequence at the NH_2-terminus is removed. The coat protein from the infecting phage and that synthesized de novo in the infected cells are functionally equivalent, and both are utilized for progeny phage assembly. The precise role of the signal sequence and its cleavage in the assembly of procoat protein into the cytoplasmic membrane is in dispute (31, 106); however, the fact that the processed coat protein can be assembled into the cytoplasmic membrane by two distinct paths and can achieve the same orientation in the same subcellular compartment strongly suggests that the assembly of coat protein as a precursor form into the inner membrane, either co-translationally or posttranslationally, is not the only mechanism for targeting a protein to its destination.

SIGNAL PEPTIDASE With the number of precursor proteins containing a transient signal sequence rapidly increasing, the question of the number and specificity of signal peptidase(s) becomes even more important and intriguing. Definitive answers can only be provided by biochemical and genetic characterization of the presumptive enzymes. Activities capable of processing the precursors of f1 coat protein, alkaline phosphatase, lipoprotein, LamB protein, and maltose-binding protein have been described (30, 97, 141, 146, 190). Whether there is in fact a single enzyme, a set of enzymes with broad specificities, or individual enzymes for each precursor protein remains to be seen. A number of observations suggest that there may be more than a single processing enzyme for the major outer membrane proteins. For instance, different concentrations of toluene or phenethyl alcohol are required to elicit the accumulation of precursors of lipoprotein, OmpF, OmpC, and OmpA proteins (75, 125); the degree of inhibition of the processing of these precursors by reduction of membrane fluidity also differs quantitatively (50). These results may reflect differential sensitivities of distinct signal peptidases towards membrane perturbations, but they may also indicate differential effects of these perturbants on the conformation of individual precursor proteins. By the same reasoning, the accumulation of the precursor form of λ-receptor in Mal^s cells induced for the export of *malE-lacZ* hybrid protein does not prove that λ-receptor protein and maltose-binding protein share a common processing enzyme. It is quite possible that jamming of a common export site or machinery prevents the λ-receptor precursor from reaching its signal peptidase. Strong suggestive evidence for a unique signal peptidase for prolipoprotein comes from studies using globomycin. This novel antibiotic appears to be a specific inhibitor for the processing of prolipoprotein (or other similar diglyceride-containing proteins) (94, 103). Although this antibiotic may yet have effects other than the inhibition of prolipoprotein processing, precursors for other major outer membrane proteins do not accumulate under conditions in which the processing of prolipoprotein is totally abolished. This observation suggests that the signal peptidase for prolipoprotein may be distinct and specific for prolipoprotein processing.

The localization of the signal peptidase(s) remains to be determined. Proteolytic activities capable of solubilizing nitrate reductase (140) and processing prolipoprotein and precursors of alkaline phosphatase and M13 coat protein have been localized in isolated outer membrane (97). On the other hand, processing activities for precursors of f1 coat protein, alkaline phosphatase, and λ-receptor have been shown in vitro using inverted inner membrane vesicles in a co-translational assay with membrane-bound polysomes (30, 146; cited in 262). These results would be consistent with the presence of the signal peptidase at the external surface of the cytoplasmic membrane. Similarly, in vivo studies suggest that processing of prolipoprotein takes place before the translocation of lipoprotein to the outer membrane (128) and that processed lipoprotein accumulates in the cytoplasmic membrane fraction of spheroplasts (112). The accumulation of diglyceride-containing prolipoprotein in the inner membrane of globomycin-treated cells (94) also suggests that the signal peptidase of prolipoprotein resides in the cytoplasmic membrane. Both in vitro and in vivo evidence suggest that signal peptidases are endopeptidases (30, 129).

OTHER COMPONENTS OF THE EXPORT MACHINERY While the primary structure of an exported protein eventually determines its destination, other cellular components must be involved in the overall process of protein export. A genetic approach to this problem has proved to be very promising. The selection of export-defective mutants based on the Mal^s phenotype of *lamB-lacZ* or *malE-lacZ* fusion should at least in theory lead to the identification of unlinked genetic loci involved in the export of these hybrid proteins. This approach has not yet been successful. On the other hand, Silhavy et al have succeeded in identifying second-site mutations that partially suppress the defective export of mutated λ-receptor proteins and result in a very low level of λ-receptor in the outer membrane (218). These mutations are co-transducible with *rpsE* (3) within a cluster of genes coding for ribosomal proteins. This suppressor mutation is not allele specific and appears to suppress several of the *malE* signal sequence mutations as well as a small deletion in the signal sequence of the λ-receptor. If biochemical evidence can be obtained that this suppressor mutation is in a gene encoding a ribosomal protein, it will provide strong suggestive evidence for a ribosome-membrane interaction during protein export, as envisaged by the co-translational model of protein secretion. It has been suggested, however, that a reduction in the rate of peptide elongation or an increased packing density of ribosome on the mRNA may allow a more efficient export (254). Both of these two parameters could be affected by a ribosomal mutation.

ENERGETICS OF PROTEIN EXPORT The source of energy for co-translational assembly of outer membrane and periplasmic proteins has been a subject of considerable interest (42, 237). Part of the energy may be derived from the energy of chain elongation on the ribosome, provided that there is a direct attachment of ribosome to the membrane such as that mediated by ribophorins in eucaryotic cells (119). In *E. coli* a direct attachment of ribosome to the cytoplasmic membrane which remains after the release of nascent polypeptide chains by puromycin is yet to be demonstrated (224, 225). Extracellular folding of the nascent chain also appears unlikely to be the energy source for protein secretion, since transfer of alkaline phosphatase across the cytoplasmic membrane was not affected by extensive modification of its primary structure (226). It is conceivable that there is an active secretory machinery in the membrane which allows an unidirectional export of proteins across the cytoplasmic membrane at the expense of metabolic energy. On the other hand, neither the processing nor the assembly of outer membrane lipoprotein appears to be affected by abolition of proton-motive force (128). Inasmuch as the rate-limiting step in the assembly of outer membrane proteins lies in the step of chain elongation, uncoupling of protein export from protein synthesis may not be possible. The apparent slower rate of synthesis of outer membrane proteins in *E. coli* may be an indication of a greater activation energy in the transmembrane extrusion of protein chains.

COMMON VS UNIQUE PATHWAYS FOR THE ASSEMBLY OF PROTEINS DESTINED FOR THE CYTOPLASMIC MEMBRANE, OUTER MEMBRANE, AND PERIPLASMIC SPACE There are four potential destinations for a given protein in *E. coli:* the cytoplasm, the inner cytoplasmic membrane, the periplasm, and the outer membrane. Whereas the original signal hypothesis was formulated to account for the co-translational segregation of secretory proteins into the lumen of rough endoplasmic reticulum, its derivative version has attempted to account for the assembly of membrane proteins in general (133, 200). Recent studies have indeed revealed such features common to a variety of cell envelope or periplasmic proteins, yet at the same time have indicated a divergence in the mechanism of assembly of these three classes of noncytoplasmic proteins.

1. Site of synthesis. Proteins shown to be synthesized on membrane-bound polysomes include λ-receptor (an outer membrane protein), maltose-binding protein, arabinose-binding protein, and alkaline phosphatase (periplasmic proteins) (26, 188, 227, 250). On the other hand, the synthesis of M13 coat protein (a cytoplasmic membrane protein) and lipoprotein (outer membrane protein) appears to occur on free polysomes (106). Whether the small size of these two proteins is responsible for this apparent anomaly remains to be seen.

2. Necessity for a precursor form with a cleavable signal sequence. Many outer membrane and periplasmic proteins are made initially in precursor forms containing transient signal sequences at their amino termini (Table 2), and the same is true of the capsid protein of the filamentous phages M13, f1, and fd which is assembled into the cytoplasmic membrane of the infected cells (31, 106). However, whether normal *E. coli* cytoplasmic membrane proteins are synthesized as precursor forms remains to be determined. The DNA sequence of *lacY* gene (25a, 238) reveals many interesting features including extreme hydrophobicity and a preponderance of β-sheets in the secondary structure of the M protein; however, a closer examination of the aminoterminal segment following the initiating methionine reveals a sequence different in kind from the known signal sequences of the exported proteins in *E. coli.* It is possible that this segment contains a functionally equivalent signal sequence. On the other hand, the assembly of inner membrane proteins may be solely dependent on the extreme hydrophobicity of the protein itself, as suggested by the unusual primary structure of the *lacY* gene product.

3. Site of assembly. Recent studies on the assembly of periplasmic and outer membrane proteins have revealed significant differences in the temporal or topological control of the assembly process. Among the outer membrane proteins, the sites of appearance of λ-receptor in the outer membrane

are different from those of OmpF and OmpC proteins (202, 223). λ-Receptor appears to be incorporated initially only at the cell septum (202). The same may also be true for the periplasmic maltose-binding protein (49). On the other hand, Smit & Nikaido (223) have shown that newly inserted porins (matrix proteins) appeared as discrete patches uniformly distributed over the cell surface; furthermore, the zones of adhesion between the cytoplasmic and outer membranes (9) were most probably the sites through which these nascent major outer membrane proteins are exported to the outer cell surface (223). This study and those reported earlier by Mühlradt et al (153, 154) suggest that two of the major components of the outer membrane, the matrix proteins (or porins) and lipopolysaccharide, are added to the cell surface by a diffuse intercalation process at the regions of membrane adhesion; the number of these adhesion sites is 200–400 per cell. A second important conclusion from the work of Smit & Nikaido is their observation that the newly inserted porins do not undergo rapid lateral diffusion, but rather form patches at the sites of insertion. This observation would suggest a continuous formation of new adhesions with a concomitant lateral displacement of existing adhesions. De Leij et al have arrived at a similar conclusion based on biochemical considerations (45). Temporal control of the synthesis of outer membrane or periplasmic proteins, either transcriptional or translational, may alter the apparent site of assembly of various exported proteins. For instance, galactose-binding protein is synthesized only during a short period before cell division, whereas alkaline phosphatase is synthesized throughout the cell cycle (216). For the final localization of the site of assembly of these proteins, such control mechanisms may operate and be superimposed upon a common biochemical mechanism of protein export.

4. Kinetics of the assembly process. The rates of assembly of nascent proteins into the cytoplasmic membrane, outer membrane, and periplasmic proteins are quite different (107). When the lipid fluidity of the membrane is reduced, this difference becomes accentuated (107). Although the biochemical basis for this apparent difference in kinetics remains obscure, it may indicate a differentiation in the assembly pathways of inner membrane, outer membrane, and periplasmic proteins.

5. Multiplicities of export machineries. Studies by Silhavy, Beckwith and co-workers using hybrid proteins have revealed an unexpected difference in the ability of *E. coli* cells to assembly β-galactosidase into inner membrane, outer membrane, and periplasm when this large soluble enzyme is fused with varying portions of the NH_2-terminal segments of proteins encoded by *malF, lamB,* and *malE* respectively (218). *MalF-lacZ* fusion brings β-galactosidase to the cytoplasmic membrane, as expected, without confer-

ring the Mal[s] phenotype. The *lamB-lacZ* fusion product may appear either in the outer membrane, as expected, or in the cytoplasmic membrane, rendering the cells Mal[s]. *MalE-lacZ* fusion fails to bring β-galactosidase to the periplasm, the fusion product accumulates in the cytoplasmic membrane, and the cells become inducer sensitive. These striking differences in the disposition of a large soluble protein when the latter protein is attached to the NH_2-terminal portions of a cytoplasmic membrane, outer membrane, or periplasmic protein, respectively, may reflect a fundamental feature of the differential compartmentalization of these proteins in *E. coli.*

A common step in the pathways for protein export has been suggested by the observations of competition between exported proteins and by identification of a pleiotropic mutation affecting the assembly of a number of proteins. Competition for export was achieved by jamming the export machineries with the synthesis of large amounts of fused proteins that cannot be efficiently exported (218). Thus, outer membrane λ-receptor protein and periplasmic maltose-binding protein may be exported at a common site, since the precursor form of λ-receptor protein accumulates in induced cultures of Mal[s] *malE-lacZ* protein fusion strains. Another reflection of competition for a common site may be reflected by the reduction of OmpF and OmpC proteins in cells containing a twofold increase in OmpA protein due to the presence of cloned *ompA* gene on pSC101-*ompA*$^+$ (88).

Wanner et al have recently identified a mutation (*perA*) that seems to affect the assembly of alkaline phosphatase into the periplasm (262). Strains carrying the *perA* alleles have reduced amounts of several other periplasmic proteins and three outer membrane proteins including OmpF protein. Further genetic analysis of pleiotropic mutations affecting the export or assembly of multiple outer membrane and periplasmic proteins may prove decisive in the unraveling of this complex process.

Regulation of the Synthesis and Assembly of Outer Membrane Proteins

The regulation of the synthesis and assembly of outer membrane proteins is one of the most promising subjects for future investigation. A number of observations suggest that a complex regulatory mechanism or supramolecular interactions operate to determine the amounts and composition of proteins to be inserted into the outer membrane. Synthesis and assembly of murein lipoprotein were affected in an *E. coli* mutant that contained an amber mutation in a gene mapped in the vicinity of 74 min of the chromosome (241, 242). Synthesis of OmpC protein is positively regulated by the *ompB* gene product at the transcriptional level (77); the absolute and relative amounts of OmpC and OmpF proteins are dependent on growth conditions. The amounts of OmpF and OmpC are greatly reduced in heptoseless mutants of *Escherichia coli* (118) and *Salmonella typhimurium* (2). The level at which the structure of the polysaccharide portion of lipopolysaccharide influences the synthesis and/or assembly of proteins into the outer membrane is unknown. The assembly of OmpF and OmpC proteins appears to be unusually sensitive to perturbation; it is inhibited by protease inhibitors (104, 105), phenethyl alcohol (50), and by a reduction of lipid fluidity in the membrane (75). The kinetics of assembly of OmpF and OmpC proteins is unusually slow, as compared to that of OmpA protein (107, 132). All these unusual features suggest the possibility of additional regulation at a transcriptional, translational, or posttranslational level.

Another level of regulation of outer membrane protein assembly is reflected in the amounts of OmpA protein in the outer membrane. No gene dosage effect is seen for wild-type homogenotes carrying additional copies of *ompA* gene as F'*ompA*$^+$ (41). Mutants lacking OmpF and OmpC proteins contain more OmpA protein (84, 210). An *ompA* strain carrying pSC101-*ompA*$^+$ plasmids (6–8 copies per chromosome) contains less OmpF and OmpC proteins but a twofold increase of OmpA protein in the cell envelope (88). These observations suggest that the total amounts of major outer membrane proteins are limited by either the space they occupy in the outer membrane or, less likely, by a rate-limiting step in the assembly process. Lipoprotein which is present in larger molar quantities in the outer membrane does not seem to be equally affected by this limitation. Homogenotes with lipoprotein gene on the F-prime contain twice as much free-form lipoprotein as the parental haploid strain (152). The amounts of lipoprotein and λ-receptor are slightly reduced in the strain producing twice as much OmpA protein (88). It is worth noting that a decrease in the amounts of these proteins in the outer membrane, because of defective lipopolysaccharide or overproduction of another protein, is not accompanied by the appearance of these outer membrane proteins in the cytoplasm. A high proportion of *ompA, ompF,* and *ompC* mutants lack these proteins in the outer membrane, rather than having structurally altered proteins (41). These considerations have led to the suggestion that the synthesis of outer membrane proteins is under a negative feedback control by these proteins at a posttranscriptional level (41). Failure to incorporate or translocate normal or structurally altered proteins into the outer membrane would result in a rapid shut-off of their synthesis. Alternatively, one may postulate a rapid degradation of outer membrane proteins that fail to be incorporated into the membrane at its site of synthesis or export. Why the hybrid proteins that accumulate in the cytoplasmic membrane are not degraded or do not negatively regulate their synthesis remains to be explained.

INDEPENDENT ASSEMBLY OF OUTER MEMBRANE COMPONENTS

The major components of the outer membrane in Gram-negative bacteria are phospholipids, lipopolysaccharides, and proteins. Both lipopolysaccharide and phospholipids are synthesized in the cytoplasmic membrane and subsequently translocated to the outer membrane (171, 174). Table 5 summarizes the common and special features of the assembly of each of these major outer membrane components. The weight of the evidence at present seems to favor an independent assembly of outer membrane components rather than a mechanism involving intermediate assembly of a subunit containing nascent phospholipids, lipopolysaccharides, and polypeptides.

1. At the cellular level, it has been shown that the synthesis and the assembly of phospholipids, lipopolysaccharides, and proteins into the outer membrane proceed independently of each other. In the absence of net protein synthesis, lipopolysaccharides and phospholipids continue to be incorporated into the outer membrane (199). Similarly, proteins and lipopolysaccharides are assembled into the outer membrane, albeit at a reduced rate, in the absence of de novo phospholipid synthesis (131, 147). Assembly of phospholipid and proteins into the outer membrane was not abolished in the conditional lethal lipid A mutant grown at the non-permissive temperature (195). All these data argue against an obligatory coupling in the assembly of phospholipid, lipopolysaccharide, and proteins into the outer membrane.

2. Kinetics. The rate of translocation of completed polypeptides to the outer membrane is extremely rapid—much faster than that of phospholipids and lipopolysaccharides. This also suggests that assembly of proteins into the outer membrane is independent of phospholipid and lipopolysaccharide translocation.

3. Site of assembly and directionality of translocation. Lipopolysaccharides and porins appear to be exported to the outer membrane at or near zones of adhesion (153, 154, 223). These same adhesion zones have been postulated as the sites of export of mucopolysaccharides as well as the ports of entry of foreign charged polymers such as DNA during phage infection (9, 10). Translocation of lipopolysaccharides and proteins to the outer membrane is unidirectional and irreversible (171, 174), which is consistent with their unique localization in vivo (172). In contrast, translocation of phospholipids is bidirectional and reversible (109, 173, 174). This apparent difference may be related to processes secondary to the primary translocation event, such as intermolecular interactions, lateral mobility, etc. Alternatively, the unidirectional translocation of proteins into the outer

Table 5 Comparison of translocation of lipopolysaccharide, phospholipid, and proteins into the outer membrane

Features of translocation	Lipopoly-saccharide	Phospholipids	Proteins
1. Site of synthesis	Cytoplasmic membrane	Cytoplasmic membrane	Membrane-bound polysomes
2. Number and location of translocation sites	Multiple, random, probably at or near zones of adhesion	Multiple, random	Multiple and random for OmpC and OmpF proteins (porins); localized for λ-receptor and maltose-binding protein
3. Reversibility and directionality	Irreversible and unidirectional	Reversible and bidirectional	Irreversible and unidirectional
4. Rate (half-life)	Rapid (~1 min)	Rapid (~3 min)	Extremely rapid (sec)
5. Energy source	Proton motive force (?)	Proton motive force (?)	Chain elongation or active export machinery

membrane may be attributed to unique features of the export machineries.

4. Energetics of translocation. Translocation of phosphatidylethanolamine to the outer membrane is not driven by ATP, nor by continued synthesis of phospholipids, but by protonmotive force (53). Likewise, the translocation of lipopolysaccharides was inhibited by energy uncouplers (170). On the other hand the processing and assembly of lipoprotein and possibly other major outer membrane proteins into the outer membrane were not prevented by the abolishment of the membrane potential with dinitrophenol or carbonyl cyanide *p*-cholorophenylhydrazone or by using an *uncA* mutant of *E. coli* (100, 128). This differential effect of energy inhibitors on the translocation of proteins, phospholipids, and lipopolysaccharides may reflect a fundamental difference in the mechanism of translocation of these components.

The mechanisms of translocation of phospholipid, lipopolysaccharide, and proteins remain totally obscure at the molecular level. Before detailed mechanisms can be formulated, more information is needed regarding the precise molecular organization of the cytoplasmic and outer membrane and their dynamics. For instance, one needs to define the topological distribution of these components between the two leaflets of the outer membrane (201) to determine the orientation of the polypeptides in the membrane and to ascertain whether these molecules undergo lateral movement or flip-flop during the process of translocation.

A MODEL FOR THE ASSEMBLY OF OUTER MEMBRANE PROTEINS

A number of models have been postulated for the assembly of nascent polypeptides into the outer membrane (44, 45, 50, 175, 218). These models differ in details and their unique features are not mutually exclusive. We summarize here those features on which there appears to be agreement and formulate a composite model as a working hypothesis.

The body of evidence appears to be heavily in favor of a process envisioned by the signal hypothesis. The processing of the precursor proteins most likely takes place in the cytoplasmic membrane and co-translationally; mechanistically speaking, the processing by the signal peptidase can be separated from the translocation of the protein through the cytoplasmic membrane. Further evidence also strongly suggests that features other than the leader sequence are involved in the second step of the assembly process, i.e. the translocation of proteins from the outer surface of the cytoplasmic membrane to the outer membrane. How these proteins end up in the outer membrane remains the biggest mystery. It is unlikely that the specificity lies solely in the primary structure of the outer membrane protein itself, even though the latter is of utmost importance. The corollary of this conclusion is that additional specificity is conferred in this second step by additional components such as an export machinery containing receptor proteins, by specific interactions with other macromolecules (e.g. lipopolysaccharides or peptidoglycan) either during or immediately following translocation, and by an additional control that may be cell-cycle dependent. Although ribosomal proteins may affect the efficiency of this process, they are unlikely to confer selectivity to proteins destined for the outer membrane.

It has been suggested that outer membrane proteins appear in the periplasm following translocation across the cytoplasmic membrane and that they are subsequently assembled into the outer membrane (75). This seems unlikely under physiological conditions in view of the observation that the rate of assembly of bulk outer membrane proteins is significantly faster than that of bulk periplasmic proteins (107). This model is energetically unfavorable unless these nascent outer membrane proteins are coated with amphipathic molecules during transit through the periplasm. Conversely, it has been postulated that periplasmic proteins first appear in the outer membrane as the precursor forms and are subsequently released into the periplasm by proteolytic processing (175).

A specific model has been suggested to account for the divergence of export of outer membrane proteins from that of periplasmic proteins (Figure 2*A*) (218). This model is ingenious in providing a reasonable explanation for the ability of cells to export a large protein like the *lamB-lacZ* hybrid protein to the outer membrane. On the other hand, it is doubtful that exocytosis via vesicle formation could be rapid enough to account for the kinetics of protein assembly into the outer membrane; nor is the known orientation of lipoprotein and OmpA protein in the outer membrane consistent with the export by budding and fusion of membrane vesicles (20, 213). The lateral diffusion model has the same problem of orientation (according to this model, without additional rearrangement all outer membrane proteins would have their COOH-termini external to the cell surface).

A model envisioning a co-translational transfer of outer membrane proteins through Bayer's zones of adhesion has many attractive features (Figure 2*B*). In the case of OmpF and OmpC proteins, it is consistent with the experimental evidence of diffuse insertion sites (13, 223). It accounts for the rapid appearance of outer membrane protein upon completion of protein synthesis (132) and allows for a feedback self-regulation of the synthesis of these proteins (41). While the assembly process could be subdivided into multiple steps, it proceeds so rapidly in vivo as to be conceived as a continuing process. Only if the connection between the inner and outer membranes was interrupted by the physical removal of bulk outer membrane during EDTA-lysozyme spheroplast formation could the assembly of proteins into the outer membrane be uncoupled from that of insertion into the cytoplas-

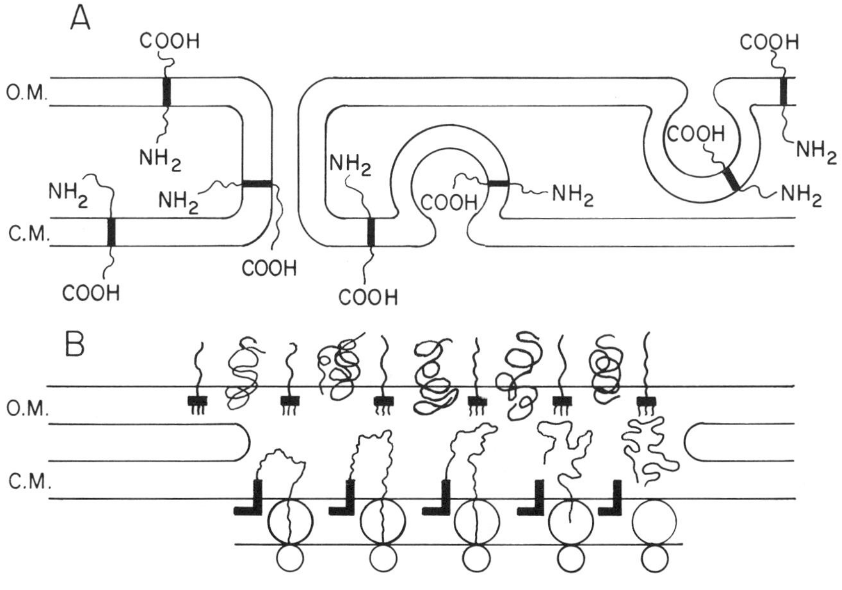

Figure 2 Models for the assembly of proteins into the outer membrane. OM = outer membrane; CM = cytoplasmic membrane.

mic membrane (112). This model would also account for the detection of nascent incomplete chains of outer membrane proteins in the cytoplasmic or outer membrane fraction, depending on whether the hypothetical zones of adhesions were enriched in the bulk inner or outer membrane fractions by the specific method of membrane separation (44, 132). Since metastable zones of adhesion appear more consistent with the observation that the insertion site rather than the nascent chain undergoes lateral diffusion (223), it is difficult to predict the buoyant densities of these insertion sites. The number of such sites may be so few that their isolation and characterization would be extremely difficult. This model would not easily account for the export of *lamB-lacZ* hybrid protein to the outer membrane (218). However, the site of export of λ-receptor appears to be different from those sites for the matrix porins. Future experiments using *ompF-lacZ* or *ompC-lacZ* hybrid proteins may ascertain whether zones of adhesion can allow export of a very large and hydrophilic hybrid protein.

In the case of OmpF, OmpC, and OmpA proteins, it is reasonable to assume that a specific interaction between the nascent polypeptides and the lipopolysaccharide and/or peptidoglycan near the insertion sites is important for continued synthesis and assembly of the protein into the outer membrane. We have already commented on the clustering of mutations selected for export-deficiency within the signal sequence of λ-receptor and maltose-binding protein; it is also known that the majority of *ompA, ompC,* or *ompF* mutants selected for resistance to phages or colicins lack these proteins, rather than having structurally altered forms in the outer membrane. Unless one assumes that receptor function is not completely lost in missense mutants, one is led to the conclusion that most missense mutant proteins are not incorporated into the outer membrane. This is also supported by studies which showed a severe reduction of incorporation of labeled amino acid into OmpF and OmpC proteins in the presence of amino acid analogues (113). A reasonable explanation for the preponderance of phage-resistant mutants lacking outer membrane proteins is as follows. While the structure of the signal sequence in an outer membrane protein is important for the initiation of the export process, mutations altering the remaining portion of the protein affect the second stage of the assembly process, i.e. interaction with lipopolysaccharide or peptidoglycan that serves as the anchorage for the nascent proteins. When this specific interaction is affected, direct or indirect feedback inhibition on the synthesis of these proteins will prevent an accumulation of these mutated proteins in the cytoplasm or in the inner membrane. This feedback control is likely to be at the translational level, since the mRNA for the outer membrane proteins appear to be unusually stable (68, 92, 126). Alternatively, unassembled membrane proteins may be rapidly degraded in the cytoplasm.

Literature Cited

1. Achtman, M., Manning, P. A., Edelbluth, C., Herrlich, P. 1979. *Proc. Natl. Acad. Sci. USA* 76:4837–41
2. Ames, G. F. L., Spudich, E. N., Nikaido, H. 1974. *J. Bacteriol.* 117: 406–16
3. Bachmann, B. J., Low, K. B. 1980. *Microbiol. Rev.* 44:1–56
4. Bassford, P. J. Jr., Beckwith, J. 1979. *Nature* 277:538–40
5. Bassford, P. J. Jr., Diedrich, D. L., Schnaitman, C. A., Reeves, P. 1977. *J. Bacteriol.* 131:608–22
6. Bassford, P. J. Jr., Emr, S. D., Silhavy, T. J., Beckwith, J., Bedouelle, H., Clement, J. M., Hedgpeth, J., Hofnung, M. 1980. In *Methods and Perspectives in Cell Biology.* Academic
7. Bassford, P. J. Jr., Silhavy, T. J., Beckwith, J. R. 1979. *J. Bacteriol.* 139:19–31
8. Bavoil, P., Nikaido, H., von Meyenburg, K. 1977. *Mol. Gen. Genet.* 158: 23–33
9. Bayer, M. E. 1975. *Membrane Biogenesis,* ed. A. Tzagaloff, pp. 393–427. New York: Plenum

9a. Bayer, M. E., Leive, L. 1977. *J. Bacteriol.* 130:1364–81

10. Bayer, M. E., Thurow, H. 1977. *J. Bacteriol.* 130:911–36
11. Beacham, I. R., Haas, P., Yagil, E. 1977. *J. Bacteriol.* 129:1034–44
12. Bedouelle, H., Bassford, P. J. Jr., Fowler, A. V., Zabin, I., Beckwith, J., Hofnung, M. 1980. *Nature* 285:78–81
13. Begg, K. J. 1978. *J. Bacteriol.* 135: 307–10
14. Benz, R., Janko, K., Boos, W., Lauger, P. 1978. *Biochim. Biophys. Acta* 511: 305–19
15. Benz, R., Janko, K., Lauger, P. 1979. *Biochim. Biophys. Acta* 511:238–47
16. Blobel, G., Dobberstein, B. 1975. *J. Cell Biol.* 67:835–51
17. Boehler-Kohler, B. A., Boos, W., Dieterle, R., Benz, R. 1979. *J. Bacteriol.* 138:33–39
18. Bonatti, S., Blobel, G. 1979. *J. Biol. Chem.* 254:12261-264
19. Bragg, P. D., Hou, C. 1972. *Biochim. Biophys. Acta* 274:478–88
20. Braun, V. 1975. *Biochim. Biophys. Acta* 415:335–77
21. Braun, V. 1978. *Symp. Soc. Gen. Microbiol.* 28:111–38
22. Braun, V., Bosch, V. 1973. *FEBS Lett.* 34:302–6
23. Braun, V., Bosch, V., Klumpp, E. R., Neff, I., Mayer, H., Schlecht, S. 1976. *Eur. J. Biochem.* 62:555–66
24. Braun, V., Krieger-Brauer, H. J. 1977. *Biochim. Biophys. Acta* 469:89–98
25. Braun, V., Rotering, H., Ohms, J.-P., Hagenmaier, H. 1976. *Eur. J. Biochem.* 70:601–10

25a. Büchel, D. E., Gronenborn, B., Müller-Hill, B. 1980. *Nature* 283:541–45

26. Cancedda, R., Schlesinger, M. J. 1974. *J. Bacteriol.* 117:290–301
27. Cashmore, A. R., Broadhurst, M. K., Gray, R. E. 1978. *Proc. Natl. Acad. Sci. USA* 75:655–59
28. Chai, T. J., Foulds, J. 1978. *J. Bacteriol.* 135:1478–85
29. Chai, T. J., Foulds, J. 1979. *J. Bacteriol.* 139:418–23
30. Chang, C. N., Blobel, G., Model, P. 1978. *Proc. Natl. Acad. Sci. USA* 75:361–65
31. Chang, C. N., Model, P., Blobel, G. 1979. *Proc. Natl. Acad. Sci. USA* 76:1251–55
32. Chattopadhyay, P. K., Lai, J. S., Wu, H. C. 1979. *J. Bacteriol.* 137:309–12
33. Chattopadhyay, P. K., Wu, H. C. 1977. *Proc. Natl. Acad. Sci. USA* 74:5318–22
34. Chen, R., Kramer, C., Schmidmayr, W., Henning, U. 1979. *Proc. Natl. Acad. Sci. USA* 76:5014–17
35. Chopra, I., Eccles, S. J. 1978. *Biochem. Biophys. Res. Commun.* 83:550–57
36. Chua, N. H., Schmidt, G. W. 1978. *Proc. Natl. Acad. Sci. USA* 75:6110–14
37. Clement, J. M., Hedgpeth, J., Hofnung, M. 1979. *C. R. Acad. Sci.* 289–1033–36
38. Cote, C., Solioz, M., Schatz, G. 1979. *J. Biol. Chem.* 254:1437–39
39. Coulton, J. W., Braun, V. 1979. *J. Gen. Microbiol.* 110:211–20
40. Datta, D. B., Arden, B., Henning, U. 1977. *J. Bacteriol.* 131:821–29
41. Datta, D. B., Kramer, C., Henning, U. 1976. *J. Bacteriol.* 128:834–41
42. Davis, B. D., Tai, P. C. 1980. *Nature.* 283:433–38
43. Decad, G. M., Nikaido, H. 1976. *J. Bacteriol.* 128:325–36
44. De Leij, L., Kingma, J., Witholt, B. 1978. *Biochim. Biophys. Acta* 512: 365–76
45. De Leij, L., Kingma, J., Witholt, B. 1979. *Biochim. Biophys. Acta* 553: 224–34
46. DeMartini, M., Inouye, M. 1978. *J. Bacteriol.* 133:329–35
47. Diedrich, D. L., Schnaitman, C. A. 1978. *Proc. Natl. Acad. Sci. USA* 75:3708–12
48. Diedrich, D. L., Summers, A. O., Schnaitman, C. A. 1977. *J. Bacteriol.* 131:598–607

49. Dietzel, I., Kolb, U., Boos, W. 1978. *Arch. Microbiol.* 118:207–18
50. DiRienzo, J. M., Inouye, M. 1979. *Cell* 17:155–61
51. DiRienzo, J. M., Nakamura, K., Inouye, M. 1978. *Ann. Rev. Biochem.* 47:481–532
52. Dobberstein, B., Blobel, G., Chua, N. H. 1977. *Proc. Natl. Acad. Sci. USA* 74:1082–85
53. Donohue-Rolfe, A. M., Schaechter, M. 1980. *Proc. Natl. Acad. Sci. USA* 77: 1867–71
53a. Earhart, C. F., Lundigran, M., Pickett, C. L., Pierce, J. R. 1979. *FEMS Microbiol. Lett.* 6:277–80
54. Emr, S. D., Clement, J. M., Silhavy, T. J., Hedgpeth, J., Hofnung, M. 1980. *Nature.* 285:82–85
55. Emr, S. D., Schwartz, M., Silhavy, T. J. 1978. *Proc. Natl. Acad. Sci. USA* 75:5802–6
56. Emr, S. D., Silhavy, T. J. 1980. Submitted to *J. Mol. Biol.*
57. Endermann, R., Henning, U. 1979. *FEBS Lett.* 97:339–42
58. Endermann, R., Krämer, C., Henning, U. 1978. *FEBS Lett.* 86:20–24
59. Engbaek, F., Kjeldgaard, N. O., Maaloe, O. 1973. *J. Mol. Biol.* 75: 109–18
59a. Fiss, E. H., Hollifield, W. C. Jr., Neilands, J. B. 1979. *Biochem. Biophys. Res. Commun.* 91:29–34
60. Forchhammer, J., Lindahl, L. 1971. *J. Mol. Biol.* 55:563–68
61. Foulds, J. 1976. *J. Bacteriol.* 128:604–8
62. Foulds, J., Chai, T.-J. 1978. *J. Bacteriol.* 133:1478–83
63. Foulds, J., Chai, T.-J. 1978. *J. Bacteriol.* 136:501–6
64. Fung, J., MacAlister, T. J., Rothfield, L. I. 1978. *J. Bacteriol.* 133:1467–71
65. Furukawa, H., Yamada, H., Mizushima, S. 1979. *J. Bacteriol.* 140: 1071–80
66. Gabay, J., Yasunaka, K. 1980. *Eur. J. Biochem.* In press
67. Gamon, K., Chen, R., Henning, U. 1978. *Mol. Gen. Genet.* 166:187–92
68. Garten, W., Henning, U. 1976. *FEBS Lett.* 67:303–5
69. Gayda, R. C., Aoni, H., Berg, P. E., Markovitz, A. 1979. *Mol. Gen. Genet.* 175:325–32
70. Gayda, R. C., Henderson, G. W., Markovitz, A. 1979. *Proc. Natl. Acad. Sci. USA* 76:2138–42
71. Gayda, R. C., Markovitz, A. 1978. *J. Bacteriol.* 136:369–80
72. Deleted in proof
73. Goldman, B. M., Blobel, G. 1978. *Proc. Natl. Acad. Sci. USA* 75:5066–70
74. Habener, J. F., Rosenblatt, M., Kemper, B., Kronenberg, H. M., Rich, A., Potts, J. T. Jr. 1978. *Proc. Natl. Acad. Sci. USA* 75:2616–20
75. Halegoua, S., Inouye, M. 1979. *J. Mol. Biol.* 130:39–61
76. Halegoua, S., Sekizawa, J., Inouye, M. 1977. *J. Biol. Chem.* 252:2324–30
77. Hall, M. N., Silhavy, T. J. 1979. *J. Bacteriol* 140:342–50
78. Hamon, Y., Paron, Y. 1966. *Ann. Inst. Pasteur Paris* 110:389–402
79. Hancock, R. E. W., Nikaido, H. 1978. *J. Bacteriol.* 136:381–90
80. Hantke, K. 1976. *FEBS Lett.* 70: 109–12
81. Hantke, K. 1978. *Mol. Gen. Genet.* 164:131–35
82. Harder, M. E., Banaszak, L. J. 1979. *Biochim. Biophys. Acta* 552:89–102
83. Hedgpeth, J., Clement, J. M., Marchal, C., Perrin, D., Hofnung, M. 1980. *Proc. Natl. Acad. Sci. USA* 77:2621–25
84. Henning, U., Haller, I. 1975. *FEBS Lett.* 55:161–64
85. Henning, U., Hindennach, I., Haller, I. 1976. *FEBS Lett.* 61:46–48
86. Henning, U., Hoehn, B., Sonntag, I. 1973. *Eur. J. Biochem.* 39:27–36
87. Henning, U., Jann, K. 1979. *J. Bacteriol.* 137:664–66
88. Henning, U., Royer, H., Teather, R. M., Hindennach, I., Hollenberg, C. P. 1979. *Proc. Natl. Acad. Sci. USA* 76:4360–64
89. Henning, U., Schmidmayr, W., Hindennach, I. 1977. *Mol. Gen. Genet.* 154:293–98
90. Henning, U., Sonntag, I., Hindennach, I. 1978. *Eur. J. Biochem.* 92:491–98
91. Highfield, P. E., Ellis, R. J. 1978. *Nature* 271:420–24
92. Hirashima, A., Childs, G., Inouye, M. 1973. *J. Mol. Biol.* 79:373–89
93. Hirota, Y., Suzuki, H., Nishimura, Y., Yasuda, S. 1977. *Proc. Natl. Acad. Sci. USA* 74:1417–20
94. Hussain, M., Ichihara, S., Mizushima, S. 1980. *J. Biol. Chem.* 255:3707–12
95. Ichihara, S., Mizushima, S. 1978. *J. Biochem. Tokyo* 83:1095–1100
96. Ichihara, S., Mizushima, S. 1979. *Eur. J. Biochem.* 100:321–28
97. Inouye, H., Beckwith, J. 1977. *Proc. Natl. Acad. Sci. USA* 74:1440–44
98. Inouye, M. 1974. *Proc. Natl. Acad. Sci. USA* 71:2396–2400
98a. Inouye, M. Personal communication
99. Inouye, M., ed. 1979. *Bacterial Outer*

Membranes: Biogenesis and Functions. New York: Wiley. 534 pp.
100. Inouye, M., Halegoua, S. 1979. See Ref. 99, pp. 67–113
101. Inouye, S., Lee, N., Inouye, M., Wu, H. C., Suzuki, H., Nishimura, Y., Iketani, H., Hirota, Y. 1977. *J. Bacteriol.* 132:308–13
102. Inouye, S., Wang, S., Sekizawa, J., Halegoua, S., Inouye, M. 1977. *Proc. Natl. Acad. Sci. USA* 74:1004–8
103. Inukai, M., Takeuchi, M., Shimizu, K., Arai, M. 1978. *J. Antibiot.* 31:1203–5
104. Ito, K. 1977. *J. Bacteriol.* 132:1021–23
105. Ito, K. 1978. *Biochem. Biophys. Res. Commun.* 82:99–107
106. Ito, K., Mandel, G., Wickner, W. 1979. *Proc. Natl. Acad. Sci. USA* 76: 1199–1203
107. Ito, K., Sato, K., Yura, T. 1977. *Cell* 11:551–59
108. Johansson, V., Aarti, A., Nurminen, M., Makela, P. H. 1978. *J. Gen. Microbiol.* 107:183–87
109. Jones, N. C., Osborn, M. J. 1977. *J. Biol. Chem.* 252:7405–12
110. Kadner, R. J., Bassford, P. J. Jr. 1978. In *Bacterial Transport,* ed. B. Rosen, pp. 413–62. New York: Dekker
111. Kamio, Y., Nikaido, H. 1977. *Biochim. Biophys. Acta* 464:589–601
112. Kanazawa, H., Wu, H. C. 1979. *J. Bacteriol.* 137:818–23
113. Kanazawa, H., Wu, H. C. Unpublished observations
114. Katz, E., Loring, D., Inouye, S., Inouye, M. 1978. *J. Bacteriol.* 134: 674–76
115. Kellermann, O., Szmelcman, S. 1974. *Eur. J. Biochem.* 47:139–49
116. Konings, R. N. H., Hulsebos, T., van den Hondel, L. A. 1975. *J. Virol.* 15:570–84
117. Konisky, J. 1979. See Ref 99, pp. 319–59
118. Koplow, J., Goldfine, H. 1974. *J. Bacteriol.* 117:527–43
119. Kreibich, G., Ulrich B. C., Sabatini, D. D. 1978. *J. Cell Biol.* 77:464–87
120. Krieger-Brauer, H. J., Braun, V. 1980. *Arch. Microbiol.* In press
121. Lazdunski, C., Baty, D., Pages, J. M. 1979. *Eur. J. Biochem.* 96:49–57
122. Lee, D. R., Schnaitman, C. A., Pugsley, A. P. 1979. *J. Bacteriol.* 138:861–70
123. Lee, N., Cheng, E., Inouye, M. 1977. *Biochim. Biophys. Acta* 465:650–56
124. Lee, N., Inouye, M. 1974. *FEBS Lett.* 39:167–70
124a. Lee, N., Inouye, M., Lauterbur, P. C. 1977. *Biochem. Biophys. Res. Commun.* 78:1211–16
125. Lee, N., Scandella, C., Inouye, M. 1978. *Proc. Natl. Acad. Sci. USA* 75:127–30
126. Levy, S. B. 1975. *Proc. Natl. Acad. Sci. USA* 72:2900–4
127. Lin, J. J. C., Kanazawa, H., Ozols, J., Wu, H. C. 1978. *Proc. Natl. Acad. Sci. USA* 75:4891–95
128. Lin, J. J. C., Giam, C. Z., Wu, H. C. 1980. *J. Biol. Chem.* 255:807–11
129. Lin, J. J. C., Kanazawa, H., Wu, H. C. 1980. *J. Biol. Chem.* 225:1160–63
130. Lin, J. J. C., Kanazawa, H., Wu, H. C. 1980. *J. Bacteriol.* 141:550–57
131. Lin, J. J. C., Wu, H. C. 1976. *J. Bacteriol.* 125:892–904
132. Lin, J. J. C., Wu, H. C. 1980. *J. Biol. Chem.* 255:802–6
133. Lingappa, V. R., Katz, F. N., Lodish, H. F., Blobel, G. 1978. *J. Biol. Chem.* 253:8667–70
134. Lingappa, V. R., Lingappa, J. R., Blobel, G. 1979. *Nature* 281:117–21
134a. Lounatmaa, K., Nurminen, M. 1977. *FEMS Microbiol. Lett.* 2:317–22
134b. Luckey, M., Nikaido, H. 1980. *Proc. Natl. Acad. Sci. USA* 77:167–71
135. Lugtenberg, B., Meijers, J., Peters, R., van der Hock, R., van Alphen, L. 1975. *FEBS Lett.* 58:254–58
136. Lugtenberg, B., Peters, R., Bernheimer, H., Berendsen, W. 1976. *Mol. Gen. Genet.* 147:251–62
137. Lugtenberg, B., van Boxtel, R., Verhoef, C., van Alphen, W. 1978. *FEBS Lett.* 96:99–101
138. Luktenhaus, J. F. 1977. *J. Bacteriol.* 131:631–37
139. Maccecchini, M. L., Rudin, Y., Blobel, G., Schatz, G. 1979. *Proc. Natl. Acad. Sci. USA* 76:343–47
140. MacGregor, C. H., Bishop, C. W., Blech, J. E. 1979. *J. Bacteriol.* 137:574–83
141. Mandel, G., Wickner, W. 1979. *Proc. Natl. Acad. Sci. USA* 76:236–40
142. Manning, P. A., Pugsley, A. P., Reeves, P. 1977. *J. Mol. Biol.* 116:285–300
143. Manning, P. A., Puspuro, A., Reeves, P. 1976. *J. Bacteriol.* 127:1080–84
144. Manning, P. A., Reeves, P. 1976. *Biochem. Biophys. Res. Commun.* 72: 694–700
145. Manning, P. A., Reeves, P. 1977. *FEMS Microbiol. Lett.* 1:275–78
146. Marchal, M., Perrin, D., Hedgpeth, J., Hofnung, M. 1980. *Proc. Natl. Acad. Sci. USA* 77:1491–95
147. McIntyre, T. M., Bell, R. M. 1975. *J. Biol. Chem.* 250:9053–59
148. Deleted in proof
149. Mirelman, D., Siegel, R. C. 1979. *J. Biol. Chem.* 254:571–74

150. Mizuno, T., Kageyama, M. 1979. *J. Biochem. Tokyo* 85:115–22
151. Moreno, F., Fowler, A. V., Hall, M., Silhavy, T. J., Zabin, I., Schwartz, M. 1980. *Nature.* In press
152. Movva, N. R., Katz, E., Asdourian, P. L., Hirota, Y., Inouye, M. 1978. *J. Bacteriol.* 133:81–84
153. Mühlradt, P. F. 1976. *J. Supramol. Struct.* 5:103–8
154. Mühlradt, P. F., Menzel, J., Golecki, J. R., Speth, V. 1973. *Eur. J. Biochem.* 35:471–81
155. Deleted in proof
156. Munch-Peterson, A., Mygind, B., Nicolaisen, A., Pihl, N.J. 1979. *J. Biol. Chem.* 254:3730–37
157. Mutoh, N., Furukawa, H., Mizushima, S. 1978. *J. Bacteriol.* 136:693–99
158. Nakae, T. 1976. *J. Biol. Chem.* 251:2176–78
159. Nakae, T. 1976. *Biochem. Biophys. Res. Commun.* 71:877–84
160. Nakae, T. 1979. *Biochem. Biophys. Res. Commun.* 88:774–81
161. Nakae, T., Ishii, J. 1978. *J. Bacteriol.* 133:1412–18
162. Nakae, T., Ishii, J., Tokunaga, M. 1979. *J. Biol. Chem.* 154:1457–61
163. Nakae, T., Nikaido, H. 1975. *J. Biol. Chem.* 250:7359–65
164. Nakamura, K., Pirtle, R. M., Inouye, M. 1979. *J. Bacteriol.* 137:595–604
165. Nikaido, H., Bavoil, P., Hirota, Y. 1977. *J. Bacteriol.* 132:1045–47
166. Nikaido, H., Song, S. A., Shaltiel, L., Nurminen, M. 1977. *J. Bacteriol.* 76: 324–30
167. Nixdorff, K., Fitzer, H., Gmeiner, J., Martin, H. H. 1977. *Eur. J. Biochem.* 81:63–69
168. Nurminen, M. 1978. *FEMS Microbiol. Lett.* 3:331–34
169. Nurminen, M., Lounatmaa, K., Sarvas, M., Mäkelä, P. H., Nakae, T. 1976. *J. Bacteriol.* 127:941–55
170. Osborn, M. J. Unpublished observations
171. Osborn, M. J., Gander, J. E., Parisi, E. 1972. *J. Biol. Chem.* 247:3973–86
172. Osborn, M. J., Gander, J. E., Parisi, E., Carson, J. 1972. *J. Biol. Chem.* 247: 3962–72
173. Osborn, M. J., Jones, N. C., Schindler, M. 1978. *Ann. NY Acad. Sci.* 308: 215–25
174. Osborn, M. J., Rick, P. D., Lehmann, V., Rupprecht, E., Singh, M. 1974. *Ann. NY Acad. Sci.* 235:52–65
175. Pages, J. M., Piovant, M., Varenne, S., Lazdunski, C. 1978. *Eur. J. Biochem.* 86:589–602
176. Palmiter, R. W., Gagnon, J., Walsh, K. A. 1978. *Proc. Natl. Acad. Sci. USA* 75:94–98
177. Palva, E. T. 1978. *J. Bacteriol.* 136:286–94
178. Palva, E. T. 1979. *Eur. J. Biochem.* 93:495–503
179. Palva, E. T. 1979. *FEMS Microbiol. Lett.* 5:72–78
180. Palva, E. T., Randall, L. L. 1976. *J. Bacteriol.* 127:1558–60
181. Palva, E. T., Randall, L. L. 1978. *J. Bacteriol.* 133:279–86
182. Palva, E. T., Randall, L. L. 1979. *J. Bacteriol.* 138:254–56
183. Palva, E. T., Westermann, P. 1979. *FEBS Lett.* 99:77–80
184. Payne, J. W., Gilvarg, C. 1968. *J. Biol. Chem.* 243:3395–3403, 6291–99
185. Piovant, M., Varenne, S., Pages, J. M., Lazdunski, C. 1978. *Mol. Gen. Genet.* 164:265–74
186. Pugsley, A. P., Schnaitman, C. A. 1978. *J. Bacteriol.* 133:1181–89
187. Pugsley, A. P., Schnaitman, C. A. 1978. *J. Bacteriol.* 135:1118–29
188. Randall, L. L., Hardy, S. J. S. 1977. *Eur. J. Biochem.* 75:43–53
189. Randall, L. L., Hardy, S. J. S., Josefsson, L. G. 1978. *Proc. Natl. Acad. Sci. USA* 75:1209–12
190. Randall, L. L., Josefsson, L. G., Hardy, S. J. S. 1978. *Eur. J. Biochem.* 92:411–15
191. Randall-Hazelbauer, L., Schwartz, M. 1973. *J. Bacteriol.* 116:1436–46
192. Reeves, P. 1979. See Ref. 99, pp. 255–91
193. Reithmeier, R. A. F., Bragg, P. D. 1977. *Can. J. Biochem.* 55:1082–90
194. Reithmeier, R. A. F., Bragg, P. D. 1977. *Biochim. Biophys. Acta* 466: 245–56
195. Rick, P. D., Osborn, M. J. 1977. *J. Biol. Chem.* 252:4895–4903
196. Robbi, M., Lazarow, P. B. 1978. *Proc. Natl. Acad. Sci. USA* 75:4344–48
197. Rosenbusch, J. P. 1974. *J. Biol. Chem.* 249:8019–29
198. Rosenbusch, J. P., Steven, A., Alkan, M., Regenass, M. 1979. In *Regular 2-D Arrays of Biomolecules: Structure Determination and Assembly,* ed. W. Baumeister. Berlin: Springer
199. Rotering, H., Braun, V. 1977. *FEBS Lett.* 83:41–44
200. Rothfield, L., Pearlman-Kothencz, M. 1969. *J. Mol. Biol.* 44:477–92
201. Rothman, J. E., Lenard, J. 1977. *Science* 195:743–53
202. Ryter, A., Shuman, H., Schwartz, M. 1975. *J. Bacteriol.* 122:295–301

203. Sanderson, K. E., Hartman, P. E. 1978. *Microbiol. Rev.* 42:471–519
204. Sarma, V., Reeves, P. 1977. *J. Bacteriol.* 132:23–27
205. Sato, T., Yura, T. 1979. *J. Bacteriol.* 139:468–77
206. Sato, T., Ito, K., Yura, T. 1977. *Eur. J. Biochem.* 78:557–67
207. Schindler, H., Rosenbusch, J. P. 1978. *Proc. Natl. Acad. Sci. USA* 75:3751–55
208. Schindler, M., Crowlesmith, I., Osborn, M. J. 1978. *Fed. Proc.* 37:1393
209. Schmidt, G. W., Devillers-Thiery, A., Desruisseaux, H., Blobel, G., Chua, N. H. 1979. *J. Cell Biol.* 83:615–22
210. Schnaitman, C. A. 1974. *J. Bacteriol.* 118:454–64
211. Schumacher, G., Bussmann, K. 1978. *J. Bacteriol.* 135:239–50
212. Schweizer, M., Henning, U. 1977. *J. Bacteriol.* 129:1651–52
213. Schweizer, M., Hindennach, I., Garten, W., Henning, U. 1978. *Eur. J. Biochem.* 82:211–17
214. Schweizer, M., Schwarz, H., Sonntag, I., Henning, U. 1976. *Biochim. Biophys. Acta* 448:474–91
215. Sekizawa, J., Inouye, S., Halegoua, S., Inouye, M. 1977. *Biochem. Biophys. Res. Commun.* 77:1126–33
216. Shen, B. H. P., Boos, W. 1973. *Proc. Natl. Acad. Sci. USA* 70:1481–85
217. Siitonen, A., Johansson, V., Nurminen, M., Mäkelä, P. H. 1977. *FEMS Microbiol. Lett.* 1:141–44
218. Silhavy, T. J., Bassford, P. J. Jr., Beckwith, J. R. 1979. See Ref. 99, pp. 203–54
219. Silhavy, T. J., Casadaban, M. J., Shuman, H. A., Beckwith, J. R. 1976. *Proc. Natl. Acad. Sci. USA* 73:3423–27
220. Silhavy, T. J., Shuman, H. A., Beckwith, J., Schwartz, M. 1977. *Proc. Natl. Acad. Sci. USA* 74:5411–15
221. Skurray, R. A., Hancock, R. E. W., Reeves, P. 1974. *J. Bacteriol.* 119:726–35
222. Smit, J., Kamio, Y., Nikaido, H. 1975. *J. Bacteriol.* 124:942–58
223. Smit, J., Nikaido, H. 1978. *J. Bacteriol.* 135:687–702
224. Smith, W. P., Tai, P. C., Davis, B. D. 1978. *Proc. Natl. Acad. Sci. USA* 75:814–17
225. Smith, W. P., Tai, P. C., Davis, B. D. 1979. *Biochemistry* 18:198–202
226. Smith, W. P., Tai, P. C., Davis, B. D. 1978. *Proc. Natl. Acad. Sci. USA* 75:5922–25
227. Smith, W. P., Tai, P. C., Thompson, R. C., Davis, B. D. 1977. *Proc. Natl. Acad. Sci. USA* 74:2830–34
228. Sonntag, I., Schwarz, H., Hirota, Y., Henning, U. 1978. *J. Bacteriol.* 136:280–85
229. Steven, A. C., Ten Heggeler, B., Muller, R., Kistler, J., Rosenbusch, J. P. 1977. *J. Cell Biol.* 72:292–301
230. Stock, J. B., Rauch, B., Roseman, S. 1977. *J. Biol. Chem.* 252:7850–61
231. Stocker, B. A. D., Nurminen, M., Mäkelä, P. H. 1979. *J. Bacteriol.* 139:376–83
232. Sugimoto, K., Sugisaki, H., Okamoto, T., Takanami, M. 1977. *J. Mol. Biol.* 111:487–507
233. Sutcliffe, J. G. 1978. *Proc. Natl. Acad. Sci. USA* 75:3737–41
234. Suzuki, H., Nishimura, Y., Yasuda, S., Nishimura, A., Yamada, M., Hirota, Y. 1978. *Mol. Gen. Genet.* 167:1–9
235. Szmelcman, S., Hofnung, M. 1975. *J. Bacteriol.* 124:112–18
236. Szmelcman, S., Schwartz, M., Silhavy, T. J., Boos, W. 1976. *Eur. J. Biochem.* 65:13–19
237. Tai, P. C., Smith, W. P., Davis, B. D. 1978. In *Limited Proteolysis in Microorganisms, Fogarty Conf., Natl. Inst. Health*, pp. 171–75
238. Teather, R. M., Müller-Hill, B., Abrutsch, U., Aichele, G., Overath, P. 1978. *Mol. Gen. Genet.* 159:239–48
239. Tokunaga, H., Tokunaga, M., Nakae, T. 1979. *Eur. J. Biochem.* 95:435–40
240. Tokunaga, M., Tokunaga, H., Okajima, Y., Nakae, T. 1979. *Eur. J. Biochem.* 95:441–48
241. Torti, S. 1977. PhD Thesis. Tufts Univ., Mass. 200 pp.
242. Torti, S. V., Park, J. T. 1976. *Nature* 263:323–26
243. Ueki, T., Mitsui, T., Nikaido, H. 1979. *J. Biochem. Tokyo* 85:173–82
244. van Alphen, L., Havekes, L., Lugtenberg, B. 1977. *FEBS Lett.* 75:285–88
245. van Alphen, L., Lugtenberg, B., van Boxtel, R., Hack, A. M., Verhoef, C., Havekes, L. 1979. *Mol. Gen. Genet.* 169:147–55
246. van Alphen, L., Lugtenberg, B., van Boxtel, R., Verhoef, K. 1977. *Biochim. Biophys. Acta* 466:257–68
247. van Alphen, L., van Alphen, W., Verkleij, A., Lugtenberg, B. 1979. *Biochim. Biophys. Acta* 556:233–43
248. van Alphen, L., Verkleij, A., Leunissen-Bijvelt, J., Lugtenberg, B. 1978. *J. Bacteriol.* 134:1089–98
249. van Alphen, W., van Selm, N., Lugtenberg, B. 1978. *Mol. Gen. Genet.* 159:75–83
250. Varenne, S., Piovant, M., Pages, J. M.,

Lazdunski, C. 1978. *Eur. J. Biochem.* 86:603–6
251. Verhoef, C., deGraaff, P. J., Lugtenberg, E. J. J. 1977. *Mol. Gen. Genet.* 150:103–5
252. Verhoef, C., Lugtenberg, B., van Boxtel, R., deGraaff, P., Verheij, H. 1979. *Mol. Gen. Genet.* 169:137–46
253. Verkleij, A., van Alphen, L., Bijvelt, J., Lugtenberg, B. 1977. *Biochim. Biophys. Acta.* 466:269–82
254. Von Heijne, G. Personal communications.
255. Von Heijne, G., Blomberg, C. 1979. *Eur. J. Biochem.* 97:175–81
256. von Meyenberg, K. 1971. *J. Bacteriol.* 107:878–88
257. von Meyenberg, K., Nikaido, H. 1977. *Biochem. Biophys. Res. Commun.* 78:1100–7
258. Wainwright, M., Beacham, I. R. 1977. *Mol. Gen. Genet.* 154:67–73
259. Walk, R. A., Hock, B. 1978. *Biochem. Biophys. Res. Commun.* 81:636–43
260. Wandersman, C., Schwartz, M. 1978. *Proc. Natl. Acad. Sci. USA* 75:5636–39
261. Wandersman, C., Schwartz, M., Ferenci, T. 1979. *J. Bacteriol.* 140:1–13
262. Wanner, B. L., Sarthy, A., Beckwith, J. 1979. *J. Bacteriol.* 140:229–39
263. Weiss, R. L. 1977. *J. Cell Biol.* 73: 505–19
264. Wickner, W. 1979. *Ann. Rev. Biochem.* 48:23–45
265. Wilson, V., Hogg, R. Personal communication
266. Wu, H. C., Hou, C., Lin, J. J. C., Yem, D. W. 1977. *Proc. Natl. Acad. Sci. USA* 74:1388–92
267. Yagil, E., Beacham, I. R., Nissim, A., Price, G. 1978. *FEBS Lett.* 85:133–36
268. Yamada, H., Mizushima, S. 1978. *J. Bacteriol.* 135:1024–31
269. Yamada, H., Mizushima, S. 1980. *Eur. J. Biochem.* 103:209–18
270. Yem, D. W., Wu, H. C. 1978. *J. Bacteriol.* 133:1419–76
271. Yu, F., Ichihara, S., Mizushima, S. 1979. *FEBS. Lett.* 100:71–74
272. Yu, F., Mizushima, S. 1977. *Biochem. Biophys. Res. Commun.* 74:1397–1403

Ann. Rev. Microbiol. 1980. 34:423–64

CHEMICAL AND FUEL PRODUCTION BY ANAEROBIC BACTERIA

❖1782

J. G. Zeikus

Department of Bacteriology, University of Wisconsin, Madison, Wisconsin 53706

CONTENTS

INTRODUCTION 423
Scope 423
Historical 424
Outlook 425
SUBSTRATE-PRODUCT RELATIONSHIPS. 428
Substrate Availability and Recalcitrance 428
Product Potentials and Limitations 430
ORGANISMAL AND CULTURAL RELATIONSHIPS 432
Species Diversity: Selection of the Model Organism 432
Acidogen, Solventogen, and Methanogen Characteristics 434
Mixed-Culture Fermentations 437
METABOLIC RELATIONSHIPS 439
Biopolymer Degradation Mechanisms 439
Hexose and Pentose Fermentation Pathways 441
One-Carbon Metabolism Pathways 447
Intra- and Inter-Species Control of End-Product Formation 450
TECHNOLOGICAL RELATIONSHIPS 457
Methane Production 457
Solvent Production 458
Acids and Other Vendable Chemical Products 459
CONCLUDING REMARKS 460

INTRODUCTION

Scope

Society is confronted today with dwindling sources of fossil fuels and chemical feedstocks and the proliferation of wastes generated by municipalities,

0066-4227/80/1001/0423$01.00

agriculture, and industries. The conversion of renewable resources (i.e. biomass) or wastes to chemicals and fuels by microbial fermentations or enzymes represents a tremendous challenge for microbiologists in the future. Indeed this challenge has helped stimulate biotechnology as a new scientific discipline. Biotechnology aims to develop novel processes that are less energy intensive and more efficient than chemical synthetic processes and that are based on abundant or renewable resources. In order to accomplish these goals, the call for a microbial revolution to stimulate biotechnology has been issued (19).

Anaerobic fermentations form the basis for microbial production of chemical, and fuel. That is, as a result of catabolizing organic matter in the absence of oxygen, a variety of reduced organic compounds (e.g. ethanol, methane, acetic acid, butanol) are produced in lieu of complete aerobic combustion to CO_2 and H_2O.

The objective of this paper is to review the fermentations of anaerobic, chemosynthetic bacteria and to assess their biotechnological potential in chemical and fuel production. Within the total group of anaerobic bacteria, three general kinds of fermentations are examined in detail. These include methane production by the methanogens, acid production by the acidogens, and alcohol and ketone production by the solventogens. Not included here are the anaerobic metabolism of phototrophic bacteria, sulfate-reducing bacteria, nitrate-reducing bacteria, and facultatively anaerobic bacteria (i.e. O_2 catabolizing).

Obligately anaerobic bacteria possess unique metabolic features that may have tremendous potential for the development of novel biotechnology. These bacteria arose very early on earth but should not be viewed as primitive organisms in the sense of catabolic function (i.e. anaerobic-metabolic energy generation). Instead, they are highly evolved and have optimally adapted under energy-stressed conditions to grow efficiently on a wide variety of substrates. As such, anaerobic bacteria may represent model systems for the study of metabolic efficiency and energy conservation. Unlike aerobic microorganisms whose anabolic features are largely exploited by biotechnology (i.e. antibiotics, single-cell protein, and amino acid production), anaerobes offer the potential for utilizing catabolic features in the large-scale production of chemicals and fuels.

Historical

Anaerobic fermentations have a long history of study in microbiology, as exemplified in alcoholic beverages, lactic acid–fermented foods, and biogas generation from organic wastes. Anaerobic bacterial fermentations for industrial scale chemical production was an interesting topic in the 1930s and 1950s when this subject was last examined in the *Annual Review of Microbiology* (83, 132).

Few industrial processes exist for chemical and fuel production that employ defined species of anaerobic bacteria. Only the acetone-butanol fermentations of Clostridia are of real historical significance. At present, acetone and butanol are the only major chemical feedstocks that are produced in significant quantities by bacterial fermentations (151, 162). In 1976, an estimated 5% of acetone and 10% of butanol were produced by fermentation; the balance was synthesized from petrochemicals. Acetone-butanol fermentation has a long career as a successful industrial fermentation process. Bacterial production of butanol was first studied by Pasteur (134). Interest in commercializing butanol production was initiated in 1909 as a means to obtain butadiene, used in the synthesis of rubber (169). In 1912, Weizmann isolated an organism that was capable of fermenting starch to acetone, butanol, and ethanol; he obtained a British patent in 1915. This organism was named *Clostridium acetobutylicum* strain Weizmann (114). The production of acetone was of great interest in World War I as a chemical feedstock used for explosives (i.e. cordite) and airplane wing dope. The demands for acetone decreased dramatically after the war, but the fermentation process continued as other needs for acetone and butanol developed. The acetone-butanol fermentation process ceased to operate in the US during the 1960s because of unfavorable economics caused by chemical synthesis of these products from petroleum-derived feedstocks. At present, there is renewed interest in utilizing the *Clostridium acetobutylicum* fermentation process as a means of producing butanol and acetone because of the higher price and limited availability of ethylene and propylene as feedstocks for the chemical-synthetic process (151).

Outlook

By and large, three factors related to our present dependence on petroleum have renewed interest in microbial fermentations for chemical and fuel production. First, is the need for new technology in the utilization of renewable resources and underdeveloped fossil reserves as raw materials for chemical and fuel production. Secondly, is the need to improve energy conservation in current waste-processing and chemical production technology. In view of the rapidly escalating costs of energy, new technologies for waste processing are required that yield vendable products (i.e. fuels, chemicals, etc.) and that do not merely consume energy. Also, the energy content of petroleum, a high molecular weight compound, should not be wasted for the production of simple low molecular weight organic compounds (with carbon chain lengths less than C_6) when microbial technologies exist for their production from renewable biomass. From a bioconversion technology standpoint, petroleum should be conserved as a starting material for synthesis of high molecular weight products that cannot be derived from biomass without excessive energy expenditure and waste. Lastly and most importantly, the economics of chemical and fuel production has changed considerably and will continue to change in favor of microbial fermentations rather than chemical synthetic routes from petroleum. The favorable economics encompass subsidized fermentations (i.e. bioethanol) that are based on lowering the import demands on petroleum as well as on lower total process costs for the production of specific chemicals via fermentations.

Primary production by photosynthetic organisms (i.e. light-driven CO_2 fixation into biomass) and its biogeochemical conversion to fossil organics yields the starting substrate (i.e. photosynthate) for chemical and fuel production technology. A general scheme for the conversion of photosynthate to chemicals, fuels and other vendable products via anaerobic fermentation is shown in Figure 1.

Certain forms of biomass (e.g. lignified tissue) and fossilized photosynthate (e.g. coal) are recalcitrant to anaerobic fermentation. Both biomass and coal can be pyrolyzed to syn-gas (CO, H_2, CO_2) and economically converted to methanol and acetic acid (23, 67, 133, 144). However, this involves tremendous loss of energy as heat. Alternatively, biomass can either be directly fermented (i.e. starches, nonlignified celluloses) or pretreated to remove lignin (98, 121) and/or convert both lignins and celluloses to easily fermentable substrates (96, 127, 166) by their depolymerization to

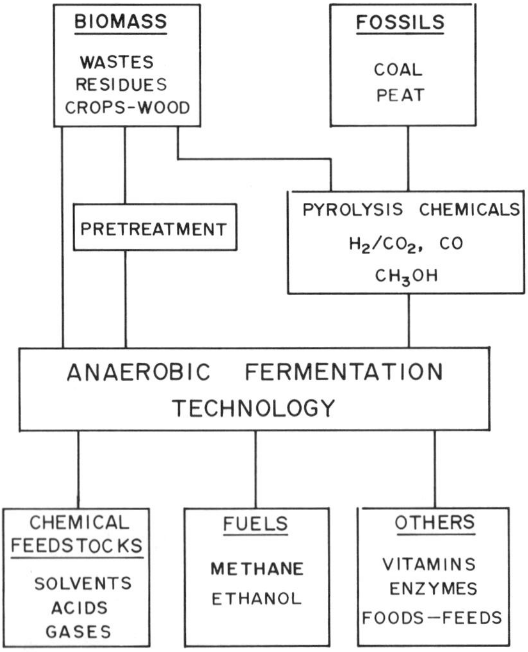

Figure 1 Bioconversion of photosynthate by anaerobic bacteria.

low molecular weight aromatics and sugars. Thus, the constituents of biomass or simple pyrolysis products are abundant substrates for the development of anaerobic fermentation technologies for chemical and fuel production. The fermentation products of anaerobic bacteria can be used directly if the compound is in high demand by chemical industries (48, 87, 163) (e.g. acetic acid, ethanol, butanol) or can be used indirectly as feedstock (48, 87, 96, 163) for the production of other chemicals (e.g. ethanol as a starting substrate for ethylene or butadiene). Some chemicals, as products of microbial fermentation, are of food-grade quality (e.g. acetic and lactic acid) or are promising fuels (e.g. ethanol). In addition, development of large-scale anaerobic bacterial fermentations will yield as byproducts vitamins, industrial enzymes, and foods or feeds that will compete economically with present methods for production of these biochemicals.

In general, anaerobic bacterial fermentations are of interest to developing biotechnology because of the wide range of products formed and substrates fermented, the high substrate-to-product conversion yields and rates, and the potential for enhanced process stability and product recovery due to physiological diversity of species (e.g. extreme thermophily, acidophily, halophily). Nevertheless, aside from the historical acetone-butanol fermentations, the biotechnological and economic feasibility of chemical and fuel production by anaerobic bacteria remains to be well established.

At present anaerobic fermentation technology is primarily focused on gasohol production—that is, producing ethanol from biomass as a liquid fuel to supplement gasoline and thus lower dependency on petroleum. Considerable debate (5, 68, 105) (by and large, political, but also scientific) has focused on whether or not production of bioethanol from biomass results in a positive net energy balance. Depending on the process employed, a positive net energy balance for ethanol from biomass can be achieved (58, 97). The majority of the energy requirements for bioethanol production come from the industrial phase (i.e. ethanol fermentation) and not the agricultural phase (i.e. biomass production) (58, 60, 97). A positive energy balance for gasohol production was achieved by selection of the appropriate biomass substrate (58, 66a, 106), by the use of biomass waste (58) or coal (22) rather than petroleum as the energy source for ethanol distillation, and by the development of novel engineering processes for ethanol recovery (60, 64, 97). Indeed, now the bioethanol debate is focused on economics and not net energy balances. The pertinent economic issues for bioethanol production concern substrate availability and price and lowering fermentation process costs. It is in this regard that anaerobic bacteria may have advantages over yeasts as the organisms of choice for bioethanol production. Only anaerobic bacteria offer the potential of less energy-intensive, thermophilic processing for the direct conversion of inexpensive biopolymers (i.e. cellulose, hemicellulose, starch) to ethanol (195).

SUBSTRATE-PRODUCT RELATIONSHIPS

Substrate Availability and Recalcitrance

The desire to replace petrochemicals and fuels by microbial fermentations requires the availability of abundant substrates that are readily bioconvertible. Although abundant but fixed sources of coals exist in the US, they are not utilizable as substrates for fermentation technology unless first pyrolyzed. Consequently, more interest has centered around biomass fermentations than coal-based fermentations because they are less energy intensive and are based upon renewable resources. Biomass and coal can be directly pyrolyzed to syn-gas and chemically converted to simple substrates (23). Thus, methanol will remain a renewable, abundant substrate for future fermentation technology (39).

In 1978, the US consumed approximately 820 million tons of oil, produced one billion tons of primary biomass (crops and wood), and generated another billion tons of biomass-derived residues (165). The greatest challenge is to develop fermentation technology that employs the underutilized biomass residues, because they are often considered as wastes and require net energy input for treatment without product gain or they are decomposed in the environment by aerobic organisms without recapturing biochemicals or biofuels. Table 1 illustrates representative forms of confined biomass in the US (i.e. produced, localized, and readily available as a resource). Primary biomass is produced with defined utilizations (i.e. foods, feeds, lumber, paper). For example, in 1977 only 1.5% of the US corn crop was processed for nonfood needs (40). Secondary biomass is produced in nearly equal amounts but has considerably lower product value. For example, in 1978 (165) corn cost $89 per ton as compared to $8–$30 per ton of wood chips (of which the primary cost involved transportation). Tertiary biomass is produced in lesser amounts and generally requires net fossil energy for processing without product gains. At present, secondary and tertiary biomass is a substrate of choice for fermentation technology because its full economic potential is not realized (57, 133, 192). In the future, new developments in silviculture, aquaculture, and agriculture may make primary biomass production more economic and the substrate of choice for fermentation technology (79, 87).

Chemical compositional analysis of biomass substrates reveals (27, 28) that most biomass, except for grains (i.e. corn, wheat, etc.), is composed primarily of lignocellulosic materials (see Table 2). The three major chemical constituents of lignocellulose are lignin, α-cellulose, and a conglomerate termed hemicellulose. The composition of hemicellulose varies considerably in biomass and consists of hexose and pentose polymers. The principal monomers of hemicellulose are xylose, arabinose, mannose, glucose, galactose and glucuronic acid. Certain forms of biomass, in addition to lignocel-

Table 1 Annual agriculture and forestry biomass in the United States.

Biomass substrate	Amount[a] (million metric tons)
Primary biomass	
Crop productivity	720
Corn	195
Wheat	85
Hay	150
Soybeans	105
Wood productivity	286
Secondary biomass	
Crop residues	430
Cereal straw	141
Stover-cobs	145
Forest residues	260
Tertiary biomass	
Feedlot manures	237
Urban refuse	150
Forest product waste	100
Industrial wastes	45
Sewage solids	15

[a]Based on 1972 figures obtained from References (73) and (154).

lulose, contain other major organic components. For example, bark contains large amounts of extractives and phenolics, whereas cattle manure contains large amounts of proteins.

A major physiochemical feature limiting the direct fermentation of biomass to chemicals and fuels is its polymeric nature. Of the major biomass polymers, α-cellulose, hemicellulose, and amylopectin are directly fermented by anaerobic bacteria, whereas lignin is totally recalcitrant (198). Most importantly, lignin physically surrounds but is not covalently bonded to celluloses in biomass. Thus lignin limits the activity of microbial cellulases and hemicellulases by stearic hindrance (27, 28). Lignin differs significantly from other biopolymers because it is synthesized via an oxidative, free-radical condensation process that yields five different major intermonomer linkages including both C-C and C-O bonds, with the β-arylether bond being quantitatively the most significant. As an anaerobic fermentation substrate, lignin does not contain any readily hydrolyzable intermonomer bonds and requires extremely oxidative conditions for biological depolymerization (30, 198). Thus, grains, which are composed mainly of amylopectin, are directly fermentable by anaerobic bacteria, whereas other forms of biomass must be pretreated (121) to remove lignin prior to fermentation.

Table 2 Chemical Composition (%) of representative dry biomass substrates[a]

	Primary biomass				Secondary biomass		Tertiary biomass
Component	Poplar	Pine	Hemlock	Corn/ wheat	Hemlock bark	Cornstalk/ stover	Feedlot manure
Lignin	21	29	29.8	1–2	15	19	7
α-Cellulose	48	41	38	3–4	26	38	17
Hemicellulose							
Total	27	27	27.5	—	16	26	19
0-Acetyl-4-0-methyl, glucurano, xylan	24	—	—	—	—	—	—
Arabino-4-0-methyl, glucurano, xylan	—	9	—	—	—	—	—
Galacto-glucomanan	3	18	—	—	—	—	—
Pectin-starch	4	3	—	80–85	—	—	—
Extractives	—	—	4.6	2–5	29	—	—
Others	—	—	—	9–12	15	17	57

[a]Data compiled from References 17, 27, 40, 67, 96.

Product Potentials and Limitations

The utilization of anaerobic fermentations to replace petroleum-derived chemicals and fuels necessitates the production of enormous volumes of product from available substrates. Large volumes of chemicals or fuels can be derived by anaerobic fermentations of biomass. For example, the fermentation of one sixth of the total US corn crop (1×10^9 bu) can yield 2.5×10^9 gal of bioethanol; this represents more than the yearly chemical-industrial use of ethanol and, as a fuel, 2.3% of the total gasoline consumed (44, 165).

Biomass can be converted to a variety of different chemicals and byproducts by anaerobic bacterial fermentations as illustrated in Table 3. These include several kinds of organic acids, solvents, and gases, as well as byproduct CO_2, enzymes, vitamins, and cell residues. The solvents and gases can be burned directly as fuels. However, when one considers the theoretical yields of these biofuels from glucose, only solvents can be produced at yields (percentage of overall weight) of 30 to 51% (163), whereas theoretical yields for methane and H_2 are 27 and 4%, respectively. Furthermore, H_2 is not considered as a significant biofuel from fermentation because only 33% of the combustible energy from glucose fermentation can be converted to H_2, whereas 85% of the combustible energy of glucose can be converted to methane by anaerobic bacterial fermentations (159). The bacterially produced solvents are also large volume industrial chemicals (44, 163) and can be converted (87, 162, 166) to other chemical feedstocks (i.e. conversion of butanol to butadiene or ethanol to ethylene).

The production of organic acids by anaerobic bacterial fermentations results in the highest theoretical substrate-to-product conversion yields. Nearly 100% of the carbohydrate fermented by certain species can be

Table 3 Representative products of anaerobic bacteria catabolism[a]

Chemicals		
Organic acids	Alcohols-ketones	Gases
Propionic	Ethanol	H_2
Acetic	Acetone	CH_4
Caproic	Butanol	CO_2
Lactic	Isopropanol	
Succinic	Glycerol	
Butyric	Methanol	
Formic		
Biochemical/Byproducts		
Enzymes	Vitamins	
Cellulase	Riboflavin	
Alcohol dehydrogenase	B_{12}	

[a]Other kinds of fermentation chemicals are produced by anaerobic bacteria. Those listed are formed in yields >0.2 mol/mol substrate fermented.

recovered as lactic, acetic, or butyric acids (e.g. 3 mol acetic/mol glucose with *Clostridium thermoaceticum*). The organic acids have a variety of uses (109, 163) ranging from large-volume industrial chemicals (i.e. acetic acid) to food chemicals (i.e. lactic acid) or feedstocks for the production of other chemicals (i.e. butyric acid).

In addition to fuels and chemicals, anaerobic bacteria produce expensive biochemicals in smaller quantities. Both riboflavin (35, 135) and Vitamin B_{12} (49) have been commercially produced via anaerobic bacterial fermentation. The future large-scale utilization of anaerobic bacterial fermentations for biofuel or biochemical production will produce tremendous amounts of byproducts that must be effectively utilized in order to make the processes economical. Such utilization may include recovery of the following products: commercial enzymes from the cells or medium, cells for vitamins or feeds, CO_2 for compressed gas or dry ice, and undigested residues for fertilizers or substrates for biomethane formation.

The potential for anaerobic fermentation products other than those listed in Table 3 is promising. In general, the microbiology and biochemistry of anaerobic bacteria have not been fully investigated. Many other species remain to be described in nature, particularly those from extreme environments (e.g. halophilic, acidophilic, and thermophilic) that may yield different products. Metabolic manipulation of known species by chemical control of fermentation parameters or by selection of mutants devoid of specific enzymatic components may result in new fermentation products from existing species (e.g. production of acrylic, malic, or fumaric acids, acetoin, acetaldehyde, polyols, etc). In this regard, it has recently been shown (3) that *Clostridium propionicum* can form acrylic acid in lieu of propionic acid.

At present, effective product recovery is a major technological factor that limits utilization of anaerobic fermentations for fuel or chemical production. A positive energy balance for bioethanol from yeast fermentation of sugar cane or corn requires utilization of nonpetroleum energy sources (e.g. biomass residues or coal) to provide the enormous quantities of heat needed to distill and recover ethanol (22, 58). Furthermore, solvent or acid production by anaerobic bacterial fermentations of biomass polymers requires improved product-tolerant strains and recovery methods. Production of methane from wastes requires treatment of biogas to remove corrosive H_2S. It is often the economics of product recovery that dictates the success of an anaerobic fermentation process.

ORGANISMAL AND CULTURAL RELATIONSHIPS

Species Diversity: Selection of the Model Organism

Relatively little is known about the entire spectrum of anaerobic bacteria that may be of importance in biofuel and biochemical production. In the past, lack of interest and technological problems associated with pure culture growth of these organisms in the absence of air prevented more detailed investigations of species diversity and metabolism. Continued studies of the general microbiology of anaerobes, especially in extreme environments (i.e. acid, thermal, and hypersaline), may yield organisms that possess novel features advantageous for industrial fermentations. These features could include enhanced process stability via fermentation with acidophilic, halophilic, or thermophilic bacteria, enhanced product recovery with thermophiles, and enhanced product yields with acidophiles.

Most anaerobic species characterized to date are mesophiles that have been isolated from near neutral gastrointestinal related environments (i.e. rumen, decomposing animal excrements) or sediments. The diversity and metabolism of anaerobic bacterial species has only been well characterized in the rumen environment (74). Here, important biopolymer-decomposing and acid, or methane-forming species often require complex media or defined mixtures of vitamins, fatty acids, and amino acids for growth (15, 110, 144). The effect of air on anaerobic bacteria that are not able to catabolize oxygen is quite varied (122). Oxygen is lethal to certain anaerobes (e.g. *Methanosarcina* species), inhibits the metabolism of *Clostridium* species, and has no effect on *Lactobacillus* species. Cultural techniques (8, 12, 32, 43, 75) have been developed so that even the most oxygen-sensitive bacteria are easily cultured. Although some anaerobic species are very oxygen sensitive, this does not present problems in large-scale industrial fermentations because oxygen is easily removed and is poorly soluble, especially at thermophilic temperatures. Indeed, aerobic organisms present the process-limiting problems of oxygen transfer; consequently, they often are not ideal organisms for large-scale fermentations.

As a result of growth at high temperature and unique macromolecular properties, obligately thermophilic bacteria can possess high metabolic rates, physically (i.e. thermal resistance) and chemically stable enzymes, and a higher end product-to-cell ratio than is found in metabolically similar mesophilic species (195). These features of thermophilic systems are of tremendous importance for the development of novel biotechnology. Thermophilic anaerobic bacteria appear to have a limited species composition but also appear to possess the major nutritional categories (i.e. chemolithotroph, chemoorganotroph, photoorganotroph, etc) and to metabolize the same substrates as mesophiles. At present, the diversity of known thermophilic anaerobes is limited but includes acidogenic (e.g. *C. thermoaceticum*), solventogenic (e.g. *C. thermohydrosulfuricum*), and methanogenic (e.g. *Methanobacterium thermoautotrophicum*) species. Thermophilic anaerobes are easily obtained (195) from a variety of self-heating environments (i.e. soil) or volcanic features (i.e. thermal springs, muds, decomposing biomass).

Obligately acidophilic anaerobic bacteria have not been described. The process stability of anaerobic fermentations with acid-tolerant microorganisms is well documented in the fermented food products industry, as exemplified by low pH-tolerant brewers yeast and lactic acid bacteria. *Propionibacterium* and *Lactobacillus* species are examples of anaerobes that can grow at moderately low pH's (i.e. pH 5). Extreme acid-tolerant (i.e. pH 2), solventogenic (i.e. the ethanol fermentation of *Sarcina ventriculi*), and acidogenic species (i.e. the butyric acid fermentation of *Sarcina maxima*) have been described (21). Acid-tolerant methanogens have not been described and low pH (<5.5) limits methane formation as exemplified by sour anaerobic digestors. The reason H_2, and not methane, is detected in sour digestors is related to process thermodynamics. For example, as the proton concentration increases, it becomes thermodynamically more favorable to reduce protons and form hydrogen than to oxidize hydrogen and form methane. Methanogens obtain cellular energy as a result of establishing proton gradients during the catabolism of H_2/CO_2 (41) and probably other one-carbon compounds and acetic acid (125). Thus, methanogens, as opposed to acidogens and solventogens, may not function at extreme pH values because of thermodynamic properties limiting their energy-yielding metabolism. Examination of the microbial ecology of acid environments (i.e. peat bogs or acid thermal areas) may yield interesting acidogenic or solventogenic species.

Investigations on the microbial ecology of anaerobic decomposition processes in hypersaline environments have been initiated in Great Salt Lake sediments that contain > 28% salinity (138). Here, H_2, and not methane, was the most abundant biogas; radioactive tracer studies demonstrated methane formation from [^{14}C] methylmercaptan and [^{14}C] methylmethionine but not from CO_2 or acetate, the common methanogen C-sources. Anaerobic bacteria, which were isolated in pure culture, fermented complex media in the presence of 30% salt; however, the potential significance of these species in acid or solvent production remains to be established.

Acidogen, Solventogen, and Methanogen Characteristics

Rates and/or yields (i.e. mole product formed/mole substrate fermented) of acid, solvent, or methane produced during anaerobic fermentations vary considerably and depend on species and strain, type of fermentation substrate, exact cultural conditions, and kinds of acids or solvents formed. Substrate-product relationships of representative acidogenic, solventogenic, and methanogenic bacteria vary considerably (Tables 4 and 5, pp. 454–56). Cultivation of most acidogenic and solventogenic species requires vitamins and/or amino acids as growth factors. One homoacetic acid producing species, *Acetobacterium woodii,* is capable of autotrophic growth (11).

Among the acidogens, the homoacid-forming species that produce either acetic, lactic, or butyric acid are the most interesting in terms of product yields. The best characterized homoacetic acid–producing bacteria are *Clostridium formicoaceticum* (6), *C. thermoaceticum* (51), and *A. woodii* (11). None of these species ferment biomass polymers, but the homoacetogens can form acetic acid from a variety of hexoses, pentoses, and lactic acid. In addition. *A. woodii* can grow on formic acid and H_2/CO_2. Product yields of 3 mol acetic acid/mol hexose fermented (6) and 1 mol/4 mol H_2 and 2 mol CO_2 (11) have been reported. It is important to note that maximal acetic acid yields depend on cultural conditions (i.e. cultural pH, substrate fermented). For example, *C. formicoaceticum* forms acetic acid as the sole product during the logarithmic growth phase but produces formic and acetic acid during the stationary phase at low pH (6).

Homolactic acid–producing bacteria ferment starch, hexoses, pentoses, and cellobiose. Depending upon the cultural conditions, the yield of lactic acid by the homolactic acid bacterium, *Lactobacillus casei,* and the heterolactic acid bacterium, *Thermoanaerobium brockii,* are nearly equivalent. In nonenergy-limited-batch culture, *L. casei* produces lactic acid as the sole end product, whereas in energy-limited, continuous culture, nearly equivalent amounts of lactic, acetic, formic, and ethanol are produced (38). Lactate is the major fermentation product of *T. brockii* grown in high yeast extract, batch cultures, whereas ethanol is the major product in low yeast extract medium (99). Certain heterolactic acid bacteria (e.g. *Lactobacillus brevis*) produce, in addition to ethanol and lactic acid, significant quantities of glycerol (190), which is an important industrial chemical.

Most butyric acid–producing bacteria ferment starch, hexose, pentose, and cellobiose and form acetic acid, in addition to butyric acid, as the major (i.e. percentage of substrate weight converted to product) fermentation product. Butyric acid production is also related to cultural conditions of the specific species. For example, *Clostridium thermosaccharolyticum* produces butyric acid as the major fermentation product during exponential growth (72). Induction of sporulation is associated with the formation of glucose 6-phosphate dehydrogenase and ethanol dehydrogenase and the production of ethanol in lieu of butyrate as a major fermentation product (72). Recently a new butyrogenic bacterium, *Butyribacterium methylotrophicum,* has been isolated [Zeikus et al (200a)]. This Gram-positive, rod-shaped species is very interesting because it can ferment methanol in addition to hexose, lactic acid, or H_2/CO_2. In batch culture, butyric acid is the only fermentation product detected during catabolism of methanol by *B. methylotrophicum,* whereas acetate is the major product on H_2/CO_2.

Homoacidogenic fermentations for propionic, succinic, and caproic acid have not been reported. Product yields (i.e. mole/mole) from hexose fermentation are greater for propionic than for succinic acid. Propionic acid bacteria metabolize hexose, pentose, or lactic acid. Two different pathways are reported for lactic acid metabolism, but only one is utilized for sugars. The ethanol-acetate fermentation of *Clostridium kluyveri* is the only significant mechanism described for caproic acid synthesis (14). This species does not ferment carbohydrates, and H_2, caproate, and butyrate are the major fermentation products (14). Succinic acid bacteria (i.e. *Ruminococcus flavofaciens* and *Bacteroides succinogenes*) are the only cellulose-fermenting species that produce high yields of acids (i.e. succinic, acetic, formic) (184).

Many anaerobic species have been described that produce ethanol as a major end product (18). Cellulose, starch, a variety of hexoses, pentoses, and cellobiose are fermentation substrates for ethanologenic anaerobes. The most interesting species for biotechnology include cellulose and starch fermentors, thermophiles, and acid-tolerant anaerobes (e.g. *Sarcina ventriculi*). *Clostridium thermocellum* and *C. thermohydrosulfuricum* strains are of particular interest because of the active extracellular cellulase (128, 129) of the former and the high ethanol (13, 195, 198a) yield (1.95 mol ethanol/mol glucose) of the latter. The ethanol yields of both of these saccharolytic species are strain-specific characteristics. For example, *C. thermohydrosulfuricum* strain 39E produces the highest ethanol yield of any described thermophilic anaerobe (13, 128, 198a), whereas other strains (178) display yields similar to that of *T. brockii* (99). Likewise, the substrates fermented by different strains of *C. thermocellum* and *C. thermohydrosulfuricum* vary (13, 71, 102, 112, 128, 148). *C. thermocellum* strain LQR1 and *C. thermohydrosulfuricum* strain 39E actively ferment saccharides at temperatures = 60°C; however, the former strain does not ferment pentoses or starch while the latter strain does not ferment cellulose, and neither strain ferments xylans or pectins. Mixed cultures of the two organisms actively ferment xylans (13).

Butanol is the only other described major alcohol produced in high yields by anaerobic fermentations other than ethanol. All butanol-producing anaerobes display a mixed-solvent fermentation. *Clostridium acetobutylicum* ferments starch, hexoses, or pentoses to butanol, acetone, and ethanol in the general ratio of 6:3:1 (151). *C. butylicum* ferments hexose or starch and produces largely butanol and smaller quantities of isopropanol. Solvent yields of butanol fermentations are dependent upon type and concentration of substrate and the specific strain utilized (24). Acetate and butyrate, but not butanol and acetone, are produced during the exponential growth phase of *C. acetobutylicum* (34, 131). "Ripe cultures" that apparently become competent for solvent production at the end of the logarithmic growth phase are required.

Methanogens display a unique species diversity that is reflected by several levels of biological analysis, including niches occupied in nature (193, 194, 197), species composition (12), morphology and ultrastructure (194, 196), macromolecular composition (53, 86, 164), and catabolic (61, 158, 182, 196) and anabolic (33, 55, 56, 158, 175–177, 197, 199) pathways. A recent review summarizes the taxonomic significance of methanogen diversity and proposes a new scheme for methanogen classification (10). Methanogens catabolize a very restricted range of substrates that include a variety of one-carbon compounds, acetate, and polymethylamines.

Methanobacterium thermoautotrophicum, Methanosarcina barkeri, and *Methanobacterium formicicum* metabolize all the known methanogen substrates and are capable of autotrophic growth (i.e. CO_2 as the sole carbon source for cell biosynthesis). *M. thermoautotrophicum* has a limited range of substrates that it can utilize as energy sources for growth (31, 202). This species proliferates rapidly (i.e. a doubling time of 2 h) on H_2/CO_2 as the sole energy and carbon sources for growth at 65°C. It can also grow very slowly (i.e. a doubling time of 30 h) on carbon monoxide (31). Carbon monoxide is neither a significant energy source in nature nor a suitable substrate to grow *M. thermoautotrophicum* in the laboratory. The reasons for this are that carbon monoxide is toxic and must be used in concentrations less than 30% of the culture gas phase and that the carbon monoxide dehydrogenase of *M. thermoautotrophicum* has low activity and low affinity for carbon monoxide (31). The thermodynamics of CO conversion to CH_4 are as favorable as for H_2/CO_2 metabolism; thus the slow growth rate of methanogens on CO is related to the kinetic properties of CO dehydrogenase. *Methanobacterium formicicum,* unlike *M. thermoautotrophicum,* ferments formate in addition to H_2/CO_2 as an energy and carbon source for growth.

M. barkeri is the most metabolically versatile methanogen and metabolizes H_2/CO_2 (152), methanol (152), acetate (150, 156, 176), CO (31, 92), methylamine (175), and polymethylamines (69). The growth yields of *M. barkeri* on these different substrates reflect the respective thermodynamic energy-yielding reactions employed. For example, the cellular growth yield on acetate is approximately one fourth of that obtained with methanol or H_2/CO_2 as an energy source (175). The growth rate of *M. barkeri* on methanol (i.e. 10–12-h doubling time) is considerably greater than on acetate (i.e. doubling time ~60 h). Kinetic properties not yet determined must explain the growth rate differences observed when *M. barkeri* is grown on different substrates (e.g. methanol versus acetate). One can speculate that a rate-limiting step in methanogen metabolism is the rate of acetate uptake into cells. An active transport system involving stoichiometric amounts of ATP for acetate uptake is not reasonable in light of the limited free energy of formation available from acetate catabolism.

In addition to unitrophic (i.e. use of H_2/CO_2, methanol, or acetate alone) growth, these three methanogenic species can grow mixotrophically on combinations of energy and/or carbon sources. All three species can metabolize H_2 and CO simultaneously (31)). Both *M. barkeri* and *M. thermoautotrophicum* assimilate acetate as a major cell carbon precursor when catabolizing H_2/CO_2 (56, 176, 201). *M. barkeri* can also catabolize H_2 and methanol simultaneously (175).

Mixed-Culture Fermentations

The production of fuels or chemicals from biomass fermentations may require mixed populations for formation of specific products (i.e. methane) or for process stability. The requirement for defined mixed cultures of anaerobic bacteria is well documented in the production of lactic acid–fermented foods. Defined mixed cultures in biofuel or biochemical production have not been well established. However, the role of mixed cultures in the bioconversion of complex organic matter to methane provides an interesting example of how mixed anaerobic populations function in nature or in anaerobic biogas digestors, and it will be reviewed here.

Bioconversion of complex organic matter into methane via bacterial fermentation is performed by a diverse microbial population whose individual metabolic activities operate at different trophic levels (i.e. different species perform different biochemical reactions). The end result of these combined chemical reactions is the production of methane and carbon dioxide from organic matter. Methane, the major final reduced fermentation product, is essentially biochemically inert anaerobically in the absence of electron acceptors, thus assuring continued organic decomposition.

Effective fermentation of organic matter to biogas is a result of the combined and coordinated metabolic activity of the anaerobic bacterial population. The population is comprised of at least four major trophic groups (16, 196) that possess different carbon-catabolizing functions: hydrolytic bacteria (group I) that catabolize saccharides, proteins, lipids, and other minor chemical constituents of biomass; hydrogen-producing acetogenic bacteria (group II) that catabolize certain fatty acids and neutral end products; homoacetogenic bacteria (group III) that catabolize unicarbon compounds (e.g. H_2/CO_2 or HCOOH) or hydrolyze multicarbon compounds to acetic acid; and methanogenic bacteria (group IV) that catabolize acetate and one-carbon compounds to methane.

Metabolic interactions between methanogenic and nonmethanogenic species are of tremendous importance in biogas production. Process stability is a reflection of species interactions that provide optimal conditions for anaerobic metabolism including the supply of essential nutrients, the removal of inhibitory process metabolites, and/or an increase in specific catabolic rates. Metabolic interactions between methanogenic and nonmethanogenic bacteria have been well established in defined mixed-culture studies (78, 145, 149, 174, 184, 185), including the recent demonstration of complete decomposition of glucose to methane and CO_2 by co-cultures of *A. woodii* and *M. barkeri* (180). Methanogens are metabolic regulators of biogas production and they ensure process stability and enhance decomposition rates (196, 197). Three kinds of regulatory functions performed by methanogens appear most significant: proton regulation, electron regulation, and nutrient regulation. Proton regulation via acetic acid catabolism by methanogens removes toxic protons and insures the optimal pH range for growth of the bacterial population. Several facts suggest that proton regulation is the ecologically most important function of methanogens in anaerobic ecosystems. Most methane formed during anaerobic decomposition is derived from acetate (111), and this substrate is only significantly catabolized by methanogenic bacteria. Also, high proton concentrations inhibit H_2 catabolism by methanogens. Electron regulation via hydrogen catabolism by methanogens appears to be most significant in creating thermodynamically favorable conditions for catabolism of multicarbon compounds (e.g. alcohols, long chain fatty acids, aromatics) by acetogenic bacteria and in increasing substrate utilization by fermentative bacteria. Nutrient regulation via synthesis and excretion of organic growth factors by certain methanogens that are needed for growth of other anaerobic species involved in anaerobic digestion remains to be well established. Recent evidence has demonstrated that diverse methanogenic species contain high levels of cobamides (93). The cells and spent fermentation liquor of *M. barkeri* contained the highest concentrations of cobamides. B_{12}-dependent metabolic interactions between *Methanosarcina* and *Eubacterium* strains obtained from sewage sludge digestors have been reported (173).

METABOLIC RELATIONSHIPS

Biopolymer Degradation Mechanisms

Anaerobic fermentations of biomass require unique bacteria that produce extracytoplasmic enzymes to solubilize biomass polymers to transportable substrates for cellular catabolism. Most previous studies of biopolymer degradation mechanisms have examined aerobic processes (4, 50, 63, 142, 143). Nonetheless, anaerobic bacteria actively ferment and solubilize homopolysaccharides including starch, cellulose, and pectin via amylases, cellulases, and pectinases. Anaerobes also ferment hemicellulose, a heteropolysaccharide, but hemicellulase activities remain to be characterized. Anaerobes can neither ferment nor hydrolyze lignin, a heterogeneous polymer that is formed by the oxidative coupling of aromatic alcohols. Maximal lignin degradation, even by aerobic organisms, requires an oxygen level greater than that available in air (90, 91a). The present understanding of the microbiology and biochemistry of aerobic lignin decomposition and the biological fate of lignin in anaerobic environments has been recently reviewed (4, 91, 198). Biopolymer-degrading organisms are important in biotechnology for direct fermentations of biomass to chemicals and fuels and also for utilizing their extracellular enzymes in solubilizing polymers to mono- and disaccharides that can be used directly as feeds or fermented to other products.

Cellulose is the most abundant biopolymer on earth and exists as a highly ordered crystalline structure composed of glucose moities linked by β1–4 bonds (28, 47). Most microbial cellulases (i.e. the cellulolytic enzyme outfit of an organism that is responsible for solubilizing cellulose to transportable sugars) are comprised of three components which when purified have readily distinguishable activities (63, 141, 142). These include the following: 1. endo-β-1, 4-glucanases that act randomly on crystalline cellulose and are assayed using carboxymethyl-cellulose as substrate; 2. exo-β-1, 4-glucanases that are either glucohydrolases or cellobiohydrolases that act on the nonreducing end of the cellulose chain and that are assayed using a variety of crystalline celluloses as substrates; 3. cellobiase or β-glucosidase, which cleaves cellobiose into glucose. The components act synergistically (189) to effectively solubilize crystalline cellulose.

The cellulolytic enzyme outfits in described anaerobic bacteria appear somewhat different from each other and from those of aerobic organisms. *Ruminococcus albus* produces two extracellular components, an affinity factor and a hydrolytic factor, that complex together to form a complete cellulase (100). In contrast, *Clostridium thermocellum* produces an active extracellular cellulase without the apparent production of an affinity factor. The cellulase of *Bacteroides succinogenes* is cell bound and not actively released into the culture medium (63). Among the anaerobes, *C. thermocellum* strains display the highest cellulolytic activity. It is worth noting that the growth rate of *C. thermocellum* on cellulose or cellobiose is greater than that of *Trichoderma viride* (i.e. *T. reeseii*) strains, but less than that of some *Thermoactinomyces* species (195).

The ability to ferment glucose, fructose or xylose and to form cellulase on cellobiose is a strain-specific property in *C. thermocellum,* as well as in other mesophilic, cellulolytic, anaerobic bacteria (74). Strains LQRI (13, 128) and AS39 (148) actively ferment cellulose and cellobiose; they can be adapted to growth on glucose in high yeast extract medium, and they produce carboxymethylcellulase during growth on these substrates.

Most interestingly, the supernatant cellulase of *C. thermocellum* differs significantly from that of *T. viride* in both the types of activities present and their specific activities. *C. thermocellum* contains both endo- and exoglucanase activities but the ratio of endoglucanase to exoglucanase is greater in *C. thermocellum* than in *T. viride* (128, 129, 148). Filter paper activity is significantly higher in *T. viride* hypercellulase mutants than in strains of *C. thermocellum* (128, 130). Recently, *C. thermocellum* mutants have been obtained that have significantly higher activity of endo- and exoglucanase than is found in the original wild type strain (148). *C. thermocellum* supernatant cellulase, unlike that of *T. viride,* lacks cellobiase activity (129) and is not as sensitive to end-product inhibition by cellobiose or glucose (128, 148). *C. thermocellum* cellulase hydrolyzes both xylans and glycans (128). The initial hydrolytic end products of *C. thermocellum* supernatant cellulase on Avicell have a larger degree of polymerization (i.e. Dp 16) than those of *T. viride* (128, 130). A major component purified 170-fold from *C. thermocellum* cellulase (128) hydrolyzes both carboxymethylcellulose and microcrystalline cellulose. Preliminary purification studies have suggested that *C. thermocellum* cellulose is a complex; however, the mechanism of action of individual components is not described (2, 128).

The activities of the extracellular cellulases of *C. thermocellum* appear uniquely coordinated with the saccharide transport activities. *C. thermocellum* contains both a cellobiose phosphorylase and a cellodextrin phosphorylase that is active on cellotriose, cellotetrose, and cellopentose (3a). Thus, the main hydrolytic products of cellulase (i.e. cellobiose and C3-C5 cellodextrins) are activated to glucose-1-phosphate without expenditure of ATP. The faster growth rate observed on cellobiose than on cellulose (129, 174) and the ability of noncellulolytic species to grow coordinately on cellulase hydrolysis products in co-culture (13, 128) suggest that both cellulose hydrolysis and the uptake of hydrolytic products are rate-limiting steps in *C. thermocellums* metabolism. In addition to cellobiose phosphorylase, cellobiase activity has been purified from the "periplasmic space" of

C. thermocellum (1). The specific end products and the significance of this activity in cellulose metabolism remain to be better established.

The microbiology and biochemistry of starch and pectin decomposition have recently been reviewed (50, 143). Starch is a glycocidic polymer linked by α1–4 and α1–6 bonds and is comprised of branched amylopectin (~ 80%) and unbranched amylose (~20%). Microbial hydrolysis of raw starch requires extracytoplasmic amylases which, when purified, contain three component activities: α-amylases that endocleave α1–4 bonds, amyloglucosidases that exocleave α1–4 and α1–6 bonds, and debranching enzymes that act on α1–6 bonds. Only α-amylase has been characterized in mesophilic starch-fermenting anaerobes (45, 54, 70, 116, 126). Pectin is a galactopyranosiduronic acid polymer linked by α1–4 bonds. The carboxylic groups of the galacturonic acid are methoxylated to a varying extent, depending on the source of the pectin. Pectins present in lignocellulosic materials are covalently linked to hemicellulose by glycosidic bonds. Pectinases contain several different component activities, including pectinesterases that form methanol and depolymerases (i.e. pectin transeliminases and pectin hydrolases) that solubilize pectin into various saccharides including hexoses and pentoses. Pectinesterases and transeliminases have been best characterized in mesophilic Clostridia (103, 118, 143).

Hexose and Pentose Fermentation Pathways

The anaerobic bacterial metabolism of hexoses and pentoses generated from biopolymer decomposition are converted into C_2 and C_3 intermediary metabolites and reduced electron carriers by a few common pathways (42, 123, 124). Most anaerobic bacteria described, except for some heterolactic acid species, employ the Embden-Meyerhof pathway (42) for hexose metabolism (i.e. glycolysis). In this pathway hexoses are converted into 2 mol of pyruvate and 2 mol of reduced pyridine nucleotide. The pathway is identified by the fructose 1,6-bisphosphate aldolase (E.C. 4.1.2.13). On the other hand, the hexose-phosphoketolase path (42) of heterolactic acid bacteria forms 1 mol of pyruvic acid, 1 mol of acetylphosphate, 1 mol of CO_2 and 2 mol of reduced pyridine nucleotide per mol of hexose. The pathway is identified by the phosphoketolase (E.C. 4.1.2.9) and phosphogluconate dehydrogenase (E.C. 1.1.1.44).

Most anaerobic bacteria described, except for some heterolactic acid species, employ the Warburg-Dickens pathway (42) for pentose metabolism (i.e. xylolysis). In this pathway pentoses are converted into pyruvate and reduced pyridine nucleotides, and the pathway is identified by transaldolase (E.C. 2.2.1.2) and transketolase (E.C. 2.2.1.1). In the pentose-phosphoketolase pathway (42) of heterolactic acid bacteria equal molar quantities of pyruvate, acetate, and reduced pyridine nucleotides are produced per mole of pentose metabolized. The pentose- and hexose-phosphoketolase pathways are recognized by the same key enzyme (E.C. 4.1.2.9).

The C_2 and C_3 intermediates and reduced pyridine nucleotides generated by these common pathways for hexolysis or pentolysis are transformed into fermentation end products by other enzymatic activities that vary tremendously in different anaerobic species. The known pathways for glucose conversion to acids and solvents are compared in Figures 2–4.

Lactic acid yields are generally highest during glycolysis via the homolactic fermentation pathway (see Figure 2). Theoretically, 2 mol of lactate and 2 mol of ATP are formed per mole of glucose fermented. Electron transfer reactions in homolactic acid bacteria are simple; they do not involve cytochromes or low redox electron carriers and they function by coupling NAD

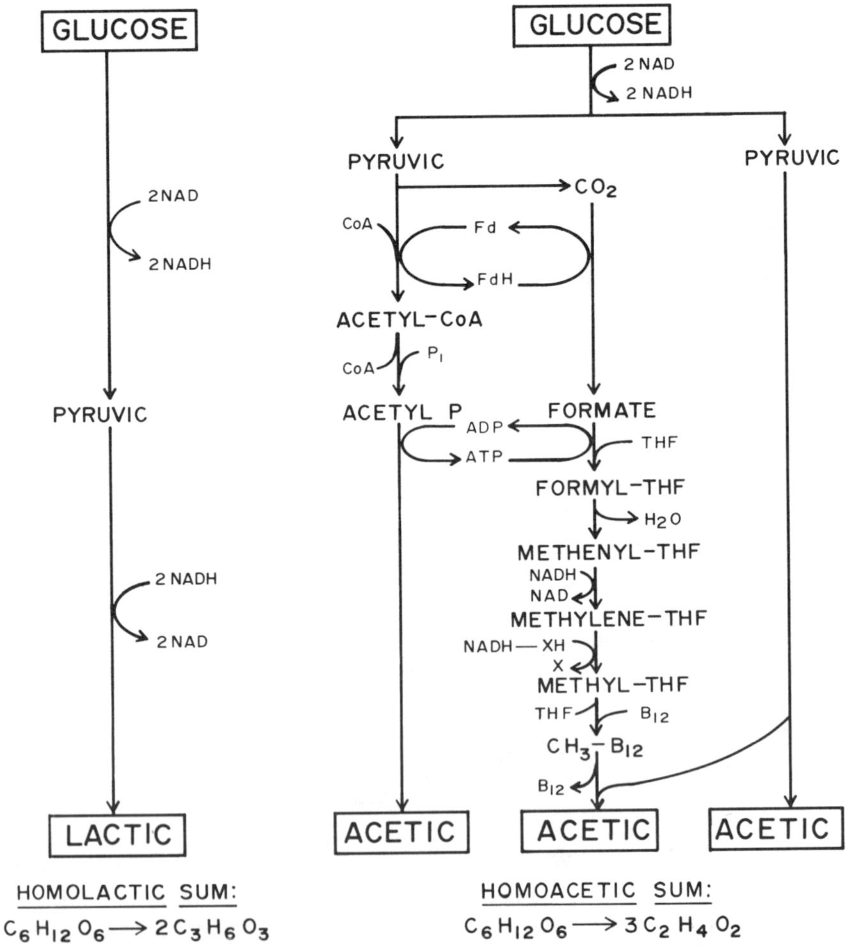

Figure 2 Homolactic and homoacetic fermentation pathways for glucose.

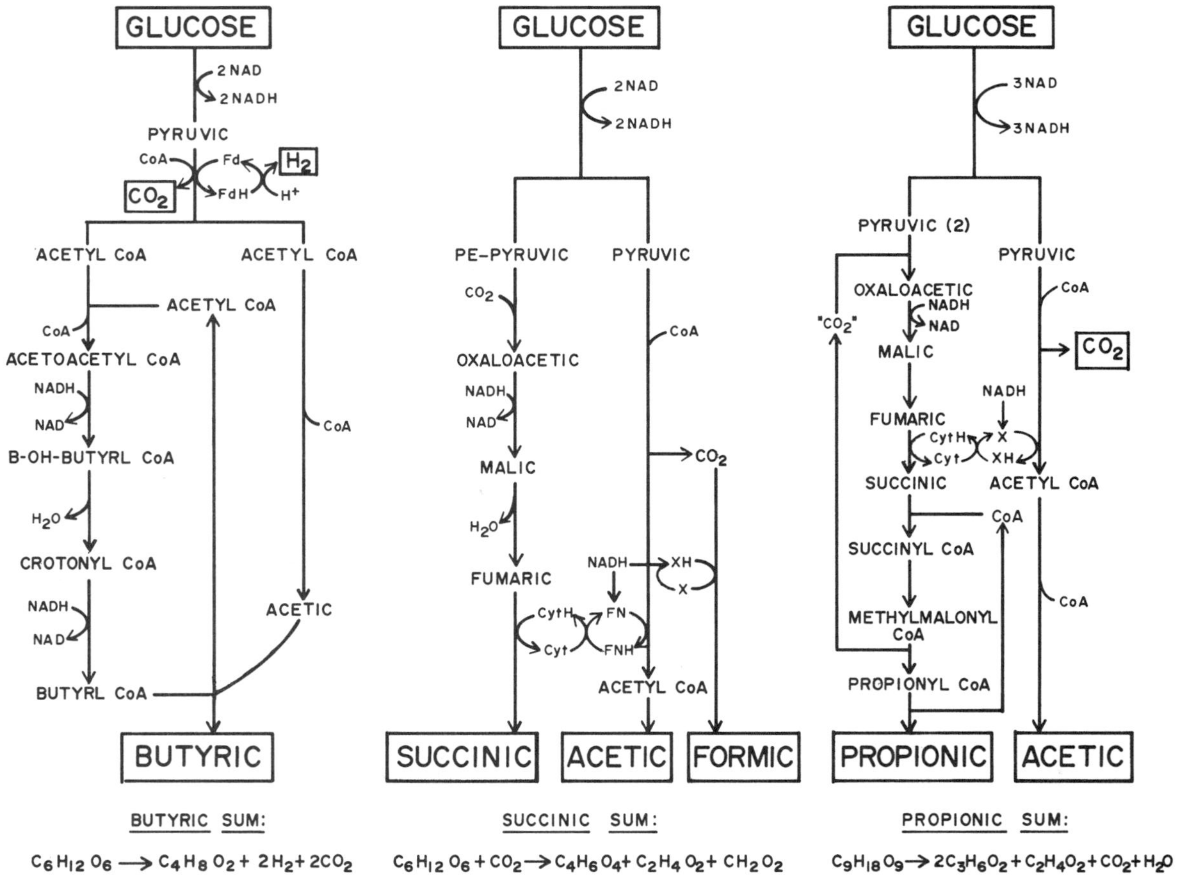

Figure 3 Heteroacidic fermentation pathways for glucose.

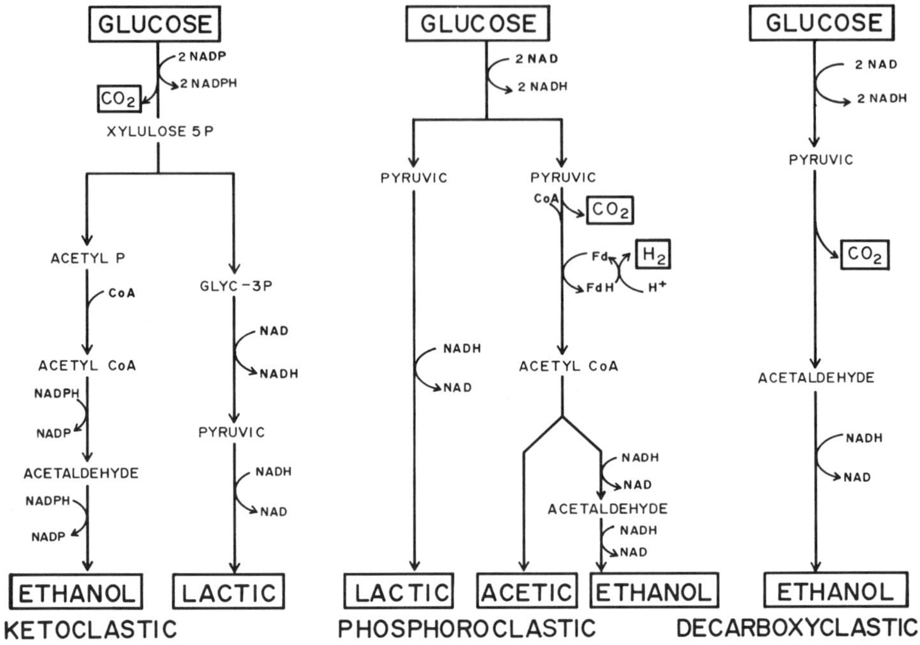

Figure 4 Ethanolic fermentation pathways for glucose.

reduction via glyceraldehyde-3-phosphate dehydrogenase to NADH oxidation via pyruvate reduction by lactate dehydrogenase. It should be noted that lactate yields in homolactic acid bacteria depend on specific growth conditions and that additional products (e.g. formic and acetic acids and ethanol) can also be formed (38, 161, 191). Recently, the theoretical ATP yield (i.e. 2 ATP/glucose) for lactic acid bacteria has been challenged, and excretion of lactate was suggested to increase the theoretical ATP yield by 30% (117). The establishment of pH gradients and ATP generation via product excretion in lactic acid bacteria is an exciting result and may be of importance to anaerobic metabolism in general. In view of these interpretations, ATP yields from different fermentation pathways will not be discussed here. ATP yields and conservation in chemosynthetic anaerobic bacteria are described in previous reviews (156, 160).

The homoacetic acid fermentation path (107, 108, 178a, 186, 187) has a theoretical yield of 3 mol acetic acid per mol of metabolized glucose (see Figure 2). The homoacetogenic fermentation is complex and involves several electron carriers and one-carbon carriers. The flow of carbon from glucose to acetate has only been established in *C. thermoaceticum* (178a) and the exact electron flow scheme is not understood. In addition to pyridine nucleotides, low redox potential electron carriers (e.g. ferredoxin) and higher redox potential electron carriers (e.g. cytochromes) are involved. The one-carbon carriers involved include tetrahydrofolate derivatives and methyl B_{12}, which are involved in the formation of 1 mol of acetate via the organism's unique one-carbon metabolism machinery. Homoacetogenic bacteria obtain ATP via both substrate level and electron transport–mediated phosphorolations (160).

Theoretical yields of 1 mol of butyrate and 2 mol of hydrogen and CO_2 are obtainable via the butyric fermentation path. Pyridine nucleotides and ferredoxins are the carriers involved in electron flow. Acetate is also formed as an intermediate and is required in high concentrations to drive the butyrl CoA-acetyl CoA transfer reaction involved in butyric acid synthesis (160).

The succinate fermentation pathway of *Bacteroides succinogenes* has recently been proposed (119). It would appear that equal molar quantities of succinate, acetate, and formate are formed per mole of glucose and CO_2 fermented. The exact nature of electron flow in this path, including both the direction and specific carriers involved, remains to be established. Likewise, the path of carbon to formic acid remains to be determined. The electron carriers detected include flavin nucleotides associated with pyruvate dehydrogenase and cytochromes linked with the fumarate reductase (119). Succinate-producing bacteria that employ this pathway obtain ATP via both substrate level and electron transport–mediated phosphorylation mechanisms.

The glycolytic pathway for propionate production in *Propionibacterium* species (81, 101, 188) is shown in Figure 3. This pathway yields 2 mol of propionic acid and 1 mol of acetic acid and CO_2 per 1.5 mol of fermented glucose. The carbon flow path is unique because of the presence of (S)-methylmalonyl-CoA-pyruvate-transcarboxylase (i.e. E.C.2.1.3.1). The electron carriers include flavoproteins, menaquinones, and cytochromes, but not ferredoxin (37, 101, 147). This pathway is also used for lactate fermentation by *Propionibacterium* species. However, a different path is employed by *Clostridium, Megasphaera,* and *Bacteroides* species (82, 95, 168). The mechanism of propionic acid formation in these bacteria involves acrylic acid as a carbon intermediate and ferredoxin as an electron carrier (101).

Three different pathways for glucose conversion to ethanol are described in anaerobic bacteria (36, 42) and they are distinguished by the mechanism of key carbon cleavage enzymes (see Figure 4). The yields of ethanol obtained from glucose fermentation by any of these pathways depend upon specific cultural conditions (i.e. substrate type and concentration, pH, and the presence of organic and inorganic cofactors) that control the intraspecies regulation of carbon and electron flow during the fermentation time course. These factors are explained below in more detail.

The ketoclastic pathway used by lactic acid bacteria (e.g. *Lactobacillus brevis*) produces ethanol from acetyl phosphate that is generated by the

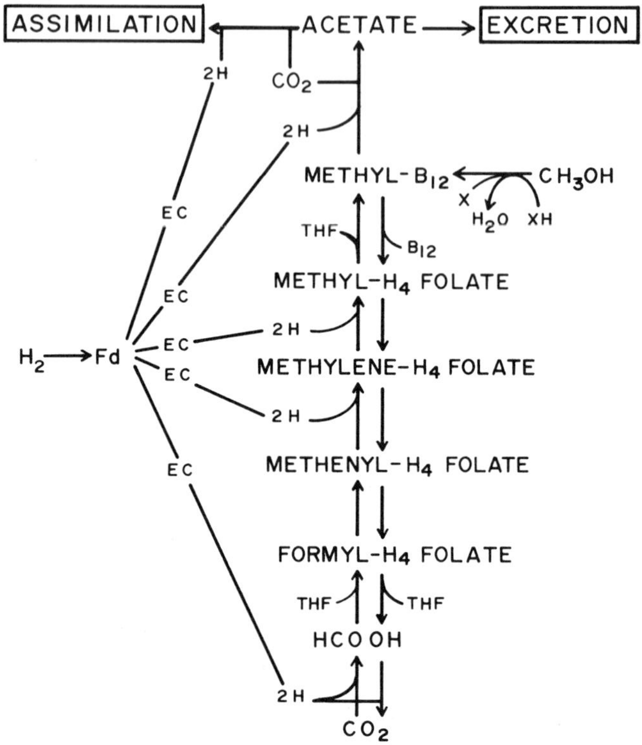

Figure 5 Proposed scheme for unification of one-carbon metabolism in homoacetogens.

phosphoketolase cleavage of xylulose-5-phosphate (42). Electron flow in this path is simple and involves pyridine nucleotide–linked reduction of acetyl CoA and pyruvate to ethanol and lactate. The phosphoroclastic path appears most common to anaerobic bacterial ethanol production and is employed by diverse genera (e.g. *Clostridium, Thermoanaerobium, Sarcina, Ruminococcus*). Acetyl CoA, reduced ferredoxin, and CO_2 are generated from pyruvate via the phosphoroclastic reaction. The reduced pyridine nucleotides generated by glycolysis and the reduced ferredoxin formed by pyruvate dehydrogenase are oxidized and coupled to the formation of lactate, H_2, and/or ethanol as the final reduced end products. *Ruminococcus albus,* which employs this pathway, does not contain lactate dehydrogenase, and it forms formate as an additional end product (120). The decarboxyclastic path present in yeasts is not common to bacteria and has only been reported in facultative *Zymononas* species (190) and in one obligately anaerobic species, *Sarcina ventriculi* (21). In this path acidaldehyde is generated directly from pyruvate decarboxylation and is reduced by pyridine nucleotides generated in glycolysis. Most notably, *S. ventriculi* contains both the decarboxyclastic and phosphoroclastic pathways (155).

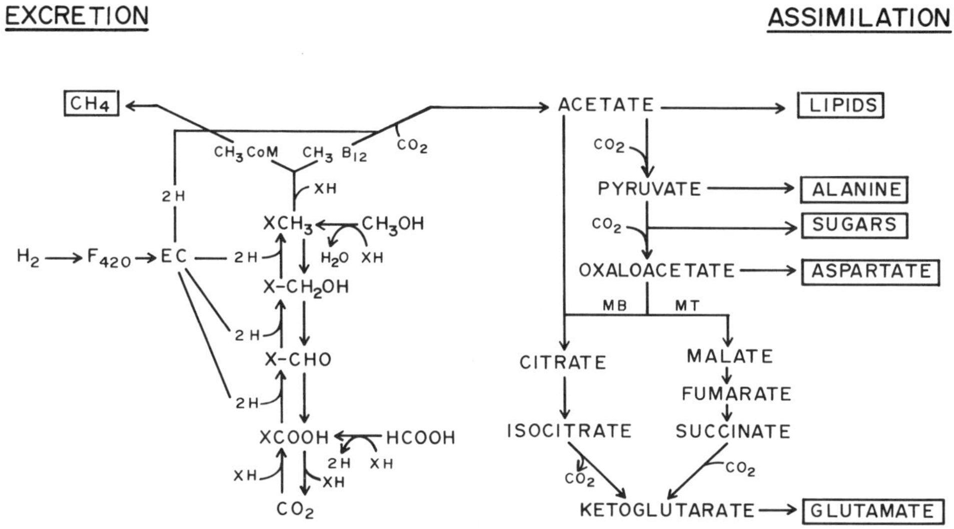

Figure 6 Proposed scheme for unification of one-carbon metabolism in methanogens. Note that the pathway for C_5 synthesis differs in *M. thermoautotrophicum* (MT) and *M. barkeri* (MB). B_{12} means corrinoid molecule.

One-Carbon Metabolism Pathways

One-carbon metabolism is of interest to chemical and fuel biotechnology because of the availability of syn-gas (i.e. H_2/CO_2, CO) and methanol. Methane, acetic acid, and butyric acid are the only known fermentation products of one-carbon metabolism in anaerobic bacteria (i.e. homoacidogen and methanogen species). Detailed studies on one-carbon metabolism in pure cultures of anaerobic bacteria were only initiated in the 1970s. Therefore, the exact catabolic or anabolic pathways employed by chemosynthetic anaerobic bacteria that grow on one-carbon compounds as the sole source of energy and/or carbon are not known. Most aerobic bacteria (i.e. the methylotrophs) that utilize one-carbon compounds as sole carbon and energy for growth contain novel pathways (139) and appear unique because initial catabolic and anabolic reactions are unified by common intermediates (i.e. methanol metabolism involves the conversion of formaldehyde to both CO_2 and cell carbon). At present, anaerobic bacteria that grow on H_2/CO_2 or methanol appear unique because known pathways (115) for one-carbon metabolism in either autotrophic species (i.e. the Calvin cycle) or methylotrophic species (i.e. the serine or hexulose phosphate pathways) have not been detected. Unifying schemes for one-carbon metabolism in homoacidogenic and methanogenic bacteria are compared in Figures 5 and 6.

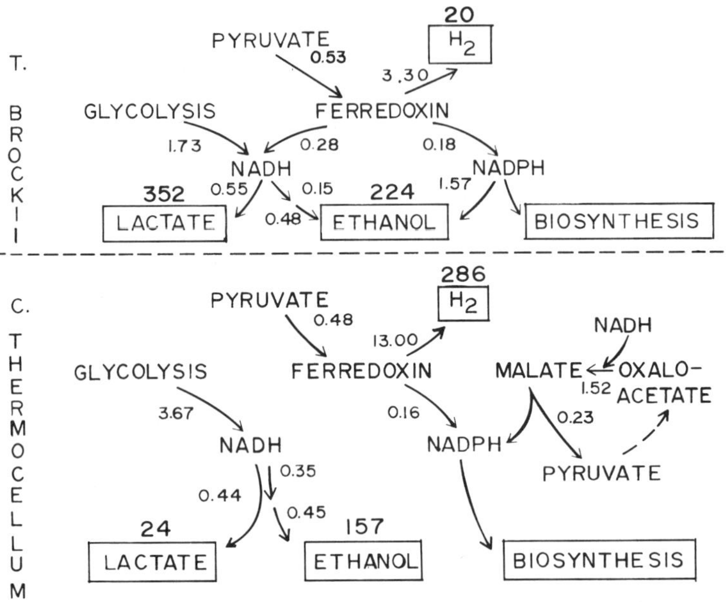

Figure 7 Relation of catabolic enzyme activities to reduced fermentation product ratios in ethanologenic thermophiles. Arrows indicate the direction of electron flow; numbers represent product ratios and the specific activities of the appropriate enzymes (see Figure 8) in μmol/min·mg protein at 40°C (99; unpublished findings).

Although the exact electron carriers and carbon intermediates involved in one-carbon metabolism in homoacidogenic bacteria that make acetic acid (i.e. *A. woodii*) or butyric acid (i.e. *B. methylotrophicum*) require documentation, these species appear to have initial metabolic reactions similar to those described for one-carbon metabolism in *C. thermoaceticum* (7, 108, 178a). Both *A. woodii* and *B. methylotrophicum* contain high levels of corrinoids (157, 200a). Cell-free extracts of *A. woodii* contain high levels of folate enzymes (157), and they actively generate acetate from H_2/CO_2 (146). However, detailed short-term radioactive tracer studies have not been reported. Methanol metabolism in homoacidogens has not been characterized but could involve corrinoids, as suggested in previous studies with methylotrophic methanogens (152). Growth of homoacetogens on H_2/CO_2 involves the hydrogen-mediated, reductive carboxylation of CO_2 to acetate (i.e. excretion) and to cell carbon (i.e. assimilation). Acetate reduction to pyruvate is a logical precursor to cell carbon synthesis in homoacetogenic bacteria, because growth of these species on hexose involves cell carbon synthesis from this intermediate.

Several lines of evidence suggest that methanogens employ one-carbon carriers for initial metabolic steps in the metabolism of one-carbon compounds. Short-term radioactive tracer studies (33) revealed the presence of

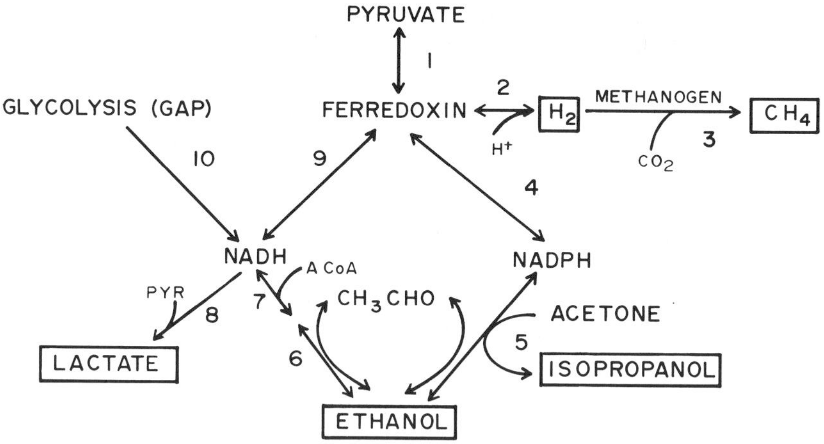

Figure 8 Metabolic control of electron flow in *T. brockii* by regulation of reversible oxidoreductases. Numbers represent the following activities: 1. Pyruvate-ferredoxin oxidoreductase; 2. H_2-ferredoxin oxidoreductase; 3. "Methanogenase"; 4. NADP-ferredoxin oxidoreductase; 5. NADP-linked alcohol-aldehyde/ketone oxidoreductase; 6. NAD-linked acetaldehyde-ethanol oxidoreductase; 7. NAD-linked acetyl CoA-acetaldehyde oxidoreductase; 8. NADH-pyruvate reductase; 9. NAD-ferredoxin oxidoreductases; 10. Glyceraldehyde-3-phosphate dehydrogenase (13; unpublished findings).

one-carbon carriers (i.e. methyl Coenzyme M and structurally unidentified one-carbon carriers) but not intermediary metabolites common to autotrophic (i.e. 3 PGA) or methyltrophic (i.e. serine or allulose phosphate) species. The first identified products of assimilatory CO_2 fixation in methanogens were the amino acids alanine, aspartate, and glutamate (33). Similarly, neither formate, formaldehyde, nor methanol are detected in culture media during growth of methanogens on H_2/CO_2. Likewise, growth of methanogens on methanol or formate is not accompanied by detection of H_2, formaldehyde, and either formate or methanol. CO metabolism is associated with the formation of H_2 and CO_2 (31). Only the terminal reactions of catabolism and anabolism in methanogens have been identified. Conversion of CO_2, methanol, or formate to methane involves one-carbon carriers, some (e.g. YFC) of which remain to be identified (33, 152, 182). Identified one-carbon carriers in methanogenic species include Coenzyme M (182) and corrinoid derivatives (93, 152). The final step in methane production from H_2/CO_2 involves CoM and not B_{12} because the purified catabolic methyl reductase in methanogens is specific for methyl CoM and not methyl B_{12} (62, 182; R. S. Wolfe, pers. commun.). The path of methanol conversion to methane has not yet been clearly elucidated, but initial enzymatic and short-term labeling studies performed with cells grown in pure culture demonstrated an involvement for CoM (33, 61). Note that other studies indicate a B_{12} involvement in methanol metabolism (152). Electron flow during methanogen growth on H_2/CO_2 involves electron carriers unique to methanogens (182). For example, the low redox electron carrier for key catabolic and anabolic reactions in methanogens (i.e. hydrogenase and pyruvate dehydrogenase) is the deazoflavin, factor F_{420}, and not ferredoxin (167, 199). Recently, cytochromes that have not been detected in methanogens grown on H_2/CO_2 have been reported in *Methanosarcina barkeri* grown on methanol (94). Two alternative hypotheses concerning cell carbon synthesis from one-carbon compounds remain viable. Namely, initial catabolic and anabolic reactions are unified by a common pathway as paralleled in methylotrophic aerobes and homoacetogens or separate pathways exist for cell carbon and methane formation. A unified pathway for one-carbon metabolism in methanogens may be unique in that anabolic synthesis of a C2 unit may not require ATP (see Figure 6). Recently, it has been shown that growth of methanogens on H_2/CO_2 or methanol is inhibited by iodopropane, a B_{12} antagonist, and that acetate addition reverses the iodopropane-dependent growth inhibition (89). This preliminary finding, and the results of short-term ^{14}C-tracer studies (33) and long term ^{14}C-acetate incorporation studies (55, 158, 177) suggest that acetate is a key intermediate in cell carbon synthesis and that corrinoids are involved in acetate synthesis. Two different pathways for acetate assimilation in methanogens have been described (55, 177). Pyruvate synthase is a key reaction in both pathways (177, 199). However, the mechanism of C_5 synthesis differs significantly in *M. barkeri* and *M. thermoautotrophicum.* The former synthesizes α-ketoglutarate via oxidative reactions of the tricarboxylic acid cycle (TCA) (177), whereas the latter involves reductive reactions of the TCA cycle (55, 199). Neither species grown on one-carbon compounds has a functional, complete TCA cycle.

Intra- and Inter-Species Control of End-Product Formation

Biotechnological exploitation of anaerobic bacteria for chemical and fuel production necessitates a knowledge of metabolic features that control the rates, yields, and kinds of fermentation products formed by both pure and mixed cultures. Regulation of end-product formation in pure cultures of anaerobic bacteria (i.e. intra-species control) and mixed cultures (i.e. inter-species control) is poorly understood and appears complex, with multiple factors interacting to control the rates and yields of specific product formation. These factors include parameters that influence the flow of carbon and electrons in a given metabolic path, as well as species tolerance to the fermentation products formed. In some instances the controlling features of a specific product have been related to the activity and regulation of a specific catabolic enzyme. Intra-species product control has been examined in solventogenic and acidogenic fermentations but not in methanogenic fermentations. On the other hand, inter-species product control has been studied in methanogenic fermentations, as cited above, but not in solventogenic or acidogenic fermentations.

Among acidogenic fermentation products, control of lactic acid formation has been most thoroughly described. In homolactic acid fermentations, cultural conditions that influence the activity of lactate dehydrogenase are most important. Lactate dehydrogenase is regulated by its allosteric effector, fructose 1, 6-bisphosphate (183). Thus, cultural parameters that influence the levels of fructose 1,6-diphosphate FDP (e.g. substrate concentration) or increase the affinity of the allosteric effector (e.g. proton concentration) control the yield of lactic acid. Thus, homolactic acid fermentations can be converted to heterolactic acid fermentations under glucose-limited conditions (161, 191). Similarly, at low glucose dilution rates the heterolactic bacterium *Lactobacillus casei* formed acetate, ethanol, and formate exclusively, whereas at high dilution rates lactate production was maximal and only traces of acetate, formate, and ethanol were detected (38). In heterolactic acid bacteria that form H_2 via ferredoxin, additional control of lactic acid production is found at the level of ferredoxin-pyridine nucleotide oxidoreductase regulation. Control of acetic acid formation in homoacetogens appears primarily related to cultural pH. None of the species described to date can grow well at pH values below 6. The detection of formate (6) or H_2 at the end of logarithmic growth of acetogens grown on hexose in non-pH–controlled batch conditions suggests that their unique one-carbon metabolism is controlled by the proton concentration. Formation of butyric acid by butyrogens requires a high acetate concentration to drive the butyrl CoA-acetyl CoA transferase reaction (160); however, it is also controlled by the regulatory properties of the pyridine nucleotide-ferredoxin oxidoreductases and the proton concentration (84, 160). Detailed studies on pyridine nucleotide-ferredoxin oxidoreductases in *Clostridium* species revealed that the function and regulatory properties of these enzymes depend on both the specific bacterial species and the specific growth conditions of a given species (84, 136). For example, when *C. tyrobutyricum* is grown on glucose, regulation of the NAD-ferredoxin oxidoreductases by NADH and acetyl CoA allows the enzymes to function co-relatively with glyceraldehyde-3-phosphate dehydrogenase and to control the levels of NAD^+ and NADH, which influence the flow of electrons from ferredoxin to H_2 or butyrate. However, when grown on pyruvate/acetate, NAD-ferredoxin reductase is not detected and only ferredoxin-NAD reductase controls the flow of electrons to butyrate (136). It appears that NAD-ferredoxin oxidoreductases in anaerobic bacteria are reversible but that the direction of the enzyme depends on the species and cultural conditions. Thus in *Clostridium acetobutylicum* this activity controls electron flow; it functions in the direction of NADH reduction when butanol is formed, and it functions in the direction of ferredoxin reduction when butyrate and H_2 are formed (136). In sum, electron flow during butyric acid formation is controlled at the level of pyridine nucleotides and by intermediary product concentrations (i.e. both acetate and H^+).

Metabolic control of alcohol production in solventogenic fermentations is complex because multiple reduced products are often formed (i.e. H_2, organic acids, alcohols, and ketones). *C. acetobutylicum* should be a model organism for fundamental studies on regulation of end-product formation in anaerobes because of its past industrial significance. However, detailed studies on catabolic regulation, especially those utilizing a chemostat to interpret the effect of pH on growth, intermediary metabolites, and solvent production, have not been performed. Analysis of *C. acetobutylicum* batch cultures (34, 131) indicates that cells are expressed for solvent production at the end of growth when the proton concentration is high (34). Notably, the same alcohol dehydrogenase that reduces acetaldehyde to ethanol during logarithmic growth functions in butyraldehyde reduction by ripe cells (42).

Metabolic control of ethanol production has been examined in *Sarcina ventriculi* (155) and thermophilic anaerobes (13). *S. ventriculi* contains both the phosphoroclastic and the decarboxyclastic pathways for ethanologenesis (155). The proton concentration determines the path used and the amount of ethanol produced. At pH 4.7, the activities of both pyruvate dehydrogenase and pyruvate decarboxylase are equivalent. Decreasing the proton concentration favors the phosphoroclastic pathway, whereas increasing the proton concentration favors the carboxyclastic pathway, probably as a result of mass action inhibition of the phosphoroclastic enzymes by acetate (155).

Metabolic control of ethanol production is greatly influenced by regulation at the pyridine nucleotide-ferredoxin oxidoreductase level as exemplified in recent studies of thermophilic anaerobes (13, 99, 128). Several ethanologenic species produce the same end products (i.e. ethanol, H_2, CO_2, lactate and acetate), but the ratios of these products in balanced fermentations can vary tremendously (see Tables 4, 5). The different fermentation product ratios observed in different ethanol-producing species that employ the phosphoroclastic pathway are related to the specific activities and regulatory properties of the catabolic enzymes that control electron flow (see Figure 7). For example, fermentation of cellobiose under identical conditions in *Thermoanaerobium brockii* strain HTD4 yields a reduced product ratio of 224 ethanol: 20 H_2:352 lactate; whereas in Clostridium thermocellum strain LQRI the ratio is 157 ethanol: 286 H_2:24 lactate (13). In *T. brockii,* ethanol yield is higher as a consequence of electron flow from pyruvate to ethanol via pyruvate-ferredoxin reductase, ferredoxin NAD and NADP reductase, and both NAD- and NADP-acetaldehyde reductase. In *C. thermocellum,* ferredoxin-NAD reductase and NADP-acetaldehyde reductase are not detectable during cellobiose fermentation. In *C. thermocellum,* H_2 yield is higher because of higher hydrogenase activity and the absence of electron flow from reduced ferredoxin or NADPH to lactate or ethanol. Higher lactate yields corresponded with the finding of 18 mmol FDP/cells in *T. brockii,* 2 mmol/gram cells in *C. thermocellum,* electron flow from pyruvate to NADH via ferredoxin NAD reductase, and significantly lower activities of glyceraldehyde-3P-dehydrogenase in *T. brockii* (13, 99).

Depending on the specific species and/or strain, the flow of electrons during catabolism of thermophilic ethanologenic bacteria can either be reversed or regulated by the addition of exogenous electron donors and/or acceptors (13, 128). These alternative channels for catabolic electron flow in *T. brockii* are summarized in Figure 8. The flow of electrons from energy source to end products in *T. brockii* is interconnected by reversible oxidoreductases and common electron carriers (i.e. ferredoxin, NAD, NADP). The addition of 1 atm of exogenous H_2 completely inhibits growth and product formation in *T. brockii* strain HTD4 but has no effect on *C. thermocellum* strain LQRI, because of specific differences in their enzyme outfits (see Figure 7). The addition of lower concentrations of exogenous H_2 (i.e. 0.3 atm) to *T. brockii* fermentations results in decreased growth rate, inhibition of acetate and H_2 production, and increased ethanol and lactate yields. Thus, electrons can flow from H_2 to the other major reduced end products in this organism. The growth inhibition by H_2 (i.e. 1 atm) in *T. brockii* fermentations is reversed by the addition of a variety of electron acceptors (e.g. acetone) that are recognized with high affinity by the organisms' unique NADP-linked alcohol dehydrogenase (99). The addition of exogenous acetone results in increased alcohol yield, decreased lactate yield, nearly stoichiometric conversion of H_2 and acetone to isopropanol, and stimulation of the growth rate, probably as a consequence of the increased rate of oxidation of reduced cellular electron carriers. In addition, *T. brockii,* but not *C. thermocellum,* can grow on ethanol, its major fermentation product, as an energy source in the presence of *M. thermoautotrophicum* (13). This indicates the reversibility of the oxidoreductases controlling electron flow in *T. brockii* fermentations. In the absence of the methanogen that catabolizes H_2, *T. brockii* is not able to grow on ethanol because H_2 is an end-product effector of the reversible oxidore-ductases. *T. brockii/M. thermoautotrophicum* co-cultures do not grow on lactate as an energy source because *T. brockii's* lactate dehydrogenase functions only in the direction of NADH oxidation (99).

Table 4 Representative fermentation substrates and product yields of selected acidogenic bacteria[a]

		Fermentation products (mmole/100 mmole hexose)										
Organism	Energy sources	Acetic	Lactic	Butyric	Propionic	Succinic	Formic	CO_2	H_2	Ethanol	Glycerol	Reference
Acetic												
C. formicoaceticum	Fructose	300[b]										6
		280[c]										
C. thermoaceticum	Hexose, pentose, lactic						40					108
A. woodii	Hexose, lactic, H_2/CO_2											11
Lactic												
L. amylophillus	Starch, hexose											126
L. casei	Hexose, pentose, cellobiose	5[d]	160				10					38
		68[e]	70				114			60		
L. brevis	Hexose, pentose	15	83					81		74	32	190
T. brockii	Starch, hexose, cellobiose	18[f]	152					80	14	65		99
		20[g]	84					131	50	95		

Butyric										
C. butyricum	Starch, hexose, pentose	42		76				188	235	190
C. thermosac-charolyticum	Hexose, pentose, cellobiose									72
S. maxima	Carbohydrates	30	21	76		5	4	149	230	21
B. methylotrophicum	Hexose, lactic, methanol H_2/CO_2									200[a]
Propionic										
C. propionicum	Lactic									190
P. arabinosum	Hexose, pentose	10			149	8		64		190
Succinic										
R. flavofaciens	Cellulose, hexose	74				95	35	37	33	184
B. succinogenes	Cellulose, hexose									184
Caproic										
C. kluvyeri	Ethanol-acetate									190

[a]Many other species of acidogenic bacteria have been described (18). Those listed here have been selected because of their high yields, metabolic rates, or substrate fermentation range. Carbon recovery for fermentation balances greater than 84%.
[b]Batch culture after 15 hr incubation.
[c]Batch culture after 30 hr incubation.
[d]Batch culture, end of growth, glucose non-limiting.
[e]Continuous culture, glucose limiting, dilution rate 0.39 hr^{-1}.
[f]Batch culture, end of growth, glucose non-limiting, 0.1% yeast extract.
[g]Batch culture, end of growth, glucose non-limiting, 0.05% yeast extract.

Table 5 Representative fermentation substrates and product yields of selected solventogenic bacteria[a]

Organism	Energy sources	Fermentation products (mmole/100 mmole hexose)										
		Ethanol	Butanol	Isopropanol	Acetone	Acetoin	Lactate	Acetate	Butyrate	CO_2	H_2	Reference
Ethanol												
Clostridium thermocellum str. LQRI	Cellulose, cellobiose	67					10	71		148	122	13, 128
Clostridium thermohydrosulfuricum str. 39E	Starch, hexose pentose, cellobiose	194					2	11		207	11	13
Thermoanaerobium brockii str. HTD4	Starch, hexose, cellobiose	95					84	20		131	50	99, 200
Sarcina ventriculi	Hexose	171				4		20		195	41	29
Ruminococcus albus	Cellulose, hexose, pentose, cellobiose	69						74		142	257	184
Butanol, Acetone-Isopropanol												
Clostridium acetobutylicum	Starch, hexose, pentose	7	56		22	6		14	4	221	135	190
Clostridium butylicum	Hexose, starch		59	12				17	17	204	78	190

[a]Many other species of solventogenic bacteria have been described (18). Those listed have been selected because of their high yields, metabolic rates, or substrate fermentation range. Carbon recovery for fermentation balances in nonenergy source–limited batch cultures was >90%.

Biotechnological optimization of ethanol yields in phosphoroclastic fermentations will require metabolic regulation of species catabolic electron flow. In this regard, fermentation control of extraneous electron acceptors and donors is necessary. The presence of hydrogen-oxidizing bacteria (i.e. the involvement of homoacetogenic or methanogenic species as fermentation contaminants) diverts electron flow from ethanol to methane or acids. Likewise, the presence of inorganic electron acceptors such as $SO_3^{=}/S_2O_3^{=}$ (13) or $NO_3^{=}$ (65) alters intra-species electron flow from ethanol to reduction of these electron acceptors. On the other hand, addition of certain electron donors (e.g. H_2) or electron acceptors (e.g. acetone) to *T. brockii* or *C. thermohydrosulfuricum* fermentations increases alcohol yield.

TECHNOLOGICAL RELATIONSHIPS

Anaerobic bacteria have potential in the production of large volume chemicals and fuels, not only because of their substrate-product relationships but also because they offer the promise of simple, efficient processes not common to previous aerobic industrial fermentations. Anaerobic bacterial fermentations offer the following advantages: larger volume reactors because of lower self-heating, simpler fermentor design requirements for mixing because of the absence of O_2-related mass transfer problems, utilization of process heat as an asset instead of the requirement for refrigeration, and decreased energy demands for volatile product recovery as a result of thermophilic fermentations. Furthermore, the potential exists to enhance bacterial product formation rates, product yields, and product recovery used in current anaerobic fermentation technology by optimizing species metabolism via strain selection and genetic techniques.

Methane Production

Methane fermentations of biomass are biologically stable processes that enable complete anaerobic mineralization of non-recalcitrant carbon. Methane, the final reduced fermentation product, is stable anaerobically and its presence does not inhibit anaerobic metabolism. At present, methane fermentations are economically feasible for treatment of concentrated organic matter in industrial wastes, municipal solids and sludge, and animal manures (76, 153). Recent technological developments have increased process rates by the use of thermal temperatures (17, 25, 26, 137, 174, 181) and new digestor designs that increase the resident microbial populations (80, 104). More emphasis has been placed on waste pretreatment (113), including chemical and physical techniques to solubilize ligneous materials to fermentable aromatic compounds (46, 66, 198). Additional emphasis has been placed on obtaining other vendable products besides methane from anaerobic waste fermentations; these products include the use of digestor effluent-solids for chemical fertilizer and feeds and the recovery of CO_2 (153). Also, the development of biomethanation technology has been initiated (181). Biomethanation involves the utilization of methanogenic bacterial populations to ferment coal gasification products (e.g. CO_2, H_2, and CO). The current status of both the fundamental and applied aspects of methane fermentation technology was presented at a recent symposium (153) and will not be discussed further here.

Solvent Production

The acetone-butanol fermentation of *C. acetobutylicum* has current industrial interest for two major reasons. First, the demand for butanol from biomass fermentations has increased because of the high cost of petroleum-based chemical feedstocks (163) and the use of butanol as an intermediate for the synthesis of butyl acetate, butyl acrylate, and other chemical products (48). Second, the organism can produce solvents from a variety of low-cost substrates, including pentose sugars derived from biomass residues (166) or from wood acid- and prehydrolyzates (67). Current process optimization involves the use of sugar concentrations below 7% because the solvents produced are highly toxic over the 2% level and the maximal solvent production yield (30% conversion) cannot be achieved at higher sugar concentrations without waste. The current process technology for the acetone-butanol fermentation has been recently reviewed (151, 169).

Several factors account for technological interest in bacterial fermentations, as opposed to yeast fermentations, for bioethanol production. Bacterial fermentations enable direct use of the cellulosic and hemicellulosic components of delignified biomass without pretreatment to depolymerize the substrates. Bacteria also have the ability to ferment both hexoses and pentoses to ethanol in high yield. Perhaps, most importantly, thermophilic fermentations lower the energy requirements for product recovery via reduced pressure distillation in a vacuum fermentor (20, 29). At present, yeasts, and not anaerobic bacteria, are used for industrial bioethanol production from soluble sugars. However, current technological developments may enable bacterial ethanol production from direct thermophilic fermentations of nonlignified biomass. Co-cultures of *Clostridium thermocellum* and either *C. thermohydrosulfuricum* or *C. thermosaccharolyticum* have been shown to actively ferment the biomass pentoses and hexoses in ground corn stover (59, 170, 171) or in delignified wood fiber (13, 128) to ethanol. The effect of a high ethanol-yielding, mono- and disaccharide-fermenting second species on *C. thermocellum's* cellulose metabolism is especially evident in co-cultures with *C. thermohydrosulfuricum* grown on Solka Floc (i.e. a wood cellulose containing both hexose and pentose moities). In mono-culture neither species ferments xylans, and only *C. thermocellum* metabolizes cellulose, whereas in co-culture xylans, glycans and mono- and disaccharides are metabolized (128). Comparison of ethanol yields at the end of the fermentation in mono- and co-cultures demonstrated that the ethanol/acetate ratio was 14-fold higher and the ethanol yield increased 2-fold in co-culture. The major process limitation with wild-type anaerobic thermophiles is low ethanol-tolerance and final solvent concentrations of $\leq 1\%$ in the fermentation liquor. Preliminary reports indicate that ethanol-tolerant (3–5%) mutant strains are selectable (13, 170, 171). The direct fermentation of corn stover to ethanol with *C. thermocellum* co-cultures (171) appears more economically favorable than the carefully investigated processes (165, 179) that combine cellulose hydrolysis by *Trichoderma viride* cellulase and ethanol production by *Saccharomyces cerevisiae* (C. L. Cooney, personal communication).

Acids and Other Vendable Chemical Products

Organic acids are used in large volume by both food and chemical industries (88, 109). Recent technological interest has focused on acid fermentations of biomass and food-processing wastes. New waste treatment processes have been developed for the production of lactic acid from fermentation of potato-processing starches and milk whey sugars by *Lactobacillus* (52, 140). Acetic acid is one of the major industrial chemicals used in large volume. The US consumed nearly 2,700 million pounds of acetic acid in 1978 (88). The high product yields of homoacetogens on biomass pentoses or hexoses and coal pyrolysis products has initiated research into the potential process applications of *C. thermoaceticum* and H_2/CO_2-metabolizing species (172). The production of butyric acid from biomass or methanol fermentations is especially intriguing; however, data on process application technology are not available. Butyric acid is not presently a large volume industrial chemical, but it has been suggested as a feedstock for ketones (64).

Production of biochemicals by anaerobic bacterial fermentations is likely to increase in order to lower process costs of current fermentation technology. Studies have been initiated to find lower cost substrates for vitamin B_{12} production (49, 85). The high yield vitamin B_{12} fermentation of *Propionibacterium* species is limited to glycerol, lactate, and sugars as substrates (49). Aerobic methanol-oxidizing B_{12}-producing species (e.g. *Klebsiella* and *Pseudomonas* species) have been suggested (85). However, anaerobic methanol fermentors (e.g. *Methanosarcina barkeri* and *Butyribacterium methylotrophicum,* may be of more a interest in B_{12} production because these species contain higher corrinoid levels (93, 200a). Similarly, enzyme production from biomass waste fermentations may provide low cost catalysts for industrial enzymes (9). In this regard, the high physiochemical stability and activity of cellulase and alcohol dehydrogenase in thermophilic anaerobes has been established (99, 128, 129).

CONCLUDING REMARKS

Undoubtedly, more research on both the fundamentals and applications of anaerobic bacterial metabolism is needed before their true utility in biofuel and biochemical production can be economically assessed. The past decade provided an active interest in fundamental research on the microbiology of anaerobes. The next decade calls for more intense study and a rebirth of anaerobic fermentation technology.

At the present time, anaerobic bacterial fermentations are economically successful processes for treatment of biomass-derived wastes with vendable products gain (i.e. biogas or lactic acid). New biotechnology for chemical feedstock and fuel production by bacterial fermentations of biomass and organic pyrolysis chemicals will have an important process feature that is not shared by chemical-synthetic technology—namely, the high efficiency of energy conservation inherent in chemical transformation reactions of anaerobes. Ultimately, maximal energy conservation in both the production and consumption of fuels and chemicals is all that society can hope to attain. In chemical-synthetic reactions the amount of substrate energy that is conserved as the needed product and that is not converted to other products or lost as heat from the system should be questioned. Anaerobic bacteria as catalysts for specific chemical transformations have had over three billion years to evolve their mechanisms of energy conservation and chemical catalysis. In anaerobic bacterial fermentations certain chemical transformations practice nearly maximal theoretical yields of product and minimal energy loss from the system.

Literature Cited

1. Ait, N., Creuzet, N., Cattaneo, J. 1979. *Biochim. Biophys. Acta* 90:537–46
2. Ait, N., Creuzet, N., Forget, P. 1979. *J. Gen. Microbiol.* 113:399–402
3. Akedo, M., Sinskey, A. J., Cooney, C. L. 1978. *Abstr. Ann. Meet. Am. Soc. Microbiol.* 042:185

3a. Alexander, J. K. 1972. *Methods Enzymol.* 28:944–53

4. Ander, P., Eriksson, K. E. 1978. *Prog. Ind. Microbiol.* 14:256–99
5. Anderson, E. V. 1978. *Chem. Eng. News,* July 31, 1978, pp. 8–15
6. Andreesen, J. R., Gottschalk, G., Schlegel, H. G. 1970. *Arch. Microbiol.* 72:154–74
7. Andreesen, J. R., Schaupp, A., Neurauter, C., Brown, A., Ljungdahl, L. 1973. *J. Bacteriol.* 114:743
8. Aranki, A., Freter, R. 1972. *Am. J. Clin. Nutr.* 25:1329–34
9. Aunstrup, K. 1978. *Annual Reports on Fermentation Processes,* ed. D. Perlman, 2:125–54. New York: Academic
10. Balch, W. E., Fox, G. E., Magrum, L. J., Woese, C. R., Wolfe, R. S. 1979. *Microbiol. Rev.* 43:260–96
11. Balch, W. E., Schoberth, S., Tanner, R. S., Wolfe, R. S. 1977. *Int. J. Syst. Bacteriol.* 27:355–61
12. Balch, W. E., Wolfe, R. S. 1976. *Appl. Environ. Microbiol.* 32:781–92
13. Ben-Bassat, A., Lamed, R., Ng, T. K., Zeikus, J. G. 1980. *Inst. Gas Technol. 2nd Ann. Symp. Fuels Biomass Wastes, Orlando, Fla.* In press
14. Borstein, B. T., Barker, H. D. 1948. *J. Biol. Chem.* 172:659–65
15. Bryant, M. P. 1973. *Fed. Proc.* 32:1809–13
16. Bryant, M. P. 1976. *Microbial Energy Conversion,* ed. H. G. Schlegel, J. Barnea, pp. 107–18, Gottingen: Goltze

17. Bryant, M. P., Varel, V. H., Frobish, R. A., Isaacson, H. R. 1976. See Ref. 16, pp. 347–60
18. Buchanan, R. E., Gibbons, N. E. 1974. *Bergey's Manual of Determinative Bacteriology.* Baltimore: Williams & Wilkins. 8th ed.
19. Bull, A., Bulock, J. D. 1979. *New Sci.,* 82:808–10
20. Bulock, J. D. 1979. *Microbial Technology: Current State, Future Prospects,* 29th Symp. Soc. Gen. Microbiol., ed. A. T. Bull, D. C. Ellwood, C. Rutledge, pp. 309–26. Oxford: Cambridge Univ. Press
21. Canale-Parola, E. 1970. *Bacteriol. Rev.* 34:82–97
22. Chambers, R. S. 1979. *Science* 206: 789–95
23. Cheremisinoff, N. P. 1979. *Gasohol for Energy Production.* Ann Arbor, Mich: Ann Arbor Sci. 140 pp.
24. Compere, A. L., Griffin, D. G. 1979. *Dev. Ind. Microbiol.* 20:509–17
25. Cooney, C. L., Ackerman, R. Y. 1975. *Eur. J. Appl. Microbiol.* 2:65–72
26. Cooney, C. L., Wise, D. L. 1975. *Biotechnol. Bioeng.* 27:1119–35
27. Cote, W. A. 1977. *Recent Adv. Phytochem.* 11:1–44
28. Cowling, E. B. 1975. *Biotechnol. Bioeng. Symp. No. 5,* pp. 163–81
29. Cysewski, G. R., Wilke, C. R. 1978. *Biotechnol. Bioeng.* 20:1421–44
30. Dagley, S. 1978. *Q. Rev. Biophys. II* 4:577–602
31. Daniels, L. D., Fuchs, G., Thauer, R. K., Zeikus, J. G. 1977. *J. Bacteriol.* 132:118–26
32. Daniels, L. D., Zeikus, J. G. 1975. *Appl. Microbiol.* 29:710–11
33. Daniels, L. D., Zeikus, J. G. 1978. *J. Bacteriol.* 136:75–84
34. Davies, R., Stephenson, M. 1941. *Biochem. J.* 35:1320–31
35. Demain, A. L. 1972. *Ann. Rev. Microbiol.* 26:369–88
36. DeMoss, R. D. 1955. *J. Cell. Comp. Physiol.* 41:207–24
37. DeVries, W., van Wyck-Kaptey, W. M., Stouthamer, A. H. 1973. *J. Gen. Microbiol.* 76:31–41
38. DeVries, W., Kapteijn, W. M., Van der Beek, E. G., Stouthamer, A. H. 1970. *J. Gen. Microbiol.* 63:333–45
39. Dimmling, W. 1976. See Ref. 16, pp. 499–514
40. Doane, W. M. 1978. *J. Coatings Technol.* 50:88–98
41. Doddema, H. J., Drift, C. van der, Vogels, G. 1979. *J. Bacteriol.* 140:1081–89
42. Doelle, W. H. 1975. *Bacteriol Metabolism.* New York: Academic. 2nd ed. 738 pp.
43. Edwards, T., McBride, B. C. 1975. *Appl. Microbiol.* 29:540–45
44. Edwards, V. H. 1975. *Biotechnol. Bioeng. Symp. No. 5,* pp. 321-38
45. Ensley, B., McHugh, J. L., Barton, L. L. 1970. *J. Gen. Appl. Microbiol.* 21:51–57
46. Evans, W. C. 1977. *Nature* 270:17–22
47. Fan, L. T., Lee, Y. H., Beadmore, D. H. 1980. *Adv. Biochem Eng.* 14:101–17
48. Flickinger, M. C., Tsao, G. T. 1978. *Annual Reports on Fermentation Processes,* ed. D. Perlman, 2:23–41. New York: Academic
49. Florent, J., Ninet, L. 1979. *Microbial Technology,* ed. H. J. Peppler, D. Perlman, 1:497–517. New York: Academic. 2nd ed.
50. Fogarty, W. M., Kelly, C. T. 1979. *Prog. Ind. Microbiol.* 15:87–150
51. Fontaine, F. E., Peterson, W. H., McCoy, E., Johnson, M. J. 1942. *J. Bacteriol.* 43:710–11
52. Formey, C. J., Reddy, C. A. 1977. *Dev. Ind. Microbiol.* 119:135–43
53. Fox, G. E., Magrum, L. J., Balch, W. E., Wolfe, R. S., Woese, C. R. 1977. *Proc. Natl. Acad. Sci. USA* 74:4537–41
54. French, P., Knapp, D. W. 1950. *J. Biol. Chem.* 187:463–70
55. Fuchs, G., Stupperich, E. 1978. *Arch. Microbiol.* 118:121–26
56. Fuchs, G., Stupperich, E., Thauer, R. K. 1978. *Arch. Microbiol.* 119:215–18
57. Golueke, C. G., McGauhey, P. H. 1976. *Ann. Rev. Energy* 1:257–77
58. Gomes Da Silva, J., Serra, G. E., Moreira, J. R., Concalves, J. C., Goldemberg, J. 1978. *Science* 201:903–6
59. Gordon, J., Jiminez, M., Cooney, C. L., Wang, D. I. L. 1978. *AIChE Symp. Ser. No. 181* 74:91–97
60. Gregor, H. P., Jeffries, T. W. 1979. *NY Acad. Sci.,* pp. 273–87
61. Gunsalus, R. P., Eirich, D., Romesser, J. A., Balch, W. E., Shapiro, S., Wolfe, R. S. 1976. In *Microbial Production and Utilization of Gases,* pp. 191–98. ed. H. Schlegel, G. Gottschalk, N. Pfennig. Gottingen: Goltze
62. Gunsalus, R. P., Romesser, J. A., Wolfe, R. S. 1978. *Biochem. J.* 17: 2374–77
63. Halliwell, G. 1979. *Prog. Ind. Microbiol.* 15:1–60
64. Hartline, F. R. 1979. *Science* 206:41–42
65. Hasan, S. M., Hall, J. B. 1975. *J. Gen. Microbiol.* 87:120–28
66. Healy, J. B., Young, L. Y. 1979. *Appl. Environ. Microbiol.* 38:84–89

66a. Hepner, E. 1976. See Ref. 16, pp. 531–54
67. Herrick, F. W., Hergert, H. L. 1977. *Recent Adv. Chem.* 11:443–515
68. Hertzmark, D. I. 1979. SERI/RR-51-292, US Dep. Commerce. 24 pp.
69. Hippe, H. P., Caspari, D., Fiebig, K., Gottschalk, G. 1979. *Proc. Natl. Acad. Sci. USA* 76:494–98
70. Hobson, P. N., MacPherson, N. 1952. *Biochem. J.* 52:671–79
71. Hollaus, F., Sleytr, U. 1972. *Arch. Mikrobiol.* 86:129–46
72. Hsu, E., Ordal, E. J. 1970. *J. Bacteriol.* 102:369–76
73. Humphrey, A. E. 1975. *Biotechnol. Bioeng. Symp. No. 5.*, pp. 49–65
74. Hungate, R. E. 1966. *The Rumen and its Microbes.* New York: Academic. 533 pp.
75. Hungate, R. E. 1969. *Methods in Microbiology,* ed. J. R. Norris, D. W. Ribbons, 30:117–32. New York: Academic
76. Hungate, R. E. 1976. See Ref. 16, pp. 339–46
77. Deleted in proof
78. Iannotti, E. L., Kafkewitz, D., Wolin, M. J., Bryant, M. P. 1973. *J. Bacteriol.* 114:1231–40
79. Jeffries, T. W., Moulthrop, P. H., Timourian, H., Ward, R. C., Berger, B. J. 1976. *UCRL-52177, Univ. Calif., Livermore.* 37 pp.
80. Jewell, W. J. 1980. See Ref. 153. In press
81. Johns, A. T. 1951. *J. Gen. Microbiol.* 5:337–45
82. Johns, A. T. 1952. *J. Gen. Microbiol.* 6:123–27
83. Johnson, M. J. 1947. *Ann. Rev. Microbiol.* 1:159–72
84. Jungerman, K., Thauer, R. K., Leimenstoll, G., Decker, K. 1973. *Biochim. Biophys. Acta* 305:268–80
85. Kamikubo, T., Hayashi, M., Nishio, N., Nagai, S. 1978. *Appl. Environ. Microbiol.* 35:971–73
86. Kandler, O., Konig, H. 1978. *Arch. Microbiol.* 118:141–52
87. Keenan, J. D. 1979. *Process Biochem.,* May, pp. 9–15
88. Keiger, D. M. 1977. *Chem. Eng. News* 55:31–32
89. Kenealy, W. R., Kryzcki, J., Zeikus, J. G. 1980. *Abstr. Ann. Meet. Am. Soc. Microbiol., Miami, Fla.* I115:103
90. Keyser, P., Kirk, J. K., Zeikus, J. G. 1978. *J. Bacteriol.* 135:790–97
91. Kirk, T. K., Connors, W., Zeikus, J. G. 1977. *Recent Adv. Phytochem.* 11:369–94
91a. Kirk, T. K., Schultz, E., Connors, W. J., Lorenz, L. F., Zeikus, J. G. 1978. *Arch. Microbiol.* 117:277–85
92. Kluyver, A. J., Schnellen, C. G. 1947. *Arch. Biochem.* 14:57–70
93. Kryzcki, J., Zeikus, J. G. 1980. *Curr. Microbiol.* 3:243–45
94. Kuhn, W., Fiebig, K., Walter, R., Gottschalk, G. 1979. *FEBS Lett.* 1:58–59
95. Ladd, J. N., Walker, D. J. 1965. *Ann. NY Acad. Sci.* 119:1038–45
96. Ladisch, M. R. 1979. *Process Biochem.* 11:21–25
97. Ladisch, M. R., Duck, K. 1979. *Science* 205:898–900
98. Ladisch, M. R., Ladisch, C. M., Tsao, G. T. 1978. *Science* 201:743–45
99. Lamed, R. J., Zeikus, J. G. 1980. *J. Bacteriol.* 141:1251–57
100. Leatherwood, T. M. 1973. *Fed. Proc.* 32:1809–13
101. Leaver, F. W., Wood, H. G., Stjernholm, R. 1955. *J. Bacteriol.* 70:521–30
102. Lee, B. H., Blackburn, T. H. 1975. *Appl. Microbiol.* 30:346–53
103. Lee, M., Miller, L., Macmillan, J. D. 1970. *J. Bacteriol.* 103:595–600
104. Lettinga, I. G., van Velsen, A. F., deZeener, I. W., Hobson, S. 1980. See Ref. 153. In press
105. Lindeman, L. R., Rocchiccioli, S. 1979. *Biotechnol. Bioeng.* 21:1107–9
106. Lipinsky, E. S. 1978. *Science* 199: 644–51
107. Ljungdahl, L. G., Sherod, D. W., Moore, M. R., Andreesen, J. R. 1975. *Symposium on Enzymes and Proteins from Thermophilic Microorganisms,* ed. H. Zuber, pp. 237–48. Basal: Birkhauser
108. Ljungdahl, L. G., Wood, H. G. 1969. *Ann. Rev. Microbiol.* 23:515–38
109. Lockwood, L. B. 1979. See Ref. 49, 1:355–88
110. Macy, J. M., Probst, I. 1979. *Ann. Rev. Microbiol.* 33:561–94
111. Mah, R. A., Ward, D. M., Baresi, L., Glass, T. L. 1977. *Ann. Rev. Microbiol.* 31:309–41
112. McBee, R. H. 1950. *Bacteriol. Rev.* 14:61–63
113. McCarty, P. L., Young, L. Y., Stuckey, D. C., Healy, J. B. 1976. See Ref. 16, pp. 179–200
114. McCoy, E., Fred, E. B., Peterson, W. H., Hastings, E. G. 1926. *J. Infect. Dis.* 39:457–83
115. McFadden, B. A. 1978. *The Bacteria,* ed. J. N. Ornston, J. R. Sokatch, 6:219–304. New York: Academic
116. McWethy, S. J., Hartman, P. A. 1977. *J. Bacteriol.* 131:890–977

117. Michels, P. A., Michels, J. P., Boonstra, J., Konings, W. M. 1979. *FEMS Microbiol. Lett.* 5:357–64
118. Miller, L., MacMillan, J. D. 1970. *J. Bacteriol.* 102:72–78
119. Miller, T. L. 1978. *Arch. Microbiol.* 117:145–52
120. Miller, T. L., Wolin, M. J. 1973. *J. Bacteriol.* 116:836–40
121. Millet, M. A., Baker, A. J., Satter, L. D. 1975. *Biotechnol. Bioeng. Symp. No. 5,* pp. 193–219
122. Morris, J. G. 1975. *Adv. Microb. Physiol.* 12:169–246
123. Mortlock, R. P. 1976. *Adv. Microb. Physiol.* 13:1–53
124. Mortlock, R. P., Fossitt, D. D., Wood, W. N. 1965. *Proc. Natl. Acad. Sci. USA* 54:572–79
125. Mountfort, D. O. 1978. *Biochem. Biophys. Res. Commun.* 85:1346–51
126. Nakamura, L. K., Crowell, C. D. 1979. *Dev. Ind. Microbiol.* 20:531–40
127. Nesse, N., Wallick, J., Harper, J. M. 1977. *Biotech. Bioeng.* 29:323–36
128. Ng, T. K., Benn-Bassat, A., Lamed, R. J., Zeikus, J. G. 1979. *Proc. US Conf. Fundam. Microb. Processes, Oct. 29, 1979, Boston, Mass. NTIS Rep.*
129. Ng, T. K., Weimer, P. J., Zeikus, J. G. 1977. *Arch. Microbiol.* 114:1–7
130. Ng, T. K., Zeikus, J. G. 1979. *Abstr. Ann. Meet. Am. Soc. Microbiol.* 08:198
131. O'Brien, R. W., Morris, J. G. 1971. *J. Gen. Microbiol.* 68:307–18
132. Owen, S. P. 1960. *Ann. Rev. Microbiol.* 14:99–120
133. Pape, M. 1976. See Ref. 16, pp. 515–30
134. Pasteur, L. 1862. *Bull. Soc. Chim. Paris 1862* (1):53
135. Perlman, P. 1979. See Ref. 49, pp. 521–27
136. Petitdemange, H., Cherrier, C., Ravel, G., Gay, R. 1976. *Biochim. Biophys. Acta* 421:334–47
137. Pfeffer, J. T. 1976. See Ref. 16, pp. 139–56
138. Phelps, T., Zeikus, J. G. 1980. *Abstr. Ann. Meet. Am. Soc. Microbiol., Miami, Fla.* I4:85
139. Quayle, J. R. 1972. *Adv. Microb. Physiol.* 1:119–203
140. Reddy, C. A., Erdman, M. D. 1975. *Proc. 1st Chem. Congr. North Am. Continent, Am. Chem. Soc. Abstr. 66*
141. Reese, E. T. 1975. *Biotechnol. Bioeng. Symp. No. 5,* pp. 77–80
142. Reese, E. T. 1977. *Recent Adv. Phytochem.* 11:311–67
143. Rexova-Benkova, L., Markovic, O. 1976. *Adv. Carbohydr. Chem. Biochem.* 33:323–85
144. Roche, C., Albertyn, H., van Gylswyk, N. I., Kistner, A. 1973. *J. Gen. Microbiol.* 78:253–60
145. Scheifinger, C. C., Wolin, M. J. 1973. *Appl. Microbiol.* 27:789–95
146. Schoberth, S. 1977. *Arch. Microbiol.* 144:143–48
147. Schwartz, A. C., Sporkenbach, J. 1975. *Arch. Microbiol.* 102:261–73
148. Shinmyo, A., Garcia-Martinez, D. V., Demain, A. L. 1979. *J. Appl. Biochem.* 1:202–9
149. Sineriz, F., Pirt, S. J. 1977. *J. Gen. Microbiol.* 101:57–64
150. Smith, M. R., Mah, R. A. 1978. *Appl. Environ. Microbiol.* 36:870–79
151. Spivey, M. J. 1978. *Process Biochem.* 10:2–25
152. Stadtman, T. C. 1967. *Ann. Rev. Microbiol.* 21:121–42
153. Stafford, D. A., ed. 1980. *Proc. 1st Int. Symp. Anaerobic Digestion, Cardiff, Wales, UK.* In press
154. Stephens, G. R., Heichel, G. H. 1975. *Biotechnol. Bioeng. Symp. No. 5,* pp. 27–42
155. Stephenson, M. P., Dawes, E. A. 1971. *J. Gen. Microbiol.* 69:331–43
156. Stouthamer, A. H. 1978. See Ref. 115, pp. 389–462
157. Tanner, R. S., Wolfe, R. S., Ljungdahl, L. G. 1978. *J. Bacteriol.* 134:668–70
158. Taylor, G. T., Kelly, D. P., Pirt, S. J. 1976. See Ref. 61, pp. 173–80
159. Thauer, R. K. 1976. See Ref. 16, pp. 201–5
160. Thauer, R. K., Jungerman, K., Decker, K. 1977. *Bacteriol. Rev.* 41:100–80
161. Thomas, T. D., Ellwood, P. C., Longyear, V. M. 1979. *J. Bacteriol.* 138:109–17
162. Tong, G. E. 1978. *Chem. Eng. Prog.* 74(4):70–74
163. Tong, G. E. 1979. *Enzyme Microb. Technol.* 1:173–79
164. Tornabene, T. G., Langworthy, J. D. 1978. *Science* 203:51–53
165. Tsao, G. T. 1978. *Process Biochem.* 10:12–14
166. Tsao, G. T., Ladisch, M., Ladisch, C., Hsu, T. A., Dale, B., Choc, T. 1978. See Ref. 9, pp. 1–22
167. Tzeng, S. F., Wolfe, R. S., Bryant, M. P. 1975. *J. Bacteriol.* 121:184–91
168. Wallnofer, P., Baldwin, R. L. 1967. *J. Bacteriol.* 93:504–5
169. Walton, M. T., Martin, J. L. 1979. See Ref. 49, pp. 187–209
170. Wang, C. C., Biocic, I., Fang, H., Wang, S. 1979. *Proc. 3rd Ann. Biomass Energy Syst., Golden, Colo.,* pp. 218–69

171. Wang, D., Cooney, C. L., Wang, S., Gordon, J., Wang, G. Y. 1978. *Proc. 2nd Ann. Symp. Fuels Biomass II,* pp. 537–48
172. Wang, D., Fleishchaker, R., Wang, G. 1978. *AIChE Symp. Ser. No. 182* 74:105–10
173. Ward, D., Mah, R. A., Kaplan, I. 1978. *Appl. Environ. Microbiol.* 35:1185–92
174. Weimer, P. J., Zeikus, J. G. 1977. *Appl. Environ. Microbiol.* 33:289–97
175. Weimer, P. J., Zeikus, J. G. 1978. *Arch. Microbiol.* 119:49–57
176. Weimer, P. J., Zeikus, J. G. 1978. *Arch. Microbiol.* 119:175–82
177. Weimer, P. J., Zeikus, J. G. 1979. *J. Bacteriol.* 137:332–39
178a. Welty, K. T., Wood, H. C. 1978. *J. Biol. Chem.* 253(16):5832–38
178. Wiegel, T., Ljungdahl, L. G., Rawson, J. R. 1979. *J. Bacteriol.* 139:800–11
179. Wilke, G. R. 1975. *Cellulose as a Chemical and Energy Resource,* Biotech. Bioengr. Symp. No. 5. New York: Wiley. 361 pp.
180. Winter, J., Wolfe, R. S. 1979. *Arch. Microbiol.* 121:97–102
181. Wise, D. L., Cooney, C. L., Augenstein, D. C. 1978. *Biotech. Bioeng.* 20:1153–72
182. Wolfe, R. S., Higgins, I. J. 1979. *Microbial Biochemistry,* ed. T. R. Quayle, 21:267–370. Baltimore: Univ. Park Press
183. Wolin, M. J. 1964. *Science* 146:775–76
184. Wolin, M. J. 1974. *Am. J. Clin. Nutr.* 27:1320–28
185. Wolin, M. J. 1976. See Ref. 61, pp. 141–50
186. Wood, H. G. 1952. *J. Biol. Chem.* 199:579–87
187. Wood, H. G. 1952. *J. Biol. Chem.* 199:905–11
188. Wood, H. G., St. Jernholm, R. 1961. *Proc. Natl. Acad. Sci. USA* 47:289–303
189. Wood, T. M. 1975. *Biotechnol. Bioeng. Symp. No. 5,* pp. 111–37
190. Wood, W. A. 1961. *The Bacteria: A Treatise on Structure and Function,* ed. I. C. Gunsalus, R. Y. Stanier, 11:59–150. New York: Academic
191. Yamada, T., Carlson, J. 1975. *J. Bacteriol.* 124:55–61
192. Young, H. E. 1976. See Ref. 16, pp. 45–58
193. Zehnder, A. B. 1978. *Water Pollution Microbiology,* ed. R. Mitchell, 2:349–76. New York: Wiley
194. Zeikus, J. G. 1977. *Bacteriol. Rev.* 41:514–41
195. Zeikus, J. G. 1979. *Enzyme Microb. Technol.* 1:243–52
196. Zeikus, J. G. 1979. See Ref. 153
197. Zeikus, J. G. 1979. *Symp. Methane Other Vendable Prod. Anim. Wastes, Orlando, Fla.* In press
198. Zeikus, J. G. 1980. In *Lignin Biodegradation: Microbiology, Chemistry, and Applications,* ed. T. K. Kirk. West Palm Beach: CRC
198a. Zeikus, J. G., Ben-Bassat, A., Hegge, P. 1980. *J. Bacteriol.* 143: In press
199. Zeikus, J. G., Fuchs, G., Kenealy, W., Thauer, R. K. 1977. *J. Bacteriol.* 132:604–13
200. Zeikus, J. G., Hegge, P. W., Anderson, M. A. 1979. *Arch. Microbiol.* 122:41–48
200a. Zeikus, J. G., Lynd, L., Thompson, T., Kryzcki, J., Weimer, P., Hegge, P. 1980. *Curr. Microbiol.* 3:381–86
201. Zeikus, J. G., Weimer, P. J., Nelson, D. R., Daniels, L. D. 1975. *Arch. Microbiol.* 104:129–34
202. Zeikus, J. G., Wolfe, R. S. 1972. *J. Bacteriol.* 109:707–13

Ann. Rev. Microbiol. 1980. 34:465–96

PLASMID-MEDIATED FACTORS ASSOCIATED WITH VIRULENCE OF BACTERIA TO ANIMALS

❖1783

Lynn P. Elwell

Department of Microbiology, Wellcome Research Laboratories, Research Triangle Park, North Carolina 27709

Patricia L. Shipley

Department of Microbiology, Medical College of Virginia, Virginia Commonwealth University, Richmond, Virginia 23298

CONTENTS

INTRODUCTION 465
VIRULENCE PLASMIDS OF ENTEROPATHOGENIC *ESCHERICHIA COLI* 466
Enterotoxin Plasmids 468
Colonization Antigen Plasmids 474
VIRULENCE PLASMIDS OF INVASIVE *ESCHERICHIA COLI* 477
ColV Plasmid 477
Vir Plasmid 482
R PLASMIDS AS VIRULENCE PLASMIDS 482
VIRULENCE PLASMIDS IN *STAPHYLOCOCCUS AUREUS* 486
Plasmids and Enterotoxin B Synthesis 486
Plasmids and Exfoliative Toxin Synthesis 487
Effect of R Plasmid Carriage on the Virulence of S. aureus 489
A POTPOURRI OF VIRULENCE PLASMIDS 490
CONCLUDING REMARKS 490

INTRODUCTION

Plasmids are extrachromosomal DNA elements of bacteria that constitute a reasonably stable, but dispensable, gene pool. Under most circumstances they are not essential for the successful growth and metabolism of their host

0066-4227/80/1001-0465$01.00

bacterium. Often, however, these genetic elements carry genes for some supplementary activity that allows their host to better survive in adverse environments or permits their host to compete more successfully with other microorganisms of the same or different species.

The best-known plasmids from the standpoint of human medicine are those that specify antibiotic resistances. It has become increasingly apparent, however, that plasmids also specify properties that directly contribute to the pathogenicity of a variety of microorganisms. These so-called virulence plasmids are the subject of this review.

In the first part of this presentation we discuss in detail those areas in which the contribution of plasmid-encoded factors, such as toxins and adherence proteins, to the virulence of certain bacteria has been well defined. In fact, many of these plasmids have been the subject of rather extensive molecular and genetic analyses. The latter part of this review is concerned with examples in which the specific contribution of plasmids to microbial pathogenicity is more speculative, albeit suggestive.

VIRULENCE PLASMIDS OF ENTEROPATHOGENIC *ESCHERICHIA COLI*

Certain strains of the common intestinal bacterium *Escherichia coli* have been identified as the causative agents of a variety of diarrheal illnesses including infantile diarrhea (156), cholera-like disease in adults (110), travelers' diarrhea (49), and colibacillosis in young domestic animals (129). Unlike *E. coli* strains isolated from healthy individuals, these enteropathogenic *E. coli* are capable of elaborating one or both of two types of enterotoxins. One toxin, designated heat labile (LT), is inactivated by heating to 60°C, whereas the other toxin, designated heat stable (ST), remains active after heating. *E. coli* LT is a high molecular weight antigenic protein that resembles cholera toxin both pharmacologically and immunologically. Like cholera toxin, *E. coli* LT binds to the GM_1 ganglioside in the target cell membrane (50) and stimulates membrane-bound adenyl cyclase (40). In addition, LT cross-reacts with antiserum directed against either the intact cholera toxin molecule (50, 53) or the isolated A and B subunits of cholera toxin (15, 61). *E. coli* ST, on the other hand, is a low molecular weight nonantigenic or weakly antigenic polypeptide (1) that may act by stimulation of guanylate cyclase (45, 63). It shows no immunological cross-reactivity with cholera toxin. Differences in the chemical and biological behavior of ST preparations suggest that there may be more than one type of *E. coli* heat-stable enterotoxin (1, 10, 67).

In addition to enterotoxin production, the enteropathogenicity of these *E. coli* strains is related to their ability to colonize intestinal epithelial surfaces. This colonization is often associated with the presence of certain pilus-like proteinaceous surface antigens called colonization or adherence antigens (39, 95, 133, 138). The colonization antigens associated with the *E. coli* strains pathogenic for different animal species are antigenically distinct, but they share a number of chemical and biological properties. In addition to enhancing retention and proliferation of enterotoxigenic *E. coli* in the upper and/or lower small intestine of infected humans or animals (38, 133), each of these adherence antigens promotes mannose-resistant hemagglutination of animal or human erythrocytes (11, 41, 66). Furthermore, all consist of protein subunits 22,000–29,500 daltons in size (36, 64, 83), that are produced only at temperatures above 18°C (37, 39, 96). The adherence antigen associated with porcine enteropathogenic strains has been designated K88 (96). Three subtypes of K88 have been described: K88ab, K88ac, and K88ad (51). Strains of bovine or ovine origin frequently carry the K99 antigen (86). K99 is also occasionally isolated from cases of porcine diarrhea (85). Two adherence antigens, designated CFAI and CFAII, have been described for enterotoxigenic *E. coli* isolated from human diarrheal disease (35, 39). Each is associated with different serogroups of *E. coli:* CFAI with 078, 015, 063, and 025; and CFAII with 06 and 08 (35). Each of these colonization antigens, as well as other *E. coli* surface antigens, may bind to specific receptors in the mammalian cell (65). In the case of the K88 antigen, the receptor on the porcine intestinal tissues appears to be determined by a single dominant genetic locus inherited in a simple Mendelian manner (47, 108). The K88 receptor has been isolated and partially characterized and appears to be a membrane glycolipid similar to the GM_1 ganglioside receptor for cholera and *E. coli* LT toxins (70). Possible receptors for the other adherence antigens have not yet been isolated. It should be noted that a number of strains isolated from both human and animal sources adhere to intestinal epithelial cells in vivo or in vitro and/or exhibit mannose-resistant hemagglutination; however, they do not possess any of the protein surface antigens so far described (94, 150, 165). It is likely, therefore, that additional colonization antigens will be described in the future.

Genetic analysis of enterotoxigenic *E. coli* strains isolated from both humans and animals indicated that the incidence of conjugative plasmids was much higher in these strains than in strains of *E. coli* isolated from healthy individuals (56, 135). Furthermore, studies with strains isolated from young pigs and calves indicated that the genetic determinants for enterotoxin production (130) and for elaboration of both the K88 (93) and K99 (138) surface antigens were transmissible, i.e. carried on plasmids. In an elegant series of experiments, Smith & Linggood (136) exploited the transmissible nature of these potential virulence factors to assess their role in the pathogenesis of porcine diarrhea. A set of strains was constructed that differed only in the presence or absence of one or more of the potential virulence factor plasmids. These strains were used to infect young pigs, and their ability to induce diarrhea was assessed. It was determined that the presence of both the enterotoxin (Ent) plasmid and the K88 plasmid was sufficient to convert some *E. coli* strains from the normal flora of healthy pigs to enteropathogenicity. The presence of either Ent or K88 alone was not sufficient to convert a strain to virulence, although strains expressing K88 could sometimes induce a mild form of diarrhea. Porcine enterotoxigenic strains are often capable of producing an hemolysin, but the gain or loss of plasmids mediating hemolysin production (Hly plasmids) appeared to have no effect on the ability of these strains to cause diarrhea. It should be noted that acquisition of the Ent and K88 plasmids was not sufficient to convert all *E. coli* strains to an enteropathogenic state. Other, as yet undefined, chromosomal or plasmid factors are apparently involved either in the expression of Ent and K88 or as additional virulence factors. In a later study, Smith & Huggins (133) found evidence that the polysaccharide K antigens and, to a lesser extent, the O somatic antigens of *E. coli* affect the expression or effectiveness of the K99 antigen in promoting colonization of pig and calf intestines. Enterotoxigenic strains of human origin have not been studied as extensively as porcine and bovine strains. However, the genetic determinants for both exterotoxin production (125, 137) and elaboration of surface antigens that promote colonization (39) have been shown to be plasmid mediated in human isolates.

It is clear that the virulence determinants of enteropathogenic *E. coli* are frequently found on plasmids, but these plasmids have been demonstrated in only a relatively small proportion of the strains tested (56). In addition, in one isolate associated with human diarrheal illness, the heat-labile enterotoxin (LT) genes were carried on a temperate bacteriophage (147). In many cases neither conjugational nor transductional transfer of the enterotoxin and colonization factor properties could be demonstrated. It is therefore not yet clear whether these genes are always located on extrachromosomal elements.

Enterotoxin Plasmids

At the time of the initial analysis of *Escherichia coli* enterotoxin plasmids, all of the human and animal strains under study produced either the ST toxin alone or both ST and LT. In ST^+LT^+ strains, both toxin genes were carried on a single plasmid molecule. Physical and genetic analysis of several of these plasmids from porcine and human strains indicated that they were relatively homogeneous with molecular weights between 55 and 61×10^6 and a mole fraction guanine plus cytosine content of 0.50 (56, 141). Furthermore, DNA-DNA hybridization studies by So et al (141, 142) showed that the porcine ST+LT plasmid P307 was highly related to other ST+LT plasmids, sharing 55% of its polynucleotide sequences with an ST+LT plasmid from a human strain and at least 87% of its sequences with two other porcine plasmids. Similar studies with representative plasmids of common incompatibility groups (141, 142) revealed significant homology between ST+LT plasmids and plasmids of the F incompatibility complex. Incompatibility tests indicated that P307 belonged to the FI incompatibility group (112, 142) while the human ST+LT plasmid SF119 was assigned to the FII group (142). Heteroduplex analysis by Santos et al (112) showed that P307 was homologous with F in four regions. Three of the regions of homology were within the genes for conjugal transfer while the fourth homologous region involved genes for replication and incompatibility. McConnell and co-workers (76) have described another ST+LT plasmid of human origin that was 55 megadaltons in size and conferred sensitivity to F-specific bacteriophages but was compatible with plasmids in incompatibility groups FI through FV. This plasmid, unlike P307 (112), is derepressed with respect to transfer. In summary, the independently isolated ST+LT plasmids from human and animal sources appear to be distinct but are highly related both to each other and to other F-like plasmids.

E. coli strains that elaborate only the heat-stable enterotoxin have been implicated in both human and animal diarrheal illness (56, 156). Unlike the ST+LT plasmids, however, the ST-only plasmids appear to be quite diverse. Gyles and co-workers (56) isolated several porcine ST-only plasmids with molecular weights ranging from 20 to 80 $\times 10^6$. DNA-DNA hybridization studies with two of these plasmids showed that they had little or no homology with either the porcine ST+LT plasmid P307 or the FII incompatibility group R factor Rldrd19 (141, 142). On the other hand, the 65-megadalton ST-only plasmid, ESF0041, from the bovine strain B41 shared 44% of its polynucleotide sequences with Rldrd19 and 33% of its sequences with F (140). Furthermore, ESF0041 showed 36% homology with ST+LT plasmids of porcine and human origin but 3% or less homology with porcine ST-only plasmids. Wachsmuth et al (156) have isolated a 30-megadalton ST-only plasmid from an *E. coli* strain associated with human infantile diarrhea. No plasmids of this size have been isolated from either bovine or porcine strains. The degree of polynucleotide sequence relatedness between this plasmid and porcine or bovine ST plasmids is not known.

Further analysis of the specific DNA segment encoding the ST toxin was carried out by So et al (140) using the techniques of molecular cloning. Insertion of a 5.7-megadalton EcoR1 fragment carrying the ST genes from ESF0041 into the multicopy ColE1 derivative cloning vector RSF2124 resulted in at least a threefold amplification of toxin production, compared to strains carrying the parent ESF0041 plasmid (140). Electron microscopic analysis of single-stranded DNA from the hybrid plasmid ESF3001 carrying the 5.7-megadalton ST^+ fragment revealed the presence of a prominent inverted repeat, flanking a short single-stranded region (145). This structure was still present on ST^+ subclones in which a 3.4 kbp (2.2 megadalton) BamHI-EcoR1 fragment from ESF3001 was inserted into the pBR322 cloning vector. Restriction mapping and sequencing data indicated that the inverted sequences were IS1. The size of the fragment carrying the ST genes was further reduced by stepwise subcloning with PstI and AluI (145). The final ST^+ subclone, pMS6, contained two contiguous AluI fragments with a combined length of 640 kbp. The complete nucleotide sequence of this DNA segment containing the ST genes flanked by 66 nucleotides of the IS1 sequence has been determined. The AluI cleavage site within this 640 kbp fragment is apparently in an area essential for ST expression. Although the structure of the DNA region containing the ST determinant resembled the structure of the antibiotic resistance transposons, the inability to select for ST^+ bacteria made it difficult to assess the transposability of ST. In order to overcome this problem a DNA fragment carrying the structural genes required for expression to tetracycline resistance, but no transposition functions, was inserted into a HincII site in the DNA segment between the IS1 repeats. Insertion into this site resulted in loss of ST expression. Transposition of the newly constructed Tc^r segment to an F factor plasmid could be easily demonstrated, indicating that the ST gene is part of a transposon (Tn *1681*) (145). The transposability of the ST gene could account for the heterogeneity of the ST plasmids. It is not yet clear, however, whether there is only a single form of ST toxin. Variation in the behavior of heat-stable toxic substances during purification (1, 10) or in animal model systems (10, 67) indicates that there may be more than one type of *E. coli* ST. With the availability of a small DNA fragment encoding in ST toxin, it should be possible to resolve this question through DNA-DNA hybridization studies.

As more enterotoxigenic strains were studied, particularly the newly recognized human pathogenic isolates, it became evident that the division of toxin plasmids into ST-only and ST and LT species was an oversimplification. In some strains that elaborated both heat-labile and heat-stable enterotoxin, for example, the ST and LT determinants were found to be on separate plasmids. Evans and co-workers (42) observed that the ability to produce ST and LT was lost independently from ST^+LT^+ strains of human origins that also carry the CFAI colonization antigen. Analysis of the plasmid content of some of these strains showed that the ST toxin gene was located on the same plasmid as the CFAI antigen determinant while the LT genes are on a smaller plasmid (127; D. J. Evans and P. L. Shipley, unpublished observations).

E. coli strains that produce only the heat-labile enterotoxin have recently been implicated as the causative agents of human diarrheal disease (157). Little is known about the genetics of toxin production in these strains. Among strains isolated from an outbreak of diarrheal illness aboard a cruise ship, the LT toxin gene appeared to be carried on a plasmid of undetermined size in some strains (157) and on a bacteriophage in others (147). A 120-megadalton recombinant plasmid carrying the LT toxin determinant and antibiotic resistance genes has been transferred out of a strain involved in infantile diarrhea (29). On the other hand, the LT-only plasmid found in strain H10407 isolated from a case of cholera-like diarrhea is 42 megadaltons in size (127). It appears likely that the LT plasmids, like the ST-only plasmids, may be quite heterogeneous. There is no direct evidence for an LT transposon. Deletion analysis of the ST+LT plasmid pCG86 by Silva and co-workers (120) indicated that both the ST and LT genes were located in or very near a region flanked by inverted repeats similar to those of the Tn10 transposon. Further analysis of this plasmid, however, using the Tn5 transposon as a molecular probe has shown that the ST gene lies on the DNA segment within the inverted repeats while the LT genes are located just outside of this region (W. K. Maas, personal communication).

In order to further characterize the specific genes involved in LT synthesis, So et al isolated the LT determinant from the porcine ST+LT plasmid P307, by molecular cloning (143). A 7.8-megadalton fragment containing the LT genes was generated by partial digestion of the P307 plasmid with the EcoR1 restriction endonuclease. This fragment was inserted into the multicopy cloning vector RSF2124 and introduced into *E. coli* K12 by selection for the ampicillin resistance property of the cloning vector. The *E. coli* K12 strains carrying the chimeric plasmid ESF3003 produced more LT than a K12 strain harboring the original P307 plasmid. The 7.8-megadalton fragment could be digested to completion with EcoR1 yielding three smaller fragments of 0.7, 2.7, and 4.4 megadaltons. Removal of the 0.7-megadalton fragment had no effect on LT expression, but both the 4.4- and 2.7-megadalton fragments were required. The LT genes were subcloned into the pBR313 vector on a 5.8-megadalton BamHI fragment containing a single EcoR1 recognition site. By introducing deletion mutations of varying lengths into the LT fragment, Dallas et al (20) showed that the maximum size of the LT region was 1.2 megadaltons. The protein products of this region were analyzed using minicells as an in vitro protein-synthesizing system. Minicells do not contain chromosomal DNA but may contain plasmid DNA and are capable of transcription and translation of that DNA. About 12 distinct plasmid-specific polypeptides are produced by minicells isolated from strains carrying the chimeric plasmid EWD299, which consists of a 1.2-megadalton LT fragment linked to the cloning vector pBR313. The LT gene-specified proteins were identified by immune precipitation with antiserum against a crude LT toxin preparation with *Staphylococcus aureus* protein A as a co-precipitant (19). Two proteins with molecular weights of 11,500 and 25,500 were found to be complexed in the presence of the anti-LT serum. The two cistrons encoding for these proteins have been located on the LT DNA region and both appear to be transcribed from the same promoter. The two proteins were also found to react with anti-cholera toxin serum and anti-cholera toxin subunit B serum. Functional analysis of these proteins showed that the 25,500-dalton protein had adenyl cyclase activating activity while the 11,500-dalton protein was required for activity in intact Y-1 adrenal cells and apparently had adsorption activity. The 11,500-dalton protein was also shown to form aggregates of 4 or 5 molecules. These results indicated that the LT toxin is a multimeric protein consisting of one molecule of the 25,500-dalton subunit (A) and 4 or 5 molecules of the 11,500-dalton subunit (B). Recently, Dorner and co-workers (27) examined the heat-labile enterotoxin synthesized in a cell-free system programmed by P307 plasmid DNA. The resultant toxin was purified by immunoprecipitation and analyzed by SDS polyacrylamide gel electrophoresis. Adenyl cyclase stimulating activity was found in a 26,000-dalton polypeptide and occasionally in a 23,000-dalton subunit. It is possible that the 26,000-dalton polypeptide is a precursor of the smaller subunit. In addition, an 11,500-dalton subunit was observed. This subunit appeared to be present in multiple copies. A similar subunit structure for LT has been suggested by recent studies of LT purified by several different protocols (18, 43, 72, 114, 148). The LT structure that emerges from these studies is strikingly similar to cholera toxin, which consists of an A subunit of 28,000 daltons that activates adenyl cyclase and a B subunit of 11,000 daltons that binds to the GM_1 ganglioside in the cell membrane and forms as aggregate of 5 molecules in the intact toxin. In light of these findings, it would be interesting to determine the degree of polynucleotide sequence homology among the DNA segments encoding LT and cholera toxin, as well as among the LT genes from different sources. A 0.5-megadalton HindIII fragment coding for the LT B subunit and for a portion of the A subunit was used as a molecular probe in filter-blot hybridization studies with plasmid DNA from LT-producing *E. coli* strains of human and animal origin and chromosomal *V. cholera* DNA (21). The results indicated identity between the LT genes from P307 and those from other *E. coli* Ent plasmids. Under stringent hybridization conditions there was no evidence of DNA sequence homology between this fragment and *V. cholera* DNA, but hybridization under less stringent conditions indicated some homology. The DNA sequence of the LT B subunit has recently been determined. Comparison of this sequence with the known amino acid sequence of the cholera toxin B subunit suggests a high degree of homology (S. Falkow, personal communication).

In the absence of a direct selection procedure or even a convenient method for screening very large numbers of isolates for toxin production, direct isolation of mutations in toxin production is very difficult. The ST+LT plasmid, pCG86, however, contains the genes for tetracycline and streptomycin resistance that can be detected by direct selection. Using this plasmid, Silva et al (120) employed the technique of co-mutagenesis to isolate LT^- and ST^- mutants. A strain carrying a Tc^s derivative of pCG86 was mutagenized with *N*-methyl-*N*'-nitro-*N*-nitrosoguanidine, and Tc^r revertants were selected. Many of their revertants had also suffered mutations in the nearby DNA region encoding the LT and ST genes. Among the LT^- mutations were amber mutants, temperature-sensitive mutants, and "leaky" mutants with reduced LT activity. Most of the LT^- mutants produced cross-reacting material that could be detected in a solid phase radioimmunoassay using antibody to cholera toxin (8, 21). The mutagenesis technique often resulted in loss of transferrability of pCG86. However, in all of the LT^- mutants where pCG86 maintained the Tra^+ phenotype, the LT^- mutation was shown to be on the plasmid. In contrast, only one transferrable ST^- mutant was isolated.

Although only the enterotoxin and colonization antigen plasmids have been shown to have a direct role in pathogenicity, enterotoxigenic *E. coli* strains routinely harbor five or more distinct plasmid species. One or more of these plasmids is frequently an antibiotic resistance plasmid. The antibiotic resistance determinants, toxin genes, and adherence antigen genes are usually found on separate plasmid species. However, several plasmids encoding both toxin production and antibiotic resistance have been reported. Gyles and co-workers (55) have isolated a naturally occurring conjugative plasmid that carries the genetic information for synthesis of both ST and LT toxin and resistance to tetracycline and streptomycin. This plasmid, isolated from a porcine enteropathogenic *E. coli* strain, was larger (about 75 megadaltons in total size) than the ST+LT plasmids described above and probably arose by recombination between and ST+LT plasmid and an R factor. Using this plasmid, pCG86, Gyles et al (54) have demonstrated the transfer of enterotoxigenicity in the intestines of newly weaned pigs. Surprisingly, no difference was observed in the extent of transfer in pigs given antibiotic-free feed and those given feed containing oxytetracycline.

Although enteropathogenic *E. coli* of human and animal origin are usually of different serotypes and carry distinct adherence antigens, the overall characteristics of diarrheagenic *E. coli* in humans and animals are the same. It is therefore important to determine the prevalence and character of *E. coli* strains in food sources of animal origin. Silver et al (121) investigated the transfer of antibiotic resistance plasmids from toxigenic *E. coli* isolated from food. A small percentage of the resistant transconjugants had also acquired the ability to produce heat-labile enterotoxin. In addition, some of these R^+, Ent^+ transconjugants contained plasmids that were larger than either the Ent or R plasmid and had apparently arisen by virtue of a recombination event. Similarly, Echeverria & Murphy (29) have described a plasmid, about 120 megadaltons in size, that specifies heat-labile enterotoxin synthesis as well as resistance to tetracycline and streptomycin. This plasmid was thought to be the result of recombination between a 60-megadalton R factor and an Ent plasmid in a strain isolated from a case of human infantile diarrhea.

Ent^+ R plasmids may also be generated by transpositional events. McConnell et al (76) have observed the transposition of ampicillin resistance from a naturally occurring R plasmid to an ST+LT enterotoxin plasmid in an *E. coli* strain of human origin. Similarly, So and co-workers (144) have reported that transposition of ampicillin resistance occurs at a relatively high frequency in a laboratory-constructed strain containing the P307 ST+LT plasmid and in a derivative of the ColE1 plasmid carrying the Tn3 ampicillin resistance transposon. Although no increase in toxin transfer has yet been documented, the occurrence of enterotoxin–drug resistance plasmids may be important in increasing the number of enterotoxigenic *E. coli* in environments where antibiotics are used as food additives or in therapy.

Colonization Antigen Plasmids

During the initial studies of the transfer of the K88 determinant, Ørskov & Ørskov (93) observed that transfer of K88 into an F^+ strain of *Escherichia coli* resulted in inhibition of F fertility. The fi^+ transfer activity, however, could be separated from the K88 genes, suggesting that the F-like transfer factor might be an independent plasmid which could mobilize the K88 plasmid or that the two properties might be part of a Class I transfer system in which plasmid cointegrates could be formed. The latter interpretation was supported by the electron microscopic studies of Bak and co-workers (5); these studies suggested that the K88 antigen and transfer genes might reside on a 50-megadalton composite plasmid that could dissociate into a 10-megadalton plasmid carrying the K88 structural gene and a 40-megadalton transfer plasmid. However, definite phenotypes could not be assigned since the different plasmids could not be isolated as a single molecular species in separate cell lines. So et al (141) reported similar molecular weights of 43 and 47 megadaltons for two K88 plasmids transferred into *E. coli* K12 host strains. Subsequent to these studies, Smith & Parsell (139) noted the association of the transfer of the ability to utilize the trisaccharide raffinose with the transfer of K88. Shipley et al (119) found that the raffinose

(Raf) and K88 genes in many porcine enteropathogenic strains were located on a single nonconjugative plasmid approximately 50 megadaltons in size. The Raf/K88 plasmids from different strains showed at least 97% polynucleotide sequence homology with a representative Raf/K88 plasmid pPS100 chosen as a standard. There did not appear to be any significant difference between the plasmids determining the K88ab and K88ac antigenic variants. DNA-DNA homology studies between pPS100 and representative plasmids of common incompatibility groups revealed 17 to 19% homology between Raf/K88 and FI and FII incompatibility group plasmids. The Raf/K88 plasmid may, therefore, belong to the F incompatibility complex, although no incompatibility was observed with FI and FII plasmids. In some cases the Raf and K88 determinants were found on a larger conjugative plasmid that appeared to be a recombinant between the Raf/K88 plasmid and transfer factor. Occasionally, plasmids carrying only the raffinose fermentation genes arose by deletion of a DNA segment of about 20 megadaltons that included the K88 antigen determinant. The mechanism of this dissociation and the DNA sequences involved is not known. Recently Schmitt et al (115) have reported IS1-mediated transposition of a Raf-K88 element. It is possible that similar mechanisms are involved in these phenomena as well as in the formation of recombinants between Raf/K88 and other plasmids.

The K88ab (84) and K88ac (118, 119) genes have been isolated by molecular cloning. In each case a HindIII fragment of 7.7–8.4 megadaltons was inserted into the vector pBR322. Mooi and co-workers (84) found that cloning of the K88ab determinant resulted in a fourfold increase in K88 production at 37°C but that expression was highly dependent upon the orientation of the K88 fragment in the chimeric plasmid. By in vitro deletion the size of the K88ab fragment was reduced to 4.3 megadaltons. The Raf genes were found to be on a 4.0-megadalton SalI fragment. Restriction mapping of the Raf/K88 plasmid showed that the Raf and K88 genes were not closely linked but were separated by about 20 megadaltons.

The proteins synthesized by the chimeric plasmid containing the K88ac determinant were analyzed in a minicell system (118; P. L. Shipley, G. M. Dougan, and S. Falkow, manuscript in preparation). The 8.4-megadalton HindIII fragment carrying K88ac encodes at least 6 polypeptides. A single 23,500-dalton polypeptide was identified by immunoprecipitation with anti-K88ac serum and *S. aureus* protein A. This molecular weight is in good agreement with the reported size of purified K88ac antigen (83). It is not yet known whether any of the other polypeptides synthesized in minicells from the chimeric plasmid are involved in K88 expression.

Only one K99 plasmid has been studied. The K99 determinant in the bovine strain B41 was found on a 52-megadalton conjugative plasmid that also carried the genes for resistance to tetracycline and streptomycin (140).

The first evidence of the plasmid location of the human colonization factor, CFAI, was obtained by comparison of a $CFAI^{+}ST^{+}LT^{+}$ strain, H10407, and a laboratory-passed derivative, H10407-P, which continued to produce LT but was $CFAI^{-}$ and ST^{-} (39). The loss of CFAI and ST production correlated with the loss of a plasmid about 60 megadaltons in size. Smith and co-workers (127) confirmed this observation and have shown that the loss of expression of CFAI and ST corresponds to the loss of a 50–61-megadalton plasmid in several other strains of the 078 serogroup. In addition, the CFAI/ST plasmid from H10407 was transferred into an *E. coli* K12 host. A CFAI/ST plasmid approximately 60 megadaltons in size was also found in human enteropathogenic strains of the 026 and 063 serogroups (P. L. Shipley, D. G. Evans, and D. J. Evans, unpublished observations). The cellular location of the CFAII antigen genes has not yet been reported.

McNeish and co-workers (77) studied the ability of human enteropathogenic *E. coli* strains to adhere to human fetal small intestinal tissue. In a strain of serotype 026:K60:H11, adherence was shown to be plasmid mediated (78). The mucosal adherence determinant was found on a 56-megadalton plasmid that also carried the genes for production of ColIb bacteriocin (165). The nature of the adherence factor is not known, but it appeared to be distinct from the CFAI and CFAII antigens described by Evans and co-workers (35, 39).

It is clear from the data presented in this part of the review, dealing with enterotoxin and colonization antigen plasmids in enteropathogenic *E. coli,* that a great deal of sophisticated molecular genetics is being applied to the problem of diarrhea. In developing countries, diarrheal disease is a major cause of mortality among infants and young children and a significant cause of morbidity in people of all ages (109). Improved sanitation has greatly reduced the incidence of diarrheal illness in the human population in industrialized countries, but it remains a threat to infants and certain high risk population groups (111) and an annoyance, at least, to travelers. In addition, diarrheal disease is recognized as a major cause of death among young domestic animals and represents a serious economic problem in the animal husbandry industry (129). Although a variety of bacterial as well as viral pathogens are known to cause this type of illness, recent epidemiological studies have implicated *E. coli* strains as a significant cause of many of these forms of disease. The recognition that two major contributing factors to pathogenicity, namely enterotoxin production and surface colonization antigens, are carried on plasmids has greatly facilitated analysis of the mechanisms of pathogenesis in this organism. For example, LT enterotoxin had long eluded purification and characterization despite the expenditure of considerable investigative effort. The application of molecular genetic techniques to this problem has now provided a clear picture of the structure of LT and is also providing clues to the molecular evolution of this determinant. The further use of this technology to study these and other virulence factors should greatly contribute to our understanding of the mechanisms of infectious disease and, hopefully, open new avenues for diagnosis, treatment, and prevention of bacterial infections.

VIRULENCE PLASMIDS OF INVASIVE *ESCHERICHIA COLI*

In addition to *Escherichia coli* isolates specifically capable of causing diarrheal disease, there exists another class of *E. coli* strains with the capacity to cause generalized, extraintestinal infections in man and domestic animals. Minshew et al (81) surveyed a series of *E. coli* strains isolated from extraintestinal infections and compared their phenotypes with those of *E. coli* isolates randomly selected from stool cultures of normal individuals. They concluded that *E. coli* implicated in extraintestinal infections were more likely to (*a*) be hemolytic, (*b*) produce colicin V (ColV), (*c*) hemagglutinate human RBCs in the presence of D-mannose, and (*d*) kill 13-day-old chick embryos—than were randomly picked fecal isolates. Powell & Finkelstein (101) had reported earlier that virulence of *E. coli* for chicken embryos was correlated with the ability to hemagglutinate chicken erythrocytes. It should be noted that the specific phenotypes previously listed, namely hemolysin production, colicin biosynthesis, and specific adherence properties, have all been shown to be plasmid-mediated characteristics in *E. coli* as well as in other bacterial species (59, 88).

What complicates this issue is the fact that not all of the *E. coli* isolates from extraintestinal sources possessed each (or any) of the aforementioned characteristics (81). In fact, it was far from clear whether these phenotypes contributed directly to the virulence of these invasive strains. Perhaps they were merely linked to a virulence property. What is becoming clear, however, is that the majority of *E. coli* strains from urinary tract infections, meningitis, peritonitis, and bacteremias possess a constellation of special virulence properties, some of which are definitely plasmid borne (80). Recently, the virulence property of a ColV plasmid has been reasonably well defined, and this most interesting example will be presented in the next section.

ColV Plasmid:

Smith (128) was the first to observe that a significant proportion of *E. coli* strains associated with bacteremia in man and animals produced colicin V. It also appeared that the ColV plasmid conferred upon its host *E. coli* a greater ability to survive in the blood, peritoneal fluid, and alimentary tracts of a variety of test animals. Thus, when human volunteers consumed mixtures of $ColV^+$ and $ColV^-$ strains of *E. coli* B188, the $ColV^+$ organisms gradually became the dominant species isolated from their feces. Eventually they were the only *E. coli* B188 organisms that could be isolated (129a). In addition, $ColV^+$ forms of *E. coli* were found to be 30 times more lethal for chickens than the $ColV^-$ forms. Similar results were also obtained in mice (129a). Subsequently, Smith & Huggins (131, 134) showed that the elimination of the ColV plasmid from human, bovine, ovine, and avian *E. coli* strains was always accompanied by a decrease in pathogenicity. Reintroduction of the ColV plasmid into cured derivative strains by conjugation restored pathogenicity to its original level. These results, therefore, established an association between plasmids specifying colicin V synthesis and a virulence-enhancing property in *E. coli.* Although colicin V itself was not thought to be toxic for animals (58, 132), Ozanne et al (97) reported that culture supernatants possessing colicin activity increased vascular permeability and produced an inflammatory response in rabbits and guinea pigs. In addition, a small dialyzable protein, identified as colicin V, exhibited inhibitory activity against macrophages (97). Hence, it remained a possibility that colicin V itself might have contributed to the observable increase in the virulence of ColV plasmid containing *E. coli.*

The relationship between colicin V activity and virulence in strains of *E. coli* was further defined by Quackenbush & Falkow (103). Their basic approach was to compare the virulence of $ColV^+$ *E. coli* with isogenic strains carrying ColV plasmids in which the genes for colicin V synthesis had been inactivated. Inhibition of colicin synthesis was accomplished by allowing the ampicillin transposon, Tn*1*, to insert into the ColV structural gene. Strains carrying the ColV plasmid but lacking ColV activity were still more virulent for mice than were $ColV^-$ strains, indicating that colicin production was not essential to virulence enhancement.

Recently, the experiments of Binns et al (7) have succeeded in defining the role of plasmid ColV in the pathogenesis of certain strains of *E. coli.* The determinants for serum resistance, increased virulence, and ColV biosynthesis were localized by cloning restriction endonuclease fragments of plasmid ColV,I-K94 into pBR322 and by isolating deletion and point mutants of plasmid ColV,I-K94. The ColV derivative plasmids originally isolated in *E. coli* K12 strains were subsequently transferred into *E. coli* KH933, a strain more suitable for testing the effects of plasmids on the pathogenicity of *E. coli* for experimental animals. Basically their findings were the following: (*a*) a cloned BamH1-generated fragment of ColV,I-94 increased the virulence of *E. coli* for 1-day-old chicks, lowering the LD_{50} 100-fold, (*b*) a genetic determinant for resistance to the bactericidal effects of fresh rabbit serum was mapped to a 5,300-kbp region within the BamH1-generated fragment, (*c*) the determinants for serum resistance and for colicin V synthesis were closely linked in ColV,K94, and (*d*) neither colicin V nor immunity to colicin V affected the pathogenicity of *E. coli* for chicks. Of interest was the fact that plasmid derivatives which greatly increased the survival of their host bacterium in serum also enhanced the pathogenicity of the strain for chicks. Hence, the characteristics of serum resistance and virulence enhancement were clearly associated. In addition, several ColV derivatives were examined for their effects on the survival of *E. coli* K12 in serum. All of the K12 transformants tested were killed more rapidly by rabbit serum than were derivatives of the more pathogenic strain, *E. coli* KH933. However, the ColV derivative plasmids that increased the pathogenicity and serum resistance of *E. coli* KH933 also increased the survival of *E. coli* K12. Not surprisingly, the mere presence of the "serum resistance/virulence enhancement" gene(s) was not sufficient to convert an innocuous K12 strain into an invasive one.

Binns et al (7), noting the close linkage of the genes for colicin V biosynthesis and virulence in plasmid ColV,I-K94, suggested that these genes may interact to their mutual selective advantage. The nature of this putative interaction is, at the moment, unclear. Nonetheless, colicin V production could be exploited as a useful marker for the detection of virulence determinants in naturally occurring *E. coli* isolates. Minshew et al (80) found 12% colicin V–producing *E. coli* among 51 strains isolated from blood and 16% among strains from other extraintestinal sites. In contrast, no ColV$^+$ strains were detected among *E. coli* isolated from feces of normal individuals. Since, however, the virulence determinant(s) functions independently of the gene for ColV biosynthesis, these quoted percentages no doubt underestimate the true incidence of this particular gene(s) for virulence/serum resistance. As soon as these specific DNA sequences are further defined, isolated, and radiolabeled they can, no doubt, be exploited as molecular probes. For example, in situ colony hybridization experiments could be carried out in order to determine the extent of dissemination of these important genetic determinants.

Recently, Williams & George (164) have reported that ColV plasmids specify an efficient iron-sequestering mechanism that may play a key role in the pathogenicity of certain *E. coli* strains. The crucial role of ferric cations in host-bacterial interactions has been well documented (99). Almost all microorganisms require iron for growth; however, in nature, iron exists either as insoluble, high molecular weight aggregates or complexed with iron-binding proteins such as transferrin in animal tissues and fluids (161). To obtain the required iron from these aggregates, aerobic microorganisms have evolved specialized iron-solubilizing and -transporting ligands that are called siderophores. Siderophores can be further split into two general categories, hydroxymate and phenolate (87). *E. coli, Salmonella typhimurium,* and perhaps other enteric bacteria secrete a phenolate-type siderophore termed enterochelin (91), or enterobactin (100).

Exogenous iron has been shown to promote infection in a variety of experimental systems. For example, iron-treated animals have been shown to be more susceptible to infection with a variety of pathogenic microorganisms, compared to untreated animals (9, 98). In addition, techniques that reduce the availability of iron increase the resistance of animal hosts to infection. For example, mice fed an iron-deficient diet have been shown to be less susceptible to infection with *Salmonella typhimurium* than control mice (102). Williams & George (164) have demonstrated an association between plasmid ColV and iron uptake in the following experiments. A defined medium containing 3 μM human transferrin (the iron-binding protein of serum) was shown to markedly limit the growth rate of a plasmid-free *E. coli* K12 strain, presumably due to the conversion of free iron to an unavailable, complexed form. The addition of excess iron relieved this growth inhibition and confirmed that the presence of transferrin in defined medium made iron relatively unavailable for normal bacterial growth. In contrast to the plasmid-free K12 strains, a number of $ColV^+$, bacteremic isolates of *E. coli* from various animal sources were not inhibited by transferrin. Two pieces of evidence suggested that the ability of these strains to salvage necessary iron from the bound form was due to the presence of a ColV plasmid: (*a*) growth of cured derivatives of invasive strains was markedly limited by the presence of transferrin, and (*b*) transfer of the plasmid from the bacteremic strain into an *E. coli* K12 recipient rendered the recipient insensitive to transferrin-induced iron stress.

Experiments to probe the possible nature of this ColV-specified iron uptake system involved *E. coli* AN1937, an *E. coli* K12 mutant deficient in enterochelin biosynthesis. This particular strain was unable to take up iron and therefore could not grow unless specific siderophores were added to the growth medium. However, derivatives of AN1937 carrying ColV plasmids were able to grow in the absence of exogenously supplied siderophores. It should be noted here that iron stress is responsible for the induction of a number of outer membrane proteins in *E. coli* K12 including two known siderophore receptors (57)—a protein of 83,000 daltons whose function is unclear, and the receptor for colicin V! Using radiolabeled iron, it was found that ferric ions efficiently entered the cells of these plasmid-containing cells. Furthermore, an analysis of bacterial membranes demonstrated that enough iron entered the $ColV^+$ strains, growing in the absence of citrate (important since the ferric-citrate complex can enter cells via a citrate-inducible transport system), to maintain repression of the major membrane proteins normally induced under conditions of iron-stress. This result can be interpreted to mean that these proteins are not required in large amounts in order to transport the ColV plasmid-specified iron-binding compound.

In summary, it has been demonstrated, in plasmid ColV,I-94, that there is a close correlation between increased pathogenicity and increased serum resistance. Neither ColV synthesis nor immunity were required for these activities. In addition, the experimental data suggested that at least one of the reasons for increased virulence of the $ColV^+$ bacteria resided in the fact that they were more resistant to host defense mechanisms, primarily those mechanisms dependent upon antibody and complement. Furthermore, it has been shown that some ColV plasmids specify a novel iron uptake system that contributed to the pathogenicity of invasive *E. coli* strains. Hence the suggestive evidence is most convincing that the increased capacity to scavenge iron and to resist the potential lethal effects of serum, conferred upon *E. coli* by plasmid ColV, are important aspects of the invasive property of certain $ColV^+$ strains (12a).

It should be noted that other investigators have also shown a link between plasmid carriage and serum resistance. For example, Timmis et al (82, 153) reported that the conjugative, multiple resistance plasmid, R6-5, endowed its *E. coli* host with high level serum resistance. The serum resistance determinant(s) was further localized on an EcoR1-generated fragment of R6-5, a fragment that carried the surface exclusion genes *traS* and *traT,* as well as the *traD* gene. Initial genetic experiments suggest that the serum resistance determinant consists partly or solely of the surface exclusion gene, *traT.* TraT protein is synthesized in large quantities in plasmid-carrying bacteria and is incorporated into the outer membrane where it constitutes a major component. Since *traT* encodes an outer membrane protein, this determinant is a tempting candidate for the serum resistance gene; whether it is or not awaits further study.

In addition, Taylor & Hughes (149) showed that a smooth *E. coli* isolate, strain C8, was killed by serum in a "delayed" fashion, i.e. only after being in contact with serum for 1 hr. Curing this strain of antibiotic resistance and colicin determinants resulted in a small but significant increase in serum sensitivity. Furthermore, inheritance by a cured derivative of plasmids from a number of laboratory strains frequently, but not invariably, led to a significant increase in serum resistance. Plasmid-mediated enhancement of serum resistance was most marked with plasmids NR1 and R1. These plasmids were not, however, able to modify the serum response of a "non-delayed" serum-sensitive *E. coli* isolate. The authors speculated that a significant portion of the lipopolysaccharide O side chain is essential for the expression of plasmid determinants that modify serum sensitivity. To this end, strains are being constructed with various permutations of O and K antigens in the hope that the relative importance of these structures on the expression of plasmid-specified serum resistance can be defined.

It remains to be determined how these plasmid-borne determinants are interrelated and how each, individually and in concert with various host cell factors, contributes to the overall virulence of particular *E. coli* strains.

Vir Plasmid

An *E. coli* plasmid, provisionally designated Vir, specifies a surface antigen as well as a heat-labile, acid-sensitive, nondialyzable toxin lethal for rabbits, mice, and especially chickens (129a). Intravenous inoculation of chickens with Vir^{+} cultures of *E. coli* caused death within 6–24 hr. Necropsy findings in chickens suggested that death was primarily due to cardiac failure. Conjugative transfer of the Vir phenotype has been demonstrated not only between *E. coli* strains but also to *Salmonella typhi* and *Shigella sonnei* (129a).

Lopez-Alvarez et al (74) have partially characterized two Vir plasmids, pJL1 and pJL2, isolated from two septicemic *E. coli* strains of divergent geographical origins. Both plasmids had a molecular weight of 92 magadaltons, and subsequent restriction endonuclease analysis and DNA duplex studies revealed that pJL1 and pJL2 were related but not identical.

At the present time, the Vir plasmid appears to be comparatively rare. The role this plasmid plays in human disease (if any) is unknown. However, as Smith has pointed out (129a), the possibility of Vir acquiring drug resistance determinants is a disquieting one, in that widespread antibiotic use could insure the dissemination of this potentially dangerous plasmid.

R PLASMIDS AS VIRULENCE PLASMIDS

During 1969 and 1970, a major pandemic of bacillary dysentery caused by the classic Shiga bacillus, *Shigella dysenteriae* 1, occurred in Mexico and Central America. Many communities in seven countries had outbreaks of unusually severe dysentery with high morbidity and mortality. Over 500,-000 clinical cases were reported in the countries involved (Guatemala, Honduras, El Salvador, Nicaragua, and Costa Rica) and hospital case-fatality rates were as high as 35% (6). In Guatemala alone, 12,500 people died in one year (46). This pandemic strain of *S. dysenteriae* was resistant to chloramphenicol (Cm), tetracycline (Tc), streptomycin (Sm), and sulfadiazine (Su)—the drugs commonly used to treat dysentery. During the first half of 1972 an extensive epidemic of typhoid fever swept through Mexico and eventually into the US, infecting 100,000 people and killing 14,000, mostly between the ages of 5 and 24 (34). Clearly, the resultant disease was more severe, more protracted, with a higher rate of complications than is usually seen with typhoid fever (48, 92). The epidemic *Salmonella typhi* had a resistance pattern identical to that of the pandemic strain of *S. dysenteriae.* It has been demonstrated by several investigators (44, 46) that the multiple drug resistance in both organisms was due to the presence of transferable R plasmids. The occurrence of these two epidemics, within a short period of time, in the same geographical region, and due to unusual organisms with identical, transferable antibiotic resistance patterns, led to the speculation that the same R plasmid may have increased the virulence of these two enteric pathogens (46).

Several groups (24, 151) compared the genetic properties of R plasmids isolated from strains of *S. dysenteriae* implicated in the 1969–1970 epidemic in Central America with those found in selected *S. typhi* strains isolated in the 1972 Mexican outbreak. It was quickly apparent that these plasmids were significantly different. Subsequent compatibility tests revealed that the R plasmids from the two epidemics belonged to different compatibility groups. Thus, Datta & Olarte (24) found that 17 *S. typhi* strains originating in the Mexican epidemic carried R plasmids of compatibility group H, whereas all of the *S. dysenteriae* isolates examined harbored compatibility group O plasmids. Clearly, therefore, the plasmids implicated in these geographically related epidemics of typhoid fever and bacillary dysentery were genetically distinct (152).

As mentioned earlier, it was speculated, based primarily on epidemiological evidence, that these plasmids might have endowed their host bacteria with enhanced virulence in addition to multiple drug resistance. Briefly, this evidence consisted of the following observations summarized by Gangarosa (46). 1. An outbreak caused by a drug-sensitive strain of *S. dysenteriae* occurred in a Guatemalan Village in 1964. No mortality was associated with this and cases were mild. The same organism, now multiply resistant, was implicated in the subsequent explosive outbreaks (in the same area of Guatemala) with resultant case-fatality ratios of 20–30% for hospitalized patients. 2. Strains of *Shigella flexneri* 2a that infect healthy adults in the US rarely cause bloody dysentery. However 9 of 11 patients infected with *S. flexneri* harboring the epidemic R plasmid had bloody diarrhea. In addition, one patient died.

Butler et al (12) attempted to determine whether the compatibility group H plasmid from *Salmonella typhi* could increase the virulence of *Salmonella typhimurium* for mice. Hence, the *S. typhi* plasmid was transferred into *S. typhimurium* LT-2 and the virulence of the R^+ strain for mice was assessed by intraperitoneal 50% lethal dose and by the number of organisms found in the spleen of infected animals. The plasmid-containing *S. typhimurium* strain did not prove to be more virulent for mice by the aforementioned criteria. It is risky to conclude, on the basis of these data alone, that the R plasmid lacks a virulence-enhancing determinant. Perhaps the use of a more sensitive in vivo model or a different recipient strain would have resulted in a different conclusion. In any event, the supposition that these epidemic R plasmids per se increased the virulence of their host bacteria lacks convincing supportive evidence. Neither, in our view has it been ruled out. Now that some of the genetic determinants specifying increased virulence and serum resistance have been localized, their presence in epidemiologically important R plasmids can be sought.

Even in a situation where the presence of DNA regions specifying virulence-enhancing properties has been excluded, it is clear that in certain circumstances R plasmids can be considered to be virulence plasmids. The concept of virulence, that is, the extent or degree of pathogenicity, in terms of human disease is extremely difficult to quantify due to the many contributing and interacting factors. There is no question, however, that the sudden and unexpected emergence of multiply drug-resistant enteric pathogens in the Mexican and Central American epidemics seriously compromised appropriate medical treatment and resulted in dramatically high morbidity and mortality. In the early months of the Guatemalan epidemic the ratio of cases to fatalities was especially high because in many instances physicians misdiagnosed and treated the illness as amebiasis. This was due, in part, to clinicians' lack of familiarity with bacillary dysentery that proved unresponsive to chloramphenicol, tetracycline, and sulfonamide, the antibiotics commonly used for treatment of this particular disease. Once the organisms's susceptibility to ampicillin was established, mortality rates drastically declined. In fact, plasmid-mediated ampicillin resistance emerged in strains of *S. dysenteriae* type 1 in 1972. An isolated outbreak of dysentery occurred in a hospital ward in which 22 children with tuberculosis were being treated; 15 of 22 developed shigellosis with at least 4 deaths (6). The ampicillin plasmid, however, appeared to be rather unstable compared to the multiply resistant O compatibility group plasmid. Presumably due to this fact, serious outbreaks of dysentery caused by the dual plasmid-containing strain of Shiga bacillus were limited. This was a fortunate happenstance. Clinicians presented with serious cases of dysentery refractory to chloramphenicol, tetracycline, streptomycin, sulfonamide, and ampicillin would have faced a most troublesome dilemma.

Another recent example in which R plasmids have drastically altered chemotherapeutic strategy was the emergence of Ap, Cm, Tc, and kanamycin resistance plasmids in *Haemophilus influenzae* (22, 23, 30, 154). *H. influenzae* type b is responsible for a number of serious infections of children, notably meningitis and epiglottis. A 1978 study of bacterial meningitis in the United States reported that 18% of *H. influenzae* isolates, causing meningitis or bacteremia, were resistant to ampicillin, compared to a 5% incidence in a similar survey in 1976–1977 (14). The 18% rate of reported resistance may be somewhat inflated by preferential reporting; nonetheless, plasmid-mediated ampicillin resistance in *H. influenzae* has assumed great significance. In fact, for serious infections presumed to be due to this organism, chloramphenicol has become the antimicrobial agent of choice in initial therapy (126), an alternative with inherent and serious risks (158).

In addition, strains of *Neisseria gonorrhoeae* harboring β-lactamase-producing plasmids were detected in 1976. Since their recognition, ampicillin-resistant gonococcal strains have been isolated in more than 15 countries, and most cases have been epidemiologically linked with either the Far East or West Africa. Resistant isolates from each source harbor R plasmids that are highly related yet physically distinguishable (33, 105). Of interest is the fact that both gonococcal R plasmids share significant (70–90%) DNA sequence homology with an ampicillin-resistant R plasmid (RSF0885) isolated two years earlier from *H. influenza* (30, 32). Dire predictions regarding the spread of these plasmid-containing strains of *N. gonorrhoeae* have not materialized, presumably because these plasmids have been shown to be unstable in the absence of selective antibiotic pressure (105). Nonetheless, resistant strains account for about 30% of all recent isolates in the Philippines and 16% in the Republic of Singapore (13). One of the factors thought to contribute to the high prevalence of R^+ strains of *N. gonorrhoeae* in these two particular areas is the widespread prophylactic use of oral penicillins, especially by prostitutes. As in the case of the emergent ampicillin plasmid in the epidemic *S. dysenteriae* type 1 strains (6), the inherent instability of both gonococcal R plasmids was extremely fortuitous. For example, had these β-lactamase-producing plasmids been as stable as the small, indigenous gonococcal plasmid (31), ampicillin therapy for this ubiquitous disease would have had to be abandoned.

Finally, the discovery of R plasmids in *Bacteroides* that can be transferred to *E. coli* (52, 75, 113) has potentially serious implications. The enormously large population of obligate anaerobes in the colon constitutes an extensive pool of resistance plasmids capable of infecting more conventional pathogens such as Salmonella and Shigella. In addition, the emergence of transferable drug resistance in *Bacteroides fragilis* will undoubtedly complicate the successful treatment of infections caused by this important anaerobic pathogen.

VIRULENCE PLASMIDS IN *STAPHYLOCOCCUS AUREUS*

Plasmids and Enterotoxin B Synthesis

The role of extrachromosomal elements in the synthesis of enterotoxin B (SEB) among food-poisoning strains of *Staphylococcus aureus* has been an area of controversy and confusion. Over ten years ago, Dornbusch et al (26) reported that the SEB determinant in *S. aureus* strain DU4916 was frequently transduced in association with methicillin resistance (*mec*^{r}). These two determinants were themselves contransduced with either a penicillinase plasmid or a tetracycline plasmid with varying frequencies (25, 117). In addition, acriflavine-treated, methicillin-sensitive *S. aureus* mutants showed a concurrent loss of SEB and β-hemolysin synthesis as well as a greater sensitivity to mercuric ions (26). Hence their data suggested that *mec*^{r} and SEB synthesis were closely linked in a single plasmid. Subsequently, Sjostrom et al (124) carried out transformation studies with DNA extracted from the methicillin-resistant strain DU4916 and showed that the *mec*^{r} locus was confined to the chromosomal DNA with no apparent *mec*^{r} gene(s) of plasmid origin. Shafer & Iandolo (116) examined the SEB locus in two *Staphylococcus aureus* food-poisoning isolates, strains S6 and S277. Strain S6, for example, was found to contain a single 17.5-megadalton plasmid. Transductional analysis showed that this plasmid encoded cadmium resistance but *not* exterotoxin B. Furthermore, elimination of cadmium resistance resulted in a plasmid-negative derivative that synthesized SEB at the same level as the parent strain. The results for *S. aureus* S277 were generally the same. It seemed clear, therefore, that in these two food-poisoning strains of *S. aureus* the SEB gene(s) was located in the chromosome.

Later, Shalita et al (117) reexamined the question of SEB synthesis in strain DU4916 of *Staphylococcus aureus.* These investigators identified a small plasmid, pSN2 (0.75 megadalton), in addition to the known tetracycline resistance plasmid, pSN1 (2.8 megadalton), and a large penicillinase plasmid. Results of co-elimination and co-transformation experiments showed that the capacity to synthesize SEB was obligatorily associated with the small plasmid, pSN2. Hence, curing a strain of pSN2 always resulted in the loss of enterotoxin B production, whereas its introduction, by unselected co-transfer with pSN1, always resulted in the ability to synthesize the toxin. Furthermore, their findings seemed to suggest that pSN2 was a satellite plasmid—that is, its maintenance relied on the presence of the 2.8 megadalton tetracycline plasmid, pSN1.

S. Kahn and R. Novick (manuscript in preparation) may have resolved the dilemma of SEB biosynthesis in *S. aureus* strain DU4916. Their approach was to evaluate the structure and coding capacity of plasmid pSN2 with respect to whether or not it contained the structural gene for enterotoxin B. The proteins specified by plasmid pSN2 were analyzed in *Bacillus subtilis* minicells. Immunodiffusion tests revealed no detectable toxin and it appeared that pSN2 encoded a single 20-kilodalton polypeptide. SEB has a molecular weight of 29 kilodaltons. These experiments were repeated using *E. coli* and *S. aureus* cell-free extracts programmed with pSN2 DNA. Two polypeptides of 12 and 20 kilodaltons were produced, but there was no immunologically detectable SEB. It was concluded, on the basis of these independent negative results, that plasmid pSN2 does not carry the structural gene for enterotoxin B.

Kahn and Novick considered two alternative interpretations of these results: 1. pSN2 encodes a portion of the SEB protein and the chromosome encodes the rest, or 2. pSN2 is involved in the control of SEB synthesis. To test the first possibility, the majority of the polynucleotide sequence of pSN2 was determined. The resultant sequence indicated that the 12- and 20-kilodalton polypeptides were made from a single mRNA. Most importantly, partial N and C terminal amino acid sequences of the two pSN2 proteins, derived from the corresponding DNA sequence, bore no resemblance to the N and C terminal regions of the SEB protein (62), making it unlikely that plasmid pSN2 carried even a part of the enterotoxin B cistron. Hence the second alternative, namely that plasmid pSN2 serves a regulatory role in SEB synthesis, is currently favored. Perhaps SEB biosynthesis involves a control mechanism in which one or both of the pSN2-specified polypeptides is a positive regulator of toxin synthesis by a structural gene in the chromosome. However, the possibility that plasmid-encoded functions play a role in toxin processing or transport has not been ruled out.

Plasmids and Exfoliative Toxin Synthesis

The affliction of the skin of newborns, called toxic epidermal necrolysis, was first described in 1878 (104). Much later it was established that the disease was due to certain strains of *Staphylococcus aureus,* and the condition was renamed scalded-skin syndrome (79). Kapral & Miller (68) isolated and partially characterized a soluble product in culture supernatants of certain staphylococcal isolates that reproduced the clinical scalded-skin syndrome when injected into suckling mice. This extracellular product was called exfoliative toxin (ET).

Warren et al (159) showed that ET synthesis and bacteriocin (Bac) production were lost at high frequencies after growth of selected strains in the presence of ethidium bromide or sodium dodecyl sulfate (SDS). The tox^+ and bac^+ markers were co-eliminated at a frequency of 92%, which suggested that the genes for ET and Bac biosynthesis were on the same plasmid. Subsequent experiments provided physical evidence for the presence of a 3.3×10^7-mol wt plasmid carrying the structural genes for exfoliative toxin and bacteriocin in a strain designated UT0007 (159). The high molecular weight plasmid present in tox^+ UT0007 was shown to be absent from a tox^--cured derivative strain after exposure to ethidium bromide (160). In addition, it was demonstrated that certain "tox^-" substrains, derived by curing naturally occurring tox^+ strains, could indeed synthesize small amounts of toxin. Exfoliative toxin was detectable in these particular strains only when their culture filtrates were concentrated 20-fold prior to injection into suckling mice (71). Later, it was demonstrated that the reason why certain tox^+ strains could not be completely cured was that they harbored both chromosomal and extrachromosomal genes for ET synthesis. For example, treatment of the tox^+ *S. aureus* strain UT0002 at 44°C yielded plasmid-negative UT0002 derivatives that had totally lost the capacity to synthesize bacteriocin and yet retained partial capacity to synthesize ET.

Wiley & Rogolsky (163) characterized the ET synthetic capabilities of *S. aureus* UT0002, a wild-type strain presumably with both plasmid and chromosomal control mechanisms governing toxin synthesis. Electrophoresis of electrofocused UT0002 ET on SDS-polyacrylamide cylindrical gels yielded a single protein band. However, when the same ET was electrophoresed on SDS-polyacrylamide *slab* gels, two separate bands were reproducibly obtained (162). Electrophoretic analysis of toxin synthesized by strain UT0007, a strain shown to specify only plasmid-controlled ET (163), consistently resulted in only a single protein band. Since the molecular weights of the two toxins differed, the possibility that they were also antigenically distinct was examined. Antisera were produced in rabbits; electrofocused plasmid-controlled and chromosome-controlled ETs were used as antigens. Ouchterlony double-diffusion tests clearly indicated that these toxins were antigenically distinguishable. At about the same time and independently, Arbuthnott et al (3, 4) detected two ET components based on differences in isoelectric points and concluded, on the basis of radial immunodiffusion tests, that purified ET in some staphylococcal strains consisted of two serologically distinct components.

In summary, therefore, the following conclusions can be made regarding the regulation and properties of exfoliative toxin in particular (i.e. phage group II) strains of *S. aureus:* (*a*) isolates exist that express only chromosome-controlled ET synthesis (107), (*b*) strains have been characterized that express only plasmid-controlled ET synthesis (160), (*c*) strains exist in which both chromosome- and plasmid-controlled mechanisms exist (106), and (*d*) on the basis of the few enzymes that have been examined, it appears that the plasmid- and chromosome-controlled ETs differ in molecular weight and antigenic specificity. As to the eventual resolution of the intricacies of the exfoliative toxin story, to quote Wiley et al., "It is clear that the fragments of this puzzle are present in several labs. . . . Whether or not the whole will make the molecular biology of the staphylococcal scalded-skin syndrome understandable remains to be seen" (163).

Effect of R Plasmid Carriage on the Virulence of S. aureus

Two examples are presented to illustrate the point that the correlation between R plasmid carriage and virulence in *Staphylococcus aureus* is far from clear. Lacey & Chopra (73) investigated the growth kinetics and virulence for the chick embryo of plasmid-positive and -negative variants of *S. aureus.* Plasmid content was verified by dye-buoyant density centrifugation. Six of eight R^+ staphylococcal strains had significantly reduced in vitro growth rates, compared to the isogenic, R^- strain. In addition, R^+ strains were found to be significantly less virulent for 10-day-old chick embryos than the corresponding plasmid-free strain. Interestingly, subsequent loss of R plasmids was not associated with a return of virulence. The reason for this was unclear. In any event, their findings suggested that, in the absence of antibiotics, plasmid carriage proved to be disadvantageous to staphylococci. This is not totally surprising, since a common feature of R^+ bacteria is that in the absence of drug pressure they tend to be at an evolutionary disadvantage compared with their sensitive counterparts (89). For example, plasmid-containing strains of *E. coli* have been shown to disappear from the feces of human volunteers more rapidly than R^- organisms (2).

In contrast to these data, however, Cutler (17) concluded on the basis of his experiments that the virulence of *S. aureus* strains *decreased* with the loss of resistance determinants. Virulence was assayed by injecting staphylococci subcutaneously into guinea pigs and determining the number of organisms required to produce skin lesions. In these experiments a multiply resistant strain of *S. aureus* was "cured" of antibiotic resistance(s) by incubating cultures at 42°C. Isolates with altered antibiograms were then compared with the parental strain in terms of virulence. It should be noted, however that there was no attempt to physically characterize the plasmid content of the "cured" variants. Loss of antibiotic resistance(s) can occur by mechanisms other than plasmid loss. For example, (*a*) two plasmids can recombine with the resultant loss of one or more resistance determinants, (*b*) a plasmid can suffer a transpositional event (90) resulting in the inactivation of one or more resistance determinants with only a slight alteration in the plasmid gene pool, or (*c*) the resistance gene, now inactivated, may have resided in the chromosome in the first place. Hence, it is difficult to draw valid conclusions regarding the contribution of R plasmids to virulence, positive or negative, in the absence of physical data as to the precise content of extrachromosomal DNA.

The quest to identify, isolate, and characterize possible virulence-enhancing genetic determinants within *S. aureus* plasmids has only begun. Perhaps the lessons that are being learned, as well as future research on the ColV plasmids of the Enterobacteriaceae, can be productively applied to the plasmids residing in other Gram-positive microorganisms, as well.

A POTPOURRI OF VIRULENCE PLASMIDS

Table 1 contains a selection of pathogenic microorganisms in which plasmids are suspected to play a role in their virulence. In many of these studies virulence plasmids were "identified" by their consistent occurrence in virulent strains and their absence from avirulent variants. However, definitive proof of the presence of a virulence plasmid requires the demonstration that a certain virulence property can be transferred from strain to strain in conjunction with a particular plasmid (118). Therefore, the presence of virulence plasmids in some of the examples cited in Table 1 is somewhat speculative.

CONCLUDING REMARKS

It has become increasingly evident that plasmids often play an important role in the pathogenic potential of a variety of microorganisms. The various technical advances that have accrued from the study of the molecular biology of R plasmids can now be directed toward the investigation of plasmid-mediated virulence factors.

For example, the discovery that the ST gene resides within a transposable DNA sequence (145) poses obvious questions regarding the transposability of other virulence-enhancing determinants. In addition, cloned virulence genes can serve as convenient hybridization probes to determine whether a specific polynucleotide sequence encoding serum-resistance or toxin production, for example, is present in the plasmid or chromosomal DNA extracted from pathogenic strains isolated from man or domestic animals (118). The isolation, amplification, and manipulation of the genetic determinants for adherence antigens and enterotoxin biosynthesis will undoubtedly lead to the production of effective vaccines. Finally, as has been mentioned several times in this review, many as yet uncharacterized chromosomal determinants appear to influence the expression of plasmid-mediated virulence factors. Recombinant DNA techniques can be exploited to define the nature of the relationships between specific chromosomal genes and plasmid-borne virulence genes.

Table 1 A group of pathogenic microorganisms in which plasmids are suspected to play a role in their virulence

Microorganism	Associated disease	Evidence for plasmid involvement in pathogenicity	Reference/comment
Vibrio cholera	Cholera	In experimental models of cholera, strains of *V. cholera* harboring plasmids P (sex factor, promoting conjugation) and V (function unknown) were *less* pathogenic than isogenic strains devoid of these plasmids. Plasmid-mediated effect was thought to be due to decreased synthesis of enterotoxin.	Sinha & Srivastava (122, 123). Authors suggested that plasmid P and/or V gene product(s) interfered with enterotoxin biosynthesis or membrane transport. It was further suggested that plasmid-bearing strains might be considered for use as live oral vaccines since they are essentially attenuated strains.
Vibrio anguillarum	Vibriosis in marine fish. Disease is characterized by hemorrhaging at the base of the fins, internal inflammation, and a generalized septicemia.	A 50-megadalton plasmid class was consistently found in high-virulent strains of *V. anguillarum*. This plasmid class was absent from the low-virulent isolates. High-virulent strains "naturally" cured of the 50-megadalton plasmid were converted to low-virulent status. DNA duplex studies revealed that all 50-megadalton plasmids were related, regardless of geographical origin.	Crosa, Schiewe, & Falkow (16). Authors hypothesized that a plasmid-specified determinant might operate by the biosynthesis of either an enterotoxin or a specific surface antigen that enables attachment of the bacteria to a specific target tissue of the infected fish.
Enterobacter hafnia	Porcine dysentery	The pathogenicity of certain strains of *E. hafnia* was shown to be co-transferred with oxytetracycline resistance to both nonvirulent *E. hafnia* and *E. coli* recipients. The pathogenic capabilities of these strains, including the *E. coli* transconjugants, appeared to be the result of toxin biosynthesis.	Swiderski, Jedrzejowski & Lachowicz (146). The putative *E. hafnia* virulence (Ent ?) plasmid was not physically characterized in this study. The relationship that this virulence plasmid has to other Ent plasmids originating in the enterobacteriaceae is unknown.
Ureolytic *E. coli* (UEC)	Urinary tract infection. Certain strains of UEC are considered to be pathogens with a marked prediliction for the urogential site. The ability to use urea and produce alkaline	A ureolytic *E. coli* clinical isolate was shown to conjugally transfer the abilities to hydrolyze urea, ferment sucrose, and resist sulfadiazine inhibition *en bloc*. The resultant *E. coli* K12 transconjugant possessed a plasmid with a molecular mass of 80–90 megadaltons. Ten of 45 UEC isolates segregated non-UEC	Wachsmuth, Davis, & Allen (155). The authors observed that the urease gene(s) appeared to be closely associated with the sucrose or raffinose genes in at least two UEC strains. This is reminiscent of the fact that the genes determining the porcine colonization factor, K88, are

Table 1 *(Continued)*

Microorganism	Associated disease	Evidence for plasmid involvement in pathogenicity	Reference/comment
	conditions can result in renal damage, stone formation, and antibiotic inactivation.	colonies, and all were found to harbor at least one plasmid of common molecular mass (65 megadaltons).	closely linked with genes for raffinose utilization.
Yersinia enterocolitica	Human yersiniosis	The presence of a 41-megadalton plasmid was found to be absolutely correlated with tissue invasiveness (positive Sereny test) in strains of *Y. enterocolitica* involved in an outbreak of human enteric disease. Many strains produced ST but ST synthesis was not associated with any particular plasmid. A 35-megadalton plasmid was harbored by many strains but, unlike the 41-megadalton species, the smaller plasmid was not associated with any invasive property in *Y. enterocolitica.* Correlated with any invasive property in *Y. enterocolitica.*	Zink, Feeley, Wells, Vanderzant, Vickery, Roof & O'Donovan (166).
Clostridium perfringens Type C	Diarrheal disease in domestic animals	β-Toxin-negative (βTox^-) mutants of *C. perfringens* type C were isolated by growing βTox^+ strains in the presence of ethidium bromide. The plasmid profiles of six cured strains were compared to those of the βTox^+ parent. A 75-megadalton plasmid species present in the parent strain was absent in all of the βTox^- derivative strains.	Duncan, Rokos, Christenson, & Rood (28). Authors concluded that β-toxin biosynthesis in *C. perfringens* type C may be under plasmid control.
Streptococcus mutans	Dental caries	All naturally occurring mucoid strains of *Streptococcus mutans* tested were found to harbor a 3-megadalton plasmid species. Ethidium bromide-cured strains of cariogenic *S. mutans* lacked the capacity to synthesize insoluble extracellular polysaccharides.	Higuchi & Araya (60) and Katayama, Ishikawa, Ando & Arai (69). These studies relied solely on phenotypic curing as a means of identifying a plasmid-mediated characteristic.

By these and numerous other approaches the molecular geneticist can be expected to contribute to a new level of understanding of the processes of microbial pathogenicity.

ACKNOWLEDGMENT

We are very grateful to the following people for providing us with unpublished data or stimulating discussions and, in some cases, both: Kay Wachsmuth, Richard Novick, Stanley Falkow, Francis Macrina, Edmund Farrar, Werner Maas, and John Bennett. We also wish to thank Coyla McCullough of the Burroughs Wellcome Library for many helpful literature searches.

Literature Cited

1. Alderete, J. F., Robertson, D. C. 1978. *Infect. Immun.* 19:1021–30
2. Anderson, J. D. 1974. *J. Med. Microbiol.* 7:85–90
3. Arbuthnott, J. P., Billcliffe, B. 1976. *J. Gen. Microbiol.* 9:191–220
4. Arbuthnott, J. P., Billcliffe, B., Thompson, W. 1974. *FEBS Lett.* 46:92–95
5. Bak, A. L., Christiansen, G., Christiansen, C., Stenderup, A. 1972. *J. Gen. Microbiol.* 73:373–85
6. Balows, A. 1977. *J. Antimicrob. Chemother.* 3:Suppl. C, pp. 3–6
7. Binns, M. M., Davies, D. L., Hardy, K. G. 1979. *Nature* 279:778–81
8. Bramucci, M. G., Silva, M. L. M., Maas, W. K., Holmes, R. K. 1977 *Abstr. 17th Intersci. Conf. Antimicrob. Agents Chemother.,* p. 399
9. Bullen, J. 1974. In *Microbial Iron Metabolism,* ed. J. Neilands, pp. 517–51. New York: Academic
10. Burgess, M. N., Bywater, R. J., Cowley, C. M., Mullan, N. A., Newsome, P. M. 1978. *Infect. Immun.* 21:526–31
11. Burrows, M. R., Sellwood, R., Gibbons, R. A. 1976. *J. Gen. Microbiol.* 96:269–75
12. Butler, T., Shuster, C. W., Franco, A. 1979. *Antimicrob. Agents Chemother.* 15:478–80
12a. Cabello, F., Timmis, K. N. 1979. In *Plasmids of Medical, Environmental and Commerical Importance,* ed. K. N. Timmis, A. Puhler, pp. 55–69. Amsterdam: Elsevier-North Holland
13. Center for Disease Control. 1979. *Morb. Mortal. Wkly Rep.* 28:85–87
14. Center for Disease Control. 1979. *Morbid. Mortal. Wkly Rep.* 28:277–79
15. Clements, J. D., Finkelstein, R. A. 1978. *Infect. Immun.* 22:709–13
16. Crosa, J. H., Schiewe, M. H., Falkow, S. 1977. *Infect. Immun.* 18:509–13
17. Cutler, R. R. 1979. *J. Med. Microbiol.* 12:55–62
18. Dafni, Z., Sack, R. B., Craig, J. P. 1978. *Infect. Immun.* 22:852–60
19. Dallas, W. S., Falkow, S. 1979. *Nature* 277:406–7
20. Dallas, W. S., Gill, D. M., Falkow, S. 1979. *J. Bacteriol.* 139:850–58
21. Dallas, W. S., Mosely, S. L., Falkow, S. 1979. *Abstr. 79th Ann. Meet. Am. Soc. Microbiol.* 47:D42
22. Dang, Van A., Bieth, G., Bouanchaud, D. H. 1975. *C. R. Acad. Sci.* 280:1323
23. Dang, Van A., Goldstein, F., Acar, J. F., Bouanchaud, D. H. 1975. *Ann. Microbiol. Paris* 126:370–99
24. Datta, N., Olarte, J. 1974. *Antimicrob. Agents Chemother.* 5:310–17
25. Dornbusch, K., Hallander, H. O. 1973. *J. Gen. Microbiol.* 76:1–11
26. Dornbusch, K., Hallander, H. O., Lofquist, F. 1969. *J. Bacteriol.* 98:351–58
27. Dorner, F., Hughes, C., Nahler, G., Hogenauer, G. 1979. *Proc. Natl. Acad. Sci. USA* 76:4832–36
28. Duncan, C. L., Rokos, E. A., Christenson, C. M., Rood, J. I. 1978. In *Microbiology 1978,* ed. D. Schlessinger, pp. 246–48. Wash. DC: Am. Soc. Microbiol.
29. Echeverria, P., Murphy, J. 1978. *Pediatr. Res.* 12:491–96
30. Elwell, L. P., de Graaff, J., Seibert, D., Falkow, S. 1975. *Infect. Immun.* 12:404–10
31. Elwell, L. P., Falkow, S. 1977. In *The Gonococcus,* ed. R. Roberts, pp. 138–54. New York: Wiley
32. Elwell, L. P., Roberts, M., Falkow, S. 1978. See Ref. 28, pp. 255–56

33. Elwell, L. P., Roberts, M., Mayer, L. W., Falkow, S. 1977. *Antimicrob. Agents Chemother.* 11:528–33
34. Eskridge, N. 1978. *BioScience* 28:249–52
35. Evans, D. G., Evans, D. J. 1978. *Infect. Immun.* 21:638–47
36. Evans, D. G., Evans, D. J., Clegg, S., Pauley, J. 1979. *Infect. Immun.* 23:336–46
37. Evans, D. G., Evans, D. J., Tjoa, W. S., DuPont, H. L. 1978. *Infect. Immun.* 19:727–36
38. Evans, D. G., Satterwhite, T. K., Evans, D. J., DuPont, H. L. 1978. *Infect. Immun.* 19:883–88
39. Evans, D. G., Silver, R. P., Evans, D. J., Chase, D. G., Gorbach, S. L. 1975. *Infect. Immun.* 12:656–67
40. Evans, D. J., Chen, L., Curlin, G., Evans, D. G. 1972. *Nature* 236:137–38
41. Evans, D. J., Evans, D. G., DuPont, H. L. 1979. *Infect. Immun.* 23:336–46
42. Evans, D. J., Evans, D. G., DuPont, H. L., Ørskov, F., Ørskov, I. 1977. *Infect. Immun.* 17:105–11
43. Evans, D. J., Evans, D. G., Gorbach, S. L. 1974. *Infect. Immun.* 10:1010–17
44. Farrar, W. E., Eidson, M. 1971. *J. Infect. Dis.* 124:327–29
45. Field, M., Graf, L. H., Laird, W. J., Smith, P. L. 1978. *Proc. Natl. Acad. Sci. USA* 75:2800–4
46. Gangarosa, E. J., Bennett, J. V., Wyatt, C., Pierce, P. E., Olarte, J., Mendoza Hernandes, P., Vazquez, V., Bessudo, D. 1972. *J. Infect. Dis.* 126:215–18
47. Gibbons, R. A., Sellwood, R., Burrows, M. R., Hunter, P. A. 1978. *Theor. Appl. Genet.* 51:65–70
48. Gonzalez-Cortes, A., Sanchez-Leyva, R., Hinojosa, M., Bessudo, D., Fragoso, R., Becerril, P. 1973. *Lancet* 2:605–7
49. Gorbach, S. L., Kean, B. H., Evans, D. G., Evans, D. J., Bessudo, D. 1975. *N. Engl. J. Med.* 292:933–36
50. Guerrant, R. L., Brunton, L. L. 1977. *J. Infect. Dis.* 135:720–28
51. Guinee, P. A., Jansen, W. H. 1979. *Infect. Immun.* 23:700–5
52. Guiney, D. G., Davis, C. E. 1978. *Nature* 274:181–82
53. Gyles, C. L. 1974. *Infect. Immun.* 9:564–70
54. Gyles, C. L., Falkow, S., Rollins, L. 1978. *Am. J. Vet. Res.* 39:1438–41
55. Gyles, C. L., Palchaudhuri, S., Maas, W. K. 1977. *Science* 198:198–99
56. Gyles, C. L., So, M., Falkow, S. 1974. *J. Infect. Dis.* 130:40–49
57. Hancock, R. E. W., Hantke, K., Braun, V. 1976. *J. Bacteriol.* 127:1370–75
58. Hardy, K. G. 1975. *Bacteriol. Rev.* 39:464–515
59. Helinski, D. R. 1973. *Ann. Rev. Microbiol.* 27:437–70
60. Higuchi, M., Araya, S. 1976. *J. Dent. Res.* 55:266–71
61. Holmgren, J., Svennerholm, A. M. 1979. *Curr. Microbiol.* 2:55–58
62. Huang, I. Y., Bergdoll, M. S. 1970. *J. Biol. Chem.* 245:3518–25
63. Hughes, J. M., Murad, F., Chang, B., Guerrant, R. L. 1978. *Nature* 271:755–56
64. Isaacson, R. E. 1977. *Infect. Immun.* 15:272–79
65. Isaacson, R. E., Fusco, P. C., Brinton, C. C., Moon, H. W. 1978. *Infect. Immun.* 21:392–97
66. Jones, G. W., Rutter, J. M. 1974. *J. Gen. Microbiol.* 84:135–44
67. Kapitany, R. A., Forsythe, G. W., Scoot, A., McKenzie, S. F., Worthington, R. W. 1977. *Infect. Immun.* 24:965–66
68. Kapral, F. A., Miller, M. M. 1971. *Infect. Immun.* 4:541–45
69. Katayama, A., Ishikawa, E., Ando, T., Arai, T. 1978. *Arch. Oral Biol.* 23:1099–1103
70. Kearns, M. J., Gibbons, R. A. 1979. *FEMS Microbiol. Lett.* 6:165–68
71. Keyhani, M., Rogolsky, M., Wiley, B. B., Glasgow, L. A. 1975. *Infect. Immun.* 12:193–97
72. Kunkel, S. L., Robertson, D. C. 1979. *Infect. Immun.* 25:586–96
73. Lacey, R. W., Chopra, I. 1975. *J. Med. Microbiol.* 8:137–47
74. Lopez-Alvarez, J., Gyles, C. L., Shipley, P., Falkow, S. 1979. *Abstr. 79th Ann. Meet. Am. Soc. Microbiol.* 139:H17
75. Mancini, C., Behme, R. J. 1977. *J. Infect. Dis.* 136:597–600
76. McConnell, M. M., Willshaw, G. A., Smith, H. R., Scotland, S. M., Rowe, B. 1979. *J. Bacteriol.* 139:346–55
77. McNeish, A. S., Turner, P., Fleming, J., Evans, N. 1975. *Lancet* 2:946–48
78. McNeish, A. S., Williams, P. H., Evans, N., Turner, P., George, R. H. 1977. *Gut* 18:A943
79. Melish, M. E., Glasgow, L. A. 1970. *N. Engl. J. Med.* 282:1114–19
80. Minshew, B. H., Jorgensen, J., Counts, G. W., Falkow, S. 1978. *J. Infect. Dis.* 20:50–54
81. Minshew, B. H., Jorgensen, J., Swanstrum, M., Grootes-Reuvecamp, G. A., Falkow, S. 1978. *J. Infect. Dis.* 137:648–54

82. Moll, A., Cabello, F., Timmis, K. N. 1979. *FEMS Microbiol. Lett.* 6:273–76
83. Mooi, F. R., de Graaf, F. K. 1979. *FEMS Microbiol. Lett.* 5:17–20
84. Mooi, F. R., de Graaf, F. K., Van Embden, J. D. 1979. *Nucleic Acids Res.* 6:849–65
85. Moon, H. W., Nagy, B., Isaacson, R. E., Ørskov, I. 1977. *Infect. Immun.* 15:614–20
86. Moon, H. W., Whipp, S. C., Skartveat, S. M. 1976. *Am. J. Vet. Res.* 37:1025–29
87. Neilands, J. 1973. In *Inorganic Biochemistry,* ed. G. Eichorn, pp. 167–202 Amersterdam:Elsevier/North Holland
88. Novick, R. 1969. *Bacteriol. Rev.* 33:210–63
89. Novick, R. 1979. *The Sciences* 19:14–17
90. Novick, R. P., Edelman, I., Schwesinger, M. D., Gruss, A. D., Swanson, E. C., Pattee, P. A. 1979. *Proc. Natl. Acad. Sci. USA* 76:400–4
91. O'Brien, I. G. Cox, G. B. Gibson, F. 1970. *Biochim. Biophys. Acta.* 201: 453–60
92. Olarte, J., Galindo, E. 1973. *Antimicrob. Agents Chemother.* 4:597–601
93. Ørskov, I., Ørskov, F. 1966. *J. Bacteriol.* 91:69–75
94. Ørskov, I., Ørskov, F. 1977. *Med. Microbiol. Immunol.* 163:99–110
95. Ørskov, I., Ørskov, F., Smith, H. W., Sojka, W. J. 1975. *Acta Pathol. Microbiol. Scand.* 83:31–36
96. Ørskov, I., Ørskov, F., Sojka, W. J., Leach, L. M. 1961. *Acta Pathol. Microbiol. Scand.* 53:404–22
97. Ozanne, G., Mathieu, L. G., Baril, J. P. 1977. *Infect. Immun.* 17:497–503
98. Payne, S. M., Finkelstein, R. A. 1975. *Infect. Immun.* 12:1313–18
99. Payne, S. M., Finkelstein, R. A. 1978. *J. Clin. Invest.* 61:1428–39
100. Pollack, J. R., Neilands, J. B. 1970. *Biochem. Biophys. Res. Commun.* 38: 989–92
101. Powell, C. J., Finkelstein, R. A. 1966. *J. Bacteriol.* 91:1410–17
102. Puschmann, M., Ganzoni, A. M. 1977. *Infect. Immun.* 17:663–64
103. Quackenbush, R., Falkow, S. 1979. *Infect. Immun.* 24:562–64
104. Ritter von Rittershain, G. 1878. *Centralbl. Z. Kinderheilkd.* 2:3–23
105. Roberts, M., Elwell, L. P., Falkow, S. 1977. *J. Bacteriol.* 131:557–63
106. Rogolsky, M., Wiley, B. B., Glasgow, L. A. 1976. *Infect. Immun.* 13:44–52
107. Rosenblum, E. D., Tyrone, S. 1976. *Infect. Immun.* 14:1259–60
108. Rutter, J. M., Burrows, M. R., Sellwood, R., Gibbons, R. A. 1975. *Nature* 257:135–36
109. Sack, R. B. 1975. *Ann. Rev. Microbiol.* 29:333–53
110. Sack, R. B., Gorbach, S. L., Banwell, J. G., Jacobs, B., Chatterjee, B. D., Mitra, R. C. 1971. *J. Infect. Dis.* 123:378–85
111. Sack, R. B., Hirschorn, N., Brownlee, I., Cash, R. A., Woodward, W. E., Sack, D. A. 1975. *N. Engl. J. Med.* 292:1041–45
112. Santos, D. S., Palchaudhuri, S., Maas, W. K. 1975. *J. Bacteriol.* 124:1240–47
113. Saunders, J. R. 1978. *Nature* 274: 113–14
114. Schenkein, I., Green, R. F., Santos, D. S., Maas, W. K. 1976. *Infect. Immun.* 13:1710–20
115. Schmitt, R., Mattes, R., Schmid, K., Altenbuchner, J. 1979. See Ref. 12a, pp. 199–210
116. Shafer, W. M., Iandolo, J. J. 1978. *Infect. Immun.* 20:273–78
117. Shalita, Z., Hertman, I., Sarid, S. 1977. *J. Bacteriol.* 129:317–25
118. Shipley, P. L., Dallas, W. S., Dougan, G., Falkow, S. 1979. In *Microbiology 1979,* ed. D. Schlessinger, pp. 176–80. Wash. DC: Am. Soc. Microbiol.
119. Shipley, P. L., Gyles, C. L., Falkow, S. 1978. *Infect. Immun.* 20:559–66
120. Silva, M. L. M., Maas, W. K., Gyles, C. L. 1978. *Proc. Natl. Acad. Sci. USA* 75:1384–88
121. Silver, R. P., Aaronson, W., Garon, C. F. 1979. *Abstr. 79th Ann. Meet. Am. Soc. Microbiol.* 18:B19
122. Sinha, V. B., Srivastava, B. S. 1978. *J. Gen. Microbiol.* 104:251–55
123. Sinha, V. B., Srivastava, B. S. 1978. *Nature* 276:708–9
124. Sjostrom, J. E., Lofdahl, S., Philipson, L. 1975. *J. Bacteriol.* 123:905–15
125. Skerman, F. J., Formal, S. B., Falkow, S. 1972. *Infect. Immun.* 5:622–24
126. Smith, A. L. 1976. *N. Engl. J. Med.* 294:1329–30
127. Smith, H. R., Cravioto, A., Willshaw, G. A., McConnell, M. M., Scotland, S. M., Gross, R. J., Rowe, B. 1979. *FEMS Microbiol. Lett.* 6:255–60
128. Smith, H. W. 1974. *J. Gen. Microbiol.* 83:95–111
129. Smith, H. W. 1976. In *Acute Diarrhoeae in Childhood, Ciba Found. Symp. 42,* pp. 45–72. Amsterdam: Elsevier/North Holland
129a. Smith, H. W. 1978. *J. Am. Vet. Med. Assoc.* 173:601-7.
130. Smith, H. W., Halls, S. 1968. *J. Gen. Microbiol.* 52:319–34

131. Smith, H. W., Huggins, M. B. 1976. *J. Gen. Microbiol.* 92:335–50
132. Smith, H. W., Huggins, M. B. 1977. *J. Med. Microbiol.* 10:479–82
133. Smith, H. W., Huggins, M. B. 1977. *J. Med. Microbiol.* 11:471–92
134. Smith, H. W., Huggins, M. B. 1978. *J. Gen. Microbiol.* 109:375–79
135. Smith, H. W., Linggood, M. A. 1970. *J. Gen. Microbiol.* 62:287–99
136. Smith, H. W., Linggood, M. A. 1971. *J. Gen. Microbiol.* 4:467–85
137. Smith, H. W., Linggood, M. A. 1971. *J. Med. Microbiol.* 4:301–5
138. Smith, H. W., Linggood, M. A. 1972. *J. Med. Microbiol.* 5:243–50
139. Smith, H. W., Parsell, Z. 1975. *J. Gen. Microbiol.* 87:129–40
140. So, M., Boyer, H. W., Betlach, M., Falkow, S. 1976. *J. Bacteriol.* 128: 463–72
141. So, M., Crandell, J. F., Crosa, J. H., Falkow, S. 1974. In *Microbiology 1974*, ed. D. Schlessinger, pp. 16–26. Wash. DC: Am. Soc. Microbiol.
142. So, M., Crosa, J. H., Falkow, S. 1975. *J. Bacteriol.* 121:234–38
143. So, M., Dallas, W. S., Falkow, S. 1978. *Infect. Immun.* 21:405–11
144. So, M., Heffron, F., Falkow, S. 1978. *J. Bacteriol.* 133:1520–23
145. So, M., Heffron, F., McCarthy, B. J. 1979. *Nature* 277:453–56
146. Swiderski, M., Jedrzejowski, A., Lachowicz, T. M. 1978. *Acta Microbiol. Pol.* 27:11–18
147. Takeda, Y., Murphy, J. R. 1978. *J. Bacteriol.* 133:172–77
148. Takeda, Y., Taga, S., Miwatani, T. 1979. *FEMS Microbiol. Lett.* 5:181–86
149. Taylor, P. W., Hughes, C. 1978. *Infect. Immun.* 22:10–17
150. Thorne, G. M., Deneke, C. F., Gorbach, S. L. 1979. *Infect. Immun.* 23:690–99
151. Thorne, G. M., Farrar, W. E. 1973. *J. Infect. Dis.* 128:132–36
152. Thorne, G. M., Farrar, W. E. 1974. *J. Infect. Dis.* 130:284–87
153. Timmis, K. N., Moll, A., Danbara, H. 1979. See Ref. 12a, pp. 145–53
154. Van Klingeren, B., Van Embden, J. D., Dessens-Kroon, M. 1977. *Antimicrob. Agents Chemother.* 11:383–87
155. Wachsmuth, I. K., Davis, B. R., Allen, S. D. 1979. *J. Clin. Microbiol.* 10:897–902
156. Wachsmuth, I. K., Falkow, S., Ryder, R. W. 1976. *Infect. Immun.* 14:404–7
157. Wachsmuth, I. K., Wells, J., Shipley, P. L., Ryder, R. 1979. *Infect. Immun.* 24:793–97
158. Wallerstein, R. O., Condit, P. K., Kasper, C. K., Brown, J. W., Morrison, F. R. 1969. *J. Am. Med. Assoc.* 208:2045–50
159. Warren, R., Rogolsky, M., Wiley, B. B., Glasgow, L. A. 1974. *J. Bacteriol.* 118:980–85
160. Warren, R., Rogolsky, M., Wiley, B. B., Glasgow, L. A. 1975. *J. Bacteriol.* 112:99–105
161. Weinberg, E. D. 1978. *Microbiol. Rev.* 42:45–66
162. Wiley, B. B., Glasgow, L. A., Rogolsky, M. 1976. *Infect. Immun.* 13:513–20
163. Wiley, B. B., Rogolsky, M. 1977. *Infect. Immun.* 18:487–94
164. Williams, P. H., George, H. K. 1979. See Ref. 12a, pp. 161–72
165. Williams, P. H., Sedgwick, M. I., Evans, N., Turner, P. J., George, R. H., McNeish, A. S. 1978. *Infect. Immun.* 22:393–402
166. Zink, D. L., Feeley, J. C., Wells, J. G., Vanderzant, C., Vickery, J. C., Roof, W. D., O'Donovan, G. A. 1980. *Nature* 283:224–26

Ann. Rev. Microbiol. 1980. 34:497–536

SOME ASPECTS OF STRUCTURE AND FUNCTION IN N_2-FIXING CYANOBACTERIA

❖1784

W. D. P. Stewart

Department of Biological Sciences, University of Dundee, Dundee, Scotland, United Kingdom

CONTENTS

INTRODUCTION	497
THE CYANOBACTERIAL VEGETATIVE CELL	498
A CAPACITY TO FIX N_2	506
CYANOBACTERIAL NITROGENASE	511
INHIBITORY EFFECTS OF OXYGEN ON NITROGENASE AND PROTECTION AGAINST THESE EFFECTS	512
AMMONIA ASSIMILATION AND THE ROLE OF GLUTAMINE SYNTHETASE IN THE REGULATION OF NITROGENASE	514
GLUTAMINE SYNTHETASE–NITROGENASE INTERACTIONS	516
REDUCTANT AND ATP FOR NITROGENASE	518
HYDROGEN METABOLISM	523
PERSPECTIVE	525

INTRODUCTION

Cyanobacteria (blue-green algae), many species of which fix N_2, are O_2-evolving photosynthetic prokaryotes. They bear a resemblance to gliding bacteria in gross morphology (see 65, 133, 140), to some photosynthetic bacteria in being able to fix both CO_2 and N_2 using light energy (69, 281), and to eukaryotic algae and higher plants in having chlorophyll *a* and in being able to photolyze water. They occupy a central niche in the probable evolution of photosynthetic organisms (121, 248), and nitrogenase is more widely distributed in cyanobacteria and photosynthetic bacteria (325, 377)

0066-4227/80/1001-0497$01.00

than in any other group of organisms. Yet cyanobacterial nitrogenase seems little different from that of other N_2-fixing prokaryotes (366). What is different is the cellular backcloth of structure, function, and molecular organization against which nitrogenase functions. This chapter summarizes some recent information on such aspects as well as on N_2 fixation. There are recent relevant reviews on cyanobacteria (64, 97, 121, 351, 352), N_2 fixation (366), and N_2-fixing cyanobacteria (37, 126, 155, 362, 363, 378).

THE CYANOBACTERIAL VEGETATIVE CELL

N_2-fixing cyanobacteria range from unicellular types to branched multicellular filamentous forms, but the basic organization and functioning of the vegetative cells are rather similar in all. These features have been admirably reviewed by Stanier (351) and Stanier & Cohen-Bazire (352). Here I shall update and mention aspects relative to N_2-fixation

The cyanobacterial cell is bounded by a rigid, multilayered peptidoglycan-containing wall as in other Gram-negative bacteria. Its ultrastructure and composition have been investigated in detail in some species (138, 139, 339). It is sensitive to penicillin and lysozyme. The former finding is useful in selecting drug-resistant strains (e.g. 86, 333), the latter in the preparation of cell-free extracts and isolated heterocysts (277). From the wall are produced the fimbriae (pili) (nonflagellar proteinaceous appendages) characteristic of certain Gram-negative bacteria. Those of *Nostoc* differ (92) in at least one character from the major fimbrial groups of other heterotrophic Gram-negative bacteria (100). Fimbriae are not essential for cyanobacterial movement since some motile forms lack them (H. L. N. Dick and W. D. P. Stewart, unpublished observations). Fimbriae are also involved in prokaryotic/eukaryotic cell recognition phenomena (181); whether they play such a role in symbiotic associations involving N_2-fixing cyanobacteria (379) is not yet established (e.g. 226).

The material external to the wall is considered as a sheath (or slime layer) if it is relatively soluble in water or if it forms a diffuse outer boundary, and as an envelope if it forms a firm, usually narrow, discrete layer. The slime layer may relate to the production of extracellular material by cyanobacteria (e.g. 120, 121, 412, 413). Not specifically associated with the slime layer, however, are many of the more interesting, recently studied extracellular products, such as anatoxin *a,* which has a rather similar structure to cocaine and acts as a postsynaptic depolarizing neuromuscular blocking agent (59, 60), the amines of *Microcystis aeruginosa* (165), the norcarotenoids that act as growth inhibitors (184), the NH_4^+ liberated by N_2-fixing symbiotic cyanobacteria (108, 372, 374), the siderophores [i.e. secondary hydroxamates and catechols of microbial origin that act as

Fe^{3+}-chelating compounds (6, 109, 237, 331)], and the extracellular peptides that may be involved in differentiation (116). Interrelations of extracellular products and associated microorganisms have been considered (52, 81, 224, 225).

The plasmalemma bounds the protoplast and may be the location of the uptake hydrogenase involved in the oxyhydrogen reaction in *Anacystis nidulans* (272). A pH gradient between cytoplasm and medium allows the cyanobacterium to accumulate weak acids and bases, depending on environmental conditions [(114, 258); for a review of membrane lipids see (352)]. In the outer protoplasmic area are the thylakoids (flattened membranous sacs with which the photosynthetic components and reactions are associated). Chlorophyll *a,* the photosynthetic reaction centers, the electron transport chain, and the accessory carotenoid pigments are membrane bound; the water-soluble phycobiliproteins, which act as light-harvesting antennae and transfer absorbed light mainly to photosystem II as well as to the photosystem I reaction centers, occur in packets (phycobilisomes) stacked on the outer thylakoid membranes. The transfer of light energy is considered to be mainly in the sequence phycoerythrin → phycocyanin → allophycocyanin → allophycocyanin B → chlorophyll *a* (134); but a direct energy transfer between phycocyanin and chlorophyll (84) and between allophycocyanin and chlorophyll (210, 282) may occur. The elusive "phycochromes" reported to be present in cyanobacteria (24–26) appear in fact to be allophycocyanin (243, 244). Phycobiliproteins have been reviewed (47, 129, 130, 134, 135, 352). Recently the molecular structure of the phycobilisomes of several cyanobacteria has been elegantly elucidated (47, 135, 234). The phycobilisomes have a triangular core of allophycocyanin assembled from three stacks of disc-shaped subunits. Radiating from each of the two sides of the core are three rods, about 12 nm in diameter, which contain the phycocyanin and, when present, the phycoerythrin (47). The detailed structures differ in different strains (135). *Gloeobacter violaceous* has no thylakoids—the pigments are associated with the plasmalemma as in Chlorobacteriaceae (293).

The photosynthetic system of cyanobacterial vegetative cells has two photosystems linked in series. Water, which serves as electron donor for NADPH production, is split in a Mn^{2+}-dependent process, and photosystem II activity is inhibited by DCMU [3'-(3,4-dichlorophenyl)-1',1'-dimethyl urea] and BNT (2-bromo-4-nitrothymol) (104). Although various workers have found that DCMU acts, as in higher plants (14) after Q near plastoquinone (9, 231, 251), evidence for *Oscillatoria chalybea* (313) and *Anabaena cylindrica* (71) suggests that in these species it may act on the water-splitting side of the photosystem II reaction center. This is based on the fact that diphenylcarbazide, while reducing the photolysis of water by thylakoid preparations, can act as a substitute electron donor in the Hill reaction and yet the diphenylcarbazide-supported activity is unaffected by DCMU. This argument assumes that the site of electron donation by diphenylcarbazide is on the reducing side of the photosystem II reaction center. It is supported by fluorescent data and by findings with isolated thylakoids that the photosystem II–mediated reduction of silicomolybdate, which accepts electrons directly from the primary acceptor of photosystem II, Q, is completely inhibited by DCMU (75). DCMU-resistant mutants are known (9).

The electron transport components from the photosystem II reaction center to the photosystem I reaction center (P700) are unexceptional (see 193), with the proportion of reaction centers I and II varying with change in environmental conditions (187). Inhibition of electron transport by DBMIB (2,5-dibromothymoquinone) (which affects plastoquinone) can be alleviated by TMPD (*N*-tetramethyl-*p*-phenylenediamine) which allows an electron flow bypass round plastoquinone (37). On the oxidizing side of photosystem I, EPR spectra of whole filaments of *Nostoc muscorum* and *Anabaena cylindrica* provide evidence for the photosystem I iron-sulfur centers A and B (both 4Fe-4S centers), for the photochemical electron acceptor of photosystem I (X) (possibly an Fe protein or one requiring Fe components for synthesis), for soluble ferredoxin, for a membrane-bound FeS protein, and for soluble storage iron (54; see also 110, 111). There is evidence against a linear electron transfer from P700 → Center B → Center A in *Phormidium laminosus,* and it may be that the electrons equilibrate between the two centers in accordance with their redox potentials (55).

Cyanobacterial ferredoxins are of the higher plant type with a single 2Fe-2S active center and a molecular weight of about 11000 (see 7, 433). They serve in vitro in cyanobacteria to donate electrons to nitrogenase (31, 344), nitrate reductase (253, 274), nitrite reductase (30, 274, 284), glutamate synthase (204), etc and are involved in $NADP^+$ photoreduction (340); they can accept electrons from pyruvate (36, 205, 341) and from NADPH (5, 31, 344). Various cyanobacteria (53, 153, 154, 167, 177, 324), but apparently not all (409), contain at least two molecular species of ferredoxin, as do other N_2-fixing prokaryotes and higher plants (see 7). Such cyanobacterial ferredoxins have similar molecular weights but have different N-terminal amino acid sequences (177) and immunological properties (392), and they may play different roles. Thus in *Nostoc* MAC ferredoxin II is most active in $NADP^+$ photoreduction while ferredoxin I is more active in pyruvate decarboxylation; they have different midpoint redox potentials (-350mV for ferredoxin I; -455mV for ferredoxin II, at pH 8; the potential varies with pH) (177). The latter value is the lowest known for any ferredoxin (see also below). Possibly the low potential cytochrome c_{549} [midpoint potential -300mV in *Nostoc* (434); -260mV in *Anacystis* (170–172)] functions as an electron carrier in conjunction with one or more of the low potential ferredoxins.

Flavodoxin, a low potential electron transport protein with flavin rather than a FeS center, develops in iron-deficient cyanobacteria (32, 83, 175, 340, 341) and can replace ferredoxin, to differing degrees, in various reactions including electron donation to nitrogenase (32). On iron-starving *Nostoc* MAC, flavodoxin is synthesized at and below 1 μM Fe, with ferredoxin II then ferredoxin I disappearing; probably flavodoxin replaces ferredoxin II in vivo (175). Ferredoxin II > flavodoxin > ferredoxin I in supporting $NADP^+$ photoreduction; ferredoxin I is best and flavodoxin poorest in supporting the phosphoroclastic cleavage of pyruvate (176). Since flavodoxin can effectively replace ferredoxin in supporting nitrogenase activity and in $NADP^+$ photoreduction but not in the phosphoroclastic cleavage of pyruvate, it may be that ferredoxin II, which also functions best in $NADP^+$ photoreduction and which has a lower midpoint redox potential than ferredoxin I (see above), serves as electron donor to nitrogenase.

Ferredoxin-$NADP^+$ oxidoreductase, which may also show NADPH diaphorase activity, transhydrogenase activity, and cytochrome *f* reductase activity in eukaryotes [see (300) for references], has been studied in various species (101, 218, 300, 382). The enzyme(s) from the nonheterocystous *Spirulina platensis, Nostoc* MAC, and the heterocystous *A. cylindrica* show various catalytically active species (five reported for *Nostoc* MAC, four at least for *A. cylindrica,* and two for *S. platensis*—some may be breakdown products!). The two for *S. platensis* and the two major ones of *A. cylindrica* appear to be very similar. Multiple forms have also been reported in higher plants (88, 123, 143, 188). Like ferredoxin, the precise roles in vivo of the different forms are equivocal.

The enzyme responsible for the net photofixation of CO_2 in cyanobacteria, other autotrophic prokaryotes (3, 220, 221, 376), and higher plants (see 132) is ribulose 1,5-bisphosphate (RUBP) carboxylase (3-phospho-D-glycerate carboxylase) (dimerizing) (RUBPCase), which carboxylates RUBP to give two molecules of 3-phosphoglycerate or oxygenates RUBP to give one molecule of phosphoglycerate and one molecule of phosphoglycolate. It is not a very efficient catalyst, a feature compensated for by the fact that it may represent 20–30% of the total cellular protein in *A. cylindrica* (G. A. Codd, personal communication). It does not seem to be a useful evolutionary marker (385).

RUBP carboxylases (molecular weight in excess of 600,000) may be O type, i.e. with only large (L) subunits (about 55,000 mol wt) or T type, i.e. with both large and small (LS) subunits (molecular weight of small subunits about 15,000). The enzyme has been characterized to different extents from

Aphanocapsa (78), *Microcystis aeruginosa* (354), *Plectonema boryanum* (391), *Anabaena variabilis* (391) (all L_8S_8), and from *A. cylindrica* where the presence (390) and absence (387) of small subunits have both been reported. The discrepancy between the results may be due to degradation of the small subunit during purification (see 77); however, using a treatment similar to that which allows the detection of both large and small subunits in *Anabaena cylindrica,* only large subunits (L_4) can be detected in *Aphanothece halophytica* (70). An L_8 structure has been reported in *Anacystis nidulans, Nostoc* MAC, and *Agmenellum quadruplicatum* (386, 387). As more strains from different typological groups are examined, a diversity of molecular structural types may become apparent. Let us hope we do not find that the types which appear different from L_8S_8 are in fact due to a loss of a basic L_8S_8 structure during purification, a view for which there is little evidence at present. The role of the small subunits is uncertain, but they are unnecessary for catalysis or activation since enzymes without them function well (295, 422).

The cyanobacterial enzymes, like other carboxylases (e.g. 68), are heat activated (246). Mg^{2+} is required (possibly for activation rather than cata lysis); activity is inhibited by 6-phosphogluconate (78), and a different effect of hydroxylamine on activated carboxylase and oxygenase activities has been reported (246).

RUBP oxygenase activity is responsible in part for the light-dependent O_2 uptake which varies with O_2 and CO_2 concentrations in cyanobacteria, although the response is not as great as found in many eukaryotes (23, 208, 213). The role of superoxide dismutase (SOD) in O_2 uptake has also been emphasized (1, 2, 76, 106, 264).

Biochemically, phosphoglycolate produced via RUBP oxygenase activity gives rise to glycolate via phosphoglycolate phosphatase. Little glycolate is usually produced extracellularly by cyanobacteria which may metabolize it both by glycine-serine (see 76) and tartronic semialdehyde pathways (76). In *A. nidulans* and *A. cylindrica,* glycolate may donate electrons to photosystem I when photosystem II activity is low and glycolate dehydrogenase activity is present in thylakoid membrane preparations of various cyanobacteria (74, 76, 144, 306). There is no published evidence yet for the presence of a photorespiratory nitrogen cycle (190) in cyanobacteria.

SOD functions to reduce O_2^- radical toxicity, generating H_2O_2 in the process (124). Cyanobacteria such as *P. boryanum, A. variabilis,* and *A. nidulans* contain Mn-SOD in thylakoids and Fe-SOD in the cytosol. The Mn-SOD may help reduce O_2^- produced by the autoxidation of the photosystem I primary electron acceptor, although its overall importance is uncertain because Mn-SOD is low relative to the total thylakoid Mn content (247). The Fe-SOD of *A. nidulans* has a molecular weight of 37,500, contains one Fe^{3+} active center per molecule, and is composed of two identical subunits (85).

Phosphoenol pyruvate (PEP) carboxylase activity has been noted in various cyanobacteria (76, 82, 95, 96, 180). Döhler (96) obtained data which suggested that in *Anacystis,* in strong light, the Calvin cycle was the main carboxylating route, whereas at low and red light PEP carboxylase and phycocyanin increased as RUBPCase activity declined. He also found high activities of PEP carboxylase, and suggested affinities with a C_4-pathway of photosynthesis (95). A *Phormidium* species similarly examined showed only a C_3-pathway. Peschek (269) who worked on *A. nidulans* in Döhler's laboratory concludes that both under oxygenic and anoxygenic conditions the Calvin cycle is the main CO_2-fixing reaction sequence. The possible role of PEP carboxylase has not been considered in the case of *Chlorogloea fritschii* and *Aphanocapsa* 6714 where dark fixation at 1% of the light rate is due in part to RUBPCase activity (183). Enzymic studies (169) and the kinetics of ^{14}C incorporation into citrulline (269) suggest that carbamoyl phosphate synthetase is an important anaplerotic route of CO_2 fixation in some cyanobacteria.

Some, not all, cyanobacteria (370) can photosynthesize when photosystem II is inhibited or inactivated and when an alternative electron donor feeds into photosystem I. The alternative electron donor may be organic compounds, sulfide, or H_2; even within the one species, different compounds act to differing extents in supporting growth.

The ability of organic compounds to support anoxygenic photosynthesis or growth depends in the first instance on the capacity of the cyanobacteria to assimilate the exogenous fixed carbon source. Some cyanobacteria do not assimilate exogenous fixed carbon at all, others do so poorly, and none show as good growth in the dark as in the light on exogenous fixed carbon; however, in light with photosystem II inhibited, growth can be as good on exogenous fixed carbon as when both photosystems are operating. Indeed at low light intensities growth may be better, possibly because then the cyanobacterium can generate sufficient ATP by photophosphorylation but cannot generate sufficient fixed carbon by photosynthesis. The subject has been recently reviewed (342) and more recent studies by Bottomley & Van Baalen (43, 44) suggest important differences in uptake and metabolism when glucose and fructose are supplied exogenously to *Nostoc* MAC in the dark. The permeases and transport systems for uptake of fixed carbon compounds by cyanobacteria urgently require elucidation [see, however, (258)]. Possibly the general lack of interest has been due to the earlier erroneous belief that an interrupted tricarboxylic acid (TCA) cycle would prevent efficient catabolism of fixed carbon. In fact the oxidative pentose phosphate pathway copes easily and efficiently with fixed carbon dissimilation. My own view is that as the oxidative pentose phosphate pathway is the major route of carbon dissimilation and yet is inhibited in light (see below), then fixed carbon, even if assimilated, cannot be readily catabolized by this route in the light, whereas in the dark, when it can be catabolized, transport of organics into the cell is limited by availability of energy, etc. In the dark, stored polyglucose is catabolized (e.g. 67, 122, 206, 235, 419).

Of course the ability to grow in the presence of fixed carbon when photosystem II is inhibited does not mean that anoxygenic photosynthesis, i.e. CO_2 fixation using ATP from cyclic photophosphorylation and electrons from fixed carbon compounds, is occurring. However, evidence that certain organic compounds do feed directly into photosystem I to support CO_2 fixation has recently been forthcoming (22, 147, 236, 345, 346).

The most detailed evidence for anoxygenic photosynthesis comes from studies using sulfide as electron donor. Early workers such as Hinze (166) and Nakamura (238) reported on sulfur droplets within the cells of Na_2S -grown *Oscillatoria,* and growth of various cyanobacteria under reducing conditions has long been known (see 256, 257). More recent studies, particularly on *Oscillatoria limnetica* at the physiological and biochemical level, have put such early reports on a firm scientific footing. There is no doubt that when DCMU inhibits photosystem II or when photosystem II is largely inactive (e.g. in red light $>$ 673 nm), then certain cyanobacteria can use sulfide as electron donor in a photosystem I-dependent reaction after a short period of adaptation and elemental sulfur is generated extracellularly. Growth on Na_2S may be as good as when water serves as electron donor. The site of electron donation to the photosynthetic electron transport chain is unclear but may be via cytochromes (18, 66, 79, 80, 249, 250, 252, 257, 403).

H_2 may also act as electron donor, but CO_2 photofixation rates supported by H_2 are only 40% of those on Na_2S for *Oscillatoria* and about 6% for *Aphanothece;* in the case of *Aphanothece,* fixation ceases after 30 h (18). Anoxygenic NO_2^- photoreduction using H_2 has also been noted in *A. cylindrica* (37, 156), and H_2-supported nitrogenase activity is considered below. Ecologically, the findings mean that if photosystem II light is limiting in the field, certain cyanobacteria can use a variety of compounds to short-circuit photosystem II and feed electrons directly into photosystem I for the subsequent reduction of CO_2, NO_3^-, N_2, etc. Such versatility may contribute significantly to the success of the group in nature. Even forms incapable of anoxygenic photosynthesis, if able to tolerate H_2S, may benefit from the reduced O_2 toxicity, for example, by protecting their nitrogenase from O_2 inactivation.

Sulfate assimilation in cyanobacteria may be of the bacterial type that uses PAPS (3'-phosphoadenosine-5'-phosphosulfate) as sulfate donor or of the eukaryotic plant type which uses APS (adenosine-5'-phosphosulfate) as sulfate donor. *Spirulina, Synechococcus,* and *Synechocystis* use PAPS with little APS activity (314), *A. cylindrica* synthesizes PAPS (308) but may also use APS (402), and *P. boryanum* uses APS as sulfate donor (314). Schmidt (314) speculates that APS and PAPS specificity may be useful taxonomic markers. Too few cyanobacteria have been examined to be sure, but the data to date do not lend much support for the idea.

In vegetative cells of cyanobacteria, the generally propounded view has been that the major route of carbon dissimilation is the oxidative pentose phosphate pathway which is highly active in dark but inactive or less active in light, that glycolysis is important although the measured enzyme activities are usually low, and that the Krebs cycle is incomplete (although a glyoxylate bypass functions) and operates mainly in a biosynthetic, rather than energy-yielding, role (see 64, 342, 352). As usual the position is more complex (and interesting) than was once supposed. First, inhibition of the oxidative pentose phosphate pathway in light was earlier attributed to RUBP allosterically inhibiting glucose-6-phosphate dehydrogenase activity, but studies using the partially purified enzyme have not confirmed this (309). NADPH and ATP may inhibit activity (4, 15, 267, 268, 305). Also, interconvertible molecular forms of the enzyme are now known (309) and there is evidence that light inhibition of glucose-6-phosphate dehydrogenase is alleviated by cyanophage attack (13). Second, isocitrate dehydrogenase activity is undetectable in vegetative cells of N_2-grown *A. cylindrica,* although it functions in vegetative cells of NH_4^+ or NO_3^--grown *A. cylindrica* and *A. nidulans* and in heterocysts of N_2-grown *A. cylindrica* (37). Since studies on the importance of the glyoxylate bypass have been carried out using cultures grown on combined nitrogen, its importance, if any, in the vegetative cells of N_2-fixing cultures will have to be reassessed. In any case, ATP pools may be as high when oxidative phosphorylation is supplying ATP as when photophosphorylation is functional in heterocystous cyanobacteria; but under conditions when fixed carbon is available and ATP pools are normal, prolonged optimum nitrogenase activity does not occur. When fermentation alone supplies ATP, nitrogenase activity is negligible (41, 42). In *O. limnetica,* polyglucose degraded in dark in the absence of O_2 can be metabolized to support growth by lactic acid fermentation or can be respired using elemental S as terminal electron acceptor. This elemental sulfur may be generated during anoxygenic photosynthesis (252, 323).

The centroplasm of the cyanobacterial vegetative cell is the major nucleic acid–containing region. Rapid progress, fortunately, is now being made in research on nucleic acid metabolism after being "in limbo" for part of the last decade; developments in this area are considered by Stanier & Cohen-Bazire (352) and in a splendid review by Doolittle (97; see also 12, 262).

Cyanobacterial plasmids have also been reviewed (200). More recently, detailed studies on genome sizes (these vary widely: 1.6–7.6 $\times 10^9$ daltons with a general increase in size on moving from unicellular to heterocystous forms) and on DNA base compositions of the major typological groups of cyanobacteria have appeared (163, 164). The use of DNA-DNA hybridization techniques as a phylogenetic index has been considered (350), and in particular the major DNA component of *A. variabilis* has been isolated in what may be a single circular chromosome that is negatively superspiralized with probably one turn per 165 base pairs (94). RNA polymerase from the N_2-fixing *Fremyella diplosiphon* has been characterized and evidence obtained that it can recognize the same lambda promoters as *Escherichia coli* ribonucleic acid polymerases (229, 230). This offers hope that on transfer of cyanobacterial genes to *E. coli* it will be possible to have these genes expressed. Studies on the oligonucleotide sequence of 16S ribosomal RNAs of various cyanobacteria suggest that the N_2-fixing *Nostoc* and *Fischerella* types probably arose from within the *Synechocystis* group (28, 29). It would have been nice if some present-day *Synechocystis* strains fixed N_2, but apparently they do not (see Table 1).

The thorny question of transcriptional control of enzyme synthesis (or possible lack of it) in cyanobacteria (e.g. 63, 174) is becoming clearer. In fact it now seems that any ideas of a general lack of transcriptional control in cyanobacteria have to be discarded; evidence in favor of it being involved in enzymic regulation in unicells (including obligate autotrophs) and filamentous forms is being accumulated for nitrogen metabolism (199), hydroxamate siderophore production (6), phycocyanin degradation and synthesis (199; see also 255), ribonucleotide reductase activity (136), phosphorus metabolism [(178); but see (404)], phycoerythrin synthesis (131), and possibly carbon metabolism (186).

Subcellular inclusion bodies (352, 361, 371) and gas vacuoles (414) are considered elsewhere.

A CAPACITY TO FIX N_2

Well over 125 strains or types of cyanobacteria are known to have nitrogenase, and N_2-fixing strains occur in all major typological groups. This number compares with one possible eukaryote (432), just over 50 photosynthetic bacteria (325), and 9 chemoautotrophic bacteria (87). Some *Rhizobium* (112) and *Derxia* (266) strains, although mainly heterotrophs, can also grow autotrophically using RUBPCase as carboxylating enzyme. The frequent possession of RUBPCase by N_2-fixing organisms seems more than evolutionary coincidence, yet interrelationships of CO_2 fixation via RUBP carboxylase and N_2 fixation via nitrogenase have scarcely been investigated.

Table 1 gives the current position regarding N_2-fixing cyanobacteria, based on an amalgamation of the taxonomic treatment of Rippka et al (289) and the literature on N_2 fixation. All heterocystous genera have an active enzyme under aerobic and anaerobic conditions. *Gloeothece* is unique among nonheterocystous cyanobacteria so far tested in axenic culture in showing aerobic nitrogenase activity; all other axenic strains show activity only under microaerobic or anaerobic conditions. Most of the nonheterocystous forms have been tested for nitrogenase activity using only the acetylene reduction technique (365), and few rates of activity have been published (289, 292). Very few strains have been shown to fix N_2, as distinct from reducing acetylene, although there is no organism yet known which has an acetylenase and not a nitrogenase. Only *Plectonema boryanum* 594 (369) among the anaerobic N_2 fixers has been shown to grow logarithmically on N_2 (299).

Among Section I cyanobacteria about 20% of the total strains tested have nitrogenase, with 50% fixing aerobically. In Table 1 the organism referred to as *Aphanothece stagnina* (336) has been included under *Synechococcus* (see 291), as has the N_2-fixing *Aphanothece castagnei* (337) although its classification as a *Synechococcus* is not yet proven. N_2 fixation by *Gloeothece* (including all N_2-fixing strains previously referred to as *Gloeocapsa*), an obligate photoautotroph, has been studied extensively by Gallon (see 126). There are two points of interest here. One is that a contaminated culture reduces C_2H_2 better than an axenic culture, even although the contaminant (probably a pseudomonad) does not fix N_2. The contaminated strain also grows better and is more O_2 tolerant than the axenic strain (see also 400). Do the bacteria remove toxins (see 52), do they help reduce O_2 levels round the cyanobacterium (see 259, 260)? How relevant are laboratory measurements on axenic cultures to what goes on in the field where every cyanobacterium is presumably contaminated? Second, the culture called *Gloeocapsa alpicola* IAM M123, although originally able to reduce C_2H_2, cannot now do so (126). Has it lost *nif*-containing plasmid(s)? Nitrogenase-containing *Synechococcus* strains occur in both subgroups of this genus (289).

Of Section II cyanobacteria tested, about 60% have nitrogenase, but under anaerobic conditions only. Such organisms are mainly marine, some N_2-fixing strains require B_{12}, and their physiology and biochemistry is the least studied of all cyanobacteria [see (417) for details of the group].

Nitrogenase activity by nonheterocystous filamentous forms was reported in the early literature (see 359); however, not until it was shown that axenic *P. boryanum* (369) reduced C_2H_2 and fixed $^{15}N_2$ anaerobically, but not in air, was their importance and similarity to the photosynthetic bacteria in this respect appreciated. Now over half of the numerous strains tested are able to do so under microaerobic or anaerobic conditions (292, 355). This may be very important ecologically because the anoxic or reduc-

Table 1 N_2-fixing cyanobacteria

Section	Genus	Strains tested	Number with nitrogenase	N_2-fixing strains[a]
I				
Unicellular forms reproducing by binary fission or budding	*Gloeobacter*	1	0	—
	Gloeothece[b]	5	5	27151 (6501); 27152 (6909); 29163 (7109); 29116 (73107); 29164 (73108)
	Gloeocapsa	4	0	—
	Synechocystis	16	0	—
	Chamaesiphon	0	0	—
	Synechococcus[c]	26	5	29155 (7424); 29403 (7335); 29141 (7425)
II				
Unicellular forms reproducing by multiple fission	*Dermocarpa*	6	2	29367 (7301); 29369 (7303)
	Xenococcus	3	1	29373 (7305)
	Dermocarpella	1	0	—
	Myxosarcina	2	1	29377 (7312)
	Chroococcidiopsis	8	8	27176 (6712); 27900 (7203); 29379 (7431); 29380 (7432); 29381 (7433); 29383 (7436); 29384 (7439); 29382 (7434)
	Pleurocapsa group	12	7	29386 (7314); 29389 (7320); 29390 (7321); 29391 (7322); 29392 (7324); 29393 (7327); 29396 (7516)
III				
Filamentous nonheterocystous forms dividing in one plane	*Spirulina*	2	0	—
	Oscillatoria	9	5	27906 (6407); 29205 (6412); 29081 (6506); 27935 (6602); 29209 (7515)

	Pseudanabaena	8	3	27183 (6802); 29210 (7403); 29118 (6406)
	LPP group[d]	24	16	29346 (7419); 29206 (7113); 29125 (7406); 29409 (7375); 29129 (7427); 29344 (7408); 29541 (7409); 27894 (6306); 27902 (6402); 29407 (73110); 29136 (7410); 29170 (7505); 27913 (7004); 29119 (6409); 29117 (7104); 29123 (7124)
IV				
Filamentous heterocystous forms dividing only in one plane[f]	*Anabaena*	+		
	Nodularia	+		
	Cylindrospermum	+		
	Nostoc[e]	+		
	Scytonema	+		
	Calothrix[g]	+		
V				
Filamentous heterocystous forms dividing in more than one plane	*Chlorogloeopsis*[h]	+		
	Fischerella[i]	+		

[a] The first number refers to ATCC numbers, but as there is sometimes difficulty in obtaining cultures from ATCC, the corresponding Paris Culture Collection numbers are bracketed.

[b] This includes what were formerly known as N_2-fixing *Gloeocapsa* strains.

[c] This includes the two strains shown by Singh (336, 337) to fix N_2 and classified as *Aphanothece* by him [see (291) and text]. Culture collection numbers, if available, have not yet been published.

[d] For simplicity, only those ATCC cultures tested have been included here, but others (see 360) have also shown nitrogenase activity in strains, some of which may not correspond to organisms listed here.

[e] *Nostoc* includes Watanabe's culture of *Anabaenopsis circularis* (CCAP 1402/1) (see 415, 416) as ATCC 27895 (PCC 6720).

[f] All heterocystous genera have aerobic nitrogenase as a characteristic feature.

[g] *Calothrix* includes Watanabe's strain of *Tolypothrix tenuis* (see 415, 416) and *Nodularia sphaerocarpa* (UTEX 583). It also includes genera previously referred to as *Rivularia, Gloeotrichia, Dichothrix,* and *Polythrix.*

[h] This includes as reference strain the cyanobacterium previously referred to as *Chlorogloea fritschii* (CCAP strain 1411/1).

[i] This includes cyanobacteria previously referred to as *Mastigocladus laminosus* and includes Fogg's strain of *M. laminosus* (CCAP strain 1447/1). Cyanobacteria previously referred to as *Hapalosiphon* (388, 389), *Westiella,* and *Westiellopsis* (e.g. 263) would presumably also be placed in the genus *Fischerella.*

ing environments where cyanobacteria often grow (see 257) may allow them to fix N_2 there, but not in air. Indeed a capacity to fix N_2 anoxygenically may be more advantageous in some habitats than a capacity to use H_2S instead of H_2O in photosynthesis. Whether or not there are nonheterocystous filamentous forms that fix N_2 in air is uncertain. *Gloeothece* does so, many nonheterocystous filamentous strains have *nif* genes, the photosynthetic bacterium *Rhodopseudomonas capsulata* reduces C_2H_2 in the presence of O_2 (228) (although once thought to fix N_2 only anaerobically), and there are early unconfirmed reports of N_2 fixation by nonheterocystous filamentous cyanobacteria under what were presumably aerobic conditions (e.g. 405). Pearson and co-workers (265) have recently demonstrated C_2H_2 reduction in aerobic cultures of the bundle-forming *Microcoleus chthonoplastes* contaminated by non-N_2-fixing bacteria. Such data must remain equivocal until nitrogenase activity in axenic cultures has been established. [Early studies failed to demonstrate nitrogenase activity in *Microcoleus vaginatus* (312), and strains in the American Type Culture Collection previously referred to as *Microcoleus* (ATCC 27930, 29126, and 29128) show no nitrogenase activity even under anaerobic conditions (289).] The early findings of nitrogenase activity by natural populations of *Trichodesmium* (99, 137) have been confirmed and expanded upon (49, 61, 62), but absolute proof that the cyanobacterium has nitrogenase again awaits the isolation of axenic cultures.

Among the heterocystous forms, if heterocysts are present the culture usually fixes N_2; when heterocysts are absent there is no aerobic nitrogenase activity. There are few exceptions, usually nitrogenaseless heterocystous mutants that have been obtained in the laboratory (but there is no aerobic N_2-fixing heterocystousless mutant). Vegetative cells of at least some heterocystous cyanobacteria have nitrogenase under anaerobic conditions (see 155, 356). Akinetes (see 327, 328, 383) do not fix N_2 aerobically (115). The availability of heterocystous N_2-fixing strains that grow with generation times of only a few hours should facilitate biochemical and enzymological studies (141). Overall, it is difficult to relate the possession of an active nitrogenase to any peculiar feature of N_2-fixing forms (apart from the presumed presence of *nif* genes!). There is only a general direct correlation with increase in morphological complexity and increase in genome size; O_2 protection does not seem overimportant, and neither do useful taxonomic markers, e.g. a heterotrophic capacity, B_{12} requirement, presence or absence of phycoerythrin, phycoerythrocyanin, etc. Either nitrogenase was characteristic of archetypal forms and has subsequently been lost in some [although data on oligonucleotide sequences of 16S ribosomal RNAs (29) provide no support for this assumption] or *nif* gene exchange (presumably mainly plasmid mediated) among existing forms probably occurs fairly readily (as was suggested some time ago for N_2-fixing prokaryotes in general (326)). Spontaneous loss of nitrogenase, with or without changes in heterocysts is well documented (e.g. 126, 157).

CYANOBACTERIAL NITROGENASE

Cyanobacterial nitrogenase like other nitrogenases (50, 366) catalyzes the reduction of various substrates including N_2, protons (37, 160), cyanide (160), and C_2H_2 (37, 126, 365). Methyl isocyanide, azide, nitrous oxide, and cyclopropene reductions await demonstration. All cyanobacterial nitrogenases so far studied—from *Anabaena cylindrica* (151, 401), *Anabaena* 7120 (286, 287), and *P. boryanum* (151)—require ATP, reductant, and Mg^{2+} (31, 159, 343) and have two O_2-sensitive components that fix N_2 only in combination (151, 286, 344, 401). The Fe protein (dinitrogen reductase) functions to bind MgATP and transfers electrons, probably one at a time (212) from the electron donor to the MoFe protein (dinitrogenase) which binds and reduces the substrate (51). Early work on cyanobacterial nitrogenase has been reviewed (357, 358). Recently, partial purifications of cyanobacterial enzymes have been achieved (151, 286, 401). The MoFe component of *A. cylindrica* is an acidic tetramer (216,000 mol wt) with nonidentical subunits 52,600 and 55,000 mol wt), its isoelectric point is between pH 4.72–4.99, and the Mo : Fe : S per mole ratio is 2.2 : 20.4 : 20.1. In amino acid composition relatedness (227) it resembles MoFe components from other N_2 fixers, particularly *Rhodospirillum rubrum* [215,000 mol wt, with 4 subunits of 56,000 mol wt and Mo : Fe : acid labile sulfide ratios of 2 : 25–30 : 19–22 (242)]. It is least like *Rhizobium japonicum* and *Klebsiella pneumoniae* MoFe proteins (151). There are no reports yet of an essential membrane-bound factor for activity (215, 216, 240, 241), for a FeMo-containing cofactor (see 102, 103) (although in *Nostoc muscorum* nitrogenase and nitrate reductase may share a common component; 334), or of two forms of nitrogenase (58) as in *R. rubrum*. The Fe protein is a highly labile dimer (60,000 mol wt; two identical subunits). The MoFe and Fe proteins of *A. cylindrica* and *P. boryanum* cross-react with 65–90% of the efficiency of homologous crosses (151); the MoFe protein of *A. cylindrica* cross-reacts with *Azotobacter* and *Clostridium* Fe proteins with 75% (151) and 50% (401) efficiency respectively. *Anabaena* and *Plectonema* Fe proteins show little cross-reactivity with the MoFe proteins from *Azotobacter vinelandii, R. rubrum* (151), and *Clostridium pasteurianum* (401). *P. boryanum* Fe protein cross-reacts with the *Anabaena* MoFe protein with 5% efficiency (151). It has been suggested (233) that nitrogenase may act as a dephosphorylase generating ATP when supplied with ADP, PO_4^{3-}, NH_4^+, and an oxidizing agent. No information is available for cyanobacterial nitrogenase.

INHIBITORY EFFECTS OF OXYGEN ON NITROGENASE AND PROTECTION AGAINST THESE EFFECTS

Cyanobacterial nitrogenases are all sensitive to O_2; in addition, high O_2 possibly inhibits nitrogenase activity indirectly (208). The effect of oxygen on nitrogenase in cyanobacteria seems to be threefold: it causes a rapid inhibition of nitrogenase activity which can be reversed in the short term (142), it can irreversibly inhibit existing nitrogenase (27, 290, 369, 370), and it irreversibly inhibits the synthesis of nitrogenase polypeptides (118). Short-term protection against O_2 has been attributed to conformational protection, and recent evidence for heterotrophs, particularly *Azotobacter,* implicates a soluble 2Fe-2S protein that may complex with nitrogenase and so protect the latter from O_2 inactivation (see 146, 296, 297, 310). To date such a protein has not been isolated from cyanobacteria. The above mechanisms of O_2 inhibition can explain why upon anaerobic incubation of forms such as *P. boryanum* after prolonged exposure to air, nitrogenase activity does not return immediately even although ATP and reductant pools remain high; these mechanisms also can account for sustained nitrogenase synthesis and activity of heterocysts in air. Other factors involved in O_2 protection in cyanobacteria include physical barriers, O_2 scavenging mechanisms, temporal barriers, and conformational protection (see also 298).

In *Gloeothece* O_2 protection of nitrogenase (see 126, 400) may be effected by a temporal separation of photosynthesis and N_2 fixation in batch culture (this is difficult to reconcile with the view that the photolysis of water supplies reductant directly to nitrogenase; 126), by SOD activity coupled with glutathione peroxidase or ascorbate to remove hydrogen peroxide, by continuous nitrogenase synthesis, and by a thick capsular sheath which acts as O_2 barrier. It would be interesting to examine the O_2 sensitivity of nonencapsulated *Gloeothece* protoplasts (the unicellular *Synechococcus,* which has no sheath, fixes only anaerobically). In *Gloeothece* Ca^{2+} deprivation causes a rapid O_2 inhibition of nitrogenase activity in light but not in dark; this has been attributed to an effect on membranes which afford O_2 protection (126, 152). Ca^{2+} limitation also rapidly inhibits O_2 evolution by membrane preparations of *Anacystis nidulans* (46).

Nonheterocystous cyanobacteria, apart from *Gloeothece,* have little protection against O_2 inhibition of nitrogenase. A temporal separation of nitrogenase activity and the photoevolution of O_2 has again been suggested (418). The bundled habits of colonial forms may be important in providing anaerobic environments in the middle of the colony; specialized paler cells, which do not fix CO_2, in the center of the filaments have been suggested as loci of nitrogenase activity in *Trichodesmium* (61), and there is some ^{13}N tracer evidence for compartmentalization in *Plectonema* (222). On Na_2S and exogenous fixed carbon, *P. boryanum* 594 can grow logarithmically and fix N_2 in light at high rates (50 nmol C_2H_4 mg protein^{-1} min^{-1}) throughout its growth cycle (299). There is also the possibility of aerobic nitrogenase in *Microcoleus* (265). Urgently needed are axenic cultures of forms like *Microcoleus* and *Trichodesmium* so that a systematic dissection of how they are organized to fix N_2 aerobically (if indeed they do) can be made.

Heterocystous cyanobacteria fix N_2 in air because heterocysts provide an O_2-protected environment for nitrogenase; early studies showing this (see 117, 358, 368), were followed by studies on how heterocysts were organized to do so (90, 367, 395, 423). More recent work has confirmed the earlier view by demonstrating higher rates of nitrogenase activity by isolated heterocysts (37, 276), showing $^{13}N_2$ incorporation into heterocysts (223, 398, 427), and quantifying the proportion of nitrogenase protein in heterocysts relative to vegetative cells by using electrophoretic studies and ^{55}Fe (279) and by examining N transport from heterocysts (398).

Central to the success of heterocysts as N_2-fixing loci in aerobic cultures are the O_2-protective mechanisms. These include the thick multilayered envelope acting as an O_2 barrier. Evidence for this comes from mutant studies: mutants deficient in certain envelope glycolipids are more O_2 sensitive (157; see also 142, 290). Indirect evidence also suggests that heterocysts provide a gaseous diffusion barrier. Thus the pC_2H_2 for nitrogenase of *A. cylindrica* is about 10-fold lower in vitro than in vivo, whereas that of the anaerobic N_2-fixer *P. boryanum* is little different in vitro and in vivo (151). Other features that may contribute are the general reducing environment (98), the uptake hydrogenase, which via an oxyhydrogen reaction provides respiratory protection (see 37), the high activities of the oxidative pentose phosphate pathway in heterocysts compared with the vegetative cells (5, 37, 367, 423), a lack of photosynthetic O_2 evolution (395, 397), enhanced SOD activities compared with the vegetative cells (162), and H_2 production in heterocysts which may protect against O_2 inactivation (for example the nitrogenase of isolated heterocysts prepared under H_2 is insensitive to a pO_2 of 0.05 atm in light; 279). It would be of interest to determine how the O_2 sensitivity of nitrogenase in heterocysts of different cyanobacteria correlates with their rates of net H_2 evolution. Heterocysts have negligible RUBP oxygenase activity and indeed synthesis of the enzyme appears to be repressed in heterocysts (72). Gotto et al (142) have recently found an, as yet inexplicable, direct correlation between O_2 sensitivity of nitrogenase in mutants and resistance of the mutants to L-methionine-DL-sulfoximine (MSX) and 7-azatryptophan.

AMMONIA ASSIMILATION AND THE ROLE OF GLUTAMINE SYNTHETASE IN THE REGULATION OF NITROGENASE

Various NH_4^+-assimilating enzymes—glutamic acid dehydrogenase, alanine dehydrogenase, glutamine synthetase, glutamate synthase and carbamoyl phosphate synthetase—occur in cyanobacteria.

Glutamic acid dehydrogenase (16, 91, 158, 239) activity is generally low in N_2-fixing cyanobacteria (< 2 nmol product formed mg protein^{-1} min^{-1}), is sometimes undetectable (e.g. in *Anabaena* 7120 and *Calothrix* 7101), and may be higher on combined nitrogen (239). In *A. cylindrica* the enzyme has a K_m for NH_4^+ of about 12.5 mM (158). It is not of major importance in primary NH_4^+ assimilation in most cyanobacteria, and especially not in those growing on N_2. In *A. nidulans* it has been reported as undetectable enzymatically (168) and also has been reported as a possible major route of glutamate production based on ^{13}N tracer kinetics (222). Clarification is needed.

Alanine dehydrogenase has been purified and characterized from *A. cylindrica* (304). It is NAD^+ specific, can function both in aminating and deaminating directions, but probably is of more importance in alanine catabolism. It may be the major route of alanine formation in *Cylindrospermum licheniforme* because alanine ^{13}N-labeling does not decrease on adding MSX or aminooxyacetate to inhibit transaminase-mediated reactions. In *Anabaena variabilis* alanine formation is probably transaminase-mediated (222).

Carbamoyl phosphate synthetase has been reported in various cyanobacteria (158, 169, 202; see also 223, 427). It may be important in dark CO_2 fixation (269), it is essential for significant citrulline and arginine production, and nitrogen incorporation via the urea cycle may be more important in NH_4^+-grown than in N_2-grown cultures. It seems not to be a major route of primary NH_4^+ assimilation in any N_2-fixing cyanobacterium, although carbamoyl phosphate may regulate nitrogenase (see 202).

Glutamine synthetase (GS) coupled with ferredoxin-linked glutamate synthase (GOGAT) in most but not all cyanobacteria [see reference (222), *A. nidulans*] is the major route of primary NH_4^+ assimilation (90, 203, 222, 301, 367, 373, 399, 427). It has been purified from *Anabaena* CA (348, 349), *A. cylindrica* (307), *P. boryanum* (303), *Nostoc* CAN (the cyanobiont of the lichen *Peltigera canina;* 303), and *A. nidulans* (107). It is a dodecamer (~ 600,000 mol wt) with the subunits (49–50,000 mol wt) arranged in two superimposed hexagonal rings. Purification requires the presence of stabilizing ligands and the enzyme may be membrane bound, with stability of the complex being pH-dependent (107).

One would expect from comparison with other Gram-negative bacteria (see 322) that the enzyme should show adenylylation-deadenylylation, but evidence for this is lacking despite exhaustive studies (90, 107, 301, 303, 349, 367). Possible alternative or complementary mechanisms include (*a*) transcriptional control in response to nitrogen availability, (*b*) end-product inhibition, (*c*) feedback inhibition by products of glutamine metabolism, (*d*) changes in energy charge, (*e*) light-dark modulation of enzyme activity, (*f*) NH_4^+ modulation of enzyme activity.

It is uncertain whether transcriptional control operates, since enzyme activity changes little with environmental variation [a 2–2.5-fold decrease in GS activity in NH_4^+-grown compared with N_2-grown cultures (301, 349)]. End-product inhibition by glutamine does not occur (90, 367). AMP inhibits by 75–80% in *A. cylindrica* (367), possibly indicating regulation by energy charge. There is feedback inhibition by various amino acids, adenylates, and unknown low molecular weight inhibitors. The latter are found in cultures grown only on combined nitrogen (349). Feedback inhibition is cumulative in mixtures involving AMP, aspartate, serine (349), and alanine in the case of *A. cylindrica* (303, 367). A reversible deactivation of purified GS from *A. cylindrica* can occur in vitro with enzyme that has been dialyzed without stabilizing ligands being inactivated and dissociating to give three subspecies (possibly a conformer of the native enzyme, a half molecule, and a dimer/trimer respectively). The subspecies can be reassociated in vitro and activity restored to a maximum of 59% by adding both 2-mercaptoethanol and substrates of the biosynthetic assay [2-mercaptoethanol, alone, reassociates but does not reactivate (307)]. This resembles the ligand-induced conformational change which has been found with certain eukaryotic GS (288, 353). Further studies (302) have shown an in vivo light-dark modulation of GS in *A. cylindrica* and *A. nidulans* [see also (288) for higher plant GS]. On darkening *A. cylindrica* cultures, GS activity drops rapidly and stabilizes at about 50% of the light activity; after adding 2-mercaptoethanol, activity is immediately restored to its original level in vitro and upon re-illumination activity is restored to its original level within 6 h in vivo. ATP does not seem to be involved directly in deactivation/reactivation, and reactivation does not require enzyme synthesis. The maintenance of activity at 50% in the short term in dark is not surprising if this is the sole NH_4^+-assimilating enzyme of importance in the organism. This finding broadly resembles the light modulation of other key cyanobacterial enzymes such as glucose-6-phosphate dehydrogenase (4, 5, 267, 309). It will be interesting to determine whether the heterocyst enzyme is so regulated.

[So far, there is no evidence for different characteristics of vegetative cell and heterocyst GS (349).] The GS of *Nostoc* CAN and *P. boryanum* (cyanobacteria that can use exogenous fixed carbon) do not respond in a similar way to light-dark change.

An inhibition of *Anabaena* GS activity also occurs after treatment with NH_4^+; the GS of NH_4^+-grown cultures shows higher K_m values for ATP, glutamate, and NH_4^+. Rowell et al (303) have evidence that the light-dark and NH_4^+ changes, which are associated with conformational changes and do not involve dissociation/reassociation of the molecule and which lead to reduced catalytic activity of the enzyme, may play a functional role equivalent to adenylylated GS in *E. coli* and thus may reduce the drain on ATP and fixed carbon in this obligate autotroph. *Anabaena* GS can be activated/deactivated by thiols (302, 303), and the in vivo regulatory mechanisms may involve soluble oxidants such as glutathione or membrane-bound oxidants in dark (48, 317) or a membrane-bound vicinal dithiol-containing factor (LEM) (see 4) and/or thioredoxin (4, 48, 410, 430) in light. Thioredoxins are proteinaceous factors involved in, among other things, the activation and regulation of various enzyme systems including ribonucleotide reductase, 3'-phosphoadenosine 5'-phosphosulfate sulfotransferase, fructose 1,6-bisphosphatase (410), malic dehydrogenase (431), and phosphoribulokinase (318). They occur in the major groups of cyanobacteria (316) and have been purified from *Synechococcus* 6301 (315) where other thioredoxins can substitute for the native one. It has been suggested that they may play a role in N_2 fixation since thioredoxin-dependent activities are higher in N_2-grown heterocystous cultures than in NO_3-grown heterocyst-less cultures (316). However, thioredoxins have not been detected in all N_2-fixing strains.

Amino transferases of various cyanobacteria have also been considered (see 158, 222, 374).

GLUTAMINE SYNTHETASE–NITROGENASE INTERACTIONS

GS and nitrogenase closely interact in cyanobacteria, and the general consensus is that GS is involved directly or indirectly in nitrogenase regulation. Evidence for an involvement comes from the fact that the inhibition of nitrogenase activity and heterocyst production which occurs on adding NH_4^+ to N_2-fixing cultures can be prevented by adding MSX and that MSX allows nitrogenase synthesis and heterocyst production in NH_4^+-grown cultures (254, 373). Hydroxylysine, another glutamate analogue, has the same effect (195), but unlike MSX [(332); see however (155)] binds reversibly.

Thus, NH_4^+ (119) is not the sole inhibitor of nitrogenase and heterocyst synthesis but GS and/or a product is also involved.

Early evidence for *Klebsiella* (321, 381) suggested that low NH_4^+ caused deadenylylation of GS, in which state the GS acted as a positive transcriptional activator allowing *nif* gene expression, but that high NH_4^+ caused adenylylation of GS and in this state the enzyme did not promote *nif* gene expression. The picture is now much more complicated. First, certain mutants may express *nif* genes independent of GS (11). Second, in *Salmonella* (194) there are present, in addition to *gln* A which codes for GS protein, two other genes, *gln* F and *gln* R, whose products function together to mediate nitrogen control. In *E. coli* (261) a regulatory gene, *gln* G, tightly linked to *gln* A mediates both activation and repression of glutamine synthetase synthesis. Third, in cyanobacteria where GS adenylylation has not been shown, changes in nitrogenase activity on adding NH_4^+ precede measurable changes in GS catalytic activity (301), and high GS activity does not always correlate with high nitrogenase activity (283, 374, 375). Fourth, in some cyanobacteria NH_4^+, although assimilated, does not completely inhibit nitrogenase (349).

In cyanobacteria, changes in nitrogenase may involve products of GS. Thus in *A. cylindrica,* changes in nitrogenase correlate inversely with changes in free glutamine pools but not in other amino acids (254, 301, 373). Exogenous glutamine rapidly inhibits nitrogenase, whereas other major pool amino acids do not (283, 301); in the symbiotic *Nostoc* of *Peltigera aphthosa,* nitrogenase activity declines when glutamine produced through eukaryotic GS accumulates in cephalodia [in this way the lichen eukaryote(s) may regulate nitrogenase activity when cyanobiont GS itself cannot do so (283)]. Lawrie (202) believes that glutamine-derived carbamoyl phosphate, which is higher in NH_4^+ than N_2-grown cultures (as is carbamoyl phosphate synthetase activity) and which inhibits nitrogenase activity in vivo and in vitro (as does cyanate, the initial decomposition product of carbamoyl phosphate), is a regulator of nitrogenase [see also (105, 319, 320) for *Clostridium*]. GS could also exert an effect on nitrogenase activity by draining the cellular pool of ATP when NH_4^+ is available (see 245). Indeed some workers do not implicate GS in nitrogenase regulation; they attribute effects of high NH_4^+ on nitrogenase to the alteration of membrane potential by NH_4^+ which in turn affects reductant supply to nitrogenase (145).

GS is unlikely to be the only factor affecting nitrogenase and heterocyst production. For example in *Anabaena* CA (an odd organism in which NO_3^- but not NH_4^+ markedly inhibits nitrogenase and heterocyst production; 40), 7-azatryptophan allows heterocyst and nitrogenase expression in cultures grown on combined nitrogen without affecting GS (347). Cyclic

AMP (see 173), or cyclic GMP independent of GS [see (211) for *Rhizobium*] may also be involved. In addition, the relationship between nitrogenase and heterocysts is uncertain. Clearly, heterocysts provide O_2 protection but they can be independent variables: nitrogenaseless mutants occur, in *Anabaena* CA MSX causes a threefold increase in activity without an increase in heterocysts (347), etc. There is controversy about whether nitrogenase is involved in the regulation of heterocyst spatial patterns, and evidence for and against an involvement has been obtained (34, 45).

REDUCTANT AND ATP FOR NITROGENASE

Possible routes of reductant supply to nitrogenase are miscellaneous; which routes operate in vivo, and under what circumstances, is uncertain. Potential sources of reductant are water that is photolyzed, fixed carbon produced endogenously by photosynthesis, supplied exogenously or stored, and H_2, or reduced sulfur compounds. Compounds that may donate electrons directly to nitrogenase are usually considered to be NADPH (by some) or reduced ferredoxin (by most). What is not known is how many pools of NADPH, for example, exist, what roles different ferredoxins play, whether more than one type of reductant can function simultaneously, and, if they can, whether their effects are additive or not, how important are membrane potentials in reductant flow to nitrogenase, etc.

In *Gloeothece* where photosynthesis and N_2 fixation occur within the same cell, Gallon concludes, on balance, that electrons from the photolysis of water probably contribute reductant directly to nitrogenase but that there are other sources of reductant (126). Evidence supporting (or rather not arguing against) direct photoreduction is a possible Emerson enhancement of nitrogenase activity (cf N_2 fixation by heterocystous cyanobacteria where there is no enhancement; 217), inhibition of C_2H_2 reduction by the ferredoxin antagonist disalicylidine propanediamine (DSPD), and inhibition of C_2H_2 reduction at a pCO_2 above 0.01 atm. However, as noted (126), the situation is uncertain. For example, the results do not show enhancement if the values for acetylene reduction in light only are used to calculate enhancement values; positive evidence is obtained only if dark rates are first subtracted from light rates, and this is doubtful practice, e.g. in *Gloeothece* if glucose-6-phosphate dehydrogenase activity is inhibited in light (see 267) and if DSPD can inhibit cyclic photophosphorylation or inhibit electron donation from dark routes of reductant supply (5). The fact that DCMU causes only a transient drop in nitrogenase activity (126) also suggests that an equally efficient alternative reductant source(s) to water is available. This could be fixed carbon compounds or H_2 feeding into photosystem I or light-independent reductant sources such as pyruvate-ferredoxin oxidoreductase or the Krebs cycle/glyoxylate shunt, possibly from isocitrate to nitrogenase (127, 128). It may be that glucose-6-phosphate dehydrogenase can function in light in DCMU-treated cells. In dark the oxidative pentose phosphate pathway is the major route of reductant supply, activities of glucose-6-phosphate dehydrogenase and 6-phosphogluconate dehydrogenase are 4–10 times higher in N_2 than in NH_4^+-grown cultures, the activities of glucose-6-phosphate dehydrogenase and nitrogenase vary in parallel, and dark-supported nitrogenase activity may occur at substantial rates (126).

The nonheterocystous forms, *Gloeothece* apart, have scarcely been studied. What can be said is that electrons from the photolysis of water or from aerobic respiration are not essential for nitrogenase activity since most of these organisms have been screened for nitrogenase activity by anaerobic incubation in the presence of DCMU (292). Good growth of *P. boryanum* occurs on N_2 in the presence of Na_2S and exogenous fixed carbon, but the organism cannot grow on Na_2S even in the presence of combined nitrogen without fixed carbon (421). Possibly, electrons for nitrogenase in *Plectonema* are generated via light-independent processes from fixed carbon compounds or, in light under the test conditions employed, N_2 competes effectively with CO_2 for photochemically produced electrons. Again it will be interesting to determine whether the oxidative pentose phosphate pathway operates in light when photosystem II is nonfunctional because of the presence of Na_2S (see 251).

In aerobically grown N_2-fixing heterocystous cyanobacteria, nitrogenase is located in heterocysts that develop from vegetative cells via proheterocysts (heterocyst differentiation and development patterns are reviewed elsewhere; 155, 196). In mature heterocysts various vegetative cell metabolic processes are shut down, probably by transcriptional control, and existing vegetative cell components such as polyphosphate bodies, glycogen granules, carboxysomes, phycocyanin, and structured granules are degraded and their material reused and reordered; the most striking morphological features of the heterocysts are their thick complex envelope (57), polar plugs of cyanophycin (197), and contorted lamellae (196).

Biochemically, heterocysts have an altered photosynthetic system, compared with vegetative cells. They do not photolyze water, but photosystem I components are present and functional. The photosystem II accessory pigments, phycocyanin, allophycocyanin (and phycoerythrin), as well as the short-wave length chlorophyll *a*, are reduced or undetectable in heterocysts (see 155, 395, 397), although in some organisms normal amounts of phycocyanin have been reported (278). Concentrations may vary with heterocyst age (397). When synthesized, harvested light energy may be transferred from phycocyanin to P700. A Mn^{2+} deficiency may contribute to the lack of O_2 evolution in *A. cylindrica* heterocysts; other components associated with photosystem II may be partially degraded, e.g. cytochrome

b_{559} is detectable in heterocysts only at 77° K. Reinman & Thornber (285) have recently reported that a chlorophyll protein complex which is present in vegetative cells and photosystem II enriched membrane fractions is not present in heterocysts. Other components detected are plastoquinone, plastocyanin, and probably cytochrome b_{554} and cytochrome b_{563} (395) (see also 93). Quantitative studies on the components are required. A difficulty is that heterocysts sampled are not in a synchronous state of development and thus vary not only in their state of differentiation but also in ease of rupture. Although electrons from the photolysis of water do not feed into photosystem I, H_2 via an uptake hydrogenase donates electrons on the reducing side of photosystem I. P700 contents are high in *A. cylindrica* relative to numbers of photosystem II reaction centers, but the extra P700 does not seem to be specifically associated with the heterocysts; it may however facilitate ATP generation in them (285). Spectroscopic evidence for reaction centers A and B and for component X [the primary electron acceptor(?), for bound and soluble ferredoxin] as well as enzymatic evidence for ferredoxin-$NADP^+$ oxidoreductase in heterocysts have been obtained (5, 54, 56).

Photofixation of CO_2 via RUBP carboxylase activity is negligible in heterocysts, the enzyme protein is not detectable immunologically, and carboxysomes are degraded as heterocysts differentiate (364). Other enzymes also show low or undetectable activities: phosphoribulokinase, which catalyzes RUBP formation via the Calvin cycle, phosphoglycolate phosphatase, which yields glycolate from phosphoglycolate formed through RUBP oxygenase activity, and glycolate dehydrogenase, which yields glyoxylate, i.e. a suite of enzymes associated with RUBP metabolism are shut down in heterocysts (72).

Heterocysts import fixed carbon from vegetative cells as Wolk (424) first showed. Experiments in which whole filaments have been exposed to ^{14}C and the ^{14}C compounds in the isolated heterocysts analyzed suggest that the major transport compound is maltose (185); preliminary evidence that it may be sucrose (425) seems less likely now (C. P. Wolk, personal communication); of various compounds presented to isolated heterocysts only erythrose supports nitrogenase activity of isolated heterocysts (426). The latter approach may tell us little of what actually happens in vivo because membranes connecting vegetative cells and heterocysts may be affected during heterocyst isolation and membrane potentials and transport systems may be altered in isolated heterocysts. The nature of the carbon compound(s) transported remains an outstanding problem.

Heterocysts show high activities of enzymes of the oxidative pentose phosphate pathway (423). This pathway probably also operates in heterocysts in light and dark (5, 207, 423), possibly because inhibitors in the light, such as RUBP, are unlikely to build up in heterocysts (phosphoribulokinase activity is negligible) (72) or (less likely) because there is no photosystem II activity (see 4). Such a pathway is almost certainly the main route of sugar catabolism in heterocysts. However, despite earlier findings (207, 423), substantial activity of NAD^+-specific glyceraldehyde-3-phosphate dehydrogenase and appreciable activities of 3-phosphoglycerate kinase, enolase, and pyruvate kinase have recently been found in heterocysts (37), indicating that glycolysis may have a more important role to play in heterocysts than previously supposed. There may be a mechanism which allows partitioning of fixed carbon catabolism between the oxidative pentose phosphate pathway and glycolysis. Perhaps the oxidative pentose phosphate pathway is most active when reductant is required and glycolysis is most active when biosynthetic processes involving organic acids are limiting. Possible factors affecting partitioning between the two pathways require study. Even more intriguing is isocitrate dehydrogenase which shows substantial activity in heterocysts and thus can provide 2-oxoglutarate required for glutamine synthesis and NADPH; its activity is negligible in vegetative cells of N_2-fixing *A. cylindrica* but not in NO_3^-- or NH_4^+-grown vegetative cells. NH_4^+ produced in heterocysts is assimilated via GS and the glutamine so produced is exported to vegetative cells where GOGAT is active (398). Glutamate may be returned from vegetative cells to heterocysts but this is debatable (see 37).

From the above it is clear that electron donation to nitrogenase could be from photosystem I–dependent reactions in light, from the oxidative pentose phosphate pathway in light or dark, and possibly from glycolysis and/or Krebs cycle in heterocysts.

Evidence that H_2 may donate electrons to nitrogenase via an uptake hydrogenase (see below) feeding into photosystem I comes from the early findings of H_2-stimulated C_2H_2 reduction by isolated heterocysts (428). More recent studies show that H_2 supports light-dependent C_2H_2 reduction in extracts and whole filaments (20, 38, 160) and feeds into photosystem I on the donor side of plastoquinone and after Q (see below). The possibility that organic compounds may feed into photosystem I and support nitrogenase activity was suggested by early work on N_2 fixation (209) and also by the finding that several organic acids donate electrons to photosystem I in lamellar fragments of whole filaments (236). However, to date, electron donation from organic acids to nitrogenase via photosystem I of heterocysts has not been demonstrated using malate, succinate, glycolate, and pyruvate (214). Indeed no glycolate dehydrogenase has been detected in heterocysts (72), although it is present in lamellar fragments from whole filaments (74, 76, 144, 306). Such data are in keeping with the studies of Bergman (22) which provide evidence of glycolate feeding into photosystem I in whole filaments of *A. cylindrica* and possibly indirectly stimulating nitrogenase activity.

Evidence that NADPH from glucose-6-phosphate dehydrogenase (5, 31, 344) or from isocitrate dehydrogenase can support nitrogenase has been obtained. Thus electron transfer from NADPH to ferredoxin has been observed in vitro, and transfer of electrons from NADPH to cytochrome *c* in a ferredoxin-dependent reaction in heterocysts has been observed in light. This would help explain the possible presence of ferredoxin-$NADP^+$ oxidoreductase in heterocysts which are unable to fix CO_2 via RUBPCase and in which functionless enzymes are usually shut down (155). It is interesting that heterocysts of *A. cylindrica* appear to have only one form of ferredoxin-$NADP^+$ oxidoreductase, whereas whole filaments have several forms (300). Others (145) argue against ferredoxin-$NADP^+$ oxidoreductase alone being implicated in electron transfer from NADPH to ferredoxin in vivo; they consider the difference in redox potential to be too large, and allude to the possible importance of reversed electron flow driven by a proton-motive force being implicated in electron flow from NADPH to nitrogenase. Bothe et al (37) rightly argue that what goes on in *Azotobacter* need not happen in heterocysts of cyanobacteria. Nevertheless the idea is a valuable one which merits serious investigation.

Cyanobacteria possess an ATP-dependent, extremely O_2-sensitive pyruvate-ferredoxin oxidoreductase that shows fivefold higher activity in N_2 compared with NH_4^+-grown cultures and that may be important if glycolysis is more active than once thought. To date, however, only low or negligible rates of pyruvate-supported nitrogenase activity have been obtained in whole cell or heterocyst extracts (73, 214), possibly because the enzyme was inactivated during filament breakage or because the pyruvate did not penetrate the heterocysts. Pyruvate dehydrogenase is undetectable in cyanobacteria (36, 205).

ATP to support nitrogenase activity may come from total photophosphorylation, cyclic photophosphorylation alone, oxidative phosphorylation, or substrate level phosphorylation (see 41, 42). It is now fairly clear that in light, cyclic photophosphorylation alone can supply the necessary ATP for maximum nitrogenase activity and that in dark when oxidative phosphorylation with O_2 as terminal electron acceptor maintains the ATP pool, nitrogenase activity is never sustained at optimum rates, although it is difficult to disentangle effects due to shortage of ATP, reductant, and change in membrane potential in dark- versus light-incubated cells. When substrate level phosphorylation alone operates, nitrogenase activity is usually low or undetectable. However in *Oscillatoria limnetica* anaerobic respiration with sulfur as terminal electron acceptor, and lactic acid fermentation may be important (252). Whether these processes support high rates of N_2 fixation in *O. limnetica* under such conditions is uncertain (see 17).

HYDROGEN METABOLISM

Cyanobacterial nitrogenase, like other nitrogenases (366), can act as an ATP-dependent hydrogenase, and this capacity of some cyanobacteria to generate H_2 from water and sunlight in air has aroused much current interest. Recent reviews cover physiology and enzymology (33, 35, 37, 149, 311), practical applications (19, 150, 311), and Russian research (113, 191, 192).

The ability of cyanobacteria to produce H_2 was known almost a century ago (179), the presence of inducible hydrogenase in cyanobacteria has long been documented (see 189), and it is now known that nitrogenase acts as a hydrogenase. However, the number of distinct hydrogenases in cyanobacteria is uncertain and the literature is confusing, partly because different workers have used different organisms, partly because there are vegetative cell and heterocyst hydrogenases to contend with, but mostly because the enzymes have not yet been purified and characterized [see, however, (148)].

Evidence that nitrogenase acts as a hydrogenase is well documented and unequivocal: the purified *A. cylindrica* enzyme can evolve H_2 (151); other nitrogenases do likewise (see 366); ATP-dependent hydrogenase activity occurs only when nitrogenase is active and does not occur in NH_4^+-grown cultures; growth, physiological, and environmental conditions affect nitrogenase and ATP-dependent hydrogenase activity similarly; like nitrogenase, ATP-dependent hydrogenase functions only in heterocysts of air-grown cultures. The amounts of H_2 produced vary with strain, on whether or not substrate reduction is occurring, on the extent of H_2 recycling via uptake hydrogenase activity, and on the nutritional status of the cyanobacterium (e.g. 20, 21, 33, 38, 39, 182, 275, 277, 280, 376, 393, 394, 420). The validity of some of the very high rates of H_2 production catalyzed by nitrogenase has been questioned (37).

There are also good data for uptake hydrogenase activity which is membrane bound. Uptake hydrogenase activity may couple to a light-dependent, O_2-independent photosystem I–mediated electron transfer chain. Activity is unaffected by DCMU (39) and BNT (104), but photosystem I components from plastoquinone to ferredoxin are probably involved. Thus the plastoquinone antagonist DBMIB inhibited light-dependent H_2-supported C_2H_2 reduction, as did metronidazole which affects low potential electron carriers such as ferredoxin and flavodoxin (37, 104). The case for ferredoxin being involved is not in fact clear cut because metronidazole has not always been found to inhibit activity (see 396). Uptake hydrogenase activity may also be associated with a DBMIB-sensitive, metronidazole-insensitive respiratory chain coupling to O_2 in an oxyhydrogen reaction (37, 396) and generating ATP [the reaction is inhibited by uncouplers (38, 39); ATP production has been measured directly (277)]. KCN also inhibits, which indicates the involvement of a cytochrome oxidase system (38). Collectively, the functions of uptake hydrogenase activity in relation to nitrogenase are to recycle H_2 lost through nitrogenase activity, provide reductant via photosystem I, generate ATP for nitrogenase via an oxyhydrogen reaction, scavenge O_2 and thus protect nitrogenase from O_2 inactivation, possibly prevent H_2 binding to nitrogenase [this is thought not to be a function in *Azotobacter* (411)], and possibly help provide a suitable membrane potential for nitrogenase to function. The above-mentioned membrane-bound hydrogenase activity has been examined mainly in heterocystous cyanobacteria; it has been suggested that both the light-dependent and O_2-dependent processes share common electron transport components and that only one uptake hydrogenase occurs (37). It has also been suggested that uptake hydrogenase activity is localized solely in heterocysts (280; see also below, however).

Others consider that there are in fact two distinct uptake hydrogenases —one linked to photoreducing activity and another to the oxygen-dependent activity of the cells. The best evidence for this has come from Peschek (270, 271–273). In *A. nidulans* he finds that 90% of the anaerobically induced uptake hydrogenase, which is DBMIB sensitive and could photoreduce various components including ferredoxin, $NADP^+$ and NO_2^-, is located in a 144,000 X g X 3 h thylakoid membrane fraction. This thylakoid membrane fraction can also evolve H_2, and is sensitive to O_2, CO, and thiol-blocking agents. In *Anacystis* in the presence of O_2 (but $<$ 10–15%) there is a second uptake hydrogenase which seems to be bound, not to the thylakoids but to the plasmalemma, and which is involved in phosphorylative electron flow from H_2 to O_2.

In addition to uptake hydrogenases, soluble inducible reversible hydrogenase activity was found equally in heterocysts and vegetative cells of cyanobacteria (149). It is induced under anaerobic conditions (125, 393) and can evolve H_2 from various artificial electron donors in dark and light. It may be involved in photoreduction but does not show an oxyhydrogen reaction. It has been partially purified from *A. cylindrica* (148). Bothe et al (37) strongly argue that the particulate hydrogenase activity and the soluble hydrogenase are expressions of a single multifunctional enzyme. They note similar patterns of induction of the oxyhydrogen-implicated uptake hydrogenase and the reversible hydrogenase (which shows photoreduction and methyl-viologen dependent activity, but not an oxyhydrogen reaction); they believe that the lack of oxyhydrogen activity is because an essential component of the respiratory chain has been lost during isolation and that only on solubilization of the membrane-bound enzyme is methyl-viologen and $Na_2S_2O_4$ accessible to the enzyme. This is an interesting concept because both Bothe's uptake hydrogenases and Peschek's uptake hydrogenases are in fact capable of H_2 evolution. Whether there is a uniform number of hydrogenases in cyanobacteria, and what the characteristics of each are, is still unclear from the literature (to me at least!). If the reader wants to start a review of the literature I suggest beginning with References (37, 270, 271, 273, 277, 311, 394). It has only been possible in the present chapter to mention a few of the many interesting papers on this subject—I apologize to authors of papers omitted. What is clear is that in N_2-fixing cyanobacteria the possession of uptake hydrogenase activity is certainly beneficial; one questions how effective strains would be if, as has been suggested, mutants were bred for enhanced H_2 production via nitrogenase that lacked an uptake hydrogenase.

PERSPECTIVE

The last decade has seen remarkable advances in our knowledge of cyanobacteria. A close inspection of the original papers reveals contributions by biologists of all sorts using the newer and more powerful experimental techniques that have become available.

Advances in the 1970s have been concerned with validating (or disproving), mainly at the cellular and biochemical level, many of the hypotheses which emanated in the 1960s (and sometimes earlier!). Aspects which are now clear include the following: the prokaryotic nature of cyanobacteria and their similarity to other Gram-negative bacteria (a new taxonomic treatment that includes physiological and biochemical as well as structural and morphological features has also emerged); confirmation that the major function of heterocysts is to fix N_2; the demonstration of N_2-fixation by nonheterocystous forms under microaerobic or anaerobic conditions as in certain photosynthetic bacteria; the importance of glutamine synthetase, often coupled with glutamate synthase, in primary NH_4^+ assimilation, metabolism, and regulation; the nature and role of cyanobacterial cellular inclusions; the fact that cyanobacteria do indeed show transcriptional control; the capacity of certain cyanobacteria to carry out anoxygenic photosynthesis; and the role of the oxidative pentose phosphate pathway as the major route of carbon dissimilation.

What is lacking from the above list is the question of cyanobacterial genetics. The sad fact is that at present our knowledge of cyanobacterial genetics is at least a decade behind what is known for organisms such as *E. coli.* Cyanobacterial geneticists missed the boat in the early 1970s and failed to capitalize on the pickings that were then available. The 1980s, if nothing else, will see rapid progress being made in this area by a new breed of geneticists reared on a diet of molecular biology. The current approaches of Doolittle, Simon, Ausubel and Bogorad, Haselkorn and Van Arkel, among others, commend themselves, and the background information for a push forward is now available.

First, cyanobacterial mutants are now easily prepared (e.g. 86) and an appreciation of the Gram-negative nature of the cell walls has facilitated the selection of antibiotic resistant isolates; many unicellular forms are available which grow rapidly, suspend homogeneously, and some fix N_2. Akinetes which germinate to give single filaments are easily purified (384), and good replica plating techniques have been developed (429). In addition, nitrogenase-less mutants, forms with altered heterocysts and O_2 sensitivities, and a capacity to grow heterotrophically (which will facilitate mutant studies on photosynthetic systems), etc, are available (86, 142, 335, 338, 380).

Second, there is some literature on mating, transformation, and possibilities for transduction in cyanobacteria, although the latter has not yet been demonstrated. These aspects have been critically assessed (89, 97, 406).

Third, substantial progress has been made recently in the plasmid biology of cyanobacteria. These extrachromosomal elements of DNA may vary widely in molecular weight and are arranged as covalently closed circles. They have been detected in numerous strains, especially of unicellular cyanobacteria (8, 161, 198, 232, 294, 329, 330, 407, 408). They have been well reviewed (200, 201).

Characterization of the plasmids present in two *A. nidulans* and in a *Synechococcus* strain has confirmed that they are indeed homologous, that spontaneous curing of cyanobacterial plasmids may occur, and that under the electron microscope the plasmids appear as supercoiled and relaxed circular molecules. The strain in which plasmid curing occurs shows no obvious changes from the others and this strain may prove to be a useful vector for self-cloning in *A. nidulans* (198). The plasmids of six strains belonging to *Synechococcus* or *Synechocystis* have also been characterized. Restriction enzyme analyses of a similar molecular weight plasmid in three of the strains (*Synechococcus* 6301, 6707, and 6908) have shown identical cleavage patterns indicating that they may be identical (407), even though the cyanobacterial strains containing them are different in genome size and base composition (163, 164). The relatively small size of the plasmids, with one cleavage site for the restriction enzyme *Endo*R *Bam*H1 which produces cohesive ends, may make them useful in preparing recombinant DNA in vitro. The function of these plasmids is unknown (407).

A comprehensive study of the plasmid DNA in 13 species spread through the major typological groups has been carried out (330). Plasmids are common in filamentous cyanobacteria; they are present in 7 out of 13 tested, and in all but *Plectonema* more than one plasmid is present. Heterocystous cyanobacteria with plasmids include various *Anabaena* strains (*A. cylindrica* has five), *Nostoc,* and *Fremyella.* No plasmids were found in *Cylin-*

drospermum, Nodularia, Tolypothrix, and *Fischerella.* In general no correlation was found with morphological type or metabolic activities, but the more complex morphological types had no extrachromosomal DNA.

Recently the construction of genetically marked cyanobacterial plasmids has been achieved, using techniques developed with *E. coli,* by introducing the ampillicin-resistant encoding transposon Tn901 into the cyanobacterial plasmid pUH24 from *A. nidulans* (408). This was done by transforming *A. nidulans* R2 with *E. coli* plasmid pR146, which contained Tn901, and then after selection for antibiotic resistance, clones were selected in which the original plasmid pUH24 was replaced by a new plasmid consisting of Tn901 inserted into pUH24. Proof of transfer was confirmed by transforming wild type *A. nidulans* R2 using pUH24:Tn 901 to yield ampillicin-resistant clones. This is the first example of expression of an *E. coli* gene in a cyanobacterial cell. Also the construction of a recombinant plasmid consisting of pUH24 in which the 5Md part of pR146 (i.e. the part which includes its streptomycin resistance gene) is inserted offers the possibility of further constructing a plasmid carrying ampicillin and streptomycin resistance genes. This would open up the way for cloning based on insertional inactivation procedures. Recently it has been shown (219) on the basis of heteroduplex mapping between *Klebsiella pneumoniae nif* fragment A and a cloned homologous fragment from *Anabaena* 7120 that a homologous region 2 kb long existed (see also 10). In the 1980s, possibly using extensions of such plasmid-mediated techniques, the transfer of genes encoding for such economically important features as N_2 fixation, toxin production, H_2 production and others will surely be achieved.

ACKNOWLEDGMENTS

I thank Drs. G. A. Codd and P. Rowell for helpful criticisms of this manuscript. My own work reported here was supported by the Science Research Council and the Natural Environment Research Council, U.K.

Literature Cited

1. Abeliovich, A., Shilo, M. 1972. *J. Bacteriol.* 111:682–89
2. Abeliovich, A., Shilo, M. 1972. *Biochim. Biophys. Acta* 283:483–91
3. Akazawa, T. 1979. See Ref. 132, pp. 208–29
4. Anderson, L. E. 1979. See Ref. 3, pp. 271–81
5. Apte, S. K., Rowell, P., Stewart, W. D. P. 1978. *Proc. R. Soc. London Ser. B* 200:1–25
6. Armstrong, J. E., Van Baalen, C. 1979. *J. Gen Microbiol.* 111:253–62
7. Arnon, D. I. 1977. In *Encyclopedia of Plant Physiology,* ed. A. Trebst, M. Avron, pp. 7–56. Berlin: Springer
8. Asato, Y., Ginoza, H. S. 1973. *Nature* 244:132–33
9. Astier, C., Vernotte, C., Der Vartanian, M., Joset-Espardellier, F. 1979. *Int. Symp. Photosynth. Prokaryotes 3rd, Oxford, U.K.,* Abstr. C5
10. Ausubel, F. M., Janssen, K. A., Ow, D. W., Riedel, G. E., Ruvkin, G. B., Cannon, F. C., Cannon, M. C. 1980. See Ref. 366. In press

11. Ausubel, F. M., Margolskee, F. R., Maizels, N. 1977. In *Recent Developments in Nitrogen Fixation,* ed. W. Newton, J. R. Postgate, C. Rodriguez-Barrueco, pp. 347–56. London: Academic
12. Bagi, G., Csatorday, K., Farkas, G. L. 1979. *Arch. Microbiol.* 123:109–11
13. Balogh, A., Borbely, G., Cseke, C., Udvandy, J., Farkas, G. L. 1979. *FEBS Lett.* 105:158–62
14. Barr, R., Crane, F. L., Giaquinta, R. T. 1975. *Plant Physiol.* 55:460–62
15. Bassham, J. A. 1979. See Ref. 3, pp. 9–30
16. Batt, T., Brown, D. H. 1974. *Planta* 116:27–37
17. Belkin, S., Cohen, Y., Padan, E. 1979. See Ref. 9, Abstr. B17
18. Belkin, S., Padan, E. 1978. *Arch. Microbiol.* 116:109–11
19. Benemann, J. R., Hallenbeck, P. C. 1978. See Ref. 311, pp. 395–413
20. Benemann, J. R., Weare, N. M. 1974. *Arch. Microbiol.* 101:401–8
21. Benemann, J. R., Weare, N. M. 1974. *Science* 184:174–75
22. Bergman, B. 1980. *Physiol. Plant.* In press
23. Birmingham, B. C., Colman, B. 1979. *Plant Physiol.* 64:892–95
24. Björn, G. S. 1978. *Physiol. Plant.* 42:321–23
25. Björn, G. S. 1979. *Physiol. Plant.* 46:281–86
26. Björn, G. S., Björn, L. O. 1976. *Physiol. Plant.* 36:297–304
27. Bone, D. H. 1972. *Arch. Mikrobiol.* 86:13–24
28. Bonen, L., Doolittle, W. F. 1978. *J. Mol. Evol.* 10:283–91
29. Bonen, L., Doolittle, W. F., Fox, G. E. 1979. *Can. J. Biochem.* 57:879–88
30. Bothe, H. 1969. *Prog. Photosynth. Res.* 3:1483–91
31. Bothe, H. 1970. *Ber. Dtsch. Bot. Ges.* 83:421–32
32. Bothe, H. 1977. See Ref. 7, pp. 217–21
33. Bothe, H., Distler, E., Eisbrenner, G. 1978. *Biochimie* 60:277–89
34. Bothe, H., Eisbrenner, G. 1977. *Biochemie Physiol. Pflanz.* 171:323–32
35. Bothe, H., Eisbrenner, G. 1978. See Ref. 19, pp. 353–69
36. Bothe, H., Falkenberg, B., Nolteernsting, U. 1974. *Arch. Microbiol.* 96:291–304
37. Bothe, H., Neuer, G., Kalbe, I., Eisbrenner, G. 1980. See Ref. 366. In press
38. Bothe, H., Tennigkeit, J., Eisbrenner, G. 1977. *Arch. Microbiol.* 114:43–49
39. Bothe, H., Tennigkeit, J., Eisbrenner, G., Yates, M. G. 1977. *Planta* 133:237–42
40. Bottomley, P. J., Grillo, J. F., Van Baalen, C., Tabita, F. R. 1979. *J. Bacteriol.* 140:938–48
41. Bottomley, P. J., Stewart, W. D. P. 1976. *Arch. Microbiol.* 108:249–58
42. Bottomley, P. J., Stewart, W. D. P. 1977. *New Phytol.* 79:625–38
43. Bottomley, P. J., Van Baalen, C. 1978. *J. Bacteriol.* 135:888–94
44. Bottomley, P. J., Van Baalen, C. 1978. *J. Gen. Microbiol.* 107:309–18
45. Bradley, S., Carr, N. G. 1976. *J. Gen. Microbiol.* 96:175–84
46. Brand, J. J. 1979. *FEBS Lett.* 103:114–17
47. Bryant, D. A., Guglielmi, G., Tandeau de Marsac, N., Castets, A-M., Cohen-Bazire, G. 1979. *Arch. Microbiol.* 123:113–28
48. Buchanan, B. B., Wolosiuk, R. A., Schürmann, P. 1979. *Trends Biochem. Sci.* 4:93–96
49. Bunt, J. S., Cooksey, K. E., Heeb, M. A., Lee, C. C., Taylor, G. C. 1970. *Nature* 227:1163–64
50. Burns, R. C., Hardy, R. W. F. 1975. *Nitrogen Fixation in Bacteria and Higher Plants.* New York: Springer 189 pp.
51. Burris, R. H., Arp, D. J., Benson, D. R., Emerich, D. W., Hageman, R. V., Ljones, T., Ludden, P. W., Sweet, W. J. 1980. See Ref. 366. In press
52. Caldwell, D. E. 1977. *Crit. Rev. Microbiol.* 3:305–70
53. Cammack, R., Rao, K. K., Bargeron, C. P., Hutson, K. G., Andrew, P. W., Rogers, L. J. 1977. *Biochem. J.* 168:205–9
54. Cammack, R., Luijk, L. J., Maguire, J. J., Fry, I. V., Packer, L. 1979. *Biochim. Biophys. Acta* 548:267–75
55. Cammack, R., Ryan, M. D., Stewart, A. C. 1979. *FEBS Lett.* 107:422–26
56. Cammack, R., Tel-Or, E., Stewart, W. D. P. 1976. *FEBS Lett.* 70:241–44
57. Cardemil, L., Wolk, C. P. 1976. *J. Biol. Chem.* 251:2967–75
58. Carithers, R. P., Yoch, D. C., Arnon, D. I. 1979. *J. Bacteriol.* 137:779–80
59. Carmichael, W. W., Biggs, D. F., Gorham, P. R. 1975. *Science* 187:542–43
60. Carmichael, W. W., Gorham, P. R. 1978. *Mitt. Int. Ver. Theor. Angew. Limnol.* 21:285–95
61. Carpenter, E. J., Price, C. C. 1976. *Science* 191:1278–80
62. Carpenter, E. J., Walsby, A. E. 1979. *J. Phycol.* 15:221–23

63. Carr, N. G. 1973. See Ref 64, pp. 39–66
64. Carr, N. G., Whitton, B. A., eds. 1973. *The Biology of Blue-green Algae.* Oxford: Blackwell. 655 pp.
65. Castenholz, R. W. 1973. See Ref. 64, pp. 320–39
66. Castenholz, R. W., Utkilen, H. C. 1979. See Ref. 9, Abstr. A9
67. Chao, L., Bowen, C. C. 1971. *J. Bacteriol.* 104:331–38
68. Chollett, R., Anderson, L. L. 1976. *Arch. Biochem. Biophys.* 176:344–51
69. Clayton, R. K., Sistrom, W. R., eds. 1978. *The Photosynthetic Bacteria.* New York/London: Plenum. 946 pp.
70. Codd, G. A., Cook, C. M., Stewart, W. D. P. 1979. *FEMS Microbiol. Lett.* 6:81–86
71. Codd, G. A., Cossar, J. D. 1978. *Biochem. Biophys. Res. Commun.* 83: 342–46
72. Codd, G. A., Okabe, K., Stewart, W. D. P. 1980. *Arch. Microbiol.* 124:149–54
73. Codd, G. A., Rowell, P., Stewart, W. D. P. 1974. *Biochem. Biophys. Res. Commun.* 61:424–31
74. Codd, G. A., Sallal, A-K. J. 1978. *Planta* 139:177–81
75. Codd, G. A., Schmid, G. H. 1980. *Z. Naturforsch.* In press
76. Codd, G. A., Stewart, W. D. P. 1973. *Arch. Mikrobiol.* 94:11–28
77. Codd, G. A., Stewart, W. D. P. 1977. *FEMS Microbiol. Lett.* 1:35–38
78. Codd, G. A., Stewart, W. D. P. 1977. *Arch. Microbiol.* 113:105–10
79. Cohen, Y., Jørgensen, B. B., Padan, E., Shilo, M. 1975. *Nature* 257:489–92
80. Cohen, Y., Padan, E., Shilo, M. 1975. *J. Bacteriol.* 123:855–61
81. Collins, M. 1978. *Microbiol. Rev.* 42:725–46
82. Colman, B., Cheng, K. H., Ingle, R. K. 1976. *Plant Sci. Lett.* 6:123–27
83. Crespi, H. L., Smith, U., Gajda, L., Tisue, T., Ammeraal, R. M. 1972. *Biochim. Biophys. Acta* 256:611–18
84. Csatorday, K., Kleinen Hammans, J. W., Goedheer, J. C. 1978. *Biochem. Biophys. Res. Commun.* 81:571–75
85. Cseke, C., Horvath, L. I., Simon, P., Borbely, G., Keszthelyi, L., Farkas, G. L. 1979. *J. Biochem. Tokyo* 85:1397–1404
86. Currier, T. C., Haury, J. F., Wolk, C. P. 1977. *J. Bacteriol.* 129:1556–62
87. Dalton, H. 1980. See Ref. 366. In press
88. Davis, D. J., San Pietro, A. 1977. *Arch. Biochem. Biophys.* 184:572–77
89. Delaney, S. F., Herdman, M., Carr, N. G. 1976. In *Genetics of the Algae,* ed. R. A. Lewin, pp. 7–28. Berkeley: Univ. Calif. Press
90. Dharmawardene, M. W. N., Haystead, A., Stewart, W. D. P. 1973. *Arch. Mikrobiol.* 90:281–95
91. Dharmawardene, M. W. N., Stewart, W. D. P., Stanley, S. O. 1972. *Planta* 108:133–45
92. Dick, H. L. N., Stewart, W. D. P. 1980. *Arch. Microbiol.* 124:107–9
93. Dietrich, W. E. Jr., Thormber, J. P. 1971. *Biochim. Biophys. Acta* 245: 482–93
94. Dmitrieva, E. Y., Lozlov, A. V. 1979. *Biokhimiya* 44:252–58
95. Döhler, G. 1974. *Planta* 118:259–69
96. Döhler, G. 1976. *Planta* 131:129–33
97. Doolittle, W. F. 1979. *Adv. Microb. Physiol.* 20:1–102
98. Drawert, H., Tischer, I. 1956. *Naturwissenschaften* 43:132
99. Dugdale, R. C., Menzel, D. W., Ryther, J. H. 1961. *Deep Sea Res.* 7:298–300
100. Duguid, J. P. 1968. *Arch. Immunol. Ther. Exp.* 16:173–88
101. Dutton, J. E., Rogers, L. J. 1979. *Biochem. Soc. Trans.* 7:1262–64
102. Eady, R. R., Imam, S., Lowe, D. J., Miller, R. W., Smith, B. E., Thorneley, R. N. F. 1980. See Ref. 366. In press
103. Eady, R. R., Smith, B. E. 1979. In *A Treatise on Dinitrogen Fixation, Section II,* ed. R. W. F. Hardy, R. C. Burns, pp. 399–490. New York: Wiley
104. Eisbrenner, G., Bothe, H. 1979. *Arch. Microbiol.* 123:37–45
105. Elliott, B. B., Mortenson, L. E. 1976. *J. Bacteriol.* 127:770–79
106. Eloff, J. N., Steinitz, Y., Shilo, M. 1976. *Appl. Environ. Microbiol.* 31:119–26
107. Emond, D., Rondeau, N., Cedergren, R. J. 1979. *Can. J. Biochem.* 57:843–51
108. Englund, B. 1978. *Ecol. Bull. Stockholm* 26:234–46
109. Estep, M., Armstrong, J. E., Van Baalen, C. 1975. *Appl. Microbiol.* 30:186–88
110. Evans, E. H., Carr, N. G., Rush, J. D., Johnson, C. E. 1977. *Biochem. J.* 166:547–51
111. Evans, E. H., Rush, J. D., Johnson, C. E., Evans, M. C. W. 1979. *Biochem. J.* 182:861–65
112. Evans, H. J., Emerich, D. W., Lepo, J. E., Maier, R. J., Carter, K. R., Hanus, F. J., Russell, S. A. 1980. See Ref. 366. In press
113. Evstigneev, V. B. 1977. In *Living Systems as Energy Convertors,* ed. R. Buvet, M. J. Allen, J. P. Massue, pp. 275–84. Amsterdam: North Holland

114. Falkner, G., Horner, F., Werden, K., Heldt, H. W. 1976. *Plant Physiol.* 58:717–18
115. Fay, P. 1969. *J. Exp. Bot.* 20:100–9
116. Fisher, R. W., Wolk, C. P. 1976. *Nature* 259:394–95
117. Fleming, H., Haselkorn, R. 1973. *Proc. Natl. Acad. Sci. USA* 70:2727–31
118. Fleming, H., Haselkorn, R. 1974. *Cell* 3:159–70
119. Fogg, G. E. 1949. *Ann. Bot. London* 14:241–59
120. Fogg, G. E. 1971. *Arch. Hydrobiol. Beih. Ergebn. Limnol.* 5:1–25
121. Fogg, G. E., Stewart, W. D. P., Fay, P., Walsby, A. E. 1973. *The Blue-green Algae,* London/New York: Academic. 459 pp.
122. Foy, R. H., Smith, R. V. 1980. *Br. Phycol. J.* In press
123. Fredricks, W. W., Gehl, J. M. 1976. *Arch. Biochem. Biophys.* 174:666–74
124. Fridovich, I. 1975. *Ann. Rev. Biochem.* 44:147–59
125. Fujita, Y., Ohmori, H., Hattori, A. 1964. *Plant Cell Physiol.* 5:305–14
126. Gallon, J. R. 1980. See Ref. 366. In press
127. Gallon, J. R., Kurz, W. G. W., LaRue, T. A. 1973. *Can. J. Microbiol.* 19: 461–65
128. Gallon, J. R., Ul-Haque, M. I., Chaplin, A. E. 1978. *J. Gen. Microbiol.* 106: 329–36
129. Gantt, E. 1975. *Bioscience* 25:781–87
130. Gantt, E., Lipschultz, C. A., Grabowski, J., Zimmermann, B. K. 1979. *Plant Physiol.* 63:615–20
131. Gendel, S., Ohad, I., Bogorad, L. 1979. *Plant Physiol.* 64:786–90
132. Gibbs, M., Latzko, E., eds. 1979. *Encyclopedia of Plant Physiology, New Series,* Vol. 6. Berlin: Springer. 578 pp.
133. Gibson, J. 1979. See Ref. 9, Abstr. A21
134. Glazer, A. N. 1977. *Mol. Cell. Biochem.* 18:125–40
135. Glazer, A. N., Williams, R. C., Yamanaka, G., Schachman, H. K. 1979. *Proc. Natl. Acad. Sci. USA* 76: 6162–66
136. Gleason, F. K. 1979. *Arch. Microbiol.* 123:15–21
137. Goering, J. J., Dugdale, R. C., Menzel, D. W. 1966. *Limnol. Oceanogr.* 11: 614–20
138. Golecki, J. R. 1977. *Arch. Microbiol.* 114:35–41
139. Golecki, J. R. 1979. *Arch. Microbiol.* 120:125–33
140. Gorlenko, V. M., Korotkov, S. A. 1979. See Ref. 9, Abstr. A16
141. Gotto, J. W., Tabita, F. R., Van Baalen, C. 1979. *Arch. Microbiol.* 121:155–59
142. Gotto, J. W., Tabita, F. R., Van Baalen, C. 1979. *J. Bacteriol.* 140:327–32
143. Gozzer, C., Zanetti, G., Galliano, M., Sacchi, G. A., Minchiotti, L., Curti, B. 1977. *Biochim. Biophys. Acta* 485: 278–90
144. Grodzinski, B., Colman, B. 1976. *Plant Physiol.* 58:199–202
145. Haaker, H., Laane, C., Veeger, C. 1980. See Ref. 366. In press
146. Haaker, H., Veeger, C. 1977. *Eur. J. Biochem.* 77:1–10
147. Halldal, P., Holmen, A. T. 1979. *Plant Cell Physiol.* 20:757–63
148. Hallenbeck, P. C., Benemann, J. R. 1978. *FEBS Lett.* 94:261–64
149. Hallenbeck, P. C., Benemann, J. R. 1979. In *Photosynthesis in Relation to Model Systems,* ed. J. Barber, pp. 331–64. Amsterdam: Elsevier/North-Holland Biomedical
150. Hallenbeck, P. C., Kochian, L. V., Weissman, J. C., Benemann, J. R. 1979. *Biotech. Bioeng. Symp.* 8:283–97
151. Hallenbeck, P. C., Kostel, P. J., Benemann, J. R. 1979. *Eur. J. Biochem.* 98:275–84
152. Hamadi, A. F., Gallon, J. R. 1979. *Biochem. Soc. Trans.* 7:1266–67
153. Hase, T., Wada, K., Matsubara, H. 1975. *J. Biochem. Tokyo* 78:605–10
154. Hase, T., Wada, K., Ohmiya, M., Matsubara, H. 1976. *J. Biochem. Tokyo* 80:993–99
155. Haselkorn, R. 1978. *Ann. Rev. Plant Physiol.* 29:319–44
156. Hattori, A. 1963. In *Studies on Microalgae and Photosynthetic Bacteria. Jpn. Soc. Plant Cell Physiol.,* pp. 485–92. Tokyo: Univ. Press
157. Haury, J. F., Wolk, C. P. 1978. *J. Bacteriol.* 136:688–92
158. Haystead, A., Dharmawardene, M. W. N., Stewart, W. D. P. 1973. *Plant Sci. Lett.* 1:439–45
159. Haystead, A., Robinson, R., Stewart, W. D. P. 1970. *Arch. Mikrobiol.* 75: 235–43
160. Haystead, A., Stewart, W. D. P. 1972. *Arch. Mikrobiol.* 82:325–36
161. Heaton, D., Frampton, E. W. 1976. *Abstr. Ann. Meet. Am. Soc. Microbiol.* 1976. I117, p. 131
162. Henry, L. E. A., Gogotov, I. N., Hall, D. O. 1978. *Biochem. J.* 174:373–77
163. Herdman, M., Janvier, M., Rippka, R., Stanier, R. Y. 1979. *J. Gen. Microbiol.* 111:73–85
164. Herdman, M., Janvier, M., Waterbury, J. B., Rippka, R., Stanier, R. Y., Man-

del, M. 1979. *J. Gen. Microbiol.* 111: 63–71
165. Herrmann, V., Jüttner, F. 1977. *Analy. Biochem.* 78:365–73
166. Hinze, G. 1903. *Ber. Dtsch. Bot. Ges.* 21:394–98
167. Ho, K. K., Ulrich, E. L., Krogmann, D. W., Gomez-Lojero, C. 1979. *Biochim. Biophys. Acta* 545:236–48
168. Hoare, D. S., Hoare, S. L., Moore, R. B. 1967. *J. Gen. Microbiol.* 49:351–70
169. Holm-Hansen, O., Brown, G. W. 1963. *Plant Cell Physiol.* 4:299–306
170. Holton, R. W., Myers, J. 1963. *Science* 142:234–35
171. Holton, R. W., Myers, J. 1967. *Biochim. Biophys. Acta* 131:375–84
172. Holton, R. W., Myers, J. 1967. *Biochim. Biophys. Acta* 131:362–74
173. Hood, E. E., Armour, S., Ownby, J. D., Handa, A. K., Bressan, R. A. 1979. *Biochim. Biophys. Acta.* 588:193–200
174. Hood, W., Leaver, A. G., Carr, N. G. 1969. *Biochem. J.* 114:12P–13P
175. Hutber, G. N., Hutson, K. G., Rogers, L. J. 1977. *FEMS Microbiol. Lett.* 1: 193–96
176. Hutber, G. N., Smith, A. J., Rogers, L. J. 1978. *Biochem. Soc. Trans.* 6: 1214–16
177. Hutson, K. G., Rogers, L. J., Haslett, B. G., Boulter, D., Cammack, R. 1978. *Biochem. J.* 172:465–77
178. Ihlenfeldt, M. J. A., Gibson, J. 1975. *Arch. Microbiol.* 102:23–28
179. Jackson, D. P., Ellms, J. W. 1896. *Rep. Mass. State Board Health*
180. Jansz, E. R., MacLean, F. I. 1973. *Can. J. Microbiol.* 19:497–504
181. Jones, G. W. 1977. *Recept. Recogn. Ser. B* 3:139–76
182. Jones, L. W., Bishop, N. I. 1976. *Plant Physiol.* 57:659–65
183. Joset-Espardellier, F., Astier, C., Evans, E. H., Carr, N. G. 1978. *FEMS Microbiol. Lett.* 4:261–64
184. Jüttner, F. 1979. *Z. Naturforsch. Teil C.* 34:186–91
185. Jüttner, F., Carr, N. G. 1976. *Int. Symp. Photosynth. Prokaryotes, 2nd, Dundee, UK,* pp. 121–23
186. Karagouni, A. D., Slater, J. H. 1979. *J. Gen. Microbiol.* 115:369–76
187. Kawamura, M., Mimura, M., Fujita, Y. 1979. *Plant Cell Physiol.* 20:697–705
188. Keirns, J. J., Wang, J. H. 1972. *J. Biol. Chem.* 247:7374–82
189. Kessler, E. 1974. In *Algal Physiology and Biochemistry,* ed. W. D. P. Stewart, Bot. Monogr., 10:456–73. Oxford: Blackwell
190. Keys, A. J., Bird, I. F., Cornelius, M. J., Lea, P. J., Wallsgrove, R. M., Miflin, B. J. 1978. *Nature* 275:741–43
191. Kondratieva, E. N. 1976. In *Microbial Energy Conversion,* ed. H. G. Schlegel, J. Barnea, pp. 205–16. Göttingen: Goltz KG
192. Krasnovsky, A. A. 1976. In *Research in Photobiology,* ed. A. Castellini. New York/London: Plenum
193. Krogmann, D. W. 1973. See Ref. 63, pp. 80–98
194. Kustu, S., Burton, D., Garcia, E., McCarter, L., McFarland, N. 1979. *Proc. Natl. Acad. Sci. USA* 76:4576–80
195. Ladha, J. K., Rowell, P., Stewart, W. D. P. 1978. *Biochem. Biophys. Res. Commun.* 83:688–96
196. Lang, N. J., Fay, P. 1971. *Proc. R. Soc. London Ser. B* 178:193–203
197. Lang, N. J., Simon, R. D., Wolk, C. P. 1972. *Arch. Microbiol.* 83:313–20
198. Lau, R. H., Doolittle, W. F. 1979. *J. Bacteriol.* 137:648–52
199. Lau, R. H., Mackenzie, M. M., Doolittle, W. F. 1977. *J. Bacteriol.* 132:771–78
200. Lau, R. H., Sapienza, C., Doolittle, W. F. 1980. In *Plasmids: Environmental Effects and Maintenance Mechanisms,* ed. K. R. Rozee, C. Stuttard. New York/London: Academic. In press
201. Lau, R. H., Sapienza, C., Doolittle, W. F. 1980. *Mol. Gen. Genet.* 178:203–11
202. Lawrie, A. C. 1979. *J. Bacteriol.* 139:115–19
203. Lawrie, A. C., Codd, G. A., Stewart, W. D. P. 1976. *Arch. Microbiol.* 107:15–24
204. Lea, P. J., Miflin, B. J. 1975. *Biochem. Soc. Trans.* 3:381–84
205. Leach, C. K., Carr, N. G. 1971. *Biochim. Biophys. Acta* 292:436–43
206. Lehmann, M., Wöber, G. 1976. *Arch. Microbiol.* 111:93–97
207. Lex, M., Carr, N. G. 1974. *Arch. Microbiol.* 101:161–67
208. Lex, M., Silvester, W. B., Stewart, W. D. P. 1972. *Proc. R. Soc. London Ser. B* 180:87–102
209. Lex, M., Stewart, W. D. P. 1973. *Biochim. Biophys. Acta* 292:436–43
210. Ley, A. C., Butler, W. L., Bryant, D. A., Glazer, A N. 1977. *Plant Physiol.* 59:974–80
211. Lim, S. T., Hennecke, H., Scott, D. B. 1979. *J. Bacteriol.* 139:256–63
212. Ljones, T., Burris, R. H. 1978. *Biochem. Biophys. Res. Commun.* 80:22–25
213. Lloyd, N. D. H., Canvin, D. T., Culver, D. A. 1977. *Plant Physiol.* 59:936–40
214. Lockau, W., Peterson, R. B., Wolk, C. P., Burris, R. H. 1978. *Biochim. Biophys. Acta* 502:298–308

215. Ludden, P. W., Burris, R. H. 1976. *Science* 194:424–26
216. Ludden, P. W., Burris, R. H. 1978. *Biochem. J.* 175:251–59
217. Lyne, R. L., Stewart, W. D. P. 1973. *Planta* 109:27–38
218. Masaki, R., Wada, K., Matsubara, H. 1979. *J. Biochem. Tokyo* 86:951–62
219. Mazur, B. J., Rice, D., Haselkorn, R. 1980. *Proc. Natl. Acad. Sci. USA* 77:186–90
220. McFadden, B. A. 1978. In *The Bacteria,* ed. N. Ornston, J. R. Sokatch, 6:219–304. New York: Academic
221. McFadden, B. A., Purohit, K. 1978. In *Photosynthetic Carbon Assimilation,* ed. H. W. Siegelman, G. Hind, pp. 179–207. New York: Plenum
222. Meeks, J. C., Wolk, C. P., Lockau, W., Schilling, N., Shaffer, P. W., Chien, W-S. 1978. *J. Bacteriol.* 134:125–30
223. Meeks, J. C., Wolk, C. P., Thomas, J., Lockau, W., Shaffer, P. W., Austin, S. M., Chien, W-S., Galonsky, A. 1977. *J. Biol. Chem.* 252:7894–7900
224. Meffert, M. A., Overbeck, J. 1979. *Arch. Hydrobiol.* 87:118–21
225. Meffert, M. A., Zimmermann-Telschow, H. 1979. *Arch. Hydrobiol.* 87: 125–38
226. Mellor, R., Hannah, F. J., Rowell, P., Stewart, W. D. P. 1980. In preparation
227. Metzer, H., Shapiro, M. B., Mosimann, J. E., Vinton, J. G. 1968. *Nature* 219:1166–68
228. Meyer, J., Kelley, B. C., Vignais, P. M. 1978. *FEBS Lett.* 85:224–28
229. Miller, S. S., Ausubel, F. M., Bogorad, L. 1979. *J. Bacteriol.* 140:246–50
230. Miller, S. S., Bogorad, L. 1978. *Plant Physiol.* 62:995–99
231. Mohanti, P., Govindjee, 1973. *Plant Cell Physiol.* 14:611–29
232. Morey, A. V., Krampitz, L. O. 1978. *Abstr. Ann. Meet. Am. Soc. Microbiol.* 1978. HI23, p. 124
233. Morowitz, L. S., Morowitz, H. J. 1978. *Biochem. Biophys. Res. Commun.* 82:727–30
234. Mörschel, E., Koller, K. P., Wehrmeyer, W., Schneider, H. 1977. *Cytobiologie Z. Exp. Zellforsch.* 16:118–29
235. Mullineaux, P. M., Chaplin, A. E., Gallon, J. R. 1979. *Biochem. Soc. Trans.* 7:1295–97
236. Murai, T., Katoh, T. 1975. *Plant Cell Physiol.* 16:789–97
237. Murphy, T. O., Lean, D. R. S., Nalewajko, C. 1976. *Science* 192:900–2
238. Nakamura, H. 1938. *Acta Phytochim.* 10:271–81
239. Neilson, A. H., Doudoroff, M. 1973. *Arch. Microbiol.* 89:15–22
240. Nordlund, S., Eriksson, U. 1979. *Biochim. Biophys. Acta* 547:429–37
241. Nordlund, S., Eriksson, U., Baltscheffsky, H. 1977. *Biochim. Biophys. Acta* 462:187–95
242. Nordlund, S., Eriksson, U., Baltscheffsky, H. 1978. *Biochim. Biophys. Acta* 504:248–54
243. Ohad, I., Clayton, R. K., Bogorad, L. 1979. *Proc. Natl. Acad. Sci. USA.* 76:5655–59
244. Ohad, I., Schneider, H. A. W., Gendel, S., Bogorad, L. 1980. *Plant Physiol.* 65:6–12
245. Ohmori, M., Hattori, A. 1978. *Arch. Microbiol.* 117:17–20
246. Okabe, K-I., Codd, G. A., Stewart, W. D. P. 1979. *Nature* 279:525–27
247. Okada, S., Kanematsu, S., Asada, K. 1979. *FEBS Lett.* 103:106–10
248. Olson, J. M. 1978. *Evol. Biol.* 11:1–37
249. Oren, A., Padan, E. 1978. *J. Bacteriol.* 133:558–63
250. Oren, A., Padan, E., Avron, M. 1977. *Proc. Natl. Acad. Sci. USA* 72:2152–56
251. Oren, A., Padan, E., Malkin, S. 1979. *Biochim. Biophys. Acta* 546:270–79
252. Oren, A., Shilo, M. 1979. *Arch. Microbiol.* 122:77–84
253. Ortego, T., Castillo, F., Cardenas, J. 1976. *Biochem. Biophys. Res. Commun.* 71:885–91
254. Ownby, J. D. 1977. *Planta* 136:277–79
255. Ownby, J. D., Shannahan, M., Hood, E. 1979. *J. Gen. Microbiol.* 110:255–61
256. Padan, E. 1979. *Ann. Rev. Plant Physiol.* 30:27–40
257. Padan, E. 1979. In *Advances in Microbial Ecology,* ed. M. Alexander, 3:1–48. New York/London: Plenum
258. Padan, E., Schuldiner, S. 1978. *J. Biol. Chem.* 253:3281–86
259. Paerl, H. W. 1978. *Microb. Ecol.* 4:215–31
260. Paerl, H. W., Kellar, P. E. 1978. In *Microbial Ecology,* ed. M. W. Loutit, J. A. R. Miles, pp. 68–75. Berlin: Springer
261. Pahel, G., Tyler, B. 1979. *Proc. Natl. Acad. Sci. USA* 76:4544–48
262. Parrott, L. M., Slater, J. H. 1980. *Arch. Microbiol.* In press
263. Pattnaik, H. 1966. *Ann. Bot. London* 30:231–38
264. Paul, J. S., Volcani, B. E. 1976. *Arch. Microbiol.* 110:247–52
265. Pearson, H. W., Howsley, R., Kjeldsen, C. K., Walsby, A. E. 1979. *FEMS Microbiol. Lett.* 5:163–67
266. Pedrosa, F. O., Dobereiner, J., Yates,

M. G. 1980. *J. Gen. Microbiol.* Submitted
267. Pelroy, R. A., Bassham, J. A. 1972. *Arch. Mikrobiol.* 86:25–38
268. Pelroy, R. A., Kirk, M. R., Bassham, J. A. 1976. *J. Bacteriol.* 128:623–32
269. Peschek, G. A. 1979. *FEBS Lett.* 106:34–38
270. Peschek, G. A. 1979. *Biochim. Biophys. Acta* 548:187–202
271. Peschek, G. A. 1979. *Biochim. Biophys. Acta* 548:203–15
272. Peschek, G. A. 1979. *Arch. Microbiol.* 123:81–92
273. Peschek, G. A. 1980. *Arch. Microbiol.* 125:123–32
274. Peschek, G. A. 1979. *FEMS Microbiol. Lett.* 6:371–74
275. Peters, G. A., Evans, W. R., Toia, R. E. 1976. *Plant Physiol.* 58:119–26
276. Peterson, R. B., Burris, R. H. 1976. *Arch. Microbiol.* 108:35–40
277. Peterson, R. B., Burris, R. H. 1978. *Arch. Microbiol.* 116:125–32
278. Peterson, R. B., Ke, B. 1979. See Ref. 9, Abstr. D9
279. Peterson, R. B., Wolk, C. P. 1978. *Proc. Natl. Acad. Sci. USA* 75:6271–75
280. Peterson, R. B., Wolk, C. P. 1978. *Plant Physiol.* 61:688–81
281. Pfennig, N. 1977. *Ann. Rev. Microbiol.* 31:275–90
282. Pullin, C. A., Brown, R. G., Evans, E. H. 1979. *FEBS Lett.* 101:110–12
283. Rai, A. N., Rowell, P., Stewart, W. D. P. 1980. *New Phytol.* In press
284. Ramirez, J. M., Del Campo, F. F., Paneque, A., Losada, M. 1966. *Biochim. Biophys. Acta* 118:58–71
285. Reinman, S., Thornber, J. P. 1979. *Biochim. Biophys. Acta* 547:188–97
286. Reynaud, P. 1977. *Cah. ORSTOM, Ser. Biol.* 12:109–16
287. Reynaud, P. 1978. *Cah. ORSTOM. Ser. Biol.* 13:143–55
288. Rhodes, D., Sims, A. P., Stewart, G. R. 1979. In *Nitrogen Assimilation of Plants,* ed. E. J. Hewitt, C. V. Cutting. pp. 501–20. New York/London: Academic
289. Rippka, R., Deruelles, J., Waterbury, J. B., Herdman, M., Stanier, R. Y. 1979. *J. Gen. Microbiol.* 111:1–61
290. Rippka, R., Stanier, R. Y. 1978. *J. Gen. Microbiol.* 105:83–94
291. Rippka, R., Stanier, R. Y. 1979. See Ref. 9, Abstr. A26
292. Rippka, R., Waterbury, J. B. 1977. *FEMS Microbiol. Lett.* 2:83–86
293. Rippka, R., Waterbury, J. B., Cohen-Bazire, G. 1974. *Arch. Microbiol.* 100:419–36
294. Roberts, T. M., Koths, K. E. 1976. *Cell* 9:551–57
295. Robinson, P. D., Martin, M. W., Tabita, F. R. 1979. *Biochemistry* 18:4453–58
296. Robson, R. L. 1979. *FEMS Microbiol. Lett.* 5:259–62
297. Robson, R. L. 1979. *Biochem. J.* 181: 569–75
298. Robson, R. L., Postgate, J. R. 1980. *Ann. Rev. Microbiol.* 34: In press
299. Rogerson, A. C. 1980. *Nature.* 284:563–65
300. Rowell, P., Diez, J., Apte, S. K., Stewart, W. D. P. 1980. *Biochim. Biophys. Acta.* Submitted
301. Rowell, P., Enticott, S., Stewart, W. D. P. 1977. *New Phytol.* 79:41–54
302. Rowell, P., Sampaio, M. J. A. M., Ladha, J. K., Stewart, W. D. P. 1979. *Arch. Microbiol.* 120:195–200
303. Rowell, P., Sampaio, M. J. A. M., Stewart, W. D. P. 1980. *Biochim. Biophys. Acta.* Submitted
304. Rowell, P., Stewart, W. D. P. 1976. *Arch. Microbiol.* 107:115–24
305. Rubin, P. M., Zetoony, E., McGovan, R. E. 1977. *Plant Physiol.* 60:407–11
306. Sallal, A-K. J., Codd, G. A. 1975. *FEBS Lett.* 56:230–34
307. Sampaio, M. J. A. M., Rowell, P., Stewart, W. D. P. 1979. *J. Gen. Microbiol.* 11:181–91
308. Sawhney, S. K., Nicholas, D. J. D. 1976. *Planta* 132:189–95
309. Schaeffer, F., Stanier, R. Y. 1978. *Arch. Microbiol.* 116:9–19
310. Scherings, G., Haaker, H., Veeger, C. 1977. *Eur. J. Biochem.* 77:621–30
311. Schlegel, H. G., Schneider, K., eds. 1978. *Hydrogenases: Their Catalytic Activity, Structure and Function.* Gottingen: Goltze KG 453 pp.
312. Schloesing, T., Laurent, E. 1892. *Ann. Inst. Pasteur Paris.* 6:824–40
313. Schmid, G. H., Lehmann-Kirk, U. 1977. *Arch. Microbiol.* 115:265–69
314. Schmidt, A. 1977. *FEMS Microbiol. Lett.* 1:137–40
315. Schmidt, A., Christen, U. 1978. *Planta* 140:239–44
316. Schmidt, A., Christen, U. 1979. *Z. Naturforsch. Teil C* 34:1272–74
317. Schurmann, P., Wolosuik, R. A. 1978. *Biochim. Biophys. Acta* 522:130–38
318. Schürmann, P., Wolosiuk, R. A., Breazeale, V. D., Buchanan, B. B. 1976. *Nature* 263:257–59
319. Seto, B. L., Mortenson, L. E. 1973. *Biochem. Biophys. Res. Commun.* 53: 419–23

320. Seto, B. L., Mortenson, L. E. 1974. *J. Bacteriol.* 117:805–12
321. Shanmugam, K. T., Streicher, S. L., Morandi, C., Ausubel, F., Goldberg, R. B., Valentine, R. E. 1976. In *Proc. 1st Int. Symp. Nitrogen Fixation,* ed. W. E. Newton, C. J. Nyman, pp. 313–26. Pullman: Wash. State Univ. Press
322. Shapiro, B. M., Stadtman, E. R. 1970. *Ann. Rev. Microbiol.* 24:501–24
323. Shilo, M., Oren, A., Friedberg, D. 1979. See Ref. 9, Abstr. A27
324. Shin, M., Sukenobu, M., Reiko, O., Kitazume, Y. 1977. *Biochim. Biophys. Acta* 460:85–93
325. Siefert, E. 1976. *Die fixierung von molekularem stickstoff bei phototrophen bakterien am beispiel von Rhodopseudomonas acidophila.* PhD thesis. Gottingen Univ. 149 pp.
326. Silver, W. S., Postgate, J. R. 1973. *J. Theor. Biol.* 40:1–10
327. Simon, R. D. 1977. *Arch. Microbiol.* 111:283–88
328. Simon, R. D. 1977. *J. Bacteriol.* 129:1154–55
329. Simon, R. D. 1977. *Abstr. Ann. Meet. Am. Soc. Microbiol.* 1977. I105, p. 172
330. Simon, R. D. 1978. *J. Bacteriol.* 136:414–18
331. Simpson, F. B., Neilands, J. B. 1976. *J. Phycol.* 12:44–48
332. Sims, A. P., Toone, J., Box, V. 1974. *J. Gen. Microbiol.* 80:485–89
333. Singer, R. A., Doolittle, W. F. 1975. *Nature* 253:650–51
334. Singh, H. N., Sonie, K. C. 1977. *Mutat. Res.* 43:205–12
335. Singh, H. N., Vaishanpayan, A., Sonie, K. C. 1978. *Mutat. Res.* 50:427–32
336. Singh, P. K. 1973. *Arch. Mikrobiol.* 92:59–62
337. Singh, P. K. 1977. *Biol. Plant* 19:156–57
338. Sinha, B. D., Kumar, H. D. 1973. *Ann. Bot. London* 37:673–79
339. Smarda, J., Cashavska, J., Komarek, J. 1979. *Arch. Hydrobiol.* Suppl. 56 (Algological Studies 23): 154–65
340. Smillie, R. M. 1965. *Plant Physiol.* 40:1124–28
341. Smillie, R. M. 1965. *Biochem. Biophys. Res. Commun.* 20:621–29
342. Smith, A. J., Hoare, D. 1977. *Bacteriol. Rev.* 41:419–48
343. Smith, R. V., Evans, M. C. W. 1970. *Nature* 225:1253–54
344. Smith, R. V., Noy, R. J., Evans, M. C. W. 1971. *Biochim. Biophys. Acta* 253:104–9
345. Sörensen, L., Halldal, P. 1977. *Photochem. Photobiol.* 26:511–18
346. Sörensen, L., Holmen, A. T., Halldal, P. 1978. *Physiol. Plant.* 42:425–27
347. Stacey, G., Bottomley, P. J., Van Baalen, C., Tabita, F. R. 1979. *J. Bacteriol.* 137:321–26
348. Stacey, G., Van Baalen, C., Tabita, F. R. 1977. *Arch. Microbiol.* 114:197–201
349. Stacey, G., Van Baalen, C., Tabita, F. R. 1977. *Arch. Biochem. Biophys.* 194:457–67
350. Stam, W. T., Venema, G. 1977. *Acta Bot. Neerl.* 26:327–42
351. Stanier, R. Y. 1977. *Carlsberg Res. Commun.* 42:77–98
352. Stanier, R. Y., Cohen-Bazire, G. 1977. *Ann. Rev. Microbiol.* 31:225–74
353. Stewart, G. R., Rhodes, D. 1977. In *Regulation of Enzyme Synthesis and Activity,* ed. H. Smith, pp. 1–22. London: Academic
354. Stewart, R., Auchterlonie, C. C., Codd, G. A. 1977. *Planta* 136:61–64
355. Stewart, W. D. P. 1971. *Plant Soil. Spec. Vol.* 1971, 377–91
356. Stewart, W. D. P. 1972. In *Taxonomy and Biology of Blue-green Algae,* ed. T. V. Desikachary, pp. 227–35. Madras: Univ. Press
357. Stewart, W. D. P. 1973. *Ann. Rev. Microbiol.* 27:283–316
358. Stewart, W. D. P. 1973. See Ref. 64, pp. 260–78
359. Stewart, W. D. P. 1974. In *The Biology of Nitrogen Fixation,* ed. A. Quispel, pp. 202–37. Amsterdam: North Holland
360. Stewart, W. D. P. 1977. In *A Treatise on Dinitrogen Fixation Section III,* ed. R. W. F. Hardy, W. S. Silver, pp. 63–123. New York: Wiley
361. Stewart, W. D. P. 1977. *Br. Phycol. J.* 12:89–115
362. Stewart, W. D. P. 1978. *Endeavour New Ser.* 2:170–79
363. Stewart, W. D. P. 1980. In *Methods for Evaluating Biological Nitrogen Fixation,* ed. F. J. Bergersen, pp. 583–635. London/New York: Wiley
364. Stewart, W. D. P., Codd, G. A. 1975. *Br. Phycol. J.* 10:273–78
365. Stewart, W. D. P., Fitzgerald, G. P., Burris, R. H. 1967. *Proc. Natl. Acad. Sci. USA* 58:2071–78
366. Stewart, W. D. P., Gallon, J. R. eds. 1980. *Nitrogen Fixation,* Ann. Proc. Phytochem. Soc. Eur. London/New York: Academic. In press
367. Stewart, W. D. P., Haystead, A., Dharmawardene, M. W. N. 1975. In *Nitrogen Fixation by Free-living Microorganisms,* ed. W. D. P. Stewart, pp. 129–58. London: Cambridge Univ. Press

368. Stewart, W. D. P., Haystead, A., Pearson, H. W. 1969. *Nature* 224:226–28
369. Stewart, W. D. P., Lex, M. 1970. *Arch. Mikrobiol.* 73:250–60
370. Stewart, W. D. P., Pearson, H. W. 1970. *Proc. R. Soc. London Ser. B* 175:293–311
371. Stewart, W. D. P., Pemble, M., Al-Ugaily, L. 1978. *Mitt. Int. Ver. Theor. Angew Limnol.* 21:224–47
372. Stewart, W. D. P., Rodgers, G. A. 1977. *New Phytol.* 78:459–71
373. Stewart, W. D. P., Rowell, P. 1975. *Biochem. Biophys. Res. Commun.* 65:846–56
374. Stewart, W. D. P., Rowell, P. 1977. *Nature* 265:371–72
375. Stewart, W. D. P., Rowell, P., Apte, S. K. 1977. See Ref. 11, pp. 287–307
376. Stewart, W. D. P., Rowell, P., Codd, G. A., Apte, S. K. 1978. *Proc. 4th Int. Congr. Photosynth. Reading, UK, 1977.* pp. 133–46
377. Stewart, W. D. P., Rowell, P., Ladha, J. K., Sampaio, M. J. A. M. 1979. In *Nitrogen Rice Symp. IRRI, Los Banos, Philippines.*, pp. 263--85
378. Stewart, W. D. P., Rowell, P., Lockhart, C. M. 1979. See Ref. 288, pp. 45–66
379. Stewart, W. D. P., Rowell, P., Rai, A. N. 1980. See Ref. 366. In press
380. Stewart, W. D. P., Singh, H. N. 1975. *Biochem. Biophys. Res. Commun.* 62:62–69
381. Streicher, S. L., Shanmugam, K. T., Ausubel, F., Morandi, C., Goldberg, R. B. 1974. *J. Bacteriol.* 120:815–21
382. Susor, W. A., Krogmann, D. W. 1966. *Biochim. Biophys. Acta* 120:65–72
383. Sutherland, J. M., Herdman, M., Stewart, W. D. P. 1979. *J. Gen. Microbiol.* 115:273–87
384. Sutherland, J. M., Reaston, J., Herdman, M. 1979. See Ref.9, Abstr. D24
385. Tabita, F. R., Gibson, J. L., Whitman, W. B., Martin, M. N., Robinson, P. D. 1979. See Ref. 9, Abstr. Ell
386. Tabita, F. R., Stevens, S. E. Jr., Gibson, J. L. 1976. *J. Bacteriol.* 125:531–39
387. Tabita, F. R., Stevens, S. E. Jr., Quijano, R. 1974. *Biochem. Biophys. Res. Commun.* 61:45–52
388. Taha, M. S. 1963. *Mikrobiologiya* 32:421–25
389. Taha, M. S. 1964. *Mikrobiologiya* 33:352–58
390. Takabe, T. 1977. *Agric. Biol. Chem.* 41:2255–60
391. Takabe, T., Nishimura, M., Akazawa, T. 1976. *Biochem. Biophys. Res. Commun.* 68:537–44
392. Tel-Or, E., Cammack, R., Rao, K. K., Rogers, L. J., Stewart, W. D. P., Hall, D. O. 1977. *Biochim. Biophys. Acta* 490:120–31
393. Tel-Or, E., Luijk, L. W., Packer, L. 1977. *FEBS Lett.* 78:49–51
394. Tel-Or, E., Luijk, L. W., Packer, L. 1978. *Arch. Biochem. Biophys.* 185:185–94
395. Tel-Or, E., Stewart, W. D. P. 1977. *Proc. R. Soc. London Ser. B* 198:61–86
396. Tetley, R. M., Bishop, N. I. 1979. *Biochim. Biophys. Acta* 546:43–53
397. Thomas, J. 1970. *Nature* 228:181–83
398. Thomas, J., Meeks, J. C., Wolk, C. P., Shaffer, P. W., Austin, S. M., Chien, W-S. 1977. *J. Bacteriol.* 129:1545–55
399. Thomas, J., Wolk, C. P., Shaffer, P. W., Austin, S. M., Galonsky, A. 1975. *Biochem. Biophys. Res. Commun.* 67:501–7
400. Tözum, S. R. D., Gallon, J. R. 1979. *J. Gen. Microbiol.* 111:313–26
401. Tsai, L. B., Mortenson, L. E. 1978. *Biochem. Biophys. Res. Commun.* 81:280–87
402. Tsang, M. L.-S., Schiff, J. A. 1975. *Plant Sci. Lett.* 4:301–7
403. Utkilen, H. C., Castenholz, R. W. 1979. See Ref. 9, Abstr. D12
404. Vaillancourt, S., Beauchemin-Newhouse, N., Cedergren, R. J. 1978. *Can. J. Microbiol.* 24:112–16
405. Van Baalen, C. 1962. *Bot. Mar.* 4:129–39
406. Van Baalen, C. 1973. See Ref. 64, pp. 201–13
407. Van den Hondel, C. A. M. J. J., Keegstra, W., Borrias, W. E., Van Arkel, G. A. 1979. *Plasmid* 2:323–33
408. Van den Hondel, C. A. M. J. J., Verbeek, S., Van der Ende, A., Weisbeek, P. J., Borrias, W. E., Van Arkel, G. A. 1980. *Proc. Natl. Acad. Sci. USA.* 77:1570–74
409. Wada, K., Hase, T., Tokunaga, H., Matsubara, H. 1975. *FEBS Lett.* 55:102–4
410. Wagner, W., Follman, H., Schmidt, A. 1978. *Z. Naturforsch. Teil C* 33:517–20
411. Walker, C. C., Yates, M. G. 1978. *Biochimie* 60:225–32
412. Walsby, A. E. 1974. *Br. Phycol. J.* 9:371–81
413. Walsby, A. E. 1974. *Br. Phycol. J.* 9:383–91
414. Walsby, A. E. 1978. *Symp. Soc. Gen. Microbiol.* 28:327–58
415. Watanabe, A. 1951. *Arch. Biochem. Biophys.* 34:50–55
416. Watanabe, A. 1959. *J. Gen. Appl. Microbiol.* 5:21–29

417. Waterbury, J. B., Stanier, R. Y. 1978. *Microbiol. Rev.* 42:2–44
418. Weare, N. M., Benemann, J. R. 1974. *J. Bacteriol.* 119:258–65
419. Weber, M., Wöber, G. 1975. *Carbohydr. Res.* 39:295–302
420. Weissman, J. C., Benemann, J. R. 1977. *Appl. Environ. Microbiol.* 33:123–31
421. White, A. W., Shilo, M. 1975. *Arch. Microbiol.* 102:123–27
422. Whitman, W. B., Martin, M. N., Tabita, F. R. 1979. *J. Biol. Chem.* 254:10184–89
423. Winkenbach, F., Wolk, C. P. 1973. *Plant Physiol.* 52:480–83
424. Wolk, C. P. 1968. *J. Bacteriol.* 96: 2138–43
425. Wolk, C. P. 1979. In *Determinants of Spatial Organisation,* pp. 247–66. New York/London: Academic
426. Wolk, C. P. 1979. See Ref. 9, Abstr. D1
427. Wolk, C. P., Thomas, J., Shaffer, P. W., Austin, S. M., Galonsky, A. 1976. *J. Biol. Chem.* 251:5027–34
428. Wolk, C. P., Wojciuch, E. 1971. *Planta* 97:126–34
429. Wolk, C. P., Wojciuch, E. 1973. *Arch. Microbiol.* 91:91–95
430. Wolosiuk, R. A., Buchanan, B. B. 1977. *Nature* 266:565–67
431. Wolosiuk, R. A., Buchanan, B. B., Crawford, N. A. 1977. *FEBS Lett.* 81:253–54
432. Yamada, T., Sakaguchi, K. 1980. *Arch. Microbiol.* 124:161–67
433. Yoch, D. C., Carithers, R. P. 1979. *Microbiol. Rev.* 43:384–421
434. Yoch, D. C., Carithers, R. P., Arnon, D. I. 1978. *J. Bacteriol.* 136:1018–26

Ann. Rev. Microbiol. 1980. 34:537–57

ANTIBIOTICS FROM *MICROMONOSPORA* ❖1785

Gerald H. Wagman

Microbiological Sciences, Schering Corporation, Kenilworth, New Jersey 07033

Marvin J. Weinstein

Microbiological Sciences, Schering Corporation, Bloomfield, New Jersey 07003

CONTENTS

INTRODUCTION 538
AMINOGLYCOSIDES 539
Gentamicins 539
Sisomicin 540
Verdamicin 541
Antibiotic G-52 542
Antibiotic G-418 542
Antibiotic JI-20 543
Fortimicins 544
Neomycin 545
Antibiotic 460 545
Sagamicin 545
MACROLIDES 546
Megalomicins 546
Rosaramicin 547
Juvenimicins 548
M-4365 Complex 548
Erythromycin B 549
ANSAMYSINS 550
Halomicins 550
Rifamycins 551
EVERNINOMICINS 552
ACTINOMYCINS 552
MISCELLANEOUS ANTIBIOTICS 553
CONCLUDING REMARKS 555

0066-4227/80/1001-0537$01.00

INTRODUCTION

There are rare occasions in science when the obvious is conspicuously avoided. An example is the neglect of a relatively well-known group of microorganisms, the micromonospora, during the halcyon period of antibiotic research. The genus *Micromonospora* was initially described by Ørskov in 1923 (42) and expanded to a total of four species in 1932 by Jensen (22). Culturing the organism was not difficult. In 1930 Jensen (21) reported seven different media for the isolation of *Micromonospora,* none more complex than starch-casein agar or dextrose-asparagine agar. Kriss in 1939 (25) isolated eight strains of *Micromonospora* from Russian soils on artificial medium. Umbreit & McCoy (1941) surveyed Lake Mendota by plating on sodium caseinate agar and showed that 16% of the wet mud population was *Micromonospora* (49). Erikson (1941) studied 20 strains of *Micromonospora* from Lake Mendota in some detail on a medium consisting of a mineral salt solution with either cellulose, lignen, or chiten (9). Growth was abundant on chiten. In 1942 Welsch (73) reported the first antibiotic activity from *Micromonospora.* Colmer & McCoy in 1943 studied the *Micromonospora* in 13 Wisconsin lakes on a simple medium consisting of starch, casein, and salts (5). Waksman et al (1942) cultured a *Micromonospora* species on starch-tryptone agar (59), and this strain was reported to produce the antibiotic micromonosporin by Waksman et al in 1947 (58). In these studies, the organism grew well on glucose-starch agar and fermented in a starch tryptone medium. Fisher et al (1951) reported the production of actinomycin from a species of *Micromonospora* grown in submerged culture in synthetic medium (10). Taira & Fujii (1952) described the antibiotics Microcin A and B produced by a *Micromonospora* grown on a starch peptone medium (48). In a 1957 patent assigned to Charles Pfizer & Co. (47), a steroid transformation by *Micromonospora chalcea* grown in a medium consisting of N-Z-Amine, dextrose, and yeast extract was described.

These early studies, prior to the discovery of gentamicin [Weinstein et al, 1963 (63)] and other antibiotics from *Micromonospora,* indicate that this genus of microorganism was not difficult to cultivate, yet no extensive evaluation of their antibiotic-producing capabilities was made.

After the discovery of gentamicin by the Schering group in 1963, this little studied group of microorganisms was never again to be ignored as a source of new antibiotics. Since that time, representatives of practically every chemical family of antibiotics have been found to be produced by members of the genus *Micromonospora.*

For purposes of orientation, Figure 1 presents a selection of antibiotic types, the organisms which produce them, and the place of the *Micromonospora* among these antibiotic producers.

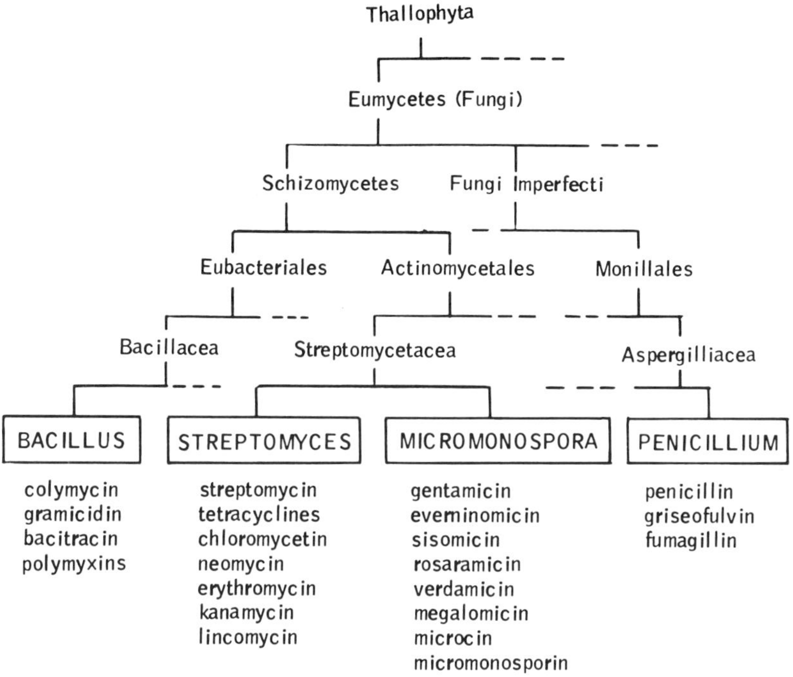

Figure 1 Place of *Micromonospora* among other antibiotic-producing organisms.

AMINOGLYCOSIDES

Gentamicins

Beginning with gentamicin, the aminoglycoside group of antibiotics has received the most attention and is discussed first. The gentamicin complex was first reported in 1963 from two newly discovered species (63), *Micromonospora purpurea* NRRL 2953 and *M. echinospora* NRRL 2985 (spiny spores) and two subspecies, *M. echinospora* subsp. *ferruginea* NRRL 2995 and subsp. *pallida* NRRL 2996. The complex was reported to consist of three components (54, 67) referred to as C_1, C_{1a}, and C_2 (Figure 2), as well as numerous minor components.

There was great interest in gentamicin, initially, because of its unusually wide spectrum of activity against Gram-positive and Gram-negative bacteria. Its outstanding characteristic is its unique potency against both *Proteus* and *Pseudomonas* species (61, 63, 71). It was superior to neomycin and kanamycin both in spectrum and safety. It was also superior to colistin, which is inactive against Gram-positive organisms as well as *Proteus* species. Gentamicin proved to be the better antibiotic, and because of its particular activity against both species of *Pseudomonas* and *Proteus*, in-

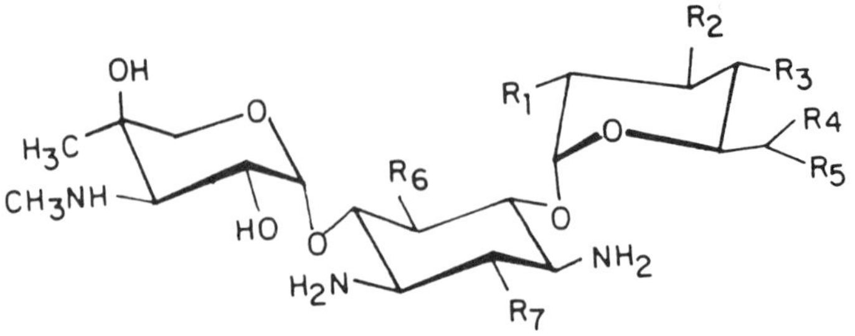

$R_1 = NH_2$; $R_6 = OH$; $R_7 = H$

	R_2	R_3	R_4	R_5
Gentamicin C_1	H	H	CH_3	$NHCH_3$
Gentamicin C_2	H	H	CH_3	NH_2
Gentamicin C_{1a}	H	H	H	NH_2
Gentamicin C_{2b} (Sagamicin)	H	H	H	$NHCH_3$
G-418	OH	OH	CH_3	OH
JI-20A	OH	OH	H	NH_2
JI-20B	OH	OH	CH_3	NH_2

Figure 2 Gentamicin and related structures.

cluding clinical strains resistant to other antibiotics, it received rapid clinical acceptance.

Since the first discovery by the Schering group of gentamicin production by *Micromonospora purpurea* and related species, gentamicin has also been reported to have been isolated from *M. purpurea* var. *violaceous* (13). *M. purpurea* var. *nigrescens* (12), and *M. sagamiensis* (39). The organisms initially found to produce gentamicin were described in 1964 by Luedemann & Brodsky (29) who established the validity of these novel species. Additional discussion is found in articles by Luedemann (27, 28).

Sisomicin

Sisomicin, an aminoglycoside antibiotic that resembles gentamicin C_{1a} but differs stereochemically and contains a double bond in one of the amino sugar constituents (Figure 3), was described by Weinstein et al (67) and Wagman et al (55) and is produced by *Micromonospora inyoensis* (NRRL 3292). This antibiotic, in contrast to gentamicin, is produced substantially as a single component. Its spectrum of activity appears to be quite similar to that of gentamicin both in vitro and in vivo. Although the acute toxicity is somewhat higher than that of gentamicin, the in vivo activity

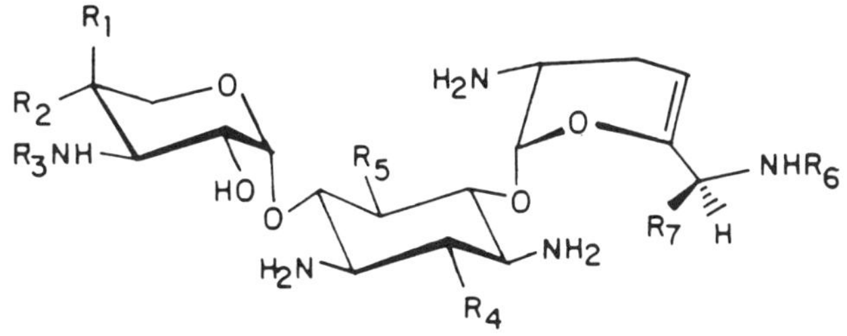

$R_1 = R_5 = OH$; $R_2 = R_3 = CH_3$; $R_4 = H$

	R_6	R_7
Sisomicin	H	H
Verdamicin	H	CH_3
G-52	CH_3	H

Figure 3 Sisomicin and related structures.

against a number of resistant organisms is better than that of the gentamicin complex.

Micromonospora inyoensis was isolated from soil obtained from the Inyo National Forest in California. Microscopic observation shows no aerial mycelia, the colonies appear viscid to poorly plicate, and growth is fair to poor on N-Z Amine agar, with a few well-developed colonies appearing late in the inoculation area. A faint reddish-brown diffusible pigment is associated with colonies on some plates. The mycelium is long, branched, regular, and nonseptate when examined by phase contrast microscopy, and it averages about 0.5 μm in diameter. Spores are occasionally borne singly on simple sporophores, 1–1.5 μm in diameter, ovoid to circular in shape, and rough walled.

Verdamicin

In 1975 Weinstein et al (70) described a new broad spectrum aminoglycoside named verdamicin which was produced by *Micromonospora grisea* (NRRL 3800). The nomenclature of the species and the name of the antibiotic were derived from the gray-green colony color that is typical of the producing organism on a variety of culture media. Under microscopic examination the mycelium of *M. grisea* appears long, sparingly branched, and averages 0.6 μm in diameter. Spores are relatively abundant and are borne singly on simple sporophores, 1–1.5 μm in diameter, which appear to be colored brown by transmitted light and to be rough walled. Sisomicin is co-produced with verdamicin by this culture. Chromatographically, verdamicin moves similarly to gentamicin C_2, but it differs from the latter by the presence of a double bond in one of the amino sugar constituents (Figure

3) and is chemically related to sisomicin. Verdamicin has a spectrum of activity similar to that of sisomicin and gentamicin or tobramycin against Gram-positive organisms in mice; it is 1.5 to over 3 times more active against Gram-negative organisms, with the exception of *Pseudomonas.* It displays slightly greater activity against *Pseudomonas* than is shown by gentamicin and somewhat less activity than is shown by tobramycin. Verdamicin was slightly more active against Gram-positive bacteria than sisomicin and was approximately as active as sisomicin against Gram-negative bacteria, with the exception of *Pseudomonas.* The major difference between verdamicin and these other antibiotics is that it was shown to be substantially less ataxic in cats than gentamicin [Weinstein et al (70)], producing ataxia in 26 days, as compared to 16 days for gentamicin at a dosage of 40 mg/kg 7 days per week.

Antibiotic G-52

Antibiotic G-52 is an aminoglycoside produced (32) by a species of *Micromonospora* named *M. zionensis* (NRRL 5466). G-52 has a spectrum of activity quite similar to that of both verdamicin and gentamicin but is differentiated from them by its increased activity against 6'-*N*-acetylating strains. The structure of antibiotic G-52 is described by Daniels et al (6) and shown in Figure 3. The producing organism, *M. zionensis,* was distinguished from other related *Micromonospora* species by color difference on a variety of media, by various chemical tests and particularly by the fact that it grows well on rhamnose as a carbohydrate source, compared to poor growth by related species. Antibiotic G-52 shows broad spectrum protection in mice but is slightly less active than gentamicin. The acute toxicity is comparable to gentamicin if administered via the intravenous and subcutaneous routes but is greater via the intraperitioneal route. As noted earlier, the organisms producing kanamycin acetyltransferase (AAC-6') are less effective against antibiotic G-52 as compared to verdamicin, sisomicin, and gentamicin, probably because of the steric hindrance at the 6th amino site of G-52. The structure/activity relationship of G-52 is discussed in the paper by Daniels (6).

Antibiotic G-418

Another aminoglycoside, antibiotic G-418, was reported by Wagman et al (56) and is produced by *Micromonospora rhodorangea* (NRRL 5326). The antibiotic has broad spectrum antibacterial activity similar to the gentamicins and other previously described aminoglycosides but is of particular interest because of its high activity against protozoa, amoeboe, tapeworm, and pinworm infections in mice.

The designation *M. rhodorangea* was based on the fact that the colonies have a red-orange appearance on a number of standard agar media. On a N-Z Amine type A-1% dextrose-1.5% agar medium, the growth of the organism is poor and spores are not produced; occasionally, chalmydospores are seen. Microscopic observation of the same culture indicates that the mycelia range from 0.4 to 0.8 μm in diameter and are sparsely branched. Although *M. rhodorangea* and *M. purpurea* are closely related, their growth responses on glucose asparagine agar, Emerson agar, tomato paste oatmeal agar, and czapek agar differ. Nitrate is reduced to nitrite by *M. rhodorangea* and by some strains of *M. purpurea.* The salt tolerance, critical for identification of Micromonosporae, is lower for *M. rhodorangea* than for *M. purpurea.* The structure of the antibiotic is shown in Figure 2.

As noted, antibiotic G-418 has activity against both protozoa and helminths. Loebenberg et al (26) described the in vitro and antiparasitic activity of G-418 against *Trichomonas vaginalis, Entamoeba histolytica, Hymenolepis nana, Sepatia obvelata,* and *Taenia* species. It was superior to paromomycin and metronidizole in cecal amebiasis. A high degree of activity, with a relatively short-term, low-dosage treatment, characterized this antibiotic. In vivo results indicated that the antibiotic was trichomonocidal at low levels but did not always effect cures. It appears to have promise as an anticestode agent because it is more active than paromomycin against *Hymenolepis nana* and is active as a single oral dose at low levels against *Taenia* species.

Antibiotic JI-20

In 1975 Ilavsky et al (20) were granted a patent on a new aminoglycoside from *M. purpurea* JI-20; the antibiotic is known as JI-20. A mutant strain of *M. purpurea* (NRRL 2953) produces the antibiotic JI-20 complex, which consists of two components, antibiotic JI-20A and antibiotic JI-20B, the structures of which are shown in Figure 2.

M. purpurea JI-20 (NRRL 5467) is similar in taxonomic and morphological properties to *M. purpurea* NRRL 2953. The major distinguishing strain characteristics are (*a*) it produces an antibiotic complex which differs substantially from that of the parent and (*b*) unlike *M. purpurea* which usually produces a purple pigment, the mutant strain may produce diffusible pigments of various shades of red, pink, yellow, brown, and gray-green.

Both antibiotics JI-20A and JI-20B have antibacterial activities similar to other aminoglycosides in this group and they have been shown to protect against a number of Gram-positive and Gram-negative infections in mice. However, the activity against certain resistant strains of *Pseudomonas* is not as high as is the activity of gentamicin, sisomicin, and related antibiotics (20).

Fortimicins

A new series of aminoglycosides known as the fortimicins, structures of which are shown in Figure 4, were described by Nara et al (37) in 1976 and in 1977 (36, 38). Data on extraction, purification of the compound, structural studies, and in vitro data were described respectively by Okachi et al (40), Egan et al (8), and Girolami (17) in 1977.

The fortimicins are produced by various strains of *Micromonospora olivoasterospora* (ATCC 21819,31010,31009). The typical strain of *M. olivoasterospora* (ATCC 21819) was originally identified as strain MK-70. This strain never forms true aerial mycelium as observed with *Streptomyces,* and on the surface of agar where there is good spore formation, there is observed an olive-green, wax-like and lustrous layer of spores. Mycelia are about 0.5 μm in diameter and are well developed and nonseptate. A single spore is formed at the end of each sporophore which is approximately 0.3–1.0 μm in length. The mature spores are circular and about 1 μm in diameter. Observation of the surfaces of the spores by electron microscopy shows an appearance like a star, since there are a large number of projections whose tip ends are somewhat round.

M. olivoasterospora has been differentiated from three gentamicin-producing strains essentially because of its olive to dark olive color and the fact that the MK-70 strain cannot utilize L-rhamnose, unlike the *M. echinospora* strains which are able to do so. The name of the species derives from the formation of oval or spherical spores with projections. Two variant strains previously mentioned are ATCC 31009 and 31010. These differ from the type strain because they have the ability to utilize D-galactose, D-fructose,

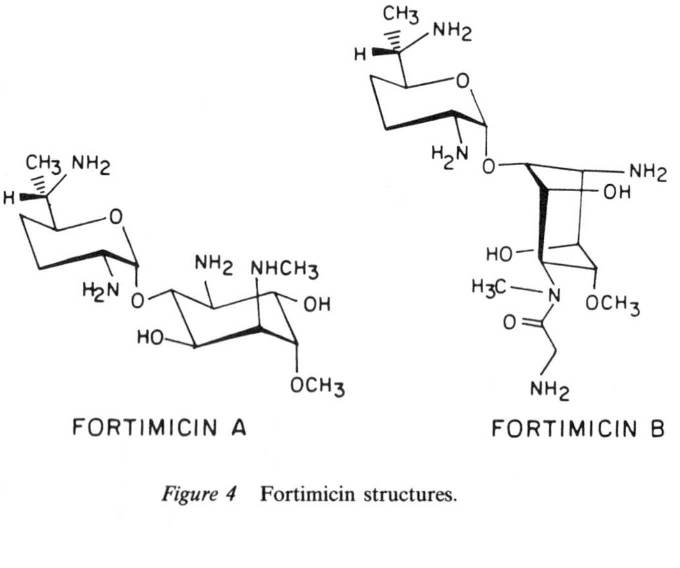

Figure 4 Fortimicin structures.

and D-xylose. Also, when cultured on various media they lack the ability to form mycelial spores.

Compared to amikacin, gentamicin, sagamicin, and tobramycin, fortimicin A appears to be the most active member of the fortimicin group against Enterobacteraciae and other organisms of medical significance. Fortimicin and amikacin had comparable levels of antimicrobial activity, although slightly lower than those of gentamicin, sagamicin, or tobramycin. Fortimicin displayed weak activity against *Pseudomonas aeruginosa* strains, although it appears to have many of the characteristics of other aminoglycoside antibiotics.

Neomycin

Wagman et al in 1973 reported (52) the production of neomycin B by a species of *Micromonospora* identified as *M.* sp. 69–683. Colonies of *M.* sp. 69–683 on an organic agar medium were plicate; initially reddish-orange, they turned a deep dark brown as abundant sporulation developed in the colony. A light yellow diffusible pigment was generally produced. The sporophore has a diameter of 0.5 μm and the spore surface appears minutely worty. Rupture of the thin cell wall facilitates release of the mature spore. Neomycin B is the first example of an important aminoglycoside produced by a *Streptomyces* species and by a *Micromonospora* species.

Antibiotic 460

The antibiotic 460 complex (66) was shown to be a group of aminoglycosides produced by a new species of *Micromonospora, M. chalcea* var. *flavida* (NRRL 3222). Microscopic examination of 21-day-old cultures of *M. chalcea* var. *flavida* on N-Z Amine-dextrose agar medium shows long, sparingly branched mycelia of approximately 0.5 μm in diameter. Spores are singly borne and not abundant. They are oval to spherical, about 1 μm in diameter, and appear brownish. The antibiotic complex has broad spectrum antimicrobial activity and is under investigation.

Sagamicin

Sagamicin, initially identified as XK-62-2, is produced as an an antibiotic complex by two strains of *Micromonospora, M. sagamiensis* ATCC 21803 and ATCC 21826 (39). Two major components, XK-62-1 and XK-62-2, were found to be identical with gentamicin C_{1a} and 6'-*N*-methyl gentamicin C_{1a}, respectively. The latter, named sagamicin, is identical to gentamicin C_{2b} (7), which is produced as a major component by a mutant of *M. purpurea,* designated as *M. purpurea* var. JI-33. The structure is shown in Figure 2.

MACROLIDES

Megalomicins

The first new micromonospora-produced macrolide antibiotic complex, which was named megalomicin, was isolated from fermentation broths of two strains of a previously undescribed species of *Micromonospora* (68, 69). The megalomicin complex consists of four components (31, 69) which have been identified as megalomicins A, B, C_1, and C_2. The structures of these compounds are shown in Figure 5.

The type species which produces the megalomicin complex is identified as *M. megalomicea* and the strains, which are natural color variants, are distinguished microscopically by the degree to which sporulation occurs (69). These strains have been designated NRRL 3274 and NRRL 3275; the former is referred to as *M. megalomicea* var. *megalomicea,* and the latter as *M. megalomicea* var. *nigra.*

Microscopic examination of 28-day-old cultures of *M. megalomicea* var. *megalomicea* on Czapek's sucrose agar indicates good growth, no aerial mycelia, and raised and plicate colonies of a soft, moist, and non-waxy

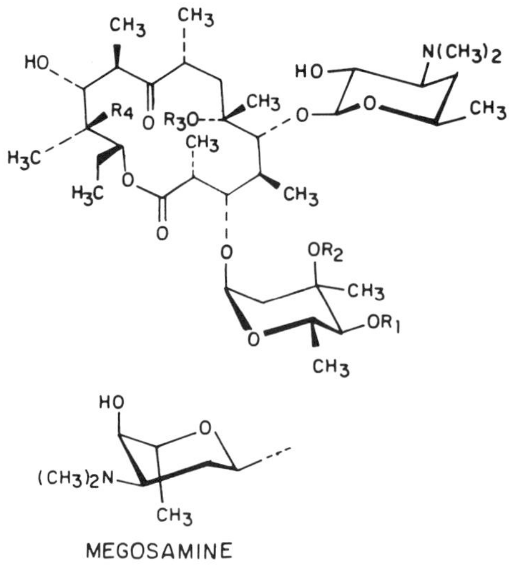

Megalomicin A	$R_1 = R_2 = H$; R_3 = megosamine; $R_4 = OH$
Megalomicin B	$R_1 = COCH_3$; $R_2 = H$; R_3 = megosamine; $R_4 = OH$
Megalomicin C_1	$R_1 = R_2 = COCH_3$; R_3 = megosamine; $R_4 = OH$
Megalomicin C_2	$R_1 = COCO_2CH_3$; $R_2 = COCH_3$; R_3 = megosamine; $R_4 = OH$

Figure 5 Megalomicin structures.

consistency producing no diffusible pigments. Microscopic examination shows a regular mycelium composed of long, branched filaments approximately 0.6 μm in diameter. Spores are infrequently found. *M. megalomicea* var. *nigra* grown in the same medium under the same conditions is characterized by good growth exhibiting the gross colony characteristics of the previous strain, except for the color, which is black (62). Microscopic observations indicate that the culture displays the same pattern as the previous strain. In this strain, however, spores are very abundant and are randomly produced throughout the mycelium. The spores are ovoid to spherical in shape, with a diameter of 0.7–1.0 μm, and are dark brown when mature.

Like other macrolides, the complex is primarily active against Gram-positive bacteria and is more active at an alkaline pH. Of the four known components, megalomicin A has been studied most extensively (69).

Megalomicin A has activity equal to or slightly less than that of erythromycin, both in vitro and in vivo. In dogs that were dosed orally, it was better tolerated and gave higher peak serum levels with a much greater duration then did erythromycin. Activity was not demonstrated in humans, however, and the antibiotic was not pursued further.

Rosaramicin

The antibiotic rosaramicin, formally named rosamicin, is a macrolide antibiotic unrelated to megalomicin but closely related to cirramycin A_1. It is produced by a newly identified species of *Micromonospora* named *M. rosaria* NRRL 3178 (57).

On an agar medium consisting of N-Z-Amine and dextrose, no aerial mycelia are evident microscopically; colonies are slightly raised, granular to weakly folded. Growth is fair, glistening, and no diffusible pigment is produced. However, on an agar medium composed of yeast extract and glucose a rose-colored diffusible pigment is produced—thus, the derivation of the antibiotic's name. The mycelia are regularly branched, averaging 10–20 μm in length and 0.6 μm in diameter; numerous chlamydospores are produced, up to 2 μm in diameter. Conidia are not observed on N-Z Amine medium. The structure of rosaramicin is shown in Figure 6.

The results of in vitro tests in which rosaramicin was compared with erythromicin and megalomicin A demonstrate that it has a broad antibacterial spectrum in vitro, with greatest activity against Gram-positive bacteria. It is also active against gonococci (43). Its activity against Gram-negative bacteria appears to be greater than that evidenced by erythomicin. It has less diminution of activity in the physiological pH range then erythromycin or megalomicin A. It also is active against a number

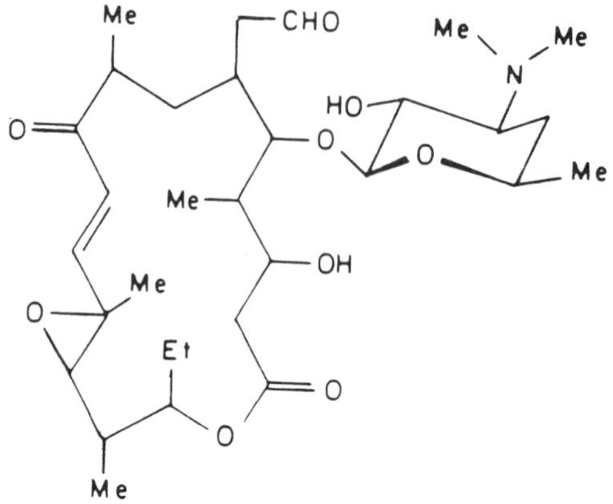

Figure 6 Rosaramicin structure.

of erythromycin-resistant strains of bacteria, as well as having much greater stability under acid conditions.

Juvenimicins

A new variety of *M. chalcea* named *M. chalcea* var. *izumensis* (ATCC 21561), isolated in Japan, has been shown to produce a group of antibiotics known as the juvenimicins, with the co-production of everninomicin (19).

From its morphological and cultural characteristics, *M. chalcea* var. *izumensis,* known as strain No. T-1124, was considered to belong to the species *Micromonspora* Φrskov. According to the taxonomic criteria of the genus *Micromonospora,* strain T-1124 resembled *M. chalcea* (Foulerton) Φrskov and *M. halophytica.*

Although the juvenimicin complex is composed of eight components, (juvenimicins A_1 through A_4 and B_1 through B_4) only A_2, A_3, A_4, B_1, and B_3 were isolated (19). Structures of some of these are shown in Figure 7. Juvenimicin A_3 showed the highest antibacterial activity against Gram-positive bacteria and some of the Gram-negative bacteria. It was inactive against a macrolide-resistant strain of *Staphylococcus aureus* FDA-209P, mycobacteria, fungi, and yeasts. The other components showed about one quarter to one twentieth of the activity of juvenimicin A_3.

M-4365 Complex

A series of basic 16-membered macrolide antibiotics, M-4365 A_1, A_2, A_3, G_1, G_2, and G_3 (11) were isolated from the culture broth of a newly discovered species of *Micromonospora, M. capillata* sp. nov. Antibiotic M-4365 A_2 and G_2 showed the strongest inhibitory activity against Gram-

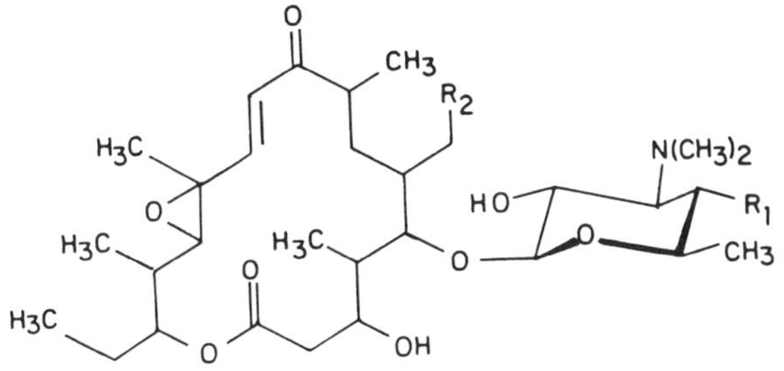

Juvenimicin A_2	$R_1 = R_2 = H$
Juvenimicin A_4	$R_1 = H; R_2 = CH_2OH$
M-4365A_1	$R_1 = H; R_2 = CH_3$

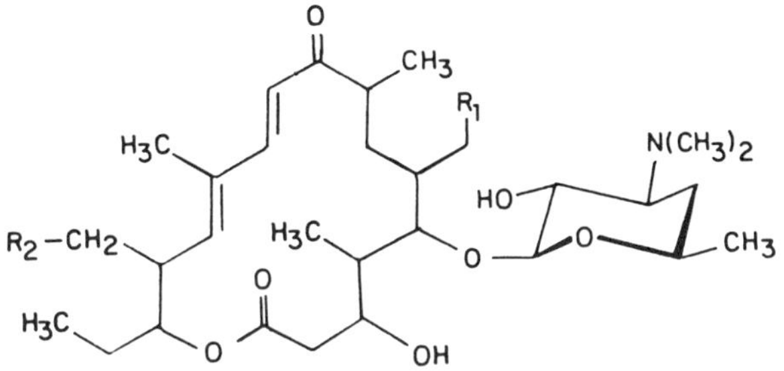

Juvenimicin B_1	$R_1 = CH_2OH; R_2 = H$
Juvenimicin B_3	$R_1 = CH_2OH; R_2 = OH$
M-4365G_1	$R_1 = CH_3; R_2 = H$
M-4365G_2	$R_1 = CHO; R_2 = H$

Figure 7 Structures of some juvenimicin and M-4365 components.

positive and Gram-negative bacteria. Structural studies indicated that A_2, A_3, and G_3 were identical with rosaramicin, juvenimicin A_4, and juvenimicin B_1 respectively, but that A_1, G_1, and G_2 were novel. Several of these structures [determined by Kinumaki et al (24)] are shown in Figure 7.

Erythromycin B

In 1976 Marquez et al (30a) reported that a new isolate, *Micromonospora* sp. 1225, produces erythromycin B. This was the first report of erythromicin production by an organism outside of the genus *Streptomyces.* The fermentation yielded an antibiotic complex that was shown to contain two minor components, one of which has been differentiated by comparative chromatography and appears to be identical to erythromycin A. A third trace component is also produced which was not identified.

ANSAMYSINS

The ansamysins are a relatively new class of antibiotics in which an aliphatic chain (ansa bridge) is connected to two nonadjacent positions of an aromatic nucleus. The halomicins and rifamycins are members of one of the two ansamycin subgroups in which the ansa bridge is attached to a substituted naphthalene or naphthoquinone moity. Both of these antibiotics have been isolated from various species of *Micromonospora.*

Halomicins

In 1967 Weinstein et al (65) described the production of halomicin, a solvent extractable antibiotic, from two previously undescribed species of *Micromonospora,* specifically *M. halophytica* (NRRL 2998) and *M. halophytica* var. *nigra* (NRRL 3097). Halomicin was said to consist of at least four components that were separable by paper chromatography and resolved by partition chromatography on Chromsorb.® Structures of some of the halomycins were reported by Ganguly et al (13a, 15) and are shown in Figure 8.

M. halophytica is characterized by a long, branched mycelium, approximately 0.5 μm in diameter, and abundant sporulation. The spores are ellipsoidal to spherical and their largest diameter averages 1.2 μm. In older cultures, the spores appear smooth walled and colored; they appear to be borne randomly on short or long sporophores. *M. halophytica* var. *nigra* is differentiated from the type species by the fact that its growth on many agar media is initially orange but, as sporulation progresses, it turns to olive-brown and eventually black. The copious black sporulation layer typical of

HALOMICINS	R_1	R_2
A	H	OH
B	H	H
C	OH	H

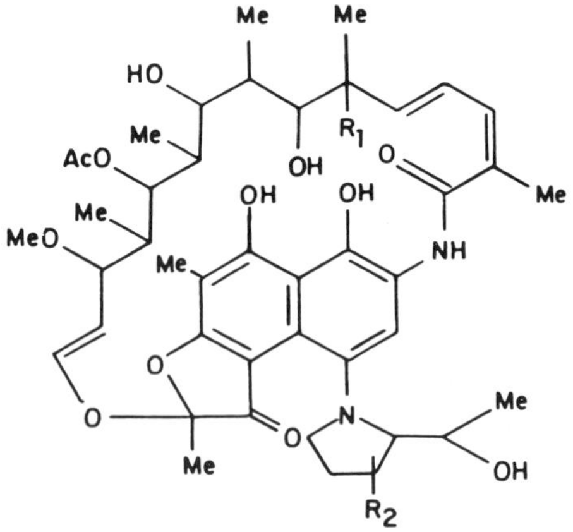

Figure 8 Halomicin structures.

this culture easily distinguishes it from the light brown to brown sporulation layer present in *M. halophytica.*

Halomicins A, B, C, and D have similar spectra against Gram-positive bacteria and *Mycobacterium tuberculosis.* They have no activity against Gram-negative bacteria. Of the four components, halomicin C appeared to be the most potent because of its activity and high stability, and it was studied in some depth in in vivo studies. Investigations are still in progress on this antibiotic complex.

Rifamycins

The rifamycin complex is produced by *Nocardia mediterraniae* (initially considered to belong to the genus *Streptomyces*), one of whose components is rifamycin B. Rifamycin B is essentially inactive against bacteria; however, when allowed to stand in aqueous solution in the presence of air, it yields rifamycin O, which can be converted under acidic pH to the highly active antibacterial compound named rifamycin S. Upon reduction using ascorbic acid, rifamycin S yields another active antibacterial compound, rifamycin SV. The structures are shown in Figure 9.

It was reported that a species of *Micromonospora, M. ellipsospora* 71372 (NRRL 8021), produces rifamycin SV when fermented under submerged aerobic conditions in the presence of a variety of assimilable sources of carbon and nitrogen (72). Initially *M. ellipsospora* was classified as a species of the genus *Micromonospora* on the basis of whole cell analysis. On the basis of growth and physiological properties, it was determined to be a new species. The whole cell analysis revealed that the microorganism contained *meso*-diaminopimelic acid, xylose, and arabinose as characteristic chemical components. The microorganism was unique at the time, because it was the

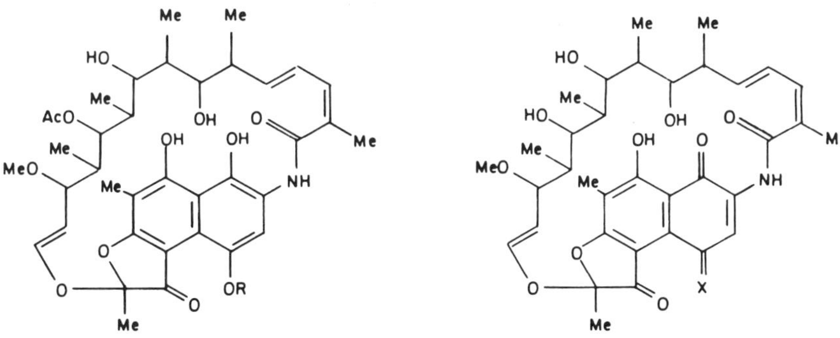

RIFAMYCIN B: R = CH_2CO_2H
RIFAMYCIN SV: R = H

RIFAMYCIN O: X = OCH_2COO
RIFAMYCIN S: X = O

Figure 9 Rifamycin structures.

only species of the genus *Micromonospora* known to produce a rifamycin.

Somewhat after the discovery of the production of rifamycin by *M. ellipsospora,* Chinese investigators reported rifamycin production by a new organism, *M. rifamycetica* (44). Celmer et al reported (4) the production of rifamycin S, SV, and the three methylthiorifamycin derivatives of rifamycin S and SV by *M. lacustris* sp. nov. Routien (ATCC 21975). Similarly, the discovery was made of the production of rifamycin S and SV by *M. chalcea* ATCC 21994 (3). Thus, it appears that a variety of species of *Micromonospora* are capable of producing the ansamycin group. Perhaps in the future, other ansamycins will be discovered from this group of organisms.

EVERNINOMICINS

Everninomicin is a solvent extractable antibiotic complex consisting of five components active against Gram-positive organisms (64). The everninomicins, labeled A through E, are oligosaccharide antibiotics and are produced by *M. carbonacea* (NRRL 2972) and *M. carbonacea* var. *aurantiaca* (NRRL 2997). The everninomicin-producing organisms are described by Ludemann & Brodsky (30) who established the validity of the species. The everninomicin complex is extracted from fermentation broth with organic solvents; the individual components can be resolved by partition chromatography (51). The structures of the everninomicins have been described by Ganguly et al (14) and are illustrated in Figure 10. The major antibiotic component of the complex, everninomicin D, is highly active against Gram-positive bacteria, including strains resistant to other antibiotics. In vivo protection in mice was obtained against lethal strains of *Streptococcus, Staphylococcus,* and *Diplococcus.* The production of the everninomicin complex by members of the genus *Micromonospora* and its chemical similarity to the antibiotic curamycin, produced by a *Streptomyces,* contributes to the speculation that other *Streptomyces*-type antibiotics of this nature may be expected to be isolated from this group of microorganisms.

ACTINOMYCINS

One of the first antibiotics isolated from a species of *Micromonospora* was initially identified as actinomycin A but probably was actinomycin D. This organism, identified as *M.* sp. 608 and isolated by Fisher et al in 1951 (10), had previously been isolated only from *Streptomyces* species. *M.* sp. 608 showed a similarity to *M. globosa.*

In 1976 Wagman et al isolated a new actinomycin complex from a *Micromonospora* species identified as *M. floridensis* NRRL 8020 which was found to produce at least 25 active components (53). *M. floridensis* can be

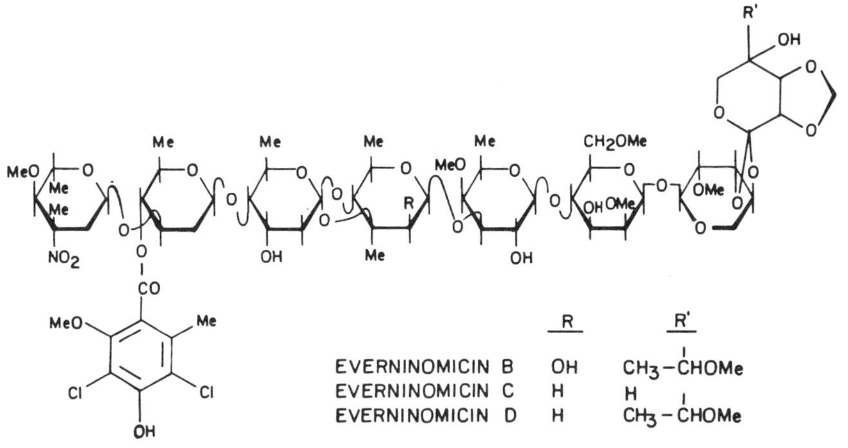

Figure 10 Everninomicin structures.

distinguished from the actinomycin-producing culture (reported to be similar to *M. globosa* by Fisher et al) by spore shape and size. Furthermore, whereas *M. globosa* was reported to be colorless, *M. floridensis* produces a yellow-orange, diffusible pigment. *M. globosa* has slender mycelia 0.7 μm in diameter with spherical conidia 1.4 μm in diameter, borne singly on short conidiophores in grape-like clusters. *M. floridensis* has much thinner mycelia, ranging from 0.4 to 0.6 μm in diameter, and the spores are borne predominantly on sympodially branched sporophores. Furthermore, the identified actinomycins produced by *M. floridensis* are different from those produced by the *Streptomyces* species, as described in the literature. Detailed studies on several of these actinomycins, specifically identified as Schering 1A, 1B, 1C, 6A, and 10, are summarized by Mauger & Katz (34). Much more work has yet to be done on these compounds. It is of interest that whereas so many new actinomycins have been produced from *Micromonospora,* none have been shown to be identical to the previously produced actinomycins from the *Streptomyces* group of organisms.

MISCELLANEOUS ANTIBIOTICS

Numerous other antibiotics have been reported recently from various species of *Micromonospora.* A very early antibiotic complex consisting of microcins A and B was reported by Taira & Fugii in 1952 (48); it was produced by an unidentified *Micromonospora* species. More recently, in 1976 Marquez et al (33) reported the production of a sulfur-containing peptide antibiotic by a new species of *Micromonospora* named *M. arborensis*

NRRL 8041. This complex, which consists of one major active component identified as SCH 18640 and at least three minor components, is extracted from the broth with a solvent such as ethyl acetate. The components are separated by preparative TLC on silica gel. SCH 18640 contains a number of amino acids (threonine, proline, alanine, cysteine, isoleucine, and tyrosine) and bears some resemblance to the thiostrepton group of antibiotics. It is highly active in vitro and has an excellent spectrum of activity against a variety of resistant Gram-positive bacteria. This antibiotic is still under investigation.

Other antibiotics have been reported in the last several years from *Micromonospora,* some of which are not well-defined chemically. These include chalcidin, produced by *M. chalcea* [Gause et al (16)]. This antibiotic is described as a complex of several components that are "probably peptides." Okuda & Awadaguchi reported that antibiotic M-92 was produced by *M. verruculosa* (41). Antibiotic 37.504 produced by *M. vividifaciens* sp. nov. Routien (1) is a solvent-extractable, amorphous yellow compound mainly active against Gram-positive organisms.

Antibiotic SF-1919, active against *Mycoplasma* and Gram-positive bacteria, was reported by Shomura et al to be produced by *M.* sp. SF-1919 (46). The active substance was extracted from the fermentation broth by solvent and was identified as a neutral white powder.

Antibiotic SF-1854 is produced by *M.* sp. SF-1854 (45). The antibiotic, an amorphous light powder, was effective against Gram-positive and Gram-negative bacteria. *M. melanogenes* PA-399 (23) produces an antibiotic that is effective against viruses and Gram-negative bacteria. Antibiotic T-43218, produced by *M. papulosus* No. T-42318 (18), is an acidic violet powder and is effective against Gram-positive and Gram-negative bacteria as well as acidophilic bacteria. It also has antitumor activity.

Another antibiotic from *Micromonospora* is primycin (50); it is produced by *M. galeriensis* isolated from the wax moth *Galeria melonella.* Bottromycin, a known antibiotic, has been isolated from a species of *M. chalcea* FERM-P1823 (35). The antibiotic was identified conclusively as bottromycin by melting point. UV spectra, elemental analysis, R_f values on silica gel and thin-layer chromatography, and amino acid analysis of the HCl hydrolysate and its antibiotic spectrum. Several antibiotics have been reported to be produced by *M. saitamica* sp. nov. Routien ATCC 31178 (2). These compounds are identified as 42,405, 42,752, 43,038, and 43,139. Antibiotic 42,405 has been determined to be identical with previously reported rubradirin produced by *Streptomyces achromogenes* var. *rubradiris* NRRL 3061. The other three antibiotic are novel. These antibiotics are active essentially against Gram-positive organisms, especially *Streptococci* and *Staphylococci.* The structures of these substances were not reported.

CONCLUDING REMARKS

It has often been stated that there are few or no new worthwhile antibiotics to be discovered because intensive screening over many years by research laboratories throughout the world has resulted in the examination of practically all antibiotic-producing soil microorganisms. It is true that many industrial and pharmaceutical companies have reinforced this misconception by reducing, if not entirely eliminating, their antibiotic screening efforts. Nevertheless, the tools and technology have been refined over the years and known antibiotics are constantly being rediscovered. Every year several new antibiotics are announced, although very few reach the clinicians' hands. Many of the recently discovered antibiotics are being utilized as "raw materials" for modification and production of substances which are active against organisms resistant to many of the antibiotics that are currently in use. Members of the genus *Micromonospora* have been known for many years, but very few species had been recognized, and even fewer species were known to produce antibiotic substances (60) until the discovery of gentamicin. Research by the Schering group has activated this very interesting genus and this review indicates that numerous antibiotics, most of which have been heretofore unknown (but including several known antibiotics), are capable of being produced by the *Micromonospora* group of organisms. We await further reports of newly discovered antibiotics from these organisms.

NOTE ADDED IN PROOF A complex of five novel macrolide antibiotics named mycinamycins have been isolated from a new species of *Micromonospora, M. griseorubida* sp. nov. (Satoi, S., Muto, N., Hayashi, M., Fujii, T., Otani, M. 1980. *J. Antibiot.* 33:364–76). This antibiotic may be of interest due to unusual in vivo absorption characteristics.

Literature Cited

1. Celmer, W. D., Cullen, W. P., Moppett, C. E., Oscarson, J. R., Routien, J. B., Shibakawa, R., Tone, J. 1976. *US Patent No. 3,991,183*
2. Celmer, W. D., Cullen, W. P., Moppett, C. E., Oscarson, J. R., Routien, J. B., Shibakawa, R., Tone, J. 1977. *US Patent No. 4,032,631*
3. Celmer, W. D., Cullen, W. P., Routien, J. B. 1975. *US Patent No. 3,884,763*
4. Celmer, W. D., Sciavolino, F. C., Cullen, W. P., Routien, J. B. 1975. *US Patent No. 3,914,218*
5. Colmer, A. R., McCoy, E. 1943. *Trans. Wis. Acad. Sci. Arts Lett.* 35:187–220
6. Daniels, P. J. L., Jaret, R. S., Nagabhushan, T. L., Turner, W. N. 1976. *J. Antibiot.* 29:488–91
7. Daniels, P. J. L., Luce, C., Nagabhushan, T. L., Jaret, R. S., Schumacher, D., Reimann, H., Ilavsky, J. 1975. *J. Antibiot.* 28:35–41
8. Egan, R. S., Stanaszek, R. S., Cirovic, M., Mueller, S. L., Tadanier, J., Martin, J. R., Collum, P., Goldstein, A. W., DeVault, R. L., Sinclair, A. C., Fager, E. E., Mitscher, L. A. 1977. *J. Antibiot.* 30:552–63
9. Erikson, D. 1941. *J. Bacteriol.* 41:277–300
10. Fisher, W. P., Charney, J., Bolhofer, W. A. 1951. *Antibiot. Chemother. Washington DC* 6:571–72

11. Fumari, T., Maezawa, I., Matsuzawa, N., Yano, S., Yamaguchi, T., Takeda, K., Okuda, T. 1977. *J. Antibiot.* 30:443–49
12. Gadó, I. 1975. *Hungary Patent No. 10, 972*
13. Ganchev, K. L. 1973. *Farmatsiya Sofia* 23:8–11
13a. Ganguly, A. K., Liu, Y. T., Sarre, O. Z., Szmulewicz, S. 1977. *J. Antibiot.* 30:625–27
14. Ganguly, A. K., Szmulewicz, S. 1975. *J. Antibiot.* 28:710–12
15. Ganguly, A. K., Szmulewicz, S., Sarre, O. Z., Greeves, D., Morton, J., McGlotten, J. 1974. *J. Chem. Soc. Chem. Commun.* pp. 395–96
16. Gause, G. F., Brazhnikova, M. G., Shorin, V. A., Maksinova, T. S., Olkhovatova, O. C., Kudinova, M. K., Vishnyakova, I. A., Pevzner, N. S., Shapovalova, S. P. 1970. *Antibiotiki Moscow* 15:483–86
17. Girolami, R. L., Stamm, J. M. 1977. *J. Antibiot.* 30:564–77
18. Hatano, K., Hasegawa, T., Higashide, E., Ito, M., Mitsuko, A. 1978. *Japan Patent No. 78,59,098*
19. Hatano, K., Higashide, E., Shibata, M. 1976. *J. Antibiot.* 30:1163–70
20. Ilavsky, J., Bayan, A. P., Charney, W., Reimann, H. 1975. *US Patent No. 3, 903,072*
21. Jensen, H. C. 1930. *Proc. Linn. Soc. N.S. W.* 55:231–48
22. Jensen, H. C. 1932. *Proc. Linn. Soc. N.S. W.* 57:173–80
23. Kawamura, Y., Mayama, S., Wakisada, Y., Matsumoto, K., Hattori, M., Matsuura, S., Shoji, J., Kondo, E. 1978. *Japan Patent No. 78,66,494*
24. Kinumaki, A., Harada, K., Suzuki, T., Suzuki, M., Okuda, T. 1977. *J. Antibiot.* 30:450–54
25. Kriss, A. E. 1939. *Mikrobiologiya* 8:178–85
26. Loebenberg, D., Counelis, M., Waitz, J. A. 1975. *Antimicrob. Agents Chemother.* 7:811–15
27. Luedemann, G. M. 1970. *Adv. Appl. Microbiol.* 11:101–33
28. Luedemann, G. M. 1971. *Trans. NY Acad. Sci.* 33:203–18
29. Luedemann, G. M., Brodsky, B. C. 1964. *Antimicrob. Agents Chemother.* 1963:116–24
30. Luedemann, G. M., Brodsky, B. C. 1965. *Antimicrob. Agents Chemother.* 1964:47–52
30a. Marquez, J. A., Kirschner, A., Truumees, I., Testa, R. T., Wagman, G. H., Weinstein, M. J. 1976. *Abstr. 172nd Am. Chem. Soc. Meet. MICR 55*
31. Marquez, J. A., Murawski, A., Wagman, G. H., Jaret, R. S., Reimann, H. 1969. *J. Antibiot.* 22:259–64
32. Marquez, J. A., Wagman, G. H., Testa, R. T., Waitz, J. A., Weinstein, M. J. 1976. *J. Antibiot.* 29:483–87
33. Marquez, J. A., Wagman, G. H., Testa, R. T., Weinstein, M. J. 1976. *Abstr. 16th Intersci. Conf. Antimicrob. Agents Chemother. No. 55*
34. Mauger, A. B., Katz, E. 1978. In *Antibiotics: Isolation, Separation and Purification,* ed. M. J. Weinstein, G. H. Wagman, pp. 1–38. Amsterdam/Oxford/New York: Elsevier. 771 pp.
35. Mizuno, K., Muto, N., Kamato, S., Asano, K. 1974. *Japan Patent No. 74, 116,297*
36. Nara, T., Okachi, R., Yamamoto, M., Mori, Y., Sato, M., Sugimoto, M., Shimizu, Y. 1977. *US Patent No. 4,048, 015*
37. Nara, T., Takasawa, S., Okachi, R., Kawamoto, I., Yamamoto, M. 1976. *US Patent No. 3,931,400*
38. Nara, T., Yamamoto, M., Kawamoto, I., Takayama, K., Okachi, R., Takasawa, S., Sato, T., Sato, S. 1977. *J. Antibiot.* 30:533–40
39. Okachi, R., Kawamoto, I., Takasawa, S., Yamamoto, M., Sato, S., Sato, T., Nara, T. 1974. *J. Antibiot.* 27:793–800
40. Okachi, R., Takasawa, S., Sato, T., Sato, S., Yamamoto, M., Kawamoto, I., Nara, T. 1977. *J. Antibiot.* 30:541–51
41. Okuda, A., Awadaguchi, S. 1976. *Japan Patent No. 76,33,195*
42. Ørskov, J. 1923. *Investigations Into the Morphology of the Ray Fungi.* Copenhagen: Levin & Munksgaard. 171 pp.
43. Sanders, C., Sanders, W. E. Jr. 1977. *Antimicrob. Agents Chemother.* 12: 293–94
44. Shanghai Res. Inst. Pharm. Ind. 1975. *Acta. Microbiol. Sin.* 15:114–18
45. Shomura, T., Ooba, K., Watanabe, H., Omoto, S., Tsuruoka, T., Kojima, M., Inoue, S., Niida, T. 1977. *Japan Patent No. 77,15,896*
46. Shomura, T., Watanabe, H., Yoshida, J., Totsugawa, K., Omoto, S., Kojima, M., Inoue, S. 1977. *Japan Patent No. 77,136,995*
47. Shull, G. 1957. *US Patent No. 2,809,919*
48. Taira, T., Fujii, S. 1952. *J. Antibiot.* 5:185–87
49. Umbreit, W. W., McCoy, E. 1941. *Symp. Hydrobiol. Madison, Wisconsin,* pp. 106–14

50. Valyi-Nagy, T., Kulcsar, G. 1969. *Acta. Biol. Acad. Sci. Hung.* 20:127–40
51. Wagman, G. H., Luedemann, G. M., Weinstein, M. J. 1965. *Antimicrob. Agents Chemother.* 1964:33–37
52. Wagman, G. H., Marquez, J. A., Watkins, P. D., Bailey, J. V., Gentile, F., Weinstein, M. J. 1973. *J. Antibiot.* 26:732–36
53. Wagman, G. H., Marquez, J. A., Watkins, P. D., Gentile, F., Murawski, A., Patel, M., Weinstein, M. J. 1976. *Antimicrob. Agents Chemother.* 9:465–69
54. Wagman, G. H., Marquez, J. A., Weinstein, M. J. 1968. *J. Chromatogr.* 34:210–15
55. Wagman, G. H., Testa, R. T., Marquez, J. A. 1970. *J. Antibiot.* 555–58
56. Wagman, G. H., Testa, R. T., Marquez, J. A., Weinstein, M. J. 1974. *Antimicrob. Agents Chemother.* 6:144–49
57. Wagman, G. H., Waitz, J. A., Marquez, J. A., Murawski, A., Oden, E. M., Testa, R. T., Weinstein, M. J. 1972. *J. Antibiot.* 25:641–45
58. Waksman, S. A., Geiger, W. B., Bugie, E. 1947. *J. Bacteriol.* 53:355–57
59. Waksman, S. A., Horning, E. S., Welsch, M., Woodruff, H. B. 1942. *Soil Sci.* 54:281–96
60. Waksman, S. A., Lechevalier, H. A. 1962. *The Actinomycetes, Vol. 3: Antibiotics of Actinomycetes,* p. 31. Baltimore, Md: Williams & Wilkins. 430 pp.
61. Weinstein, M. J. 1967. *1st Int. Gentamicin Symp.* Pt. 3:9–18
62. Weinstein, M. J., Luedemann, G. M. 1972. *US Patent No. 3,632,750*
63. Weinstein, M. J., Luedemann, G. M., Oden, E. M., Wagman, G. H. 1964. *Antimicrob. Agents Chemother.* 1963:1–7
64. Weinstein, M. J., Luedemann, G. M., Oden, E. M., Wagman, G. H. 1965. *Antimicrob. Agents Chemother.* 1964: 24–32
65. Weinstein, M. J., Luedemann, G. M., Oden, E. M., Wagman, G. H. 1968. *Antimicrob. Agents Chemother.* 1967: 435–41
66. Weinstein, M. J., Luedemann, G. M., Wagman, G. H., Marquez, J. A. 1969. *US Patent No. 3,454,696*
67. Weinstein, M. J., Marquez, J. A., Testa, R. T., Wagman, G. H., Oden, E. M., Waitz, J.A. 1970. *J. Antibiot.* 23:551–54
68. Weinstein, M. J., Wagman, G. H., Marquez, J. A., Oden, E. M., Testa, R. T., Waitz, J. A. 1969. *Antimicrob. Agents Chemother.* 1968:260–61
69. Weinstein, M. J., Wagman, G. H., Marquez, J. A., Testa, R. T., Oden, E. M., Waitz, J. A. 1969. *J. Antibiot.* 22:253–58
70. Weinstein, M. J., Wagman, G. H., Marquez, J. A., Testa, R. T., Waitz, J. A. 1975. *Antimicrob. Agents Chemother.* 7:246–49
71. Weinstein, M. J., Wagman, G. H., Oden, E. M., Marquez, J. A. 1967. *J. Bacteriol.* 94:789–90
72. Weinstein, M. J., Wagman, G. H., Patel, M. G., Marquez, J. A. 1975. *US Patent No. 3,901,764*
73. Welsch, M. 1942. *J. Bacteriol.* 44: 571–88

Ann. Rev. Microbiol. 1980. 34:559–92

NATURAL POPULATIONS OF THE GENUS *STAPHYLOCOCCUS*

❖1786

Wesley E. Kloos

Department of Genetics, North Carolina State University, Raleigh, North Carolina 27650

CONTENTS

INTRODUCTION ... 559
DEVELOPMENT OF TAXONOMIC CONCEPTS ... 560
Early Classification and the Micrococcus-Staphylococcus Controversy ... 561
Baird-Parker's Schemes and the Species-Biotype Concept ... 564
Subdivision of Staphylococcus aureus into Subspecies or Biotypes ... 566
MODERN TAXONOMY ... 567
Development of a Species Concept ... 567
Identity of Staphylococcus Species on the Basis of Simple Character Determinations ... 568
Cell Wall Composition ... 570
Electrophoretic Comparison of Iso-Functional Enzymes ... 571
Immunological Relationship of Proteins ... 572
DNA Relatedness ... 573
NATURAL HABITATS ... 576
Transient Versus Resident Populations ... 576
Populations on Primates ... 578
Populations on Domestic Ungulates ... 581
Populations on Carnivora ... 582
Populations on Rodents and Lagomorpha ... 583
Populations on Marsupials ... 583
Populations on Birds ... 584
CONCEPTS OF SPECIATION ... 584
Mechanisms of Adaptation ... 584
Hypothesis of Conjugate Evolution of Host and Parasite ... 586

INTRODUCTION

Staphylococci have received a great deal of attention over the past century. They cause a large number of infections in man and animals. Few, if any, of us have escaped some form of "staph" infection. These organisms are also

0066-4227/80/1001-0559$01.00

one of the major groups of bacteria inhabiting skin (98, 118, 137). The relationship between staphylococci and their hosts is an intimate one that cannot be ignored, especially when natural barriers are compromised through injury or by medical practices involving surgery, implantation of artificial prostheses, or immunosuppressive therapy.

Most research has been conducted with the pathogenic species *Staphylococcus aureus.* Comprehensive reviews of this species have been presented by Elek (43), Cohen (27), Jeljaszewicz (89, 90), and Noble & Somerville (137). Interest in other *Staphylococcus* species is now gaining considerable momentum and our view of the genus *Staphylococcus* is continuing to expand as more habitats are explored and more species and subspecies are discovered. The taxonomy of this group has undergone revision several times in the past decade, as a result of renewed interest and the availability of new tools to estimate phenotypic and genetic relationships. In this regard, the systematics of staphylococci has largely kept pace with taxonomic advances made with many other bacteria.

This article attempts to familarize the reader with taxonomic developments that have been made over the past century and then bring to focus an emerging new classification based on molecular approaches. It also presents the fragmentary information currently available on the structure of natural populations. This information is used in conjunction with nucleic acid hybridization data to formulate a concept for speciation.

DEVELOPMENT OF TAXONOMIC CONCEPTS

Events leading to Ogston's (154) discovery of the role of "grouped-micrococci" or staphylococci in suppuration are eloquently portrayed by Elek in his book, *Staphylococcus pyogenes and Its Relation to Disease* (43). Anyone interested in a comprehensive historical survey of the staphylococci should read his account. In 1881 Ogston used the word *staphylococcus* as a common name. Several others before him used such terms as *micrococci, microsporon,* or *monads* to identify the round organisms in pus. Rosenbach (175) is given credit for introducing the generic name *Staphylococcus* to accommodate these cluster-forming cocci. His work, published in 1884, marked the beginning of *Staphylococcus* systematics. Within a short time, it became apparent that the classification of staphylococci would be met with considerable difficulty and frustration. Elek (43) clearly demonstrated his understanding of one of the major problems facing the future of *Staphylococcus* systematics, and in particular their taxonomy, when he made the statement, "The medical bacteriologist is not very concerned as a rule with classification or nomenclature. To him the broad division into pathogens and nonpathogens overrides other considerations, and further subdivision matters only if it aids the recognition of a pathogen or enables him to trace the source of infection. The biologist aims to fit the pathogen into the general order of living creatures, caring little about disease and the microbial features that enter into its causation . . .The classification of staphylococci is much bedevilled by this fundamental difference in aim."

Early Classification and the Micrococcus-Staphylococcus Controversy

Rosenbach (175) classified species of staphylococci on the basis of colony color, a rather obvious and simple character to identify at the time. Elek (43) suggested that the underlying interest in color was due to Verneuil's (211) claim connecting the yellow appearance of pus with the color of growth of the infecting staphylococci, a connection also suggested by Ogston (155). Rosenbach called the orange-yellow staphylococci *Staphylococcus aureus* (or *S. pyogenes aureus*) and white staphylococci *S. albus* (or *S. pyogenes albus*). Passet (160) added the lemon-colored species *S. citreus.* Pigment as the sole criterion for species classification proved later to be unsatisfactory, mainly because it was not a genetically stable character in many strains.

It became readily apparent by the beginning of the twentieth century that staphylococci were not found solely in infections but were rather widespread in nature and were especially common on the skin of humans and a variety of animals (41, 66, 214, 224). As early as 1882 Ogston (155) was aware of the presence of staphylococci on the surfaces of the human body and questioned their innocence. For practical reasons at the time, medical bacteriologists placed major emphasis on distinguishing the recognized pathogenic species *S. aureus* from the presumed commensal staphylococci, first referred to as *S. albus* (175) and then later as *S. epidermidis albus* (214) or *S. epidermidis* (81). The distinction was of considerable importance, since the host and clinical specimens often carried both types of organisms. Contamination by the commensal group was facilitated by the occurrence of large populations extending over much of the body surface and by their presence in air and dust surrounding areas of host activity (66, 135, 136). The distinguishing characters used to identify *S. aureus* at the turn of the century were not completely reliable, though the most satisfactory criterion, *i.e.* their ability to clot blood plasma, was available but not noticed (116, 133). Von Darányi (212) drew attention to the practical value of the coagulating principle (coagulase) test to identify *S. aureus,* but the test did not gain general acceptance until later in the 1930s when the correlation between coagulase reaction and pathogenicity became apparent. Several other properties of *S. aureus* that were suspected of playing a role in pathogenicity—such as toxins, hemolysins, and leucocidin—were also investigated at the turn of the century, but had limited taxonomic value. A variety of biochemical tests including liquefaction of gelatin, clotting of milk, nitrate reduction, and carbohydrate fermentations were examined for their use in distinguishing pathogenic from nonpathogenic staphylococci and in subdividing staphylococci isolated from various habitats (41, 66, 223). Of these, fermentation of mannitol showed some degree of correlation with pathogenicity.

While medical bacteriologists were focusing their attention on a utilitarian classification to satisfy their objectives, other bacteriologists with presumably less bias were attempting to classify staphylococci according to their biological relationships and to fit them into the general order of bacteria. Even without an obvious bias or limited interest, the "pure" taxonomists did little to enhance our understanding of the natural relationships of staphylococci prior to the last two decades. By the end of the nineteenth century, all cocci were included in the one family Coccaceae. Flügge (58) placed the staphylococci, streptococci, and gonococci into one subdivision and the saprophytic micrococci into another subdivision. Migula (127) divided the family into the genera *Streptococcus, Micrococcus, Sarcina, Planococcus,* and *Planosarcina.* In his classification, staphylococci were grouped together with micrococci in the genus *Micrococcus,* first described by Cohn (28). This genus was subdivided on the basis of colony color and included some 200 species. Winslow & Rogers (222) divided the Coccaceae into two subfamilies: the Paracoccaceae, composed of staphylococci and streptococci, and the Metacoccaceae, composed of micrococci and sarcinas. Paracoccaceae were regarded as parasitic facultative anaerobes and Metacoccaceae as mainly aerobic saprophytes. The valid separation of staphylococci from micrococci made by these early taxonomists was not appreciated until the mid-1950s. Taxonomists following in their footsteps, during the period 1924–1951, added confusion to classification by lumping the two together, first into the genus *Micrococcus* (85, 86) and then into the genus *Staphylococcus* (193). In 1948 Abd-El-Malek & Gibson (1) concluded that dairy staphylococci and micrococci formed a continuous series, from the biochemically active pathogenic staphylococci, at one extreme, to the relatively inactive, saprophytic micrococci, at the other. They considered these organisms as members of a large group designated the *Staphylococcus-Micrococcus* complex. This concept influenced the course of future taxonomic studies for two decades.

Evans et al (51) were not satisfied with the lumping of staphylococci and micrococci into a single genus or complex, and they proposed separating these organisms on the basis of their relation to oxygen. Species that were facultative were placed in the genus *Staphylococcus;* species that were obligate aerobes were considered as *Micrococcus.* Their views completed a full cycle in the history of opinions concerning the relationship of staphylococci and micrococci and placed systematics once again on a fruitful course. Hill (80) later supported the separation of the two genera on the basis of an Adansonian analysis (198). In 1965 at the first meeting of the subcommittee on staphylococci and micrococci set up by the International Association of Microbiological Societies, a standard test for separating staphylococci from micrococci was introduced. It was based on the ability of staphylococci to grow and produce acid anaerobically from glucose in a peptone-yeast extract medium containing the pH indicator bromo-cresol purple (203). Thomas & Schuhardt (204) supported this separation, based on the susceptibility of these organisms to lysostaphin. Anaerobic glucose-fermenting staphylococci were attacked by this enzyme preparation, whereas aerobic glucose-negative micrococci and sarcinas were not attacked. The separation of aerobic, cubical packet-forming sarcinas from micrococci eventually lost the support of the taxonomists, who felt that packet formation, a somewhat variable character, should not be used as sole criterion to differentiate the two genera *Micrococcus* and *Sarcina* (49, 95, 110). The genus *Sarcina* currently contains only strict anaerobic species (21).

In the mid-1960s several investigators, including Silvestri & Hill (194), Bohacek et al (15), Auletta & Kennedy (6), and Rosypal et al (178), presented exciting data indicating that members of the genus *Staphylococcus* have a guanine plus cytosine (G+C) content in DNA within the range of 30 to 39 mol% and that members of the genus *Micrococcus* have a G+C content in DNA within the range of 63 to 73 mol%. Their studies presented very convincing evidence that these genera are not closely related. The fact that they are both composed of Gram-positive, catalase-positive cocci clearly does not, in itself, provide evidence of a close relationship. In general, there existed a good correlation between DNA base composition and acid formation from glucose of staphylococci and micrococci (132); however, some notable exceptions became evident, especially as new species populations were discovered and characterized (101, 102, 106, 183–186). Today, several new criteria, which correlate highly with DNA base composition, have been included in taxonomic schemes to separate staphylococci from micrococci. These include the chemical composition of cell walls (106, 183–186) and their serological differentiation (190, 191), the presence of aliphatic hydrocarbons in neutral lipids (in micrococci) (106), menaquinone patterns (88), growth in the presence of nitrofuran (by micrococci) (30), and susceptibility to lysostaphin and acid from glycerol in the presence of erythromycin (by staphylococci) (183, 185). The latter two criteria can form the basis for a simple test system to be used in the routine laboratory.

The very different DNA base composition, as reflected by G+C contents of near opposite extreme values tolerated by living organisms, would suggest that the genera *Staphylococcus* and *Micrococcus* should not be placed in the same family if organisms in one family are to be regarded as being more closely related to one another than to members of another family. The current family Micrococcaceae Pribram (14), which includes the genera *Staphylococcus, Micrococcus,* and *Planococcus,* in all probability should be disbanded. The relationship of each of these genera to genera in certain other families should be evaluated more closely. Stackebrandt & Woese (201) have recently compared the 16S ribosomal RNA sequences of several representative strains of Micrococcaceae to other bacteria and demonstrated a close relationship between *Micrococcus* and *Arthrobacter* of the coryneform group, a relationship previously speculated upon by others (106, 182). Their studies indicate clearly that *Staphylococcus, Micrococcus,* and *Planococcus* bear no special relationship to one another. It would be of interest to compare the nucleotide sequence relationships of *Staphylococcus* to members of the family Streptococcaceae, which would be a likely candidate for a parent group.

Baird-Parker's Schemes and the Species-Biotype Concept

During the 1960s while efforts were largely aimed at solving the *Micrococcus-Staphylococcus* controversy, several investigators were also engaged in designing taxonomic schemes to further subdivide each genus. We focus our discussion here on proposals made to divide the genus *Staphylococcus.* Hill (80), on the basis of an Adansonian classification and using names according to the Shaw et al (193) scheme, supported the inclusion of the two species *S. aureus* and *S. saprophyticus* in the genus *Staphylococcus.* He doubted the correctness of the name *S. saprophyticus,* as the group of strains examined corresponded to *S. epidermidis* (48). Furthermore, it was generally agreed at the time by medical and food bacteriologists that staphylococci should be divided into two species. *S. aureus* was largely defined as a staphylococcus that produced coagulase and could produce acid from mannitol anaerobically, whereas *S. epidermidis* was coagulase negative and unable to ferment mannitol (47, 48, 92).

Baird-Parker (9–12) conducted some of the most comprehensive taxonomic studies to emerge from this period. He examined many different characters in a large number of strains of staphylococci and micrococci isolated from a variety of sources such as foods, soil, water, air, humans, and various domestic animals. He first proposed dividing the staphylococci into six subgroups and the micrococci into seven subgroups (10). In a following study, he added an eighth subgroup to the micrococci to accommodate pink-pigmented strains (11). The characters chosen to delineate *Staphylococcus* subgroups included the coagulase reaction, phosphatase activity, aerobic and anaerobic acid production from mannitol, aerobic acid production from lactose and maltose, acetoin production, and growth at 10°C. Subgroup I contained the species *S. aureus* which was coagulase and phosphatase positive and usually produced acid from mannitol, aerobically and anaerobically. Baird-Parker did not originally assign a species name to the other subgroups (II through VI) (10, 11) but later included them under the name *S. epidermidis* and changed the subgroups to biotypes (12). Subgroup II (*S. epidermidis* biotype I) was composed of strains that were coagulase and mannitol negative, phosphatase, acetoin, and maltose positive, and usually lactose positive. Members of this biotype were isolated from human surfaces and household dust. This biotype, though redefined today by additional criteria, essentially became the species *S. epidermidis* sensu stricto (184, 186). Subgroup III (biotype 2) contained strains that were isolated frequently from pig skin and could be distinguished from biotype 1 strains by being acetoin and maltose negative. A number of pig and other animal strains fitting into this biotype are recognized today as coagulase-negative strains of *S. hyicus* (37). Subgroup IV (biotype 3) was acetoin positive and coagulase, phosphatase, lactose, and mannitol negative. Subgroup V (biotype 4) was acetoin, lactose, and maltose positive and coagulase, phosphatase, and mannitol negative. Subgroup VI (biotype 5) was acetoin positive and was usually mannitol positive and coagulase and phosphatase negative. This biotype could be further subdivided on the basis of aerobic acid production from lactose and maltose. In a much later scheme, Baird-Parker (13, 14) condensed the *S. epidermidis* biotypes 1 and 4 into biotype 1. Although strains in biotype 4 were phosphatase negative on the plate test (10), they were usually phosphatase positive by the more sensitive tube test of Pennock & Huddy (163), currently recommended for use. His original biotype 5 then became biotype 4.

After some debate by systematists that was largely initiated by the influx of data on the DNA base and cell wall composition of these organisms, Baird-Parker (13, 14) moved his original *Micrococcus* subgroups 1 through 4 into the genus *Staphylococcus* under the species *S. saprophyticus* and changed the subgroups into biotypes. Many of the strains that he included in *S. saprophyticus* biotype 3 are members of the currently recognized species *S. saprophyticus,* which has been recently amended (184). At least some of the strains included in *S. saprophyticus* biotype 4 are now recognized as members of the new species *S. xylosus* (184). Baird-Parker (12) considered the possibility that the rather discontinuous groups or biotypes listed under *S. epidermidis* (and perhaps also under *S. saprophyticus*) might deserve species rank; however, he chose at the time to take a conservative stance and not "further confuse the classification of staphylococci by giving these species names." His work was recognized by many bacteriologists as a reasonable approach to the classification of these organisms, and it served to provide the groundwork from which much of our current taxonomy followed.

Subdivision of Staphylococcus aureus into Subspecies or Biotypes

Meyer (124, 125) proposed that the species *S. aureus* could be subdivided into at least three varieties or subspecies according to the natural host origin. Those strains living on humans were designated *S. aureus var. hominis;* those from cattle, *S. aureus var. bovis;* and those from dogs, *S. aureus var. canis.* The characters chosen to differentiate the varieties included coagulase type (reaction with human or bovine plasma), crystal violet type, hemolysin type, nutrient markers (amino acid requirements), and phage pattern (172).

Hajek & Marsalek (73, 74) chose to use a modification of Baird-Parker's classification (10, 11), and they divided the species *S. aureus* into six biotypes, three of which corresponded closely to the varieties suggested by Meyer. These investigators together with Oeding and co-workers (148–153) demonstrated that on each different host species one biotype was predominant. Most *S. aureus* strains from humans were biotype A. They could be distinguished from strains of all other biotypes by being fibrinolysin positive, usually β-hemolysin negative, and typable by human, but not bovine, phages. Poultry and pig strains were usually biotype B. They were fibrinolysin negative, unable to coagulate bovine plasma, crystal violet type A, usually α- and β-hemolysin positive, and typable by human phages. Some pig strains are also typable by bovine phages and some poultry strains by poultry phages. Cattle and sheep strains were placed in biotype C. They could be distinguished from strains in biotype B by their ability to coagulate bovine plasma. Strains isolated from hares were placed in biotype D. They could be recognized by their lack of fibrinolysin activity, their inability to coagulate bovine plasma, and crystal violet type C. The predominant strains isolated from dogs, mink, and horses were placed in biotype E and those isolated from pigeons and foxes were placed in biotype F. Both of these biotypes included strains that failed to produce pigment or fibrinolysin, that were crystal violet type E, and that were not typable by human or bovine phages. Canine strains of biotype E could be typed by canine phages, and these and other strains in this biotype failed to coagulate human plasma. Strains of biotype E and F did not contain the cell wall β-*N*-acetylglucosaminyl ribitol teichoic acid (polysaccharide Aβ) found in strains of other biotypes. They were clearly set apart from *S. aureus* strains in the other biotypes and were eventually reclassified as members of the new species *S. intermedius* (69, 189).

The finding that certain populations of staphylococci tend to be rather host specific, as inferred earlier by Baird-Parker (9, 10) and brought to fruition in the above studies, provided some insight into the adaptability and complexity of the genus *Staphylococcus.* In a short time, other systematists began studying different host-adapted populations, which resulted in the discovery and introduction of new species and subspecies.

MODERN TAXONOMY

Development of a Species Concept

Bacterial species are defined without regard to the criterion of reproductive isolation, used extensively in the definition of species of sexually reproducing, higher organisms. Bacteria reproduce primarily by asexual means and for this reason alone we might expect that discontinuities would be promoted by the natural selection of various mutations accumulating in clones. Genetic exchange between bacteria, although perhaps a relatively infrequent event in nature, offers the possibility of another source of variation. Until we understand the modes of speciation utilized by bacteria, we will have some difficulty correlating bacterial species with those of higher organisms. For the time being, bacterial species are defined somewhat subjectively by estimating genetic divergence according to phenotypic character analysis and nucleic acid sequence relationships. Deoxyribonucleotide sequence divergence [e.g. determined by relative DNA binding or the thermal stability of DNA duplexes (17, 18)] is the most reliable criterion currently available. The choice of phenotypic characters used to define or identify a species may vary between certain genera or families, but all such characters should have a high predictive value in resolving DNA homology groups. Debate continues on just how much divergence should be required for a separate species status. Generally, organisms placed in separate species demonstrate relative DNA-binding values of less than 70% at an optimal criterion (nonrestrictive conditions) and usually more than 50% reduction in binding from these values at a stringent criterion (restrictive conditions) (17, 33, 91), though in certain genera these values may be slightly higher or lower (174, 192). Subpopulations of a species that can be distinguished on the basis of phenotypic characters and small, but significant, differences in DNA-binding values would be good candidates for subspecies ranking. For higher organisms, Mayr (120) defines a subspecies as an aggregate of local populations of a species, inhabiting a geographic subdivision of the range of the species, and differing taxonomically from other populations of the species. In the case of parasites, host range takes the place of the geographic range. A correspondence here to certain staphylococci and other host-adapted bacteria seems quite appropriate.

Not all bacteria may fall into discontinuous DNA homology groups for a variety of reasons. For example, they may represent evolutionary remnant populations exhibiting varying degrees of divergence, species (or even generic) hybrids produced by genetic exchange of large blocks of DNA or accumulations of DNA by multiple exchanges, or very rare species where the probability of finding more than one isolate in nature is rather low. The frequency of such "intermediate" organisms in natural populations is likely to be low compared to the species populations currently recognized, and their existence should not pose a threat to a sound species concept.

Today only a relatively small number of laboratories have the capability to conduct DNA hybridization studies to identify species or subspecies. Where such a capability does not exist, the investigator is often forced to make an identification solely on the basis of key phenotypic characters. In the routine laboratory or in large ecological studies, the characters selected may have to be relatively simple to test and small in number. Such restrictions may limit the degree of accuracy in identification, especially if one has to take into consideration the resolution of a relatively large number of species or subspecies. This situation often creates a conflict between the systematist and the applied bacteriologist as to what is an acceptable taxonomic scheme. Fortunately, in the case of the staphylococci, many of the characters used to distinguish species have a relatively high predictive value in identifying DNA homology groups, especially when used in specific combinations (37, 69, 101, 104, 105). Some of the taxonomic characters in use today were employed earlier to resolve *S. aureus* from other staphylococci or to resolve *S. epidermidis* or *S. saprophyticus* biotypes (9–14), but others have been added to the list to resolve additional species.

Identity of Staphylococcus Species on the Basis of Simple Character Determinations

The amended human species *S. epidermidis* and *S. saprophyticus* and the new human species *S. haemolyticus, S. hominis, S. warneri, S. capitis, S. cohnii, S. xylosus,* and *S. simulans* were recognized originally as representing discontinuous clusters of staphylococci on the basis of an extensive phenotypic character analysis (42, 44, 45, 50, 101, 102, 104, 184, 227, 228) and were confirmed later by DNA-DNA hybridization studies (96, 107, 168, 176, 187; K. H. Schleifer, personal communication; W. E. Kloos, unpublished data). Shortly after the formal designation of these species, Kloos & Schleifer (101) prepared a simplified taxonomic scheme for application in the routine laboratory. The key characters used in this scheme could be determined by simple tests and included coagulase activity, hemolysis, nitrate reduction, and aerobic acid production from β-D(-) fructose, D(+)xylose, L(+)arabinose, D(-)ribose, maltose, α-lactose, sucrose, D(+)-

trehalose, D-mannitol, and xylitol. Susceptibility to novobiocin and lysostaphin, phosphatase activity, anaerobic growth pattern in thioglycolate, and colony morphology were useful as secondary characters to improve accuracy in identification. The combination of characters used to identify species has been quite accurate in predicting correct DNA homology groups. Recently, several other simplified taxonomic schemes that identify fewer species and/or combine several into a single taxonomic unit have been proposed (55, 147, 209, 210). These are primarily designed to reduce the amount of effort required to identify those species or species groups of special medical interest. Some modification of existing schemes was necessary for identification of the new species *S. sciuri, S. intermedius,* and *S. hyicus* found on other mammals and/or birds (37, 69, 105, 189).

One must always be careful to avoid contamination and to use only pure cultures when making any of the character analyses. This is an important issue because staphylococci are often found associated with other genera and as mixed species populations in their natural habitats. This point may seem academic, but on several occasions our laboratory has received mixed cultures of two different species and even genera from clinical specimens that were submitted as a single isolate or species. Here, one of the problems may be that of recognizing a particular organism by its colony. If well isolated *Staphylococcus* colonies are allowed to grow on certain agars for three days at 34°C and 2 additional days at room temperature, they will develop features [e.g. profile, size, edge, internal structure, and pigment (when present)] that tend to be species specific (102, 104, 105, 184). Some experience and adequate controls are required for making an identification on the basis of colony morphology alone. By comparing colony morphology on P agar (106), on 5% bovine blood agar (101), and on 1% maltose agar (101), the accuracy in making a species identification is quite high. If a culture demonstrates more than one colony type, inocula should be taken from each one separately, whether or not the observer feels confident in making a species identification or if the colonies are suspected of being the same species.

As early as 1965, Evans (49) and Baird-Parker (11) expressed the need to expand the range of characters used for the taxonomy of staphylococci. They suggested probing different levels of cellular organization, from the molecular to the population level—an approach that was being pursued in the systematics of several other bacteria (29, 59, 117). Evans made the comment, "We need to . . . include (in taxonomy) such items as cell structure and composition, metabolic pathways for obtaining energy and synthesizing cell constituents, antigenic components, genetic composition and compatibility, as well as environmental effects. This will require application of both the concepts and methods of modern cytochemistry, serology, genetics, and molecular biology." Evans thereby showed considerable insight into what later proved to be useful taxonomic characters for the genus *Staphylococcus.* A few of the most useful complex biochemical characters used to distinguish species are discussed briefly in subsequent sections. Their complete application may not be feasible in most routine laboratories, but they are of considerable value to the research systematist with access to an appropriately equipped laboratory.

Cell Wall Composition

Staphylococcus species can be distinguished on the basis of their cell wall peptidoglycan and teichoic acid composition (37, 69, 102, 105, 145, 184, 189). Most early investigations into the cell wall composition of staphylococci were conducted in the laboratories of Archibald (4, 5), Baddiley (7, 8), Ghuysen (61, 62), and Tipper (206, 207). These biochemists introduced peptidoglycan and teichoic acid types as promising characters to identify *S. aureus* and several other staphylococcus groups. Later, Schleifer and co-workers (37, 69, 94, 102, 105, 183–186, 188) conducted comprehensive studies on the cell wall peptidoglycans and teichoic acids of all currently recognized species and clearly demonstrated the taxonomic value of these diverse characters. Their work played an important role in the discovery and definition of many new species.

The peptidoglycan type L-Lys-Gly$_{5-6}$ is found in *S. aureus, S. hyicus, S. simulans, S. cohnii,* and *S. xylosus* (37, 102, 184, 189). These species can be separated from one another on the basis of teichoic acid composition. *S. aureus* contains *N*-acetylglucosaminyl ribitol teichoic acid, *S. hyicus* contains *N*-acetylglucosaminyl glycerol teichoic acid, *S. simulans* contains glycerol teichoic acid with galactosamine as the glycosyl substituent, *S. cohnii* strains usually contain glycerol teichoic acid with glucose and glucosamine, and *S. xylosus* contains both ribitol and glycerol teichoic acids with glucosamine or occasionally glucose.

The peptidoglycan type L-Lys-Gly$_{3-5}$, L-Ser is characterized by having about 0.3 to 1.5 mol of glycine/mole of glutamic acid replaced by L-serine. This type is found in *S. intermedius, S. epidermidis, S. haemolyticus, S. hominis, S. warneri, S. capitis,* and *S. saprophyticus* (69, 102, 184, 189). Some of these species can be separated by their teichoic acids. *S. intermedius* contains glycerol teichoic acid with glucose or glucosamine as glycosyl substituents. The glucosamine residues are *N*-acetylated (69, 189). *S. epidermidis* and *S. warneri* contain glycerol teichoic acid with glucose, and *S. haemolyticus* and *S. hominis* contain glycerol teichoic acid with glucosamine. *S. capitis* contains glycerol teichoic acid without a detectable neutral sugar or additional amino sugar. Cell walls of this species contain rather low amounts of teichoic acid and have additional glutamic acid, probably in the form of a glutamic acid polymer. *S. saprophyticus* contains ribitol and glycerol teichoic acids with glucosamine or occasionally glucose.

The peptidoglycan type L-Lys-L-Ala-Gly_4 is found in *S. sciuri* subsp. *sciuri* and *S. sciuri* subsp. *lentus.* Based on recent DNA-DNA hybridization data, these subspecies should be given a separate species status and probably renamed *S. sciuri* and *S. lentus,* respectively (to be discussed in the section on DNA-DNA hybridization). In most strains of *S. sciuri,* small amounts (0.1 to 0.4 mol/mol of glutamic acid) of glycine are replaced by L-serine in the peptidoglycan. Both proposed species usually contain a glycerol teichoic acid with glucosamine as the glycosyl substituent, but in *S. sciuri* the concentration of free glycerol is usually low, which might indicate the presence of an atypical teichoic acid (4, 32).

The immunological properties of cell wall peptidoglycans and teichoic acids may be exploited for the serological differentiation of *Staphylococcus* species (40, 146,190, 191).

Electrophoretic Comparison of Iso-Functional Enzymes

Schleifer and co-workers (37, 102, 105, 184, 189) have suggested that the configuration of lactic acid, which is formed from glucose by fermentation, is a useful taxonomic character. Their data indicate that *S. epidermidis, S. simulans, S. intermedius, S. hyicus, S. capitis, S. xylosus, S. saprophyticus, S. cohnii,* and *S. sciuri* form predominantly the L-(+)-lactate isomer. *S. xylosus, S. saprophyticus, S. cohnii,* and *S. sciuri,* however, produce only small amounts of lactate compared to the other species. *S. hominis* and *S. haemolyticus* form predominantly the D-(-)-lactate isomer, though a small percentage of *S. hominis* strains produce both isomers in near equal amounts. *S. warneri* and *S. aureus* form both L-(+)- and D-(-)- lactate in sizable amounts.

Stockland & San Clemente (202) and Gotz & Schleifer (67, 68) have reported that the lactate dehydrogenase (LDH) enzymes responsible for the formation of lactate in staphylococci may exist as several different electrophoretic forms or isoenzymes. Gotz & Schleifer conducted their preliminary investigations with special reference to taxonomic implications and were able to demonstrate the presence of a single, but different, electrophoretic form of L-LDH in each of the species *S. epidermidis, S. intermedius, S. aureus,* and *S. warneri.* In contrast to the others, *S. epidermidis* and *S. intermedius* produced a fructose-1,6-diphosphate (FDP) activated L-LDH (67, 68, 186). Each of the species *S. aureus, S. warneri,* and *S. hominis* exhibits a different electrophoretic form of D-LDH. *S. hominis* and *S. haemolyticus* type strains contain D-LDHs with similar electrophoretic ability, but their enzymes can be distinguished on the basis of heat stability in the presence of NAD, NADH, and other stabilizing compounds.

Zimmerman & Kloos (228) reported that the species *S. simulans, S. capitis, S. epidermidis, S. hominis, S. aureus,* and *S. intermedius* (denoted in the reference as *Staphylococcus* sp. 1) could be distinguished from one another by the electrophoretic mobility of their esterases hydrolyzing α-naphthylacetate. The first four species demonstrate similar slow-migrating esterases but have different esterases appearing in the mid-region of gels. *S. capitis* may be distinguished further from *S. hominis* and *S. epidermidis* by its production of a faint, fast-migrating esterase band. The three species *S. haemolyticus, S. warneri,* and *S. sciuri* demonstrate only single, fast-migrating esterase bands of similar electrophoretic mobility, and, therefore, could not be distinguished from one another. *S. cohnii* and *S. xylosus* showed considerable esterase polytypism and polymorphism. Schleifer et al (189) determined that the complex esterase pattern of *S. intermedius* could distinguish this species from *S. aureus,* and in some cases could even distinguish strains of *S. intermedius* obtained from different host sources.

Several of the species can be identified by the electrophoretic mobility of their catalases (227). *S. hominis, S. warneri, S. epidermidis, S. capitis,* and *S. simulans* demonstrated distinctly different catalases. *S. xylosus, S. sciuri,* and *S. lentus* produced catalases of rather similar electrophoretic mobility.

Immunological Relationship of Proteins

Immunological studies aimed at determining structural homologies may provide information on isoenzyme identity and, in addition, may offer clues on phylogenetic relationships (60, 181). Protein homology studies have been commonly used by systematists to estimate phylogenetic relationships of higher organisms (24, 64, 65), and one would hope that the examination of selected bacterial proteins will also be successful in predicting prokaryotic evolutionary divergence. Schleifer et al (187) have recently reported on some studies that determined the immunological relatedness of catalases of various *Staphylococcus* species using double immunodiffusion and micro-complement fixation techniques. Their data indicate that the staphylococci form a well-defined genus with immunological distances not exceeding 90 ImD units. The catalases of *S. epidermidis, S. capitis,* and *S. warneri* were separated by less than 30 ImD units. The catalases from *S. xylosus* and *S. saprophyticus* are separated by a very low immunological distance of 5, whereas the catalase of *S. cohnii* is separated from that of *S. xylosus* by a distance of 40 ImD units. *S. simulans* and *S. sciuri* formed separate catalase homology groups, distinct from each other and other reference species, with immunological distances of 50 to 68 and 68 to 80 ImD units respectively. The immunological relationships determined for catalases of the various species correlated rather well with the genomic relationships determined by DNA-DNA hybridization studies.

DNA Relatedness

Recent DNA-DNA hybridization studies have estimated the genomic relationships of various staphylococci and have confirmed the existence of at least fifteen species (or widely divergent homology groups) within the genus *Staphylococcus* (Figure 1). Results obtained by several different laboratories using either the hydroxyapatite procedures of Brenner and co-workers (16, 17) or the nitrocellulose filter techniques of Gillespie & Spiegelman (63), as later modified by Denhardt (34), have been comparable and reproducible (37, 96, 107, 123, 176, 187).

Meyer & Schleifer (123) and Rosenblum & Tyrone (176) have determined that *S. aureus* (biotypes A to D) strains form a closely related group displaying over 75% relative binding (DNA homology) under restrictive conditions. *S. intermedius* (previously *S. aureus* biotypes E and F), another coagulase-positive species, demonstrates less than 15% DNA homology to *S. aureus* under the same conditions. Furthermore, it has been shown recently that *S. intermedius* contains a catalase that demonstrates only partial identity and high immunological distance values when compared to the catalase of *S. aureus* strains, which adds epigenetic evidence for a separate species status (M. Rupprecht and K. H. Schleifer, unpublished data). *S. hyicus,* a partial coagulase-positive species, can be distinguished on the basis of phenotypic characters and DNA homology (37, 164). This species has less than 20% DNA homology to *S. aureus* or *S. intermedius* under restrictive conditions. Several different subspecies populations can be discerned in *S. intermedius* and *S. hyicus* on the basis of DNA reassociation reactions, but not in *S. aureus* (37, 108, 123; W. E. Kloos and W. E. Phillips, unpublished data). Schleifer et al (187) and Kloos & Wolfshohl (96, 107, 108) have indicated that each of the coagulase-negative species *S. epidermidis, S. hominis, S. haemolyticus, S. capitis, S. warneri, S. saprophyticus, S. xylosus, S. cohnii, S. simulans,* and *S. sciuri* form separate DNA homology groups. Schleifer and co-workers showed that the above species had DNA homology values of 32% or less when compared to one another under restrictive conditions. Using somewhat different procedures and reassociation buffers to obtain restrictive conditions, Kloos and co-workers were able to demonstrate DNA homology values of less than 20%. Results in both laboratories have made it quite clear that the status of each species is sound. Some of the species are more closely related than others and may form species groups (103, 104). The *S. epidermidis* species group is composed of *S. epidermidis, S. haemolyticus, S. hominis, S. warneri* and *S. capitis;* the *S. saprophyticus* species group is composed of *S. saprophyticus, S. xylosus,* and *S. cohnii.* Schleifer et al (187) have suggested that the *S. epidermidis* species group can be further divided into one subgroup contain-

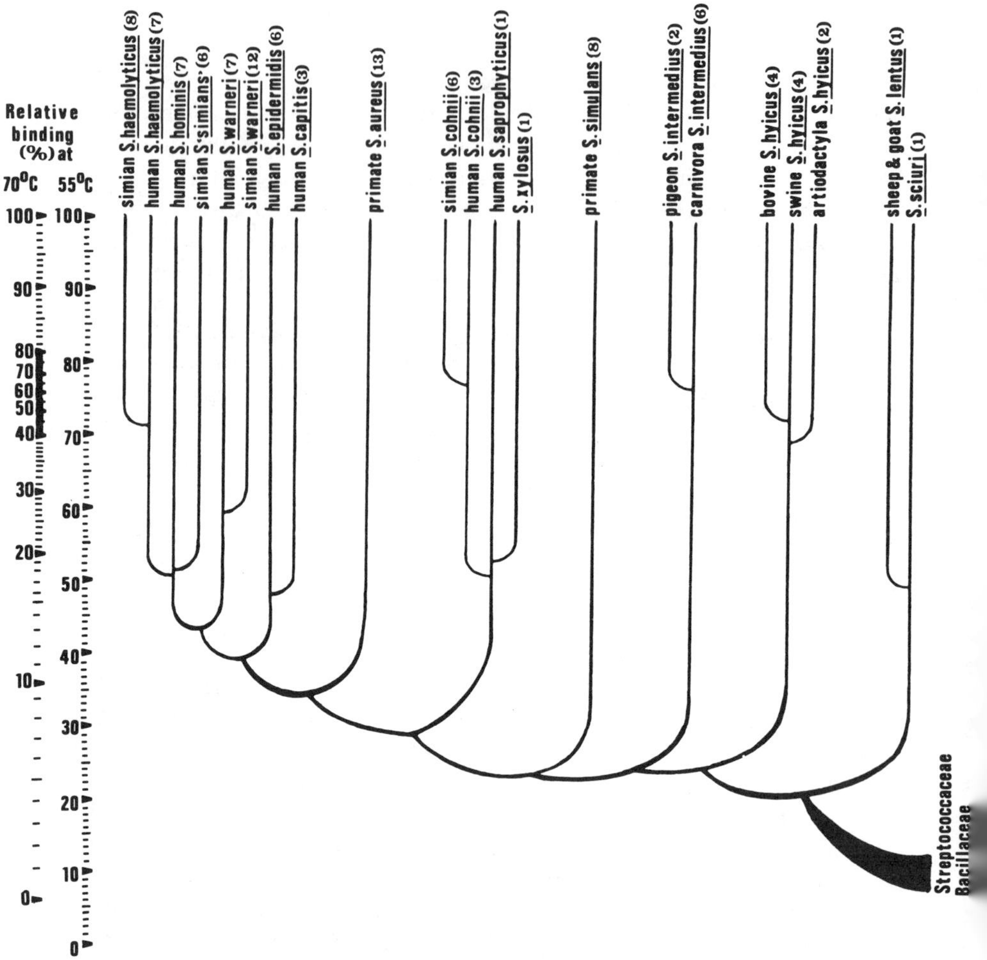

Figure 1 DNA homologies of known *Staphylococcus* species and subspecies based on relative DNA-binding values determined at nonrestrictive (55°C) and restrictive (70°C) conditions (17, 18). Results of reassociation reactions using pigeon and carnivora *S. intermedius* DNA and artiodactyla *S. hyicus* (subsp. *chromogenes*) DNA are from the work of Meyer & Schleifer (123) and Devriese et al (37), respectively. Other results were obtained by Kloos and co-workers (96, 107, 108; W. E. Kloos and J. F. Wolfshohl, unpublished data). The major natural host(s) is indicated before each species' name and indicates the source of strains. The *S. lentus* type strain was from a goat, the *S. sciuri* type strain was from a squirrel, and the *S. xylosus* type strain was from a human. The number of strains examined for each species or subspecies is shown in parentheses.

ing the species *S. epidermidis, S. warneri,* and *S. capitis* and another containing the species *S. hominis* and *S. haemolyticus.*

DNA-DNA hybridization studies have indicated the presence of human and nonhuman primate subspecies populations in the species *S. haemolyticus, S. warneri,* and *S. cohnii.* Kloos & Wolfshohl (107) determined that the mean homology of human and nonhuman primate *S. haemolyticus* DNA in reciprocal reactions under nonrestrictive conditions is 72 ± 3% and at restrictive conditions is 43 ± 6%, whereas between human and nonhuman primate *S. warneri* DNA homology values are 59 ± 6% and 26 ± 5%, respectively. The thermal stability of heterologous DNA duplexes formed by the DNA of each subspecies is significantly reduced (*S. haemolyticus* subspecies $\Delta T_{m(e)}$=9.2; *S. warneri* subspecies $\Delta T_{m(e)}$=12.0). The DNA divergence between human and nonhuman primate *S. warneri* strains is about borderline for what would be expected for a separate species status. They are, however, clearly more closely related to one another than to any other recognized species, and for this reason we choose to take a conservative stand and call them subspecies. Human and nonhuman primate *S. cohnii* strains appear to have diverged only slightly, as indicated by a mean DNA homology of 64 ± 11% at restrictive conditions (W. E. Kloos and J. F. Wolfshohl, unpublished data).

The few discrepancies in DNA relatedness reported for certain strains identified as *S. hominis, S. capitis, S. warneri,* and *S. cohnii* (168) have not been substantiated in our laboratory. We find that the reference strains *S. warneri* ATCC 27836 (AW25), *S. warneri* ATCC 27837 (RM130), *S. hominis* ATCC 27846 (MK129), *S. capitis* ATCC 27842 (MCSA11), and *S. cohnii* ATCC 29973 (DSM 20261, AW81) that have been questioned are correctly named according to phenotypic characterizations and DNA-DNA hybridization studies (W. E. Kloos, unpublished data). The reason for the discrepancies is unclear, though it is sometimes possible that, during processing, cultures may be mislabeled or become contaminated by other staphylococci. As an extra precaution, cultures may be checked for purity and compliance to original descriptions (when available) when they are first received and at the last step in processing, just prior to DNA isolation. Some investigators (55, 134) view the few alleged discrepancies as indications that a very close DNA homology exists between some of the species or that key phenotypic characters used to differentiate the coagulase-negative species are not satisfactory.

Preliminary studies on the DNA relatedness of *S. sciuri* subsp. *sciuri* and *S. sciuri* subsp. *lentus* indicate that these two subspecies should be given a separate species status (W. E. Kloos and J. F. Wolfshohl, unpublished data). Reassociation reactions performed under restrictive conditions between DNAs of these two groups have shown homologies of 20% or less; under nonrestrictive conditions DNA homologies were less than 50%. These species are more closely related to one another than to other staphylococci. Feltham (55) has suggested that *S. sciuri* (designated as groups P and R) be moved into a new genus *Cellobiosococcus* because of some unique phenotypic characters, including production of acid from D–(+)-cellobiose, amygdalin, and arbutin, oxidase activity and menaquinone pattern. However, DNA homologies with other species under nonrestrictive conditions and catalase immunological relationships do not clearly support this proposal.

Several new species of staphylococci are currently under investigation. DNA-DNA hybridization studies have identified a new species (tentatively designated *S. "simians"*), found living on nonhuman primates, that is a member of the large *S. epidermidis* species group and that displays a slightly closer relationship to *S. haemolyticus* and *S. hominis* than to other species of the group (W. E. Kloos and J. F. Wolfshohl, unpublished data). In support of the proposal of Schleifer et al (187), it would appear that *S. haemolyticus, S. hominis,* and *S. "simians"* form a distinctive subgroup. Recent studies by Schleifer and co-workers (94; K. H. Schleifer, personal communication) have shown that strains identified as *Peptococcus saccharolyticus* are actually anaerobic staphylococci that may constitute a new species. A clear relationship to other members of the genus *Staphylococcus* was established on the basis of immunological cross-reactions of catalases, DNA-DNA homology, and DNA-rRNA homology. It is of interest that the lysostaphin-producing strain labeled *S. staphylolyticus* can be included in the species *S. simulans* on the basis of DNA homology (W. E. Kloos and G. L. Sloan, unpublished data). Perhaps as more natural habitats are explored, some additional species and subspecies will be discovered and brought to our attention.

NATURAL HABITATS

Transient Versus Resident Populations

Mammalian skin (including the anterior nares) forms one of the major habitats of staphylococci (22, 98, 107, 109, 118, 137) (Table 1). Some staphylococci may be found in other regions of the body such as the throat, mouth, mammary glands, and intestinal tract, but usually less frequently and/or in smaller numbers than on skin. Staphylococci have been isolated from birds (36, 39, 71), though information on avian populations is very incomplete and one cannot be certain they constitute a major natural reservoir as compared to mammals.

Table 1 Major natural hosts of *Staphylococcus* species

Species	Host(s)
S. haemolyticus	Humans and nonhuman primates (e.g. *Pan, Macaca, Cercocebus, Erythrocebus, Microcebus, Lemur*)
S. hominis	Humans
S. "simians"	Nonhuman primates (e.g. *Pan, Gorilla, Pongo, Papio, Alouatta*)
S. warneri	Humans and nonhuman primates (e.g. *Pan, Gorilla, Pongo, Papio, Cercopithecus, Cercocebus, Erythrocebus, Macaca, Presbytix, Alouatta, Ateles, Lagothrix, Saimiri, Lemur, Microcebus, Galago*)
S. epidermidis	Humans
S. capitis	Humans
S. aureus	Humans and nonhuman primates (e.g. same list as above for *S. warneri*); infections in a variety of mammals and birds; specific subspecies or ecotypes for certain domestic animals–residency status questionable
S. cohnii	Humans, nonhuman primates (e.g. same list as above for *S. warneri*), tree shrews (*Tupaia*)
S. saprophyticus	Humans and nonhuman primates (residency status on various nonhuman primate host genera undetermined)
S. xylosus	Primates, Carnivora, Artiodactyla, Perissodactyla, Rodentia, Marsupialia (all Mammalia orders examined to date); residency status not clear
S. simulans	Humans and nonhuman primates (residency status on various nonhuman primate host genera undetermined)
S. intermedius	Carnivora (e.g. *Canis, Mustela, Vulpes, Procyon*); residency status on horses, rodents, and pigeons not clear
S. hyicus	Artiodactyla (e.g. *Bos, Sus*); residency status on poultry not clear
S. sciuri (*S. sciuri* subsp. *sciuri*)	All Mammalia orders examined to date (same list as above for *S. xylosus*); residents on Rodentia, residency status on other orders not clear
S. lentus (*S. sciuri* subsp. *lentus*)	Artiodactyla (*Ovis* and *Capra*)

Price (165) identified those bacteria that are relatively rare on clean, unexposed skin, but occur more frequently on exposed skin and may be easily washed away as transients. Residents, on the other hand, are bacteria that produce relatively stable populations and increase in numbers mainly by multiplication of those already present. According to Price, transients come from extraneous sources; residents are indigenous to the host. Noble & Somerville (137) proposed three categories of skin microbes according to their host relationship: (*a*) transients, contaminating organisms that do not multiply; (*b*) temporary residents, contaminants that multiply and persist for short periods of time; and (*c*) residents, the natural inhabitants of the skin. These ecological concepts are important to understand when we choose to define the natural habitats of staphylococci. Staphylococci are spread widely throughout our ecosystem and contaminants can be maintained on surfaces or in certain materials for relatively long periods of time. Some species are unusually resistant to drying. Because staphylococci are rather ubiquitous in nature, one must use stringent criteria based on temporal studies and population size to determine major natural habitats (22, 98, 137). Determinations of natural host range should be made with host organisms that are not in frequent contact with other host species. Cross-contamination of staphylococci can occur readily, but where host specificity is high, the contaminating species will usually be eliminated within several hours or days, unless defense barriers are broken (e.g. in infections). Although staphylococci may be found growing in large numbers in foods and animal products (e.g. milk, cheese, eggs, meat, etc), it is generally believed that the primary sources are human handlers or animals. The species *S. xylosus* and *S. sciuri* have been occasionally isolated from soil, beach sand, natural waters, and marsh grass (103), but one wonders whether they are more free-living than other species or are deposited in habitats frequented by local mammals and/or birds.

In any ecological study, the investigator must use care in sampling techniques and the processing of specimens and cultures so as not to introduce contaminants, especially from her or his own body. Noble (135) has taken the arbitrary level of six or more colonies of *S. aureus* on an agar plate inoculated from a skin swab as indicating resident carriage or a noncontaminant status. Contamination by this or other species on healthy skin seldom exceeds the limit proposed by Noble, unless the host has been in recent contact with another primary source or sampling techniques are inadequate.

Populations on Primates

Many reports have been made on the staphylococci inhabiting human skin and most have dealt with the most potentially pathogenic species *S. aureus.* Noble & Somerville (137) have made a comprehensive review of the literature on the skin carriage of this species. *S. aureus* may be isolated from the nares in less than 10% to more than 40% of adults outside of hospitals, depending upon the population sampled. Nasal carrier rates may increase considerably with prolonged hospitalization (139). The populations of *S. aureus* found living in the nares may be quite large and persist for variable periods of time. For *S. aureus,* the anterior nares are generally regarded as the headquarter region. This species can be isolated from other regions of the body, though usually not as consistently or in as large a number as found in the nares (138, 199, 217). In preadolescent children the carriage rate for *S. aureus* is often higher than in adults and populations are often more dispersed over the child's body (98, 217).

Comprehensive reviews on the nature of human infections caused by *S. aureus* can be found in texts prepared by Elek (43), Cohen (27), Jeljaszewicz (89, 90), and Noble & Somerville (137). Some of the more common infections include furuncles (boils), carbuncles, impetigo, toxic epidermal necrolysis of the skin, pneumonia, osteomyelitis, endocarditis, mastitis, bacteremia, and various abscesses. Food poisoning is often due to staphylococcal enterotoxin. This species may also produce infections in a wide variety of other animals (157, 200, 220).

The major natural hosts for *S. aureus* appear to be primates, based on this species' population size and frequency of occurrence on normal primate skin (98; W. E. Kloos, unpublished data). *S. aureus* can, however, be isolated occasionally from other mammals and also from birds, especially when contact with humans is frequent and/or infections are present. The specific biotypes of *S. aureus* found living on different domestic animals would suggest some host species adaptation or selection. In this regard, one can raise the questions: did *S. aureus* live on the skin of these animals prior to contact with man, e.g. prior to domestication, or was this species transferred to animals from man and did it become modified slightly by association with its new hosts? Other explanations may also be possible. Epidemiological studies have shown that some strains of *S. aureus* can spread rapidly among human or animal populations and tend to be epidemic in character (130, 167, 218). Because of the epidemic nature of this species, it is often difficult to identify major primary sources, though phage typing has greatly facilitated this search (159, 215, 219). With the advent of phage-typing procedures, it became evident that human *S. aureus* strains could be divided into three main phage groups and that these groups exhibited some distinct ecological differences (112, 137).

Preliminary results of DNA-DNA hybridization studies have indicated no significant DNA divergence between *S. aureus* strains isolated from various sources or representing different phage groups (108, 123, 176).

The most prevalent and persistent *Staphylococcus* species on human skin are *S. epidermidis* sensu stricto and *S. hominis* (22, 98, 102). Nearly everyone carries them. *S. epidermidis* usually makes up from 90 to 100% of the staphylococci isolated from the nares when the sympatric species *S. aureus* is not present. In the presence of a dominant *S. aureus* strain, populations of *S. epidermidis* may be greatly reduced in size in the nares. *S. epidermidis* and *S. hominis* produce large populations in the axillae and perineum, where habitats are moist and supplied with a rich source of nutrients. Both of these species usually comprise more than 65% of the staphylococci found on normal glabrous skin which accounts for most of the skin area. Their natural host range appears to be largely limited to humans. They were not isolated from nonhuman primates living either in captivity, open ranges, or in the wild (W. E. Kloos, unpublished data). Furthermore, they were not isolated from woodland and swamp mammals (including squirrels, raccoons, rats, and opossums) captured in North Carolina (99, 109) and the Canal Zone (W. E. Kloos, unpublished data). *S. epidermidis* has been isolated in very small numbers from the normal skin of less than 5% of domestic animals sampled in one study (109) and from teats and milk of cows with mastitis (35, 82). Here we would suspect that this species was transferred to domestic animals mainly by human contact or activity.

S. epidermidis and *S. hominis* may occur in human infections. Of the coagulase-negative species, *S. epidermidis* is the one most frequently associated with bacteremia, endocarditis, wounds, and colonization of artificial prostheses (83, 140, 158, 169).

S. haemolyticus usually comprises from 1 to 30% of the staphylococci isolated from normal human glabrous skin (98). It is less frequently isolated from the nares and axillae and when present it usually occurs in small numbers. In one study, 31 of 40 individuals (78%) demonstrated the presence of this species on normal skin and 50% maintained relatively persistent populations over the one-year sampling period. A different subspecies of *S. haemolyticus* is found on nonhuman primate skin where it is present in small- to moderate-size populations. One encounters some difficulty in distinguishing *S. haemolyticus*, on the basis of simple phenotypic characters, from a sibling species, tentatively named *S. "simians,"* living on nonhuman primate skin. *S. haemolyticus* is also found in some human and animal infections, but usually less frequently than *S. epidermidis* (35, 57, 140). The natural hosts for this species appear to be primates (98, 107). It has been only rarely isolated from the normal skin of some domestic animals (109).

S. warneri has been isolated in very small numbers from the normal skin of 21 of 40 individuals (52%) sampled in one study (98). This species usually comprises less than 1% of the total staphylococci found on humans. A different subspecies is found living on the skin of most nonhuman primates and comprises from 8 to 69% of the total staphylococci present (107); it and *S. aureus* are the major species found on most nonhuman primates. Like other members of the *S. epidermidis* species group, *S. warneri* is found primarily on primates. Other rare hosts appear to be only temporary. *S.*

warneri has been seldom found in human (57, 140, 147) and animal infections (35).

S. capitis produces moderate-size populations on the human head, especially in adults, and may be found occasionally in relatively small populations on other regions of the skin. It has been isolated only from humans and in one study was isolated from the normal skin of 26 of 40 individuals (65%) sampled (98). This species usually comprises from 1 to 30% of the total aerobic staphylococci present. *S. capitis* has been seldom found in human infections (57, 140, 147) and, so far, has not been identified from animal infections. Preliminary studies indicate that the human forehead may also carry large populations of an anaerobic *Staphylococcus* (94), previously identified as *Peptococcus saccharolyticus* (46). More comprehensive ecological studies will need to be performed before the niche preference(s) and/or host range of this very interesting group is clearly identified.

S. simulans, S. saprophyticus, S. cohnii, and *S. xylosus* are only occasionally isolated from normal human skin (98). The population size of these species may be quite variable, depending on the individual carrying them. Of these species, *S. saprophyticus* is the most frequently isolated and *S. simulans* and *S. xylosus* are the least frequently isolated. A few individuals carry relatively persistent populations of *S. simulans,* but most carry only sporadic transient populations of *S. xylosus. S. saprophyticus* is most frequently isolated from human urinary tract infections (129, 140, 169, 173). It, *S. cohnii,* and *S. simulans* have been occasionally isolated from several other types of infections (57, 140, 147). *S. simulans, S. xylosus,* and *S. cohnii* have been isolated from the udders and milk of cows with mastitis (35). *S. simulans* is mainly found on the skin of primates, and preliminary DNA-DNA hybridization studies have not indicated a clear DNA divergence between human and nonhuman primate strains (98, 108). *S. saprophyticus, S. cohnii,* and *S. xylosus* are also found on nonhuman primates, but *S. xylosus* is even more widespread in nature and occurs on animals representing several different orders. *S. sciuri* is very rarely isolated from humans and is occasionally isolated from nonhuman primates (99, 103).

Populations on Domestic Ungulates

Many reports have been made on the staphylococci isolated from domestic ungulates; however, few studies have estimated carrier rates, residency status, or population size in the cutaneous habitat. Until rather recently, many of the staphylococci and micrococci isolated from animals were misclassified, making data difficult to interpret in light of today's developments in taxonomy. Most attention has focused on the characterization of coagulase-positive strains isolated from infections.

Cattle can support populations of *S. aureus* on udders, in teat canals, and in quarter milk, especially if they have mastitis or are in contact with afflicted animals (70, 115, 200, 213). *S. aureus* is infrequently isolated from the nares of cattle (43, 109, 130). The occurrence in other cutaneous areas is not adequately assessed. The bovine biotype C is the more usual one found on cattle and, as mentioned earlier, can be distinguished from other biotypes on the basis of immunological, biochemical, and phage-typing properties (73, 74, 145, 152). *S. hyicus* subsp. *hyicus* and *chromogenes* have also been isolated from the udders and milk of cows suffering from mastitis (35). The distribution and carriage of this species on normal skin also has not been adequately assessed. In preliminary studies, Kloos et al (99, 109) have indicated that *S. xylosus* is a major species found on the normal skin of cattle and other ungulates. Other natural species populations have received little attention to date.

The staphylococci of pigs have not been studied in much detail, though *S. hyicus* and *S. aureus* populations have been identified on these animals and have been shown to be occasionally involved in infections (9, 37, 39, 109). *S. hyicus* appears to be quite common in the nares and on the hairy cutaneous areas of pigs. Sometimes small transient populations of *S. epidermidis* sensu stricto, *S. haemolyticus,* and *S. saprophyticus* have been discovered on normal pig skin, which may indicate limited acquisition and survival of human staphylococci (109).

S. aureus has been occasionally isolated from the nares and udders of sheep and, when found, is usually biotype C, the major biotype also found in cattle (73, 74, 150). Both sheep and goats carry relatively large cutaneous populations of *S. xylosus* and *S. sciuri* subsp. *lentus* (proposed to be renamed *S. lentus*) (103, 109). *S. lentus* appears to be rather host specific; to date, populations of this species have been isolated only from sheep and goats.

Horses can carry populations of *S. aureus* and *S. intermedius,* though the residency status of these species is still unclear (74, 149). They may carry large populations of *S. xylosus* on normal skin (99, 109). The other coagulase-negative species occurring on horses have not been adequately assessed.

Populations on Carnivora

Most studies of the staphylococci of carnivora have been concerned with coagulase-positive species isolated from the domestic dog (*Canis familiarus*). Dogs may occasionally carry populations of *S. aureus,* but these are usually of the human biotype A (39, 73, 189), which most likely come from human handlers. The major coagulase-positive species of dogs is *S. inter-*

medius (69, 189). This species appears also to be indigenous to a variety of other carnivora, including mink (*Mustela lutreola*) (75, 148), foxes (*Volpes* sp.) (74), and raccoons (*Procyon lotor*) (99, 109). *S. intermedius* has also been isolated from horses and pigeons (73, 74), though the residency status of this species on these animals and birds is uncertain. Natural populations of coagulase-negative species living on carnivora have not yet been studied in much detail. However, some preliminary studies indicate that dogs and raccoons occasionally carry small populations of *S. sciuri* and usually carry medium-size to large populations of *S. xylosus* (99, 109; W. E. Kloos, unpublished data). Dogs kept in the home may occasionally carry small numbers of viable coagulase-negative staphylococci obtained from their human handlers (W. E. Kloos and B. R. Kimbro, unpublished data).

Populations on Rodents and Lagomorpha

Natural populations of staphylococci have been isolated from a variety of common laboratory rodents including the mouse (*Mus muscelus*), rat (*Rattus norvegicus*), guinea pig (*Cavia porcellus*), and hamster (*Cricetus mesocricetus*) (20, 76, 180, 208). However, classification was not complete or made according to current criteria. Mice and rabbits have served as useful experimental animals for various induced staphylococcal infections (137, 180, 197, 205).

In a preliminary study by Kloos et al (99, 103, 109), very small numbers of *S. aureus* and *S. intermedius* were isolated from a small percentage of wild Eastern gray squirrels (*Sciurus carolinensis*). The predominant species found living on the skin of Eastern gray squirrels, Southern flying squirrels (*Glaucomys volans*), the Central American squirrel *Sciurus granatensis*, and spiny rats (*Proechimys semispinosus*) were *S. sciuri*, *S. xylosus*, and an unnamed species included in the *S. saprophyticus* species group.

S. aureus has been isolated from infections in wild and domestic rabbits (*Sylvilagus* and *Oryctolagus* spp.) (2, 25, 122). Occasionally, *S. aureus* may be isolated from the nares of European hares (72, 73, 148). Most strains have been classified as belonging to biotype D, which appears to be unique to hares. The coagulase-negative species living on rabbits and hares have not been adequately examined.

Populations on Marsupials

In preliminary studies, Kloos et al (99, 103, 109; W. E. Kloos, unpublished data) have indicated that opossums (*Didelphis marsupialis*) from North Carolina and the Canal Zone carry relatively small populations of *S. sciuri*, *S. xylosus*, and two unnamed species included in the *S. saprophyticus* species group. In addition, opossums carry large populations of an unnamed species that so far has been found only on marsupials. This species is currently under investigation.

Our understanding of natural populations of staphylococci is far from complete; very little effort has been made in examining these organisms from mammals other than those already mentioned in the sections above. A few isolated reports have been made on coagulase-positive staphylococci isolated from infections in some wild and captive exotic mammals, but other groups or species of staphylococci have not been given much consideration.

Populations on Birds

Several major reports have been made on the coagulase-positive staphylococci of chickens (38, 39, 73, 196). *S. aureus* strains representing biotypes A (human) and B (pigs and poultry) have been isolated occasionally from chickens, although their primary sources are not always clear. Devriese and co-workers (37, 38) have isolated and characterized strains of *S. hyicus* from chickens. Other clearly defined species have not been reported on to date.

Pigeons have been shown to carry *S. intermedius* in their nares (39, 71, 151, 189); appropriate ecological studies have not yet been conducted to clarify the residency status of this species and other staphylococci on this avian host.

The staphylococci of birds have received little attention in the past and should provide a challenge to systematic bacteriologists. It remains to be proven that birds have unique natural populations of staphylococci that have specifically adapted to their cutaneous habitats.

CONCEPTS OF SPECIATION

Mechanisms of Adaptation

Although intrinsic gene mutations may play a role in the adaptation and evolution of bacteria, other sources of variation (e.g. extrachromosomal elements) may be more important. The introduction of new gene mutations into natural populations is largely prevented by such inherent factors as DNA polymerases and other repair enzymes that reduce random errors in DNA (19, 84). Furthermore, gene mutations in bacteria probably often fail to increase adaptive value or fitness, since most involve a loss in genetic function. However, it is possible that loss of "nonessential" genetic information may provide some selective advantage in certain niches (e.g. auxotrophs growing in the presence of an essential metabolite) (54, 226).

Disadvantageous or selectively neutral mutations present in low frequencies can be important in the adaptation of small or founder populations because of genetic drift (156). In this regard, it is interesting that *Staphylococcus xylosus,* which is widely dispersed in nature and often found living in small populations, is clearly one of the most polytypic and polymorphic species in the genus.

Reanney (170), in his excellent treatise on extrachromosomal elements as possible agents of adaptation and development, took the position that extrachromosomal elements, and not stochastic mutations, provide the prime vehicle of adaptive change for cell evolution. I would tend to agree with such a position, as it is becoming more apparent that many extrachromosomal elements are specifically designed to take part in the exchange of blocks of genetic information with the aid of insertion sequences (78, 166, 171). They, in effect, constitute a mobile reservoir of genes that may be called upon as the need arises. Under laboratory conditions, extrachromosomal elements, such as phage genomes and plasmids, have been successfully transferred between certain bacteria (e.g. by transfection, transduction, transformation, or conjugation), but the frequency with which transfer occurs in natural populations still remains to be determined. Evidence for genetic transfer in natural populations of bacteria is rather scanty and has not always been conclusive (3, 53, 195). Clearly, more vigorous investigation into natural genetic exchange needs to be pursued before mechanisms of speciation can be elucidated.

Considerable progress has been made in the study of staphylococcal phages and plasmids, to the point that their transfer in natural populations should be monitored with reasonable success. Transduction (131, 141, 161) and transformation (114, 162) have been well documented in this organism. Novick & Morse (143) and Lacey and co-workers (111, 113) have demonstrated the transfer of plasmids between implanted *S. aureus* strains growing on mice and humans, respectively. Although the identification and characterization of extrachromosomal elements has been largely confined to those occurring in *S. aureus* (87, 112, 142, 144), some information is accumulating on the phages and plasmids of other species (97, 128, 177, 221, 225). Staphylococci are commonly polylysogens and may harbor up to five or more different prophages (56, 143, 179). Recent studies by Kloos et al (97, 100) indicate that many of the species are composed of a high percentage of strains carrying plasmids. For example, 64% of *S. aureus,* 75% of *S. epidermidis,* 78% of *S. warneri,* 85% of *S. capitis,* 90% of *S. xylosus,* 95% of *S. haemolyticus,* and 100% of *S. hominis, S. saprophyticus,* and *S. cohnii* strains tested (20 to 40 per species) contained plasmids in the size range of 15 to 25 megadaltons. The percentage of strains carrying plasmids is even higher in some of the above species when the very common smaller plasmids are taken into consideration. The demonstration of transduction between *S. aureus* and *S. epidermidis* by Yu & Baldwin (225) suggests that at least some of the species may exchange genetic information. Plasmid exchange between the widely divergent species *S. aureus* and *S. epidermidis* is perhaps implied by the high DNA relatedness of certain of their Tc^r (87) or penicillinase plasmids (23). However, here one must distinguish between interspecies transfer and conservation of plasmid nucleotide sequences. It is expected that new applications of agarose gel electrophoresis (97, 126), restriction endonuclease analyses (87, 97), heteroduplex analyses (31, 87), and nucleic acid hybridization techniques (87, 216) should greatly facilitate the analysis of extrachromosomal element transfer in natural populations, especially with regard to determining plasmid identity and localizing exchange events. Hopefully, a number of investigators will take up the challenge.

Hypothesis of Conjugate Evolution of Host and Parasite

The demonstration of niche and host preferences by certain of the *Staphylococcus* species leads one to consider the possibility that these organisms may have evolved concurrently with their hosts. The idea, itself, is not new. Kellog (93) in studying the Mallophaga (biting lice) of birds suggested that parasitic louse species living on closely related birds have persisted unchanged and are derived from a common ancestor. This would explain the occurrence of lice common to the European and American counterparts of avocets, coots, or bitterns. Harrison (77) believed that the cestode and nematode parasites of the ostriches of Africa and rheas of South American have evolved from a common ancestor and so also must the birds themselves. Ewing (52) studied the host distribution of the head lice *Pediculus* and concluded that in America two distinct groups exist, one confined to man and one to monkeys. The monkey pediculids of America fall into distinct species according to the hosts they infect, which suggested to Ewing a parallel host and parasite phylogeny. Hegner (79) was impressed by the similarity of protozoan parasites of monkeys and man, compared with those of other animals associated with man, and proposed that close relationships of parasites indicate a common ancestry of their hosts. Most of the early ideas on host-parasite conjugate evolution were reported prior to 1930. More recently, Mayes (119) investigated the monogenetic nematodes of the genus *Urocleidus* from centrarchid fishes of the genera *Acantharchus, Enneacanthus,* and *Eclassoma;* he concluded that the similarity between the hosts and their monogenean parasites suggested yet another case of conjugate evolution.

The hypothesis of conjugate evolution might be extended to certain bacteria as well, particularly to those that tend to be parasitic or have a restricted natural host range. Isolation on specific host species could lead to the formation of new bacterial species or subspecies in much the same way that free-living animals may speciate during isolation on islands (26, 121). Bacteria could evolve through adaptations to the changing environment brought about by changes in the evolution of the host. In support of this view, Kloos & Wolfshohl (107), using DNA-DNA hybridization techniques, have shown that human and nonhuman primate strains of the related species *S. haemolyticus* and *S. warneri* are closely related to one another and form distinct DNA homology groups. Furthermore, as mentioned earlier, natural populations of *S. haemolyticus* and *S. warneri,* as well as other species of the *S. epidermidis* species group, appear to be restricted to primate hosts (98, 103). On rare occasions transient populations may be found on other mammals, but these are presumably due to contact with humans. Members of the *S. epidermidis* species group are also more closely related to one another than to species living primarily on lower mammals.

We may question the evolutionary course taken by such widespread species as *S. xylosus* and *S. sciuri,* which may be capable of a free-living existence. These species do not require an organic source of nitrogen and have been isolated occasionally from soil and natural waters (44, 45, 103). One could speculate that ancestral populations of these species came in contact with the skin of vertebrates and eventually became adapted to the cutaneous habitat. During the course of evolution, it might be expected that staphylococci would adapt to different niches in the cutaneous habitat, which, if effectively isolated, could promote the multiplication of species. Based on the relatively large number of species found living on humans, it would appear that adaptive radiation of staphylococci reached a peak during primate evolution. The relatively large natural populations of *S. epidermidis, S. hominis,* and *S. capitis* that are restricted to humans may be products of recent radiations. The small size of populations of *S. warneri* and *S. haemolyticus* occurring on humans may be providing an additional clue to their long primate history, i.e. they may represent remnants of ancient radiations. The advanced cutaneous adaptation of members of the *S. epidermidis* species group is probably reflected, in part, by their complex amino acid requirements, many of which are not revertable and are perhaps represented by multi-site mutations or deletions (44, 45).

One could even speculate that staphylococci and streptococci shared a common ancestor and that whereas staphylococci became adapted to the cutaneous habitat, certain streptococci became adapted to the oral cavity and intestinal tract.

ACKNOWLEDGMENTS

Work from this laboratory was supported by NIH Biomedical Research Support Grant RR7071 and National Science Foundation Grant DEB77-16078. Paper No. 6356 of the Journal Series of the North Carolina Agricultural Research Service, Raleigh, North Carolina.

Literature Cited

1. Abd-El-Malek, Y., Gibson, T. 1948. *J. Dairy Res.* 15:249–60
2. Adlam, C., Thorley, C. M., Ward, P. D., Collins, M. 1976. In *Staphylococci and Staphylococcal Diseases,* ed. J. Jeljaszewicz, pp. 761–71. Stuttgart/New York: G. Fisher
3. Anderson, J. D., Gillespie, W. A., Richmond, M. H. 1973. *J. Med. Microbiol.* 6:461–73
4. Archibald, A. R., Baddiley, J., Button, D. 1968. *Biochem. J.* 110:543–57
5. Archibald, A. R., Baddiley, J., Shankat, G. A. 1968. *Biochem. J.* 110:583–88
6. Auletta, A. E., Kennedy, E. R. 1966. *J. Bacteriol.* 92:28–34
7. Baddiley, J., Buchanan, J. G., Hardy, F. E., Martin, R. O., Rajbhandary, U. L., Sanderson, A. R. 1961. *Biochim. Biophys. Acta* 52:406–7
8. Baddiley, J., Buchanan, J. G., Rajbhandary, U. L., Sanderson, A. R. 1962. *Biochem. J.* 82:439–48
9. Baird-Parker, A. C. 1962. *J. Appl. Bacteriol.* 25:352–61
10. Baird-Parker, A. C. 1963 *J. Gen. Microbiol.* 30:409–27
11. Baird-Parker, A. C. 1965. *J. Gen. Microbiol.* 38:363–87
12. Baird-Parker, A. C. 1965. *Ann. NY Acad. Sci.* 128:4–25
13. Baird-Parker, A. C. 1974. *Ann. NY Acad. Sci.* 236:7–14
14. Baird-Parker, A. C. 1974. In *Bergey's Manual of Determinative Bacteriology,* ed. R. E. Buchanan, N. E. Gibbons, pp. 478–90. Baltimore: Williams & Wilkins. 8th ed.
15. Bohacek, J., Kocur, M., Martinec, T. 1965. *Publ. Fac. Sci. Univ. J. E. Purkyne, Brno K35,* pp. 318–22
16. Brenner, D. J., Fanning, G. R., Rake, A., Johnson, K. E. 1969. *Anal. Biochem.* 28:447–59
17. Brenner, D. J., Fanning, G. R., Skerman, F. J., Falkow, S. 1972. *J. Bacteriol.* 109:953–65
18. Brenner, D. J., Fanning, G. R., Steigerwalt, A. G. 1974. *Int. J. Syst. Bacteriol.* 24:197–204
19. Brutlag, D., Kornberg, A. 1972. *J. Biol. Chem.* 247:241–48
20. Buhles, W. C. 1969. *Lab. Anim. Care* 19:465–69
21. Canale-Parola, E. 1974. See Ref. 14, pp. 527–28
22. Carr, D. L., Kloos, W. E. 1977. *Appl. Environ. Microbiol.* 34:673–80
23. Chabbert, Y. A., Bouanchaud, D. H., Courvalin, P., Horodniceanu, T. 1978. *Abstr. 12th Int. Congr. Microbiol., München,* 5 (Abstr.)
24. Champion, A. B., Prager, E. M., Wachter, D., Wilson, A. C. 1974. In *Biochemical and Immunological Taxonomy of Animals,* ed. C. A. Wright, pp. 397–416. London: Academic
25. Cheatum, E. L. 1941. *J. Wildl. Manage.* 5:304–8
26. Clay, T. 1949. *Evolution* 3:279–99
27. Cohen, J. O., ed. 1972. *The Staphylococci.* New York: Wiley. 548 pp.
28. Cohn, F. 1872. *Bacteria The Smallest of Living Organisms.* Transl. C. S. Dolley, 1881. *Bull. Hist. Med.* (Repr., 1939) 7:49–92
29. Cummins, C. S. 1962. *J. Gen. Microbiol.* 28:35–50
30. Curry, J. C., Borovian, G. E. 1976. *J. Clin. Microbiol.* 4:455–57
31. Davis, R. W., Simon, M., Davidson, N. 1971. In *Methods in Enzymology,* ed. L. Grossman, K. Moldave, 21D:413–28. New York: Academic
32. Davison, A. L. 1968. *Biochem. J.* 110:557–58
33. DeLey, J., Park, I. W., Tijtgat, R., Van Ermengem, J. 1966. *J. Gen. Microbiol.* 42:43–56
34. Denhardt, D. T. 1966. *Biochem. Biophys. Res. Commun.* 23:641–46
35. Devriese, L. A. 1979. *Res. Vet. Sci.* 27:313–20
36. Devriese, L. A., Devos, A. H., Beumer, J., Maes, R. 1972. *Poult. Sci.* 51:389–97
37. Devriese, L. A., Hajek, V., Oeding, P., Meyer, S. A., Schleifer, K. H. 1978. *Int. J. Syst. Bacteriol.* 28:482–90
38. Devriese, L. A., Oeding, P. 1975. *J. Appl. Bacteriol.* 39:197–207

39. Devriese, L. A., Oeding, P. 1976. *Res. Vet. Sci.* 21:284–91
40. Digranes, A., Oeding, P. 1975. *Acta Pathol. Microbiol. Scand.* 83:373–81
41. Dudgeon, L. S. 1908. *J. Pathol. Bacteriol.* 12:242–57
42. Durham, D. R., Kloos, W. E. 1978. *Int. J. Syst. Bacteriol.* 28:223–28
43. Elek, S. D. 1959. *Staphylococcus pyogenes and its Relation to Disease.* London: Livingstone. 767 pp.
44. Emmett, M., Kloos, W. E. 1975. *Can. J. Microbiol.* 21:729–33
45. Emmett, M., Kloos, W. E. 1979. *J. Gen. Microbiol.* 110:305–14
46. Evans, C. A., Mattern, K. L., Hallam, S. L. 1978. *J. Clin. Microbiol.* 7:261–64
47. Evans, J. B. 1947. *J. Bacteriol.* 54:266
48. Evans, J. B. 1957. In *Bergey's Manual of Determinative Bacteriology,* ed. R. S. Breed, E. G. D. Murray, N. R. Smith, pp. 464–66. Baltimore: Williams & Wilkins. 7th ed.
49. Evans, J. B. 1965. *Int. Bull. Bacteriol. Taxon.* 15:111–12
50. Evans, J. B. 1976. *Int. J. Syst. Bacteriol.* 26:17–21
51. Evans, J. B., Bradford, W. L., Niven, C. F. 1955. *Int. Bull. Bacteriol. Nomenl. Taxon.* 5:61–66
52. Ewing, H. E. 1926. *Proc. US Natl. Mus. 68*
53. Farrar, W. E., Eidson, M., Guerry, P., Falkow, S., Drusin, L. M., Roberts, R. B. 1972. *J. Infect. Dis.* 126:27–33
54. Farrior, J. W., Kloos, W. E. 1976. *Can. J. Microbiol.* 22:1680–90
55. Feltham, R. K. A. 1979. *J. Appl. Bacteriol.* 47:243–45
56. Fisk, R. T. 1942. *J. Infect. Dis.* 71: 153–60
57. Fleurette, J., Brun, Y. 1977. *Staphylocoques: Abstr. Meet. Soc. Francaise Microbiol.* 13–14 (Abstr.)
58. Flügge, C. 1890. *Microorganisms with Special References to the Etiology of the Infectious Diseases.* London: New Sydenham Soc.
59. Friedman, S., De Ley, J. 1965. *J. Bacteriol.* 89:95–100
60. Gasser, F., Gasser, C. 1971. *J. Bacteriol.* 106:113–25
61. Ghuysen, J. M., Strominger, J. L. 1963. *Biochemistry* 2:1110–19
62. Ghuysen, J. M., Strominger, J. L. 1963. *Biochemistry* 2:1119–25
63. Gillespie, D., Spiegelman, S. 1965. *J. Mol. Biol.* 12:829–42
64. Goodman, M. 1962. *Ann. NY Acad. Sci.* 102:219–34
65. Goodman, M., Moore, G. W. 1971. *Syst. Zool.* 20:19–62
66. Gordon, M. H. 1904–1905. *34th Ann. Rep. Med. Off. Local Gov. Board London,* pp. 387–409
67. Gotz, F., Schleifer, K. H. 1975. *Arch. Microbiol.* 105:303–12
68. Gotz, F., Schleifer, K. H. 1976. See Ref. 2, pp. 245–52
69. Hajek, V. 1976. *Int. J. Syst. Bacteriol.* 26:401–8
70. Hajek, V., Marsalek, E. 1969. *Zentralbl. Bakteriol. Parasitenkd. Infektionskr. Hyg. Abt. 1 Orig.* 209:154–60
71. Hajek, V., Marsalek, E. 1969. *Zentralbl. Bakteriol. Parasitenkd. Infektionskr. Hyg. Abt. Orig. 1* 212:67–73
72. Hajek, V., Marsalek, E. 1971. *Zentralbl. Bakteriol. Parasitenkd. Infektionskr. Hyg. Abt. Orig. A1* 216:168–74
73. Hajek, V., Marsalek, E. 1971. *Zentralbl. Bakteriol. Parasitenkd. Infektionskr. Hyg. Abt. Orig. A1* 217:176–82
74. Hajek, V., Marsalek, E. 1976. See Ref. 2, pp. 11–21
75. Hajek, V., Marsalek, E., Hubacek, J. 1972. *Zentralbl. Bakteriol. Parasitenkd. Infektionskr. Hyg. Abt. 1 Orig. A* 222:194–99
76. Hard, G. C. 1966. *Lab. Anim. Care* 16:421–29
77. Harrison, L. 1928. *Proc. Linn. Soc. N. S. W.* 53:ix–xxxii
78. Heffron, F., Rubens, C., Falkow, S. 1975. *Proc. Natl. Acad. Sci. USA* 72:3623–27
79. Hegner, R. W. 1928. *Q. Rev. Biol.* 3:225–44
80. Hill, L. R. 1959. *J. Gen. Microbiol.* 20:277–83
81. Hine, T. G. M. 1922. *Lancet* 2:1380–82
82. Holmberg, O. 1973. *Acta. Vet. Scand. Suppl.* 45:1–144
83. Holt, R. J. 1972. *Br. J. Dermatol.* 86: Suppl. 8, pp. 42–49
84. Hopfield, J. J. 1974. *Proc. Natl. Acad. Sci. USA* 71:4135–39
85. Hucker, G. J. 1924. *Tech. Bull. NY State Agric. Exp. Stn. No. 100*
86. Hucker, G. J. 1948. In *Bergey's Manual of Determinative Bacteriology,* ed. R. S. Breed, E. G. D. Murray, A. P. Hitchens, pp. 235–94. London: Bailliere, Tindall & Cox. 6th ed.
87. Iordanescu, S., Surdeanu, M., Latta, P. D., Novick, R. P. 1978. *Plasmid* 1:468–79
88. Jeffries, L., Cawthorne, M. A., Harris, M., Cook, B., Diplock, A. T. 1969. *J. Gen. Microbiol.* 54:365–80
89. Jeljaszewicz, J., ed. 1973. *Staphylococci and Staphylococcal Infections.* Basel: Karger. 658 pp.

90. Jeljaszewicz, J., ed. 1976. *Staphylococci and Staphylococcal Diseases.* Stuttgart-/New York: Fischer. 1137 pp.
91. Johnson, J. L. 1973. *Int. J. Syst. Bacteriol.* 23:308–15
92. Jones, D., Deibel, R. H., Niven, C. F. Jr. 1963. *J. Bacteriol.* 85:62–67
93. Kellog, V. L. 1896. *Proc. Calif. Acad. Sci.* 6:31–168
94. Kilpper, R., Schleifer, K. H. 1978. *Abstr. 12th Int. Congr. Microbiol., München,* 86 (Abstr.)
95. Kloos, W. E. 1969. *J. Gen. Microbiol.* 59:247–55
96. Kloos, W. E. 1978. *Abstr. Ann. Meet. Am. Soc. Microbiol.* 82 (Abstr.)
97. Kloos, W. E., Kopp, U., Orban, B. S., Blobel, H. 1979. *Curr. Microbiol.* 2:333–38
98. Kloos, W. E., Musselwhite, M. S. 1975. *Appl. Microbiol.* 30:381–95
99. Kloos, W. E., Musselwhite, M. S., Zimmerman, R. J. 1976. See Ref. 2, pp. 967–73
100. Kloos, W. E., Orban, B. S., Walker, D. D. 1980. *Abstr. Ann. Meet. Am. Soc. Microbiol.* 120 (Abstr.)
101. Kloos, W. E., Schleifer, K. H. 1975. *J. Clin. Microbiol.* 1:82–88
102. Kloos, W. E., Schleifer, K. H. 1975. *Int. J. Syst. Bacteriol.* 25:62–79
103. Kloos, W. E., Schleifer, K. H. 1981. In *The Prokaryotes,* ed. M. P. Starr, H. Stolp, H. G. Truper, A. Balows, H. G. Schlegel. Berlin/Heidelberg/-New York: Springer Verlag. In press
104. Kloos, W. E., Schleifer, K. H., Noble, W. C. 1976. See Ref. 2, pp. 23–41
105. Kloos, W. E., Schleifer, K. H., Smith, R. F. 1976. *Int. J. Syst. Bacteriol.* 26:22–37
106. Kloos, W. E., Tornabene, T. G., Schleifer, K. H. 1974. *Int. J. Syst. Bacteriol.* 24:79–101
107. Kloos, W. E., Wolfshohl, J. F. 1979. *Curr. Microbiol.* 3:167–72
108. Kloos, W. E., Wolfshohl, J. F. 1980. *Abstr. Ann. Meet. Am. Soc. Microbiol.* 94 (Abstr.)
109. Kloos, W. E., Zimmerman, R. J., Smith, R. F. 1976. *Appl. Environ. Microbiol.* 31:53–59
110. Kocur, M., Martinec, T. 1965. *Int. Bull. Bacteriol. Nomencl. Taxon.* 15:113–14
111. Lacey, R. W. 1971. *J. Med. Microbiol.* 4:73–84
112. Lacey, R. W. 1975. *Bacteriol. Rev.* 39:1–32
113. Lacey, R. W., Richmond, M. H. 1974. *Ann. NY Acad. Sci.* 236:395–412
114. Lindberg, M., Novick, R. P. 1973. *J. Bacteriol.* 115:139–45
115. Live, I. 1972. In *The Staphylococci,* ed. J. O. Cohen, pp. 443–56. New York: Wiley-Interscience
116. Loeb, L. 1903–1904. *J. Med. Res.* 10:407–19
117. Marmur, J., Seaman, E., Levine, J. 1963. *J. Bacteriol.* 85:461–67
118. Marples, M. J. 1965. *The Ecology of the Human Skin.* Springfield: Thomas. 970 pp.
119. Mayes, M. A. 1973. *Trans. Am. Microsc. Soc.* 92:280–84
120. Mayr, E. 1963. *Animal Species and Evolution.* Cambridge: Belknap Press of Harvard Univ. Press. 797 pp.
121. Mayr, E. 1970. *Populations, Species, and Evolution.* Cambridge: Belknap Press of Harvard Univ. Press. 453 pp.
122. McCoy, R. H., Steenbergen, F. 1969. *Bull. Wildl. Dis. Assoc.* 5:11
123. Meyer, S. A., Schleifer, K. H. 1978. *Arch. Microbiol.* 117:183–88
124. Meyer, W. 1966. *Postepy Mikrobiol.* 5:435–39
125. Meyer, W. 1967. *Int. J. Syst. Bacteriol.* 17:387–89
126. Meyers, J. A., Sanchez, D., Elwell, L. P., Falkow, S. 1976. *J. Bacteriol.* 127:1529–37
127. Migula, W. 1900. *System der Bakterien. 2. Specielle Systematik der Bakterien.* Jena, Germany: Fischer. 1068 pp.
128. Minshew, B., Rosenblum, E. D. 1973. *Antimicrob. Agents Chemother.* 3:568–74
129. Mitchell, R. G. 1968. *J. Clin. Pathol.* 21:93–96
130. Moeller, R. W., Smith, I. M., Shoemaker, A. C., Tjalma, R. A. 1963. *J. Am. Vet. Med. Assoc.* 142:613–17
131. Morse, M. L. 1959. *Proc. Natl. Acad. Sci. USA* 45:722–27
132. Mortensen, N., Kocur, M. 1967. *Acta Pathol. Microbiol. Scand.* 69:445–57
133. Much, H. 1908. *Biochem. Z.* 14:143–55
134. Namavar, F., DeGraaff, J., MacLaren, D. M. 1978. *Antonie van Leeuwenhoek J. Microbiol. Serol.* 44:425–34
135. Noble, W. C. 1969. *J. Clin. Pathol.* 22:249–53
136. Noble, W. C., Lidwell, O. M., Kingston, D. 1963. *J. Hyg.* 61:385–91
137. Noble, W. C., Somerville, D. A. 1974. *Microbiology of Human Skin.* London: Saunders. 341 pp.
138. Noble, W. C., Valkenburg, H. A., Wolters, C. H. L. 1967. *J. Hyg.* 65:567–73
139. Noble, W. C., Williams, R. E. O., Jevons, M. P., Shooter, R. A. 1964. *J. Clin. Pathol.* 17:79–83
140. Nord, C. E., Holta-Oie, S., Ljungh, A., Wadstrom, T. 1976. See Ref. 2, pp. 105–11

141. Novick, R. P. 1963. *J. Gen. Microbiol.* 33:121–36
142. Novick, R. P. 1967. *Fed. Proc.* 27: 29–38
143. Novick, R. P., Morse, S. I. 1967. *J. Exp. Med.* 125:45–59
144. Novick, R. P., Murphy, E., Gryczan, T. J., Baron, E., Edelman, I. 1979. *Plasmid* 2:109–29
145. Oeding, P. 1973. *Acta Pathol. Microbiol. Scand.* 81:327–36
146. Oeding, P. 1974. *Ann. NY Acad. Sci.* 236:15–21
147. Oeding, P., Digranes, A. 1977. *Acta Pathol. Microbiol. Scand.* 85:136–42
148. Oeding, P., Hajek, V., Marsalek, E. 1973. *Acta Pathol. Microbiol. Scand.* 81:567–70
149. Oeding, P., Hajek, V., Marsalek, E. 1974. *Acta Pathol. Microbiol. Scand.* 82:899–903
150. Oeding, P., Hajek, V., Marsalek, E. 1976. *Acta Pathol. Microbiol. Scand.* 84:61–65
151. Oeding, P., Marandon, J. L., Hajek, V., Marsalek, E. 1970. *Acta Pathol. Microbiol. Scand.* 78:414–20
152. Oeding, P., Marandon, J. L., Hajek, V., Marsalek, E. 1971. *Acta Pathol. Microbiol. Scand.* 79:357–64
153. Oeding, P., Marandon, J. L., Meyer, W., Hajek, V., Marsalek, E. 1972. *Acta Pathol. Microbiol. Scand.* 80:515–33
154. Ogston, A. 1881. *Br. Med. J.* 1:369–75
155. Ogston, A. 1882. *J. Anat.* 17:24–58
156. Ohta, T. 1973. *Nature* 252:351–54
157. Pargaonker, V. N., Coles, E. H., Eisenstark, A. 1962. *Am. J. Vet. Res.* 23:1205–12
158. Parisi, J. T. 1973. *Mo. Med.* 70: 243–44
159. Parker, M. T. 1962. *J. Appl. Bacteriol.* 25:389–402
160. Passet, J. 1885. *Fortschr. Med.* 3:33–43
161. Pattee, P. A., Baldwin, J. N. 1961. *J. Bacteriol.* 82:875–81
162. Pattee, P. A., Thompson, N. E., Haubrich, D., Novick, R. P. 1977. *Plasmid* 1:38–51
163. Pennock, C. A., Huddy, R. B. 1967. *J. Pathol. Bacteriol.* 93:685–88
164. Phillips, W. E., King, R. E., Kloos, W. E. 1980. *Am. J. Vet. Res.* 41:274–76
165. Price, P. B. 1938. *J. Infect. Dis.* 63: 301–18
166. Ptashne, K., Cohen, S. N. 1975. *J. Bacteriol.* 122:776–81
167. Pulverer, G., Gho, C., Spieckerman, C. 1971. In *Bayer-Symposium III. Bacterial Infections,* ed. M. Finland, W. Marget, K. Bartman, pp. 31–35. New York/Heidelberg/Berlin: Springer
168. Pulverer, G., Mordarski, M., Tkacz, A., Szyba, K., Heczko, P., Goodfellow, M. 1978. *FEMS Microbiol. Lett.* 3:51–56
169. Pulverer, G., Pillich, J. 1971. See Ref. 167, pp. 91–96
170. Reanney, D. C. 1976. *Bacteriol. Rev.* 40:552–90
171. Richmond, M. H., Wiedman, B. 1974. In *Evolution in the Microbial World. Soc. Gen. Microbiol. Symp.* ed. M. J. Carlile, J. J. Skehel, 24:59–85. Cambridge: Cambridge Univ. Press
172. Rische, H., Meyer, W., Tschape, H., Voigt, W., Ziomek, D., Hummel, R. 1973. In *Staphylococci and Staphylococcal Infections,* ed. J. Jeljaszewicz, pp. 24–29. Basel: Karger
173. Roberts, A. P. 1967. *J. Clin. Pathol.* 20:631–32
174. Roop, D. R., Mundt, J. O., Riggsby, W. S. 1974. *Int. J. Syst. Bacteriol.* 24: 330–37
175. Rosenbach, F. J. 1884. *Micro-organismen bei den Wund-Infections-Krankheiten des Menschen.* Wiesbaden: Bergmann. 122 pp.
176. Rosenblum, E. D., Tyrone, S. 1979. *Curr. Microbiol.* 2:171–74
177. Rosendorf, L. L., Kayser, F. H. 1974. *J. Bacteriol.* 120:679–86
178. Rosypal, S., Rosypalova, A.. Horejs, J. 1966. *J. Gen. Microbiol.* 44:281–92
179. Rountree, P. M. 1949. *J. Gen. Microbiol.* 3:153–63
180. Rountree, P. M., Freeman, B. H., Johnston, K. G. 1956. *J. Pathol. Bacteriol.* 72:319–21
181. Rupprecht, M., Schleifer, K. H. 1977. *Arch. Microbiol.* 114:61–66
182. Schleifer, K. H., Kandler, O. 1972. *Bacteriol. Rev.* 36:407–77
183. Schleifer, K. H., Kloos, W. E. 1975. *J. Clin. Microbiol.* 1:337–38
184. Schleifer, K. H., Kloos, W. E. 1975. *Int. J. Syst. Bacteriol.* 25:50–61
185. Schleifer, K. H., Kloos, W. E. 1976. See Ref. 2, pp. 3–9
186. Schleifer, K. H., Kocur, M. 1973. *Arch. Mikrobiol.* 93:65–85
187. Schleifer, K. H., Meyer, S. A., Rupprecht, M. 1979. *Arch. Microbiol.* 122:93–101
188. Schleifer, K. H., Reid, M., Kandler, O. 1968. *Arch. Mikrobiol.* 62:198–208
189. Schleifer, K. H., Schumacher-Perdreau, F., Gotz, F., Popp, B. 1976. *Arch. Microbiol.* 110:263–70
190. Schleifer, K. H., Seidl, P. H. 1977. In *Microbiology 1977,* ed. D. Schlessinger, pp. 339–43. Washington DC: Am. Soc. Microbiol.
191. Seidl, P. H., Schleifer, K. H. 1978. *Appl. Environ. Microbiol.* 35:479–82

192. Seki, T., Oshima, T., Oshima, Y. 1975. *Int. J. Syst. Bacteriol.* 25:258–70
193. Shaw, C., Stitt, J. M., Cowan, S. T. 1951. *J. Gen. Microbiol.* 5:1010–23
194. Silvestri, L. G., Hill, L. R. 1965. *J. Bacteriol.* 90:136–40
195. Smith, H. W. 1969. *Lancet* 1:1174–76
196. Smith, H. W., Crab, W. E. 1960. *J. Pathol. Bacteriol.* 79:243–49
197. Smith, I. M., Warren, G. H., Johnson, V. L. 1976. See Ref. 2, pp. 791–808
198. Sneath, P. H. A. 1957. *J. Gen. Microbiol.* 17:201–26
199. Solberg, C. O. 1965. *Acta Med. Scand. Suppl. 1* 178:1–96
200. Stableforth, A. W., Galloway, I. A. 1959. *Infectious Diseases of Animals, Vol. 2: Diseases Due to Bacteria.* New York: Academic. 810 pp.
201. Stackebrandt, E., Woese, C. R. 1979. *Curr. Microbiol.* 2:317–22
202. Stockland, A. E., San Clemente, C. L. 1969. *J. Bacteriol.* 100:347–53
203. Subcommittee on Taxonomy of Staphylococci and Micrococci. 1965. *Int. Bull. Bacteriol. Nomencl. Taxon.* 15:107–8
204. Thomas, E. T., Schuhardt, V. T. 1964. *Bacteriol. Proc.* 23 (Abstr.)
205. Thorig, L., Thompson, J., Eulderink, F. 1977. *Infect. Immun.* 17:504–9
206. Tipper, D. J. 1969. *Biochemistry* 8:2192–2202
207. Tipper, D. J., Strominger, J. L., Ensign, J. C. 1967. *Biochemistry* 6:906–20
208. Totten, M. 1958. *J. Hyg.* 56:190–96
209. Veraldo, P. E., Satta, G. 1978. *Int. J. Syst. Bacteriol.* 28:148–53
210. Veraldo, P. E., Satta, G., Grazi, G., Romanzi, C. A. 1978. *Int. J. Syst. Bacteriol.* 28:141–47
211. Verneuil. 1880. *Arch. Gen. Med.* 146:641–54
212. Von Dáranyi, J. 1925. *Arch. Hyg.* 96:182–84
213. Wallace, G. D., Quisenberry, W. B., Tanimoto, R. H., Lynd, T. T. 1962. *Am. J. Public Health* 52:1309–17
214. Welch, W. H. 1891. *Am. J. Med. Sci.* 102:439–65
215. Wentworth, B. B. 1963. *Bacteriol. Rev.* 27:253–72
216. Wetmur, J. G., Davidson, N. 1968. *J. Mol. Biol.* 31:349–70
217. Williams, R. E. O. 1963. *Bacteriol. Rev.* 27:56–71
218. Williams, R. E. O. 1971. See Ref. 167, pp. 99–109
219. Williams, R. E. O., Rippon, J. E. 1952. *J. Hyg.* 50:320–53
220. Williams-Smith, H. 1947. *J. Comp. Pathol.* 57:98–115
221. Wilson, C. R., Totten, P. A., Baldwin, J. N. 1978. *Appl. Environ. Microbiol.* 36:368–74
222. Winslow, C. E. A., Rogers, A. F. 1906. *J. Infect. Dis.* 3:485–546
223. Winslow, C. E. A., Rothberg, W., Parsons, E. I. 1920. *J. Bacteriol.* 5:145–67
224. Winslow, C. E. A., Winslow, A. R. 1908. *The Systematic Relationships of the Coccaceae.* New York: Wiley. 300 pp.
225. Yu, L., Baldwin, J. N. 1971. *Can. J. Microbiol.* 17:767–73
226. Zamenhof, S., Eichorn, H. H. 1967. *Bacteriol. Proc.* 59 (Abstr.)
227. Zimmerman, R. J. 1976. *Can. J. Microbiol.* 22:1691–98
228. Zimmerman, R. J., Kloos, W. E. 1976. *Can. J. Microbiol.* 22:771–79

Ann. Rev. Microbiol. 1980. 34:593–618

CHEMICALLY DEFINED ANTIVIRAL VACCINES

❖1787

Ruth Arnon

Department of Chemical Immunology, The Weizmann Institute of Science, Rehovot, Israel

CONTENTS

INTRODUCTION 593
Virology and Immunology 593
Historical Aspects of Antiviral Vaccines 594
CONSIDERATIONS IN VACCINE PREPARATION 595
Cellular vs Humoral Immune Response 595
Attenuated vs Killed Viral Vaccines 596
Immune Neutralization of Biological Activity 597
Inactivation of Viruses by Antibodies 598
Genetic Control of Immune Response to Viral Antigens 599
ANTIGENICITY OF PROTEINS AND VIRAL ANTIGENS 600
CHEMICALLY DEFINED ANTIGENIC DETERMINANTS 602
Defined Determinants in Proteins 602
Synthetic Antigens With Protein Specificity 603
Synthetic Approach to Vaccination 605
ANTIVIRAL RESPONSE INDUCED BY SNYTHETIC ANTIGENS 606
Tobacco Mosaic Virus (TMV) 606
MS-2 Coliphage 607
CELLULAR VS HUMORAL RESPONSE TO SYNTHETIC VACCINES 611
EFFECT OF ADJUVANTS ON EFFICACY OF VACCINES; SYNTHETIC ADJUVANTS 612
CONCLUDING REMARKS—PROSPECTS FOR THE FUTURE 614

INTRODUCTION

Virology and Immunology

Virology and immunology have been closely linked. That immunity against various infectious agents, including viruses, is a consequence of recovery from disease has been common knowledge for centuries; however, one can

0066-4227/80/1001-0593$01.00

say that, as scientific disciplines, virology and immunology were woven together only at the end of the 17th century, when Jenner introduced vaccination with cowpox to protect against the related disease smallpox. Contained within this discovery were three components: (*a*) the recognition of a contagious viral disease, (*b*) an appreciation of cross-reactivity between related viruses, and (*c*) the concept of active immunization. The two fields continued to advance together when, almost a century later, Pasteur deliberately attenuated virulent rabies virus, thus introducing a new concept, which persists till the present time—namely, the use of certain live virus vaccines.

Since these early events, both virology and immunology developed at a fast pace, with many areas of contact between them over the years. Two such areas worth mentioning are, on the one hand, the concept that viruses induce not only systemic immunity but also local immunity which is manifested in secretory immunoglobulins, and, on the other hand, the notion that immune responses are sometimes responsible for the pathological results associated with viral infections such as, for example, the slow virus infections. This latter concept has gained impetus recently, as it is now realized that many autoimmune and neurological disorders such as multiple sclerosis, for example, stem from a cell-mediated immune response triggered initially by an early viral exposure.

The actual process as well as the success of immunization or vaccination against viral diseases depends on achieving an appropriate and adequate immune response towards protective viral antigens. The efficacy of immunization is evaluated in terms of the potency and amount of induced antibodies, the time required for production, the potential for their recall, and the location of antibody in relation to its capacity to influence the key steps in the pathogenesis of the infecting virus. Efforts towards this end were made in many laboratories; as a result, several antiviral vaccines are available today.

Historical Aspects of Antiviral Vaccines

It is of some interest that the real advances in the development of antiviral vaccines have been sporadic and have always depended upon a major breakthrough. The first major breakthrough was Jenner's recognition of the protective effect of cowpox infection against smallpox, and its actual use for vaccination of humans. The second breakthrough, which was the first to be based on immunological principles—namely, the attenuation of a virus by serial passage in a new host (the rabbit)—led to Pasteur's rabies vaccine. Essentially, this method of preparing live attenuated vaccines is used to this date. From that period on, the major problem has been how to grow the virus. The first half of the present century saw two major developments: the employment of the embryonated hen's egg and of the laboratory mouse for viral propagation. These led to the development of yellow fever, influenza, and Japanese B encephalitis vaccines. Cell culture techniques were introduced in the late 1940s (35), leading to the quick development of killed and live poliovaccines and of an adenovirus vaccine in the 1950s. The licensing of the Salk vaccine in 1955 signaled the start of modern vaccination against viral diseases. With cell culture technology well established, live measles, mumps, and rubella virus vaccines were developed in the following decade; more recently, in the 1970s, efforts were directed largely to the improvement of existing vaccines and to the production of more efficient vaccines against newly arising viral strains, such as those of influenza.

While it is clear that existing vaccines have diminished the incidence, morbidity, and mortality of a number of infectious or communicable diseases, a general solution to the control and prevention of viral infections is not yet available, for several reasons. First, not all viruses can be cultured and developed into effective vaccines; second, many of the previously prevalent viral diseases that have been almost overcome are being replaced by other diseases, thus requiring the continuous development of new vaccines. Our increased understanding of the molecular biology of viral infection and growth can be expected to contribute to the resolution of problems associated with development of new vaccines. However, recent events (for example, the swine flu vaccination program in the USA) have highlighted some of the difficulties and complexities that are involved in these efforts. Consequently, it is not at all surprising that increased attention is being devoted to the search for new approaches, including the development of chemically defined and synthetic materials to be used in vaccination. The last approach is the main topic of this review.

CONSIDERATIONS IN VACCINE PREPARATION

Cellular vs Humoral Immune Response

Protection against infection, afforded by vaccination, seems to operate primarily through the humoral arm of the immune response, with the participation of all major classes of immunoglobulins: IgM, IgA, and IgG (79). Less attention has been paid to the role of the cellular response in recovery from viral infections and in the inhibition of viral growth, partly because antibody seemed to be an obvious mechanism. However, in recent years evidence is rapidly accumulating concerning the role of cell-mediated immunity and its crucial effect on both the type and the intensity of the immune response (23, 82), as discussed below.

Some evidence about the respective roles of antibody and cell-mediated immunity in recovery from viral infections is provided by certain "experiments of nature" in the form of patients in whom either antibody production or cell-mediated immunity is deficient. For example, it has been observed that patients with agammaglobulinemia, who fail to produce immunoglobulins, respond normally to smallpox vaccination, and recover normally from measles and most other viral infections (42). In contrast, patients with thymic aplasia, who generally show normal antibody responses but fail to develop cell-mediated immunity, suffer from recurring and often fatal infections with various viruses. Vaccination of such patients with smallpox vaccine may lead to disseminated vaccinia (45). Similarly, infection with varicella or Zoster, which is trivial in normal children, may prove fatal in leukemic children who are treated with immunosuppressive drugs and are deficient in their cell-mediated immunity (103, 104).

Experimental evidence also points to the role of cell-mediated immunity in recovery from certain viral infections. Thus, in animal models it has been possible to demonstrate that thymic impairment, either by neonatal-thymectomy or by treatment with antithymus globulin, can increase susceptibility to some viruses, such as ectromelia (22) or vaccinia (46). This is not a general phenomenon, since the same treatment had no effect on susceptibility to other viruses such as enteroviruses or yellow fever virus (115).

It is clear that the emphasis in the future development of antiviral vaccines should be directed toward eliciting both humoral and cell-mediated immune response. It should also be borne in mind that in some cases cellular immunity may play a crucial role in achieving effective immunity.

Attenuated vs Killed Viral Vaccines

A question that often arises is which type of preparation is most suitable for use as a vaccine for immunoprophylaxis of viral infections—that is, should the vaccine consist of live attenuated virus or inactivated killed virus? Both types of vaccines are available and in use; for some viruses killed vaccines may provide adequate immunity, but for others it is essential to use the live attenuated vaccine. For example, in the case of poliovirus, a live attenuated vaccine provides both protection and resistance to reinfection, whereas an inactivated vaccine, which protects against disease, is considerably less effective in inducing resistance. In the case of rubella, on the other hand, even an attenuated live vaccine is effective only in preventing disease and does not induce effective resistance to reinfection. The general belief is that live attenuated vaccines could be advantageous, since the virus, although nonvirulent, may proliferate in vivo, resulting in greater efficacy. However, killed vaccines have other advantages, and thus the question of choosing between these two types of vaccine has not yet been resolved.

The efficacy of killed versus attenuated vaccine, or the protection they provide, is determined by the process of neutralization or inactivation of the virus by the relevant antibodies and immunocompetent cells, since neutralization, by definition, is the loss of virus infectivity brought about by the course of immunization. The mechanism of this neutralization is quite complex and still controversial. The complexity is due mainly to the size of the virus (on a molecular scale) and the fact that the neutralization involves three components: virus, immune constituent, and host cell. In order to gain more insight into this crucial problem, less complicated systems of biologically active materials have been investigated, as described in the following section.

Immune Neutralization of Biological Activity

The interaction of antibodies with biologically active antigens, and the resulting neutralization of their activity, were among the earliest observations in the history of modern immunology (toxins and antitoxins). The category of biologically active materials includes a very broad spectrum of molecules such as enzymes, hormones, toxins, etc. The immunochemistry of many such materials has been explored; however, in studies that concern the mechanism of neutralization by antibodies, the most investigated substances are the enzymes, and the findings obtained with them can be applied to other systems as well.

The interaction between enzymes and their respective antibodies generally leads to a reduction in enzyme activity (7). In some cases the enzyme is completely inhibited; in others, only partially. Attempts to elucidate the mechanism of inactivation of different enzymes indicate that neutralization can occur via three mechanisms: (*a*) direct interaction of the antibodies with the active site; (*b*) interaction of the antibodies with regions contiguous or adjacent to the active site, i.e. steric hindrance; and (*c*) interaction with other regions in a manner that induces conformational changes in the molecule, leading to loss of activity. The prevailing mechanism is steric hindrance (28, 94). For all three mechanisms it is clear that the antibodies effective in inhibition are only a fraction of the total heterogeneous antibody population—that is, they are the only antibodies reactive with antigenic determinants related to the active site (7). In the case of several enzymes, such as lysozyme or papain, it has been possible to isolate exclusively the fractions of such inhibitory antibodies (14, 37, 48).

In these studies enzymes served as model systems; however, the results obtained are significant and they are relevant to this review, in view of the findings that similar diversity in antibody population is observed among antibodies induced by viruses (100). In this case as well, heterogeneity was reflected in differences in the neutralizing capacity observed for different antibody fractions.

The neutralization of toxins by antitoxins seems to occur by very similar mechanisms. A case in point is cholera toxin, a molecule consisting of subunits A and B that are distinct from each other chemically and that differ in their biological activity. Antibodies specific for determinants of the B subunit (which is identical with the natural toxoid of the toxin) are responsible for the toxin neutralization in vivo (64, 82).

The fact that only a small percentage of the antibodies participates in the neutralization process has a fundamental implication: If it were feasible to identify the antigenic determinants involved in the biological activity and, consequently, to immunize with them exclusively, only neutralizing antibodies would be elicited, thus providing much more efficient protective immunity against any biological agent, including viruses.

Inactivation of Viruses by Antibodies

That antibodies can neutralize viruses is a well-documented phenomenon, as manifested primarily by the protective effect exerted by serum of patients who had recovered from viral infections. This neutralization capacity, in serum of both humans and experimental animals, has been demonstrated for various viral diseases, not only following natural convalescence but also as a result of active immunization. For example, serum antibody was shown to be effective against influenza in mice (85, 91, 106); thus, passively administered antibodies provided protection against lethal viral infections. Infection with foot-and-mouth disease virus also induces humoral response characterized by development of neutralizing antibodies in both cattle (43) and guinea pigs (52). In the case of turkey herpesvirus it is possible to induce virus-neutralizing antibodies not only by vaccination with the intact virus (49) but also by immunization with glycoproteins isolated from chicken cells infected with the virus (110).

The introduction of cell cultures as host systems for viral growth aided greatly in the study of neutralization of viruses by antibodies, since it allowed quantitative in vitro assays of the interaction and subsequent studies on the mechanism of neutralization. A survey of the literature, however, indicates that although it is clear that antibody and virus do combine (and as a result the virus infectivity is reduced), the mechanism of neutralization is not yet understood. As mentioned by Mandel (61), there are several possible mechanisms.

There is no evidence that antibody can influence the viral replicative process after viral uncoating has occurred. Hence, the focus of interest on how antibody functions is restricted either to the direct effect of antibody on the integrity of the virion or to the subversion of one of the early stages in the replication cycle. Neutralization can be the final manifestation of several phenomena that are fundamentally different. At the most elementary level, one can envision a morphologically simple virion (with several copies of a single antigen uniformly distributed throughout the capsid), at a very low concentration, interacting with one or several molecules of a homogeneous antibody population and, as a result, losing its infectious capability. At the other extreme, one can envision a morphologically complex virus composed of several different antigens in a topographically complex distribution; some antigens may be virus specific and other host specific, some may react with one class of antibody and others with a different class. In addition, if the relative concentrations of virus and antibody are adjusted appropriately, secondary interactions leading to the formation of large aggregates may occur. The reaction that represents the critical neutralizing event cannot readily be isolated from those concurrent reactions that may also lead to neutralization, but for superficial reasons. In any event, the specificity of the antibodies, as related to particular antigenic determinants of the virus, plays an important role in the neutralization process.

Genetic Control of Immune Response to Viral Antigens

A parameter of increasing importance that might influence the efficacy of viral vaccines is genetic control of immune responses toward viral antigens. The notion that the immune response may be controlled genetically was proposed over 60 years ago for the phenomenon of hypersensitivity (29), but only in recent years have data become available for the molecular and cellular mechanisms of this process. Genetic differences in sensitivity and resistance to viral infection in guinea pigs and mice have also been described for many viral systems (24). The two phenomena are based on one mechanism—the existence of immune response (Ir) genes that control the recognition of and response to various antigenic determinants on various molecules including viral components. The antigens employed in studies on the genetic control of the immune response were mainly synthetic (68, 75), but some information is available on several proteins with defined antigenic structure and on alloantigens that have a very limited number of potentially immunogenic determinants.

The results indicate the immune response is controlled by a quantitative unigenic dominant gene that is linked to the major histocompatibility complex. Thus the capacity of an antigen to provoke an immune response is dependent not merely on its structure and specificity but also on major histocompatibility restriction (112, 114), probably involving dual recognition sites (33, 113). A case in point is the genetic control of different insulin molecules (51). Bovine insulin differs from porcine insulin in two amino acid residues (at position 8 and 10) that are located in the intra-chain "loop" of the A chain. The response to the two antigens in mice has been shown to be genetically controlled, in H-2-linked fashion. Thus H-2^d mice showed high response to both insulins, H-2^b mice responded only to the bovine insulin, whereas mice carrying H-2^k are low responders to both.

The response to hen egg-white lysozyme was also shown to be under H-2-linked control. In this case it was feasible to elicit and detect the response to a defined antigenic determinant (loop) of the molecule (13). The results demonstrated that whereas all mouse strains tested responded well to the whole lysozyme, only a few strains responded to the loop determinant (65, 73), thus indicating that the immune response to different determinants of proteins is under separate genetic control. Moreover, in many cases the "carrier" may play an important role in the control of the response (74).

Immunity to viral diseases is similarly under genetic control. Hereditary resistance to various viral diseases has been documented (24). Most knowledge on this topic comes from the study of resistance to selected agents in various inbred strains of mice and chicken; such studies point, however, to strain differences in resistance to many viral diseases. These included the arboviruses, mouse hepatitis virus, influenza in mice, scrapie, and slow virus diseases of the central nervous system. Although the mechanism of the effects of genetic resistance in heterozygous populations in not yet known, it has been shown that for all viruses (at least all those that produce in vitro measurable cytotoxicity) the response is MHC restricted (33, 112)—namely, it is definitely linked to the histocompatibility complex.

ANTIGENICITY OF PROTEINS AND VIRAL ANTIGENS

In the course of an immune response two distinct reactivities, which may not necessarily coincide, are exhibited. The first is *immunogenicity,* that is, the capacity of the antigenic substrate to elicit an immune response manifested either by producing antibodies or by provoking cell-mediated immunity. The second characteristic, *antigenic specificity,* refers to the antigen's capacity to react in a specific manner with antibodies or with immune lymphocytes, regardless of how these have been raised. The regions in the antigen molecule that come into direct contact with the active site of the antibodies or with the cell receptors are defined as antigenic determinants.

Proteins, viral components, and other macromolecules may carry a large number and variety of possible antigenic determinants that dictate their antigenic specificy. However, only a limited number of the potential antigenic sites are immunogenic or immunodominant. In viral antigens, even a smaller number of determinants are involved in inducing the neutralizing immunity. The antigenic complexity of proteins stems both from their primary structure and from their three-dimensional conformation. This is true for intact viral structures, as well. Studies on the antigenic properties of proteins have included elucidation of the role of various molecular parameters in the antigenic functions, as well as attempts to identify specific antigenic determinants. Whereas the detailed description of defined antigenic determinants that have been identified in several proteins is included in the following section, some general consideration of the immunological properties of proteins is given here.

As discussed by Arnon & Geiger (10), the parameters that are most crucial for the immunological properties are the molecular size of the immunogen, the spatial conformation, and the accessibility of the antigenic determinants. The molecular size is important first for immunogenicity. Consequently, small molecules are often nonimmunogenic, but they can become immunogenic by coupling to carriers. The assumption that a minimal size is a prerequisite for immunogenicity is not borne out by experimental data; however, in most cases, when a small molecule is by itself immunogenic, the response it elicits can be augmented by aggregation into a polymeric form. This phenomenon was best illustrated with cytochrome *c* (87) and with the system of flagellin (78).

The molecular size is also important for the individual antigenic determinants; the sizes of a large variety of determinants have been reported to be quite similar, and probably correspond to the sizes of the antibody-combining sites (50).

The spatial conformation is crucial in determining the antigenic specificity of proteins, as discussed in detail in a review by Arnon & Geiger (10). It has thus been documented that a drastic change in antigenic properties occurs upon denaturation of native proteins or unfolding of their polypeptide chains. In many instances more subtle conformational alterations are also accompanied by a change in the antigenic reactivity; the best example of this is the role of the heam group in the antigenic specificity of sperm whale myoglobin (32). This observation led to the conclusion that most of the antigenic determinants of proteins, including the viral proteins, are conformational determinants—namely, they result from the steric conformation and may include residues that are remote in the unfolded peptide chain but occupy juxtapositions in the native molecule. Thus, in most globular and structural proteins antigenicity is dependent almost exclusively on the three-dimensional conformation.

The last parameter to be discussed is accessibility. The interactions of individual antigenic determinants with either antibodies or specific receptors of the immunocompetent cells (which are, by definition, the requirements for antigenicity) necessitate their exposure on the surface of the antigenic molecule. Indeed, for both synthetic models and native proteins the accessibility of determinants has proved to be crucial (10). In native proteins the best example is sperm whale myoglobin, which has been antigenically mapped. Its antigenic determinants consist of segments that are at the "corners" of the folded polypeptide chain and are fully or partly exposed on the surface of the protein molecule (15). This parameter may be an even stronger influence in intact viruses in which the coat proteins are packed in a characteristic ordered pattern that could allow the exclusive exposure of particular regions (which may consequently serve as the immunodominant characteristics).

CHEMICALLY DEFINED ANTIGENIC DETERMINANTS

Defined Determinants in Proteins

Several proteins have been antigenically mapped and the antigenic determinants in them have been identified in whole or in part. This topic has been reviewed recently (10) and is described below in very brief form, with a few examples. Most antigenic determinants of native proteins are conformation dependent. Identification of such determinants is usually accomplished by fragmentation of the protein, either by chemical cleavage adjacent to specific residues or by controlled proteolysis. The resultant fragments are then screened for immunologically active components that can bind to the antibodies and interfere with their interaction with the intact antigen.

The first example is the *protein* of *tobacco masaic virus* (TMVP). This protein is the only constitutent of the protein coat of tobacco mosaic virus; 2200 identical subunits of the protein are packed in an orderly assembly into the coat surrounding the RNA viral core. The protein consists of one polypeptide chain of 158 amino acid residues, the sequence of which has been determined (105). Immunochemical studies with this protein demonstrated that an icosapeptide, comprising the residues 93–112 of the protein, possesses the total inhibitory activity of a tryptic digest and thus encompasses the single antigenic determinant of the protein (20). Detailed studies have demonstrated that most of the activity resides in its three terminal residues Ala-Thr-Arg (19), pinpointing to a very small and defined antigenic determinant.

In *staphylococcal nuclease,* on the other hand, several antigenic determinants have been identified, and although the protein lacks disulfide bonds to stabilize its three dimentional structure, the determinants are conformation dependent. The three identified determinants are present within the residues 18–47, 99–126, and 127–149 (90). According to the three-dimensional structure of the molecule (30), each of these regions occupies corner(s) of the folded polypeptide chain, is therefore exposed on the surface of the native protein, and consequently possesses conformation specificity.

Sperm whale myoglobin is a protein for which the full antigenic mapping has been accomplished (15) using several approaches and methodologies. The data, in this case as well, indicate that a relatively large proportion of the antimyoglobin antibody population is directed towards a comparatively small portion of the total surface of the antigen. Five independent determinants have been identified and all of them are localized in the corners of the molecule that separate the helical regions. The antigenic determinants comprise the sequences 16–21, 56–62, 94–99, 113–119, and 146—153. All these defined determinants are small, consisting of only five to seven amino acid residues, but they are all exposed on the surface of the molecule (15).

The last example to be mentioned here is hen *egg-white lysozyme.* Two independent antigenic regions have been identified in this protein; both are conformation dependent and contain a disulfide bond that stabilizes the structure and is crucial for the antigenic specificity. One of these defined determinants contains the C- and N-terminal segments 1–27 and 122–129 linked by a disulfide bond between cysteins 6 and 127 (41). The second region is a larger one, comprising residues 57–104 and containing two disulfide bonds; it encompasses more than one antigenic determinant. The region can be further split to yield a smaller immunologically active peptide with the amino acid sequence 60–83, containing a single disulfide bond between cysteines 64 and 80 which is denoted a "loop" (13). From the three dimensional structure of lysozyme it becomes clear that this region is located at one edge of the molecule and that it lies exposed on the surface of the molecule. It is possible to prepare antibodies which are specific exclusively to this determinant, the specificity of which is entirely conformation dependent (81).

Synthetic Antigens With Protein Specificity

As documented earlier in this section, it has been possible to identify antigenic determinants of several proteins. In most cases the determinants consisted of a relatively small number of amino acid residues with known sequences. With the present peptide synthesis methodology (40, 69), such peptide fragments can be readily synthesized and used for the preparation of appropriate immunogenic conjugates. This approach has been employed in the case of several protein antigens and has led to the production of synthetic antigens capable of eliciting antiprotein-specific immune response. A few examples illustrate this point.

The first example is collagen, the main protein constituent of connective tissue and probably the most abundant protein in animals. The collagen of vertebrates is composed of three polypeptide chains: two identical α_1 chains and one α_2 chain, which are supercoiled in the form of a characteristic triple helix (31). Collagen as such is a weak immunogen, and immunization with the native protein leads mainly to antibodies directed towards the N- and C-terminal nonhelical regions of both types of chains (83), which show considerable interspecies differences (17, 71).

The helical region of collagen has been conserved during evolution to a greater extent than other parts, yet some interspecies differences have been observed in this region as well, and they are expressed in some conformation-dependent antigenic determinants (102). This assumption was confirmed by the synthetic approach: A synthetic periodic polypeptide $(ProGlyPro)_n$, which was shown to have a collagen-like triple-helical structure (36), was found to be immunogenic in guinea pigs (25). Immunization with this co-polymer elicited antibodies that, in addition to their reaction with the homologous polymer, reacted also with native collagens of several species (62, 63). This cross-reaction is by virtue of the triple-helical conformation, which is common to the synthetic material and the various collagens.

Thus, when the structure or, in this case, the conformation of a particular region in a protein is known, a synthetic molecule having a similar structure can be prepared and is indeed capable of provoking antibodies reactive with the intact native protein.

The second example is tobacco mosaic virus protein (TMVP). The antigenic activity of this protein has been located in an icosapeptide (20), mainly in its three terminal residues Ala-Thr-Arg (111). Since these peptides are relatively small, an attempt has been made to synthesize them for the preparation of synthetic immunogens. The direct immunization of experimental animals with such synthetic analogs has been unsuccessful because the antibodies elicited by them did not react with the intact TMVP. Neither could intact TMVP inhibit the reaction between the peptides and their antibodies (97). However, the synthetic peptides could elicit specific delayed and immediate skin reactions in TMVP-sensitized guinea pigs. This demonstrates the structural differences between antigenic specificity and immunogenicity of various antigenic determinants and emphasizes the importance of the choice of material used for immunization. Nonetheless, it indicates that synthetic materials are capable of eliciting an immune response towards a native protein.

In the case of hen egg-white lysozyme, one of its defined antigenic determinants consists of the residues 60–83 in the amino acid sequence and contains a disulfide bond (13). This peptide "loop," when attached to a macromolecular carrier, elicited antibodies with restricted heterogeneity which were reactive with intact lysozyme (66), although they did not inhibit its enzymatic activity. Moreover, these antibodies were directed towards a conformation-dependent determinant, the structure of which is typical for the native enzyme (81).

In later studies (11), it was shown that the "loop" peptide can be synthesized chemically. Attachment of the resultant peptide to a synthetic carrier yields a completely synthetic conjugate which can elicit antibodies that are reactive with native lysozyme and can still recognize the conformational determinant of the intact molecule (8). Thus, at least in the case of lysozyme, a synthetic antigen was shown capable of immunizing against the native protein. Regrettably, in this case, the anti-"loop" antibodies did not exert an inhibitory effect on the catalytic activity of the enzyme. However, it should be feasible in similar studies to use fragments that will elicit inactivating antibodies.

The last example is a protein of great interest, namely the carcinoembryonic antigen (CEA) of the colon. A glycoprotein of about 200,000 mol wt, it is characteristic of many types of cancer tissues (54). Antibodies against it are used in a radioimmunoassay for detection of cancer. The synthetic approach has been employed in this case as well: A peptide corresponding to the 11 amino acid residues of the NH_2-terminal portion of the sequence of CEA has been synthesized by the solid-phase technique (69). The synthetic CEA (1–11) peptide was chemically attached both to a synthetic carrier and to bovine serum albumin. Both macromolecular conjugates provoked antipeptide antibodies in rabbits (9). Investigation of the specificity of this immunological system by two different techniques has revealed that the peptide reacted not only with its homologous antibodies but also with anti-CEA sera. Likewise, the antiserum against the peptide reacted with intact CEA, since semipurified CEA could inhibit the interaction of CEA peptide with its specific antiserum. This reaction, using a synthetic antigen, served as the basis for a viroimmunoassay to detect CEA levels in sera of cancer patients (12).

Synthetic Approach to Vaccination

As seen from the above mentioned examples, synthetic antigens that contain immunoreactive region(s) of protein molecules can give rise to an immune response towards the intact protein. There is no reason why this should be limited to purified proteins or enzymes. It should be feasible to use a similar approach for components of viruses and bacteria, with the purpose of inducing antibodies reactive with the intact virus and hopefully leading to its neutralization. A prerequisite for this research is a detailed knowledge of the structure of the viral components (proteins) and the elucidation of their involvement in the process of neutralization by antibodies. Only regions that take part in such activity might be able to elicit neutralizing antibodies.

Until now, very few attempts have been made in this interesting and promising direction. These will be summarized in the next section.

ANTIVIRAL RESPONSE INDUCED BY SYNTHETIC ANTIGENS

Tobacco Mosaic Virus (TMV)

The first report of a synthetic fragment that induced an antiviral response was by Anderer (1), describing his work on tobacco mosaic virus. This virus is a rod-like particle of molecular weight 40×10^6; it is composed of 5% RNA core surrounded by a coat of 2200 identical protein subunits that form 95% of the virus and are packed in a characteristic ordered pattern (4). The interaction of TMV with antiserum raised against the intact virus results in neutralization of the virus infectivity. Anderer (1) observed that peptides isolated from enzymatic digests of TMV protein had the capacity to partially inhibit the quantitative precipitation of the TMV by its rabbit antibodies. In this interaction the icosapeptide, which is immunologically active in TMVP, was not inhibitory; apparently only a few peptides were active, all of them originating from the C-terminus of the viral coat protein (3). These results led to the conclusion that the only immunologically active region of the TMVP in the interaction of the whole virus with the antibodies, is the C-terminal hexapeptide. This phenomenon is probably due to the exclusive exposure of this peptide on the surface of the virus, as a result of the packing of the protein subunits around the RNA core (4, 18). This orderly arrangement leads to the formation of conformation-dependent determinants, as evidenced by the accessibility of this region in the intact virus to proteolytic enzymes (44).

Based on the above finding, namely that the C-terminal hexapeptide of TMVP is the sole immunologically active region of the virus, an artificial antigen has been prepared and tested for its relatedness to TMV (2). In this study the C-terminal hexapeptide Thr-Ser-Gly-Pro-Ala-Thr was isolated from TMVP enzymatic digest; it was then N-acylated and converted to the *p*-aminobenzoyl derivative. The diazotized sample of this peptide was reacted with cross-linked bovine serum albumin and the resultant conjugate, containing 1 mg of peptide bound to 27 mg of protein, was used for the immunization of rabbits.

The derived antiserum contained antibodies that could precipitate with the homologous antigen, as well as (although to a much lesser extent) with the intact tobacco mosaic virus. The specificity of the reaction was demonstrated by the capacity of the hexapeptide to inhibit the immune precipitation of the antibodies by the homologous conjugate (albeit to a low degree).

The most important observation of that study, as emphasized by Anderer (2), is that the antiserum raised towards the artificial conjugate, when mixed in large excess with tobacco mosaic virus, inhibited the appearance of lesions when it was applied to tobacco plants. Thus, the serum against the hexapeptide antigen was effective in inhibiting the infectivity of the virus, and its effect was similar to that of the homologous anti-TMV serum.

Although the hexapeptide used in this study and the shorter peptides derived from it (5) were obtained from an enzyme digest of the native protein, they can still be considered within the class of synthetic materials, since, with the advanced methodology of peptide synthesis available today, such peptides can be easily prepared by chemical synthesis. The drawbacks of this system, however, in the case of the antiviral immune response, are the limited reactivity of the peptide—namely, that the inhibition of the intact TMV–anti-TMV reaction by the peptide is only partial—and the requirement of a large excess of antipeptide antibodies (as compared to anti-TMV antibodies) for neutralizing the infectivity of the virus.

MS-2 Coliphage

In a more recent study an immunologically active synthetic peptide that is analogous to a fragment of another virus, MS-2 coliphage, was described. A conjugate containing this peptide provoked in rabbits and in guinea pigs antibodies capable of *efficiently* inactivating the native bacteriophage. The MS-2 phage is an RNA-containing virus with icosahedral symmetry. The viral capsid consists of 180 identical coat-protein subunits, with a molecular weight of 13,700 each, and a single molecule of another protein, denoted A protein (80). Each coat-protein subunit consists of a single polypeptide chain with 129 amino acid residues, the sequence of which has been determined (60, 107).

Immunochemical studies on this phage indicated that antisera prepared against the total phage are capable of neutralizing its activity (86, 88, 96). Moreover, monomeric units of the coat proteins which can be readily isolated (38) can also yield, upon immunization, the formation of antisera that are efficient in neutralizing the intact phage (55). Efforts were therefore made to locate and identify the region(s) in the molecule that participates in the immunological activity and neutralizing process in order to explore the possibility of using synthetic materials that would provoke neutralizing antibodies.

The first step was the isolation and characterization of the coat protein. Its purity was established by analytical ultracentrifugation, which yielded a single peak, and by amino acid analysis, the results of which corresponded well with the known amino acid sequence of the protein. Further characterization related to the possible presence of disulfide bonds in the protein.

Their absence was evidenced by the diagonal high voltage electrophoresis technique in which no off-diagonal peptides appeared after tryptic hydrolysis and performic acid oxidation. These findings are significant since they ensure that enzymatic or chemical cleavage of the protein will yield fragments that are not linked together by disulfide bridges.

The second step was to prepare antisera that would inactivate the virus. Indeed, the viability of MS-2 phage was totally neutralized by antiserum induced by the intact phage. The specificity of this inactivation is due to a large extent to the coat protein, since the latter is capable of causing 50% inhibition of the neutralization. A further indication that the coat protein is an important component in the neutralization process is the finding that antiserum prepared by immunization against the isolated monomeric coat protein is capable of neutralizing the phage to an extent similar to that brought about by the antiphage serum, when both sera were used in the same dilution.

To locate the region(s) in the molecule that participates in the neutralization process, the coat protein was cleaved with CNBr and the resulting fragments were screened for their inhibitory activity in the neutralization assay (56). According to the amino acid sequence of the coat protein, the cleavage points are at the two methionine residues at positions 88 and 108, respectively (60). Consequently, three fragments are expected: one fragment of about 10,000 daltons and two fragments, each about 2000 daltons. Therefore, separation of the fragments by gel filtration yielded, as expected, only two fractions: the first peak containing the large fragment, denoted P_1, and the second peak containing a mixture of the two small peptides (P_2 and P_3). Amino acid composition of the material under the two peaks confirmed the expected results (56).

The relevance of these two separated fractions in the neutralization process was studied by phage inactivation experiments. The large fragment, P_1, served for immunization of rabbits. The P_1 antiserum was capable of partially inactivating the intact phage, but not as efficiently as antiserum against phage whole coat protein; thus, P_1 antiserium could effect neutralization of up to 80%, but only when used at a relatively high concentration. This fragment, due to its large size, is of limited interest since it does not provide any advantage over the entire protein.

The mixture of the two small fragments, P_2 and P_3, was used in inhibition studies and was found to be capable of effectively inhibiting the neutralization of MS-2 phage by antiserum against the whole phage. The extent of inhibition was almost 40%, close to the value of 50% obtained with the intact coat protein. Efforts to separate P_2 and P_3 from the mixture were unsuccessful, due to the negligible difference in their molecular size, as well as their almost equal net electrical charge.

In order to determine which of these two small fragments is active in exerting the inhibitory effect on the phage neutralization, synthesis was undertaken of two peptides that correspond to the sequences of the fragments P_2 and P_3 of the coat protein. The synthesis was carried out by the solid phase technique of Merrifield (69). The amino acid composition of the resultant synthesized peptides was in agreement with the expected values, according to the amino acid sequence of the coat protein.

The two synthetic peptides were evaluated for their inhibitory effect on the neutralization of MS-2 phage by antiserum to the whole phage. The results showed that the synthetic P_3 did not exhibit inhibitory activity. On the other hand, the synthetic P_2, corresponding to sequence 89–108, possessed high inhibitory activity, almost identical to the inhibition effected by a similar concentration of the mixture of the native P_2 and P_3 fragments resulting from the cleavage of the intact coat protein. This indicates that P_2 is the inhibitory active fragment.

A prerequisite for the preparation of synthetic vaccines is the identification and availability of a molecular fragment(s) that is involved in the neutralization process and hence has a chance of evoking neutralizing antibodies. It appears that in the case of MS-2 not only has such a fragment been identified but a synthetic peptide corresponding to its sequence retains the capacity to inhibit the neutralization of the phage by antiphage serum, in a manner similar to the native peptide. This system appears, therefore, amenable for studying the synthetic approach to vaccination.

For the purpose of immunization, conjugates were prepared, in which the two peptides P_2 and P_3, respectively, were attached to a synthetic carrier, multichain poly-DL alanine. The conjugate prepared with the P_2 peptide (P_2-A--L) contained 9.7% (wt/wt) of P_2, and the conjugate prepared from P_3 (P_3-A--L) contained 5.7% (wt/wt) of the peptide. Rabbits were immunized with these two conjugates and the resultant antisera were tested for their capacity to neutralize MS-2 phage. The results are depicted in Figure 1. All the plates contained the same number of plaque-forming units of phage (*A*). This number is not affected by the presence of normal rabbit serum (*B*). However, a drastic decrease is observed when the phage is incubated with antiserum against the intact phage (*C*), and almost the same neutralization is effected by antiserum evoked by the synthetic conjugate P_2A--L (*D*). A quantitative description of the neutralization process is shown in the right part of the figure, which demonstrates that while antiserum raised by the P_3-A--L conjugate had essentially no neutralizing activity, the antiserum against P_2-A--L had neutralizing capacity to the extent of 85%, comparable to that obtained by the anticoat protein serum.

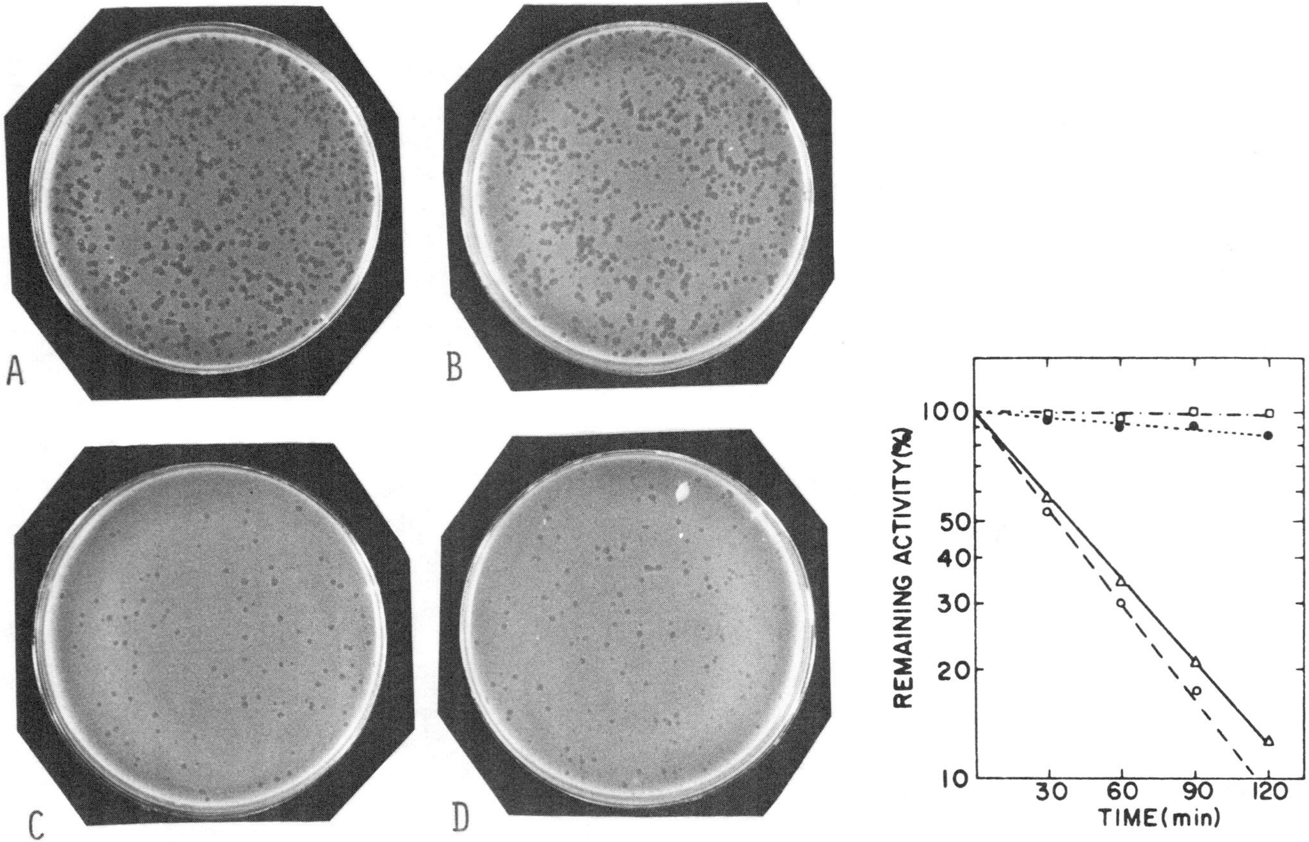

Figure 1 Neutralization of MS-2 coliphage by antisera. (*Left*) Plates containing 500 plaque-forming units of MS-2 preincubated with (*A*) PBS; (*B*) normal rabbit serum; (*C*) anti-MS-2; (*D*) anti-P_2-A--L. (*Right*) Quantitative expression of the neutralization of MS-2 coliphage by antiserum against coat protein (●– –●); antiserum against P_2-A--L (Δ-Δ); antiserum against P_3-A--L (○– –○); normal serum (□-·-·-□).

Since information is not available regarding the three dimensional structure of the MS-2 coat protein, nor is it known what conformation the coat protein assumes in the intact capsid, it is difficult to interpret the role of the structural conformation of the P_2 peptide (as it appears in the intact virus) in the antigenic properties of MS-2. However, the results obtained so far provide evidence that a synthetic peptide corresponding to a region involved in viral neutralization can be utilized for eliciting antiviral activity.

CELLULAR VS HUMORAL RESPONSE TO SYNTHETIC VACCINES

Cellular immunity (CMI) often plays a paramount role in protection against viral infection. This is true when protection occurs during or after convalescence and when it is achieved by vaccination. In recent years mounting evidence points to the involvement of CMI in the immune response towards various viruses. For example, in a recent study on vaccination of humans with influenza virus, CMI responses to the hemagglutinin and the neuraminidase were observed (27), as well as to the intact virus (89). Both responses were probably relevant for the protective effect. The immune response to foot-and-mouth disease has also been shown to involve cellular immunity (52). Similarly, CMI was observed after immunization with many other viral vaccines, such as rubella (98), or as a result of viral infections such as hepatitis (21) or sendai virus (6). Moreover, mice infected with sendai virus could be treated with thymic hormone, an agent which enhances the CMI (84). The role of T-lymphocytes in the host defense has not yet been clarified. The duration of the CMI is usually short; however, it may be involved in factors other than antibody formation and may contribute to changes in the pathogenesis of various viral infections. Corroboration of this assumption comes from the recent findings that in leukemic children, who are treated with immunosuppressive drugs and consequently exhibit extremely low level of CMI, even trivial viral infections, such as varicella or Zoster, can become fatal. The viral infection in this case could be overcome with the enhancement of the CMI by agents such as levamisol or thymic hormone (103, 104).

It thus seems that upon immunization with viruses, humoral- and cell-mediated immunity are induced concomitantly. In the case of proteins and some other defined antigens, however, it has been shown that the humoral and cellular responses do not necessarily parallel each other in their specificity or manifestation. (67, 93, 101). In view of the findings (reported in the previous section) that the synthetic material P_2-A--L elicited humoral antibodies with capacity to neutralize the viable phage and in view of the relevance of this finding to the potential of vaccine preparation, it was of interest to follow the cellular immune response toward MS-2 phage which is elicited by the P_2-A--L conjugate.

The cellular immune response toward intact MS-2 and toward P_2-A--L was evaluated in guinea pigs, after sensitization with either antigen, by both in vivo (delayed hypersensitivity) and in vitro (lymphocyte transformation) methods. The results with both techniques were quite similar and demonstrated that, whereas each of these two antigens is capable of inducing high homologous cellular reaction, the degree of cross-reactivity between them on the cellular level was not significantly high (58). Thus, by sensitizing with the P_2-A--L conjugate, only a low degree of cellular reactivity toward intact MS-2 was observed. This indicates that the specificity of the cellular reactivity in this case is not parallel to that of the humoral response.

The results in this study relate only to immunological cross-reactivity and do not rule out the possibility that, in spite of the low cross-reactivity, some protective effect toward MS-2 on the cellular level may still be achieved as a result of immunization with the synthetic conjugate P_2-A--L under optimal conditions. However, this study emphasizes the necessity (in each case where a synthetic material is considered for vaccination against a particular organism) to evaluate the cross-reactivity, on both the humoral and the cellular levels, between any fragment used for vaccination and the intact organism.

EFFECT OF ADJUVANTS ON EFFICACY OF VACCINES; SYNTHETIC ADJUVANTS

An important consideration in all vaccines is the adjuvant they contain in order to augment the immunogenicity of the primary agent. This point is even more crucial when synthetic vaccines are considered, since most of these substances are water soluble and tend to be less immunogenic than particulate materials. For experimental immunization in laboratory animals the most commonly used adjuvant is Freund's complete adjuvant (FCA), which contains killed mycobacteria dispersed in water-in-oil emulsion (39). It usually evokes high-level and long-lasting immunity. This adjuvant, however, is too problematic and is not adequate for use in humans since it induces local reactions, probably due to the very slow metabolic removal, if any, of the mineral oil and to the inflammation caused by the mycobacteria. Efforts are being made, on the one hand, to replace the mineral oil with mixtures of readily metabolizable components, or to eliminate it completely, and on the other hand, to replace the mycobacteria with less damaging materials.

In the search for the active components of the mycobacteria, which could replace the intact bacteria in the adjuvant without inflicting damaging effects, attention was focused mainly on the cell walls (59) or on Wax D (109). More recently it has been reported that water-soluble fractions can also substitute for mycobacterial cell walls in enhancing immunogenicity (47, 72, 77, 99, 108). In these studies it became apparent that the polysaccharide peptidoglycans extracted from bacterial cells had the capacity to enhance the immune response toward various antigens, such as ovalbumin, influenza virus, or staphylococcal infection.

In the series of experiments (described above) dealing with the synthetic conjugate P_2-A--L which could induce neutralizing antibodies toward intact MS-2 bacteriophage, all immunizations were carried out with FCA; in view of the accumulation of data on water-soluble adjuvants (as mentioned above) and their activity, it seemed of interest to explore whether one of these materials could replace FCA in the immunization with P_2-A--L for eliciting neutralizing antibodies. The material used was the peptidoglycan isolated form *Bacillus megaterium* (76, 77). The sole criterion for evaluating the efficacy of the immune response it elicited was the capacity of the resultant antisera to neutralize the MS-2 phage, namely, to reduce its viability (57).

Evaluation of the effectiveness of the soluble adjuvants was performed in guinea pigs. By analogy with most studies carried out with the peptidoglycans or with other water-soluble adjuvants, in the first step the peptidoglycan was mixed with the antigen and administered either in aqueous medium or in water-in-oil emulsion. Under these conditions no significant enhancement of the immune response was observed (Figure 2). In the second stage the peptidoglycan was covalently linked to the synthetic P_2-A--L, and the conjugate was again injected either in physiological saline or in water-in-oil emulsion Freund's incomplete adjuvant (FIA). As depicted, the antiserum raised by the conjugate when administered in the oily emulsion had neutralizing titer almost identical to that obtained by immunizing the guinea pigs with P_2-A--L in FCA. In these experiments the amount of peptidoglycan injected per guinea pig was 50 μg when injected in a mixture, and 5–10 μg when injected in a chemically bound form—amounts that are less than optimal for the adjuvant effect of this material. Hence, the results obtained can be considered minimal effects and could probably be improved by increasing the dose of the peptidoglycan or by otherwise optimalizing the system.

In the development of water-soluble adjuvants it was observed initially that various water-soluble fractions of the mycobacterial cell wall can substitute for the intact cells in Freund's complete adjuvant. With all these

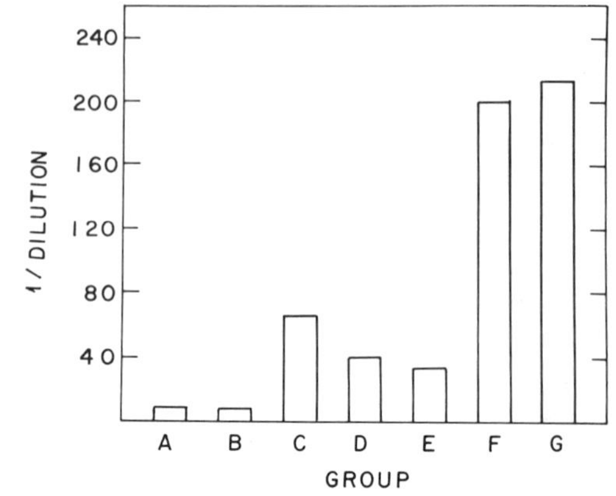

Figure 2 Adjuvant effect of water-soluble peptidoglycan on the neutralizing capacity of antisera towards MS-2 coliphage. The bars designate the reciprocal dilution effecting 50% inactivation of the virus of antisera obtained by immunization with (*A*) P_2-A--L in saline; (*B*) P_2-A--L in FIA; (*C*) P_2-A--L + peptidoglycan in saline; (*D*) P_2-A--L + peptidoglycan in FIA; (*E*) P_2-A--L – peptidoglycan conjugate in saline; (*F*) P_2-A--L + peptidoglycan conjugate in FIA; (*G*) P_2-A--L in FCA.

materials, the augmentation of antigenicity could be observed only when the adjuvant and the antigen were injected together with mineral oil (76). But, it was subsequently shown that several *synthetic* materials with similar adjuvant activity can be used. The synthetic *N*-acetylmuramyl-L-alanyl-D-isoglutamine (34, 53, 70) was found to have the minimal structure required for the adjuvanticity. More recently Audibert et al (16) and Chedid et al (26), have demonstrated that this synthetic material and several of its analogs, e.g. N-acetylmuramyl-L-alanyl-D-glutamic acid (MDP), are advantageous to the natural water-soluble adjuvant preparations and can increase the humoral immune response even when given in aqueous media instead of the water-in-oil emulsions. Indeed, preliminary investigations indicate that a conjugate containing MDP covalently attached to P_2-A--L elicits efficient neutralizing antibodies in rabbits, even when injected in aqueous saline solution (92).

In view of these results it is believed that the use of the most suitable synthetic adjuvant, in a sufficiently high dose and chemically linked to the antigen, will result in an optimal adjuvant that can be used in man.

CONCLUDING REMARKS—PROSPECTS FOR THE FUTURE

The theme of this review is the description of chemically defined vaccines and the exploration of the possibility of inducing antiviral immune response by utilizing synthetic antigens that comprise definite regions of a virus.

When such a region(s) is involved in the process of viral neutralization, it is envisaged that the antibodies induced by the respective artificial antigen will have neutralizing activity. It is hoped that this approach may lead to the production of synthetic vaccines.

The use of synthetic materials in the field of vaccination against viruses may have several advantages over the use of intact, attenuated, or killed viruses. First, theoretically it should be possible to attach several peptides, representing the relevant portions of different viruses, to the same carrier molecule. Thus, each adequately designed synthetic antigen will be multivalent and will be capable of replacing several narrowly specific vaccines. Second, this approach might eliminate immunization against many irrelevant antigenic determinants of the virus or of irrelevant proteins that contaminate the viral preparation used for vaccination. Thus, frequently occurring and undesired side-reactions might be avoided. Third, for many vaccines the addition of an adjuvant is required in order to initiate or to augment an immune response, and some of these adjuvants are not suitable for human use. In a synthetic macromolecule this problem of adjuvanticity may find its solution by introduction of certain groups that enhance antigenicity. Antigens so designed may possess built-in adjuvanticity and may prove less hazardous.

The two latter features have indeed proven feasible in antiviral vaccination as outlined in this review. Thus, synthetic antigens induced narrowly specific antibodies reactive with a limited region of a virus (TMV or MS-2) while still exerting a neutralizing effect on its viability. Moreover, water-soluble adjuvants had a dramatic effect in augmenting the immunogenicity of a synthetic antigen which elicits antiviral response, when covalently attached to it.

Another advantage of the synthetic approach is the possibility of designing the molecule according to the purpose desired. For example, it was mentioned that the immune response is genetically controlled (68)—a control that is partly dependent on the structure of the macromolecular carrier (95) and in many cases is linked to the main histocompatibility locus of the host (75). It may thus be foreseen that the efficiency of synthetic materials for different individuals could depend on the macromolecular carrier used for their preparation. A detailed study of this correlation might enable the selection of the most efficient vaccine to be used for different individuals according to their tissue typing.

The prerequisite for the preparation of synthetic vaccines is the availability of immunologically active fragments that are involved in neutralization. To achieve this end, more information on the structure of various pathogens and their components is essential. Indeed, considerable effort devoted to this area in the recent years is leading to the elucidation of viral structures.

Within this scope the results obtained, as summarized in this chapter, are encouraging, since they demonstrate the feasibility of the chemical approach and provide the conceptual tools for the development of synthetic antiviral vaccines in the future.

Literature Cited

1. Anderer, F. A. 1963. *Z. Naturforsch. Teil B* 18:1010–14
2. Anderer, F. A. 1963. *Biochim. Biophys. Acta* 71:246–48
3. Anderer, F. A., Handschuh, D. 1962. *Z. Naturforsch. Teil B* 17:536–43
4. Anderer, F. A., Handschuh, D. 1963. *Z. Naturforsch. Teil B* 18:1015–21
5. Anderer, F. A., Schlumberger, H. D. 1965. *Biochim. Biophys. Acta* 97:503–9
6. Anderson, M. J., Bainbridge, D. R., Pattison, J. R., Heath, R. B. 1977. *Infect. Immun.* 15:239–44
7. Arnon, R. 1973. In *The Antigens,* ed. M. Sela, I:87–159. New York: Academic
8. Arnon, R. 1976. In *Immunochemistry of Enzymes and Their Antibodies,* ed. R. J. Salton, pp. 1–28. New York: Wiley
9. Arnon, R., Bustin, M., Calef, E., Chaitchik, S., Haimovich, J., Novik, N., Sela, M. 1976. *Proc. Natl. Acad. Sci. USA* 73:2123–27
10. Arnon, R., Geiger, B. 1977. In *Immunochemistry,* ed. L. E. Glynn, pp. 307–63. New York: Wiley
11. Arnon, R., Maron, E., Sela, M., Anfinsen, C. B. 1971. *Proc. Natl. Acad. Sci. USA* 68:1450–55
12. Arnon, R., Novik, J., Haimovich, S., Chaitchik, S. 1977. *Isr. J. Med. Sci.* 13:1022–27
13. Arnon, R., Sela, M. 1969. *Proc. natl. Acad. Sci. USA* 62:163–70
14. Arnon, R., Shapira, E. 1967. *Biochemistry* 6:3942–50
15. Atassi, M. Z. 1975. *Immunochemistry* 12:423–38
16. Audibert, F., Chedid, L., Lefrancier, P., Choay, J. 1976. *Cell. Immunol.* 21:243–49
17. Becker, U., Timpl, R., Kuhn, K. 1972. *Eur. J. Biochem.* 28:221–31
18. Benjamini, E., Michaeli, D., Young, J. D. 1972 *Curr. Top. Microbiol. Immunol.* 58:85–134
19. Benjamini, E., Shimizu, M., Young, J. D., Leung, C. Y. 1969. *Biochemistry* 8:2242–46
20. Benjamini, E., Young, J. D., Peterson, W. T., Leung, C. Y., Shimizu, M. 1965. *Biochemistry* 4:2081–85
21. Beutner, R. K., Tiku, M. L., Ogra, P. L. 1978. *Infect. Immun.* 21:480–888
22. Blanden, R. V. 1970. *J. Exp. Med.* 132:1035–54
23. Bloom, B. R., Rager-Zisman, B. 1975. In *Viral Immunology and Immunopathology,* ed. A. L. Notkins, pp. 13–136. New York: Academic
24. Bong, F. B. 1978. *Adv. Virus Res.* 23:269–348
25. Borek, F., Kurtz, J., Sela, M. 1969. *Biochim. Biophys. Acta* 188:314–23
26. Chedid, L., Audibert, F., Lefrancier, P., Choay, J., Lederer, E. 1976. *Proc. Natl. Acad. Sci. USA* 73:2472–75
27. Chow, T. C., Beutner, K. R., Ogra, P. L. 1979. *Infect. Immun.* 25:103–9
28. Cinader, B. 1967. In *Antibodies to Biologically Active Molecules,* ed. B. Cinader, pp. 85–137. New York: Academic
29. Cook, R. A., van Dear, A. 1916. *J. Immunol.* 1:201–11
30. Cotton, F. A., Hazen, E. E. 1971. *The Enzymes,* ed. D. D. Boyer, 4:153–75 New York/London: Academic. 3rd ed.
31. Cowan, P. M., McGavin, S., North, A. C. T. 1955. *Nature* 176:1062–64
32. Crumpton, M. J., Wilkinson, J. M. 1966. *Biochem. J.* 100:223–32
33. Doherty, P. C., Blanden, R. V., Zinkernagel, R. M. 1976. *Transplant. Rev.* 29:89–124
34. Ellouz, F., Adam, A., Ciorbaru, R., Lederer, E. 1974. *Biochem. Biophys. Res. Commun.* 59:1317–25
35. Enders, T. F., Weller, T. H., Robbins, F. C. 1949. *Science* 109:85–87
36. Engel, J., Kurtz, J., Katchalski, E., Berger, A. 1966. *J. Mol. Biol.* 17:255–72
37. Fellerberg, R. von, Levine, L. 1967. *Immunochemistry* 4:363–65
38. Fraenkel-Conrat, H. 1957. *Virology* 4:1–4
39. Freund, J. 1947. *Ann. Rev. Microbiol.* 1:291–308
40. Fridkin, M., Patchornik, A. 1974. *Ann. Rev. Biochem.* 43:419–43
41. Fujio, H., Imanishi, M., Nishioka, K., Amano, T. 1968. *Biken J.* 11:207–18
42. Fulginiti, V. A., Kempe, C. H., Hathaway, W. E., Pearlman, D. S., Sieber, O.

F., Eller, J. J., Joyner, J. J., Robinson, A. 1968. In *Immunologic Deficiency Diseases in Man,* ed. D. Bergsma, pp. 129–51. Washington DC: Natl. Found.
43. Greaves, J. H., McKercher, P. D., Callis, J. J. 1972. *Am. J. Vet. Res.* 33:765–68
44. Harris, J. I., Knight, C. A. 1955. *J. Biol. Chem.* 214:215–30
45. Hathaway, W. E., Githens, J. H., Blackburn, W. R., Fulginiti, V., Kempe, C. H. 1965. *N. Engl. J. Med.* 273:953–58
46. Hirsch, M. S., Nahmias, A. J., Murphy, F. H., Kramer, J. H. 1968. *J. Exp. Med.* 128:121–32
47. Hiu, I. J. 1972. *Nature New Biol.* 238:241–42
48. Imanishi, M., Miyagawa, N., Fujio, H., Amano, T. 1969. *Biken J.* 12:85–96
49. Kaaden, O.-R., Dietzschold, B., Ueberschar, S. 1974. *Med Microbiol. Immunol.* 159:261–69
50. Kabat, E. A. 1967. *Structural Concepts in Immunology and Immunochemistry,* pp. 82–111. New York: Holt, Rinehart & Winston
51. Keck, K. 1977. *Nature* 254:78–80
52. Knudsen, R. C., Groocock, C. M., Andersen, A. A. 1979. *Infect. Immun.* 24:782–92
53. Kotani, S., Watanabe, Y., Kinoshita, F., Shimono, T., Morizaki, L., Sluba, T., Kusamoto, S., Tarumi, Y., Ikenaka, K. 1975. *Biken J.* 18:105–11
54. Krupey, J., Gold, P., Freedman, S. O. 1968. *J. Exp. Med.* 128:387–98
55. Langbeheim, H., Arnon, R. 1974. *Isr. J. Med. Sci.* 10:1173
56. Langbeheim, H., Arnon, R., Sela, M. 1976. *Proc. Natl. Acad. Sci. USA* 73:4636–40
57. Langbeheim, H., Arnon, R., Sela, M. 1978. *Immunology* 35:573–79
58. Langbeheim, H., Teitelbaum, D., Arnon, R. 1978. *Cell. Immunol.* 38:193–97
59. Larson, C. L., Bell, J. F., List, R. H., Ribi, E., Wicht, W. C. 1963. *Bacteriol. Rev.* 27:341–51
60. Liu, U. Y., Tsung, Ch. M., Fraenkel-Conrat, H. 1967. *J. Mol. Biol.* 24:1–14
61. Mandel, B. 1978. *Adv. Virus Res.* 23:205–68
62. Maoz, A., Fuchs, S., Sela, M. 1973. *Biochemistry* 12:4238–45
63. Maoz, A., Fuchs, S., Sela, M. 1973. *Biochemistry* 12:4246–52
64. Markel, D. E., Hejtmancik, K. E., Peterson, J. W., Martin, F. B., Kurosky, A. 1979. *Infect. Immun.* 25:615–26
65. Maron, E., Sher, H. I., Mozes, E., Arnon, R., Sela, M. 1973. *J. Immunol.* 111:101–5
66. Maron, E., Shiozawa, C., Arnon, R., Sela, M. 1971. *Biochemistry* 10:763–71
67. Maron, E., Webb, C., Teitelbaum, D., Arnon, R. 1972. *Eur. J. Immunol.* 2:294–99
68. McDevitt, H. O., Benacerraf, B. 1965. *Adv. Immunol.* 11:31–74
69. Merrifield, B. B. 1965. *Science* 150: 178–85
70. Merser, C., Sinay, P., Adam, A. 1975. *Biochem. Biophys. Res. Commun.* 66:1316–22
71. Michaeli, D., Martin, G. R., Kettman, J., Benjamini, E., Leung, C. Y., Blatt, B. A. 1969. *Science* 166:1522–23
72. Migliore-Samour, D., Jollès, P. 1972. *FEBS Lett.* 25:301–4
73. Mozes, E., Maron, E., Arnon, R., Sela, M. 1971. *J. Immunol.* 106:862–64
74. Mozes, E., McDevitt, H. O., Jaton, J.-C., Sela, M. 1969 *J. Exp. Med.* 130:1263–78
75. Mozes, E., Shearer, G. M. 1972. *Curr. Top. Microbiol. Immunol.* 59:167–200
76. Nauciel, C., Fleck, J., Martin, J. P., Mock, M., Nguyen-Huy, H. 1974. *Eur. J. Immunol.* 4:352–56
77. Nguyen-Huy, N., Nauciel, C., Wermuth, C. G. 1976. *Eur. J. Biochem.* 66:79–84
78. Nossal, G. J. V., Austin, C. M., Ada, G. L. 1965. *Immunology* 9:333–48
79. Ogra, P. L., Morag, A., Tiku, M. L. 1975. See Ref. 23, pp. 57–77
80. Osborn, M., Weiner, A. M., Weber, K. 1970. *Eur. J. Biochem.* 17:63–67
81. Pecht, I., Maron, E., Arnon, R., Sela, M. 1971. *Eur. J. Biochem.* 19:368–71
82. Peterson, J. W., Hejtmancik, K. E., Markel, D. E., Craig, J. P., Kurosky, A. 1979. *Infect. Immun.* 24:774–79
83. Piez, K. A., Bladen, H. A., Land, J. M., Miller, E. J., Bornstein, P., Butler, W. T., Kang, A. H. 1968. *Brookhaven Symp. Biol.* 21(1):345–51
84. Rager-Zisman, Z., Harish, Z., Rotter, V., Yakir, Y., Trainin, N. 1979. In *Proc. 10th Int. Congr. Allergology.* Oxford: Pergamon. In press
85. Ramphal, R., Cogliano, R. C., Shands, J. W. Jr., Small, P. A. Jr. 1979. *Infect. Immun.* 25:992–97
86. Rappaport, I. 1970. *J. Gen. Virol.* 6:25–32
87. Reichlin, M., Nisonoff, A., Margoliash, E. 1970. *J. Biol. Chem.* 245:947–54
88. Rohrmann, G. F., Krueger, R. G. 1970. *J. Immunol.* 104:353–58

89. Ruben, F. L., Jackson, G. G., Gotoff, S. P. 1973. *Infect. Immun.* 7:594–96
90. Sachs, D. H., Schechter, A. N., Eastlake, A., Anfinsen, C. B. 1972. *J. Immunol.* 109:1300–10
91. Schulman, J. L., Khakpour, M., Kilbourne, E. D. 1968. *J. Virol.* 2:778–86
92. Sela, M., Mozes, E., Arnon, R. 1979. *J. Infect. Dis.* In press
93. Senyk, G. W., Williams, E. B., Nitecki, D. E., Goodman, J. W. 1971 *J. Exp. Med.* 133:1294–1308
94. Shapira, E., Arnon, R. 1967. *Biochemistry* 6:3951–56
95. Shearer, G. M., Mozes, E., Sela, M. 1972. *J. Exp. Med.* 135:1009–27
96. Snippe, H., de Reuver, M. J., Belder, M., Willers, J. M. 1976. *Int. Arch. Allergy Appl. Immunol.* 50:111–22
97. Spitler, L., Benjamini, E., Young, J. D., Kaplan, H., Fudenberg, H. H. 1970. *J. Exp. Med.* 131:133–48
98. Steele, R. W., Hense, S. R., Vincent, M. M. 1974. *J. Infect. Dis.* 130:449–53
99. Stewart-Tull, D. E. S., Shimono, Y., Kotani, S., Kato, M., O'Gawa, Y., Yamamura, Y., Koga, T., Pearson, C. M. 1975. *Immunology* 29:1–15
100. Svehang, S.-E. 1967. In *Antibodies to Biologically Active Molecules,* ed. B. Cinader, pp. 301–48. New York: Academic
101. Thompson, K., Harris, M., Benjamini, E., Mitchell, G., Noble, M. 1972. *Nature New Biol.* 238:20–21
102. Timpl, R., Beil, W., Furthmayr, H., Meigel, W., Pontz, B. 1971. *Immunology* 21:1017–30
103. Trainin, N., Rotter, V., Yakir, Y., Leve, R., Handzel, Z. T., Shohat, B., Zaizov, R. 1980. *Ann. NY Acad. Sci. Conf., Subcellular Factors in Immunity, 1979.* 332:9–22
104. Trainin, N., Zaizov, R., Pecht, M., Shohat, B., Yakir, Y. 1980. *Symp. New Trends Human Immunol. Cancer Immunother., 1980, Montpellier.* In press
105. Tsugita, A., Gish, D., Young, J., Fraenkel-Conrat, H., Knight, C. A., Stanley, W. M. 1960. *Proc. Natl. Acad. Sci. USA* 46:1463–69
106. Virelizier, J. L. 1975. *J. Immunol.* 115:434–39
107. Weber, K., Koenigsberg, W. 1975. In *RNA-Phages, Cold Spring Harbor Symp.,* ed. Zinder, N. D., pp. 51–84
108. Werner, G. H., Marah, R., Floch, F., Migliore-Samour, D., Jollés, P. 1975. *Biomedicine* 22:440–52
109. White, R. G., Bernstock, L., Johns, R. G. S., Lederer, E. 1958. *Immunology* 1:54–66
110. Wyn-Jones, A. P., Kaaden, O. R. 1979. *Infect. Immun.* 25:54–59
111. Young, J. D., Benjamini, E., Leung, C. Y. 1968. *Biochemistry* 7:3113–19
112. Zinkernagel, R. M. 1977. *Immune System: Genetics and Regulation. ICN-UCLA Symp. Mol. Cell. Biol.,* 4:593–98
113. Zinkernagel, R. M., Doherty, P. C. 1974. *Nature* 251:547–48
114. Zinkernagel, R. M., Doherty, P. C. 1979. *Adv. Immunol.* 27:51–177
115. Zisman, B., Wheelock, E. F., Allison, A. C. 1971. *J. Immunol.* 107:236–43

Ann. Rev. Microbiol. 1980. 34:619–44

DEFECTIVE INTERFERING INFLUENZA VIRUSES[1]

❖1788

Debi P. Nayak

Department of Microbiology and Immunology, UCLA School of Medicine
Los Angeles, California 90024

CONTENTS

INTRODUCTION 620
NOMENCLATURE 620
PRODUCTION OF INFLUENZA DI VIRUS 621
ASSAY OF INFLUENZA DI VIRUS 621
PROPERTIES OF INFLUENZA DI VIRUS 623
GENOME OF INFLUENZA DI VIRUS 624
Standard Virus RNAs 625
DI Viral RNAs 626
ROLE OF DI RNA IN VIRAL INTERFERENCE 627
ORIGIN OF DI RNA 629
Oligonucleotide Mapping 629
Nucleotide Sequencing 633
Influenza DI RNA is Formed by Internal Deletion of Progenitor RNA 634
MECHANISM OF DI VIRUS-MEDIATED INTERFERENCE 636
EFFECT OF HOST ON INFLUENZA DI VIRUS FORMATION 637
EFFECT OF DI VIRUS ON HOST 639
Establishment of Persistently Infected Cultures of Influenza Virus 639
CONCLUSION 642

[1]Abbreviations used in this review are as follows: cDNA (complementary DNA), cpe (cytopathic effect), cRNA (complementary RNA), DI (defective interfering), DIU (defective interfering unit), HA (hemagglutinin), HAU (hemagglutinin unit), M (M protein), m (multiplicity), NA (neuraminidase), NDV (New Castle disease virus), NP (nucleoprotein), NS (nonstructural protein), P (polymerase), p- (passage), PAGE (polyacrylamide gel electrophoresis), PFU (plaque forming unit), Pi cells (persistently infected cells), RNP (ribonucleoprotein), SV40 virus 40), ts^-(temperature sensitive), ts^+ (wild type), UV (ultraviolet), vRNA (viral RNA), VSV (vesicular stomatitis virus).

0066-4227/80/1001-0619$01.00

INTRODUCTION

von Magnus (74, 75) first observed the formation of incomplete or noninfectious virus in 1951 when he serially passed undiluted influenza virus in embryonated chicken eggs. Since then, such noninfectious virus particles have been found in almost all animal virus systems that have been carefully analyzed (see 37). In 1970 the term *defective interfering virus* (or DI virus) was proposed to describe these noninfectious viruses (36)—that is, they are defective and require the helper function of homologous infectious virus for replication, but, in turn, they can interfere with the replication of infectious or standard virus. Although DI virus was first demonstrated with influenza virus (74), much progress has been made in elucidating the nature of DI particles from other viruses (see 36). In fact, until recently little definitive information was available concerning the nature of the influenza DI virus. Progress was severely limited because of (*a*) difficulty in resolving the segmented influenza viral genome, (*b*) lack of an appropriate cell-virus system for growing high titer influenza DI virus in a controlled environment, (*c*) inability to separate influenza DI virus from infectious virus, and (*d*) lack of a suitable assay for quantifying influenza DI virus.

Over the last few years, though, many of these problems have been overcome. For example, major advances have been made in elucidating the segmented nature of the viral genome and its role in viral pathogenesis and epidemiology (59, 69). Also, a cell-virus system is now available for growing high titer infectious (9) as well as DI virus (55). Consequently, during the last few years a serious effort has been made to understand the nature of the influenza DI virus.

This review attempts to summarize our current knowledge of the influenza DI virus. Other aspects of the biology of influenza virus (including viral genome, replication, transcription and epidemiology) have been recently reviewed (44, 54, 57, 69) and are not covered extensively in this review.

NOMENCLATURE

In the literature of influenza and other viruses, a number of terms have been alternately applied to describe DI viruses: noninfectious virus, defective virus, deleted virus, incomplete virus, immature particles, defective interfering (DI) virus, von Magnus virus, etc. (37). Among these, the name DI virus best describes the properties of the von Magnus virus. Other terms, although innocuous for nonsegmented DI viruses, may be completely misleading for segmented viruses, particularly influenza DI virus. For example, one can obtain defective, noninfectious, deleted, or incomplete influenza virus (29) if one or more viral RNA segment is missing; however, these virus particles will not be interfering and therefore must not be called defective interfering influenza virus.

PRODUCTION OF INFLUENZA DI VIRUS

Since von Magnus (74) observed the formation of noninfectious virus after repeated passages of influenza virus at high multiplicity, a number of workers have confirmed the same observation both in embryonated chicken eggs and in cell cultures (see 37, 54). However, after the third or fourth serially undiluted passage (p-3 or p-4), the total virus production is also greatly reduced. Very little DI virus is obtained for any extensive biological characterization or for biochemical analysis. Recently, the problem of low yield of influenza DI virus has been overcome by coinfecting cells with DI virus and standard influenza viruses (termed *amplification*) (40). A similar procedure has been used for amplifying other DI viruses (33).

When serially undiluted WSN (H0N1) influenza virus is passaged in MDBK cells, DI virus replaces over 99% of infectious virus particles by p-3 to p-5 (55). DI particles can be generated and amplified with either ts^+ (wild type) or ts^- (temperature sensitive) viruses. DI particles generated from either ts^+ or ts^- virus can replicate (as well as interfere with the replication of infectious virus) both at permissive and nonpermissive temperatures if the helper is ts^+, but can replicate only at permissive temperatures if the helper virus is ts^-. Amplification of a particular DI virus in MDBK cells in the presence of homologous infectious virus also helps in maintaining the same quality of a DI virus preparation in a number of studies because the nature of the DI viruses generated from individual viral clones varies widely (39).

ASSAY OF INFLUENZA DI VIRUS

The direct assay of DI virus in a given preparation has been a difficult problem; in virus systems where DI virus can be separated from infectious virus based on a size or density difference, various gradient techniques have been used for the identification of DI particles. Further quantification has been achieved through the use of optical density and/or radioactivity. Amplification has also been used as an aid for demonstrating the presence of a relatively small amount of DI virus in the original preparation (32). The analysis and quantification of the DI genome via various gel systems has often been employed for assaying DI virus. In addition, the lack of infectivity in a given viral preparation has also been used to determine the amount of DI virus in the preparation. In the case of influenza virus, a reduction in the PFU/HA ratio has been frequently used for determining the amount of noninfectious virus in a given preparation. Although the loss of infectivity without a concomitant loss of particle production can be equated to the amount of DI particles in most virus systems, this alone, for reasons discussed earlier, may not always represent the amount of influenza DI virus particles. Additionally, PFU/HA ratio is not sensitive enough to detect a relatively small amount of DI virus present in an infectious virus preparation. Recently, a direct assay system for quantitating influenza DI virus particles by using an infectious center reduction assay has been developed (39). In this procedure, which is similar to that used for quantifying Sindbis DI virus (41), cells are first infected with varying amounts of the DI virus preparation to be tested and are subsequently coninfected with a known amount of standard virus (usually 4 PFU/cell), such that each cell becomes infected with infectious virus. Subsequently these cells are trypsinized and varying numbers of cells are plated on a monolayer of uninfected cells and are overlaid with agar. Plaques are counted on the third and fourth days and the percentage of reduction due to interference by the DI virus is calculated. The fraction of cells uninfected by DI virus is determined by comparing directly the yield of infectious centers at different DI virus concentrations to the infectious center yield of infectious virus alone. The assumption is that infected cells not receiving DI virus will produce infectious centers, whereas cells receiving one or more DI virus will not produce an infectious center when superinfected with infectious virus. The multiplicity of DI virus can be calculated using the formula of the Poisson distribution: $P(O) = e^{-m}$ or $m = -\ln P(O)$ where m is the multiplicity of DI virus/cell and $P(O)$ is the fraction of cells not receiving DI virus as determined from the infectious center yield. Using this assay the concentration of biologically active DI particles can be measured directly as the defective interfering unit (DIU/ml) in a given preparation.

Several conclusions have been drawn from such analyses. (*a*) Influenza DI virus can inhibit infectious centers (or plaques) produced by homologous infectious virus. (*b*) m (multiplicity of DI virus/cell) is directly proportional to the amount of DI virus, suggesting that a single DI particle is capable of inhibiting infectious center formation by infectious virus. (*c*) DIU/ml can be determined directly from the multiplicity (m) of DI virus. The amount of DI virus obtained from different clones after repeated passage varies from 2 to 4.6×10^6 DIU/m1 while the DIU/PFU ratio varies from 27 to 1500 (39). (*d*) DIU/PFU ratio is generally increased when the PFU/HA ratio is decreased. The absolute amount of DIU/ml is not affected by the amount of contaminating infectious virus. In fact, usually a higher yield of DIU/ml is observed when the preparation also contains a relatively greater amount of infectious virus (PFU/ml) and hemagglutinin

(HA/ml). This is expected, since some replication of infectious virus is required for the amplification of DI virus. A high multiplicity of DI virus tends to suppress the total yield of DIU/ml, PFU/ml, and HA/ml as well. (*e*) In the p-4 virus, DIU/HA ratio is quantitatively comparable to the PFU/HA ratio in the stock virus, suggesting that in the DI virus preparation the entire loss of infectivity can be accounted for by the DI virus. Therefore, very little if any additional randomly incomplete, noninfectious and noninterfering virus is formed during serially undiluted passages. (*f*) Since interfering activity is much more resistant to UV light than infectivity (55), any contaminating infectious virus can be reduced greatly by exposing the sample to UV light before using it in the infectious center reduction assay. Thus aliquots of the same sample can be used for determining PFU/ml and DIU/ml as well as HA/ml.

The lack of visible infectious centers does not indicate complete inhibition of virus production. Since multiple cycles of infection are required for plaque formation and since DI virus tends to suppress cytopathic effect in coinfected cells (38), cells coinfected with both infectious and DI virus may produce both infectious and DI virus without producing visible plaques. The development of this direct assay for quantifying influenza DI virus has been very useful for studying the biology of these DI viruses.

PROPERTIES OF INFLUENZA DI VIRUS

In addition to the biological properties of interference and loss of infectivity, DI particles of a number of viruses have been studied in order to compare their structural proteins, antigenicity, morphology, genomic content, and other biophysical and biochemical properties to those of homologous infectious viruses. Many DI virus particles are shorter and less dense than the standard virus particles and can be separated either by density or velocity gradient centrifugation, e.g. VSV or Sendai DI viruses. On the other hand, influenza, polio, and reo DI viruses are not easily distinguishable by either centrifugation or electronmicroscopy. The qualitative nature of the structural proteins as determined by their antigenicity and PAGE analysis appears indistinguishable from that of homologous infectious virus, although their relative proportions may vary. Proteins of various DI viruses also have been shown to display normal biological activity, e.g. hemagglutinin (75), neuraminidase (48), transcriptase (22), and even transformation (73).

In the case of influenza virus, definitive studies on the biophysical and biochemical properties of the DI virus have not been possible because of the difficulty in obtaining pure, separate populations of DI virus and infectious virus. Although some investigators have reported a clear separation of DI virus from infectious virus via density gradient centrifugation (77), such a separation has not been reproducible in many laboratories. We find that the two peaks often observed in density gradients do not represent pure DI and infectious virus populations because they contain essentially similar RNA profiles by gel analysis as well as similar PFU/HA ratios (Nayak, unpublished data). Although it is difficult to obtain a pure population of influenza DI virus, recent studies (10, 48, 52) have shown that virus populations containing >99% DI virus and <1% infectious virus can be obtained by repeated undiluted passages. In addition, it has been difficult to obtain a pure population of infectious influenza virus using chick embryo fibroblasts and embryonated chicken eggs. Both cells produce significant amounts of "incomplete" or DI virus, even in diluted passages. Repeated cloning of WSN virus in MDBK cells produces a population consisting mostly of infectious virus particles (11, 39). Even with this procedure, some clones may contain significant amounts of DI virus already present in the plaque (39). Therefore, any standard virus preparation used for biochemical analysis must also be screened for contaminating DI virus.

With these limitations in mind, the data obtained using DI virus produced by repeated passages in MDBK cells and standard virus grown in MDBK cells show that the structural proteins of the DI and standard influenza virus are qualitatively the same. It does appear, though, that the amount of nucleoprotein (NP) is reduced (48, 52) in the DI virus compared to the NP in infectious virus. This may reflect the reduced amount of nucleic acid content in DI virus. Minor differences in glycoprotein or M protein content of DI and standard viruses have also been found (48, 52). Differences in lipid content of DI and infectious viruses also have been reported (7). Morphological differences have been noted in the electron micrographs of DI and standard virus preparations. More pleomorphic particles were present in the DI virus preparations (3, 43, 48, 52).

GENOME OF INFLUENZA DI VIRUS

It is well established that DI viruses are noninfectious because they do not contain the complete viral genome. In all DI viruses studied to date, a portion of the genome of standard virus appears to have been deleted. The amount of deletion may vary greatly, ranging from 15 to 20% or less in poliovirus (12, 50) to 90% or more in Sendai, VSV, or influenza viruses (16, 45, 60). In DNA viruses small supercoiled DNA circles result from the deletion in the SV40 or polyoma genomes (6). In the case of SV40, deletions may also be replaced by insertions of covalently linked host DNA (47). Hybridization studies have shown that DI nucleic acids are derived from the parental viral genome (27). Sequence homology data from the kinetics of hybridization and oligonucleotide mapping of various RNA viruses suggest that similarly generated DI RNAs possess large amounts of sequence homology (16, 42). However, some DI RNAs possess both plus- and minus-strand RNA. These are double-stranded, snapback molecules with a hairpin-like structure (60).

Influenza DI viruses produced in high multiplicity serial passages have been shown to contain less RNA (1, 2) and RNP (48) compared to that present in standard virus particles. Analyses of the DI viral RNAs by sucrose gradients and gel electrophoresis indicate that larger viral RNA segment(s) may be reduced (10, 21, 53). The recent observation (55) that DI influenza virus contains new, small characteristic RNA segments (DI RNA) in addition to the standard vRNA segments has helped to elucidate the nature of the influenza DI viral RNA. Others have reported similar findings of smaller RNA molecules in influenza DI virus preparations (14, 39, 51, 68). Small RNA segments, different from the eight standard vRNA segments, had been found in earlier preparations (10, 59) but their association with influenza DI virus was not clearly established until it was shown that standard virus free from small RNA segments can be isolated and that these standard viral clones will consistently generate defective interfering virus particles as well as DI RNA upon undiluted passages (39, 55).

Standard Virus RNAs

Although it had been suspected for a long time that influenza viral RNA was segmented, only during the last few years has it been unambiguosly proven that the influenza viral RNA is composed of eight RNA segments. The proteins coded by each RNA segment have also been identified (57, 69), including a ninth protein (NS_2) which is coded by the same gene as NS_1, possibly using a different reading frame (46). A profile of standard viral RNA of WSN strain (HON1) is shown in Figure 1. The protein coded by each RNA segment has been determined (58). Although there is a significant variation in the mobility of different RNA segments from different viral strains in polyacrylamide/urea gels, such variations, except for HA and NA gene, are not observed after complete denaturation of viral RNA by glyoxal treatment (17). For all influenza viruses the order of genes (named by the protein for which they code) is P3, P1, P2, HA, NP, NA, M, and NS with respective molecular weights of 0.89, 0.89, 0.86, 0.66, 0.56, 0.48, 0.28, and 0.21 million daltons (17). The respective number of bases is 2400–2500 for the P, 1920–1940 for the HA, 1680–1730 for the NP, 1550–1580 for the NA, 1100 for the M, and 930–970 for the NS genes (23). These estimates may be in error by 100–200 bases as shown for the HA gene of fowl plague virus which has been completely sequenced and is 1742 nucleotides in length (63).

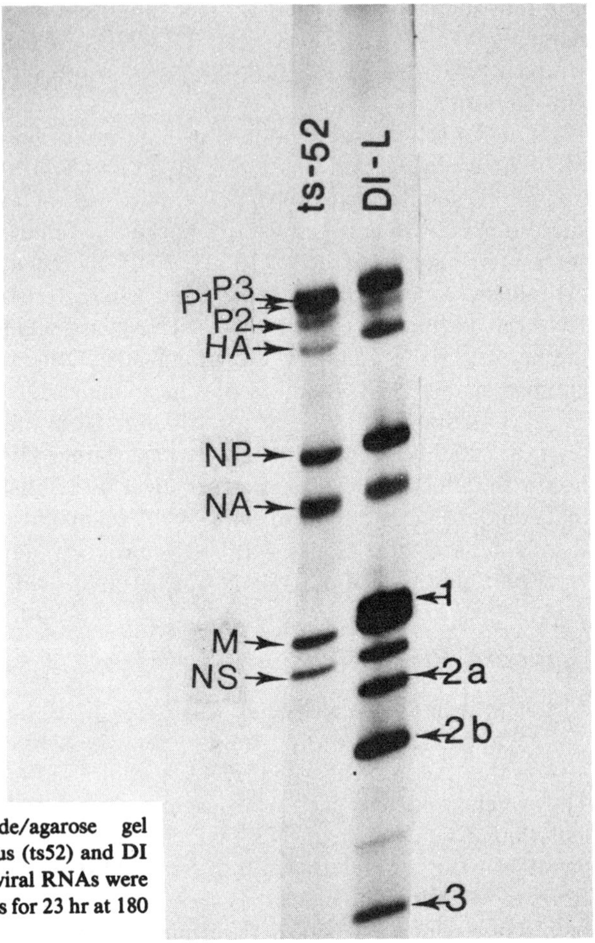

Figure 1 **Polyacrylamide/agarose gel electrophoresis of infectious (ts52) and DI (DI-L) RNA. ^{32}P-labeled viral RNAs were analyzed by electrophoresis for 23 hr at 180 V and 4°C (16).**

DI Viral RNAs

Analysis of the RNA of DI influenza virus preparations consistently demonstrates new, smaller RNA segments not present in standard viral RNA preparations (Figure 1). In addition, as reported earlier, there is greater reduction (and sometimes almost complete loss) of P and HA genes in the DI RNA preparation compared to that in the standard viral RNA preparation (10). However, as reported by Bean & Simpson (5), the loss of a specific RNA segment in the DI preparation cannot account for the total loss of infectivity in the DI virus preparation. Furthermore, the specific loss of any one RNA segment is not observed consistently, even though there is a drastic reduction of infectivity in all DI virus preparations. By analyzing the RNA at each serially undiluted passage of virus, it can be shown that a number of small RNA segments appear after p-1 or p-2 and become further pronounced with each undiluted passage. It is also apparent that all of these DI RNA segments are not present in an equimolar ratio. Furthermore, each clonal stock of infectious virus gives rise to a unique set of DI RNAs, suggesting that, as with other negative strand viruses, influenza DI viruses are probably randomly formed and present in clonal stocks (even after repeated cloning) or in plaques (39). Once formed, these DI viruses breed true and can be amplified in subsequent passages with the help of infectious virus, giving rise to the predominant DI virus species in a given preparation.

ROLE OF DI RNA IN VIRAL INTERFERENCE

Although the mechanism of interference by DI virus remains to be determined, it is well established in a number of virus systems that the deleted viral genome present in the DI virus is responsible for the interference of infectious viral genome replication. Such definitive studies have been possible in many virus systems because of the availability of separate, relatively pure DI virus and infectious virus populations and also because the DI virus contains only the shortened nucleic acid. Using such relatively pure DI virus preparations, one can show that the DI virus does cause interference of standard virus replication. However, such direct experimental evidence of DI-mediated interference of standard virus replication is not possible with influenza virus particles because influenza DI particles cannot be physically separated from standard virus particles. Furthermore, since the influenza viral genome is segmented, the influenza DI virus is likely to contain, in addition to the DI RNA segments, some of the standard vRNA segments. Several lines of evidence do suggest, however, that these small deleted RNA segments, and not any of the vRNA segments, are responsible for the interference of infectious virus replication. First, DI RNAs are present only in the DI virus preparation and are absent in the cloned infectious virus preparation. Even small RNAs that have been found as contaminants in many standard virus preparations can be removed by repeated cloning of infectious virus and are not required for maintaining infectivity (28, 59; Nayak, unpublished data). Second, during high multiplicity passages of infectious WSN virus in MDBK, HeLa, and CEF cells DI RNAs consistently appear in progeny virus particles and amplify in subsequent passages. The appearance and the amount of DI RNAs correlate fairly well with the interfering activity (DIU/ml) of the DI virus preparation. We have never found a DI virus preparation that does not contain one or more visible DI RNA segment(s). Third, UV sensitivity data suggest that the target size of the interfering molecule is approximately 1/40th the size of the infectious viral genome, a size which approximates the size of the predominant small RNA segment present in the specific DI virus preparation tested (55). Finally, direct experimental evidence that the small RNAs present in DI virus preparations are the interfering molecule(s) has been obtained by demonstrating that RNP complexes containing DI RNA(s) are interfering while RNP complexes containing only vRNA segment(s) are not interfering (40). In this experiment RNP complexes were isolated from infectious and DI virus preparations and analyzed in glycerol velocity gradients (67). RNP complexes enriched in P and HA genes (Class I), NA and NP genes (Class II), and M and NS genes (Class III) can be separated (13). RNA analysis of RNP complexes shows that Class 1 RNP complexes are completely free from Class III RNP complexes. In the RNP preparation of the DI virus the Class III RNP complexes containing M and NS genes also contain DI RNA segments. Using the infectious center reduction assay, it has been shown that none of the RNP complexes (Class I, II, or III) from infectious virus possess any interfering activity, whereas only the Class III RNP complexes containing DI RNA(s) isolated from DI virus cause interference. The other DI viral RNP fractions that do not contain DI RNAs, e.g. P gene RNP complexes from DI virus, do not possess any interfering activity. The peak of the interfering activity in the gradient also coincides with the expected peak of the RNP containing DI RNAs. Interfering activity is also sensitive to RNase. Dilution experiments suggest that a single DI RNP is capable of causing interference of plaque formation by an infectious virus. These results suggest strongly that DI RNAs which arise during high multiplicity passages and which can be amplified by coinfection with homologous infectious helper virus are responsible for interference in segmented negative strand virus replication.

Although it is certain that the DI RNA(s) present in DI viruses is responsible for the interference, the genomic content of individual DI particles remains undetermined. For example, whether one or more DI RNA is present in a single DI particle is unknown. Since a DI virus preparation often contains two or more DI RNA segments which are not in equimolar ratio, DI virus particles are heterogeneous relative to their DI RNA content. Similarly since vRNA segments are also not in equimolar ratio, the vRNA content of DI virus particles will also be heterogeneous. The exact genomic content of individual DI virus as well as infectious virus particles remains unknown at present. The answer to both these questions will depend on the elucidation of the process of selection (random vs specific) of RNA segments during maturation, assembly, and the final budding process of virions.

DI influenza virus thus appears to contain less than a full complement of viral genome. In addition, one or more DI RNAs are present in DI virus and are responsible for interference. Thus the presence of DI RNA may explain the loss of multiplicity-dependent reactivation, as well as marker rescue of any influenza DI viruses. For either of these phenomena to occur, cells must be infected with one or more DI viruses; these cells, because of the presence of one or more DI RNAs, will not produce plaque. Recently, partial expression of viral genes at higher multiplicity of DI viruses (42a) supports the above hypothesis (55).

ORIGIN OF DI RNA

The nature and the origin of the DI nucleic acid and its relationship to the parental virus genome has been studied for a number of RNA and DNA viruses. Of the negative strand RNA viruses, the DI RNA of VSV and Sendai virus has been explored in detail. The majority of these DI RNAs appear to be viral RNAs from which sequences have been deleted. Varying lengths are deleted from the 3'-end of viral RNA while the 5'-end of vRNA is preserved. In VSV a sequence of approximately 46 nucleotides from the 3'-end of DI RNA is complementary to the 5'-end of viral RNA and is believed to be formed by a copy-back mechanism (34, 45). Recently Lazzarini and his colleagues (70) have suggested that a specific polymerase recognition site (GGUCUU) which is proximal to the "stem" (complementary, RNase resistant ends) of a number of VSV DI RNAs may be involved in such a process.

Influenza DI RNAs have similarly been shown to be of the same polarity as vRNA because they hybridize to cDNA but not to vRNA (15). However, unlike the case with VSV or Sendai, the RNase sensitivity data suggest that complementarity within an influenza DI RNA species is absent or less than a sequence of twenty nucleotides. This suggests that influenza might not utilize the same copy-back mechanism found in other negative strand viruses. Further sequence relationships among the DI RNAs and their relationships to the progenitor RNAs have been determined by the two approaches described below.

Oligonucleotide Mapping

Since influenza viruses contain eight distinct RNA segments and a number of DI RNAs have been found, the technique of oligonucleotide mapping has been used in determining the progenitor vRNA(s) of DI RNA(s) and the interrelationship among the DI RNAs. The oligonucleotide maps of the total and individual vRNA segments as determined by two dimensional gel electrophoresis (19) are shown in Figures 2 and 3 (16). Subsequently, oligonucleotide maps of individual DI RNAs from a number of viral preparations have been determined and compared (Table 1). A number of important conclusions can be drawn from these data.

1. All of the DI RNAs examined to date appear to arise from the polymerase (P) genes (P1, P2, P3). The significance of this observation is not yet understood. One possibility is that since three P genes represent approximately 54% of the mass of total viral RNA, they are likely to yield the most DI RNA species if formed at random. Some of the arguments against this hypothesis are (*a*) DI RNAs are not generated at random, since vRNA ends are preserved (discussed below), and (*b*) the intracellular or intravirion molar concentration of P genes is not in excess compared to other vRNA segments. Alternatively, only the P genes may be capable of yielding DI RNAs. For example, it is possible that a unique secondary structure or the increased length of these genes makes them more vulnerable to replication or transcription defects giving rise to DI RNAs. A detailed sequence and secondary structure analysis of P gene and DI RNAs will be required to test this hypothesis. Additionally, a translational product could be involved in interference. A defective P gene product would be an efficient interfering molecule in blocking the replication and transcription of vRNA. There is, however, no experimental support for this hypothesis. Influenza DI viruses like VSV and Sendai DI viruses appear to contain less endogenous transcriptase activity (11). However, it is not known if this lack of transcription in vitro represents a defect in the template viral RNA, as in VSV (22), or a defect in the transcriptase itself.

2. Some DI viral preparations obtained from a single clone contain a number of DI RNAs which arise from one or more P genes, suggesting that these DI RNAs arise independently.

3. DI RNAs that arise from the same gene but are from different viral preparations often contain a number of identical oligonucleotide spots. This suggests that DI RNAs are not formed at random and that some specific segment(s) of the progenitor gene is preserved in DI RNAs.

4. Some new spots (for example, a, b, c, or d in Table 1) that are not present in vRNA segments are found in DI RNA. The origin of these new spots is not known, but they may be formed by the deletion of an internal sequence(s) either creating a totally new spot or modifying an old spot.

5. Two types of DI RNAs appear to be present among the multiple sets of DI RNAs arising from the same progenitor RNA. In the first type, larger DI RNA contains all the spots present in a smaller DI RNA (for example,

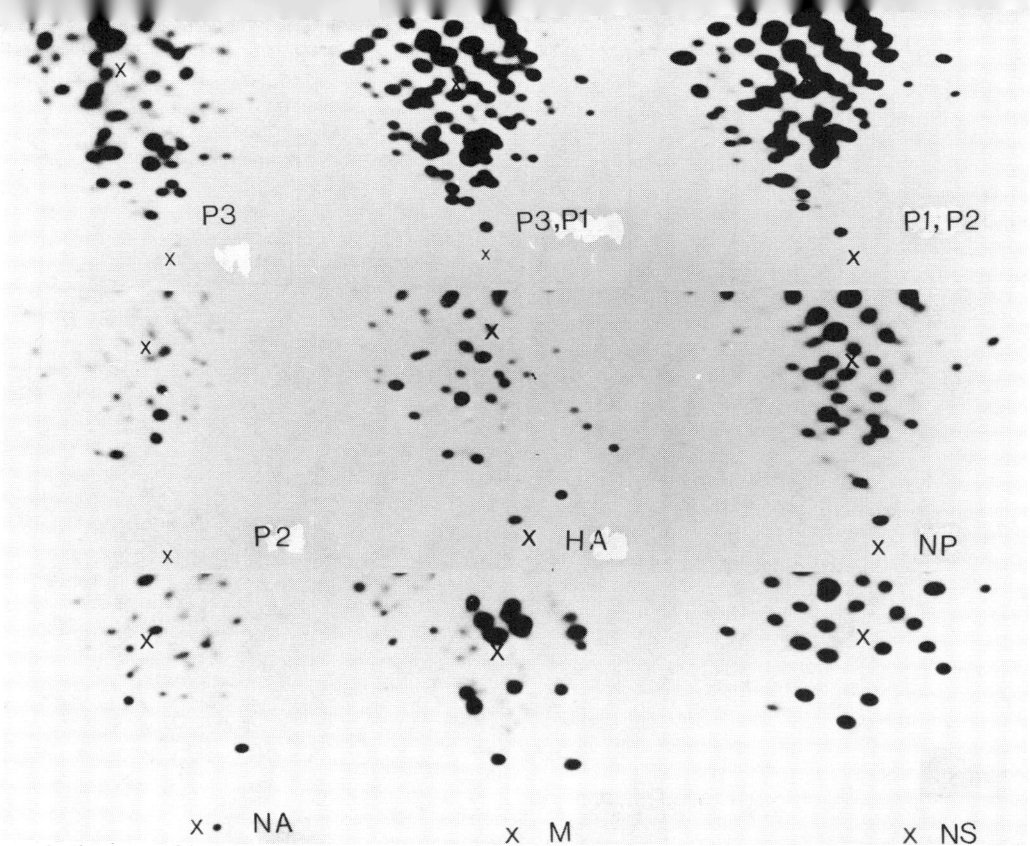

Figure 2 Oligonucleotide map of individual vRNA segments of WSN (HON1) virus. Individual vRNA segments were isolated from polyacrylamide/agarose gel either at 4 or 22°C (16), treated with T1 RNase and analyzed by two dimensional gel electrophoresis. P3 (22°C), P3, P1 (4°C), P1, P2 (22°C), P2 (4°C), HA (4°C), NP (22°C), NA (22°C), M (22°C), NS (22°C). First dimension, right to left; second dimension, bottom to top. The positions of xylene cyanol (*lower*) and bromophenol blue (*upper*) are marked by Xs.

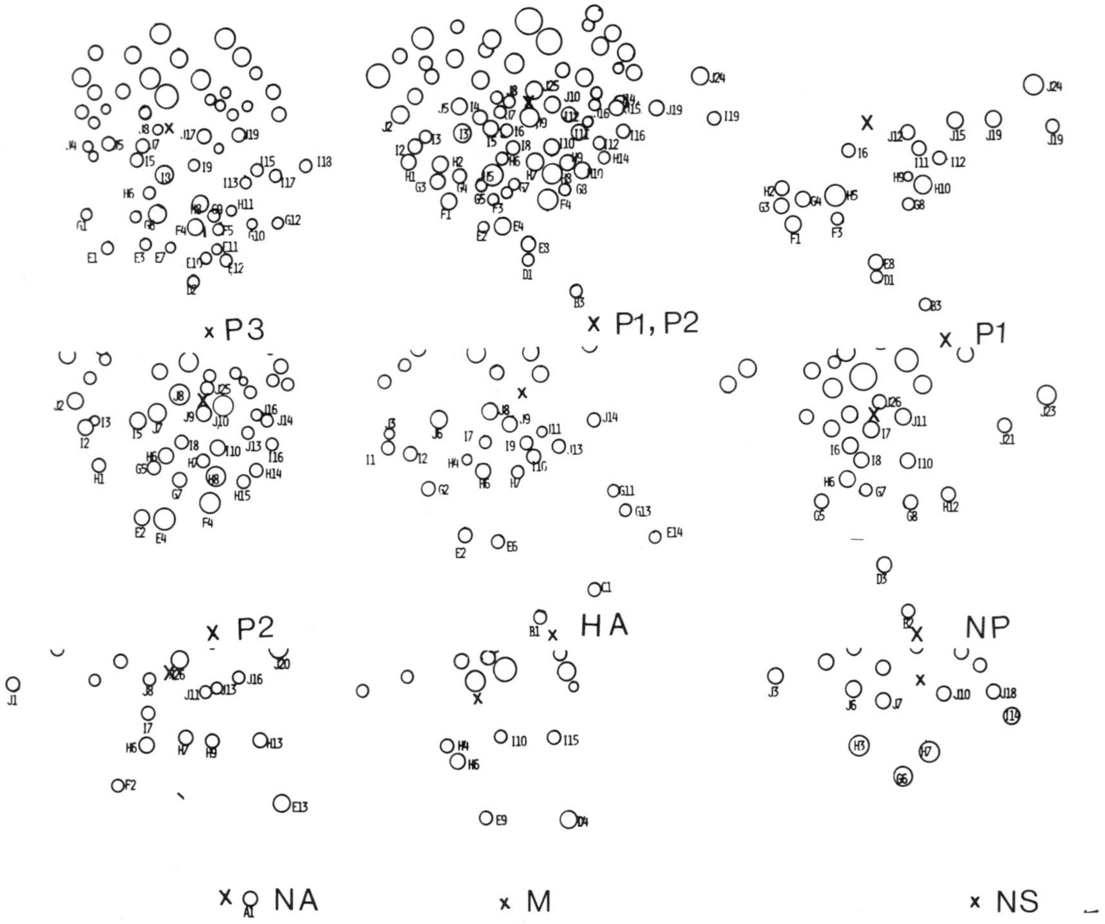

Figure 3 Tracing and identification of characteristic oligonucleotide spots of vRNA segments shown in Figure 2. Oligonucleotide map of P2 was deduced from Figure 2 since P3 could not be separated.

Table 1 Oligonucleotide maps of DI RNAs

DI RNA	Spot number[a]	vRNA origin
L1	H11 J4 I5 J7 E1 E7 G1 I8 I15 J17 d	(P3)
L2a	H11 J4 I5 J7 E11 J8 G6 J5	(P3)
P2	H11 J4 I5 E11 J8	(P3)
ts^+2a	H11 J4 I5 E11 J8	(P3)
DIa	H11 J4 I5 E11 J8 J7 E7	(P3)
DIb	H11 I5 E11	(P3)
ts^+3	H11 J4 H8	(P3)
B1	D1 G4 H5 I6 I11 J15 H10 J12 a	(P1)
P1	D1 G4 H5 I6 I11 J15 J12 b	(P1)
L2b	D1 G4 H5 I6 I11 J15 J12 c	(P1)
ts^+1	D1 G4 H5 I6 I11 J15 H10	(P1)
L3	D1 G4 H5 I6 I11 J15	(P1)
ts^+2b	E4 H7 H14 J10 J16 J25	(P2)

[a]Spots present in more than one DI RNA are underlined (16).

B1, P1, L3 in Table 1). The oligonucleotide sequence of the smaller DI RNA appears to be a subset of the larger DI RNA. Such completely overlapping DI RNAs have also been found in VSV DI RNAs. In the second type, some of the DI RNAs that arise from the same gene (P1 and ts^+1; L2b and ts^+1; ts^+2a and ts^+3; L1 and L2a) contain both overlapping and non-overlapping sequences. The latter classes of DI RNA cannot be explained by a common initiation or termination point and a simple deletion from the other end as has been proposed for most negative strand DI virus RNAs (35, 49). They must be formed by a different mechanism.

Nucleotide Sequencing

Since the oligonucleotide analysis of DI and viral RNAs suggested that the formation of some of the influenza DI RNAs may be different from that observed for the majority of other negative strand DI RNAs, further sequence relationships among the influenza DI RNAs and their progenitors were studied by direct RNA sequencing. Two types of analytical procedures were used. In the first either 5'- or 3'-end-labeled viral or DI RNA was subjected to partial nuclease digestion using base specific nucleases and was analyzed by electrophoresis in 20% polyacrylamide gels containing 7M urea (24). In the second procedure terminally labeled RNAs were partially digested with either alkali or formamide and subjected to two dimensional slab gel electrophoresis. This technique permits sequencing based upon net charge at pH 3.5 in the first dimension and upon fragment chain length in the second dimension (16).

The 5'- and 3'-terminal sequences of combined polymerase genes (P1+P-2+P3) and three DI RNAs are shown in Table 2. The first 13 nucleotides at the 5'-end and the last 12 nucleotides at the 3'-end of all DI RNAs are the same and are also identical to those of the P genes. The sequence beyond the first 13 nucleotides at the 5'-end and before the last 12 nucleotides at the 3'-end appears to diverge in the different vRNA segments (18).

Influenza DI RNA is Formed by Internal Deletion of Progenitor RNA

The 3'- and 5'-terminal sequences of defective interfering RNAs are identical to the 3'- and 5'-terminal sequences of their progenitor polymerase RNA. The common sequence of the DI RNAs and the progenitor vRNAs is 5'AGUAGAAACAAGG——CCUGCUUUCGCU–OH3'. The terminal sequences are essentially the same for all eight vRNA segments, except for one nucleotide change from C to U at the fourth position from the 3'-terminus for HA and NP genes (18). Thus the 3'- and 5'-terminal sequences do not show complete inverted complementarity. Comparing the 12 nucleotides at both ends, there are five mismatches at positions 3 (G→U), 4 (C→A), 5 (U→G), 8 (C→A), and 11 (C→A). Therefore, influenza DI RNAs cannot be formed by copy-back synthesis on the nascent replicative intermediate which would result in the formation of 3' and 5' complementary termini. In the majority of the DI RNAs found in VSV and Sendai, the 5'- end is the same as that of the genomic RNA and the 3'-end is complementary to the 5'-end. The model for the generation of DI RNAs for both VSV and Sendai virus implies that the sequence at the 5'-end is preserved and that the 3'-terminal sequence of the DI RNA is generated by a copy-back mechanism (35, 49). The absence of complementarity of the ends of influenza DI viral RNAs and the identity of the DI RNA ends to the ends of progenitor genomic RNA do not allow such a mechanism for the formation of influenza DI RNA. The majority of influenza viral DI RNAs, therefore, are formed by internal deletion. In this respect influenza DI RNAs may be similar to the DI RNAs present in positive strand virus. For example, the DI RNAs of Semliki forest virus (43, 72), Sindbis virus (20), and poliovirus (49) share common 3'- and 5'-ends with their progenitor RNA and are formed by internal deletion. Similar mechanisms, although infrequent, may also take place in the formation of some VSV DI RNAs. Recently, two DI RNAs derived from a heat-resistant strain of VSV have been shown to be formed by internal deletion (25, 61).

Table 2 Nucleotide sequences of the 3′– and 5′–end of defective interfering viral RNAs and combined polymerase genes (P1 + P2 + P3)

3′–End	1 5 10 15 20
	G A A
P1 + P2 + P3	U–C–G–C–U–U–U–C–G– U – C – C– A – (U)– G – (–)[b] – G –G– (U)– A – A –(–)
	G (C)[a] (U) (C) U
	(C)
L1	U–C–G–C–U–U–U–C–G–U –C – C –A – G –(–)–(–)– A –(–)–(–)– A – (–) A
L2	U–C–G–C–U–U–U–C–G–U – C – C –G – G –(–)–(–)– G – G –(–)– A – (–) A
L3	U–C–G–C–U–U–U–C–G –U – C – C –G – (–)–(–)–(–)– G – G –(U)– A – A (–)
	(C)
5′–End	1 5 10 15 20 25
P1 + P2 + P3	A–G–U–A–G–A–A–A–C –A – A – G –G– U – A – G – U – U – U – U – (–)–(–)– A – A – (–)– (–) – (–)–(–)–(–)–(–)
	C G
L1	A–G–U–A–G–A–A–A–C –A – A – G –G– U – A – G – U – U – U –(U)– (U)–(U)– A – A – G – (–) – A – G – G – G
	(C) (C) (C)
L2	A–G–U–A–G–A–A–A–C– A – A – G – G – (A)–(A) – G – U – U – U –(–)– (–)–(–)–(–)–(–)– G – (–) – (–)– G – G – G
	(C) (C)
L3	A–G–U–A–G–A–A–A–C– A – A – G – G – (A)–(A) – G – U – U – U – U – U –(A)–(A)–(A)– G – (A) – (A)– G – G – G
	(C) (C) (C) (C) (C) (C) (C)

[a]Parentheses indicate that only one of the two nucleotides is present. The presence of more than one nucleotide at a given position indicates divergence of P1, P2, and P3 genes (14a).
[b]Not determined.

MECHANISM OF DI VIRUS-MEDIATED INTERFERENCE

Although it is well established that the DI viral genome (or DI RNA) is responsible for the interference of infectious virus replication, the mechanism of this interference is not well understood. It is known that the interference mediated by DI virus is effective only against homologous or closely related viruses and therfore is not mediated via interferon. It is also known that the interference is not via blocking the cell surface receptors for virus. Rather, an intracellular event involving primarily viral RNA replication is affected (35). Any effect on viral transcription or translation is believed secondary to the interference of vRNA synthesis. The mechanism by which DI RNA interferes with vRNA synthesis is not well understood; however, it is believed that the interference is due to a competitive advantage of the smaller DI RNA molecules for the limited number of polymerase (replicase) molecules present in infected cells. It has been further postulated that since most of the DI RNAs of VSV and Sendai virus possess the 5' vRNA terminus (and not the 3' vRNA terminus), the replicase recognition site will be generated at the 3'-end of both plus and minus strands of DI RNAs. Since DI RNAs lack the transcriptase recognition site, the DI RNA will only function in replication and may out-compete standard vRNAs that possess a replication recognition site at one end and the transcription recognition site at the other end (62). This hypothesis does not postulate the inhibitory role of any transcriptional or translational product of DI RNA in interference. Recently, however, Rao & Huang (66) have found that s 40–60 nucleotide RNA similar to one synthesized in vitro is also synthesized in DI virus infected cells. The role of this small plus strand RNA in interference remains undetermined at present.

In the case of influenza DI virus, interference also appears to be an early intracellular event since DI virus must be present within two hours of infection by the standard virus to cause interference of standard virus replication (55). However, the mechanism of interference by influenza DI virus may be different from that of VSV or Sendai DI viruses. Unlike the majority of VSV or Sendai DI viral RNAs, influenza viral DI RNA is formed by an internal deletion possessing both 5'- and 3'-ends of vRNA. Since influenza DI RNAs do not possess ends complementary to each other and since both vRNA ends are preserved, such DI RNAs would not possess any additional replicative advantage, other than their smaller size, over standard vRNA segments. It is also evident that size is not the sole factor in providing a competitive edge in replication because all of the DI RNAs in a given preparation are not present in equimolar ratio and the most abundant species may not be the smallest one (Figure 1). Furthermore, during long-term coinfection experiments the population of DI virus gradually changes, with the emergence of the smaller DI RNAs over the larger DI RNAs. It is not clear if these smaller DI RNAs are newly generated or are already present as a minor component in earlier passages. All of the predominant DI RNAs analyzed to date appear to be of P gene origin. It is also to be noted that the replication of P genes appears to be primarily affected in most DI virus preparation. Whether this interference is specific for the progenitor genes of DI RNA as observed in some DI virus preparation (39, 51, 62a) or is nonspecific and merely represents a size dependence i.e. the largest genes being affected most, is not clear. Finally, the molecular mechanism of interference mediated by influenza DI virus remains undetermined. Since both 5'- and 3'-ends are present in influenza DI RNA, such DI RNAs, unlike VSV DI RNA, should be capable of undergoing full-length transcription and possible translation in coinfected cells. In summary, although the outcome of influenza DI virus appears to be similar to that of VSV DI virus, the structure of influenza DI RNA appears to be different from that of the majority of VSV DI RNAs and thus the mechanism of interference may be different from that of other negative strand DI viruses.

EFFECT OF HOST ON INFLUENZA DI VIRUS FORMATION

For a number of viruses, the generation and amplification of DI viruses have been shown to be strongly dependent on host function. For example, the same clonal stock of VSV produces different DI viruses in different cells, although it will produce the same DI virus(es) in a given cell type (32, 42). Stark & Kennedy (72) have reported a strong host influence in the generation and propagation of Semliki forest DI virus. Kang et al (42) have further reported that a host factor is required for the generation of VSV DI genome and that cells treated with actinomycin D do not generate VSV DI viruses.

Influenza viruses vary greatly in their host range in nature as well as in the laboratory. WSN virus has been shown to possess a differential growth potential in different host cells. For example, WSN virus produces largely infectious virus in MDBK cells, predominantly incomplete virus in chick embryo fibroblast (CEF) cells, and only abortive infection with little or no virus production in HeLa cells (9). Upon serial undiluted passages of WSN virus, in these three types of cells, the yield of infectious and DI virus varies greatly as expected.

MDBK cells also produce the maximum amount of infectious virus which is reduced 10,000 fold by p-5. In CEF cells, the yield of infectious virus at p-0 and p-1 is essentially the same as in MDBK cells, but upon subsequent passages the yield of infectious virus in CEF cells is precipitously reduced. HeLa cells produce at least 50-fold less infectious virus than either MDBK or CEF cells at p-0 and hardly any infectious virus at all after p-3.

The amount of DI virus produced at different passages also varies greatly in different cells. DI virus is not detectable at p-0 in MDBK, CEF, or HeLa cells. However, at subsequent undiluted passages, the amount of DI virus increases with a maximum yield of DI virus at p-5, p-4, and p-3 in MDBK, CEF, and HeLA cells, respectively. Again, MDBK cells produce the greatest amount of DI virus whereas HeLa cells in which infectious virus replication is restricted, also yield a lower amount of DI virus. This is not unexpected since the growth and amplification of DI virus depends on the replication of infectious helper virus. If the formation of DI virus essentially requires the same steps of replication as needed for infectious virus, the yield of DI virus will be reduced in cells with a defect in viral replication e.g. HeLa cells (8). It is also seen that even in the same MDBK cells, different clones produce different amounts of DI virus. The higher yield of DI virus (DIU/ml) is observed when the amount of contaminating infectious virus is also higher in the preparation (39).

Although these three types of cells produce significantly different amounts of DI virus upon serial undiluted passages, the quality of the DI RNA generated in these cells appears identical. Two types of experiments, namely (*a*) analysis of RNA by slab gels and (*b*) sequence relationship among these DI RNAs by oligonucleotide fingerprinting, yielded similar results. The major DI RNA components in all these types of cells have identical mobility and the same oligonucleotide spots.

When DI viruses are amplified over many passages by adding infectious virus in each passage, the amount of DIU per ml increases until p-9; thereafter, an equilibrium between DIU and PFU is established. However, during these passages, a gradual change in the nature of the DI virus RNA is observed. A smaller molecular weight DI RNA is selected over the larger DI RNA. Again, these smaller DI RNAs produced in all three types of cells are essentially identical. Thus our data suggest that although different host cells have a profound effect on the replication of infectious as well as DI influenza viruses, the quality of DI virus in all three types of cells is essentially the same. These results, although apparently different from those observed for VSV (32, 42), are not totally unexpected. Even with VSV, the host factors do not appear to be absolutely selective because (*a*) some of the DI viruses produced in different types of cells are identical and (*b*) any predominant DI virus can replicate in a given cell, including HeLa cells that fail to generate VSV DI virus (32). It appears that the varying proportion of DI virus in a clonal stock may influence the selective advantage of one

DI virus over others in a given type of cell. These results suggest that the nature of the influenza DI virus is primarily determined in the clonal stock and that cells like MDBK, CEF, and HeLa cells do not produce great selective pressure in the amplification of a particular influenza DI virus.

EFFECT OF DI VIRUS ON HOST

Huang & Baltimore (36) postulate a significant role for DI virus particles in acute and chronic viral infections, although definitive evidence is still lacking. DI viruses may be involved in the establishment and maintenance of persistent and chronic infections. Since DI viruses reduce excessive virus growth and inhibit the cell-killing effect of homologous lytic virus (31), they are believed to aid in prolonging an acute infection that would normally end in the elimination of the virus either by stimulating host defense or by killing the host. To understand the mechanism of chronic debilitating viral infection in man and animals (76), the mechanism of viral persistence in cell culture has been studied intensively. At least four possible mechanisms have been postulated in the establishment of persistent infection in cell culture. 1. Interferon-mediated persistent infection: Interferon induced by agents including DI particles or mutant viruses (i.e. less virulent) may reduce the cell-killing effect of the virus and thus establish persistent infection (56, 65). 2. Proviral DNA-mediated viral persistence: Although the integration of viral DNA in many DNA viruses and of proviral DNA in retroviruses is well established, the formation of such proviral DNA for lytic RNA viruses and its integration with host cell DNA may be a rare event and has been reported by some, but not by others (26). 3. Temperature-sensitive mutation-mediated viral persistence: Preble & Younger (64) have advocated the important role of temperature-sensitive mutants in establishing and maintaining persistent infection in restrictive or semi-restrictive temperatures. 4. DI virus-mediated persistent infection: A large number of studies have implicated the role of DI particles in establishing and maintaining persistent infection (26, 30).

Establishment of Persistently Infected Cultures of Influenza Virus

Attempts to obtain persistently infected (Pi) cultures of MDBK and HeLa cells by infecting cells with wild type (ts^+) WSN virus, alone, at varying multiplicities (0.1 to 1 PFU/cell) or coinfecting with DI virus have been largely unsuccessful. After infection with ts^+ virus, cytopathic effect (cpe) is severe in these cultures. A few resistant colonies of cells occasionally observed can not be maintained beyond two or three initial passages. Attempts to obtain persistently infected cells using ts52 WSN virus (0.1 to 1

PFU/cell), alone, have been almost equally futile. Only one out of four attempts have yielded cells that could be grown and maintained for a maximum of seven passages.

On the other hand, Pi MDBK and Pi HeLa cell cultures can be routinely established by simultaneously infecting cells with standard ts52 virus and DI virus. Initially coinfected cultures show a moderate amount of cpe (40–50%). All dead cells are removed by a thorough wash, and the medium is replaced every day until residual viable cells form a confluent monolayer in 2–3 weeks. Subsequently, cultures are split every 3–4 days except when they undergo crisis, at which time the medium is changed every day until the crisis is over. Cells after p-9 or p-10 do not show any further signs of crisis.

At early passages ($<$p-7), Pi cells show a typical cyclical pattern of cpe and virus production. Immediately after subculture, Pi cells usually show the greatest amount of cpe and virus production, which gradually diminishes upon daily washing with fresh medium until the cultures become confluent again. These Pi cells appear more rounded and refractile than the uninfected cells and are easily trypsinizable.

Such Pi cells can grow and multiply as well as produce a relatively small amount of virus. There are two possible explanations for these results: (*a*) a small percentage of the cells in cultures are infected and are producing virus at a given time or (*b*) the majority, if not all, of the cells are infected and contain viral genome, but either some or all of them are producing small amounts of virus. A number of experiments suggest the latter to be the case.

First, these Pi cells (both Pi MDBK and Pi HeLa) are resistant to superinfection by homologous but not heterologous viruses. Both early (p-10) and late (p-30) passaged Pi MDBK and Pi HeLa cells, after superinfection with WSN virus, show little cell destruction ($<$15% cpe), as well as markedly reduced virus production. Control MDBK cells when infected with ts52 or ts^+ WSN virus produce 2048 HAU/ml and 30×10^7 PFU/ml, whereas Pi MDBK cells (MP2 and MP3) produce only 32 HAU/ml and $3–5 \times 10^3$ PFU/ml upon superinfection. Thus, there is over a 90% reduction in infectious virus yield in Pi cells compared to that in normal cells. Similar reduction in cpe and virus production is also observed after superinfection of Pi HeLa cells with WSN virus when compared to normal HeLa cells. However, when a heterologous virus (NDV) is used for superinfection, both normal cells and persistently infected cells are equally susceptible. Over 80% of cells undergo cpe within 24 hours after infection, and a high HAU titer (4096–8194 HAU/ml in MDBK cells, 1024 HAU/ml in HeLa cells) and infectious virus titer ($50–70 \times 10^6$ PFU/ml for MDBK and 4–5 $\times 10^6$ PFU/ml for HeLa cells) are obtained in both normal and Pi cultures.

Second, viral antigens are present in almost all Pi cells. Persistently infected as well as acutely infected cultures of both MDBK and HeLa cells have been examined by indirect immunofluorescence using antisera against WSN virus. After acetone fixation, acutely infected MDBK cells show an intense fluorescence, as expected, throughout the cell cytoplasm and nucleus. Pi MDBK cells (MP2 and MP3) when analyzed under similar conditions show a specific immunofluorescence in 70–80% of cells, suggesting the expression of viral antigens in nearly all cells. Intensity of fluorescence in Pi cultures is much less, compared to that present in acutely infected cells. In Pi cells, fluorescence is often more pronounced in the cytoplasm and cellular membrane than in the nucleus (10). When live cells in suspension are used for immunofluorescence, about 80% of Pi cells appear positive, although the intensity of fluorescence is much reduced compared to that present in acutely infected cells. Thus, immunofluorescence studies show that nearly all of Pi MDBK and Pi HeLa cells contain viral antigen.

Third, an infectious center assay has been used to determine the presence of viral genome in persistently infected cells. Pi MDBK and Pi HeLa cells show a 70–90% plating efficiency compared to the plating efficiency of acutely infected MDBK and HeLa cells. This slightly lower plating efficiency of persistently infected cells can be due either to DI virus present in some Pi cells and preventing plaque formation or to some cells not producing any infectious virus at all. Although one can not distinguish between these two possibilities, these results confirm that the majority of, if not all, cells contain infectious virus genome.

Viruses released by persistently infected cells are temperature sensitive as reported by others. Surprisingly, however, DI viruses have not been detected in persistently infected cultures (Nayak, unpublished data). To determine the nature of the viral genome the virus particles released from Pi cells have been amplified using fresh uninfected MDBK cells. PAGE analysis of the released virus shows that only standard viral RNAs have replicated with no appreciable amount of DI RNAs, even though DI viruses had been used to initiate these Pi cultures.

The role of temperature-sensitive mutants in both establishing persistent infection and maintaining the persistent infection has been further examined by two types of experiments. In one, attempts have been made to establish persistent infection by using the ts mutant virus alone at restricted (39° C), semirestricted (37° C), or permissive (34° C) temperatures. Results show that at permissive and semipermissive temperatures, over 99% of cells are destroyed in three days compared to only 40–50% cpe in cells incubated at the restrictive temperature. However, eventually all cells undergo lysis, and persistent infection could not be established in these cells at the restrictive temperature. In the second type of experiments, Pi cultures established and maintained at 37° C are shifted to 34° C. Following shift down, these Pi cultures do not show any crisis nor do they produce an increased amount of infectious virus compared to the Pi cultures kept at 37° C. These Pi cultures contain no detectable interferon.

Thus it appears that both DI virus and ts^- influenza mutants when present together greatly facilitate the establishment of Pi cultures; but once established, ts^- mutants alone appear to maintain the state of Pi infection in cultured cells. However, it is not possible to rule out the presence of intracellular DI RNA or a small amount of DI virus in the Pi culture supernatant. Holland and his colleagues (30, 71) have recently done an elegant series of studies showing the occurrence of extensive mutational changes in both infectious and DI virus shed by VSV persistently infected cells. Meinkoth & Kennedy (50a) have reported the involvement of at least three factors, i.e. DI particles, interferon, and genetic evolution of carrier viruses, in the establishment and maintenance of persistent infection. Further studies to elucidate the process of viral persistence are required.

In nature as well as in the laboratory, there appears to be a continuous evolution of influenza viruses. These changes are not limited to HA and NA genes and cannot be attributed solely to immunological pressure. Occurrence of DI virus is a relatively common phenomenon in influenza virus replication, and the DI viruses are often present in plaques. These DI viruses may further aid in the selection of variants and thus help in the evolution of viruses and the creation of diversity among the virus population.

CONCLUSION

1. Although DI viruses were first discovered during undiluted passaging of influenza viruses (74), only recently has it been possible to study influenza viruses in detail (55). Like other DI viruses, influenza DI viruses can be generated by high multiplicity passages in a permissive cell (MDBK for WSN virus) and subsequently can be amplified by the helper homologous infectious virus (39).
2. A sensitive assay for quantitating DI viruses using an infectious center reduction assay has been developed (39).
3. Influenza DI viruses, like other DI viruses, greatly facilitate the formation of persistent infection in cell cultures, and the viral genome is present in the majority of Pi cells even after 20 subcultures.
4. Like other DI viruses, influenza DI viruses contain new small RNA molecules (DI RNA) that are absent in infectious virus (14, 55).
5. These DI RNAs vary from clone to clone, but once generated these DI RNA species become predominant and amplified in the presence of helper infectious virus (39).

6. A direct interference assay with DI RNP complexes shows that these newly generated DI RNAs are responsible for the interference of homologous infectious virus replication (40).
7. Influenza DI RNA species are predominantly generated from the three polymerase genes (P1, P2, and P3) (16).
8. Certain sequences of progenitor vRNAs of varying complexities are preserved in the DI RNAs.
9. Influenza DI RNAs possess identical 5'- and 3'-termini of the progenitor vRNAs and, therefore, are formed by internal deletion (14a). Thus, influenza DI RNAs are generated by a mechanism different from that postulated for other negative strand DI viruses (35, 45). Influenza DI RNAs may therefore interfere by a mechanism different from that postulated for other negative strand viruses.

ACKNOWLEDGMENT

This work was supported by grants from the National Institute of Allergy and Infectious Diseases (AI 12749) and The National Science Foundation (PCM 7823220).

Literature Cited

1. Ada, G. L., Perry, B. T. 1955. *Nature* 175:209–10
2. Ada, G. L., Perry, B. T. 1956. *J. Gen. Microbiol.* 14:623
3. Almeida, J. D., Waterson, A. P. 1969. In *The Biology of Large RNA Viruses*, ed. R. D. Barry, B. W. J. Mahy, Academic New York: pp. 27–51
4. Barry, R. D. 1961. *Virology* 14:389–97
5. Bean, W. J. Jr., Simpson, R. W. 1976. *J. Virol.* 18:365–69
6. Blackstein, M. E., Stanners, C. P., Farmilo, A. J. 1969. *J. Mol. Biol.* 42:301
7. Blough, H. A., Merlie, J. D. 1970. *Virology* 40:685–92
8. Caliguiri, L. A., Holmes, K. V. 1979. *Virology* 92:15–30
9. Choppin, P. W. 1969. *Virology* 39:130–34
10. Choppin, P. W., Pons, M. W. 1970. *Virology* 42:603–10
11. Chow, N. L., Simpson, R. W. 1971. *Proc. Natl. Acad. Sci. USA* 68:752
12. Cole, C. N., Baltimore, D. 1973. *J. Mol. Biol.* 76:325
13. Compans, R. W., Content, J., Duesberg, P. 1972. *J. Virol.* 10:795–800
14. Crumpton, W. M., Dimmock, N. J., Minor, P. D., Avery, R. J. 1978. *Virology* 90:370–73
14a. Davis, A. R., Hiti, A. L., Nayak, D. P. 1980. *Proc. Natl. Acad. Sci. USA* 77:215–19
15. Davis, A. R., Nayak, D. P. 1977. *J. Virol.* 23:263–71
16. Davis, A. R., Nayak, D. P. 1979. *Proc. Natl. Acad. Sci. USA* 76:3092–96
17. Desselberger, U., Palese, P. 1978. *Virology* 88:394–99
18. Desselberger, U., Racaniello, V. R., Zazra, J. J., Palese, P. 1980. *Gene* 8:315–28
19. DeWatcher, R., Fliers, W. 1971. *Methods Enzymol.* 21:167–78
20. Dohner, D., Monroe, S., Weiss, B., Schlesinger, S. 1979. *J. Virol.* 29:794–98
21. Duesberg, P. H. 1968. *Proc. Natl. Acad. Sci. USA* 59:930–37
22. Emerson, S. U., Wagner, R. R. 1972. *J. Virol.* 10:297–309
23. Emtage, J. S., Catlin, G. H., Carey, N. H. 1979. *Nucleic Acids Res.* 6:1221–39
24. England, T. E., Uhlenbeck, O. C. 1978. *Nature* 275:560–61
25. Epstein, D. A., Herman, R. C., Chien, I., Lazzarini, R. A. 1979. *J. Virol.* In press
26. Friedman, R. M., Ramseur, J. M. 1979. *Arch. Virol.* 60:83–103
27. Guild, G. M., Flores, L., Stollar, V. 1977. *Virology* 77:158–74
28. Hay, A. J., Lomniczi, B., Bellamy, A.

R., Skehel, J. J. 1977. *Virology* 83: 337–55
29. Hirst, G. K., Pons, M. W. 1973. *Virology* 56:620–31
30. Holland, J. J., Grabau, E. A., Jones, C. L., Semler, B. L. 1978. *Cell* 16:495–504
31. Holland, J. J., Villarreal, L. P. 1974. *Proc. Natl. Acad. Sci. USA* 71:2956–60
32. Holland, J. J., Villarreal, L. P. 1975. *Virology* 67:438–49
33. Holland, J. J., Villarreal, L. P., Breindl, M. 1976. *J. Virol.* 17:805–15
34. Huang, A. S. 1973. *Ann. Rev. Microbiol.* 27:101–17
35. Huang, A. S. 1977. *Bacteriol. Rev.* 41:811–21
36. Huang, A. S., Baltimore, D. 1970. *Nature* 226:325–27
37. Huang, A. S., Baltimore, D. 1977. *Compr. Virol.* 10:73–116
38. Huang, A. S., Little, S. P., Oldstone, M. B. A., Rao, D. 1978. In *Persistent Viruses,* pp. 399–408. New York: Academic
39. Janda, J. M., Davis, A. R., Nayak, D. P., De, B. K. 1979. *Virology* 95:48–58
40. Janda, J. M., Nayak, D. P. 1979. *J. Virol.* 32:697–702
41. Johnston, R. E., Tovell, D. R., Brown, D. T., Faulkner, P. 1975. *J. Virol.* 16:951–58
42. Kang, C. Y., Glimp, T., Clewley, J. P., Bishop, D. H. L. 1978. *Virology* 84: 142–52
42a. Kavern, N., Kolomietz, L., Rudneva, I. 1980. *J. Virol.* 34:506–11
43. Kennedy, S. I. T. 1976. *J. Mol. Biol.* 108:491–511
44. Kilbourne, E. D. 1975. In *The Influenza Viruses.* New York: Academic
45. Kolakofsky, D. 1976. *Cell* 8:547–55
46. Lamb, R. A., Choppin, P. W. 1979. *Proc. Natl. Acad. Sci. USA* 76:4908–12
47. Lavi, S., Winocour, E. 1972. *J. Virol.* 9:309–16
48. Lenard, J., Compans, R. W. 1975. *Virology* 65:418–26
49. Leppert, M., Kort, L., Kolakofsky, D. 1977. *Cell* 12:539–52
50. Lundquist, R. E., Sullivan, M., Maizel, J. F. Jr. 1979. *Cell* 18:759–69
50a. Meinkoth, J., Kennedy, S. I. T. 1980. *Virology* 100:141–55
51. Nakajima, K., Ueda, M. Sugiura, A. 1979. *J. Virol.* 29:1142–48
52. Nayak, D. P. 1969. *Fed. Proc.* 28: 1858–65
53. Nayak, D. P. 1972. *J. Gen. Virol.* 14: 63–67
54. Nayak, D. P. 1977. In *The Molecular Biology of Animal Viruses,* ed. D. P. Nayak, 1:281–348. New York: Dekker
55. Nayak, D. P., Tobita, K., Janda, J. M., Davis, A. R., De, B. K. 1978. *J. Virol.* 28:375–86
56. Nishiyama, Y. 1972. *J. Gen. Virol.* 35:265–79
57. Palese, P. 1977. *Cell* 10:1–10
58. Palese, P., Ritchey, M. B., Schulman, J. L. 1977. *J. Virol.* 21:1187–95
59. Palese, P., Schulman, J. L. 1976. *J. Virol.* 17:876–84
60. Perrault, J. 1976. *Virology* 70:360–71
61. Perrault, J., Semler, B. L. 1979. *Proc. Natl. Acad. Sci. USA.* 76:6191–95
62. Perrault, J., Semler, B. L., Leavitt, R. W., Holland, J. J. 1978. In *Negative Strand Viruses and the Host Cells,* ed. B. W. J. Mahy, R. D. Barry, pp. 527–38. New York: Academic
62a. Pons, M. W. 1980. *Virology* 100:43–52
63. Porter, A. G., Barber, C., Carey, N. H., Hallewell, R. A., Threefall, G., Emtage, J. S. 1979. *J. Mol. Biol.* In press
64. Preble, O. T., Younger, J. S. 1975. *J. Inf. Dis.* 131:467–73
65. Ramseur, J. M., Friedman, R. M. 1977. *J. Gen. Virol.* 37:523–33
66. Rao, D. D., Huang, A. S. 1979. *Proc. Natl. Acad. Sci. USA* 76:3742–45
67. Rochovansky, O. M., Hirst, G. K. 1976. *Virology* 73:339–49
68. Rohde, W., Boschek, C. B., Harms, E., Rott, R., Scholtissek, C. 1979. *Arch. Virol.* In press
69. Scholtissek, C. 1978. *Curr. Top. Microbiol. Immunol.* 80:139–69
70. Schubert, M., Kenne, J. D., Lazzarini, R. A. 1979. *Cell* 18:749–57
71. Semler, B. L., Holland, J. J. 1979. *J. Virol.* 32:420–28
72. Stark, C., Kennedy, S. I. T. 1978. *Virology* 89:285–99
73. Uchida, S., Watanabe, S. 1969. *Virology* 39:721
74. von Magnus, P. 1951. *Acta. Pathol. Microbiol. Scand.* 29:157
75. von Magnus, P. 1954. *Adv. Virus Res.* 2:59–78
76. Welsh, R. M., Oldstone, M. B. A. 1977. *J. Exp. Med.* 145:1449–68
77. Yoshishita, T., Kawai, K., Fukai, K., Ito, R. 1959. *Biken J.* 2:25

Ann. Rev. Microbiol. 1980. 34:645–76

GENETICS OF *ERWINIA* SPECIES

◆1789

Arun K. Chatterjee

Department of Plant Pathology, Kansas State University, Manhattan, Kansas 66506

Mortimer P. Starr

Department of Bacteriology, University of California, Davis, California 95616

CONTENTS

INTRODUCTION AND SCOPE 646
TAXONOMIC CONSIDERATIONS 647
PLASMID INHERITANCE 649
Foreign Plasmids 649
Resident Plasmids 650
BACTERIOPHAGES 651
GENETIC SYSTEMS 652
Conjugation 652
Hfr donors 652
R plasmid-mediated chromosomal gene transfer 653
Transduction 655
Transformation 656
CHROMOSOMAL HOMOLOGY 656
DETERMINANTS OF BACTERIAL PHYTOPATHOGENICITY 658
Cell Envelope Components 658
Capsule 659
Lipopolysaccharide and outer membrane proteins 660
Amylovorin 662
Extracellular Enzymes 664
Polygalacturonic Acid Catabolism 665
Location of pectolytic activity 666
Regulation of PATE production 666
Mapping of the pat locus 668
Degradation of oligouronides and catabolism of monomeric derivatives 670
PROSPECTS 671

0066-4227/80/1001-0645$01.00

INTRODUCTION AND SCOPE

Living plants—both lower and higher forms—are preferred habitats for many sorts of bacteria. These organismic associations (178) exhibit a variety of formats. One aspect usually considered in categorizing such relationships between organisms deals with the perceived benefit or harm each component creature receives from the association. Associations between plants and bacteria belong to every conceivable category with respect to the benefit or harm (or neither) that is perceived (by the human observer) as received or given by each associant.

The organismic association (178) that mainly concerns us here is when bacteria harm (antagonize) plants in the progressive manner regarded as disease. Antagonistic bacteria causing frank disease are conventionally termed pathogens; the harmed plant is usually called the host (a sardonic contravention of the usual meaning of the word). Some bacteria—those called epiphytic—regularly colonize plant surfaces (54). Only rarely do epiphytic bacteria elicit overt pathological responses on plants or plant parts, and, when they do, they behave somewhat like the opportunistic or emerging pathogens (179) of medical interest. The term "plant-associated bacteria" will sometimes be used here to refer to the entire assemblage of bacteria that live upon, within, and around plants—without reference to the concepts of benefit or harm to either organism.

The most common bacteria known to be associated antagonistically with plants (180) are otherwise rather ordinary heterotrophic bacteria (agrobacteria, corynebacteria, erwinias, pseudomonads, rhizobia, streptomycetes, xanthomonads); there are also some less ordinary forms (such as the wall-less spiroplasmas and mycoplasmas, and the "rickettsia-like" and other fastidious bacterial sorts). All of these phytopathogenic bacteria—with the possible exception of the osmotically fragile (wall-less) ones—seem capable of sustaining a bimodal life style; that is, they can live in association with the host plant or, as free-living forms, apart from the host.

In this context, it is necessary to keep in mind that the ability of a phytopathogenic bacterium to exist in a successful association with its plant host requires that the phytopathogen have the capacity (*a*) to establish itself within or upon the plant host and (*b*) to proliferate at the expense of the host; in addition, inherent in the usual concept of disease is (*c*) the capacity of the phytopathogen to produce some factor(s) that can harm (antagonize) the host. The nature of a bacterial association with a plant results from the cumulative outcome of successive events determined by the genetic constitutions of both organisms and subject to the prevailing environmental conditions. Although this notion has prevailed among all biologists—plant pathologists as well as bacteriologists—no systematic effort was made until recently to investigate the genetics of the bacterial determinants that enable antagonistic associations with host plants. The primary cause of this lack of effort has been the unavailability of technology for genetic manipulations in phytopathogenic bacteria.

During the past few decades, remarkable developments have occurred in genetic technologies; during the 1970s, these advances have generated an interest in the genetics and molecular biology of phytopathogenic bacteria. Consequently, efficient gene transfer systems are now available in various phytopathogenic bacteria; determinants of phytopathogenicity are being genetically analyzed; and molecular, genetic, and biophysical properties of plasmids are being unraveled in relation to phytopathogens. Originally, we had hoped to be able to provide an overview covering the genetics of all plant-associated bacteria; however, because of space limitations we decided to center our discussion on the genetics of *Erwinia* species—with only occasional glances elsewhere. Our regret is assuaged somewhat by the availability of several excellent review articles (39, 59, 125, 165) on agrobacterial tumor-inducing (Ti) plasmids and the summary (117) on genetic systems of phytopathogenic bacteria.

Thus, we propose (*a*) to review briefly the properties of genetic systems currently available in *Erwinia* spp., (*b*) to assess the genomic homology between phytopathogenic and nonphytopathogenic enterobacteria, (*c*) to discuss the functional and structural characteristics of bacterial phytopathogenic determinants, and (*d*) to project the future uses of genetic technologies in studies on plant-associated bacteria. Other review articles (25, 28, 52, 53, 77, 87, 127, 142, 145, 164, 177, 180, 181, 186, 187, 189) collectively summarize various facets of the present knowledge on phytopathogenic bacteria. Because of the circumscribed scope of this essay, we have restricted our discussion to specific examples that, in our view, are clearly relevant to this truncated topic. The exploration by us of some of these research areas over the past decade has provided a mutually prized intellectual and personal association.

TAXONOMIC CONSIDERATIONS

The bacteria presently assigned to the genus *Erwinia* have both practical and theoretical importance. *Erwinia* species cause important diseases of plants (181); erwinias form a significant component of the nonphytopathogenic epiphytic microflora (54, 77); and some *Erwinia* strains are opportunistic pathogens of man and other animals (166, 179, 190). The genus *Erwinia* was proposed originally by a committee (197) as a repository solely for those phytopathogenic bacteria that are Gram-negative and peritrichously flagellated; the committee noted quite candidly that there was insufficient information about bacterial phytopathogens to enable a more rational nomenclatural action. This taxonomic segregation of the phytopathogenic bacteria—that is, solely because they are plant-associated—stemmed not only from the lack of scientific facts but also from disciplinal insularity (179, 181), an intellectual gap that existed (and still exists) because of the completely separate developments of plant and animal bacteriology.

The genus *Erwinia* is heterogenous, falling into several phenotypic clusters that correlate loosely with groupings based on their phytopathogenicity and molecular genetics (21–23, 72, 138). The natural groups depicted by Dye (60–63) are generally accepted by phytobacteriologists (121). One group (60, 87), which is similar in many bacteriological traits to the *Enterobacter-Klebsiella-Serratia* generic complex, consists of *Erwinia* species, most of which possess strong pectolytic capacities that enable them to cause tissue-macerating plant diseases and storage rots; this group is called the "carotovora group" or the "soft-rot group" or the "pectolytic group" or the genus *Pectobacterium* (23, 56, 193). Another of Dye's (62) *Erwinia* groups consists of erwinias that usually produce a yellow, water-insoluble pigmentation (carotenoids; see 180); such organisms are associated with plants as nonphytopathogenic epiphytes or phytopathogens (88). When considered as a group, these erwinias are called the "herbicola group" or the "herbicola-lathyri group" or the "yellow-pigmented *Erwinia* group" (77, 82, 179). Yellow-pigmented and related nonpigmented *Erwinia* strains isolated from diseases in man and other animals (166, 181) are generally considered as belonging to the herbicola-lathyri group; we call them "human clinical erwinias" or "*Erwinia herbicola*"; they are also called *Enterobacter agglomerans* (69) and are known by many other names (88, 166, 190). The third of Dye's (60) *Erwinia* groups, the members of which form neither pectolytic enzymes nor yellow pigments but do cause necrotic and/or wilt diseases of plants, is often typified by *Erwinia amylovora* and is called the "amylovora group" (and, sometimes, "white nonpectolytic erwinias", "*Erwinia sensu stricto*", or "true erwinias"). The miscellaneous assemblage that forms Dye's (63) "atypical erwinias" group has in recent years been distributed into other genera (161).

Other taxonomic arrangements of these plant and animal enterobacteria are indicated by the results of various comparative studies (21, 31–34, 72, 119, 138, 161, 182, 183). Many arrangements have in fact been suggested, including placement of most erwinias into other enterobacterial genera; however, there does not yet seem to be a consensus concerning the most reasonable arrangement. The current "compromise" treatment of these bacteria (121) is begging for taxonomic revision!

PLASMID INHERITANCE

Foreign Plasmids

Prior to 1972, no report documented the inheritance of enterobacterial or other plasmids by *Erwinia* spp., although other enterobacteria (such as *Salmonella* spp., *Proteus* spp., *Serratia* spp., *Yersinia* spp.) were known to inherit plasmids (R factors and F-prime plasmids) originating in *Escherichia coli.* Our earliest work (32, 33) clearly demonstrated that several *Erwinia* spp. were receptive to enterobacterial plasmids such as R factors or F-prime plasmids; these plasmids were retained in a stable state in most of their bacterial hosts and the plasmid-bearing strains were donors of plasmid markers. The donor ability of plasmid-bearing erwinias was not restricted to *Erwinia* spp. (such as *E. amylovora, E. chrysanthemi, E. herbicola*), but extended to other enterobacteria (such as *Escherichia coli, Salmonella typhimurium,* and *Shigella dysenteriae*). Based upon these in vitro observations, we had predicted that genetic interaction, particularly via plasmid transfer, might also occur between phytopathogenic and non-phytopathogenic enterobacteria in the wild (33, 181). The fact that multiply drug-resistant (R factor-bearing) strains of *Erwinia herbicola* (= *Enterobacter agglomerans*) have now emerged in clinical situations (171, 176) lends credence to this notion.

Subsequently, IncP and other plasmids were introduced into various *Erwinia* spp. (29, 37, 40, 44, 78, 91, 116, 147). In some of these studies, a differential expression of the fertility genes of certain plasmids was apparent (29, 44, 78). For example, Gibbins et al (78) made an interesting observation concerning the expression of sex factor genes of the plasmid RP1 in a strain of *E. herbicola.* Although the drug-resistance genes were fully expressed in the plasmid-bearing strain, this strain failed to transfer plasmid markers by conjugation to *E. coli* or *Pseudomonas aeruginosa;* it also was insensitive to the sex factor–specific phages (141). That the host (*E. herbicola*) strain contained the plasmid genome was indicated by the presence of plasmid-specific ccc-DNA; transformation of an *E. coli* strain using DNA preparations produced drug-resistant clones that were donors. These observations suggest that—in *E. herbicola,* at least—the plasmid genome, particularly those regions that specify sex factor activity, was not modified (by excision and/or deletion), but rather was repressed. The molecular mechanism of this repression remains to be elucidated. A somewhat similar situation also prevailed in a strain of *E. stewartii* harboring RP1 (78). In this case, the RP1-bearing strain, although sensitive to P-specific phages, was unable to transfer the drug-resistance genes to *E. coli* or *P. aeruginosa* recipient strains.

As opposed to this pattern of expression of RP1 in certain strains belonging to the herbicola group, we (29, 37) as well as others (40, 44, 91, 116, 147) have noted normal expression of IncP plasmids in other *Erwinia* spp. (such as *E. amylovora, E. carotovora, E. chrysanthemi, E. stewartii*). These observations, therefore, implicate a differential expression of the fertility genes of IncP plasmids in certain species of *Erwinia* but not in others. Since several *Erwinia* spp. have been shown to carry "cryptic" resident plasmids (see below), some interaction between the resident and incoming plasmid is feasible.

Resident Plasmids

In several bacteria pathogenic to animals and man, plasmid genomes specify some of the pathogenic determinants. Noteworthy in this context is the plasmid location of genes that specify the production of enterotoxin, hemolysin, and cell surface (K antigen) properties in *Escherichia coli* (70). Findings such as these have generated much interest concerning the involvement of plasmids in host associations—including pathogenicity of plant bacteria. Indeed, recent studies have demonstrated a requirement for the presence (as well as expression) of plasmid DNA in the phytopathogenicity of *Agrobacterium tumefaciens* and *Pseudomonas syringae.*

In *A. tumefaciens,* the Ti plasmid determines oncogenicity, synthesis and catabolism of opines, fertility, sensitivity to bacteriocin [agrocin (84)], and exclusion of bacteriophage AP1. Moreover, there is now good evidence for the presence and expression of a segment of the Ti genome in plant tumor cells [for comprehensive treatments of this fascinating subject, see (39, 59, 125, 165)]. In *P. syringae,* Gonzalez & Vidaver (80, 81) detected an association between the presence of a plasmid and toxinogenesis; however, toxinogenesis might be chromosomally determined in certain strains of this bacterial species (A. K. Chatterjee, unpublished). A plasmid may possibly be involved in production of phaseotoxin by *P. phaseolicola* (71).

One to several resident plasmids have been detected in each of several *Erwinia* species: in *E. amylovora* (143; A. K. Chatterjee, unpublished; E. N. Lawson and M. P. Starr, in preparation), *E. chrysanthemi* (175), *E. herbicola* (30, 35, 78, 171, 176), and *E. stewartii* (46). However, none of these plasmids has yet been convincingly shown to be involved in the phytopathogenicity or capacity for plant association of these bacteria. Judging from what is now known in pathogenic as well as in free-living bacteria (157), it seems reasonable to predict that the presence in bacteria of one or more extrachromosomal genomes is a generalized feature rather than an exceptional trait. In that light, it is desirable to make a concerted effort to identify the phenotypes associated with a plasmid genome, now that available technologies (112) make this task much simpler; the use of transposons is a particularly attractive approach. Indeed, Schell and his associates (94) have used this genetic tool to identify some of the phenotypes associated with the tumor-inducing (Ti) plasmid of *Agrobacterium tumefaciens.* Using a similar approach, Coplin & Rowan (46) associated sex factor activity with a "cryptic" resident plasmid in *Erwinia stewartii.* An extension of this finding might prove useful in developing a conjugational genetic system in this bacterial phytopathogen.

Transmissible plasmids have been detected in human clinical isolates of *Erwinia herbicola* (30, 35, 171, 176). One of these plasmids, E-*lac*$^+$, carries genes for lactose fermentation, is transmissible (albeit at a low frequency) to a variety of enterobacteria (other *Erwinia* species, *Escherichia coli, Paracolobactrum arizonae, Salmonella typhimurium,* and *Shigella dysenteriae*), and is remarkably stable in all these hosts (30, 35). Thus far, this E-*lac*$^+$ plasmid has been found compatible with (hence unrelated to) representative plasmids belonging to all tested compatibility groups (13, 30). It is noteworthy that E-*lac*$^+$ is stable in certain species of the carotovora group such as *Erwinia aroideae* and *E. atroseptica,* which—at least in our hands—are either nonreceptive to a variety of F-prime or R plasmids or lose the inherited plasmids at a very high frequency. Mutants of E-*lac*$^+$ derepressed in fertility function might prove useful in developing conjugational genetic systems in these bacteria—a notion we are presently exploring.

BACTERIOPHAGES

Though bacteriophages active against certain *Erwinia* spp. (such as *E. amylovora* and *E. herbicola*) are readily obtained from soil, sewage, or infected plant material (77, 158, 159, 181), phages against other species (e.g. *E. carotovora* or *E. chrysanthemi*) are rarely isolated from such sources (146; A. K. Chatterjee and M. P. Starr, unpublished). The mechanism underlying this unusual resistance ("immunity") is unclear. However, ultraviolet (UV) irradiation or mitomycin treatment of the exponential cultures of *E. carotovora* and *E. chrysanthemi* causes bacterial lysis (A. K. Chatterjee and M. A. Brown, in preparation). Electron microscopic studies of *E. carotovora* lysates have revealed the presence of structures resembling bacteriophage tails, which could very well represent bacteriocins (181). On the other hand, mitomycin-treated culture lysates of *E. chrysanthemi* have been found to contain bacteriophages (A. K. Chatterjee and M. A. Brown, in preparation). Paulin & Nassan (146) also have detected spontaneous bacteriophage production in strains of *E. chrysanthemi,* and the production of bacteriocins by *E. chrysanthemi* has recently been reported (64).

Despite the sporadic reports documenting the occurrence of bacteriophages of *Erwinia* spp., no systematic attempt has in general been made to characterize these bacteriophages fully, to employ them in typing of bacteria, or to use them for transduction. There are exceptions: several *E. amylovora* and *E. herbicola* phages have been characterized in some detail (4, 90, 92, 159); and *E. chrysanthemi* phage(s), which seem to differentiate bacterial strains on the basis of their host-plant origin (146; A. K. Chatterjee and M. A. Brown, in preparation) and can mediate generalized transduction, are known (see below). The availability of bacteriophages that are capsule specific and can depolymerize extracellular polysaccharide material of *E. amylovora* (4, 158, 159) is particularly interesting in terms of isolation of capsular mutants of the phytopathogen and structural investigations on the polysaccharide material (see below for details). We anticipate that future work also will be directed towards identifying bacteriophage receptor sites, such as lipopolysaccharide or outer membrane proteins. With the availability of such knowledge, it would be feasible to isolate mutants having altered cell surface properties and thereby facilitate investigations on the role of outer membrane components in bacterial associations with the host plants.

GENETIC SYSTEMS

Conjugation

Soon after we learned (32, 33) that *Erwinia* spp. could inherit enterobacterial plasmids, it became apparent that these plasmids could be used to mobilize chromosomal genomes of these bacteria. Subsequently, this mobilization has been accomplished by applying two approaches: (*a*) isolating Hfr strains using F-prime plasmids originating in *Escherichia coli,* and (*b*) using R factors derepressed in sex factor activity.

HFR DONORS Hfr donors are available in both *Erwinia amylovora* and *E. chrysanthemi* (35–38, 154, 155). Genetic evidence—such as a gradient and a fixed origin of marker transfer, inheritance of sex factor genes in recombinants of terminal markers but not of proximal markers, and the insensitivity to "curing" of plasmid genomes by agents such as acridine dyes —strongly suggests that the F-prime plasmids have integrated into the genomes of these bacteria, resulting in the Hfr state (34, 36, 154, 155). Moreover, in *E. amylovora,* molecular analysis has revealed the presence of plasmid DNA (i.e. ccc-DNA) in the F-prime bearing strain but its absence in the Hfr strains (154). The Hfr strains of these bacterial species have been used to map chromosomal genes by the time of entry, by gradient of transmission, and by linkage analysis (see below).

From what has been accomplished in *E. amylovora* and *E. chrysanthemi,* it seems reasonable to predict that different Hfr strains (i.e. strains with different origins of chromosome transfer) could be obtained by using different F-prime plasmids. For example, in *E. amylovora* Hfr 99 and Hfr 159 strains which have resulted from the integration of F'*lac*$^+$ and F'*his*$^+$ plasmids, respectively, markers are transferred with different polarity: Hfr 99 transfers *cys*$^+$ and *ser*$^+$ as proximal markers and *ilv*$^+$ as a distal marker (35), and Hfr 159 transfers *ilv*$^+$ as a proximal marker and *ser*$^+$ as a distal marker (155). Such differences in transfer origins can be explained by postulating that the F genes have integrated into different regions of the *E. amylovora* chromosome. These results also suggest that the integration of F' plasmids in these Hfr strains depends, at least in part, upon the homology between the chromosomal DNA of *Escherichia coli* (where chromosomal *lac*$^+$ and *his*$^+$ are linked to F genes) and *Erwinia amylovora.* In spite of repeated attempts, we have thus far not succeeded in isolating an Hfr strain of *E. amylovora* derived from an F'*lac*$^+$ plasmid that transfers *his*$^+$ as a proximal marker, or an Hfr strain derived from an F'*his*$^+$ plasmid that transfers *cys*$^+$ or *ser*$^+$ as a proximal marker.

A similar situation seems to prevail in the formation of Hfr strains in *E. chrysanthemi:* the integration of F'*lac*$^+$ has consistently produced Hfr strains that transfer *leu*$^+$ as a proximal marker. It seems likely that F'*lac*+ has integrated into the *Erwinia chrysanthemi* chromosomal segment corresponding to the putative homologous *lac-pro* region (7–9 min) of *Escherichia coli* (6), and that the chromosomal genes are transferred in a clockwise manner. As opposed to this behavior, the integration of F'*his*$^+$ produced a strain that transferred *trp*$^+$ as a proximal marker (A. K. Chatterjee, unpublished data). The data on DNA-DNA hybridization between *Erwinia* species and *E. coli* obtained in our laboratory (138) and elsewhere (21–23, 72) reveal a limited polynucleotide sequence homology between genomes of these bacteria. Such homology, albeit small, might explain the recombinational events between the F-prime plasmid and the corresponding homologous regions on *Erwinia* chromosomes. If this interpretation is valid, it could be predicted that the integration of other F-prime plasmids (126) into the chromosomes of *Erwinia* spp. should result in Hfr strains with different origins of transfer. This notion remains to be experimentally tested.

R PLASMID-MEDIATED CHROMOSOMAL GENE TRANSFER R plasmids have been used in mobilizing chromosomal genes in many bacteria, including some that cause diseases in plants (98). In *Erwinia amylovora,* R100*drd*-56 (an F-like R plasmid) was found to mobilize certain chromosomal markers, albeit at a low frequency (A. K. Chatterjee and M. P. Starr, unpublished). As opposed to this behavior, R68.45 (an IncP1 R plasmid) which mobilizes chromosomal genes in many bacteria (98)—including *Er-*

winia carotovora (147) and *E. chrysanthemi* (29)—did not transfer chromosomal genes in *E. amylovora* crosses, although the plasmid markers were readily transferred (29). The chromosomal mobilization ability (Cma) of plasmid R68.45 is believed to be dependent upon the presence in the plasmid genome of a segment of the *Pseudomonas aeruginosa* chromosome, perhaps an insertion sequence (98, 108). It is possible that, while R68.45 can interact with the chromosomes of *E. carotovora* and *E. chrysanthemi,* it is unable to do so in *E. amylovora.*

Pérombelon & Boucher (147) detected R68.45-mediated transfer of chromosomal markers in *Erwinia carotovora.* While certain markers (such as *leu* and *trp*) were transferred at a relatively high frequency ($\sim 10^{-5}$ recombinants per donor cell), other marker (such as *his*) was transferred at a somewhat lower frequency ($\sim 10^{-7}$ recombinants per donor cell). Their data do suggest a generalized Cma of R68.45 in *E. carotovora.* In our studies (29), in which we employed strain ICPB EC153 of *E. carotovora,* the transfer of R68.45 from *Escherichia coli* did not occur. This apparent discrepancy might simply reflect differential recipient-ability and R68.45-expression in strains of *E. carotovora.* The frequency of marker transfer observed by Pérombelon & Boucher (147) is quite respectable, and it should now permit genetic studies on this important phytopathogen.

In addition to the Hfr strains currently available (see above), various R plasmids (RP1, R68.45, Rts1, RK2) can mobilize chromosomal markers in *E. chrysanthemi* (29, 91, 116). Although Guimaraes et al (91) detected efficient transfer of certain chromosomal markers, no attempt was made to exploit the system in mapping chromosomal genes including those that specify phytopathogenicity. Using R68.45, we (29) have established linkage between *thr-leu-lys-ade* and between *trp* and *his* in *E. chrysanthemi,* thus confirming our earlier findings (36–38) with Hfr donor cells. Moreover, our data clearly demonstrate the usefulness of R68.45 in strain construction and in reciprocal crosses.

Differences were apparent between the processes of chromosomal transfer in *E. chrysanthemi* brought about (*a*) by the donor strain harboring R68.45 in an extrachromosomal state (29) and (*b*) by the Hfr strain resulting from chromosomal integration of F' lac^+ (36). The donors differed with respect to the frequency and gradient of gene transfer, the extent of linkage between markers, and the inheritance of plasmid markers among recombinants of chromosomal genes. Based upon these findings, we concluded (29) that plasmid R68.45 mediates transfer of chromosomal segments considerably shorter than those transferred by the Hfr strain and that it is capable of interacting with the chromosome of *E. chrysanthemi* at various regions.

The same R plasmid (R68.45) has recently been introduced into *E.*

chrysanthemi strains originating from different plant hosts (such as chrysanthemum, dieffenbachia, and dianthus). Most of the plasmid-bearing strains are donors of both chromosomal and plasmid markers (A. K. Chatterjee, in preparation). Lacy (116) reported RP1-mediated mobilization of chromosomal genes in *E. chrysanthemi* strains originating on corn. These findings are significant in terms of the genetic analysis of compatibility of *E. chrysanthemi* in various plant hosts.

Transduction

Despite the occurrence of both virulent and temperate bacteriophages in *Erwinia* spp. and other phytopathogenic bacteria (see above), the transductional mode of gene transfer was unavailable, until recently, in any phytobacterial species. We (A. K. Chatterjee and M. A. Brown, in preparation) have now documented that a temperate phage of *Erwinia chrysanthemi* mediates generalized transduction in a strain (ICPB EC183) of this bacterial species. The bacteriophage, Erch 12, transferred an array of chromosomal genes (*ade, arg, ilv, leu, his, rif, ser, thr, trp, ura*) to appropriate recipient strains derived from *E. chrysanthemi* strain EC183. The frequency of recombinant formation was stimulated by UV irradiation. Maximal stimulation (5- to 100-fold, depending on the test marker) occurred at about 60–99% inactivation of the bacteriophage particles; at higher UV dosage, which caused greater inactivation of the phage, there was a concomitant drop in the frequency of transductants. It is noteworthy that the enhancement of transductional frequency following UV irradiation has been observed in other bacterial systems, such as *Escherichia coli* (1, 57, 58, 196), *Myxococcus xanthus* (27), *Pseudomonas aeruginosa* (99), *Rhizobium leguminosarum* (26), and *Salmonella typhimurium* (17, 74). In other bacterial systems, stimulation of transductional efficiency seems to result either from the activity of the host recombination system(s) or from the inactivation of the killing effects of the bacteriophages. The data available for *E. chrysanthemi* do not yet allow us to discount either possibility. By performing two-factor crosses, we have established linkage between chromosomal markers (*rif* and *ade; thr* and *ser*) in *E. chrysanthemi* and have mapped several closely linked mutations in *ser* with respect to *thr*. This system, used in conjunction with R68.45 donors, should prove highly efficient in mapping the chromosome of *E. chrysanthemi*.

Various coliphage::R plasmid cointegrates (such as P1CM*clr*100, P1KM*clr*100, RP4::Mu*cts*62, or R68::$c^{+}\Delta$445-7) have been introduced into *Erwinia* spp.—namely, *E. amylovora, E. carotovora,* and *E. stewartii* (45, 79, 147). Although this introduction has not yet yielded efficient gene transfer systems, the findings are significant in terms of the generation of transpositional mutants, particularly of the bacteriophage Mu. Indeed, there is evidence that Mu interacts with the chromosomes of *E. carotovora* (147) and *E. stewartii* (45).

Transformation

Although more than two decades have elapsed since transformation was detected in *Agrobacterium tumefaciens* by Klein & Klein (113, 114) and in *Xanthomonas phaseoli* by Corey & Starr (47, 48), this mode of gene transfer has generally remained unexplored in *Erwinia* spp. and other phytopathogenic bacteria. One noteworthy exception is the efficient transformation of chromosomal markers in *Pseudomonas solanacearum* (120). Lacy & Sparks (118) have shown transformation of plasmid (pBR322) markers in *Erwinia herbicola.* Their protocol, if successful with phytopathogenic *Erwinia* spp., might prove useful in probing the phenotypes specified by "cryptic" resident plasmids.

CHROMOSOMAL HOMOLOGY

Since Hfr strains became available in *Erwinia* spp., chromosomal genes have been mapped in both *E. amylovora* and *E. chrysanthemi* by interrupted matings, by gradient of transmission, and by linkage analysis (35, 36, 154, 155). Moreover, in *E. chrysanthemi* the extent of linkage between various markers also has been determined by performing transductional and R68.45-mediated crosses (29; A. K. Chatterjee and M. A. Brown, in preparation). From the little that we have done in mapping chromosomal gene arrangement in *Erwinia* spp., an overall resemblance to the *Escherichia coli* gene order (6) is evident. The data (116) for a corn strain of *Erwinia chrysanthemi,* although also preliminary in nature, also suggest a similarity in chromosomal gene order in this strain and *Escherichia coli.* It should be emphasized that the location of certain markers on *Erwinia* chromosomes is at present tentative. Moreover, for a better estimate of homology, it is also essential to demonstrate that the gene products are isofunctional.

It is noteworthy that, in *Erwinia amylovora,* there is an inversion (relative to *Escherichia coli*) in chromosomal regions involving *ilv* and *rbs.* In *E. coli,* these gene sequences (in clockwise direction) are *his-rbs-ilv;* in *E. amylovora,* the order is *his-ilv-rbs* (155). It also should be noted that—despite the overall similarity in linkage maps of *Escherichia coli* (6) and *Salmonella typhimurium* (163)—there is a chromosomal region at about 4 o'clock on the maps showing inversion between the two genera (162).

A functional similarity in gene products is indicated by complementation of metabolic defects in *Erwinia* spp. by F-prime plasmids originating in

Escherichia coli (32, 36, 155; A. K. Chatterjee, in preparation). Recently, F-prime plasmids of *E. coli* carrying isofunctional genes have been shown (131) to complement various gene loci (such as *ilv, leu, met, arg*) of *Pseudomonas fluorescens* biotype IV. Moreover, this study documented functional expression of *E. coli* tRNA in *P. fluorescens,* as well as interactions between RNA polymerases of these bacteria. In light of these findings, it was scarcely unexpected to learn that F-prime plasmids complement isofunctional genes of *Erwinia* spp.—which, after all, are related to *Escherichia coli* and other enterobacteria by various other criteria as summarized by us elsewhere (180, 181).

Gene transfer followed by recombination indicates relatedness between two bacteria, and this process is considered analogous to the formation of fertile hybrids in eukaryotes (162). Sanderson (162) has recently summarized the extent of recombinational homology among various enterobacteria. Subsequently, Wu et al (199) demonstrated recombinational homology in *trpB* and *trpD* genes of *Erwinia amylovora* and *Salmonella typhimurium; trp*$^+$ genes of *E. amylovora,* mobilized by F'*lac*$^+$, were shown to integrate at the selected sites of the *S. typhimurium* chromosome, resulting in phenotypically stable *trp*$^+$ hybrids. Transductional analysis revealed that the hybrids (*a*) lacked a cryptic *trp* allele selected against in the female parent and (*b*) had high genetic values (132) in the tryptophan region. In crosses between *E. amylovora* F'*lac*$^+$ and *S. typhimurium* it should be noted that *trp*$^+$ recombinants were recovered in only three out of the six female parents with single-site mutations and in none of the nine female parents with multiple-site mutations; the genetic and molecular bases for the locus- or loci-specific integration remain to be clarified. In our studies we have been consistently unable over the past decade to transfer chromosomal genes from *Escherichia coli* to *Erwinia* spp. (A. K. Chatterjee and M. P. Starr, unpublished data). Noteworthy in this context is the finding that certain *E. coli* chromosomal genes can be transferred to *Proteus* spp. (42, 162) which, like some *Erwinia* spp., are distantly related to *E. coli* (162). Clearly, much remains to be learned concerning recombinational homology between *Erwinia* spp. and other enterobacteria, as well as functional similarities in products of both biosynthetic and catabolic genes.

Such ignorance notwithstanding, the existing evidence on homology in gene order on chromosomes of various enterobacteria belonging to the genera *Escherichia, Salmonella, Shigella,* and *Yersinia* (162)—taken together with what is known in *Erwinia* spp. (see above)—suggests a common evolutionary origin of these bacteria. Moreover, it is likely that these bacteria—despite the present evolutionary divergence, particularly in terms of their preferred habitats—have not been subjected to extensive genomic rearrangements and gene shuffling. It therefore follows that the genetic information required for association of these bacteria with their preferred hosts (plants, animals, or humans) was acquired later in their evolution; perhaps it is superimposed on what constitutes the core genetic material that is homologous in all of these bacteria.

DETERMINANTS OF BACTERIAL PHYTOPATHOGENICITY

Although host plants are continually exposed to myriads of bacteria and other microorganisms, only a few organisms can successfully colonize the plant and even fewer elicit disease symptoms typical of some antagonistic associations. It now is apparent that nonphytopathogenic (saprophytic) or certain avirulent bacteria may be recognized by a plant host as incompatible. In such cases, the incompatible bacterial cells might be immobilized and subsequently eliminated from the host, or the host metabolites (both constitutive and induced) might suppress the physiological activities of the pathogen. Conceivably, both of the host responses, structural and physiological, can operate concomitantly and thereby render the incoming bacterium ineffective as a pathogen. As opposed to this situation, a virulent bacterium in a compatible plant host can overcome the host's innate defense systems and initiate pathogenic responses that eventually culminate in a diseased plant. Thus, a phytopathogenic bacterium, as opposed to its nonphytopathogenic counterpart, possesses genetically determined traits permitting establishment of a compatible relationship with the plant host, multiplication and translocation within the host tissue, and the production of cytotoxic virulence factors. For a better understanding of bacterial pathogenic mechanisms, we need to know which bacterial traits elicit these discrete pathogenic events. The available literature indeed suggests that significant roles are played in host associations by bacterial cell surface components and various bacterial metabolic activities. In the following narrative, we intend to examine what is now known of bacterial determinants of phytopathogenicity and how genetic approaches might facilitate investigations of the related phytopathogenic mechanisms.

Cell Envelope Components

The Gram-negative cell envelope consists of three layers: the inner cytoplasmic membrane, the peptidoglycan layer, and the outer lipopolysaccharide layer (49). The Gram-positive envelope differs from the Gram-negative envelope in many respects, including the absence of the unit outer membrane, the presence of teichoic acid and a much thicker peptidoglycan layer, and the relative lipid content. Both types of cells may contain a capsule or a slime layer that is outermost to the cell and in certain instances may be excreted into the environment. In initial interactions between bacterial and host cells, the exposed cell surface components—such as capsule, lipopolysaccharide, teichoic acid, or proteins—might be of greater significance. Indeed, findings with several phytopathogenic bacteria (discussed below) suggest that capsule and lipopolysaccharide may play important roles in host associations. Lipoteichoic acid, which in many biological properties resembles lipopolysaccharide of Gram-negative bacteria (195), might be relevant to pathogenicity of Gram-positive phytopathogenic corynebacteria; however, teichoic acid may be absent from some.

CAPSULE The significance of capsular material in bacterial phytopathogenicity has been realized both from avirulence of noncapsular mutants and pathological responses induced by fractionated capsular material. Laboratory mutants or natural isolates defective in capsular material have been obtained in various phytopathogenic bacteria including *Erwinia amylovora* (4, 15, 16, 20; A. K. Chatterjee, K. K. Thurn, and J. G. Wyman, in preparation), *Pseudomonas solanacearum* (106, 109; T. C. Currier, personal communication), *Xanthomonas citri* (198), *X. oryzae* (86), and *X. phaseoli* (47, 48). The isolation of capsular mutants has been effected by looking for clones either with altered colony morphology on various media or with bacteriophage resistance. However, in no instance, has the gene locus or loci been mapped. In *P. solanacearum,* spontaneous noncapsular [extracellular polysaccharide (EPS)-deficient] variants appear at a high frequency; the conditions that permit the enrichment of noncapsular forms have been defined (109, 110). Although the high frequency of appearance of noncapsular variants suggests the involvement of plasmid(s), the genetic determinants of EPS have yet to be located.

In *Erwinia amylovora* (103), *Pseudomonas pisi* (85), and *Pseudomonas solanacearum* (168, 169), electron microscopy of thin sections of infected plant materials has revealed that noncapsular or incompatible strains are encapsulated by fibrillar material, probably of host origin, and consequently are immobilized. Sing & Schroth (172) noted similar encapsulation of nonphytopathogenic (saprophytic) bacteria but not of virulent compatible phytopathogens. Although host lectins have been implicated (53, 83, 168), the molecular mechanisms underlying the recognition and elimination of bacterial cells remain to be elucidated.

El-Banoby & Rudolph (67, 68) have demonstrated that EPS of various *Pseudomonas* and *Xanthomonas* species caused water congestion (water-soaking) of the mesophyll. The hydrosis, indicative of changes in host cell permeability, was thought to promote the multiplication of the pathogen.

Based upon these findings, it could be postulated that capsules of phytopathogenic bacteria might contribute to bacterial virulence (*a*) by masking the chemical entities (binding sites) usually present on the bacterial cell envelope, which might be recognized by the host-cell components (such as lectins); (*b*) by preventing interactions between host cells and bacterial elicitor(s) of defense reactions; and (*c*) by creating an environment conducive to the multiplication and translocation of the pathogen. Genetically modified strains and capsular materials fractionated from them should prove valuable in further testing the validity of these hypotheses. Moreover, investigations of pathogenic roles of capsular material should be facilitated by generating fundamental knowledge concerning the monomeric composition, structure, immunological characteristics, and genetics and regulation of synthesis of capsular material.

LIPOPOLYSACCHARIDE AND OUTER MEMBRANE PROTEINS The lipopolysaccharide (LPS) molecule of certain phytopathogenic bacteria—such as *Agrobacterium tumefaciens, Erwinia chrysanthemi,* and *Pseudomonas solanacearum*—seems to influence bacterial phytopathogenicity. Likewise, there is some preliminary evidence for a role of outer membrane (OM) proteins in *Pseudomonas* species. The available data suggest that LPS molecules might determine bacterial attachment to plant cells. In *A. tumefaciens* this attachment appears to be an important pathogenic event; the lack of bacterial attachment due to changes in the LPS (and perhaps also OM proteins) results in the loss of tumorigenesis (123, 124, 194). As opposed to this behavior, in other phytopathogenic bacteria (including *E. amylovora* and *P. solanacearum*) bacterial attachment to plant cells leads to abortive infections.

In *P. solanacearum,* bacterial attachment has occurred in the absence of EPS but not in its presence, thus suggesting an interaction between the exposed OM components and the host (tobacco) cell wall. Sequeira & Graham (170), using purified lectin, demonstrated that while avirulent isolates (lacking EPS) strongly agglutinated with the lectin, the virulent isolates (possessing EPS) either did not agglutinate or agglutinated weakly at much higher lectin concentrations. Upon removal of the EPS by repeated washing, the virulent cells did agglutinate with lectin. Likewise, adding EPS to avirulent cells or washed cells of virulent bacteria prevented agglutination. Moreover, LPS purified from avirulent cells precipitated when treated with the purified potato lectin, and the binding site of the lectin appeared to reside in the lipid A portion (*N*-acetylglucosamine residues) of the LPS.

It should be recalled that the lipid A portion of the LPS molecule is usually embedded in the outer membrane (49, 55). If that is the case also in *P. solanacearum,* the agglutination of whole cells by potato lectin could be explained by invoking the presence of *N*-acetylglucosamine residues in the OM components (proteins and polysaccharides) in addition to the LPS. Such a hypothesis would be supported if lectin(s) can agglutinate OM fractionated by applying gentle procedures; isolation procedures now are available for various phytopathogenic bacteria such as *E. amylovora, E.*

chrysanthemi, and *P. syringae* (K. K. Thurn, A. J. Trainer, and A. K. Chatterjee, in preparation). Moreover, by using that approach, it might be possible to isolate the lectin receptor present on the bacterial outer membrane.

The available evidence also suggests that LPS or LPS-protein complex derived from virulent, avirulent, and nonphytopathogenic bacteria can induce disease resistance in various plant hosts (89, 129, 168, 172). The findings of Graham et al (89) associate inducer activity with the lipid A portion of the LPS molecule. From these studies, two interesting features are apparent: (*a*) LPS of a wide variety of bacteria can bind to the plant cell wall, which might very well account for the immobilization in the host tissue of avirulent or nonphytopathogenic bacterial cells (see above for the EPS effect on bacterial attachment to host cells); and (*b*) the induction of disease resistance occurs subsequent to the binding of the LPS molecule to the host cell wall.

If the inducer role of lipid A—as detected in *P. solanacearum* (89)—is confirmed in other bacterial systems, such a finding would raise the issue of the accessibility of this moiety to the plant cells. The following plausible model might explain the apparent paradox. The incompatible bacteria might possess on their cell surfaces chemical groups (such as *N*-acetylglucosamine in the case of *P. solanacearum*) that are complementary to molecules (= lectins) present on plant cell walls, thus promoting the attachment of bacterial cells by the host cells. Once attached, the bacterial cells are enveloped by fibrillar material of host origin. During the process the bacterial cells might undergo partial or complete autolysis, or the OM components (such as LPS) might be selectively released; host degradative enzymes, bacterial autolytic enzymes, or both, might trigger such a response. The LPS molecule thus released might have an exposed lipid A moiety, which could then interact with the host cell wall and thereby trigger the host defense reactions.

It is noteworthy, in this connection, that ultrastructural studies (97) on interactions of various bacteria with bean plants led to the postulation that fibrillar material implicated in pathogen entrapment was not formed in response to bacteria but rather resulted from physical forces involved in the evaporation of water from intercellular spaces. Moreover, these data (97) suggest that bacterial attachment to the bean plant cell wall is not an active process. Obviously, a great deal remains to be learned before we can fully delineate the temporal sequence of events in bacterial association with compatible and noncompatible hosts and elucidate the underlying molecular interactions.

The OM proteins of Gram-negative phytopathogens have received relatively little attention. In *Pseudomonas morsprunorum* and *P. phaseolicola,* Hignett & Quirk (96) detected phytotoxicity in an LPS-associated protein.

As opposed to this finding, OM of *Erwinia amylovora* strains did not cause phytotoxicity in pear seedlings (K. K. Thurn, A. J. Trainer, and A. K. Chatterjee, in preparation). Our ongoing studies on genetically modified strains of *E. amylovora* should reveal whether or not some OM component(s) can induce resistance in apples and pears.

It should be emphasized that well-characterized mutants of phytopathogenic bacteria defective in LPS or OM protein have seldom been used in pathobiological studies. One notable exception is the finding (76) that *P. morsprunorum* mutants resistant to bacteriophage A7 were avirulent. Because LPS was found to be the bacteriophage-receptor site, it is likely that this OM component is involved in eliciting the disease in stone fruits. By adopting a similar approach, we should be able to obtain mutants defective in LPS or OM protein in other phytopathogenic bacteria. Investigations with such mutants should greatly add to our understanding of the role of bacterial cell surface components in phytopathogenicity. However, we caution about interpreting the findings of such studies, particularly if the mutants have not been fully characterized. Cell surface of certain LPS or OM protein mutants might differ architecturally; alterations in pathogenic response might result from this secondary phenotypic change rather than a specific defect on the OM component. Some OM mutants might also have defects in synthesis and assembly of capsular material and leakage of periplasmic proteins; these defects might in turn influence bacterial plant pathogenicity.

Amylovorin

Goodman and his associates (84, 100) reported production by *Erwinia amylovora* of a wilt-inducing toxin, amylovorin, within the susceptible host plant, plant parts, and apple cell suspension cultures. Subsequently, Ayers et al (5) concluded that amylovorin induced both wilt and browning-necrosis symptoms. An alternative viewpoint was presented by Sjulin & Beer (173) who reported that the infection of the host by *E. amylovora* caused an alteration of cell permeability, whereas amylovorin caused wilting of the host plants by a nonspecific restriction of water movement. Such findings cast doubt on the alleged specific phytotoxic role of amylovorin in the fire blight disease. Recent evidence suggests that amylovorin is perhaps a galactose-rich capsular material produced by virulent strains of the pathogen. Beer and his colleagues (12) demonstrated the in vitro production by *E. amylovora* of a polysaccharide that appeared to be homologous to Goodman's amylovorin—as judged by chemical, immunological, and biological criteria. Eden-Green & Knee (65) have also documented the production of a galactose-rich polysaccharide by *E. amylovora* in the presence or absence of the host. More recently, Bennett & Billing (16) detected the in vitro production by *E. amylovora* of two distinct polysaccharides; one was galactose-rich and resembled amylovorin in composition, and the other contained only fructose.

Although the toxic role of amylovorin in fire blight disease is questionable, it is possible that this macromolecule, which is perhaps equivalent to the capsular material produced by other virulent bacteria, functions in other capacities, such as in the establishment of the pathogen within the host. This notion is supported by several sorts of evidence. Goodman and his associates (103) showed that an avirulent strain of *E. amylovora*—one which does not produce amylovorin (i.e. lacks exopolysaccharide)—did not translocate from Jonathan apple petioles (the site of inoculation) to the stem as did the virulent exopolysaccharide (amylovorin)-producing strain; the failure was ascribed to the susceptibility of the avirulent strain to host defense systems. Using bacteriophage-resistant mutants, Ayers et al (4) have documented avirulence in *E. amylovora* strains deficient in capsular polysaccharide. Bennett & Billing (15) also noted acquisition of virulence in capsular mutants originating from a noncapsulated avirulent strain. [See above for the role of extracellular polysaccharide (EPS) on bacterial pathogenicity.]

The EPS (probably the same as amylovorin) of *E. amylovora* is composed predominantly ($\sim$ 75%) of galactose and, to a lesser degree, of glucose, uronic acid, and mannose (16, 65, 187). Huang (101) reported the presence of a galactosyltransferase in *E. amylovora.* The specificity of the transfer of galactose from UDP-galactose to various primers suggests an important role of the enzyme in producing EPS or amylovorin. Genetic and physiological investigations on mutants deficient in galactosyltransferase should establish the role of the enzyme in the synthesis of EPS and the contribution of the polysaccharide to bacterial virulence.

If amylovorin, the extracellular polysaccharide substance, is indeed involved only in the establishment of the pathogen and not in primary host cytotoxicity, there should exist an additional bacterial component that induces the extensive necrosis so typical of the fire blight disease. A recent report (14) suggests that additional virulence factors can be found. Experimental support of these notions is starting to surface: the formation of relatively small (i.e. dialyzable), possibly phytotoxic molecules in pear cell suspension cultures (PCSC) inoculated with virulent *E. amylovora* has been shown; cells of avirulent strains of *E. amylovora* or of nonphytopathogens did not elicit the formation of such molecules; the dialyzable substance(s) seemed to cause necrosis of pear seedlings, inhibited growth of pear callus, plasmolyzed and disintegrated pear cells in PCSC, and produced some browning of pear callus (G. E. Buchanan and M. P. Starr, in preparation). These preliminary and highly tentative observations suggest that such molecules might indeed play a role in the necrotic symptoms characteristic of the fire blight disease. Chemical, phytopathological, and genetic approaches are being used in further explorations (G. E. Buchanan and M. P. Starr, in progress) of the putative necrotoxin(s).

Extracellular Enzymes

Most members of the carotovora group of the genus *Erwinia* produce extracellular enzymes such as pectinases, proteases, cellulases, and phospholipases (10, 11, 181). A concerted activity of all or some of these enzymes might be necessary in the bacterial induction of plant tissue maceration and the production of soft-rot disease (18, 19). Recent biochemical studies (8, 9, 75, 136, 184) have revealed that one of the pectolytic enzymes, polygalacturonic acid *trans*-eliminase (PATE), plays an essential role in plant tissue maceration.

We have obtained, in *E. chrysanthemi,* Pat^- mutants deficient in PATE activity (see below for the details). These mutant strains do not macerate plant tissues. Moreover, we showed that Pat^+ recombinants (but not Pat^- recombinants), derived from crosses between an Hfr donor strain and Pat^- polyauxotrophic recipient strains (irrespective of the auxotrophic markers), macerated plant tissues such as potato tubers. These observations, which provide genetic evidence for an essential role of the extracellular PATE in plant tissue maceration, are consistent with the biochemical findings of others.

The physiological and/or pathological functions of other extracellular enzymes of the soft-rot erwinias remain to be elucidated. In our laboratories, recently perfected methods now permit us to readily isolate mutants deficient in hydrolytic polygalacturonase (M. P. Starr, P. R. Dong, and G. E. Buchanan, in preparation) and in protease and phospholipase (A. K. Chatterjee, in preparation). Preliminary trials in which these mutants were used suggest that PATE has a dual function—i.e. both cytolytic (cell separation and cell death) and catabolic (nutritional)—whereas other enzymes might have purely catabolic, and no directly cytolytic, function.

In the development of fire blight disease, the bacteria are predominantly intercellular in early stages of infection; during the later stages, lysogenous cavities are formed (102, 122) and the pathogen (*Erwinia amylovora*) is detected within plant cells. This shift in location (inter- to intra-cellular) of the phytopathogenic bacteria might result from a degeneration of the host cell wall or through the process of endocytosis. Early work of Miller (133) had also revealed larger intracellular spaces within the infected tissue and localized openings of cell walls. The mechanism by which the host cell wall is damaged or digested is not evident. Pectolytic enzymes, likely candidates in host tissue or cell degeneration, are undetectable under in vitro conditions (60, 167, 182). Moreover, Seemuller & Beer (167) failed to detect pectolytic, cellulolytic, or xylulolytic activities in extracts of infected shoots or in ooze produced during infection of pear fruits. All of these findings tend to support the notion that the pathogen, by itself, is perhaps unable to mediate the host cell wall degradation. How, then, might the formation of lysogenous cavities be explained? A possibility, which remains to be tested rigorously, is that the host, as a result of bacterial infection, is induced to produce certain autolytic enzymes that might not cause extensive tissue maceration but would generate localized openings in host cell wall. It should be noted that *E. amylovora* produces extracellular proteases (167; A. K. Chatterjee, unpublished) and aminopeptidases (130). These enzymes, although by themselves unable to digest host cell wall, might very well exert a modifying effect on host-enzymes and thus perhaps trigger the autolytic event. Protease-deficient mutants have been obtained by us in virulent parent strains of *E. amylovora,* and we are currently examining the pathogenic response(s) induced by these genetically marked strains. Clearly, additional studies are necessary to explain the occurrence of lysogenous cavities that have been consistently observed during pathogenesis of *E. amylovora.*

Polygalacturonic Acid Catabolism

Most members of the carotovora group of the genus *Erwinia* possess enzymes that cause the breakdown of polygalacturonic acid (PGA; pectic acid); the monomeric products are utilized by these organisms as sources of carbon and energy [for a detailed treatment of this subject, see (181)]. Briefly, the α-1,4-glycosidic bond of PGA can be broken by a hydrolytic polygalacturonase (HPG) activity or by a *trans*-eliminase (lyase) reaction mediated by polygalacturonic acid *trans*-eliminase (PATE; sometimes referred to as pectate lyase). These two activities can be of the exo sort (which removes the terminal units) or the endo sort (which produces a random in-chain splitting of the glycosidic bonds) (11, 93). Similar enzymes (polymethylgalacturonase and pectin methyl *trans*-eliminase) in some fungi and bacteria are known to cleave polymethylgalacturonic acid (pectin) (41, 66); generally, however, the bacterial enzymes, including those produced by *Erwinia* spp., preferentially cleave demethoxylated polygalacturonic acid (41, 73, 181). Our earlier findings [see (181) for a summary] revealed that the primary products of HPG activity are D-galacturonic acid and digalacturonic acid, whereas those of PATE activity are unsaturated digalacturonic acid [*O*-(4-deoxy-β-L-5-*threo*-hexopyranos-4-enyluronic acid)-(1→4)-D-galacturonic acid] and lesser amounts of unsaturated trigalacturonic acid and of saturated mono- and digalacturonic acids.

It should be noted that the production of HPG and PATE by the enterobacteria is not confined only to *Erwinia* spp. as previously thought (51). Recent reports clearly document that the pectolytic activity in members of other enterobacterial genera, such as *Klebsiella* and *Yersinia* (182, 191, 192), results from the production of these enzymes (7, 31, 182). This observation revives taxonomic issues concerning segregation of the carotovora group of the genus *Erwinia* from other enterobacterial genera solely on the grounds of their pectolytic activity; it certainly renders unacceptable the proposed delineation of a genus *Pectobacterium* solely on the basis of pectolytic ability (22, 56, 193).

Since the development of genetic research on polypectate catabolism is intimately associated with physiological findings on these metabolic processes, a brief discussion of the relevant aspects is appropriate.

LOCATION OF PECTOLYTIC ACTIVITY Various enterobacteria clearly differ in terms of the location of PATE activity (31). In a strain of *Erwinia chrysanthemi,* PATE is an extracellular enzyme and is totally excreted; in strains of *Yersinia enterocolitica* and *Y. pseudotuberculosis,* PATE activity is periplasmic and cytoplasmic; in a strain of *Erwinia carotovora,* PATE activity is extracellular, periplasmic, and cytoplasmic; in an "oxytocum" strain of *Klebsiella pneumoniae,* PATE is entirely cytoplasmic, with little or no activity detectable in periplasm or culture supernatants. Osmotic shock experiments have revealed the periplasmic location of PATE in *E. rubrifaciens* (73). The excretion of the PATE molecule in *E. carotovora* and *E. chrysanthemi* is independent of cellular lysis and the release of periplasmic enzyme. As opposed to this route operative in *Erwinia* spp., in other enterobacteria (such as *Klebsiella* and *Yersinia*) very little of this activity is present external to the cell during exponential growth. Such differential excretion patterns seem to result from structural differences in PATE molecules produced by these bacteria rather than from a nonspecific permeability of the cell envelope. In a recent comparative study, Bagley & Starr (7) noted structural differences in PATE molecules produced by erwinias, klebsiellas, and yersinias. Our genetic studies (see below) tend to support this notion.

REGULATION OF PATE PRODUCTION PATE is inducible in both *Erwinia carotovora* and *E. chrysanthemi* (31, 43, 104, 135, 181, 188, 200, 201). In some of the early studies on regulation, the extracellular but not the cytoplasmic PATE was considered. However, recent reports have documented different regulatory responses of cytoplasmic and extracellular enzymes in *E. carotovora* and in *E. chrysanthemi.* During exponential growth, all or most of the induced PATE activity is excreted in *E. chrysanthemi.* On the other hand, most of the induced (as well as uninduced) activity in *E. carotovora* remains cell bound (31). Similar findings have been reported for another strain of *E. carotovora* (188).

Based on the differential kinetics of induction of intracellular PATE of *E. carotovora* by PGA and by unsaturated digalacturonic acid (UDG), Tsuyumu (188) suggested that the inducer might be the product of the catalytic activity, i.e. UDG. Hubbard & Mount (104) also reported that both the unsaturated di- and tri-galacturonic acid residues were more effective than the native sodium polygalacturonate in inducing PATE activity in *E. carotovora.* In *E. chrysanthemi* our recent kinetic studies (M. W. Ferguson and A. K. Chatterjee, in preparation) revealed a relatively more rapid induction of PATE with UDG than with PGA. However, much higher levels of PATE were synthesized in the presence of PGA (0.1% wt/vol) than with a similar concentration of UDG in the bacterial growth medium. These differential effects probably reflect the relative concentrations of the inducer in the growth medium and in the cell. Obviously, genetic and additional physiological studies are necessary to establish that the unsaturated derivative(s) and not some other metabolic product(s) (see below for details) is (are) the inducer(s) of this activity. In such studies, it also would be necessary to assess the role of oligogalacturonide *trans*-eliminase (OGTE; 134) in the formation of the inducer molecule. The findings of Collmer & Bateman (43) implicate HPG activity in the production of the inducer of PATE. HPG or α-galacturonidase activity on PGA can generate saturated oligouronic acids, which could be acted upon by OGTE with the production of the unsaturated product(s), the inducer of PATE. We now have initiated genetic studies on OGTE; with the availability of OGTE-deficient mutants of *E. chrysanthemi,* it should be possible to test this notion rigorously.

PATE production in both *E. carotovora* and *E. chrysanthemi* is also subject to catabolite repression (31, 36, 43, 105, 135). The early findings of Moran & Starr (135) concerning the repressive effect of glucose have been confirmed and extended (31); both studies used the same strain of *E. carotovora.* We showed that the intracellular activity of PATE, in cells grown on glucose and sucrose, was severely decreased compared with the levels of activity in cells grown on galacturonate, gluconate, or glycerol. On the other hand, the levels of extracellular activity were comparable when cells were grown on each of these substrates including glucose and sucrose. The results suggest a preferential repressive effect of glucose or sucrose on the intracellular, but not on the extracellular, enzyme. The teleological significance of this behavior might reside in the formation of the putative inducer molecule. If a product of PATE activity (such as unsaturated digalacturonic acid) acts as an inducer, the production of extracellular activity under all growth conditions ensures the formation of this inducer when the bacterium is presented with the seemingly impermeable substrate (polygalacturonic acid).

As expected, the repressive effect of glucose in these *Erwinia* spp. seemed to result from a decrease in the intracellular concentration of adenosine 3',5'-cyclic monophosphate (cAMP). Hubbard et al (105) could reverse the repressive effect by supplying exogenous cAMP to cultures of *E. carotovora.* Moreover, the intracellular concentration of cAMP was found to decrease during glucose repression and to increase in induced cultures (105). Subsequent observations (137) with a cAMP-deficient mutant of *E. carotovora* also suggested a regulatory role of the cyclic nucleotide in the synthesis of PATE. These findings, taken together with those of Ide (107), implicate cAMP and cAMP-receptor protein (CRP) in the expression of the gene (*pat*) that specifies the production of PATE in *E. carotovora.*

To establish rigorously this mode of control in the expression of *pat* as well as other gene loci involved in pathogenicity, we have, in our *E. chrysanthemi* system, adopted genetic approaches similar to those applied in other bacteria (24, 144). One class of our mutants (36) exhibited a pleiotropic-negative phenotype; they failed to grow on glycerol, arabinose, ribose, xylose, galactose, galacturonate, and polygalacturonate either in the presence or absence of exogenous cAMP. Moreover, the mutants failed to degrade polygalacturonic acid. By Hfr matings, the relevant locus *mcu,* which is distinct from *pat,* has been mapped on the chromosome of *E. chrysanthemi.* Using an F'*crp*$^+$ that originates in *E. coli,* we are now attempting the complementation of the metabolic defect in *E. chrysanthemi.* If our ongoing genetic as well as physiological studies further confirm this idea, it would clearly establish the influence of the cAMP-CRP system in the expression of genes that specify the production of PATE as well as other extracellular enzymes and phytopathogenicity in this bacterial species.

MAPPING OF THE *PAT* LOCUS In the past, genetics of PATE production has been hampered by the lack of a recombinational system in these bacteria. With the development of conjugational and transductional systems in soft-rot erwinias (see above), it became possible to systematically examine the genetics of production of this as well as other extracellular enzymes and to associate catabolic and/or cytolytic functions with these activities.

We have developed a simple procedure (36) that allows rapid screening of mutants defective in extracellular PATE activity. As already noted, *E. chrysanthemi* and other soft-rot erwinias produce a variety of pectolytic enzymes including HPG and PATE. Moreover, the reaction products of either activity can support the growth of the bacterium (see below). Initially, this equivalence posed a problem in isolating mutants defective in one or the other activity. We resolved this issue by taking advantage of the vastly different pH optima of these activities; HPG is most active at pH 5.5, whereas PATE has optimal activity at pH 8.5–9.0. The degradation of polygalacturonic acid, visualized by flooding the medium with hydrochloric acid, can result either from PATE activity or from HPG activity, depending on the pH of the medium. Using this procedure, we have obtained a number of independent mutants with defects in PATE (36) or HPG (M. P. Starr, P. R. Dong, and G. E. Buchanan, in preparation) activity. Enzymological studies (M. W. Ferguson and A. K. Chatterjee, in preparation) reveal that the Pat$^-$ mutants fall into two classes: class I mutants have considerably higher intracellular activity but much less extracellular activity than do the parent strains; class II mutants have much reduced intra- and extracellular activities. It is possible that the structure of the PATE molecule in the class I mutants has been altered such that it no longer is transported across the membranes. Class II mutants, however, might synthesize lower PATE levels or synthesize catalytically altered PATE molecules.

It is noteworthy that in our search for Pat$^-$ mutations we have deliberately looked for clones that do not degrade PGA on agar media (36; A. K. Chatterjee, unpublished). Both *E. carotovora* and *E. chrysanthemi* synthesize various isozymes of PATE (7, 75, 128, 156), and the pectolytic reaction on agar medium containing PGA probably results from the cumulative activities of all of these isozymes. If polypeptides of PATE isozymes are specified by different genes, some of our "tight" Pat$^-$ mutants would have to be defective in multiple structural genes or in a regulatory locus that controls the production of all of the isozymes. The genetic data (see below) tend to support the latter hypothesis. Several independent *pat* mutations have been mapped by linkage analysis of recombinants derived from Hfr matings. The frequency of coinheritance of *pat* with selectable markers (such as *trp, his, thr*) clearly indicates that *pat* is located on the *E. chrysanthemi* chromosome and that it is closer to *his* than to *thr* and *trp* (36, 38; A. K. Chatterjee, unpublished data). At present, it is unclear whether these mutations (which yield distinct enzymological classes, yet map in one region) are in regulator, structural, or "modifier" genes. We now have perfected techniques that allow fractionation of the isozymes on polyacrylamide gels (M. W. Ferguson and A. K. Chatterjee, in preparation) and thus should facilitate rapid determination of the isozyme profiles in Pat$^-$ and Pat^{leaky} mutants. This information, in conjunction with the fine structure map deduced from transductional and R68.45-mediated crosses, should clarify the organization and regulation of the genes for production of PATE isozymes in *E. chrysanthemi.*

DEGRADATION OF OLIGOURONIDES AND CATABOLISM OF MONOMERIC DERIVATIVES Catabolism of saturated or unsaturated di- and oligouronides requires another activity, oligouronide *trans*-eliminase (OGTE; 93, 134). OGTE degrades unsaturated digalacturonic acid into two molecules of 4-deoxy-L-*threo*-5-hexoseulose uronic acid (deoxyketouronic acid), and it degrades saturated digalacturonic acid into one molecule of D-galacturonic acid and one molecule of deoxyketouronic acid—indicating a *trans*-eliminase reaction. By observing the sequential activities of isomerase, dehydrogenase, kinase, and aldolase enzymes, Preiss & Ashwell (151–153) have established the following pathway in the catabolism of ketouronic acid in a "soil pseudomonad": 4-deoxy-L-*threo*-5-hexoseulose uronic acid →3-deoxy-D-glycero-2,5-hexodiulosonic acid → 2-keto-3-deoxy-D-gluconic acid → 2-keto-3-deoxy-6-phospho-D-gluconic acid → pyruvate + glyceraldehyde-3-phosphate. Using cell-free extracts of *E. carotovora,* Moran et al (134) have detected the formation of 2-keto-3-deoxy-D-gluconic acid from deoxyketouronic acid in the presence of NADH. This finding tentatively suggests a similar route in the catabolism of deoxyketouronic acid by *Erwinia* spp.; the full characterization of the individual steps of the pathway awaits further study.

D-Galacturonic acid—a product of HPG, PATE, and OGTE activities —is metabolized by *Erwinia carotovora* (111, 115) and by *Escherichia coli* (3, 50, 95, 139, 174) through the sequential formation of the following intermediates (and enzyme activities): D-tagaturonate (uronate isomerase), D-altronate (altronate oxidoreductase), 2-keto-3-deoxy-D-gluconate (altronate hydrolyase), 2-keto-3-deoxy-6-phospho-D-gluconate (2-keto-3-deoxygluconate kinase), and pyruvate + triose-3-phosphate (2-keto-3-deoxy-6-phosphogluconate aldolase). An overall similarity is also apparent between *Erwinia carotovora* and *Escherichia coli* with regard to the steps in the catabolism of D-glucuronate (2, 111, 139).

The genetics of catabolism of these substrates in *Erwinia* spp. is of considerable interest, in that this system might unravel interlocking regulatory mechanisms controlling the degradation of the polymer (PGA), cleavage of the dimers (unsaturated and saturated digalacturonic acid), and the subsequent catabolism of monomeric residues (D-galacturonic acid and deoxyketouronic acid). Moreover, because some of these degradative processes are intimately associated with pathogenicity of these bacteria, an elucidation of the regulatory mechanism is relevant in terms of the expression of bacterial virulence. In addition, excretion of PATE in *Erwinia* spp. is a useful model system for investigating the molecular aspects of secretion of enzymes in Gram-negative bacteria, a subject that has received relatively little attention.

In *Escherichia coli,* where the genetics and physiological aspects of D-glucuronate and D-galacturonate catabolism have been intensively studied, gene products of the following regulatory units have been shown to be involved (6, 139, 140, 148–150, 160, 185):

1. The *exu* (the symbol for functions involved in both glucuronate and galacturonate metabolism) regulon which includes three operons: the *uxaC-uxaA* operon (67 min), the *uxaB* operon (52 min), and the *exuT* operon (67 min). The *exu* regulon is under negative control of the product of the regulatory gene, *exuR* (67 min).
2. The *uxu* operon (98 min) consists of *uxuB* and *uxuA* which are negatively controlled by the products of two regulatory genes, *exuR* (67 min) and *uxuR* (98 min).
3. The *kdg* regulon is composed of *eda* (41 min), *kdgR* (40 min), *kdgK* (78 min), and *kdgP* and *kdgT* (88 min), and it is negatively controlled by the *kdgR* product.

Obviously much remains to be accomplished in *Erwinia* spp. before we can even begin to evaluate critically the homologies that might prevail in these seemingly identical catabolic processes occurring in members of two enterobacterial genera. The aforementioned investigations in *E. coli* serve as an admirable model for our ongoing studies with *Erwinia* spp.

PROSPECTS

It is apparent that genetic approaches can be extremely useful in understanding overall biological processes, including those that determine associations between plants and members of the bacterial genus *Erwinia* (as well as other phytopathogenic bacteria not dealt with here). In the context of phytopathogenic mechanisms, genetic technologies are particularly attractive for elucidating the role of bacterial cell surface components in pathogen establishment, bacterial host specificity, and induction of the host's defense reactions. Another area in which genetic technologies can effectively be applied is bacterial production of virulence factors such as toxins and enzymes—specifically, the organization and expression of the genes that control the underlying metabolic processes. It also is conceivable that genetic tools might be applied to modify plant or bacterial genomes and thereby suppress in vivo activities of phytopathogenic bacteria.

At this juncture, it is important to recognize that, for various reasons [see Starr & Chatterjee (181) for a historical perspective], phytopathogenic bacteria as a group have rarely been investigated thoroughly and systematically. Consequently, their biology is poorly understood, the available knowledge is sketchy, and little effort is ordinarily expended in comparative studies of phytopathogens and possibly related nonphytopathogens. Unfortunately, this evaluation is true even for those species that have attracted relatively more attention. A better understanding of phytopathogens and the diseases they cause can emerge only from concerted genetic, biochemical, physiological, and pathobiological studies—in which disciplinal barriers (179) are breached by comparative approaches. Because of the nature and inherent complexity of associations between bacteria and plants, elucidation of interaction mechanisms necessitates an interdisciplinary approach. Knowledge concerning the host and the pathogen must evolve simultaneously; one without the other would defeat the purpose.

It is our hope that specialists in related disciplines will share this viewpoint and that collaborative endeavor will lead all of us to a better overall understanding of the various facets of host-pathogen associations and to the realization of the ultimate goal: healthier plants. Such diligent collaboration already has contributed to the knowledge of genetics, physiology, cell surface components, and plasmid biology of phytopathogenic bacteria. Therefore, we remain optimistic that some of the "bigger" issues will be resolved by such concerted effort during the 1980s.

ACKNOWLEDGMENTS

Research in our laboratories is supported by the National Science Foundation (grant PCM-7910923 to AKC), the Science and Education Administration of the US Department of Agriculture (grant 5901-0410-8-0008-0 to AKC, from the Competitive Research Grants Office), and the National Institutes of Health, US Public Health Service (grant AI-08426 to MPS).

This report is Contribution No. 80-320-R, Department of Plant Pathology, Kansas Agricultural Experiment Station, Kansas State University, Manhattan, Kansas 66506.

Literature Cited

1. Arber, W. 1958. *Arch. Sci.* 11:259–338
2. Ashwell, G. 1962. In *Methods in Enzymology,* ed. S. P. Colowick, N. O. Kaplan, 5:190–208. New York/London: Academic
3. Ashwell, G., Wahba, A. J., Hickman, J. 1960. *J. Biol. Chem.* 235:1559–65
4. Ayers, A. R., Ayers, S. B., Goodman, R. N. 1979. *Appl. Environ. Microbiol.* 38:659–66
5. Ayers, A. R., Goodman, R. N., Ayers, S. B., White, J. A. 1977. *Proc. Am. Phytopathol. Soc.* 4:107
6. Bachmann, B. J., Low, K. B. 1980. *Microbiol. Rev.* 44:1–56
7. Bagley, S. T., Starr, M. P. 1979. *Curr. Microbiol.* 2:381–86
8. Basham, H. G., Bateman, D. F. 1975. *Phytopathology* 65:141–53
9. Basham, H. G., Bateman, D. F. 1975. *Physiol. Plant Pathol.* 5:249–62
10. Bateman, D. F., Basham, H. G. 1976. In *Physiological Plant Pathology,* ed. R. Heitefuss, P. H. Williams, pp. 316–55. Berlin/Heidelberg/New York: Springer-Verlag

11. Bateman, D. F., Millar, R. L. 1966. *Ann. Rev. Phytopathol.* 4:119–46
12. Beer, S. V., Barker, C. J., Woods, A. C., Sjulin, T. M. 1977. *Proc. Am. Phytopathol. Soc.* 4:182–83
13. Behrens, M. K., Starr, M. P. 1979. *Abstr. Ann. Meet. Am. Soc. Microbiol. H80,* p. 132
14. Bennett, R. A. 1980. *J. Gen. Microbiol.* 116:351–56
15. Bennett, R. A., Billing, E. 1978. *Ann. Appl. Biol.* 89:41–45
16. Bennett, R. A., Billing, E. 1980. *J. Gen. Microbiol.* 116:341–49
17. Benzinger, R., Hartman, P. E. 1962. *Virology* 18:614–26
18. Beraha, L., Garber, E. D. 1971. *Phytopathol. Z.* 70:335–44
19. Beraha, L., Garber, E. D., Billeter, B. A. 1974. *Phytopathol. Z.* 81:15–22
20. Billing, E. 1960. *Nature* 186:819–20
21. Brenner, D. J., Fanning, G. R., Steigerwalt, A. G. 1972. *J. Bacteriol.* 110:12–17
22. Brenner, D. J., Fanning, G. R., Steigerwalt, A. G. 1974. *Int. J. Syst. Bacteriol.* 24:197–204
23. Brenner, D. J., Steigerwalt, A. G., Miklos, G. V., Fanning, G. R. 1973. *Int. J. Syst. Bacteriol.* 23:205–16
24. Brickman, E., Soll, L., Beckwith, J. 1973. *J. Bacteriol.* 116:582–87
25. Brinkerhoff, L. A. 1970. *Ann. Rev. Phytopathol.* 8:85–110
26. Buchanan-Wollston, V. 1979. *J. Gen. Microbiol.* 112:135–42
27. Campos, J. M., Geisselsoder, J., Zusman, D. R. 1978. *J. Mol. Biol.* 119:167–78
28. Chatterjee, A. K. 1979. *Proc. Int. Conf. Plant Pathog. Bacteria, 4th, Angers, 1978,* ed. Station de Pathologie Végétale et Phytobactériologie, pp. 3–16. Beaucouzé: Inst. Natl. Rech. Agron.
29. Chatterjee, A. K. 1980. *J. Bacteriol.* 142:111–19
30. Chatterjee, A. K., Behrens, M. K., Starr, M. P. 1979. See Ref. 28, pp. 75–79
31. Chatterjee, A. K., Buchanan, G. E., Behrens, M. K., Starr, M. P. 1979. *Can. J. Microbiol.* 25:94–102
32. Chatterjee, A. K., Starr, M. P. 1972. *J. Bacteriol.* 11:169–76
33. Chatterjee, A. K., Starr, M. P. 1972. *J. Bacteriol.* 112:576–84
34. Chatterjee, A. K., Starr, M. P. 1973. *Infect. Immun.* 8:563–72
35. Chatterjee, A. K., Starr, M. P. 1973. *J. Bacteriol.* 116:1100–6
36. Chatterjee, A. K., Starr, M. P. 1977. *J. Bacteriol.* 132:862–69
37. Chatterjee, A. K., Starr, M. P. 1979. See Ref. 28, pp. 81–88
38. Chatterjee, A. K., Starr, M. P. 1979. See Ref. 28, pp. 89–94
39. Chilton, M.-D., Drummond, M. H., Merlo, D. J., Sciaky, D., Montoya, A. L., Gordon, M. P., Nester, E. W. 1977. *Cell* 11:263–71
40. Cho, J. J., Panopoulos, N. J., Schroth, M. N. 1975. *J. Bacteriol.* 122:192–98
41. Codner, R. C. 1971. *J. Appl. Bacteriol.* 34:147–60
42. Coetzee, J. N. 1972. *Ann. Rev. Microbiol.* 26:23–54
43. Collmer, A., Bateman, D. F. 1979. *Phytopathology* 69:1025
44. Coplin, D. L. 1978. *Phytopathology* 68:1637–43
45. Coplin, D. L. 1979. *J. Gen. Microbiol.* 113:181–84
46. Coplin, D. L., Rowan, R. G. 1979. See Ref. 28, pp. 67–73
47. Corey, R. R., Starr, M. P. 1957. *J. Bacteriol.* 74:141–45
48. Corey, R. R., Starr, M. P. 1957. *J. Bacteriol.* 74:146–50
49. Costerton, J. W., Ingram, J. M., Cheng, K.-J. 1974. *Bacteriol. Rev.* 38:87–110
50. Cynkin, M. A., Ashwell, G. 1960. *J. Biol. Chem.* 235:1576–79
51. Davis, B. R., Ewing, W. H. 1964. *J. Bacteriol.* 88:16–19
52. De Ley, J. 1968. *Ann. Rev. Phytopathol.* 6:63–90
53. DeVay, J. E., Adler, H. E. 1976. *Ann. Rev. Microbiol.* 30:147–68
54. Dickinson, C. H., Preece, T. F., eds. 1976. *Microbiology of Aerial Plant Surfaces.* London/New York: Academic
55. DiRienzo, J. M., Nakamura, K., Inouye, M. 1978. *Ann. Rev. Biochem.* 47:481–532
56. Dowson, W. J. 1957. *Plant Diseases Due to Bacteria.* Cambridge: Cambridge Univ. Press. 2nd ed.
57. Drexler, H. 1970. *Proc. Natl. Acad. Sci. USA* 66:1083–88
58. Drexler, H., Kylberg, K. J. 1975. *J. Virol.* 16:263–66
59. Drummond, M. 1979. *Nature* 281:343–47
60. Dye, D. W. 1968. *N. Z. J. Sci.* 11:590–607
61. Dye, D. W. 1969. *N. Z. J. Sci.* 12:81–97
62. Dye, D. W. 1969. *N. Z. J. Sci.* 12:223–36
63. Dye, D. W. 1969. *N. Z. J. Sci.* 12:833–39
64. Echandi, E., Moyer, J. W. 1979. *Phytopathology* 69:1204–7
65. Eden-Green, S. J., Knee, M. 1974. *J. Gen. Microbiol.* 81:509–12

66. Edstrom, R. D., Phaff, H. J. 1964. *J. Biol. Chem.* 239:2409–15
67. El-Banoby, F. E., Rudolph, K. 1979. *Phytopathol. Z.* 95:38–50
68. El-Banoby, F. E., Rudolph, K. 1979. *Physiol. Plant Pathol.* 15:341–49
69. Ewing, W. H., Fife, M. A. 1972. *Int. J. Syst. Bacteriol.* 22:4–11
70. Falkow, S. 1975. *Infectious Multiple Drug Resistance.* London: Pion Ltd.
71. Gantotti, B. V., Patil, S. S., Mandel, M. 1979. *Appl. Environ. Microbiol.* 37:511–16
72. Gardner, J. M., Kado, C. I. 1972. *Int. J. Syst. Bacteriol.* 22:201–9
73. Gardner, J. M., Kado, C. I. 1976. *J. Bacteriol.* 127:451–60
74. Garen, A., Zinder, N. D. 1955. *Virology* 1:347–76
75. Garibaldi, A., Bateman, D. F. 1971. *Physiol. Plant Pathol.* 1:25–40
76. Garrett, C. M. E., Crosse, J. E., Sletten, A. 1974. *J. Gen. Microbiol.* 80:475–83
77. Gibbins, L. N. 1979. See Ref. 28, pp. 403–31
78. Gibbins, L. N., Bennett, P. M., Saunders, J. R., Grinsted, J., Connolly, J. C. 1976. *J. Bacteriol.* 128:309–16
79. Goldberg, R. B., Bender, R. A., Streicher, S. L. 1974. *J. Bacteriol.* 118:810–14
80. Gonzalez, C. F., Vidaver, A. K. 1979. See Ref. 28, pp. 31–38
81. Gonzalez, C. F., Vidaver, A. K. 1979. *Curr. Microbiol.* 2:75–80
82. Goodfellow, M., Austin, B., Dickinson, C. H. 1976. *J. Gen. Microbiol.* 97:219–33
83. Goodman, R. N. 1978. *Mycopathologia* 65:107–13
84. Goodman, R. N., Huang, J.-S., Huang, P.-Y. 1974. *Science* 183:1081–82
85. Goodman, R. N., Huang, P.-Y., White, J. A. 1976. *Phytopathology* 66:754–64
86. Goto, M. 1972. *J. Appl. Bacteriol.* 35:505–15
87. Graham, D. C. 1964. *Ann. Rev. Phytopathol.* 2:13–42
88. Graham, D. C., Hodgkiss, W. 1967. *J. Appl. Bacteriol.* 30:175–89
89. Graham, T. L., Sequeira, L., Huang, T.-S. R. 1977. *Appl. Environ. Microbiol.* 34:424–32
90. Grimont, F., Grimont, P. A. D., du Pasquier, P. 1978. *Curr. Microbiol.* 1:37–40
91. Guimaraes, W. V., Panopoulos, N. J., Schroth, M. N. 1979. See Ref. 28, pp. 53–65
92. Harrison, A., Gibbins, L. N. 1975. *Can. J. Microbiol.* 21:937–44
93. Hatanaka, C., Ozawa, J. 1971. *Agric. Biol. Chem.* 35:1617–24
94. Hernalsteens, J. P., De Greve, H., Van Montagu, M., Schell, J. 1978. *Plasmid* 1:218–25
95. Hickman, J., Ashwell, G. 1960. *J. Biol. Chem.* 235:1566–70
96. Hignett, R. C., Quirk, A. V. 1979. *J. Gen. Microbiol.* 110:77–81
97. Hildebrand, D. C., Alosi, M. C., Schroth, M. N. 1980. *Phytopathology* 70:98–109
98. Holloway, B. W. 1979. *Plasmid* 2:1–19
99. Holloway, B. W., Monk, M. 1961. *Proc. Australasian Conf. Radiobiol., 3rd,* ed. P. L. T. Ilbery, pp. 231–37. London: Butterworths
100. Hsu, S.-T., Goodman, R. N. 1978. *Phytopathology* 68:351–54
101. Huang, J.-S. 1979. *Physiol. Plant Pathol.* 15:193–200
102. Huang, P.-Y., Goodman, R. N. 1976. *Phytopathology* 66:269–76
103. Huang, P.-Y., Huang, J.-S., Goodman, R. N. 1975. *Physiol. Plant Pathol.* 6:283–87
104. Hubbard, J. P., Mount, M. S. 1978. *Am. Phytopathol. Soc. Newslett., Abstr. NE-20,* p. 236
105. Hubbard, J. P., Williams, J. D., Niles, R. M., Mount, M. S. 1978. *Phytopathology* 68:95–99
106. Husain, K., Kelman, A. 1958. *Phytopathology* 48:155–65
107. Ide, M. 1971. *Arch. Biochem. Biophys.* 144:262–68
108. Jacob, A. E., Cresswell, J. M., Hedges, R. W. 1977. *FEMS Microbiol. Lett.* 1:71–74
109. Kelman, A. 1954. *Phytopathology* 44:693–95
110. Kelman, A., Hruschka, J. 1973. *J. Gen. Microbiol.* 76:177–88
111. Kilgore, W. W., Starr, M. P. 1959. *J. Biol. Chem.* 234:2227–35
112. Kleckner, N., Roth, J., Botstein, D. 1977. *J. Mol. Biol.* 116:125–59
113. Klein, D. T., Klein, R. M. 1953. *J. Bacteriol.* 66:220–28
114. Klein, D. T., Klein, R. M. 1956. *J. Bacteriol.* 72:308–13
115. Kraght, A. J., Starr, M. P. 1952. *J. Bacteriol.* 64:259–64
116. Lacy, G. H. 1978. *Phytopathology* 68:1323–30
117. Lacy, G. H., Leary, J. V. 1979. *Ann. Rev. Phytopathol.* 17:181–202
118. Lacy, G. H., Sparks, R. B. Jr. 1979. *Phytopathology* 69:1293–97
119. Lakso, J. U., Starr, M. P. 1970. *J. Appl. Bacteriol.* 33:692–707

120. Lê, T. K. T., Leccas, D., Boucher, C. 1979. See Ref. 28, pp. 819–22
121. Lelliott, R. A. 1974. In *Bergey's Manual of Determinative Bacteriology,* ed. R. E. Buchanan, N. E. Gibbons, pp. 332–40. Baltimore: Williams & Wilkins. 8th ed.
122. Lewis, S., Goodman, R. N. 1965. *Phytopathology* 55:719–23
123. Liao, C. H., Heberlein, G. T. 1979. *Can. J. Microbiol.* 25:185–91
124. Lippincott, B. B., Whatley, M. H., Lippincott, J. A. 1977. *Plant Physiol.* 59:388–90
125. Lippincott, J. A., Lippincott, B. B. 1975. *Ann. Rev. Microbiol.* 29:377–405
126. Low, K. B. 1972. *Bacteriol. Rev.* 36:587–607
127. Maramorosch, K. 1974. *Ann. Rev. Microbiol.* 28:301–24
128. Mazzucchi, U., Alberghina, A., Garibaldi, A. 1974. *Phytopathol. Mediterr.* 13:27–35
129. Mazzucchi, U., Pupillo, P. 1976. *Physiol. Plant Pathol.* 9:101–12
130. McIntyre, J. L., Huber, D., Kuć, J., Williams, E. B. 1975. *Phytopathology* 65:1206–12
131. Mergeay, M., Gertis, J. 1978. *J. Bacteriol.* 135:18–28
132. Middleton, R. B., Mojica-a, T. 1971. *Adv. Genet.* 16:53–79
133. Miller, P. W. 1929. *J. Agric. Res.* 39:579–621
134. Moran, F., Nasuno, S., Starr, M. P. 1968. *Arch. Biochem. Biophys.* 125:734–41
135. Moran, F., Starr, M. P. 1969. *Eur. J. Biochem.* 11:291–95
136. Mount, M. S., Bateman, D. F., Basham, H. G. 1970. *Phytopathology* 60:924–31
137. Mount, M. S., Berman, P. M., Mortlock, R. P., Hubbard, J. P. 1979. *Phytopathology* 69:117–20
138. Murata, N., Starr, M. P. 1974. *Can. J. Microbiol.* 20:1545–65
139. Némoz, G., Robert-Baudouy, J., Stoeber, F. 1976. *J. Bacteriol.* 127:706–18
140. Novel, M., Novel, G. 1974. *C. R. Acad. Sci. Ser. D* 279:695–98
141. Olsen, R. H., Thomas, D. D. 1973. *J. Virol.* 12:1560–67
142. Palleroni, N. J., Doudoroff, M. 1972. *Ann. Rev. Phytopathol.* 10:73–100
143. Panopoulos, N. J., Guimaraes, W. V., Hua, S.-S., Sabersky-Lehman, C., Resnik, S., Lai, M., Shaffer, S. 1978. In *Microbiology 1978,* ed. D. Schlessinger, pp. 238–41. Washington DC: Am. Soc. Microbiol.
144. Pastan, I., Adhya, S. 1976. *Bacteriol. Rev.* 40:527–51
145. Patil, S. S. 1974. *Ann. Rev. Phytopathol.* 12:259–79
146. Paulin, J. P., Nassan, N. A. 1979. See Ref. 28, pp. 539–45
147. Pérombelon, M. C. M., Boucher, C. 1979. See Ref. 28, pp. 47–52
148. Portalier, R. C., Robert-Baudouy, J. M., Némoz, G. M. 1974. *Mol. Gen. Genet.* 128:301–19
149. Portalier, R. C., Robert-Baudouy, J. M., Stoeber, F. R. 1972. *Mol. Gen. Genet.* 118:335–50
150. Pouyssegur, J., Stoeber, F. 1974. *J. Bacteriol.* 117:641–51
151. Preiss, J., Ashwell, G. 1962. *J. Biol. Chem.* 237:309–16
152. Preiss, J., Ashwell, G. 1962. *J. Biol. Chem.* 237:317–21
153. Preiss, J., Ashwell, G. 1963. *J. Biol. Chem.* 238:1577–83
154. Pugashetti, B. K. 1976. *Genetics and physiology of virulence in Erwinia amylovora.* PhD thesis. Univ. Calif., Davis. 135 pp.
155. Pugashetti, B. K., Chatterjee, A. K., Starr, M. P. 1978. *Can. J. Microbiol.* 24:448–54
156. Pupillo, P., Mazzucchi, U., Pierini, G. 1976. *Physiol. Plant Pathol.* 9:113–20
157. Reanney, D. 1976. *Bacteriol. Rev.* 40:552–90
158. Ritchie, D. F., Klos, E. J. 1977. *Phytopathology* 67:101–4
159. Ritchie, D. F., Klos, E. J. 1979. *Phytopathology* 69:1078–83
160. Robert-Baudouy, J. M., Jimeno-Abendano, J., Stoeber, F. R. 1975. *Biochimie* 57:1–8
161. Sakazaki, R., Tamura, K., Johnson, R., Colwell, R. R. 1976. *Int. J. Syst. Bacteriol.* 26:158–79
162. Sanderson, K. E. 1976. *Ann. Rev. Microbiol.* 30:327–49
163. Sanderson, K. E., Hartman, P. E. 1978. *Microbiol. Rev.* 42:471–519
164. Schaad, N. W. 1979. *Ann. Rev. Phytopathol.* 17:123–47
165. Schell, J. 1979. See Ref. 28, pp. 115–26
166. Schneierson, S. S., Bottone, E. J. 1973. *Crit. Rev. Clin. Lab. Sci.* 4:341–55
167. Seemuller, E. A., Beer, S. V. 1976. *Phytopathology* 66:433–36
168. Sequeira, L. 1979. In *Host-Parasite Interfaces,* ed. B. B. Nickol, pp. 71–84. New York/San Francisco/London: Academic
169. Sequeira, L., Gaard, G., De Zoeten, G. A. 1977. *Physiol. Plant Pathol.* 10:43–50
170. Sequeira, L., Graham, T. L. 1977. *Physiol. Plant Pathol.* 11:43–54

171. Shuster, C. W., Stark, J., O'Neil, J. 1978. *Abstr. Ann. Meet. Am. Soc. Microbiol. H38,* p. 110
172. Sing, V. O., Schroth, M. N. 1977. *Science* 197:759–61
173. Sjulin, T. M., Beer, S. V. 1978. *Phytopathology* 68:89–94
174. Smiley, J. O., Ashwell, G. 1960. *J. Biol. Chem.* 235:1571–75
175. Sparks, R. B., Lacy, G. H. 1977. *Proc. Am. Phytopathol. Soc.* 4:198
176. Stark, J., O'Neil, J., Nishimune, T., Shuster, C. W. 1978. *Abstr. Ann. Meet. Am. Soc. Microbiol. A3,* p. 1
177. Starr, M. P. 1959. *Ann. Rev. Microbiol.* 13:211–38
178. Starr, M. P. 1975. *Symp. Soc. Exp. Biol.* 29:1–20
179. Starr, M. P. 1979. *Ann. Intern. Med.* 90:708–10
180. Starr, M. P. 1981. In *The Prokaryotes. A Handbook on Habitats, Isolation, and Identification of Bacteria,* ed. M. P. Starr, H. Stolp, H. G. Trüper, A. Balows, H. G. Schlegel, Chap. 4, 102. New York/Heidelberg/Berlin: Springer Verlag
181. Starr, M. P., Chatterjee, A. K. 1972. *Ann. Rev. Microbiol.* 26:389–426
182. Starr, M. P., Chatterjee, A. K., Starr, P. B., Buchanan, G. E. 1977. *J. Clin. Microbiol.* 6:379–86
183. Starr, M. P., Mandel, M. 1969. *J. Gen. Microbiol.* 56:113–23
184. Stephens, G. J., Wood, R. K. S. 1975. *Physiol. Plant Pathol.* 5:165–81
185. Stoeber, F., Lagarde, A., Némoz, G., Novel, G., Novel, M., Portalier, R., Pouyssegur, J., Robert-Baudouy, J. 1974. *Biochimie* 56:199–213
186. Stolp, H., Starr, M. P., Baigent, N. L. 1965. *Ann. Rev. Phytopathol.* 3:231–64
187. Strobel, G. A. 1977. *Ann. Rev. Microbiol.* 31:205–24
188. Tsuyumu, S. 1977. *Nature* 269:237–38
189. Vidaver, A. K. 1976. *Ann. Rev. Phytopathol.* 14:451–65
190. von Graevenitz, A. 1977. *Ann. Rev. Microbiol.* 31:447–71
191. von Riesen, V. L. 1975. *J. Clin. Microbiol.* 2:552–53
192. von Riesen, V. L. 1976. *Int. J. Syst. Bacteriol.* 26:143–45
193. Waldee, E. L. 1945. *Iowa State Coll. J. Sci.* 19:435–84
194. Whatley, M. H., Bodwin, J. S., Lippincott, B. B., Lippincott, J. A. 1976. *Infect. Immun.* 13:1080–83
195. Wicken, A. J., Knox, K. W. 1977. In *Microbiology 1977,* ed. D. Schlessinger, pp. 360–65. Washington DC: Am. Soc. Microbiol.
196. Wilson, D. E. 1960. *Virology* 11:533–46
197. Winslow, C.-E. A., Broadhurst, J., Buchanan, R. E., Krumwiede, C. Jr., Rogers, L. A., Smith, G. H. 1917. *J. Bacteriol.* 2:505–66
198. Wu, W. C. 1972. *Ann. Phytopathol. Soc. Jpn.* 38:333–41
199. Wu, W. C., Middleton, R. B., Hsu, W. H. 1977. *Chin. J. Microbiol.* 10:37–47
200. Zucker, M., Hankin, L. 1970. *J. Bacteriol.* 104:13–18
201. Zucker, M., Hankin, L., Sands, D. 1972. *Physiol. Plant Pathol.* 2:59–67

Ann. Rev. Microbiol. 1980. 34:677–709

THE GENUS *SPIROPLASMA*[1] ❖1790

Robert F. Whitcomb

US Department of Agriculture, Science and Education Administration, Agricultural Research, Plant Protection Institute, Insect Pathology Laboratory, Beltsville, Maryland 20705

CONTENTS

INTRODUCTION 678
CLASSIFICATION AND PHYLOGENY 679
Higher Classification 679
Species Concept 681
SPIROPLASMA PROPERTIES RELEVANT TO SPECIES TAXONOMY 681
Serology 681
Polyacrylamide Gel Electrophoresis of Cell Proteins 683
Substrate Utilization 684
THE SPIROPLASMA GENOME 686
SPIROPLASMA SPECIES AND SPECIES CANDIDATES 687
Spiroplasma citri: Classical Serovar (Group I-1) 688
Spiroplasma citri: Honey Bee Serovar (Group I-2) 688
Spiroplasma citri: Corn Stunt Serovar (CSS) (Group I-3) 689
Spiroplasma citri: 277F Serovar (Group I-4) 689
Sex Ratio Organisms (SROs) (Group II) 690
Flower Spiroplasma (Group III) 690
Flower Spiroplasma (Group IV) 690
Suckling Mouse Cataract Agent (SMCA) Spiroplasma (Group V) 690
Green Leaf Bug Spiroplasma (Group VI) 691
THE ASTER YELLOWS GROUP: NEW SPIROPLASMAS? 691
CULTIVATION OF SPIROPLASMAS 692
Media 692
Measurement of Growth 692
Direct Quantitation 693
Indirect Quantitation 695
Growth Rates and Yields 695
SPIROPLASMA MORPHOLOGY 696
SPIROPLASMA MOTILITY 699
THE SPIROPLASMA MEMBRANE 701

Sterol and Lipid Metabolism 701
Carbohydrates 702
Proteins 702
SPIROPLASMAVIRUSES 702
SPIROPLASMA BIOLOGY: HOST RANGE AND PATHOGENESIS 703
SUMMARY AND CONCLUSIONS 705

INTRODUCTION

Spiroplasmas (Class Mollicutes, Order Mycoplasmatales, Family Spiroplasmataceae) were first recognized as helical wall-less prokaryotes in 1972 (48, 52). The motility of the organisms was recognized in 1973 by Davis & Worley (49), who gave them the trivial name spiroplasma. Shortly thereafter, an organism that had been cultivated in 1971 (61, 62, 131, 132) and that later was shown (100, 122) to induce citrus stubborn disease was named *Spiroplasma citri* (133). These events were an aftermath of the historic reports by Doi et al (53) and Ishiie et al (77) that plant diseases of the "yellows" type were not caused by viruses, as had previously been supposed, but instead were caused by prokaryotic, probably wall-less, microorganisms. This discovery by the Japanese workers led to thin section electron microscopic observation of the citrus stubborn (74, 87) and corn stunt spiroplasmas (CSS: 67, 68) in vivo, which in turn enabled the unique nature of spiroplasmas to be recognized, once their helical nature was observed by phase and dark-field microscopy.

Discovery of the microbial identity of spiroplasmas was postponed for more than a decade after the organisms were first envisioned. Spiroplasmas were first observed microscopically by Poulson & Sakaguchi in 1961 (118). These organisms (sex ratio organisms: SROs) were associated with a trait in some populations of certain *Drosophila* species that was characterized by the absence of males in the broods of infected females (172). However, because the organisms were helical and motile, they were thought to be spirochetes. Similarly, a spiroplasma (277F) from the rabbit tick, *Haemaphysalis leporispalustris,* was cultivated in the chick embryo in 1967 (117) and envisioned by dark-field microscopy, but was also misidentified as a spirochete.

In 1964, the suckling mouse cataract agent (SMCA) was isolated from rabbit ticks in the course of searches for rickettsiae (25). For many years this agent was thought to be a virus because of its filterability through small pores (26). In fact, misidentification of wall-less prokaryotes as viruses was almost the rule in the early history of pathogenic mycoplasmas; all of the plant agents had been misidentified, as had the pathogenic mycoplasmas of certain avian diseases (79), swine enzootic pneumonia (165), and human primary atypical pneumonia (16).

Today, spiroplasmas (5, 42, 46, 151, 160) are well recognized pathogens, and fundamental misidentification of new spiroplasmas as spirochetes or viruses seems unlikely. Indeed, spiroplasmas are now so widely recognized that one wonders whether a newly discovered spirochete in a plant or insect would be correctly identified; although many spirochetes are significantly larger than spiroplasmas, some are not. Also, despite their apparent independent evolution (56) and serological distinctiveness (7), spirochetes and spiroplasmas have similar shapes and modes of motility (13). Therefore, careful electron microscopic study of the ultrastructure of the bounding wall or membrane and periplasmic fibrils (= axial filament; 13) (if any) of a newly discovered helical organism, coupled with data on penicillin sensitivity, would be essential for its definitive identification (7).

Many new spiroplasma strains and serotypes have recently been discovered.[2] Serological studies have revealed at least six groups that may warrant description as species; some of these groups may be large clusters of more or less closely related strains. Furthermore, the very existence of helicity and motility in wall-less organisms has raised fundamental questions about the nature of membrane structure and the mechanisms of microorganismal motility (7). Thus, in less than a decade since the discovery of its microbial identity, the genus *Spiroplasma* has become a well-established taxon that offers significant opportunities as a model for studies of basic microbial biology.

CLASSIFICATION AND PHYLOGENY

Higher Classification

The term mycoplasma has been established (143) by common usage as the trivial name for members of the class Mollicutes *sensu* Edward & Freundt (54). Acceptance of the class Mollicutes is reflected in the eighth edition of Bergey's manual (11). On the other hand, the implications of a recent proposal (66) to elevate the Mollicutes to the status of a division of the Procaryotae are not yet clear. Spiroplasmas can be readily classified as mycoplasmas (4, 7, 134) by virtue of their ability, under many conditions, to form fried egg (umbonate) colonies on solid media, their ability to pass through filters with 0.22 μm pores, their complete failure to revert to walled bacterial forms, their absolute resistance to penicillin, and the absence of cell wall or murein cell wall precursors. At present, the ordinal concept in

[2]The number of new isolates cannot be determined because lack of full publication of important data regarding spiroplasmas has become an extremely unfortunate aspect of the spiroplasma literature. In recent years, the literature has been afflicted by an "abstractitis" that reflects in part the rapid expansion of knowledge in the field but also in part an overreliance on abstracts to secure priority and publication of discoveries.

Mollicutes is identical with the class concept, in that a single order (Mycoplasmatales) is recognized. Informal discussions have been held by the Subcommittee on Taxonomy of the Class Mollicutes[3] (hereafter referred to as the Subcommittee) regarding the creation of a new order for members of the Acholeplasmataceae, but it was recommended (144) that such a division should be postponed. Therefore, *Spiroplasma* will remain in the Mycoplasmatales for the foreseeable future.

The recent work of Woese and his collaborators (55, 56) utilizing the comparative cataloging of 16S rRNA as a tool for investigating prokaryote phylogeny has important implications for mycoplasma taxonomy. The rRNA cataloging technique has recently been applied (177) to *Mycoplasma gallisepticum, Mycoplasma capricolum, Acholeplasma laidlawii, Spiroplasma citri,* and *Thermoplasma acidophilum.* All these organisms, except *Thermoplasma,* cluster with *Clostridia* in a branch of prokaryote evolution that includes the Gram-positive bacteria. Oligonucleotide catalogs of *Spiroplasma* and *Mycoplasma* species suggests that, despite a twofold difference in the genome size, the two genera constitute a natural cluster. However, the data also suggest that *Acholeplasma* is relatively distant from the *Mycoplasma-Spiroplasma* cluster. *Thermoplasma,* on the other hand, appears to be most closely related to the Archaebacteria (2). Refinement of these important indications about spiroplasma phylogeny, together with other data on mycoplasma phylogeny (110, 111, 158), no doubt will eventually lead to improvement in higher classification.

The major differences that separate spiroplasmas from other mycoplasmas are presently used to distinguish the two groups at the family level. In 1974, Skripal proposed (136) that the genus *Spiroplasma* be elevated to the rank of a family on the basis of (*a*) Gram-positivity (*b*) helicity and motility, (*c*) possession of a "main body" on the helical spiroplasma cells, and (*d*) moderate sensitivity to digitonin, amphotericin B, and sodium polyanethol sulphate. In 1977, the Subcommittee (142) concluded that Skripal's proposal had been validly published and agreed with the principle and concept of a new family of mycoplasmas. However, the Subcommittee also expressed serious reservations, not only about the application of Gram-staining techniques to wall-less organisms but also about the significance of the "main bodies" that are sometimes visualized emanating from spiroplasma cells. Subsequent research makes it clear that certain other features of spiroplasmas merit consideration in descriptions of their higher taxonomy. These include (7) a genome size of 1×10^9 daltons (133), a G+C ratio of 26–31 mol% (7, 82), and localization of reduced nicotinamide adenine

[3]A subcommittee of the International Committee on Systematic Bacteriology of the International Association of Microbiological Societies.

dinucleotide (NADH) oxidase in the cytoplasm (83) rather than on the membrane, as in acholeplasmas. The presence of a phosphoenol pyruvate phosphotransferase system in spiroplasmas (24) also distinguishes them from acholeplasmas. Furthermore, the presence of other ultrastructural features of spiroplasma cells such as intracellular fibrils has now been established (168, 172). In all, an updated family description, such as that which would be provided by future revisions of Bergey's manual (11), seems warranted.

The generic concept of *Spiroplasma* at present is identical with the family concept, since the described family contains the single genus *Spiroplasma*. *Spiroplasma* spp. are distinguished from *Mycoplasma* spp. on the basis of their morphology and motility and from *Ureaplasma* spp. by morphology, motility, and absence of urease activity (143).

Species Concept

At present there is no formalized species concept in *Spiroplasma*. The Subcommittee, in a recent emendation of earlier proposals for minimal standards for description of new species of the class Mollicutes, defined mycoplasma species ideally, as "clusters of morphologically similar isolates whose genomes exhibit a high degree of relatedness" (143). However, the Subcommittee recognized that extensive hybridization studies require specialized and expensive technology and that alternative techniques such as determination of G+C values, serology, gel electrophoresis of cellular proteins, or biochemical tests would often be sufficient for separation and description of species. Although biochemical tests have not proved to be useful for spiroplasma taxonomy, other alternative techniques, especially serology, have great promise.

SPIROPLASMA PROPERTIES RELEVANT TO SPECIES TAXONOMY

Serology

Several serological tests (169) have been investigated as possible techniques for the separation of spiroplasma isolates. These include growth inhibition (21, 47, 127a, 152, 153), deformation (173, 176), metabolism inhibition (21, 47, 150, 173), complement fixation (153), precipitin ring (152, 153), immunoelectrophoresis (182), and enzyme-linked immunosorbent assays (ELISA) (27, 135, 150). As in other mycoplasma serology, despite variations due to immunization schedules or immunized animals (18), each test has a characteristic specificity and sensitivity. For general mycoplasma taxonomy, immunofluorescence, growth inhibition, and metabolic inhibition have been the most generally useful tests (143). Immunofluorescence has not been applied in depth to spiroplasma taxonomy. In contrast, the growth inhibition test, employed in the same manner as in conventional mycoplasma studies (30, 179), has been applied in several studies. Early observations of heterologous crossing between *S. citri* and the corn stunt spiroplasma (CSS) (21, 152, 175) suggested that the growth inhibition test might be less useful for spiroplasmas than it had been for mycoplasmas because it was then generally considered that these two spiroplasmas would turn out to be different species. However, the current weight of evidence now suggests that *S. citri* and the CSS are too closely related to warrant description as separate species (7, 82, 105, 144). Broader application of the test has shown that no reciprocal crossing occurs between clearly distinct serogroups. For example, Davis and his colleagues recently used the growth inhibition test in conjunction with metabolic inhibition and deformation tests (47) to separate four distinct serological groups. Presumably, such groupings form a contemporary basis for classifying taxonomic units that will eventually be regarded as species (47). Finally, a recent comprehensive assessment of the growth inhibition test, in which a large assortment of spiroplasma isolates and antisera were used, indicated that the test may possess an ideal combination of specificity and sensitivity for separation of spiroplasma species (127a).

A comprehensive assessment of spiroplasma serogroups was provided by the studies of Williamson et al (173) which utilized both deformation and metabolic inhibition tests to assess interrelationships between 13 spiroplasma isolates. The deformation test employed was a modification of a test reported earlier (174, 176) in which the limiting dilution of antibodies that causes microscopically visible deformation (bleb formation or rounding) of spiroplasma cells is recorded. The metabolic inhibition test was very similar to classical techniques that have been applied to mycoplasmas (145, 178). Combination of the two tests permitted the separation of four serologically distinct groups of spiroplasmas, including the noncultivable SROs from *Drosophila* (173).

The results of the two independent, contemporaneous serological studies of Davis et al (47) and Williamson et al (173) are in close accord; when synthesized with the work of Lei, Su & Chen (91, 141) on the green leaf bug spiroplasma and Tully et al (150) on flower spiroplasmas, they define six spiroplasma serogroups that are unrelated in growth inhibition, metabolic inhibition, and deformation tests. A more recent study (82) has formalized this concept and demonstrated that the serological groupings correlate well with data on G+C values, and DNA-DNA homologies (Table 1).

Most or all antigens involved in growth inhibition, deformation, or metabolic inhibition tests are located on the spiroplasma cell surface. There does exist a class of antigens that are shared among spiroplasma serogroups,

Table 1 Spiroplasma serogroups[a]

Species or serogroup[b]	Subgroup (serovar)	Principal strains	G + C (mol %)	DNA–DNA homology[c]	Principal host	Disease incited	Reference
I *Spiroplasma citri*	I–1	R8A2, C189 Israel	25–27	100%	Dicots, leaf-hoppers	Citrus stubborn	41, 62, 133
	I–2	AS–576, BC–3, KC–3, B63	25–27	65%	Honey bee[d]	Honey bee spiroplasmosis	28, 50, 173
	I–3	I–747, E–275, Miss. E, B655	25–27	53%	Maize, leaf-hoppers	Corn stunt	21, 173, 175
	I–4	277F	25–27	4%	Rabbit tick[d]	None known	10, 117
II (SROs)		WSRO, NSRO, ESRO	25–27	nd[e]	*Drosophila*	Sex-ratio trait	172
III		OBMG, BNR1, 23–6	25–27	0%	Isolated from flowers	None known	29, 44, 47, 173
IV		SR–3, PPS1	29–31	0%	Isolated from flowers	None known	44, 47, 103, 150, 157
V		SMCA, GT–48, TP–2	29–31	0%	Rabbit tick	Suckling mouse cataract syndrome	26, 153
VI		LB–12	nd	nd	Green leaf bug[d]	None known	91, 141

[a]Modified from Junca et al (82), with additional data from other studies (47, 91, 173).
[b]Serogroups assigned on the basis of failure to cross-react in growth inhibition (47, 153), metabolic inhibition (47, 173), and deformation (47, 173) tests.
[c]DNA–DNA homology tested (82) against a probe against *Spiroplasma citri* (R8A2).
[d]Latin binomials for insect species: honey bee, *Apis mellifera*; rabbit tick, *Haemaphysalis leporis-palustris*; green leaf bug, *Trigonotylus ruficornis*.
[e]nd = not done.

most or all of which appear to be cytoplasmic. These can be identified by complement fixation or precipitin techniques (153). More intensive study of this aspect of spiroplasma serology is urgently needed, because the identification of nonhelical spiroplasmas, if such spiroplasmas exist, would depend largely upon the availability of serological tests for specific group antigens.

Polyacrylamide Gel Electrophoresis of Cell Proteins

Three types of gel electrophoresis have been utilized in spiroplasma taxonomy. The first is one-dimensional electrophoresis. Patterns obtained from such gels were utilized for the description of the type species *S. citri* (133) and for its comparison with other spiroplasmas (114). Such one-dimensional patterns have been in general use in mycoplasma taxonomy (43, 143) since their introduction by Razin & Rottem in 1967 (125).

Recently, important modifications of gel electrophoresis have been introduced. For example, use of slab gels (104, 105) permits a more refined one-dimensional separation of cellular proteins and particularly facilitates two-dimensional electrophoretic analyses. Mouches et al (104, 105) recently analyzed spiroplasma protein patterns by a two-dimensional procedure. The first dimension was provided by isoelectric focusing in cylindrical gels in glass tubes, whereas the second dimension was provided by separation according to electrophoretic mobilities in sodium docecyl sulfate (SDS) slab gels. About 150 co-migrating proteins were common to all *S. citri* isolates, but non-co-migrating proteins could also be demonstrated. Some of these proteins were present in only one *S. citri* strain. Others consisted of sets of presumably homologous proteins with similar, but not identical, electrophoretic mobilities. As might be expected from the results of other taxonomic comparisons of SMCA and *S. citri,* analysis by two-dimensional electrophoresis showed that these spiroplasmas shared very few co-migrating proteins. By contrast, although *S. citri* and the CSS shared few common proteins, they did share a large number of presumably homologous proteins. Thus, the results from two-dimensional electrophoresis (105) confirmed results from serology and DNA-DNA hybridization that suggested a moderate degree of relationship between *S. citri* and CSS. In independent studies, Rodwell & Rodwell (126) analyzed other mycoplasmas by two-dimensional electrophoresis. In these studies, degrees of relatedness of the compared strains were expressed by a similarity index. If a similar statistical device for expression of relatedness could be incorporated into the technique of Mouches et al (104, 105), the utility of two-dimensional electrophoresis in spiroplasma taxonomy would be greatly increased.

Substrate Utilization

In the past, great emphasis has been placed upon utilization of substrates (especially carbohydrates) in mycoplasma taxonomy. Today, at least three tests are mandatory for all descriptions of mycoplasma species (143). Enzymatic hydrolysis of urea is a unique characteristic of members of the genus *Ureaplasma.* Within the genus *Mycoplasma,* ability of an isolate to ferment glucose with acid production and/or the ability of the isolate to catabolize arginine with production of ammonia (and a consequent increase in pH) are critical properties (58). None of the spiroplasmas isolated has been shown to lack the enzymatic machinery for glucose fermentation and arginine hydrolysis, but none have been shown to possess ureases.

Although carbohydrate utilization patterns have been reported for several spiroplasma isolates (75, 130, 133) they are of little comparative value at present, and have led to problems in interpretation. In particular, the utility of such carbohydrate utilization tests in spiroplasma taxonomy has been diminished by the unavailability of a minimal medium that supports growth of all spiroplasmas. Demonstration of a particular pathway for carbohydrate utilization by spiroplasmas depends upon (*a*) the degree of cultural adaptation of the strain and (*b*) the growth rate of the strain in the chosen medium. Well-adapted spiroplasmas growing on rich media ferment substances present in the yeast derivatives (or other undefined components), even in the absence of a defined amount of carbohydrate. Thus, truly "carbohydrate-free" controls are difficult to incorporate into experimental designs. If simple media (e.g. without yeast derivatives, etc) could be used, such problems might be solved; but fastidious spiroplasmas such as SMCA must be grown in media that are rich, compared to minimal media that are satisfactory for fast-growing spiroplasmas such as the BNR1 isolate. Minimal media may also be inadequate for the demonstration of comparatively weak pathways or patterns of metabolic activity that are mediated by adaptive enzymes. Difficulties such as these may explain some of the observed discrepancies (130) in spiroplasma utilization tests. In any event, there is at present no single medium that can be used for characterization of all spiroplasma isolates. Rather, a new minimal medium must be developed for each spiroplasma isolate.

Evaluation of amino acid metabolism by spiroplasmas is made especially difficult by the rich constituency of the complex components of culture media, many of which contain substrate levels of free amino acids. Nevertheless, several important clues suggest that amino acids are important metabolic building blocks for spiroplasmas. For example, growth of *S. citri* (78, 88) and SMCA (R. F. Whitcomb, unpublished data) is stimulated by addition of free amino acids. The amino acid fraction from Schneider's Drosophila medium was especially stimulatory to *S. citri* (78). The balance of acids is important, since addition of glutamine to *S. citri* media in amounts equimolar to the total amino acid content of Schneider's medium does not produce this growth enhancement (R. F. Whitcomb, unpublished data). On the other hand, *S. citri* cultures that had been adapted to a medium in which glutamine was present at substrate levels, in the absence of defined amounts of carbohydrates, exhibited a lengthened lag phase when transferred to medium without glutamine (R. F. Whitcomb, unpublished data). Such results suggest that this amino acid, which is present in large amounts in plants and insects (134), plays a dispensable but significant role in spiroplasma metabolism.

The ability of spiroplasmas to utilize arginine has been well documented (76, 146) and constitutes an important taxonomic characteristic. Spiroplasma cultures, when provided both a fermentable carbohydrate and arginine, first acidify the media. Arginine catabolism becomes evident as the pH of the culture gradually increases with the release of ammonia into the medium (146). Although arginine catabolism is most readily demonstrated in media that have been supplemented with fermentable carbohydrates, well-adapted cultures in modified M1A medium (serum replaced by bovine serum fraction) catabolize arginine even without the addition of defined amounts of glucose or other fermentable carbohydrates (R. F. Whitcomb, unpublished data). Indications of growth stimulation by cysteine (89) are difficult to evaluate in the light of the strong reducing potential of the acid. However, the ability of asparagine to replace yeastolate in a complex medium (15) suggests a metabolic role for this amino acid. In all, it is likely that amino acids other than arginine and glutamine are also of critical importance in spiroplasma metabolism; however, unequivocal demonstration of the metabolic role of any amino acid must await development of minimal media or isolation of the enzymes that mediate its utilization.

THE SPIROPLASMA GENOME

In recent years, there has been an increasing tendency to resort to DNA-DNA homology experiments for decisions on the taxonomic status of mycoplasma strains suspected to be partially related on the basis of serological or gel electrophoretic analyses. A particularly relevant example is the case of the subspecies of *Mycoplasma mycoides,* which are inadequately separated by conventional taxonomic techniques (144). In this case, even DNA-DNA homology studies failed to resolve the difficult questions raised, since the results of serology, nucleic acid hybridization, and two-dimensional gel electrophoresis do not completely correspond (1, 126).

Unfortunately, the difficulties encountered with *M. mycoides* may recur with all ramifications (or more) with spiroplasmas. Serological classifications (Table 1) indicate that at least two large clusters of partially related spiroplasma strains exist. These are the *S. citri* cluster (82, 173) and a second cluster (150) consisting, in part, of the SR-3 (47) and Powder Puff (PPS1) (103) spiroplasmas, but also including other strains from diverse geographic origins and habitats (157). Species separations are especially difficult in the *S. citri* complex, since estimates of homologies (82) indicate that there may be a gradient of relatedness among isolates.

Added to the difficulties posed by the existence of a homology gradient are difficulties in the technique itself. For example, considerable effort has been expended in attempts to determine the DNA-DNA homologies between *S. citri* and the CSS. Christiansen et al (23) estimated the level of hybridization between *S. citri* and the CSS to be about 30%. However, work in other laboratories, utilizing different techniques and strains with different passage histories, has given somewhat higher values (82, 90, 93, 119). At present, it is unknown whether the presence or absence of extrachromosomal DNA (7, 123) (especially of viral orgin) may significantly affect DNA homology data. Because numbers of intracellular virions of spiroplasma viruses, for reasons that are poorly understood, fluctuate greatly at different stages during cultural history and from passage to passage, the quantity of viral DNA may vary greatly from one culture to another. Also, there is an intrinsic problem with homologies in the range of 30–70%. Because the variance of a fraction is maximal at 0.50, small differences in observed counts have an exaggerated effect on computed percentages as homology values approach 50%. For example, the same percentage difference between 5 and 10% homologies would have a completely different taxonomic interpretation than a difference between 30 and 60% homologies.

Data on spiroplasma G+C values have, by contrast, been reproducible and consistent, even if different methods have been used for their determination. For example, values of 29–31 mol% for the G+C value for SMCA, obtained in independent studies (7, 23), are in good agreement and indicate that *S. citri* and SMCA must be regarded as different spiroplasma species. Similarly, recent evidence indicates that members of the SR-3-PPS1 serogroup also have values of 29–31 mol% (82). All other G+C values cluster tightly in the range of about 25–27 mol% (7, 82). Thus, the experience in spiroplasma research reinforces general experience in microbial classification: G+C values are of use in species taxonomy only if different species have significantly different values. In recognition of the many cases in which G+C determinations have proved useful, the Subcommittee made such determination an obligatory requirement in mycoplasma species taxonomy (143).

The genome size of *S. citri* is about 10^9 daltons (133). This fact is of utmost importance in the taxonomic separation of the Spiroplasmataceae from the Mycoplasmataceae. Presumably, the genome sizes of other spiroplasmas will prove to be similar to that of *S. citri.*

None of the techniques discussed above for spiroplasma taxonomy have the potential for identification or separation at the strain or isolate level. A promising technique for this purpose is gel electrophoresis of spiroplasma DNA after treatment with restriction endonuclease EcoRI. Using this method, Bové & Saillard (7) were able to distinguish individual patterns for many isolates of the classical serovar of *S. citri.*

SPIROPLASMA SPECIES AND SPECIES CANDIDATES

Only one spiroplasma (*S. citri*) has been given a Latin binomial (133). Five other spiroplasmas, or groups of spiroplasmas, are candidates for eventual designation as species (82, 91). The *S. citri* group consists of four subgroups (= serovars). The eight significantly different spiroplasma groups [scheme of Junca et al (82), Table 1] are briefly described below.

Spiroplasma citri: Classical Serovar (Group I-1)

The type strain of *Spiroplasma* (Moroccan isolate = R8A2 = Maroc = ATTC 27556) was isolated in 1971 from a Washington navel sweet orange tree afflicted with stubborn disease (131, 132). Subsequent characterization (133) established that the isolate was serologically (133) and morphologically (35) distinct from previously recognized mycoplasmas. In addition, *S. citri* was shown to have a G+C ratio of about 26 mol% (133) and a characteristic protein profile as assessed by one- and two-dimensional gel electrophoresis (104, 105). A second strain, the C189 strain, was isolated independently from citrus in California (61, 62) and was deposited in the ATTC (27563 and 27665) during the early period of research on spiroplasma cultivation. Its properties are similar to those of R8A2 (75). Cultured spiroplasmas such as R8A2 or C189 show typical spectra of antibiotic sensitivities (8, 75, 133). A third isolate of historical importance is the Israel isolate (NCPPB 2565) from citrus affected with "little leaf" disease (41). This isolate was derived from the isolate used in the first demonstration of infectivity of a cultured plant mycoplasma for insect and plant hosts (100), a study that fulfilled the requirements of Koch's postulates. Other isolates of the classical serovar of *S. citri* have assumed importance because of their role in the study of spiroplasma biology. For example, isolates have been obtained from the leafhoppers *Scaphytopius nitridus* and *Circulifer tenellus;* other insects in the Mediterranean region have also served as sources (6). An unusual nonhelical variant (ASP-1, NCPPB 2565) discovered (148) by Townsend and his colleagues has been studied as a model organism for elucidating mechanisms underlying helicity and motility (147). Many *S. citri* isolates have been obtained from the Mediterranean region and the western United States. The stubborn disease is known from these areas, as well as Mexico and South America, and may be of worldwide occurrence (85).

Spiroplasma citri: Honey Bee Serovar (Group I-2)

In 1976, T. B. Clark discovered and cultivated a spiroplasma from diseased honey bees, *Apis mellifera* (28). Further study of this organism showed, surprisingly, that it was serologically closely related to, but distinguishable from, the classical *S. citri* serovar (47, 173). The AS-576 isolate (ATCC 29416) has been studied and characterized by Davis and his colleagues (47, 50), and the BC-3 isolate (ATCC 33219) has been extensively studied (82, 161, 173). Other triply cloned isolates, including strains from Hawaii

(KC-3), Florida, and Morocco are available. Preliminary serological studies suggest that these strains, although of diverse geographic origin, are relatively homogeneous serologically.

Spiroplasma citri: Corn Stunt Serovar (CSS) (Group I-3)

The first cultivated corn stunt spiroplasmas (21, 175) were derived from a strain maintained in leafhoppers and plants in the laboratory for many years after collection in Mexico in 1955 (97). In 1970, the CSS was isolated and maintained in primary isolation by Chen & Granados (20). Definitive cultivation and fulfillment of Koch's postulates for the cultivated organism were achieved simultaneously and independently by two groups (21, 175) in 1975. The I-747 isolate (ATCC 29051) and E275 isolate (ATCC 29320) were derived from originally pathogenic lines. However, both of these triply cloned lines, in the course of their cultural history, have apparently lost their ability to complete the natural biological cycle. A pathogenic but uncloned isolate (strain E:ATCC 27954) has been lyophilized and is available for general distribution. A second triply cloned isolate of Rio Grande corn stunt is the Mississippi E. isolate (78). A Peruvian isolate obtained by Nault et al (108) was cultivated (47) and compared with other spiroplasma isolates, but has not been triply cloned. Finally, CSS isolates were obtained by S. Eden Green from stunted maize in Jamaica. One of these (ATCC 33289) was subsequently triply cloned and shown to be serologically similar or identical with I-747 and E275 (S. Eden Green, unpublished data). A second uncloned isolate in early passage was also deposited by Eden Green (ATCC 33109). Because the corn stunt disease is widespread in the Neotropics, it is likely that many other geographical isolates will eventually be available.

Spiroplasma citri: 277F Serovar (Group I-4)

This serovar of *S. citri* (ATCC 29761) is represented by a single isolate (277 F-W) obtained from the rabbit tick in 1967 (117). Originally thought to be a spirochete, the isolate was later identified as a spiroplasma (10). The original isolate was cultivated in, and apparently at one time was pathogenic to, embryonated eggs (117). Further reexamination of the isolate revealed, surprisingly, that it was serologically unrelated to another spiroplasma (SMCA) isolated from the rabbit tick. Instead it cross-reacted to some extent with *S. citri* and the CSS (137, 173). In contrast to its serological crosses, only 4% DNA-DNA homology was noted when 277F was tested against an *S. citri* probe (82). If reciprocal tests also show low values, 277F would qualify as a candidate for species description. Because the agent has been isolated only once, further study of its ecological status is needed.

Sex Ratio Organisms (SROs) (Group II)

Junca et al (82) showed that the noncultivable (172) sex ratio organisms (SROs) of *Drosophila,* a distinct serological group (173) parallel to *S. citri* and candidate species, have a G+C ratio of 25–27 mol%.

Flower Spiroplasma (Group III)

Flower spiroplasmas of this group, which emerged as unexpected byproducts of T. B. Clark's discovery of spiroplasmas in the bee-flower habitat, have been isolated only from Maryland. Davis's surveys revealed several isolates, of which 23-6 (ATCC 29989) was chosen as a representative. The OBMG (ATCC 33221) and BNR1 (ATCC 33220) isolates, chosen by Clark from his flower isolations (29), were utilized experimentally in deformation and metabolic inhibition studies (173) and were used for a study of spiroplasma morphology during different parts of the growth cycle (161). These strains were shown (82) to have G+C values of about 25–27 mol%, and are serologically distinct from other spiroplasma species (47, 173). Clarification of the taxonomic status of this putative species awaits discovery of other geographical isolates and proper characterization.

Flower Spiroplasma (Group IV)

Flower spiroplasmas of this group have been obtained from diverse geographical areas. The SR-3 isolate was obtained from tulip tree (*Liriodendron tulipifera*) in Connecticut and identified as a representative of a fourth putative spiroplasma species (44). The PPS1 spiroplasma, on the other hand, was isolated from flowers of a tropical tree, Powder Puff (*Calliandra haematocephala*), in Florida (103). These two isolates have been most extensively studied. Recent study of other isolates (157) from honey bees, froghoppers (Cercopidae), and flowers in the Mediterranean region have revealed other spiroplasmas that cross-react (150) to various degrees with SR-3 and PPS1. Some of the new isolates may be significantly different from PPS1 and/or SR-3. Strains of this putative spiroplasma species, although they have a G+C value of 29–31 mol% (82), differ profoundly from SMCA in their antigenic composition (150) and protein compositions as indicated by two-dimensional gel electrophoresis. Because these strains may be part of a complex whose members share various degrees of serological affinity, extensive further study may be necessary before the nature of the SR-3-PPS1 group of spiroplasmas can be defined (150).

Suckling Mouse Cataract Agent (SMCA) Spiroplasma (Group V)

The suckling mouse cataract agent is a spiroplasma represented by a single serovar that has been collected from rabbit ticks in Georgia and Maryland.

The type isolate (SMCA: ATCC 29335) was isolated by H Fred Clark in 1964 in Georgia, in the course of searches for rickettsiae, by inoculation of tick extracts into the embryonated egg (25). The agent was recognized as a mycoplasma in 1974 (184), as a spiroplasma in 1976 (154), and was subsequently cultivated (153) and shown to induce the ocular pathology in rodents that gives the agent its common name of suckling mouse cataract agent (SMCA). The GT-48 strain (ATCC 29334) was isolated in the course of the same rickettsial survey, but has different pathogenic properties (26, 153, 154). The TP-2 strain was isolated from rabbit ticks in Maryland in 1978 by direct inoculation of tick suspensions into the SP-4 spiroplasma medium (140). Strains of SMCA differ serologically from *S. citri* strains in their G+C values of 29–31 mol%, in their protein patterns in gel electrophoresis, and by their low levels of DNA-DNA hybridization with *S. citri* (7, 23, 82, 105, 153).

Green Leaf Bug Spiroplasma (Group VI)

Serological studies by Lei et al (91) suggest that a spiroplasma isolated (141) in Taiwan from the green leaf bug *Trigonontylus ruficornis* may represent a putative spiroplasma species.

THE ASTER YELLOWS GROUP: NEW SPIROPLASMAS?

The aster yellows (AY) group (22, 101) of plant pathogens is a long studied, well-recognized group of leafhopper-borne pathogens that affects a wide variety of plants. Most or all members of the group induce virescence and proliferative symptoms such as witches'-broom. The great majority of plant diseases caused by mycoplasma-like organisms appear to be caused by members of this group. Previous claims from one laboratory (63) that yellows agents were cultivable mycoplasmas, such as *Acholeplasma* or *Mycoplasma* spp., contradicted published negative results (72) and could not be confirmed in other laboratories (14, 37). Although further claims have been published from the same laboratory (64, 65), a recent critique (134) of this work appears to remain valid.

Claims (17, 86, 96, 98, 120, 121) from several other laboratories suggest that yellows diseases may be caused not by acholeplasmas, or members of the genus *Mycoplasma,* but instead by spiroplasmas that appear, when they are serologically typed (121, 173), to be similar or identical to *S. citri.* Electron microscopy of AY organisms in vivo, however, shows no hint of helical morphology (71), an observation that contrasts with reports for *S. citri* (60) and CSS (49). Also, these claims have not been accompanied by convincing proof that the isolated organisms produce the typical symptoms that are the pathogenic hallmarks of the yellows group. In one case, three years have elapsed since initial claims (86) of cultivation. The assessment of such claims, therefore, must be held in abeyance until evidence of fulfillment of Koch's postulates finally becomes available.

CULTIVATION OF SPIROPLASMAS

Media

Spiroplasma media (7, 19, 160) contain combinations of 10–20% serum, beef heart infusion, peptones and tryptones, carbohydrates, and amino acids. Other complex additives may include fresh yeast extract, yeast hydrolysates, and rich tissue culture media such as CMRL-1066 or Schneider's Drosophila medium. Carbohydrates such as sucrose or sorbitol may be used to achieve high osmolarities. Simplified formulations, in which serum is replaced with bovine serum fraction or in which some but not all complex additives have been deleted, are suitable for some spiroplasmas. Nevertheless, if maximum growth rates and growth yields are to be achieved, complex formulations are required. This is also true for many approaches to primary isolation (151, 160).

Measurement of Growth

Spiroplasma cultivation inevitably requires qualitative and quantitative assessments of growth. Qualitative monitoring of growth is important, not only during primary isolation but also during continuous passage (19). The presence of helical, motile, short spiroplasma cells is a reliable first indication of successful primary isolation and is a useful indicator of optimal growth conditions during continued maintenance. Abnormal spiroplasma growth and morphology may result from suboptimal temperatures, pH, or osmolarity (19, 59, 94). Erratically slow growth of spiroplasma isolates is often accompanied by overt spiroplasmavirus infection (34).

Routine passage of spiroplasmas can usually be monitored by observation of acid production (78), because cultures entering stationary phase reach a minimal pH. Especially when cultivating spiroplasmas that enter death phase rapidly, it is important to pass cultures as soon as possible after, or in some cases before, maximum acidification. SMCA, for example, is slow to acidify media, especially during early passages after primary isolation. For this reason, it is important to monitor cultures of this spiroplasma microscopically.

No discussion of spiroplasma growth would be complete without emphasizing the importance of cultural history. Spiroplasmas transferred from one medium to another commonly undergo several changes in growth rates.

The first observed change (78) is a subtle reduction that is probably related to alterations in nutrition, pH, osmolarity, etc. This first slow change occurs during a period when essential nutrients (e.g. sterols) from the initial medium may still be present as part of the inoculum.

Initial subtle reductions in spiroplasma growth can be better understood in the light of experience with other experimental systems. For example, it is commonly observed that washed cells in animal tissue culture systems, transferred in the absence of any unbound extracellular nutrients, may also show only slow reductions in growth rates during the first 1–5 passages in a new medium. Eventually, however, if the new medium is deficient, there will be a drastic slump during which the growth rate decreases precipitously. Also, insect cells, like bacteria, may exhibit shortened lag phases if partially spent media is transferred with the cells (156). This is circumstantial evidence for the importance of extracellular factors in cell growth, but it is also possible that intra- as well as extracellular pools of nutrients are involved in survival of cultures during early passages after transfer to a new medium (J. Vaughn, personal communication).

Precipitous declines in growth rates are often observed with spiroplasma cultures and constitute a second phase after transfer into a new growth medium. Often, however, it proves possible to "resuscitate" a slumped culture in a minimal or nutritionally simplified medium; after prolonged adaptation a third phase begins in which growth rates may increase or, in some instances, return to the original level. The eventual outcome of the adjustment of growth rates in new media depends upon at least two critical factors: (*a*) the absolute ability of the new medium to support the organism, (*b*) the patience of the investigator in monitoring successive passages during the "collapse phase" in order to determine suitable intervals for passage into fresh medium. Thus, because adaptation to new media cannot be accomplished by a standardized technique, it is difficult to make quantitative assessments of the relative merit of different media for spiroplasma cultivation (78).

Direct Quantitation

Direct microscopic enumeration of helical microorganisms under dark-field microscopy, long employed for spirochetes (155), was adapted for spiroplasmas by Williamson (167) during his studies of SROs and later for CSS and other spiroplasmas (163). Subsequently, the method was extended by Liao & Chen and used for such purposes as the determination of spiroplasma growth curves (92).

Although microscopic enumeration is useful for cultures that are growing optimally in logarithmic phase, it is inadequate for measurement of viable but nonhelical cells. Whatever the reason for their morphological alteration, the presence of viable but nonhelical cells means that direct measurement must be made on culture media.

Although, conceptually, the most accurate technique for counting viable cells involves recording the numbers of colonies produced on solid media (colony forming units: CFUs), problems often arise in practical application. For example, viable cells from older cultures are less likely to form colonies than those of log phase cells (161). Further, variations in the composition of solid media affect the ability of spiroplasmas to form colonies; in this respect, agar concentration is particularly important. Because solid mycoplasma media are poured at relatively cool temperatures (about 56°C) to protect sensitive ingredients, agar concentrations may vary from plate to plate. Therefore, even plates from the same lot may vary in their ability to support colony formation. Also, colony size, and perhaps the probability that colonies will appear at all, is greatly affected by colony numbers, even at very low colony densities. Furthermore, spiroplasmas vary in their ability to form colonies on solid media. For example, although some isolates of the CSS form umbonate colonies under restricted conditions on solid media (73), most colonies produced by this spiroplasma are granular. The CSS and other spiroplasmas often produce small satellite colonies in the vicinity of primary colonies. These satellites almost certainly arise from cells that are the progeny of a founding cell at a primary colony site but that were able to move through the agar to a peripheral site where, for some reason, they became anchored and founded a secondary colony. Such satellite colonies, of course, cannot be included in quantitative counts; but unless there are fewer than about 30 colonies per plate (5 cm in diameter), there is often uncertainty about the status of small colonies that are not obvious satellites of primary colonies. Some spiroplasmas, perhaps by virtue of their small size or, especially, their dynamic motility, form extremely diffuse colonies, even when the agar concentration is as high as 2.25%. A final difficulty is that colony formation by many isolates requires incubation in a gaseous environment of 95% N_2 and 5% CO_2 for as long as 14–20 days (7, 19). For all these reasons, measurement of CFUs has not become a routine procedure for counting viable spiroplasma cells.

Some of the difficulties with CFU measurements can be avoided by use of titrations involving dilution series. In such titrations, the highest dilution that shows spiroplasma growth is considered to contain one color changing unit (CCU). The titer of the undiluted culture is then the reciprocal of the dilution at the endpoint (78). For example, the dilution tubes from CFU platings, if incubated, form a CCU titration. The problem with single dilution series is that they are statistically crude estimates of numbers of viable spiroplasma cells. An observed CCU endpoint is actually an estimate of the Poisson probability of presence or absence of a viable cell (CCU) in the endpoint tube. This is most dramatically illustrated by the occasional occurrence of a ++-+- pattern at the endpoint, an occurrence which should theoretically be observed at a small fraction of endpoints. Of course, the statistical variance in CCU titrations could theoretically be lowered by reducing the dilution factor and by replicating the series; however, the labor and materials required for such an enterprise would usually be prohibitive. Despite its deficiencies, the CCU method does have the advantage of recording viable spiroplasma cells, regardless of their specific activity in forming agar colonies. For purposes such as the determination of growth curves, in which total differences of 9–10 $\log_{10}$ CCUs are involved, such a procedure may be the method of choice.

Indirect Quantitation

Growth has also been measured by several indirect means. Although absorbance at 660 nm was used by Lee (88) to measure growth of *S. citri*, measurements of absorbance or turbidity in most spiroplasma cultures are made difficult by nonspecific changes in the growth media, not all of which are necessarily growth related. Measurement of the incorporation of radioactive precursors into spiroplasmal nucleic acids has proved to be useful for measurement of *S. citri* growth (7). Because this technique measures the radioactivity of trichloracteic acid (TCA)-insoluble precipitates, it is much less subject to artifacts than other indirect methods. ATP, total adenylate pools, and amounts of incorporated radioactive thymidine and phenylalanine also increase exponentially during logarithmic growth (129). However, none of the indirect means of measurement so far employed parallels the loss of spiroplasma viability during death phase.

Growth Rates and Yields

Spiroplasma growth rates do not depend solely on temperature and medium composition (19, 44, 60, 94) but also vary among the major groups. In general, different isolates of each of the various serological subgroups tend to have characteristic and similar growth rates in a given medium. These growth rates appear to correspond closely with the generality of the habitat requirements of the spiroplasmas. Organisms that are found on flower surfaces [groups III and IV of Junca et al (82)] have rapid growth rates, with doubling times of about 1.8 hr (161). *Spiroplasma citri*, which exhibits considerable generality in its insect and plant host ranges, grows less rapidly, with a doubling time of about 5–6 hr (129). The CSS, which has a specialized habitat in maize and in the leafhoppers that inhabit maize, grows slowly (doubling time 20 hr) (92). The suckling mouse cataract agent, which is tick associated, also grows slowly.

Growth yields of spiroplasmas usually exceed 10^8/ml and may reach 10^{10}/ml in the case of well-adapted isolates growing in rich media. Yields may be improved by incorporation of buffers such as HEPES (7, 88), which prevents attainment of a low limiting pH in the culture before exhaustion of critical nutrients. Growth yields in vivo may exceed those attainable in vitro. In *Drosophila,* yields of SROs may exceed 10^{11}/ml (172), presumably because hemolymph is a dynamic tissue that is capable of importing nutrients and exporting toxins.

SPIROPLASMA MORPHOLOGY

Spiroplasma cells, under certain conditions at least, display all the pleomorphic features that characterize members of the class Mollicutes (143). In addition, however, all but deficient strains (147, 148) have the capability of existing as motile, helical filaments (35, 36, 49, 51). The presence of motility and helicity in organisms that lack cell walls, periplasmic fibrils, or flagellae focuses special attention on the study of spiroplasma morphology.

Spiroplasma cells that are envisioned by dark-field microscopy are often seen to be helically coiled filaments of variable length, 0.08 to 0.2 μm in diameter (35). In logarithmic phase, the filaments may be 2–4 μm in length, but in stationary phase they may be much longer. Filaments seen in vivo tend to be of diverse lengths, with many cells much longer than those envisioned in logarithmic phase cultures. For example, cells of CSS expressed from infected maize were 3–15 μm in length (52). Cells of the SRO in *Drosophila* hemolymph (172) are more homogeneous, measuring 3–5 μm in length, and appear to be somewhat narrower (0.1 μm, 0.2 μm) than the cells of *S. citri* or CSS. Cells of SMCA are also narrower in appearance (153).

Early studies on spiroplasma morphology took special note of "main bodies" attached to the helical filaments (35, 52). These bodies are, however, best interpreted as blebs that arise on older, nonviable cells (124). For example, they never appear to be attached to the short cells that dominate spiroplasma populations during logarithmic phase (7). Rather, they become more numerous as the cultures age (124). Blebs also appear if spiroplasmas are stressed by transfer to deficient media or to unusual insect hosts (R. F. Whitcomb and D. L. Williamson, unpublished data). Thus, suggestions that blebs may participate in the spiroplasma reproductive process seem unfounded.

The morphology of spiroplasma cells changes markedly during growth of the culture. During log phase, all or nearly all cells are short helical filaments (7, 35, 44, 161). The replication of *S. citri* cells was studied in detail by M. Garnier, M. T. Clerc, and J. M. Bové [cited by Bové & Saillard (7)], who used a collodion membrane transfer technique to count the morphotypes in cultures of various ages. Helices of 2–4 turns predominated during logarithmic growth. Numbers of helices with more than 5 turns increased in stationary phase, whether or not the medium contained HEPES buffer. Therefore, elongation of helices in older cultures was associated with nutritional changes in the medium, rather than with acidification. The ends of short, helical, filamentous spiroplasma cells, in confirmation of previous observations (174), were often noted to be different; one end appeared blunt, the other end, tapered. Electron micrographs of helices with 6–8 turns occasionally showed constrictions. Autoradiographic analyses showed that such cells possessed multiple genomes at the time the constrictions appeared. Although semiconservative DNA replication would be expected to yield even numbers of genomes, some helices with three nascent, short (2 turns) helices were observed. This probably indicates that a certain degree of asynchrony exists between replication of genomes, formation of constrictions, and the liberation of new, short helical cells (7).

Spiroplasma morphology always changes drastically during stationary and/or death phase, but the details vary widely among the serological subgroups. For example, in M1A medium, *S. citri* cells in stationary phase are long filaments, many of which have lost their helicity; by this time, viability has also declined dramatically (7, 161). The closely related honey bee spiroplasma retains helicity and viability for a much longer time in stationary phase cultures that have achieved a similar low pH (161). The BNR1 spiroplasma, by contrast, quickly loses both viability and its characteristic morphology in stationary phase (although not at the same rate); its cells become irregularly blebbed or round off to large nonviable spherical bodies (161). The ability of these deformed bodies to regain helicity upon transfer to fresh medium (161) is reminiscent of the restoration of helicity of *S. citri* cells in C3-G medium after transfer to hypertonic medium (95). However, the deformation of BNR1 cells cannot be explained by pH or osmotic changes alone (161). Completely deformed and absolutely nonviable bodies may remain intact in spent media for at least 30 days, and probably for an indefinite period. This observation parallels the finding of Saglio et al (129) that levels of incorporated [^{14}C]thymidine or [^{3}H] phenylalanine, after following an exponential course during logarithmic growth of *S. citri*, were maintained indefinitely during death phase.

Spiroplasmas have been examined by several different electron microscopic techniques. Negative stains were applied to spiroplasmas by Granados (67), who identified the even-calibered filaments of the CSS after staining with phosphotungstic acid (PTA). Such preparations, although diagnostic for CSS, showed many severely deformed cells. These artifacts were also encountered by Cole et al (35) when *S. citri* was examined by PTA staining. On the other hand, staining by 2% ammonium molybdate (AMB) enhanced preservation of cellular helicity, particularly if the stain was adjusted to the approximate osmolarity of the culture medium (35).

When spiroplasmas are sectioned, attention must be paid to section thickness and to the fixation and staining procedures. In properly fixed material, helices are best envisioned in thick (0.3–1.0 μm) sections (49, 62). For example, Davis & Worley (49) found CSS helices in thick sections of the vascular tissue of stunted corn. Reliance on thinner sections for wall-less prokaryotes in vivo has been shown to lead to underestimation of pleomorphism (159). Cole et al (35) arrived at a fixation technique that employed 3.35% glutaraldehyde or 10% formalin prior to post-fixation in 1% osmium tetroxide. Comparisons of fixation methods emphasized the effect of preparative techniques on apparent filament diameters; diameters of helices fixed in glutaraldehyde, alone, were relatively uniform, measuring 104–170 nm, whereas diameters of cells fixed by the conventional cacodylate-glutaraldehyde method ranged from 90 to more than 250 nm in width (35). When properly fixed, the helical cells contained coarse and compact DNA strands, but discrete nucleoids were absent. Ribosomes about 17 nm in diameter were uniformly present, and the bounding membrane of the cells was 6.7 to 8.7 nm in width (35).

Conventional electron microscopy has also revealed inner and outer layers abutting the spiroplasma membrane. The outer layer, in the form of a delicate "nap" 5 to 7 nm in width, was best envisioned by negative staining and consisted of short projections that often appeared periodic (35). An external coating was also envisioned on the 277F spiroplasma (138). Negatively stained filaments also showed (especially if the cells were large or irregular) surface areas with a barred periodicity of units about 4 nm in width and with a center-to-center distance of about 5 nm (35). The significance of these structures is unknown, as is the significance of an internal layer, envisioned in sectioned material, that was about 6.7 nm wide and that abutted the membrane of certain cells (35). The internal layer, unlike the external structures, occurred most often in cells in which infection with spiroplasma virus SVC2 was readily apparent.

Most features of spiroplasma cells seen by negative staining and sectioning techniques have also been envisioned by freeze etching techniques. For example, "main bodies" or blebs could be envisioned not only in preparations from cultures but also in vivo (52). A layer external to the cell membrane could often be demonstrated in freeze-fractured specimens (124). Freeze etching techniques were especially appropriate for envisioning particles (about 10 nm in diameter) associated with both convex and concave fracture faces of the membrane (124). A report (138) that the membrane of the CSS was in fact longitudinally banded with regions that varied in the content of membrane particles was published only as an abstract; documentary micrographs are not available.

SPIROPLASMA MOTILITY

Mechanisms of motility, common among prokaryotes, are of special interest in the case of helical organisms because of the unusual configuration of their cells. For example, careful study of the motility of spirochetes (13) reveals that three types occur in liquid environments. These are translational motion, rotation about the longitudinal axis, and flexing (13). Flexing motions, which frequently interrupt linear translational motion, may correspond to the "tumbles" exhibited by flagellated bacteria (69). Spiroplasmas have been shown, under some circumstances at least, to exhibit all of these types of motility (35, 46, 49, 88). In this regard, they differ profoundly from other mycoplasmas, which either are nonmotile or may have capacities for gliding movement conferred by specialized organelles (9). As viewed under dark-field microscopy, spiroplasma movement in liquid media is not readily distinguishable from that of similarly sized spirochetes (E. P. Greenberg, personal communication). If the two taxa differ, it is in their capacity for translational movement in media of low viscocity. Although the translational motility of spirochetes may be enhanced in media of high viscocity (70), it does not appear to depend on such media. Spiroplasmas show little translational movement at low viscocity, but they exhibit translational movement in semisolid agar media (51) when cells are in contact with a solid surface (44) or in liquid media with elevated viscocity (44). Active motility in viscous solutions may enable helical organisms to inhabit niches unavailable to other prokaryotes. The active chemotaxis recently demonstrated for spiroplasmas (40a) suggests an important role for motility in their natural competition.

Various factors are inhibitory to spiroplasmal motility. For example, deformation by antibody may incapacitate a helical cell at one end, but may leave the other end free to exhibit flexing motion; higher titers of antibody deform the entire cell and render it nonmotile (176). The ability of *S. citri* to pass through filters of small pore size (0.2 μm) was blocked at low temperatures (3°C) or by 0.001 M iodoacetate, suggesting that motility depends upon energy obtained from glycolysis (128). On the other hand, 2,4-dinitrophenol, which uncouples oxidative phosphorylation, did not affect helicity or motility (128).

Because spiroplasmas lack flagellae and periplasmic fibrils and have no trace of peptidoglycan cell wall, their motility is especially intriguing. Several observations suggest that helicity is important for spiroplasmal motility. In media adjusted to high osmolarity and viscocity (e. g. 1 M sucrose), spiroplasma cells simultaneously lost helicity and motility; these properties were regained on reintroduction into C-3G medium (95). Townsend et al (147, 148) studied a nonhelical *S. citri* mutant (ASP-1) that had been obtained from diseased sweet orange trees. The mutant was stable not only during subculturing but also during reintroduction into plants and insects. In polyacrylamide gel electrophoresis, it was found to differ from other *S. citri* strains in the absence of one protein. The ASP-1 strain retained the ability to twitch erratically, but it did not exhibit typical vigorous rotational or flexing motility. One consequence of this loss of motility was the appearance of unusually well defined umbonate colonies. Interestingly, helicity has also been considered to be important for spirochetal motility. Although the degree of coiling of spirochete strains appeared to be correlated with their capacity for translational motility through viscous media (70), nonhelical mutants were not completely nonmotile (70).

Although helicity may play an important role in the motility of both spiroplasmas and spirochetes, the structural basis for helicity apparently differs in the two taxa. In the spirochetes, helicity is maintained by the peptidoglycan layer (80, 81). This was evidenced by the retention of helicity in purified peptidoglycan (80) and by the destruction of helicity by substances, such as lysozyme and penicillin, that affected the integrity or synthesis of cell wall (81). Spiroplasmal helicity, of course, cannot depend on peptidoglycan since none is present (4).

Treatment of spirochete cells with sodium deoxycholate (DOC) does not destroy helicity, but spiroplasmas are lysed by such treatment (168). Under some conditions, DOC-lysed cells show microfibrils 3.6 nm in width, with repeat intervals of 9 nm along their lengths (168, 174). That such fibrils are not artifacts of the DOC technique was unequivocally demonstrated by the visualization of similar fibrils in SROs undergoing lysis by SRO viruses (172). In the 277F spiroplasma such fibrils were apparently associated with the membrane and possibly lay in the plane of the membrane's exterior layer (137). Recently (146a), techniques have been developed for purification of the fibrils. It would be surprising if these membrane-associated fibrils were not involved, in some way, in spiroplasmal motility. In this regard, the recent demonstration (115) of the role of the periplasmic fibrils in the motility of spirochetes is of special interest.

Recently, interest has turned to microbial relatives of actin-like proteins that appear to be of wide occurrence in both eukaryotic and prokaryotic cells. Neimark (109) extracted an actin-like protein from *Mycoplasma pneumoniae* and furthermore reported finding such a protein in *S. citri.* Williamson et al (170) showed that an antiserum prepared against SDS-denatured invertebrate actin coupled to horseradish peroxidase specifically stained cells of *S. citri.* Mouches et al [cited in Bové & Saillard (7)] studied a protein of about 42,000 daltons that co-migrated with muscle actin in one dimensional electrophoresis, but the protein was not otherwise identified.

In summary, although studies of spiroplasma morphology have revealed numerous bits of evidence that the limiting structures of spiroplasma cells are ultrastructurally complex, and that internal or membrane-associated fibrils may be present, no firm ultrastructural basis has been found to account for the observed motility and helical shape of their cells.

THE SPIROPLASMA MEMBRANE

Sterol and Lipid Metabolism

The universal presence of serum in spiroplasma growth media reflects the dependence of these organisms on sterol for growth (133). Analysis of membranes from *S. citri* (124) show that about 30% of the total dry weight of the membrane is lipid. Of this membrane lipid, more than 20% is cholesterol (124). Cholesterol, provided with bovine serum albumin and palmitic acid as a medium supplement, is directly incorporated by *S. citri* in preference to cholesteryl ester (57). Growth of *S. citri* also occurred when β-sitosterol or, to a lesser degree, ergosterol or stigmasterol were provided as supplements (57).

Spiroplasmas, like most mycoplasmas, are unable to synthesize fatty acids from acetate (57). *S. citri,* however, readily and selectively incorporates palmitic acid from growth media. Oleic, linoleic, and linolenic acids are also incorporated, although active discrimination against linolenic acid has been noted (106). The fate of [16-^{14}C] palmitic acid after incorporation by *S. citri* has been determined [(57); B. Roy, cited in (7)]. More than 90% of the radioactivity was membrane associated, and more than 70% resided in phosphatidyl- and diphosphatidylglycerol, which are therefore major phospholipids synthesized by the organism. Glycolipids are also present in spiroplasmas, although in small amounts (116, 137). Sphingomyelin and phosphatidylcholine are also incorporated; the latter phospholipid was shown to favor typical growth and morphology when added as a medium supplement (88). Spiroplasmas differ from other mycoplasmas in their ability to regulate incorporation from media that differ widely in their content of these substances.

The lipid compositions of whole cells (116) or fractionated membranes (107) of *S. citri* and CSS were similar. However, it is now evident that these spiroplasmas are related members of the *S. citri* complex (Table 1), so the true diversity of lipid compositions of spiroplasmas is unknown.

Carbohydrates

About 2.2% of the spiroplasma membrane consists of carbohydrates. The presence of glucose, galactose, and mannose has been determined directly (83), and the presence of free hexose residues on the membrane surface was shown by binding of concanavalin A and *Ricinus communis* agglutinin (84). The presence of *N*-acetylglucosamine in the membrane could be demonstrated by binding of wheat germ agglutinin after pronase treatment. Hexosamines (124), glucosamine (4), and galactosamine (83) have also been identified as membrane components.

Proteins

About 48% of the dry weight of the *S. citri* membrane is protein (124). Some of the proteins have been studied functionally in terms of their enzymatic activities. For example, ATPase (83, 106), *p*-nitrophenyl phosphatase (83, 106), and DNAse (83) are located on the membrane.

Only one membrane protein of *S. citri* has been studied in depth. Spiralin is the dominant member of a set of 16 membrane proteins demonstrable by gel electrophoresis (183) and comprises more than 22% of total membrane protein. The protein could be quantitatively solubilized in the presence of deoxycholate but could not be solubilized in the absence of of detergents. Therefore, it was considered to be an intrinsic membrane protein of *S. citri* (180, 181). Spiralin has a distinctive amino acid composition that differed significantly from that of whole membranes of *S. citri* (183). Apparently the hydrophilic part of the protein forms part of the spiroplasma cell surface, since antispiralin antibodies deform *S. citri* and inhibit growth of the organism (180). The functional role of spiralin in transport, maintenance of structural integrity, or shape of the membrane has not been determined.

SPIROPLASMAVIRUSES

The earliest morphological studies (35, 36) of *S. citri* revealed, surprisingly, that its cells contained particles reminiscent of a type B tailed bacterial virus. Further morphological studies have shown that these particles may at times be associated with lytic infection. They are therefore assumed to be viruses, functionally as well as structurally. The virus (SVC2) has since been found in many strains of *S. citri,* including representatives from diverse geographic areas. Its morphology has recently (31, 32) been described in detail (Table 2). In the course of ultrastructural searches for SVC2 virus, two further viruses were discovered in spiroplasmas (Table 2). Like SVC2, these viruses are morphologically reminiscent of previously described bacterial viruses. One of the new viruses is rod shaped and is frequently envisioned attached to the outer envelope of spiroplasma cells (31, 32). This

Table 2 Spiroplasmaviruses[a]

Group	Dimensions	Host range	Infection type
SVC1	10–15 × 230–280 nm	SMCA, 277F, CSS, SRO	Nonlytic
SVC2	Head: 48–51 nm (between flat sides) 25–28 nm between vertices Tail: 78–83 × 6–8 nm	Many strains of *Spiroplasma citri*	Lytic
SVC3	Head: 37–44 × 35–37 nm Tail: 13–18 × 6–7 nm	All spiroplasmas examined	Lytic

[a]Adapted from descriptions by Cole (31, 32).

virus (SVC1) has been found in four spiroplasmas, including the SROs. A third virus (SVC3), whose virions are polyhedrons with short tails (31, 32), has been found ubiquitously in all spiroplasma isolates examined; in fact, no isolate or clone is known to be virus-free. In SROs (171), and in some cultivable spiroplasmas, the SVC3 viruses produce lytic cross-infections. These are detected, for example, by the production of plaques on lawns of *S. citri* strain 750 by SVC3 virions from SMCA or strain 608 of *S. citri* (33). Because the indicator strain harbors an SVC3 virus of its own, it is clear that infection is not invariably lytic. The state of carriage of SVC3 and all other spiroplasmaviruses is essentially unknown. Recently, a fourth virus (SpV4) with isometric (diameter 25 nm) virions was discovered in an isolate of honey bee spiroplasma from Morocco (125a). Propagation of SVC3/608 and SVC3/SMCA in strain 750 yielded virions that had a buoyant density of 1.26 g/cm^3 in metrizamide gradients (33). The virus contained five structural proteins ranging in molecular weight from 38,000 to 130,000 daltons (33). The DNA, which was presumed to be double stranded, on the basis of enzymatic digestion experiments, showed contour lengths of 7.2 $\pm$ 0.32 μm. These lengths correspond to a molecular weight of about 14 $\times 10^6$ daltons. The viral DNA contrasts with a group of covalently closed, circular DNA molecules of various sizes found in 10 spiroplasma isolates. These molecules, for which no function has been demonstrated, were termed cryptic plasmids (123).

SPIROPLASMA BIOLOGY: HOST RANGE AND PATHOGENESIS

Spiroplasmas appear to be universally associated with arthropod reservoirs. Perhaps the oldest of the known associations is that between SROs and members of the *Drosophila willistoni* species complex (172). Although these vertically transmitted spiroplasmas eliminate male progeny from broods of infected females, it is not clear that the processes involved represent true pathogenesis (166). Other spiroplasmas that may be vertically transmitted occur in *Drosophila hydei* in Japan (113) and in the leafhopper *Oncometopia nigricans* in Florida (102).

A second, more thoroughly studied spiroplasma habitat consists, in part, of plant phloem and, in part, of the hemocoele of leafhoppers (Homoptera: Cicadellidae) and other sap-sucking insects that feed in phloem by means of highly adapted sylets. In the course of such feeding, the insects secrete salivary fluids into the phloem and, in the process, introduce spiroplasmas into the plant (99). Pathogenicity of spiroplasmas is invariably observed in infected plant hosts (38, 39, 40). For example, *S. citri* occurs naturally and causes symptoms in a wide range of weed hosts (12, 112) as well as in citrus, in which its pathogenicity is an important economic problem (85). Spiroplasmas may also be pathogenic for some of the insects that transmit them (162, 164).

A third major spiroplasma habitat involves flowers. As noted, in 1976 T. B. Clark discovered (28) spiroplasmas in honey bees in his experimental hives. Ecological evidence suggested that the spiroplasmas were disseminated in the foraging habitats of the bees as well as in the hive. A search in flowers revealed that not only the honey bee spiroplasma (45) but also an assemblage of helical and nonhelical wall-less prokaryotes (29, 44, 103, 157) occurred on flower surfaces. Presumably the spiroplasmas of flowers are carried by insects; some of the new agents, like honey bee spiroplasma, may eventually be found to be potent insect pathogens. Recent evidence suggests that spiroplasmas from this habitat adapt readily to simple spiroplasma media and that such cultured organisms are pathogenic for the embryonated egg (127) and for cultured mammalian cells (139).

A fourth major spiroplasma habitat concerns ticks. Two serologically distinct spiroplasmas have been isolated from the rabbit tick. Because the 277F agent (10, 117, 137) has been isolated only once, its ecological relationships remain in doubt. On the other hand, independent isolations from two separate geographic locations—Georgia (25) and Maryland (140)—support the suggestion that SMCA is specifically associated with the rabbit tick. Because this tick is associated with rodents and birds as well as with its primary host, it is possible that the biology of the SMCA spiroplasma is complex (140).

The SMCA agent induces experimental ocular disease in rodents (25, 26, 153, 154) but has not been demonstrated to be associated with vertebrates in nature. However, the inferred association with vertebrate hosts has initiated speculation about a possible role of spiroplasmas in human disease. For example, preliminary screening of sera from patients with neurological syndromes of unknown etiology showed an increase in antispiroplasmal complement-fixing antibody that bordered on statistical significance (149).

Recently, Bastian (3) observed helical structures resembling spiroplasmas in autopsied brain material from patients that had succumbed to the Creutzfeld-Jacob disease. Because of their demonstrated potential for experimental vertebrate pathogenesis, spiroplasmas will probably continue to be screened as candidates for causative agents of neurological diseases of obscure etiology.

SUMMARY AND CONCLUSIONS

Less than a decade ago, spiroplasmas were unknown. Today, it is recognized that members of the genus occur in a wide range of habitats and are pathogenic to insects, plants, and vertebrates. Thus, although nearly a century has passed since Erwin F. Smith and Robert Koch discovered that prokaryotes incite disease in eukaryotic organisms, the study of disease etiology is as exciting as ever!

ACKNOWLEDGMENTS

I am indebted to J. G. Tully and J. Vaughn for thoughtful reading and discussion of the manuscript.

Literature Cited

1. Askaa, G., Ernø, H., Ojo, M. O. 1978. *Acta Vet. Scand.* 19:166–78
2. Balch, W. E., Fox, G. E., Magrum, L. J., Woese, C. R., Wolfe, R. S. 1979. *Microbiol. Rev.* 43:260–96
3. Bastian, F. O. 1979. *Arch. Pathol. Lab. Med.* 103:665–69
4. Bebear, C., Latrille, J., Fleck, J., Roy, B., Bové, J. M. 1974. *Colloq. Inst. Natl. Sante Rech. Med.* 33:35–42
5. Bové, J. M. 1980. In *C. R. Journees Francaises sur les Maladies des Plantes. Assoc. Coord. Tech. Agric., Paris.* In press
6. Bové, J. M., Moutous, G., Saillard, C., Fos, A., Bonfils, J., Vignault, J. C., Nhami, A., Abassi, M., Kabbage, K., Hafidi, B., Mouches, C., Viennot-Bourgin, G. 1979. *C. R. Acad. Sci. Ser. D* 288:335–38
7. Bové, J. M., Saillard, C. 1979. In *The Mycoplasmas,* ed. R. F. Whitcomb, J. G. Tully, 3:83–153. New York: Academic
8. Bowyer, J. W., Calavan, E. C. 1974. *Phytopathology* 64:346–49
9. Bredt, W. 1979. In *The Mycoplasmas,* ed. M. Barile, S. Razin, 1:141–55. New York: Academic
10. Brinton, L. P., Burgdorfer, W. 1976. *Int. J. Syst. Bacteriol.* 26:554–60
11. Buchanan, R. E., Gibbons, N. E., eds. 1974. *Bergey's Manual of Determinative Bacteriology.* Baltimore: Williams & Wilkens. 1268 pp. 8th ed.
12. Calavan, E. C., Oldfield, G. N. 1979. See Ref. 7, pp. 37–64
13. Canale-Parola, E. 1978. *Ann. Rev. Microbiol.* 32:69–99
14. Caudwell, A., Kuszala, C., Larrue, J. 1974. *Ann. Phytopathol.* 6:173–90
15. Chang, C. J., Chen, T. A. 1979. *9th Int. Congr. Plant Prot.* (Abstr.)
16. Chanock, R. M., Hayflick, L., Barile, M. F. 1962. *Proc. Natl. Acad. Sci.* 48:41–49
17. Charbonneaux, D. L., Hawthorne, J. D., Ghiorse, W. C., Vandemark, P. J. 1979. *Am. Soc. Microbiol. Ann. Meet. G21* (Abstr.)
18. Chen, C. S., Chen, T. A. 1980. *Phytopathology* 70:279–82
19. Chen, T. A., Davis, R. E. 1979. See Ref. 7, pp. 65–82
20. Chen, T. A., Granados, R. R. 1970. *Science* 167:1633–36
21. Chen, T. A., Liao, C. H. 1975. *Science* 188:1015–17
22. Chiykowski, L. 1974. *Colloq. Inst. Natl. Sante Rech. Med.* 33:291–97
23. Christiansen, C., Askaa, G., Freundt,

E. A., Whitcomb, R. F. 1979. *Curr. Microbiol.* 2:323–26
24. Cirillo, V. P. 1979. See Ref. 9, pp. 323–49
25. Clark, H F. 1964. *J. Infect. Dis.* 114:476–87
26. Clark, H F., Rorke, L. B. 1979. See Ref. 7, pp. 155–74
27. Clark, M. F., Flegg, C. L., Bar-Joseph, M., Rottem, S. 1978. *Phytopathol. Z.* 92:332–37
28. Clark, T. B. 1977. *J. Invertebr. Pathol.* 29:112–13
29. Clark, T. B. 1978. *Am. Bee J.* 118:18–19, 23
30. Clyde, W. A. Jr. 1964. *J. Immunol.* 92:958–65
31. Cole, R. M. 1977. In *The Atlas of Insect and Plant Viruses Including Mycoplasma Viruses and Viroids,* ed. K. Maramorosch, pp. 451–64. New York: Academic
32. Cole, R. M. 1979. See Ref. 9, pp. 385–410
33. Cole, R. M., Mitchell, W. O., Garon, C. F. 1977. *Science* 198:1262–63
34. Cole, R. M., Tully, J. G., Popkin, T. J. 1974. *Colloq. Inst. Natl. Sante Rech. Med.* 33:125–32
35. Cole, R. M., Tully, J. G., Popkin, T. J., Bové, J. M. 1973. *J. Bacteriol.* 115:367–86
36. Cole, R. M., Tully, J. G., Popkin, T. J., Bové, J. M. 1973. *Ann. NY Acad. Sci.* 225:471–93
37. Cousin, M. T., Perreau, P., Kartha, K. K. 1974. *Ann. Phytopathol.* 6:277–84
38. Daniels, M. J. 1979. *Zentralbl. Bakteriol. Parasitenkd. Infektionskr. Hyg. Abt. 1 Orig. Reihe A* 245:184–99
39. Daniels, M. J. 1979. See Ref. 7, pp. 209–27
40. Daniels, M. J. 1979. *J. Gen. Microbiol.* 114:323–28
40a. Daniels, M. J., Longland, J. M., Gilbart, J. 1980. *J. Gen. Microbiol.* 118:pt. 2. In press
41. Daniels, M. J., Markham, P. G., Meddins, B. M., Plaskitt, A. K., Townsend, R., Bar-Joseph, M. 1973. *Nature* 244:523–24
42. Daniels, M. J., Markham, P. G., Townsend, R. 1979. In *Soc. Appl. Bacteriol. Tech. Ser. Plant Pathogens,* pp. 61–81. London: Academic
43. Daniels, M. J., Meddins, B. M. 1973. *J. Gen. Microbiol.* 76:239–42
44. Davis, R. E. 1978. *Can. J. Microbiol.* 24:954–59
45. Davis, R. E. 1978. *Phytopathol. News* 12(7):PO–7 (Abstr.)
46. Davis, R. E. 1979. In *Leafhopper Vectors and Plant Disease Agents,* ed. K. Maramorosch, K. F. Harris, pp. 451–84. New York: Academic
47. Davis, R. E., Lee, I. M., Basciano, L. K. 1979. *Can. J. Microbiol.* 25:861–66
48. Davis, R. E., Whitcomb, R. F., Chen, T. A., Granados, R. R. 1972. In *Pathogenic Mycoplasmas, Ciba Found. Symp.* ed. K. Elliott, J. Birch Jr., pp. 205–14. New York: Associated Scientific Publ.
49. Davis, R. E., Worley, J. F. 1973. *Phytopathology* 63:403–8
50. Davis, R. E., Worley, J. F., Clark, T. B., Moseley, M. 1976. *Proc. Am. Phytopathol. Soc.* 3:304 (Abstr.)
51. Davis, R. E., Worley, J. F., Moseley, M. 1975. *Proc. Am. Phytopathol. Soc.* 2:56 (Abstr.)
52. Davis, R. E., Worley, J. F., Whitcomb, R. F., Ishijima, T., Steere, R. L. 1972. *Science* 176:521–23
53. Doi, Y., Teranaka, M., Yora, K., Asuyama, H. 1967. *Ann. Phytopathol. Soc. Jpn.* 33:259–66
54. Edward, D. G. ff., Freundt, E. A. 1967. *Int. J. Syst. Bacteriol.* 17:267–68
55. Fox, G. E., Pechman, K. R., Woese, C. R. 1977. *Int. J. Syst. Bacteriol.* 27:44–57
56. Fox, G. E., Stackebrandt, E., Hespell, R. B., Gibson, J., Maniloff, J., Dyer, T., Wolfe, R. S., Balch, W., Tanner, R., Magrum, L., Zablen, L. B., Blakemore, R., Gupta, R., Bonen, L., Lewis, B. J., Chen, K. N., Woese, C. R. 1980. *Science* 209:457–63
57. Freeman, B. A., Sissenstein, R., McManus, T. T., Woodward, J. E., Lee, I. M., Mudd, J. B. 1976. *J. Bacteriol.* 125: 946–54
58. Freundt, E. A., Edward, D. G. ff. 1979. See Ref. 9, pp. 1–41
59. Fudl-Allah, A. E.-S. A., Calavan, E. C. 1973. *Phytopathology* 63:256–59
60. Fudl-Allah, A. E.-S. A., Calavan, E. C. 1974. *Phytopathology* 64:1309–13
61. Fudl-Allah, A. E.-S. A., Calavan, E. C. Igwegbe, E. C. K. 1971. *Phytopathology* 61:1321 (Abstr.)
62. Fudl-Allah, A. E.-S. A., Calavan, E. C., Igwegbe, E. C. K. 1972. *Phytopathology* 62:729–31
63. Giannotti, J. 1974. *Colloq. Inst. Natl. Sante Rech. Med.* 33:99–106
64. Giannotti, J., Giannotti, D. 1978. *Ann. Phytopathol.* 10:489–92
65. Giannotti, J., Vago, C., Giannotti, D. 1979. *C. R. Acad. Sci. Ser. D* 288:85–87
66. Gibbons, N. E., Murray, R. G. E. 1978. *Int. J. Syst. Bacteriol.* 28:1–6
67. Granados, R. R. 1969. *Contrib. Boyce Thompson Inst.* 24:173–88

68. Granados, R. R., Maramorosch, K., Shikata, E. 1968. *Proc. Natl. Acad. Sci. USA* 60:841–44
69. Greenberg, E. P., Canale-Parola, E. 1977. *J. Bacteriol.* 130:485–94
70. Greenberg, E. P., Canale-Parola, E. 1977. *J. Bacteriol.* 131:960–69
71. Haggis, G. H., Sinha, R. C. 1978. *Phytopathology* 68:677–80
72. Hayflick, L., Arai, S. 1973. *Ann. NY Acad. Sci.* 225:494–502
73. Igwegbe, E. C. K. 1978. *Phytopathology* 68:1530–34
74. Igwegbe, E. C. K., Calavan, E. C. 1970. *Phytopathology* 60:1525–26
75. Igwegbe, E. C. K., Stevens, C., Hollis, J. J. Jr. 1979. *Can. J. Microbiol.* 25:1125–32
76. Igwegbe, E. C. K., Thomas, C. 1978. *J. Gen. Appl. Microbiol.* 24:261–69
77. Ishiie, T., Doi, Y., Yora, K., Asuyama, H. 1967. *Ann. Phytopathol. Soc. Jpn.* 33:267–75
78. Jones, A. L., Whitcomb, R. F., Williamson, D. L., Coan, M. E. 1977. *Phytopathology* 67:738–46
79. Jordan, F. T. W. 1979. In *The Mycoplasmas,* ed. J. G. Tully, R. F. Whitcomb, 2:1–48. New York: Academic
80. Joseph, R., Canale-Parola, E. 1972. *Arch. Mikrobiol.* 81:146–68
81. Joseph, R., Holt, S. C., Canale-Parole, E. 1973. *J. Bacteriol.* 115:426–35
82. Junca, P., Saillard, C., Tully, J., Garcia-Jurado, O., Degorge-Dumas, J.-R., Mouches, C., Vignault, J. C., Vogel, R., McCoy, R., Whitcomb, R., Williamson, D., Latrille, J., Bové, J. M. 1980. *C. R. Acad. Sci. Ser. D.* 290:1209–12
83. Kahane, I., Greenstein, S., Razin, S. 1977. *J. Gen. Microbiol.* 101:173–76
84. Kahane, I., Tully, J. G., 1976. *J. Bacteriol.* 128:1–7
85. Klotz, L. J., Calavan, E. C., Weathers, L. G. 1972. *Virus and Viruslike Diseases of Citrus, Calif. Agric. Exp. Stn. Ext. Ser. Cir. 559.* 42pp.
86. Kondo, F., Maramorosch, K., McIntosh, A. H., Varney, E. H. 1977. *Proc. Am. Phytopathol. Soc.* 4:190 (Abstr.)
87. Laflèche, D., Bové, J. M. 1970. *Fruits* 25:455–65
88. Lee, I. M. 1977. PhD thesis. Univ. Calif, Riverside. 98pp.
89. Lee, I. M., Davis, R. E. 1978. *Phytopathol. News* 12(9):215 (Abstr.)
90. Lee, I. M., Davis, R. E. 1980. *Phytopatholology* 70:464 (Abstr.)
91. Lei, J. D., Su, H. J., Chen, T. A. 1979. In *Proc. R.O.C. US Coop. Sci. Semin. Mycoplasma Dis. Plants. NSC Symp. Ser. I,* pp. 89–97. Taipei: Nat. Sci. Counc.
92. Liao, C. H., Chen, T. A. 1977. *Phytopathology* 67:802–7
93. Liao, C. H., Chen, T. A. 1980. *Phytopathology* 70:465 (Abstr.)
94. Liao, C. H., Chen, T. A. 1978. *Can. J. Microbiol.* 24:325–29
95. Liao, C. H., Cotty, P. J., Chen, T. A. 1979. See Ref. 91, pp. 83–87
96. Lowe, S. K., Raju, B. C. 1978. *Phytopathol. News* 12(9):216 (Abstr.)
97. Maramorosch, K. 1955. *Plant Dis. Rep.* 39:896–98
98. Maramorosch, K., Kondo, F. 1978. *Zentralbl. Bakteriol. Parasitenkd. Infektionskr. Hyg. Abt. 1 Orig. Reihe A* 241:196 (Abstr.)
99. Markham, P. G., Townsend, R. 1974. *Colloq. Inst. Natl. Sante Rech. Med.* 33:201–6
100. Markham, P. G., Townsend, R., Bar-Joseph, M., Daniels, M. J., Plaskitt, A., Meddins, B. M. 1974. *Ann. Appl. Biol.* 78:49–57
101. McCoy, R. E. 1979. See Ref. 7, pp. 229–64
102. McCoy, R. E., Tsai, J. H., Thomas, D. L. 1978. *Phytopathol. News* 12(9):217 (Abstr.)
103. McCoy, R. E., Williams, D. S., Thomas, D. L. 1979. See Ref. 91, pp. 75–81
104. Mouches, C., Duthil, P., Vignault, J. C., Protopapadakis, F., Nhami, A., Tully, J. G., Bové, J. M. 1980. In *Proc. 8th Conf. Int. Organ. Citrus Virol.,* ed. E. C. Calavan. Australia: Univ. Calif. Press. In press
105. Mouches, C., Vignault, J. C., Tully, J. G., Whitcomb, R. F. Bové, J. M. 1979. *Curr. Microbiol.* 2:69–74
106. Mudd, J. B., Ittig, M., Roy, B., Latrille, J., Bové, J. M. 1977. *J. Bacteriol.* 129:1250–56
107. Mudd, J. B., Lee, I. M., Liu, H. Y., Calavan, E. C. 1979. *J. Bacteriol.* 137:1056–58
108. Nault, L. R., Gordon, D. T., Gingery, R. E., Bradfute, O. E., Loayza, J. C. 1979. *Phytopathology* 69:824–28
109. Neimark, H. C. 1977. *Proc. Natl. Acad. Sci. USA* 74:4041–45
110. Neimark, H. 1979. See Ref. 9, pp. 43–61
111. Neimark, H., Tung, M. C. 1973. *J. Bacteriol.* 114:1025–33
112. Oldfield, G. N., Kaloostian, G. H. 1979. See Ref. 91, pp. 119–25
113. Ota, T., Kawabe, M., Oishi, K., Poulson, D. F. 1979. *J. Hered.* 70:211–13
114. Padhi, S. B., McIntosh, A. H.,

Maramorosch, K. 1977. *Phytopathol. Z.* 90:268–72
115. Paster, B. J., Canale-Parola, E. 1980. *J. Bacteriol.* 141:359–64
116. Patel, K. R., Smith, P. F., Mayberry, W. R. 1978. *J. Bacteriol.* 136:829–31
117. Pickens, E. G., Gerloff, R. K., Burgdorfer, W. 1968. *J. Bacteriol.* 95:291–99
118. Poulson, D. F., Sakaguchi, B. 1961. *Science* 133:1489–90
119. Rahimian, H., Gumpf, D. J. 1980. *Int. J. Syst. Bacteriol.* 30: In press
120. Raju, B. C., Nyland, G. 1978. *Phytopathology News* 12(9):216 (Abstr.)
121. Raju, B. C., Purcell, A. H., Nyland, G. 1979. *Proc. 4th Meet. Int. Counc. Lethal Yellowing, Ft. Lauderdale,* p.12 (Abstr.)
122. Rana, G. L., Kaloostian, G. H., Oldfield, G. N., Granett, A. L., Calavan, E. C., Pierce, H. D., Lee, I. M., Gumpf, D. J. 1975. *Phytopathology* 65:1143–45
123. Ranhand, J. M., Mitchell, W. O., Popkin, T. J., Cole, R. M. 1980. *J. Bacteriol.* 143: In press
124. Razin, S., Hasin, M., Ne'eman, Z., Rottem, S. 1973. *J. Bacteriol.* 116:1421–35
125. Razin, S., Rottem, S. 1967. *J. Bacteriol.* 94:1807–10
125a. Ricard, B., Garnier, M., Bové, J. M. 1980. *Proc. 3rd. Int. Meet. Int. Org. Mycoplasm., Custer, S. Dak., Sept. 1980, Abstr. 91*
126. Rodwell, A. W., Rodwell, E. S. 1978. *J. Gen. Microbiol.* 109:259–63
127. Rose, D. L., Tully, J. G., Whitcomb, R. F. 1979. *Am. Soc. Microbiol. Ann. Meet. Abstr. G 10*
127a. Rose, D. L., Whitcomb, R. F., Tully, J. G. 1980. *Proc. 3rd. Int. Meet. Int. Org. Mycoplasm., Custer, S. Dak., Sept. 1980, Abstr. 64*
128. Saglio, P. H. M. 1979. *Plant Dis. Rep.* 63:293–96
129. Saglio, P. H. M., Daniels, M. J., Pradet, A. 1979. *J. Gen. Microbiol.* 110:13–20
130. Saglio, P., Davis, R. E., Dalibart, R., Dupont, G., Bové, J. M. 1974. *Colloq. Inst. Natl. Sante Rech. Med.* 33:27–34
131. Saglio, P., Laflèche, D., Bonissol, C., Bové, J. M. 1971. *Physiol. Veg.* 9:569–82
132. Saglio, P., Laflèche, D., Bonissol, C., Bové, J. M. 1971. *C. R. Acad. Sci. Ser. D* 272:1387–90
133. Saglio, P., L'Hospital, M., Laflèche, D., Dupont, G., Bove, J. M., Tully, J. G., Freundt, E. A. 1973. *Int. J. Syst. Bacteriol.* 23:191–204
134. Saglio, P. H. M., Whitcomb, R. F. 1979. See Ref. 7, pp. 1–36
135. Saillard, C., Dunez, J., Garcia-Jurado, O., Nhami, A., Bové, J. M. 1978. *C. R. Acad. Sci. Ser. D* 286:1245–48
136. Skripal, I. G. 1974. *Mikrobiol. Zh. Kiev* 36:462–67
137. Stalheim, O. H. V., Ritchie, A. E., Whitcomb, R. F. 1978. *Curr. Microbiol.* 1:365–70
138. Steere, R. L., Davis, R. E. 1972. *Phytopathology* 62:672 (Abstr.)
139. Steiner, T., Gamon, L., Levine, E., McGarrity, G. 1980. *In Vitro* 16: (Abstr.) In press
140. Stiller, D., Whitcomb, R. F., Coan, M. E. 1978. *Am. Soc. Microbiol. Ann. Meet. G7* (Abstr.)
141. Su, H. J., Lei, J. D., Chen, T. A. 1978. In *Plant Diseases Due to Mycoplasma-like Organisms,* pp. 158–65. Taipei: Food Fert. Tech. Cent. Asian Pac. Reg.
142. Subcommittee on the Taxonomy of *Mycoplasmatales.* 1977. *Int. J. Syst. Bacteriol.* 27:392–94
143. Subcommittee on the Taxonomy of *Mollicutes.* 1979. *Int. J. Syst. Bacteriol.* 29:172–80
144. Subcommittee on the Taxonomy of *Mollicutes.* 1980. *Int. J. Syst. Bacteriol.* 30: In press
145. Taylor-Robinson, D., Purcell, D. C., Wong, D. C., Chanock, R. M. 1966. *J. Hyg.* 64:91–104
146. Townsend, R. 1976. *J. Gen. Microbiol.* 94:417–20
146a. Townsend, R., Archer, D. B., Plaskitt, K. A. 1980. *J. Bacteriol.* 142:694–700
147. Townsend, R., Burgess, J., Plaskitt, K. A. 1980. *J. Bacteriol.* 142:973–81
148. Townsend, R., Markham, P. G., Plaskitt, K. A., Daniels, M. J. 1977. *J. Gen. Microbiol.* 100:15–21
149. Tully, J. G. 1978. *Zentralbl. Bakteriol. Parasitenkd. Infektionskr. Hyg. Abt. 1 Orig. Reihe A* 241:191 (Abstr.)
150. Tully, J. G., Rose, D. L., Vignault, J. C., Saillard, C., Bové, J. M., Garcia-Jurado, O., McCoy, R. E., Williamson, D. L. 1980. *Curr. Microbiol.* 3:369–72
151. Tully, J. G., Whitcomb, R. F. 1981. In *The Prokaryotes,* ed. M. P. Starr, H. Stolp, H. G. Truper, A. Balows, H. G. Schlegel, Ch. 12. New York: Springer-Verlag. In press
152. Tully, J. G., Whitcomb, R. F., Bové, J. M., Saglio, P. 1973. *Science* 182:827–29
153. Tully, J. G., Whitcomb, R. F., Clark, H F., Williamson, D. L. 1977. *Science* 195:892–94
154. Tully, J. G., Whitcomb, R. F., Williamson, D. L., Clark, H F. 1976. *Nature* 259:117–20

155. Turner, T. B., Hollander, D. H. 1957. *Biology of The Treponematoses, World Health Org. Monogr. Ser. No. 35*
156. Vaughn, J. L. 1973. *Proc. 3rd Int. Colloq. Invertebr. Tissue Cult,* ed. J. Rehacek, D. Blaskovic, W. F. Hink, pp. 209–19. Bratislava: Publ. House Slovak Acad. Sci.
157. Vignault, J.-C., Bové, J. M., Saillard, C., Vogel, R., Farro, A., Venegas, L., Stemmer, W., Aoki, S., McCoy, R., Al-Beldri, A. S., Larue, M., Tuzcu, O., Ozsam, M., Nhami, A., Abassi, M., Bonfils, J., Moutous, G., Fos, A., Poutiers, F., Viennot-Bourgin, B. 1980. *C. R. Acad. Sci. Ser. D.* 290:775–78
158. Walker, R. T. 1976. In *Proc. Int. Conf. Synth. Struct. Chem. tRNAs Compon. Poznan, Poland,* pp. 291–305
159. Waters, H., Hunt, P. 1980. *J. Gen. Microbiol.* 116:111–31
160. Whitcomb, R. F. 1981. *Ann. Rev. Entomol.* 26: In preparation
161. Whitcomb, R. F., Coan, M. E. 1980. *Am. Soc. Microbiol. Ann. Meet. Abstr. G18*
162. Whitcomb, R. F., Tully, J. G., Bové, J. M., Saglio, P. 1973. *Science* 182:1251–53
163. Whitcomb, R. F., Williamson, D. L. 1975. *Ann. NY Acad. Sci.* 266:260–75
164. Whitcomb, R. F., Williamson, D. L. 1979. *Zentralbl. Bakteriol. Parasitenkd. Infektionskr. Hyg. Abt. 1 Orig. Reihe A* 245:200–21
165. Whittlestone, P. 1979. See Ref. 79, pp. 133–76
166. Williamson, D. L. 1965. *J. Invertebr. Pathol.* 7:493–501
167. Williamson, D. L. 1969. *Jpn. J. Genet. 44; Suppl.* 1, pp. 36–41
168. Williamson, D. L. 1974. *J. Bacteriol.* 117:904–6
169. Williamson, D. L. 1980. In *Practical Techniques for the Study of Plant and Insect Mycoplasmas,* ed. M. J. Daniels, P. G., Markham. Croom Helm Ltd. In press
170. Williamson, D. L., Blaustein, D. I., Levine, R. J. C., Elfvin, M. J. 1979. *Curr. Microbiol.* 2:143–45
171. Williamson, D. L., Oishi, K., Poulson, D. F. 1977. See Ref. 31, pp. 465–72
172. Williamson, D. L., Poulson, D. F. 1979. See Ref. 7, pp. 175–208
173. Williamson, D. L., Tully, J. G., Whitcomb, R. F. 1979. *Int. J. Syst. Bacteriol.* 29:345–51
174. Williamson, D. L., Whitcomb, R. F. 1974. *Colloq. Inst. Natl. Sante Rech. Med.* 33:283–90
175. Williamson, D. L., Whitcomb, R. F. 1975. *Science* 188:1018–20
176. Williamson, D. L., Whitcomb, R. F., Tully, J. G. 1978. *Curr. Microbiol.* 1:203–7
177. Woese, C. R., Maniloff, J., Zablen, L. B. 1980. *Proc. Natl. Acad. Sci. USA* 77:494–98
178. Working Group of the FAO/WHO Programme on Comparative Mycoplasmology. 1975. *The Metabolism-inhibition Test, World Health Organ. Working Doc. VPH/MIC/75.6*
179. Working Group of the FAO/WHO Programme on Comparative Mycoplasmology. 1976. *The Growth Inhibition Test, World Health Organ. Work. Doc. VPH/MIC/76.7*
180. Wroblewski, H. 1978. *Zentralbl. Bakteriol. Parasitenkd. Infektionskr. Hyg. Abt. 1 Orig. Reihe A* 241:179–80 (Abstr.)
181. Wroblewski, H. 1979. *J. Bacteriol.* 140:738–41
182. Wroblewski, H., Johansson, K. E., Burlot, R. 1977. *Int. J. Syst. Bacteriol.* 27:97–103
183. Wroblewski, H., Johansson, K. E., Hjerten, S. 1977. *Biochim. Biophys. Acta* 465:275–89
184. Zeigel, R. F., Clark, H F. 1974. *Infect. Immun.* 9:430–43

AUTHOR INDEX

(Names appearing in capital letters indicate authors of chapters in this volume.)

A

Aaronson, W., 473
Aarti, A., 376
Aasa, R., 268
Abassi, M., 683, 686, 688, 690, 704
Abd-El-Malek, Y., 562
Al-Beldri, A. S., 683, 686, 690, 704
Abeliovich, A., 502
Abelson, J., 153
Aberhart, D. J., 165, 166
Abraham, E. P., 160-67, 169, 170, 213, 222
Abraham, G., 88
Abrutsch, U., 408
Acar, J. F., 485
Achtman, M., 402
Acker, G., 79, 98, 99
Ackerman, R. Y., 457
Ackrell, B. A. C., 187, 188
Acs, G., 63
Ada, G. L., 601, 625, 640
Adam, A., 313, 317-19, 322, 323, 325, 327, 330, 614
Adams, G. A., 10
Adams, J. M., 57
Adams, R. D., 328
Adhya, S., 217, 250, 668, 671
Adlam, C., 583
Adler, H. E., 647, 659
Adler, J., 52, 53, 57, 58, 70, 86, 88, 90, 92-94, 98
Adriaens, P., 165, 177
Agabian, N., 84, 87
AHARONOWITZ, Y., 209-33; 210, 211, 213, 220-22, 227, 228
Ahmed, Q. S., 346, 348, 349
Aiba, S., 187, 275
Aichele, G., 408
Ainsworth, G. C., 128, 130
Ait, N., 440, 441
Aita, S., 78
Aizawa, S. I., 85
Ajello, L., 117, 124, 129, 130
Akazawa, T., 501, 502
Akedo, M., 431
Akiyama, K., 328
Aladegbami, S. L., 193
Al-Aidroos, K., 50
Alaoui, R., 63
Alberghina, A., 669
Albers-Schönberg, G., 173, 175
Albertyn, H., 426, 432
Albrecht, S. L., 192, 193, 200, 201
Alden, C. J., 151, 152
Alderete, J. F., 466, 470
Aldova, E., 346, 350
Aleem, A. R. M. A., 352, 354, 357
Alegria, A. H., 138, 145
Alexander, E. R., 287, 290, 296, 298-302, 305
Alexander, J. J., 293
Alexander, J. K., 440
Alexandruschkina, N. I., 138, 141
Alexopoulos, C. J., 112, 115, 129
Alford, R. H., 177
Alkan, M., 379, 381-83, 391
Allaman, J., 290, 301, 302
Allegra, D. T., 364
Allison, A. C., 596
Allweiss, B., 97
Almeida, J. D., 624
Alosi, M. C., 661
Alper, M. D., 225
Alpert, S. S., 76, 77
Altenbuchner, J., 475
Al-Ugaily, L., 506
Amako, K., 78
Amano, T., 597, 603
Amar, C., 317
Ames, B. N., 225, 236, 251
Ames, G. F., 84
Ames, G. F.-L., 225, 411
Ammann, R., 300
Ammer, S., 88
Ammeraal, R. M., 501
Anagnostakis, S. L., 51
Ander, P., 439
Anderer, F. A., 606, 607
Anderka, M., 290, 301, 302
Andersen, A. A., 598, 611
Andersen, J. E., 274
Anderson, D. R., 291
Anderson, E. V., 427
Anderson, J. B., 290, 298, 300
Anderson, J. D., 489, 585
Anderson, L. E., 505, 515, 516, 521
Anderson, L. L., 502
Anderson, M. A., 456
Anderson, M. J., 611
Anderson, R., 273, 280
Anderson, R. A., 89, 98
Ando, T., 492
Andrea, J., 238
Andreesen, J. R., 434, 444, 448, 451, 454
Andrew, P. W., 500
Anfinsen, C. B., 602, 605
Anne, J., 177
Ansel, J., 287, 290, 299
Antonson, K., 245
AOKI, H., 159-81; 160, 170-72
Aoki, S., 683, 686, 690, 704
Aoni, H., 387
Aplin, R. T., 170
Aposhian, H. V., 150
Appelbaum, P. C., 347, 349, 350
Appleby, C. A., 194
Apte, S. K., 500, 501, 513, 515, 517, 518, 520, 522, 523
Aragno, M., 80
Arai, M., 238, 393, 394, 406
Arai, S., 691
Arai, T., 492
Aranki, A., 432
Araya, S., 492
Arber, W., 655
Arbuthnott, J. P., 488
Archer, D. B., 700
Archer, L. J., 195
Archibald, A. R., 570, 571
Arden, B., 389, 391
Arends, J. J. A., 99, 100
Arison, B. H., 173, 175
Arita, M., 354
Armitage, J. P., 78, 92, 93
Armour, S., 518
Armstrong, J. E., 499, 506
Arnaud, L. E., 315
Arnon, D. E., 500
Arnon, D. I., 501, 511
ARNON, R., 593-619; 597, 600-5, 607, 608, 611-14
Arnott, S., 59
Arnstein, H. R. V., 165, 213
Aronson, A. T., 227
Arp, D. J., 511
Arst, H. N., 219, 220, 225, 229
Arth, C., 301
Artman, M., 165
Asada, K., 502
Asakura, S., 72, 74, 77, 81-85, 88, 90
Asano, K., 554
Asato, Y., 526
Asdourian, P. L., 386, 411
Asher, Y., 290, 293, 294
Ashoor, S. A., 237
Ashwell, G., 670
Askaa, G., 686, 687, 691
Asquith, P., 314
Asselineau, J., 315
Astier, C., 499, 500, 503
Asuyama, H., 678
Atassi, M. Z., 602, 603
Atkins, A. S., 273
Atwood, G., 299
Aubert, J.-P., 228

Auchterlonie, C. C., 502
Audibert, F., 317, 323-27, 329, 614
Audsley, A., 278
Augenstein, D. C., 457, 458
Auletta, A. E., 563
Aunstrup, K., 459
Austin, B., 648, 659
Austin, C. M., 601
Austin, S. M., 513, 514, 521
Austwick, P. K. C., 130
Ausubel, F., 219, 227, 517
Ausubel, F. M., 506, 517, 527
Autrup, H., 255
Avery, R. J., 625, 635, 642
Avron, M., 504
Awadaguchi, S., 554
Awakura, S., 85
Ax, H. A., 160
Ayers, A. R., 652, 659, 662, 663
Ayers, J. L., 242
Ayers, S. B., 652, 659, 662, 663
Aziz, K. M. S., 363
Azuma, H., 99
Azuma, I., 313, 315, 318, 323, 324, 327, 329-31, 333, 334

B

Bachmann, B. J., 371, 373, 385, 407, 653, 656, 671
Back, E., 347, 350
Baddiley, J., 570, 571
Dader, J. P., 292
Bagi, G., 505
Bagley, S. T., 666, 669
Bahl, H., 200
Baigent, N. L., 647
Bailey, J. M., 57
Bailey, J. V., 545
Bailone, A., 250, 251
Baimai, V., 250
Bainbridge, D. R., 611
Baird-Parker, A. C., 564-69, 582
Bak, A. L., 474
Baker, A. J., 426, 429
Baker, C. E., 218
Baker, C. N., 177, 344, 353, 357, 358, 360
Baker, W., 160, 162
Balch, W., 679, 680
Balch, W. E., 432, 434, 436, 449, 454, 680
Baldwin, J. E., 166
Baldwin, J. N., 585, 586
Baldwin, R. L., 445
Ball, E. J., 328
Ball, T. S., 220, 229
Ballard, R. W., 39
Balogh, A., 505
Balows, A., 343, 351, 482, 484, 485
Baltimore, D., 52, 53, 60, 62, 620, 621, 624, 639
Baltscheffsky, H., 511
Baltz, R. H., 152
Bamberger, I., 79, 99
Banaszak, L. J., 390
Bancroft, J., 238
Banerjee, M., 353, 356
Banks, G., 76, 77
Banks, J., 288, 289, 303
Banti, G., 121
Banwell, J. G., 466
Barash, I., 224
Barber, C., 625
Baresi, L., 438
Bargeron, C. P., 500
Barich, D., 238
Barich, L. L., 238
Baril, J. P., 467
Barile, M. F., 291, 678
Bar-Joseph, M., 678, 683, 688
Barker, C. J., 662
Barker, H. D., 435
Barker, L. J., 242, 243, 249, 255, 256
Barker, S. A., 265
Barker, W. H. Jr., 352, 355-57
Barlow, A. J. E., 130
Barnes, W. S., 257
Barnett, J. A., 112
Baron, E., 585
Baross, J., 362
Barr, R., 499
Barrctt, T. J., 364
Barron, A. L., 290, 295, 306
Barron, G. L., 115
Bartlett, G. L., 330
Bartnicki-Garcia, S., 112, 115, 129
Bartnik, E., 219
Barton, L. L., 441
Bärwolff, D., 154
Basciano, L. K., 681-83, 686, 688-90
Basham, H. G., 664
Bashford, D. J., 348
Bassford, P. J. Jr., 370, 373-75, 377, 381, 384, 395, 397-401, 403-5, 407, 409, 410, 414, 416
Bassham, J. A., 505, 515, 518
Bast, R. C., 332
Bastian, F. O., 705
Batchelor, F. R., 162
Bateman, D. F., 664-67, 669
Batt, T., 514
Baty, D., 393
Bauer, K., 162, 165
Baumann, L., 357
Baumann, P., 19, 39, 357
Baumgarten, J., 191, 195
Bavoil, P., 375, 377-80, 388
Bayan, A. P., 543
Bayer, M. E., 390, 409, 412
Beacham, I. R., 373, 379, 394
Beadmore, D. H., 439
Beall, J. R., 238
Bean, W. J. Jr., 626
Beauchemin-Newhouse, N., 506
Beauclerk, A. A. D., 44
Bebear, C., 679, 700, 702
Becerril, P., 483
Beck, J. F., 271, 274, 276, 277
Beck, J. V., 265, 267, 269, 271, 272, 274, 276, 277
Becker, U., 604
Becker, Y., 286, 290, 293, 294
Beckwith, A. C., 238, 240
Beckwith, J., 374, 389, 393, 395, 397, 399-401, 403-6, 410, 668
Beckwith, J. R., 397, 398, 405, 407, 409, 410, 414, 416
Bednár, B., 329
Bedouelle, H., 395, 397, 399-401, 403, 404
Beem, M. O., 301, 305
Beer, S. V., 662, 665
Begg, K. J., 415
Behme, R. J., 485
Behrens, M. K., 648, 650, 651, 666, 667
Behrens, O. K., 161, 163
Beil, W., 604
Beinert, H., 189
Bejba, N., 237
Dckierkunst, A., 331, 333
Belder, M., 607
Belkin, S., 504, 522
Bell, J. F., 613
Bell, R. M., 412
Bell, S. D., 290, 296
Bellamy, A. R., 627
Belly, R. T., 273
Belyakova, T. N., 92
Benacerraf, B., 599, 615
Ben-Bassat, A., 435, 436, 440, 452, 453, 456-59
Bender, R. A., 218, 655
Benemann, J. R., 202, 511-13, 521, 523, 524
Benenson, A. S., 346, 350
Benjamin, R. K., 129, 131
Benjamini, E., 602, 604, 606, 611
Benn-Bassat, A., 435, 440, 452, 453, 456, 458, 459
Bennett, J. C., 265
Bennett, J. E., 117
Bennett, J. V., 482, 483
Bennett, P. M., 81, 82, 649, 650
Bennett, R. A., 659, 662, 663
Benoki, M., 355

Benson, D. R., 511
Benson, P. M., 239, 241, 245
Benz, R., 378-80, 383
Benzinger, R., 655
Beraha, L., 664
Berdy, J., 212, 230
Berendsen, W., 374, 375, 387
Berg, H. C., 70, 73, 90, 91, 98, 101
Berg, P. E., 387
Bergdoll, M. S., 487
Berger, A., 604
Berger, B. J., 428
Berger, F. M., 317, 327
Berger, R. E., 287, 290, 299
Bergersen, F. J., 190, 192, 193, 195
Berglund, O., 143
Bergman, B., 504, 521
Berkhout, M., 116
Berkner, K. L., 141, 148, 149
Berlese, A. N., 116
Berlier, Y., 200
Berman, P. M., 668
Bernard, C., 328
Bernard, P. D., 84
Berndt, H., 193, 200, 201
Bernheim, B. C., 291
Bernheimer, H., 374, 375, 387
Bernlohr, R. W., 228
Bernstein, I. D., 330
Bernstock, L., 315, 317, 613
Berry, E. A., 50, 52, 56
Berry, V. K., 265
Bertin, G., 245
Bessman, M. J., 143
Bessudo, D., 466, 482, 483
Betlach, M., 469, 470, 475
Beug, A., 153
Beukman, W., 144
Beumer, J., 576
Beutner, K. R., 611
Beutner, R. K., 611
Bevan, E. A., 50-59, 62-64
Bezdek, M., 95
Bezer, A. E., 328
Bhattacharji, L. M., 351
Biddle, C., 100
Bieth, G., 485
Biggins, D. R., 191, 193
Biggs, D. F., 498, 511
Bijvelt, J., 390
Billcliffe, B., 488
Billeter, B. A., 664
Billing, E., 659, 662, 663
Binford, C. H., 120, 121, 130
Bingham, P. M., 152
Binns, M. M., 478, 479
Biocic, I., 458, 459
Biozzi, G., 330
Birch-Anderson, A., 87
Bird, I. F., 502
Birmingham, B. C., 502
Birnbaum, J., 173-75
Birrien, J. L., 334
Bisgaard, M., 347
Bishop, C. C. Jr., 140
Bishop, C. W., 406
Bishop, D. H. L., 625, 637, 638
Bishop, N. I., 523
Bishop, P. E., 190
Bistner, S. I., 238
Björn, G. S., 499
Björn, L. O., 499
Black, F. T., 87, 90
Black, H. S., 244, 250, 253
Black, R., 343
Blackburn, T. H., 435
Blackburn, W. R., 596
Blackstein, M. E., 624
Bladen, H. A., 604
Blake, P., 357
BLAKE, P. A., 341-67; 355, 357-60, 364
Blakemore, R., 95, 679, 680
Blakemore, R. P., 95
Blakesly, R. W., 151
Blanden, R. V., 596, 599, 600
Blatt, B. A., 604
Blaustein, D. I., 700
Bleaney, R. C., 165
Blech, J. E., 406
Blobel, G., 62, 396, 402, 404-6, 408
Blobel, H., 585, 586
Blomberg, C., 404
Bloom, B. R., 595
Bloomfield, V., 152
Blough, H. A., 624
Blount, J. F., 160
Blumer, S., 125
Blyth, A. A., 239
Boccardo, G., 63
Bocker, H., 221, 222
Bode, W., 78, 83
Bodey, G. P., 175
Bodwin, J. S., 660
Boeck, L. D., 161, 164, 168, 169
Boehler-Kohler, B. A., 378, 380, 383
Boghosian, A., 147, 150
Bogorad, L., 499, 506
Bohacek, J., 563
Bohlke, K. W., 55
Bolen, J. L., 354
Bolewska, K., 152
Bolhofer, W. A., 538, 552
Bolle, A., 153
Bollum, F. J., 140
Bona, C., 333, 334
Bonaly, R., 313
Bonanto, M. V., 314
Bonatti, S., 402
Bone, D. H., 512
Bonen, L., 506, 510, 679, 680
Bonfils, J., 683, 686, 688, 690, 704
Bong, F. B., 599, 600
Bonissol, C., 678, 688
Boon, J. P., 77
Boonstra, J., 444
Boos, W., 378-80, 383, 398, 409
Booth, C., 114
Borbely, G., 503, 505
Bordeleau, L. M., 192, 193
Borek, F., 604
Borelli, D., 121
Borichewski, R. M., 275
Bornstein, P., 604
Borovian, G. E., 563
Borrias, W. E., 526, 527
Borsos, T., 332
Borstein, B. T., 435
Bosch, V., 390, 396
Boschek, C. B., 625
Bose, B., 351
Bose, R., 227
Bose, R. J., 140
Bose, S. K., 227, 290
Bosselia, A. A., 245
Bost, P. E., 165
Bostian, K. A., 50-53, 55, 56, 61, 62, 65
Bothe, H., 195, 199, 201, 202, 498-501, 504, 505, 511, 513, 518, 521-25
Botstein, D., 650
Bott, K., 141, 142
Bott, K. F., 228
Bottomley, P. J., 503, 505, 517, 518, 522
Bottomly, F., 184
Bottone, E. J., 647, 648
Bouanchaud, D. H., 485, 586
Boucher, C., 649, 650, 654-56
Bouhet, J. C., 239, 241, 252
Boulter, D., 500
Boutibonnes, P., 241
Bové, J. M., 678-92, 694-704
Bowen, C. C., 504
Bowen, R. A., 290, 300
Bowmer, E. J., 353
Bowyer, J. W., 688
Box, S. J., 174, 176
Box, V., 516
Boxer, D. H., 268
Boyce, J. M., 352, 354, 357
Boyd, M. F., 114
Boyer, H. W., 469, 470, 475
Boyle, T. T., 170
Bozarth, R. F., 51-53, 56-58
Bradford, W. L., 562
Bradfute, O. E., 689
Bradley, C. H., 166
Bradley, D., 153
Bradley, S., 518

Bragg, P. D., 372, 382, 384, 385, 389, 390
Braley, S. A., 273
Bramucci, M. G., 473
Brand, J. J., 512
Brandl, E., 161, 163
Brandon, C., 140-42, 154
Brandon, C. R., 138
Branion, R. M. R., 272-74
Brannon, D. R., 165, 168, 170
Brault, J., 125
Braun, V., 370, 377-79, 384, 385, 388, 390, 395-97, 408, 412, 415, 480
Bray, R. C., 185
Brazhnikova, M. G., 554
Breazeale, V. D., 516
Bredt, W., 699
Breeze, R. H., 189
Breindl, M., 621
Brenchley, J. E., 218
Brennan, V., 57, 60, 62, 65
Brenner, D. J., 351, 363, 567, 573, 574, 648, 653, 666
Bressen, R. A., 518
Brewer, S. J., 166, 170
Brice, J. M., 187
Brickman, E., 668
Brierley, C. L., 264, 267, 268, 271, 273-75, 278
Brierley, J. A., 264, 267, 273
Brill, W. J., 185, 189, 190
Brillinger, G. V., 211
Briman, A., 224
Brinkerhoff, L. A., 647
Brinton, C. C., 467
Brinton, L. P., 683, 689, 704
Broadhurst, J., 647
Broadhurst, M. K., 404
Brock, K. M., 273
Brock, T. D., 267, 268, 273, 279
Brodsky, B. C., 540, 552
Brotzu, G., 162
Brown, A., 290, 448
Brown, A. G., 173-77
Brown, B. L., 95
Brown, C. M., 217, 226, 227
Brown, D. A., 73
Brown, D. G., 265
Brown, D. H., 514
Brown, D. T., 622
Brown, G. W., 503, 514
Brown, J. P., 244
Brown, J. W., 485, 487
Brown, R. G., 499
Brown, S. L., 146
Brownlee, I., 476
Brox, L., 239, 253
Bruenn, J., 56-62, 65
BRUENN, J. A., 49-68; 50, 53-55, 60-62, 65
Brumpt, E., 125
Brun, Y., 580, 581
Brunton, L. L., 466
Brutlag, D., 584
Bruynesteyn, A., 267, 272, 274-76
Bryant, D. A., 45, 499
Bryant, M. P., 430, 432, 438, 450, 457
Bryner, L. C., 271, 273, 274, 276, 277, 280
Buc, H., 315
Buchanan, B. B., 516
Buchanan, G. E., 648, 666, 667
Buchanan, J. G., 570
Buchanan, R. E., 435, 647, 679, 681
Buchanan, T. M., 290, 299
Buchanan-Wollston, V., 655
Büchel, D. E., 384, 395, 408
Büchi, G., 244, 245, 249, 255, 256
Buck, K. W., 50, 52, 53, 55, 56, 58, 63
Buckley, H., 112
Bugie, E., 538
Buhles, W. C., 583
Bulen, W. A., 189, 195-98
Bull, A., 424
Bullen, J., 480
Bullivant, S., 86
Bu'Lock, J. D., 211, 226, 273, 424, 458
Bültmann, B., 314, 329
Bunt, J. S., 510
Burd, J. F., 151
Burdash, N. M., 71
Burdette, W. J., 236
Burgdorfer, W., 678, 683, 689, 704
Burger, M. M., 327
Burgess, B. K., 196
Burgess, J., 688, 696, 700
Burgess, M. N., 466, 470
Burk, D., 186
Burlot, R., 681
Burnett, J. P., 56, 63
Burns, M. J., 360, 362
Burns, R. C., 184, 185, 196-98, 201, 511
Burris, R. H., 184, 187, 192, 193, 195, 198, 498, 507, 511, 513, 521-25
Burrows, M. R., 467
Burton, C. E., 224
Burton, D., 517
Burton, K., 144
Busby, W. F. Jr., 249, 254-56
Bush, J. A., 193
Bussey, H., 50, 51, 62
Bussmann, K., 393
Bustin, M., 605
Butler, T., 483
Butler, W. H., 242
Butler, W. L., 499
Butler, W. T., 604
Butterworth, D., 162, 174, 176
Button, D., 570, 571
Byrne, G. I., 289, 290
Bywater, R. J., 466, 470

C

Cabello, F., 481
Cacciari, I., 192, 193
Calavan, E. C., 678, 683, 688, 691, 692, 695, 698, 701, 704
Caldwell, D. E., 499, 507
CALDWELL, H. D., 285-309; 290, 295, 296
Calef, E., 605
Calia, F. M., 354
Caliguiri, L. A., 638
Calladine, C. R., 78, 89, 90
Callen, D. F., 236, 251
Callis, J. J., 598
Cameronwood, J., 162
Cammack, R., 500, 520
Camp, L. B., 125
Campbell, A., 53
Campbell, C. T., 237
Campbell, F. C., 187, 199
Campbell, J. L., 148
Campbell, N. E. R., 200
Campbell, P. A., 333
Campbell, T. C., 237
Campos, J. M., 655
Canale-Parola, E., 70, 100, 101, 433, 446, 455, 563, 679, 681, 699, 700
Cancedda, R., 396, 404, 408
Cannon, F. C., 527
Cannon, M. C., 527
Cánovas, J. L., 23
Canvin, D. T., 502
Capco, G. R., 144
Capone, J. J., 161, 166
Caraway, B. H., 90, 91, 95
Caraway, C. T., 364
Carbonelle, E., 239
Cardemil, L., 519
Cardenas, J., 500
Carelli, C., 326
Carey, K. E., 97
Carey, N. H., 625
Carithers, R. P., 500, 501, 511
Carlson, F. D., 77
Carlson, J., 444, 451
Carlson, K., 148
Carmichael, J. W., 119-21, 123-26, 128
Carmichael, W. W., 498, 511
Caroli, G., 362
Carpenter, E. J., 194, 510, 513
Carr, D. L., 576, 578, 579

Carr, N. G., 498, 500, 503, 505, 506, 518, 520-22, 526
Carrington, G. O., 353, 360-62
Carrión, A. L., 123
Carruthers, M. M., 354, 355
Carson, J., 412
Carter, I. S., 188
Carter, K. R., 200, 506
Carter, S. B., 239
Casadaban, M. J., 397
Casella, E., 147, 154
Cash, R. A., 476
Cashavska, J., 498
Cashmore, A. R., 404
Caspari, D., 437
Caspary, E. A., 328
Cassidy, P., 173
Cassidy, P. J., 173, 175
Castellani, A., 127
Castenholz, R. W., 497, 504
Castets, A. M., 45, 499
Castillo, F., 500
Catlin, G. H., 625
Cattaneo, J., 441
Caudwell, A., 691
Cawthorne, M. A., 563
Cedergren, R. J., 506, 514, 515
Celada, J., 273
Celmer, W. D., 552, 554
Celozzi, E., 170
Chabbert, Y. A., 586
Chai, T. J., 373-78, 381
Chain, E., 160, 162
Chain, E. B., 56, 162
Chaitchik, S., 605
Chalcroft, J. P., 86
Chalmers, A. J., 127
Chambers, L. A., 273
Chambers, R. S., 427, 432
Champion, A. B., 572
Chan, H. W., 151
Chan, J. A., 165
Chan, P. K., 238, 239
Chandler, J. W., 290, 301, 302
Chang, B., 466
Chang, C. J., 214, 215, 686
Chang, C. N., 405, 406, 408
Chang, J. Y., 82
Chanock, R. M., 678, 682
Chany, E., 245
Chao, J., 143, 144
Chao, L., 504
Chaplin, A. E., 504, 519
Charbonneaux, D. L., 691
Charney, J., 538, 552
Charney, W., 543
Chase, D. G., 467, 468, 476
Chater, K. F., 63
Chatt, J., 196-98
Chattaway, W. F., 216
CHATTERJEE, A. K., 645-76; 647-54, 656, 657, 664-69, 671
Chatterjee, B. D., 102, 466
Chatton, E., 41
Chattopadhyay, P. K., 388
Cheatum, E. L., 583
Chedid, L., 312, 315, 317, 323-27, 329-31, 333, 334, 614
Chen, C. H., 195
Chen, C. S., 681
Chen, J. S., 185, 199
Chen, K. N., 679, 680
Chen, L., 466
Chen, R., 375, 384
Chen, S. H., 76, 77, 99
Chen, T. A., 678, 681-83, 686-89, 691-95, 697, 700
Chen, Y., 215
Cheng, E., 390
Cheng, K. H., 503
Cheng, K.-J., 658, 660
Cheng, Y. E., 227
Chenu, E., 319
Cheremisinoff, N. P., 426, 428
Cherrier, C., 451, 452
Chesson, A., 118
Chiang, W. T., 290, 302
Chien, I., 634
Chien, W-S., 513, 514, 516, 521
Child, J. J., 192
Childs, G., 394, 416
Chilton, M.-D., 647, 650
Chimori, M., 320
Chinn, J. S., 296
Chipley, J. R., 250
Chisnel, J. R., 185
Chiu, C.-S., 143, 144
Chiykowski, L., 691
Cho, J. J., 649, 650
Choay, J., 317, 324, 614
Choc, T., 426, 430, 458
Choi, E., 236, 251
Chollett, R., 502
Choppin, P. W., 620, 624-26, 637, 641
Chopra, I., 379, 489
Chow, N. L., 57, 624, 630
Chow, T. C., 611
Christ, W., 238
Christen, U., 516
Christenson, C. M., 492
Christiansen, C., 87, 90, 474, 686, 687, 691
Christiansen, G., 474
Christman, J. K., 63
Chu, F. S., 237, 245, 250
Chu, J. Y. R., 166
Chua, N. H., 404
Chun, D., 353
Chung, J. K., 353
Chuong, P. P. V., 252
Chupp, C., 126
Ciegler, A., 238, 240, 250
Ciferri, R., 120, 123
Cinader, B., 597
Ciorbaru, R., 317-19, 322, 323, 325, 327, 614
Cirillo, V. P., 681
Cirovic, M., 544
Clark, H F., 678, 681, 683, 691, 696, 704
Clark, R. H., 273
Clark, S., 150
Clark, T. B., 683, 688, 690, 704
Clark, W. A., 71, 110, 357
Clarke, S. K. R., 300
Clay, T., 587
Clayton, R. K., 497, 499
Clegg, S., 467
Clement, J. M., 394, 395, 397, 399-401, 403, 404
Clements, J. D., 466
Clewell, D. B., 95
Clewley, J. P., 625, 637, 638
Clifford, J. I., 253
Cline, J. C., 239
Clyde, W. A. Jr., 682
Coan, M. E., 685, 688-97, 704
Cobley, J. G., 268
Codd, G. A., 499-503, 513, 514, 520-23
Codner, R. C., 118, 665
Coetzee, J. N., 657
Cogliano, R. C., 598
Cohen, B. L., 219
Cohen, J. J., 333
Cohen, J. O., 560, 579
Cohen, S. N., 585
Cohen, S. S., 138, 140, 141, 143
Cohen, Y., 504, 522
Cohen-Bazire, G., 24, 27-31, 44, 45, 498, 499, 505, 506
Cohn, F., 562
Cohn, M., 19
Cohn, M. S., 64
Cole, C. N., 624
Cole, G. T., 112, 113, 115, 126, 129
Cole, M., 162, 174, 176, 177
Cole, R. M., 687, 688, 692, 696, 698, 699, 702, 703
Coles, E. H., 579
Collins, A. R., 290, 295
Collins, M., 499, 583
Collinsworth, W. L., 143
Collmer, A., 666, 667
Collum, P., 544
Colman, B., 502, 503, 521
Colmer, A. R., 267, 538
Colover, J., 328
Colwell, R. R., 348, 353, 359, 364, 648
Compans, R. W., 623-25, 628
Compere, A. L., 436
Concalves, J. C., 427, 432
Condit, P. K., 485, 487

Connolly, J. C., 649, 650
Connors, W. J., 439
Consden, R., 328
Constantin, M., 119
Content, J., 628
Conti, S. F., 94
Contopoulou, R., 33, 34, 40
Cook, B., 563
Cook, C. M., 502
Cook, J. H., 71
Cook, K. A., 185
Cook, R. A., 599
Cook, S. J., 150
Cooke, W. B., 119
Cooksey, K. E., 510
Coon, J., 318
Cooney, C. L., 431, 457-59
Coot, J. G., 228
Coplin, D. L., 649-51, 655, 656
Corbett, D. F., 173-75
Corbin, J. L., 196
Corey, R. R., 656, 659
Cornelius, M. J., 502
Corrans, I. J., 263
Corrick, J. D., 271, 272
Corse, J., 161, 163
Cory, S., 57
Cossar, J. D., 499
Costerton, J. W., 658, 660
Cote, C., 404
Cote, W. A., 428-30
Cotton, F. A., 602
Cotty, P. J., 697, 700
Coulton, J. W., 86, 385
Counelis, M., 543
Counts, G. W., 477, 479
Courvalin, P., 586
Cousin, M. T., 691
Cove, D. J., 219, 220, 225, 229
Cowan, P. M., 603
Cowan, S. T., 562, 564
Cowley, C. M., 466, 470
Cowling, E. B., 428, 429, 439
Cox, B. S., 53, 55
Cox, G. B., 480
Cox, J. C., 268
Crab, W. E., 584
Craig, J. P., 364, 472, 595, 598
Cramer, S. P., 185
Crandell, J. F., 468, 469, 474
Crane, F. L., 499
Crang, R. E., 119
Cravioto, A., 470, 471, 476
Crawford, N. A., 516
Creech, W. B., 355
Crespi, H. L., 501
Cresswell, J. M., 654
Creuzet, N., 440, 441
Crist, M. Y., 129, 130
Crokaert, F., 347, 350, 360-62
Crosa, J. H., 468, 469, 474, 491
Crosby, L. K., 144
Crosse, J. E., 662
Crothers, D. M., 152
Crowell, C. D., 441, 454
Crowlesmith, I., 391
Croy, R. G., 249, 254-56
Cruickshank, C. N. D., 130
Crumpton, M. J., 601
Crumpton, W. M., 625, 635, 642
Csatorday, K., 499, 505
Cseke, C., 503, 505
Cullen, W. P., 552, 554
Culver, D. A., 502
Cummins, C. S., 315, 327, 569
Curlin, G., 466
Curlin, G. T., 352, 354, 357
Currie, S. A., 168, 169, 173-75
Currier, R. W., 286, 290, 303
Currier, T. C., 498, 526
Curry, J. C., 563
Curti, B., 501
Curtis, C., 255
Cutchfield, E. D., 114
Cutler, R. R., 489
Cynkin, M. A., 670
Cysewski, G. R., 456, 458
Czajkowski, J., 78

D

Dabinett, P. E., 112, 115, 130
Daborne, G. R., 278
Dabrowa, N., 125
Dafni, Z., 472
Dagley, S., 429
Dahlquist, F. W., 73
Dahms, R. P., 242
Dakin, W. P. H., 346, 350
Dale, B., 426, 430, 458
Dalibart, R., 684, 685
Dallas, W. S., 471-73, 475, 490
Dalton, H., 185-88, 192, 193, 506
Damais, C., 324, 325, 333, 334
D'Amato, R. F., 117, 343
Danbara, H., 481
D'Andrea, A. D., 255, 256
Dang, Van A., 485
Daniel, R. M., 190
Daniel, R. R., 346, 348, 349
Daniels, L. D., 432, 436, 437, 448-50
Daniels, M. J., 678, 679, 683, 684, 688, 695-97, 699, 700, 704
Daniels, P. J. L., 542, 545
Dantzig, A. H., 220, 229
Daoust, D., 173
Daoust, D. R., 170
Darila, G., 224
Darland, G. K., 268, 273
Darling, S. T., 124
Darlington, A. J., 219
Darnell, J. E., 49, 53
da Rocha-Lima, H., 124
Darougar, S., 290, 299, 300
Das, A., 250
Datta, D. B., 386, 389, 391, 411, 415
Datta, N., 483
Daum, S. J., 214, 229
Dave, C. V., 255
Davidson, N., 57, 586
Davies, D. L., 478, 479
Davies, J. A., 290, 300
Davies, M., 314, 333
Davies, R., 436, 452
Davis, A. R., 620-31, 633, 634, 636-38, 642, 643
Davis, B. D., 404, 407, 408
Davis, B. R., 351, 666
Davis, C. E., 485
Davis, D. B., 271, 274, 276, 277
Davis, D. H., 39
Davis, D. J., 501
Davis, J., 353, 357
Davis, N. E., 161, 164
Davis, R. E., 678, 679, 681-92, 694-96, 698, 699, 704
Davis, R. W., 586
Davison, A. L., 571
Dawes, E. A., 188, 446, 452
Dawson, C. R., 286, 288, 293, 297, 298, 301-4
Day, P. R., 51
De, B. K., 620-25, 627-29, 636-38, 642
De, S. P., 352, 353, 356
de Almeida, F., 125
Dean, D. F., 129, 130
Dean, W., 268
Deb, B. C., 352, 353, 356
de Bertoldi, M., 115
de Beurmann, L., 128
De Boer, W. E., 101-3
De Bont, J. A. M., 191, 192
Decad, G. M., 377, 379
Decker, K., 444, 445, 451
Defranco, A. L., 90
Degorge-Dumas, J.-R., 680, 682, 686-91, 695
de Graaf, F. K., 467, 475
de Graaff, J., 485, 575
deGraaff, P., 373, 374
deGraaff, P. J., 373, 389
De Greve, H., 651
de Hoog, G. S., 112, 115, 119, 122, 123, 127, 128
Deibel, R. H., 564
Deighton, F. C., 126
De Jong, M. H., 92, 99, 100
de La Hunt, A., 238
Delaney, S. F., 526
Delange, R. J., 82
Del Campo, F. F., 500
De Leij, L., 409, 414, 416

DeLeo, A. B., 218
DeLey, J., 567, 569, 647
De Long, C. W., 213
DeLong, D. C., 239
Demain, A. L., 163, 165, 166, 168, 210-14, 216, 220, 227, 239, 241, 244, 245, 254, 255, 431, 435, 440
Demarco, P. V., 172
DeMartini, M., 381
Demasius, I. P. C., 239, 241-45, 250, 251, 253
De Matteis, F., 238
Demny, T. C., 160
de Monbreun, W. A., 124
DeMoss, R. D., 445
Demoulin, V., 110
den Dooren de Jong, L. E., 38
Deneke, C. F., 467
Denhardt, D. T., 573
DePamphilis, M. L., 86, 90
de Reuver, M. J., 607
DeRosa, M., 273
Derry, R., 271, 278
Deruelles, J., 45, 507, 510
Dervartanian, D. V., 188, 189
Der Vartanian, M., 499, 500
Desruisseaux, H., 404
Desselberger, U., 625, 634
Dessens-Kroon, M., 485
Destombes, P., 114
DeVault, R. L., 544
DeVay, J. E., 647, 659
Devillers-Thiery, A., 404
Devoret, R., 250, 251
Devos, A. H., 576
DeVries, W., 434, 444, 445, 451, 454
Devriese, L. A., 565, 568-71, 573, 574, 576, 580-82, 584
de Waard, A., 144
DeWatcher, R., 630
deZeener, I. W., 457
De Zoeten, G. A., 659
Dharmawardene, M. W. N., 512-16
Dhir, S. P., 290, 294, 295, 297
Dick, H. L. N., 498
Dickens, F., 238, 240, 242
Dickinson, C. H., 646-48, 659
DiCosmo, F., 112
Diedrich, D. L., 373-75, 381, 385
Dieterle, R., 378, 380, 383
Dietrich, P. S., 244
Dietzel, I., 409
Dietzschold, B., 598
Diez, J., 501, 522, 524
Digranes, A., 569, 571, 581
Dilworth, M. J., 192, 194
Dimmitt, K., 84
Dimmling, W., 428
Dimmock, N. J., 625, 635, 642
Din, G. A., 269
Dinarello, C. A., 329
Dingman, C. W., 250, 253
DiPaolo, J. A., 250
Diplock, A. T., 563
DiRenzo, A. B., 144
DiRienzo, J. M., 370, 372, 388, 390, 393, 394, 402, 406, 411, 414, 660
Distler, E., 195, 199, 523
Dixon, R., 191
Dixon, R. O. D., 200-2
Dmitrieva, E. Y., 506
Doane, W. M., 428, 430
Dobberstein, B., 396, 404
Dobereiner, J., 506
Dodd, H., 125
Doddema, H. J., 433
Dodgson, J. B., 151
Doelle, W. H., 441, 445, 446, 452
DOETSCH, R. N., 69-108; 74-76, 91, 93, 96, 100, 101
Doherty, P. C., 599, 600
Döhler, G., 503
Dohner, D., 634
Doi, R. H., 227
Doi, Y., 56, 678
Dolimpio, D. A., 250
Dondero, N. C., 95
Donnelly, A. J., 238
Donohue, T. J., 228
Donohue-Rolfe, A. M., 413
Donovan, T. J., 343, 345, 348, 362, 363
Donta, S. T., 354
Doolin, L. E., 169, 216
Doolittle, W. F., 498, 505, 506, 510, 526
Dornbusch, K., 486
Dorner, F., 472
Dosmar, M., 147, 150, 154
Dostal, J., 97
Doster, R. C., 238
Doty, P., 139, 141
Doudoroff, M., 19, 33, 34, 39, 40, 101, 102, 514, 647
Dougan, G., 475, 490
Douglas, C. W. I., 74
Douthart, R. J., 56, 63
Dow, C. S., 270
Downs, A. J., 187
Dowson, W. J., 648, 666
Doyle, F. P., 162
Drake, J. W., 152
Drapier, J-C., 331
Drawert, H., 513
Drechsler, C., 130, 131
Drew, S. W., 210, 216
Drexler, H., 655
Drift, C. van der, 433
Drozd, J., 187, 189
Drozd, J. W., 187, 189
Drummond, M., 647, 650
Drummond, M. H., 647, 650
Drusin, L. M., 585
Dubois, E., 219, 225
Duck, K., 427
Dudgeon, L. S., 561, 562
Dudman, W. F., 190, 192, 193
Duesberg, P., 628
Duesberg, P. H., 625
Du Four, E. H., 319
Dugan, P. R., 267, 275
Dugdale, R. C., 510
Duguid, J. P., 498
Dukes, D., 315
Dulaney, E. L., 212
Dumon, L., 177
Duncan, B. K., 145, 150, 152, 153
Duncan, C. L., 492
Duncan, D. W., 265-68, 271, 274-76, 279
Duncan, J., 145
Dunez, J., 681
Dunham, L. F., 145, 149, 150, 153
Dunlop, E. M. C., 290, 299
Dunlop, P., 224
Dunn, E., 219
Dunn, J., 61
Dunn-Coleman, N. S., 220
Dunny, G. M., 95
du Pasquier, P., 652
Dupont, G., 678, 680, 683-85, 687, 688, 701
DuPont, H. L., 467, 470
DuPreez, N. P., 239
du Rand, M., 244
Durfee, P. T., 286, 290, 303
Durham, D. R., 568
Durkin, J. P., 177
Durston, W. E., 236
Duthil, P., 684, 688
Dutrizac, J. E., 266, 273, 274
Dutton, J. E., 501
Dye, D. W., 648, 665
Dyer, T., 679, 680

E

Eady, R., 191
Eady, R. R., 185, 190, 196-98, 511
Earhart, C. F., 386
Eastlake, A., 602
Eccles, S. J., 379
Eccleston, M., 270, 273
Echandi, E., 651
Echeverria, P., 471, 474
Eddie, B., 289, 290, 303
Edelbluth, C., 85, 402
Edelman, I., 489, 585
Eden-Green, S. J., 662, 663
Edlin, G. J., 153

Edstrom, R. D., 665
Edward, D. G., 679, 684
Edwards, G. S., 240, 242
Edwards, J. P., 161, 163
Edwards, T., 432
Edwards, T. F., 97
Edwards, V. H., 430
Egan, R. S., 544
Eglington, A. J., 173-75
Ehle, H., 225
Ehrenkranz, N. J., 353, 357
Ehrlich, H. K., 266
Ehrlich, H. L., 267, 269, 271, 275, 279, 280
Ehrlich, K., 141, 146
Ehrlich, M., 140-42, 146, 154
Eichorn, H. H., 584
Eidam, E., 130, 131
Eidson, M., 483, 585
Eirich, D., 436, 449
Eisbrenner, G., 195, 199, 201, 202, 498-500, 504, 505, 511, 513, 518, 521-25
Eisele, T. A., 255
Eisenstark, A., 579
Eissa, M. H., 245
Elander, R. P., 163
El-Banoby, F. E., 659
Elek, S. D., 560, 561, 579, 582
Elfvin, M. J., 700
Elin, R. J., 329
Elis, J., 250
El-Kady, I., 250
El-Kammah, B., 245
Elkan, G. H., 219
El-Kirdassi, Z. H. M., 245
Eller, J. J., 596
Elliott, B. B., 517
Elliott, J., 192
Ellis, J. J., 129
Ellis, L. F., 56, 63
Ellis, M. B., 123
Ellis, R. J., 404
Ellms, J. W., 523
Ellouz, F., 319, 322, 323, 614
Ellwood, P. C., 444, 451
Eloff, J. N., 502
Elson, S. W., 176
Elvidge, J. A., 22
ELWELL, L. P., 465-96; 485, 586
Ely, B., 87
El-Zawahri, M., 250
Emerich, D. W., 200-2, 506, 511
Emerson, S. U., 84, 623, 630
Emmett, M., 568, 587
Emmons, C. W., 120, 121, 123, 126, 130
Emond, D., 514, 515
Emr, S. D., 397, 399-401, 403, 404
Emtage, J. S., 625
Ende, D., 147, 150
Endermann, R., 385, 388, 389, 392
Enders, T. F., 595
Eng, N. T., 126, 130
Engbaek, F., 397
Engel, J., 78, 604
Engelke, J. A., 200
England, T. E., 633
English, M., 290, 301, 302
English, M. G., 290, 301
English, V. L., 360-62
Englund, B., 498
Enomoto, M., 236, 238-40
Ensign, J. C., 570
Ensley, B., 441
Enticott, S., 514, 515, 517
Epstein, D. A., 634
Epstein, R. H., 153
Epstein, S. S., 238
Erdman, M. D., 459
Erickson, J., 245
Erickson, S. K., 188
Erikson, D., 538
Erikson, R. L., 144
Eriksson, K. E., 439
Eriksson, U., 197, 511
Erno, H., 686
Ernst, A., 524
Eschenbach, D. A., 290, 299
Eskridge, N., 483
Esmon, B., 225
Espin, G., 223, 224, 229
Essigmann, J. M., 242, 243, 249, 254-56
Estep, M., 499
Eubanks, E. R., 79
Eulderink, F., 583
Eustace, G. C., 162
Evans, C. A., 581
Evans, D. G., 466-68, 470, 472, 476
Evans, D. J., 466-68, 470, 472, 476
Evans, E. H., 499, 503
Evans, H. J., 190, 192, 200-2, 506
Evans, J. B., 562-64, 568, 569
Evans, L. G., 271, 272, 274
Evans, M. A., 241
Evans, M. C. W., 92, 93, 185, 500, 511, 522
Evans, N., 467, 476
Evans, W. C., 19, 22, 457
Evans, W. R., 523
Even, H. L., 223, 224
Evstigneev, V. B., 523
Ewing, H. E., 586
Ewing, W. H., 648, 666
Eyssen, H., 165, 177

F

Fabry, L., 239
Fager, E. E., 544
Fahlbusch, K., 219
Falkenberg, B., 500, 522
Falkner, G., 499
Falkow, S., 288, 466-75, 477-79, 482, 485, 490, 491, 567, 573, 574, 585, 586, 650
Fan, L. T., 439
Fan, V. S. C., 290, 293
Fang, H., 458, 459
Fanning, G. R., 567, 573, 574, 648, 653, 666
Farkas, G. L., 503, 505
Farmer, J. J. III, 357
Farmilo, A. J., 624
Farrah, S. R., 95
Farran, J. D., 168
Farrar, W. E., 483, 585
Farrior, J. W., 584
Farro, A., 683, 686, 690, 704
Farthing, J. E., 166
Faulkner, P., 622
Faure, J. P., 329
Fawcett, P., 166
Fawcett, P. A., 165, 166
Fay, P., 497, 498, 510, 519
Fearrington, E. L., 347, 350
Fedorov, M. W., 191
Feeley, J. C., 343, 346, 350, 364, 492
Fein, J. E., 87
Feldman, R. A., 364
Fellerberg, R. von, 597
Feltham, R. K. A., 569, 575, 576
Feng, T. Y., 146
Fennell, D. I., 112
Ferenci, T., 378-80, 393
Fernandez, C. R., 357, 359
Fevrier, M., 334
Fiebig, K., 437, 450
Field, E. J., 328
Field, M., 466
Fife, M. A., 648
Filippi, S., 362
Filloy, L., 350
Fink, G. R., 50, 51, 55-60, 62, 64
Finkelstein, R. A., 466, 477, 479, 480
Fischer, I., 57, 65
Fisher, J. R., 278
Fisher, R. J., 189
Fisher, R. W., 499
Fisher, W. P., 538, 552
Fisk, R. T., 585
Fiss, E. H., 386, 387
Fitzer, H., 379
Fitzgerald, G. P., 498, 507, 511
Fitzpatrick, T. B., 32
Flanegan, J. B., 143, 144
Fleck, J., 319, 322, 325, 326, 333, 334, 613, 614, 679, 700, 702

Fleischman, R. A., 148
Fleishchaker, R., 459
Fleming, A., 160, 162
Fleming, H., 512, 513
Fleming, J., 476
Fleming, R. H., 96
Fleming, W. H., 143
Fletcher, A. W., 271
Fletcher, C. M., 162
Fleurette, J., 580, 581
Flickinger, M. C., 427, 458
Fliers, W., 630
Floc'h, F., 318, 320, 322, 331, 613
Florent, J., 431, 459
Flores, L., 624
Florey, H. W., 162
Floss, H. G., 214-16
Flügge, C., 562
Flynn, E. H., 161, 166
Fogarty, W. M., 439, 441
Fogg, G. E., 497, 498, 517
Foit, B., 225
Foley, G. E., 239
Folk, W. R., 141, 148, 149
Follman, H., 516
Fontaine, F. E., 434
Forchhammer, J., 397
Forgan-Smith, W. R., 353, 360-62
Forget, P., 440
Formal, S. B., 468
Formey, C. J., 459
Forsyth, P. S., 290, 299
Forsyth, W. G. C., 33
Forsythe, G. W., 466, 470
Fos, A., 683, 686, 688, 690, 704
Fossitt, D. D., 441
Foster, J. W., 192
Foulds, J., 372-79, 381
Fowler, A. V., 395, 399-401, 403, 404
Fowler, K. W., 242, 243, 249, 255, 256
Fox, G. E., 436, 506, 510, 679, 680
Fox, S. I., 275
Foy, R. H., 504
Frabotta, M., 149
Fraenkel-Conrat, H., 602, 607, 608
Fragoso, R., 483
Frampton, E. W., 526
Francisco, M. A., 242, 243, 249, 255, 256
Franco, A., 483
Frank, H. K., 238
Franke, R. G., 112
Frankel, R. B., 95
Franklin, R. M., 56, 59
Franklin, T. J., 239
Frappier, A., 332
Frato, J., 145, 150, 154
Frayssinet, C., 245
Fred, E. B., 425
Fredericks, W. W., 501
Freed, H. J., 250
Freedman, S. O., 605
Freeman, B. A., 79, 701
Freeman, B. H., 583
Freese, E., 228
Freimuth, F., 71
French, C. S., 24
French, P., 441
Frenkel, A. W., 25
Freter, R., 97, 432
Freund, J., 314, 328, 329, 612
Freundt, E. A., 87, 90, 678-80, 683, 684, 686-88, 691, 701
Fridkin, M., 603
Fridovich, I., 502
Fried, H. M., 56-60
Fried, M. L., 360, 362
Friedberg, D., 505
Friedberg, E., 145
Friedberg, E. C., 145, 153
Friedman, H., 334
Friedman, L., 129, 131
Friedman, M., 150
Friedman, R. M., 639
Friedman, S., 569
Friedrich, B., 218, 219
Friedrich, C. G., 218, 219, 221, 222
Friesen, J. D., 55
Friis, R. R., 290
Fritzberg, A., 166
Frobish, R. A., 430, 457
Fromageot, P., 239, 241, 252
Frommell, G. T., 290, 301, 302
Fry, I. V., 500, 520
Fuchs, G., 436, 437, 449, 450
Fuchs, L. A., 353
Fuchs, S., 315, 317, 604
Fudenberg, H. H., 604
Fudl-Allah, A. E.-S. A., 678, 683, 688, 691, 692, 695, 698
Fujii, A., 160
Fujii, S., 538, 553
Fugii, T., 555
Fujime, S., 77
Fujimoto, S., 253
Fujio, H., 597, 603
Fujisawa, Y., 161, 164-66
Fujita, Y., 500, 524
Fukada, K., 153
Fukada, S., 173
Fukagawa, Y., 174-76
Fukai, K., 623
Fukasawa, T., 148
Fukase, H., 168, 169
Fukita, T., 161, 164
Fukuda, A., 98
Fukumi, H., 349
Fukushima, K., 239
Fukuyoshi, S., 349
Fulginiti, V., 596
Fulginiti, V. A., 596
Fuller, W., 59
Fumari, T., 548
Fung, J., 387, 392
Furman, D. P., 290, 303
Furniss, A. L., 343, 345, 348, 362, 363
Furthmayr, H., 604
Furukawa, H., 391
Fusco, P. C., 467
Fuska, J., 245
Fuson, G. B., 112

G

Gaard, G., 659
Gabay, J., 381
Gabinskaya, K. N., 186
Gabra, G. G., 275, 278
Gado, I., 540
Gaffron, H., 34
Gagnon, J., 402
Gaidarjiev, S. S., 271
Gajda, L., 501
Gale, N. L., 269
Galgolev, A. N., 92
Galindo, E., 483
Galliano, M., 501
Galliers, E. M., 228
Gallo, M., 211
Gallon, J. R., 184, 194, 498, 504, 507, 511, 512, 518, 519, 523
Gallop, P. M., 140, 141
Galloway, I. A., 579, 582
Galonsky, A., 513, 514
Galtier, P., 238
Gambocorta, A., 273
Gamon, K., 375
Gamon, L., 704
Gams, W., 118, 119
Ganchev, K. L., 540
Gander, J. E., 112, 412
Gandy, C., 201
Ganesan, A. K., 145, 153
Ganesan, A. T., 150
Gangarosa, E. J., 347, 350-52, 482, 483
Ganguly, A. K., 550, 552
Gantotti, B. V., 650
Gantt, E., 499
Ganzoni, A. M., 480
Garber, E. D., 664
Garcia, E., 517
Garcia-Jurado, O., 680-83, 686-91, 695
Garcia-Martinez, D. V., 435, 440
Gardner, A. D., 162
Gardner, J., 276, 278
Gardner, J. M., 648, 653, 665, 666
Garen, A., 655

Garibaldi, A., 664, 669
Garland, P. B., 268
Garner, R. C., 249, 251
Garnier, M., 703
Garon, C. F., 473, 703
Garrett, A. J., 290, 293
Garrett, C. M. E., 662
Garrett, K. H., 271, 278
Garrison, L., 161, 163
Garrison, R. G., 125
Garten, W., 384, 385, 389, 391, 415, 416
Gasser, C., 572
Gasser, F., 572
Gaur, P. K., 124, 125
Gause, G. F., 554
Gay, R., 451, 452
Gayda, R. C., 387, 393
Gehl, J. M., 501
Geiduschek, E. P., 149
Geiger, B., 601, 602
Geiger, W. B., 538
Geisselsoder, J., 655
Genchev, F. N., 271
Gendel, S., 499, 506
Gentile, F., 545, 552
Gentles, J. C., 130
Georg, L. K., 125
George, H. K., 436
George, R. H., 467, 476, 479, 480
George, T. A., 195
Gepts-Friedenreich, E., 357, 359
Gerloff, R. K., 289, 290, 678, 683, 689, 704
Gersbach, H., 252
Gerster, R., 200
Gertis, J., 657
Gest, H., 24, 184, 219
Ghiorse, W. C., 691
Gho, C., 579
Ghosh, A., 352, 353, 356
Ghosh, A. C., 239, 241, 245
Ghosh, A. K., 352
Ghuysen, J. M., 313, 570
Giam, C. Z., 397, 404, 406, 407, 413
Giambiagi, N., 186
Giannotti, D., 691
Giannotti, J., 691
Giaquinta, R. T., 499
Gibbins, L. N., 647-52
Gibbons, N. E., 435, 679, 681
Gibbons, R. A., 467
Gibbs, M., 501
Gibel, W., 245
Gibson, A. H., 190, 192, 193
Gibson, F., 480
Gibson, J., 497, 506, 679, 680
Gibson, J. L., 501, 502
Gibson, T., 562
Gilani, S. H., 238
Gilbart, J., 699
Gilbert, R. J., 351
Gilbert, W., 151
Gilchrist, T. C., 119, 121
Gill, D. M., 471
Gill, J. E., 140
Gillespie, D., 573
Gillespie, W. A., 585
Gillum, W. O., 185
Gilvarg, C., 379, 380
Gingery, R. E., 689
Ginoza, H. S., 526
Ginther, C. L., 227
Girolami, R. L., 544
Giroud, J-P., 327
Gish, D., 602
Githens, J. H., 596
Glasgow, L. A., 487, 488
Glass, T. L., 438
Glauert, A. M., 79
Glazer, A. N., 45, 82, 84, 499
Gleason, F. H., 129
Gleason, F. K., 506
Glimp, T., 625, 637, 638
Gmeiner, J., 379
Godfrey, O. W., 169, 216
Godzeski, C. W., 168
Goedheer, J. C., 499
Goegelman, R., 173-75
Goering, J. J., 510
Goetz, I. E., 238, 239
Gogotov, I. N., 513
Gogotov, J. N., 191
Gohda, A., 354
Gold, L., 153
Gold, P., 605
Goldberg, E. B., 144
Goldberg, I. D., 141
Goldberg, R. B., 219, 227, 517, 655
Goldblum, A., 151
Goldemberg, J., 427, 432
Goldfarb, D. M., 138
Goldfine, H., 411
Goldman, B. M., 404
Goldmeier, D., 290, 299
Goldstein, A. W., 544
Goldstein, F., 485
Golecki, J. R., 389, 409, 412, 498
Golten, C., 101-3
Golueke, C. G., 428
Gomatos, P. J., 58, 59
Gomes Da Silva, J., 427, 432
Gomez-Lojero, C., 500
Gonzalez, C. F., 650
Gonzalez-Cortes, A., 483
Gooden, D., 220
Goodfellow, M., 568, 575, 648, 659
Gooding, C. A., 301
Goodman, J. W., 611
Goodman, M., 572
Goodman, R. N., 650, 652, 659, 662-64
Goodner, E., 301, 302, 305
Goodner, K., 351
Gorbach, S. L., 175, 466-68, 472, 476
Gordon, D. T., 689
Gordon, F. B., 293
Gordon, J., 458, 459
Gordon, M. A., 118
Gordon, M. H., 561, 562
Gordon, M. P., 647, 650
Goren, M. B., 318
Gorham, M. E., 120, 121
Gorham, P. R., 498, 511
Gorlenko, V. M., 497
Gorman, M., 164, 168, 169
Goshima, K., 354
Goto, M., 659
Goto, S., 172, 173
Gotoff, S. P., 611
Gots, J. S., 99
Gotschlich, E. C., 313, 315
Gottesman, M., 250
Gotto, J. W., 510, 512, 513, 526
Gottschalk, G., 434, 437, 450, 451, 454
Gotz, F., 566, 569-72, 582-84
Gougerot, H., 128
Goulden, S. A., 216
Govindjee, 499
Gow, W. A., 264, 271-73, 277, 278
Goze, A., 251
Gozzer, C., 501
Grabau, E. A., 61, 639, 642
Grabowski, J., 499
Graessle, O. E., 166
Graf, L. H., 466
Gräfe, U., 221, 222
Graham, D. C., 647, 648
Graham, T. L., 660, 661
Granados, R. R., 678, 689, 697
Granboulan, N., 59
Granett, A. L., 678
Grant, P. T., 165, 213
Gratt, R. H., 220
Gray, C. T., 184
Gray, P. H. H., 71
Gray, R. E., 404
Grayston, J. T., 286, 288, 290, 294-99, 305
Grazi, G., 569
Greaves, J. H., 598
Grebenyuk, M. V., 71
Green, R. F., 472
Green, S., 250
Greenberg, E. P., 100, 101, 699, 700
Greenberg, G. R., 143, 144
Greenblatt, M., 242

Greenough, W. B. III, 346, 350, 354
Greenstein, S., 681, 702
Greenway, J. C., 244
Greenwood, R. C., 353
Greer, D. L., 129, 131
Greeves, D., 550
Gregor, H. P., 427
Grenson, M., 219, 225
Greuter, W., 110
Griffin, D. G., 436
Griffith, A. H., 332
Griffiths, D. A., 129
Griffiths, M., 29
Grimes, J. E., 290, 303
Grimont, F., 652
Grimont, P. A. D., 652
Grinsted, J., 649, 650
Grodzinski, B., 502, 521
Groen, F. J., 362
Gromova, L. A., 273
Gronenborn, B., 384, 395, 408
Groner, Y., 57
Groocock, C. M., 598, 611
Groopman, J. D., 254, 255
Grootes-Reuvecamp, G. A., 477
Gros, C., 326, 327
Gross, R. J., 470, 471, 476
Grossman, M., 301, 302, 305
Groudev, S. N., 271
Gruss, A. D., 489
Grutman, G., 239
Grutzner, J. B., 166
Gryczan, T. J., 585
Guay, R., 270-75, 277, 278
Guého, E., 115
Guengerich, F. P., 249
Guerrant, R. L., 466
Guerry, P., 64, 585
Guglielmi, G., 45, 499
Guild, G. M., 61, 624
Guimaraes, W. V., 649, 650, 654
Guinee, P. A., 467
Guiney, D. G., 485
Gumpf, D. J., 678
Gunsalus, C. F., 23
Gunsalus, I. C., 23
Gunsalus, R. P., 436, 449
Gupta, R., 679, 680
Gurtoo, H. L., 237, 242, 255
Gustafson, J., 267, 273, 279
Gutterman, J. U., 332
Guttman, B. S., 150, 152, 153
Guttman, N., 62
Guzewska, J., 219
Gvozdyak, R. I., 71
Gyles, C. L., 466-69, 471, 473-75, 482
Gyllenberg, H. G., 267, 274

H

Haaker, H., 187-90, 200, 512, 517, 522
Haas, P., 373, 379
Habashi, F., 276-78
Habener, J. F., 394, 404
Hack, A. M., 375, 376, 380
Hackette, S. L., 224
Haddock, B. A., 187, 268
Hadfield, K. L., 195, 196, 198
Haferkamp, O., 314, 329
Hafidi, B., 688
Hageman, R. V., 511
Hagenmaier, H., 384, 390, 395, 408
Hagerman, R. V., 184
Haggis, G. H., 691
Hagimoto, D., 318
Haimovich, J., 605
Haimovich, S., 605
Hajek, V., 565, 566, 568-71, 573, 574, 582-84
Hakamura, A., 354
Hakomori, S., 290, 294
Halegoua, S., 388, 393-95, 402, 404, 405, 411, 413, 414
Hall, D. H., 144
Hall, D. O., 500, 513
Hall, H. E., 352, 360
Hall, J. B., 457
Hall, M., 399, 400
Hall, M. N., 373, 410
Hall, R. H., 138
Hallam, S. L., 581
Hallander, H. O., 486
Halldal, P., 504
Hallenbeck, P. C., 511, 513, 523, 524
Hallenbeck, P. S., 523
Haller, I., 373, 385, 389, 411
Hallewell, R. A., 625
Halling, P. J., 268
Halliwell, G., 439, 440
Halls, S., 467
Halpern, B. N., 330
Halpern, Y. S., 219
Hamada, M., 174
Hamadi, A. F., 512
Hamill, R. L., 161, 164, 168, 169
Hamilton, L., 145
Hammerschlag, M. R., 290, 301, 302
Hamon, Y., 385
Hampton, R. O., 190
Hanawalt, P. C., 251, 252
Hancock, R. E. W., 379, 385, 389, 480
Handa, A. K., 518
Handschuh, D., 606
Handsfield, H. H., 290, 298, 300
Handzel, Z. T., 596, 611
Hanert, H., 267
Hankin, L., 51, 666
Hanna, L., 290, 294, 296
Hannah, F. J., 498
Hanscomb, G., 174, 176
Hansen, W., 347, 350, 357, 359-62
Hantke, K., 373, 377, 378, 391, 480
Hanus, F. J., 200, 202, 506
Hanus, J., 200, 201
Harada, K., 315, 329, 549
Harayama, S., 95
Harber, L. C., 32
Harbison, R. D., 240, 241
Hard, G. C., 583
Harder, M. E., 390
Hardies, S. C., 151
Hardy, F. E., 570
Hardy, K. G., 478, 479
Hardy, R. W. F., 184, 185, 196, 198, 201, 511
Hardy, S. J. S., 393, 396, 404, 405, 408
Harish, Z., 611
Harms, E., 625
Harold, F. M., 91, 92
Harper, J. M., 426
Harris, B., 263
Harris, H., 315
Harris, J. I., 606
Harris, L. F., 177
Harris, M., 563, 611
Harris, M. S., 50, 56, 60
Harrison, A., 652
Harrison, D. E. F., 187
Harrison, H. R., 290, 301
Harrison, L., 586
Harrison, M. J., 290, 293
Harrison, V. F., 264, 271-73, 277, 278
Hart, L. T., 79
Hart, M. V., 162
Hartline, F. R., 427, 459
Hartman, P. A., 441
Hartman, P. E., 371, 655, 656
Hasan, S. M., 457
Hase, T., 500
Hasegawa, T., 168, 169, 554
Haselkorn, R., 498, 510, 512, 513, 516, 519, 522, 527
Haseltine, W. A., 255, 256
Hash, J., 320
Hashimoto, K., 21
Hashimoto, M., 160, 170
Hashimoto, S., 315, 320
Hasibuan, M. A., 354
Hasin, M., 696, 698, 701, 702
Haslam, E. A., 145
Haslett, B. G., 500
Hassan, S. I., 346, 350
Hastie, N., 62

Hastie, N. D., 62, 65
Hastings, E. G., 425
Hatanaka, C., 665, 670
Hatano, K., 168, 169, 548, 554
Hatch, T. P., 290, 293
Hathaway, W. E., 596
Hattman, S., 148
Hattori, A., 504, 517, 524
Hattori, M., 554
Haubrich, D., 585
Haury, J. F., 511, 513
Hauser, D. C. R., 95
Havekes, L., 375, 376, 380, 385, 391
Havens, P. L., 129
Hawksworth, D. L., 114
Hawthorne, J. D., 691
Hay, A. J., 627
Hayaishi, O., 20-22
Hayashi, H., 140, 141
Hayashi, M., 459, 555
Hayat, M., 319
Hayes, A. W., 237-41, 245, 252
Hayes, J. R., 237
Hayflick, L., 678, 691
Haystead, A., 511-16, 521
Hayward, A. C., 33
Hazarika, U. R., 347
Hazen, E. E., 602
Healy, J. B., 457
Heath, H. E., 239, 241, 245
Heath, R. B., 611
Heatley, N. G., 162
Heaton, D., 526
Heberlein, G. T., 660
Heczko, P., 568, 575
Hedges, R. W., 654
Hedgpeth, J., 394, 395, 397, 399-401, 403-6
Heeb, M. A., 510
Heffron, F., 470, 473, 490, 585
Hegeman, G. D., 23
Hegge, P., 435, 459
Hegge, P. W., 456
Hegner, R. W., 586
Heiberg, B., 342, 351
Heichel, G. H., 429
Heidelberger, C., 238, 252
Heinze, J. E., 228
Hejtmancik, K. E., 595, 598
Hektoen, L., 127
Heldt, H. W., 499
Helinski, D. R., 477
Hemphill, H. E., 138, 144, 149
Henderson, G. W., 387, 393
Henderson, J. F., 239, 253
Hendlin, D., 168-70, 173-75
Hennebert, G. L., 111
Hennecke, H., 518
Henning, U., 372-75, 384-86, 388-93, 410, 411, 415, 416
Henrichsen, J., 70
Henrici, A. T., 35
Henry, L. E. A., 513
Hense, S. R., 611
Hepner, E., 427
Herchen, S., 166
Herdman, M., 45, 506, 507, 510, 526
Hergert, H. L., 426, 430, 458
Herman, R. C., 634
Hermanides-Nijhof, E. J., 115, 119, 122, 123, 127, 128
Hernalsteens, J. P., 651
Hernandez, S., 168, 169, 173-75
Herrick, F. W., 426, 430, 458
Herring, A. J., 50, 52-58, 62-64
Herrlich, P., 402
Herrmann, V., 498
Hersh, E. M., 332
Hertman, I., 486
Hertzmark, D. I., 427
Herzog, W., 239
Hespell, R. B., 679, 680
Hesseltine, C. W., 129
Heublein, P. C., 357-60
Heymer, B., 314, 326, 327, 329, 332
Hickman, J., 670
Hiepko, P., 110
Higa, H., 360, 362
Higashide, E., 548, 554
Higgens, C. E., 161, 164, 168, 169
Higgins, I. J., 192, 436, 449, 450
Highfield, P. E., 404
Hignett, R. C., 661
Higuchi, M., 492
Hildebrand, D. C., 661
Hill, L. R., 563, 564
Hill, S., 189, 191, 192, 195, 201
Hillmer, P., 219
Hilmen, M., 84
Hilton, A. L., 300
Himmel, N., 290, 294
Himmelweit, F., 56
Hindennach, I., 373-75, 384-86, 389, 391, 393, 410, 411, 415
Hine, P. W., 193
Hine, T. G. M., 561
Hinkle, M. F., 267
Hinojosa, M., 483
Hinze, G., 504
Hippe, H. P., 437
Hirao, K., 238
Hirashima, A., 394, 416
Hirata, S., 174, 175
Hirota, Y., 378, 385-88, 390, 392, 393, 411
Hirsch, M. S., 596
Hirschorn, N., 476
Hirst, G. K., 621, 628
Hiti, A. L., 643
Hitzeman, R., 150
Hitzeman, R. A., 145, 146, 150
Hiu, I. J., 317, 318, 331, 613
Hjelm, H., 327
Hjerten, S., 702
Hnilica, V. S., 215
Ho, K. K., 500
Hoare, D., 44, 503, 505
Hoare, D. S., 313, 514
Hoare, S. L., 514
Hobo, K., 353
Hobson, D., 290, 300
Hobson, P. N., 441
Hobson, S., 457
Hoch, G. E., 195
Hock, B., 404
Hodgkin, D. C., 163
Hodgkiss, W., 648
Hodgson, A., 59
Hodgson, K. O., 185
Hoehn, B., 372, 384
Hoehn, M. M., 161, 164, 168, 169
Hoeniger, J. F. M., 86, 87
Hoffman, P. S., 188
Hofnung, M., 377-79, 394, 395, 399-401, 403-6
Hogenauer, G., 472
Hogg, R., 395
Holland, J. J., 61, 621, 636-39, 642
Holland, L. E., 56-59
Hollander, D. H., 693
Hollaus, F., 435
Hollenberg, C. P., 386, 393, 410, 411
Hollifield, W. C. Jr., 386, 387
Hollis, D., 357
HOLLIS, D. G., 341-67; 344, 347, 350, 351, 353, 357-60
Hollis, J. J. Jr., 684, 688
Holloway, B. W., 653-55
Holm, C., 53, 55
Holm, C. A., 56-59
Holmberg, O., 580
Holmen, A. T., 504
Holmes, K. K., 287, 288, 290, 298-302
Holmes, K. V., 638
Holmes, R. K., 473
Holmgren, J., 466
Holm-Hansen, O., 503, 514
Holt, J., 301, 302, 305
Holt, R. J., 580
Holt, S. C., 700
Holta-Oie, S., 580, 581
Holton, J. B., 316
Holton, R. W., 501
Honda, T., 102, 354
Hood, E. E., 518
Hood, J. D., 174, 176
Hood, R. D., 238, 240
Hood, W., 506
Hopfield, J. J., 584

Hopper, J. E., 50-53, 55, 56, 61, 62, 65
Hopps, H. E., 291
Hopwood, D. A., 210
Horejs, J., 563
Hori, K., 174
Hori, S., 176
Horn, G. T., 151
Hornemann, U., 215
Horner, F., 499
Horning, E. S., 538
Horodniceanu, T., 586
Horoschak, K. D., 290
Horton, D. R., 168
Horvath, L. I., 503
Hosoda, J., 153, 160, 168-72
Hotani, H., 72, 78, 83, 84
Hotnung, M., 397, 399, 400, 403
Hou, C., 372, 384, 388, 400
Houchins, J. P., 193
Howard, B. H., 86
Howard, L. V., 290, 296
Howarth, T. T., 173-75, 177
Howell, D. J., 346, 350
Howsley, R., 510, 513
Hruschka, J., 659
Hsieh, D. P. H., 239, 241-43, 245, 255
Hsu, E., 435, 455
Hsu, S.-T., 662
Hsu, T. A., 426, 430, 458
Hsu, W. H., 657
Hua, S.-S., 650
Huang, A. S., 52, 60, 620, 621, 623, 629, 633, 634, 636, 639, 643
Huang, F-C., 165, 166
Huang, I. Y., 487
Huang, J. S., 315, 650, 659, 662, 663
Huang, P.-Y., 650, 659, 662-64
Huang, T.-C., 141, 185
Huang, T.-S. R., 661
Hubacek, J., 583
Hubbard, J. P., 666-68
Huber, D., 665
Huberman, E., 250
Hucker, G. J., 562
Huddleston, J. A., 165, 166
Huddy, R. B., 565
Huggins, M. B., 467, 468, 478
Hugh, R., 38, 344, 346
Hughes, C., 472, 481
Hughes, J. H., 355
Hughes, J. M., 347, 350-52, 354, 357, 466
Hughes, S. J., 111, 115, 126-29
Hughson, M. R., 272, 278
Hui, S. P., 225
Hulsebos, T., 393, 396
Hummel, R., 566
Humphrey, A. E., 275, 429
Humphreys, J. D., 265
Hungate, R. E., 432, 440, 457
Hunt, N. A., 166
Hunt, P., 698
Hunt, S. D., 273, 278
Hunter, B. I., 141
Hunter, P. A., 467
Hunter, R., 318
Huppert, M., 121
Huq, A., 346, 348, 349
Huq, I., 343
Huq, M. I., 363
Huray, J. F., 498, 526
Hurst, W. E., 238
Hurwitz, J., 148
Husain, K., 659
Hussain, M., 393, 394, 406
Hutber, G. N., 501
Hutchison, J. A., 131
Hutson, K. G., 500, 501
Hwang, J. C., 195
Hynes, M. J., 219

I

Iaccarino, M., 191
Iandolo, J. J., 486
Iannotti, E. L., 438
Iba, H., 98
Ichihara, S., 373, 381, 382, 391, 393, 394, 406
Icho, T., 97, 98
Ide, M., 668
Igarasi, S., 238, 239
Iguchi, E., 170
Iguchi, H., 176
Igwegbe, E. C. K., 678, 683-85, 688, 694, 698
Ihlenfeldt, M. J. A., 506
Iino, T., 70, 81-83, 85, 95, 97, 98
Iinuma, K., 174
Iitor, Y., 239
Iizuka, H., 129, 130
Ikawa, M., 313
Ikeda, T., 357, 359
Ikenaka, K., 323, 614
Iketani, H., 388, 390
Ikewaka, K., 333, 334
Ikkai, T., 74
Ikuta, F., 328
Ilavsky, J., 543, 545
Ilus, T., 241, 244
Imae, Y., 76, 96
Imai, K., 273, 274, 277
Imam, S., 511
Imanaka, H., 160, 168-72
Imanishi, M., 597, 603
Ingle, R. K., 503
Ingledew, W., 268
Ingledew, W. J., 268
Ingraham, J. L., 22
Ingram, J. M., 658, 660
Innes, J. E., 240
Inniss, W. E., 71
Inoue, S., 168, 169, 554
Inouye, H., 393, 405, 406
Inouye, M., 370, 372, 381, 386-88, 390, 393-96, 402, 404-6, 411, 413, 414, 416, 660
Inouye, S., 387, 388, 390, 393, 395
Inui, T., 129, 130
Inukai, M., 393, 394, 406
Iordanescu, S., 585, 586
Irwin, R. S., 129, 130
Isaacson, H. R., 430, 457
Isaacson, M., 347, 349, 350
Isaacson, R. E., 467
Isani, B., 77
Ishibashi, T., 315
Ishii, J., 379, 381, 382, 391
Ishiie, T., 678
Ishijima, T., 678, 696, 698
Ishikawa, E., 492
Ishiko, T., 238, 239
Ishikura, T., 174-76
Issack, R., 190
Ito, J., 149
Ito, K., 384, 396, 404, 405, 408, 409, 411, 414
Ito, M., 554
Ito, R., 623
Ito, T., 239, 242, 243, 250, 355
Itoh, H., 211, 213
Ittig, M., 701, 702
Itzkovitch, I. J., 275
Ivarson, K. C., 274, 276-78
Iwanaga, M., 293
Iwasaki, H., 168, 169
Iwata, S., 315, 317, 319
Iyobe, S., 174

J

Jackson, D. M., 314, 333
Jackson, D. P., 523
Jackson, F. A., 188
Jackson, G. G., 611
Jackson, L. K., 238, 240
Jackson, M., 168, 169, 173-75
Jackson, R. T., 177
Jacob, A. E., 654
Jacobs, B., 466
Jacobson, A., 61
Jacobson, C., 250
Jacobson, C. B., 250
Jacobus, N. V., 175
Jacquemin, J. M., 63
Janda, J. M., 620-25, 627-29, 636-38, 642
Janko, K., 379, 383
Jann, K., 391
Janot, M-M., 319, 323
Jansen, W. H., 467

Janssen, K. A., 527
Jansz, E. R., 503
Janvier, M., 45, 506, 526
Jaret, R. S., 542, 545, 546
Jarosch, R., 74
Jaton, J.-C., 600
Jawetz, E., 290, 294, 296
Jedrzejowski, A., 491
Jeffries, L., 563
Jeffries, T. W., 427, 428
Jeljaszewicz, J., 560, 579
Jenkin, H. M., 290, 293
Jennings, M. A., 162
Jennings, N. T., 200, 201
Jensen, H. C., 538
Jensen, H. L., 9
Jensen, K. F., 151
Jensen, L., 153
Jensen, S. L., 31, 32
Jerusalimsky, N. D., 186
Jevons, M. P., 578
Jewell, W. J., 457
Jimeno-Abendano, J., 671
Jiminez, M., 458
Jinguji, Y., 354
Jirgensons, B., 244, 250, 253
Joe, L. K., 126, 130
Joffe, A. Z., 240
Johansson, I-B., 327
Johansson, K. E., 681, 702
Johansson, V., 376
Johns, A. T., 445
Johns, R. G. S., 315, 317, 613
Johnson, B. F., 23
Johnson, D. E., 35, 354
Johnson, K. E., 573
Johnson, L. D., 61
Johnson, M. J., 186, 424, 434
Johnson, M. W., 96
Johnson, R., 648
Johnson, R. C., 87
Johnson, V. L., 583
Johnsrud, L., 151
Johnston, K. G., 583
Johnston, R. E., 622
Joklik, W. K., 63
Jolivet, M., 326
Jollès, P., 315, 317, 318, 320, 322, 323, 327, 328, 331, 613
Jollick, J. D., 98
Jomon, K., 168-70
Jones, A. L., 685, 689, 692-94
Jones, B. L., 219
Jones, B. R., 290, 298, 299
Jones, C. A., 273, 275
Jones, C. L., 61, 639, 642
Jones, C. W., 186-88, 190
Jones, D., 564
Jones, D. F., 239
Jones, G. W., 97, 467, 498
Jones, H. E. H., 238, 240, 242
Jones, K. W., 129, 130
Jones, L. W., 523
Jones, N. C., 412
Jones, R. G., 161, 163
Jones, R. W., 268
Jong, S. C., 117, 124
Jordan, F. T. W., 678
Jørgensen, B. B., 504
Jorgensen, J., 477, 479
Josefsson, L. G., 393, 405
Joseph, R., 700
Joseph, S. W., 348
Joset-Espardellier, F., 499, 500, 503
Joshi, S., 238
Joyner, J. J., 596
Joys, T. M., 78
Junca, P., 680, 682, 686-91, 695
Jungerman, K., 444, 445, 451
Jüttner, F., 498, 520

K

Kaaden, O.-R., 598
Kabat, E. A., 328, 601
Kabbage, K., 688
Kada, T., 239, 241-43, 245
Kada, Y., 327
Kader, M. M. A., 245
Kadner, R. J., 370, 377, 384
Kado, C. I., 648, 653, 665, 666
Kafkewitz, D., 438
Kagawa, H., 83-85
Kageyama, M., 387
Kahan, F. M., 138, 145, 173-75
Kahan, J. S., 173-75
Kahane, I., 681, 702
Kahn, M., 363
Kalbe, I., 498, 500, 504, 505, 511, 513, 521-25
Kalininskaya, T. A., 191
Kallen, R. G., 140, 141, 152
Kaloostian, G. H., 678, 704
Kamato, S., 554
Kamikubo, T., 459
Kamio, Y., 385, 389, 390
Kamiya, R., 72, 81, 83, 84, 88, 90
Kamiya, T., 160, 170
Kampelmacher, E. H., 362
Kanazawa, H., 388, 390, 394, 400, 402, 403, 406, 416
Kandel, J. S., 51, 52
Kandler, O., 313, 320, 436, 564, 570
Kane, W., 50, 53-61
Kaneko, T., 353, 359
Kanematsu, S., 502
Kanetsuna, F., 313, 315, 327
Kang, A. H., 604
Kang, C. Y., 625, 637, 638
Kano, K., 128
Kanzaki, T., 161, 164-66
Kaper, J., 348, 364
Kapitany, R. A., 466, 470
Kaplan, D. A., 148
Kaplan, H., 604
Kaplan, I., 438
Kaplan, W., 130
Kapral, F. A., 487
Kapteijn, W. M., 434, 444, 451, 454
Karagouni, A. D., 506
Karam, J., 143, 144
Karavaiko, G. I., 273
Karayiannis, P., 290, 300
Karrer, E., 148
Kartha, K. K., 691
Kasper, C. K., 485, 487
Kass, E. H., 32
Kastner, R. E., 168
Katagiri, M., 22
Katamoto, K., 161, 164
Katayama, A., 492
Katchalski, E., 604
Kato, K., 315, 317, 319, 320, 322-24
Kato, M., 315, 317-19, 327, 328, 331, 613
Kato, T., 353
Katoh, H., 356
Katoh, T., 504, 521
Katterman, F., 50, 51, 55-58, 60, 62
Katz, B., 113
Katz, E., 24, 211, 213, 214, 227, 386, 387, 411, 553
Katz, F. N., 408
Katz, G. E., 145
Kaufman, L., 120, 124, 125, 129, 130
Kaufmann, W., 162
Kavern, N., 629
Kawabe, M., 704
Kawai, K., 623
Kawamoto, I., 540, 544, 545
Kawamura, M., 500
Kawamura, Y., 554
Kawata, S., 315, 317, 319, 320, 322, 323
Kayser, F. H., 585
Kazekawa, I., 320
Kazuno, Y., 354
Ke, B., 189, 519
Kean, B. H., 466
Kearns, M. J., 467
Keck, K., 599
Keegstra, W., 526
Keenan, J. D., 427, 428, 430
Keene, J. D., 61
Keiger, D. M., 459
Keirns, J. J., 501
Keister, D. L., 192
Keitz, B., 56, 57
Kellar, P. E., 507
Keller, S. R., 74

Kellermann, O., 398
Kellett, M., 160
Kelley, B. C., 199, 201, 202, 510
Kelln, R. A., 148, 227
Kellog, V. L., 586
Kellogg, K. R., 290
Kelly, C. T., 439, 441
Kelly, D. P., 264, 266, 267, 270, 273-75, 278, 436, 450
Kelly, M., 185, 189, 196, 198
Kelly, M. T., 333
Kelman, A., 659
Kemp, M. B., 23
Kempe, C. H., 596
Kemper, B., 394, 404
Kempson-Jones, G. F., 55
Kendrick, B., 112, 115, 126, 129
Kenealy, W., 436, 450
Kenealy, W. R., 450
Kenne, J. D., 629
Kennedy, B. P. C., 245
Kennedy, C., 190, 191, 197
Kennedy, E. R., 563
Kennedy, J. F., 265
Kennedy, S. I. T., 61, 624, 634, 637, 642
Kennel, Y. M., 210, 211
Kennings, N. T., 200
Kenny, G. E., 290, 294-96
Kenyon, C. N., 45
Kerjan, P., 149
Kertopati, S., 126
Keshishyan, H. L., 290, 294
Kessler, E., 523
Keszthelyi, L., 503
Kettman, J., 604
Keyhani, M., 488
Keyl, A. C., 242
Keys, A. J., 502
Keyser, P., 439
Khakpour, M., 598
Khan, M. U., 363
Khan, S., 90
Khmel, I. A., 186, 187
Khudyakov, I. Y., 141
Kibrya, A. K. M. G., 343
Kida, M., 161, 164-66
Kidby, D. K., 112
Kikuchi, M., 166
Kikuchi, T., 160
Kilbourne, E. D., 598, 620
Kilby, B. A., 19
Kilgore, W. M., 670
Kilpper, R., 570, 576, 581
Kim, H., 78
Kim, S.-H., 151, 152
Kimura, H., 242
Kind, D. P., 333
King, A. M. Q., 253
King, D. S., 117, 124, 131
King, R. E., 573
King, T. J., 177
Kinghorn, J. R., 219, 224
Kingma, J., 273, 279, 280, 409, 414, 416
Kingsbury, D. T., 289, 290
Kingsley, V. V., 87
Kingston, D., 561
Kinoshita, F., 315, 317, 319, 320, 322-24, 614
Kinosita, R., 238, 239
Kintaka, K., 161, 164
Kinumaki, A., 549
Kirk, J. K., 439
Kirk, J. T. O., 140
Kirk, M. R., 505
Kirk, T. K., 439
Kirkpatrick, J. R., 169, 216
Kirnos, M. D., 138, 141
Kirschner, A., 549
Kistler, J., 381-83
Kistner, A., 426, 432
Kitano, K., 161, 164, 166
Kitaura, T., 315
Kitazume, Y., 500
Kjeldgaard, N. O., 397
Kjeldsen, C. K., 510, 513
Klaus, D., 191
Kleckner, N., 650
Klein, D. T., 656
Klein, R. M., 656
Kleinen Hammans, J. W., 499
Kleiner, D., 219
Kleinschmidt, J. A., 219
Klekowski, E., 257
Klemme, J. H., 202
Klin, M. F., 238
KLOOS, W. E., 559-92; 560, 563-65, 568-76, 578-87
Klos, E. J., 651, 652
Klotz, L. C., 141
Klotz, L. J., 688, 704
Klucas, R., 192
Kluender, H., 166
Klumpp, E. R., 390
Kluyver, A. J., 199, 437
Knapp, D. W., 441
Knee, M., 662, 663
Knight, C. A., 602, 606
Knights, B. A., 335
Knoblauch, M., 300
Knowles, C. J., 187
Knowles, R., 192, 193
Knox, K. W., 327, 659
Knudsen, R. C., 598, 611
Knudson, A. G., 236
Kobayashi, Y., 238
Kobayasi, S., 76
Kobbe, B., 244, 245
Kobori, J., 236
Kochian, L. V., 523
Kocur, M., 563, 565, 570, 571
Koenigsberg, W., 607
Koerner, J. F., 148
Koff, R. S., 364
Koga, T., 315, 317, 319, 327, 328, 331, 613
Kogami, J., 320
Kohn, L. M., 111
Kohno, S., 357, 359
Kohsaka, M., 166, 170
Kojami, J., 315
Kojima, M., 168, 169, 554
Kojo, H., 172, 173
Koki, A., 174
Kolakofsky, D., 61, 624, 629, 633, 634, 643
Kolb, U., 409
Koller, K. P., 499
Kolomietz, L., 629
Koltin, Y., 51, 52, 64
Komarek, J., 498
Kominek, L. A., 212, 215
Komitowaski, D., 238
Komori, T., 170, 172
Kondo, E., 554
Kondo, F., 691, 692
Kondo, S., 174
Kondo, Y., 168, 169
Kondoh, H., 78, 82, 84
Kondratieva, E. N., 523
Konetzka, W. A., 95
Konig, H., 436
Konigsberg, W., 153
Konings, R. N. H., 393, 396
Konings, W. M., 444
Konisky, J., 377, 384
Konomi, T., 166, 170-72
Konvicka, J., 140-42, 154
Koornhof, H. J., 347, 349, 350
Kopeloff, L. M., 328
Kopeloff, N., 328
Koplow, J., 411
Kopp, U., 585, 586
Korf, R. P., 111
Kornberg, A., 584
Koronzis, M., 320
Korotkov, S. A., 497
Kort, E. N., 88
Kort, L., 61, 633, 634
Koshakji, R. P., 240
Koshland, D. E. Jr., 71, 73, 75, 88-92, 96, 99
Kostel, P. J., 511, 513, 523
Kotani, S., 315, 317, 319, 320, 322-24, 327-29, 331, 333-35, 613, 614
Koths, K. E., 526
Kouno, K., 174, 175
Kozak, Y. de, 329
Kozloff, L. M., 144
Kraght, A. J., 670
Krajewska, E., 141, 152
Kramer, C., 384-86, 389, 392, 411, 415
Kramer, J. H., 596
Kramer, M. J., 293

Krampitz, L. O., 526
Krasnovsky, A. A., 523
Krause, R. M., 326, 327
Kreger-van Rij, N. J. W., 116
Kreibich, G., 407
Krieg, N. R., 77, 90, 91, 95
Krieger-Brauer, H. J., 378, 379
Krishna Rao, K., 500
Kriss, A. E., 538
Kristensen, K. K., 362
Krogmann, D. W., 500, 501
Kronenberg, H. M., 394, 404
Kropinski, A. M. B., 140
Krueger, R. G., 607
Krumwiede, C. Jr., 647
Krupey, J., 605
Krupinski, V. M., 216
Kryzcki, J., 435, 438, 449, 450, 459
Kubochi, Y., 170
Kubota, K., 239, 241-43, 245, 250, 251
Kuć, J., 665
Kuczuk, M., 239, 241, 245
Kudinova, M. K., 554
Kudo, Y., 355
Kuge, S., 170
Kuhn, K., 604
Kuhn, W., 450
Kulcsar, G., 554
Kumar, H. D., 526
Kumazawa, Y., 317, 319
Kunisawa, R., 24, 28, 32-34, 40
Kunkel, S. L., 472
Kunugita, K., 160, 170, 172
Kuo, C. C., 288, 290, 295, 296
Kuo, T.-T., 141, 146
Kurahashi, K., 211, 213
Kurata, T., 354
Kurita, M., 170
Kuroiwa, T., 81, 82, 85
Kurosky, A., 595, 598
Kurtz, J., 604
Kurz, W. G. W., 188, 192, 194, 519
Kusama, T., 324, 329, 331
Kusamoto, S., 614
Kustu, S., 517
Kustu, S. G., 225
Kusumoto, S., 315, 317, 319, 322-24, 328, 329, 331, 333, 334
Kuszala, C., 691
Kutter, E., 153
Kutter, E. M., 150, 152, 153
Kuwahara, S., 172, 173
Kwon-Chung, K. J., 113, 114, 117, 121, 130
Kylberg, K. J., 655

L

Laane, C., 187-89, 200, 517, 522
Labia, R., 177
Lacey, R. W., 489, 579, 585
Lachance, M., 112
Lachowicz, T. M., 491
Lacy, G. H., 647, 649, 650, 654-56
Ladd, J. N., 445
Ladha, J. K., 497, 498, 515, 516
Ladisch, C., 426, 430, 458
Ladisch, C. M., 426
Ladisch, M., 426, 430, 458
Ladisch, M. R., 426, 427, 430
Laflèche, D., 678, 680, 683, 684, 687, 688, 701
Lafont, J., 245
Lafont, P., 245
Lagarde, A., 671
Lagenaur, C., 84, 87
Lai, J. S., 388
Lai, M., 650
Laidlaw, R. H., 362
Laird, W. J., 466
Lakso, J. U., 648
Lalucat, J., 193
Lamb, R. A., 625
Lambrecht, F. L., 290, 303
Lamed, R., 435, 436, 440, 452, 453, 456-59
Lamed, R. J., 434, 435, 440, 452-54, 456, 458, 459
Lamensans, A., 317, 327, 330, 331
Lammli, J., 300
Lamoureux, G., 328
Land, J. M., 604
Landau, J. W., 125
Landers, M. K., 242
Landesman, J., 265, 268, 276
Lang, E., 121
Lang, G., 185
Lang, N. J., 519
Langbeheim, H., 607, 608, 612, 613
Langen, P., 154
Langenbach, R., 250
Langheinrich, W., 225, 226
Langridge, R., 58, 59
Langridge, R. J., 152
Langworthy, J. D., 436
Lapage, S. P., 110
Lapshinskaya, O. A., 244
Lara, S. L., 129
Lara-Gomez, J., 273
Larimore, F., 225
Larimore, F. L., 224
Larrue, J., 691
Larsen, S. H., 88, 239
Larson, A. D., 79
Larson, C. L., 613
Larson, J. E., 151
Larue, M., 683, 686, 690, 704
LaRue, T. A., 188, 192, 194, 519
Lascelles, J., 28
Latrille, J., 679, 680, 682, 686-91, 695, 700-2
Latta, P. D., 585, 586
Latzko, E., 501
Lau, R. H., 506, 526
Lauer, G. D., 141
Läuger, P., 90, 92, 379, 383
Laughon, B. E., 77
Laurent, E., 510
Lauterbur, P. C., 390
Lavi, S., 624
Lawn, A. M., 80, 84
Lawrence, D. N., 355
Lawrie, A. C., 514, 517
Lawton, W. D., 141
Lazarow, P. B., 404
Lazdunski, C., 393, 394, 408, 414
Laznickova, K., 346, 350
Lazzarini, R. A., 61, 629, 634
Lê, T. K. T., 656
Lea, P. J., 500, 502
Leach, C. K., 500, 522
Leach, L. M., 426, 427, 430
Leach, M., 143, 144
Leadbetter, E. R., 192
Lean, D. R. S., 499
Leary, J. V., 647
Leathen, W. W., 273
Leatherwood, T. M., 439
Leaver, A. G., 506
Leaver, F. W., 445
Leavitt, R. W., 636
Lebar, R., 328
LeBlanc, B. M., 175
Leccas, D., 656
Lechevalier, H. A., 230, 555
LeClair, R. A., 353, 360
Leclerc, C., 323, 331, 334
LeComte, J. R., 189, 197
Lederer, E., 312, 313, 315, 317-19, 321-25, 327, 330, 331, 613, 614
Ledingham, G. A., 10
Lee, B. H., 435
Lee, C. C., 510
Lee, C. K., 290, 301
Lee, D. J., 238, 242
Lee, D. R., 371, 372, 375, 376
Lee, F. D., 236
Lee, H. C., 238
Lee, I. M., 678, 681-83, 685-90, 695, 696, 699, 701
Lee, J. V., 343, 345, 348, 362-64
Lee, K., 360, 362
Lee, M., 441
Lee, N., 388, 390, 396, 405
Lee, S. B., 199
Lee, Y. F., 61
Lee, Y. H., 439
Lees, H., 186, 188, 191, 193, 269

Lefrancier, P., 317, 324, 614
Legator, M., 250
Legator, M. S., 239
Legault, G., 266, 276, 279
Lehman, I. R., 138, 144
Lehmann, M., 504
Lehmann, V., 412
Lehmann-Kirk, U., 499
Lei, J. D., 682, 683, 688, 691
Leibowitz, M. J., 51, 55, 57, 58, 62-65
Leifson, E., 38, 71
Leighton, T. G., 227
Leimenstoll, G., 451
Lein, J., 174-76
Leisinger, T., 213
Leitjen, M. W. N., 191
Lelliott, R. A., 648
Lemke, J. R., 214, 229
Lemke, P. A., 49, 55, 56, 63, 165, 166
Lemoigne, M., 33
Lenard, J., 413, 623-25
Léonard, A., 239
Leonard, B. J., 239
Lepo, J. E., 506
Leppert, M., 61, 633, 634
LeRoux, N. W., 267, 271, 273, 278
Lespinat, P. A., 200
Lessel, E. F., 110
Lettinga, I. G., 457
Leung, C. Y., 602, 604
Leunissen-Bijvelt, J., 390
Levandowsky, M., 95
Leve, R., 596, 611
Levij, I. S., 331
Levin, D. E., 257
Levine, A., 250
Levine, E., 704
Levine, J., 569
Levine, L., 597
Levine, R. J. C., 700
Levinthal, C., 153
Levy, J. S., 225
Levy, N. J., 290
Levy, S. B., 416
Lewis, A., 160
Lewis, A. L., 112
Lewis, B. J., 679, 680
Lewis, H. A., 141, 142
Lewis, S., 664
Lex, M., 192, 502, 507, 512, 520, 521
Ley, A. C., 499
Lhoas, P., 50, 52, 53, 55
L'Hospital, M., 678, 680, 683, 684, 687, 688, 701
Li, M., 125
Liacopoulos, P., 334
Liao, C. H., 660, 681-83, 687, 689, 692, 693, 695, 697, 700
Libby, L. M., 255
Lichtwardt, R. W., 124, 125
Lidwell, O. M., 561
Liebhaber, H., 290
Liersch, M., 166
Lietava, J., 346, 350
Lijinsky, W., 242
Lillehoj, E. B., 250
Lim, S. T., 200, 518
Lin, F.-S., 146
Lin, J. J. C., 388, 390, 394, 396, 397, 400, 402-4, 406, 407, 411-13, 415, 416
Lin, J. K., 249, 256
Lin, J. S., 290, 299
Lin, L. J., 166
Linczevski, I. A., 110
Lindahl, L., 397
Lindahl, T., 145, 152, 153
Lindberg, M., 585
Lindberg, R. B., 360-62
Lindeman, L. R., 427
Lindner, R., 52, 53, 55
Lindroth, S., 239, 241
Lingappa, J. R., 402
Lingappa, V. R., 402, 408
Linggood, M. A., 467, 468
Linn, D. M., 77
Linnaeus, C., 110
Linnainmaa, K., 241, 244
Linnemann, G., 130
Linstead, R. P., 22
Lipinsky, E. S., 427
Lippi, D., 192, 193
Lippincott, B. B., 647, 650, 660
Lippincott, J. A., 647, 650, 660
Lipschultz, C. A., 499
Lipton, M. M., 329
Liras, P., 211
Lisenkova, L. L., 187
List, R. H., 613
Liston, J., 362
Little, S. P., 623
Liu, H. Y., 701
Liu, T. Y., 313, 315
Liu, U. Y., 607, 608
Liu, Y. T., 550
Live, I., 582
Lively, D. H., 239
Ljones, T., 511
Ljungdahl, L., 448
Ljungdahl, L. G., 435, 444, 448, 454
Ljunggren, A., 347, 350
Ljungh, A., 580, 581
Ljungquist, S., 145, 152
Lloyd, N. D. H., 502
Loayza, J. C., 689
Lockau, W., 513, 514, 516, 521, 522
Lockhart, C. M., 498
Lockman, H., 348
Lockwood, L. B., 431, 459
Lockwood, S. J., 267, 273
Lodder, J., 112, 116, 117
Loder, P. B., 165
Lodish, H. F., 62, 408
Loeb, L., 561
Loebenberg, D., 543
Loeffler, W., 122
Lofdahl, S., 486
Lofquist, F., 486
Loh, P., 57
Lombardi, K., 150
Lomniczi, B., 627
London, J., 44
Longland, J. M., 699
Longyear, V. M., 444, 451
Lopez-Alvarez, J., 482
Loquet, C., 241
Lorenz, L. F., 439
Loring, D., 387
Losada, M., 500
Losick, R., 150
Lotz, W., 98, 99
Lounatmaa, K., 376, 390, 393
Loveland, L. M., 255
Lovely, P. S., 73
Lovett, M.A., 288
Loviny, T., 51, 57
Low, K. B., 371, 373, 385, 407, 653, 656, 671
Lowe, D. J., 185, 196, 197, 511
Lowe, E. A., 271, 279
Lowe, J. K., 239, 253
Lowe, S. K., 691
Löwy, I., 334
Lozlov, A. V., 506
Lubimenko, V., 24
Lucas, B. H., 264, 272, 273, 278
Luce, C., 545
Luckenbach, G. A., 333
Luckey, M., 380, 381
Ludden, P. W., 511
Ludwig, R. A., 219
Luedemann, G. M., 538-40, 545, 547, 550, 552
Lugano, J. M., 216
Lugtenberg, B., 372-76, 378-81, 385-87, 390, 391
Lugtenberg, E. J. J., 373, 389
Luijk, L. J., 500, 520
Luijk, L. W., 523, 524
Luktenhaus, J. F., 375, 377, 379
Lum, L., 301
Lund, Z., 679
LUNDGREN, D. G., 263-83; 265, 268-70, 272-75, 278
Lundh, N. P., 98
Lundigran, M., 386
Lundquist, R. E., 624
Lunt, M. R., 144
Luria, S. E., 49, 53, 148, 149, 152
Lute, M., 144
Luttrell, E. S., 110, 112
Lutz, A., 125

Lvov, N. P., 191
Lyalikova, N. N., 279
Lynd, L., 435, 448, 459
Lynd, T. T., 435, 459, 582

M

Maaloe, O., 397
Maas, W. K., 214, 469, 471-73
Mabe, J. A., 168, 170
MacAlister, T. J., 387, 392
Maccecchini, M. L., 404
MacDonald, A. B., 297
MacDonald, D. G., 273
MacDonald, D. L., 20, 22
MacDonald, R. J. C., 266, 273, 274
MacGregor, C. H., 406
MacGregor, R. A., 272, 278
Maciag, W. J., 269
Mackenzie, D. W. R., 130
Mackenzie, M. M., 506
Mackintosh, M. E., 192
MacLaren, D. M., 575
MacLean, F. I., 503
MacLeod, R. A., 8
Macmillan, J. D., 441
Macnab, R. M., 70-73, 84, 85, 88-92, 96, 99
MacPherson, N., 441
Macsai, S., 97
Macy, J. M., 432
Madelin, M. F., 115
Madgwick, J. C., 267
Maeda, K., 76, 96, 160, 174
Maes, R., 576
Maezawa, I., 548
Magasanik, B., 217-20, 223
Magradze, N. M., 138
Magrum, L., 679, 680
Magrum, L. J., 436, 680
Maguire, J. J., 500, 520
Mah, R. A., 437, 438
Maher, V. M., 250, 253
Maia, J. C. C., 149
Maier, R. J., 200-2, 506
Mainigi, K. D., 237
Maizel, J. F. Jr., 624
Maizel, J. V., 87
Maizels, N., 517
Makela, P. H., 376, 385, 386, 389, 390
Makino, S., 293
Makower, M., 50, 51, 59
Maksinova, T. S., 554
Malik, K. A., 191
Malkin, S., 519
Malloch, D., 112, 114, 115
Malmstrom, B. G., 268
Malouf, E. E., 271, 273, 276, 279
Manchee, R. J., 264, 271, 278
Mancini, C., 485
Mandel, B., 598
Mandel, G., 404, 405, 408
Mandel, M., 39, 45, 101, 102, 140-42, 146, 147, 154, 506, 526, 648, 650
Mandelstam, J., 229
Maniloff, J., 679, 680
Manire, G. P., 290, 291, 293, 296
Manmade, A., 239, 241, 245
Manning, P. A., 378, 385, 387, 389, 402
Manson, M. D., 91
Mantel, N., 238
Manten, A., 199
Maoz, A., 604
Marah, R., 613
Maral, R., 318, 320, 322, 331
Maramorosch, K., 647, 678, 683, 689, 691, 692, 700
Marandon, J. L., 566, 582, 584
Marasas, W. F. O., 241, 245
Marcano, C., 121
Marchal, C., 394, 395
Marchal, M., 405, 406
Marchlenwitz, B., 272, 274
Marcus, L., 189
Marcus, M., 145, 149, 150, 152, 153
Mardh, P-A., 299, 300, 305
Margalith, P., 275
Margoliash, E., 601
Margolskee, F. R., 517
Margraff, R., 213
Margreiter, H., 161, 163
Margulis, L., 109
Marino, W., 88
Markel, D. E., 595, 598
Markewych, O., 147, 150, 154
Markham, P. G., 678, 679, 683, 688, 696, 700, 704
Markham, R., 242, 248
Markovic, O., 439, 441
Markovitz, A., 387, 393
Marligit, G., 332
Marmur, J., 139-42, 152, 154, 569
Maron, E., 600, 603-5, 611
Maron, R., 315, 317
Marples, M. J., 560, 576
Marquez, J. A., 539-42, 545-47, 549, 551-53
Marquis, R. E., 100
Marsalek, E., 566, 582-84
Marshall, A. H. E., 328
Martin, F. B., 598
Martin, G. R., 604
Martin, H. H., 379
Martin, J. F., 210-12, 216
Martin, J. L., 425, 458
Martin, J-P., 319, 325, 326, 333, 334, 613, 614
Martin, J. R., 544
Martin, M. N., 501, 502
Martin, M. W., 502
Martin, R. O., 570
Martinec, T., 563
Martinez, R. J., 82, 84, 98
Maruyama, H. B., 99
Maruyama, M., 77
Maruyama, Y., 200
Marwah, S. M., 347
Masaki, R., 501
Mascaretti, O., 214, 215
Maslen, E. N., 163
Mason, E. W., 123
Mason, K. T., 214
Masurekar, P. S., 216
Mata, J. M., 168, 169, 173
Matern, H., 211
Mathé, G., 332
Mathews, C. K., 138, 143, 144
Mathews, M. M., 32
Mathews-Roth, M. M., 32
Mathieu, L. G., 467
Matic, M., 278
Matsubara, H., 500, 501
Matsubara, T., 315, 320
Matsuguchi, M., 78
Matsumoto, A., 291
Matsumoto, K., 554
Matsuo, K., 244, 245
Matsuo, T., 357, 359
Matsushima, T., 236, 237, 241
Matsuura, S., 554
Matsuzawa, N., 548
Matter, B. E., 239
Mattern, K. L., 581
Mattes, R., 475
Mattson, T., 153
Matz, L., 189
Mauger, A. B., 553
Mayama, S., 554
Mayberry, W. R., 701
Mayer, F., 79, 80, 85, 99
Mayer, H., 390
Mayer, L. W., 485
Mayer, W. M., 239
Mayes, M. A., 586
Mayfield, C. I., 71
Mayo, J. A., 141, 146
Mayr, E., 567, 587
Mazam, A., 151
Mazrimas, J. A., 140
Mazumder, D. N. G., 352
Mazur, B. J., 527
Mazzucchi, U., 661, 669
McBee, R. H., 435
McBride, B. C., 432
McCann, J., 236, 251
McCarter, L., 517
McCarthy, B. J., 470, 490
McCarty, P. L., 457
McClelland, D. B. L., 314
McComb, D., 290, 301, 302
McComb, D. E., 296

McComb, J. A., 192
McConnell, M. M., 469-71, 474, 476
McCormack, G., 287, 290, 299
McCormack, W. M., 290, 299, 301, 302
McCoy, E., 425, 434, 538
McCoy, R., 680, 682, 683, 686-91, 695, 704
McCoy, R. E., 681-83, 686, 690, 691, 704
McCoy, R. H., 583
McCready, S. J., 53, 55
McCreedy, H. H., 264, 271-73, 278
McDermott, J., 223
McDermott, K., 314
McDevitt, H. O., 599, 600, 615
McDonough, E. S., 112
McDonough, M. W., 84
McElroy, R. O., 272, 274
McFadden, B. A., 447, 501
McFarland, L., 364
McFarland, N., 517
McFarland, N. C., 225
McGarrity, G., 704
McGauhey, P. H., 428
McGavin, S., 603
MCGINNIS, M. R., 109-35; 110, 113, 120-23, 125, 127, 128
McGlotten, J., 550
McGovan, R. E., 505
McHugh, J. L., 441
McIntosh, A. H., 683, 691, 692, 700
McIntosh, K., 290, 301, 302
McIntyre, J. L., 665
McIntyre, L. D., 273
McIntyre, O. R., 346, 350
McIntyre, T. M., 412
McKenzie, S. F., 466, 470
McKercher, P. D., 598
McLaughlin, C. S., 53, 55-59
McManus, T. T., 701
McNamara, V. M., 264, 272, 273, 278
McNeish, A. S., 467, 476
McNicol, L. A., 144
McSweeney, R. J., 353, 360-62
McVaugh, R., 110
McWethy, S. J., 441
Meadows, P. S., 97, 102
Meddins, B. M., 678, 683, 684, 688
Medlar, E. M., 126
Meeks, J. C., 513, 514, 516, 521
Meers, J. L., 217, 226, 227
Meesschaert, B., 165
Meffert, M. A., 499
Meganathan, R., 100
Mégnin, M., 122
Meigel, W., 604
Meijers, L., 372, 375, 386
Meikle, R. D., 110
Meinkoth, J., 642
Melin, E., 123
Melish, M. E., 487
Mellor, R., 498
Mendoza Hernandes, P., 482, 483
Menien, M. A., 245
Menzel, D. W., 510
Menzel, J., 389, 409, 412
Mergeay, M., 657
Merlie, J. D., 624
Merlo, D. J., 647, 650
Merrick, M., 191
Merrick, M. J., 210
Merrifield, B. B., 603, 605, 609
Merser, C., 323, 614
Merson, M. H., 343, 357-60
Mertens, A., 357, 359
Mesibov, R., 94
Metchnikoff, E., 312
Metzer, H., 511
Metzner, P., 90, 91, 95
Meuzelaar, H. L. C., 129
Mewborn, A., 347, 350
Meyer, C., 201
Meyer, F., 193
Meyer, J., 199, 202, 510
Meyer, K. F., 286, 289, 290, 296, 303
Meyer, S. A., 117, 565, 568-74, 576, 579, 582, 584
Meyer, T., 330
Meyer, T. J., 330
Meyer, W., 566
Meyerhof, O., 186
Meyers, J. A., 586
Meynell, E. W., 98
Michaeli, D., 604, 606
Michels, J. P., 444
Michels, P. A., 444
Middleton, R. B., 657
Miflin, B. J., 500, 502
Migliore, D., 315
Migliore-Samour, D., 317, 318, 320, 322, 327, 328, 331, 613
Migula, W., 562
Miklos, G. V., 648, 653
Mikulik, K., 210
Millar, R. L., 664, 665
Miller, A. K., 170, 173-75
Miller, C. G., 228
Miller, E. C., 236, 249, 252, 256
Miller, E. J., 604
Miller, J. A., 236, 249, 252, 256
Miller, J. B., 92
Miller, J. M., 177
Miller, L., 441
Miller, M. M., 487
Miller, P. W., 664
Miller, R. C. Jr., 141, 142
Miller, R. P., 278
Miller, R. W., 197, 511
Miller, S. S., 506
Miller, T. L., 445, 446
Miller, T. W., 173-75
Millet, M. A., 426, 429
Millis, N. F., 275
Mills, J., 301, 302, 305
Mills, S. D., 239
Mimura, M., 500
Minchiotti, L., 501
Minck, R., 319, 322
Mine, Y., 172, 173
Minor, P. D., 625, 635, 642
Minshew, B., 585
Minshew, B. H., 477, 479
Minton, K., 145, 153
Mintzlaff, H. J., 238
Minuth, J. N., 357
Mirelis, B., 347, 350
Mirelman, D., 385
Mirzabekov, A., 151
Misaki, A., 315
Mitani, M., 98
Mitchell, D. J., 50, 56-58, 60-62, 64
Mitchell, G., 611
Mitchell, R., 267
Mitchell, R. G., 581
Mitchell, W. O., 687, 703
Mitchison, N. A., 314
Mitra, R. C., 466
Mitscher, L. A., 544
Mitsuhashi, S., 174
Mitsui, T., 390
Mitsuko, A., 554
Miura, K. I., 57
Miwatani, T., 102, 352-57, 472,
Miyagawa, N., 597
Miyairi, N., 170
Miyakawa, K., 98
Miyake, M., 238
Miyaki, K., 238
Mizoguchi, T., 265
Mizumoto, K., 239, 241, 252
Mizuno, K., 554
Mizuno, T., 387
Mizunoe, K., 317, 319
Mizushima, S., 372, 373, 381, 382, 391, 393, 394, 406
Mochales, S., 168, 169, 173-75
Mock, M., 319, 322, 325, 326, 613, 614
Model, P., 405, 406, 408
Modolell, M., 333
Moeller, R. W., 579, 582
Moench, T. T., 95
Mohanti, P., 499

Mohn, G. R., 236
Mojica-a, T., 657
Molitor, H., 166
Moll, A., 481
Møllgaard, H., 145, 146
Monaghan, R. L., 173
Monda, G. D., 287, 290, 299
Monk, M., 655
Monod, J., 19
Monroe, S., 634
Montague, T. S., 353, 360
Montemartini, A., 120
Montgomery, D. L., 149
Montoya, A. L., 647, 650
Monty, K. J., 219
Mooi, F. R., 467, 475
Moon, H. W., 467
Moore, G. W., 572
Moore, M. R., 444
Moore, R. B., 514
Moppett, C. E., 554
Mora, J., 223, 224, 229
Morad, M., 250
Morag, A., 595
Moran, F., 666, 667, 670
Morandi, C., 219, 227, 517
Mordarski, M., 568, 575
Mordhorst, C. H., 298, 299, 305
Moré, J., 238
Moreau, P., 250, 251
Moreau, P. L., 250
Morecombe, D. J., 166
Moreira, J. R., 427, 432
Moreno, F., 399, 400
Morey, A. V., 526
Morgan, D. H., 63
Morgan, H. R., 292
Morgan, I. M., 328
Morgan, J. J., 118
Morgan, T. V., 188
Mori, S., 171
Mori, Y., 320, 544
Moriarty, D. J. W., 270
Morino, D., 168, 169
Morisaki, I., 323, 324
Morizaki, L., 614
Morooka, N., 238
Morowitz, H. J., 511
Morowitz, L. S., 511
Morris, D., 165
Morris, G. K., 343
Morris, J. A., 185
Morris, J. G., 432, 436, 452
Morrison, F. R., 485, 487
Mörschel, E., 499
Morse, M. L., 585
Morse, S. I., 585
Mortensen, N., 563
Mortenson, L. E., 184, 185, 195, 197, 201, 511, 517
Mortlock, R. P., 441, 668
Morton, D., 150, 152, 153
Morton, J., 550
Moseley, M., 683, 688, 696, 699
Mosely, S. L., 472, 473
Mosher, R. A., 144
Mosimann, J. E., 511
Mosley, W. H., 351
Moss, J. F., 274
Mossel, D. A. A., 362
Moubasher, A., 250
Mouches, C., 680, 682, 684, 686-91, 695
Moulder, J. W., 286, 287, 290, 293
Moulé, Y., 251
Moulthrop, P. H., 428
Mount, M. S., 664, 666-68
Mountfort, D. O., 433
Mouton, D., 330
Moutous, G., 683, 686, 688, 690, 704
Movitz, J., 327
Movva, N. R., 386, 411
Moyer, J. W., 651
Mozes, E., 315, 317, 599, 600, 614, 615
Mrost, M., 278
Much, H., 561
Mudd, J. B., 701, 702
Mueller, S. L., 544
Mühlradt, P. F., 389, 409, 412
Mukherjee, P. K., 227
Mulder, E. G., 192
Mulder, J. L., 126
Mulholland, A., 79
Mullan, N. A., 466, 470
Müller, E., 112
Muller, G., 348
Muller, H. E., 348
Muller, R., 381-83
Müller-Hill, B., 384, 395, 408
Muller-Schoop, J., 300
Mullineaux, P. M., 504
Multani, J. S., 185
Munch-Peterson, A., 378
Munder, P. G., 333
Mundt, J. O., 567
Murad, F., 439, 440
Murai, T., 504, 521
Muraoka, Y., 160
Murata, N., 648, 653
Murawski, A., 546, 547, 552
Murphy, E., 585
Murphy, F. H., 596
Murphy, J., 471, 474
Murphy, J. R., 468, 471
Murphy, T. O., 499
Murr, L. E., 264, 265, 267
Murray, E. S., 290, 296
Murray, N. E., 153
Murray, R. G. E., 86, 87, 679
Musher, D. N., 357
Musselwhite, M. S., 560, 576, 578-83, 587
Muto, N., 554, 555
Mutoh, N., 391
Myers, J., 501
Mygind, B., 378

N

Nadzan, A. M., 249, 255, 256
Nagabhushan, T. L., 542, 545
Nagai, S., 187, 459
Nagai, Y., 328
Naganawa, H., 174
Nagao, M., 236, 237, 239, 241
Nagao, S., 334
Nagaoka, K., 214
Nagarajan, R., 161, 164, 166, 168, 169, 172
Nagasaki, M., 355
Nagel, D., 245
Nagler, J., 357, 359
Nagy, B., 467
Nahler, G., 472
Nahmias, A. J., 596
Nakae, T., 376-82, 390, 391
Nakahara, K., 172
Nakajima, K., 625, 637
Nakajima, M., 239, 241
Nakamura, H., 504
Nakamura, K., 370, 372, 387, 388, 390, 402, 660
Nakamura, L. K., 441, 454
Nakamura, Y., 239, 242, 243, 250
Nakanishi, K., 140, 141, 238
Nakano, N., 238
Nakao, Y., 161, 164
Nakata, M., 252
Nakayama, T. O. M., 31
Nalewajko, C., 499
Namavar, F., 575
Namba, K., 81
Nannfeldt, J. A., 123
Napier, E., 273, 278
Nara, K., 161, 164, 166
Nara, T., 540, 544, 545
Narita, T., 315, 317, 319, 322, 323, 327
Nash, C. H., 55, 56, 63, 166
Nason, A., 220, 229
Nassan, N. A., 651, 652
Nasuno, S., 667, 670
Nauciel, C., 319, 322, 325, 326, 333, 334, 613, 614
Naughton, M. J., 238
Nault, L. R., 689
NAYAK, D. P., 619-44; 620-31, 633, 634, 636-38, 642, 643
Naylor, J. H. C., 161, 162
Neely, W. C., 241, 252

Ne'eman, Z., 696, 698, 701, 702
Neff, I., 390
Negroni, P., 123
Neilands, J., 480
Neilands, J. B., 386, 387, 480, 499
Neilson, A. H., 514
Neimark, H., 680
Neimark, H. C., 700
Nelson, D. R., 437
Nelson, L. M., 192, 193
Némoz, G., 670, 671
Nes, I. F., 151
Neser, M. L., 88
Nesheim, S., 238
Nesse, N., 426
Nester, E. W., 647, 650
Neubort, S., 140-42, 154
Neuer, G., 498, 500, 504, 505, 511, 513, 521-25
Neuhard, J., 145, 146
Neurauter, C., 448
Neuss, N., 166
Newberne, P. M., 237, 240, 242
Newcomer, V. D., 125
Newkirk, J. F., 168
Newlon, M. C., 145, 149, 150, 152, 153
Newman, A. M., 56-59
Newman, L. W., 289
Newsome, P. M., 466, 470
Newton, A., 84
Newton, G. G. F., 160, 162-64, 213, 222
Newton, W., 184, 185, 194
Newton, W. E., 184, 194, 196
Ng, T. K., 435, 436, 440, 452, 453, 456-59
Nguyen-Dang, T., 319, 323
Nguyen-Huy, H., 319, 325, 326, 613, 614
Nguyen-Trung-Luong-Cros, H., 315
Nhami, A., 681, 683, 684, 686, 690, 704
Nicholas, D. J. D., 270, 505
Nicholls, D. G., 268
Nichols, R. L., 296
Nicholson, B. H., 253
Nickerson, M. A., 131
Nicol, C. S., 300
Nicolaisen, A., 378
Nicolaisen, B., 148
Nielsen, A. M., 276, 277
Niemela, S. I., 267, 274
Nierlich, D. P., 148
Niida, T., 168, 169, 554
Nikaido, H., 84, 375, 377-81, 385, 388-91, 409, 411, 412, 415, 416
Nikonova, L. A., 198
Niles, R. M., 667, 668
Ninet, L., 431, 459
Ninomiya, H., 357, 359
Nisbet, J. J., 165
Nishida, M., 172, 173
Nishihara, M., 150
Nishimune, T., 649-51
Nishimura, A., 387, 392
Nishimura, M., 502
Nishimura, Y., 387, 388, 390, 392
Nishio, N., 459
Nishioka, K., 603
Nishiyama, Y., 639
Nishizawa, Y., 187
Niskanen, A., 245
Nisonoff, A., 601
Nissim, A., 379
Nitecki, D. E., 611
Niven, C. F., 562
Niven, C. F. Jr., 564
Nixdorff, K., 379
Nixon, J. E., 255
Noble, M., 611
Noble, W. C., 560, 561, 568, 569, 573, 576-79, 583
Noguchi, Y., 238, 249
Nolteernsting, U., 500, 522
Nomoto, A., 61
Nondasuta, A., 250
Nonoyama, S., 172, 173
Nord, C. E., 580, 581
Nordlund, S., 197, 511
Norris, P. R., 267
North, A. C. T., 603
North, T. W., 143, 144
Nossal, G. J. V., 601
Nossal, R., 76, 77, 99
Nottebrock, H., 129
Novel, G., 671
Novel, M., 671
Novick, R., 477, 489
Novick, R. P., 489, 585, 586
Novik, J., 605
Novik, N., 605
Noy, R. J., 500, 511, 522
Nüesch, J., 161, 164, 166
Nurminen, M., 376, 377, 379, 380, 385, 386, 389, 390, 393
Nyberg, B., 145, 152
Nyland, G., 691
Nyman, C. J., 184

O

Obara, Y., 353
O'Brien, E. J., 81, 82
O'Brien, I. G., 480
O'Brien, P. C. M., 97
O'Brien, R. W., 436, 452
Oda, Y., 20
Oden, E. M., 538-40, 546, 547, 550, 552
O'Donnell, M. J., 196
O'Donovan, G. A., 492
Oeding, P., 565, 566, 568-71, 573, 574, 576, 581-84
Officer, J. E., 290
Ogawa, Y., 168, 169, 315, 317, 319, 327, 328, 331, 613
Ogawara, H., 174
Ogra, P. L., 595, 611
Ogston, A., 560, 561
Oguchi, T., 81, 82
Ohad, I., 499, 506
Ohashi, M., 349, 355
Ohba, Y., 252, 253
Ohmiya, M., 500
Ohmori, H., 524
Ohmori, M., 517
Ohms, J.-P., 384, 390, 395, 408
Ohno, M., 174
Ohsawa, S., 171, 172
Ohta, K., 353, 355, 360
Ohta, T., 585
Ohtsubo, K., 239, 242
Oishi, K., 703, 704
Ojo, O. O., 686
Okabe, K., 513, 520, 521
Okabe, K-I., 502
Okabe, M., 174
Okabe, T., 265
Okachi, R., 540, 544, 545
Okada, S., 323, 324, 329, 331, 333, 334, 502
Okada, Y., 98
Okajima, Y., 376, 379, 381, 382
Okamoto, K., 102, 103
Okamoto, R., 174
Okamoto, T., 394, 395
Okamura, K., 174-76
Okamura, Y., 349
O'Keefe, M. F., 346, 350
Okon, Y., 192, 193
Okubo, S., 141
Okuda, A., 554
Okuda, T., 548, 549
OKUHARA, M., 159-81
Okumura, Y., 174, 175
Okunaga, T., 324
Olarte, J., 350, 480, 482, 483
Oldfield, G. N., 678, 704
Oldstone, M. B. A., 623, 639
Olive, L., 128
Oliver, J. D., 359
Oliver, R. S., 176
Oliver, S. G., 53, 55-59
Olkhovatova, O. C., 554
Olsen, H., 353, 360-62
Olsen, R. H., 649
Olson, J. M., 497
Omoto, S., 554
O'Neil, J., 649-51
Ong, T-M., 236, 242, 249-51
Onishi, H. R., 170
Onodera, M., 187

Ooba, K., 554
Oosawa, F., 96
Opitz, R., 191, 195
Oppenheim, J., 189
Orban, B. S., 585, 586
Ordal, E. J., 435, 455
Oren, A., 499, 504, 505, 519, 522
Oriel, J. D., 300
Orkin, B. A. J., 22
Orme-Johnson, W. H., 184, 189, 194, 198
Ornston, L. N., 22, 23
Ornston, M. K., 89
Orr, I., 290, 301, 302
Ørskov, F., 80, 467, 470, 474
Ørskov, I., 80, 467, 470, 474
Ørskov, J., 538
Ortego, T., 500
Osato, Y., 174
Osborn, M., 607
OSBORN, M. J., 369-422; 391, 412, 413
Oscarson, J. R., 554
Oshima, T., 567
Oshima, Y., 567
Osswald, H., 238
Ostler, B., 301
Ostler, H. B., 303
Ostwal, K. P., 193
O'Sullivan, J., 170
Ota, T., 704
Otani, M., 555
Ott, J. L., 160, 168
Overath, P., 408
Overbeck, J., 499
Overman, T. L., 343
Ow, D. W., 527
Owaribe, K., 84
Owen, S. P., 424
Ownby, J. D., 516-18
Ozanne, G., 467
Ozawa, J., 665, 670
Ozols, J., 388, 390, 394, 400, 403
Ozsam, M., 683, 686, 690, 704

P

Paavonen, J., 299
Packer, L., 500, 520, 523, 524
Padan, E., 92, 499, 503, 504, 510, 519, 522
Padhi, S. B., 683, 700
Padhye, A. A., 112, 120-22
Paerl, H. W., 507
Pagan, J. D., 192
Page, L. A., 287
Pages, J. M., 393, 394, 408, 414
Paget, G. E., 238
Paglialunga, S., 241, 242
Pahel, G., 517
Paigen, B., 242
Paisley, J. W., 177
Pal, S. C., 352, 353, 356
Palacios, R., 223, 224, 229
Palchaudhuri, S., 466, 469, 473
Palese, P., 620, 625, 627, 634
Palfree, G. E., 51, 62
Palleroni, N. J., 39, 40, 94, 101, 102, 647
Palmer, G., 185
Palmiter, R. W., 402
Palva, E. T., 376, 378, 382, 385, 390
Pan, F. L., 228
Panda, F. A., 271, 273
Paneque, A., 500
Pankey, G. A., 357, 359
Pankhurst, R. J., 112
Panopoulos, N. J., 98, 649, 650, 654
Pape, H., 211
Pape, M., 426, 428
Parant, F., 312, 317, 324, 327, 330
Parant, M., 312, 317, 324, 325, 327, 330, 333, 334
Pardee, A. B., 9, 23, 24
Pargaonker, V. N., 579
Parisi, E., 412
Parisi, J. T., 580
Park, I. W., 567
Park, J. T., 313, 326, 410
Parker, C. A., 186
Parker, M. T., 579
Parker, R. L., 286, 290, 303
Parkin, D. M., 314
Parkinson, J. S., 70
Paron, Y., 385
Parrott, L. M., 505
Parsell, Z., 474
Parshall, G. W., 185, 198
Parsons, E. I., 562
Partridge, C. D. P., 187, 199
Passet, J., 561
Pastan, I., 217, 668, 671
Paster, B. J., 681
Pasteur, L., 425
Patchornik, A., 603
Pate, J. L., 189
Patel, K. R., 701
Patel, M., 552
Patel, M. G., 551
Pateman, J. A., 219, 224
Pathak, M. A., 32
Patil, K., 245
Patil, L. G., 218
Patil, S. S., 647, 650
Pattee, P. A., 489, 585
Patterson-Delafield, J., 84
Pattison, J. R., 611
Pattnaik, H., 509
Paul, J. S., 502
Pauley, J., 467
Paulin, J. P., 651, 652
Paulus, H., 227
Pavey, D., 168
Pawlowski, N. E., 255
Payen, J., 245
Payne, J. W., 379, 380
Payne, S. M., 479, 480
Pearlman, D. S., 596
Pearlman-Kothencz, M., 408
Pearson, C. M., 315, 317, 319, 327, 328, 331, 613
Pearson, H. W., 503, 510, 512, 513
Peberdy, J. F., 129
Pechak, D. G., 119
Pechman, K. R., 680
Pecht, I., 603, 604
Pecht, M., 596, 611
Pedrosa, F. O., 506
Peduzzi, J., 177
Pelak, B. A., 170
Pelroy, R. A., 44, 505, 515, 518
Pemble, M., 506
Pengra, R. M., 190
Pennock, C. A., 565
Perahia, D., 151
Pereira-Continho, L., 242, 248
Pereverzew, N. A., 273
Perez-Miravete, A., 350
Pericas, R., 347, 350
Perkins, C. F., 127
Perkins, H. R., 319, 320
Perlman, P., 431
Perlman, P. S., 50
Pero, J., 150
Pérombelon, M. C. M., 649, 650, 654-56
Perrault, J., 624, 625, 634, 636
Perreau, P., 691
Perrin, D., 394, 395, 405, 406
Perry, B. T., 625, 640
Perry, C., 360, 362
Peschek, G. A., 499, 500, 503, 514, 524, 525
Peters, G. A., 523
Peters, R., 372, 374, 375, 386, 387
Peterson, J. W., 595, 598
Peterson, R. B., 498, 513, 519, 521-25
Peterson, W. H., 425, 434
Peterson, W. T., 602, 604
Petit, J-F., 312, 313, 317, 318, 322, 325, 327, 330, 331
Petitdemange, H., 451, 452
Petrylak, D., 95
Petter, H. F. M., 41
Pevzner, N. S., 554
Pezzlo, M., 360, 362
Pfeffer, J. T., 457
Pfennig, N., 199, 497
Phaff, H. J., 112, 665

Pheiffer, T. A., 290, 301, 302
Phelps, H. L., 250, 253
Phelps, T., 434
Philipson, L., 486
Phillips, D. H., 186
Phillips, W. E., 573
Philliskirk, G., 50
Philpot, C. M., 125
Pickens, E. G., 678, 683, 689, 704
Pickett, C. L., 386
Pien, F., 360, 362
Pierce, H. D., 678
Pierce, J. R., 386
Pierce, P. E., 482, 483
Pierini, G., 669
Pietras, D., 50, 53-55, 60, 61
Pietras, D. F., 53-55
Pietrzykowska, I., 140
Piez, K. A., 604
Pihl, N.J., 378
Pijper, A., 88, 89
Pilgram, W. K., 94
Pillich, J., 580, 581
Pillot, J., 679
Pinkwart, M., 200
Piovant, M., 394, 408, 414
Piret, J. M., 227
Pirt, S. J., 436, 438, 450
Pirtle, R. M., 387
Pisani, T. M., 328
Planque, K., 185, 193
Plaskitt, A., 678, 688
Plaskitt, A. K., 683, 688
Plaskitt, K. A., 688, 696, 700
Platel, A., 239, 241, 252
Plesiewicz, E., 152
Pohan, A., 126, 130
Poindexter, J. S., 37
Pollack, J. R., 480
Pollock, H. M., 290, 299
Pollock, M. R., 19
Polonsky, J., 245
Pomerantz, M. J., 145
Poncelet, F., 239
Pons, M. W., 621, 624-26, 637, 641
Pontz, B., 604
Poole, M. D., 359
Poore, G. A., 239
Popkin, T. J., 687, 688, 692, 696, 698, 699, 702, 703
Popp, B., 566, 569-72, 582-84
Pore, R. S., 117
Porres, J. M., 353
Portalier, R. C., 671
Porter, A. G., 625
POSTGATE, J. R., 183-207; 184-91, 193, 194, 196, 197, 199-201, 511, 512
Potts, J. T. Jr., 394, 404
Poulson, D. F., 678, 681, 683, 690, 696, 700, 703, 704
Poutiers, F., 683, 686, 690, 704
Pouyssegur, J., 671
Powell, A. J., 211, 226
Powell, C. J., 447
Pradet, A., 695, 697
Prager, E. M., 572
Prater, J. D., 271, 273, 276, 279
Prats, G., 347, 350
Pratt, E. A., 138, 144
Preble, O. T., 639
Preece, T. F., 646, 647
Preiss, J., 670
Premakumar, R., 220
Price, A. R., 145, 146, 149, 150, 153, 154
Price, C. C., 194, 510, 513
Price, C. W., 112
Price, G., 379
Price, K. E., 160
Price, P. B., 577
Prival, M. J., 218, 219
Probst, I., 432
Prociv, P., 360-62
Promchainant, C., 250
Proska, B., 245
Proteau, G., 270
Protopapadakis, F., 684, 688
Pruess, D. L., 160
Prutton, I., 59
Ptashne, K., 585
Pugashetti, B. K., 652, 653, 656, 657
Pugsley, A. P., 371, 372, 375-78, 380, 381, 385
Puhalla, J. E., 51
Puhr, N. D., 364
Pullen, M. M., 286, 290, 303
Pullin, C. A., 499
Pullman, A., 151
Pulverer, G., 568, 575, 579-81
Pupillo, P., 661, 669
Purcell, A. H., 691
Purcell, D. C., 682
Purcell, E. M., 70
Purchase, I. F. H., 238, 242, 248
Purohit, K., 501
Puschmann, M., 480
Pushkaran, M., 118
Puspuro, A., 385, 389
Pyysalo, H., 245

Q

Quackenbush, R., 480
Quail, A., 148
Quayle, J. R., 192, 447
Queener, S. W., 161, 166, 210, 223
Quijano, R., 502
Quirk, A. V., 661
Quisenberry, W. B., 582

R

Rabussay, D., 149
Racaniello, V. R., 634
Raczynska-Bojanowska, K., 219, 222
Radue, A. B., 223
Rae, P. M. M., 154
Rafalski, A., 222
Raffel, S., 315
Rager-Zisman, B., 595
Rager-Zisman, Z., 611
Rahimian, H., 687
Rahman, A. S. M. M., 352, 354, 357
Rai, A. N., 498, 517
Raimondo, L. H., 98
Rajbhandary, U. L., 570
Raju, B. C., 691
Rake, A., 573
Ralph, B. J., 263, 264, 266-68, 270, 279
Ralston, E., 39
Ramirez, J. M., 500
Ramphal, R., 598
Ramseur, J. M., 639
Rana, G. L., 678
Rand, C. H. Jr., 347, 350
Rand, M. J., 239
Randall, L. L., 382, 390, 393, 396, 404, 405, 408
Randall-Hazelbauer, L., 398
Ranhand, J. M., 687, 703
Rank, R. G., 306
Rantz, L. A., 18
Rao, D., 623
Rao, D. D., 636
Rapp, H. J., 330, 332
Rappaport, I., 607
Raska, I., 79, 80, 85
Ratcliffe, H. D., 190
Ratti, G., 58, 63
Rattray, J. B. M., 112
Rauch, B., 384
Raude, A. B., 161, 166
Raveed, D., 189
Ravel, G., 451, 452
Rawson, J. R., 435
Ray, B., 227
Razin, S., 681, 684, 696, 698, 701, 702
Razzell, W. E., 271, 273, 276
Read, S., 327
Reader, R. W., 88
Reading, C., 176, 177
Reali, D., 362
Reanney, D., 650
Reanney, D. C., 585
Reaston, J., 510, 526
Rebell, G., 125
Redaelli, P., 123
Reddy, C. A., 459
Reddy, C. S., 238, 239

Reddy, G. V. P., 143, 144
Redfearn, E. R., 187
Redfearn, M. S., 39
Reed, D. W., 189
Reefschläger, J., 154
Rees, E., 290, 300
Rees, K. R., 253
Reese, E. T., 439
Reeve, P., 300
Reeves, P., 371-75, 378, 381, 385, 387, 389
Regamey, R. H., 332
Regenass, M., 379, 381-83, 391
Reichelt, J. L., 357
Reichert, C., 326
Reichlin, M., 601
Reid, M., 570
Reiko, O., 500
Reily, M., 238
Reimann, H., 543, 545, 546
Reimer, M., 200
Reinhardt, D. J., 130
Reinhardt, G., 221, 222
Reinhold, V. N., 242, 243, 249, 254-56
Reinman, S., 520
Reiss, J., 239, 241
Reithmeier, R. A. F., 382, 384, 385, 389, 390
Resnick, A. D., 219
Resnik, S., 650
Revel, H. R., 148, 149, 152
Revet, B., 138, 141
Revilla, G., 216
Rexova-Benkova, L., 439, 441
Reynaud, P., 511
Reysset, G., 228
Rhodes, D., 515
Rhodes, M. E., 71
Ribi, E., 330, 613
Ribi, E. E., 330
Ricard, B., 703
Rice, D., 527
Rice, E. H., 121
Rich, A., 394, 404
Richards, M., 162
Richards, R. L., 196
Richardson, C. C., 148
Richer G., 328
Richmond, M. H., 585
Richmond, S. J., 300
Rick, P. D., 412
Rickenberg, H. V., 217
Riedel, G. E., 527
Rietschel, E. T., 329
Riggsby, W. S., 567
Riis, R. C., 238
Rima, B. K., 146, 149
Rinehart, K. L., 214, 219
Ring, K., 225, 226
Ripa, K. T., 300, 305
Ripa, T., 299
Rippel-Baldes, A., 186
Rippka, R., 44, 45, 499, 506, 507, 509, 510, 519, 526
Rippon, J. E., 579
Ris, H., 98
Rische, H., 566
Ritcey, G. M., 264, 272, 273, 278
Ritchey, M. B., 625
Ritchie, A. E., 689, 700, 701, 704
Ritchie, D. F., 651, 652
Ritchie, M. I., 276, 278
Ritter, D. B., 289, 290
Ritter von Rittershain, G., 487
Rivera-Ortez, J. M., 198
Rixford, E., 121
Robbers, J. E., 216
Robbi, M., 404
Robbins, F. C., 595
Robert-Baudouy, J., 670, 671
Robert-Baudouy, J. M., 671
Roberts, A. P., 581
Roberts, D., 351
Roberts, G. T., 239
Roberts, J. R., 33
Roberts, M., 485
Roberts, R. B., 585
Roberts, R. J., 149
Roberts, T. M., 526
Robertson, D. C., 466, 470, 472
Robins-Browne, R. M., 347, 349, 350
Robinson, A., 596
Robinson, P. D., 501, 502
Robinson, R., 160, 162
ROBSON, R. L., 183-207; 189, 190, 512
Rocchiccioli, S., 427
Roche, C., 426, 432
Rochovansky, O. M., 628
Rodgers, G. A., 498
Rodrigues de Miranda, L., 116, 124
Rodriguez, G. E., 333
Rodriguez-Barrueco, C., 184, 194
Rodwell, A. W., 684, 686
Rodwell, E. S., 684, 686
Roebuck, B. D., 249, 256
Rogers, A. F., 562
Rogers, D. P., 116
Rogers, D. T., 50, 51, 55, 56, 62, 65
Rogers, G. T., 138
Rogers, L. A., 647
Rogers, L. J., 500, 501
Rogerson, A. C., 507, 513
Rogolsky, M., 488, 489
Rohde, W., 625
Rohrmann, G. F., 607
Rokos, E. A., 492
Roland, F. P., 353, 357
Rolicka, M., 326
Rolinson, G. N., 162, 174, 176
Rolland., 119
Rollins, L., 466, 473
Rollins, R. C., 110
Romanzi, C. A., 569
Romesser, J. A., 436, 449
Rondeau, N., 514, 515
Rood, J. I., 492
Roof, W. D., 492
Rook, G. A. W., 333, 334
Roon, R. J., 223-25
Roop, D. R., 567
Rorke, L. B., 683, 691, 704
Roscoe, D. H., 145, 149, 150, 153
Rose, D. L., 681-83, 686, 690, 704
Rose, L., 290, 296
Roseman, S., 384
Rosenbach, F. J., 560, 561
Rosenberg, E., 141
Rosenberg, M., 61
Rosenblatt, M., 394, 404
Rosenblum, E. D., 488, 568, 573, 579, 585
Rosenbusch, J. P., 371, 379, 381-84, 389, 391
Rosendorf, L. L., 585
Ross, R., 110
Rosselet, J. P., 317, 327
Rosypal, S., 563
Rosypalova, A.., 563
Roszkowski, J., 222
Rotering, H., 384, 388, 390, 395, 408, 412
Roth, J., 650
Rothberg, W., 562
Rothenberg, R., 290, 301, 302
Rothfield, L., 408
Rothfield, L. I., 387, 392
Rothman, J. E., 413
Rott, R., 625
Rotta, J., 329
Rottem, S., 684, 696, 698, 701, 702
Rottenberg, H., 92
Rotter, V., 596, 611
Rountree, P. M., 583, 585
Routien, J. B., 552, 554
Rowan, R. G., 650, 651
Rowbury, R. J., 78
Rowe, B., 469-71, 474, 476
Rowe, L. B., 50, 52, 53, 55, 56, 61, 62
Rowell, P., 497, 498, 500, 501, 513-18, 520, 522-24
Rowley, B. I., 188
Roy, B., 679, 700-2
Royer, H., 386, 393, 410, 411
Ruben, F. L., 611
Rubens, C., 585
Rubik, B. A., 90

Rubin, P. M., 505
Rubin, S. J., 344, 360-62
Rudin, Y., 404
Rudneva, I., 629
Rudolph, K., 659
Ruet, A., 239, 241, 252
Ruettinger, T., 143
Ruger, M., 212
Ruiz-Argueso, T., 200-2
Runge, W. J., 238
Rupprecht, E., 412
Rupprecht, M., 568, 572, 573, 576
Russell, S. A., 200, 201, 506
Rutter, J. M., 467
Ruvkin, G. B., 527
Ryan, M. D., 500
Ryan, W. J., 360-62
Ryder, R., 471
Ryder, R. W., 466, 469
Ryter, A., 409
Ryther, J. H., 510

S

Saad, A., 346, 350
Sabatini, D. D., 407
Sabersky-Lehman, C., 650
Sabouraud, R., 122
Saccardo, P. A., 114-16, 120, 127
Sacchi, G. A., 501
Sache, E., 324
Sachs, D. H., 602
Sack, D. A., 346, 348, 349, 476
Sack, R. B., 347, 466, 472, 476
Sacks, D. L., 297
Sadaie, Y., 239, 241-43, 245
Sadoff, H. L., 227, 228
Sadowski, P. D., 148
Saglio, P., 678-85, 687, 688, 701, 704
Saglio, P. H. M., 679, 685, 691, 695, 697, 699
Saiki, I., 324, 329, 331
Saillard, C., 679-83, 686-92, 694-97, 701, 704
Saito, K., 168, 169
Saito, M., 238, 239, 241, 242
Saito, N., 236, 238, 240
Saito, R., 318, 324, 334
Sakaguchi, B., 678
Sakaguchi, H., 266, 272-74, 276, 277, 279
Sakaguchi, K., 506
Sakai, F., 238, 249
Sakai, H., 168-70
Sakai, S., 355
Sakakibara, Y., 238
Sakamoto, M., 176
Sakazaki, R., 344, 347, 351, 353, 354, 648
Saksena, K. N., 49, 55, 56
Sakurai, J., 354
Sallal, A-K. J., 502, 521
Salton, M. R. J., 313
Samour, D., 315, 317, 323
Sampaio, M. J. A. M., 497, 498, 514-16
Samson, R. A., 112, 113, 115, 126, 129, 130
Samson, R. R., 314
San Blas, G., 315
Sanchez, D., 586
Sanchez, F., 224
Sanchez-Leyva, R., 483
San Clemente, C. L., 571
Sanders, C., 547
Sanders, W. E. Jr., 547
Sanderson, A. R., 570
Sanderson, K. E., 371, 656, 657
Sands, D., 666
Sands, T. H., 161, 164
San Pietro, A., 501
Santos, D. S., 469, 472
Sanwal, B. D., 223
Sanyal, S. C., 347, 356
Sapienza, C., 506, 526
Sarasin, A., 251
Sarasin, A. R., 251, 252
Sarid, S., 486
Sarma, V., 373, 374
Sarre, O. Z., 550
Sarthy, A., 374, 410
Saruwatari, K., 357, 359
Sarvas, M., 376, 390
Sassiver, M. L., 160
Sato, K., 396, 409, 411, 414
Sato, M., 270, 544
Sato, S., 540, 544, 545
Sato, T., 265, 373, 376, 384, 540, 544, 545
Satoi, S., 555
Satta, G., 569
Satter, L. D., 426, 429
Satterwhite, T. K., 467
Saunders, J. R., 95, 485, 649, 650
Sawhney, S. K., 505
Saxon, E., 301
Saxon, E. M., 301, 305
Scandella, C., 390, 405
Scannell, J. P., 160
Scazzocchio, O., 219
Schaad, N. W., 647
Schachenmayr, W., 314
Schachman, H. K., 9, 23, 24, 499
SCHACHTER, J., 285-309; 286, 288, 289, 293, 297-99, 301-5
Schachtschabel, D. O., 239
Schade, S. A., 98
Schaechter, M., 413
Schaefer, D. W., 76, 77
Schaeffer, F., 505, 515
Schaffer, P., 229
Schalch, W., 83
Schatz, G., 404
Schaupp, A., 448
Schechter, A. N., 602
Schechter, E. M., 293
Schechter, Y., 125
Scheffers, W. A., 101-3
Scheifinger, C. C., 438
Schell, J., 647, 650, 651
Schenkein, I., 472
Scherings, G., 189, 190, 512
Schibeci, A., 112
Schiewe, M. H., 491
Schiff, J. A., 505
Schildkraut, C. L., 139, 141
Schilling, N., 513, 514, 516
Schindler, H., 379, 381, 383
Schindler, M., 391, 412
Schipper, M. A. A., 129, 130
Schlapfer, H. U., 300
Schlecht, S., 390
Schlegel, H. G., 80, 191, 193, 195, 434, 451, 454, 523, 525
Schleifer, K. H., 313, 320, 326, 327, 563-66, 568-74, 576, 578, 579, 581-84, 587
Schlesinger, M. J., 396, 404, 408
Schlesinger, S., 634
Schloesing, T., 510
Schlumberger, H. D., 607
Schmid, G. H., 499, 500
Schmid, K., 475
Schmidmayr, W., 373-75, 384, 389
Schmidt, A., 505, 516
Schmidt, G. W., 404
Schmidt, J. M., 37
Schmidt, W. C., 314
Schmidt-Lorenz, W., 186
Schmitt, R., 79, 80, 85, 98, 99, 475
Schnaitman, C. A., 274, 371-78, 380, 381, 384-87, 411
Schneider, H., 499
Schneider, H. A. W., 499
Schneider, K., 195, 523, 525
Schneider, K. C., 195
Schneider, W. R., 75, 76, 96, 100, 101
Schneierson, S. S., 647, 648
Schnellen, C. G., 437
Schnoes, H., 166
Schoberth, S., 434, 448, 454
Schoenhard, G. L., 242
Schoental, R., 236, 240
Scholer, H. J., 129
Schol-Schwarz, M. B., 123, 126
Scholtissek, C., 620, 625
Schopf, J. M., 110

Schramek, S., 289
Schrank, G. D., 79
Schrauzer, G. N., 196, 198
Schroth, M. N., 98, 649, 650, 654, 659-61
Schubert, K. R., 200
Schubert, M., 61, 629
Schuhardt, V. T., 563
Schuldiner, S., 499, 503
Schulman, J. L., 598, 620, 625, 627
Schultz, E., 439
Schumacher, D., 545
Schumacher, G., 393
Schumacher-Perdreau, F., 566, 569-72, 582-84
Schumann, C., 193
Schürmann, P., 516
Schutz, R. D., 238
Schwab, J. H., 316
Schwartz, A. C., 445
Schwartz, M., 374, 378-80, 389, 393, 397-401, 409
Schwartz, W., 264, 272, 274
Schwarz, H., 385, 390, 392, 393
Schwarz, J., 238
Schweizer, M., 384, 385, 389-91, 415
Schwesinger, M. D., 489
Sciaky, D., 647, 650
Sciavolino, F. C., 552
Scoot, A., 466, 470
Scotland, S. M., 469, 470, 471, 474, 476
Scott, D. B., 518
Scott, F. W., 238
Scott, P. M., 245
Scowcroft, W. R., 192
Scragg, J. N., 347, 349, 350
Seaman, E., 569
Sear, H. S., 364
Sebek, O. K., 166, 210
Sedgwick, M. I., 467, 476
Sedgwick, S. G., 250
Seegers, J. C., 239
Seeliger, H. P. R., 101, 110
Seemuller, E. A., 665
Segel, H., 224
Segretain, G., 114
Seibert, D., 485
Seibert, F. B., 319
Seidel, G. E., 290, 300
Seidl, H. P., 327
Seidl, P. H., 326, 327, 563, 571
Seki, T., 567
Sekizawa, J., 393, 395
Sela, M., 315, 317, 600, 603-5, 608, 613-15
Sellwood, R., 467
Selsing, E., 151
Selzer, G., 153
Semancik, J. S., 58
Semine, D. Z., 290, 301, 302
Semler, B. L., 61, 634, 636, 639, 642
Sen, D., 353, 356
Sen, P. C., 347, 356
Sen, P. K., 166
Sengupta, P. G., 353, 356
Senior, P. J., 188
Sentein, R., 239
Sentenac, A., 239, 241, 252
Senyk, G. W., 611
Seol, S. Y., 353
Sequeira, L., 659, 661
Serra, G. E., 427, 432
Seto, B. L., 517
Seto, T., 238, 239
Shafer, W. M., 486
Shaffer, P. W., 513, 514, 516, 521
Shaffer, S., 650
Shafia, F. M., 274
Shah, V. K., 185, 189, 190
Shalita, Z., 486
Shalitin, C., 57, 65
Shaltiel, L., 377, 379, 380
Shands, J. W. Jr., 598
Shankat, G. A., 570
Shanmugam, K. T., 200, 219, 227, 517
Shaper, J. H., 82, 84
Shapira, E., 597
Shapiro, B. M., 515
Shapiro, L., 87, 88
Shapiro, M. B., 511
Shapiro, S., 436, 449
Shapovalova, S. P., 554
Sharp, J. T., 327
Shatkin, A. J., 57
Shaw, C., 562, 564
Shaw, C. R., 129
Shaw, E. R., 189
Shear, C. L., 114, 127
Shearer, G. M., 599, 615
Shearman, D. J. C., 314
Sheffer, H. W., 271, 272, 274
Sheffery, M., 84
Shen, B. H. P., 409
Shepard, T. H., 244
Shepherd, D., 211
Sher, H. I., 600
Sherman, D., 51
Sherod, D. W., 444
Shethna, Y. I., 189
Shewan, J. M., 343
Shiba, T., 315, 317, 319, 322-24, 328, 329, 331, 333, 334
Shibakawa, R., 554
Shibamoto, N., 174
Shibata, M., 548
Shibusawa, A., 317, 319
Shields, D., 62
Shikata, E., 678
Shikata, T., 238
Shilo, M., 499, 502, 504, 505, 519, 522
Shilov, A. E., 198
Shimada, K., 74, 88, 214, 215
Shimada, T., 347, 349, 351
Shimauchi, Y., 174, 175
Shimizu, K., 393, 394, 406
Shimizu, M., 354, 602, 604
Shimizu, Y., 544
Shimono, T., 315, 317, 319, 322-24, 327-29, 331, 335, 614
Shimono, Y., 613
Shin, M., 500
Shinmyo, A., 435, 440
Shinoda, S., 102, 103
Shinohara, Y., 238
Shioi, J-I., 96
Shiozawa, C., 604
Shipley, P., 482
SHIPLEY, P. L., 465-96, 471, 474, 475, 490
Shirafuji, H., 161, 164-66
Shoeb, Z. E., 245
Shoemaker, A. C., 579, 582
Shoesmith, J. G., 100, 101
Shohat, B., 596, 611
Shoji, J., 554
Shomura, T., 168, 169, 554
Shooter, R. A., 578
Shorin, V. A., 554
Shub, D., 153
Shugar, D., 140, 141, 152
Shull, G., 538
Shuman, H., 409
Shuman, H. A., 389, 397
Shuster, C. W., 483, 649-51
Sieber, O. F., 596
Siebke, J.-C., 144
Siefert, E., 199, 497, 498, 506
Siegel, R. C., 385
Siegel, W. G., 249, 256
Siegert, W., 145, 152
Siepmann, R., 130
Sigler, L., 120, 121, 123-25
Sih, C. J., 165, 166
Siitonen, A., 376
Sil, J., 353, 356
Silhavy, T. J., 373, 378, 379, 389, 397-401, 403-5, 407, 409, 410, 414, 416
Silva, M. L. M., 471, 473
SILVER, M., 263-83; 270-80
Silver, R. P., 467, 468, 473, 476
Silver, W. S., 511
Silverman, M., 70, 84, 85, 88, 97
Silverman, M. P., 265, 266, 273
Silverstein, S. C., 63
Silvester, W. B., 502, 512
Silvestri, L. G., 563

Simon, E. J., 239, 241, 252
Simon, M., 84, 88, 97, 140, 141, 152, 586
Simon, M. I., 70, 84, 85
Simon, P., 503
Simon, R. D., 510, 519, 526
Simonetti, S., 362
Simpson, F., 200, 201
Simpson, F. B., 200, 499
Simpson, R. W., 624, 626, 630
Sims, A. P., 515, 516
Sims, P., 22
Sinay, P., 313, 323, 614
Sinclair, A. C., 544
Sineriz, F., 438
Sing, V. O., 659, 660
Singer, B., 256
Singer, G., 95
Singer, P. C., 266
Singer, R. A., 498
Singh, A., 143
Singh, H., 347
Singh, H. N., 526
Singh, H. W., 526
Singh, M., 412
Singh, P., 166
Singh, P. K., 507, 509
Singh, R., 242, 243
Singh, S. J., 347
Sinha, B. D., 526
Sinha, R. C., 691
Sinha, V. B., 491
Sinnhuber, R. O., 238, 242, 255
Sinskey, A. J., 431
Sipe, J. D., 57
Siraj, M. Y., 241, 252
Sirkar, B. K., 352, 353, 356
Sissenstein, R., 701
Sistrom, W. R., 27, 29, 32, 497
SJOBLAD, R. D., 69-108
Sjöquist, J., 327
Sjostrom, J. E., 486
Sjulin, T. M., 662
Skartveat, S. M., 467
Skehel, J. J., 627
Skerman, F. J., 468, 567, 573, 574
Skerman, V. B. D., 110
Skipper, N., 50, 51
Skopek, T. R., 254, 255
Skripal, I. G., 680
Skulachev, V. P., 92
Skurray, R. A., 385, 389
Skye, G. E., 224
Slater, J. H., 505, 506
Sleeper, B. P., 20
Sletten, A., 662
Sleytr, U., 435
Sleytr, U. B., 79
Sluba, T., 614
Sluss, R., 153
Small, P. A. Jr., 598
Smalley, E. B., 245
Smarda, J., 498
Smiley, J. O., 670
Smillie, R. M., 500, 501
Smit, J., 389, 390, 409, 412, 415, 416
Smith, A. J., 44, 501, 503, 505
Smith, A. L., 485
Smith, B. E., 185, 196, 197, 511
Smith, B. S. W., 22
Smith, C. A., 252
Smith, D. G., 78
Smith, D. M., 354
Smith, G. H., 647
Smith, H. Jr., 347, 350
Smith, H. L. Jr., 351
Smith, H. R., 469-71, 474, 476
Smith, H. W., 466-68, 474, 476-78, 482, 584, 585
Smith, I. M., 579, 582, 583
Smith, J. L., 93
Smith, L. A., 201
Smith, L. B., 241, 252
Smith, M. R., 437
Smith, M. T., 116, 124
Smith, P. F., 701
Smith, P. L., 466
Smith, R. F., 568-71, 576, 580, 582, 583
Smith, R. V., 185, 500, 504, 511, 522
Smith, S. E., 84, 271, 278
Smith, U., 501
Smith, W. P., 404, 407, 408
Sneath, P. H. A., 110, 563
Snell, E. E., 313
Snippe, H., 607
Snoke, J. E., 213
Snustad, D. P., 148
Snyder, J. C., 290, 296
Snyder, J. D., 364
Snyder, L., 153
Snyder, L. R., 149
So, M., 467-71, 473-75, 490
Sober, H. A., 53
Sojka, W. J., 467
Solanes, R. E., 101, 102
Solberg, C. O., 579
Solioz, M., 404
Soljanto, P., 277
Soll, L., 668
Soloff, B. L., 306
Soltesz, V., 78
Somers, J. M., 50, 51, 59-62, 64
Somerville, D. A., 560, 576-79, 583
Song, S. A., 377, 379, 380
Sonie, K. C., 526
Sonntag, I., 372, 384, 385, 389, 390, 392, 393
Soper, Q. F., 161, 163
Sörensen, L., 504
Sorger, G. J., 220
Soroff, S., 237
Sorsa, M., 241, 244
Soska, J., 95
Soto-Figueroa, E., 319
Soulic, M.-O., 138, 141
Southern, P. M., 71
Spanel, R., 314
Spark, R. P., 360, 362
Sparks, R. B., 650
Sparks, R. B. Jr., 656
Spaulding, P. L., 352, 360
Spears, P., 290, 300, 303
Specter, S., 334
Spector, S., 301
Sperens, B., 145, 152
Speth, V., 389, 409, 412
Spieckerman, C., 579
Spiegelman, S., 19, 573
Spingarn, N. E., 236
Spira, W. M., 346, 348, 349
Spitler, L., 604
Spivey, M. J., 425, 436, 458
Splendore, A., 125
Sporkenbach, J., 445
Sporn, M. B., 250, 253
Spotts, C. R., 9, 35
Spudich, E. N., 84, 411
Spudich, J. L., 75, 91
Sripati, C. E., 57
Srivastava, B. S., 491
Stableforth, A. W., 579, 582
Stacey, G., 514-18
Stachow, C. S., 223
Stackebrandt, E., 564, 679, 680
Stadler, G. R., 239
Stadtman, E. R., 515
Stadtman, T. C., 437, 448, 449
Stafford, D. A., 457, 458
Stafford, M. E., 143
Stafleu, F. A., 110
Stalheim, O. H. V., 689, 700, 701, 704
Stam, W. T., 506
Stamm, J. M., 544
Stanaszek, R. S., 544
Standard, P., 120
Standard, P. G., 124
Stanford, G. K., 238, 240
Stang, W. J., 362
STANIER, R. Y., 1-48; 8-11, 19-24, 27-35, 37, 39, 41, 42, 44, 45, 101, 102, 498, 499, 505-7, 509, 510, 515, 526
Stanley, S. O., 226, 514
Stanley, W. M., 602
Stanners, C. P., 624
Stanton, M. F., 332
Staplers, J. A., 129, 130
Stapley, E. O., 168-70, 173-75
STARK, A. A., 235-62; 239, 241, 244, 245, 254, 255

Stark, C., 634, 637
Stark, J., 649-51
Stark, W. M., 164, 168, 169
STARR, M. P., 645-76; 646-54, 656, 657, 659, 664-72
Starr, P. B., 648, 665, 666
Steele, R. W., 611
Steenbergen, F., 583
Steere, R. L., 678, 696, 698
Steigerwalt, A. G., 357, 567, 574, 648, 653, 666
Steiner, T., 704
Steinitz, Y., 502
Stemmer, W., 683, 686, 690, 704
Stempel, A., 160
Stenderup, A., 474
Stent, G. S., 138
Stepankova, E., 346, 350
Stephens, G. J., 664
Stephens, G. R., 429
Stephenson, M., 436, 452
Stephenson, M. P., 188, 446, 452
Stepien, E., 152
Stern, E. R., 328
Steven, A., 379, 381-83, 391
Steven, A. C., 381-83
Stevens, C., 684, 688
Stevens, C. M., 213
Stevens, D. M., 170
Stevens, S. E. Jr., 502
Stewart, A. C., 500
Stewart, G. R., 515
Stewart, R., 502
STEWART, W. D. P., 497-536; 184, 192, 497, 498, 500-3, 505-7, 510-26
Stewart, W. W., 160
STEWART-TULL, D. E. S., 311-40; 314, 315, 317, 319, 322, 323, 327, 328, 331, 333-35, 613
Steyn, P. S., 239
Stiefel, E. I., 185, 196
Stiffel, C., 330
Stigliani, R., 121
Still, C. S., 347, 349, 350
Still, G. G., 188
Still, P. E., 245
Stiller, D., 691, 704
Stitt, J. M., 562, 564
Stjernholm, R., 445
St. John, R. T., 190
Stock, G. B., 77
Stock, J. B., 384
Stockdale, P. M., 130
Stocker, B. A. D., 376, 385, 386, 389
Stockland, A. E., 571
Stodolsky, M., 141
Stoeber, F., 670, 671
Stoeber, F. R., 671
Stokes, J. L., 86
Stokes, W. R., 119
Stollar, V., 61, 624
Stolp, H., 647
Stone, J. C., 141, 142
Storck, R., 112, 115, 129
Storz, J., 290, 300, 303
Stout, D. L., 129
Stouthamer, A. H., 434, 437, 444, 445, 451, 454
Stove, J. L., 37
Straley, S. C., 94
Strauss, B., 141, 142
Street, B. K., 50, 52, 53, 55
Streicher, S. L., 219, 227, 517, 655
Strength, W. J., 77
Strobel, G. A., 647, 663
Strominger, J. L., 570
Strong, F. M., 245
Stroshane, R. M., 214, 219
Stuckey, D. C., 457
Stumm, C., 99, 100
Stumm, W., 266
Stupperich, E., 436, 437, 450
Styles, C. A., 50, 64
Su, H. J., 682, 683, 688, 691
Subramanian, C. V., 115, 118, 119
Subramanian, K. N., 279
Suda, M., 20
Sugg, N., 289, 303, 304
Sugihara, S., 238
Sugimoto, K., 394, 395
Sugimoto, M., 544
Sugimura, K., 324, 329, 331, 333, 334
Sugimura, T., 236, 237, 241
Sugino, Y., 354
Sugio, T., 273, 274, 277
Sugisaki, H., 394, 395
Sugiura, A., 625, 637
Sugiura, M., 57
Sugiyama, K., 315, 318, 324
Sugiyama, S., 238, 239
Sukenobu, M., 500
Sullivan, M., 624
Summers, A. O., 375, 381
Summers, W. C., 250, 253
Sun, S. H., 121
Sung, M., 289, 303, 304
Surdeanu, M., 585, 586
Susor, W. A., 501
Sutcliffe, J. G., 394, 395
Sutherland, J. M., 510, 526
Sutherland, P. A., 53, 55
Sutton, J. A., 271, 272
Sutton, R. G. A., 346, 350
Suzuki, H., 387, 388, 390, 392
Suzuki, I., 269
Suzuki, K., 328
Suzuki, M., 549
Suzuki, N., 252
Suzuki, S., 161, 164, 238
Suzuki, T., 81, 200, 317, 319, 549
Svehang, S.-E., 597
Svennerholm, A. M., 466
Svensson, L., 299, 300
Sverdrup, H. U., 96
Swank, R. T., 187
Swanson, E. C., 489
Swanstrum, M., 477
Sweeney, M. J., 239
Sweeney, T. K., 56-60
Sweet, R., 301, 302, 305
Sweet, W. J., 511
Swenson, D. H., 249, 256
Swiderski, M., 491
Sydow, P., 114
Szekely, M., 51, 57
Szer, W., 140
Szmelcman, S., 92, 377-79, 398
Szmulewicz, S., 550, 552
Szulmajster, F., 149
Szulmajster, J., 228
Szyba, K., 568, 575
Szybalski, W., 144

T

Tabita, F. R., 501, 502, 510, 512-18, 526
Tabita, R., 270
Tabor, C. W., 64
Tabor, H., 64
Tadanier, J., 544
Taga, S., 354, 472
Taha, M. S., 509
Tai, P. C., 404, 407, 408
Taira, T., 538, 553
Tak, R., 353
Takabe, T., 502
Takada, H., 324, 333, 334
Takahashi, I., 98, 138, 141, 145, 146, 149, 152, 153
Takahashi, K., 238
Takahashi, N., 84
Takahashi, S., 174
Takanami, M., 394, 395
Takasawa, S., 540, 544, 545
Takashima, T., 327
Takayama, K., 544
Takeda, K., 548
Takeda, S., 328
Takeda, T., 354
Takeda, Y., 102, 129, 130, 352-57, 468, 471, 472
Takeuchi, M., 393, 394, 406
Takeya, K., 78
Takita, T., 160
Tally, F. P., 175
Tamura, A., 291, 293
Tamura, K., 353, 354, 648
Tanaka, A., 315, 318, 324, 327, 334

Tanaka, K., 318
Tandeau de Marsac, N., 45, 499
Tani, N., 170-72
Taniguchi, M., 329
Tanimoto, R. H., 582
Taniyama, T., 324, 331, 333, 334
Tanner, R., 679, 680
Tanner, R. S., 434, 448, 454
Tano, T., 265, 270, 273, 274, 277
Tanyashin, V. I., 153
Taplin, D., 125
Tarumi, Y., 315, 317, 319, 322, 323, 333, 334, 614
Tate, A., 56-60
Tatsuno, M., 238, 249
Tatsuno, T., 238, 239, 241, 252
Tauschel, H. D., 86
Tay, L., 353, 354, 356
Taylor, B. L., 75, 88, 96
Taylor, G. C., 510
Taylor, G. T., 436, 450
Taylor, H. J., 141
Taylor, J. J., 128
Taylor, M. J., 152
Taylor, P. W., 481
Taylor-Robinson, D., 679, 682
Teather, R. M., 386, 393, 408, 410, 411
Tedesco, P., 91
Tedesco, P. M., 73
Teitelbaum, D., 611, 612
Telfer, A., 185
Tel-Or, E., 500, 513, 519, 520, 523-25
Tempest, D. W., 217, 226, 227
Teng, M.-H., 141
Ten Heggeler, B., 381-83
Tennigkeit, J., 201, 202, 521, 523, 524
Teranaka, M., 678
Terayama, T., 355
Testa, R. T., 539-42, 546, 547, 549, 553
Tetley, R. M., 523
Thauer, R. K., 430, 436, 437, 444, 445, 449-51
Theodore, T. S., 117
Thibeault, G., 328
Thiel, P. G., 239, 241-45, 250, 251, 253
Thielmann, H. W., 252
Thillaye B., 329
Thomas, B. J., 300
Thomas, C., 685
Thomas, D. D., 649
Thomas, D. L., 683, 686, 690, 704
Thomas, D. W., 313
Thomas, E. T., 563
Thomas, J., 513, 514, 519, 521
Thomas, P., 346, 350
Thomas, T. D., 444, 451
Thompson, G. E., 329
Thompson, J., 583
Thompson, K., 611
Thompson, M., 328
Thompson, N. E., 585
Thompson, R. B., 332
Thompson, R. C., 404, 408
Thompson, R. K., 120, 121
Thompson, T., 435, 459
Thompson, T. L., 138
Thompson, W., 488
Thorig, L., 583
Thorley, C. M., 583
Thornber, J. P., 520
Thorne, C. B., 152
Thorne, G. M., 467, 483
Thorneley, R. N. F., 184, 185, 196-98, 511
Thornsberry, C., 177, 344, 353, 357, 358, 360
Thorsteinsson, S. B., 357
Threefall, G., 625
Thrum, H., 221, 222
Thurow, H., 412
Thygeson, P., 290, 296
Tijtgat, R., 567
Tiku, M. L., 595, 611
Tilton, R. C., 344, 360-62
Timmis, K. N., 481
Timourian, H., 428
Timpl, R., 604
Timsit, J., 327
Tinoco, I. Jr., 152
Tipper, D. J., 50-53, 55, 56, 61, 62, 65, 313, 320, 570
Tipple, M., 301
Tipple, M. A., 301
Tischer, I., 513
Tisue, T., 501
Tiwari, I. C., 347
Tjalma, R. A., 579, 582
Tjepkema, J., 192
Tjoa, W. S., 467
Tkacz, A., 568, 575
Tobita, K., 620, 621, 623, 625, 628, 629, 636, 642
Toh-E, A., 64
Toia, R. E., 189, 523
Tokunaga, H., 376, 379, 381, 382, 500
Tokunaga, M., 376, 379, 381, 382, 391
Tomasz, A., 160
Tomfohrde, K. M., 343
Tomich, P. K., 143, 144
Tomino, S., 211, 213
Tomita, F., 145, 146, 153
Tomizuka, N., 273, 274, 278, 279
Toms, E. J., 165
Tomsett, A. B., 220
Tone, J., 554
Tong, G. E., 425, 427, 430, 431, 458
Toone, J., 516
Torma, A. E., 264, 266, 268, 270-80
Tornabene, T. G., 436, 563, 564, 569
Torti, S., 410
Torti, S. V., 410
Toth, B., 245
Totsugawa, K., 554
Totten, M., 583
Totten, P. A., 585
Toullet, F., 327, 329
Tovell, D. R., 622
Townsend, D., 293
Townsend, J. M., 239, 241, 245
Townsend, R., 678, 679, 683, 685, 686, 688, 696, 700, 704
Tözum, S. R. D., 507, 512
Trainin, N., 596, 611
Traxler, P., 161, 164
Treharne, J. D., 300
Treichler, H. J., 161, 164, 166
Tributsch, H., 265
Trudinger, P. A., 264
Truffaut, N., 138, 141
Trump, B. F., 255
Trussell, P. C., 271, 273, 275, 276, 279
Truumees, I., 549
Tsai, J. C., 193
Tsai, J. H., 704
Tsai, L. B., 511
Tsang, M. L.-S., 505
Tsao, G. T., 426-28, 430, 458, 459
Tschape, H., 566
Tschapek, M., 186
Tso, W-W., 88, 93
Tsuchida, M., 20, 21
Tsuchimoto, I., 239
Tsuchiya, H. M., 271, 273
Tsugita, A., 602
Tsujimoto, M., 324
Tsukioka, M., 238, 249
Tsung, C. M., 607, 608
Tsuno, M., 355
Tsunoda, H., 238, 239
Tsuruoka, T., 554
Tsuruta, O., 242
Tsutsui, T., 239, 241
Tsuyumu, S., 666, 667
Tu, J., 146
Tubaki, K., 115
Tucker, R. G., 145
Tully, J., 680, 682, 686-88, 690, 691, 695
Tully, J. G., 678-84, 686-92, 696, 698, 699, 701, 702, 704

Tunac, J. B., 173
Tung, M. C., 680
Tuovinen, O. H., 264, 266, 267, 270, 271, 273-75, 277, 278
Turck, M., 290, 298, 300
Turner, G. L., 190, 192, 193
Turner, L., 101
Turner, M., 129
Turner, M. K., 166, 170
Turner, P., 476
Turner, P. J., 467, 476
Turner, R. W., 239
Turner, T. B., 693
Turner, W. B., 239
Turner, W. N., 542
Tutikawa, K., 239, 241-43, 245
Tuttle, A. L., 24
Tuttle, J. H., 275
Tuzcu, O., 683, 686, 690, 704
Twedt, R. M., 352, 360
Tyler, B., 217, 218, 223, 229, 517
Tyreyar, F. J., 141
Tyrone, S., 488, 568, 573, 579
Tyrrell, D., 131
Tytgat, F., 319, 322
Tzen, J. C., 50, 60-62
Tzeng, S. F., 450

U

Ubbink, T. E. C. M., 144
Uchida, N., 238
Uchida, S., 623
Udvandy, J., 505
Ueberschar, S., 598
Ueda, I., 168, 169
Ueda, M., 625, 637
Ueki, T., 390
Uemiya, M., 324, 329, 331
Ueno, I., 237-39, 241, 252
Ueno, Y., 237, 239, 241-43, 245, 250-52
Uhlenbeck, O. C., 633
Ulbricht, T. L. V., 138
Ul-Hague, M. I., 519
Ulitzur, S., 102, 103
Ulrich, E. L., 500
Ulrich B. C., 407
Umbreit, W. W., 538
Umeda, A., 78
Umeda, M., 239, 241
Umezawa, H., 160, 174
Unz, R. F., 95
Upchurch, R. G., 219
Uraguchi, K., 238, 249
Usher, J. J., 165, 166
Utahara, R., 174
Utkilen, H. C., 504
Utz, J. P., 121, 130
Uyeo, S., 160

V

Vago, C., 691
Vaillancourt, S., 506
Vaishanpayan, A., 526
Vaituzis, Z., 74
Valadon, L. R. G., 112
Valentine, R. E., 517
Valentyne, J. R., 272
Valkenburg, H. A., 579
Valter, P. J., 360, 362
Valyi-Nagy, T., 554
Van Abeele, F. R., 161, 163
van Alphen, L., 372, 373, 375, 376, 380, 385, 386, 390, 391
van Alphen, W., 375, 378-81, 390
Van Arkel, G. A., 526, 527
Van Baalen, C., 499, 503, 506, 510, 512-18, 526
van Boxtel, R., 373-76, 380, 381
Vandamme, E. J., 165, 212
van Dear, A., 599
Vandemark, P. J., 691
Van den Hondel, C. A. M. J. J., 526, 527
van den Hondel, L. A., 393, 396
Van der Beek, E. G., 434, 444, 451, 454
van der Drift, C., 91, 92, 99, 100
Van der Ende, A., 526, 527
Vanderhaeghe, H., 165
van der Hock, R., 372, 375, 386
van der Meulen, A., 126
van der Meulen, H., 130
Vandermolen, G. E., 77, 78
van der Walt, J. P., 116
Van der Watt, J. J., 238, 242, 248
Van der Werf, A., 187, 199, 200
Vanderzant, C., 492
Vanek, Z., 210
Van Embden, J. D., 475, 485
Van Ermengem, J., 567
Van Etten, J. L., 58
Van Franke, R. M., 56, 63
van Gylswyk, N. I., 426, 432
van Houwe, G., 153
Van Klingeren, B., 485
Van Montagu, M., 651
van Niel, C. B., 8, 10, 25, 41
Van Noorle Jansen, L. M., 362
Van Rensburg, S. J., 239, 241-45, 248, 250, 251, 253
van Selm, N., 375, 378-80
van Uden, N., 112
van Velsen, A. F., 457
van Warmelo, K. T., 111
van Wyck-Kaptey, W. M., 445
Vanyushin, B. F., 138, 141
Van Zeeland-Wolbers, L., 189
Varel, V. H., 430, 457
Varela, G., 350
Varenne, S., 394, 408, 414
Varney, E. H., 691, 692
Vasconcelos, G. J., 362
Vaughn, J. L., 693
Vaughn-Jackson, J. D., 290, 299
Vazquez, V., 482, 483
Vedros, N. A., 295
Veeger, C., 187-90, 200, 512, 517, 522
Veeger, D., 189
Vela, G. R., 193
Velten, J., 153
Venegas, L., 683, 686, 690, 704
Venema, G., 506
Veraldo, P. E., 569
Verall, M. S., 174, 176
Verbeek, S., 526, 527
Verger, G., 347, 350
Verheij, H., 373, 374
Verhoef, C., 373-76, 380, 381, 389
Verhoef, K., 373
Verkleij, A., 390
Verneuil, 561
Vernon, M., 343
Vernotte, C., 499, 500
Vézina, C., 166, 210
Vickery, J. C., 492
Vidal-Leiria, M., 112
Vidaver, A. K., 58, 647, 650
Viennot-Bourgin, B., 683, 686, 690, 704
Viennot-Bourgin, G., 688
Vignais, P., 201
Vignais, P. M., 195, 199, 202, 510
Vignault, J. C., 680-84, 686-91 695, 704
Vilkas, E., 317, 331
Villa-Komaroff, L., 62
Villaneuva, J. R., 211, 216
Villarreal, L. P., 621, 637-39
Vincent, M. M., 611
Vinther, O., 87, 90
Vinton, J. G., 511
Virelizier, J. L., 598
Vishnyakova, I. A., 554
Viswanatha, T., 177
Vitkovic, L., 227, 228
Vleggaar, R., 239
Vodkin, M., 50, 51, 55-58, 60-62, 65
Vodkin, M. H., 50, 56

Vogel, R., 680, 682, 683, 686-91, 695, 704
Vogels, G., 433
Vogels, G. D., 92
Voigt, W., 566
Voisin, G. A., 327-29
Volcani, B. E., 502
von Arx, J. A., 112, 114-16, 122, 124
Von Dáranyi, J., 561
Von Graevenitz, A., 353, 360-62, 647, 648
Von Heijne, G., 402, 404, 407
von Magnus, P., 620, 621, 623, 642
von Meyenberg, K., 375, 377-80
von Riesen, V. L., 666
Von Schmidt, B., 301
von Wright, A., 239, 241, 245
Voss, E. G., 110

W

Wachsmuth, I. K., 466, 469, 471
Wachter, D., 572
Wada, K., 500, 501
Wadstrom, T., 580, 581
Wadsworth, M. E., 272
WAGMAN, G. H., 537-57; 538-42, 545-47, 549-53
Wagner, E. K., 56-59
Wagner, R. R., 623, 630
Wagner, W., 516
Wahba, A. J., 670
Wainwright, M., 373, 394
Waitz, J.A., 539-43, 546, 547
Wakabayashi, K., 81, 83
Wakerley, D. S., 273, 278
Wakisada, Y., 554
Waksman, B. H., 327, 328
Waksman, S. A., 538, 555
Walc-Pokrzywnicki, Z., 71
Waldee, E. L., 648, 666
Walden, C. C., 265, 266, 268, 271-76, 279
Wales, J. H., 238, 242
Walk, R. A., 404
Walker, C., 195, 198, 199, 202
Walker, C. C., 187, 199, 201, 202, 524
Walker, D. D., 585
Walker, D. J., 445
Walker, G. A., 185
Walker, G. C., 251
Walker, J. B., 211, 214-16, 218
Walker, M., 185
Walker, M. N., 185
Walker, M. S., 138, 146, 147, 154, 214-16, 218
Walker, R. T., 680
Wall, J. D., 219
Wall, M., 129
Wallace, G. D., 582
Wallerstein, R. O., 485, 487
Wallick, H., 170
Wallick, J., 426
Wallnofer, P., 445
Wallsgrove, R. M., 502
Walsby, A. E., 497, 498, 506, 510, 513
Walsh, F., 267
Walsh, K. A., 402
Walsh, M. P., 87
Walter, R., 450
Walther-Maurschat, A., 80
Walton, M. T., 425, 458
Wandersman, C., 374, 378-80, 393
Wang, C. C., 458, 459
Wang, C. H., 188
Wang, C. J. K., 126, 127
Wang, D., 458, 459
Wang, D. I. L., 458
Wang, G., 459
Wang, G. Y., 458, 459
Wang, J. H., 501
Wang, L., 331, 333
Wang, S., 393, 395, 458, 459
Wang, S-P., 286, 288, 290, 295-302, 305
Wanner, B. L., 374, 410
Ward, A. C., 188
Ward, D., 438
Ward, D. M., 438
Ward, P. D., 583
Ward, R. C., 428
Ware, D. A., 195
Warner, H. R., 145, 150, 152, 153
Warner, J. R., 57
Warner, R. C., 56-59
Warren, A. J., 227
Warren, G. H., 583
Warren, R., 488
WARREN, R. A. J., 137-58; 140-42, 148
Wartell, R. M., 151
Waschke, S., 154
Washington, J. A. II., 177
Wassink, E. C., 24
Watabe, T., 78
Watanabe, A., 509
Watanabe, H., 168, 169, 554
Watanabe, K., 57
Watanabe, S., 623
Watanabe, Y., 315, 317, 319, 320, 322-24, 328, 329, 614
Waterbury, J. B., 45, 499, 506, 507, 510, 519, 526
Waters, H., 698
Waterson, A. P., 624
Watkins, C., 360, 362
Watkins, P. D., 545, 552
Watson, R. O., 289, 290
Watson, S. A., 241, 252
Watt, G. D., 196
Waynforth, H. B., 240, 242
Weare, N. M., 202, 512, 521, 523
Weathers, L. G., 688, 704
Weaver, R., 357
WEAVER, R. E., 341-67; 344, 347, 350, 351, 353, 357-60
Weaver, S. S., 175
Webb, C., 611
Webber, J. A., 160
Weber, H., 52, 53, 55
Weber, K., 239, 607
Weber, M., 504
Weglenski, P., 219
Wegner, K., 245
Wehland, J., 239
Wehner, F. C., 239, 241-45, 250, 251, 253
Wehrmeyer, W., 499
Weibull, C., 78, 88
Weijman, A. C. M., 112, 115, 124, 129
Weimer, P., 435, 459
Weimer, P. J., 435-38, 440, 450, 457, 459
Wein, R. D., 245
Weinberg, E. D., 479
Weiner, A. M., 607
WEINSTEIN, M. J., 537-57; 538-42, 545-47, 549-53
Weisbeek, P. J., 526, 527
Weiss, B., 634
Weiss, E., 289
Weiss, F., 160
Weiss, R. L., 273, 390
Weissman, J. C., 523
Weitzman, I., 129, 130
Welch, W. H., 561
Weller, T. H., 595
Wellman, A. M., 112, 115, 130
Wells, J., 471
Wells, J. G., 352, 354, 355, 357, 492
Wells, R. A., 278
Wells, R. D., 151
Welsch, M., 538
Welsh, J. D., 62, 63
Welsh, R. M., 639
Welshimer, H. J., 101
Welty, K. T., 444, 448
Wentworth, B. B., 290, 298-300, 305, 579
Werden, K., 499
Weresub, L. K., 111
Wermuth, C-G., 326, 613
Werner, G. H., 318, 320, 322, 331, 613
West, M., 71

Westall, F. C., 328
Westermann, P., 376, 382
Westrom, L., 299, 300
Wetmur, J. G., 586
Whatley, M. H., 660
Wheat, R. P., 18
Wheeler, W. J., 161
Wheelis, M., 23
Wheelis, M. L., 23
Wheelock, E. F., 596
Wherland, S., 196
Whipp, S. C., 467
Whitcomb, R., 680, 682, 686-88, 690, 691, 695
WHITCOMB, R. F., 677-709; 678, 679, 681-701, 704
White, A. W., 519
White, H. J., 306
White, J. A., 659, 662
White, R. G., 315, 317, 323, 328, 333, 613
Whitehead, C. W., 161, 163
Whiteley, H. R., 138, 144, 149
Whitman, W. B., 501, 502
Whitney, D. J., 168, 170
Whitney, J. G., 164, 168, 169
Whittaker, B. L., 250
Whittaker, R. H., 109
Whittenbury, R., 192
Whittlestone, P., 678
Whitton, B. S., 498, 505
Wiame, J. M., 33, 219, 225
Wiberg, J. S., 153
Wicht, W. C., 613
Wicken, A. J., 327, 659
Wicker, K. J., 168, 170
Wickner, R. B., 50, 51, 55, 57, 58, 60, 61, 64, 65
Wickner, W., 370, 404, 405, 408
Wiedman, B., 585
Wiegel, J., 191, 195
Wiegel, T., 435
Wierzchowski, K. L., 152
Wietzerbin, J., 331
Wietzerbin-Falszpan, J., 313
Wilcockson, J., 193
Wildner, G. P., 245
Wiley, B. B., 488, 489
Wilke, C. R., 456, 458
Wilke, D., 191, 195
Wilke, G. R., 459
Wilkerson, J., 347, 350
Wilkins, T. D., 177
Wilkinson, J. F., 33
Wilkinson, J. M., 601
Wilkinson, P. C., 333
Willers, J. M., 607
Williams, A. M., 187
Williams, D. S., 683, 686, 690, 704
Williams, E. B., 611, 665
Williams, F. D., 77, 78, 94
Williams, J. D., 667, 668
Williams, P. H., 467, 476, 479, 480
Williams, R. C., 499
Williams, R. E. O., 578, 579
Williams, R. H., 239
Williams, T. H., 160
Williams, W. K., 213
Williamson, D., 680, 682, 686-91, 695
Williamson, D. H., 33
Williamson, D. L., 678, 681-83, 685, 686, 688-97, 699, 700, 703, 704
Williams-Smith, H., 579
Willshaw, G. A., 469-71, 474, 476
Wilson, A. C., 572
Wilson, B. J., 239-41
Wilson, C. R., 585
Wilson, D. E., 655
Wilson, D. G., 271, 274, 276, 277
Wilson, G. G., 153
Wilson, J. J., 98
Wilson, N. N., 289
Wilson, P. W., 187, 189, 190, 193, 195, 199
Wilson, V., 395
Wimmer, E., 61
Winet, H., 74
Winkenbach, F., 513, 520, 521
Winklmair, D., 78
Winocour, E., 624
Winogradsky, S., 8
Winslow, A. R., 561
Winslow, C. E. A., 561, 562, 647
Winstanley, D. J., 211, 216
Winston, V., 138
Winter, H., 238
Winter, H. C., 184
Winter, J., 438
Wintersgill, C., 290, 301, 302
Wise, D. L., 457, 458
Withers, R. E. G., 239
Witholt, B., 409, 414, 416
Witmer, H., 147, 150, 154
Wöber, G., 504
Woese, C. R., 436, 564, 679, 680
Wogan, G. N., 236, 239-45, 248-50, 253-56
Wojciuch, E., 202, 521, 526
Wolf, A., 328
Wolfe, R. S., 95, 432, 434, 436, 438, 448-50, 454, 679, 680
Wolff, S. M., 329
Wölfle, D., 200, 201
Wolfshohl, J. F., 568, 573-76, 579-81, 587
Wolin, M. J., 435, 438, 446, 451, 455, 456
Wolk, C. P., 202, 498, 499, 511, 513, 514, 516, 519-24, 526
Wolosiuk, R. A., 516
Wolters, C. H. L., 579
Wong, D. C., 682
Wong, J. J., 239, 241-43, 245, 255
Wood, D. R., 51
Wood, F. D., 327
Wood, H. A., 51-53, 55-58
Wood, H. C., 444, 448
Wood, H. G., 444, 445, 448, 454
Wood, M. A., 185
Wood, R. G., 273
Wood, R. K. S., 664
Wood, T. M., 439
Wood, W. A., 434, 446, 454-56
Wood, W. N., 441
Woodruff, H. B., 168, 169, 173-75, 212, 538
Woodruff, M. F. A., 332
Woods, A. C., 662
Woodward, J. E., 701
Woodward, W. E., 476
Woollacott, P. J. V., 353
Work, E., 313
Worley, J. F., 678, 683, 688, 691, 696, 698, 699
Worthington, R. W., 466, 470
Wovcha, M. G., 143, 144
Wright, A., 313, 320
Wright, B. L., 98
Wright, L. M., 251
Wright, V., 187
Wroblewski, H., 681, 702
Wu, H. C., 388, 390, 392, 394, 396, 397, 400, 402-4, 406, 407, 411-13, 415, 416
WU, H. C. P., 369-422
Wu, W. C., 657, 659
Wüst, J., 177
Wuyts, W., 165
Wyatt, C., 482, 483
Wyatt, G. R., 138, 140, 141
Wycoff, R. W. G., 276
Wyn-Jones, A. P., 598

Y

Yagen, B., 240
Yagil, E., 373, 379
Yagisawa, M., 273, 274, 278, 279
Yajima, T., 214
Yakir, Y., 596, 611
Yakuta, T., 99
Yamada, H., 381, 391
Yamada, M., 211, 213, 387, 392
Yamada, T., 444, 451, 506
Yamada, Y., 168, 169

Yamagishi, H., 141
Yamaguchi, S., 85
Yamaguchi, T., 83, 548
Yamai, S., 353
Yamamoto, J., 239, 241
Yamamoto, M., 540, 544, 545
Yamamura, Y., 315, 317-19, 323, 324, 327-29, 331, 333, 334, 613
Yamanaka, G., 499
Yamasaki, E., 236, 251
Yamashita, S., 56
Yamaura, Y., 324
Yamawaki, M., 324, 329, 331, 333, 334
Yamazaki, M., 238
Yamazaki, S., 174
Yanagida, M., 82
Yanai, M., 239, 241
Yang, G. C. H., 79
Yano, S., 548
Yapo, A., 312
Yarkoni, E., 331, 333
Yarrow, D., 116, 117, 124
Yashuk, J. C., 355
Yasuda, S., 387, 392
Yasunaka, K., 381
Yates, G., 197
Yates, M. G., 185-90, 193, 195, 197-202, 506, 523, 524
Yehle, C. O., 150
Yem, D. W., 388, 392, 400
Yoch, D. C., 500, 501, 511
Yokogawa, K., 315, 317, 319, 320, 322, 323, 329
Yokota, T., 172
Yoneda, M., 161, 164-66, 168
Yong, E. C., 296
Yora, K., 56, 678
Yoshida, J., 554
Yoshida, M., 166
Yoshida, T., 74
Yoshikazu, Y., 252
Yoshimura, Y., 320
Yoshioka, T., 160
Yoshishita, T., 623
Young, D. W., 166
Young, H. E., 428
Young, J., 602
Young, J. D., 602, 604, 606
Young, K. K. Y., 153
Young, L. Y., 457
Young, R. A., 50
Young, T. W., 50
Younger, J. S., 639
Yourassowsky, E., 347, 350, 360-62
Yu, F., 372, 381, 382, 391
Yu, F-L., 237
Yu, H. M., 293
Yu, L., 585, 586
Yu, M., 353, 354, 356
Yura, T., 373, 376, 384, 396, 409, 411, 414
Yusuf, A., 346, 348, 349

Z

Zabin, I., 395, 399-401, 403, 404
Zablen, L. B., 679, 680
Zaboura, M., 219
Zabriskie, J. B., 327
Zähner, H., 214
Zaizov, R., 596, 611
Zakay-Rones, Z., 290, 294
Zaki, A. H., 245
Zamchuk, L. A., 138
Zamenhof, S., 584
Zamiska, S. A., 354
Zanetti, G., 501
Zazra, J. J., 634
Zbar, B., 330, 332
Zee, L., 215
Zehnder, A. B., 436
Zeigel, R. F., 691
ZEIKUS, J. G., 423-64; 427, 429, 432-40, 448-50, 452-54, 456-59
Zen-Yoji, H., 353, 355, 360
Zetoony, E., 505
Zheleznyak, L. D., 351
Zide, N., 353, 357
Zilberstein, D., 92
Zilliken, F., 239
Zimm, B. H., 141
Zimmerman, R. J., 568, 572, 576, 580-83
Zimmerman, S. B., 168-70, 173, 175
Zimmermann, B. K., 499
Zimmermann-Telschow, H., 499
Zimmern, D., 57
Zinder, N. D., 655
Zink, D. L., 492
Zinkernagel, R. M., 599, 600
Zinnaka, Y., 349
Ziomek, D., 566
Zisman, B., 596
Zmudzka, B., 140
Zubko, V. I., 351
Zucker, M., 666
Zuckerman, A., 18
Zumft, W. G., 185
Zurowski, W. K., 220, 229
Zusman, D. R., 655
Zweibel, S. M., 126
Zycha, H., 130

SUBJECT INDEX

A

Absidia, 129
corymbifera, 129
ramosa, 129
Acetate
photometabolism of, 34
Acetobacterium woodii
autotrophic growth of, 434
glucose decomposition and, 438
Acetone-butanol fermentation, 425
Acetylcholine
Escherichia coli migration and, 99–100
N-Acetylthienamycin, 173–76
Acholeplasma laidlawii
rRNA cataloging technique and, 680
Acidogenic bacteria, 433–37
fermentation substrates and product yields of, 454–55
Acinetobacter calcoaceticus, 19
Acremonium, 118–19, 127
falciforme, 118
kiliense, 118
potronii, 118
recifei, 118
roseo-griseum, 118
Acrotheca, 123
Actinomycin, 552–53
repression in trophophase, 211
Actinomycin D
production of, 213
Actinoplanes brasiliensis
positive chemotaxis and, 94
Adenovirus vaccine, 595
Aeromonas hydrophila, 343–44
Aflatoxin B_1 (AFB_1)
carcinogenicity of
species specificity of, 254–55
liver cancer and, 248
sterigmatocystin-DNA adducts and, 255–57
Aflatoxins, 248–52
carcinogenicity of, 242–43
mutagenicity of, 250–51
cellular functions and, 251–52
sterigmatocystin and, 253–54
AfV
see Aspergillus foetidus virus
Agammaglobulinemia, 596
Agaricus bisporus
genetic activity of, 245
Agmenellum quadruplicatum, 502
Agrobacterium tumefaciens, 650–51
chromosomal marker transformation in, 656
lipopolysaccharide of, 660
Ajellomyces, 112–13
capsulatus, 113, 125
dermatitidis, 113
Alanine dehydrogenase
in cyanobacteria, 514
Alcaligenes eutrophus
flagellar filaments of, 79
Alcaligenes faecalis
motility of, 100
Alcaligenes paradoxus
flagellar filaments of, 80
Alcaligenes ruhlandii
flagellar filaments of, 80
Amebiasis
antibiotic G-418 and, 543
Amikacin, 545
Amino acids
Escherichia coli and, 94
transport in bacteria, 224–27
7-Aminocephalosporanic acid (7-ACA), 160–63
Aminoglycosides, 539–45
6-Aminopenicillanic acid (6-APA), 160
Ammonia
nitrogen catabolic reactions in fungi and, 219–20
Ammonia assimilation
cyanobacterial nitrogenase and, 514–16
Ammonium
amino acid transport in fungi and, 225
antibiotic production and, 224
Ampicillin
bicillary dysentery and, 484
Amylovorin, 662–64
Anabaena cylindrica, 499–502
Anabaena GS
activation/deactivation of, 516
Anabaena variabilis, 502
nitrogen fixation and, 202
Anacystis cylindrica
alanine dehydrogenase in, 514
glutamine synthetase-nitrogenase interactions in, 51
Anacystis nidulans
glutamic acid dehydrogenase in, 514
oxyhydrogen reaction in, 499
Anaerobic bacteria
acidogenic, 433–37
bioconversion of photosynthate by, 426
chemical and fuel production by, 423–60
methanogenic, 433–37
oxygen and, 432–33
solventogenic, 433–37
Anaerobic bacterial fermentation
biochemicals produced by, 459–60
biopolymer degradation mechanisms and, 439–41
hexose and pentose pathways in, 441–46
intra- and inter-species control of end-product formation in, 450–57
methane production and, 457–58
mixed-culture, 437–38
one-carbon metabolism pathways in, 447–50
product potentials and limitations in, 430–32
solvent production and, 458–59
species diversity and, 432–34
substrate availability and recalcitrance in, 428–29
Anatoxin a, 498
Ansamysins, 550–52
Anthraquinones
antitumor activity of, 245
Antibiotic, 460, 545
Antibiotic biosynthesis, 219–29
in fungi, 222–24
nitrogen metabolism and, 212–20
in streptomycetes, 220–22
Antibiotic G-52, 542
Antibiotic G-418, 542–43
Antibiotic JI-20, 543
Antibiotic production, 227–29
nitrogen metabolite regulation in, 220–24
Antibiotics
from Micromonospora, 538–54
see also specific type
Antibiotic SF-1854, 554
Antibiotic SF-1919, 554
Antibiotic T-43218, 554
Antibodies
antigenic interaction with, 597–98

synthesis of
humoral immune response and, 313–14
virus inactivation by, 598–99
Antigenicity, 600–2
Antigenic specificity, 600–2
Antigens
antibody interaction with, 597–98
carcinoembryonic, 605
chlamydial, 294–97
synthetic
antiviral response induced by, 606–11
with protein specificity, 603–5
viral
immune response and, 599–600
protein antigenicity and, 600–2
Antimicrobial agents
chlamydiae and, 293–94
Antiprotein-specific immune response, 603–4
Antitoxins
toxins and, 598
Antiviral response
synthetic antigens inducing, 606–11
Antiviral vaccines, 593–614
attenuated live, 596–97
killed, 596–97
synthetic, 606
cellular vs humoral response to, 611–12
synthetic adjuvants and, 612–14
Aphanocapsa, 502
Aphanothece halophytica, 502
Aquaspirillum autotrophicum
flagellar filaments of, 80
Aquaspirillum fasciculus
flagellar fascicle of, 77
Aromatic substrates
dissimilation of, 19–23
Arthrobacter atrocyaneus
peptidoglycan and, 320
Arthroderma, 113
Ascomycetes, 112–14
Ascomycota, 110
Aspergillus foetidus virus (AfV), 55
dsRNAs of, 58
Aspergillus nidulans
ammonia and nitrogen catabolic reactions in, 219–20
ammonium transport in, 224
Aspergillus niger virus, 55
ATP
nitrogenase in cyanobacteria and, 518–22
Aureobasidium, 119
pullulans, 119
Autoimmune disease
induction of, 328–29
Azospirillaceae
nitrogen fixation and, 191–92
Azotobacter
nitrogen fixation and, 185–196, 201
Azotobacter beijerinckii
nitrogen fixation and, 188
Azotobacter chroococcum
nitrogen fixation and, 185–202
Axotobacter vinelandii
nitrogen fixation and, 185–200

B

Bacillus brevis
antibiotic production and, 227
gramicidin S production and, 212–13
Bacillus cereus
antibiotic production and, 227
Bacillus lichenformis
bacitracin production and, 213
flagellar morphogenesis in, 87
motility of, 100
sporulation and, 228
Bacillus megaterium
peptidoglycan and, 319–20, 323
polyarthritis in rats and, 327
prophage induction in, 250
sporulation and, 228
viral vaccines and, 613
Bacillus polymyxa, 10
nitrogenase synthesis in, 184
Bacillus subtilis
DNA polymerase of, 150
DNA transformation in, 250
ϕe-infected
hmUra biosynthesis in, 144–45
flagellar basal structure of, 86
flagellar morphogenesis in, 87
flagellar motility inhibition in, 92
flagellin and, 78, 82–84
membrane potential and, 92
mycotoxin assay and, 240–44
PBS2-infected, 145
phage PBS-1 of, 98
sporulation and, 228
Bacitracin
ornithine in, 218
production of, 213
Bacteria
amino acid transport in, 224–27
bacteriophages adsorbing to, 98
ore leaching by, 263–80
virulence of
plasmid-mediated factors and, 465–90
see also specific type
Bacterial leaching, 253–60
medium composition and, 273–75
oxidation-reduction potential and, 273
particle size and substrate concentration and, 275
pH and, 273
temperature and, 272–73
Bacterial motility, 93–103
Bacterial peptidoglycans, 311–35
Bacteriochlorophyll
synthesis of, 27–28
Bacteriophage
adsorption to motile bacteria, 98
Erwinia spp. and, 651–52
Bacteriophage DNAs, 137–55
modified bases in, 138–39
biological consequences of, 148–54
biosynthesis and, 142–48
detection and identification of, 139–40
Bacteriophage ϕe, 138–54
Bacteriophage ϕ29, 149
Bacteriophage ϕW14, 140–42, 147–52
Bacteriophage PBS2, 140, 145–54
Bacteriophage S2L, 142
Bacteriophage SPO1, 138
Bacteriophage SP8, 138, 152
Bacteriophage SP82G, 138
Bacteriophage SP10, 142, 147–50
Bacteriophage SP15, 140–54
Bacteriophage T3, 140
Bacteriophage T4, 138–54
Bacteriophage XP12, 140, 146, 151–53
Bacteroides fragilis
transferable drug resistance in, 485
Bacteroides spp.
lactate fermentation by, 445
Bacteroides succinogenes
cellulase of, 439–40
succinate fermentation pathway of, 445
Bartholinitis
chlamydial, 287

Basidiobolus, 130–31
haptosporus, 130–31
heterosporus, 131
lacertae, 130–31
magnus, 131
meristosporus, 130–31
microsporus, 131
myxophilus, 131
philippinensis, 131
ranarum, 130–31
Basidiomycetes, 114–15
Basidiomycota, 110
Bdellovibrio
flagellar filaments in, 79
Bdellovibrio bacteriovorus
chemotaxis and, 94
Beneckea vulnifica, 357
Benzylpenicillin, 161, 166–68
Bioethanol
production of, 427
Biomass
anaerobic fermentation of, 426–32
polymeric nature of, 429
production of, 428
substrates of
composition of, 428–29
Blastomyces, 119–20
dermatitidis, 112–13, 119–20, 125
luteus, 119
Blastomycetes, 116–18
Bleomycins, 160
Bottromycin, 554
Butanol
anaerobic bacteria producing, 436
Butyribacterium
methylotrophicum, 435, 448
Butyric acid
anaerobic bacteria producing, 435, 459

C

Cadmium
bacterial oxidation of, 279
Cancer
immunotherapy of, 330–32
Candicin
synthesis of, 211
Candida, 114–17
Candida pseudotropicalis, 111
Caproic acid synthesis
anaerobic bacteria and, 435
Carbamoyl phosphate synthetase
in cyanobacteria, 514
Carcinoembryonic antigen (CEA), 605
β-Carotene
erythropoietic protoporphyria and, 32–33
Carotenogenesis
inhibition of
diphenylalamine and, 30–32
Carotenoid biosynthesis, 30–32
Carotenoid pigments, 29–33
photoprotection of
chemoheterotrophs and, 32–33
Carotenotherapy, 32–33
Caulbacter
cellular differentiation in, 35–37
Caulbacter crescentus, 36
flagellar basal structure of, 87
flagellin of, 84
polyhook mutants of, 84
surface structure formation in, 87–88
Cell-mediated immunity
immune response and, 595–96
Cellular immunity
synthetic antiviral vaccines and, 611–12
Cephalosporin C
biosynthesis of, 222–23
Cephalosporins, 161–68
biosynthesis of, 216
clavulanic acid and, 177
production of, 213
nitrogen metabolism and, 220–21
Cephalosporium, 118, 161–65
Cephalosporium acremonium, 118, 162–66
cephalosporin C biosynthesis in, 216, 222–23
penicillin N production and, 211
Cephalosporium boydii, 114, 127
Cephamycin C
synthesis of, 227
Cephamycins, 168–70
Ceratocystis, 112, 128
Cercospora, 126
Cervicitis
chlamydial, 299
Chaetomium mollicellum
mutagenic to Salmonella, 244
Chalara, 112
Chalcidin, 554
Chlamydiae, 286–304
antigens, 294–97
growth cycle of, 291–94
infections and, 297–302
gonococcal, 300
initiation of, 289–91
laboratory isolation of, 305–6
properties of, 288, 292
taxonomy of, 287–89
Chlamydia psittaci, 286–304
epidemiology of, 302–4
infections and, 297
Chlamydia trachomatis, 286–306
epidemiology of, 204–5
infections and, 298–302
laboratory isolation of, 305–6
nongonococcal urethritis and, 286, 298
Chloramphenicol, 211
bacillary dysentery and, 482–84
Chlorogloea fritschii, 503
Cholera, 342
toxin, 598
Chromatography
taxonomy of Fungi Imperfecti and, 115
Chromatophore concept, 23–27
Chromobacterium violaceum, 344
Chromoblastomycosis, 123
Chrysosporium, 113, 125–26
dermatitidis, 120
merdarium, 119
parvum, 120
pruinosum, 120
Chytridiomycota, 110
Cinematography
bacterial motion and, 74
Cirramycin A-1, 547
Citrinin
carcinogenicity of, 238–39
Cladosporium, 110, 120–23
bantianum, 120–21
castellanii, 121
chlorocephalum, 123
trichoides, 120–21
werneckii, 122
Clavulanic acid, 176–77
Clostridium acetobutylicum
acetone-butanol fermentation of, 425
butanol-producing, 436
metabolic control of alcohol production in, 452
Clostridium brockii
ethanol yield in, 453
Clostridium butylicum
butanol-producing, 436
Clostridium formicoaceticum
homoacetic acid-producing, 434
Clostridium kluyveri
caproic acid synthesis and, 435
Clostridium pasteurianum
hydrogenase in, 184
nitrogen fixation and, 185, 193–99
Clostridium propionicum
acrylic acid formation and, 432

Clostridium spp.
acetone-butanol fermentations of, 425
lactate fermentation by, 445
oxygen and, 432
Clostridium thermoaceticum
carbon flow from glucose to acetate in, 444–45
homoacetic acid-producing, 434
one-carbon metabolism in, 448
Clostridium thermocellum
cellulolytic activity of, 439–40
ethanol-producing, 435, 453
Clostridium thermohydrosulfuricum
ethanol-producing, 435
flagellar filaments of, 79
Clostridium thermosaccharolyticum
butyric acid-producing, 435
Cobalt
bacterial oxidation of, 279
Coccidioides, 120–21
immitis, 121
Colicin V
Escherichia coli and, 477–82
Collagen
antiprotein-specific immune response and, 603–4
Comamonas terrigena, 174
Conidiobolus coronatus, 131
Conidiobolus incongruus, 131
Conjunctivitis
inclusion, 298
neonatal chlamydial, 301–2
Copper
Bacterial oxidation of, 275–77
Corynebacterium
mitogenic, 333
Corynebacterium autotrophicum
flagellar filaments of, 80
Corynebacterium betae
peptidoglycan and, 320
Corynebacterium diphtheriae
polyarthritis in rats and, 327
Corynebacterium insidiosum
peptidoglycan and, 320
Corynebacterium parvum
peptidoglycan and, 319, 323
Corynebacterium poinsettiae
carotenoid pigmentation and, 32
peptidoglycan and, 319–20, 326
Creutzfeld-Jacob disease
Spiroplasma and, 705
Cryptococcus, 114–15
bacillispora, 117
neoformans, 114, 117
CsCl density gradient centrifugation
ScV and, 54–55
Cunninghamella, 130
bertholletiae, 130
elegans, 130
Cyanobacteria
axenization of, 44
genetic and cytoplasmic characteristics of, 43
genetics of, 525–26
glutamine synthetase-nitrogenase interactions in, 516–18
hydrogen metabolism and, 523–24
nif genes and, 42
nitrogenase, 511–16
ATP and, 518–22
nitrogen-fixing, 497–527
obligate autotrophy and, 44
oxygenic photosynthesis and, 42–43
vegetative cells of, 498–506
Cyanobacterial nitrogenase
ammonia assimilation and, 514–16
glutamine synthetase and, 514–16
oxygen and, 512–13
cyclic AMP (cAMP)
bacterial motility and, 100
flagella synthesis of bacteria and, 99
Cyclochlorotin
carcinogenicity of, 238–39
Cycloheximide
killer character of ScV and, 50
Cytophaga
purification of, 8–9
Cytophaga johnsonae, 11

D

Dark-field microscopy
bacterial flagella and, 72
Defective interfering (DI) influenza viruses, 620–42
assay of, 621–23
formation of
host and, 637–39
genome of, 624–27
host and, 639–42
production of, 621
properties of, 623–24
RNA of, 625–27
origin of, 629–35
viral interference and, 627–29
Defective interfering (DI) virus-mediated interference
mechanism of, 636–37
Defective interfering (DI) particles
viral pathogenesis and, 52
Dendrostilbella boydii, 114, 127
Derxia gummosa
nitrogen fixation and, 192–93
Desulfovibrio
hydrogenase in, 184
Desulfovibrio desulfuricans
nitrogen fixation and, 193, 199
Deuteromycota, 110
Diarrheal disease
Escherichia coli and, 466–73
Diketopiperazines
antitumor activity and, 245
Diphenylamine
Rhodospirillum rubrum carotenogenesis inhibition and, 30–32
Dipodascus, 124
DNA
conformation of, 151–52
physical-chemical properties of
modified bases and, 140–42
see also Bacteriophage DNAs
DNA/DNA reassociation, 39–40
Dopamine
Escherichia coli migration and, 99
Doxycycline
nongonococcal urethritis and, 299
Dysentery
bacillary
antibiotic-resistant, 482–84

E

Ectromelia, 596
Egg-white lysozyme
antigenic regions in, 603
antiprotein-specific immune response and, 604
Electron microscopy
bacterial flagellar structure and, 77–88
ScV RNAs and, 57
Electrophoresis
taxonomy of Fungi Imperfecti and, 115
Emericellopsis, 161, 165
Emmonsia, 120
brasiliensis, 120
ciferrina, 120
crescens, 120
parva, 120
Emmonsiella, 113
capsulata, 113
Encephalitis vaccine
Japanese B, 595

Encephalomyelitis
demyelinating, 328
Entamoeba histolytica
antibiotic G-418 and, 543
Enterobacter agglomerans, 648
Enterobacter cloaccae
clavulanic acid and, 177
Enterobacteriaceae spp.
fortimicin A and, 545
murein lipoprotein in, 387
Vibrio differentiated from, 343
Entomophthora, 131
Entomophthoromycosis, 129
Enzymes
antibody interaction with, 597
extracellular
of Erwinia spp., 664–65
Epidermidophyton, 121–22
floccosum, 122
gallinae, 122
stockdaleae, 122
Epididymitis
chlamydial, 287
Ergot alkaloids
carcinogenicity of, 238–39
Erwinia amylovora, 648–65
capsular material in, 659
Hfr donors in, 652–53
isolation procedures for, 660
R plasmid-mediated chromosomal gene transfer in, 653–56
transductional gene transfer in, 655–56
Erwinia carotovora, 651–71
R plasmid-mediated chromosomal gene transfer in, 654
transductional gene transfer in, 655–56
Erwinia chrysanthemi, 650–68
Hfr donors in, 652–53
isolation procedures in, 660–61
lipopolysaccharide of, 660
R plasmid-mediated chromosomal gene transfer in, 654–55
Erwinia herbicola, 648–56
chromosomal marker transformation in, 656
Erwinia spp., 646–72
bacteriophages and, 651–52
cell envelope components of, 658–62
chromosomal homology of, 656–58
extracellular enzymes of, 664–65
flagella of, 71
genetic systems of, 652–56
phytopathogenicity of, 658–71
plasmid inheritance in, 649–51
polygalacturonic acid catabolism of, 665–71
Erwinia stewartii, 649–55
transductional gene transfer in, 655–56
Erythromycin
biosynthesis of, 222
chlamydiae and, 293
nongonococcal urethritis and, 299
Vibrio alginolyticus infection and, 361
Erythromycin B, 549
Erythropoietic protoporphyria
carotenotherapy and, 32–33
Escherichia coli, 170–72
amino acids and, 94
bacteriophage T4 and, 149
body rotation of, 88
cephamycin C and, 170
chemotactic inhibition in, 97
chemotactic responses of, 73
clavulanic acid and, 177
colonization antigen plasmids of, 474–77
ColV plasmids of, 477–82
enterotoxin plasmids of, 468–74
flagellar basal structure of, 86
flagellar motility inhibition in, 92
flagellin of, 84
D-galacturonic acid metabolism and, 670
helical flagellar filaments of, 81–82
hook protein of, 84
invasive
virulence plasmids of, 477–82
matrix proteins of, 371–75
membrane potential in, 92
migration of
neurotransmitters and, 99–100
mitogenic, 333
motility of, 96–101
new membrane proteins of, 375–76
nocardicin A and, 172
OmpA protein of, 384–85
outer membrane proteins of, 372
peptidoglycan and, 319, 326
phage χ system, 98
phototaxis in, 96
polyhook mutants of, 85
prophage induction in, 250–51
protein export in, 398–410
energetics of, 407
signal peptidase and, 405–6
signal sequence in, 398–405
pyrogenicity of, 329
RNA polymerase of, 149–50
RNAP-lac promotor complex in, 151
sexual recombination in, 41
streptomycin and, 35
tethered
rate and direction of, 76
thermotaxis in, 96
transductional gene transfer in, 655
Vir plasmid of, 482
virulence plasmids of, 466–77
Ethanol
anaerobic bacteria producing, 435
Eubacteria
flagellar structure and function in, 69–104
Eubacterium limosum
peptidoglycan and, 320
Eukaryotes
functional attributes of, 41–42
genetic and cytoplasmic characteristics of, 43
Eurotiopsis gayoni, 114
Everninomicins, 552
Exfoliative toxin (ET), 487–89
Exoascus, 115
Exophilia, 119, 122, 128
jeanselmei, 122
spinifera, 122
werneckii, 122

F

Filobasidiella, 114–15, 124
bacillispora, 117
Filobasidium, 114–15, 124
Fimbriae
prokaryotic/eukaryotic cell recognition phenomenon and, 498
Fissuricella filamenta, 117
Flagella
bacterial
basal structure of, 85–88
biomechanics of, 88–93
filament of, 77–84
hook of, 84–85
motility of, 93–103
organelle of, 70–73

proton-motive force and, 91–92
structure of, 77–88
Flagellin 77–78, 82–84
filament polymorphism and, 82
Fonsecaea, 123, 128
compacta, 123
pedrosoi, 123
Food poisoning
Staphylococcus aureus causing, 486–87
Vibrio parahaemolyticus-associated, 356
Foot-and-mouth disease
cellular immunity and, 611
Fortimicins, 544–45
Freund adjuvant, 314–16, 612
Fungi
amino acid transport in, 225
ammonia and nitrogen catabolic reactions in, 219–20
β-lactam antibiotic biosynthesis in, 222–24
medically important, 109–32
metabolites of
antitumor activity of, 245
see also specific type
Fungi Imperfecti, 110, 115–28
Fusarenon-X
carcinogenicity of, 238–39

G

Gallionella, 267
Gasohol
anaerobic fermentation and, 427
Gastroenteritis
Vibrio causing, 342, 347, 352–56
Gel electrophoresis
ScV RNAs and, 57–59
Spiroplasma and, 683–84
Genes
immune response, 599
see also specific type
Genital tract disease
chlamydiae and, 286–87, 298–300
Gentamicin, 539–40, 545
Geotrichum, 123–24
candidum, 124
capitatum, 124
fermentans, 124
penicillatum, 124
Gliomastix, 118
Gloeobacter violaceous, 499
Gloeocapsa
nitrogen fixation and, 194
Glucose
ethanolic fermentation pathways for, 444
heteracidic fermentation pathways for, 443
homolactic and homoacetic fermentation pathways for, 442
Glutamic acid dehydrogenase
in cyanobacteria, 514
L-Glutamine
motile bacteria and, 99
Glutamine synthetase
in cyanobacteria, 514
cyanobacterial nitrogenase and, 514–16
Gonococci
chlamydial infections and, 300
rosaramicin and, 547
Gramicidin
repression in trophophase in, 211
Gramicidin S
production of, 212–13
Gram-negative bacteria
outer membrane of
components of, 412–13
outer membrane proteins of, 370–416
amino terminal sequence of, 395
assembly of, 414–16
biosynthesis of, 393–97
genetic determinants of the localization of, 397–98
molecular organization of, 388–93
verdamicin and, 542
Graphium, 112–14
Griseofulvin
carcinogenicity of, 238–39
Gyrodinium cohnii, 154
Gryomytra esculenta
genetic activity of, 245

H

Haemophilus inflenzae
antibiotic-resistant, 485
Haemophysalis leporispalustris, 676
Halobacterium
gas vacuoles in, 41
Halomicins, 550–52
Haplosporangium, 120
parva, 120
Helminths
antibiotic G-418 and, 543
Hepatitis
cellular immunity and, 611
Hexose
fermentation pathways of, 441–46
Histamine
Escherichia coli migration and, 99
Histoplasma, 120–21
capsulatum, 113, 124–25
capsulatum var. capsulatum, 113, 124
capsulatum var. duboisii, 113, 124
farciminosum, 124
Homoacetic acid
anaerobic bacteria producing, 434
Hormiscium dermatitidis, 128
Hormodendrum pedrosoi, 123
Hormonema, 119
Hydrogen
cyanobacteria and, 523–24
nitrogen fixation and, 194–202
poly-β-Hydroxybutyrate, 33
prokaryotic synthesis of, 42
Hymenolepsis nana
antibiotic G-418 and, 543
Hyphomycetes, 118–28

I

IFS
see Intensity fluctuation spectroscopy
Immune response
antiprotein-specific, 603–4
cell-mediated immunity and, 595–96
humoral
antibody synthesis and, 313–14
viral antigens and, 599–600
Immune response (Ir) genes, 599
Immunity
cellular
synthetic antiviral vaccines and, 611–12
Immunotherapy
of cancer, 330–32
Indolmycin
production of, 215
Infertility
chlamydiae and, 300
Influenza vaccine, 595
Influenza viruses
defective interfering (DI), 620–42
Intensity fluctuation spectroscopy (IFS), 76–77

J

Juvenimicins, 548

K

Kanagawa phenomenon, 353–55
Keratoconjunctivitis, 286
β-Ketoadipate
  isolation of, 19–20
  pathway of, 22–25
Klebsiella aerogenes, 218–19
Klebsiella pneumoniae
  clavulanic acid and, 177
  nitrogenase synthesis in, 184
  nitrogen fixation and, 184, 190–99
  peptidoglycan and, 324
Kluyveromyces marxianus, 111
Kojic acid
  carcinogenicity of, 238–39
Krebs cycle, 20

L

Labyrinthulids, 110
β-Lactam antibiotics, 160–78
  cephalosporins, 161–68
  cephamycins, 168–70
  classification of, 161
  clavulanic acid, 176–77
  nocardicins, 170–73
  olivanic acids, 173–76
  penicillins, 161–68
  thienamycins, 173–76
Lactic acid
  anaerobic bacteria producing, 434–35
Lactobacillus casei
  lactic acid yielding, 434
Lactobacillus plantarum
  mitogenic, 333
  peptidoglycan and, 320–21
  polyarthritis in rats and, 327
Lactobacillus spp.
  low pH and growth of, 433
  oxygen and, 432
Lactones
  antitumor activity of, 245
Lead
  bacterial oxidation of, 279
Leucosporidium, 114
Light microscopy
  flagellar distribution and morphology and, 70–72
Lignin
  anaerobic bacterial fermentation and, 429
Lipopolysaccharide
  of phytopathogenic bacteria, 660–62
Listeria monocytogenes
  macrophages killing, 333
  mitogenic, 333
Liver cancer
  aflatoxin B_1 and, 248
Luteoskyrin
  carcinogenicity of, 238–39
Lymphogranuloma venereum (LGV), 286–90
  sulfonamide resistance in, 287

M

Macrolides, 546–49
  antitumor activity of, 245
Madurella, 125
  mycetomatis, 125
Magnetotaxis, 95
Malassezia, 117–18
  furfur, 118, 122
  pachydermatis, 118
Malbranchea, 120–21
Mandelate
  pathway of, 23
Mass spectrometry
  taxonomy of Fungi Imperfecti and, 115
Measles vaccine, 595
Megalomicins, 546–47
Megasphaera spp.
  lactate fermentation by, 445
Metallogenium, 267
Methane
  production of, 457–58
Methanobacterium formicicum, 436
Methanobacterium thermoautotrophicum, 436–37
Methanogenic bacteria, 433–37
Methanosarcina barkeri, 436–37
  glucose decomposition and, 438
Methanosarcina spp.
  oxygen and, 432
Methanotrophs
  nitrogen fixation and, 192
7-Methoxycephalosporins, 168–70
7-Methoxycephem compounds, 169
Methylospira capsulatus
  nitrogen fixation and, 192
Metronidizole, 543
Microbacterium lacticum
  peptidoglycan and, 320
Micrococcus luteus
  peptidoglycan and, 319, 326
  polyarthritis in rats and, 327
Microcystis aeruginosa, 498, 502
Micromonospora
  antibiotics from, 538–54
  arborensis, 553–54
  capillata, 548
  carbonacea, 552
  chalcea var. flavida, 545
  chalcea var. izumensis, 548
  echinospora, 539, 544
  ellipsospora, 551–52
  floridensis, 552–53
  galeriensis, 554
  globosa, 553
  grisea, 541
  halophytica, 550–51
  halophytica var. nigra, 550
  inyoensis, 540–41
  lacustris, 552
  megalomicea var. megalomicea, 546
  megalomicea var. nigra, 546
  melanogenes, 554
  olivoasterospora, 544
  papulosus, 554
  purpurea, 539–43
  rhodorangea, 542–43
  rifamycetica, 552
  rosaria, 547
  sagamiensis, 540, 545
  saitamica, 554
  verruculosa, 554
  vividifaciens, 554
  zionensis, 542
Microsporum, 110–13, 125–26
  gallinae, 122
  mansonii, 122–23
Minocycline
  nongonococcal urethritis and, 299
Monascus, 114
Monilia, 116
Monosporium apiospermum, 127
Moraxella glucidolytica
  peptidoglycan and, 319, 326
MS-2 coliphage
  antiviral response induction and, 607–11
Muconic acid
  third geometrical isomer of, 22
Mucor, 129
  pusillus, 130
Mucormycosis, 129
Mumps vaccine, 595
Murein lipoprotein, 387–88
Mycetoma, 127
Mycetozoans, 110
Mycobacillin
  production of, 227
Mycobacteria
  viral vaccines and, 612–13
Mycobacterium
  mitogenic, 333
Mycobacterium bovis, 317–19
  polyarthritis in rats and, 327
  tumor suppression and, 330
Mycobacterium kansasii
  tumor suppression and, 330

Mycobacterium phlei, 317
Mycobacterium smegmatis, 317
polyarthritis in rats and, 327
Mycobacterium tuberculosis, 315–18
autoimmune disease induction and, 328
halomicin and, 551
polymorphonuclear leukocytes and, 312
tumor suppression and, 330
Mycocentrospora, 126
acerina, 126
Mycophenolic acid
carcinogenicity of, 238–39
Mycoplasma, 679–81
Mycoplasma capricolum
rRNA cataloging technique and, 680
Mycoplasma gallisepticum
rRNA cataloging technique and, 680
Mycoses, 129
Mycotoxins
carcinogenicity of, 237–47
genetic activity of, 244–47
nucleic acid binding and, 252–57
structures of, 246–47
Myxococcus xanthus
transductional gene transfer in, 655

N

Nannizzia, 113
Neisseria gonorrhoeae
antibiotic-resistant, 485
Neisseria perflava
peptidoglycan and, 319, 326
Neomycin, 545
Neotestudina, 114
rosatii, 114
Neurospora crassa, 223–24
aflatoxin B_1 and, 250
ammonia and nitrogen catabolic reactions in, 219–20
Neurotransmitters
Escherichia coli migration and, 99–100
Nickel
bacterial oxidation of, 279
nif genes
encoding of, 42
Nitrogen
antibiotic biosynthesis and, 212–24
microbial assimilatory mechanisms, 217
transfer reactions, 214–16
Nitrogen fixation, 184–202
cyanobacterial, 497–527
prokaryotic, 42
Nivalenol
carcinogenicity of, 238–39
NMR spectroscopy
taxonomy of Fungi Imperfecti and, 115
Nocardia
mediterraniae, 551
mitogenic, 333
rubra, 333
uniformis subsp. tsuyamanensis, 170–71
Nocardicins, 170–73
Nongonococcal urethritis (NGU), 286, 298
Nonsulfur bacteria
purple, 23–29
nif genes encoded by, 42
pigment synthesis regulation in, 26–29
Nostoc MAC
enzymes from, 501
Nourseothricin
production of, 221–22
Nucleic acid binding
mycotoxins and, 252–57
Nucleotide sequencing
of DI influenza viral RNA, 629–33

O

Ochratoxin A
carcinogenicity of, 238–39
Oidium albicans, 116
Oligonucleotide mapping
of DI influenza viral RNA, 629–33
Olivanic acids, 173–76
OmpA protein, 384–86
Oomycetes, 110
Ophiostoma, 112
Organic acids
anaerobic bacterial fermentation producing, 430–31
Organic substrates
photoheterotrophy and, 33–34
Organotropism
species specificity of AFB_1 and, 254–55
Oscillatoria chalybea, 499
Otitis media
neonatal, 301
Oxygen
anaerobic bacteria and, 432–33
cyanobacterial nitrogenase and, 512–13
nitrogen fixation and, 184–94

P

Pachysandra terminalis, 160
Paecilomyces, 118–19
Paracoccidioides, 120–121, 125
Paracoccus denitrificans
flagellar filaments of, 80
Paromomycin, 543
Patulin
carcinogenicity of, 238–39
Patulin-cystein adduct
carcinogenicity of, 240–41
PcV
see Penicillium chrysogenum virus
Pectobacterium, 648
Peltigera aphthosa
nitrogenase activity in, 517
Penicillic acid
carcinogenicity of, 240–41
Penicillin, 161–68
chlamydiae and, 293
cyanobacteria and, 498
postgonococcal urethritis and, 300
production of, 211, 223–24
sterility and, 10
Penicillium camemberti
genetic activity of, 245
Penicillium chrysogenum, 161–66, 223–24
ammonium uptake in, 224
penicillin overproduction in, 216
Penicillium chrysogenum virus (PcV)
capsid polypeptides in, 56
Penicillium notatum, 160–62
Penicillium roqueforti
genetic activity of, 245
Penicillium stoloniferum virus
S RNA polymerase of, 63
structure of, 55
Pentenylpenicillin, 161
Pentose
fermentation pathways of, 441–46
Peptides
antitumor activity of, 245
Peptidoglycans, 311–35
adjuvants, 316–25
antigenicity of, 326–27
cell activation by, 332–34
Freund adjuvant and, 314–16
immunopotentiating effects of, 314–25
pyrogenicity of, 329–30
structure of, 312–13
Perihepatitis
chlamydial, 287
Petriellidium, 114
boydii, 127
Phaeococcus, 119

Phaeohyphomycosis
  cerebral, 120–21
Phages
  flagellotropic, 98
  staphylococcal, 585–86
Phagocytosis
  chlamydiae and, 290
  eukaryotic, 42
Phenoxymethylpenicillin, 166
Phialophora, 125–28
  americana, 126
  gougerotii, 122
  heteromorpha, 127
  hoffmannii, 127
  jeanselmei, 122
  spinifera, 122
  verrucosa, 123, 126
Phleomycins, 160
Phormidium laminosus, 499
Photoheterotrophy
  organic substrates and, 33–34
Photophosphorylation, 25
Photosynthate
  bioconversion of, 426
Photosynthesis
  anoxygenic, 33
  oxygenic
    cyanobacteria and, 42–43
Phototrophs
  nitrogen fixation and, 192
Pinocytosis
  eukaryotic, 42
Pityosporum, 117–18
  orbiculare, 118
  ovale, 118
  pachydermatis, 118
Plasmids
  of Erwinia spp., 649–51
  of staphylococci, 585–86
  virulent microorganisms and, 491–92
  see also Virulence plasmids
Plasmodiophoromycetes, 110
Plectonema boryanum, 502
  nitrogen fixation and, 192
Plesiomonas shigelloides, 344
Pneumonia
  chlamydial neonatal, 301–2
Poliovaccine, 595
Polyarthritis
  in rats, 327–28
Polygalacturonic acid
  catabolism of
    Erwinia spp. and, 665–71
Polymorphonuclear leukocytes
  Mycobacterium tuberculosis and, 312
Polypeptides
  capsid
    in PcV, 56
    in ScV, 55–56
Porin proteins, 371–84
  of Escherichia coli, 371–76
  of Salmonella typhimurium, 376
  structure and function of, 376–84
Porter-Lincoln sequence, 30–31
Postgonococcal urethritis (PGU), 300
Primycin, 554
Proctitis
  chlamydial, 299
Prokaryotes
  definition of, 40–45
  functional attributes of, 42
  genetic and cytoplasmic characteristics of, 43
  motile
    aerotaxis and, 95
    phototaxis and, 95–96
Prokaryotic/eukaryotic cell recognition phenomenon, 498
Propionibacterium spp.
  glycolytic pathway for propionate production in, 445–46
  lactate fermentation by, 445
  low pH and growth of, 433
  vitamin B_{12} yield of, 459
Protein antigenicity
  determinants in, 602–5
  viral proteins and, 600–2
Proteins
  tobacco mosaic virus, 602
  see also specific type
Proteolysis
  antibiotic production and, 227–29
Proteus mirabilis
  chemotaxis in, 94
  clavulanic acid and, 177
  flagella of, 78
  motility of
    pressure and, 100
  murein lipoprotein in, 387
  OmpA protein of, 386
  outer membrane proteins of, 378–79
Proteus spp.
  cephamycin C and, 170
  flagellin protomers in, 78
  gentamicin and, 539–40
  nocardicin A and, 172
  swarming phenomenon in, 74
Proteus vulgaris
  peptidoglycan and, 319, 326
Proton-motive force
  flagellar motility and, 91–92
Prototheca filamenta, 117
Providencia
  cephamycin C and, 170
Pseudomonads
  fluorescent, 19–20
Pseudomonas acidovorans, 148
Pseudomonas aeruginosa, 38, 170–72
  clavulanic acid and, 177
  flagella of
    helical, 78
  murein lipoprotein in, 387
  nocardicin A and, 172
  outer membrane proteins of, 379
  transductional gene transfer in, 655
Pseudomonas citronellolis
  body rotation of, 88
  phototaxis in, 96
Pseudomonas facilis
  flagellar filaments of, 80
Pseudomonas flava
  flagellar filaments of, 80
Pseudomonas fluorescens, 38
  motility of
    alcohol and, 100
Pseudomonas mendocina
  flagellar diversity in, 101
Pseudomonas morsprunorum
  outer membrane proteins of, 661–62
Pseudomonas phaseolicola
  motility and plant invasiveness and, 97–98
  outer membrane proteins of, 661–62
  phaseotoxin produced by, 650
Pseudomonas pseudoflava
  flagellar filaments of, 80
Pseudomonas rhodos
  flagella of, 79–80
  flagellar hooks of, 85
Pseudomonas solanacearum
  capsular material in, 659
  chromosomal marker transformation in, 656
  lipopolysaccharide of, 660
Pseudomonas, spp.
  aerobic
    taxonomic structure of, 37–40
  cinematographic analysis of, 74–75
  flagella of, 71
  gentamicin and, 539–40
  pyrolnitrin produced by, 213–14
  verdamicin and, 542
Pseudomonas stutzeri
  flagella of, 72
  flagellar diversity in, 101
Pseudomonas syringae, 650
  isolation procedures for, 661
Pseudomonas tabaci, 160
Psittacosis, 286, 297
Pullularia, 119
Puromycin, 214

Pyrolnitrin
production of, 213–14

R

Rabies, 594
Renispora flavissima, 124–25
Reovirus dsRNAs
sizing of, 57–58
Rhinocladiella, 122–23, 128
Rhizobiaceae
nitrogen fixation and, 192
Rhizobium 32H1
nitrogen fixation and, 190
Rhizobium japonicum
nitrogen fixation and, 185, 190, 200–2
Rhizobium leguminosarum
nitrogen fixation and, 200–2
tranductional gene transfer in, 655
Rhizobium lupini
flagellar filament structure of, 79
phage 7-7-1 of, 98–99
Rhizomucor pusillus, 130
Rhizophlyctis rosea, 9
Rhizopus nigricans, 130
Rhizopus stolonifer, 130
Rhodopseudomonas capsulata
nitrogen fixation and, 192, 199, 202, 510
Rhodopseudomonas sphaeroides
membrane potential in, 92
pigment synthesis regulation in, 27–29
Rhodospirillum rubrum
carotenogenesis by
diphenylalamine inhibiting, 30–32
flagellar motility inhibition in, 92, 100
nitrogen fixation and, 197–99
particulate structure of, 24
photophosphorylation and, 25
phototaxis in, 95–96
pigment synthesis regulation in, 27–29
Rhodosporidium, 114
Rhodotorula, 114
Riboflavin
anaerobic bacterial fermentation producing, 431
Rifampicin
chlamydiae and, 294
Rifamycins, 551–52
RNA
influenza viral, 625–27
origin of, 629–35
viral interference and, 627–29
reovirus
sizing of, 57–58
ScV, 56–61
RNA polymerase, 149–50
fungal virus, 63
ScV, 62–63
dsRNA viruses, 52
Rosaramicin, 547–48
Rubella virus
cellular immunity and, 611
vaccine, 595
Rubradirin, 554
Rubratoxin-B
carcinogenicity of, 240–41
Rugulosin
carcinogenicity of, 240–41
Ruminococcus albus
cellulase of, 439

S

Saccharomyces cerevisiae
ammonium uptake in, 224
Saccharomyces cerevisiae provirus, 65
Saccharomyces cerevisiae virus (ScV), 50–66
capsid polypeptides in, 55–56
CsCl density gradient centrifugation and, 54–55
cytoplasmic genotypes of, 51
killer character of, 50–52
nuclear mutations and, 64–65
physical properties of, 52–55
replication of, 63
RNA polymerase of, 62–63
RNAs of, 56–61
defective interfering, 59–61
translation products of, 61–62
Saccharomyces ellipsoideus, 116
Sagamicin, 545
Sagenomella, 119
Sagrahamala, 118
Salk vaccine, 595
Salmonella enteritidis, 97
Salmonella spp.
Chaetomium mollicellum mutagenic to, 244
cinematographic analysis of, 74–75
flagellar filaments of, 72, 77
helical, 81
flagellin and, 78, 83–84
LH flagella of, 88–89
Salmonella typhi
antibiotic-resistant, 483
Vir plasmid transfer to, 482
Salmonella typhimurium
amino acid transport in, 225–26
chemotactic inhibition in, 97
filaments of
LH helical, 88
mutants from, 81
phase 2, 81–82
helical, 78
luteoskyrin and rugulosin mutagenizing, 253
OmpA protein of, 385–86
outer membrane proteins of, 372
phototaxis in, 96
polyhook mutants of, 84
porins of, 376
sex attractants and, 95
stroboscopy and, 75
transductional gene transfer in, 655
Salmonella typhosa
motility of, 100
Salpingitis
chlamydial, 287, 299
Sandai virus
cellular immunity and, 611
Sarcina lutea
carotenoid pigmentation and, 32
Sarcina ventriculi
decarboxyclastic path of, 446
metabolic control of ethanol production in, 452
Sarcinosporon inkin, 117
Scalded-skin syndrome, 487–89
Scanning electron microscopy (SEM), 78
taxonomy of Fungi Imperfecti and, 115
Scedosporium, 114, 127
apiospermum, 127
ScV
see Saccharomyces cerevisiae virus
Scytalidium, 119
Selenomonas ruminantium
flagellar tuft of, 86
SEM
see Scanning electron microscopy
Sepatia obvelata
antibiotic G-418 and, 543
Sepedonium, 120, 125
Serratia marcescens, 18
murein lipoprotein of, 387
nocardicin A and, 172
Serratia marinorubra
motility of, 100
Sexually transmitted diseases (STDs), 286–87
Shigella
bacteriophage T4 and, 149
Shigella dysenteriae, 482–85

Shigella flexneri
R plasmid and, 483
Shigella sonnei
Shigellosis, 484
Sisomicin, 540–41
Smallpox, 594
Solventogenic bacteria, 433–37
fermentation substrates and product yields of, 456
Spectrophotometry
taxonomy of Fungi Imperfecti and, 115
Sperm whale myoglobin
antigenic mappin for, 603
Sphaerotilus natans
polar organelle of, 86
Spirillum
helical swimming in, 74
Spirillum serpens
pyrogenicity of, 329
Spirillum volutans
flagellar motility in, 90–91
phototaxis in, 95
Spiroplasma, 678–705
classification of, 679–81
cultivation of, 692–96
gel electrophoresis of, 683–84
genome of, 686–87
membrane of, 701–2
morphology of, 696–99
motility of, 699–701
pathogenicity of, 703–5
serology of, 681–83
species candidates for, 687–91
substrate utilization in, 684–86
Spiroplasma citri, 678–713
Spiroplasmaviruses, 702–3
Spirulina platensis
enzymes from, 501
Sporothrix, 112, 127–28
Sporothrix schenckii, 122, 128
Sporotrichum aureum, 128
Sporulation
antibiotic production and, 227–28
Staphylococcal nuclease
antigenic determinants in, 602
Staphylococcal scalded-skin syndrome, 487–89
Staphylococci, 559–87
adaptation mechanisms of, 584–86
cell wall composition of, 570–71
conjugate evolution of, 586–87
DNA relatedness in, 573–76
immunological relationship of proteins in, 572
iso-functional enzymes of, 571–72
natural habitats of, 576–84
penicillin-resistant, 167
plasmids of, 585–86
Staphylococcus albus, 561
Staphylococcus aureus, 560–87
clavulanic acid and, 177
mitogenic, 333
nocardicin A and, 172
penicillin-resistant, 167
peptidoglycan and, 319–21
polyarthritis in rats and, 327
prophage induction in, 250
pyrogenicity of, 329
R plasmid carriage and, 489–90
virulence plasmids in, 486–90
Staphylococcus capitis, 568, 579–87
Staphylococcus citreus, 561
Staphylococcus cohnii, 568, 587
Staphylococcus epidermidis, 561–87
mitogenic, 333
peptidoglycan and, 319
pyrogenicity of, 329
Staphylococcus haemolyticus, 568–87
Staphylococcus hominis, 568–87
Staphylococcus hyicus, 565–87
Staphylococcus intermedius, 565–87
Staphylococcus lentus, 571
Staphylococcus pyogenes, 560
Staphylococcus saprophyticus, 556, 587
Staphylococcus sciuri, 568–87
Staphylococcus simulans, 568–87
Staphylococcus warneri, 568–87
Staphylococcus xylosus, 565–87
Stenella araguata, 121
Sterigmatocystin
aflatoxins and, 253–54
Sterigmatocystin-DNA adducts
aflatoxin B_1 and, 255–57
Stibiobacter senarmontii, 278–79
Stibnite
bacterial oxidation of, 278–79
Streptidine
repression in trophophase in, 211
Streptococcus
flagellar motility inhibition in, 91
Streptococcus faecalis
peptidoglycan and, 320
sex attractants and, 95
Streptococcus mutans
mitogenic, 333
peptidoglycan and, 319–20
pyrogenicity of, 329
Streptococcus pneumoniae
pyrogenicity of, 329
Streptococcus pyogenes
peptidoglycan and, 319–20
polyarthritis in rats and, 327
Streptococcus salivarius
mitogenic, 333
peptidoglycan and, 320
Streptococcus sanguis
mitogenic, 333
Streptomutin, 214
Streptomyces, 160–64
β-lactam antibiotics and, 168–70
Streptomyces achromogenes var. rubradiris, 554
Streptomyces alcalophilus
nocardicins and, 171
Streptomyces antibioticus, 213
Streptomyces bikiniensis, 215
Streptomyces cattleya
thienamycin and, 173–74
Streptomyces clavuligerus, 168–70
cephalosporins and, 213
nitrogen metabolism and, 220–21
clavulanic acid and, 176
β-lactam antibiotics and, 211–12
Streptomyces coelicolor, 9
Streptomyces cremeus subsp. auratilis
thienamycin and, 174
Streptomyces erythreus
erythromycin and, 222
Streptomyces flavorgriseus
thienamycin and, 173–74
Streptomyces fradiae
polyarthritis in rats and, 327
Streptomyces griseus
candicin synthesis and, 211
indolmycin biosynthesis and, 215
streptomycin and, 212
Streptomyces heteromorphus, 168
Streptomyces hydrogenans
amino acid transport in, 225–26
Streptomyces lactamdurans
cephamycin C synthesis and, 227
Streptomyces lavendulae
polyarthritis in rats and, 327
Streptomyces lipmanni, 168–69
Streptomyces niveus, 212
Streptomyces noursei
nourseothricin and, 221–22
Streptomyces olivaceus
thienamycin and, 173–74

Streptomyces panayensis, 168
Streptomyces parvulus
actinomycin D and, 213
Streptomyces verticillus
anticancer antibiotics and, 160
Streptomycetes
antibiotic biosynthesis and, 220–22
Streptomycin
bacillary dysentery and, 482–84
mechanism of action of, 34–35
production of, 212
Stroboscopy
bacterial motion and, 75
Successive adaptation, 20
Sulfadiazine
bacillary dysentery and, 482–84
Sulfonamides
chlamydia and, 294
lymphogranuloma venereum and, 287
nongonococcal urethritis and, 299
Swine flu vaccine, 595
Syringospora, 116–17
albicans, 117
robinii, 116

T

T-2 toxin
carcinogenicity of, 240–41
Taenia spp.
antibiotic G-418 and, 543
Taphrina, 115
T cells
antibody formation and, 313–14
host defense and, 611
Tetracycline
bacillary dysentery and, 482–84
chlamydiae and, 293
gonorrhea and, 300
nongonoccocal urethritis and, 298
Vibrio alginolyticus infection and, 361
T_1 fingerprint analysis
ScV RNAs and, 57
Thermoactinomyces spp.
growth rate on cellulose, 440
Thermoanaerobium brockii
lactic acid yielded by, 434
Thermoplasma acidophilum
flagellar motility in, 87, 90
rRNA cataloging technique and, 680
Thienamycins, 173–76
Thiobacilli
iron-oxidizing, 267–71
Thiobacillus acidophilus
mineral leaching and, 270
Thiobacillus ferrooxidans
mineral leaching and, 267–80
nitrogen fixation and, 192
Thiobacillus thioparus
positive chemotaxis in, 94
Thiospirillum jenense
flagellar fascicle form of, 77
Thraustochytrids, 110
Tobacco mosaic virus (TMV)
antiviral response induced by, 606–7
Tobacco mosaic virus protein (TMVP), 602
antiprotein-specific immune response and, 604
Tobramycin, 545
Torula bantiana, 120–21
Torula luzulae, 118
Torulopsis, 114–17
colliculosa, 116
rosea, 116
Toxic epidermal necrolysis, 487
Toxins
antitoxin neutralization of, 598
Trachoma, 286, 298, 304
Transmission electron microscopy
taxonomy of Fungi Imperfecti and, 115
Trichoderma viride
growth rate on cellulose, 440
Trichodesmium
nitrogen fixation and, 194
nitrogenase activity and, 510
Trichomonas vaginalis
antibiotic G-418 and, 543
Trichophyton, 113, 125–26
soudanense, 125–26
yaoundei, 125–26
Trichosporon, 124
capitatum, 124
fermentans, 124
penicillatum, 124
Tricothecenes
antitumor activity of, 245
Tryptophan
dissimilatory metabolism of, 20–21
Tylosin
repression in trophophase in, 211
Typhoid fever, 483

U

Uranium
bacterial oxidation of, 277–78
Ureaplasma urealyticum, 298
Urethritis
see specific type
Ustilago maydis
killer system in, 51–52

V

Vaccines
preparation of, 595–600
see also specific type
Vaccinia
disseminated, 596
Variola infection
leukemic children and, 596
Verdamicin, 541–42
Verticillium, 118
Vibrio alginolyticus, 342–44, 360–62
flagellar diversity in, 101–2
Vibrio anguillarum, 344–46
Vibrio cholerae
chemotactic inhibition in, 97
differentiation of, 343–44
flagellar filaments of, 79
non-O group 1, 346–52
O-group 1, 342
Vibrio metschnikovii, 342–46, 363
Vibrio parahaemolyticus, 342–44, 352–57
flagellar diversity in, 102–3
Vibrio spp.
group F, 362–63
infection prevention and, 364–65
isolation and identification of, 342–36
Vibrio vulnificus, 342–44, 357–60
Viral antigens
immune response and, 599–600
protein antigenicity and, 600–2
Viral disease
immunity to, 600
Viral vaccines
see Antiviral vaccines
Virulence plasmids
of enteropathogenic Escherichia coli, 466–77
of invasive Escherichia coli, 477–82
R, 482–85
of Staphylococcus aureus, 486–90
Viruses
antibodies inactivating, 598–99
properties of, 288
see also specific type

Vitamin B_{12}
anaerobic bacterial
fermentation producing, 431, 459

W

Wangiella, 119, 123, 128
dermatitidis, 128
Warburg vessels, 19

X

Xanthobacter
nitrogen fixation and, 191
Xanthobacter autotrophicus
nitrogen fixation and, 195, 200–1
Xanthomonas phaseoli
chromosomal marker
transformation in, 656
Xanthomonas spp.
capsular material in, 659
Xeroderm apigmentosum, 252
X-ray diffraction
bacterial flagella and, 79
taxonomy of Fungi
Imperfecti and, 115
Xylohypha, 123
curta, 123

Y

Yeasts
ascomycetous, 112
virus-like particles of, 49–66
see also specific type
Yellow fever vaccine, 595

Z

Zeralenone
carcinogenicity of, 240–41
Zinc
bacterial oxidation of, 276
Zoogloea, 95
Zopfia, 114
rosatii, 114
Zoster infection
leukemic children and, 596
Zygomycetes, 128–31
Zygomycosis, 129
Zygomycota, 110
Zymonema brasiliense, 125
Zymononas spp.
decarboxyclastic path of, 446

CUMULATIVE INDEXES

CONTRIBUTING AUTHORS, VOLUMES 30–34

A

Abdelal, A. T., 33:139–68
Achong, B. G., 31:421–45
Adler, H. E., 30:147–68
Aharonowitz, Y., 34:209–33
Ahearn, D. G., 32:59–68
Alford, C. A., 32:285–300
Anderson, R. P., 31:473–505
Anilionis, A., 32:519–60
Aoki, H., 34:159–81
Arnon, R., 34:593–618

B

Baresi, L., 31:309–41
Baumann, L., 31:39–61
Baumann, P., 31:39–61
Belser, L. W., 33:309–33
Blake, P. A., 34:341–67
Bradley, S. G., 33:67–94
Bruenn, J. A., 34:49–68
Bryan, B. A., 30:241–62

C

Caldwell, H. D., 34:285–309
Canale-Parola, E., 32:69–99
Cerdá-Olmedo, E., 31:535–47
Chatterjee, A. K., 34:645–76
Chet, I., 30:221–39
Cohen-Bazire, G., 31:225–74
Colby, J., 33:481–517
Coronelli, C., 33:389–411
Costerton, J. W., 33:459–79
Curtiss, R. III, 30:507–33

D

Dalton, H., 33:481–517
Daum, S. J., 33:241–65
Davies, J., 32:469–518
Delwiche, C. C., 30:241–62
Demain, A. L., 31:343–56
DeVay, J. E., 30:147–68
Doetsch, R. N., 34:69–108
Douglas, S. D., 33:267–307
Drew, S. W., 31:343–56
Drews, G., 33:215–39
Dubinina, G. A., 33:377–87
Dworkin, M., 33:595–639

E

Elwell, L. P., 34:465–96
Ensign, J. C., 32:185–219
Epstein, M. A., 31:421–45

F

Farley, J., 32:143–54
Fredrickson, A. G., 31:63–87
Fulton, C., 31:597–629

G

Gander, J. E., 33:169–99
Gerba, C. P., 33:413–37
Glass, T. L., 31:309–41
Glenn, A. R., 30:41–62
Goodfellow, M., 31:159–80
Goren, M. B., 31:507–33
Grimont, F., 32:221–48
Grimont, P. A. D., 32:221–48
Grunert, R. R., 33:335–53
Gutnick, D. L., 31:379–96

H

Harold, F. M., 31:181–203
Hastings, J. W., 31:549–95
Heidelberger, M., 31:1–12
Henriksen, S. D., 30:63–83
Hollis, D. G., 34:341–67
Hopwood, D. A., 32:373–92
Horgen, P. A., 32:249–84
Hungate, R. E., 33:1–20
Hylemon, P. B., 30:303–25

I

Isenberg, H. D., 30:483–505

J

Jensen, R. A., 30:409–25
Johnson, R. C., 31:89–106
Juni, E., 32:349–71

K

Kagan, I. G., 32:329–47
Kaiser, D., 33:595–639
Kharatyan, S. G., 32:301–27
Kingsbury, D. W., 30:21–39
Kloos, W. E., 34:559–92
Kobayashi, G. S., 31:291–308
Krieg, N. R., 30:303–25
Krulwich, T. A., 33:95–111
Kuznetsov, G. A., 33:377–87

L

Lapteva, N. A., 33:377–87
Lemke, J. R., 33:241–65
Lemke, P. A., 30:105–45
Lin, E. C. C., 30:535–78
Lobel, H. O., 32:329–47
London, J., 30:279–301
Lumb, J. R., 33:439–57
Lundgren, D. G., 34:263–83

M

MacLowry, J. D., 30:483–505
Macy, J. M., 33:561–94
Mah, R. A., 31:309–41
Manoil, C., 33:595–639
Martín, J.-F., 31:13–38
Matin, A., 32:433–68
Mayer, H., 33:215–39
McElroy, W. D., 30:1–20
McGinnis, M. R., 34:109–35
Medoff, G., 31:291–308
Melnick, J. L., 33:413–37
Minnikin, D. E., 31:159–80
Mitchell, R., 30:221–39

N

Nayak, D. P., 34:619–44
Nealson, K. H., 31:549–95
Nierlich, D. P., 32:393–432

O

Okuhara, M., 34:159–81
Osborn, M. J., 34:369–422
Owen, P., 30:451–82

P

Parenti, F., 33:389–411
Payne, W. J., 32:155–83
Peberdy, J. F., 33:21–39
Pelliccione, N. J., 33:95–111
Pfennig, N., 31:275–90
Pike, R. M., 33:41–66
Postgate, J. R., 34:183–207
Probst, I., 33:561–94

Q

Queener, S. W., 32:593–636

R

Raghow, R., 30:21–39
Riley, M., 32:519–60
Robinson, W. S., 31:357–77
Robson, R. L., 34:183–207
Rosenberg, E., 31:379–96
Roth, J. R., 31:473–505

S

Salton, M. R. J., 30:451–82
Sanderson, K. E., 30:327–49
Savage, D. C., 31:107–33
Schachter, J., 34:285–309
Schmidt, E. L., 33:355–76
Schwarzhoff, R. H., 32:101–22
Scott, W. A., 30:85–104
Sebek, O. K., 32:593–636
Shapiro, L., 30:377–407
Shipley, P. L., 34:465–96
Silver, J. C., 32:249–84
Silver, M., 34:263–83
Silver, S., 32:637–72
Silverman, M., 31:397–419
Simon, M. I., 31:397–419
Sjoblad, R. D., 34:69–108
Smibert, R. M., 32:673–709
Smith, D. I., 32:469–518
Stanbridge, E. J., 30:169–87
Stanier, R. Y., 31:225–74
Stanier, R. Y., 34:1–48
Stark, A.-A., 34:235–62
Starr, M. P., 34:645–76
Steinfeld, J. L., 30:427–50
Stewart, W. D. P., 34:497–536
Stewart-Tull, D. E. S., 34:311–40
Strobel, G. A., 31:205–24
Summers, A. O., 32:637–72
Switzer, R. L., 31:135–57

T

Taber, W. A., 30:263–77
Tachibana, D. K., 30:351–75
Tomasz, A., 33:113–37
Tonn, S. J., 33:169–99
Trentini, W. C., 32:123–41
Troy, F. A., 33:519–60

V

van Oss, C. J., 32:19–39
Vézina, C., 32:593–636
von Graevenitz, A., 31:447–71

W

Wagman, G. H., 34:537–57
Wallis, C., 33:413–37
Wang, L.-H., 32:561–92
Ward, D. M., 31:309–41
Warren, R. A. J., 34:137–58
Weaver, R. E., 34:341–67
Weckesser, J., 33:215–39
Weinstein, M. J., 34: 537–57
Weisman, R. A., 30:189–219
Whitcomb, R. F., 34:677–709
White, R. G., 30:579–600
Whitley, R. J., 32:285–300
Whittenbury, R., 33:481–517
Wiebe, W. J., 32:155–83
Wilkinson, H. W., 32:41–57
Williams, F. D., 32:101–22
Williams, R. C., 32:1–18
Wishnow, R. M., 30:427–50
Wu, H. C. P., 34:369–422

Z

Zeikus, J. G., 34:423–64
Zinkernagel, R. M., 33:201–13
Zuckerman, S. H., 33:267–307

CHAPTER TITLES, VOLUMES 30–34

PREFATORY CHAPTERS

From the Precise to the Ambiguous: Light, Bonding, and Administration	W. D. McElroy	30:1–20
A "Pure" Organic Chemist's Downward Path	M. Heidelberger	31:1–12
Spectroscopes, Telescopes, Microscopes	R. C. Williams	32:1–18
Evolution of a Microbial Ecologist	R. E. Hungate	33:1–20
The Journey, not the Arrival, Matters	R. Y. Stanier	34:1–48

DIVERSITY AND SYSTEMATICS

Moraxella, Neisseria, Branhamella, and Acinetobacter	S. D. Henriksen	30:63–83
The Taxonomy of the Chemoheterotrophic Spirilla	N. R. Krieg, P. B. Hylemon	30:303–25
Genetic Relatedness in the Family Enterobacteriaceae	K. E. Sanderson	30:327–49
Biology of the Marine Enterobacteria: Genera Beneckea and Photobacterium	P. Baumann, L. Baumann	31:39–61
The Spirochetes	R. C. Johnson	31:89–106
Nocardioform Bacteria	M. Goodfellow, D. E. Minnikin	31:159–80
Phototrophic Prokaryotes: The Cyanobacteria	R. Y. Stanier, G. Cohen-Bazire	31:225–74
Phototrophic Green and Purple Bacteria: A Comparative, Systematic Survey	N. Pfennig	31:275–90
Group B Streptococcal Infection in Humans	H. W. Wilkinson	32:41–57
Medically Important Yeasts	D. G. Ahearn	32:59–68
Motility and Chemotaxis of Spirochetes	E. Canale-Parola	32:69–99
Nature of the Swarming Phenomenon in Proteus	F. D. Williams, R. H. Schwarzhoff	32:101–22
Biology of the Genus Caryophanon	W. G. Trentini	32:123–41
Formation, Properties, and Germination of Actinomycete Spores	J. C. Ensign	32:185–219
The Genus Serratia	P. A. D. Grimont, F. Grimont	32:221–48
Genetics and Physiology of Acinetobacter	E. Juni	32:349–71
Organic Nutrition of Chemolithotrophic Bacteria	A. Matin	32:433–68
The Genus Campylobacter	R. M. Smibert	32:673–709
Catabolic Pathways of Coryneforms, Nocardia, and Mycobacteria	T. A. Krulwich, N. J. Pelliccione	33:95–111
Lipopolysaccharides of Photosynthetic Prokaryotes	J. Weckesser, G. Drews, H. Mayer	33:215–39
Population Ecology of Nitrifying Bacteria	L. W. Belser	33:309–33
Biology of Oligotrophic Bacteria	S. I. Kuznetsov, G. A. Dubinina, N. A. Lapteva	33:377–87
Members of the Genus Actinoplanes and their Antibiotics	F. Parenti, C. Coronelli	33:389–411
Biological and Biochemical Aspects of Microbial Growth on C_1 Compounds	J. Colby, H. Dalton, R. Whittenbury	33:481–517
The Biology of Gastrointestinal Bacteroides	J. M. Macy, L. Probst	33:561–94
Recent Taxonomic Developments and Changes in Medical Mycology	M. R. McGinnis	34:109–35
Chlamydiae	J. Schachter, H. D. Caldwell	34:285–309
Some Aspects of Structure and Function in N_2-Fixing Cyanobacteria	W. D. P. Stewart	34:497–536

Natural Populations of the Genus Staphylococcus	W. E. Kloos	34:559–92
The Genus Spiroplasma	R. F. Whitcomb	34:677–709

MORPHOLOGY, ULTRASTRUCTURE, AND DIFFERENTIATION

Biochemical Genetics of Morphogenesis in Neurospora	W. A. Scott	30:85–104
Differentiation in Acanthamoeba castellanii	R. A. Weisman	30:189–219
Ecological Aspects of Microbial Chemotactic Behavior	L. Chet, R. Mitchell	30:221–39
Differentiation in the Caulobacter Cell Cycle	L. Shapiro	30:377–407
Bacterial Membrane Structure	M. R. J. Salton, P. Owen	30:451–82
Bacterial Flagella	M. Silverman, M. I. Simon	31:397–419
Cell Differentiation in Naegleria gruberi	C. Fulton	31:597–629
Motility and Chemotaxis of Spirochetes	E. Canale-Parola	32:69–99
Nature of the Swarming Phenomenon in Proteus	F. D. Williams, R. H. Schwarzhoff	32:101–22
Formation, Properties, and Germination of Actinomycete Spores	J. C. Ensign	32:185–219
Fungal Protoplasts: Isolation, Reversion, and Fusion	J. F. Peberdy	33:21–39
Lipopolysaccharides of Photosynthetic Prokaryotes	J. Weckesser, G. Drews, H. Mayer	33:215–39
The Role of Electron Microscopy in the Elucidation of Bacterial Structure and Function	J. W. Costerton	33:459–79
Flagellar Structure and Function in Eubacteria	R. N. Doetsch, R. D. Sjoblad	34:69–108
The Immunological Activities of Bacterial Peptidoglycans	D. E. S. Stewart-Tull	34:311–40
Proteins of the Outer Membrane of Gram-Negative Bacteria	M. J. Osborn, H. C. P. Wu	34:369–422
Some Aspects of Structure and Function in N_2-Fixing Cyanobacteria	W. D. P. Stewart	34:497–536

ANIMAL PATHOGENS AND DISEASES

A Reevaluation of the Role of Mycoplasmas in Human Disease	E. J. Stanbridge	30:169–87
Microbiology of the Foot	D. K. Tachibana	30:351–75
The Conquest of the Major Infectious Diseases in the United States: A Bicentennial Retrospect	R. M. Wishnow, J. L. Steinfeld	30:427–50
Automated Methods and Data Handling in Bacteriology	H. D. Isenberg, J. D. MacLowry	30:483–505
Recent Progress in Epstein-Barr Virus Research	M. A. Epstein, B. G. Achong	31:421–45
The Role of Opportunistic Bacteria in Human Disease	A. von Graevenitz	31:447–71
Group B Streptococcal Infection in Humans	H. W. Wilkinson	32:41–57
Medically Important Yeasts	D. G. Ahearn	32:59–68
The Genus Serratia	P. A. D. Grimmont, F. Grimont	32:221–48
The Genus Campylobacter	R. M. Smibert	32:673–709
Laboratory-Associated Infections: Incidence, Fatalities, Causes, and Prevention	R. M. Pike	33:41–66
Cellular and Molecular Mechanisms of Action of Bacterial Endotoxins	S. G. Bradley	33:67–94
Associations Between Major Histocompatibility Antigens and Susceptibility to Disease	R. M. Zinkernagel	33:201–13
Recent Taxonomic Developments and Changes in Medical Mycology	M. R. McGinnis	34:109–35
Chlamydiae	J. Schachter, H. D. Caldwell	34:285–309

Diseases of Humans (Other Than Cholera) Caused by Vibrios	P. A. Blake, R. E. Weaver, D. G. Hollis	34:341–67
Plasmid-Mediated Factors Associated With Virulence of Bacteria to Animals	L. P. Elwell, P. L. Shipley	34:465–96
PLANT PATHOGENS AND DISEASES		
Antigens Common to Hosts and Parasites	J. E. DeVay, H. E. Adler	30:147–68
Bacterial Phytotoxins	G. A. Strobel	31:205–24
Initiation of Plant Root–Microbe Interactions	E. L. Schmidt	33:355–76
Genetics of Erwinia Species	A. K. Chatterjee, M. P. Starr	34:645–76
The Genus Spiroplasma	R. F. Whitcomb	34:677–709
IMMUNOLOGY		
Antigens Common to Hosts and Parasites	J. E. DeVay, H. E. Adler	30:147–68
The Adjuvant Effect of Microbial Products on the Immune Response	R. G. White	30:579–600
Phagocyte Lysosomes: Interactions with Infectious Agents, Phagosomes, and Experimental Perturbations in Function	M. B. Goren	31:507–33
Phagocytosis as a Surface Phenomenon	C. J. van Oss	32:19–39
Group B Streptococcal Infection in Humans	H. W. Wilkinson	32:41–57
Seroepidemiology of Parasitic Diseases	H. O. Lobel, I. G. Kagan	32:329–47
Dynamics of the Macrophage Plasma Membrane	S. H. Zuckerman, S. D. Douglas	33:267–307
Perspectives on the In Vivo Location of Cellular Interactions in the Humoral Immune Response	J. R. Lumb	33:439–57
The Immunological Activities of Bacterial Peptidoglycans	D. E. S. Stewart-Tull	34:311–40
Chemically Defined Antiviral Vaccines	R. Arnon	34:593–618
VIROLOGY		
Endogenous Viral Enzymes Involved in Messenger RNA Production	R. Raghow, D. W. Kingsbury	30:21–39
Viruses of Eukaryotic Microorganisms	P. A. Lemke	30:105–45
The Genome of Hepatitis B Virus	W. S. Robinson	31:357–77
Recent Progress in Epstein-Barr Virus Research	M. A. Epstein, B. G. Achong	31:421–45
Developmental Aspects of Selected Antiviral Chemotherapeutic Agents	R. J. Whitley, C. A. Alford	32:285–300
The Gene Order of Avian RNA Tumor Viruses Derived from Biochemical Analyses of Deletion Mutants and Viral Recombinants	L.-H. Wang	32:561–92
Search for Antiviral Agents	R. R. Grunert	33:335–53
Concentration of Viruses from Water by Membrane Chromatography	C. Wallis, J. L. Melnick, C. P. Gerba	33:413–37
Virus-Like Particles of Yeast	J. A. Bruenn	34:49–68
Modified Bases in Bacteriophage DNAs	R. A. J. Warren	34:137–58
Chemically Defined Antiviral Vaccines	R. Arnon	34:593–618
Defective Interfering Influenza Viruses	D. P. Nayak	34:619–44
CHEMOTHERAPY AND CHEMOTHERAPEUTIC AGENTS		
The Conquest of the Major Infectious Diseases in the United States: A Bicentennial Retrospect	R. M. Wishnow, J. L. Steinfeld	30:427–50
Biosynthesis of Polyene Macrolide Antibiotics	J.-F. Martin	31:13–38
Antifungal Agents: Recent Developments	G. S. Kobayashi, G. Medoff	31:291–308
Developmental Aspects of Selected Antiviral Chemotherapeutic Agents	R. J. Whitley, C. A. Alford	32:285–300
Extrachromosomally Determined Antibiotic Production	D. A. Hopwood	32:373–92

Plasmid-Determined Resistance to Antimicrobial Agents	J. Davies, D. I. Smith	32:469–518
Mutants Blocked in Antibiotic Synthesis	S. W. Queener, O. K. Sebek, C. Vézina	32:593–636
The Mechanism of the Irreversible Antimicrobial Effects of Penicillins: How the Beta-Lactam Antibiotics Kill and Lyse Bacteria	A. Tomasz	33:113–37
Mutational Biosynthesis of New Antibiotics	S. J. Daum, J. R. Lemke	33:241–65
Search for Antiviral Agents	R. R. Grunert	33:335–53
Members of the Genus Actinoplanes and their Antibiotics	F. Parenti, C. Coronelli	33:389–411
Natural β-Lactam Antibiotics	H. Aoki, M. Okuhara	34:159–81
Nitrogen Metabolite Regulation of Antibiotic Biosynthesis	Y. Aharonowitz	34:209–33
Antibiotics From Micromonospora	G. H. Wagman, M. J. Weinstein	34:537–57

GENETICS

Biochemical Genetics of Morphogenesis in Neurospora	W. A. Scott	30:85–104
Genetic Relatedness in the Family Enterobacteriaceae	K. E. Sanderson	30:327–49
Enzyme Recruitment in Evolution of New Function	R. A. Jensen	30:409–25
Genetic Manipulation of Microorganisms: Potential Benefits and Biohazards	R. Curtiss III	30:507–33
Tandem Genetic Duplications in Phage and Bacteria	R. P. Anderson, J. R. Roth	31:473–505
Behavioral Genetics of Phycomyces	E. Cerdá-Olmedo	31:535–47
Chromatin in Eukaryotic Microbes	P. A. Horgen, J. C. Silver	32:249–84
Genetics and Physiology of Acinetobacter	E. Juni	32:349–71
Extrachromosomally Determined Antibiotic Production	D. A. Hopwood	32:373–92
Regulation of Bacterial Growth, RNA, and Protein Synthesis	D. P. Nierlich	32:393–432
Plasmid-Determined Resistance to Antimicrobial Agents	J. Davies, D. I. Smith	32:469–518
Evolution of the Bacterial Genome	M. Riley, A. Anilionis	32:519–60
The Gene Order of Avian RNA Tumor Viruses Derived from Biochemical Analyses of Deletion Mutants and Viral Recombinants	L.-H. Wang	32:561–92
Mutants Blocked in Antibiotic Synthesis	S. W. Queener, O. K. Sebek, C. Vézina	32:593–636
Associations Between Major Histocompatibility Antigens and Susceptibility to Disease	R. M. Zinkernagel	33:201–13
Myxobacteria: Cell Interactions, Genetics, and Development	D. Kaiser, C. Manoil, M. Dworkin	33:595–639
Modified Bases in Bacteriophage DNAs	R. A. J. Warren	34:137–58
Mutagenicity and Carcinogenicity of Mycotoxins: DNA Binding as a Possible Mode of Action	A. A. Stark	34:235–62
Plasmid-Mediated Factors Associated With Virulence of Bacteria to Animals	L. P. Elwell, P. L. Shipley	34:465–96
Genetics of Erwinia Species	A. K. Chatterjee, M. P. Starr	34:645–76

GROWTH AND NUTRITION

Production of Extracellular Proteins by Bacteria	A. R. Glenn	30:41–62
Behavior of Mixed Cultures of Microorganisms	A. G. Fredrickson	31:63–87

Growth Yield and Efficiency in Chemosynthetic Microorganisms	W. J. Payne, W. J. Wiebe	32:155–83
Microbes as Food for Humans	S. G. Kharatyan	32:301–27
Regulation of Bacterial Growth, RNA, and Protein Synthesis	D. P. Nierlich	32:393–432
Organic Nutrition of Chemolithotrophic Bacteria	A. Matin	32:433–68
Mutational Biosynthesis of New Antibiotics	S. J. Daum, J. R. Lemke	33:241–65

METABOLISM, BIOCHEMISTRY, AND REGULATION

Production of Extracellular Proteins by Bacteria	A. R. Glenn	30:41–62
Ecological Aspects of Microbial Chemotactic Behavior	I. Chet, R. Mitchell	30:221–39
Denitrification	C. C. Delwiche, B. A. Bryan	30:241–62
Enzyme Recruitment in Evolution of New Function	R. A. Jensen	30:409–25
Glycerol Dissimilation and Its Regulation in Bacteria	E. C. C. Lin	30:535–78
The Inactivation of Microbial Enzymes In Vivo	R. L. Switzer	31:135–57
Ion Currents and Physiological Functions in Microorganisms	F. M. Harold	31:181–203
Biogenesis of Methane	R. A. Mah, D. M. Ward, L. Baresi, T. L. Glass	31:309–41
Effect of Primary Metabolites on Secondary Metabolism	S. W. Drew, A. L. Demain	31:343–56
Oil Tankers and Pollution: A Microbiological Approach	D. L. Gutnick, E. Rosenberg	31:379–96
Motility and Chemotaxis of Spirochetes	E. Canale-Parola	32:69–99
Nature of the Swarming Phenomenon in Proteus	F. D. Williams, R. H. Schwarzhoff	32:101–22
Genetics and Physiology of Acinetobacter	E. Juni	32:239–71
Regulation of Bacterial Growth, RNA, and Protein Synthesis	D. P. Nierlich	32:393–432
Plasmid-Determined Resistance to Antimicrobial Agents	J. Davies, D. I. Smith	32:469–518
Microbial Transformations of Metals	A. O. Summers, S. Silver	32:637–72
Catabolic Pathways of Coryneforms, Nocardia, and Mycobacteria	T. A. Krulwich, N. J. Pelliccione	33:95–111
Arginine Catabolism by Microorganisms	A. T. Abdelal	33:139–68
Biosynthesis of Polysaccharides by Prokaryotes	S. J. Tonn, J. E. Gander	33:169–99
Lipopolysaccharides of Photosynthetic Prokaryotes	J. Weckesser, G. Drews, H. Mayer	33:215–39
Mutational Biosynthesis of New Antibiotics	S. J. Daum, J. R. Lemke	33:241–65
Biological and Biochemical Aspects of Microbial Growth on C_1 Compounds	J. Colby, H. Dalton, R. Whittenbury	33:481–517
The Chemistry and Biosynthesis of Selected Bacterial Capsular Polymers	F. A. Troy II	33:519–60
The Biology of Gastrointestinal Bacteroides	J. M. Macy, I. Probst	33:561–94
Flagellar Structure and Function in Eubacteria	R. N. Doetsch, R. D. Sjoblad	34:69–108
Oxygen and Hydrogen in Biological Nitrogen Fixation	R. L. Robson, J. R. Postgate	34:183–207
Nitrogen Metabolite Regulation of Antibiotic Biosynthesis	Y. Aharonowitz	34:209–33
Proteins of the Outer Membrane of Gram-Negative Bacteria	M. J. Osborn, H. C. P. Wu	34:369–422
Chemical and Fuel Production by Anaerobic Bacteria	J. G. Zeikus	34:423–64
Some Aspects of Structure and Function in N_2-Fixing Cyanobacteria	W. D. P. Stewart	34:497–536

APPLIED MICROBIOLOGY AND ECOLOGY

Production of Extracellular Proteins by Bacteria	A. R. Glenn	30:41–62
Antigens Common to Hosts and Parasites	J. E. DeVay, H. E. Adler	30:147–68
Ecological Aspects of Microbial Chemotactic Behavior	I. Chet, R. Mitchell	30:221–39
Denitrification	C. C. Delwiche, B. A. Bryan	30:241–62
Wastewater Microbiology	W. A. Taber	30:263–77
The Ecology and Taxonomic Status of the Lactobacilli	J. London	30:279–301
Automated Methods and Data Handling in Bacteriology	H. D. Isenberg, J. D. MacLowry	30:483–505
Genetics Manipulation of Microorganisms: Potential Benefits and Biohazards	R. Curtiss III	30:507–33
Biology of the Marine Enterobacteria: Genera Beneckea and Photobacterium	P. Baumann, L. Baumann	31:39–61
Behavior of Mixed Cultures of Microorganisms	A. G. Fredrickson	31:63–87
Microbial Ecology of the Gastrointestinal Tract	D. C. Savage	31:107–33
The Inactivation of Microbial Enzymes in Vivo	R. L. Switzer	31:135–57
Biogenesis of Methane	R. A. Mah, D. M. Ward, L. Baresi, T. L. Glass	31:309–41
Effect of Primary Metabolites on Secondary Metabolism	S. W. Drew, A. L. Demain	31:343–56
Oil Tankers and Pollution: A Microbiological Approach	D. L. Gutnick, E. Rosenberg	31:379–96
Bacterial Bioluminescence	J. W. Hastings, K. H. Nealson	31:549–95
The Genus Serratia	P. A. D. Grimont, F. Grimont	32:221–48
Microbes as Food for Humans	S. G. Kharatyan	32:301–27
Microbial Transformations of Metals	A. O. Summers, S. Silver	32:637–72
Population Ecology of Nitrifying Bacteria	L. W. Belser	33:309–33
Initiation of Plant Root–Microbe Interactions	E. L. Schmidt	33:355–76
Biology of Oligotrophic Bacteria	S. I. Kuznetsov, G. A. Dubinina, N. A. Lapteva	33:377–87
Concentration of Viruses from Water by Membrane Chromatography	C. Wallis, J. L. Melnick, C. P. Gerba	33:413–37
Mutagenicity and Carcinogenicity of Mycotoxins: DNA Binding as a Possible Mode of Action	A. A. Stark	34:235–62
Ore Leaching By Bacteria	D. G. Lundgren, M. Silver	34:263–83
Chemical and Fuel Production by Anaerobic Bacteria	J. G. Zeikus	34:423–64

OTHER

The Social, Political, and Religious Background to the Work of Louis Pasteur	J. Farley	32:143–54
Evolution of the Bacterial Genome	M. Riley, A. Anilionis	32:519–60
Laboratory-Associated Infections: Incidence, Fatalities, Causes, and Prevention	R. M. Pike	33:41–66
The Role of Electron Microscopy in the Elucidation of Bacterial Structure and Function	J. W. Costerton	33:459–79

ORDER FORM ANNUAL REVIEWS INC.

Please list on the order blank on the reverse side the volumes you wish to order and whether you wish a standing order (the latest volume sent to you automatically upon publication each year). Volumes not yet published will be shipped in month and year indicated. Prices subject to change without notice. Out of print volumes subject to special order.

NEW TITLES FOR 1980

ANNUAL REVIEW OF PUBLIC HEALTH — ISSN 0163-7525
Vol. 1 (avail. May 1980): $17.00 (USA), $17.50 (elsewhere) per copy

ANNUAL REVIEWS REPRINTS: IMMUNOLOGY, 1977–1979 — ISBN 0-8243-2502-8
A collection of articles reprinted from recent *Annual Review* series
Avail. Mar. 1980 Soft cover: $12.00 (USA), $12.50 (elsewhere) per copy

SPECIAL PUBLICATIONS

ANNUAL REVIEWS REPRINTS: CELL MEMBRANES, 1975–1977 — ISBN 0-8243-2501-X
A collection of articles reprinted from recent *Annual Review* series
Published 1978 Soft cover: $12.00 (USA), $12.50 (elsewhere) per copy

THE EXCITEMENT AND FASCINATION OF SCIENCE, VOLUME 1 — ISBN 0-8243-1602-9
A collection of autobiographical and philosophical articles by leading scientists
Published 1965 Clothbound: $6.50 (USA), $7.00 (elsewhere) per copy

THE EXCITEMENT AND FASCINATION OF SCIENCE, VOLUME 2: Reflections by Eminent Scientists
Published 1978 Hard cover: $12.00 (USA), $12.50 (elsewhere) per copy — ISBN 0-8243-2601-6
Soft cover: $10.00 (USA), $10.50 (elsewhere) per copy — ISBN 0-8243-2602-4

THE HISTORY OF ENTOMOLOGY — ISBN 0-8243-2101-7
A special supplement to the *Annual Review of Entomology* series
Published 1973 Clothbound: $10.00 (USA), $10.50 (elsewhere) per copy

ANNUAL REVIEW SERIES

Annual Review of ANTHROPOLOGY — ISSN 0084-6570
Vols. 1–8 (1972–79): $17.00 (USA), $17.50 (elsewhere) per copy
Vol. 9 (avail. Oct. 1980): $20.00 (USA), $21.00 (elsewhere) per copy

Annual Review of ASTRONOMY AND ASTROPHYSICS — ISSN 0066-4146
Vols. 1–17 (1963–79): $17.00 (USA), $17.50 (elsewhere) per copy
Vol. 18 (avail. Sept. 1980): $20.00 (USA), $21.00 (elsewhere) per copy

Annual Review of BIOCHEMISTRY — ISSN 0066-4154
Vols. 28–48 (1959–79): $18.00 (USA), $18.50 (elsewhere) per copy
Vol. 49 (avail. July 1980): $21.00 (USA), $22.00 (elsewhere) per copy

Annual Review of BIOPHYSICS AND BIOENGINEERING* — ISSN 0084-6589
Vols. 1–8 (1972–79): $17.00 (USA), $17.50 (elsewhere) per copy
Vol. 9 (avail. June 1980): $17.00 (USA), $17.50 (elsewhere) per copy

Annual Review of EARTH AND PLANETARY SCIENCES* — ISSN 0084-6597
Vols. 1–7 (1973–79): $17.00 (USA), $17.50 (elsewhere) per copy
Vol. 8 (avail. May 1980): $17.00 (USA), $17.50 (elsewhere) per copy

Annual Review of ECOLOGY AND SYSTEMATICS — ISSN 0066-4162
Vols. 1–10 (1970–79): $17.00 (USA), $17.50 (elsewhere) per copy
Vol. 11 (avail. Nov. 1980): $20.00 (USA), $21.00 (elsewhere) per copy

Annual Review of ENERGY — ISSN 0362-1626
Vols. 1–4 (1976–79): $17.00 (USA), $17.50 (elsewhere) per copy
Vol. 5 (avail. Oct. 1980): $20.00 (USA), $21.00 (elsewhere) per copy

Annual Review of ENTOMOLOGY* — ISSN 0066-4170
Vols. 7–24 (1962–79): $17.00 (USA), $17.50 (elsewhere) per copy
Vol. 25 (avail. Jan. 1980): $17.00 (USA), $17.50 (elsewhere) per copy

Annual Review of FLUID MECHANICS* — ISSN 0066-4189
Vols. 1–11 (1969–79): $17.00 (USA), $17.50 (elsewhere) per copy
Vol. 12 (avail. Jan. 1980): $17.00 (USA), $17.50 (elsewhere) per copy

Annual Review of GENETICS — ISSN 0066-4197
Vols. 1–13 (1967–79): $17.00 (USA), $17.50 (elsewhere) per copy
Vol. 14 (avail. Dec. 1980): $20.00 (USA), $21.00 (elsewhere) per copy

Annual Review of MATERIALS SCIENCE — ISSN 0084-6600
Vol. 1–9 (1971–79): $17.00 (USA), $17.50 (elsewhere) per copy
Vol. 10 (avail. Aug. 1980): $20.00 (USA), $21.00 (elsewhere) per copy

(continued on reverse)

*Price will be increased to $20.00 (USA), $21.00 (elsewhere) per copy effective with the 1981 volume.